LaunchPad macmillan learning with LearningCurve

for *Psychology*, Eighth Edition

Available April 2018 at launchpadworks.com

Each chapter in LaunchPad for *Psychology*, Eighth Edition, features a collection of activities carefully chosen to help master the major concepts. The site serves students as a comprehensive online study guide, available any time, with opportunities for self-quizzing with instant feedback, exam preparation, and further explorations of topics from the textbook. For instructors, all units and activities can be instantly assigned and students' results and analytics are collected in the Gradebook.

For Students

- Full e-Book of *Psychology*, Eighth Edition
- LearningCurve Quizzing
- Student Video Activities
- Concept Practice Activities
- PsychSim 6.0 by Thomas Ludwig and John Krantz
- *Scientific American* Newsfeed

For Instructors

- Gradebook
- Presentation Slides
- Instructor's Resource Guide
- Test Bank
- Electronic Figures, Photos, and Tables
- Correlation of *Psychology*, Eighth Edition, to APA Learning Goals
- Correlation of *Psychology*, Eighth Edition, to MCAT Topics

LearningCurve

What Is LearningCurve? LearningCurve is a cutting-edge study tool designed to increase your understanding and memory of the core concepts in every chapter. Based on insights from the latest learning and memory research, the LearningCurve system pairs multiple-choice and fill-in-the-blank questions with instantaneous feedback and a rich array of study tools including videos, animations, and lab simulations. The LearningCurve system is adaptive, so the quiz you take is customized to your level of understanding. The more questions you answer correctly, the more challenging the questions become. Best of all, the e-Book of *Psychology*, Eighth Edition, is fully integrated, so you can easily review the text as you study and answer questions. LearningCurve is a smart and fun way to study each chapter.

LearningCurve is available as part of **LaunchPad** for *Psychology*, **Eighth Edition**.

To find out more or purchase access, go to **launchpadworks.com**

Psychology

EIGHTH EDITION

Peter Gray
Boston College

David F. Bjorklund
Florida Atlantic University

worth publishers
Macmillan Learning
New York

Vice President, Social Sciences: Charles Linsmeier

Director of Content and Assessment, Social Sciences: Shani Fisher

Executive Program Manager: Christine Cardone

Developmental Editor: Elsa Peterson

Assistant Editor: Melissa Rostek

Executive Marketing Manager: Katherine Nurre

Marketing Assistant: Morgan Ratner

Director of Media Editorial, Social Sciences: Noel Hohnstine

Senior Media Editor: Laura Burden

Assistant Media Editor: Nik Toner

Director, Content Management Enhancement: Tracey Kuehn

Managing Editor: Lisa Kinne

Senior Content Project Manager: Kerry O'Shaughnessy

Lead Media Project Manager: Eve Conte

Senior Workflow Project Manager: Paul Rohloff

Permissions Manager: Jennifer MacMillan

Photo Researcher: Krystyna Borgen

Director of Design, Content Management: Diana Blume

Cover and Interior Design: Lumina Datamatics, Inc.

Art Manager: Matthew McAdams

Illustrations: DragonFly Studios, Matthew Holt, Hans Neuhart, Evelyn Pence, and Matthew McAdams

Composition: Lumina Datamatics, Inc.

Printing and Binding: LSC Communications

Cover credits: Jasper James/Getty Images and sumroeng chinnapan/Shutterstock

Library of Congress Control Number: 2017944643

ISBN-13: 978-1-319-01589-3
ISBN-10: 1-319-01589-1

Printed in the United States of America
First printing

Worth Publishers
One New York Plaza
Suite 4500
New York, NY 10004-1562
www.macmillanlearning.com

For

Hari Kirin Kaur Khalsa (aka Diane Pingeton)

and

Barbara Bjorklund

About the Authors

Peter Gray, Ph.D., was a full-time professor of psychology at Boston College for 30 years, where he served his department at various times as Department Chair, Undergraduate Program Director, and Graduate Program Director. He has published research in biological, evolutionary, cultural, developmental, and educational psychology; published articles on innovative teaching methods; taught more than 20 different undergraduate courses, including, most regularly, introductory psychology; helped develop a university-wide program to improve students' study and learning skills; and developed a program of research practicum courses. He is now retired from regular teaching but maintains a position as Research Professor at Boston College. Most of his current research and academic writing has to do with the value of play, especially free age-mixed play, in children's development. He is also author of *Free to Learn: Why Unleashing the Instinct to Play Will Make Our Children Happier, More Self-Reliant, and Better Students for Life* (Basic Books) and writes a popular blog for *Psychology Today* magazine entitled *Freedom to Learn: The Roles of Play and Curiosity as Foundations for Learning.*

Before joining Boston College, Peter Gray studied psychology as an undergraduate at Columbia University and earned a Ph.D. in biological sciences at the Rockefeller University. He earned his way through college by coaching basketball and working with youth groups in New York City. As a graduate student, he directed a summer biology program for talented high school students from impoverished neighborhoods. His avocations today include long distance bicycling, kayaking, backwoods skiing, and vegetable gardening.

David F. Bjorklund, Ph.D., is a Professor of Psychology at Florida Atlantic University, where he has taught graduate and undergraduate courses in developmental and evolutionary psychology since 1976. He received a B.A. in psychology from the University of Massachusetts, an M.A. in psychology from the University of Dayton, and a Ph.D. in developmental psychology from the University of North Carolina at Chapel Hill. He has received numerous teaching and research awards from Florida Atlantic University and is the recipient of an Alexander von Humboldt Research Award.

David Bjorklund served as Associate Editor of *Child Development* (1997–2001) and is currently serving as Editor of the *Journal of Experimental Child Psychology*. He has served on the editorial boards of numerous journals and also served as a contributing editor to *Parents Magazine*. He has published more than 200 scholarly articles on various topics relating to child development and evolutionary psychology and has received financial support for his research from the National Science Foundation, the Spencer Foundation, and the German Research Foundation. David Bjorklund's other books include *Children's Thinking: Cognitive Development and Individual Differences*, now in its sixth edition (with Kayla Causey, 2018, Sage); *Why Youth Is Not Wasted on the Young* (2007, Blackwell); *Child and Adolescent Development: An Integrative Approach* (with Carlos Hernández Blasi, 2012, Cengage); *Looking at Children: An Introduction to Child Development* (with Barbara Bjorklund, 1992, Brooks/Cole); *Parents Book of Discipline* (with Barbara Bjorklund, 1990, Ballantine); *Applied Child Study* (with Anthony Pellegrini, 1998, Erlbaum); *The Origins of Human Nature: Evolutionary Developmental Psychology* (with Anthony Pellegrini, 2002, American Psychological Association); *Children's Strategies: Contemporary Views of Cognitive Development* (1990, Erlbaum); *False-Memory Creation in Children and Adults: Theory, Research, and Implications* (2000, Erlbaum); and *Origins of the Social Mind: Evolutionary Psychology and Child Development* (with Bruce Ellis, 2005, Guilford). His current research interests include children's cognitive development and evolutionary developmental psychology. He lives in Jupiter, Florida, with his wife Barbara and enjoys traveling, cooking, playing basketball, and kayaking. He welcomes sincere feedback concerning this textbook from students as well as faculty, and can be reached by email at dbjorklu@fau.edu.

Brief Contents

Contents

PART I

Foundations for the Study of Psychology

PART II

The Biological Bases of Behavior

PART V
Growth of the Mind and Person

PART VI
Social and Personality Psychology

PART VII

Psychological Disorders and Treatment

An Introduction and Note From Peter Gray

The best and worst thing about authoring a psychology textbook is that it is a continuous work in progress. Psychology is such a dynamic field that whenever an author comes close to capturing it, it shape-morphs, sprints ahead, and laughs. For nearly three decades, this pursuit was my greatest academic challenge and pleasure. When I finally decided to drop this chase, after the sixth edition, and devote more time to new pursuits, Worth Publishers pressed on to find a new author. In my conceit, I said, in effect, "You'll never find someone whose vision of psychology is close enough to mine and whose drive for this pursuit is sufficient to maintain the book's spirit." But they didn't listen; and when they found David F. Bjorklund—a superb researcher, thinker, and writer whose work I already greatly admired—I was glad they hadn't listened. How flattering it was to know that he was interested in taking over this chase, and how grateful I am that he has continued it so beautifully.

David is the perfect choice as a coauthor for this book. We have long admired each other's research and writing and we share similar perspectives about psychology, how to teach it, and how to write about it.

Thank you, David, for continuing on with our shared vision to engage students in the big ideas in psychology. I can't imagine anyone more qualified than you for this pursuit.

Peter Gray

An Introduction and Note From David Bjorklund

When I received an e-mail from Worth editor Christine Cardone about taking over a general psychology textbook, my immediate reaction was, "No thanks." Writing an introductory psychology text was not on my bucket list of professional things to do, and in fact I had never considered it. But Chris had served as editor for an earlier book of mine, and I thought it only polite to listen to what she had to say. Then she told me it was Peter Gray's *Psychology* book, and I had to reconsider. Peter and I hold similar views about the "big picture" of psychology, and he had written six editions of an introductory psychology textbook that covered all important topics, but did so in a way that organized the field around the theme of adaptation. It was a wonderful book, the best on the market I thought, and so I said "yes," and I haven't been sorry.

By coincidence, just a week before Christine asked if I wanted to write a note for the eighth edition to accompany Peter's, I sent Peter this e-mail:

Dear Peter,

I'm in the middle of production of the 8th edition of our *Psychology* text and have just finished proofing the first five chapters. In doing so, I realized how much I really like the book! It's easy to get caught up in the details of revising diverse chapters and lose sight of the big picture. The big picture is that you bequeathed to me a book that organizes the field of psychology in a wonderful way, one that can have a profound effect on how beginning students (and their instructors) view psychology and therefore life. I thought I'd take the time to thank you again for the opportunity to take over the book. I'm proud to be associated with it. I hope this finds you well.

Best,

Dave

That about says it all. I've completed two editions of this text now, and the spirit and themes of Peter's original book are maintained, and I hope to be able to continue his vision of psychology and how it should be taught.

David F. Bjorklund

Preface

Long-Standing Goals for the Book

The primary purpose of a liberal arts education is to gain experience in thinking critically about ideas. Information today is available at everyone's fingertips; we don't need to store a lot of it in our heads. We do, however, need to use our heads to evaluate information and apply it logically to larger ideas. As authors, we hope that students who are introduced to psychology through our book will almost reflexively ask, upon hearing of some new idea in psychology, "What is the evidence?" and will feel empowered to think logically and critically about that evidence.

Even if this book's goal were merely to teach students the main concepts of psychology, the best means would still be one that stimulates thought. As cognitive psychologists have shown repeatedly, the human mind is not particularly good at absorbing and remembering miscellaneous pieces of information. It is designed for thinking, figuring out, and understanding, and it remembers what it understands. In the absence of some knowledge of the logic and evidence behind them, the concepts in psychology are words devoid of meaning.

In this book, critical thinking does not come in separate boxes. It is—if we have done our job—woven through almost every paragraph of the text. We have entered each domain of psychology to identify its main questions, its main approaches to answering questions, its main discoveries, and the most durable ideas and theories that have resulted from those discoveries. In writing each edition of this book, we have constantly imagined ourselves carrying on a dialogue with an inquiring, thinking, appropriately skeptical student.

One of our dearest aims has been to achieve some small measure of the personal touch that William James accomplished so masterfully in *The Principles of Psychology*—the book that still stands, in our minds, as the best introduction to psychology ever written. While reading James, one constantly senses a mind at work, a mind that is honestly struggling to understand the big issues in psychology and that invites readers into the process. We also confess to sharing two of James's biases: rationalism and functionalism. As rationalists, we are uncomfortable presenting findings and facts without trying to make sense of them. Sometimes instruction in psychology overplays the methods for gathering and analyzing data and underplays the value of logical thought. As functionalists, we want to know why, in terms of survival or other benefits, people behave as they do.

The functionalist theme runs through the book and is particularly emphasized in Chapter 3, where we introduce Darwin's theory of evolution by natural selection and its relevance for understanding behavior, and Chapter 8, where we discuss the psychology of learning. Natural selection and learning are the two reasons behavior is functional, and it is important that students know something about those processes and their interaction. The functionalist orientation also leads us, throughout the book, to pay more than the usual amount of attention to cross-cultural research and to behavioral processes as they operate in the contexts of people's everyday lives.

Goals for the Eighth Edition

Our two main goals in each revision of the book are (1) to keep the book current and accurate, and (2) to make the book more enjoyable and useful to all who read it.

Keeping the Book Current and Accurate

Most of the work and fun of each revision lies in our own continued learning and rethinking of each realm of psychology. In producing this revision, we skimmed thousands of new research articles and chapters and read hundreds carefully to determine which new developments warrant inclusion in the introductory course. The result was not so much the discovery of new ideas as the determination of how long-standing ideas are playing themselves out in current research and debate. This edition contains more than 400 new references to research, mainly to works published within the past 5 years, out of a total reference list of approximately 2,350. On average, 18% of the references in each chapter are new. By including the most recent research and controversies, we can convey to students the understanding that psychology is a continuously advancing, dynamic, contemporary human activity, not a stale collection of facts.

The hundreds of new references represent only a small portion of the thousands of research papers that have been published since the previous edition of this book. It would be tempting simply to add the new research to what was already in the earlier edition, but this soon leads to a book that is too lengthy and unwieldy for an undergraduate student (and for the authors). Knowing this, we have carefully reviewed the research and citations, deleting nearly 500 references, and streamlined the book, reducing it from 17 to 16 chapters and by nearly 20,000 words relative to the seventh edition. Six of the 16 chapters in this book are shorter than they were in the seventh edition, with the most prominent change resulting from combining the seventh edition's two chapters on social psychology into a single chapter in the eighth edition. Our goal is not to simplify psychology, but rather to make the major points about this fascinating discipline easier to understand and more enjoyable to read about.

When we compare this new edition of *Psychology* with the first edition, we see the great progress psychology has made in the past 25 years. What a pleasure it has been to keep pace with it! The progress has come on all fronts and is not easily summarized, but we are pleased to see that the general theme of adaptation, which was central to Peter's initial conception of the book, is even more central to psychology today. As humans, our basic behavioral machinery is adapted by natural selection to the general, long-standing conditions of life. That machinery, however, is itself shaped by natural selection to be adaptive to the conditions of life under which each of us develops. An enormous amount of research over the past few years, in all areas of psychology and neuroscience, elaborates on the theme of adaptation. That work is well represented in this new edition.

What's New in This Edition

Here are a few examples of new or expanded discussions in this edition that reflect our increased understanding of adaptive mechanisms:

- Chapter 2, *Methods of Psychology*, includes a new section titled *Replicating Earlier Studies* that discusses the importance of replicating, or reproducing, the results of previous research.
- Chapter 3, *Genetics and Evolutionary Foundations of Behavior*, expands the section on *Epigenetics* and how it may play a role in both evolution and development.
- Chapter 4, *The Neural Control of Behavior*, adds a section on *Hormonal Influences on Sex Drive*.
- Chapter 5, *Mechanisms of Motivation and Emotion*, discusses sleep in hunter-gatherers and its implications for modern people's sleep habits.
- Chapter 6, *Smell, Taste, Pain, Hearing, and Psychophysics*, expands the role of olfaction in sexual attraction and shortens the section on *Psychophysics*.

- Chapter 7, *The Psychology of Vision,* discusses research on how people recognize faces, including brain regions involved in face recognition.
- Chapter 8, *Basic Processes of Learning,* expands discussion of how children learn through play and includes a section on possible sexual imprinting (the Westermarck effect).
- Chapter 9, *Memory, Attention, and Consciousness,* brings back to the book an explicit discussion of consciousness in human thinking and examines people's impressive abilities to visually recognize thousands of objects.
- Chapter 10, *Solving Problems: Reasoning and Intelligence,* discusses the neurological basis of analogical reasoning, including suggestions on how to instruct students to use analogical reasoning.
- Chapter 11, *The Development of Body, Thought, and Language,* expands research on children's symbolic development, Piaget's description of cognitive development over childhood, and Vygotsky's sociocultural theory.
- Chapter 12, *Social Development,* expands coverage of attachment and adds a discussion of emerging adulthood.
- Chapter 13, *Social Psychology,* combines two chapters from the seventh edition, *Social Perception and Attitudes* and *Social Influences on Behavior,* into a single chapter in the eighth edition, streamlining the coverage of social psychology.
- Chapter 14, *Personality,* introduces a new section on *Grit and the Dark Triad,* as well as a discussion of how researchers define situations and how situations, in interaction with personality traits, affect behavior.
- Chapter 15, *Psychological Disorders,* documents the relationship between executive function/emotional regulation and psychopathology and expands the discussion of posttraumatic stress disorder.
- Chapter 16, *Treatment of Psychological Disorders,* expands on several new approaches, such as mindfulness-based cognitive therapy, that are used to treat psychological disorders.

Making the Book More Enjoyable and Useful to All Who Use It

A book becomes more useful and enjoyable not by being "dumbed down" but by being "smartened up." The clearer the logic and the more precisely it is expressed, the easier a book is to understand and the more engaging it becomes. With each revision—and with feedback from adopters, students, and editors—we continually try new ways to make difficult ideas clearer without ignoring their inherent subtlety or complexity. Our efforts toward clarity have been greatly facilitated by our developmental editor, Elsa Peterson. Elsa read the entire manuscript for the first time, as a student would, and helped very much to sharpen the wording and even suggested new research for us to consider.

In every revision we have endeavored to make the book more accessible to the full range of students. For example, we structured Chapter 1 as an orientation to the textbook and how to use its study features, as well as an orientation to psychology as a discipline. Within each chapter we included *focus questions*, placed in the margins and intended to stimulate inquisitive reading of each new idea, as well as *hierarchical review charts,* which serve as a review aid at the end of each major section. The value of these focus questions and section reviews is described in the "Pedagogical Features" section of this Preface and again, more fully, on pp. 21–23 of Chapter 1. As reviewer feedback indicated that these features have been useful in helping students to learn from the book, they have been retained and improved upon for this edition. The current edition adds *Learning Outcomes* at the beginning of each chapter, listing for students what they should know and be able to do after studying the chapter; and a section titled *Thinking Critically About* . . . at the end of each chapter to foster additional critical thinking about the material just read. We hope these features will further help students to understand and appreciate the information covered in each chapter.

General Organization of the Book

The book is divided into seven parts, each comprising two or three chapters. This edition features a new and improved chapter organization, detailed below.

Part I, *Foundations for the Study of Psychology,* has two relatively brief chapters. Chapter 1, *Background to the Study of Psychology,* is an orientation both to psychology as a discipline and to the book. It presents three major historical ideas that underlie contemporary psychology. It outlines the scope of contemporary psychology, and it offers students some advice about studying this book. Chapter 2, *Methods of Psychology,* lays out some general elements of psychological research that will be useful to students in later chapters. (This can be supplemented with the first three sections of the *Statistical Appendix,* found at the back of the book.)

Part II, *The Biological Bases of Behavior,* introduces the functionalist theme that reappears throughout the book as well as the genetic and neural mechanisms of behavior. Chapter 3, *Genetics and Evolutionary Foundations of Behavior,* includes the idea that even behaviors that are most highly prepared by evolution must develop in the individual through interaction with the environment. Chapter 4, *The Neural Control of Behavior,* examines the structure of the nervous system and its principles of operation; and Chapter 5, *Mechanisms of Motivation and Emotion,* is concerned with the neural and hormonal mechanisms underlying motivation and emotion.

Part III, *Sensation and Perception,* is about the processes through which the brain and mind gather information about the outside world. It contains Chapter 6, *Smell, Taste, Pain, Hearing, and Psychophysics;* and Chapter 7, *The Psychology of Vision.* The main question for both chapters is this: How does our nervous system respond to and make sense of the patterns of energy in the physical world? In both chapters the discussion of sensory and perceptual mechanisms is placed in a functionalist context. The senses are understood as survival mechanisms that evolved not to provide full, objective accounts of the world's physical properties, but rather to provide the specific kinds of information that are needed to survive and reproduce.

Part IV, *Learning and Thinking,* is about learning and the ability of the brain and mind to acquire and store information and use it to solve problems. Chapter 8, *Basic Processes of Learning,* discusses the traditional topics of classical and operant conditioning; learning through play, exploration, and observation; and specialized learning abilities, such as those involved in learning what to eat. Chapter 9, *Memory, Attention, and Consciousness,* focuses on the roles of both unconscious and conscious mechanisms in attention, memory encoding, and memory retrieval, as well as how information is represented in memory. The chapter includes an analysis of the multiple memory systems that have evolved to serve different adaptive functions. Chapter 10, *Solving Problems: Reasoning and Intelligence,* deals with the cognitive processes by which people solve problems, both in everyday life and on structured tests, and with the measurement of intelligence and controversies associated with such measurement. Throughout Chapters 9 and 10, the information-processing perspective is highlighted, but is tempered by ecological discussions that draw attention to the functions of each mental process and the environmental contexts within which they operate.

In sum, Parts III and IV are concerned with basic psychological processes—processes of sensation, perception, learning, attention, memory, and problem solving—and each process is discussed in a manner that integrates ideas about its mechanisms with ideas about its adaptive functions. The remaining three parts of the book are concerned with understanding the whole person and the person's relationships to the social environment.

Part V, *Growth of the Mind and Person,* is about developmental psychology. Its two chapters develop the functionalist perspective further by emphasizing the interactions between evolved human tendencies and environmental experiences in shaping a person's behavior. Chapter 11, *The Development of Body, Thought, and Language,* is concerned with the traditional topics of physical, cognitive, and language development. Chapter 12, *Social Development,* explores the changes in social relationships and life tasks that occur throughout the life span and the ways in which these relationships and tasks vary across cultures. Chapter 12 also sets the stage for the next chapter.

Part VI, *Social and Personality Psychology,* examines humans as social beings and as unique individuals with our own particular styles of interacting with the world. Chapter 13, *Social Psychology,* is concerned with the mental processes involved in forming judgments of other people, perceiving and presenting the self in the social environment, compliance, obedience, conformity, cooperation, competition, group decision making, conflict, and the social regulatory roles of emotions. A theme of this chapter is the contrast between normative and informational influences. Chapter 14, *Personality,* describes trait theories of personality; the functionalist idea of personality as adaptation to life conditions; and the psychodynamic, humanistic, and social-cognitive approaches to personality. This unit on social and personality psychology is placed before the one on psychological disorders because the insights of social psychology—especially those pertaining to social cognition—contribute to ways of understanding and treating psychological disorders.

Part VII, *Psychological Disorders and Treatment,* incorporates material from the *Diagnostic and Statistical Manual of Mental Disorders, Fifth Edition* (DSM-5, American Psychiatric Association, 2013) and consists of two chapters on topics that students tend to identify most strongly as "psychology" before they enter the course. Chapter 15, *Psychological Disorders,* begins by discussing the problems involved in categorizing and diagnosing disorders and then, through the discussion of specific disorders, emphasizes the idea of multiple causation and the theme that the symptoms characterizing disorders are different in degree, not in kind, from normal psychological experiences and processes. Chapter 16, *Treatment of Psychological Disorders,* offers an opportunity to recapitulate many of the main ideas of earlier chapters—now in the context of their application to therapy. Such themes reappear in the discussions of biological, behavioral, and cognitive therapies, and ideas from the personality chapter reappear in the discussions of psychodynamic and humanistic therapies.

Although this ordering of topics makes the most sense to us, each chapter is written so that it can be read as a separate entity, independent of others. Links are often made to material presented in another chapter, but most of these cross-references are spelled out in enough detail to be understood by students who have not read the other chapter. The only major exception falls in the biological bases unit: Chapter 5, on motivation, sleep, and emotion, assumes that the student has learned some of the basic information presented in Chapter 4, on the nervous system.

Pedagogical Features of the Book

The main pedagogical feature of this or any other textbook is, of course, the narrative itself, which should be clear, logical, and interesting. Everything else is secondary. We have attempted through every page of every chapter to produce as logical and clear a flow of ideas as we possibly can. We have avoided the kinds of boxes and inserts that are often found in introductory psychology texts, because such digressions distract from the flow of thought and add to the impression that psychology is a jumble of topics that don't fit together very well.

We want students to read and think about the ideas of this book, not attempt to memorize bits and pieces of isolated information. Toward that end we have developed study aids that help students to focus their attention on the arguments and think about individual findings and terms in relation to those arguments.

Learning Outcomes

Learning Outcomes appear at the beginning of each chapter to help guide students in their learning. They help specify what students will learn, be able to do, identify, or demonstrate when they have finished reading each chapter.

Focus Questions

The most useful study aids in this book—in our judgment and that of many students who have provided feedback—are the *focus questions*, which appear in the margins throughout the text at an average frequency of about one question per page. Each question is designed to direct students' attention to the main idea, argument, or evidence addressed in the adjacent paragraphs of text. In Chapter 1 (on pp. 21–23) we spell out more fully the rationale behind the focus questions and offer advice to students for using them to guide both their initial reading and their review of each main section of each chapter. We ask students to develop the habit of reading and thinking about each focus question as they come to it, before they read the paragraph or paragraphs of text that answer that question. Most students, once they get used to this method of study, find that it helps them greatly in focusing their attention, stimulating their thought, and increasing their understanding of what they are reading. We have even had students tell us that they find themselves writing their own focus questions in the margins of their other textbooks. We urge instructors to reinforce the value of the focus questions by talking about ways of using them in an early lecture and perhaps also by modeling their use with a think-aloud exercise.

The focus questions also offer instructors a means to make selective assignments within any chapter. The questions are numbered so instructors can easily let students know, with a list of numbers, which questions will be fair game for exams. The multiple-choice questions in the *Test Bank* are keyed by number to the focus questions. When we teach the course, we tell students that tests will consist of multiple-choice and brief essay questions that are derived from the book's focus questions. This makes clear what students must do to prepare. If they can answer the focus questions, they will do well on the test.

Hierarchical Section Reviews

At the end of each major section of each chapter, we provide a *section review,* which depicts explicitly the hierarchical structure that relates the section's main idea to its subordinate ideas and to specific observations and concepts that are relevant to those ideas. The primary purpose of this feature is to help students to review each section before moving on to the next. Here they can see, in one organized picture, the structure of the argument that they have just read. Some students may also find these charts useful as previews. By looking ahead at the section review before reading each new section, students can get a coherent overview, which should help them to read with greater focus and thought.

In Chapter 1 (p. 23) we advise students how to use the section reviews, but, as with the focus questions, we urge instructors to encourage their use by offering their own advice and, perhaps, by demonstrating in an early lecture how to use them.

Thinking Critically About . . . , Reflections and Connections, and Find Out More

Thinking Critically About . . . questions at the end of each chapter encourage students to consider or analyze the "big questions" raised in the chapter. They can also be used for class discussion or short essay assignments.

Because the focus questions and section reviews make a traditional end-of-chapter review unnecessary, we end each chapter with a section called *Reflections and Connections* that expands on the broad themes of the chapter, points out relations to ideas discussed in other chapters, and raises new ideas for students to consider as they reflect on the chapter. In many cases these thoughts are aimed at helping students to see connections between ideas from different sections of the chapter that were not tied together in the section reviews.

A brief section called *Find Out More* contains thumbnail reviews of several relevant and interesting books, websites, and content from various media that are sufficiently nontechnical to be read by first-year students. The kinds of students who continue in psychology or in related disciplines, who become the next crop of professors or professional psychologists, are the ones who take most advantage of this feature.

MCAT Guidelines

Beginning in 2015, the Medical College Admission Test (MCAT) is devoting 25% of its questions to the "Psychological, Social, and Biological Foundations of Behavior." The exam recognizes the importance of the sociocultural and behavioral determinants of health. The exam's psychology section covers the breadth of topics in this text. A full pairing of content can be found in the resources section of LaunchPad.

Media and Supplements

Worth Publishers offers a rich suite of media and supplements to support our textbook.

LaunchPad with LearningCurve Quizzing: A Comprehensive Web Resource for Teaching and Learning Psychology

LaunchPad combines Worth Publishers' award-winning media with an innovative platform for easy navigation. For students, it is the ultimate online study guide, with rich interactive tutorials and videos, as well as an e-Book and the Learning-Curve adaptive quizzing system. For instructors, LaunchPad is a full course space where class documents can be posted, quizzes easily assigned and graded, and students' progress assessed and recorded. Whether you are looking for the most effective study tools or robust platform for an online course, LaunchPad is a powerful way to enhance teaching and learning. LaunchPad for *Psychology,* Eighth Edition, includes all the following resources:

- **LearningCurve** quizzing system is based on the latest findings from learning and memory research. It combines adaptive question selection, immediate and valuable feedback, and a gamelike interface to engage students in a learning experience that is unique to them. Each LearningCurve quiz is fully integrated with other resources in LaunchPad through the Personalized Study Plan, so students will be able to review using Worth's extensive library of videos and activities. And state-of-the-art question analysis reports allow instructors to track the progress of individual students as well as their class as a whole.

- **An interactive e-Book** allows students to highlight, bookmark, and add their own notes on the e-Book page, just as they would in a printed textbook.

- **Video Activities** comprise more than 100 engaging video modules that instructors can easily assign and customize for student assessment. Videos cover classic experiments, current news footage, and cutting-edge research, all of which are sure to spark discussion and encourage critical thinking. Each activity includes a quiz to check students' understanding.

- The award-winning tutorials in **PsychSim 6.0** by Tom Ludwig (Hope College) and John Krantz (Hanover College) give students an engaging, interactive

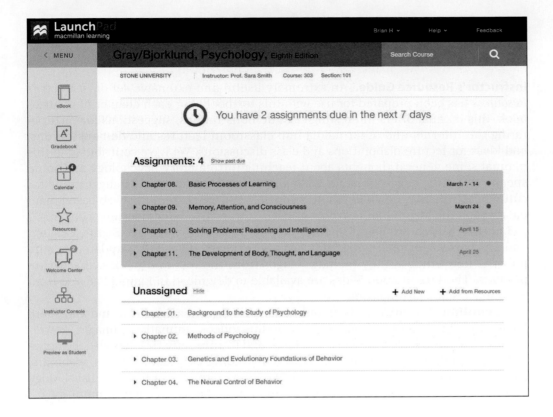

introduction to psychological phenomena, integrating demonstrations and experimental tasks. In addition, each activity includes integrated formative and summative assessment questions.

- NEW! **Concept Practice** activities by Tom Ludwig (Hope College) allow students to practice their understanding of individual concepts in less than five minutes. All the activities feature new art and assessment features to deepen students' interaction with the material.

- The *Scientific American* **Newsfeed** delivers weekly articles, podcasts, and news briefs on the very latest developments in psychology from the first name in popular-science journalism.

- **Deep integration** is available between LaunchPad products and most learning management systems including Blackboard, Brightspace by D2L, Canvas, and Moodle. These deep integrations offer educators single sign-on and Gradebook sync, now with auto refresh. These best-in-class integrations offer deep linking to all Macmillan digital content at the chapter and asset levels, giving professors maximum flexibility within their LMS.

Assessment and Other Instructor Resources

Test Bank (in online Instructor's Resources and Diploma Computerized version). A Test Bank containing approximately 2,000 multiple-choice questions has been prepared for this edition. The multiple-choice questions are keyed to the focus questions in the text, so instructors can easily identify questions that correspond with the focus questions that they have asked students to emphasize in their studies. In addition, each test bank question is tagged to one of the levels of Bloom's Taxonomy of Learning Objectives as well as the Learning Goals and Outcomes of the American Psychological Association Guidelines for the Undergraduate Psychology Major 2.0, allowing instructors to further control the desired learning outcome of each question.

The Test Bank is available as a download from the Macmillan Learning catalog at www.macmillanlearning.com. Previous editions of the Test Bank have been much praised by its users.

Instructor's Resource Guide. An extremely useful and extensive set of *Instructor's Resources* has been prepared for use with this textbook. For each chapter of the textbook, this manual offers interesting class demonstrations, suggestions for incorporating the Internet and other media into classroom lectures and demonstrations, and ideas for lecture elaborations and class discussions. We have contributed to this manual some general thoughts about teaching introductory psychology and some specific teaching suggestions for each chapter, including specific suggestions for cutting each chapter down for shorter courses. You can access this web-based manual through the Macmillan Learning Catalog at www.macmillanlearning.com.

Lecture Slides are complimentary to adopters of *Psychology,* Eighth Edition, and are perfect for technology novices and experts alike. Fully updated to support the new edition, they include images from the text and in-class discussion prompts. The Presentation Slides are available to download in LaunchPad and from www.macmillanlearning.com.

Macmillan Community is an online forum where teachers can find and share favorite teaching ideas and materials, including videos, animations, images, Power-Point slides, news stories, articles, web links, and lecture activities. It is also the home of Worth's abundant social media content, including tweets, blog posts, webinars, and more! Browse the site and share your favorite materials for teaching psychology at https://community.macmillan.com/community/the-psychology-community.

Additional Student Supplements

Macmillan offers a wide variety of texts to supplement students' first course in psychology.

Find out more about these titles or request an examination copy at www .macmillanlearning.com.

Pursuing Human Strengths: A Positive Psychology Guide, **Second Edition,** by Martin Bolt (Calvin College) and Dana S. Dunn (Moravian College), is a perfect way to introduce students to both the amazing field of positive psychology and their own personal strengths.

The Psychology Major's Companion: Everything You Need to Know to Get Where You Want to Go, by Dana S. Dunn (Moravian College) and Jane S. Halonen (University of West Florida), helps students to declare the psychology major if it is in their best interests to do so, to learn strategies regarding how to produce optimal gains in the major experience, and to prepare for either graduate school or a psychology-related professional life.

Psychology and the Real World: Essays Illustrating Fundamental Contributions to Society, **Second Edition,** is a superb collection of essays by major researchers that describe their landmark studies. Published in association with the not-for-profit FABBS Foundation, the new edition of this engaging reader includes Alan Kazdin's reflections on his research on treating children with severe aggressive behavior, Adam Grant's look at work and motivation, and Steven Hayes's research on mindfulness and acceptance and commitment therapy. A portion of all proceeds is donated to FABBS to support societies of cognitive, psychological, behavioral, and brain sciences.

The Critical Thinking Companion for Introductory Psychology, **Third Edition,** by Jane S. Halonen (University of West Florida) and Cynthia Gray (Beloit College), contains a guide to critical thinking strategies as well as exercises in pattern recognition, practical problem solving, creative problem solving, scientific problem solving, psychological reasoning, and perspective taking.

The Worth Expert Guide to Scientific Literacy: Thinking Like a Psychological Scientist, by Kenneth D. Keith (University of San Diego) and Bernard Beins (Ithaca College), helps students foster solid habits of scientific thought, learning to apply an empirical attitude and data-driven decision making in their lives. With this increased level of scientific literacy, students will be better able to make sense of complex scientific information and to recognize pseudoscientific claims that are not only invalid but also potentially harmful.

Acknowledgments

This edition, as we noted earlier, has been much improved by the excellent editing of Elsa Peterson. Also, this book wouldn't have happened at all if it hadn't been for Christine Cardone, the editor who brought Peter and David together and who made important contributions to every stage of the process in producing this book.

Nobody writes a textbook alone. Countless people have contributed directly or indirectly to the development and revisions of this one. We thank and acknowledge them here:

Stephanie Afful,
Lindenwood University

Erik Altmann,
Michigan State University

April Bleske-Rechek,
University of Wisconsin-Eau Claire

John Broida,
University of Southern Maine

Evangelia Chrysikou,
University of Kansas

Lauren Dattilo,
University of South Carolina

Stephanie Dennison,
University of Waterloo

Jop Groeneweg,
Leiden University

Russell Hamer,
Florida Atlantic University

Robert Hampton,
Emory University

Natalie Harrison,
The University of Alabama

Wido la Heij,
Leiden University

Nathaniel Herr,
American University

Ramona Houmanfar,
University of Nevada, Reno

Michelle Kitchen,
University of South Carolina

Michael Kitchens,
Lebanon Valley College

Steven Krauss,
Villanova University

Rachael Lapidis,
University of California San Diego

Bruce Mangan,
University of California, Berkeley

Chris Miller,
Syracuse University

Dennis Miller,
University of Missouri

Kevin Moore,
DePauw University

Barbara Oswald,
Miami University

Darrell Rudmann,
Shawnee State University

Alan Scott,
Elon University

Lisa Thomassen,
Indiana University

Anna Yocom,
The Ohio State University

Many others contributed their expertise to the development and production of this edition and deserve our heartfelt thanks. Among them are Chuck Linsmeier, V.P. of Social Sciences; Kate Nurre, Executive Marketing Manager; Melissa Rostek, Assistant Editor; Diana Blume, Design Manager; Tracey Kuehn, Director of Content Management Enhancement; Lisa Kinne, Managing Editor; Jeanne Busemeyer, of Hyde Park Publishing Services; Laura Burden, Senior Media Editor; Kerry O'Shaughnessy, Senior Content Project Manager; Paul Rohloff, Senior Workflow Project Manager; Jennifer MacMillan, Permissions Manager; Krystyna Borgen, Photo Researcher; and Matthew McAdams, Art Manager.

This book has also profited from the input, over the years, of more than 300 scholars who have contributed their thoughts to the development of previous editions. Among the many researchers who have made such contributions are (in alphabetical order): Michael Atkinson, Alan Baddeley, Robert Bell, Sharon Brehm, Nathan Brody, Stephen Ceci, Robert Cialdini, Stanley Coren, Martin Daly, Patricia Devine, John Dovidio, Nancy Eisenberg, Anders Ericsson, Victor Ferreira, Bennett Galef, Dedre Gentner, Daniel Gilbert, Norma Graham, David Z. Hambrick, Jill Hooley, David Hothersall, Philip Johnson-Laird, Annette Karmiloff-Smith, Lloyd Kaufman, Mark Leary, Joseph LeDoux, Brian Malley, Dan McAdams, Matt McGue, William Miller, Susan Mineka, Irene Miura, Gilda Morelli, Darwin Muir, Randy Nelson, Randolph Nesse, Julie Norem, Michael Numan, Hal Pashler, Holly Prigerson, Dennis Proffitt, Robert Rescorla, Emilie Rissman, Tony Robertson, David Rowe, Shepard Siegel, Robert Siegler, Anne Treisman, Harry Triandis, David Uttal, George C. Van Dyne, Connie Varnhagen, Kevin Weinfurt, and Leslie Zebrowitz.

In closing, we would like to thank our wives, Hari Kirin Kaur Khalsa and Barbara Bjorklund. Without their support and encouragement we would not have undertaken this revision or seen it through.

Peter Gray
Department of Psychology, Boston College
grayp@bc.edu
David F. Bjorklund
Department of Psychology, Florida Atlantic University
dbjorklu@fau.edu

Psychology

PART I

Foundations for the Study of Psychology

"Know thyself." These two words were inscribed on the shrine of the Oracle of Apollo at Delphi, Greece, in the sixth century BCE. Throughout recorded history, people have striven to understand the nature of being human, to fathom the mysteries of the human mind and human behavior. Today that endeavor is pursued as a science, the science of psychology. In this first, background unit, we examine some ideas that helped to bring about a science of psychology, and we preview some of the methods that help to make psychology a science.

CHAPTER

Background to the Study of Psychology

1

LEARNING OUTCOMES

After studying this chapter, you should be able to:

- Summarize three fundamental ideas for psychology.
- Define psychology and explain how it relates to other scholarly fields.
- Explain how this book is organized and how to use its learning tools.

CHAPTER OUTLINE

Three Fundamental Ideas for Psychology: A Historical Overview

The Scope of Psychology

Thoughts About Using This Book and Its Special Features

Thinking Critically About the Study of Psychology

Reflections and Connections

Key Terms

Find Out More

The human being, as far as we can tell, is the only creature that contemplates itself. Humans not only think, feel, dream, and act but also wonder how and why we do these things. Such contemplation has taken many forms, ranging from just plain wondering to folk tales and popular songs, to poetry and literature, to formal theologies and philosophies. In the late 1800s, human self-contemplation took a scientific turn, and we call that science psychology.

Welcome! Welcome to *Psychology* and to psychology—that is, to this book and to the field of study it is about. We hope you will enjoy them both. The principal questions of psychology are among the most fascinating that anyone can ask: Why do people feel, think, and behave as they do? Are we the result of our genes or our experiences, or both? How important are our goals versus our past in determining what we do? Is there a separation between mind and body? This book describes many ways by which psychologists go about exploring such questions, and many findings and ideas that help to answer them.

Let's begin with a formal definition of our subject: **Psychology** is the *science* of *behavior* and the *mind*. In this definition, **behavior** refers to the observable actions of a person or an animal. **Mind** refers to an individual's sensations, perceptions, memories, thoughts, dreams, motives, emotions, and other subjective experiences. It also refers to all of the unconscious knowledge and operating rules that are built into or stored in the brain and that provide the foundation for organizing behavior and conscious experience. **Science** refers to all attempts to answer questions through the systematic collection and logical analysis of objectively observable data. Most of the data in psychology are based on observations of behavior, because behavior is directly observable and mind is not; but psychologists often use those data to make inferences about the mind.

Psychology is also an applied discipline—one of the "helping professions." Clinical psychologists and others who work in applied areas of psychology often help people cope with everyday problems. They may also see clients with more serious mental or behavioral problems such as phobias (unreasonable fears), excessive anxiety, obsessive-compulsive behavior and thought, or depression. We will talk more of the different disciplines within psychology toward the end of this chapter and discuss mental disorders and their treatment in Chapters 15 and 16. It's worth noting that this book will generally deal with *typical* behavior and thought: how most people think and behave most of the time and the factors that influence such actions. We will also examine individual differences in thought and behavior. In some cases we will look at differences within the typical, or normal, range of functioning, such as some people being more outgoing than others, or sex differences in aggression or sensory abilities. In other cases we will examine atypical thought and behavior, such as in autism, schizophrenia, or extreme reactions to stress such as posttraumatic stress disorder (PTSD).

In this opening chapter, we do three things, all aimed at helping to prepare you for the rest of the book. First, we present a brief overview of the history and philosophy that predate and underlie modern psychology, focusing on the historical origins of three ideas that are so basic to our science that we refer to them as "fundamental ideas for psychology." Second, we describe the scope of modern psychology, especially the various explanatory concepts, or levels of analysis, that psychologists use in their attempts to understand behavior and mind. Third, we describe the features of this book and how you can use them to maximize your enjoyment of it and your ability to learn from it.

Right now, however, there is one feature of the book that we want you to notice. In the margins of the text, throughout the book, you will find numbered focus questions. The first focus question appears in the margin next to this paragraph. These are the questions that the text tries to answer, and they are also good self-test questions. An effective way to study this book is to read and think about each focus question as you come to it, before you read the adjacent paragraphs of text. This will help you focus as you read and will also help you understand and remember what you have read. Reading with the active intention of answering the focus questions is a more effective learning strategy than just passively trying to "learn" or "absorb" the material. Then, after reading the whole chapter or a section of it, review and check your knowledge by rereading each focus question and answering it in your own words.

FOCUS 1

How will you use the focus questions (such as this one) in the text's margins as a guide to reading this book?

Three Fundamental Ideas for Psychology: A Historical Overview

The founding of psychology as a formal, recognized, scientific discipline dates back to 1879, when Wilhelm Wundt opened the first university-based psychology laboratory in Leipzig, Germany. At about that same time, Wundt also authored the first psychology textbook and began mentoring psychology's first official graduate students. The first people to earn PhD degrees in psychology were Wundt's students.

But the roots of psychology predate Wundt. They were developed by people who called themselves philosophers, physicists, physiologists, and naturalists. In this section, we examine three fundamental ideas of psychology, all of which were conceived of and debated before psychology was recognized as a scientific discipline. Briefly, the ideas are these:

1. Behavior and mental experiences have physical causes that can be studied scientifically.

2. The way people behave, think, and feel is modified over time by their experiences in their environment.

3. The body's machinery, which produces behavior and mental experiences, is a product of evolution by natural selection.

The Idea of Physical Causation of Behavior

Before a science of psychology could emerge, people had to conceive of and accept the idea that questions about human behavior and the mind can, in principle, be answered scientifically. Seeds for this idea can be found in some writings of the ancient Greeks, who speculated about the senses, human intellect, and the physical basis of the mind in ways that seem remarkably modern. But these seeds lay dormant through the Middle Ages and did not begin to sprout again until the fifteenth century (the Renaissance) or to take firm hold until the eighteenth century (the Enlightenment).

Until the eighteenth century, Western philosophy was tightly bound to and constrained by religion. The church maintained that each human being consists of two distinct but intimately conjoined entities, a material body and an immaterial soul—a view referred to today as *dualism*. The body is part of the natural world and can be studied scientifically, just as inanimate matter can be studied. The soul, in contrast, is a supernatural entity that operates according to its own free will, not natural law, and therefore cannot be studied scientifically. This was the accepted religious doctrine, which—at least in most of Europe—could not be challenged publicly without risk of a charge of heresy and possible death. Yet the doctrine left some room for play, and one who played dangerously near the limits was the great French mathematician, physiologist, and philosopher René Descartes (1596–1650).

Descartes' Version of Dualism: Focus on the Body

Before Descartes, most dualists assigned the interesting qualities of the human being to the soul. The soul was deemed responsible for the body's heat, for its ability to move, for life itself. Descartes challenged this view in *Treatise of Man* (1637/1972), and even more explicitly in *The Passions of the Soul* (1649/1985). He was familiar with research on the flow of blood, and began to regard the body as an intricate, complex machine that generates its own heat and is capable of moving even without the influence of the soul. Although little was known about the nervous system in his time, Descartes' conception of the mechanical control of movement resembles our modern understanding of reflexes, which are involuntary responses to stimuli (see **Figure 1.1**).

Descartes believed that even very complex behaviors can occur through purely mechanical means, without involvement of the soul. Consistent with church doctrine, he contended that nonhuman animals do not have souls, and he pointed out a logical implication of this contention: Any activity performed by humans that is qualitatively no different from the behavior of a nonhuman animal can, in theory, occur without the soul. If my dog (who can do some wondrous things) is just a machine, then a good deal of what we do—such as eating, drinking, sleeping, running, panting, and occasionally going in circles—might occur purely mechanically as well.

In Descartes' view, the one essential ability that humans have but dogs do not is *thought,* which Descartes defined as conscious deliberation and judgment. Previous philosophers ascribed many functions to the soul, but Descartes ascribed just one—thought. Still, even in his discussion of thought, Descartes tended to focus on the body's machinery. To be useful, thought must be responsive to the sensory input channeled into the body through the eyes, ears, and other sense organs, and it must be capable of directing the body's movements by acting on the muscles.

FOCUS 2

What was Descartes' version of dualism? How did it help pave the way for a science of psychology?

FIGURE 1.1 Descartes' depiction of a reflex Descartes believed that reflexes occur through purely mechanical means. In describing this figure, Descartes (1637/1972) suggested that the fire causes movement in the nearby particles of skin, pulling on a "thread" (that runs "C" to "C" along the back) going to the brain, which, in turn, causes a pore to open in the brain, allowing fluid to flow through a "small conduit" to the muscles that withdraw the foot. What Descartes called a "thread" and a "small conduit" are today called nerves, and we now know that nerves operate through electrical means, not through physical pulling or the shunting of fluids.

FIGURE 1.2 Descartes' depiction of how the soul receives information through the eyes Descartes believed that the human soul is housed in the pineal gland, depicted here as the tear-shaped structure in the center of the head. In describing this figure, Descartes (1637/1972) suggested that light from the arrow enters the eyes and opens pores in structures that we now know as the optic nerves. Fluid flows from the eyes through the opened pores, causing movement in the pineal gland, which, in Descartes' words, "renders the idea" of the arrow to the soul.

Published in Descartes, R. (1972). *Treatise of Man.* Cambridge, MA: Harvard University Press.

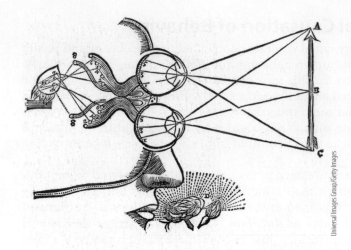

Universal Images Group/Getty Images

How can the thinking soul interact with the physical machine—the senses, organs, muscles, and other parts of the body? Descartes suggested that the soul, though not physical, acts on the body at a particular physical location: a small organ (now known as the pineal body) buried between the two hemispheres (halves) of the brain (see **Figure 1.2**).

Threadlike structures, which we now call nerves or neurons, bring sensory information by physical means into the brain, where the soul receives the information and, by nonphysical means, thinks about it. On the basis of those thoughts, the soul then wills movements to occur and executes its will by triggering physical actions in nerves that, in turn, act on muscles. Descartes' dualism, with its heavy emphasis on the body, certainly helped open the door for a science of psychology.

Descartes' theory is popular among nonscientists even today, because it acknowledges the roles of sense organs, nerves, and muscles in behavior without violating people's religious beliefs or intuitive feelings that conscious thought occurs on a nonphysical plane. But it has serious limitations, both as a philosophy and as a foundation for a science of psychology. As a philosophy, it stumbles on the question of how a nonmaterial entity (the soul) can have a material effect (movement of the body), or how the body can follow natural law and yet be moved by a soul that does not (Campbell, 1970). As a foundation for psychology, the theory sets strict limits, which few psychologists would accept today, on what can and cannot be understood scientifically. The whole realm of thought, and all behaviors that are guided by thought, are out of bounds for scientific analysis if they are the products of a willful soul.

FOCUS 3

What reasons can you think of for why Descartes' theory, despite its intuitive appeal, was unsuitable for a complete psychology?

FOCUS 4

How did Hobbes's materialism help lay the groundwork for a science of psychology?

Thomas Hobbes and the Philosophy of Materialism

Around the same time that Descartes was developing his machine-oriented version of dualism, English philosopher Thomas Hobbes (1588–1679) was going much further. In his book *Leviathan,* and in a shorter work called *Human Nature,* Hobbes argued that spirit, or soul, is a meaningless concept and that nothing exists but matter and energy, a philosophy now known as ***materialism*** (Hobbes, 1651/2010). In Hobbes's view, all human behavior, including the seemingly voluntary choices we make, can be understood in terms of physical processes in the body, especially the brain. Conscious thought, he maintained, is purely a product of the brain's machinery and therefore subject to natural law. This philosophy places no theoretical limit on what psychologists might study scientifically. Most of Hobbes's work was directed toward politics and government, but his ideas helped inspire a school of thought about the mind known as empiricism, which we will discuss below.

Nineteenth-Century Physiology: Learning About the Machine

The idea that the body, including the brain, is a machine helped to promote the science of physiology—the study of the body's machinery. By the early 1800s, considerable progress had been made in this endeavor, and during the ensuing decades discoveries were made about the nervous system that contributed significantly to the origins of scientific psychology.

Increased Understanding of Reflexes   One especially important development for the emergence of psychology was an increased understanding of reflexes. The basic arrangement of the nervous system—consisting of a central nervous system (brain and spinal cord) and peripheral nerves that connect the central nervous system to sense organs and muscles—was well understood by the beginning of the nineteenth century. In 1822, the French physiologist François Magendie demonstrated that nerves entering the spinal cord contain two separate pathways: one for carrying messages into the central nervous system from the skin's sensory receptors and one for carrying messages out to operate muscles. Through experiments with animals, scientists began to learn about the neural connections that underlie simple reflexes, such as the automatic withdrawal response to a pinprick. They also found that certain brain areas, when active, could either enhance or inhibit such reflexes.

Some of these physiologists began to suggest that all human behavior occurs through reflexes—that even so-called voluntary actions are actually complex reflexes involving higher parts of the brain. One of the most eloquent proponents of this view, known as *reflexology,* was the Russian physiologist I. M. Sechenov. In his monograph *Reflexes of the Brain,* Sechenov (1863/1935) argued that every human action, "[b]e it a child laughing at the sight of toys, or . . . Newton enunciating universal laws and writing them on paper," can in theory be understood as a reflex. All human actions, he claimed, are initiated by stimuli in the environment. The stimuli act on a person's sensory receptors, setting in motion a chain of events in the nervous system that culminates in the muscle movements that constitute the action. Sechenov's work inspired another Russian physiologist, Ivan Pavlov (1849–1936), whose work on reflexes (discussed in Chapter 8) played a crucial role in the development of a scientific psychology.

The Concept of Localization of Function in the Brain   Another important advance in nineteenth-century physiology was the concept of localization of function, the idea that specific parts of the brain serve specific functions in the production of mental experience and behavior. In Germany, Johannes Müller (1838/1965) proposed that the different qualities of sensory experience come about because the nerves from different sense organs excite different parts of the brain. Thus we experience vision when one part of the brain is active, hearing when another part is active, and so on. In France, Pierre Flourens (1824/1965) performed experiments with animals showing that damage to different parts of the brain produces different kinds of deficits in animals' abilities to move. And Paul Broca (1861/1965), also in France, published evidence that people who suffer injury to a very specific area of the brain's left hemisphere lose the ability to speak but do not lose other mental abilities.

■ **A seventeenth-century mechanical man**   Mechanical clocks represented the pinnacle of technological achievement of the seventeenth century, comparable to computers today. For amusement, clock-like mechanisms were used to operate robotic, humanoid figures, as illustrated here. Such mechanical men helped to inspire, in Descartes and Hobbes, the idea that actual human beings might also operate by mechanical means, not requiring a nonmaterial spirit to move them.

Bering Center, Division of Work & Industry, National Museum of American History, Smithsonian Institution

FOCUS 5

How did the nineteenth-century understanding of the nervous system inspire a theory of behavior called reflexology?

FOCUS 6

How did discoveries of localization of function in the brain help establish the idea that the mind can be studied scientifically?

■ **Localization of function taken to the extreme** Work by Broca and others showed that particular cognitive functions, such as language, are controlled by specific areas of the brain. This led to the popular belief that all aspects of thought, emotion, and personality can be located in the brain, culminating in the pseudoscience known as *phrenology*, developed by the German physician Franz Joseph Gall. Gall and his followers believed that the mind consists of mental faculties that are located at specific sites in the brain. By feeling bumps on the skull, phrenologists claimed they could infer the size of various areas and describe a person's psychological characteristics. Although soundly discredited, phrenology influenced nineteenth-century psychiatry and is broadly consistent with modern neuroscience's idea of localization of function.

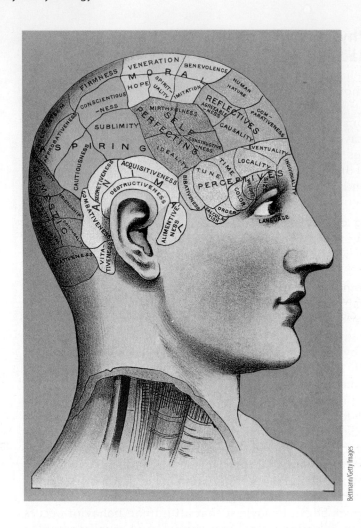

Bettmann/Getty Images

All such evidence about the relationships between mind and brain helped to lay the groundwork for a scientific psychology, because it gave substance to the idea of a material basis for mental processes.

The Idea That the Mind and Behavior Are Shaped by Experience

Besides helping to inspire research in physiology, the materialist philosophy of seventeenth-century England led quite directly to a school of thought about the mind known as *British empiricism,* carried on by such British philosophers as John Locke (1632–1704), David Hartley (1705–1759), James Mill (1773–1836), and John Stuart Mill (1806–1873). *Empiricism*, in this context, refers to the idea that human knowledge and thought derive ultimately from sensory experience (vision, hearing, touch, and so forth). If we are machines, we are machines that learn. Our senses provide the input that allows us to acquire knowledge of the world around us, and this knowledge allows us to think about that world and behave adaptively within it. The essence of empiricist philosophy is poetically expressed in the following often-quoted passage from Locke's *An Essay Concerning Human Understanding* (1690/1975, p. 104):

> Let us suppose the mind to be, as we say, white paper, void of all characters, without any ideas; how comes it to be furnished? Whence comes it by that vast store, which the busy and boundless fancy of man has painted on it, with an almost endless variety? Whence has it all the materials of reason and knowledge? To this I answer, in one word, from experience. In that, all our knowledge is founded; and from that it ultimately derives itself.

Locke viewed a child's mind as a *tabula rasa*, or *blank slate*, and believed it is experience that serves as the chalk that writes on and fills the slate. The human brain has limitations, of course—we can't detect objects using echolocation as bats and dolphins can, for instance. But Locke argued that, outside of these extremes, children are born with no dispositions or preferences to influence how they learn and develop. From this perspective, there is no "human nature" other than an ability to adapt one's behavior to the demands of the environment.

The Empiricist Concept of Association by Contiguity

In keeping with materialist philosophy, Locke and the other British empiricists argued that thoughts are not products of free will but rather reflections of a person's experiences in the physical and social environment. All the contents of the mind derive from, and relate directly to, the environment. According to the empiricists, the fundamental units of the mind are elementary ideas that come directly from sensory experiences and are linked together to form complex ideas and thoughts.

The most basic operating principle of the mind's machinery, according to the empiricists, is the law of ***association by contiguity***, an idea originally proposed by Aristotle in the fourth century BCE. *Contiguity* refers to closeness in space or time, and the law of association by contiguity can be stated as follows: If a person experiences two environmental events (stimuli, or sensations) at the same time or one right after the other (contiguously), those two events will become associated (bound together) in the person's mind, such that the thought of one event will, in the future, tend to elicit the thought of the other.

As a simple illustration, consider a child's experiences when seeing and biting into an apple. In doing so, the child receives a set of sensations that produce in her mind such elementary ideas as red color, spherical shape, and sweet, tart taste. The child may also, at the same time, hear the sound *apple* uttered by a nearby adult. Because all these sensations are experienced together, they become associated in the child's mind. Together, they form the complex idea "apple." Because of association by contiguity, the thought of any of the apple's sensory qualities will tend to call forth the thought of all its other sensory qualities. Thus, when the child hears *apple,* she will think of the red color, the spherical shape, and the sweet, tart taste. Or, when the child sees an apple, she will think of the sound *apple* and imagine the taste.

The empiricists contended that even their own most complex philosophical ponderings could, in theory, be understood as amalgams of elementary ideas that became linked together in their minds as a result of contiguities in their experiences. John Stuart Mill (1843/1875) referred to this sort of analysis of the mind as mental chemistry. Complex ideas and thoughts are formed from combinations of elementary ideas, much as chemical compounds are formed from combinations of chemical elements.

As you will discover in Chapters 8 and 9, the law of association by contiguity is still regarded as a fundamental principle of learning and memory. More broadly, most of psychology—throughout its history—has studied the effects of people's environmental experiences on their thoughts, feelings, and behavior. The impact of empiricist philosophy on psychology has been enormous.

The Nativist Response to Empiricism

For every philosophy that contains part of the truth, there is an opposite philosophy that contains another part of it. The opposite of empiricism is **nativism**, the view that the most basic forms of human knowledge and the basic operating

FOCUS 7

How would you explain the origin of complex ideas and thoughts according to British empiricism? What role did the law of association by contiguity play in this philosophy?

■ **A complex idea** To the empiricist philosophers, even as simple a concept as that of "apple" is a complex idea, consisting of a set of elementary sensations—of shape, color, and taste—that become associated in the person's mind through experiences with apples.

Amelia Fox/Shutterstock

FOCUS 8

How would you describe the influence that empiricist philosophy has had on psychology?

FOCUS 9

Why is the ability to learn dependent on inborn knowledge? In Kant's nativist philosophy, what is the distinction between *a priori* knowledge and *a posteriori* knowledge?

A fun robot that can learn This computer-driven robot, designed by researchers at the University of California, San Diego, can keep track of some of its previous interactions with children and incorporate them into its future responses to the children. Such machines can learn only the kinds of information that they are programmed to learn. Similarly, according to nativist philosophers, human learning is limited by the information and operating rules that are genetically programmed into the human brain.

Alan Decker

characteristics of the mind, which provide the foundation for human nature, are native to the human mind—that is, are inborn and do not have to be acquired from experience.

Take a sheet of white paper and present it with all the learning experiences that a normal human child might encounter (a suggestion made by Ornstein, 1991). The paper will learn nothing. Talk to it, sing to it, give it apples and oranges, take it for trips in the country, hug it and kiss it; it will learn nothing about language, music, fruit, nature, or love. To learn anything, any entity must contain some initial machinery already built into it. At a minimum, that machinery must include an ability to sense some aspects of the environment, some means of interpreting and recording those sensations, some rules for storing and combining those sensory records, and some rules for recalling them when needed. The mind, contrary to Locke's poetic assertion, must come with some initial furnishings in order for it to be furnished further through experience.

While empiricist philosophy flourished in England, nativist philosophy took root in Germany, led by such thinkers as Gottfried Wilhelm von Leibniz (1646–1716) and Immanuel Kant (1724–1804). In his *Critique of Pure Reason* (1781/1908), Kant distinguished between *a priori* knowledge, which is built into the human brain and does not have to be learned, and *a posteriori* knowledge, which one gains from experience in the environment. Without the first, argued the nativists, a person could not acquire the second. As an illustration, Kant referred to a child's learning of language. The specific words and grammar that the child acquires are *a posteriori* knowledge, but the child's ability to learn a language depends on *a priori* knowledge. The latter includes built-in rules about what to attend to and how to store and organize the linguistic sounds that are heard, in ways that allow the child eventually to make sense of the sounds. Kant also argued that to make sense of the physical world, the child must already have certain fundamental physical concepts, such as the concepts of space and time, built into his or her mind. Without such built-in concepts, a child would have no capacity for seeing an apple as spherical or for detecting the temporal contiguity of two events.

The Idea That the Machinery of Behavior and Mind Evolved Through Natural Selection

Kant understood that the human mind has some innate furnishings, but he had no scientific explanation of how those furnishings could have been built or why they function as they do. That understanding finally came in 1859 when the English naturalist Charles Darwin (1809–1882) published *The Origin of Species,* a book that was destined to revolutionize biology, mark a new age in philosophy, and provide, along with the developments in physiology, a biological grounding for psychology.

Natural Selection and the Analysis of the Functions of Behavior

Darwin's fundamental idea (explained more fully in Chapter 3) was that living things evolve gradually, over generations, by a process of natural selection. Individuals whose inherited characteristics are well adapted to their local environment are more likely to survive and reproduce than are other, less-well adapted individuals. At each generation, random changes in the hereditary material produce variations in offspring, and those variations that improve the chance of survival and reproduction are passed from generation to generation in increasing numbers.

FOCUS 10

How did Darwin's theory of natural selection offer a scientific foundation for explaining behavior by describing its functions? How did it provide a basis for understanding the origin of *a priori* knowledge?

Because of natural selection, species of plants and animals change gradually over time in ways that allow them to meet the changing demands of their environments. Because of evolution, the innate characteristics of any given species of plant or animal can be examined for the functions they serve in helping the individuals to survive and reproduce. For example, to understand why finches have stout beaks and warblers have slender beaks, one must know what foods the birds eat and how they use their beaks to obtain those foods. The same principle that applies to anatomy applies to behavior. Through natural selection, living things have acquired tendencies to behave in ways that promote their survival and reproduction. A key word here is *function*. While physiologists were examining the neural mechanisms of behavior, and empiricist philosophers were analyzing lawful relationships between behavior and the environment, Darwin was studying the functions of behavior—the ways in which an organism's behavior helps it to survive and reproduce.

Applying Darwin's Ideas to Psychology

In *The Origin of Species*, Darwin discussed only plants and nonhuman animals, but in later writings he made it clear that he viewed humans as no exception. We humans also evolved through natural selection, and our anatomy and behavior can be analyzed in the same ways as those of other living things. In fact, Darwin can be thought of as the first evolutionary psychologist, writing in 1859, "In the distant future . . . psychology will be based on a new foundation, that of the necessary acquirement of each mental power and capacity by gradation. Light will be thrown on the origins of man and his history" (p. 488).

In a book titled *The Expression of the Emotions in Man and Animals*, Darwin (1872/1965) illustrated how evolutionary thinking can contribute to a scientific understanding of human behavior. He argued that the basic forms of human emotional expressions (such as laughing and crying) are inherited, as are those of other animals, and may have evolved because the ability to communicate one's emotions or intentions improves one's chances of survival. Darwin's work provided psychology with a scientific way of thinking about all the inborn universal tendencies that constitute human nature. The inherited mechanisms underlying human emotions, drives, perception, learning, and reasoning came about gradually because they promoted the survival and reproduction of our ancestors. One approach to understanding such characteristics is to analyze their evolutionary functions—the specific ways in which they promote survival and reproduction.

If Kant had been privy to Darwin's insight, he would likely have said that the inherent furnishings of the mind, which make it possible for children to learn language, to learn about the physical world, to experience human drives and emotions, and, more generally, to behave as human beings and not as blank sheets of paper, came about through the process of natural selection, which gradually built all these capacities into the brain's machinery. Darwin, perhaps more than anyone else, helped convince scholars that we humans, despite our pretensions, are part of the natural world and can be understood through the methods of science. In this way he helped make the world ripe for psychology.

We have now reached the end of the first section of the chapter, and, before moving on, we want to point out a second feature of the book that is designed to help you study it. At the end of each major section of each chapter is a *section review* chart that summarizes the section's main ideas. The chart is organized hierarchically: the main idea or topic of the section is at the top, the sub-ideas or subtopics are at the next level down, and specific facts and lines of evidence pertaining to each sub-idea or subtopic fill the lower parts. A good way to review, before going on, is to read each item in the chart and think about it. Start at the top and think about the main idea or purpose of the whole section. How would you explain it to another person? Then go down each column, one by one; think about how the idea

■ **Charles Darwin with his eldest child, William.** Darwin's principle of evolution by natural selection helped provide a scientific footing for psychology. The principle links humans to the rest of the biological world and explains the origin of brain mechanisms that promote the individual's survival and reproduction.Taking the opportunity to learn from his own family, Darwin recorded detailed observations of his children's behavior in infancy.

Public domain

FOCUS 11

How can you use the reviews at the end of each major section to guide your thought and review before going on to the next section?

or topic heading the column pertains to the larger idea or topic above it and how it is supported or elaborated upon by the more specific statements below it. If you are unsure of the meaning of any item in the chart, or can't elaborate on that item in a meaningful way, go back and read the relevant part of the chapter again before moving on. Another way to review is to reread the focus questions in the margins and make sure you can answer each of them.

SECTION REVIEW

Psychology—the science of behavior and the mind—rests on prior intellectual developments.

Physical Causation of Behavior	The Role of Experience	The Evolutionary Basis of Mind and Behavior
▪ Descartes' dualism placed more emphasis on the role of the body than had previous versions of dualism. Hobbes's materialism held that behavior is completely a product of the body and thus physically caused. ▪ To the degree that behavior and the mind have a physical basis, they are open to study just like the rest of the natural world. ▪ Nineteenth-century physiological studies of reflexes and localization of function in the brain demonstrated the applicability of science to mental processes and behavior.	▪ The British empiricists claimed that all thought and knowledge are rooted in sensory experience. ▪ Empiricists used the law of association by contiguity to explain how sensory experiences can combine to form complex thoughts. ▪ In contrast to empiricism, nativism asserts that some knowledge is innate and that such knowledge provides the foundation for human nature, including the human abilities to learn.	▪ Darwin proposed that natural selection underlies the evolution of behavioral tendencies (along with anatomical characteristics) that promote survival and reproduction. ▪ Darwin's thinking led to a focus on the functions of behavior. ▪ Natural selection also offered a scientific foundation for nativist views of the mind.

The Scope of Psychology

Psychology is a vast and diverse field. Every question about behavior and mental experience that is potentially answerable by scientific means is within its scope. One way to become oriented to this grand science is to preview the various kinds of explanatory concepts that psychologists use.

Varieties of Explanations in Psychology and Their Application to Sexual Jealousy

Psychologists strive to *explain* mental experiences and behavior. To explain is to identify causes. What causes us to do what we do, feel what we feel, perceive what we perceive, or believe what we believe? What causes us to eat in some conditions and not in others; to cooperate sometimes and to cheat at other times; to feel angry, frightened, happy, or guilty; to dream; to hate or love; to see red as different from blue; to remember or forget; to suddenly see solutions to problems that we couldn't see before; to learn our native language so easily when we are very young; to become depressed or anxious? This is a sample of the kinds of questions that psychologists try to answer and that are addressed in this book.

The causes of mental experiences and behavior are complex and can be analyzed at various levels. The term **level of analysis**, as used in psychology and other sciences, refers to the level, or type, of causal process that is studied. More specifically, in psychology, a person's behavior or mental experience can be examined at these levels:

- *neural* (brain as cause),
- *physiological* (internal chemical functions, such as hormones, as cause),

- *genetic* (genes as cause),
- *evolutionary* (natural selection as cause),
- *learning* (the individual's prior experiences with the environment as cause),
- *cognitive* (the individual's knowledge or beliefs as cause),
- *social* (the influence of other people as cause),
- *cultural* (the culture in which the person develops as cause),
- *developmental* (age-related changes as cause).

You will find many examples of each of these nine levels of analysis in this book. Now, as an overview, we'll describe each of them very briefly. For the purpose of organization of this presentation, it is convenient to group the nine levels of analysis into two clusters. The first cluster—consisting of neural, physiological, genetic, and evolutionary explanations—is most directly biological. The second cluster, consisting of all of the remaining levels, is less directly biological and has to do with effects of experiences and knowledge.

Any given type of behavior or mental experience can, in principle, be analyzed at any of the nine levels. As you will see, the different levels of analysis correspond with different research specialties in psychology. To illustrate the different levels of analysis and research specialties in a real-world context, in the following paragraphs we will apply them to the phenomenon of sexual jealousy. For our purposes here, *sexual jealousy* can be defined as the set of emotions and behaviors that result when a person believes that his or her relationship with a sexual partner or potential sexual partner is threatened by the partner's involvement with another person.

■ **Sexual jealousy in humans** Like any common human behavioral predisposition, sexual jealousy can be studied at the neural, physiological, genetic, evolutionary, learning, cognitive, social, cultural, and developmental levels of analysis.

Explanations That Focus on Biological Processes

We can find biological explanations at many different levels, from the actions of neurons and hormones, to the functions of genes, and—taking a really big-picture perspective—the role of evolution.

Neural Explanations All behaviors and mental experiences are products of the nervous system. Therefore, one logical route to understanding is to explore how the nervous system produces a particular behavior or experience. The research specialty that centers on this level of explanation is **behavioral neuroscience**. In recent years, all areas of psychology have realized the importance of the brain in explaining behavior, and you will often see reference to more specific fields of neuroscience, including **cognitive neuroscience**, developmental neuroscience, social neuroscience, and clinical neuroscience.

Some behavioral neuroscientists study individual neurons (nerve cells) or small groups of neurons to determine how their characteristics contribute to particular psychological processes, such as learning. Others map out and study larger brain regions and pathways that are directly involved in particular categories of behavior or experience. For example, they might identify brain regions that are most involved in speaking grammatically, or in perceiving the shapes of objects, or in experiencing an emotion such as fear.

In one of the few studies to investigate neurological correlates of jealousy in humans, male college students induced to feel jealous showed greater activation in the left frontal cortex of their brains, as measured by electroencephalogram (EEG) recordings (described in Chapter 4) toward their "sexually" desired partner (Harmon-Jones et al., 2009). Previous research had shown that activation of the left frontal cortex is associated with approach-motivation, typically associated with pleasurable activities, whereas activation in the right frontal cortex is associated with withdrawal-motivation, typically corresponding to avoidance of negative stimuli.

FOCUS 12

How do neural, physiological, genetic, and evolutionary explanations differ from one another? How would you apply these explanations toward an understanding of jealousy?

■ **Viewing the active brain** In recent years, the field of behavioral neuroscience has advanced greatly, due in part to new techniques for assessing the amount of activity that occurs in specific brain locations as a person performs mental tasks. These neuroimaging techniques are discussed in Chapter 4.

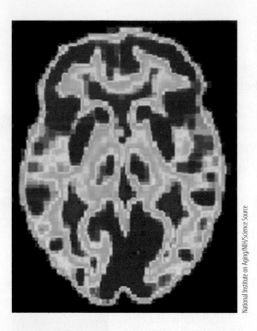

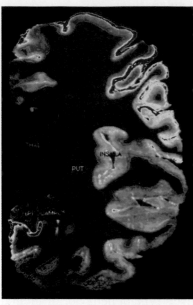

The researchers suggested that, at least initially, the primary motivational state in jealousy is one of approach, possibly aimed at preventing a threatening liaison between the target of one's jealousy and another person, or at re-establishing their primary relationship. Other researchers have found sex differences in the brain's reaction to statements depicting sexual and emotional jealousy, with men showing greater activation than women in brain regions associated with aggression, such as the amygdala (Takahashi et al., 2006).

Jealousy can also be studied in nonhuman animals, and at least one neuro-imaging study has been conducted with macaque monkeys (Rilling et al., 2004). The researchers made male monkeys jealous by exposing each one to the sight of a female, with which he had previously mated, being courted by another male. During this experience, the researchers measured the male monkey's brain activity using a technique called positron emission tomography (PET, described in Chapter 4). The result was a preliminary mapping of specific brain areas that become especially active during the experience of sexual jealousy in male macaques.

A next step in this line of research might be to try to increase or decrease jealous behavior in monkeys by artificially activating or inactivating those same areas of the brain. Researchers might also examine people who have, through strokes or other accidents, suffered damage to those brain areas to determine if they have any deficits in the experience of jealousy. These are the kinds of techniques regularly used by behavioral neuroscientists.

Physiological Explanations Closely related to behavioral neuroscience is the specialty of *physiological psychology*, or **biopsychology**. Biopsychologists study the ways hormones and drugs act on the brain to alter behavior and experience, either in humans or in nonhuman animals. For example, we're all familiar with the role that hormones play during puberty, influencing bodily growth and emotions; another example is the role of the steroid hormone cortisol in response to stress. Might hormones play a role in jealousy? Several studies suggest that they do (Cobey et al., 2011; Geary et al., 2001). For example, David Geary and his colleagues (2001) investigated this in a pair of studies, focusing mainly on young women. Geary reported that levels of the hormone estradiol were related to intensity of jealousy feelings, especially during the time of high fertility in women's menstrual cycle. Estradiol, along with progesterone, is found in many common hormone-based birth-control methods. The connection between jealousy and estradiol suggests that some of women's reproductive-related behaviors and emotions may be significantly influenced by hormones, which may be disrupted by the use of hormone-based birth control.

Genetic Explanations Genes are the units of heredity that provide the codes for building the entire body, including the brain. Differences among individuals in the genes they inherit can cause differences in the brain and, therefore, differences in mental experiences and behavior. The research specialty that attempts to explain psychological differences among individuals in terms of differences in their genes is called *behavioral genetics*.

Some behavioral geneticists study nonhuman animals. For example, they may deliberately modify animals' genes to observe the effects on behavior. Others study people. To estimate the role of genes in differences among people in some psychological trait, researchers might assess the degree to which people's genetic relatedness correlates with their degree of similarity in that trait. A finding that close genetic relatives are more similar in the trait than are more distant relatives is evidence that genes contribute to variation in the trait. Behavioral geneticists might also try to identify specific genes that contribute to a trait by comparing the DNA (genetic material) of people who differ in that trait.

People differ in the degree to which they are prone to sexual jealousy. Some become jealous with much less provocation than do others. To measure the role of genetic differences in such behavioral differences, researchers might assess sexual jealousy in twins. If identical twins, who share all their genes with each other, are much more similar in jealousy than are same-sex fraternal twins, who are no more closely related than are other siblings, that would indicate that much of the variation among people in sexual jealousy is caused by variation in genes. A next step might be to find out just which genes are involved in these differences and how they act on the brain to influence jealousy. So far, to our knowledge, only one behavioral genetic study has been conducted to explore this question; it involves data from 3,197 twin pairs of the Swedish Twin Registry (Walum et al., 2013). The researchers reported that about 32% of individual differences in self-reported sexual jealousy could be accounted for by genes. Much more behavioral genetic research has been done on the topics of intelligence, personality, and mental disorders, and will be described in Chapters 10, 14, and 15.

Evolutionary Explanations All the basic biological machinery underlying behavior and mental experience is a product of evolution by natural selection. One way to explain universal human characteristics, therefore, is to explain how or why they came about in the course of evolution. The research specialty concerned with this level of analysis is called *evolutionary psychology*.

Some evolutionary psychologists are interested in the actual routes by which particular behavioral capacities or tendencies evolved. For instance, researchers studying the evolution of smiling have gained clues about how smiling originated

■ **Sexual jealousy in ducks** Ducks, such as these blue-winged teals, form monogamous pair bonds, at least for the duration of the breeding season. When an intruder encroaches, the member of the pair that is the same sex as the intruder drives the intruder away. Such jealous-like behavior helps to keep the mated pair intact.

Cliff Beittel

in our ancestors by examining smile-like behaviors in other primates, including chimpanzees (discussed in Chapter 3). Most evolutionary psychologists are interested in identifying the evolutionary functions—that is, the survival or reproductive benefits—of the types of behaviors and mental experiences that they study. In later chapters we will discuss evolutionary, functional explanations of many human behavioral tendencies, drives, and emotions.

Evolutionary psychologists have examined the forms and consequences of human jealousy in some detail to identify its possible benefits for reproduction (Buss, 2000; Easton & Shackelford, 2009). They have also studied behaviors in various animals that appear to be similar to human jealousy. Such research supports the view that jealousy functions to promote long-term mating bonds. All animals that form long-term bonds exhibit jealous-like behaviors (Panksepp, 2013); they behave in ways that seem designed to drive off, or in other ways discourage, any individuals that would lure away their mates.

Explanations That Focus on Environmental Experiences, Knowledge, and Development

Humans, perhaps more than any other animal, are sensitive to conditions of their environment and change their behavior as a result of experience. Psychologists have developed different ways of explaining how people (as well as nonhuman animals) change in response to their environment, including learning (changes in overt behavior), cognition (changes in thinking), social, cultural (changes due to living with others), and development (changes over time).

Learning Explanations Essentially all forms of human behavior and mental experience are modifiable by learning; that is, they can be influenced by prior experiences. Such experiences can affect our emotions, drives, perceptions, thoughts, skills, and habits. Most psychologists are interested in the ways that learning can influence the types of behavior that they study. The psychological specialty that is most directly and exclusively concerned with explaining behavior in terms of learning is appropriately called **learning psychology**. For historical reasons (explained in Chapter 8), this specialty is also called *behavioral psychology*.

Learning psychologists might, for example, attempt to explain compulsive gambling in terms of patterns of rewards that the person has experienced in the past while gambling. They also might seek to explain a person's fears in terms of the person's previous experiences with the feared objects or situations. They might also conduct research, with animals or with people, to understand the most efficient ways to learn new skills (discussed in Chapter 8).

As stated earlier, differences in sexual jealousy among individuals derive partly from genetic differences. Learning psychology has found that they also derive partly from differences in past experiences. Jealous reactions that prove to be effective in obtaining rewards (e.g., that succeed in repelling competitors or attracting renewed affection from the mate) may increase in frequency with experience, and ineffective reactions may decrease. People and animals may also learn, through experience, what sorts of cues are potential signs of infidelity in their mates, and those cues may come to trigger jealous reactions. The intensity of sexual jealousy, the specific manner in which it is expressed, and the environmental cues that trigger it can all be influenced, in many ways, by learning. A learning psychologist might study any of those effects.

Cognitive Explanations The term *cognition* refers to information in the mind—that is, to information that is somehow stored and activated by the workings of the brain. Such information includes thoughts, beliefs, and all forms of memories. Some information

FOCUS 13

How do learning and cognitive explanations differ? How would you apply each of them toward an understanding of jealousy?

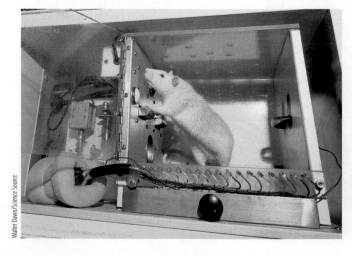

■ **Rat learning to press a button** To identify basic principles of learning, some learning psychologists study the processes by which animals learn simple responses for rewards. This thirsty rat receives a drop of water to drink each time it presses the button.

Walter Dawn/Science Source

is conscious, in the sense that the person is aware of it and can describe it, and other information is unconscious but can still influence one's conscious experiences and behavior. One way to explain any behavioral action or mental experience is to relate it to the cognitions (items of mental information) that underlie that action or experience. Note that cognition, unlike learning, is never measured directly but is inferred from observable behaviors. The specialty focusing on this level of analysis is called *cognitive psychology*.

Think of mental information as analogous to a computer's software and data, which influence the way the computer responds to new input. Cognitive psychologists are interested in specifying the types of mental information that underlie and make possible the behaviors they study. For instance, a cognitive psychologist who is interested in reasoning might seek to understand the rules by which people manipulate information in their minds in order to solve particular kinds of problems (discussed in Chapter 10). A cognitive psychologist who is interested in racial prejudice might attempt to specify the particular beliefs—including unconscious as well as conscious beliefs—that promote prejudiced behavior (discussed in Chapter 13). Cognitive psychologists are also interested in the basic processes by which learned information is stored and organized in the mind, which means that they are particularly interested in memory (discussed in Chapter 9).

Snapshots

"I don't care that you slept with him, Claire, but how dare you laugh at his jokes!"

In general, cognitive psychology differs from the psychology of learning in its focus on the mind. Learning psychologists typically relate learning experiences directly to behavioral changes and are relatively unconcerned with the mental processes that mediate such relationships. To a learning psychologist, experience in the environment leads to change in behavior. To a cognitive psychologist, experience in the environment leads to *change in knowledge or beliefs,* which in turn leads to change in behavior.

In studying jealousy, a cognitive psychologist would define jealousy as a set of beliefs—beliefs about the behavior of one's mate and some third party, about the vulnerability of one's own relationship with the mate, and about the appropriateness or inappropriateness of possible ways to react. One way to study jealousy, from a cognitive perspective, is to ask people to recall episodes of jealousy from their own lives and to describe the thoughts that went through their minds, the emotions they felt, and the actions they took. A wide variety of thoughts can enter one's mind in the jealous state, which can lead to actions ranging from romantic expressions of love, to increased attention to potential sexual competitors, to murderous violence (Maner et al., 2009). Psychotherapists who use cognitive methods to treat cases of pathological jealousy try to help their clients change their thought patterns, so they will no longer misperceive every instance of attention that their mate pays to someone else as a threat to their relationship, and so they will focus on constructive rather than destructive ways of reacting to actual threats (Ecker, 2012).

Social Explanations We humans are, by nature, social animals. We need to cooperate and get along with others in order to survive and reproduce. For this reason, our behavior is strongly influenced by our perceptions of others. We use others as models of how to behave, and we often strive, consciously or unconsciously, to behave in ways that will lead others to approve of us. One way to explain mental experiences and behavior, therefore, is to identify how they are influenced by other people or by one's beliefs about other people. The specialty focusing on this level of explanation is called *social psychology* (discussed in Chapter 13).

An often-quoted definition of social psychology describes it as "the attempt to understand and explain how the thought, feeling, and behavior of individuals are influenced by the actual, imagined, or implied presence of others" (Allport, 1968, p. 3).

 FOCUS 14

How do social and cultural explanations differ? How would you apply each of them toward an understanding of jealousy?

Social psychologists commonly attempt to explain behavior in terms of *social pressure* influences such as conformity to social norms, obedience to authority, or living up to others' expectations.

Social-psychological explanations are often phrased in terms of people's conscious or unconscious beliefs about the potential social consequences of acting in a particular way. This means that many social-psychological explanations are also cognitive explanations. Indeed, many of today's social psychologists refer to their specialty as *social cognition*. A social psychologist interested in physical fitness, for example, might attempt to explain how people's willingness to exercise is influenced by their beliefs about the degree to which other people exercise and their beliefs about how others will react to them if they do or do not exercise.

A social psychologist interested in jealousy might focus on the norms and beliefs concerning romance, mating, and jealousy that surround and influence the jealous person. Are the beloved's flirtations with a third person within or outside the realm of what is considered acceptable by other dating or married couples? How do others react in similar situations? Would others approve or disapprove of a given type of revenge? Implicitly or explicitly, the answers to such questions influence the way the jealous person feels and behaves. An understanding of such influences constitutes a social-psychological explanation of the person's feelings and behavior.

Cultural Explanations We can predict some aspects of a person's behavior by knowing about the *culture*—the general customs and beliefs of a social group—in which that person grew up. Cultures vary in language or dialect, in the values and attitudes they foster, and in the kinds of behaviors and emotions they encourage or discourage. Researchers have found consistent cultural differences even in the ways that people perceive, remember, and think about aspects of their physical environment (discussed in Chapters 9 and 10). The psychological specialty that explains mental experiences and behavior in terms of a person's cultural background is called *cultural psychology*.

Cultural and social psychology are closely related, but they differ in emphasis. While social psychologists emphasize the immediate social influences that act on individuals and groups, cultural psychologists strive to characterize entire cultures in terms of the typical ways that people within them feel, think, and act. Social psychologists use concepts such as conformity and obedience to explain behavior, whereas cultural psychologists more often refer to the unique history, economy, and religious or philosophical traditions of a culture to explain the values, norms, and habits of its people. For example, a cultural psychologist might contend that the frontier history of North America, in which individuals and families often had to struggle on their own, with little established social support, helps explain why North Americans value independence and individuality so strongly.

Concerning jealousy, a cultural psychologist would point to significant cultural differences in romantic and sexual mores. For example, some cultures are more tolerant of extramarital affairs than are others, and this difference affects the degree and quality of jealousy that is experienced. Some cultures have a strong double standard that condemns women far more harshly than men for sexual infidelity, and in those cultures violent revenge on the part of a jealous man toward his mate may be socially sanctioned (Vandello & Cohen, 2008). In other cultures, the same violence would dishonor the perpetrator and land him in jail. A full cultural analysis would include an account of the cultures' histories, which led to differences in the ways that infidelity is understood and treated.

Developmental Explanations Knowing a person's age enables us to predict some aspects of that person's behavior. Four-year-olds behave differently from 2-year-olds, and middle-aged adults differently from adolescents. The psychological specialty that documents and describes the typical age differences in how people feel, think, and act is called *developmental psychology*. Developmental psychologists may describe the sequence of changes that occur, from infancy to adulthood, for any

FOCUS 15

What constitutes a developmental explanation? How would you apply a developmental explanation toward an understanding of jealousy?

given type of behavior or mental capacity. For example, developmental psychologists who study language have described a sequence of stages in speech production that goes from cooing to babbling, then to first recognizable words, to frequent one-word utterances, to two-word utterances, and so on, with each stage beginning, on average, at a certain

■ Although true sexual jealousy is not seen until adolescence, children can become jealous over the potential loss of friendship. (Sally Forth, November 16, 2012)

age. At a superficial level, then, age itself can be an explanation: "She talks in such-and-such a way because she is 3 years old, and that is how most 3-year-olds talk."

Looking deeper, developmental psychologists are also interested in the processes that produce the age-related changes they document. Those processes include physical maturation of the body (including the brain), behavioral tendencies that are genetically timed to emerge at particular ages, the accumulated effects of many learning experiences, and new pressures and opportunities provided by the social environment or the cultural milieu as one gets older. At this deeper level, then, developmental psychology is an approach that brings together the other levels of analysis. Neural, physiological, genetic, evolutionary, learning, cognitive, social, and cultural explanations might all be brought to bear on the task of explaining behavioral changes that occur with age. Developmental psychologists are particularly interested in understanding how experiences at any given stage of development can influence behavior at later stages.

A developmental analysis of jealousy might begin with a description of age-related changes in jealousy that correspond with age-related changes in social relationships. Infants become jealous when their mother or other primary caregiver devotes extended attention to another baby (Hart, 2015). Children of middle-school age, especially girls, often become jealous when their same-sex "best friend" becomes best friends with someone else (Parker et al., 2005). These early forms of jealousy are similar in form and function to sexual jealousy, which typically emerges along with the first serious romantic attachment, in adolescence or young adulthood. Researchers have found evidence of continuity between early attachments to parents and friends and later attachments to romantic partners (discussed in Chapter 12). People who develop secure relationships with their parents and friends in childhood also tend, later on, to develop secure relationships with romantic partners, relatively untroubled by jealousy (Main et al., 2005).

Levels of Analysis Are Complementary

These various levels of analysis provide different ways of asking questions about any psychological phenomenon, such as jealousy. However, these should not be viewed as alternative approaches to understanding, but rather as complementary approaches that, when combined, provide us a more complete picture of important aspects of psychology. Although you may hear debates over the relative importance of genetic versus cultural influences on any behavior, even these most extreme levels of analysis should be viewed as complementary to one another, not as opposing poles of a philosophical argument. Genes are always expressed in a context, and culture constitutes an important component in that context. Wherever possible, throughout this book we will try to integrate findings from the various levels of analysis.

A Comment on Psychological Specialties

Because of psychology's vast scope, research psychologists generally identify their work as belonging to specific subfields, or specialties. To some degree, as indicated in the foregoing discussion, different psychological research specialties correspond

 FOCUS 16

What are some research specialties in psychology that are not defined primarily by the level of analysis employed?

to different levels of analysis. This is most true of the nine specialties already described: *behavioral neuroscience, biopsychology, behavioral genetics, evolutionary psychology, learning psychology, cognitive psychology, social psychology, cultural psychology,* and *developmental psychology*.

Other specialties, however, are defined more in terms of topics studied than level of analysis. For example, *sensory psychology* is the study of basic abilities to see, hear, touch, taste, and smell the environment; and *perceptual psychology* is the study of how people and animals make sense of, or interpret, the input they receive through their senses. Similarly, some psychologists identify their specialty as the *psychology of motivation* or the *psychology of emotion*. These specialists might use any or all of psychology's modes of explanation to understand particular phenomena related to the topics they study. And of course, many psychologists combine specialties and may describe themselves as cognitive cultural psychologists, social neuroscientists, or evolutionary developmental psychologists, for example.

Two major specialties, which are closely related to each other, are devoted to the task of understanding individual differences among people. One of these is *personality psychology* (discussed in Chapter 14), which is concerned with normal differences in people's general ways of thinking, feeling, and behaving—referred to as personality traits. The other is *abnormal psychology* (discussed in Chapter 15), which is concerned with variations in psychological traits that are sufficiently extreme and disruptive to people's lives as to be classified as mental disorders. Personality psychologists and abnormal psychologists use various levels of analysis. Differences in the nervous system, in hormones, in genes, in learning experiences, in beliefs, in social pressures, or in cultural milieu may all contribute to an understanding of differences in personality and in susceptibility to particular mental disorders.

Closely related to abnormal psychology is *clinical psychology* (discussed in Chapter 16), which focuses on helping people who have mental disorders or less serious psychological problems. Most clinical psychologists are practitioners rather than researchers. They offer psychotherapy or drug treatments, or both, to help people cope with or overcome their disorders or problems. Clinical psychologists who conduct research are usually interested in identifying or developing better treatment methods.

Research specialties in psychology are not rigidly defined. Generally speaking, they are simply convenient labels aimed at roughly classifying the different levels of analysis and topics of study that characterize the work of different research psychologists. Good researchers—regardless of what they call themselves—often use several different levels of analysis in their research and may study a variety of topics. Our main reason for listing and briefly describing some of the specialties here is to give you an overview of the broad scope of psychological science.

Psychology Connects With Other Scholarly Fields

FOCUS 17

What are the three main divisions of academic studies? How does psychology link them together?

Another way to characterize psychology is to picture its place in the spectrum of disciplines that are taught in a typical college of arts and sciences. The disciplines are divided into three broad areas. One division is the natural sciences—biology, chemistry, and physics. The second division is the social sciences, including sociology, anthropology, political science, and economics. The third division is the humanities, which includes languages, philosophy, art, and music. The humanities represent things that humans do. Humans, unlike other animals, talk to one another, develop philosophies, and create art and music.

Where does psychology fit into this scheme? Directly in the center, tied to all three of the broad divisions (see **Figure 1.3**). On the natural science end, it is tied most directly to biology by way of behavioral neuroscience, behavioral genetics, and evolutionary psychology. On the social science end, it is tied most directly to sociology

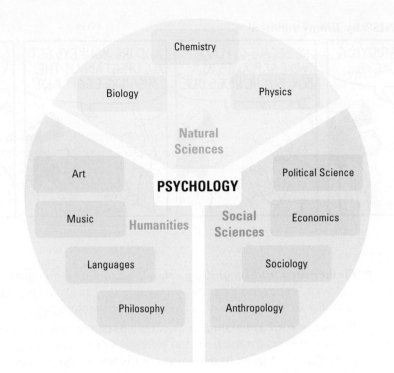

FIGURE 1.3 Psychology is a hub science Psychology has strong connections with the natural and social sciences and the humanities; it can be viewed as a hub that lies in the center of the academic pursuits of the university.

and anthropology by way of social and cultural psychology. In addition to bridging the natural and social sciences, psychology ties the whole spectrum of sciences to the humanities through its interest in how people produce and understand languages, philosophies, art, and music. It is no surprise that psychology has such meaningful connections to other disciplines: Psychology is the study of all that people do. No wonder it is very often chosen as a second major, or as a minor, by students who are majoring in other fields. In fact, psychology is one of the *hub sciences*: "a discipline in which scientific research is cited by scientists in many other fields" (Cacioppo, 2007). Kevin Boyack and colleagues analyzed publications in 7,121 scientific journals according to how frequently a research article is cited in other articles. They found strong connections between the hub of psychology and the subdisciplines of psychiatry, gerontology, biomedicine, neuroscience, public health, and education, and to the hubs of medicine and social science (Boyack, Klavans, & Börner, 2005).

Many students reading this book are planning to major in psychology, but many others are majoring in other subjects. No matter what you have chosen as your major field, you are likely to find meaningful connections between that field and psychology. Psychology has more connections to other subjects taught in the university than does any other single discipline (Gray, 2008).

Psychology as a Profession

Psychology is not only an academic discipline but also a profession. The profession includes both academic psychologists, who are engaged in research and teaching, and practicing psychologists, who apply psychological knowledge and ideas in clinics, businesses, and other settings. The majority of professional psychologists in the United States hold doctoral degrees in psychology, and most of the rest hold master's degrees (Landrum et al., 2009). The main settings in which they work, and the kinds of services they perform in those settings, are:

- *Academic departments in universities and colleges* Academic psychologists are employed to conduct basic research, such as that which fills this book, and to teach psychology courses.

- *Clinical settings* Clinical and counseling psychologists work with clients who have psychological problems or disorders, in independent practice or in hospitals, mental health centers, clinics, and counseling or guidance centers.

ARLO & JANIS® by Jimmy Johnson

- *Elementary and secondary schools* School psychologists administer psychological tests, supervise programs for children who have special needs, and may help teachers develop more effective classroom techniques.

- *Business and government* Psychologists are hired by businesses and government agencies for such varied purposes as conducting research, screening job candidates, helping to design more pleasant and efficient work environments, and counseling employees with work-related problems.

The decision to major in psychology as an undergraduate does not necessarily imply a choice of psychology as a career. Most students who major in psychology do so primarily because they find the subject fun to learn and think about. Most go on to careers in other fields—such as social work, law, education, and business—where their psychology background will be helpful (Kuther & Morgan, 2012; Landrum et al., 2009). If you are considering psychology as a career, you might want to look at the psychology career resources listed in the Find Out More section at the end of this chapter.

SECTION REVIEW

Psychology is a broad, diverse field of research, and it is a profession.

Levels of Causal Analysis and Topics of Study in Psychology

- Four types of biological causal explanations are used in psychology: neural, physiological, genetic, and evolutionary explanations.

- Five other types of causal explanations in psychology are learning, cognitive, social, cultural, and developmental explanations.

- As demonstrated with jealousy, each level of analysis can be applied to any given type of behavior or mental experience.

- Some subfields in psychology are defined primarily by the level of analysis; others are defined more by the topics studied.

A Discipline Among Disciplines

- Scholarly disciplines can be broadly classified as belonging to natural sciences, social sciences, or humanities.

- Psychology has strong connections with each class of disciplines and is a hub science.

The Profession of Psychology

- The profession includes academic psychologists, who teach and do research, and practicing psychologists, who apply psychological knowledge and principles to real-world issues.

- Psychologists work in various settings— including universities, clinical settings, and businesses—and typically hold advanced degrees.

Thoughts About Using This Book and Its Special Features

This final section of this chapter normally would go in a preface; it's about how to study this book. We've put it here because we've found that many people don't read prefaces, and we'd like you to read this. The suggestions here have proven helpful to thousands of previous students, and we want you to benefit from them. You are probably reading this book because it was assigned to you as part of a college course. You are reading it not because you chose it, but because someone chose it for you. This creates a special difficulty. When you read nonfiction outside of a course, you usually choose to do so because you are curious about some issue. In that case you read actively, constantly thinking about what you read to see if it helps answer your questions. But when reading is assigned to you for a course, you do not necessarily have particular questions in mind that you want to answer, and you may understand your job rather vaguely as that of "learning the material." This often leads to a passive and rather ineffective mode of reading, aimed more at memorizing than at thinking and understanding.

Our minds are not designed for memorizing what we don't understand or what we have not thought about actively. Our mental machinery evolved for the purpose of making sense of things, and we don't remember much of what doesn't make sense to us. So, when we read for the passive purpose of "learning" or "absorbing" the material, our minds often wander. We often find that we have read long passages—or, rather, that our eyes have moved across the lines of text—without having any idea what we just read.

Our sympathies are with you. We've been there before ourselves. We really want you to enjoy this book. We want you to read it actively, to question it, argue with it, and get excited by the ideas in it. Toward that end, we have done our best to present psychology as a set of ideas to think about, not as a set of facts to memorize. We have tried to give you enough information about each idea, enough of the evidence and logic supporting it, to enable you to have something to think about and argue with. Most of all, we do not want you to read this book as Truth with a capital *T*. Psychology is a science, and the essence of science is this: We do not accept anything on authority. It doesn't matter who says that something is or isn't true; what matters is the evidence and logic behind the statement. Each page of this book is offered for your consideration, not for your unquestioned acceptance.

Using the Focus Questions to Guide Your Study

In the introduction to this chapter, we pointed out the *focus questions* that appear in the book's margins. We suggested how to use these questions to guide both your initial reading and your review of the text. Here we'll elaborate on their use.

Each focus question is the main question that we are trying to answer in the portion of text that immediately follows the question. You can make your reading of the text more interesting and active if you reflect on each focus question as you come to it, before reading the paragraphs aimed at answering it. One way to approach the question is to formulate a preliminary, possible answer based on what you already know or believe. You might also put the question into your own words, to make it *your* question rather than ours. This will prepare you to read the relevant portion of text with a clear purpose in mind—finding out how we answer the question, and how our answer compares with your preliminary thoughts about it.

As an illustration, consider Focus Question 2, on page 3 of this chapter. This question consists of two parts: *What was Descartes' version of dualism? How did it help pave the way for a science of psychology?* When you first came to this question, you already had some good grounds for forming a preliminary answer. You had just read a definition of dualism in the previous paragraph, in which that term appeared

FOCUS 18
Why is it often more difficult to read a textbook for a course than to read nonfiction that you have chosen on your own?

FOCUS 19
How can you use the focus questions to make your reading of this textbook more thought-provoking and effective?

in boldface italics. You had read that dualism distinguishes between the body, which is physical and can be studied scientifically, and the soul, which is supernatural and cannot be studied scientifically. You may have also noticed that the section heading near the focus question reads *Descartes' Version of Dualism: Focus on the Body*, and that the larger section heading above that (on page 3) reads, *The Idea of Physical Causation of Behavior*. So, in thinking about Focus Question 2, you might have said something to yourself like: "Okay, maybe Descartes' version of dualism placed greater emphasis on the physical body and less emphasis on the soul than did previous versions. Now, I wonder if that guess is correct. If it is correct, I wonder just how Descartes developed and supported this view. What attributes did he ascribe to the body that had previously been ascribed to the soul, and why?" Having said all this to yourself, you would be ready to read the adjacent portion of text with great understanding.

After reading the portion of text that is relevant to answering a given focus question, it's a good idea to stop and think about that question again and how you would answer it. You might jot down, next to the question, the gist of the answer you would now give. If you aren't sure how to answer it, you might want to read that portion again. If you still aren't sure after that, you might want to mark that question as one to ask of your course instructor or study companions. Perhaps we didn't answer the question sufficiently clearly in the text, and perhaps a discussion with others will shed some light on it.

In later chapters, you will discover that many focus questions ask about the evidence for or against some idea. Be sure to think especially carefully about the answers you will read to those questions, and ask yourself whether or not the evidence seems convincing.

Admittedly, this approach to study will slow down your initial reading of each chapter. At first, stopping to think about each focus question may seem awkward and annoying. But most students we have taught, using previous editions of this book, have told us on course surveys that the focus-question approach begins to seem natural with practice and that it improves their comprehension, enjoyment, and test performance. In the long run, for most students, it saves study time. Having understood and thought about the material the first time through, later study and review become relatively easy. Some students have told us that they transfer this study skill to their reading of textbooks in other courses. In those books they do not find focus questions already written for them, but they use section headings and opening sentences to generate their own focus questions as they read. For more information about this study method, turn to page 340, in Chapter 9, where textbook reading is discussed in the context of a more general discussion of ways to improve memory.

■ **Example of a student's notes (see page 34)** Don't be afraid to write your own notes in the margin of this textbook. Your note taking will help you think about what you are reading and will be useful for review.

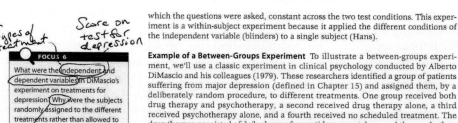

which the questions were asked, constant across the two test conditions. This experiment is a within-subject experiment because it applied the different conditions of the independent variable (blinders) to a single subject (Hans).

Example of a Between-Groups Experiment To illustrate a between-groups experiment, we'll use a classic experiment in clinical psychology conducted by Alberto DiMascio and his colleagues (1979). These researchers identified a group of patients suffering from major depression (defined in Chapter 15) and assigned them, by a deliberately random procedure, to different treatments. One group received both drug therapy and psychotherapy, a second received drug therapy alone, a third received psychotherapy alone, and a fourth received no scheduled treatment. The drug therapy consisted of daily doses of an antidepressant drug, and the psychotherapy consisted of weekly talk sessions with a psychiatrist that focused on the person's social relationships. After 16 weeks of treatment, the researchers rated each patient's degree of depression using a standard set of questions about mood and behavior. In this experiment, the independent variable was the kind of treatment given, and the dependent variable was the degree of depression after 16 weeks of

We should add, however, that a few students—roughly 10% of those we have taught—are able to read very actively, thoughtfully, and effectively without the aid of the focus questions. These are students who naturally remain focused and form questions as they read. If you are one of those few, then you may find the focus questions most useful as a review after you have finished each major section.

Using the Headings and Section Reviews to See the Hierarchical Structure of Ideas

Textbooks are always hierarchically organized. Each main heading refers to some major idea or argument, each subheading refers to a more limited idea that is part of the larger one, and each sub-subheading refers to a still more limited idea or observation that is part of the subheading's idea. In this book we have tried to compose all headings in such a way as to give you a pretty good idea of what each section, subsection, and sub-subsection is about. By looking ahead and reading all the headings within a main section before you read that section, you can preview the material and give yourself a head start toward thinking about it. You will see the basic structure of the argument that you are about to read, which will help you make sense of it as you read. Just as importantly, it will help you generate your own set of questions to try to answer as you read.

Each main section of this book ends with a *section review,* which reflects the hierarchical organization of the ideas and observations described in that section. We already described (on p. 9) how to use these charts for review. Reviewing in this way allows you to reflect back on each observation and idea as it relates to the larger idea to which it pertains. It helps you to see the individual elements of the section not as separate nuggets to memorize but as integral parts of a larger argument that helps you to make sense of them and remember them. A common mistake many students make is to study only the key terms and their definitions. That method causes the student to lose track of the larger arguments, which tie the various elements together and make them interesting and memorable. The section review charts offer you an alternative way to view the key ideas—a way that maintains their relationships to one another.

For example, the section review on page 10 of this chapter depicts the organization of our argument that scientific psychology was historically preceded by three fundamental ideas—physical causation of behavior, the role of experience, and the evolutionary basis of mind and behavior—and that these ideas provided a conceptual base on which psychology could build. That review chart should help you think about the individual concepts, such as *empiricism* and *nativism,* in relation to the argument instead of just memorizing definitions out of context. Your main goal is not to memorize definitions of these terms, but rather to think about how these philosophical ideas helped to provide a foundation for the emergence of a science of psychology.

Using the Book's Other Features

Throughout each chapter are many numbered figures and tables, as well as photos and cartoons, and boldface italicized key terms that are defined in the Glossary. At the end of each chapter you will find a set of study aids including critical thinking questions, Reflections and Connections, Find Out More, and LaunchPad. You can use the References in the back of the book to find the full citation for a study that is cited in the text. The Name Index and Subject Index enable you to find the page numbers where specific topics, researchers, and studies are covered.

Numbered Figures and Unnumbered Illustrations   As you read each chapter, pay attention to the *numbered figures.* Whenever the text refers you to a figure, take a few moments to study the figure and read its caption. Many figures are graphs of

FOCUS 20

How can you use the section and subsection headings, and the section review charts, to preview and review each major idea or argument? Why is the hierarchical organization of these study tools useful?

FOCUS 21

What purposes are served by the numbered figures and unnumbered illustrations, the terms that are set in boldface italics, the *Glossary,* the *Thinking Critically About...,* *Reflections and Connections,* and *Find Out More* sections, the reference citations and *Name Index,* and the *Subject Index* in this book?

data that support an idea presented in the text. Others are photographs or drawings designed to illustrate a point that would be difficult to describe in words alone. You will also notice unnumbered photographs, cartoons, and other images. These are included to illustrate the chapter concepts and, in many cases, to make them more concrete by applying a concept to a real-life situation or a memorable joke.

Boldface Italicized Terms and Glossary Throughout the text you will notice the use of *boldface italics* to highlight key terms: technical terms that are likely to be new to many students. We suggest that you not devote much effort, on your first reading, to learning the definitions of these key terms. Rather, read with the aim of understanding and thinking about the chapter's main ideas and the lines of evidence for or against them. This will help you learn most of the terms, in the context of the ideas, without consciously memorizing them. The boldface italics will be more useful in your later review. We suggest you also look for each of the key terms in bold italics and check your knowledge of its meaning as you review the focus questions. The key terms are listed at the end of each chapter and also defined in the *Glossary* at the back of the book. If an important term has been defined in an earlier chapter, it is sometimes, but not always, defined again when it reappears. If it is not defined in a given chapter, you can use the *Glossary* to find both the term's definition and the page number where it was first introduced.

Thinking Critically About... At the end of each chapter is a set of questions designed to promote critical inquiry about topics in the chapter. What is the evidence for a certain concept? How would we test a certain hypothesis? What information would be needed to evaluate a certain claim?

Reflections and Connections Section Each chapter includes a section called *Reflections and Connections*. This is not a summary; rather, it presents ideas, analogies, and integrating themes that are implicit in the chapter or that emerge from reflecting back on the chapter content. It also may suggest alternative ways to think about the chapter as you review it. *Reflections and Connections* is intended to deepen your understanding of psychology by connecting themes in a chapter to other concepts you will encounter elsewhere in the book and in the study of psychology as a whole. In this first chapter, for example, you will find a discussion of the concept of mind in *Reflections and Connections* that may be especially useful.

Find Out More Section You will also find, at the very end of each chapter, a section called *Find Out More,* which provides brief reviews of interesting resources (books and articles, films and videos, podcasts, websites, and more) that pertain to topics discussed in the chapter. The *Find Out More* resources are useful for deepening and expanding your knowledge of chapter topics, whether you refer to them on your own, in a study group, or to contribute to a class discussion. They may also be valuable starting points for an assignment such as a report, term paper, or class project.

Reference Citations, Name Index, and Subject Index Like most other books and articles on psychology, this book uses *reference citations*. This first chapter has relatively few of them, but in most chapters you will find them on nearly every page. Each citation consists of the name of one or more researchers followed by a year. Sometimes both the name (or names) and the year are in parentheses, such as "(Garcia & Williams, 2011)"; at other times, when the name or names are part of the sentence, only the year is in parentheses, such as "According to Alice Jones (2009), . . ." In either case, the year refers to the year of publication of an article or book, by the person or persons named, which describes more fully the idea or the research study being mentioned or discussed. When there are three or more authors, we use the convention of citing the first author's name followed by "et al.," a Latin abbreviation for "and others" (for example, Johnson et al., 2014). The full reference to that article or book can be found in the *References* section at the back of the textbook, which is arranged alphabetically by authors' last names. Don't let these citations disrupt the flow of your reading. Their purpose is not only to give credit to the people whose work or ideas are being described, but also to give you the opportunity to look up and read more about any particularly interesting ideas or research findings. Further, when you encounter a citation for a researcher whose work intrigues you, you can use the *Name Index* to find other places in this book where that individual is mentioned. Using both the *References* and the *Name Index* can give you a fuller picture of the career and life's work of a given individual.

Many students save their introductory psychology textbook and use it, after the course is over, as a reference to review topics that are relevant to other courses they take. The *Subject Index* at the back of the book, which lists topics alphabetically along with the pages where they are discussed, is very useful for this purpose. Looking up topics in the *Subject Index* can give you an advantage not just in psychology courses, but also in other social science courses, education courses, business courses, nursing courses, and some courses in other disciplines such as biology, philosophy, and English. Students who decide to apply to graduate programs in psychology often use the book to help prepare for the Graduate Record Examination in Psychology, and reviewing important topics by using the *Subject Index* can be a successful study technique for such exams.

SECTION REVIEW

Using this book's special features can markedly increase your learning.

Focus Questions

- The focus questions in the margins are designed to help you read in an active, thoughtful way; this in turn will help you understand and remember what you have read.

- The focus questions are also very useful in reviewing and testing your knowledge after you have read a section or chapter.

Headings and Section Reviews

- The book's hierarchically arranged headings can help you quickly preview a section and prepare an organized way of thinking about it.

- Section reviews can help you to check your understanding of content, visualize relationships among the ideas and facts discussed, and consolidate your learning.

Other Features

- Examining the numbered figures and unnumbered images, checking your understanding of bold italicized terms, and referring to the Glossary as needed can also benefit your study.

- Answering the *Thinking Critically About…* questions can deepen your understanding of key concepts in the chapter.

- Considering the integrative discussions in *Reflections and Connections* and taking advantage of the resources in the *Find Out More* sections can expand and deepen your understanding of topics that interest you.

- Reference citations, the *Name Index*, and the *Subject Index* can help you access material of interest to you within and beyond the book.

Thinking Critically About The Study of Psychology

1. Why might a knowledge of the history of philosophical thought about human behavior benefit an understanding of modern psychology?

2. What, if anything, connects the various areas of psychology together? Is it reasonable to think of psychology as a single discipline or does it make more sense to view it as a collection of different scientific disciplines?

3. The biologist E. O. Wilson referred to consilience as "the intrinsic unity of knowledge . . . the linkage of the sciences and humanities." How might psychology fit into Wilson's scheme for the integration of knowledge from physics to the humanities?

Reflections and Connections

This *Reflections and Connections* section, which you will find at the end of each chapter, is intended to expand or delve more deeply into one or more ideas that were implicit in the chapter or that emerge in reflecting back on the chapter as a whole. It may also draw connections with other ideas in psychology. Consider the following two thoughts in relation to the chapter you have just read.

1. Psychology as the study of normal behavior In the world outside of colleges and universities, people often associate psychology with the study of mental problems or disorders and the clinical practice of helping people overcome them. Popular television shows and self-help books also promote this "helping" view of psychology. When people "go to see a psychologist," they are seeking help. But, as shown in this chapter, psychology as a research field is primarily aimed at understanding normal human ways of feeling, thinking, and behaving.

From an intellectual point of view, the problem of how any entity normally works—whether it is an automobile, a computer, or a human being—is much more interesting than the problem of how it breaks down. Philosophers such as Descartes, Hobbes, and the British empiricists were fascinated by the workings of the normal human mind, and that is what fascinates most academic psychologists today. The normal mental experiences we take for granted in our everyday lives—such as our ability to see the color red, or to remember events, or to learn our native language—become intriguing mysteries when we stop to think about them.

As you go through this book, we hope you will allow yourself to become fascinated by all the normal things that you and other human beings do. If your ultimate interest is clinical psychology, keep in mind that some knowledge of normal functioning is essential background for figuring out where a breakdown has occurred and how normality might be restored. After all, automobile mechanics and computer repair specialists need to understand the normal operations of the machines they fix.

2. The concept of the mind as a product of the brain After reading this chapter, you may be puzzled about the meaning of the term *mind*. Join the club. Even today, *mind* ranks as perhaps the most debated of all philosophical concepts. Psychologists use the term in two quite different ways. In one use, it refers to people's *conscious experiences*—to the sensations, perceptions, memories, thoughts, desires, and emotions that run through our conscious awareness such that we can describe

them to ourselves and to others. This is the usage that generates the most debate in philosophy, because it is hard to imagine just what "consciousness" is or how it emerges from physical matter. This difficulty leads some philosophers even today to be dualists. In psychology we usually sidestep that philosophical mystery by defining consciousness as whatever it is that a person can tell us about his or her experiences. If a person can tell us about a memory, or about something that he or she is looking at, then we say that the person's mind is conscious of that memory or that visual perception.

In its other use, *mind* refers to all of the *knowledge and operating rules* that are somehow built into or stored in the brain and that provide the foundation for organizing behavior and conscious experiences. By this definition, mind is analogous to the data and software that are programmed into a computer to organize its ability to calculate and perform all the operations we expect of it. In this usage, mind is not equated with consciousness. People are not aware of most of the inner knowledge and processes that organize their feelings, thoughts, and behavior, any more than a computer is aware of its software programs.

We have used the term *mind* in both of these ways in various parts of this book, and it should be clear from the context which meaning we are using at any given time. Many psychologists in the past, and a few even today, have argued that we should avoid the concept of mind entirely. They point out that by either definition, *mind* refers to something that we cannot see directly. What we observe is people's behavior, including their verbal reports of their thoughts and feelings. With modern techniques of monitoring the brain, we can also observe physical changes in the brain—but, again, that is not the same as observing the mind. According to some psychologists, therefore, we should define our science as the study of behavior, or as the study of the brain and behavior, and leave the unobservable mind out of it. Most psychologists, however, find the concept of mind to be very useful and believe that a psychological level of analysis provides a different understanding of human behavior than a biological one. Having a theory of the brain does not replace having a theory of the mind (Bjorklund, 1997a). We can *infer* characteristics of the mind by observing behavior, and then we can use those inferences to make predictions about further behavior. Gravity can't be seen directly, either—it is inferred by observing the behavior of physical entities; yet physicists find the concept of gravity to be very useful.

Key Terms

association by contiguity 7	cognitive neuroscience 11	empiricism 6	mind 1
behavior 1	cognitive psychology 15	evolutionary psychology 13	nativism 7
behavioral genetics 13	cultural psychology 16	learning psychology 14	psychology 1
behavioral neuroscience 11	developmental psychology 16	level of analysis 10	science 1
biopsychology 12	dualism 3	materialism 4	social psychology 15

Find Out More

Christopher D. Green (1997–2017). Classics in the History of Psychology. http://psychclassics.yorku.ca/index.htm

York University professor Christopher Green has assembled a fascinating collection of articles that played important roles in the founding of psychological science, published from the mid-1800s to the early 1900s. Explore!

Ludy T. Benjamin (2014). *A brief history of modern psychology* (2nd ed.). Hoboken, NJ: Wiley.

Ludy Benjamin is a leading historian in psychology. In this concise volume, he brings the history of both the science and the practice of psychology to life, starting with the establishment of the first experimental psychology laboratory in 1879.

Charles Darwin (1877). A biographical sketch of an infant. *Mind, 2,* 285–294. Oxford University Press.

Available at Classics in the History of Psychology, http://psychclassics.yorku.ca/Darwin/infant.htm

Darwin was endlessly curious about all creatures, including human infants. After the birth of his first child, William, he kept a detailed diary of the baby's behavior, including reflexes, eye movements, and much more. As William grew older, his father also kept notes on the child's expression of emotions, memory, ability to learn, and moral development. Decades later, Charles Darwin published his observations in the newly introduced journal, *Mind,* which was dedicated to recording advances in psychology.

Dana S. Dunn & Jane Halonen (2016). *The psychology major's companion: Everything you need to know to get you where you want to go.* New York, NY: Worth Publishers.

If you are considering psychology as a major, this brief book can help you decide. If you have already chosen to major in psychology, it can help guide you through your years of study and beyond. It is packed with practical information and suggestions—from academic (such as how to do psychology research and apply to grad school) to career-related (such as job opportunities with undergraduate or graduate degrees, and how to write a résumé).

American Psychological Association, Careers in Psychology

http://www.apa.org/careers/resources/guides/careers.aspx

In the APA Careers section, you can learn about various psychology careers, the common areas of study, and what you can do with a degree in psychology.

American Psychological Association, gradPSYCH Blog

http://www.gradpsychblog.org/

Run by the American Psychological Association of Graduate Students (APAGS), this blog features posts by both current and former students about the world of psychology. It provides tips for finding internships, job interviews, possible career paths, and more. Readers can also submit their own posts about psychology-related topics to share with fellow psychology students.

LaunchPad
macmillan learning

Visit LaunchPad for Psychology 8e launchpadworks.com to access the e-book, videos, activities, additional resources, and LearningCurve quizzes, as well as study aids including flash cards and web quizzes.

Methods of Psychology

2

LEARNING OUTCOMES

After studying this chapter, you should be able to:

- Explain how Clever Hans appeared to have intellectual abilities that he actually did not have.

- Distinguish between an experiment and a correlational or descriptive study; a field setting and a laboratory setting; and self-report methods and observational methods.

- Describe the basics of descriptive statistics and inferential statistics.

- Define bias, reliability and validity, observer expectancy and subject expectancy, and replication.

- Identify key ethical issues in research with humans and with non-human animals.

In Chapter 1, *psychology* was defined as the *science* of behavior and the mind. But what does it mean to say that psychology is a science? Science is the attempt to answer questions through the systematic collection and analysis of objective, publicly observable data (data that all observers can agree on). The science of psychology attempts not only to describe behavior but also to explain it. Once the results of a scientific experiment are collected and analyzed, they need to be explained in natural cause-and-effect terms. Thus, concluding that a person behaves in a certain way because the stars aligned just so at the time of his or her birth does not qualify as a scientific explanation because no natural mechanism is proposed between the presumed cause (the position of the stars at one's birth) and effect (one's behavior or personality). Even if the person's behavior is described objectively and is reliably recorded and replicable, this explanation of the behavior goes beyond the natural world and is not within the realm of science.

In psychology, the data are usually measures or descriptions of some form of behavior produced by humans or other animals. Challenges exist in choosing what data to collect, collecting the data, and drawing conclusions from them. If we fail to deal with those problems carefully and intelligently, the answers we arrive at will not enlighten us, but mislead us.

This chapter is about scientific methods as applied to psychology. You will read sections on the research strategies psychologists use to answer questions, the statistical procedures they use to analyze data, the safeguards they employ to avoid biased results, and the ethical protections they provide to human and animal research subjects. But first, to ease ourselves into the topic, here is a story about a horse and a psychologist.

Lessons From Clever Hans

This is a true story that took place in Germany in the early twentieth century. The horse was Clever Hans, famous throughout Europe for his ability to answer questions, and the psychologist was Oskar Pfungst. In a preface to the original account

(Pfungst, 1911/1965), James Angell wrote, "Were it offered as fiction, it would take high rank as a work of imagination. Being in reality a sober fact, it verges on the miraculous." We tell the story here because of the lessons it teaches about scientific attitude and methods.

The Mystery

Hans's owner, a Mr. von Osten, was a retired schoolteacher and devoted horseman who had long believed that horses would prove to be as intelligent as people if only they were given a proper education. To test his theory, von Osten spent 4 years tutoring Hans in the manner employed in the most reputable German schools for children. Using flash cards, counting frames, and the like, he set about teaching his horse reading, arithmetic, history, and other scholarly disciplines. He always began with simple problems and worked toward more complex ones, and he rewarded Hans frequently with praise as well as carrots. Recognizing that horses lack the vocal apparatus needed for speech, von Osten taught Hans to spell out words using a code in which the letters of the alphabet were translated into hoof taps and to answer yes–no questions by tossing his head up and down for "yes" and back and forth for "no." After 4 years of this training, Hans was able to answer practically any question that was put to him in either spoken or written German, whether about geography, history, science, literature, mathematics, or current events. Remarkably, he could also answer questions put to him in other languages, even though he had never been trained in them.

Now, you might think that von Osten was a charlatan, but he wasn't. He genuinely believed that his horse could read and understand a variety of languages, could perform mathematical calculations, and had acquired a vast store of knowledge. He never charged admission or sought other personal gain for displaying Hans, and he actively sought out scientists to study the animal's accomplishments. Indeed, many scientists, including some eminent zoologists and psychologists, came to the conclusion that von Osten's claims were true. The evidence that most convinced them was Hans's ability to answer questions even when von Osten was not present, a finding that seemed to rule out the possibility that the horse depended on secret signals from his master. Moreover, several circus trainers, who specialized in training animals to give the appearance of answering questions, studied Hans and could find no evidence of trickery.

■ **Clever Hans at a mathematics lesson** Mr. von Osten believed that his horse was intellectually gifted, and so did many other people until psychologist Oskar Pfungst performed some simple experiments.

FOCUS 1

How did Clever Hans give the appearance of answering questions, and how did Oskar Pfungst unveil Hans's methods?

The Solution

The downfall of the idea that the horse could count finally came when psychologist Oskar Pfungst performed a few simple experiments. Pfungst theorized that Hans answered questions not through understanding them and knowing the answers but through responding to visual signals inadvertently produced by the questioner or other observers. Consistent with this theory, Pfungst found that the animal failed to answer questions when he was fitted with blinders so that he could not see anyone, and that even without blinders he could not answer questions unless at least one person in his sight knew the answer. With further study, Pfungst discovered just what the signals were.

Immediately after asking a question that demanded a hoof-tap answer, the questioner and other observers would naturally move their heads down just a bit to observe the horse's hoof. This, it turned out, was the signal for Hans to start tapping. To determine whether Hans would be correct or not, the questioner and other observers would then count the taps and, unintentionally, make another response as soon as the correct number had been reached. This response varied from person to person, but a common component was a slight upward movement of either the whole head or some facial feature, such as the eyebrows. This, it turned out, was the signal for Hans to stop tapping. Hans's yes–no headshake responses were also controlled by visual signals. Questioners and observers would unconsciously produce slight up-and-down head movements when they expected the horse to answer yes and slight back-and-forth head movements when they expected him to answer no, and Hans would shake his head accordingly.

All the signals that controlled Hans's responses were so subtle that even the most astute observers had failed to notice them until Pfungst pointed them out. And Pfungst himself reported that the signals occurred so naturally that, even after he had learned what they were, he had to make a conscious effort to prevent himself from sending them after asking a question. For 4 years, von Osten had believed that he was communicating scholarly information to Hans, when all he had really done was teach the horse to make a few simple responses to a few simple, though minute, gestures.

■ **Cues from the audience** When members of the audience knew the answer to a question asked of Clever Hans, they inadvertently signaled to the horse through their own head movements as to when to start and stop tapping or which way to shake his head.

Observations, Theories, and Hypotheses

The story of Clever Hans illustrates the roles of observations, theories, and hypotheses in scientific research. An *observation* is an objective statement that reasonable observers agree is true. In psychology, observations are usually particular behaviors, or reliable patterns of behaviors, of persons or animals. When Hans was tested in the manner typically employed by von Osten, the horse's hoof taps or headshakes gave the appearance that he was answering questions correctly. That is an observation, which no one involved with Hans disputed.

A ***theory*** is an idea, or a conceptual model, that is designed to explain existing observations and make predictions about new observations that might be discovered. Any prediction about new observations that is made from a theory is called a ***hypothesis***. Nobody knows what observations (or perhaps delusions) led von Osten to develop his theory that horses have humanlike intelligence. However, once he conceived his theory, he used it to hypothesize that his horse, Hans, could learn to give correct answers to verbally stated problems and questions. The psychologist, Pfungst, had a very different theory of equine intelligence: Horses don't think like humans and can't understand human language. In keeping with this theory, and to explain the observation that Hans seemed to answer questions correctly, Pfungst developed the more specific theory that the horse responded to visual cues produced by people who were present and knew the answers. This theory led Pfungst to hypothesize that Hans would not answer questions correctly if fitted with blinders or if asked questions to which nobody present knew the answer.

Observations lead to theories, which lead to hypotheses, which are tested with experiments or other research studies; these in turn lead to new observations, which sometimes lead to new theories, which . . . . This is the cycle of science, whether we are speaking of psychology, biology, physics, or any other scientific endeavor. As a colleague of ours likes to say, "Science walks on two legs: theory and observations." Theory without observations is merely speculation, and observations without theory are simply data without explanations.

FOCUS 2

How are observations, theories, and hypotheses related to one another in scientific research?

The Lessons

In addition to illustrating the roles of observation, theory, and hypothesis, the story contains three more specific lessons about scientific research:

FOCUS 3

How does the Clever Hans story illustrate (1) the value of skepticism, (2) the value of controlled experimentation, and (3) the need for researchers to avoid communicating their expectations to subjects?

1. *The value of skepticism.* People are fascinated by extraordinary claims and often act as though they want to believe them. This is as true today as it was in the time of Clever Hans. We have no trouble at all finding otherwise rational people who believe in astrology, psychokinesis, water divining, telepathy, or other occult phenomena, despite the fact that all these have consistently failed when subjected to controlled tests (Smith, 2010). Von Osten clearly wanted to believe that his horse could do amazing things, and to a lesser degree, the same may have been true of the scholars who had studied the horse before Pfungst. Pfungst learned the truth partly because he was highly skeptical of such claims. Instead of setting out to prove them correct, he set out to prove them wrong. His skepticism led him to look more carefully; to notice what others had missed. Skepticism alone was not enough for Pfungst to figure out how Hans was answering the questions, however. Pfungst also needed to engage in *critical thinking*, using his knowledge of the world to develop alternative perspectives and then develop tests to evaluate them.

   In general, the more extraordinary a claim is—the more it deviates from accepted scientific principles—the stronger the evidence for the new theory needs to be. To suggest a complex, extraordinary explanation of some behavior requires that all simple and conventional explanations be considered first and judged inadequate. Moreover, the simpler the explanation is, the better it tends to be. This is referred to as *parsimony,* or *Occam's razor* (after the medieval philosopher William of Ockham). According to the principle of parsimony, when there are two or more explanations that are equally able to account for a phenomenon, the simplest explanation is usually preferred.

   Skepticism should be applied not only to extraordinary theories that come from outside of science but also to the theories produced by scientists themselves. Ideally, a scientist always tries to disprove theories, even those that are his or her own. The theories that scientists accept as correct, or most likely to be correct, are those that could potentially be disproved but have survived all attempts so far to disprove them.

2. *The value of careful observations under controlled conditions.* Pfungst solved the mystery of Clever Hans by identifying the conditions under which the horse could and could not respond correctly to questions. He tested Hans repeatedly, with and without blinders, and recorded the percentage of correct answers in each condition. The results were consistent with the theory that the animal relied on visual signals. Pfungst then pursued the theory further by carefully observing Hans's examiners to see what cues they might be sending. And when he had an idea what the cues might be, he performed further experiments, in which he deliberately produced or withheld the signals and recorded their effects on Hans's hoof-tapping and head-shaking responses. Careful observation under controlled conditions is a hallmark of the scientific method.

3. *The problem of observer-expectancy effects.* In studies of humans and other sentient animals the observers (the people conducting the research) may unintentionally communicate to subjects (the individuals being studied) their expectations about how they "should" behave, and the subjects, intentionally or not, may respond by doing just what the researchers expect. The same is true in any situation in which one person administers a test to another. Have you ever taken an oral quiz and found that you could tell whether you were on the right track by noting the facial expression of your examiner? By tentatively trying various tracks, you may have finally hit on just the answer that your examiner wanted. Clever Hans's entire ability depended on his picking up such cues. We will discuss the general problem of expectancy effects later in this chapter (in the section on avoiding bias).

SECTION REVIEW

The case of the horse named Clever Hans illustrates several issues fundamental to scientific research.

Observations, Theories, and Hypotheses	The Importance of Skepticism	Observation and Control	Observer-Expectancy Effects
■ Objective observations of behavior lead psychologists to create conceptual models or explanations (theories), which give rise to specific, testable predictions (hypotheses). ■ Pfungst drew testable hypotheses from his theory that Hans was guided by visual cues from onlookers.	■ Skeptics seek to disprove claims. This is the logical foundation of scientific testing. ■ A scientific theory becomes more believable as repeated, genuine attempts to disprove it fail. ■ Pfungst's skepticism caused him to test rather than simply accept claims about Hans's abilities.	■ To test hypotheses, scientists control the conditions in which they make observations, so as to rule out alternative explanations. ■ Pfungst measured Hans's performance in conditions arranged specifically to test his hypothesis—with and without blinders, for example.	■ Science is carried out by people who come to their research with certain expectations. ■ In psychology, the subjects—the people and animals under study—may perceive the observer's expectations and behave accordingly. ■ Cues from observers led Hans to give responses that many misinterpreted as signs of vast knowledge.

Types of Research Strategies

In their quest to understand the mind and behavior of humans and other animals, psychologists employ a variety of research strategies. Pfungst's strategy was to observe Clever Hans's behavior in controlled experiments. But not all research studies done by psychologists are experiments. A useful way to categorize the various research strategies used by psychologists is to think of them as varying along the following three dimensions (Hendricks et al., 1990):

1. The *research design,* of which there are three basic types: experiments, correlational studies, and descriptive studies.

2. The *setting* in which the study is conducted, of which there are two basic types: field and laboratory.

3. The *data-collection method,* of which there are two basic types: self-report and observation.

Each of these dimensions can vary independently from the others, resulting in any possible combination of design, setting, and data-collection method. Here we first describe the three types of research designs and then, more briefly, the other two dimensions.

Research Designs

The first dimension of a research strategy is the research design, which can be an experiment, a correlational study, or a descriptive study. Researchers design a study to test a hypothesis, choosing the design that best fits the conditions they want to control.

Experiments

An experiment is the most direct and conclusive approach to testing a hypothesis about a cause–effect relationship between two variables. A **variable** is anything that can change or assume different values. It might be a condition of the environment, such as temperature or amount of noise; or it might be a measure of behavior, such as a score on a test. In describing an experiment, the variable that is hypothesized

FOCUS 4

How can an experiment demonstrate the existence of a cause–effect relation between two variables?

to cause some effect on another variable is called the ***independent variable***, and the variable that is hypothesized to be affected is called the ***dependent variable***. The aim of any experiment is to learn whether and how the dependent variable is affected by (depends on) the independent variable. In psychology, dependent variables are usually measures of behavior, and independent variables are factors that are hypothesized to influence those measures.

More specifically, an ***experiment*** can be defined as a procedure in which a researcher systematically manipulates (varies) one or more independent variables and looks for changes in one or more dependent variables, *while keeping all other variables constant*. If all other variables are kept constant and only the independent variable is changed, then the experimenter can reasonably conclude that any change observed in the dependent variable *is caused by* the change in the independent variable.

The people or animals that are studied in any research study are referred to as the *subjects* of the study. (Many psychologists today prefer to call them *participants* rather than subjects, because "subject" is felt to have undesirable connotations of subordination and passivity [Kimmel, 2007], but the American Psychological Association [2010] approves both terms, and in general we prefer the more traditional and precise term *subjects*.)

In some experiments, called *within-subject* experiments (or sometimes *repeated-measures experiments*), each subject is tested in each of the different conditions of the independent variable (that is, the subject is repeatedly tested). In other experiments, called *between-groups experiments* (or sometimes, *between-subjects experiments*), there is a separate group of subjects for each different condition of the independent variable.

FOCUS 5

What were the independent and dependent variables in Pfungst's experiment with Clever Hans?

Example of a Within-Subject Experiment In most within-subject experiments, a number of subjects are each tested in each condition of the independent variable. But within-subject experiments can be conducted with just one subject. In Pfungst's experiments with Clever Hans, there was just one subject, Hans. In each experiment, Pfungst tested Hans repeatedly, under varying conditions of the independent variable.

In one experiment, to determine whether or not visual cues were critical to Hans's ability to respond correctly to questions, Pfungst tested the horse sometimes with blinders and sometimes without. In that experiment the independent variable was the presence or absence of blinders, and the dependent variable was the percentage of questions the horse answered correctly. The experiment could be described as a study of the effect of blinders (independent variable) on Hans's percentage of correct responses to questions (dependent variable). Pfungst took care to keep other variables, such as the difficulty of the questions and the setting in which the questions were asked, constant across the two test conditions. This experiment is a within-subject experiment because it applied the different conditions of the independent variable (blinders) to a single subject (Hans).

FOCUS 6

What were the independent and dependent variables in DiMascio's experiment on treatments for depression? Why were the subjects randomly assigned to the different treatments rather than allowed to choose their own treatment?

Example of a Between-Groups Experiment To illustrate a between-groups experiment, we'll use a classic experiment in clinical psychology conducted by Alberto DiMascio and his colleagues (1979). These researchers identified a group of patients suffering from major depression (defined in Chapter 15) and assigned them, by a deliberately random procedure, to different treatments. One group received both drug therapy and psychotherapy, a second received drug therapy alone, a third received psychotherapy alone, and a fourth received no scheduled treatment. The drug therapy consisted of daily doses of an antidepressant drug, and the psychotherapy consisted of weekly talk sessions with a psychiatrist that focused on the person's social relationships. After 16 weeks of treatment, the researchers rated each patient's degree of depression using a standard set of questions about mood and behavior. In this experiment, the independent variable was the kind of treatment given, and the dependent variable was the degree of depression after 16 weeks of treatment. This is a between-groups experiment because the manipulations of the independent variable (that is, the different treatments used) were applied to different groups of subjects.

Notice that the researchers used a random method (a method relying only on chance) to assign the subjects to the treatment groups. *Random assignment* is regularly used in between-group experiments to ensure that the subjects are not assigned in a way that could bias the results. If DiMascio and his colleagues had allowed the subjects to choose their own treatment group, those who were most likely to improve even without treatment—maybe because they were more motivated to improve—might have disproportionately chosen one treatment condition over the others. In that case we would have no way to know whether the greater improvement of one group compared with the others resulted from the treatment or from preexisting differences in the subjects. With random assignment, any differences among the groups that do not stem from the differing treatments must be the result of chance, and, as you will see later, researchers have statistical tools for taking chance into account in analyzing their data.

The results of this experiment are shown in **Figure 2.1**. Following a common convention in graphing experimental results, which is used throughout this book, the figure depicts variation in the independent variable along the horizontal axis (known as the x-axis) and variation in the dependent variable along the vertical axis (the y-axis). As you can see in the figure, those in the drug-plus-psychotherapy group were the least depressed after the 16-week period, and those in the no-treatment group were the most depressed. The results support the hypothesis that both drug therapy and psychotherapy help relieve depression and that the two treatments together have a greater effect than either alone.

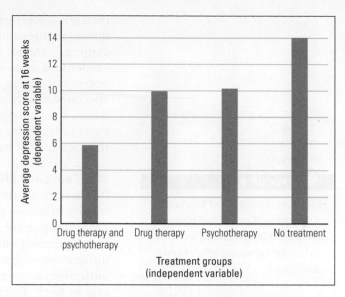

FIGURE 2.1 Effect of treatment condition on depression Subjects who received both drugs and psychotherapy were the least depressed at the end of the 16-week treatment period (according to the results of a standard interview procedure scored on a 17-point scale). In contrast, subjects who received no treatment were the most depressed. (Data from DiMascio et al., 1979.)

Correlational Studies

Often in psychology it is impossible to conduct experiments to answer certain questions because we cannot—for practical or ethical reasons—assign subjects to particular experimental conditions and control their experiences. Suppose, for example, that you are interested in the relationship between the disciplinary styles of parents and the psychological development of children. Perhaps you entertain the idea that frequent punishment is harmful, that it promotes aggressiveness or other unwanted characteristics. To test that hypothesis with an experiment, you would have to manipulate the discipline variable and then measure some aspect of the children's behavior. You might consider randomly assigning some families to a strict punishment condition and others to other conditions. The parents would then have to raise their children in the manners you prescribe. But you know that you cannot control families that way; it's not practical, not legal, and not ethical. So, instead, you conduct a correlational study.

A *correlational study* can be defined as a study in which the researcher does not manipulate any variable, but observes or measures two or more already existing dependent variables to find relationships between them. Correlational studies can identify relationships between variables, which allow us to make predictions about one variable based on knowledge of another; but such studies do not tell us in any direct way whether change in one variable is the cause of change in another.

Example of a Correlational Study A classic example of a correlational study is Diana Baumrind's (1971) study of the relationship between parents' disciplinary styles and children's behavioral development. Instead of manipulating disciplinary styles (e.g., having one group of parents discipline their children harshly and another group discipline their children more leniently), she observed and assessed differences in

FOCUS 7

What are the differences in procedure between a correlational study and an experiment? How do the types of conclusions that can be drawn differ between a correlational study and an experiment?

disciplinary styles that already existed between different sets of parents. Through questionnaires and home observations, Baumrind classified disciplinary styles into three categories: *authoritarian* (high exertion of parental power), *authoritative* (a kinder and more democratic style, but with the parents still clearly in charge), and *permissive* (parental laxity in the face of their children's disruptive behaviors). She also rated the children on various aspects of behavior, such as cooperation and friendliness, through observations in their nursery schools. The main finding (discussed more fully in Chapter 12) was that children of authoritative parents scored better on the measures of behavior than did children of authoritarian or permissive parents.

FOCUS 8

How does an analysis of Baumrind's classic study of parental disciplinary styles illustrate the difficulty of trying to infer cause and effect from a correlation?

Why Cause and Effect Cannot Be Determined From a Correlational Study It is tempting to treat Baumrind's study as though it were an experiment and interpret the results in cause–effect terms. More specifically, it is tempting to think of the parents' disciplinary style as the independent variable and the children's behavior as the dependent variable and to conclude that differences in the former caused the differences in the latter. Thus, if parents would simply raise their children using an authoritative parenting style, their children would be more cooperative, friendly, and so forth. But because the study was not an experiment, we cannot justifiably come to that conclusion. The researcher did not control either variable, so we cannot be sure what was cause and what was effect. Maybe the differences in the parents' styles did cause the differences in the children's behavior, but other interpretations are possible. Here are some of these possibilities:

- Differences in children's behavior may cause differences in parents' disciplinary style, rather than the other way around. Some children may be better behaved than others for reasons quite separate from parental style, and parents with well-behaved children may simply glide into an authoritative mode of parenting, while parents with more difficult children fall into one of the other two approaches as a way of coping.

- The causal relationship may go in both directions, with parents and children influencing each other's behavior. For example, children's disruptive behavior may promote authoritarian parenting, which may promote even more disruptive behavior.

- A third variable, not measured in Baumrind's study, may influence both parental style and children's behavior in such a way as to cause the observed correlation. For example, anything that makes families feel good about themselves (such as having good neighbors, good health, and an adequate income) might promote an authoritative style in parents and, quite independently, also lead children to behave well. Or maybe the causal variable has to do with the fact that children are genetically similar to their parents and therefore have similar personalities: The same genes that predispose parents to behave in a kind but firm manner may predispose children to behave well, and the same genes that predispose parents to be either highly punitive or neglectful may predispose children to misbehave.

If you understand and remain aware of this limitation of correlational studies, you will not only be a stronger psychology student, but a much smarter consumer of media reports about research results. All too frequently, people—including even scientists who sometimes forget what they should know—use correlations to make unjustified claims of causal relationships on subjects including not only psychology, but health, economics, and more.

The important take-home message is that "correlation does not imply causality." This is clearly seen by some significant correlations that simply make no sense. For example, the number of people who drown in their swimming pools in the United States is correlated with the number of films Nicolas Cage appeared in, and the number of people who died by becoming entangled in their bedsheets is correlated with the per capita consumption of cheese. These are obvious *spurious correlations*, but they warn us to be cautious in assuming causality when all we have is correlation.

In some correlational studies, one causal hypothesis may be deemed more plausible than others. For example, we might be tempted to infer a cause–effect relationship between children's violent behavior and the amount of time they spend watching violent television programs. Although this is one plausible explanation, it is also possible that children who are violent seek out violent television, or perhaps both violent behavior and watching violent television are related to a third factor, such as lack of parental supervision. As another example, if we found a correlation between brain damage to a certain part of the brain, due to accidents, and the onset of a certain type of mental disorder immediately following the accident, we would probably be correct in inferring that the brain damage caused the mental disorder. That possibility seems far more plausible than any other possible explanation of the relationship between the two variables.

In Baumrind's study, one variable (parents' disciplinary style) was used to place subjects into separate groups, and then the groups were compared to see how they differed in the other variable (the children's behavior). Many correlational studies are analyzed in that way, and those are the ones most likely to be confused with experiments. In many other correlational studies, however, both variables are measured numerically and neither is used to assign subjects to groups. For example, a researcher might be interested in the correlation between the height of tenth-grade boys (measured in centimeters or inches) and their popularity (measured by counting the number of classmates who list the boy as a friend). In such cases, the data are assessed by a statistic called the *correlation coefficient,* which will be discussed in the section on statistical methods later in this chapter.

■ **What causes what?** Although many correlational studies have found a relationship between the viewing of televised violence and the displaying of aggressive behavior, such studies cannot tell us whether television inspires the aggressive behavior or whether aggressive individuals are more likely than others to watch violent television programs.

Descriptive Studies

Sometimes the aim of research is to describe the behavior of an individual or set of individuals without assessing relationships between different variables. A study of this sort is called a ***descriptive study***. Descriptive studies may or may not make use of numbers. As an example of one involving numbers, researchers might survey the members of a given community to determine the percentage who suffer from various mental disorders. This is a descriptive study if its aim is simply to describe the prevalence of each disorder without correlating the disorders to other characteristics of the community's members. As an example of a descriptive study not

 FOCUS 9

How do descriptive studies differ, in method and purpose, from experiments and from correlational studies?

■ **Jane Goodall and other primatologists** have described the complex social behavior of chimpanzees.

involving numbers, an animal behaviorist might observe the courtship behaviors of mallard ducks to describe in detail the sequence of movements that are involved.

Some descriptive studies are narrow in focus, concentrating on one specific aspect of behavior, and others are broad, aiming to learn as much as possible about the habits of a particular group of people or species of animal. One of the most extensive and heroic descriptive bodies of research ever conducted is Jane Goodall's work on wild chimpanzees in Africa. She observed the apes' behavior over a period of 30 years and provided a wealth of information about every aspect of their lives (Goodall, 1986, 1988).

Research Settings

The second dimension of research strategy is the research setting, which can be either the laboratory or the field. A *laboratory study* is any research study in which the subjects are brought to a specially designated area that has been set up to facilitate the researcher's collection of data or control over environmental conditions. Laboratory studies can be conducted in any location where a researcher has control over what experiences the subject has at that time. This is often in specially constructed rooms at universities, but in educational and child development research, for example, the "laboratory" may be a small room in a school or daycare center.

In contrast to laboratory studies, a *field study* is any research study conducted in a setting where the researcher does not have control over the subjects' experiences. Field studies in psychology may be conducted in people's homes, at their workplaces, at shopping malls, or in any place that is part of the subjects' natural environment.

Laboratory and field settings offer opposite sets of advantages and disadvantages. The laboratory allows the researcher to collect data under more uniform, controlled conditions than are possible in the field. However, the strangeness or artificiality of the laboratory may induce behaviors that obscure those the researcher wants to study. A laboratory study of parent-child interactions, for example, may produce results that reflect not so much the subjects' normal ways of interacting as their reactions to a strange environment and their awareness that they are being observed. To counteract such problems, some researchers combine laboratory and field studies. It often happens that the same conclusions emerge from tightly controlled laboratory studies and less controlled but more natural field studies. In such cases, researchers can be reasonably confident that the conclusions are meaningful (Anderson et al., 1999).

In terms of how research settings relate to the three kinds of research designs discussed earlier, experiments are most often conducted in the laboratory because greater control of variables is possible in that setting, and correlational and descriptive studies are more often conducted in the field. But these relationships between research design and setting are by no means inevitable. Experiments are sometimes performed in the field, and correlational and descriptive studies are sometimes carried out in the laboratory.

As an example of a field experiment, psychologist Robert Cialdini (2003) wondered about the effectiveness of signs in public places, such as national parks, depicting undesired behaviors that visitors are asked to avoid. Do such signs reduce the behaviors they are designed to reduce? As a test, on different days Cialdini varied the signs placed along trails in Petrified Forest National Park intended to discourage visitors from picking up and taking pieces of petrified wood. He then measured, by observation, the amount of theft of petrified wood that occurred. We discuss Cialdini's study and its results in Chapter 13.

Data-Collection Methods

The third dimension of research is the data-collection method, of which there are two broad categories: self-report methods and observational methods. *Self-report*

FOCUS 10

What are the relative advantages and disadvantages of laboratory studies and field studies?

FOCUS 11

How do self-report methods, naturalistic observations, and tests differ from one another? What are some advantages and disadvantages of each?

methods are procedures in which people are asked to rate or describe their own behavior or mental state in some way. For example, in a study of generosity, subjects might be asked to respond to questions pertaining to their own degree of generosity. This might be done through a written *questionnaire,* in which people check off items on a printed list that apply to them, indicate the degree to which certain statements are true or not true of them, or write answers to brief essay questions about themselves. Or it might be done through an interview, in which people describe themselves orally in a dialogue with the interviewer. An interview may be tightly structured, with the interviewer asking questions according to a completely planned sequence, or it may be more loosely structured, with the interviewer following up on some of the subjects' responses with additional questions. In some cases, people are asked to make assessments of *other people*, such as parents or teachers asked to evaluate children in terms of aggression or agreeableness, or individuals asked to evaluate their romantic partners' tendencies toward jealousy.

One form of self-report is **introspection**, the personal observations of one's thoughts, perceptions, and feelings. This was a method used by the founders of modern psychology, especially Wilhelm Wundt. Although Wundt used exacting controls in his introspection experiments permitting them to be replicated in other laboratories, it is impossible to confirm another person's thoughts, feelings, or perceptions. The highly subjective nature of introspection made it a target of criticism for early psychologists who believed that the science of psychology should be based on observable behavior, not on what people say they "feel." Nonetheless, such sensory, cognitive, and emotional states are of great importance to the individual experiencing them and are very much "real." Modern methods for measuring neural activity (discussed in Chapter 4 and elsewhere in this book) are able to correlate people's introspections with what's happening in the brain, providing more objective, "observable behavior" than was available to the pioneers of psychology.

Observational methods include all procedures by which researchers observe and record the behavior of interest rather than relying on subjects' self-reports. In one subcategory, **tests**, the researcher deliberately presents problems, tasks, or situations to which the subject responds. For example, to test generosity a researcher might allow subjects to win a certain amount of money in a game and then allow them to donate whatever amount they wish to other subjects or to some cause. In the other subcategory, **naturalistic observation**, the researcher avoids interfering with the subjects' behavior. For example, a researcher studying generosity might unobtrusively watch people passing by a charity booth outside of a grocery store to see who gives and who doesn't.

Consider a naturalistic research study conducted by Laura Berk (1986). Berk observed first- and third-grade children during daily math periods and related their behavior (particularly the incidence of talking to themselves) to their school performance. She reported that the older children were more likely to talk to themselves while they solved problems than were the younger children. The older children often quietly engaged in inaudible mutters and movements of their lips, apparently using language to guide their problem solving (for example, "Six plus six is twelve, carry the one . . ."). But those first-grade children who did talk to themselves while doing math problems tended to be the brighter children, apparently realizing before their peers that there was something they could do to make their job easier. These and other findings would have been difficult to assess in a laboratory situation.

One important caution about naturalistic observation research is called for here. Although it is sometimes possible to observe subjects unobtrusively, such as documenting how many people put money in a Salvation Army collection pot outside a grocery store, at other times, such as in the Berk study, subjects know they are being watched. Might the knowledge that someone is watching you affect how you behave? We know that it can. Thus, an obstacle to naturalistic observation is that the researchers may inadvertently, by their mere presence, influence the behavior they are observing.

In a classic study performed in the 1930s at the Hawthorne Plant of Western Electric in Cicero, Illinois (Roethlisberger & Dickson, 1939), researchers investigated various techniques to improve workers' productivity. These ranged from pay incentives, to different lighting conditions, to different work schedules. In all cases, the employees knew they were being observed. To the researchers' surprise, most manipulations they tried resulted in enhanced performance, at least initially. This result, however, was not due to the specific factor being changed (better lighting, for example), but simply to the subjects' knowledge that they were being watched and their belief that they were receiving special treatment. Changes in subjects' behavior as a result of knowing they are being watched has come to be known as the *Hawthorne effect*, and it is something that every researcher doing observational work needs to be aware of.

One technique for minimizing the Hawthorne effect takes advantage of the phenomenon of *habituation*, a decline in response when a stimulus is repeatedly or continuously present. Thus, over time, subjects may habituate to the presence of the researcher and go about their daily activities more naturally than they would if suddenly placed under observation.

None of these data-collection methods is inherently superior to another; each has its purposes, advantages, and limitations. Questionnaires and interviews can provide information that researchers would not be able to obtain by watching subjects directly. However, the validity of such data is limited by the subjects' ability to observe and remember their own behaviors or moods and by their willingness to report those observations frankly, without distorting them to look good or to please the researcher. Naturalistic observations allow researchers to learn firsthand about their subjects' natural behaviors, but the practicality of such methods is limited by the great amount of time they take, the difficulty of observing ongoing behavior without interfering with it, and the difficulty of coding results in a form that can be used for statistical analysis. Tests are convenient and easily scored but are by nature artificial, and their relevance to everyday behavior is not always clear. What is the relationship between a person's charitable giving in a laboratory test and that person's charitable giving in real life? Or between a score on an IQ test and the ability to solve real-life problems? These are the kinds of questions that psychologists must address whenever they wish to use test results to draw conclusions about behaviors outside of the testing situation.

■ **Observing without interfering** To minimize the impact of her presence on children's behavior, this researcher unobtrusively observes children in their classroom. She makes observations of their spontaneous behavior and may examine videos of their behavior at a later time.

Spencer Grant/Science Source

SECTION REVIEW

Research strategies used by psychologists vary in their design, setting, and data-collection method.

Research Designs

- In an experiment (such as the experiment on treatments for depression), the researcher can test hypotheses about causation by manipulating the independent variable(s) and looking for corresponding differences in the dependent variable(s), while keeping all other variables constant.

- In a correlational study, a researcher measures two or more variables to see if there are systematic relationships among them. Such studies do not tell us about causation.

- Descriptive studies are designed only to characterize and record what is observed, not to test hypotheses about relationships among variables.

Research Settings

- Laboratory settings allow researchers the greatest control over variables, but they may interfere with the behavior being studied by virtue of being unfamiliar or artificial.

- Field studies, done in "real-life" settings, have the opposite advantages and disadvantages, offering less control but the likelihood of more natural behavior.

Data-Collection Methods

- Self-report methods ask the people being studied to rate or describe themselves, usually in questionnaires or interviews.

- Observational methods require the researcher to observe and record the subjects' behavior through naturalistic observation or some form of test.

- Each data-collection method has advantages and disadvantages.

Statistical Methods in Psychology

To make sense of the data collected in a research study, we must have some way of summarizing the data and some way to determine the likelihood that observed patterns in the data are (or are not) simply the results of chance. The statistical procedures used for these purposes can be divided into two categories: (1) *descriptive statistics*, which are used to summarize sets of data, and (2) *inferential statistics*, which help researchers decide how confident they can be in judging whether the results observed are due to chance. We look briefly here at some commonly used descriptive statistics and then at the rationale behind inferential statistics. A more detailed discussion of some of these procedures, with examples, can be found in the *Statistical Appendix* at the back of this book.

Descriptive Statistics

Descriptive statistics include all numerical methods for summarizing a set of data. There are a number of relatively simple statistics that are commonly used to describe a set of data. These include the mean, median, and a measure of variability.

Describing a Set of Scores

If our data were a set of numerical measurements (such as ratings from 1 to 10 on how generous people were in their charitable giving), we might summarize these measurements by calculating either the mean or the median. The **mean** is simply the arithmetic average, determined by adding the scores and dividing the sum by the number of scores. The **median** is the center score, determined by arranging the scores from highest to lowest and finding the score that has the same number

Savage Chickens

YOU'RE THREE STANDARD DEVIATIONS ABOVE THE NORM

UM...THANKS?

LOVE LETTER FROM A STATISTICIAN

Doug Savage www.savagechickens.com

www.savagechickens.com

FOCUS 12

How do the mean, median, and standard deviation help describe a set of numbers?

TABLE 2.1 Two sets of data, with the same mean but different amounts of variability

Set A	Set B
7	2
7	4
8	8
11	9
12	14
12	16
13	17
Median = 11	Median = 9
Total = 70	Total = 70
Mean = 70/7 = 10	Mean = 70/7 = 10
Standard deviation = 2.39	Standard deviation = 5.42

of scores above it as below it, that is, the score representing the 50th percentile. (The *Statistical Appendix* explains when the mean or the median is the more appropriate statistic.)

For certain kinds of comparisons, researchers need to describe not only the central tendency (the mean or median) but also the variability of a set of numbers. *Variability* refers to the degree to which the numbers in the set differ from one another and from their mean. In **Table 2.1** you can see two sets of numbers that have identical means but different variabilities. In set A, the scores cluster close to the mean (low variability); in set B, they differ widely from the mean (high variability). A common measure of variability is the **standard deviation**, which is calculated by a formula described in the *Statistical Appendix*. As illustrated in Table 2.1, the farther most individual scores are from the mean, the greater is the standard deviation.

Describing a Correlation

FOCUS 13

How does a correlation coefficient describe the direction and strength of a correlation? How can correlations be depicted in scatter plots?

Correlational studies, as discussed earlier in this chapter, examine two or more variables to determine whether or not a nonrandom relationship exists between them. When both variables are measured numerically, the strength and direction of the relationship can be assessed by a statistic called the **correlation coefficient**. Correlation coefficients are calculated by a formula (described in the *Statistical Appendix*) that produces a result ranging from –1.00 to +1.00. The sign (+ or –) indicates the direction of the correlation (positive or negative). In a *positive correlation,* an increase in one variable coincides with a tendency for the other variable to increase; in a *negative correlation,* an increase in one variable coincides with a tendency for the other variable to decrease. The absolute value of the correlation coefficient (the value with sign removed) indicates the *strength* of the correlation. To the degree that a correlation is strong (close to +1.00 or –1.00), you can predict the value of one variable by knowing the other. A correlation close to zero (0) means that the two variables are statistically unrelated, that is, knowing the value of one variable does not help you predict the value of the other.

As an example, consider a hypothetical research study conducted with 10 students in a college course, aimed at assessing the correlation between the students' most recent test score and each of four other variables: (1) the hours they spent studying for the test; (2) the score they got on the previous test; (3) their level of psychological depression, measured a day before the test; and (4) their height in centimeters. Suppose the data collected in the study are recorded in tabular format, as shown in **Table 2.2**. Each horizontal row in the table shows the data for a different student, and the students are rank-ordered in accordance with their scores on the test.

To visualize the relationship between the test score and any of the other four variables, the researcher might produce a *scatter plot,* in which each student's test score and that student's value for one of the other measurements are designated by a single point on the graph. The scatter plots relating test score to each of the other variables are shown in **Figure 2.2**:

- Plot A illustrates the relation between test score and hours of study. Notice that each point represents both the test score and the hours of study for a single student. Thus, the point indicated by the red arrow denotes a student whose score is 85 and who spent 9 hours studying. By looking at the whole constellation of points, you can see that, in general, higher test scores correspond with more hours spent studying. This is what makes the correlation positive. But the correlation is far from perfect. It can be described as a *moderate positive correlation.* (The calculated correlation coefficient is +.51.)

TABLE 2.2 Examples of correlations, using made-up data
The most recent test score and four other measures for each of 10 students in a college course are recorded in tabular format. At the bottom of each of the four right-hand columns is the correlation coefficient relating the data of that column to the test score. (The study is fictitious and the data were made up for illustrative purposes.)

Student ranked by test score	Test score	Hrs of study	Previous test score	Depression	Height (cm)
1	100	9	85	8	177
2	97	11	88	4	160
3	85	9	70	3	171
4	80	14	79	1	158
5	78	8	62	10	184
6	78	5	65	11	152
7	62	3	44	6	176
8	54	6	30	12	165
9	38	10	20	14	159
10	22	3	30	7	176
Correlation with test score		+ .51	+ .93	– .43	– .04

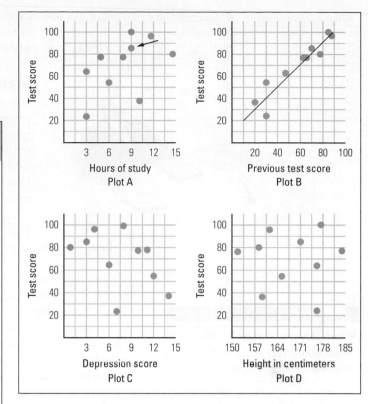

FIGURE 2.2 Scatter plots of correlations The four scatter plots depict, separately, the correlation between the test score and each of the four other measures. By comparing the plots, you can see the difference between weaker and stronger correlations and between positive and negative correlations.

- Plot B, which relates this test score to the score on the previous test, illustrates a *strong positive correlation.* Notice that in this plot the points fall very close to an upwardly slanted line. The closer the points are to forming a straight line, the stronger is the correlation between the two variables. In this study, the score on the previous test is an excellent predictor of the score on the new test. (The correlation coefficient is + .93.)

- Plot C, which shows the relation between test score and depression, illustrates a *moderate negative correlation.* Test scores tend to decrease as depression increases. (The correlation coefficient here is –.43.)

- Plot D, which shows the relation between test score and height, illustrates uncorrelated data with a correlation coefficient close to or equal to 0. Knowing a person's height provides no help in predicting the person's test score. (The correlation coefficient here is –.04.)

A correlation is actually a form of *inferential statistics,* which we turn to now.

Inferential Statistics

Any set of data collected in a research study contains some degree of variability that can be attributed to chance. That is the essential reason why inferential statistics are necessary. In the experiment comparing treatments for depression summarized back in Figure 2.1, the average depression scores obtained for the four groups reflect not just the effects of treatment but also random effects caused by uncontrollable variables. For example, more patients who were predisposed to improve could by chance have been assigned to one treatment group rather than to another. Or measurement error stemming from imperfections in the rating procedure could have contributed to differences in the depression scores. If the experiment were repeated several times, the results would be somewhat different each time because of such uncontrollable random variables. Given that results can vary as a result of

FOCUS 14

Why is it necessary to perform inferential statistics before drawing conclusions from the data in a research study?

chance, how confident can a researcher be in inferring a general conclusion from the study's data? Inferential statistics are ways of answering that question using the laws of probability.

Statistical Significance

When two groups of subjects in an experiment have different mean scores, the difference might be meaningful, or it might be just the result of chance. Similarly, a nonzero correlation coefficient in a correlational study might indicate a meaningful relationship between two variables, or it might be just the result of chance, such as flipping a coin 10 times and coming up with heads on seven of them. Seven is more than you would expect from chance if it's a fair coin (that would be 5), but with only 10 tosses you could have been "just lucky" in getting seven heads. If you got heads on 70 out of 100 flips (or 700 out of 1,000), you'd be justified in thinking that the coin is not "fair." Inferential statistical methods, applied to either an experiment or a correlational study, are procedures for calculating the probability that the observed results could derive from chance alone.

Using such methods, researchers calculate a statistic referred to as p (for *probability*), or the *level of significance*. When two means are being compared, the p value is the probability that a difference as great as or greater than that observed would occur by chance if, in the larger population, there were no difference between the two means. ("Larger population" here means the entire set of scores that would be obtained if the experiment were repeated an infinite number of times with all possible subjects.) In other words, in the case of comparing two means in an experiment, the p value is the probability that a difference as large as or larger than that observed would occur if the independent variable had no real effect on the scores. In the case of a correlational study, p is the probability that a correlation coefficient as large as or larger than that observed (in absolute value) would occur by chance if, in the larger population, the two variables were truly uncorrelated. By convention, results are usually labeled as ***statistically significant*** if the p value is less than .05 (5%). To say that results are statistically significant is to say that the probability is acceptably small (generally less than 5%) that they could be caused by chance alone. All of the results of experiments and correlational studies discussed in this textbook are statistically significant at the .05 level or better.

FOCUS 15

What does it mean to say that a result from a research study is statistically significant at the 5% level?

The Components of a Test of Statistical Significance

The precise formulas used to calculate p values for various kinds of research studies are beyond the scope of this discussion, but it is worthwhile to think a bit about the elements that go into such calculations. They are:

1. *The size of the observed effect.* Other things being equal, a large effect is more likely to be significant than a small one. For example, the larger the difference found between the mean scores for one group compared to another in an experiment, or the larger the absolute value of the correlation coefficient in a correlational study, the more likely it is that the effect is statistically significant. A large effect is less likely to be caused just by chance than is a small one.

2. *The number of individual subjects or observations in the study.* Other things being equal, results are more likely to be significant the more subjects or observations included in a research study. Large samples of data are less distorted by chance than are small samples. The larger the sample is, the more accurately an observed mean (or an observed correlation coefficient) reflects the true mean (or correlation coefficient) of the population from which it was drawn. If the number of subjects or observations is huge, then even very small effects will be statistically significant, that is, reflect a "true" difference in the population.

FOCUS 16

How is statistical significance affected by the size of the effect, the number of subjects or observations, and the variability of the scores within each group?

---

3. *The variability of the data within each group.* This element applies to cases in which group means are compared to one another and an index of variability, such as the standard deviation, can be calculated for each group. Variability can be described as an index of the degree to which uncontrolled, chance factors influence the scores in a set of data. For example, in the experiment assessing treatments for depression, greater variability in the depression scores within each treatment group would indicate greater randomness attributable to chance. Other things being equal, the *less* the variability is within each group, the more likely the results are to be significant. If all of the scores within each group are close to the group mean, then even a small difference between the means of different groups may be significant.

In short, a large observed effect, a large number of observations, and a small degree of variability in scores within groups all reduce the likelihood that the effect is due to chance and increase the likelihood that a difference between two means, or a correlation between two variables, will be statistically significant.

Statistical significance tells us that a result probably did not come about by chance, but it does not, by itself, tell us that the result has practical value. Don't confuse statistical significance with practical significance. If we were to test a new weight-loss drug in an experiment that compared 10,000 people taking the drug with a similar number not taking it, we might find a high degree of statistical significance even if the drug produced an average weight loss of only a few ounces. In that case, most people would agree that, despite the high statistical significance, the drug has no practical significance in a weight-loss program.

SECTION REVIEW

Researchers use statistics to analyze and interpret the results of their studies.

Descriptive Statistics

- Descriptive statistics help to summarize sets of data.

- The central tendency of a set of data can be represented with the mean (the arithmetic average) or the median (the middle score, or score representing the 50th percentile).

- The standard deviation is a measure of variability, the extent to which scores in a set of data differ from the mean.

Inferential Statistics

- Correlation coefficients represent the strength and direction of a relationship between two numerical variables.

- Inferential statistics help us assess the likelihood that relationships observed are real and repeatable or due merely to chance.

- Statistically significant results are those in which the observed relationships are very unlikely to be merely the result of chance.

- Researchers calculate a statistic called p, which must generally be .05 or lower (indicating a 5% or lower probability that the results are due to chance) before the results are considered to be statistically significant.

- The calculation of a p value takes into account the size of the observed effect, the number of subjects or observations, and the variability of data within each group.

Minimizing Bias in Psychological Research

Good scientists strive to minimize bias in their research. ***Bias***, as a technical term, refers to nonrandom (directed) effects caused by some factor or factors extraneous to the research hypothesis. The difference between bias and random variation in behavior can be visualized by thinking of the difference between the sets of holes produced by two archers engaged in target practice. One is a novice. He hasn't learned to hold the bow steady, so it wavers randomly as he shoots. The arrows

FOCUS 17

What is the difference between random variation in behavior and bias, and why is bias the more serious problem?

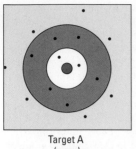  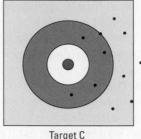

Target A   Target B   Target C
(error)   (bias)   (error and bias)

FIGURE 2.3 Random variation, bias, and both The difference between random variation in behavior and bias in research is like the difference between the sets of target holes produced by a novice archer (target A) and by a skilled archer whose bow sights are misaligned (target B). Target C shows the results from a novice archer using misaligned bow sights.

rarely hit the bull's-eye but scatter randomly around it (target A of **Figure 2.3**). His average shot, calculated as the average geometric location of his entire set of shots, is on or near the bull's-eye, even if few or none of his individual shots are on or near it. The distance between each arrow and the bull's-eye in this case exemplifies random variation. The other archer is experienced, but the sights on her bow are out of alignment. Because of that defect, all her arrows strike the target some distance to the right of the bull's-eye (target B). Those misses exemplify bias, and they are not correctable by averaging. No matter how many times the archer shoots or how carefully she aims, the average location of the whole set of arrows will be off the bull's-eye. Of course, random variation and bias can occur together, as would happen if a novice archer were given a defective bow sight (target C). In that case, the arrows would be widely scattered around a center that was some distance away from the bull's-eye.

Bias is a very serious problem in research because statistical techniques cannot identify it or correct for it. Whereas error only reduces the chance that researchers will find statistically significant results (by increasing the variability of the data), bias can lead researchers to the false conclusion that their hypothesis has been supported when, in fact, some factor irrelevant to the hypothesis has caused the observed results.

Avoiding Biased Samples

● **FOCUS 18**

How can a nonrepresentative selection of research subjects introduce bias into (a) an experiment and (b) a descriptive study?

Biased samples are one form of bias that impacts research results. If the members of a particular group are initially different from those of another group in some systematic way, or are different from the larger population that the researcher is interested in, then that group is a **biased sample**. Conducting research with a biased sample is like shooting with a bow whose sights are misaligned. No matter how large the sample is, the results will be off target.

Suppose that in the experiment on depression (Figure 2.1) the researchers had not randomly assigned the subjects to the different treatments but had allowed them to choose their own. In that case, biased samples could have resulted, because people's choices might have been based on preexisting differences among them. For example, those who felt most motivated to overcome their depression might have been particularly likely to choose the psychotherapy condition. Thus, any greater improvement by those in psychotherapy compared with the others might have resulted not from the psychotherapy but from the preexisting difference in motivation. When subjects are assigned randomly to groups, their individual differences are merely a source of error (and can be taken into account by inferential statistics); but when subjects are not assigned randomly, their differences can be a source of bias as well as error.

A sample is biased when it is not representative of the larger population that the researchers are trying to describe. A classic example of the effect of a biased sample in descriptive research is the *Literary Digest*'s poll of U.S. voters in 1936, which led the *Digest* to announce that Alf Landon would beat Franklin D. Roosevelt in the presidential election by a margin of 2 to 1 (Huff, 1954). It turned out that the publication's conclusion could not have been more mistaken—Roosevelt won by a landslide. The *Literary Digest* had conducted its poll by telephoning its subscribers. In 1936, in the midst of the Great Depression, people who could afford magazine subscriptions and telephones may indeed have favored Landon, but the great majority of voters, as the election showed, did not.

In terms of biased samples, one problem psychological scientists encounter is that the human subjects who are easily available to be studied may not be

■ Because most psychological research is conducted with people from Western, Educated, Industrialized, Rich, and Democratic (WEIRD) societies, it is difficult to generalize to all of humanity. Developmental psychologist Gilda Morelli (at left) spent many months living among the Efe in Africa, studying the sociocultural and ecological aspects of infants' and young children's development. Studies like hers contribute to a broader understanding of human behavior.

representative of the greater population. For instance, social and cognitive psychologists frequently test college students enrolled in Introductory Psychology classes and generalize their findings to the broader population. That is, they presume that what is true of college students is true of the population in general. Of course, college students are rarely representative of adults in a country: They are, on average, better educated (or at least on their way to being better educated), from more affluent backgrounds, and younger than typical adults. This makes generalizing results obtained with college students to the entire adult population of a nation a bit suspect. However, even when researchers go outside the confines of academia to get their samples by advertising for subjects online or testing specific groups of people, they still rarely get a sample that is representative of humankind in general.

Joseph Henrich and his colleagues (2010) pointed out that most psychological research is drawn from samples from Western, Educated, Industrialized, Rich, and Democratic (WEIRD) societies, and that this greatly limits what we can say about any universal characteristics we may uncover. The solution to this dilemma, of course, is to include non-WEIRD people in samples whenever possible, but this is often more easily said than done. For now, you should just be aware of some of the biases that are inherent in selecting research subjects and be cautious when interpreting a researcher's claims of uncovering a universal feature of humanity.

Reliability and Validity of Measurements

Psychological researchers must give careful thought to their measures of behavior. A good measure is both reliable and valid. What do we mean by "reliable" and "valid"?

Reliability

Reliability has to do with measurement error, not bias. A measure is reliable to the degree that it yields similar results each time it is used with a particular subject under a particular set of conditions, sometimes referred to as *replicability*. Measuring height with a cloth measuring tape is not as reliable as measuring it with a metal measuring tape because the elasticity of the cloth may cause the results to vary from one time to the next. A psychological test is not reliable if the scores are greatly affected by the momentary whims of the research subjects. Because it is a source of error, low reliability decreases the chance of finding statistical significance in a research study.

FOCUS 19

What is the difference between the reliability and the validity of a measurement procedure? How can lack of validity contribute to bias?

The drug has, however, proved more effective than traditional psychoanalysis.

A second type of reliability is *interobserver (or inter-rater) reliability*: the same behavior seen by one observer is also seen by a second observer. This requires that the behavior in question be carefully defined ahead of time. This is done by generating an **operational definition**, specifying exactly what constitutes an example of your dependent measure. An operational definition defines something in terms of the identifiable and repeatable procedures, or operations, by which it can be observed and measured. For instance, an operational definition of aggression could be based on specific behaviors in a specific context (a child hits, kicks, or pushes other children on the playground) or the results of a questionnaire designed to measure aggression. In the study discussed earlier by Baumrind (1971) assessing the relation between parenting styles (authoritarian, authoritative, and permissive) and the psychological outcomes of children (for instance, how friendly, happy, cooperative, and disruptive they were), Baumrind used operational definitions for the various parenting styles, as well as for children's psychological characteristics. Baumrind and her associates used observations of parents in their homes, noting several different categories of behavior that she believed were related to parenting styles. For example, some of Baumrind's measures for the category of "Firm Enforcement" included *Cannot be coerced by the child, Forces confrontation when child disobeys, Disapproves of defiant stance,* and *Requires child to pay attention.*

Even when operational definitions are agreed upon, it is a challenge to ensure that different observers record the behaviors similarly. To ensure interobserver reliability, most investigations require that at least two independent observers record the target behavior, and these recordings are then compared statistically to determine if the two people are seeing the same things. Interobserver reliability in Baumrind's study was generally high, suggesting that the operational definitions of the various behaviors were clear.

Validity

Validity is an even more critical issue than reliability because lack of validity can be a source of bias. A measurement procedure is valid if it measures or predicts what it is intended to measure or predict. A procedure may be reliable and yet not be valid. For example, suppose we decided to assess personality in adults by measuring thumb length. This procedure is highly reliable (we would get nearly the same thumb length score for a given person each time) but almost certainly not valid (thumb length is almost assuredly unrelated to personality). This invalid measure exemplifies bias because it would produce false conclusions, such as the conclusion that tall people (who would have longer thumbs) have different personalities than short people. If the measurement procedure appears to assess the variable that it is supposed to measure, we say the procedure has *face validity*. A test that assesses the degree to which a person is outgoing or shy has face validity as a measure of personality, but thumb length does not.

A more certain way to gauge the validity of a measurement procedure is to correlate its scores with another, more direct index of the characteristic that we wish to measure or predict. In that case, the more direct index is called the *criterion,* and the validity is called *criterion validity.* For example, suppose we operationally defined intelligence as the quality of mind that allows a person to achieve greatness in any of various realms, including business, diplomacy, science, literature, and art. With this definition, we might use the actual achievement of such greatness as our criterion for intelligence. We might identify a group of people who have achieved such greatness and a group who, despite similar environmental opportunities, have

FOCUS 20

How can we assess the validity of a measurement procedure?

not, and assess the degree to which they differ on various potential measures of intelligence. The more the two groups differ on any of the measures, the greater the correlation between that measure and our criterion for intelligence, and the more valid the test. As you can see from this example, the assessment of validity requires a clear operational definition of the characteristic to be measured or predicted. If your definition of intelligence differs from ours, you will choose a different criterion from us for assessing the validity of possible intelligence tests.

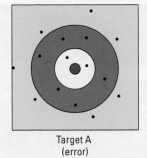  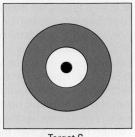

Target A
(error)   Target B
(bias)   Target C
(reliability and validity)

FIGURE 2.4 Reliability and validity Continuing the analogy of archers shooting arrows at targets, the pattern in target A reflects an unreliable measure: The different measurements (arrows) are distributed randomly. The pattern in target B reflects a reliable measure: All the shots are clustered in one area, but it is not valid (assuming the bull's-eye reflects the "real concept"). Finally, target C reflects both reliability (consistency) and validity (all shots in the "right" place).

To illustrate both reliability and validity, let's return to the analogy of archers shooting arrows at a target we used to illustrate bias. **Figure 2.4** shows three targets. In the first (A), shots are scattered randomly across the target. This reflects an unreliable measure. In the second (B), most of the shots are clustered in a single area, reflecting high reliability. However, the cluster is located far from the bull's-eye, which, for our purposes, represents the "true" concept we're trying to measure. This reflects high reliability but low validity. In the third (C), all of the shots are located in the bull's-eye, reflecting both high reliability and high validity.

Avoiding Observer-Expectancy and Subject-Expectancy Effects

A third source of bias can come from expectations of the experimenters themselves. Being human, researchers inevitably have wishes and expectations that can affect how they behave and what they observe when recording data. The resulting biases are called *observer-expectancy effects*, discussed earlier in this chapter in the case of Clever Hans. A researcher who wants or expects a subject to respond in a particular way may unintentionally communicate that expectation and thereby influence the subject's behavior. As you recall, Pfungst discovered that this sort of effect provided the entire basis for Clever Hans's apparent ability to answer questions. That episode occurred more than a century ago, but the power of observer expectancies to delude us is as strong today as ever. A dramatic example concerns a technique designed to enable people with autism to communicate.

The Facilitated-Communication Debacle

Autism is a disorder characterized by a deficit in the ability to form emotional bonds and to communicate with other people; it typically manifests before age 3. Some people with autism are almost completely unable to use either spoken or written language. Some years ago, in the prestigious *Harvard Educational Review,* Douglas Biklen (1990) described an apparently remarkable discovery, made originally by Rosemary Crossley in Australia. The discovery was that people with severe autism, who had previously shown almost no language ability, could type meaningful statements with one finger on a keyboard. They could answer questions intelligently, describe their feelings, display humor, and even write emotionally moving poetry by typing. To do this, however, a "facilitator" had to help by holding the typing hand and finger of the autistic person. According to Crossley and Biklen, the handholding was needed to calm the person, to keep the typing hand steady, and to prevent repeated typing of the same letter. (People with autism tend to repeat their actions.)

The community concerned with autism—including special educators and parents of children with autism—responded with great excitement to this apparent discovery. It takes enormous dedication and emotional strength to care for and work with people who don't communicate their thoughts and feelings, so you can imagine the thrill that parents and teachers felt when their autistic children typed, for the first time, something like "I love you." The motivation to believe in this new method was

FOCUS 21

How can the supposed phenomenon of facilitated communication by people with autism be explained as an observer-expectancy effect?

■ **Who is typing the message?** In the technique of facilitated communication, a facilitator holds the hand of the disabled person in order to "help" that person type a message on a keyboard. Experiments have shown that when this technique is used with autistic individuals, it is the facilitator, not the autistic person, who composes the message and controls the typing, even though the facilitator is not conscious of doing so.

Glenn Asakawa/Getty Images

enormous. Workshops were held to teach people to be facilitators, and thousands of teachers and parents learned the technique. By 1993, over $100 million a year was being spent by the U.S. educational system on equipment and personnel for facilitated communication (Levine et al., 1994).

Yet, from the beginning, there were skeptics. The credulity of some was strained by the sudden appearance of literary skills and erudition in people who had never previously shown evidence that they could read, write, or speak, or even understand much of what others said. As an alternative theory, the skeptics proposed that the messages were not communications from the autistic persons but unconscious creations of the facilitators (Dillon, 1993; Levine et al., 1994). The skeptics suggested that hand movements, made unconsciously by the facilitator, guided the autistic person's finger to the keys. Consistent with this view, some skeptics noticed that the persons with autism often did not even look at the keyboard as they ostensibly did their typing, while the facilitators always looked. The issue soon became important for moral and legal reasons as well as educational and scientific ones. Some autistic children, working with facilitators, typed out messages that accused parents or other caregivers of sexually abusing them (Heckler, 1994). Could facilitated messages be used by child-welfare authorities as a basis for taking a child into protective custody, or even prosecuting the accused?

Partly in response to court cases, many experiments were performed in the 1990s to test whether facilitated messages are creations of the autistic person or of the facilitator. In a typical experiment, pairs consisting of a facilitator and a person with autism, chosen because of their experience working together and their putative skill at the technique, were tested under two conditions. In one condition, the item of information that the autistic person was asked to communicate was also shown to the facilitator, and in the other condition it was not. For example, the autistic person might be shown a picture of a common object (e.g., an apple or a dog) and asked to type the name of that object, under conditions in which the facilitator either saw the object or did not. The result was that many correct responses were typed in the first condition (in which the facilitator was shown what the autistic person was shown), but not in the second condition. When the facilitator did not know what object the autistic person was shown, the number of correct responses was consistently no more than what would be produced by random guessing (Jacobson et al., 1995; Mostert, 2001). Subsequent research revealed directly that, in fact, facilitators unconsciously control the other person's hand movements (Wegner et al., 2003). It does not feel to them as if they are creating the messages and controlling the typing, even though they are.

The original observers, advocates, and practitioners of facilitated communication were deluded by a powerful effect of their own expectations. To understand that effect, imagine you are a practitioner who truly believes that the autistic person you are helping can type meaningful messages. At any given time during the facilitation, you have an idea (perhaps unconsciously) of what the autistic person is trying to type and what letter should come next. Your expectation that a particular letter will be typed leads you to feel that the autistic person's finger is moving toward that letter on the keyboard. You experience yourself as merely "facilitating" that movement, but you are actually guiding it and creating it. Moreover, the desire to enhance the communication of people with severe disabilities represents another strong bias. This bias can help to account for the fact that facilitated communication still persists in some quarters (Cardinal & Falvey, 2014) despite repeated evidence that it reflects the mind and behavior of the facilitator and not the person with autism (Travers et al., 2014).

Avoiding Observer-Expectancy Effects in Typical Experiments

In the experiments testing the validity of facilitated communication, the influence of observer expectancy was the focus of study and was assessed by varying the observers' (in this case, the facilitators') knowledge about what was supposed to be communicated. In a more typical psychological experiment, the objective is not to study observer-expectancy effects but to eliminate them in order to observe other effects without this form of bias.

Suppose you are conducting an experiment to test the hypothesis that subjects given treatment A will smile more than those given treatment B. Your expectation of more smiling by the former than the latter might cause you, unconsciously, to behave differently toward the two groups of subjects, in ways that could produce the results you expect. For example, you might unconsciously smile more yourself at the A subjects than at the B subjects, causing them to smile more in return. In that case, you would end up believing that treatment A caused the increased smiling, when in fact it was your own smiling that caused it.

In addition to influencing subjects' behavior, observers' expectations can influence observers' perceptions or judgments concerning that behavior. In the smiling experiment, for example, your expectation of seeing more smiles in one condition than in another might lead you to interpret ambiguous facial expressions as smiles in the one condition and as something else in the other.

The best way to prevent observer-expectancy effects is to keep the observer *blind*—that is, uninformed—about those aspects of the study's design that could lead him or her to form potentially biasing expectations. Thus, in a between-groups experiment, a blind observer would not be told which subjects received which treatment, so the observer would have no basis for expecting particular subjects to behave differently from other subjects. In our hypothetical experiment on smiling, you, as the blind observer, would not know who got which treatment, so you would have no basis for knowing which subjects "should" smile more or less than others. In DiMascio's study of treatments for depression (refer back to Figure 2.1), the clinicians who evaluated the patients' depression at the end of the treatment period were blind to treatment condition. To keep them blind, patients were instructed not to say anything about their treatment during the evaluation interviews.

Avoiding Subject-Expectancy Effects

Subjects also have expectations. If different treatments in an experiment induce different expectations in subjects, then those expectations, rather than anything else about the treatments, may account for observed differences in how the subjects respond. Effects of this sort are called *subject-expectancy effects*. For example, people who take a drug may subsequently behave or feel a certain way simply because they believe the drug causes such a behavior or feeling. Similarly, subjects who receive psychotherapy may improve simply because they believe psychotherapy will help them. (Recall our discussion of the Hawthorne effect earlier in this chapter.)

FOCUS 22

What are two ways by which an observer's expectations can bias results in a typical experiment? How does blind observation prevent such bias?

FOCUS 23

How can subjects' expectancies bias the results of an experiment? How does a double-blind procedure control both subjects' and observers' expectancies?

"IT WAS MORE OF A 'TRIPLE-BLIND' TEST. THE PATIENTS DIDN'T KNOW WHICH ONES WERE GETTING THE REAL DRUG, THE DOCTORS DIDN'T KNOW, AND, I'M AFRAID, NOBODY KNEW."

Ideally, to prevent bias from subject expectancy, subjects should be kept blind about the treatment they are receiving. Any experiment in which both the observer and the subjects are kept blind in this way is called a **double-blind experiment**. For example, in double-blind drug experiments, some subjects receive the drug while others receive a **placebo**, an inactive substance that looks like the drug, and neither the subjects nor the observers know who received the drug and who did not. Consequently, any observed difference between those who got the drug and those who did not must be due to the drug's chemical qualities, not to the subjects' or observers' expectancies.

Subjects cannot always be kept blind concerning their treatment. For instance, it is impossible to administer psychotherapy to people without their knowing it. As a partial control in some psychotherapy experiments, subjects in the nonpsychotherapy group are given a fake form of therapy designed to induce subject expectancies equivalent to those induced by actual psychotherapy (Boot et al., 2013). In DiMascio's depression experiment described earlier, subjects were not blind about their treatment. Those in the nondrug groups did not receive a placebo, and those in the nonpsychotherapy groups did not receive fake psychotherapy. Therefore, the results depicted in Figure 2.1 might possibly be placebo effects—that is, subject-expectancy effects caused by subjects' beliefs that the treatment would help them.

Replicating Earlier Studies

Earlier, we mentioned *replicability* with respect to the reliability of a measure: A measure is reliable/replicable to the degree that it yields similar results each time it is used with a particular subject under particular conditions. Replicability can also refer to reproducing, or replicating, the results of an entire study. If a study is performed a second time, following as closely as possible the same procedures as were used in the original study, will the same results be found? It is unusual for a researcher to conduct an exact replication of an earlier study without adding some new twist. Science advances by learning new things. Yet, it is critical for studies that find their way into the scientific literature to be reliable, and there has been much debate among psychologists (and scientists in general) about the need for replication of major findings (Pashler & Wagenmakers, 2012).

In 2015 a group of psychologists undertook the task of replicating 100 experiments published in one of three top psychology journals in 2008 (Open Science Collaboration, 2015). The results were somewhat startling, in that only slightly more than one third of the replications produced results statistically similar to the original studies. What can we make of these findings? Do they mean we can't trust the scientific literature? We don't think so. First, most of the replications produced results similar to those reported in the original studies. In fact, when the data of the original and replication studies were combined, 68% yielded significant findings. But why not 100%?

One reason is that the convention in science is to consider an effect as significant, in a statistical sense, if it is more likely to be correct than not at a certain level of probability. Recall that in psychology that probability is 95%, meaning that we are willing to take a 5% chance that an effect may have occurred by chance. Thus, we should not be surprised that a few studies produced significant results just by chance and we would not expect those to replicate.

Second, one robust finding in psychological research is the effect of context. Subtle differences in how an experiment is conducted or who the subjects were can make a difference in the outcome. For example, a sample of students from an elite university might yield results different from those obtained from a random sample of adults in a community. It is important to know about these differences, and once a finding is in the literature, other scientists will test the generality of that finding (that is, under what conditions or contexts will it be found). Although the replications were performed following the original study as closely as possible, minor differences in the context or subjects could be responsible for the different outcomes. One replication, for example, was done with subjects from Italy whereas the original study was done with subjects from the United States.

Third, science in general is a conservative institution, being cautious to accept theories or findings that depart too far from what we already know. Truly novel findings (think of facilitated communication) get tested repeatedly before they are accepted or—in the case of facilitated communication—rejected. Furthermore, among the institutions of science, textbooks tend to be the most conservative. Writers of textbooks, while wanting to bring readers the most up-to-date information in their disciplines, are hesitant to introduce truly novel findings that have not yet been widely accepted by the field. The findings of any one study are rarely taken too seriously by textbook authors unless they fit with an already established literature or until other studies using a variety of methods find consistent results.

Does this mean that all the results of every study we present in this textbook are absolutely replicable? We can only wish it were so. All sciences advance as new hypotheses are tested, new data are gathered, and new theories replace or refine old ones. However, we can say that most of the findings discussed in this book are well established and form the foundations of modern psychological science.

SECTION REVIEW

Bias—nonrandom effects caused by extraneous factors—must be avoided.

Biased Samples	Measurement Error and Bias	Expectancy Effects	Replicating Earlier Studies
■ Unless subjects in a between-groups experiment are assigned to groups randomly, an observed difference in the dependent variable may be caused by systematic differences between the groups rather than by the independent variable.	■ A good measure is reliable—able to yield similar results with repeated use on the same subjects under the same conditions.	■ A researcher's expectations about a study's results can influence those results. This is observer-expectancy bias.	■ Scientific ideas are tested by reproducing, or replicating, the results of prior studies.
■ Bias and false conclusions can occur if the subjects in a study are not representative of the group to which the researcher wants to generalize the results.	■ An operational definition specifies exactly what constitutes an example of your dependent measure, defining something in terms of the operations by which it could be observed and measured.	■ Subjects' expectations as to how they should respond can also influence results. This is subject-expectancy bias.	■ Recent research has shown that many findings published in prominent psychology journals do not replicate, although most replication studies produced the same pattern as the original studies.
■ Most psychological research with people is done from samples from Western, Educated, Industrialized, Rich, and Democratic (WEIRD) societies, which are not representative of humans.	■ Unreliable measurement produces random variability that makes it more difficult to establish statistical significance.	■ Such expectancy effects can occur without intention or even awareness.	■ Science is a conservative institution, and textbook writers in particular are likely to include only well-established findings.
	■ A good measure is also valid—able to measure what it is intended to measure. Invalid measures are sources of bias.	■ In observer-blind studies, the observer is deliberately kept ignorant of information that could create expectancies. In double-blind studies, both observers and subjects are kept ignorant of such information.	
	■ A measurement procedure that appears to assess the variable construct that it is supposed to measure has face validity. A measure that correlates significantly with another, more direct measure of the variable has criterion validity.		

Ethical Issues in Psychological Research

In designing their studies, psychologists must consider not just scientific issues but also ethical ones—issues of morality, or what is right. As an example, recall the experiment on treatments for depression by DiMascio and colleagues. From a scientific viewpoint, these researchers could have improved their study by using a placebo in the nondrug conditions and a fake form of psychotherapy in the nonpsychotherapy conditions. This would have reduced differences among the groups in subject expectancies. But from an ethical viewpoint, the researchers felt that their subjects should know which form of treatment they were receiving so that they could make an informed decision about whether or not to participate and could understand any side effects that might arise as treatment progressed.

Research With Humans

In research with humans, ethics dictate that subjects must provide their *informed consent* before participating in most studies. Informed consent means subjects must be told what the study is about and any risks it might entail. Additional ethical considerations revolve around three interrelated issues:

FOCUS 24

What are the ethical concerns pertaining to privacy, discomfort, deception, and animal welfare in psychological research? How do researchers strive to minimize problems related to these concerns?

1. *The person's right to privacy.* Common safeguards to protect privacy include informing subjects that they do not have to share any information about themselves that they do not wish to share, and keeping reports and records in ways that ensure anonymity.

2. *The possibility of discomfort or harm.* In reality, the great majority of psychological studies involve completely harmless procedures, such as reading rapidly flashed letters, memorizing lists of terms, or carrying on a discussion with other research participants. However, if a planned study involves some risk of discomfort or harm to subjects, researchers are obliged to determine whether the same research question can be answered through a design that involves less risk. If the answer is no, a determination must be made that the risk is minimal and is outweighed by the human benefits of the study. In addition, in any research study, human subjects must be advised that they are free to quit at any time.

3. *The use of deception.* This is the most controversial ethical issue in human psychological research. In some experiments, the independent variable involves a lie. Subjects may be falsely told or led to believe that something is happening, or is going to happen, so that the researcher can study the effects of that belief. Some psychologists are opposed to all use of deception. They argue that deception (a) is intrinsically unethical and (b) undermines the possibility of obtaining truly informed consent (Bersoff, 2008). Others, however, justify the use of deception on the grounds that some psychological processes cannot be studied effectively without it. These psychologists contend, further, that research deception usually takes the form of benign "white lies," and that these are cleared up during *debriefing*, in which subjects are informed of the true nature of the study after the session has ended (Benham, 2008). They also point out that informed consent can still be obtained by telling subjects about any realistic dangers they will face and by stating that some details of the study must be withheld until the data have been collected. Special consideration must be given when subjects are children, people of limited intellectual capacity, or those who have limited abilities to make their own decisions, such as prisoners.

Research With Nonhuman Animals

The use of nonhuman animals in research presents another area of ethical controversy. Most scientists agree that some procedures that would be unethical to use with humans can be used ethically with other animal species. For example, researchers may breed animals in controlled ways, raise them in controlled environments,

■ **A rat with an electrode in its brain** Experiments in behavioral neuroscience frequently involve operations on animal brains. For scientific as well as ethical reasons, conscientious researchers are scrupulous about minimizing discomfort to the animals. Discomfort can produce behaviors that interfere with those that the researcher wishes to study.

and surgically intervene in their physiology for research purposes. Because basic biological mechanisms underlying animal behavior are similar to those underlying human behavior, animal research contributes to our understanding of humans as well as the species studied. Still, research on nonhuman animals can sometimes cause them to suffer. Researchers who employ animals as subjects have an ethical obligation to balance the animals' suffering against the potential benefits of the research. Animals must be well cared for and not subjected to unnecessary deprivation or pain.

The knowledge gained from animal research has led to enormous reduction in human (and animal) suffering. For example, as we discuss in Chapter 8, research on learning with rats and pigeons (Skinner, 1953) has led to teaching techniques for children and adults with intellectual disabilities that improved their day-to-day functioning. Basic research on animal brains has led to greater understanding of human brains and ways to compensate for brain damage (Squire et al., 2013). Although some people question whether subjecting animals to pain or deprivation for research purposes is ever justifiable, others have turned the ethical question around. In the words of one (Miller, 1986): "Is it morally justifiable to prolong human (and animal) suffering in order to reduce suffering by experimental animals?" Nevertheless, research with chimpanzees, humans' closest genetic relatives, has caused special concern. Several countries have entirely banned biomedical research with chimpanzees. The United States ended biomedical research with chimpanzees in 2015, as they were classified as an endangered species (Grimm, 2015).

Formal Principles and Safeguards for Ethical Research

The American Psychological Association (2002, 2010) has established a set of ethical principles for psychological research, which researchers must follow if they are to publish their results in the research journals of that association. Moreover, the United States, Canada, and many other countries have laws that require publicly funded research institutions to establish ethics review panels, commonly called Institutional Review Boards (IRBs). An IRB's task is to evaluate all proposed research studies that have any potential for ethical controversy. IRBs today often turn down research proposals that may have been regarded as quite acceptable in the past. A few studies that are considered classics and are cited in most general psychology textbooks, including this one, would not be approved today. As you read about psychological research in the chapters that follow, questions of ethics may well occur to you from time to time. Such questions are always legitimate, as are those about the scientific merit of a study's design and the interpretation of its results. Psychology needs and usually welcomes people who raise those questions.

SECTION REVIEW

Psychologists must deal with ethical concerns in conducting research.

Human Subjects	Animal Subjects

Human Subjects

- A human subject's right to privacy must be protected.
- The risk of discomfort or harm to human subjects must be minimal.
- Deceiving subjects about some aspect of a study is both common and controversial.
- Routine measures to protect subjects include obtaining informed consent, letting subjects know they can quit at any time, ensuring anonymity in results, and debriefing subjects about deception after the study ends.

Animal Subjects

- Many procedures that would be unethical with humans—such as controlled breeding and surgical interventions—are performed with animals.
- The benefits of the knowledge gained from such research are the primary ethical justification for them, since common biological mechanisms often enable us to apply findings from animal studies to humans.
- Animals used in research must be well cared for, must not suffer unnecessary deprivation or pain, and must have their suffering balanced against the potential value of the knowledge gained.

Thinking Critically About Methods of Psychology

1. If we know that correlation does not imply causality, is there any scientific benefit of correlational research?

2. Thomas Jefferson stated, "An educated citizenry is a vital requisite for our survival as a free people." How might an understanding of research methodology play a role in today's "educated citizenry"?

Reflections and Connections

As you review and think about the concepts in this chapter, you might also consider the following two questions.

1. How does science compare with everyday observation and thought? No sharp dividing line exists between science and the kinds of observation and thought we all use every day to learn about the world around us. In our everyday learning, we begin with the data of our senses and use those data to draw tentative conclusions (make inferences) about specific aspects of our world. For example, suppose we observe someone from town X acting politely and someone from town Y acting rudely; we infer from those observations that people from X are more polite than people from Y. Most of us make such inferences all the time, often on scarcely more evidence than that. Science is simply the attempt to improve on our natural ways of learning. When we employ science, we systematize our data-collection procedures, control conditions to be more certain about which variables are having which effects, strive to eliminate sources of bias, deliberately think of alternative explanations, and use statistical procedures to assess the degree of confidence we should have in our tentative conclusions.

As you review each of the main concepts discussed in the sections on research strategies, statistical methods, and sources of bias in this chapter, think about how that concept applies to the distinctions between good and poor observation and thought in everyday life. We are observing and thinking poorly when we draw firm conclusions from too little evidence, or neglect to think about alternative explanations, or fail to see what is really there because of our biased expectations.

2. What is a science of psychology for? I (PG) remember, as a college freshman on my first visit home, expressing pride about an *A* that I had received in calculus. My mother, hearing me boast and having a knack for fostering humility and putting things into perspective, asked a simple question: "What is calculus for?" I was floored. I could rattle off terms and equations about calculus, and I could solve the problems as they were given to me in the class, but I had no understanding at all of what calculus was for. Perhaps that is why, by a few months after the class had ended, I had completely forgotten the terms, the equations, and the way to solve them. So what is a science of psychology for?

Many people think of psychology as a means of solving human problems. From that perspective, it is easy to appreciate the study on treatments for depression (illustrated in Figure 2.1) but more difficult to appreciate research motivated by the desire for knowledge and understanding, such as the evolutionary origins of human intelligence or why adults find infants' faces so cute.

For the most part, people go into psychological research, or any other research field, because they are curious or because they are thrilled by the prospect of being the first to uncover some mystery of nature, large or small. So psychology, like any other science, has two purposes: to solve practical problems and to satisfy the human quest for knowledge. It is hard to separate the two, however, because research undertaken to satisfy curiosity very often reveals solutions to practical problems, even though a connection with the research was not initially obvious. As you read the remaining chapters of this book, we hope you will allow yourself to become engaged by the questions for their own sake, regardless of whether you think they have practical applications. Each chapter contains mysteries—some solved, some not.

Key Terms

autism 49	double-blind experiment 52	mean 41	self-report methods 39
bias 45	experiment 34	median 41	standard deviation 42
biased sample 46	field study 38	naturalistic observation 39	statistically significant 44
blind 51	Hawthorne effect 40	observational methods 39	subject-expectancy effects 51
correlation coefficient 42	hypothesis 31	observer-expectancy effects 49	tests 39
correlational study 35	independent variable 34		theory 31
dependent variable 34	inferential statistics 41	operational definition 48	validity 48
descriptive statistics 41	introspection 39	placebo 52	variability 42
descriptive study 37	laboratory study 38	reliability 47	variable 33

Find Out More

Kenneth Keith & Bernard Beins (2017). *Worth expert guide to scientific literacy: Thinking like a psychological scientist.* New York, NY: Worth.

By presenting the research psychologist as having an empirical, data-driven mindset, this book uses both classic and current experiments to discuss research methods in psychology. It deals with the core principles of the research process: forming hypotheses or questions, designing research studies, considering ethical issues, and more. It further delves into the role of research in understanding social behavior.

Thomas Heinzen & Susan Nolan (2015). *The horse that won't go away: Clever Hans, facilitated communication, and the need for clear thinking.* New York, NY: Worth.

Does facilitated communication enable a child with autism to really communicate? This provocative book deals with popular misconceptions about psychological phenomena and the faulty uses of evidence and logic that lead to such

misconceptions. From Clever Hans to the exaggerated fear parents have of their child being kidnapped, this book looks at the need for science over pseudoscience, as well as addresses the deficits in human intuition that lead to faulty thinking and decision making.

Jonathan C. Smith (2010). *Pseudoscience and extraordinary claims of the paranormal: A critical thinker's toolkit.* Malden, MA: Wiley-Blackwell.

This is a book about the "evidence" and (sometimes) trickery that lead many people to believe in phenomena that violate our normal expectations of how the world works. Among the beliefs discussed are those concerning psychic readings, prophetic dreams, astrology, superstitions, UFOs, and creationism. Central to the book is the "Critical Thinker's Toolkit" that readers can use in their everyday lives.

Jane Halonen & Cynthia Gray (2016). *The critical thinking companion* (3rd ed.). New York, NY: Worth.

This workbook is designed for active learning of critical thinking. It includes exercises to empower readers to think for themselves, to question the evidence, and to be especially skeptical of claims that defy common sense. Each chapter corresponds to the chapters in Introductory Psychology textbooks, allowing you to think critically about the information presented as you go through the course.

Michael Shermer (Ed.), *Skeptic* http://www.skeptic.com/

This long-running magazine investigates a variety of pseudoscientific, paranormal, and many other controversies. Each issue is themed to a particular topic, and a variety of scholars, scientists, journalists, and teachers critically examine the claims and evidence around that topic. Visit their website to sign up for their free weekly newsletter *eSkeptic*, preview the magazine, or subscribe to receive digital issues.

LaunchPad
macmillan learning

Visit LaunchPad for Psychology 8e launchpadworks.com to access the e-book, videos, activities, additional resources, and LearningCurve quizzes, as well as study aids including flash cards and web quizzes.

PART II

The Biological Bases of Behavior

Although we've always known that behavior and thought are products of the brain, over the past several decades it has become increasingly clear that understanding the mind and behavior requires an understanding of biology. Genes, of course, influence the development and functioning of the brain, each of which have been shaped by millions of years of evolution, adapting us to the general conditions of human life on earth. In this unit, Chapter 3 examines the role of genes and evolution in the underlying mechanisms of behavior; Chapter 4 examines the structure of the nervous system and its principles of operation; and Chapter 5 is concerned with the neural and hormonal mechanisms underlying motivation and emotion.

CHAPTER

Genetics and Evolutionary Foundations of Behavior

3

LEARNING OUTCOMES

After studying this chapter, you should be able to:

- Identify some basic genetic mechanisms and describe how they work.

- Describe the influence of heredity on behavioral traits.

- Explain the theory of evolution by natural selection.

- Describe the functionalist approach to explaining behavior.

- Explain how natural selection relates to species-typical behaviors.

- Explain how patterns of mating, hurting, and helping can be understood in the context of evolution.

Have you ever spent time watching chimpanzees in their enclosure at a zoo? If not, we recommend seizing the next opportunity to do so, as the experience will undoubtedly convey a strong sense of the animal's kinship to us. Its facial expressions, its curiosity, even its sense of humor, are so like ours that we intuitively see it as a hairy, long-armed cousin. Indeed, the chimpanzee *is* our cousin. Along with the bonobo, a chimp-like ape discussed later in this chapter, it is one of our two closest animal relatives. Geneticists have lined up the DNA molecules of chimpanzees against those of humans and found that they match at 98.8% of their individual base units (The Chimpanzee Sequencing and Analysis Consortium, 2005). In genetic material, we are just 1.2% different from a chimpanzee. Humans' language and culture, and the knowledge these have given us, have in some ways separated us markedly from our non-human cousins. But in our genes—and in our basic drives, emotions, perceptual processes, and ways of learning—we are kin not just to chimpanzees, but in varying degrees to all of the mammals, and in lesser degrees to other animals as well.

More than 150 years ago, in *The Origin of Species,* Charles Darwin (1859/1963) presented a theory of evolution that explains both the similarities and the differences among the animal species. According to Darwin, all species are similar to one another because of common ancestry, and all species are unique because natural selection has adapted each species to the aspects peculiar to the environment in which it lives and reproduces. Darwin presented massive amounts of evidence for his theory, and essentially everything that scientists have learned since, about our own and other species, is consistent with it.

This chapter is primarily about the application of evolutionary theory to the behavior of humans and other animals. *Evolution* is the long-term adaptive process, spanning generations, that equips each species for life in its ever-changing natural habitat.

Darwin developed his theory of evolution before genes were discovered, but the theory is best understood today in the light of our knowledge of genes. This chapter begins by discussing genetic mechanisms and their implications for the inheritance of behavioral characteristics. The rest of the chapter is concerned with the evolution of behavior and how we can learn about our own behavior by comparing it to that of our animal relatives. Among other things, we examine patterns of mating, aggression, and helping, in our species and in others, from an evolutionary perspective.

Review of Basic Genetic Mechanisms

You have probably studied the mechanisms of gene action and reproduction in a biology course, but we will review them briefly here, focusing on their implications for psychology.

How Genes Affect Behavior

FOCUS 1

How can genes affect behavioral traits through their role in protein synthesis?

Researchers sometimes use a sort of shorthand, speaking of genes "for" particular behavioral traits. For example, they might speak of genes *for* singing ability, *for* aggression, or *for* cooperation. However, it is important to realize that genes never produce or control behavior directly; more accurately, genes are *associated* with behavior. All the effects that genes have on behavior occur through their role in building and modifying the physical structures of the body. Those structures, interacting with the environment, produce behavior. Thus, a gene might influence singing ability by promoting the development of a brain system that analyzes sounds, or by promoting certain physical aspects of the vocal cords. Similarly, a gene might affect aggressiveness by fostering the growth of brain systems that organize aggressive behavior in response to irritating stimuli. In a sense, all genes that contribute to the body's development are "for" behavior, since all parts of the body are involved in behavior. Especially relevant for behavior, however, are genes that contribute to the development of sensory systems, motor systems (muscles and other organs involved in movement), and, most especially, the nervous system (which includes the brain).

Genes Provide the Codes for Proteins

Genes affect the body's development through their influence on the production of protein molecules. Biologically speaking, we are what we are because of our proteins. A class of proteins called *structural proteins* forms the structure of every cell of the body. Another, much larger class called *enzymes* controls the rate of every chemical reaction in every cell.

Physically, **genes** are components of extremely long molecules of a substance called **DNA** (deoxyribonucleic acid). These molecules exist in the egg and sperm cells that join to form a new individual, and they replicate themselves during each cell division in the course of the body's growth and development. A replica of your whole unique set of DNA molecules exists in the nucleus of each of your body's cells, where it serves to code for and regulate the production of protein molecules.

Each protein molecule consists of a long chain of smaller molecules called amino acids. A single protein molecule may contain anywhere from several hundred up to many thousand amino acids in its chain. There are a total of 20 distinct amino acids in every form of life on earth, and they can be arranged in countless sequences to form different protein molecules. Some portions of the DNA in your cells serve as templates (molds or patterns) for producing another molecular substance called

RNA (ribonucleic acid), which in turn serves as a template for producing protein molecules. Scientists often describe a gene as a segment of a DNA molecule that contains the code that dictates the particular sequence of amino acids for a single type of protein. With that definition, geneticists have determined that human beings (and also chimpanzees and mice) have about 20,000 genes (International Human Genome Sequencing Consortium, 2004).

Recent molecular work has led many geneticists to change their definition of a gene, so that it includes portions of DNA that have other functions, not just the coding of protein molecules (ENCODE Project Consortium, 2012). Most of the DNA in human cells does not code for proteins. Although much of this noncoding DNA was once called "junk DNA" because scientists believed it had no purpose, recent evidence indicates that about 80% of DNA serves some function, such as regulating the activity of the coding DNA (ENCODE Project Consortium, 2012). Geneticists now distinguish between *coding genes,* which code for unique protein molecules, and *regulatory genes,* which work through various biological means to help activate or suppress specific coding genes and thereby influence the body's development. Recent research comparing human and chimpanzee DNA suggests that the biggest genetic differences between the two species lie in certain regulatory genes that affect the development of the brain (Prabhakar et al., 2006; McClean et al., 2011).

Genes Work Only Through Interaction With the Environment

At every level, from biochemical to behavioral, the effects of genes and environment are entwined. *Environment,* as used in this context, refers to every aspect of an individual and his or her surroundings except the genes themselves. It includes the nourishing womb and maternal bloodstream before birth; the internal chemical environment of the individual; and all the events, objects, and other individuals encountered after birth. Foods—a part of the environment—supply genes with amino acids, which are needed to manufacture proteins. Environmental effects also help to turn genes "on" and "off," resulting in bodily changes that alter the individual's behavioral capacity. Such changes can occur in adulthood as well as earlier in development. For example, physical exercise modifies the chemical environment of muscle cells, activating genes that promote further growth of the muscle. One's body and behavioral capacities result from a continuous, complex interplay between genes and environment (see **Figure 3.1**). One is no more basic than the other—genes are always expressed in a context.

The world of reptiles provides a fascinating example of the role of context in gene expression. In mammals, being male or female is a matter of genes, but this is not the case for many reptiles. Sex in many turtles, alligators, and crocodiles is determined not by differences in genes but by differences in the temperature at

FOCUS 2

What does it mean to say that genes can influence behavioral traits only through interaction with the environment? How are genes involved in long-term behavioral changes derived from experience?

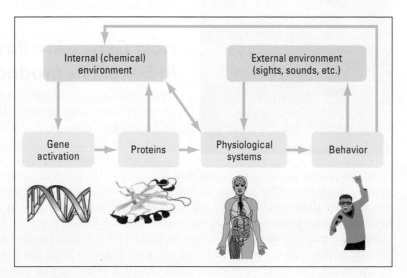

FIGURE 3.1 Route through which genes affect behavior Genes build proteins, which form or alter the body's physiological systems (including brain systems), which, in turn, produce behavior. Each step in this process involves interaction with the environment. Aspects of the internal environment control gene activation, and aspects of both the internal and the external environments act on physiological systems to control behavior. Behavior, in turn, can affect gene activation through direct and indirect effects on the internal environment.

"So, how do you want to play this? Nature, nurture, or a bit of both?"

which the eggs are incubated. Theoretically, we could have genetically identical twin reptiles, one male and one female. Genes still provide the critical instructions for developing into a male or female animal, but the context in which the genes are expressed (a warm versus a cool temperature) determines the sex that will form. A tour guide in the Galápagos Islands (about 600 miles off the coast of Ecuador) told how he remembered which temperature produces which sex for the Galápagos giant tortoises: "Hot chicks and cool dudes."

Researchers have studied specific mechanisms through which experiences can activate genes and thereby alter the individual's brain and behavior. For example, adult mice and rats that have not given birth will normally avoid newborns of their species that are placed in their cage. However, if exposed to newborns continuously for several hours or more, they gradually begin to care for them. Why? The sight, sound, or smell of newborns activates a particular gene. The activated gene produces a protein molecule that stimulates activity in a specific cluster of brain cells that are known to be crucial for the motivation and organization of such behaviors as retrieving young to a nest and hovering over them. The result is that a mouse or rat that previously did not take care of young is transformed into a mouse or rat that does. This type of behavior change is known as environmental induction of gene activity (Brown et al., 1996; Numan, 2007).

There is good reason to believe that prolonged behavioral effects that derive from experience, including those that we call "learning," involve the activation of genes (Spencer et al., 2009). Experiences activate genes, which produce proteins, which in turn alter the function of some of the neural circuits in the brain and thereby change the individual's behavior.

Distinction Between Genotype and Phenotype

The term **genotype** refers to the set of genes that the individual inherits, whereas the term **phenotype** refers to the observable properties of the body and behavioral traits. The same genes can have different effects, depending on the environment and the mix of other genes. Two individuals with the same genotype can be quite different in phenotype as a result of differences in their environments. Genetically identical rats will differ phenotypically in their behavior toward infant rats if one has been previously exposed to infant rats and the other has not. Genetically identical human twins will differ in size if they have been exposed differently to growth-promoting factors in their environments (see **Figure 3.2**), and they will differ in behavior if they have been subjected to different learning experiences.

FOCUS 3

How can the same genotype produce various phenotypes?

FIGURE 3.2 Identical twins These 13-year-old girls have the same genotype, but they obviously differ in at least one aspect of their phenotype. It is uncertain what caused this difference. It may have derived from their occupying different positions in the womb such that one received more early nutrition than the other, which activated genes promoting more growth.

How Genes Are Passed Along in Sexual Reproduction

Genes not only provide the codes for building proteins; they also serve as the biological units of heredity. They are replicated and passed along from parents to offspring.

To understand how genes are passed along in sexual reproduction, it is useful to know how they are arranged within cells. The genetic material (DNA) exists in each cell in structures called **chromosomes**, which are usually dispersed throughout the cell nucleus. Just prior to cell division, however, the chromosomes condense into compact forms that can be stained, viewed through a microscope, and photographed. The normal human cell has 23 pairs of chromosomes. Twenty-two of these are true pairs in both the male and the female, in the sense that each chromosome looks like its mate and contains similar genes.

The remaining pair is made up of the sex chromosomes. In the normal human male cell, that "pair" consists of a large chromosome labeled X and a small chromosome labeled Y (see **Figure 3.3**). Genetically, the only difference between the sexes is that females have two X chromosomes (XX—a true pair) rather than the XY of the male.

The Production of Genetically Diverse Egg and Sperm Cells

When cells divide to produce new cells other than egg or sperm cells, they do so by a process called **mitosis**. In mitosis, each chromosome precisely replicates itself and then the cell divides, with one copy of each chromosome moving into each of the two cell nuclei thus formed. Because of the faithful copying of genetic material in mitosis, all your body's cells, except your egg or sperm cells, are genetically identical to one another. The differences among cells in your body— such as muscle cells and skin cells—arise from the differential activation of their genes, not from different gene content.

When cells divide to produce egg or sperm cells, they do so by a different process, called **meiosis**, which results in cells that are not genetically alike (see **Figure 3.4**). During meiosis, each chromosome replicates itself once, but then the cell divides twice. Before the first cell division, the chromosomes of each pair line up next to one another and exchange genetic material in a random manner. Although the chromosomes in each pair look the same, they do not contain precisely the same genes. The result of this random exchange of genetic material and of the subsequent cell divisions is that each egg or sperm cell produced is genetically different from any other egg or sperm cell and contains only half of the full number of chromosomes (one member of each of the 23 pairs).

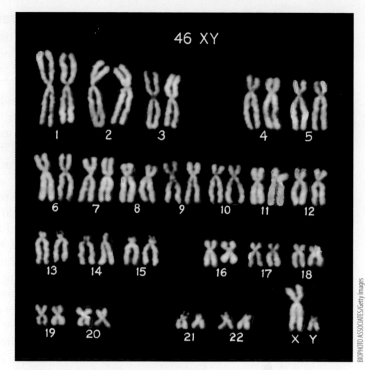

FIGURE 3.3 Chromosomes of a normal human male cell The 22 numbered pairs of chromosomes are the same in a normal female cell as they are in a normal male cell. The remaining two, labeled X and Y, are the sex chromosomes. The normal human female cell (not shown) has a second X chromosome instead of a Y.

BIOPHOTO ASSOCIATES/Getty Images

FOCUS 4

How does meiosis produce egg or sperm cells that are all genetically different from one another?

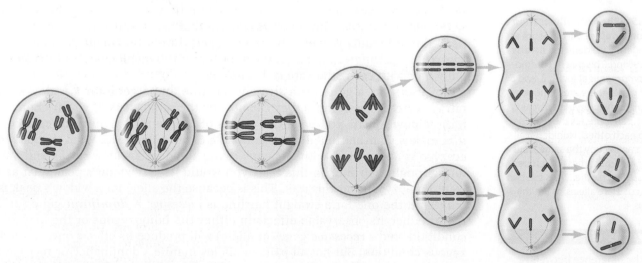

FIGURE 3.4 Schematic illustration of meiosis in sperm production This illustration is for a creature that has only three pairs of chromosomes rather than the 23 pairs that humans have. At the beginning (left), each chromosome has already replicated itself and remains attached to its replica. The pairs of replicated chromosomes (one blue and one red in each pair in the diagram) then line up next to one another and exchange genetic material through a process called *crossing over*. The cell then divides twice, resulting in four sperm cells, each with just one member of each pair of chromosomes. Notice that each sperm cell is genetically different from the others, having a different mix of the original (blue and red) material from the parental pairs of chromosomes. The diagram greatly oversimplifies the effects of crossing over. In fact, each chromosome would cross over many times with its paired mate, resulting in a random mixing of genetic material. Meiosis in egg production is similar to that in sperm production, but only one of the two cells produced at each division survives.

The Genetic Diversity of Offspring

It may seem ironic that the very cells you use for "reproduction" are the only cells in your body that cannot, in theory, reproduce you. They are the only cells in your body that do not have all your genes. In sexual reproduction you are, of course, not really reproducing yourself. Rather, you are creating a genetically unique individual who has half of your genes and half of your partner's genes. When a sperm and an egg unite, the result is a single new cell, the ***zygote***, which contains the full complement of 23 paired chromosomes. One member of each of these pairs comes from each parent. The zygote then grows, through mitosis, into a new person. Because each sperm or egg is different from any other sperm or egg (even from the same parent), each zygote is unique.

The value of sex, as opposed to simple cloning (the asexual production of genetically identical offspring), lies in the production of genetically diverse offspring. In a continually changing environment, genes have a better chance of surviving if they are rearranged at each generation in many different ways, to produce different kinds of bodies, than if they are all put into the same kind of body—an almost literal example of the old saying, "Don't put all your eggs in one basket." By producing diverse offspring, parents reduce the risk that all of their offspring will die as a result of some unforeseen change in the environment.

There are, however, people who are genetically identical to each other: ***identical twins***. They are formed when two bundles of cells separate from each other during the early mitotic divisions following the formation of a zygote. Because they originate from one zygote, identical twins are also known as *monozygotic twins*. ***Fraternal twins***, or *dizygotic twins*, originate from two zygotes, each formed from different egg and sperm cells. Fraternal twins have the same degree of genetic similarity as any two non-twin siblings. In later chapters, you will see how psychologists make use of twins in research to understand how much of the variability in certain psychological traits results from differences in people's genes, as opposed to differences in their environments.

Consequences of the Fact That Genes Come in Pairs

You have seen that genes exist on long DNA strands in chromosomes, rather like beads on a string, and that chromosomes come in pairs. The two genes that occupy the same *locus* (location; plural *loci*) on a pair of chromosomes are sometimes identical to each other and sometimes not. When they are identical, the individual is said to be *homozygous* [**home**-oh-**zai**-gus] at that locus, and when they are not identical, the individual is said to be *heterozygous* [**het**-er-oh-**zai**-gus] at that locus (see **Figure 3.5**). Different genes that can occupy the same locus, and thus can potentially pair with each other, are called ***alleles***.

For example, a gene for a straight hairline and a gene for a widow's peak in humans are alleles because they can occupy the same locus. If you are homozygous for a widow's peak, you have two copies of a gene that manufactures an enzyme that makes your hairline dip in the middle of your forehead. What if you were heterozygous for hairline, with one copy of the allele for a widow's peak and one copy for a straight hairline? In this case, you would have a widow's peak, just as if you were homozygous for this trait. This is because the allele for a widow's peak is *dominant* and the one for a straight hairline is *recessive*. A ***dominant*** gene (or allele) will produce its observable effects in either the homozygous or the heterozygous condition, and a ***recessive*** gene (or allele) will produce its effects only in the homozygous condition. But not all pairs of alleles manifest dominance or recessiveness. Some pairs blend their effects. For example, if you cross red snapdragons (a kind of flower) with white snapdragons, the offspring will have pink flowers, because neither the red nor the white allele is dominant over the other.

Mendelian Pattern of Heredity

The idea that the units of heredity come in pairs and that one member of a pair can be dominant over the other was developed in the mid-nineteenth century by

FOCUS 5

What is the advantage of producing genetically diverse offspring?

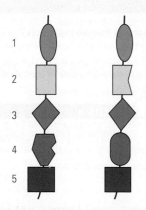

FIGURE 3.5 Schematic illustration of gene loci on a pair of chromosomes Successive genes are depicted here as beads on a string. This pair of chromosomes is *homozygous* at loci 1, 3, and 5 (the paired genes there are identical to each other) and *heterozygous* at loci 2 and 4 (the paired genes there are not identical to each other). Nonidentical genes that can occupy the same locus on a pair of chromosomes are referred to as alleles of each other. Thus the two genes at locus 2 are alleles, as are the two at locus 4.

FOCUS 6

What is the difference between a dominant and a recessive gene (or allele)?

an Austrian monk named Gregor Mendel. In a typical experiment, Mendel would start with two purebred strains of pea plants that differed in one or more easily observed traits. He could cross-pollinate them to observe the traits of the offspring, called the *F1* (first filial) generation. Then he would pollinate the *F1* peas with pollen from other *F1* peas to produce the *F2* (second filial) generation.

In one experiment, for example, Mendel cross-pollinated a strain of pea plants that regularly produced round seeds with a strain that regularly produced wrinkled seeds. His famous findings were that (a) all of the *F1* generation had round seeds and (b) three-fourths of the *F2* generation had round seeds and one-fourth had wrinkled seeds.

Mendel's findings make perfect sense if we assume that seed texture is controlled by a single pair of genes, with the allele for round dominant over that for wrinkled. To illustrate this, let us use the capital letter *R* to stand for the dominant, round-producing allele, and the small letter *r* for the recessive, wrinkle-producing allele. The purebred round strain is homozygous for the "round" allele (*RR*), and the purebred wrinkled strain is homozygous for the "wrinkled" allele (*rr*). (Purebred strains are homozygous for all traits.) Because one allele must come from each parent, the only possible result for the *F1* generation, produced by crossing the two purebred strains, is the heterozygous condition (*Rr*). This explains why all the *F1* peas in Mendel's experiment were round. At the next step, when *Rr* peas receive pollen from other *Rr* peas to produce the *F2* generation, four equally likely combinations can occur: (1) an *R* from each parent (*RR*), (2) an *R* from the female parent and an *r* from the male (*Rr*), (3) an *r* from the female parent and an *R* from the male (*rR*), and (4) an *r* from each parent (*rr*). (See **Figure 3.6**.) Since only one of these possible outcomes (*rr*) is wrinkled, the expectation is that one-fourth of the *F2* generation will be wrinkled and the other three-fourths round. This is just what Mendel found.

Whenever a trait is inherited in a pattern like that observed by Mendel, we can assume that the trait results from variation in alleles at a single gene locus that interact in a dominant-recessive manner.

The Double-Edged Sword of Sickle-Cell Anemia

A few hereditary diseases are caused by a single pair of recessive genes that lead to an early death (or were deadly before the advent of modern medicine). Among these is *sickle-cell anemia*, a disease that interferes with the transport of oxygen in the blood. In healthy individuals, the red blood cells that carry the oxygen are usually disk shaped. In patients with sickle-cell anemia, the blood cells are distorted, shaped like a sickle, or crescent moon. Because of their shape, the sickled cells tend to pile up and block small blood vessels, resulting in pain and destruction of tissue, as well as other complications that can be fatal. Given that natural selection is supposed to favor characteristics that enhance the chances of an individual surviving, and that genes that essentially kill their host do not get passed on to future generations, why haven't sickle-cell-anemia genes been eliminated?

The answer is that although having two recessive genes for sickled cells was often a death sentence before the advent of modern medicine, having just one recessive gene and one normal, dominant gene (that is, being heterozygous at that locus) provided some benefit. The genes associated with sickle-cell anemia originated in areas of the globe where malaria was common, chiefly in Africa. People with a single sickle-cell gene are less likely to die of malaria because their red blood cells are poor at supporting the growth of the malaria parasite. People who have one recessive gene (carriers) living in these areas are thus more likely to live to reproduce than noncarriers, keeping the recessive and potentially deadly gene in the gene pool. The benefit is not to those who have the disease, but to those who are carriers (Desai & Dhanani, 2004).

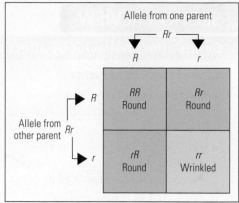

FIGURE 3.6 Explanation of Mendel's 3:1 ratio When a pea plant that is heterozygous for round versus wrinkled seeds is pollinated by another pea plant that is similarly heterozygous, four possible gene combinations occur in the offspring. Here *R* stands for the dominant, round-producing allele, and *r* for the recessive, wrinkle-producing allele. The phenotype of three of the offspring will be round and that of one wrinkled. This 3:1 ratio was Mendel's famous finding.

FOCUS 7

Why do three-fourths of the offspring of two heterozygous parents show the dominant trait and one-fourth show the recessive trait?

FOCUS 8

Why might a disease caused by two recessive genes persist in the gene pool?

Genes affect behavior by affecting the bodily structures involved in behavior.

Nature of Genetic Influence

- Through their influence on protein synthesis, genes affect bodily structures and behavior.
- Genes act in concert with the environment, not in isolation. For example, environmental cues can activate genes that make rats or mice nurturant to newborns.

Meiosis and Sexual Reproduction

- Meiosis results in egg and sperm cells that are genetically unique and contain only half the full number of chromosomes.
- Meiosis involves random assortment of paired genes.
- Genetic diversity produced by sexual reproduction promotes survival of genes by reducing the chance that all offspring will die.

Gene Pairing

- Paired genes, which occupy the same locus (location) on a pair of chromosomes, may be identical (homozygous) or different (heterozygous). Gene variations that can occupy the same locus are called alleles.
- Mendel's discovery of consistent ratios of traits in offspring of cross-pollinated strains of peas led to the gene concept and to the concepts of dominance and recessiveness.
- Some genetic conditions, such as sickle-cell anemia, carry both risks and benefits for the individuals born with them.

Inheritance of Behavioral Traits

Variation in genes contributes to variation in behavior. Some behavioral characteristics are inherited in accordance with the same pattern that Mendel observed in plants, indicative of control by a single pair of genes. Most behavioral characteristics, however, depend on many genes. In this section, we look first at two examples of single-gene traits and then at traits that are affected by many genes.

Examples of Single-Gene (Mendelian) Behavioral Traits

Mendelian Inheritance of Fearfulness in Dogs

One of the first demonstrations of single-gene control of a behavioral trait in dogs was published more than 50 years ago. In pioneering research on the role of genes in behavior, John Paul Scott and John Fuller (1965) studied the behavior of basenji hounds, cocker spaniels, and their mixed-breed offspring. Basenjis are timid dogs, showing fear of people until they have received much gentle handling. Cockers, in contrast, show little fear under normal rearing conditions. In a standard test with 5-week-old puppies, Scott and Fuller found that all the basenji puppies yelped and/or ran away when approached by a stranger, whereas only a few of the cocker puppies showed these reactions. When cockers and basenjis were crossbred, the offspring (*F1* hybrids) were like basenjis in this test: All showed signs of fear when approached. Since this was as true of hybrids raised by cocker mothers as of those raised by basenji mothers, Scott and Fuller concluded that the effect stemmed from the hybrid dogs' genes and not from anything they learned from their mothers.

The fact that the *F1* hybrids were as fearful as the purebred basenjis suggested to Scott and Fuller that the difference in fearfulness between the two purebred strains might be controlled by a single gene locus, with the allele promoting fear dominant over that promoting confidence. If this were so, then mating *F1* hybrids with each other should produce a group of offspring (*F2* generation) in which three-fourths would show basenji-like fear and one-fourth would show cocker-like confidence—the same ratios that Mendel had found with seed texture in pea plants. Scott and

FOCUS 9

How did Scott and Fuller show that the difference in fearfulness between cocker spaniels and basenji hounds is controlled by a single gene locus, with the "fear" allele dominant over the "non-fear" allele?

Fuller did this experiment and, indeed, found ratios very close to those predicted. As additional evidence, they also mated *F1* hybrids with purebred cockers. About half the offspring of those backcrosses were basenji-like in fear, and the other half were cocker-like in confidence—just as can be expected if the "fear" allele is dominant over the "non-fear" allele. (see **Figure 3.7**)

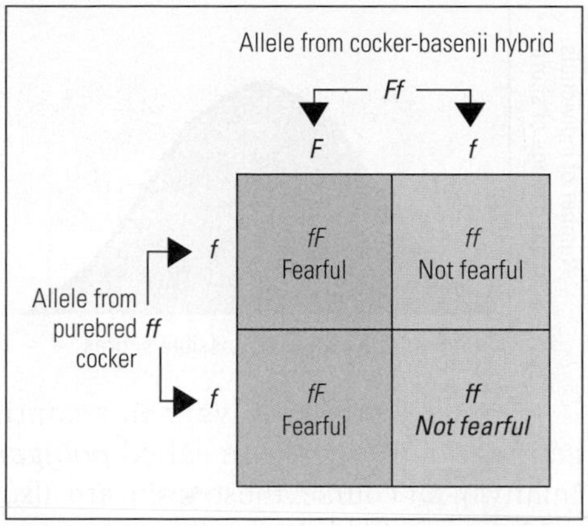

From this research, can we conclude that fear in all its various forms is controlled by a single gene? No. Scott and Fuller's work demonstrates only that the difference between cocker spaniels and basenji hounds in a particular test of fear is controlled by a single gene. In a broader context, many different genes must contribute to building the complex neural structure needed to experience fear and express it in behavior. Recognize also that Scott and Fuller could detect the effect of a specific gene pair because they raised all the dogs in similar environments; their studies do not diminish the role of environmental influences. In other research, Scott (1963) showed that any puppy isolated from people for the first 4 months of life will be fearful of humans. Had Scott and Fuller isolated the cockers from all human contact and given the basenjis lots of kind handling before the behavioral test, they might well have found the cockers to be more fearful than the basenjis, despite the genetic predispositions toward the opposite behavior.

FIGURE 3.7 Explanation of Scott and Fuller's results of mating basenji-cocker hybrids with purebred cockers The finding that half the offspring were fearful and half were not makes sense if fearfulness results from a dominant allele (*F*) and lack of fearfulness results from a recessive allele (*f*). Because half the offspring receive *F* from their hybrid parent and all receive *f* from the pure-bred parent, half the offspring will be *Ff* (phenotypically fearful) and the other half *ff* (not fearful).

Allele from cocker-basenji hybrid

Ff

	F	f
f	fF Fearful	ff Not fearful
f	fF Fearful	ff *Not fearful*

Allele from purebred *ff* cocker

FOCUS 10

Why would it be a mistake to conclude, from Scott and Fuller's work, that fear in dogs is caused just by one gene or that it is caused just by genes and not by the environment?

Mendelian Inheritance and Expression of Genetic Disorders

Most of the behaviorally relevant traits in humans that derive from alteration at a single gene locus are brain disorders, caused by relatively rare, mutant, malfunctioning genes passed from generation to generation. For example, in *phenylketonuria*, or *PKU*, infants inherit two recessive genes involved in the processing of the amino acid phenylalanine. The presence of these genes causes the amino acid to accumulate in the brain, resulting in intellectual disorders. However, PKU only has its detrimental effects if the person consumes foods that contain phenylalanine. (Phenylalanine is found in many foods and is a principal ingredient in some artificial sweeteners made with Aspartame®.) Newborns are routinely screened for the ability to process phenylalanine, and when babies who have the PKU genes are placed on a phenylalanine-free diet they develop normally. Moreover, by adulthood, people with PKU can consume phenylalanine without any negative consequences. Genes themselves, then, do not "cause" PKU – excessive phenylalanine in the diet does. However, the inability to process phenylalanine is "caused" by defective genes. Thus, even in this prototypical case of a genetic disease, genes and environment clearly interact (Widaman, 2009).

FOCUS 11

How do genes and the environment interact to affect individuals with PKU?

Polygenic Characteristics and Selective Breeding

Characteristics that derive from variation at a single gene locus are typically *categorical* in nature. That is, they are characteristics that sharply differentiate one group from another. Peas are either round or wrinkled; mixed-breed basenji-cockers differ so sharply from one another in fearfulness that they can be categorized into two distinct groups; newborn babies either have or do not have PKU (none of them "sort of have it").

But most anatomical and behavioral differences among individuals of any species are measurable in degree, not type. They are *continuous* rather than categorical. That is, the measures taken from individuals do not fall into two or more distinct groups but can lie anywhere within the observed range of scores. Most often, the set of

FOCUS 12

How does the distribution of scores for a polygenic trait differ from that usually obtained for a single-gene trait?

FIGURE 3.8 Normal distribution
When many individuals are tested for a polygenic characteristic, the majority usually fall in the middle of the range of scores and the frequency tapers off toward zero at the extremes. Mathematically, this defines a normal curve. (For a more complete description, see the *Statistical Appendix* at the end of the book.)

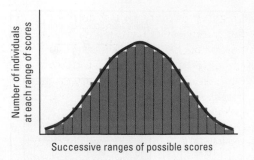

Number of individuals at each range of scores

Successive ranges of possible scores

scores obtained on such measures approximate a **normal distribution**, meaning that most scores fall near the middle of the range and the frequency tapers off toward the two extremes (see **Figure 3.8**). Measures of aggressiveness in mice, of maze learning in rats, and of conscientiousness in people are just a few of the behavioral measures that are consistently found to fit a normal distribution.

Characteristics that vary in a continuous way are generally affected by many genes and are therefore called **polygenic characteristics** (the prefix *poly-* means "many"). Of course, these traits are also influenced by variation in the environment, so the variability observed in a graph such as Figure 3.8 results from a combination of genetic differences at many gene loci and environmental differences. In animals the role of genes in polygenic traits is studied through the procedure of selective breeding.

Selective Breeding for Behavioral Characteristics in Animals

FOCUS 13

How are the characteristics of animals shaped through selective breeding?

To the degree that individuals within a species differ in any measurable characteristic because of differences in their genes, that characteristic can be modified over successive generations through **selective breeding**. This procedure involves the mating of individuals that lie toward the same extreme on the measure in question. For single-gene characteristics the effects of selective breeding are immediate, but for polygenic characteristics the effects are gradual and cumulative over generations.

The basic procedure of selective breeding is by no means new. For thousands of years, plant and animal breeders have used selective breeding to produce new and better strains of every sort of domesticated species. Grains were bred for plumper seeds; cows, for docility and greater milk production; horses, along separate lines for working and racing; canaries, for their song; and dogs, along dozens of different lines for such purposes as following a trail, herding sheep, and guarding property.

The procedure in every case was essentially the same: The members of each generation that best approximated the desired type were mated to produce the next generation, resulting in a continuous genetic molding toward the varieties we see today.

Under controlled laboratory conditions, researchers have used selective breeding to produce many behaviorally specialized strains of animals, usually to better understand the biological foundations of the behaviors in question. Fruit flies have been bred to move either toward or away from a source of light, mice to be either more or less inclined to fight, rats to either prefer or not prefer alcohol over water, and foxes to be either highly aggressive or extraordinarily docile and friendly toward humans (Kukekova et al., 2008; Wimer & Wimer, 1985). It should come as no surprise that selective breeding can influence essentially any behavioral trait: Behaviors depend on particular sensory, motor, and neural structures, all of which are built from proteins whose production depends on genes.

Selective Breeding for Maze Learning: Tryon's Classic Research

The first long-term, systematic study of selective breeding in psychology was begun in the 1920s by Robert Tryon (1942). Tryon wanted to demonstrate that a type of behavior frequently studied by psychologists could be strongly influenced by variation in genes.

■ **A fox bred for tameness** Since 1959, researchers in Russia have been selectively breeding silver foxes for tameness. At each generation, only those foxes that show the least fear and aggression and the most affection to humans have been bred. The result, after more than 30 generations, is a breed of foxes that are as friendly to humans as are dogs (Kukekova et al., 2008; Trut, 1999).

Tryon began by testing a genetically diverse group of rats for their ability to learn a particular maze. Then he mated the males and females that had made the fewest errors in the maze to begin what he called the "maze bright" strain and those that had made the most errors to begin the "maze dull" strain. When the offspring of succeeding generations reached adulthood, he tested them in the same maze and mated the best-performing members of the bright strain, and the worst-performing members of the dull strain, to continue the two lines.

Some of his results are shown in **Figure 3.9**. With each generation the two strains became increasingly distinct, until by the seventh there was almost no overlap between them. Almost all seventh-generation bright rats made fewer errors in the maze than even the best dull rats. To control for the possibility that the offspring were somehow learning to be bright or dull from their mothers, Tryon cross-fostered the rats so that some of the offspring from each strain were raised by mothers in the other strain. He found that rats in the bright strain were equally good in the maze, and those in the dull strain equally poor, regardless of which mothers raised them.

Once a strain has been bred to show some behavioral characteristic, the question arises as to what other behavioral or physiological changes accompany it. Tryon referred to his two strains of rats as "bright" and "dull," but all he had measured was their performance in a particular type of maze. Performance in the maze no doubt depended on many sensory, motor, motivational, and learning processes, and specific changes in any of them could in theory have mediated the effects that Tryon

FOCUS 14

How did Tryon produce "maze bright" and "maze dull" strains of rats? How did he show that the difference was the result of genes, not rearing?

FOCUS 15

Why is the strain difference produced by Tryon not properly characterized in terms of "brightness" or "dullness"?

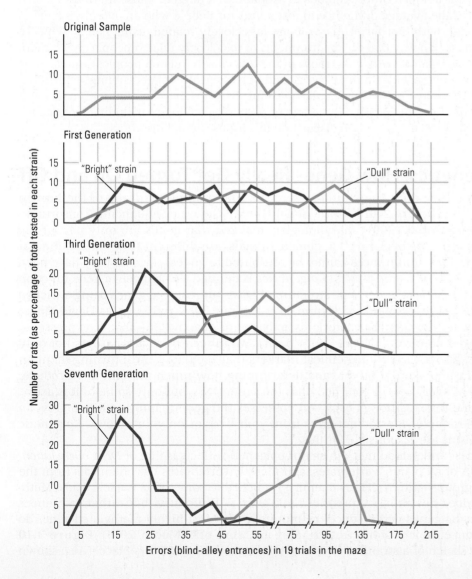

FIGURE 3.9 Selective breeding for "maze brightness" and "maze dullness" in rats The top graph shows, for the original parent stock, the distribution of rats according to the number of errors they made in the maze. Subsequent graphs show this distribution separately for the rats bred to be "bright" or "dull." With successive generations of selective breeding, an increasing percentage in the "bright" strain made few errors and an increasing percentage in the "dull" strain made many errors. (Data from Tryon, 1942.)

observed. In theory, Tryon's "dull" rats could simply have been those that had less acute vision, or were less interested in the variety of food used as a reward, or were more interested in exploring the maze's blind alleys.

In later studies, another researcher found that Tryon's "dull" rats were as good as the "bright" ones, and sometimes even better, at other learning tasks (Searle, 1949). We do not know what underlying abilities or dispositions changed in Tryon's two strains of rats to produce their difference in maze performance, but the change was apparently not one of general learning ability. This problem still occurs in modern behavioral genetics research, in which new strains of animals (usually mice) are created by adding, deleting, or modifying known genes using sophisticated genetic-engineering methods. The behavioral differences between two strains found in one laboratory often fail to occur in another laboratory, apparently because of subtle differences in the way the animals are housed or tested (Cabib et al., 2000; Crabbe et al., 1999).

Polygenic Behavioral Characteristics in Humans

Most of the measures of human traits that interest psychologists—such as scores on personality tests—are continuous and normally distributed, and are affected by many genes as well as by environmental variables. Some psychologists are interested in the degree to which the differences in such scores, for a particular group of people, are the result of differences in their genes or differences in their environmental experiences. Of course, psychologists can't perform selective breeding studies with humans, but they have developed other methods to estimate that degree. Those methods involve comparing the average difference in test scores for people who are closely related to one another with that for people who are less closely related, using people who are chosen in such a way that the environments of the closely related people are no more similar to one another than are those of the less closely related people. Comparisons of identical twins with fraternal twins, and of biologically related siblings with adoptive siblings, have proven particularly useful. In later chapters you will read about such methods as they apply to a variety of psychological topics including intelligence tests, personality tests, and predisposition to various mental disorders.

Epigenetics: How Genes Really Get Turned On and Off

FOCUS 16

How might a better understanding of epigenetics change the way we view genetic inheritance?

It was not long after the publication of the first "complete" drafts of the human genome in February 2001 (International Human Genome Sequencing Consortium, 2001; Venter et al., 2001) that biologists realized that genes are only part of the story. Identical twins, and even cloned animals, are different from one another at birth, and these differences cannot be attributed to genes. Instead, they have been attributed to epigenetic effects. *Epigenetics* is defined as "changes in gene function that do not alter its underlying structure of DNA but result in genes being switched on or off in a reversible way" (Puumala & Hoyme, 2015, p. 15), or, as David Moore describes it, "how genetic material is activated or deactivated—that is, expressed—in different contexts" (Moore, 2015, p. 14). We inherit from our parents not only DNA but also a variety of chemical markers that regulate genes, turning them on at certain times, off at others, and determining how much protein they produce. Recall that every cell in your body has the same DNA, but only some of it is active at any one time. Although each cell possesses the genetic information to grow an eye, for example, eyes do not grow from your liver or on your elbows. Epigenetic mechanisms are responsible for this.

The best understood mechanism for epigenetic effects is that of *DNA methylation*. The DNA of all plants, vertebrates, and many invertebrates has chemicals from the methyl group (written CH_3 by chemists) attached to some of its nucleic acids. Methylation does not alter the protein that a gene will produce, but rather influences whether the genes will produce the protein at all. Most highly methylated genes do not produce their proteins; that is, they are "shut off" (Moore, 2015). **Figure 3.10** shows a sketch of a strand of DNA and where methylation takes place. (Also shown in the figure is another epigenetic mechanism, *histone modification,* which typically results in activating DNA.)

Processes of DNA methylation seem highly regulated and similar across individuals. For example, in early development, genes that govern the building of an eye become methylated and "turn off" in all tissues except those that will eventually develop into eyes. However, DNA methylation can also be influenced by experience; indeed, it seems to be the primary mechanism by which experience modifies gene action and thus behavior. And these effects can last for years. For example, researchers in Canada assessed pregnant women's experience of hardship as a result of a major ice storm in Quebec in 1998. Thirteen years later they looked for epigenetic effects in immune-system cells of the children born of these pregnancies. They reported that mothers' ratings of hardship during pregnancy were related to subsequent levels of DNA methylation in their children's genes associated with the immune system (Cao-Lei et al., 2014). In other research, 11- to 14-year-old children who had been exposed to physical maltreatment showed greater methylation to a gene associated with stress regulation and to a gene associated with nerve growth factor than nonmaltreated children (Romens et al., 2015). Recent research using placental blood (Kertes, et al., 2016) or saliva (Parades et al., 2016) has shown that early stress is related to the methylation of genes associated with the expression of the stress hormone cortisol and related to subsequent internalizing behavior. Whether these effects help children better adapt to difficult environments or contribute to mental and physical disorders is debatable, but they do clearly demonstrate a chemical mechanism for how experience affects gene expression.

Some of the epigenetic markers created by methylation can be inherited, along with the behavior they influence, as shown in the following example. Mother rats groom their infant pups, mostly by licking them. Pups that have "high-licking mothers" grow up to be less vulnerable to stress than pups with "low-licking mothers." When the female pups mature and become mothers themselves, they show the same licking pattern as their mothers. This is true even when the pups are cross-fostered (that is, when a pup born to a low-licking mother is raised by a high-licking mother or vice versa). As adults, they show the pattern of their foster mother, not their genetic mother, and this pattern continues for at least several generations (Francis et al., 1999; Meaney, 2010, 2013). Michael Meaney and his colleagues documented the biochemical mechanisms responsible for these transgenerational effects, showing how early experience can alter behavior and be transmitted to future generations, all without any changes in the genes themselves.

Something similar seems to happen in humans. For example, excessive childhood stress in the form of abuse or neglect is associated with poor mental health in later life including personality disorders, depression, anxiety disorders, and substance abuse (Cicchetti & Toth, 2006). The hormone cortisol is associated with such stress, and complex interactions between cortisol, brain activity, and experience over the course of development are related to how people respond to stress (Carpenter et al., 2004; Lee et al., 2005). Discerning the chemical causes of behavior is difficult in humans (few people allow the chemicals in their brains to be assayed while they are still alive). However, research with nonhuman animals suggests that the way the human brain "learns" to react to stress through the production and processing of the hormone cortisol is likely governed by epigenetic mechanisms (Moore, 2015).

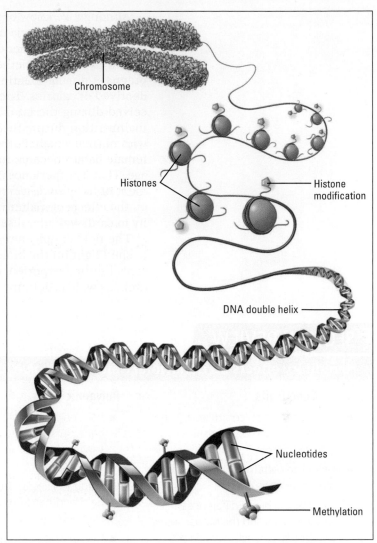

FIGURE 3.10 A schematic diagram of DNA pulled from a chromosome, showing nucleotide bases, the double helix wrapped around histones, and some epigenetic modifications to the DNA.

Although we know of no studies showing the transmission of behavior across generations in humans via epigenetic mechanisms, there is such evidence in the realm of physical development from survivors of the Dutch Hunger Winter. During World War II, parts of the Netherlands experienced extreme famine. For women who were pregnant during this time, not only they but their unborn children were severely deprived of calories. The Dutch government followed these children who were conceived during the famine, as well as the next generation. When women suffered malnutrition during their first three months of pregnancy, their babies were born with normal weight but were at high risk for obesity as adults. Moreover, when these female babies became mothers themselves, their offspring were heavier than average. That is, experiences of the grandmother while pregnant influenced the development of her *grandchildren* (Lumey, 1998). A similar phenomenon has been reported on the effects of malnutrition on the subsequent growth rate and health (susceptibility to cardiovascular disease) for a sample of Swedish *men* (Kaati et al., 2002).

The field of epigenetics is just coming into its own, but new discoveries promise to shed light on the biological basis of inheritance, including ways in which a person's lifetime experiences might influence the phenotype of his or her grandchildren, as well as defining more clearly the nature of gene-environment interactions.

SECTION REVIEW

Hereditary effects on behavioral traits can involve just one gene, but usually involve many.

Single-Gene Traits	Polygenic Traits	Epigenetics
■ Single-gene traits (controlled by one pair of genes) are categorical (all or none) in nature.	■ Polygenic traits (influenced by many gene pairs) are continuous (present in varying degrees) and often fit a normal distribution.	■ Experiences cause biochemical changes that affect the activation of genes.
■ Mendelian patterns of inheritance indicate single-gene control.	■ Through selective breeding, a trait can be strengthened or weakened gradually over generations.	■ The best understood mechanism for epigenetic effects is that of DNA methylation.
■ Examples are breed differences in fearfulness in dogs and the human hereditary disorder phenylketonuria (PKU).	■ Examples include Tryon's breeding of rats for maze ability and the Russian program of breeding foxes for tameness.	■ Experiences early in life can produce effects that persist years later.
		■ In some situations, epigenetic effects can be transmitted to children and grandchildren without any changes in the genes themselves.

Evolution by Natural Selection

Lady Ashley, a pillar of London society in the 1850s, is purported to have said upon hearing Darwin's ideas that humans evolved from apes, "Let's hope it's not true; but if it is true, let's hope that it does not become widely known." Lady Ashley's wish did not come true, as Darwin's theory is widely known today and serves as the foundation for modern biology and is also of central importance for understanding human psychology.

Darwin's Insight: Selective Breeding Occurs in Nature

FOCUS 17

What insight led Darwin to his theory of evolution? How is natural selection similar to and different from artificial selection?

In the first chapter of *The Origin of Species,* Darwin (1859/1963) used the term ***artificial selection*** to refer to human-controlled selective breeding, and he reminded readers of the enormously diverse varieties of plants and animals that had been produced through that procedure. He then pointed out—and this was his true, original insight—that breeding in nature is also selective and can also produce changes in living things over generations.

NON SEQUITUR by Wiley

HOW NATURAL SELECTION REALLY WORKS...

WELL, I'M NOT MOVING UNTIL SOMEONE CAN EXPLAIN WHY *WE* SHOULD RUN WHEN WE HAVE HIM OUT-NUMBERED...

Non-Sequitur by Wiley copyright 1997 Washington Post Writers Group/Andrews McMeel Syndication

Selective breeding in nature, which Darwin labeled **natural selection**, is dictated not by the needs and whims of humans but by the obstacles to survival and reproduction that are imposed by the natural environment. Those obstacles include predators, limited food supplies, temperature extremes, difficulty in finding and attracting mates for sexual reproduction—anything that can cut life short or otherwise prevent an organism from producing offspring. Animals and plants that have characteristics that help them overcome such obstacles are, by definition, more likely to have offspring than those that lack such characteristics.

Darwin's concept of natural selection is a simple one, having four core concepts (see **Table 3.1**). First, more individuals are born in a generation than will survive. Second, not all members of a generation are the same—there is *variation* in features or traits. Third, these individual differences are inherited, passed from one generation to the next. Fourth, individuals with collections of traits that fit well with the local environment are more apt to survive and have more offspring than individuals whose traits do not fit as well with the local environment. Any inherited trait that increases the number of offspring an individual produces is automatically "selected for," as the trait is passed on to those offspring. Conversely, any inherited trait that decreases the number of one's offspring is automatically "selected against," appearing in fewer members of the next generation. Thus, as long as inheritable differences exist among individuals in an interbreeding population, and as long as some of those differences affect survival and reproduction, evolution will occur.

TABLE 3.1 Core concepts of Darwin's theory of natural selection

- There is overproduction of offspring in each generation.
- There is *variation* in features or traits within members of a generation.
- Individual differences are inherited from one generation to the next.
- Individuals with collections of traits that fit well with the local environment are more apt to survive and have more offspring than individuals whose traits do not fit as well with the local environment.

Genetic Diversity Provides the Material for Natural Selection

Darwin realized that something, passed along through eggs and sperm, must provide the hereditary foundation for evolution, but he knew nothing of genes. Mendel's work, which was the first step toward our modern knowledge of genes, was unknown to most scientists until about 1900, long after Darwin's death. Today we know that genes are the units of heredity and that evolution entails generational changes in the frequencies of particular genes in an interbreeding population. Genes that improve an individual's ability to survive and reproduce in the existing environment increase from generation to generation, and genes that impede this ability decrease over the generations.

The genetic variability on which natural selection acts has two main sources: (1) the reshuffling of genes that occurs in sexual reproduction (already discussed) and (2) mutations. **Mutations** are errors that occasionally and unpredictably occur during DNA replication, causing the "replica" to be not quite identical to the original. In the long run of evolution, mutation is the ultimate source of all genetic variation.

FOCUS 18

How are genes involved in evolution? What are the sources of genetic diversity on which natural selection acts?

New mutations are more often harmful than helpful, and natural selection usually weeds them out. But occasionally a mutation is useful, producing a protein that affects the organism's development in a way that increases its ability to reproduce. Because of its effect on reproduction, the gene arising from such a mutation increases in frequency from generation to generation. At the level of the gene, this is evolution.

Prior to the modern understanding of genes, many people believed that changes in an individual that stem from practice or experience could be inherited and therefore provide a basis for evolution. For example, some argued that early giraffes, by frequently stretching their necks to reach leaves in trees, slightly elongated their necks in the course of their lives and that this change was passed on to their offspring—resulting, over many generations, in the long-necked giraffes we see today. That idea, referred to as the inheritance of acquired characteristics, is most often attributed to Jean-Baptiste de Lamarck (1744–1829), although many other evolutionists, both before and after Lamarck, held the same view (Futuyma, 1997). Even Darwin did not reject that idea, but he added to it the concepts of random variation and natural selection.

The biologist August Weismann established that what happens to the body cells during the life of an animal does not affect that animal's gametes (egg and sperm), a principle known as the doctrine of the separation of the germ (sex cells) and somatic (body cells) lines. No matter how many generations of mice have their tails snipped off, their offspring continue to be born with tails. Today, evolution is defined as changes in gene frequency between populations of individuals, with changes in genes being the "cause" of forming new species. However, animals inherit more than just their genes. They inherit chemicals within the egg and some cellular machinery, as well as a species-typical environment (a womb in mammals, for example). Although genes remain the focus of evolutionary change, as we saw in the earlier section on epigenetics, experiences within an animal's lifetime can sometimes result in inheritance of features across generations.

Environmental Change Provides the Force for Natural Selection

FOCUS 19

How does change in the environment affect the direction and speed of evolution? How did a study of finches illustrate the role of environmental change in evolution?

Evolution is spurred by changes in the environment: Climates change, sources of food change, predators change, and so on. When the conditions of life change, what was previously a useful characteristic may become harmful, and vice versa.

Darwin viewed evolution as a slow and steady process. But today we know that it can occur rapidly, slowly, or almost not at all, depending on the rate and nature of environmental change and on the degree to which genetic variability already exists in a population (Gould & Eldredge, 1993). Environmental change spurs evolution not by causing the appropriate mutations to occur but by promoting natural selection. Some mutations that previously would not have been advantageous and would have gradually been weeded out by natural selection are advantageous in the new environment, so they are passed along in increasing numbers from generation to generation. Evolution sometimes occurs so quickly that people can see it happen. In fact, scientists since Darwin's time have reported more than a hundred different examples of observed evolution (Endler, 1986).

Some of the best-documented examples of observed evolution come from the work of Peter and Rosemary Grant, who for more than 30 years studied a species of finch, the *medium ground finch,* on one of the Galápagos Islands (Grant & Grant, 2008). The Grants found that the members of this species differ somewhat in the thickness of their beaks, that the variation is inheritable, and that environmental changes can result in rapid evolution toward either thicker or thinner beaks. In the 1970s, a severe drought lasting several years caused most of the finches to die because the plants that produce the seeds they eat failed to grow. The birds that survived and produced offspring were those that happened to have thicker, more powerful beaks—powerful enough to crack open the large, hard-shelled seeds that remained after the smaller seeds had been eaten (see **Figure 3.11**).

Two decades later, another species of ground finch, the *large ground finch,* established a breeding colony on the island and began competing with the medium ground finch for food. The intruders were much better adapted for eating the large, hard-shelled seeds than were the medium ground finches, but they were less well adapted for eating the small seeds. The result, for the medium ground finches, was depletion in the supply of large seeds but not of small seeds. Under this condition, the medium ground finches with thinner bills, better adapted for eating the small seeds, were more likely to survive and produce offspring than were those with thicker bills. Within a few generations under this new set of conditions, the average beak thickness of the medium ground finches declined considerably (Grant & Grant, 2006).

The evolution of simple or small changes, such as in skin pigmentation or in beak thickness, can occur in a few generations when selection conditions are strong, but more complex changes require much more time. The difference between, say, a chimpanzee brain and a human brain could not have come about in a few generations, as it must have involved many mutations, each conveying a slight selective advantage to the chimpanzee (in its environment) or to the human (in our environment). When evolutionists talk about "rapid" evolution of complex changes, they are usually talking about periods measured in hundreds of thousands of years (Gould & Eldredge, 1993). **Figure 3.12** provides a simplified sketch of how evolution by natural selection works to produce new forms and functions.

FIGURE 3.11 Rapid evolution During years of drought, natural selection quickly produced the thicker beak, shown at left, in the medium ground finches studied by Peter and Rosemary Grant. During years of competition with a larger thick-billed species, natural selection quickly produced the thinner beak, shown at the right.

Evolution Has No Foresight

People sometimes mistakenly think of evolution as a mystical force working toward a predetermined end. One manifestation of this belief is the idea that evolution could produce changes for some future purpose, even though they are useless or harmful at the time that the change occurs. But evolution has no foresight. The finches studied by the Grants could not have evolved thicker beaks in anticipation of drought, or thinner ones in anticipation of thick-beaked competitors. Only genetic changes that increase survival and reproduction in the immediate environment can proliferate through natural selection.

Another manifestation of the belief in foresight is the idea that present-day organisms can be ranked according to the distance they have moved along a set evolutionary route, toward some planned end (Gee, 2002). For example, some may think of humans as the "most evolved" creatures, with chimpanzees next and amoebas way down on the list. But evolution has no set route or planned end. Humans, chimps, and amoebas have their different forms and behavioral characteristics because of chance events that resulted in them occupying different niches in the environment, where the selection criteria differed. The present-day amoeba is not an early step toward humans but rather a creature that is at least as well adapted to its environment as we are to ours. The amoeba has no more chance of evolving to become like us than we have of evolving to become like it.

A third manifestation of the belief in foresight is the idea that natural selection is a moral force, that its operation and its products are in some sense right or good. In everyday talk, people sometimes imply that whatever is natural (including natural selection) is good and that evil stems from society or human contrivances that go beyond nature. If natural selection promotes a self-interested struggle among individuals, for example, then selfishness is right. Such equations are logically indefensible because nature itself is neither moral nor immoral except as judged so by us. This is referred to as the ***naturalistic fallacy***, and it is precisely that, a fallacy. Nature is neither good nor bad, moral nor immoral. To say that natural selection led to a given characteristic does not lend any moral virtue to that characteristic. Fighting, for example, is as much a product of evolution as is cooperation, but that is no reason to consider them morally equivalent.

 FOCUS 20

What are three mistaken beliefs about evolution, all related to the misconception that foresight is involved?

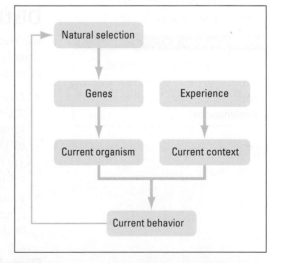

FIGURE 3.12 Natural selection over time Genes and experience combine to produce an animal's current structure and its behavior. That behavior is then the target for natural selection, continuing the cycle.

SECTION REVIEW

Natural selection is the driving force of evolutionary change.

How Natural Selection Works

- To the degree that a trait enhances survival and reproduction, genes producing that trait are passed on to offspring. The result is that such genes become more frequent over generations.

- Mutations and reshuffling of genes in sexual reproduction provide genetic diversity on which natural selection operates.

Role of Environmental Change

- The rate and nature of environmental change affect the rate and course of evolution.

- Examples are the effects of drought and of competition from another species on the evolution of beak thickness in finches.

- Complex changes, requiring many mutations, require a long time to evolve.

Evolution Lacks Foresight

- Natural selection can only lead to changes that are immediately adaptive; it cannot anticipate future needs.

- There is no preset pathway for evolution.

- The naturalistic fallacy is the error of equating "natural" with "moral" or "right." Natural selection is not a moral force.

Natural Selection as a Foundation for Functionalism

FOCUS 21

How does an understanding of evolution provide a basis for functionalism in psychology?

The mechanisms underlying behavior are products of natural selection; they came about because they promoted survival and reproduction. Just as Tryon used artificial selection to breed rats to be better at learning a particular maze, natural selection automatically breeds animals to be better at doing what they must to survive and reproduce in their natural environments. This idea provides a foundation for the psychological approach known as *functionalism*—the attempt to explain behavior in terms of what it accomplishes for the behaving individual.

The functionalist approach to explaining behavior is essentially the same as the functionalist approach to explaining anatomy: Why do giraffes have long necks? Why do humans lack fur? Why do male songbirds sing in the spring? Why do humans have such an irrepressible ability to learn language? The anatomist trying to answer the first two questions, and the behavioral researcher or psychologist trying to answer the latter two, would look for ways by which each trait helped ancestral members of the species to survive and reproduce.

Distal and Proximate Explanations of Behavior

FOCUS 22

How are distal explanations of behavior different from, but complementary to, proximate explanations?

Biologists and psychologists who think in evolutionary terms find it useful to distinguish between two kinds of explanations of behavior—distal and proximate, both of which are needed to properly understand a behavior (Scott-Phillips et al., 2011).

- *Distal explanations* (as in "distant") are explanations at the evolutionary level. They are statements of the role that the behavior has played in the animal's survival and reproduction over evolutionary time. Viewed from the vantage point of the gene, they are statements of how the behavior helped the individual's ancestor's genes make it into the next generation. Distal causation is sometimes referred to as *ultimate causation*.

- *Proximate explanations* (as in "proximity") are explanations that deal not with function but with mechanism; they are statements of the immediate conditions, both inside and outside the animal, that elicit the behavior.

Distal and Proximate Explanations Complement Each Other

Consider how distal and proximate explanations might be applied to the question of why male songbirds of many species sing in the spring. A *distal explanation* might look like this (Koodsma & Byers, 1991): Over the course of evolution, songbirds have adapted to a mating system that takes place in the spring. The male's song serves to attract a female for mating and to warn other males to stay away from the singer's territory in order to avoid a fight. In the evolution of these birds, males whose genes promoted such singing produced more offspring (more copies of their genes) than did males whose genes failed to promote such singing.

A *proximate explanation,* in contrast, might go as follows (Ball & Hulse, 1998): Through the birds' visual system, the increased period of daylight in the spring triggers a physiological mechanism that leads to the increased production of the sex hormone testosterone, which in turn acts on certain areas of the brain (which we might call the "song areas"), promoting the drive to sing.

Notice the complementary nature of these explanations. The distal explanation states the survival or reproductive value of the behavior, and the proximate explanation states the stimuli and physiological mechanisms through which the behavior occurs.

■ **A redwing blackbird at home** This male's singing warns other males of the species to stay away.

The Search for Distal Explanations in Human Psychology

Evolution by natural selection is the basis of all of the complex biological mechanisms underlying human behavior and experience—including perception, learning, memory, thought, motivation, and emotion. They all came about because each small step in their evolution tended to promote our ancestors' survival and reproduction. Thus, for any basic psychological characteristic that is part of human nature, it is legitimate to ask: How did this characteristic improve the survival and reproductive chances of our ancestors? How did it help our ancestors get their genes into the next generation?

The distal explanations of some human traits (especially those we share with all other mammals) are relatively obvious. We have strong drives to breathe air, drink fluids, and consume foods because our bodies need these things to remain alive. We have strong drives to engage in sex because that is the means by which our genes transfer from one generation to the next. Individuals who lacked such drives are ancestors to nobody today; their genes died with them.

The distal explanations of some other human traits, however, are not so obvious. It is not obvious, for example, why humans everywhere tend to sleep about eight hours each night, or why humans everywhere under certain conditions experience the disturbing emotion of guilt.

Limitations on Functionalist Thinking

Before we go deeper into discussions of distal functions, it is useful to acknowledge the limitations of functionalist thinking. Not every detail of every trait serves a useful function, and some traits that were once functional may not be so today. Here are four reasons why a particular trait or behavior may not be functional.

Some Traits Are Vestigial

Some traits that evolved because they served the needs of our ancestors are no longer functional today, yet they remain. These remnants of our past are called ***vestigial characteristics***.

As an example, consider the grasp reflex by which newborn infants close their fingers tightly around objects in their hands. This reflex may well be useful today in the development of the infant's ability to hold and manipulate objects, but that does not explain why prematurely born infants grasp so strongly that they can support their own weight, why they grasp with their toes as well as their hands, and why the best stimulus for eliciting this reflex is a clump of hair (Eibl-Eibesfeldt, 1975). These aspects of the reflex make more sense when we observe them in other primates. To survive, infant monkeys and apes cling tightly with hands and feet to their mother's fur while she swings in trees or goes about her other daily business. In the course of

FOCUS 23

What are four reasons for the existence of traits or behaviors that do not serve survival and reproductive functions?

our evolution from ape-like ancestors, we lost our fur, so our infants can no longer cling to us in this way, but the reflex remains.

The concept of vestigial traits becomes especially relevant to psychologists when applied to our inherited drives. Because of culture, our habitats and lifestyles have changed dramatically in just a few centuries, a speck on the evolutionary time scale. Essentially all of our evolution as a species occurred in conditions that were quite different from those of today, and some of our inherited tendencies may be harmful, rather than helpful, in the habitat we now occupy. An example is our great appetite for sugar. In the world of our ancestors, sugar was a rare and valuable commodity. It existed primarily in fruits and provided energy needed for vigorous physical activity. But today sugar is readily available in most areas of the world, and life (for many of us) is less physically strenuous. Yet our preference for sugar persists as strong as ever, despite such negative consequences as tooth decay and obesity.

Some Traits Are Side Effects of Natural Selection for Other Traits

Useless changes can come about in evolution as by-products of natural selection for other, useful changes. A simple example in humans is the navel, or belly button (Buss et al., 1998). To the best of anyone's knowledge, the navel serves no function related to survival or reproduction. It is simply a remnant left from the umbilical cord. The umbilical cord, of course, does serve a survival and reproductive function: It conveys nutrients from the mother to the developing fetus. As such, we refer to the umbilical cord as an *adaptation*. It is a universal and reliably developing inherited feature that arose as a result of natural selection and helped to solve some problem of survival. But navels are simply the necessary by-products of umbilical cords and have no function themselves. An anatomist from Mars who observed belly buttons on adult earthlings, but who never observed a fetus or the birth process, would be at a loss to explain why such a structure would have evolved.

It is possible that some human psychological capacities, even some that are so general that we would consider them to be part of human nature, came about as side effects of the evolution of other capacities. For example, are the universal human proclivities for art and music direct effects of natural selection, or side effects? Perhaps these proclivities served to attract mates during much of our evolutionary history (as they seem to today), and were therefore selected for directly, much as song was selected for in birds. Or perhaps they emerged simply as by-products of selection for other proclivities, such as those for planning, constructing tools, and communicating through language. A third possibility, combining the first two, is that proclivities for art and music may have initially emerged as by-products and then been selected for because of their usefulness for attracting mates or other helpers. At present, we do not have evidence to support strongly any of these theories over the others.

Some Traits Result Simply From Chance

Some inheritable characteristics that result from just one or two mutations are inconsequential for survival and reproduction. Different races of people have somewhat differently shaped noses. Maybe that variation is caused by natural selection. Perhaps one shape worked best in one climate and another worked best in another climate, so natural selection molded the noses differently. But we can't assume that. The different shapes might be a result of mutations that didn't matter and therefore were never weeded out by natural selection. Maybe the small group of people who migrated to a specific part of the world, and who were the ancestors of a particular racial group, just happened to carry along genes for a nose shape that was different from the average for the group they left. Such variation, due to chance alone without selection, is called *genetic drift.*

Many years ago, researchers discovered that the incidence of schizophrenia (a serious mental disorder, discussed in Chapter 15) is three times greater among people living in northern Sweden, above the Arctic Circle, than among people in most other parts of the world (Huxley et al., 1964). There are at least three possible explanations of this observation: (a) Environmental conditions, such as the harsh climate or the isolation it produces, might tend to bring on schizophrenia in people who are prone to it. (b) Natural selection might have increased the frequency of schizophrenia-promoting genes among these people, perhaps because such genes help protect people from harmful effects of physical stressors such as cold climate. (This was the hypothesis suggested by Huxley and his colleagues.) (c) The Arctic population may have been founded by a small group of Swedish migrants who, just by chance, had a higher proportion of schizophrenia-promoting genes than the population at large. This last possibility (also mentioned by Huxley and his colleagues) would be an example of genetic drift. To this day, scientists are unsure which of these theories is correct.

Evolved Mechanisms Cannot Deal Effectively With Every Situation

Our basic drives, emotions, and other behavioral tendencies came about in evolution because, on balance, they promoted survival and reproduction more often than they interfered with survival and reproduction. That does not mean, however, that every instance of activation of such a drive, emotion, or tendency serves survival or reproductive ends. The emotion of guilt serves the distal function of helping us to preserve our relationships with people whose help we need for survival and reproduction. When we hurt someone we depend on, we feel guilty, which motivates us to make amends and patch up the relationship. That does not mean, however, that every manifestation of guilt in every person serves that function. Sometimes guilt can be crippling; our capacity for guilt can be exploited by others for their ends at our expense. The best that natural selection could do was to develop a guilt mechanism that is triggered by certain general conditions. It could not build a mechanism capable of distinguishing every possible condition from every other one and triggering guilt only when it is useful. The same is true for all of our other evolved emotions and drives.

SECTION REVIEW

The concept of natural selection provides a secure footing for functionalism.

The Functionalist Approach

- Functionalism is an approach to psychology that focuses on the usefulness of a particular behavior to the individual engaging in it.

- Distal explanations are functional explanations, examining the role that specific behaviors play in survival and reproduction.

- Proximate explanations are complementary to distal explanations; they are concerned with mechanisms that bring about behavior.

Limitations of Functionalism

- Some traits are vestigial; they once served a function but no longer do.

- Some traits, such as the umbilical cord, are adaptations; whereas others, such as the navel, are side effects, or by-products, of other traits that arose through natural selection.

- Some traits are products just of chance, not natural selection.

- Even evolved mechanisms, such as that for guilt, are not useful in every situation in which they are active.

Natural Selection as a Foundation for Understanding Species-Typical Behaviors

Suppose you saw an animal that looked exactly like a dog, but it meowed, climbed trees, and ignored the mail carrier. Would you call it a dog or a cat? Clearly, we identify animals as much by their behavior as by their anatomy. Every species of animal has certain characteristic ways of behaving. These are commonly called *instincts*, but a more technical term for them is ***species-typical behaviors***. Meowing, tree climbing, and acting aloof are species-typical behaviors of cats. Dam building is species-typical of beavers. Smiling, talking, and two-legged walking are species-typical behaviors of humans.

Many psychologists (particularly developmental psychologists) avoid using the word "instinct" and the related term "innate" for two reasons. First, they imply "no experience necessary" and this is associated with *genetic determinism*, the belief that genes "determine" behavior independent of experience. The mistake here is assuming or implying that genes influence behavior directly, rather than through the indirect means of working with the environment to build or modify biological structures that then, in interplay with the environment, produce behavior. Some popular books on human evolution have exhibited the deterministic fallacy by implying that one form of behavior or another—such as fighting for territories—is unavoidable because it is controlled by our genes. That implication is unreasonable even when applied to nonhuman animals. Territorial birds, for example, defend territories only when the environmental conditions are ripe for them to do so. We humans can control our environment and thereby control ourselves. We can either enhance or reduce the environmental ingredients needed for a particular behavioral tendency to develop and manifest itself.

The second reason psychologists avoid the word "instinct" is because it is not easily defined. And, as Patrick Bateson wrote (2002, p. 2212):

> Apart from its colloquial uses, the term instinct has at least nine scientific meanings: present at birth (or at a particular stage of development), not learned, developed before it can be used, unchanged once developed, shared by all members of the species (or at least of the same sex and age), organized into a distinct behavioral system (such as foraging), served by a distinct neural module, adapted during evolution, and differences among individuals that are due to their possession of different genes. One does not necessarily imply another even though people often assume, without evidence, that it does.

For these reasons, we will avoid the term "instinct" in this book, using the more descriptive term "species-typical behaviors."

Species-Typical Behaviors in Humans

Species-typical behaviors are products of evolution, but that does not mean they are necessarily rigid in form or uninfluenced by learning. To understand more fully the concept of species-typical behaviors, let us examine some examples in human beings.

Human Emotional Expressions as Examples of Species-Typical Behaviors

FOCUS 24

What evidence supports the idea that many human emotional expressions are examples of species-typical behaviors?

Darwin noted that humans, like other animals, automatically communicate moods and behavioral intentions to one another through body postures, movements, and facial expressions. In his book *The Expression of the Emotions in Man and Animals,* Darwin (1872/1965) argued that specific facial expressions accompany specific emotional states in humans and that these expressions are universal, occurring in people throughout the world and even in people who were born blind and thus could not have learned them through observation.

In an extension of Darwin's pioneering work, Paul Ekman and Wallace Friesen (1975, 1982) developed an atlas that describes and depicts the exact facial-muscle movements that make up each of six basic emotional expressions in people: surprise, fear, disgust, anger, happiness, and sadness (see **Figure 3.13**). They then showed photographs of each expression to individuals in many different cultures, including members of a preliterate tribe in the highlands of New Guinea who had little previous contact with other cultures. They found that people in every culture described each depicted emotion in a way that was consistent with descriptions in

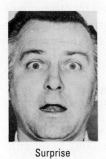
Surprise

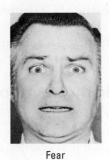
Fear

Disgust

Anger

Happiness

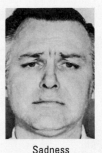
Sadness

FIGURE 3.13 Six basic human emotional expressions These expressions, taken from Ekman and Friesen's atlas of emotional expressions, were produced by a model who was asked to move specific facial muscles in specific ways. As you study each figure, try to describe the positions of the facial features for each expression. For example, surprise can be described as follows: The brows are pulled upward, producing horizontal wrinkles across the forehead; the eyes are opened wide, revealing white above the iris; and the lower jaw is dropped, with no tension around the mouth.

the United States (Ekman, 1973; Ekman et al., 1987). In a reversal of this procedure, they also photographed members of the New Guinea tribe who had been asked to act out various emotions and showed the photographs to college students in the United States. The college students were quite accurate in labeling the emotions portrayed by the New Guineans.

In a further extension of Darwin's work, Irenäus Eibl-Eibesfeldt (1989) documented the cross-cultural universality of many nonverbal signals, including one that he labeled the *eyebrow flash,* a momentary raising of the eyebrows lasting about one sixth of a second, usually accompanied by a smile and an upward nod of the head (see **Figure 3.14**). He observed this expression in every culture he studied—including those in New Guinea, Samoa, and various parts of Africa, Asia, South America, and Europe—and concluded that it is a universal sign of greeting among friends. Raised eyebrows are also a component of the emotional expression of surprise (look at Figure 3.13 again), so the eyebrow flash with its accompanying smile might be interpreted as a nonverbal way of saying, "What a happy surprise to see you!"

Eibl-Eibesfeldt (1975) also filmed children who were born blind, or both blind and deaf, and found that they manifest emotions in the same basic ways as sighted children do (see **Figure 3.15**). Such observations provide the most direct evidence that at least some human expressions do not have to be learned through observing them in others or hearing descriptions of them.

Taking all the evidence together, there can be little doubt that we are biologically predisposed to express certain emotions in certain species-typical ways. It is also clear, however, that we can control and modify our emotional expressions and learn new ones. Even researchers who focus on universal expressions are quick to point out cross-cultural differences. For example, Eibl-Eibesfeldt (1975) found that despite its cross-cultural similarity in form and general meaning, large cultural differences exist in the use of the eyebrow flash. The Japanese, who are reserved in social expressions among adults, use it mainly when greeting young children, whereas Samoans greet nearly everyone in this way. More recently, researchers have shown that cultural dialects occur in the emotional expressions that Ekman and Friesen included in their atlas. In general, people can identify each emotion

FOCUS 25

How do human emotional expressions illustrate the point that species-typical behaviors can be modified by learning?

FIGURE 3.14 The eyebrow flash This universal signal of greeting is shown in adjacent frames from films of (a) a French woman and (b) a Yanomami man (of the Brazil-Venezuela border).

(a)

(b)

FIGURE 3.15 Some emotional expressions need not be learned through observation This child, manifesting joy, has been blind and deaf since birth.

FOCUS 26

How do the examples of two-legged walking and language in humans, and singing in white-crowned sparrows, illustrate the point that species-typical behaviors may depend on learning?

FOCUS 27

How is the concept of biological preparedness related to that of species-typical behavior? How do the examples of human walking and talking illustrate biological preparedness?

---

more easily and accurately when it is expressed by other members of their own culture than when it is expressed by members of a very different culture (Elfenbein & Amady, 2003; Elfenbein et al., 2007).

The Role of Learning in the Development of Species-Typical Behaviors

To say that a behavior is species-typical is not to say that it is unaffected by learning. As we just pointed out, our basic emotional expressions are species-typical, but cultural differences among them are learned. The role of learning is even more obvious in two of our most characteristic species-specific behaviors—our manner of walking and our use of language.

A scientist from Mars would almost certainly point to two-legged walking and use of a grammar-based language as among the defining behavioral characteristics of the human species. These characterize humans everywhere and clearly depend on inherited predispositions, yet their development also clearly depends on learning.

During the peak months of learning to walk (generally during the second year of life), toddlers spend an average of about 6 hours per day practicing balancing and walking and, on a typical day, take about 9,000 walking steps and travel the length of 29 football fields (Adolph et al., 2003). For the most part they are not trying to get to any particular place; they are just walking for the sake of walking. By the time they are proficient walkers, they have spent thousands of hours practicing, on their own initiative. During those same months, infants also, on their own initiative, intensely practice talking. With language, infants do not just learn the motor coordination needed to produce the sounds; they also learn the basic vocabulary and grammar of the language that they hear around them. Talking and two-legged walking are species-typical behaviors in humans, but a human raised in an environment where either of these capacities was impossible to practice would not develop that capacity. Such an inhuman environment would not produce a normal human being.

Learning plays crucial roles in the development of species-specific behaviors in other animals as well. For example, white-crowned sparrows develop the ability to sing their species-typical song only if they are permitted to hear it during the first summer after hatching (Marler, 1970). Indeed, populations of the species living in different areas have somewhat different dialects, and young birds learn to sing the dialect that they hear (Nelson et al., 2004). Yet the range of possible songs that the birds can learn is limited by their biology. No matter what its environmental experiences, a white-crowned sparrow cannot learn to sing like a canary or like any species other than a white-crowned sparrow.

Biological Preparedness as the Basis for Species-Typical Behaviors

The difference between behaviors that we call instinctive, or species-typical, and those that we do not so label has to do with their degree of *biological preparedness*. Natural selection has equipped each species with anatomical structures that ensure that normal individuals of the species, who grow up in a normal environment for that species, will be physically able to perform their species-typical behaviors and will be motivated to learn what they must for adequate performance.

We humans come into the world biologically prepared to learn to walk on two legs. Natural selection has provided us with anatomical features—such as strong hindlimbs with feet, weaker forelimbs without feet, an upwardly tilted pelvis, and a short, stiff neck—that combine to make it more convenient for us to walk upright than on all fours. Moreover, we are born with neural systems in the brain and spinal cord that enable us to move our legs correctly for coordinated two-legged walking and with neural structures that motivate us to practice this behavior at the appropriate stage in our development. Consider the difference between two-legged walking

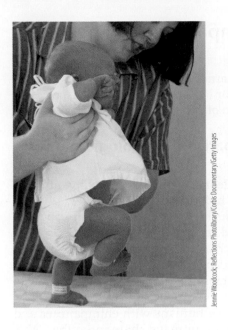

■ **Biological preparedness** Infants are born with a "stepping reflex," which shows that they have, inborn, the neural mechanisms for two-legged walking. Perfecting that behavior, however, requires extensive practice during the toddling stage, when the legs have become strong enough to support the child's weight.

in humans and in dogs. Dogs are capable of learning to walk on two legs, and much is made of that fact by circus trainers, but they are never very good at it. They do not have the appropriate muscular and skeletal systems to coordinate the behavior properly, and they have no natural impulse to walk in this manner. A dog, unlike a human child, will practice two-legged walking only if it receives immediate rewards, such as food, for doing so. Thus, two-legged walking is not a species-typical behavior in dogs.

The same is true for talking. Humans are born with anatomical structures, including a larynx and a flexible tongue, that can produce a wide range of sounds and with a brain that has special neural centers for understanding and producing language. Infants begin talking at a certain stage even if they receive little encouragement from those around them. Chimpanzees can be taught to simulate some aspects of human language, just as dogs can be taught to walk on their hind legs, but they require lots of encouragement and are never very good at it.

Species-Typical Behavior Is a Relative Concept

Having characterized the concept of species-typical behavior in terms of biological preparedness, we must now add that the concept is relative rather than absolute. No behavior stems just from biological preparedness; some sort of experience with the environment is always involved. Conversely, any behavior that an individual can produce—no matter how artificial it may seem or how much training is required—must make use of the individual's inherited biological capacities. The concept of species-typical behavior is useful as long as we accept it as relative and do not argue about whether a given behavior really should or should not be called species-typical.

The question to ask when we study a particular behavior is not, Is this a species-typical behavior? Rather, the meaningful questions are these:

- What are the environmental conditions needed for the full development of this behavior?
- What internal mechanisms are involved in producing this behavior?
- What consequences does this behavior have in the individual's daily life?
- In the course of evolution, why would the genes that make this behavior possible have been favored by natural selection?

These questions can be asked of any behavior, regardless of whether it is thought of as species-typical.

FOCUS 28

Why is the concept of species-typical behavior relative rather than absolute?

What is the difference between a homology and an analogy, and how can researchers tell whether a similarity between two species in some trait is one or the other?

The Value of Cross-Species Comparisons of Species-Typical Behaviors

In psychology as well as biology, scientists have learned a lot about our species by comparing us to other animals. The basic rationales for learning about any one species by comparing it with others are found in the principle of evolution by natural selection.

Two Forms of Cross-Species Comparison: Homologies and Analogies

An understanding of evolution makes it clear that two conceptually different classes of similarities exist across species: homologies and analogies.

A ***homology*** is any similarity that exists because of the different species' common ancestry. All animals originated from a common ancestor, so it is not surprising that some homologies—such as those in the basic structure of DNA molecules and of certain enzymes—can be found between any two species. But the more closely related two species are, the more homologies they show.

Much research has been done contrasting humans with chimpanzees and bonobos. As we noted earlier in this chapter, humans share more than 98% of their DNA with each of these great apes, making them our closest genetic relatives. However, it is *not* the case that humans evolved from chimpanzees or bonobos. Rather, we shared a common ancestor with these animals, which lived in Africa between 5 and 7 million years ago. That ancestor was likely very chimp-like, but over the course of the next several million years evolved into at least three lines that eventually led to modern humans, chimpanzees, and bonobos. **Figure 3.16** shows the evolutionary relationship of humans to the great apes and Old World monkeys.

An ***analogy***, in contrast, is any similarity that stems not from common ancestry but from *convergent evolution.* Convergent evolution occurs when different species, because of some similarity in their habitats or lifestyles, independently evolve a common characteristic.

Consider some comparisons among species that can fly. Flying has arisen separately in three taxonomic groups: birds, some insects (such as butterflies), and some mammals (bats). Similarities across these three groups in their flying motions, and in the anatomical structures that permit flight, are examples of analogies because they do not result from common ancestry (see **Figure 3.17**). However, similarities in flight and wings among species within any of these groups, such as between crows and sparrows, are likely to be homologies. The last common ancestor between a crow and a sparrow was itself a bird with wings, but the last common ancestor between a crow and a butterfly, or between a crow and a bat, did not have wings.

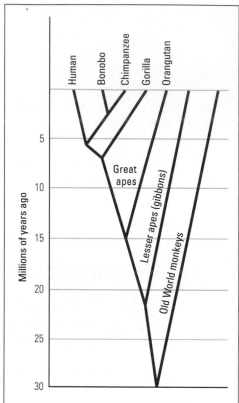

FIGURE 3.16 Relationship of humans to apes and Old World monkeys The ancestral line leading to humans split off from that leading to Old World monkeys 30 million years ago, and it split off from that leading to bonobos and chimpanzees about 6 million years ago. (Data from Corballis, 1999.)

(a)   (b)   (c)

FIGURE 3.17 Analogous wings Similarities in the wings and flying behavior of birds, bats, and butterflies are considered to be analogies, not homologies, because they arose independently in evolution.

(a)

(b)

FIGURE 3.18 Cells built by honeybees and bumblebees Honeybees build hives with hexagonally shaped cells (a), the optimal shape for storing large amounts of honey and larvae using the least amount of precious wax. To understand how such behavior might have come about through natural selection, Darwin studied homologous but simpler storage structures of related bee species. The simplest, produced by bumblebees (b), consists simply of a cluster of spherical cells, which the bees easily build by sweeping their abdomens compass-like to carve out the spheres. Other species build intermediate structures, with spherical cells that intersect and are patched up with flat wax walls at the places of intersection. Darwin suggested that ancestors of modern honeybees built their hives in a way similar to that of modern bumblebees but, through evolution, began making their cells ever closer together and more regularly spaced and patching up the intersections, resulting eventually in hexagonal cells.

The Value for Psychology of Studying Homologies

Homologies are useful for research on the physiological mechanisms of behavior (that is, research on how the brain and other biological structures operate to produce the behavior being studied). Because convergent evolution can produce similar behaviors that operate through different mechanisms, researchers who seek to understand the physiological mechanism of some behavior in humans through experiments on other species must study species in which the relevant behavior is homologous, not analogous, to that in humans. Many basic mechanisms of learning, motivation (such as hunger), and sensation (such as vision) are homologous across all or at least most species of mammals, and we have learned much about these by studying them in mice, rats, cats, and other laboratory mammals.

Homologies are also useful for inferring the pathways along which species-typical behaviors evolved. By comparing the different forms of a particular species-typical behavior in closely related species, it is often possible to reconstruct how the more complex of these forms evolved through a series of steps from the simpler form. Darwin (1859/1963) himself used this method to figure out the evolutionary steps through which honeybees acquired their marvelous ability to construct complex hives consisting of wax combs of closely fitting hexagonal cells in which to store honey and larvae (see **Figure 3.18**).

Homologies as Clues to the Evolutionary Origins of Two Human Smiles

In research that is more directly relevant to psychology, Darwin also used homologies to understand the origins of species-typical emotional expressions in humans. He watched monkeys and apes at the London Zoo and noted that a number of their expressions seemed to be homologous to human expressions, including the smile (Darwin, 1872/1965). Research following up on Darwin's work has suggested that people may produce two kinds of smiles, which may have separate evolutionary origins.

People smile in two quite different contexts: (1) when genuinely happy and (2) when wishing to show another person that they are favorably disposed toward that person. The latter situation need not entail happiness at all; in fact, people are especially likely to smile at others in potentially tense circumstances, apparently as a

---

FOCUS 30

How are homologies used for learning about (a) the physiological mechanisms and (b) the evolutionary pathways of species-typical traits?

means of reducing the tension (Goldenthal et al., 1981). Darwin (1872/1965) pointed out that these two smiles are anatomically distinct. The happy smile involves not just the turning up of the corners of the lips but also the pulling in of the skin near the outside corners of the eyes. This creates the creases called crow's feet, which radiate from the eyes and seem to make them sparkle. The other smile, in contrast, typically involves the lips alone, without the eyes—let's call it the *greeting smile*—and can be used to mask one's true feelings. This distinction has been confirmed in many studies with both adults and young children (Ekman, 1992; Sarra & Otta, 2001). In one study, for example, 10-month-old infants smiled with eyes and mouth when approached by their mother (presumably a happy situation) but smiled with mouth alone when approached by a stranger (a possibly tense situation) (Fox & Davidson, 1988).

Nonhuman primates manifest two distinct smile-like displays. The one that seems most clearly to be homologous to the human greeting smile is the *silent bared-teeth display* (see **Figure 3.19**a). This facial expression involves contraction of the same facial muscles as are involved in the human greeting smile (Parr et al., 2007). In macaque monkeys this display seems to have evolved as a means for a more submissive ape to look at a more dominant one without provoking a fight. If it could be translated into words, it might be rendered as, "I'm looking at you but I'm not going to attack, so please don't attack me." This type of display takes on a new function in chimpanzees, something more similar to that of the human smile of greeting (van Hooff, 1976). Both the more submissive and the more dominant of two chimpanzees show the display upon meeting, and it usually precedes friendly interaction between them. As used by the more submissive individual, it may retain its original meaning, "Please don't attack me," but as used by the more dominant, it may mean, "Rest assured, I won't attack," and as used by both it may mean, "Let's be friends."

FOCUS 31

How do studies of homologies between humans and other primates support the view that the human greeting smile and the human happy smile have separate evolutionary origins?

FIGURE 3.19 Possible homologues to two types of human smiles The silent bared-teeth display (a) is believed to be homologous to the human greeting smile, and the relaxed open-mouth display (b) is believed to be homologous to the human laugh and happy smile. The animals in both photos are chimpanzees.

(a)

(b)

The other primate smile-like expression is the *relaxed open-mouth display,* or *play face* (see Figure 3.19b), which occurs mostly in young primates during playful fighting and chasing and is most clearly homologous to human laughter. It involves the same facial muscles as are involved in human laughter (Parr et al., 2007), and in chimpanzees it is often accompanied by a vocalized *ahh ahh ahh,* which sounds like a throaty human laugh. This display apparently originated as a means for young primates to signal to each other that their aggressive-like behavior is not to be taken seriously; nobody will really get hurt. Interestingly, in human children, laughter occurs during playful fighting and chasing more reliably than during any other form of play (Blurton-Jones, 1967). Thus, our laughter is not only similar in form to the relaxed open-mouth display of other primates but also, at least in some cases, seems to serve a similar function.

The Value for Psychology of Studying Analogies

FOCUS 32

How can we use analogies to make inferences about the distal functions of species-typical traits?

You have just seen examples of how homologies can be used to make inferences about the evolutionary origins of species-typical behaviors. Analogies, in contrast, are not useful for tracing evolutionary origins, but are useful for making inferences about the distal functions of species-typical behaviors. If different species have independently evolved a particular behavioral trait, then comparing the species may reveal commonalities of habitat and lifestyle that are clues to the distal function of that trait. You will see examples of this use of analogies in the remaining sections of this chapter, as applied to patterns of mating, patterns of aggression, and patterns of helping.

SECTION REVIEW

Species-typical behaviors have come to exist through natural selection.

Species-Typical Behaviors

- Species-typical behaviors are ways of behaving that characterize a species—such as cats meowing and humans walking upright.

- They may be influenced by learning or even require learning, as exemplified by cultural differences in the eyebrow flash, human language learning, and white-crowned sparrows' song development.

- They depend on biological preparedness—that is, having anatomical structures that permit and motivate the behavior.

Homologies and Analogies

- Homologies are similarities due to common ancestry. They are useful for studying underlying mechanisms and for tracing the evolutionary course of species-typical behaviors, exemplified by research on the greeting smile and happy smile in humans.

- Analogies are similarities due to convergent evolution (independent evolution of similar traits). They are useful for inferring distal functions.

Evolutionary Analyses of Mating, Aggression, and Helping

Evolutionary theory is concerned with a handful of core issues including survival, mating, kin, and social relationships. In this section we examine three topics related to some of these issues: mating, aggression, and helping.

A Theory Relating Mating Patterns to Parental Investment

From an evolutionary perspective, no behavior is more important than mating. Mating is the means by which all sexually reproducing animals get their genes into the next generation. Mating is also the most basic form of social behavior. If females and males did not need to come together to reproduce, members of a species could, in theory, go through life completely oblivious to one another.

Countless varieties of male–female arrangements for sexual reproduction have evolved in different species of animals. One way to classify them is according to the number of partners a male or female typically mates with over a given period of time, such as a breeding season. Four broad classes are generally recognized: ***polygyny*** [pah-**li**-ji-nee], in which one male mates with more than one female; ***polyandry*** [pah-lee-**an**-dree], in which one female mates with more than one male; ***monogamy***, in which one male mates with one female; and ***promiscuity***, in which members of a group consisting of more than one male and more than one female mate with one another (Shuster & Wade, 2009). (These terms are easy to remember if you know that *poly-* means "many"; *mono-,* "one"; *-gyn,* "female"; and *-andr,* "male"; for example, polyandry means "many males.") As illustrated in **Figure 3.20**, a feature of both polygyny and polyandry is that some individuals are necessarily deprived of a mating opportunity—a state of affairs associated with considerable conflict.

In a now-classic article, Robert Trivers (1972) outlined *parental investment theory.* ***Parental investment*** can be defined roughly as the time, energy, and risk to survival that are involved in producing, feeding, and otherwise caring for each offspring. Trivers proposed that in sexually reproducing species there is a conflict between mating effort (time/effort expended in finding and keeping a mate) and parenting effort (time/effort expended in raising offspring). Trivers proposed that, in general, the sex that invests more in parenting will be more selective in choosing a mate than the less-investing sex, whereas the less-investing sex will compete more vigorously for access to the more investing sex.

To illustrate and elaborate on this theory—and to see how it is supported by cross-species comparisons focusing on analogies—let us apply it to each of the four general classes of mating patterns.

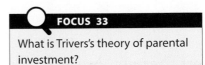

FEMALE GENETICISTS HAVE BEEN WORKING AROUND THE CLOCK SINCE THE DISCOVERY THAT **MALE** SEAHORSES GET PREGNANT

Mark Parisi, offthemark.com

FOCUS 33

What is Trivers's theory of parental investment?

FIGURE 3.20 Four mating systems In a polygynous system (common in mammals), the unmated males are a threat to the mated male, and in a polyandrous system (present in some birds and fishes), the unmated females are a threat to the mated female. Threat is reduced by monogamy and promiscuity because with those systems most individuals find mates.

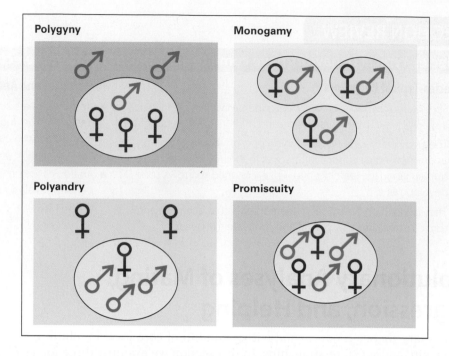

FOCUS 34

Based on Trivers's theory of parental investment, why does high investment by the female lead to (a) polygyny, (b) large size of males, and (c) high selectivity in the female's choice of mate?

Polygyny Is Related to High Female and Low Male Parental Investment

Most species of mammals are polygynous, and Trivers's theory helps explain why. Mammalian reproductive physiology is such that the female necessarily invests a great deal in the offspring she bears. The young must first develop within her body and then she must nourish them by providing milk. Because of the female's high investment, the number of offspring she can produce in a breeding season or a lifetime is limited. A human female's gestation and lactation periods are such that she can have, at most, approximately one infant per year regardless of how many different males she mates with.

Things are different for the male. His involvement with offspring is, at minimum, simply the production of sperm cells and the act of copulation. These require little time and energy, so his maximum reproductive potential is limited not by parental investment but by the number of fertile females he mates with. A male who mates with 20 females can in theory produce 20 offspring a year. When the evolutionary advantage in mating with multiple partners is greater for males than for females, a pattern evolves in which males compete with one another to mate with as many females as they can.

Among mammals, males' competition for females often involves one-on-one battles, which the larger and stronger combatant most often wins. This leads to a selective advantage for increased size and strength in males, up to some maximum beyond which the size advantage in obtaining mates is outweighed by disadvantages, such as difficulty in finding sufficient food to support the large size. In general, the more polygynous a species, the greater is the average size difference between males and females. An extreme example is the elephant seal. Males of this species fight one another, sometimes to the death, for mating rights to groups averaging about 50 females, and the males outweigh females several-fold (Hoelzel et al., 1999). In the evolution of elephant seals, those males whose genes made them large, strong, and ferocious enough to defeat other males sent many copies of their genes on to the next generation, while their weaker or less aggressive opponents sent few or none.

For the same reason that the female mammal usually has less evolutionary incentive than the male to mate with many individuals, she has more incentive to be discriminating in her choice of mate. Because she invests so much, risking her life and decreasing her future reproductive potential whenever she becomes pregnant, her genetic interests lie in producing offspring that will have the highest possible

■ **Who's bigger and stronger?** These male elephant seals are sizing each other up for possible battle over mating rights to the many females in the background. Because the larger combatant usually wins, male elephant seals have through natural selection become huge compared with females.

chance to survive and reproduce (Campbell & Cross, 2012). To the degree that the male affects the young, either through his genes or through other resources he provides, females would be expected to select males whose contribution will be most beneficial. In elephant seals, it is presumably to the female's evolutionary advantage to mate with the winner of battles. The male victor's genes increase the chance that the female's sons will win battles in the future and produce many young themselves.

Polyandry Is Related to High Male and Low Female Parental Investment

Polyandry is not the primary mating pattern for any species of mammal, but it is for some species of fishes and birds (Andersson, 2005). Polyandry is more likely to evolve in egg-laying species than in mammals, because a smaller proportion of an egg layer's reproductive cycle is tied to the female's body. Once the eggs are laid, they can be cared for by either parent, and, depending on other conditions, evolution can lead to greater male than female parental investment. Polyandry seems to come about in cases where the female can produce more eggs during a single breeding season than either she alone or she and one male can care for (Andersson, 2005). Her best strategy then becomes that of mating with multiple males and leaving each batch of fertilized eggs with the father, who becomes the main or sole caretaker.

> **FOCUS 35**
>
> What conditions promote the evolution of polyandry? How do sex differences within polyandrous species support Trivers's theory?

Consistent with Trivers's theory, females of polyandrous species are the more active and aggressive courters, and they have evolved to be larger, stronger, and in some cases more brightly colored than the males (Berglund & Rosenqvist, 2001). An example is the spotted sandpiper, a common freshwater shorebird. A female spotted sandpiper can lay up to three clutches of eggs in rapid succession, each cared for by a different male that has mated with her (Oring, 1995). At the beginning of the breeding season, the females—which outweigh the males by about 20% and have somewhat more conspicuous spots—stake out territories where they actively court males and drive out other females.

■ **An aggressive female** The spotted sandpiper is a polyandrous species. The female mates with several males and defends her territory from invading females. This female is stretching her wings in a threat display.

Monogamy Is Related to Equivalent Male and Female Parental Investment

FOCUS 36

What conditions promote the evolution of monogamy? Why are sex differences in size and strength generally lacking in monogamous species?

According to Trivers's theory, when the two sexes make approximately equal investments in their young, their degree of competition for mates will also be approximately equal, and monogamy will prevail. Equal parental investment is most likely to come about when conditions make it impossible for a single adult to raise the young but quite possible for two to raise them. Under these circumstances, if either parent leaves, the young fail to survive, so natural selection favors genes that lead parents to stay together and care for the young together. Because neither sex has a much greater likelihood of fighting over mates, there is little or no natural selection for sex differences in size and strength, and, in general, males and females of monogamous species are nearly identical in these characteristics.

Consistent with the view that monogamy arises from the need for more than one adult to care for offspring, over 90% of bird species are predominantly monogamous (Cézilly & Zayan, 2000). Among most species of birds, unlike most mammals, a single parent would usually not be able to raise the young. Birds must incubate and protect their eggs until they hatch, then must guard the hatchlings and fetch food for them until they can fly. One parent alone cannot simultaneously guard the nest and leave it to get food, but two together can. Among mammals, monogamy has arisen in some species that are like birds in the sense that their young must be given food other than milk, of a type that the male can provide. The best-known examples are certain carnivores, including foxes and coyotes (Malcolm, 1985). Young carnivores must be fed meat until they have acquired the necessary strength, agility, and skills to hunt on their own, and two parents are much better than one at accomplishing this task. Monogamy also occurs in several species of rodents, where the male may play a crucial role in protecting the young from predators while the mother forages (Sommer, 2000), and some South American monkeys (i.e., owl, Goeldi's, and titi monkeys), where the father actually engages in more childcare than the mother (Schradin et al., 2003).

■ **A not-so-faithful couple** The superb fairy wren is socially but not sexually monogamous. The male (at the left) and the female stay together at the nest and raise the young together, but DNA testing has shown that about 75% of the offspring, on average, are sired by neighboring males.

With modern DNA techniques to determine paternity, researchers have learned that *social monogamy* (the faithful pairing of female and male for raising young) does not necessarily imply *sexual monogamy* (fidelity in copulation between that female and male). Researchers commonly find that between 5 and 35% of offspring in socially monogamous birds are sired by a neighboring male rather than by the male at the nest (Birkhead & Moller, 1992); for one species, the superb fairy wren, that average is 75% (Mulder, 1994).

FOCUS 37

For what evolutionary reasons might monogamously mated females and males sometimes copulate with partners other than their mates?

Why does such extra-mate copulation occur? From the female's evolutionary perspective, copulation with a male that is genetically superior to her own mate (as manifested in song and feathers) results in genetically superior young, and copulation with any additional male increases the chance that all her eggs will be fertilized by viable sperm (Zeh & Zeh, 2001). For the male, evolutionary advantage rests in driving neighboring males away from his own mate whenever possible and in copulating with neighboring females whenever possible. Genes that build brain mechanisms that promote such behaviors are passed along to more offspring than are genes that do not.

Promiscuity Is Related to Investment in the Group

FOCUS 38

What appear to be the evolutionary advantages of promiscuity for chimpanzees and bonobos? In what ways is promiscuity more fully developed for bonobos than for chimpanzees?

Among the clearest examples of promiscuous species are chimpanzees and bonobos, which happen to be our two closest animal relatives (refer back to Figure 3.16). Bonobos are similar in appearance to chimpanzees but are rarer and have only recently been studied in the wild. The basic social structure of both species is the troop, which consists usually of two to three dozen adults of both sexes and their offspring. When the female is ovulating, she develops on her rump a prominent pink swelling, which she actively displays to advertise her condition. During the time of this swelling, which lasts about a week in chimps and three weeks in bonobos, she is likely to mate with most of the adult males of the troop, though she

■ **Bonobo sex** Bonobos seem to live by the motto, "Make love, not war." Research suggests that they are the most sexually active and the most peaceful of all primates. Here a male has mounted a female in a face-to-face position—a position long thought to be unique to humans. But bonobo sex occurs in all possible partner combinations (homosexual as well as heterosexual) and essentially all imaginable positions.

may actively choose to mate with some more often than with others, especially at the point in her cycle when she is most fertile (Goodall, 1986; Kano, 1992).

Promiscuity has apparently evolved in these ape species because it permits a group of adult males and females to live together in relative harmony, without too much fighting over who mates with whom. A related advantage, from the female's perspective, is paternity confusion (Hrdy, 2009). Among many species of primates, males kill young that are not their own, and such behavior has been observed in chimpanzees when a female migrates into a troop bringing with her an infant that was sired elsewhere (Wrangham, 1993). Because almost any chimp or bonobo male in the colony could be the father of any infant born within the troop, each male's evolutionary interest lies not in attacking the young but in helping to protect and care for the group as a whole.

Promiscuity seems to be more fully developed in bonobos than in chimps. Male chimps sometimes use force to monopolize the sexual activity of a female throughout her ovulatory cycle or during the period of peak receptivity (Goodall, 1986; Wrangham, 1993), but this does not appear to occur among bonobos (Hohmann & Fruth, 2003; Wrangham, 1993). In fact, among bonobos sex appears to be more a reducer of aggression than a cause of it (Parish & de Waal, 2000; Wrangham, 1993). Unlike any other apes, female bonobos copulate at all times of their reproductive cycle, not just near the time of ovulation. In addition to their frequent heterosexual activity, bonobos of the same sex often rub their genitals together, and genital stimulation of all types occurs most often following conflict and in situations that could potentially elicit conflict, such as when a favorite food is discovered (Hohmann & Fruth, 2000). Field studies suggest that bonobos are the most peaceful of primates and that their frequent promiscuous sexual activity helps keep them that way (de Waal, 2005; Kano, 1992).

What About Human Mating Patterns?
A Largely Monogamous, Partly Polygynous Species
When we apply the same criteria that are used to classify the mating systems of other species, we find that humans fall on the boundary between monogamy and polygyny (Dewsbury, 1988). In no culture are human beings as sexually promiscuous as are our closest ape relatives, the chimpanzees and bonobos. In every culture, people form

 FOCUS 39

What evidence suggests that humans evolved as a partly monogamous, partly polygynous species? How is this consistent with Trivers's parental investment theory?

long-term mating bonds, which are usually legitimized through some sort of culturally recognized marriage contract. Anthropologists have found that the great majority of non-Western cultures, where Western influence has not made polygyny illegal, practice a mixture of monogamy and polygyny (Marlowe, 2000; Murdock, 1981). In such cultures, men who have sufficient wealth or status have two or more wives, while the great majority of men have one wife and a few have none. Thus, even in cultures that permit and idealize polygyny, most marriages are monogamous.

Human children, more so than the young of any other primates, require an extended period of care before they can play full adult roles in activities such as food gathering. Cross-cultural research shows that in every culture mothers provide most of the direct physical care of children, but fathers contribute in various ways, which is rare among mammals. Humans are among the 5% of mammals in which the male provides some support to his offspring (Clutton-Brock, 1991). In many cultures—especially in hunter-gatherer cultures—fathers share to some degree in the physical care of their offspring (Marlowe, 2000), and in nearly all cultures fathers provide indirect care in the form of food and other material provisions. In fact, in 77% of the cultures for which data are available, fathers contribute more of the provisions for young than do mothers (Marlowe, 2000). Taking both direct and indirect care into account, humans are a species in which fathers typically lag somewhat behind mothers, but not greatly behind them, in degree of parental investment. This, in line with Trivers's parental investment theory, is consistent with our being a primarily monogamous but moderately polygynous species.

The moderate size difference between men and women is also consistent with this conclusion (Dewsbury, 1988). The average size difference between males and females in humans is nowhere near that observed in highly polygynous species, such as elephant seals and gorillas, but is greater than that observed in monogamous species.

Another clue to *Homo sapiens'* prehistorical mating patterns comes from a comparative analysis of the different types of white blood cells—which play an important role in the immune system—between humans and other primates with different types of mating systems (Nunn et al., 2000). Sexually transmitted diseases can be a problem not just for humans but for other species as well, and the more sex partners one has, the stronger one's immune system needs to be to combat infection. Nunn and his colleagues found that sexually promiscuous species, such as chimpanzees and bonobos, had more types of white blood cells than monogamous species, such as owl monkeys. Humans' immune system was between those of the polygynous, harem-based gorilla and the monogamous gibbon (a lesser ape). This suggests that the marginally monogamous/marginally polygynous relationships that characterize modern and historic humans also characterized our species' prehistoric ancestors.

Roles of Emotions in Human Mating Systems

The biological equipment that predisposes humans for mating bonds includes brain mechanisms that promote the twin emotions of romantic love and sexual jealousy. These emotions are found in people of every culture that has been studied (Buss, 2011; Fisher, 2004). People everywhere develop strong emotional ties to those toward whom they are sexually drawn. The predominant feeling is a need to be regularly near the other person. People everywhere also feel intensely jealous when "their" mates appear to be sexually drawn to others. While love tends to create mating bonds, jealousy tends to preserve such bonds by motivating each member of a mated pair to act in ways designed to prevent the other from involvement with someone else.

Other animals that form long-term mating bonds show evidence of emotions that are functionally similar to human love and jealousy (e.g., Lazarus et al., 2004). In this

FOCUS 40

From an evolutionary perspective, what are the functions of romantic love and sexual jealousy, and how is this supported by cross-species comparisons? How is sexual unfaithfulness explained?

sense, we are more like monogamous birds than we are like our closest ape relatives. The similarities between humans and birds in sexual love and jealousy are clearly analogies, not homologies. They evolved separately in humans and birds as means to create and preserve mating bonds that are durable enough to enable biparental care of offspring. Unlike humans and monogamous birds, chimpanzees and bonobos (especially the latter) can engage in open, promiscuous sex with little emotional consequence because they have not evolved strong emotions of sexual love and jealousy. The difference has to do with species differences in the need for care from both parents.

Although love and jealousy tend to promote bonding, there is another product of evolution—lust—that tends to motivate both men and women to engage surreptitiously in sex outside of such bonds. In this sense we are like those socially monogamous birds that are sexually unfaithful. A man who can inseminate women beyond his wife may send more copies of his genes into the next generation than a completely faithful man. A woman who has sex with men other than her husband may also benefit evolutionarily. Such escapades may (a) increase her chances of conception by serving as a hedge against the possibility that her husband's sperm are not viable or are genetically incompatible with her eggs; (b) increase the evolutionary fitness of her offspring if she mates with a man whose genes are evolutionarily superior to those of her husband; and/or (c) result in provisions from more than one man (Hrdy, 2009). And so the human soap opera continues, much like that of the superb fairy wren, though not to such an extreme. Studies involving DNA testing, in cultures ranging from hunter-gatherer groups to modern Western societies, suggest that somewhere between 2 and 10% of children in socially monogamous families are sired by someone other than the mother's husband (Marlowe, 2000).

What about polyandry—one woman and several men? Do humans ever engage in it? Not typically, but it is not unheard of. Polyandry occurs in some cultures when one man cannot secure enough resources to support a wife and her children. When it does happen, usually two brothers will share a wife. In this way, a man can be assured that any child the woman conceives shares at least some of his genes: 50% if he's the father and 25% if his brother is the father. When one of the brothers acquires enough resources to support a wife on his own, he often does so, leaving the polyandrous family (Schmitt, 2005).

A special form of polyandry occurs in some South American hunter-gatherer groups, who believe that a child possesses some of the characteristics of any man the mother has sex with approximately 10 months before birth, termed *partible paternity*. Although a woman may have a husband and be in a monogamous relationship, a pregnant woman may initiate affairs with other, often high-status men. As a result, these men may protect or even provide resources to "their" child, resulting in a higher survival rate for children compared to those without "multiple fathers" (Beckerman & Valentine, 2002).

Sex Differences in Aggression

From an evolutionary perspective, other members of one's species are competitors for food, mates, safe places to live, and other limited resources. Ultimately, such competition is the foundation of aggression.

Aggression, as the term is used here, is defined as behavior intended to harm another member of the same species. Brain mechanisms that motivate and organize such behavior have evolved because they help animals acquire and retain resources needed to survive and reproduce. As you saw in the previous section, much animal aggression centers on mating. Polygynous males and polyandrous females fight for mates; monogamous males fight to prevent other males from copulating with their mates; monogamous females fight to keep other females from leading their mates away; and promiscuous females fight to keep immigrating females from competing for resources (Kahlenberg et al., 2008; Tobias & Seddon, 2000). Aggression can also serve to protect a feeding ground for oneself and one's

"If anyone calls, I'll be downstairs thumping my chest at the younger apes."

offspring, to drive away individuals that may be a threat to one's young, and to elevate one's status within a social group. Much could be said from an evolutionary perspective about all aspects of aggression, but here we will focus just on sex differences in how aggression is manifested.

Why Male Primates Are Generally More Violent Than Female Primates

Among most species of mammals, and especially among primates, males are much more violently aggressive than are females. Female primates are not unaggressive, but their aggression is typically aimed directly toward obtaining resources and defending their young. When they have achieved their ends, they stop fighting. Male primates, in contrast, seem at times to go out of their way to pick fights, and they are far more likely to maim or kill their opponents than are females.

Most of the violence perpetrated by male primates has to do directly or indirectly with sex. Male monkeys of several species have been observed to kill infants fathered by others, apparently as a means to get the females to stop lactating so they will ovulate again and become sexually active. Males also fight with one another, sometimes brutally, to gain access to a particular female or to raise their rank in the dominance hierarchy of the troop. High rank generally increases both their attractiveness to females and their ability to intimidate sexual rivals (Cowlishaw & Dunbar, 1991). Males are also often violent toward females; they use violence to force copulation or to prevent the female from copulating with other males. All of these behaviors have been observed in chimpanzees and many other primate species (Goodall, 1986).

Evolution, remember, is not a moral force; it merely promotes those behaviors that tend to get one's genes passed on to the next generation. Female primates don't need to fight to get the opposite sex interested in them. Moreover, aggression may have a higher cost for females than for males: The female at battle risks not just her life but also that of any fetus she is gestating or young she is nursing—the repositories of her genes (Campbell, 1999). The male at battle risks just himself; in the calculus of evolution, his life isn't worth anything unless he can get a female to mate with him. Genes that promote mating, by whatever means, proliferate, and genes that fail to promote it vanish.

 FOCUS 41

How is male violence toward infants, toward other males, and toward females explained from an evolutionary perspective?

MICHAEL NICHOLS/National Geographic Creative

■ **Tough young males** Male mammals of many species compete with one another for dominance. Much of their competition, however, involves threat and bluff rather than bloodshed, as illustrated by these two young mountain gorillas.

Male Violence in Humans

Humans are no exception to the usual primate rule. Cross-cultural studies show that men are more violent, more likely to maim or kill, than are women. In fact, in a survey of cross-cultural data on this issue, Martin Daly and Margo Wilson (1988) were unable to find any society in which the number of women who killed other women was even one tenth as great as the number of men who killed other men. On average, in the data they examined, male–male killings outnumbered female–female killings by more than 30 to 1. One might construe a scenario through which such a difference in violence would be purely a product of learning in every culture, but the hypothesis that the difference resides at least partly in inherited sex differences seems more plausible.

According to Daly and Wilson's analyses, the apparent motives underlying male violence and homicide are very much in accord with predictions from evolutionary theory. Among the leading motives for murder among men in every culture is sexual jealousy. Some cultures have traditionally expected men to attack or even kill other men who have sex with their wives (Buss, 2000; Symons, 1979), and in others, such murders are common even though they are illegal (Daly & Wilson, 1988). Men also fight over status, which can affect their degree of success in mating (Kruger & Fitzgerald, 2012). One man insults another and then the two fight it out—with fists, knives, or guns. And, like many male monkeys and apes, men often use violence to control females. Across cultures, between 19% and 75% of women experience violence at the hands of their intimate partners (Garcia-Moreno et al., 2006). Analyses of domestic violence cases indicate that they frequently have to do with the man's belief (often unfounded) that his partner has been or might become sexually unfaithful (Goetz, 2008; Goetz & Romero, 2012).

Patterns of Helping

Although humans and other animals may use aggression to get what they need and want, at the same time, others of one's kind are potential helpmates. Many life-promoting tasks can be better accomplished by two or more together than by one struggling alone. The human drama, like that of other social species, involves the balancing of competitiveness with the need for others' help.

From an evolutionary perspective, *helping* can be defined as any behavior that increases the survival chance or reproductive capacity of another individual. Given this definition, it is useful to distinguish between two categories of helping: cooperation and altruism.

Cooperation occurs when an individual helps another while helping itself. This sort of helping happens all the time in the animal world and is easy to understand from an evolutionary perspective. It occurs when a mated pair of foxes work together to raise their young, a pack of wolves work together to kill an antelope, or a group of chimpanzees work together to chase off a predator or a rival group of chimpanzees. Most of the advantages of social living lie in cooperation. By working with others for common ends, each individual has a better chance of survival and reproduction than it would have alone. Whatever costs accrue are more than repaid by the benefits. Human beings everywhere live in social groups and derive the benefits of cooperation. Those who live as our ancestors did cooperate in hunting and gathering food, caring for children, building dwellings, defending against predators and human invaders, and, most human of all, in exchanging, through language, information that bears on all aspects of the struggle for survival. Cooperation, and behaving fairly toward other people in general, develops quite early in life, suggesting that it is not simply a reflection of children bowing to the requests and admonishments of their parents, but an aspect of sociality that runs deep in human nature (Tomasello, 2009; Warneken & Melis, 2012).

Altruism, in contrast, occurs when an individual helps another while decreasing its own survival chance or reproductive capacity. This is less common than cooperation, but many animals do behave in ways that at least appear to be altruistic. For example, some animals, including female ground squirrels, emit a loud, distinctive call when they spot an approaching predator. The cry warns others of the predator's approach and, at the same time, tends to attract the predator's attention to the caller (Sherman, 1977). (See **Figure 3.21**.) The selfish response would be to remain quiet and hidden or to move away quietly, rather than risk being detected by warning others. How can such behavior be explained from an evolutionary perspective? As Trivers (1971) pointed out long ago, any evolutionary account of apparent altruism must operate by showing that from a broader perspective, focusing on the propagation of one's genes, the behavior is not truly altruistic. Evolutionists have developed two broad theories to account for ostensible altruism in animals: the kin selection theory and the reciprocity theory.

The Kin Selection Theory of Altruism

The *kin selection theory* holds that behavior that seems to be altruistic came about through natural selection because it preferentially helps close relatives, who are genetically most similar to the helper (Hamilton, 1964). What actually survives over evolutionary time, of course, is not the individual but the individual's genes. Any gene that promotes the production and preservation of copies of itself can be a fit

FIGURE 3.21 An alarm-calling ground squirrel When they spot a predator, female ground squirrels often emit an alarm call, especially if they are living in a group of close kin. Males are less likely to live near close kin and do not show this response.

FOCUS 42

How do the kin selection and reciprocity theories take the altruism out of "altruism"? What observations show that both theories apply to humans as well as to other animals?

gene, from the vantage point of natural selection, even if it reduces the survival chances of a particular carrier of the gene.

Imagine a ground squirrel with a rare gene that promotes the behavior of calling out when a predator is near. The mathematics of inheritance are such that, on average, one-half of the offspring or siblings of the individual with this gene would be expected to have the same gene, as would one-fourth of the nieces or nephews and one-eighth of the cousins. Thus, if the altruist incurred a small risk (Δ) to its own life while increasing an offspring's or a sibling's chances of survival by more than 2Δ, a niece's or nephew's by more than 4Δ, or a cousin's by more than 8Δ, the gene would increase in the population from one generation to the next.

Many research studies have shown that animals do help kin more than nonkin. For example, ground squirrels living with kin are more likely to emit alarm calls than are those living with nonkin (Sherman, 1977). Chimpanzees and other primates are more likely to help kin than nonkin in all sorts of ways, including sharing food, providing assistance in fights, and helping take care of young (Goodall, 1986; Nishida, 1990). Consistent with the mathematics of genetic relatedness, macaque monkeys have been observed to help their brothers and sisters more readily than their cousins and their cousins more readily than more distant relatives (Silk, 2002). In these examples, the helpers can apparently distinguish kin from nonkin, and this ability allows them to direct help selectively to kin (Pfennig & Sherman, 1995; Silk, 2002). In theory, however, altruistic behavior can evolve through kin selection even without such discrimination. An indiscriminate tendency to help any member of one's species can evolve if the animal's living arrangements are such that, by chance alone, a high percentage of help is directed toward kin.

Cross-cultural research shows that among humans the selective helping of kin more than nonkin is widespread (Essock-Vitale & McGuire, 1980; Stewart-Williams, 2007). If a mother dies or for other reasons is unable to care for a child, the child's grandmother, aunt, or other close relative is by far the most likely adopter (Kurland, 1979). Close kin are also most likely to share dwellings or land, hunt together, or form other collaborative arrangements. Genetic kin living in the same household are also less often violent toward one another than are nonkin living in the same household (Daly & Wilson, 1988), and studies in non-Western cultures have shown that villages in which most people are closely related have less internal friction than those in which people are less closely related (Chagnon, 1979). People report feeling emotionally closer to their kin than to their nonkin friends, even if they live farther away from kin and see them less often than nonkin (Neyer & Lang, 2003).

When leaders call for patriotic sacrifice or universal cooperation, they commonly employ kinship terms (Johnson, 1987). At times of war, political leaders ask citizens to fight for the "motherland" or "fatherland"; at other times, religious leaders and humanists strive to promote world peace by speaking of our "brothers and sisters" everywhere. The terms appeal to our tendencies to be kind to relatives. Our imagination and intelligence allow us to extend our concept of kinship to all humanity.

The Reciprocity Theory of Apparent Altruism

The *reciprocity theory* provides an account of how acts of apparent altruism can arise even among nonkin. According to this theory, behaviors that seem to be altruistic are actually forms of long-term cooperation (Trivers, 1971). Computer simulations of evolution have shown that a genetically induced tendency to help nonkin can evolve if it is tempered by (a) an ability to remember which individuals have reciprocated such help in the past and (b) a tendency not to help those who failed to reciprocate previous help. Under these conditions, helping another is selfish because it increases the chance of receiving help from that other in the future.

Behavior fitting this pattern is found in various niches of the animal world. As one example, vampire bats frequently share food with unrelated members of their species that have shared food with them in the past (Wilkinson, 1988). As another example, bonobo females that establish friendship coalitions are often unrelated to one another, having immigrated from different natal troops (Kano, 1992; Parish & de Waal, 2000). The help each gives the others, in such acts as chasing off offending males, is reciprocated at another time.

The greatest reciprocal helpers of all, by far, are human beings. People in every culture feel a strong drive to return help that is given to them (Hill, 2002). Humans, more than any other species, can keep track of help given, remember it over a long period of time, and think of a wide variety of ways of reciprocating. Moreover, to ensure reciprocity, people everywhere have a highly developed sense of fairness and behave in ways that punish those who fail to fulfill their parts in reciprocal relationships (Baumard et al., 2013; Fehr & Fischbacher, 2003).

In one study, Canadian college students reported that they exchanged help more with close relatives (siblings) than more distant relatives (cousins), consistent with kin-selection theory. However, consistent with reciprocity theory, they reported that they received as much or more help from friends as kin (Stewart-Williams, 2007). People's willingness to help kin versus friends varied with the cost of helping, however: For low-cost help, people helped friends more than kin; for medium-cost help they helped kin and friends equally; and for high-cost help they helped kin more than friends.

Certain human emotions seem to be well designed by natural selection to promote reciprocity. We feel gratitude toward those who help us, pride when we return such help, guilt when we fail to return help, and anger when someone fails repeatedly to return help we have given. Humans also help others, including others who may never be able to reciprocate, in order to develop a good reputation in the community at large, and those with a good reputation are valued and helped by the community (Fehr & Fischbacher, 2003).

Gunter Ziesler/Getty Images

■ **Helpful little demons** Vampire bats are gregarious mammals that demonstrate reciprocal altruism. After gorging itself on a blood meal, a bat will share some of what it has ingested with another bat, usually one that has fed it in the past.

SECTION REVIEW

An evolutionary perspective offers functionalist explanations of mating, aggression, and helping.

Relation of Mating Patterns to Parental Investment	Human Mating Patterns	Male Violence	Helping
■ Trivers theorized that sex differences in parental investment (time, energy, risk involved in bearing and raising young) explain mating patterns and sex differences in size, aggressiveness, competition for mates, and selectivity in choosing mates.	■ Parental investment is somewhat lower for human fathers than for mothers, consistent with the human mix of monogamy and polygyny.	■ Male primates, including men, are generally more violent than are females of their species.	■ Helping (promoting another's survival or reproduction) takes two forms: cooperation and altruism.
■ Consistent with Trivers's theory, polygyny is associated with high female and low male parental investment; polyandry is associated with the opposite; monogamy is associated with approximately equal investment by the two sexes; and promiscuity, common to chimps and bonobos, seems to be associated with high investment in the group.	■ Romantic love and jealousy help promote and preserve bonding of mates, permitting two-parent care of offspring. ■ Both sexual faithfulness and unfaithfulness can be evolutionarily adaptive, depending on conditions.	■ Most aggression and violence in male primates relate directly or indirectly to sex. Genes that promote violence are passed to offspring to the degree that they increase reproduction.	■ Cooperation (helping others while also helping oneself, as in the case of wolves hunting together) is easy to understand evolutionarily. ■ Apparent acts of altruism (helping others at a net cost to oneself) make evolutionary sense if explained by the kin selection or reciprocity theories.

Thinking Critically About Genetics and Evolution

1. Many scientists believed that once we had a full description of the human genome we would be able to understand human functioning, including human thought and psychopathology. Few believe this now. Why the change? What are the advantages and limitations of genetic knowledge on understanding human thought and behavior?

2. Does an evolutionary perspective of human thought and behavior imply genetic determinism? Why or why not?

Reflections and Connections

1. **The indirect nature of genetic influences on behavior** Genes are simply DNA molecules that provide the code for building the body's proteins. But genes never produce behaviors directly—they work in conjunction with the environment, so their effects depend on environmental conditions. Our behavior results from an interplay between the environment in which we live and our bodies' biological mechanisms, which themselves were built through an interplay between genes and environment. We need to keep in mind the complex interaction of genes and environment when trying to make sense of people's behavior: A person's behavior is not determined solely by genes, and neither can a group of people be described as genetically predisposed to behaving in one way versus another.

2. **The unconscious nature of distal functions** Sigmund Freud (discussed in Chapters 14 and 16) is famous for his claim that we are often unconscious of the real reasons for our actions. On that point, at least, modern evolutionary psychologists and Freud agree. Our species-typical drives and behavioral tendencies evolved to promote functions related to survival and reproduction, but we rarely think of those functions, and we are often completely unaware of them.

Infants babble and attempt to stand and walk because it is "fun" to do so, without any thought about the value of such play in learning to talk and walk. We all smile, automatically or because it seems like the right thing to do, when we are happy or when we meet someone, without thinking about the functions that smiling might serve. When we fall in love, we are far more likely to attribute that feeling to the sweet, charming, and irresistible nature of the beloved person than to anything having to do with the value of bonding for producing and raising children. When we feel jealous because of attention another is paying to our beloved, we think angry thoughts about betrayal and unfaithfulness, not about the role of jealousy in preserving monogamy. When we help a person in need, we do it out of felt sympathy and compassion; we do not coldly, consciously calculate the costs and long-term benefits to ourselves.

The reasons we give ourselves for what we do are an aspect of the *proximate causation* of our behavior. We are often no more aware of the *distal functions* of our actions than the cabbage butterfly is of why it is irresistibly drawn to plants of the cabbage family as the only proper place to lay its eggs.

3. **Evolution as an integrative theme in psychology** The evolutionary perspective provides the broadest view we can take in psychology. It is concerned with the origins and distal functions of all aspects of human nature (and the nature of other animals). It is a perspective that can be applied to the whole vast range of topics related to psychology (see the many chapters in *The Handbook of Evolutionary Psychology*, Buss, 2016). The complex biological mechanisms that underlie our psychological nature came about because they helped our ancestors to survive and reproduce. We can expect, therefore, that all of our basic motivational and emotional mechanisms are biased toward generating behaviors that promote survival and reproduction; and we can expect that our sensory, perceptual, memory, and reasoning mechanisms are biased toward picking up and using information essential to those purposes. We are not general learning or thinking machines that indiscriminately analyze all information available; we are biological survival machines designed to use information selectively to achieve our ends. As you go through the rest of this book, crossing the whole range of psychology, you will see this idea applied in every chapter.

Key Terms

adaptation 78

aggression 93

alleles 64

altruism 95

analogy 84

artificial selection 72

chromosomes 62

cooperation 95

distal explanations 76

DNA 60

dominant 64

epigenetics 70

evolution 60

fraternal twins 64

functionalism 76

genes 60

genotype 62

helping 95

homology 84

identical twins 64

kin selection theory 95

meiosis 63

mitosis 63

monogamy 87

mutations 73

natural selection 73

naturalistic fallacy 75

normal distribution 68

parental investment 87

phenotype 62

polyandry 87

polygenic characteristics 68

polygyny 87

promiscuity 87

proximate explanations 76

recessive 64

reciprocity theory 96

selective breeding 68

species-typical behaviors 80

vestigial characteristics 77

zygote 64

Find Out More

Charles Darwin (1859; reprinted 1963). *The origin of species*. New York, NY: Washington Square Press.

Darwin was an engaging writer as well as a brilliant thinker. Why not read at least part of this book, which revolutionized the intellectual world? The most relevant chapter for psychologists is Chapter 8, Instinct, which includes Darwin's research on hive building in bees and many other insights about the behavior of wild and domesticated animals. This is a free download on both iTunes and Amazon.

David Sloan Wilson (2007). *Evolution for everyone: How Darwin's theory can change the way we think about our lives*. New York, NY: Delacorte Press.

Wilson is a brilliant biologist, a broad-ranging philosopher, a great storyteller, and a self-described optimist. His goal in this book is to prove how all of us can benefit by understanding evolutionary theory and applying it in our everyday thinking. Wilson shows how evolutionary theory sheds insight on topics ranging from species of beetles, to Abraham Lincoln, to organized religions.

Robert M. Sapolsky (2017). *Behave: The biology of humans at our best and worst*. New York, NY: Penguin Press.

Writing with clarity and humor, Robert Sapolsky—a behavioral neuroscientist, primatologist, and recipient of a MacArthur Foundation genius award—guides readers through the fascinating, complex, nuanced, and context-dependent relations between brains, hormones, and behaviors, focusing the some of the best (love, compassion, morality) and worst (aggression, xenophobia) aspects of human behavior.

Susan M. Schneider (2012). *The science of consequences: How they affect genes, change the brain, and impact our world*. Amherst, NY: Prometheus Books.

Schneider takes complex and challenging scientific concepts and presents them in an everyday manner. This often humorous book connects several levels of analysis from the long-standing science of biology and genetics to current investigations in learning psychology. Schneider explores how consequences change who we are as a species, how we got to be this way, and how individual experience changes what we do.

David S. Moore (2015). *The developing genome: An introduction to behavioral epigenetics*. New York, NY: Oxford University Press.

Epigenetics has emerged as a hot and important topic. This engaging and accessible book uses clear examples to show the relevance of epigenetics to human behavior. It can be easily understood by students and consumers.

Jane Goodall (2002, March). What separates us from chimpanzees? Monterey, CA: TED 2002. https://www.ted.com/talks/jane_goodall_on_what_separates_us_from_the_apes

The highly acclaimed primatologist Jane Goodall discusses the difference between the great apes and humans in this compelling talk. She makes the argument that language is the great separator between human phylogeny and apes, and encourages us all to use this gift to better the world.

The Evolution Institute https://evolution-institute.org

The Evolution Institute "connects the world of evolutionary science to the world of public policy formulation." On its website you will find dozens of articles relating evolutionary research and theory to contemporary issues in biology, psychology, culture, and politics. There is virtually something for everyone.

Visit LaunchPad for Psychology 8e launchpadworks.com to access the e-book, videos, activities, additional resources, and LearningCurve quizzes, as well as study aids including flash cards and web quizzes.

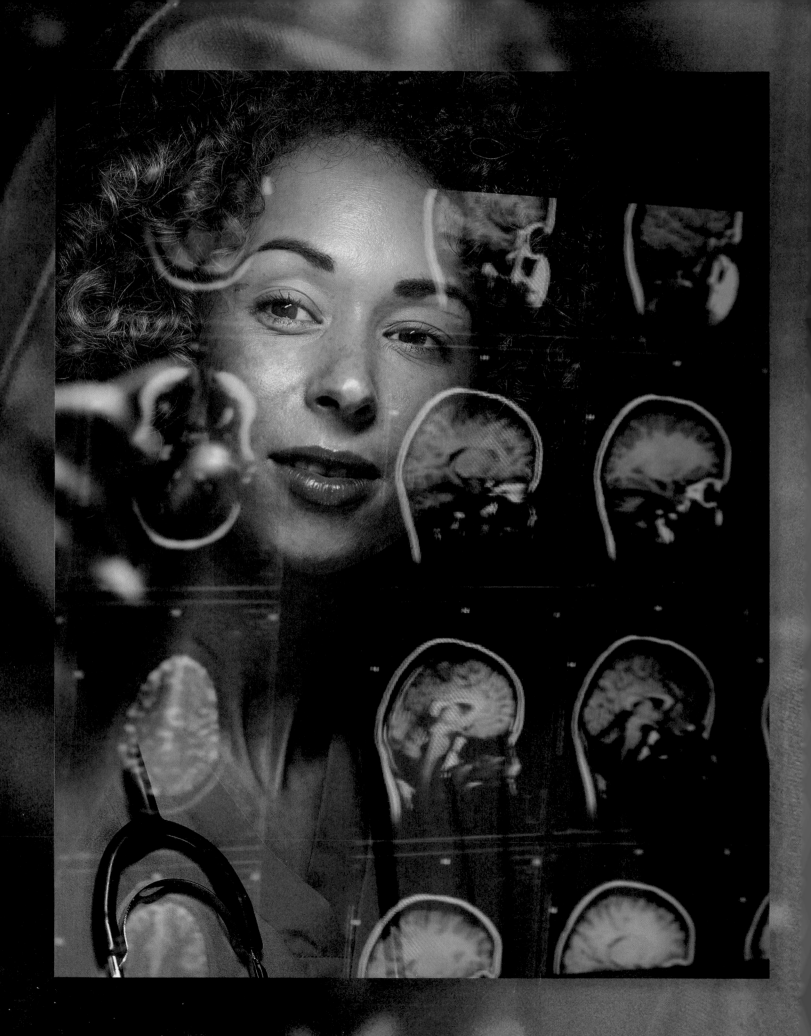

The Neural Control of Behavior

4

LEARNING OUTCOMES

After studying this chapter, you should be able to:

- Explain what neurons are and how they work.
- Describe some methods of studying the brains of humans and other animals.
- Describe how the nervous system is organized.
- Give some examples of how hormones interact with the nervous system.
- Identify some brain functions that are affected by hemispheric asymmetry.
- Explain how the brain changes and grows over time.

A human brain is, we must admit, somewhat disappointing in appearance. It's about the size and shape of a cantaloupe, but more gnarled. As described by Rita Carter in her book *Mapping the Mind* (1999), it is "as big as a coconut, the shape of a walnut, the color of uncooked liver, and the consistency of chilled butter" (p. 15). To the eye it seems relatively dormant, even when viewed in a living person. Aristotle and many other ancient Greeks—who were among the first to try to figure out what the various parts of the body are for—were not much impressed by the brain. Noticing that the blood vessels leading into it are larger than those entering other organs, they suggested that the brain's main function was to cool the blood. They were much more impressed by the heart, an obviously dynamic organ, and proposed that the heart and blood are the source of feelings, thoughts, and all else that we today call "psychological."

Not all of the ancients agreed with the heart theory of psychology, however. One who didn't was the Greek physician Hippocrates, whose observations of the effects of head injuries on people's thoughts and actions led him to focus on the brain. In the fourth century BCE, Hippocrates (1923) wrote: "From the brain, and from the brain only, arise our pleasures, joys, laughter and jests, as well as our sorrows, pains, griefs and tears. Through it, in particular, we think, see, hear. . . . Eyes, ears, tongue, hands and feet act in accordance with the discernment of the brain" (p. 175).

Hippocrates was right, of course, and that is why nearly every introductory psychology text, from William James's (1890/1950) classic on, contains a chapter about the nervous system, especially the brain. As psychologists and neuroscientists learn more about the brain, the nervous-system chapter becomes ever more meaningfully connected to the rest of the book, and material on the brain spills ever more copiously out of that chapter into others. In a real sense, psychology is the study of the nervous system; indeed, psychology focuses on the most complex aspects of what the nervous system does.

Every chapter of this book is at least indirectly about the nervous system, and this chapter is directly about it. As discussed in Chapter 1, the research specialty that studies the brain is referred to as **neuroscience**, and the subfield that studies the relation between brain and

sturti/Getty Images

behavior is *behavioral neuroscience*. In recent years, researchers in all fields of psychology have begun to study the brain more directly, resulting in more specific subfields of neuroscience, including cognitive neuroscience, developmental neuroscience, social neuroscience, and clinical neuroscience.

The chapter begins with the basic units of the nervous system—individual neurons. In the next section, it describes how we are able to study the brain. Then it describes the larger structures of the nervous system, focusing on their roles in controlling behavior. The final sections deal with the brain's higher functions and the ways in which the brain changes over time. This chapter provides essential background for many discussions of brain processes that you will come across in later chapters.

Neurons: The Building Blocks of the Brain

The brain may look inactive to the naked eye, but at a microscopic level it is the most dynamic organ of the body. It makes up about 2% of our body weight, but consumes about 20% of our metabolic energy (Magistretti, 2008). The brain requires even more energy during early childhood, with the brain metabolism of 4- and 5-year-old children being about 150% of adults', falling to adult levels around age 9 (Chugani et al., 1987). It is by far the most complex and compact computing machine in the known universe. **Figure 4.1** provides three different views of the adult brain.

The human brain contains roughly 86 *billion* nerve cells, or **neurons** (Herculano-Houze, 2012). Unlike most other cells in the human body, neurons are not compressed together but are separated; yet neurons communicate with one another. They do this through connections called synapses, of which there are roughly 100 *trillion*. Neurons are constantly active, and their collective activity monitors our internal and external environments, creates all of our mental experiences, and controls all of our behavior.

The seeming magic of the nervous system—its abilities to analyze sensory data, create mental experiences, and control movements in adaptive ways—lies not in the individual neurons, but in the organization of their multitudes. Yet each neuron is itself a complex decision-making machine. Each neuron receives information from multiple sources, integrates that information, and sends its response out to many other neurons or, in some cases, to muscle cells or glands. In this section we examine the structure and functions of individual neurons as a prelude to examining the larger structures and functions of the nervous system as a whole.

Three Basic Varieties of Neurons, and Structures Common to Them

The overall layout of the human nervous system is sketched in **Figure 4.2**. The *brain and spinal cord* (which extends from the brain down through the bones of the spinal column) make up the ***central nervous system***, which integrates and synthesizes neural information. Extensions from the central nervous system, called *nerves*, make up the ***peripheral nervous system***, which relays information to and from the brain from other parts of the body.

Don't confuse the terms *neuron* and *nerve*. A neuron is a single cell of the nervous system. A **nerve** is a bundle of many neurons—or, more precisely, a bundle consisting of the axons (defined below) of many neurons—within the peripheral nervous system. Nerves connect the central nervous system to the body's sensory organs, muscles, and glands. Note also that despite their names, the central and peripheral nervous systems are not two separate systems, but are parts of an integrated whole.

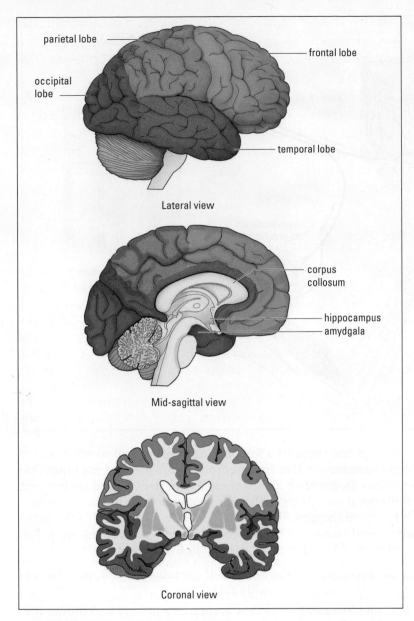

parietal lobe

frontal lobe

occipital lobe

temporal lobe

Lateral view

corpus collosum

hippocampus
amydgala

Mid-sagittal view

Coronal view

FIGURE 4.1 The human brain and some of its structures, shown in three different views (lateral, mid-sagital, and coronal).

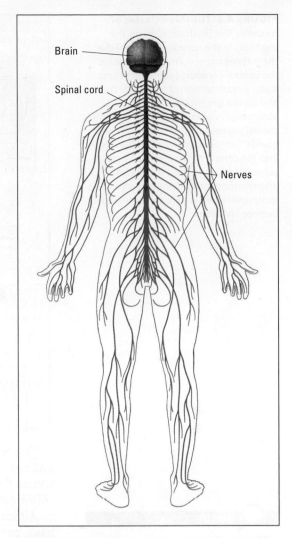

Brain

Spinal cord

Nerves

FIGURE 4.2 Human nervous system The central nervous system consists of the brain and the spinal cord, which runs through the bones of the spinal column down the center of the back. The peripheral nervous system consists of the entire set of nerves, which connect the brain and spinal cord to the sensory organs, muscles, and glands.

Neurons come in a wide variety of shapes and sizes and serve countless specific functions. At the broadest level of analysis, they can be grouped into three categories according to their functions and their locations in the overall layout of the nervous system (see **Figure 4.3**):

1. *Sensory neurons*, bundled together to form nerves, carry information from sensory organs (including the eyes, ears, nose, tongue, and skin) into the central nervous system.

2. *Motor neurons*, also bundled into nerves, carry messages out from the central nervous system to operate muscles and glands.

3. *Interneurons* exist entirely within the central nervous system and carry messages from one set of neurons to another. Interneurons collect, organize, and integrate messages from various sources. They vastly outnumber the other two types.

FOCUS 1

What are three types of neurons, and what is the function of each?

FIGURE 4.3 The three classes of neurons This illustration shows the positions in the nervous system of the three types of neurons. On the right is the central nervous system (more specifically, a cross section of the spinal cord), and on the left are muscles and skin. Motor neurons send messages from the central nervous system to muscles and glands. Sensory neurons send messages into the central nervous system from sensory organs, such as the skin. And interneurons, located entirely within the central nervous system, carry messages between neurons.

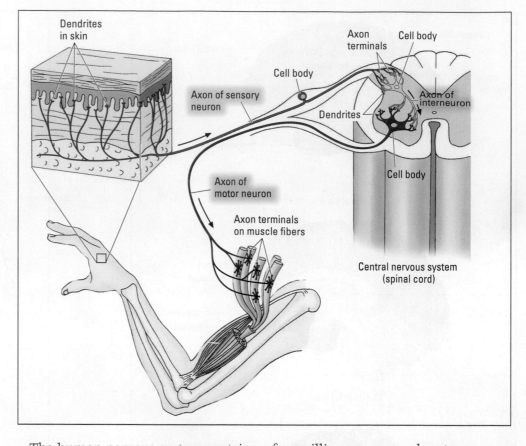

🔍 **FOCUS 2**

What are the main parts common to all or most neurons, and what is the function of each part?

The human nervous system contains a few million sensory and motor neurons and roughly 86 *billion* interneurons. Our interneurons make sense of the input that comes from sensory neurons, generate all our mental experiences, and initiate and coordinate all our behavioral actions through their connections to motor neurons.

Although neurons vary tremendously in shape and size, most contain the same basic parts. The parts, listed below, are labeled for all three types of neurons in Figure 4.3 and illustrated more fully for a motor neuron in **Figure 4.4**.

● The *cell body* is the widest part of the neuron. It contains the cell **nucleus** and other basic machinery common to all bodily cells.

● *Dendrites* are thin, tubelike extensions that branch extensively and function to receive input to the neuron. In motor neurons and interneurons, the dendrites extend directly off the cell body and generally branch out from it, forming bush-like structures. These structures increase the surface area of the cell and thereby allow for receipt of signals from many other neurons. In sensory neurons, dendrites branch out from one end of the axon, rather than directly from the cell body. They extend into a sensory organ and respond to sensory signals, such as sound waves in the ear or touch on the skin (shown for skin in Figure 4.3).

● The *axon* is another thin, tubelike extension from the cell body. Its function is to carry messages to other neurons or, in the case of motor neurons, to muscle cells. Although microscopically thin, some axons are extremely long. You have axons of sensory neurons reaching all the way from your big toe into your spinal cord and onward up to the base of your brain—a distance of 5 feet or more. Most axons form many branches some distance away from the cell body, and each branch ends with a small swelling called an *axon terminal*. Axon terminals are designed to release chemical transmitter molecules onto other neurons or, in the case of motor neurons, onto muscle cells or glandular cells. The axons of some neurons are surrounded by a casing called a *myelin sheath*. *Myelin* is a fatty substance produced by supportive brain cells called *glial cells*. As will be described later, this sheath helps to speed up the movement of neural impulses along the axon.

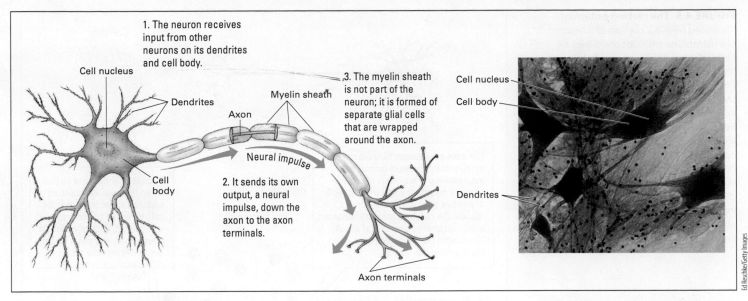

1. The neuron receives input from other neurons on its dendrites and cell body.

Cell nucleus

Dendrites

Myelin sheath

Axon

3. The myelin sheath is not part of the neuron; it is formed of separate glial cells that are wrapped around the axon.

Neural impulse

Cell body

2. It sends its own output, a neural impulse, down the axon to the axon terminals.

Cell nucleus

Cell body

Dendrites

Axon terminals

Ed Reschke/Getty Images

FIGURE 4.4 A motor neuron The parts common to many neurons can be seen in this diagram of a motor neuron. The neuron receives input from other neurons on its dendrites and cell body and sends its own output down the axon to the axon terminals. The myelin sheath is not part of the neuron; it is formed of separate cells that are wrapped tightly around the axon.

How Neurons Send Messages Along Their Axons

Neurons exert their influence on other neurons and muscle cells by firing off all-or-none impulses called ***action potentials***. In motor neurons and interneurons, action potentials are triggered at the junction between the cell body and the axon, and they travel rapidly down the axon to the axon terminals. In sensory neurons they are triggered at the dendritic end of the axon (at upper left in Figure 4.3) and travel through or past the cell body to the axon terminals.

Action potentials are described as "all or none" because they either occur or don't occur; that is, they don't occur partially or in different sizes or gradations. Each action potential produced by a given neuron is the same strength as any other action potential produced by that neuron, and each action potential retains its full strength all the way down the axon. Although each action potential is all or none, a neuron can convey varying degrees of intensity in its message by varying its rate of producing action potentials. A given neuron might fire off action potentials at a rate anywhere from less than 1 per second to as many as 1,000 per second. By varying its rate of action potentials, a neuron varies the strength of its effect on other neurons or muscle cells.

The Resting Neuron Has a Constant Electrical Charge Across Its Membrane

To understand how action potentials travel down the axon, you have to know something about the functioning of the ***cell membrane*** that encloses each neuron. The membrane is a porous "skin" that permits certain chemicals to flow into and out of the cell, while blocking others. Think of the neuron as a tube, the walls of which are the cell membrane. The tube is filled with a solution of water and dissolved chemicals called *intracellular fluid* and is bathed on the outside by another solution of water and dissolved chemicals called *extracellular fluid*.

Among the various chemicals dissolved in the intracellular and extracellular fluids are some that have electrical charges. These include *soluble protein molecules* (A^-), which have negative charges and exist only in the intracellular fluid; *potassium ions* (K^+), which are more concentrated in the intracellular than the extracellular fluid; and *sodium ions* (Na^+) and *chloride ions* (Cl^-), which are more concentrated in the extracellular than the intracellular fluid. For the reasons described in **Figure 4.5**, more negatively charged particles exist inside the cell than outside. This imbalance results in an electrical charge across the membrane, with the inside

FOCUS 3

How does the resting potential arise from the distribution of ions across the cell membrane?

FIGURE 4.5 The resting potential

Illustrated here is a portion of a neuron's cell membrane with dissolved ions on each side. Negatively charged protein molecules (A⁻) exist only inside the cell. Potassium ions (K⁺) exist mostly inside the cell. Sodium ions (Na⁺) and chloride ions (Cl⁻) exist mostly outside the cell. Because channels in the membrane that are permeable to potassium remain open, some potassium ions diffuse out, resulting in a surplus of positive charges outside the cell and a deficit of positive charges inside. For this reason, the resting membrane has an electrical charge across it of about 70 mV, with the inside negative compared to the outside.

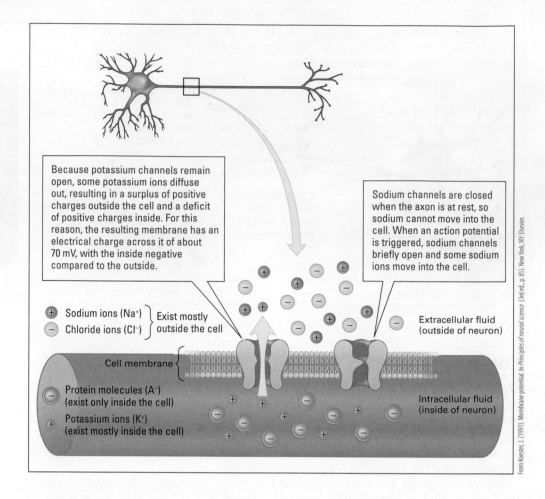

Because potassium channels remain open, some potassium ions diffuse out, resulting in a surplus of positive charges outside the cell and a deficit of positive charges inside. For this reason, the resulting membrane has an electrical charge across it of about 70 mV, with the inside negative compared to the outside.

Sodium channels are closed when the axon is at rest, so sodium cannot move into the cell. When an action potential is triggered, sodium channels briefly open and some sodium ions move into the cell.

+ Sodium ions (Na⁺) } Exist mostly
− Chloride ions (Cl⁻) } outside the cell

Extracellular fluid (outside of neuron)

Cell membrane {

Protein molecules (A⁻) (exist only inside the cell)

Potassium ions (K⁺) (exist mostly inside the cell)

Intracellular fluid (inside of neuron)

From Koester, J. (1991). Membrane potential. In *Principles of neural science* (3rd ed., p. 85). New York, NY: Elsevier.

typically about −70 millivolts (a millivolt [mV] is one-thousandth of a volt) relative to the outside. This charge across the membrane of an inactive neuron is called its *resting potential*. Just as the charge between the negative and positive poles of a battery is the source of electrical energy in a flashlight, so the resting potential is the source of electrical energy that makes an action potential possible.

The Action Potential Is Elicited by a Brief Change in Membrane Permeability

The action potential is a wave of change in the electrical charge across the axon membrane, and it moves rapidly from one end of the axon to the other. **Figure 4.6** depicts an electrical recording of the action potential, over time, at a given location on the axon.

The action potential is initiated by a change in the structure of the cell membrane at one end of the axon: Thousands of tiny channels that permit sodium ions to pass through open up (Figure 4.5). As a result, enough sodium moves inward to cause the electrical charge across the membrane to reverse itself and become momentarily positive inside relative to outside. This sudden shift constitutes the *depolarization phase* of the action potential (the rising part of the wave shown in Figure 4.6).

As soon as depolarization occurs, the channels that permitted sodium to pass through close, but channels that permit potassium to pass through remain open. Because potassium ions are more concentrated inside the cell than outside, and because they are repelled by the temporarily positive environment inside the cell,

FOCUS 4

How do the two phases of the action potential (depolarization and repolarization) result from the successive opening and closing of two kinds of channels in the cell membrane?

they are pushed outward. In this process, enough positively charged potassium ions move out of the cell to reestablish the original resting potential. This constitutes the *repolarization phase* of the action potential. As shown in Figure 4.6, the entire action potential, from depolarization to repolarization, takes about one millisecond (one-thousandth of a second).

With each action potential, a small amount of sodium enters the cell and a small amount of potassium leaves it. To maintain the original balance of these ions across the membrane, each portion of the membrane contains a chemical mechanism, the *sodium-potassium pump,* that continuously moves sodium out of the cell and potassium into it.

The Action Potential Regenerates Itself From Point to Point Along the Axon

Action potentials are triggered at one end of an axon by influences that reduce the electrical charge across the cell membrane. Sensory neurons are influenced by sensory stimuli acting on the dendrites; motor neurons are influenced by other neurons acting on the axon at its junction with the cell body.

The axon's membrane is constructed so that its sodium channels open in response to depolarization (reduction in charge across the membrane) to some critical value; this triggers an action potential. This critical value (e.g., −65 millivolts inside, compared with a resting potential of −70 millivolts inside) is called the cell's *threshold.* Once an action potential occurs at one location on the axon, it depolarizes the area of the axon just ahead of where it is occurring, thus triggering the sodium channels to open there. In this way the action potential keeps renewing itself and moves continuously along the axon. When an axon branches, the action potential follows each branch and thus reaches each of the possibly thousands of axon terminals.

The speed at which an action potential moves down an axon is affected by the axon's diameter. Large-diameter axons present less resistance to the spread of electric currents and therefore conduct action potentials faster than thin ones. Another feature that speeds up the rate of conduction in many axons is the myelin sheath (refer back to Figure 4.4). Like the plastic cover of an electric wire, myelin protects and insulates axons, speeding the rate at which nervous impulses can be sent and reducing interference from other neurons. Aided by the myelin sheath, each action potential skips down the axon, from one node to the next, faster than it could move as a continuous wave.

The thickest and most thoroughly myelinated axons in the nervous system can conduct action potentials at a velocity of about 100 meters per second. Thus, it takes about one-hundredth of a second for an action potential to run along that kind of axon from the central nervous system to a muscle about 1 meter away (a finger muscle, for example). Very thin axons without myelin sheaths, in contrast, may conduct at rates as slow as 1 or 2 meters per second. When you poke your finger with a pin, you feel the pressure of the pin before you feel the pain. That is partly because the sensory neurons for pressure are large and myelinated, while those for pain are thin and mostly unmyelinated.

The process of developing myelin, called *myelination,* begins before a child is born but is not complete until some time in adulthood, during the third decade of life or beyond. Neurons in the sensory system are the first to be myelinated, with most sensory structures being completely myelinated before a child's first birthday. This is followed by myelination of neurons in the motor area, which is nearly complete within the second year of life. The last areas to become fully myelinated are the associative areas in the frontal cortex—the "thinking" area of the brain—which are not completely myelinated until early adulthood (Stiles et al., 2015).

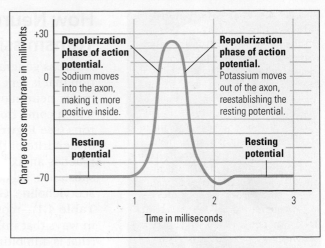

FIGURE 4.6 Electrical change during an action potential This graph depicts the change, with time, in the electrical charge across a given point on the axon membrane as an action potential passes through that point.

FOCUS 5

How is an axon's conduction speed related to its diameter and to the presence or absence of a myelin sheath?

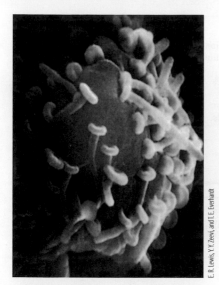

E. R. Lewis, Y. Y. Zeevi, and T. E. Everhardt

FIGURE 4.7 Axon terminals This electron micrograph shows the terminals of many axons forming synapses on a portion of the cell body of a single neuron. Synaptic vesicles, filled with neurotransmitter molecules, reside within the button-like swelling of each axon terminal. In the central nervous system, the cell bodies and dendrites of motor neurons and some interneurons are covered with tens of thousands of such terminals.

FOCUS 6

How do neurotransmitters at excitatory and inhibitory synapses affect the rate at which action potentials are produced in the postsynaptic neuron?

How Neurons Influence Other Neurons: Synaptic Transmission

Neurons generate action potentials at rates that are influenced by all the information that is sent to them from other neurons. The cell body and dendrites of a typical motor neuron or interneuron are blanketed by tens of thousands of axon terminals, which come from the branching axons of hundreds or thousands of different neurons (see **Figure 4.7**). The junction between each axon terminal and the cell body or dendrite of the receiving neuron is called a *synapse*. When an action potential reaches an axon terminal, it causes the terminal to release packets of a chemical substance, called a *neurotransmitter*. Neurotransmitters—which include dopamine, acetylcholine, GABA (gamma-aminobutyric acid), and serotonin, among others (see **Table 4.1**)—move across the space between the cells and alter the receiving neuron in ways that influence its production of action potentials, increasing or decreasing (that is, inhibiting) the likelihood that a neuron will fire.

Individuals who have too much or too little of some of these neurotransmitters may experience physical and psychological disorders. For example, Parkinson's disease—characterized by muscle tremors and severe difficulty in initiating and coordinating movements—is caused by the degeneration of dopamine-producing neurons whose axons originate and terminate in specific brain areas. Dopamine is also involved in the brain's reward system and may play an important role in schizophrenia. Other neurotransmitters have similarly been shown to be linked with certain psychological disorders, including serotonin with depression and GABA with anxiety. We will discuss the role of neurotransmitters in psychological disorders in later chapters.

The most fully studied and best-understood synapses are those that exist between axon terminals and muscle cells or between axon terminals and the dendrites of other neurons (see **Figure 4.8**). A very narrow gap, the *synaptic cleft,* separates the axon terminal from the membrane of the cell that it influences. The membrane of the axon terminal that abuts the cleft is the *presynaptic membrane,* and that of the cell on the other side of the cleft is the *postsynaptic membrane.* Within the axon terminal are hundreds of tiny globe-like *vesicles,* each of which contains several thousand molecules of a chemical neurotransmitter.

When an action potential reaches an axon terminal, it causes some of the vesicles to spill their neurotransmitter molecules into the cleft. The molecules then diffuse through the fluid in the cleft, and some become attached to special receptors on the postsynaptic membrane. Each neurotransmitter molecule can be thought of as

TABLE 4.1 Neurotransmitters Neurotransmitters are chemicals released by one neuron at the axon terminal to influence the action of an adjacent neuron. More than 100 neurotransmitters have been identified; a few of the better-studied neurotransmitters and their functions are listed here.

Neurotransmitter	Functions
Dopamine	Influences movement and reward-motivated behavior. Low levels of dopamine are associated with Parkinson's disease and high levels are implicated in some forms of schizophrenia.
Acetylcholine	Is released at neuromuscular junction and associated with the activation of muscles. Within the brain, acetylcholine functions to alter the way other brain structures process information (a neuromodulator).
Serotonin	Influences many behaviors, including sleep and mood and is implicated in depression.
GABA (gamma-aminobutyric acid)	An inhibitory neurotransmitter, which weakens or slows down signals; plays an important role in anxiety.

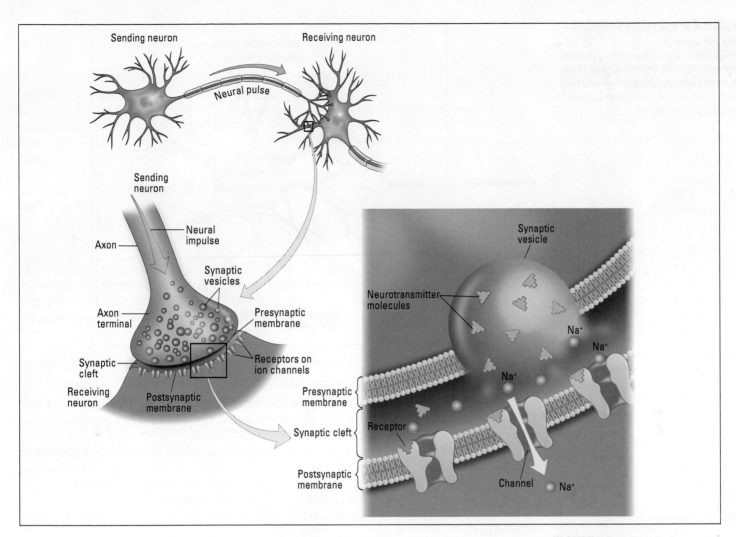

a key, and each receptor can be thought of as a lock. A molecular key entering a receptor lock opens a gate in the channel, allowing ions to pass through. If the postsynaptic cell is a muscle cell, this flow of ions triggers a biochemical process that causes the cell to contract. If the postsynaptic cell is a neuron, the result is a change in the polarization of that neuron, but the direction of change depends on whether the synapse is excitatory or inhibitory (Byrne, 2003).

At an **excitatory synapse** (as shown in Figure 4.8), the transmitter opens sodium (Na^+) channels in the postsynaptic membrane. The movement of the positively charged sodium ions into the cell causes a slight *depolarization* of the receiving neuron (the neuron becomes less negative inside), which tends to increase the rate of action potentials triggered in that neuron. At an **inhibitory synapse**, the transmitter opens either chloride (Cl^-) channels or potassium (K^+) channels. The movement of negatively charged chloride ions into the cell or of positively charged potassium ions out of the cell causes a slight *hyperpolarization* of the receiving neuron (the neuron becomes even more negative inside than it was before). Hyperpolarization tends to decrease the rate of action potentials triggered in that neuron.

Postsynaptic Neurons Integrate Their Excitatory and Inhibitory Inputs

At any given moment, a single neuron may receive input at dozens, hundreds, or even thousands of its synapses. Some of these synapses are excitatory and some inhibitory (see **Figure 4.9**). At each excitatory synapse the transmitter causes a slight depolarization, and at each inhibitory synapse the transmitter causes a slight

FIGURE 4.8 Transmission across the synapse When an action potential reaches an axon terminal, it causes some of the synaptic vesicles to spill their transmitter molecules into the synaptic cleft. Some of the molecules diffuse across the cleft and bind at special receptors on the postsynaptic membrane, where they open channels that permit ions to flow through the membrane. At an excitatory synapse (as in this example), channels permeable to sodium ions (Na^+) open, allowing an influx of positive charges into the receiving neuron. At an inhibitory synapse, channels permeable to chloride ions (Cl^-) open, allowing an influx of negative charges.

FIGURE 4.9 Excitatory and inhibitory synapses Neurons in the central nervous system receive many synaptic connections from other neurons, some excitatory and some inhibitory. All synapses from any single neuron are either excitatory or inhibitory.

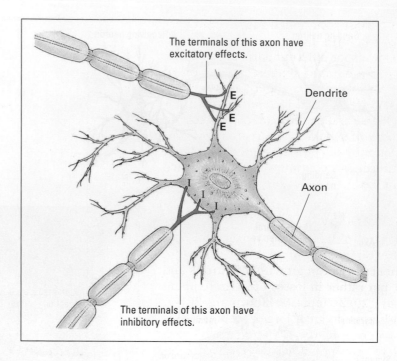

The terminals of this axon have excitatory effects.

Dendrite

Axon

The terminals of this axon have inhibitory effects.

hyperpolarization. These effects spread passively through the dendrites and cell body, combining to have an integrated effect on the electrical charge across the membrane of the axon at its junction with the cell body.

Recall that whenever the axon membrane is depolarized below the critical value, action potentials are triggered. The greater the degree of depolarization below that value, the greater the number of action potentials per second. Thus, the rate of action potentials in the postsynaptic neuron's axon depends on the net effect of the depolarizing and hyperpolarizing influences from excitatory and inhibitory synapses.

The Development of Neurons

As infants and children get older, their heads and brains get bigger, and they are increasingly able to use their brains to solve problems. It is tempting to think that the number of neurons increases with age, accounting for the increase in brain size and cognition. This is not the case, however. In fact, newborns have more neurons in their brains than adults do.

Neurogenesis

FOCUS 7

When are most neurons "born" and when do they begin to form synapses?

The process of creating new neurons is referred to as **neurogenesis** (literally, birth of neurons), and it occurs during the first 20 weeks after conception, peaking in the third and fourth months of gestation (Lenroot & Giedd, 2007). During its peak, the fetal brain generates several hundred thousand neurons *each minute* (Nelson et al., 2006). Decades ago, it was believed that all the neurons a person would ever have were generated during the prenatal period. We now know that neurogenesis continues after birth well into adulthood, particularly in the hippocampus, an area involved in memory (Eriksson et al., 1998). We will have more to say about the hippocampus later in this chapter.

FOCUS 8

How does the metaphor of sculpting apply to brain development?

Once neurons are "born," they migrate to their permanent position in the brain (Bronner & Hatten, 2012). Beginning about 20 weeks after conception, they enter the last stage of their development, termed *differentiation*. During this time, neurons grow in size and increase their numbers of dendrites and axon terminals, as well as the number of synapses they form. Differentiation doesn't stop at birth. Synapse formation is most rapid in the months immediately following birth, but the peak of synapse formation varies for different parts of the brain. For example, a burst of synapse formation in the visual cortex begins at about 3 or 4 months and peaks between 4 and 12 months. A similar pattern is found in the prefrontal cortex, but the peak number of synapses is not attained until about 24 months of age (Huttenlocher, 1994), and synaptogenesis continues at a slower pace throughout life.

Cell Death and Synaptic Pruning

Beginning late in the prenatal period and continuing after birth, the primary changes in brain development are not in growth of neurons and synapses, but rather in losses of them (Oppenheim et al., 2012; Tapia & Lichtman, 2012). Although brains do grow larger with age, this increase is due primarily to the increasing size of individual neurons and myelination of axons, not to the generation of new neurons (Lenroot & Giedd, 2007).

In fact, both the number of neurons and the number of synapses actually *decrease* over early development. At its peak during prenatal development, up to 250,000 synapses are being formed per minute. Yet, 40 to 50% of these synapses will be lost, or pruned. Furthermore, it's not just synapses that are lost; neurons themselves also die in a process, known as **selective cell death**, or **apoptosis** [a-pəp-tō′-səs], which begins before birth and continues well into the teen years (Spear, 2007; Stiles et al., 2015).

Cell death and synaptic pruning occur at different rates for different parts of the brain. For instance, children attain the adult density of visual cortex synapses at 2 to 4 years of age; in contrast, in the prefrontal areas, children continue to have more neurons and synapses than adults into their teen years (Huttenlocher & Dabholkar, 1997; Spear, 2007; see **Figure 4.10**). Thus, overall, adolescents have fewer but stronger and more effective neuronal connections than they had as children.

Rather than thinking of brain development as simple increases in size and complexity, a better metaphor may be that of sculpting. The brain first overproduces neurons and synapses, but then, just as a sculptor chisels away at extra stone to produce his or her work of art, so too do experience, hormones, and genetic signals shape the brain.

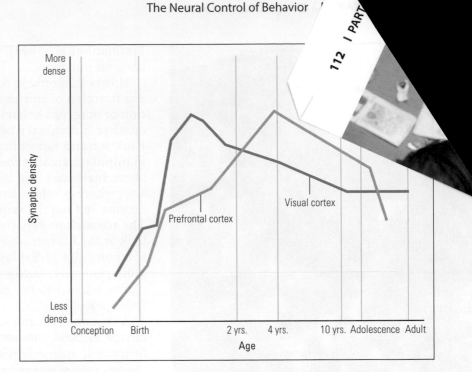

FIGURE 4.10 Age differences in synapse production and pruning in the prefrontal and visual cortex The number of synapses show sharp increases early in development but then experience "pruning," as the brain gets sculpted to its eventual adult form. Note the particularly sharp decline in synapses in the prefrontal cortex in adolescence.

(Data from Huttenlocher & Dabholkar, 1997.)

Mirror Neurons: A Means of Social Learning?

Neuroscientists have discovered that the brains of human beings and of at least some nonhuman primates contain organized systems of neurons that seem to be well designed to foster social learning (Iacoboni & Dapretto, 2006; Jaffe, 2007). These are referred to as **mirror neurons** because they are believed to help us behave in ways that mirror (mimic) what we observe or experience. They are found in various parts of the **cerebral cortex** of monkeys and humans. Mirror neurons are active both when a subject engages in a behavior, such as grasping a piece of food, and when the subject observes someone else perform a similar action. Mirror neurons were first discovered in monkeys using recordings from single neurons through electrodes placed in the monkeys' brains (Rizzolatti & Craighero, 2004;

FOCUS 9

What role might mirror neurons play in social learning?

■ **Mirror neurons** are active both when a subject watches someone perform an action and when the subject tries to imitate the action.

Rizzolatti et al., 1996). Such neurons, it was proposed, may serve as a basis for imitation.

However, monkeys do not engage in true imitation. Rather, the apparent function of mirror neurons in monkeys is not to guide reproduction of observed behavior, but to enable the monkey to *recognize* when another individual's behavior matches its own. For instance, Annika Paukner and her colleagues (2005) had both monkeys and humans manipulate small cubes with either their hands or their mouths. In some instances, the human imitated the exact behaviors of a monkey, whereas other times the person merely engaged in monkey-like actions, but not the same actions that the monkey was currently doing. The researchers reported that, in most cases, the monkeys preferred to look at the human who was copying them, apparently recognizing that someone else is displaying behavior identical or similar to their own. More generally, mirror neurons reflect an individual being "able to recognize when another is doing something that the self can do" (Byrne, 2005, p. R499).

Although one cannot implant electrodes in people's brains to detect mirror neurons, the use of transcranial magnetic stimulation (TMS) and functional magnetic resonance imaging (fMRI) (discussed later in this chapter) allow researchers to look for mirror neurons in humans and discern their purpose. Mirror neurons have indeed been found in humans, and their function seems to be somewhat different from that in monkeys. One important difference is that, unlike those of monkeys, humans' mirror neurons seem to code for movements *forming* an action and not only for the action itself (Rizzolatti & Craighero, 2004). This suggests that they are important in imitative learning, where the specific behaviors a model performs (the "means") are as important as the goal the model attains (the "ends"). The importance of mirror neurons in imitative learning is apparent in a study in which people watched an expert guitarist as he played guitar chords (Buccino et al., 2004). Using fMRI recordings, the researchers found that mirror neurons became activated when subjects watched the expert play chords, but became even more active when they tried to copy the movements.

There is considerable debate about the importance of mirror neurons in social learning (Gallese et al., 2011). Researchers have reported evidence for mirror neurons in 10- to 14-year-old children for emotional expressions (Dapretto et al., 2006), in children as young as 3 years of age for the observation and execution of hand movements (Fecteau et al., 2004; Lepage & Theoret, 2006), and for 9-month-old infants based on changes in EEG patterns when reaching or watching someone else reach for an object (Southgate et al., 2009). Some believe mirror neurons represent a brain-based mechanism for identifying with others (Ramachandran & Oberman, 2006), which is the basis of imitative learning (Iacoboni, 2005), speech perception (D'Ausilio et al., 2009), empathy (Gazzola et al., 2006), and even language (Aziz-Zadeh et al., 2006). A number of researchers have proposed that the difficulties people with autism have understanding social relations, imitating the actions of others, and developing a distinction between self and others are due to malfunctioning mirror neurons (Cascio et al., 2012; Kana et al., 2011; Oberman et al., 2005).

Mirror neurons may allow you to understand another's intentions, which, as we'll see in subsequent chapters, is the foundation for advanced forms of social cognition (Gallese et al., 2011). One provocative idea is that changes in the mirror-neuron system permitted greater social-learning abilities in our ancient ancestors, setting the stage for the revolutionary changes in thinking and lifestyle that occurred over relatively brief periods of evolutionary time (Ramachandran & Oberman, 2006; Rizzolatti & Craighero, 2004).

Javier Larrea/Getty Images

SECTION REVIEW

Neurons—individual nerve cells—"fire" electrochemically and communicate at synapses.

Basic Neural Anatomy

- Interneurons exist entirely within the central nervous system (brain and spinal cord) and carry messages from one set of neurons to another.

- Sensory neurons carry information from sensory organs into the central nervous system.

- Motor neurons carry messages out from the central nervous system to operate muscles and glands.

- A typical neuron has a cell body, dendrites (which receive input to the neuron), and an axon (which carries the neuron's output).

Basic Functioning of the Neuron

- The resting potential is an electrical imbalance that exists across the neural cell membrane when the neuron is not firing; the inside of the cell is negative relative to the outside.

- An action potential involves a very brief reversal of polarization across the cell membrane, followed by a return to the resting state. These changes sweep down the axon; their speed is determined by the axon's diameter and myelination.

- Action potentials are all or none; they do not vary in strength in a given neuron. A neuron's rate of action potentials does vary, however.

Synapses

- Neurotransmitter molecules released from an axon terminal cross the synaptic cleft to affect another neuron, a gland, or a muscle cell.

- Most synapses have brief, immediate effects—either excitatory or inhibitory—on the postsynaptic neuron.

Neural Development

- Neurogenesis and synaptogenesis begin prenatally, and newborns have more neurons in their brains than adults.

- Synaptic pruning and selective death of neurons begins prenatally and continues after birth.

Mirror Neurons

- Mirror neurons are found in the cortex of monkeys and humans and are active both when a subject engages in a behavior and when it observes someone else perform a similar action.

- Mirror neurons may be the neurological basis for imitation and social learning.

Methods of Mapping the Brain's Behavioral Functions

With its billions of neurons and trillions of synapses, the brain is a daunting subject of study. It would be hopeless, with present technology, to try to work out all of the details of its wiring, as one might with a human-made machine such as a television or a computer. Fortunately, though, for those of us who want to understand as much as we can of it, patterns exist in the brain's trillions of connections.

Methods Used for Studying the Human Brain

Psychologists and other neuroscientists have developed a number of methods of identifying the functions of specific brain areas. The methods fall into three general categories: (1) observing behavioral deficits that occur when a part of the brain is destroyed or is temporarily inactivated; (2) observing behavioral effects of artificially stimulating specific parts of the brain; and (3) recording changes in neural activity that occur in specific parts of the brain when a person or animal is engaged in a particular mental or behavioral task. **Table 4.2** provides a partial list of some of the imaging techniques in use today. What follows are brief descriptions of the most common methods used within each of these three categories. We'll look first at methods used

"It never ceases to amaze me what little brains people have."

- Although it is capable of amazing feats, the human brain is not much to look at.

TABLE 4.2 Some techniques for studying the brain

Analyzing Electrical Brain Activity
Electroencephalography (EEG) Recording of the electrical activity of the cortex using multiple scalp electrodes. *Event-Related Potentials (ERPs)* An encephalographic measure of local changes in the brain electrical activity in response to specific stimuli. *Magnetoencephalography (MEG)* Detects the magnetic field changes produced by the cortical electrical activity. *Transcranial Magnetic Stimulation (TMS)* The localization of a brain function by temporarily blocking the electrical activity of an area by exposure to a magnetic field. *Transcranial Direct Current Stimulation* (tDCS) The localization of brain function by temporarily stimulating electrical activity directing weak electrical currents to specific areas of the brain.
Analyzing Anatomical Structure
Magnetic Resonance Imaging (MRI) High-resolution image of brain anatomy measuring energy changes of brain tissue after an exposure to a strong magnetic field. *Diffusion Tension Imaging (DTI)* Measures the diffusion of water in the brain tissue, permitting the imaging of the white matter tracts.
Analyzing Functional Metabolic Activity
Positron Emission Tomography (PET) Assesses the metabolic activity of glucose or oxygen in the brain by following the path of a radioactive tracer injected intravenously. *Functional Magnetic Resonance Imaging (fMRI)* Assesses indirectly the metabolic activity of the brain through measuring the changes of the blood flow.

in studying the brains of humans and then, in the next section, at more intrusive methods used in studying the brains of nonhuman animals.

Observing Effects of Localized Brain Damage

FOCUS 10

How do researchers identify functions of areas of the human brain through (a) studying the effects of brain damage, (b) using a magnetic field to interrupt normal brain activity, (c) recording electrical activity that passes through the skull and scalp, and (d) creating images that depict patterns of blood flow?

At the height of his career, the Russian composer V. G. Shebalin suffered a stroke (a rupturing of blood vessels in the brain) that damaged a portion of his left cerebral cortex (the highest outermost part of the brain). From then on, he had great difficulty expressing himself in words or understanding what others were saying, but he continued to create great music. His Fifth Symphony, composed after his stroke, was described by the composer Dmitri Shostakovich as "a brilliant work, filled with highest emotions, optimistic and full of life" (Gardner, 1982, p. 327).

As illustrated by this case, brain damage often leaves a person deficient in some areas of mental functioning yet fully capable, or nearly so, in others. By studying many people who have damage in the same general area of the brain, psychologists can draw reasonable inferences about the behavioral and mental functions of that area. The logic is that if some abilities are missing and other abilities remain when a part of the brain is missing, then that brain part must contribute in some essential way to the missing abilities but not to those that remain. As you will discover later in this chapter and elsewhere in the book, much has been learned about the human brain through systematic studies of people who have suffered brain damage.

However, one must be cautious when interpreting the effects of brain damage on psychological functioning. Brain damage can rarely be narrowed to one area and frequently involves complications beyond that of simple lesions, or areas of specific damage. Lesions in one area of the brain can also lead to changes in other brain areas (Fuster, 1989). Nevertheless, much can be learned about brain functioning from studying brain damage, especially when viewed in combination with other sources of data.

Observing Effects of Magnetic Interference with Normal Brain Activity

A relatively new procedure for localizing functions in the human brain is ***transcranial magnetic stimulation***, or ***TMS*** (Pascual-Leone et al., 2005). In this procedure, a pulse of electricity is sent through a small copper coil, inducing a magnetic field around the coil. The coil is held just above a person's scalp so that the magnetic field passes through the scalp and skull and induces an electric current in the neurons immediately below the coil. Repetitive pulses cause a temporary loss in those neurons' abilities to fire normally. The effect is comparable to that of lesioning a small area of the brain, with the advantage that the effect is temporary and reversible. For instance, if the coil is held over an area of the brain that is crucial for fluent speech, the person becomes unable to speak fluently while the current is on, but then resumes fluent speech soon after the current is turned off. Because the magnetic field affects only that part of the brain lying immediately below the skull, TMS can be used for mapping the functions only of the outermost yet largest part of the brain, the cerebral cortex.

A good example of research using TMS is found in the work of Sara Torriero and her colleagues (2007) in Italy. These researchers were interested in the neural foundations of observational learning (learning from watching others). In one of these experiments, subjects observed another person solve a problem in which a series of squares had to be pressed in a specified order. Different groups of subjects received TMS over different parts of the brain just prior to the observation. The result was that those who received the TMS directly over a portion of the brain called the *dorsolateral prefrontal cortex* failed to benefit from observing the problem's solution. Even though the TMS did not interfere with their vision, it took these subjects as long to learn the sequence they had observed—by trial and error—as it took them to learn a new sequence they had never observed. This study now constitutes part of the evidence that a system of *mirror neurons* (discussed earlier in this chapter) exists in this part of the cerebral cortex, which is crucial for translating observed actions into self-produced actions.

Although TMS is usually used to study the effects of temporary *inactivation* of a brain area, it can also be used to study the effects of temporary *activation*. A single pulse of electrical current can cause the sets of neurons just below the coil to send a burst of action potentials through their axons. When the coil is held over an area of the brain responsible for controlling the body's muscle movements, the result is a brief muscle twitch somewhere in the body—such as in the thumb of one hand. In this way, TMS can be used to produce a map showing the functional connections between specific areas within movement-control portions of the cerebral cortex and the muscles controlled by those areas. A somewhat similar technique called *transcranial direct current stimulation* (tDCS) involves directing weak electrical currents to specific areas of the brain; it has been found to alter perceptual, cognitive, and motor functioning. Useful as a tool for investigating brain functioning, tDCS has also been effective in alleviating some brain disorders (Nitche et al., 2008; Russowsky Brunoni et al., 2012).

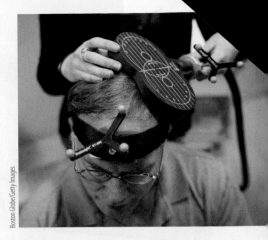

■ **Transcranial magnetic stimulation (TMS)** The electrical coil placed over the subject's skull induces a magnetic field. Repetitive pulses of the magnetic field inhibit the activity of underlying neurons. Single brief pulses activate neurons.

Recording Brain Activity Electrically, Through the Scalp

The constant activity of the brain's billions of neurons produces continuous electrical "chatter," which to some degree penetrates the skull and scalp. By placing electrodes on a person's scalp, researchers can detect and amplify these signals. The resulting record of brain activity is referred to as an ***electroencephalogram*** [i-lĕk´-trō-in-**sĕf**´-ə-lō-grăm] (abbreviated ***EEG***). Patterns in the EEG can be used as an index of whether a person is highly aroused, or relaxed, or asleep and can be used to identify various stages of sleep.

With computer technology, it is possible to record and analyze brain activity simultaneously from many electrodes, each at a different location on the scalp, to see how brain activity varies from place to place as well as from instant to instant

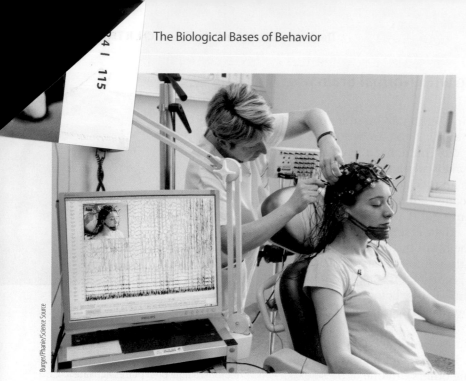

Burger/Phanie/Science Source

FIGURE 4.11 Electroencephalography The brain waves depicted on the screen reflect the electrical activity of neurons existing below each of the areas of the scalp where electrodes have been placed.

(see **Figure 4.11**). In some of these studies, subjects are asked to respond to stimuli that are presented to them as their brain activity is being recorded. For instance, a person might be presented with sets of letters flashed on a screen and instructed to push a button if and only if the letters spell out an English word. The brief change in the EEG record immediately following the stimulus is referred to as an *event-related potential,* or *ERP*. By testing the person repeatedly in such a task and averaging the EEG records obtained, it is possible to produce an average ERP for each electrode location. Comparison of the average ERPs recorded at different scalp locations reveals the pattern of activity in the brain as the person detects and responds to the stimulus. For the task just described, areas of the brain that are involved in seeing the letters would respond first, and areas that are involved in reading and making judgments would respond a split second later.

Viewing Brain Activity With Imaging Methods Sensitive to Blood Flow

Some methods for localizing brain activity rely on the fact that increased neural activity in any area of the brain is accompanied by increased blood flow to that area. Like other bodily tissues, the brain is permeated by tiny blood vessels. When a portion of the brain becomes more active, blood vessels there immediately enlarge, so more blood enters that portion. The blood carries oxygen and glucose, which are the sources of energy required to sustain the increased neural activity. Using technically complex methods, researchers can create three-dimensional pictures, or *neuroimages,* that depict the relative amount of blood flowing through each part of the brain. Thus, increased blood flow reflects increased neural activity (Logothetis, 2008).

The first of these neuroimaging methods (developed in the 1970s) was *positron emission tomography* [tō-**mȯg**´-rə-fē], or *PET*. This method involves injecting a radioactive substance into the blood (in an amount that is not dangerous to the subject) and measuring the radioactivity that is emitted from each portion of the brain. Another method (first used extensively in the 1990s) is *functional magnetic resonance imaging,* or *fMRI*. This method involves the creation of a magnetic field around a person's head, causing hemoglobin molecules that are carrying oxygen in the blood to give off radio waves of a certain frequency; these waves can be detected and used to assess the amount of blood in each part of the brain. Unlike the EEG, both PET and fMRI can depict activity anywhere in the brain, not just on the surface near the skull. These methods also produce a more fine-grained picture of the spatial locations of activity than is possible with EEG. Today fMRI is used much more often than PET, partly because it shows better spatial resolution.

With either PET or fMRI, the person's head must be surrounded by a set of sensors. With fMRI, magnetic coils are also used (see **Figure 4.12**). During the procedure, the person can communicate with the experimenter through a microphone and can respond to visual stimuli presented on a screen inside the scanning device. With either PET or fMRI, a computer is used to generate a three-dimensional image of the brain that depicts variations in amount of blood flow as variations in color. Research using fMRI since the mid-1990s has transformed how scientists can study living and "thinking" brains, although making sense of imaging data is not without some debate (see papers in Mather et al., 2013).

At any given time, the brain is doing many things, and all portions of it are always active to some degree. (Don't believe the often-heard statement that people only use 10% of their brains! People use all of their brains all of the time.) In using either PET or fMRI to determine which brain areas are most directly involved in a particular task, researchers need to employ an appropriate control condition. By subtracting the amount of activity measured in each brain area in the control condition (when the person is not performing the specific task) from the amount measured in the same areas in the experimental condition (when the person is performing the task), the researcher can determine which areas show the greatest increase in activity during the task. (For an example of such an experiment, and to see sample PET images, look ahead to Figure 4.32 on p. 140.)

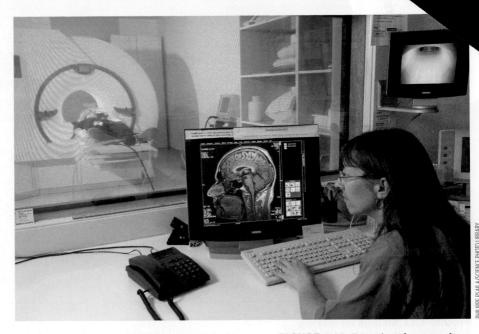

FIGURE 4.12 Functional magnetic resonance imaging (fMRI) When the subject is in the scanner, the researchers will be able to communicate with him using an intercom and visual projection system. The image of the brain depicts the amount of blood flow in each part of the brain, which indicates the amount of neural activity in each part.

There are, of course, limitations to such methods, and we must not confuse knowing which areas "light up" when a subject performs a particular task (recalling a word, for example) with actually understanding what the neurological and psychological processes are that underlie the action. For example, if we know that the brain areas that "light up" in fMRIs of children with intellectual disabilities are different from those that light up in fMRIs of typically developing children, this by itself does not tell us anything about the origins of the impairment or how to deal with such children. Yet there is a tendency for the public, including policy makers, to believe that the results of psychological studies involving brain images are more convincing than studies without brain images (Beck, 2010). The new technologies of neuroimaging are providing a window into the brain that can help us get a better understanding of human thought and behavior, but such results will be most useful when accompanied by behavioral assessment and experimental studies (Decety & Cacioppo, 2010).

Methods Used for Studying the Brains of Nonhuman Animals

When researchers study nonhuman animals, they can localize brain functions using methods that are more intrusive than those used with humans. They can destroy, stimulate, or record neural activity in small, well-localized areas anywhere in the brain in order to assess the behavioral functions of those areas.

Observing Effects of Deliberately Placed Brain Lesions

Areas of damage (referred to as lesions) can be produced in the brains of rats or other laboratory animals by either electrical or chemical means. To produce a lesion electrically, a thin wire electrode, insulated everywhere except at its tip, is surgically inserted into the brain with the help of a *stereotaxic instrument* (see **Figure 4.13**), and enough current is sent through the electrode to destroy the neurons adjacent to its tip. To produce a lesion chemically, a tiny tube called a *cannula* is inserted into the brain, again using a stereotaxic instrument, and a small amount of a chemical is injected through the cannula, destroying neurons whose cell bodies are located near the cannula's tip. The lesions produced by such means can be as small as one-fourth of a millimeter in diameter. By varying the precise location of the damage in different groups of animals, and then comparing the groups in behavioral tests, researchers can identify precise areas of the brain that are crucial for specific types of behaviors.

FOCUS 11

How do researchers damage, stimulate, and record from neurons in specific areas of nonhuman animal brains to learn about the functions of those brain areas?

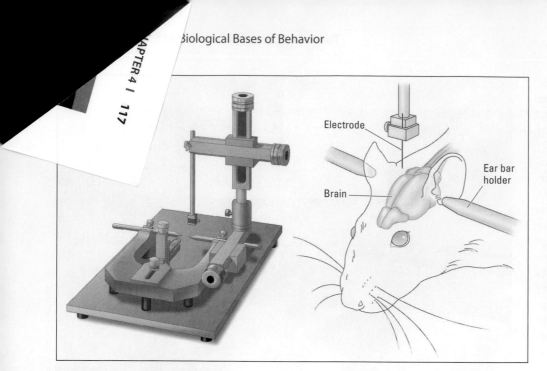

Electrode

Ear bar holder

Brain

FIGURE 4.13 Method for making lesions in or stimulating a rat's brain A stereotaxic instrument (left) is used to insert an electrode into a precise location in the anesthetized (unconscious) animal's brain (right). To produce a lesion, an electric current that is strong enough to destroy neurons near the tip is sent through the electrode, and then the electrode is removed. To prepare the animal for electrical brain stimulation, the electrode is cemented in place so that it can be stimulated through wire leads during behavioral tests after the animal has recovered from surgery.

In most such studies, the lesions are made in deep, primitive areas of the animal's brain, whose functions are similar for all mammals, including humans. Such studies have helped researchers identify specific brain nuclei that are crucial for basic motivational and emotional states, such as hunger, sexual drive, and fear—topics we will discuss in Chapter 5.

Effects of Stimulating Specific Areas of the Brain

Stimulation of specific areas of an animal's brain can also be accomplished either electrically or chemically. To stimulate neurons electrically, a wire electrode is lowered into the brain using the same surgical method as that used to produce a lesion. The electrode is then cemented in place (as shown in Figure 4.13) and can be activated at any time after surgery through a wire connection or by radio waves. The electrical current used for stimulation is much weaker than that used for producing a lesion; it is strong enough to induce action potentials in, but not destroy, neurons near the electrode tip. To stimulate neurons chemically, a cannula is permanently implanted in the brain, and shortly before behavioral testing a tiny amount of a neurotransmitter substance or other chemical known to activate neurons is injected through it.

Electrical or chemical stimulation in certain deep areas of the brain can cause an animal to exhibit drive states or emotional states that last only as long as the period of stimulation. For instance, stimulation in one area causes a previously sated animal to eat, and stimulation in another area causes a previously calm animal to behave as if frightened, as long as the stimulation continues.

Electrical Recording From Single Neurons

Electrodes can be used not just to destroy or stimulate specific brain areas, but also to record neural activity in specific areas as the animal engages in some behavioral task. Extremely thin microelectrodes, with very fine points that can penetrate into the cell bodies of single neurons, can be permanently implanted in the brain. In some experiments many such electrodes are inserted at once, each able to record the activity of a different single neuron.

Experiments using this technique have revealed some remarkable correlations between an animal's behavior and the rate of action potentials produced by individual neurons. For example, certain neurons in one area of the brain (the hippocampus, discussed later in the chapter) fire rapidly when, and only when, the animal (usually a rat) faces in a specific direction within the environment in which it is tested (Moser et al., 2008). If the entire test environment (such as an enclosed box with a maze in it) is rotated, the preferred orientations of these neurons rotate, too. Thus, a cell that originally fired whenever the animal faced north will fire whenever the animal faces south after the apparatus is turned 180 degrees. Apparently, these neurons, called *place cells,* help animals keep track of the direction they are facing within familiar environments. If the area of the brain in which these cells are located is destroyed, animals lose their ability to find their way through mazes or to locate objects easily in environments that they have explored.

Functional Organization of the Nervous System

So far in this chapter we have examined the basic workings of individual neurons and have overviewed the main methods for learning about the functions of large groups of neurons in the brain. Now it is time to tour the whole nervous system. We will look into each of its major divisions with an eye toward understanding its role in the broad task of governing the person's behavior. The section will conclude with an examination of how hormones interact with the nervous system.

It is helpful to keep in mind that the nervous system is hierarchically organized. Indeed, it contains two distinct but interacting hierarchies. One, the *sensory-perceptual hierarchy,* is involved in data processing. It receives sensory data about a person's internal and external environment, and it analyzes those data to make decisions about the person's bodily needs and about threats and opportunities in the outside world. The flow of information in this hierarchy is primarily from bottom (sensory receptors) to top (perceptual centers in the brain). The other hierarchy, the *motor-control hierarchy,* is involved in control of movement. The flow of information here is primarily from top to bottom. At the top of this hierarchy are executive centers that make decisions about the activities that the person as a whole should engage in, and at lower levels are centers that translate those decisions into specific patterns of muscle movement.

Most of the large anatomical divisions of the nervous system are involved in both hierarchies, so we will examine both at once. We'll pay most attention here, though, to the motor hierarchy; the sensory-perceptual system is discussed in detail in Chapters 6 and 7. Let's start at the bottom and work our way upward. The bottom parts of the hierarchy are evolutionarily the most primitive and are most directly tied to the muscles and the sensory organs.

Peripheral Nerves: The Nervous System's Interface With the World

The peripheral nervous system, as you may recall, consists of the entire set of nerves, which connect the central nervous system to the body's sensory organs, muscles, and glands (refer back to Figure 4.2). Nerves are divided into two classes that correspond to the portion of the central nervous system from which they protrude. **Cranial nerves** project directly from the brain. **Spinal nerves** project from the spinal cord. Like most other structures in the body, nerves exist in pairs; there is a right and a left member in each pair. Humans have 12 pairs of cranial nerves and 31 pairs of spinal nerves. With their many branches, these nerves extend to all portions of the body.

Sensory Neurons Provide Data Needed for Governing Behavior

As noted earlier, sensory neurons are activated at their dendritic ends by the effects of sensory stimuli (such as light in the eye, chemicals on the tongue or in the nose, sound waves in the ear, or pressure on the skin). They send their action potentials all the way into the central nervous system by way of their very long axons. The rates and patterns of action potentials in sensory neurons are the data that perceptual areas of the central nervous system use to figure out the state of the external and internal environment. Without such input, the central nervous system would have no information on which to base its behavior-controlling decisions.

Sensory input from the specialized sensory organs of the head—the eyes, ears, nose, and tongue—enters the brain by way of cranial nerves. Sensory input that comes from the rest of the body—from the skin, muscles, tendons, and various internal organs—enters the central nervous system by way of all of the spinal nerves and some of the cranial nerves. The sensations conveyed by these inputs, which include touch and pain, are referred to collectively as *somatosensation*. *Soma* means "body," and *somatosensation* is the set of sensations that derive from the whole body as opposed to those that come just from the special sensory organs of the head. (A full discussion of the processes of sensation and perception is found in Chapters 6 and 7.)

Motor Neurons Are the "Final Common Path" for Control of Behavior

Motor neurons, as noted earlier, have their cell bodies in the central nervous system and send their long axons out, by way of cranial or spinal nerves, to terminate on muscles or glands. All of the behavioral decisions of the nervous system are translated into patterns of action potentials in the axons of motor neurons, and those patterns determine our behavior. Only through them can the nervous system control behavior. All of the brain's calculations—including those that we experience consciously as perceptions, thoughts, emotions, desires, and intentions—would be useless if they could not act on muscles and glands. The 86 billion neurons of the central nervous system are all involved in controlling the 2 or 3 million motor neurons, which in turn control behavior. For a wonderful example of how knowledge of motor neurons has been put to medical use, see **Figure 4.14** and its caption.

The Motor System Includes Somatic and Autonomic Divisions

FOCUS 12

How do the autonomic and somatic motor systems differ from one another in function? How do the sympathetic and parasympathetic divisions of the autonomic system differ from one another in function?

Motor neurons act on two broad classes of structures. One class consists of the *skeletal muscles,* the muscles that are attached to bones and produce externally observable movements of the body when contracted. The other class consists of the visceral muscles and glands. Visceral muscles are muscles that are not attached to bones and do not move the skeleton when they contract. They form the walls of such structures as the heart, arteries, stomach, and intestines. Glands are structures that produce secretions, such as the salivary glands and sweat glands. Neurons that act on skeletal muscles make up the *somatic (body)* portion of the peripheral motor system. Those that act on visceral muscles and glands make up the *autonomic* portion.

Whereas skeletal motor neurons initiate activity in the skeletal muscles, autonomic motor neurons typically *modulate* (modify) rather than initiate activity in the visceral muscles. Skeletal muscles are completely inactive in the absence of neural input, but visceral muscles have built-in, nonneural mechanisms for generating activity. The heart continues to beat and the muscular walls of such structures as the intestines and arteries continue to contract in response to local influences, even

MATTHEW CAVANAUGH/Newscom/European Pressphoto Agency/WASHINGTON/DISTRICT OF COLUMBIA/United States

FIGURE 4.14 Artificial limb controlled by rewired nerves Jesse Sullivan (left) and Claudia Mitchell (right) are the first man and first woman, respectively, to be fitted with a thought-controlled bionic arm. Surgeons reconnected the nerves that formerly went to the arm and hand to muscles in the chest. After that, the patient could make different chest muscles twitch by thinking about moving the missing arm or fingers. The next step was to use the signals from those muscle twitches, amplified and analyzed by a tiny computer, to operate the new artificial arm and fingers. Sullivan and Mitchell are able to move their artificial arms and fingers in a wide variety of useful ways, just by thinking about doing so. For example, by willing oneself to reach out and grasp an object with the artificial limb, one can make the artificial limb reach and grasp, just as the biological limb did before it was lost (Kiuken et al., 2007).

if all the nerves to these organs are destroyed. Most visceral muscles and glands receive two sets of neurons, which produce opposite effects and come from two anatomically distinct divisions of the autonomic system: *sympathetic* and *parasympathetic* (see **Figure 4.15**).

The **sympathetic division** responds especially to stressful stimulation and helps prepare the body for possible "fight or flight." Among its effects are (a) increased heart rate and blood pressure, (b) the release of energy molecules (sugars and fats) from storage deposits to permit high energy expenditure, (c) increased blood flow to the skeletal muscles (to help prepare them for action), and (d) inhibition of digestive processes (which helps explain why a heated argument at the dinner table can lead to a stomachache). Conversely, the **parasympathetic division** serves regenerative, growth-promoting, and energy-conserving functions through effects that include the opposites of those just listed for the sympathetic division. If you are relaxed while reading this book, your parasympathetic activity probably predominates over your sympathetic, so your heart is beating at a slow, normal rate and your digestion is working fine. If you are cramming for a test that is coming up in an hour or so, the opposite may be true.

The Spinal Cord: A Conduit and an Organizer of Simple Behaviors

The spinal cord (depicted in Figure 4.2 on p. 103) connects the spinal nerves to the brain. It also organizes some simple reflexes and rhythmic movements.

The Spinal Cord Contains Pathways to and From the Brain

The spinal cord contains *ascending tracts,* which carry somatosensory information brought in by the spinal nerves up to the brain, and *descending tracts,* which carry motor control commands down from the brain to be transmitted out by spinal nerves to muscles. A person whose spinal cord is completely severed will be completely paralyzed and lacking in sensation in those parts of the body that are innervated by nerves that come from below the place of injury. The closer the place of injury is to the head, the greater the number of spinal nerves that are cut off from

FOCUS 13

What are three categories of functions of the spinal cord?

FIGURE 4.15 Divisions of the motor portion of the peripheral nervous system The motor portion of the peripheral nervous system consists of the somatic and autonomic systems, and the autonomic system consists of the sympathetic and parasympathetic systems.

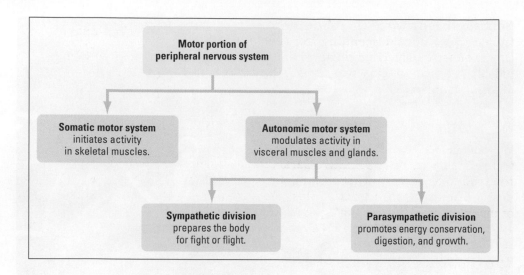

■ **New hope for spinal cord regeneration** Researchers are making progress in learning how to use stem cells to generate damaged spinal cord pathways. Ten-year-old Jesse Farquharson (shown with his therapy dog) is celebrating the 10th anniversary of Jesse's experimental surgery at SickKids Hospital in Toronto, where he became their first patient to receive a stem cell transplant using banked blood from his umbilical cord.

the brain and the greater the extent of paralysis and insensitivity. Thus, an injury that severs the spinal cord just below the brain will result in paralysis and insensitivity including the arms, trunk, and legs; but if the injury is farther down, only the legs may be paralyzed.

The Spinal Cord Organizes Simple Reflexes

Some reflexive behaviors do not require the brain; they are organized by the spinal cord alone. Such reflexes are most clearly demonstrated in animals whose spinal cords have been surgically separated from the brain. (Experiments of this sort may seem cruel, but the knowledge gained from them has been extremely valuable in helping people who have spinal cord injuries.) Animals that have had this operation—referred to as *spinal animals*—still have both a brain and a spinal cord, but these structures no longer communicate with each other.

If the paw of a spinal cat is pricked with a pin, the animal does not hiss or show facial signs of pain, as a normal cat would, because the stimulus input cannot reach the pain and vocalization centers of the brain. The cat cannot feel sensations from below the neck because feeling is mediated by the brain. Nevertheless, the animal's paw quickly withdraws from the pin. This reflex is called the *flexion reflex* because it involves contraction of the flexor muscles—the muscles that bend the limb at each joint, causing it to be pulled inward (flexed) toward the body. The adaptive advantage of the flexion reflex is obvious: It quickly and automatically moves the limb away from potentially damaging stimuli. In the intact, normal cat, this reflex occurs quickly, even before the cat shows evidence of feeling pain. It occurs quickly precisely because it occurs at the level of the spinal cord and does not require that messages be sent up to the brain for further processing and then be sent back down again.

The Spinal Cord Contains Pattern Generators for Locomotion

The old saying "running around like a chicken with its head cut off" refers to the fact that a freshly decapitated chicken will flap its wings and run around the barnyard if not restrained. This demonstrates that the spinal cord is capable of generating sustained, organized movements without the involvement of the brain. The spinal cord contains networks of neurons that stimulate one another in a cyclic manner and thereby produce bursts of action potentials that wax and wane in a regular, repeating rhythm (Kiehn, 2006). These networks, called **pattern generators**, activate motor neurons in the spinal cord in such a way as to produce the rhythmic sequence of muscle movements that results in walking, running, flying (in birds), or swimming (in fish). In some animals (but not in humans), the pattern generators become active when released from the brain's inhibitory control over them, which accounts for the wing flapping and running motions of the headless chicken.

Normally, in intact animals, pattern generators are controlled by neurons descending from the brain. They can be either inhibited, producing a motionless animal, or activated to varying degrees, producing varying rates of locomotion.

Subcortical Structures of the Brain

We now leave the spinal cord and enter the brain itself. The lower, more primitive parts of the brain are referred to as *subcortical* structures because of their position beneath the cerebral cortex, the topmost part of the brain. Working our way upward from the bottom, we begin our tour of the brain with the brainstem.

The Brainstem Organizes Species-Typical Behavior Patterns

As it enters the head, the spinal cord enlarges and becomes the **brainstem**. The parts of the brainstem, beginning closest to the spinal cord and going upward toward the top of the head, are the **medulla** [mə-du´-la], **pons**, and **midbrain** (see **Figure 4.16**). The brainstem is functionally and anatomically similar to the spinal cord, but is more elaborate. The spinal cord is the site of entry of spinal nerves, and the brainstem is the site of entry of most (10 of the 12 pairs) of the cranial nerves. Both the spinal cord and the brainstem contain ascending (sensory) and descending (motor) tracts that communicate between nerves and higher parts of the brain. Also like the spinal cord, the brainstem has some neural centers that organize reflexes and certain species-typical behavior patterns.

The medulla and pons organize reflexes that are more complex and sustained than spinal reflexes. They include *postural reflexes,* which help an animal maintain balance while standing or moving, and certain so-called *vital reflexes,* such as those that regulate breathing rate and heart rate in response to input signaling the body's metabolic needs. The midbrain contains neural centers that help govern most of an animal's species-typical movement patterns, such as those involved in eating, drinking, attacking, or copulating (Klemm, 1990). Also in the midbrain are neurons that act on pattern generators in the spinal cord to increase or decrease the speed of locomotion (Pearson & Gordon, 2000).

An animal (such as a cat) whose central nervous system is cut completely through just above the brainstem, referred to as a *brainstem animal,* is a fascinating creature to watch. It can produce most of the species-typical behaviors that a normal animal can produce (Klemm, 1990). It can walk, run, jump, climb, groom itself, attack, produce copulatory movements, chew, swallow, and so on. Unlike a normal animal, however, it makes these responses only when provoked by immediate stimuli; it does not behave in either a spontaneous or a goal-directed manner. If placed on a pole, for example, the animal automatically climbs, but it does not itself *choose* to climb a pole that has food at the top or avoid one that does not. The animal behaves like a machine that responds to certain triggers rather than like an intelligent, decision-making mammal. Such behavior indicates that the midbrain and the structures below it contain neural systems that organize species-typical patterns of movement but do not contain neural systems that permit deliberate decisions to move or refrain from moving in accordance with the animal's long-term interests or needs.

The Cerebellum and the Basal Ganglia Help to Coordinate Skilled Movements

We move now to two portions of the brain that are anatomically distinct but closely related in function—the cerebellum and the basal ganglia (see **Figure 4.17**).

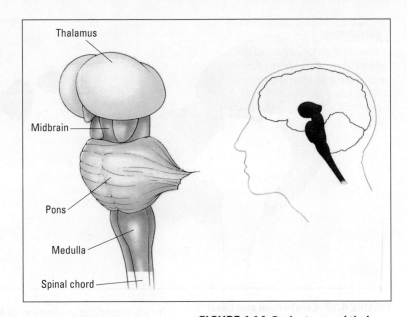

FIGURE 4.16 Brainstem and thalamus This figure makes clear why the medulla, pons, and midbrain are collectively called the *brainstem*. They form a stem-like continuation from the spinal cord, to which other brain structures are connected. The thalamus is attached to the top of the brainstem.

 FOCUS 14

How is the brainstem similar to and different from the spinal cord? What role does the brainstem play in the control of behavior?

FOCUS 15

What are the functional similarities and differences between the cerebellum and the basal ganglia?

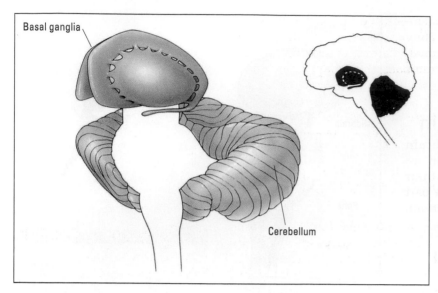

FIGURE 4.17 Cerebellum and basal ganglia These two structures are critically involved in the initiation and coordination of movement.

■ **The cerebellum in action** The cerebellum is involved in well-coordinated, precisely timed movements, which occur too fast to be controlled by sensory feedback.

Sue Bennett / Alamy

FOCUS 16

What are the main functions of the thalamus?

Cerebellum [sĕr´-ə-**bĕl´**-um] means "little brain" in Latin, and indeed this structure looks something like a smaller version of the rest of the brain, riding piggyback on the rear of the brainstem. The *basal ganglia* [bā´-səl **găng´**-lē-a] are a set of interconnected structures lying on each side of the thalamus. Damage to either the cerebellum or the basal ganglia can greatly interfere with a person's ability to produce learned, skilled, well-coordinated movements.

Damage to the cerebellum is especially associated with loss in ability to behave in ways that require rapid, well-timed sequences of muscle movements, such as pitching a baseball, leaping over a hurdle, playing a musical instrument, or typing a series of words at a computer (Bagnall et al., 2013). In contrast, damage to the basal ganglia is especially associated with loss of ability to coordinate slower, deliberate movements, such as reaching out to pick up an object (Mink, 2013).

Both structures are specialized to use sensory information to guide movements, but they apparently use that information in different ways. The basal ganglia appear to use sensory information primarily in a *feedback* manner. In other words, sensory input pertaining to an ongoing movement (such as the sight of how the hand is moving) feeds back into the basal ganglia and is used to adjust the movement as it progresses. The cerebellum, in contrast, uses sensory information primarily in a *feed-forward* manner (Ohyama et al., 2003). That is, it uses sensory information to program the appropriate force and timing of a movement before the movement is initiated. That is why the cerebellum is especially crucial for movements that occur too rapidly to be modified once they are in progress.

These characterizations are useful, but they do not describe the full range of functions of these large brain structures. People with damage in either the cerebellum or the basal ganglia can show a wide range of motor deficits, depending on the precise location of damage. Moreover, neuroimaging studies (using PET and fMRI) show that portions of the cerebellum, basal ganglia, and certain motor-planning areas of the cerebral cortex become active not just when people are producing movements but also when they are *imagining* themselves producing movements (Houk & Mugnaini, 2003). Perhaps when divers, gymnasts, or pianists "visualize" their performance before they act, what they are doing, partly, is warming up specific neurons in these motor areas, thereby setting up the neural programs that will eventuate in their best performance.

The Thalamus Is a Relay Station for Sensory, Motor, and Arousal Pathways

Directly atop the brainstem is the *thalamus* [thă´-lə-məs] (Figure 4.16). This structure, seated squarely in the middle of the brain, is most conveniently thought of as a relay station that connects various parts of the brain with one another. Most of the sensory tracts that ascend through the brainstem terminate in special nuclei in the thalamus; those nuclei, in turn, send their output to specific areas in the cerebral cortex. The thalamus also has nuclei that relay messages from higher parts of the brain to movement-control centers in the brainstem.

In addition to relaying specific sensory and motor signals, the thalamus also plays a role in the arousal of the brain as a whole. Arousal pathways in the midbrain converge in the center of the thalamus and then project diffusely to all areas of the cerebral cortex. The arousal function of the thalamus made it possible for medical researchers to awaken a patient who, because of a brain injury, had spent the previous 6 years in a minimally conscious state (Schiff et al., 2007; Personal Communication, Nicholas D. Schiff, October, 2016). The researchers implanted electrodes deep into the central nuclei of the patient's thalamus. In response to prolonged weak electrical stimulation through those electrodes, the patient would open his eyes, respond to simple requests, recognize and respond to family members, chew and swallow food placed in his mouth, and could begin a course of physical therapy that had previously been impossible. The patient maintained all gains and advanced his language capabilities over the next 6 years until his death from lung infection (Fins, 2015).

The Limbic System and the Hypothalamus Play Essential Roles in Motivation and Emotion

The term limbic comes from the Latin word *limbus,* meaning "border." The *limbic system* can be thought of as the border dividing the evolutionarily older parts of the brain below it from the newest part (the cerebral cortex), above it. The limbic system consists of several distinct structures that interconnect with one another in a circuit wrapped around the thalamus and basal ganglia (see **Figure 4.18**). Some of these structures—including especially the *amygdala* [ə-**mig**´-də-lə]—are involved in the regulation of basic drives and emotions. But the limbic system also plays other roles. One of its most prominent structures, the *hippocampus,* is crucial for keeping track of spatial location (the direction-sensitive place cells, noted earlier in the chapter, are located there) and for encoding certain kinds of memories.

The limbic system is believed to have evolved originally as a system for the sophisticated analysis of input from the sense of smell (Thompson, 1985), and its connections with the nose remain strong. This may help explain the special influence that olfactory input—such as the aroma of good food or perfume, or the stench of vomit, or the scent of freshly mown grass—can have on drives, emotions, and memories. But the limbic system also receives input from all the other sensory organs. In addition, it is intimately connected to the basal ganglia, and that connection is believed to help translate emotions and drives into actions.

The *hypothalamus* [hī-pō-**thăl**´-ə-məs] is a small but vitally important structure. Its name derives from its position directly underneath the thalamus (*hypo* in this case means "beneath"). The hypothalamus is not technically part of the limbic system, but is intimately connected to all the structures of that system (see Figure 4.18). Its primary task is to help regulate the internal environment of the body. This it accomplishes by (a) influencing the activity of the autonomic nervous system, (b) controlling the release of certain hormones (to be described later), and (c) affecting certain drive states, such as hunger and thirst. In addition, through its connections with the limbic system, the hypothalamus helps to regulate emotional states, such as fear and anger.

The hypothalamus plays a major role in the regulation of basic drives important to survival, including the so-called "four Fs": fighting, fleeing, feeding, and (to put it politely) fornicating. If you had to give up a cubic millimeter of tissue from some part your brain, the last place you would want it taken from is the hypothalamus. Depending on just which part was taken, you could be left without one or more of your basic drives, without a normal cycle of sleep and wakefulness, or without the ability to regulate your rate of metabolism. We will discuss the hypothalamus's role in drives and emotions in greater detail in Chapter 5.

FOCUS 17

Why is the limbic system so named, and what functions does it perform?

FOCUS 18

What are three ways by which the hypothalamus controls the body's internal environment?

FIGURE 4.18 Limbic system and hypothalamus The most conspicuous structures of the limbic system are the hippocampus and the amygdala, which have strong connections to the hypothalamus. The pituitary gland is strongly tied to the hypothalamus and is controlled by it.

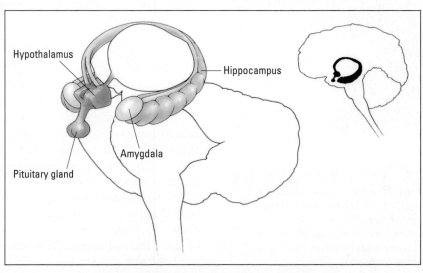

Hypothalamus

Hippocampus

Amygdala

Pituitary gland

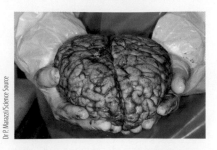

■ **A human brain** Only about one third of the surface area of the brain's cortex is visible from the outside. The remaining two thirds is hidden in the folds.

FOCUS 19

What are the four lobes of the cortex, and what are three functional categories of areas within these lobes?

The Cerebral Cortex

We now move up to the anatomically outermost and evolutionarily newest part of the brain, the *cerebral cortex*. *Cerebrum* is the Latin word for "brain," and the term generally refers to all parts of the brain other than the brainstem and cerebellum. *Cortex* is the Latin word for "bark," and in anatomical usage it refers to the outside layer of any structure. So, the cerebral cortex is the outside layer of the major portion of the brain. It is by far the largest part of the human brain, accounting for approximately 80% of its total volume (Kolb & Whishaw, 2009). Its surface area is much greater than it appears because it folds inward in many places. If the cortex were unfolded and spread out as a single sheet, it would be only 2 to 3 millimeters thick and would occupy a surface area equivalent to a square that is half a meter long on each side (Kolb & Whishaw, 2009).

The entire folded cerebral cortex is divided into left and right *hemispheres,* and each hemisphere is further divided into four lobes, or segments, demarcated by rather prominent inwardly folding creases, or *fissures.* The lobes are, from back to front, the **occipital** [ŏk-**sĭ**´-pə-təl], **temporal**, **parietal** [pa-**rĭ**´-ə-təl], and **frontal** lobes (see **Figure 4.19**).

The Cortex Includes Sensory, Motor, and Association Areas

Researchers who study the functions of the cortex divide it into three categories of functional regions, or areas. One category consists of the ***primary sensory areas***, which receive signals from sensory nerves and tracts by way of relay nuclei in the thalamus. As shown in Figure 4.19, primary sensory areas include the visual area in the occipital lobe, the auditory area in the temporal lobe, and the somatosensory area in the parietal lobe. A second category is the ***primary motor area***, which sends axons down to motor neurons in the brainstem and spinal cord. As shown in Figure 4.19, this area occupies the rear portion of the frontal lobe, directly in front of the somatosensory area. The third category consists of all the remaining parts of the cortex, which are called ***association areas***. These areas receive input from the sensory areas and lower parts of the brain and are involved in the complex processes that we call perception, thought, and decision making.

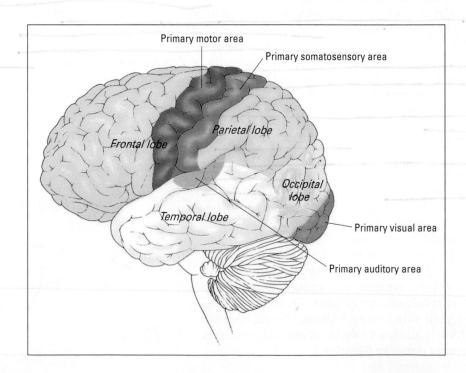

FIGURE 4.19 Cerebral cortex This figure shows the four lobes of the cortex, as well as the locations of the primary motor area and the primary sensory areas for vision, hearing, and somatosensation.

The Primary Sensory and Motor Areas Are Topographically Organized

The primary sensory and motor areas of the cortex are organized in such a way that adjacent neurons receive signals from or send signals to adjacent portions of the sensory or muscular tissue to which they are ultimately connected. This fact is referred to as the *principle of topographic organization*. For example, neurons that are near one another in the visual cortex receive signals from receptor cells that are near one another in the retina of the eye. Similarly, neurons that are near one another in the somatosensory cortex receive signals from adjacent areas of the skin, and neurons that are near one another in the primary motor cortex send signals to adjacent sets of muscle fibers. It is possible to map onto the somatosensory cortex the parts of the body from which each portion of somatosensory cortex receives its signals, and onto the motor cortex the part of the body to which each portion of motor cortex sends its signals.

The resulting maps, depicted in **Figure 4.20**, show a distorted view of the human body. This is because the amount of cortex devoted to each part of the body corresponds not to the size of the body part but to the degree of sensitivity of that part (in the case of the sensory map) or the fineness of its movements (in the case of the motor map). As you can see, huge areas of the human primary motor cortex are devoted to control of the fingers and vocal apparatus, where fine control is needed (Grillner, 2012). In other animals, other body parts have greater representation, depending on the range and delicacy of their movements. In a cat, for example, large portions of the somatosensory and primary motor areas of the cortex are devoted to the whiskers. In a spider monkey—which uses its tail as a fifth arm and hand—large areas are devoted to the tail (Walker, 1973).

FOCUS 20

What does it mean to say that cortical sensory and motor areas in the cortex are topographically organized?

FIGURE 4.20 Topographic organization of the somatosensory and primary motor areas Proportionately more cortical tissue is devoted to the more sensitive and delicately controlled body parts than to other parts.

(Information from Penfield & Rasmussen, 1950.)

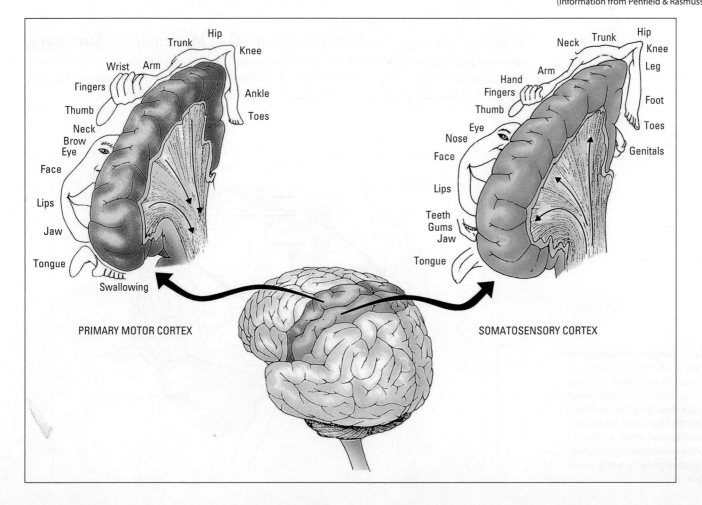

PRIMARY MOTOR CORTEX

SOMATOSENSORY CORTEX

Directly in front of the primary motor area lies a set of other cortical areas devoted to motor control, referred to collectively as ***premotor areas*** (see **Figure 4.21**). These areas set up neural programs for producing organized movements or patterns of movements. To choose what program to set up, they use information sent to them from anterior (forward) portions of the frontal lobe that are involved in overall behavioral planning. To execute an action program they send information out to the cerebellum, basal ganglia, and motor cortex, which refine the program further before sending messages down toward the muscles.

Prefrontal Association Areas Create General Plans for Action

The portion of the cerebral cortex that has expanded the most in human beings compared to other animals is the ***prefrontal cortex***, consisting of the entire frontal lobe anterior to (in front of) the premotor areas (see Figure 4.21). This part of the brain is involved in *executive function*: the processes involved in regulating attention and in determining what to do with information just gathered or retrieved from long-term memory. It plays a central role in planning and behaving flexibly, particularly when dealing with novel information (Miyake et al., 2000). We'll examine executive function in later chapters.

The arrows in Figure 4.21 indicate the general flow of information in the cortex involved in the control of movement. Association areas in the rear parts of the cortex, especially in the parietal and temporal lobes, analyze information that comes to them from sensory areas. These areas, in turn, send output to prefrontal association areas, which also receive information about the internal environment through strong connections with the limbic system. Combining all this information, the prefrontal areas set up general plans for action that can be put into effect through connections to the motor cortex and through downward links to the basal ganglia and cerebellum.

Hierarchical Organization in the Control of Movement: A Summary

We have ascended the nervous system, from bottom to top, and glimpsed the functions of each of its divisions in the overall task of controlling behavior. The parts, as we said at the outset, work together in a hierarchical manner. To review the movement-control functions of the various parts and to visualize their hierarchical organization, look

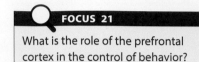

FOCUS 21

What is the role of the prefrontal cortex in the control of behavior?

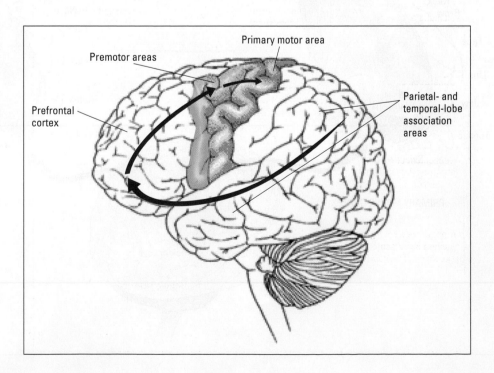

FIGURE 4.21 Control of movement by the cerebral cortex The prefrontal cortex integrates information received from other association areas and makes a general plan for action. The premotor areas convert this plan into neural programs for movement, which are then executed through connections to the cerebellum, basal ganglia, and primary motor cortex.

at **Figure 4.22**. Structures are organized there according to their general roles in controlling movement, not according to their anatomical positions. The highest structures are involved in motivation and planning, and the lower structures are involved in refining and executing the plans, turning them into action. Notice that both subcortical and cortical structures (shown, respectively, on the left and right sides of the diagram) are involved at each of the top three levels in the hierarchy.

To illustrate the hierarchy further, imagine what might occur in the nervous system of a person who has not eaten in a while and sees some fresh cherries. At the top of the hierarchy, the limbic system (which most directly monitors the internal state of the body) senses that food is needed and sends a message of "hunger" to cortical association areas with which it is connected. These areas, which share the top of the hierarchy with the limbic system, analyze information coming to them from the visual cortex and determine that fresh cherries are available in a bowl across the room. Other information is also considered by the association areas, including memories about the taste of fresh cherries, the propriety of eating them in this room at this time, and how to eat them, including seeking a receptacle for disposing of the stems and pits. Such information, integrated by prefrontal association areas, leads to a decision to cross the room, pick up some cherries, and eat them.

At the second level, the basal ganglia, cerebellum, and premotor cortex receive the program of planned action from the limbic system and prefrontal cortex. They also receive somatosensory input about the exact position of parts of the body and visual input about the exact location of the cherries. They use this information to refine the motor program—that is, to work out the specific timing and patterning of the movements to be made.

At the third level, the motor program is conveyed through two pathways for further refinement. The program for larger movements, such as walking toward the cherries, is sent directly down to a set of motor nuclei in the upper part of the brainstem. The program for delicate movements, such as those needed for removing the stems and eating the fruit while avoiding swallowing the pits, is conveyed to the motor cortex, which, in turn, sends its output down to the brainstem and spinal cord.

Finally, at the fourth level of the hierarchy, in the lower brainstem and spinal cord, are motor neurons—the final common pathway in control of behavior. Somatic

FOCUS 22

How are the movement-control functions of the nervous system summarized as a hierarchical, top-down flow of information? How is the hierarchy illustrated by an imaginative tour through the nervous system of a person who decides to eat some fresh cherries?

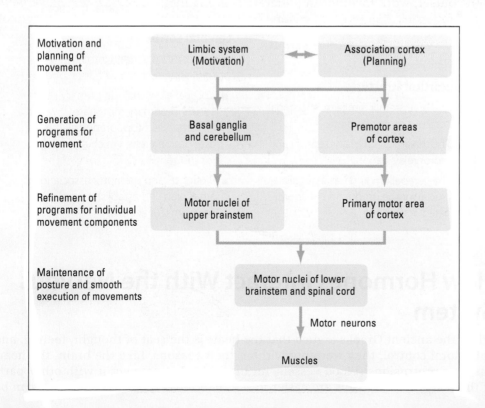

FIGURE 4.22 Hierarchy of motor control This figure summarizes the broad functions of various structures of the nervous system in the control of movement. The structures shown higher up are involved in the more global aspects of an action, and those shown farther down are involved in the finer details of carrying it out. Notice that both subcortical and cortical structures exist at each of the top three levels of the hierarchy. Although this portrayal does not show all the known pathways, it provides a useful way to think about the neural flow of information from the planning of an action to its execution. (Information from Ghez & Krakauer, 2000; Schmidt, 1986.)

motor neurons send their messages out to the skeletal muscles of the body to trigger all the movements needed to reach the cherries, pick up a handful, and put them in the mouth. Autonomic motor neurons (of the parasympathetic division) send their messages out to the salivary glands and muscular walls of the gastrointestinal system to prepare the digestive tract to receive the cherries.

A Word of Caution

The hierarchical model just described is useful as a first approach to understanding the nervous system, and it is consistent with the kinds of behavioral deficits that occur when different parts of the nervous system are damaged. However, there is a possible danger in this portrayal: It can seduce us into believing we know more than we actually do.

Specifically, the knowledge that certain parts of the brain are essential for certain aspects of behavioral control can be mistaken for knowledge about *how* those processes are accomplished. The discovery of "where" does not explain "how." In illustrating the hierarchy, we spoke of "decisions" made in prefrontal areas of the cortex and of programs for action developed and refined by other brain areas. What do such statements mean? They mean only that individuals who suffer damage in one part of the brain lose the ability to make reasonable choices for action, and that those who suffer damage in another part retain the ability to make reasonable choices but lose the ability to carry them out in a coordinated manner. It is important to remember that such statements don't address the far more difficult question of how the association cortex makes decisions or how various other structures develop and refine programs for action.

FOCUS 23

What is the difference between knowing *where* a brain function occurs and knowing *how* it occurs?

SECTION REVIEW

Divisions of the nervous system are organized hierarchically to control behavior.

Peripheral Nervous System

- This division consists of spinal and cranial nerves and their various branches, which contain sensory and motor neurons.

- Motor neurons include somatic motor neurons, which contract skeletal muscles, and sympathetic and parasympathetic autonomic motor neurons, which act in opposing ways on internal organs.

Spinal Cord

- The spinal cord acts as a conduit, carrying somatosensory information to the brain and motor commands from the brain.

- It also organizes spinal reflexes and contains pattern generators that produce rhythmic movement sequences, such as walking.

Subcortical Structures

- The brainstem is similar to the spinal cord but more elaborate.

- The thalamus is a major sensory and motor relay station.

- The cerebellum and basal ganglia are crucial for the production of coordinated actions.

- The hypothalamus and limbic system are critically involved in motivation and emotion as well as other functions.

Cerebral Cortex

- The cortex is divided into two hemispheres, each with four lobes.

- Cortical areas include primary sensory and primary motor areas, which are organized topographically, and association areas, which are crucial for thought.

- Prefrontal and premotor association areas plan and establish neural programs for actions.

How Hormones Interact With the Nervous System

When the ancient Greeks argued that the heart is the seat of thought, feeling, and behavioral control, they were not without their reasons. Like the brain, the heart has long protrusions (blood vessels, in this case) that connect it with other parts of the body. Blood vessels are easier to see than nerves, and because they can be found in all the sense organs and muscles, as well as in other tissues, early theorists believed that blood vessels were the conduits of sensory and motor messages. Today we know that the circulatory system does indeed play a vital communicative role in the body, though not the one envisioned by the ancients. A slower messenger system than the nervous system, it carries chemicals that affect both physical growth and behavior. Among these chemicals are hormones, which are secreted naturally into the bloodstream, and drugs, which may enter the bloodstream artificially through various routes.

Hormones are chemical messengers that are secreted into the blood. They are carried by the blood to all parts of the body, where they act on specific *target tissues*. Dozens of hormones have been identified. The classic hormones—the first to be identified and the best understood—are secreted by special hormone-producing glands called *endocrine glands* (see **Figure 4.23**). But many other hormones are secreted by organs that are not usually classified as endocrine glands, such as the stomach, intestines, kidneys, and brain.

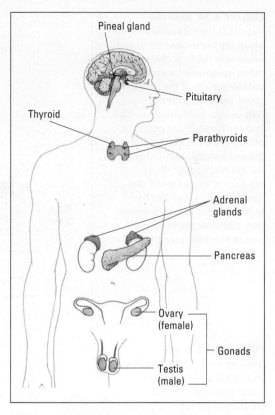

How Hormones Affect Behavior

Hormones influence behavior in many ways. They affect the growth of peripheral bodily structures, including muscles and bones, and in that way influence behavioral capacity. Hormones also affect metabolic processes throughout the body and thereby influence the amount of energy that is available for action. Of greatest interest to psychologists is the fact that hormones also act in the brain in ways that influence drives and moods.

Some effects of hormones are long term or irreversible, and some of these occur before birth. For example, almost all the anatomical differences between newborn boys and girls are caused by *androgens*, a class of hormones, including testosterone, that are found in higher levels in males than females. These anatomical differences are evident in the brain as well as in the genitals, and the brain differences provide one basis for sex differences in behavior throughout life. At puberty, the increased production of sex hormones—especially testosterone in the male and estrogen in the female—stimulates a new set of growth processes that further differentiate males and females anatomically and thereby influence their behavior.

The short-term effects of hormones range in duration from a few minutes to many days. In response to stressful stimulation, for example, the adrenal cortex (the external layer of the adrenal gland) secretes various hormones, including cortisol, that are sometimes called stress hormones. These hormones produce a variety of effects throughout the body that help in a stressful situation. For example, they release sugar and fat molecules into the blood to supply extra energy for possible "fight or flight," and they suppress inflammation caused by wounds. These hormones are also taken up by neurons in certain parts of the brain and apparently act there to help the animal adapt behaviorally to the stressful situation (McEwen, 1989).

How Hormones Are Controlled by the Brain

The pituitary, which sits at the base of the brain, is sometimes called the master endocrine gland because it produces hormones that, in turn, stimulate the production of other hormones in other glands, including the adrenal cortex and the gonads (ovaries in the female and testes in the male).

To visualize the intimate relationship between the brain and the pituitary, look at **Figure 4.24**. The rear part of the pituitary, the *posterior lobe,* is in fact a part of the brain. The posterior lobe consists mainly of modified neurons, referred to as *neurosecretory cells,* which extend down from the hypothalamus. When these neurosecretory cells are activated, by brain neurons that lie above them, they release their hormones

FIGURE 4.23 Endocrine glands These are some of the glands that secrete hormones into the bloodstream. The pituitary, which is controlled by the brain, secretes hormones that, in turn, control the production of hormones by the thyroid, adrenals, and ovaries or testes.

FOCUS 24

What are some examples of long-term and short-term effects of hormones?

FOCUS 25

How does the brain control the release of hormones from the two lobes of the pituitary and thereby control the release of other hormones as well?

FIGURE 4.24 How the hypothalamus controls pituitary hormones Specialized neurons in the hypothalamus, called neurosecretory cells, control the activity of the pituitary gland. Some neurosecretory cells secrete hormones directly into capillaries in the posterior pituitary, where they enter the general bloodstream. Others secrete hormones called *releasing factors* into a special capillary system that carries them to the anterior pituitary, where they stimulate the release of hormones manufactured there.

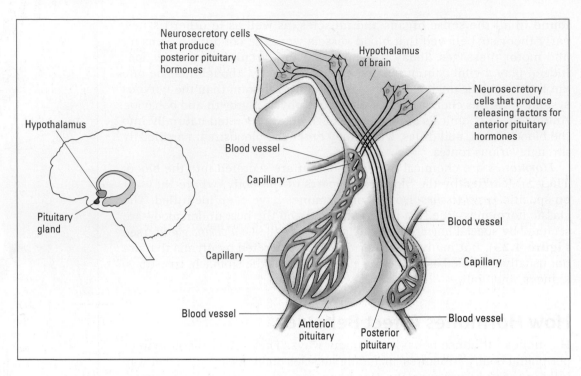

FIGURE 4.25 Brain-pituitary-adrenal response to a fearful stimulus This is one example of a brain-mediated hormonal response to sensory stimulation.

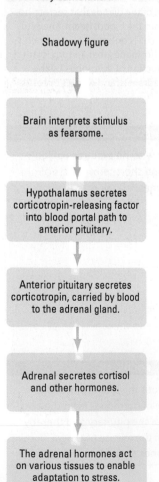

into a bed of capillaries. Once these hormones enter the capillaries, they are transported into the rest of the circulatory system to affect various parts of the body.

The remainder of the pituitary, the *anterior lobe,* is not part of the brain (no neurons descend into it) but is intimately connected to the brain by a specialized set of capillaries, as shown in Figure 4.24. Neurosecretory cells in the brain's hypothalamus produce *releasing factors,* hormones that are secreted into the special capillary system and are carried to the anterior pituitary, where they stimulate the anterior pituitary cells to synthesize and release hormones into capillaries that carry the hormones into the bloodstream. Different releasing factors, produced by different sets of neurosecretory cells in the hypothalamus, act selectively to stimulate the production of different anterior pituitary hormones.

Consider the sequence of hormonal events, triggered by the brain, that is diagrammed in **Figure 4.25**: (1) A shadowy figure is seen at night, and the brain interprets it as fearsome. (2) The association cortex sends a neural message to the viewer's hypothalamus that causes it to secrete *corticotropin-releasing factor.* (3) The specialized capillary system transports this releasing factor to the anterior pituitary, where it stimulates the release of another hormone, *corticotropin,* into the bloodstream. (4) From the bloodstream, corticotropin enters the adrenal cortex, where it causes the release of adrenal cortical hormones, including cortisol. (5) These adrenal hormones are carried throughout the body to help prepare it for a possible emergency. At the same time, many other brain-controlled effects are also occurring to deal with the possible emergency suggested by the sight of the shadowy figure. They range from the activation of the sympathetic portion of the autonomic nervous system to the development of a plan to escape.

Hormonal Influences on Sex Drive

Human sexuality is quite complex. People don't just copulate; they fall in love, compose romantic sonnets, gaze into each other's eyes over candlelit dinners, swear by the moon to be faithful, have affairs, suffer guilt, and engage in long, intimate discussions with their beloved. However, as with other mammals, hormones play a role in motivating sexual desire and behavior, with the hormones and their effects being different in males and females.

Hormonal Influences on Male Sex Drive

Although sexual desire and response are influenced by a number of different hormones, in male mammals, the most crucial hormone for the maintenance of the sexual drive is *testosterone,* a form of androgen, produced by the testes.

In male animals, castration (removal of the testes, and hence of the main supply of testosterone) causes a marked decline in the sex drive—not all at once, but gradually (Feder, 1984). It takes days to occur in rats, weeks in dogs, sometimes months in monkeys. The injection of testosterone into the bloodstream of castrated animals gradually but eventually fully restores their drive.

The sex drive can also be restored in castrated male animals by implanting a tiny crystal of testosterone into an area of the hypothalamus called the *medial preoptic area* (see **Figure 4.26**) (Davidson, 1980). Neurons in this area contain many receptor sites for testosterone, and small lesions there abolish sexual behavior in male rats (Meisel & Sachs, 1994).

Many experiments have shown that the amount of testosterone that men secrete into their blood is affected by psychological conditions. In general, conditions that would seem to promote self-confidence tend to increase a man's production of testosterone. For example, winning a game, even a sedentary game like chess, or a contrived speed-based button-pressing competition, commonly results in increased blood levels of testosterone in men, detectable within minutes of the victory (Archer, 2006; Gladue et al., 1989), and winning such contests, relative to losing them, is also associated with increased sexual interest in women (Gorelik & Bjorklund, 2015). Even driving a luxury automobile is associated with increases in men's testosterone (Saad & Vongas 2009), as are pleasant social encounters with women (Roney et al., 2007).

Hormonal Influences on Female Sex Drive

After puberty, a female's ovaries begin to secrete the female hormones *estrogen* and *progesterone* in a cyclic pattern over time, producing the cycle of physiological changes referred to as the *menstrual cycle* in humans and the *estrous cycle* in most other mammals. In both humans and nonhumans, this cycle controls ovulation (the release of one or more eggs so that pregnancy can occur). This cycle of hormones also influences sexual drive.

In most mammals, female sexual drive and behavior are tightly controlled by the estrous cycle. The female will seek out opportunities for mating, and will copulate, only at that time in the cycle when she is ovulating and hence capable of becoming pregnant. Removal of the ovaries completely abolishes sexual behavior in most nonhuman female mammals, and injection of hormones, particularly in the *ventromedial area of the hypothalamus* (see Figure 4.26), can fully restore it (Blaustein, 2008; Pleim & Barfield, 1988; Schwartz-Giblin et al., 1989). For some species an injection of estrogen alone is most effective, and for others (including rats) a sequence of estrogen followed 2 or 3 days later by progesterone is most effective, a sequence that mimics the natural change of hormones during the estrous cycle.

Unlike most other mammals, human females can experience a high or low sex drive at any time in their hormone cycle. Apparently, in women, hormonal activation of the drive has been taken over largely by adrenal androgens. The term ***androgen*** refers to a category of hormones, including testosterone, which are produced by the testes in male animals and are normally thought of as "male hormones." These hormones are also produced at lower levels by the adrenal glands, in females as well as in males. In clinical studies, women whose ovaries have been removed do not generally report a decline in sexual drive, but most women whose adrenals have been removed do report such a decline; and long-term treatment with testosterone reliably increases sexual desire and satisfaction in such women (de Paula et al., 2007; Guay, 2001).

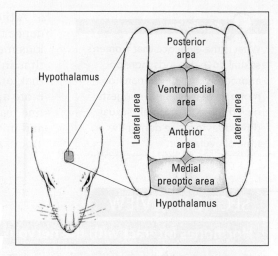

FIGURE 4.26 Hypothalamic areas where hormones activate sexual behavior In rats, testosterone promotes male sexual behavior by activating neurons in the medial preoptic area of the hypothalamus, and estrogen promotes female sexual behavior by activating neurons in the ventromedial area of the hypothalamus.

 FOCUS 26

What is some evidence that testosterone is needed to maintain the male's sex drive?

 FOCUS 27

What kinds of experiences have been shown to increase testosterone production in men? What effects might such increased testosterone have on a man's subsequent behavior?

 FOCUS 28

What evidence indicates that ovarian hormones act directly on the brain to activate the sexual drive in female rats? How do female primates differ from female rats concerning the regulation of sexual drive?

FOCUS 29

What is the evidence that women's sexual drive depends more on androgens than on ovarian hormones? What evidence suggests, nevertheless, that female sexual drive does increase during the time of ovulation?

Although the ovarian cycle does not control women's sexual drive, there is evidence that the cycle does influence it to some degree. A number of studies, using various measures, indicate that women are significantly more motivated sexually at the time in their cycle when they are fertile than at other times. The studies have shown that, on average, women during the fertile phase dress more provocatively, speak in more appealing tones of voice, are relatively more drawn to men with highly masculine features, feel themselves to be more sexually attractive and sexually motivated, and initiate sex more frequently than at other times of their menstrual cycle (Beall & Tracy, 2013; Gangestad et al., 2004; Gildersleeve et al., 2014).

SECTION REVIEW

Hormones interact with the nervous system.

Hormones and Behavior

- Hormones are chemical messengers secreted into the bloodstream.

- Hormones can influence behavior by affecting bodily growth, metabolism, and brain activity, including brain activity responsible for drives and moods.

- Hormonal effects can be long term or even permanent, as in the case of prenatal testosterone's effects on brain development. They can also be short term, as in the case of stress hormones' effects in preparing for an emergency.

Brain Controls Hormones

- The pituitary gland controls hormone production by other glands, but is itself controlled by the brain.

Sex Drive

- Testosterone maintains male sex drive over the long term. In rats, at least, this occurs by action on the preoptic area of the hypothalamus.

- Confidence-boosting events cause increased testosterone secretion in men, which may increase their tendency toward competitiveness or aggression.

- In most nonhuman female mammals, ovarian hormones promote sexual drive at the time of fertility, apparently through action on the ventromedial hypothalamus.

- In women and some other female primates, adrenal androgens promote sexual receptivity throughout the ovarian cycle. But sexual proceptivity appears to increase at the time of fertility, perhaps because of increased androgen production at that time.

Hemispheric Differences in the Cerebral Cortex

Nearly every part of the brain exists in duplicate. We have a right and a left member of each anatomical portion of the brainstem, thalamus, cerebellum, and so on. The part of the brain in which the right-left division is most evident, however, is the cerebral cortex. Each half of the cortex folds inward where it would abut the other half, forming a deep, fore-to-aft midline fissure that divides the cortex into distinct right and left hemispheres. The two hemispheres are connected by a massive bundle of axons called the ***corpus callosum*** [ka-lō-səm], which is located below that fissure (see **Figure 4.27**).

The two hemispheres are quite symmetrical in their primary sensory and motor functions. Each does the same job, but for a different half of the body. Most of the neural paths between the primary sensory and motor areas of the cortex and the parts of the body to which they connect are crossed, or *contralateral*. Thus, sensory neurons that arise from the skin on the right side of the body send their signals to the somatosensory area of the left hemisphere, and vice versa. Similarly, neurons in the primary motor area of the left hemisphere send their signals to muscles on the right side of the body. Such symmetry breaks down, however, in the association areas.

The most obvious distinction between the two cortical hemispheres in humans is that large areas in the left are specialized for language and comparable areas in the right are specialized for nonverbal, visuospatial analysis of information. The earliest

FOCUS 30

In what ways are the two hemispheres of the cerebral cortex symmetrical, and in what ways are they asymmetrical?

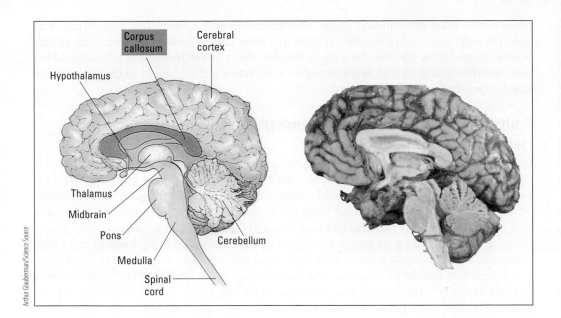

Arthur Glauberman/Science Source

Arthur Glauberman/Science Source

FIGURE 4.27 Corpus callosum The corpus callosum is a huge bundle of axons that connects the right and left hemispheres of the cerebral cortex. You can see it here in an inside view of the right hemisphere of a human brain that has been cut in half. This photograph and the matched diagram also give you an inside view of other brain structures.

evidence of this difference came from observing people who had suffered strokes or other injuries that affected just one hemisphere. In general, damage to the left hemisphere results in deficits in using and comprehending language, and damage to the right results in deficits in such tasks as recognizing faces, reading maps, and drawing geometric shapes, all of which depend on perceiving spatial relationships.

Effects of Surgical Separation of the Hemispheres: Split Brain, Split Mind

Dramatic further evidence of the separate abilities of the two hemispheres appeared in the 1960s, when Roger Sperry, Michael Gazzaniga, and their colleagues began to study patients with "split brains": people who, as a last-resort treatment for epilepsy, had undergone surgery to separate the two hemispheres by cutting the corpus callosum.

Earlier, more casual observations had revealed no remarkable deficits in people who had undergone this operation. The operation was generally successful in reducing or eliminating epileptic seizures, and, after a period of recovery, there is usually no drop in measured IQ, in ability to carry on conversations, or even in ability to coordinate the two sides of the body in skilled tasks. But Gazzaniga (1967, 1998) showed that under special test conditions, in which information is provided to just one hemisphere or the other, patients with split brains behave as though they have two separate minds with different abilities.

How Each Hemisphere Can Be Tested Separately After the Split-Brain Operation

Split-brain studies examine the crossed sensory and motor connections between the brain and peripheral parts of the body. Recall that each hemisphere most directly controls movement in, and receives somatosensory information from, the opposite half of the body. In addition, as illustrated in **Figure 4.28**, connections from the eyes to the brain are such that input from the right-hand half of a person's field of view goes first to the left hemisphere, while input from the left visual field goes first to the right hemisphere. In the normal brain, all information that goes to either hemisphere subsequently travels to the other through the corpus callosum. But split-brain surgery destroys those connections. Therefore, with the testing apparatus shown in **Figure 4.29** and with patients with split brains as subjects, it is possible

FOCUS 31

How is it possible to test each hemisphere separately in people whose corpus callosum has been cut? How do such tests confirm that the left hemisphere controls speech and the right hemisphere has superior spatial ability?

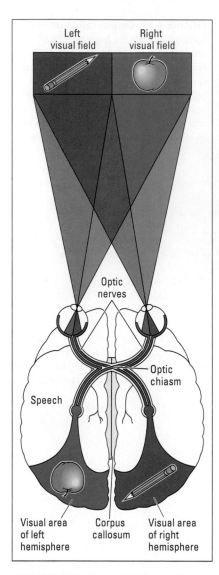

FIGURE 4.28 Neural pathways from the eyes to the right and left hemispheres of the cortex Neurons of the optic nerves either cross or don't cross at the optic chiasm. The pattern of crossing is such that neurons on the right side of either retina, which receive input from the left visual field, go to the right hemisphere of the brain, and vice versa.

FIGURE 4.29 Testing apparatus for split-brain subjects With this apparatus, it is possible to flash a stimulus in either visual field (or in both at once) and to ask the person to identify objects by touch with either hand. With the image of a pencil flashed in his left visual field, this split-brain subject will be able to identify the pencil by touch with his left hand. Vocally, however, he will report having seen an apple on the screen, as that was flashed in his right visual field, which projects to his left, speaking hemisphere.

to (a) send visual information to just one hemisphere by presenting the stimulus in only the opposite half of the visual field, (b) send tactile (touch) information to just one hemisphere by having the subject feel an object with the opposite hand, and (c) test the knowledge of just one hemisphere by having the subject respond with the hand opposite to that hemisphere.

Split-Brain Evidence for Left-Hemisphere Language and Right-Hemisphere Spatial Ability

In a typical experiment, Gazzaniga flashed pictures of common objects to either the right or the left visual field of a patient with a split brain (see Figure 4.29). When a picture was flashed in the right field (projecting to the left hemisphere), the patient described it as well as someone with an intact brain would; but when a picture was flashed in the left field (projecting to the right hemisphere), the patient either claimed to see nothing or made a random guess. Then Gazzaniga asked the same person to reach under a barrier with one hand or the other and identify, by touch, the object that had been flashed. The fascinating result was that the person could reliably identify with the left hand (but not with the right) the same object that he or she had just vocally denied having seen (Gazzaniga, 1967). For example, if the object flashed to the right hemisphere was a pencil, the subject's left hand picked out the pencil from a set of objects even while the subject's voice was continuing to say that nothing had been flashed. Such findings are consistent with the conclusion that only the left hemisphere can generate speech and that neither hemisphere has direct access to what the other one knows.

Research of this sort also revealed large individual differences among patients with split brains in the degree to which the right hemisphere can comprehend speech. Some show essentially no right-hemisphere comprehension. They cannot participate in experiments such as that just described because their right hemispheres don't understand such instructions as "Pick up the object that you saw on the screen." Others have reasonably good right-hemisphere comprehension, although their right hemisphere is still unable to generate speech; and a few show a reversal, with the right hemisphere superior to the left in language comprehension and production. Additional research, with people whose corpus callosum has not been cut, has shown that about 4% of right-handed individuals and 15% of left-handed individuals have their speech centers located in the right hemisphere rather than the left (Rasmussen & Milner, 1977).

Other experiments with patients with split brains revealed that although the right hemisphere is unable to generate speech, it is much better than the left in solving visuospatial problems. When asked to arrange puzzle pieces to match a

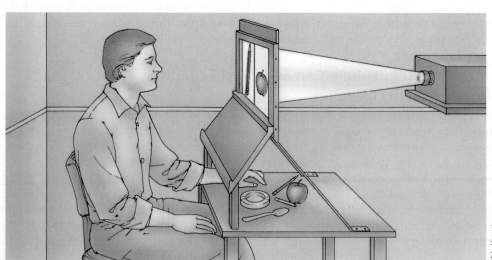

Michael Gazzaniga

particular design or to copy three-dimensional pictures, each subject performed far better with the left hand (controlled by the right hemisphere) than with the right hand (controlled by the left hemisphere), even though all of the subjects were right-handed (see **Figure 4.30**). In more recent experiments, patients with split brains were asked to judge small differences between visual stimuli presented as pairs to either hemisphere. The results showed that the left hemisphere is as good as the right in judging nonspatial differences, such as differences in brightness or in color, but not as good as the right in judging spatial differences, such as differences in size or in the slant of two lines (Corballis, 2003).

How Patients With Split Brains Cope as Well as They Do

How do people who have had the split-brain operation get along in the world as well as they do? What keeps their two hemispheres from going off in opposite directions and creating continuous conflict between the two halves of the body? In some instances, especially shortly after the surgery, conflict does occur. One man described a situation in which, while he was dressing in the morning, his right hand was trying to pull his pants on while his left hand was trying to pull them back off (Gazzaniga, 1970); apparently, his right hemisphere wanted to go back to bed. But such conflicts are rare, and when they do occur, the left hemisphere (right hand) usually wins.

The patient's ability to coordinate the two hemispheres probably involves several mechanisms. First, only the cerebral cortex and some parts of the limbic system are divided when the corpus callosum is cut. Motor centers that control movements of the larger muscles, such as those of the legs and arms (but not the fingers) lie in the lower, undivided parts, and some sensory information also passes from one hemisphere to the other by way of those lower routes (Reuter-Lorenz & Miller, 1998). The intact connections also apparently allow each hemisphere to inhibit the motor output of the other, so the more competent hemisphere can take control of any given task (Reuter-Lorenz & Miller, 1998). In addition, under normal conditions, when the eyes can move around and things can be felt with both hands, the two hemispheres can receive the same or similar information through their separate channels. Finally, each hemisphere apparently learns to communicate indirectly with the other by observing and responding to the behavior that the other produces, a process that Gazzaniga (1967) labeled *cross-cueing*. For example, the right hemisphere may perceive something unpleasant and precipitate a frown, and the left may feel the frown and say, "I'm displeased."

Split-Brain Insight Into Consciousness: The Left-Hemisphere Interpreter

One of the most fascinating findings from studies of patients with split brains is that they rarely express surprise or confusion concerning the seemingly contradictory actions that their two hemispheres generate. When asked to explain some behavior triggered by the right hemisphere, the person (speaking from the left hemisphere) usually generates quickly and confidently a seemingly logical (but often false) explanation.

For instance, in one experiment a patient with a split brain was presented simultaneously with a picture of a chicken claw shown to the left hemisphere and a picture of a snow scene shown to the right hemisphere (Gazzaniga, 2000). Then he was shown (in a way that could be seen by both hemispheres) a set of pictured objects and was asked to point with both hands to the one most closely related to what he had seen on the screen. He immediately pointed with his right hand to the chicken (clearly related to the chicken claw) and with his left hand to the snow shovel (clearly related to the snow scene). When asked why he was pointing to these two objects, his left-speaking hemisphere responded, "Oh, that's simple. The chicken claw goes with the chicken, and you need a shovel to clean out the chicken shed."

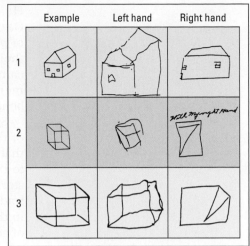

FIGURE 4.30 Evidence for right-hemisphere superiority in spatial representation Although the split-brain patient who produced these drawings was right-handed, he could copy geometric figures much better with his left hand (controlled by his right hemisphere) than with his right hand.

FOCUS 32

How do studies of split-brain patients tend to confirm and extend an idea about the nature of consciousness that was developed long ago by Sigmund Freud?

He seemed completely satisfied by this explanation. In other experiments, Gazzaniga and his colleagues found that they could induce states of annoyance or of pleasure in patients with a split brain by flashing annoying or pleasant scenes to their right hemispheres. When asked to explain their feelings, the patients always came up with plausible (but clearly false) answers. For example, they might comment on some aspect of the experimental equipment—or of the experimenter's behavior—that was either annoying them or pleasing them.

Such observations led Gazzaniga (2000) to posit that one of the natural functions of the left hemisphere is to interpret, or try to make logical sense of, everything that the person does. You might think of this *left-hemisphere interpreter* as analogous to the public relations department of a business or government. Its role is to tell stories, both to the self and to others, designed to make sense of the seemingly contradictory and irrational things that the person does. The idea of such an interpreter in the human brain or mind is by no means new. It was the centerpiece of a theory of consciousness proposed by Sigmund Freud (1912/1932) more than 100 years ago. According to Freud, we do things because unconscious decision-making processes in our mind make us do them. But one part of our mind observes what we do and tells a running story about it; that story constitutes our conscious understanding of our actions and the reasons for them. The split-brain studies indicate that the neural mechanism for generating such stories is located in the left hemisphere and is intimately connected with the brain areas that generate speech.

Language Areas of the Left Hemisphere

Perhaps the most distinctively human behavioral ability is that of producing and understanding a complex, grammar-based language. Much of the left hemisphere of the human cortex is involved with language. Damage anywhere within large portions of the left hemisphere disrupts language ability, and the nature of the disruption depends on just where the destruction occurs.

Any loss of language ability resulting from brain damage is called *aphasia* [ə-fā´-zhiə]. Aphasias have been classified into a number of types, depending on the specific nature and degree of loss (Dronkers et al., 2000). The best known and most fully studied of these are two that were first described by nineteenth-century neurologists—one by Paul Broca and the other by Carl Wernicke.

Effects of Damage to Broca's Area

Broca (1861/1965) observed that people who had brain damage that included an area of the left frontal lobe now called *Broca's area,* just anterior to the primary motor area (see **Figure 4.31**), suffered from a type of aphasia in which speech becomes labored and *telegraphic,* meaning that the minimum number of words are used to convey the message. The speech consists mostly of nouns and verbs, and a sentence is rarely more than three or four words long. If you ask a person with this disorder what he or she did today, the answer might be, "Buy bread store." This disorder is now called **Broca's aphasia** or, more descriptively, *nonfluent aphasia.* The lack of fluency in Broca's aphasia suggests that neurons in Broca's area are crucial for setting up the motor programs that are involved in fluent speech production. This conclusion is also consistent with the observation that Broca's area lies very near to the region of the primary motor cortex that controls movements of the tongue and other speech muscles.

Research since Broca's time indicates that people with damage to Broca's area also have difficulty understanding language. They become confused by grammatically complex sentences—for example, by sentences in which the agent and object of an action are reversed from the usual word order and the meaning cannot be inferred from the individual word meanings alone (Grodzinsky, 2000). Thus, they easily understand *The boy pushed the girl* (a simple, active sentence) or *The apple*

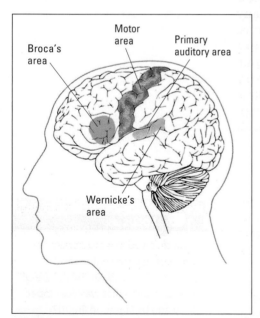

FIGURE 4.31 Left-hemisphere language areas Damage to Broca's area leads to a loss of the ability to generate fluid, grammatically complete sentences but not to a loss of the ability to supply the words needed to convey the main content of the sentence. Damage to Wernicke's area has the opposite effect on speech production and greatly impairs speech comprehension.

Motor area
Broca's area
Primary auditory area
Wernicke's area

was eaten by the boy (which can be understood just from word meanings because apples don't eat boys), but *The girl was pushed by the boy* leaves them unsure as to who pushed whom. Research suggests that people with an intact Broca's area understand that last sentence by transforming it mentally into its simpler, active equivalent—*The boy pushed the girl*. People lacking Broca's area apparently fail to produce such transformations.

In sum, studies of people with damage to Broca's area suggest that neurons in and around this area are crucial for at least two seemingly distinct language functions: (1) articulating words and sentences in a fluent manner and (2) transforming grammatically complex sentences that are heard into simpler ones in order to extract the meaning.

Effects of Damage to Wernicke's Area

Wernicke (1874/1977) observed that people who had damage to a certain area of the left temporal lobe, now called *Wernicke's area*, suffered from a type of aphasia quite different from that described by Broca. Later research found that Wernicke's area is located near the primary auditory area (see Figure 4.31). Wernicke's patients, unlike Broca's aphasics, had difficulty understanding the meanings of words they heard and also had difficulty finding the appropriate words to express the meanings they wanted to convey.

The speech of patients with damage in Wernicke's area is almost the opposite of that of Broca's aphasics. It is rich in the little words that serve primarily to form the grammatical structure of a sentence—the articles (*a, the*), prepositions (such as *of, on*), and conjunctions (*and, but*). However, it is markedly deficient in the nouns, verbs, and adjectives that give a sentence its meaning. One such patient, asked to describe the contents of a simple picture, said: "Nothing the keesereez the, these are davereez and these and this one and these are living. This one's right in and these are . . . uh . . . and that's nothing, that's nothing" (Schwartz, 1987). The inability to come up with the correct names of objects and actions leads to a heavy use of pronouns and nonsense words as substitutes. The speech retains its fluency and grammatical structure but loses its meaning.

This disorder is now called **Wernicke's aphasia**, or, more descriptively, *fluent aphasia*. Theories to explain it generally center on the idea that neurons in and near Wernicke's area are crucially involved in translating the sounds of words into their meanings and in locating, through connections to other cortical association areas, the words needed to express intended meanings (Dronkers et al., 2000). Its location near the primary auditory area is also consistent with the role of translating sounds into meaningful words (Geschwind, 1972).

Identifying Language Areas Through Neuroimaging

With PET or fMRI it is possible to determine which areas of the brain become more active when a person engages in a language-related task. Such studies tend in some ways to confirm the theories about the functions of Broca's and Wernicke's areas that arose from studies of people with brain damage, but in other ways to challenge those theories.

One of the earliest and most often cited of such studies was conducted by Steven Petersen and his colleagues (1989). These researchers used PET to image the brains of people as they carried out four types of language-related tasks that varied stepwise in level of complexity. At the first level (simplest task), the subjects simply gazed at a spot marked by crosshairs in the center of a video screen. At the second level, they continued to gaze at the crosshairs while they either saw (superimposed on the crosshairs) or heard (through earphones) a series of common English nouns. The third level was just like the second, except that now they were asked to speak aloud each word that they saw or heard. The fourth level was like the third, except that instead of simply repeating each noun, they were asked to think of and say aloud a verb that represented an action appropriate to the noun (e.g., in response to *hammer,* they might say "pound").

FOCUS 33

What are the differences between Broca's and Wernicke's aphasias in (a) language production, (b) language comprehension, and (c) areas of the brain damaged?

FOCUS 34

How was PET used to identify brain areas involved in word perception and production?

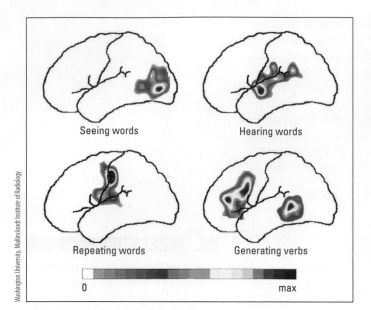

Washington University, Mallinckrodt Institute of Radiology

FIGURE 4.32 Brain activity during word-processing tasks, as revealed by PET Each figure shows the amount of activity in each part of the left hemisphere during the performance of the indicated task, relative to the amount of activity in that part during the performance of the task one level below it in the hierarchy. The colors violet, blue, green, yellow, and red, in that order, represent increasing amounts of activity.

In order to identify the brain areas brought into play by each type of task, the researchers computed, for each small area of the brain, the difference between the average amount of activity during that task and the average amount during the task that ranked one level below that task. The results are depicted in **Figure 4.32** and can be summarized as follows:

• Viewing or hearing words, without having to act on them in any way, resulted (as expected) in high activity in the relevant sensory areas—visual areas of the occipital lobe for viewing and auditory areas of the temporal lobe for hearing.

• Repeating aloud words that were seen or heard resulted in high activity in areas of the primary motor cortex that are involved in control of the vocal apparatus.

• Generating appropriate verbs in response to seen or heard nouns resulted in high activity in an area of the frontal lobe that encompassed Broca's area and in a portion of the temporal lobe somewhat behind Wernicke's area.

Notice that these results are not completely consistent with the theories about Broca's and Wernicke's areas developed from the brain-damage studies. Those theories would predict that Broca's area should be involved in speaking words that have just been seen or heard as well as in speaking words that are mentally generated, and that Wernicke's area, rather than the spot behind it, should be involved in generating words with the appropriate meaning. Neuroimaging studies are leading to new theories that implicate many cortical regions, not just Broca's and Wernicke's areas, in language comprehension and production (Caplan & Gould, 2013; Grodzinsky & Friederici, 2006).

SECTION REVIEW

The right and left hemispheres are specialized for different higher functions.

Split-Brain Studies

■ Split-brain patients enable researchers to study the functioning of each hemisphere independent of the other.

■ Results indicate that only the left hemisphere produces language in most people, while the right hemisphere is superior in visuospatial tasks.

■ Split-brain studies also suggest that the verbal left hemisphere interprets a person's own behavior, making "sense" of it even when the two hemispheres produce contradictory actions.

Language and the Left Hemisphere

■ Much of the left hemisphere is devoted to language use.

■ Aphasia is any language deficit due to brain damage. Deficits observed in Broca's and Wernicke's aphasia are used to infer functions of the corresponding brain areas.

■ Results of neuroimaging studies are only partly consistent with aphasia research and have led to more extensive mapping of language areas in the brain.

Changes in the Brain Over Time

People sometimes speak of the "wiring" of the nervous system, or even of its "hardwiring." This metaphor is useful for some purposes, but it has its limits. The nervous system is not hardwired like a computer or other human-made devices. Neurons are soft, pliable living cells. They can change their sizes, shapes, excitabilities, and patterns of connections in ways that help adapt their possessors to life's ever-changing circumstances. Every day you grow millions of new synapses and lose millions of others, and at least some of that change depends on the unique experiences you had that day. Furthermore, the brain not only changes during the span of an individual's life; it has also changed over the course of evolution.

If You Use It, It Will Grow

Like muscles, regions of the brain tend to grow when used and to atrophy when not used. Here is some of the evidence for that statement.

Effects of Deprived and Enriched Environments on the Brain

Early evidence that experience can change the structure of the brain arose from experiments, conducted in the 1960s and later, in which rats were housed in either enriched or deprived environments (Greenough & Black, 1992; Rosenzweig et al., 1972). The enriched environments were large cages in which rats lived with others and had many objects to explore. ("Enriched" is a relative term. These environments were enriched compared to the typical barren cages of laboratory rats but not compared to, say, a garbage dump, where wild rats might live.) The deprived environments were small cages in which each rat lived alone and had no objects except food and a water bottle. After weeks in these environments, the brains of the two groups showed many differences. The brains of the enriched group had thicker cerebral cortexes, larger cortical neurons, more acetylcholine (a prominent neurotransmitter in the cortex), more synapses per neuron, and thicker, more fully developed synapses than did those of the deprived group. Correlated with these brain differences were marked increases in learning ability in the enriched-environment animals compared to their deprived-environment counterparts.

The researchers who performed these early experiments assumed that the brain growth they observed must derive solely from modifications of existing neurons and possibly the addition of new glial cells (the nonneural cells in the brain that

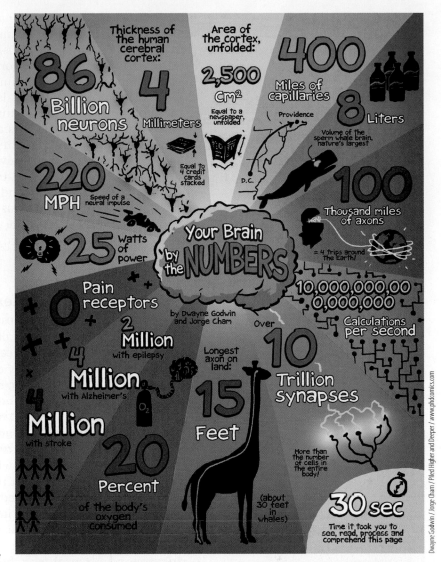

Dwayne Godwin / Jorge Cham / Piled Higher and Deeper / www.phdcomics.com

FOCUS 35

What brain changes have been observed in rats and mice caged in enriched environments?

Carolyn A. McKeone/Science Source

■ **A playground for mice** In mice, as well as in other mammals, experience in an enriched environment enhances growth in the brain.

provide structural and nutritional support to neurons). As we mentioned earlier, it was believed then that the mammalian brain is incapable of producing new neurons after birth. In the late 1990s, however, researchers using new techniques found ample evidence that new neurons are constantly being generated in some parts of the brain, including the adult human brain (Eriksson et al., 1998).

Generation of new neurons is most apparent in the hippocampus, a structure known to be involved in learning and memory. New hippocampal neurons are generated more rapidly in rats and mice housed in enriched environments than in those housed in deprived environments (Brown et al., 2003; Prickaerts et al., 2004). These new neurons develop functional synapses with already-existing neurons in the hippocampus and appear to contribute significantly to the animals' capacities for learning and memory (Ge et al., 2007; Toni et al., 2007). Other research shows that many areas of the brain, not just the hippocampus, generate new neurons in response to brain injury (Ming & Song, 2005). These new neurons may well play a role in the gradual recovery of behavioral functions that can occur after brain injury.

Restructuring of the Cortex During Skill Development

○ **FOCUS 36**

What evidence shows that practice at a skill alters neural connections so that more neurons become devoted to that skill?

As an animal or person develops skill at a task, ever more neurons in the brain are recruited into the performance of that skill. In one of the first clear demonstrations of this phenomenon, Gregg Recanzone and his colleagues (1992) trained monkeys to discriminate between subtly different rates of vibration applied to a particular patch of skin on one finger. The monkeys received banana pellets for making a certain response each time the vibration rate increased even slightly above 20 cycles per second. Other, "untrained" monkeys received the same vibrations to the skin but were not required to discriminate among them for a food reward. Subsequently, the researchers mapped the somatosensory area of the cortex of all the monkeys by touching points on the skin with a thin probe while recording the activity of cortical neurons. They found that in the trained monkeys the area of the cortex that received input from the "trained" spot of skin was, on average, two to three times larger than the equivalent area in untrained monkeys. Apparently, the brain reorganization resulted not from the skin stimulation per se, but rather from the monkeys' use of that stimulation to guide their behavior.

Subsequently, researchers have found comparable brain changes in visual or auditory sensory areas when animals are trained to discriminate among subtly different sights or sounds (Bakin et al., 1996; Zohary et al., 1994). Research using PET and fMRI neuroimaging has shown that effects like these occur for people, too (Pascual-Leone et al., 2005). In one such study with stringed-instrument players (six violinists, two cellists, and a guitarist), unusually large areas of the somatosensory cortex responded to stimulation of the fingers of the left hand—the same fingers that the musicians had used for years in fingering the strings of their instruments (Elbert et al., 1995).

Some of the most dramatic evidence of the brain's ability to restructure itself comes from studies of blind people. In sighted people, the whole occipital lobe of the cortex is used for analyzing visual input. Neuroimaging studies have shown that in blind people the occipital lobe becomes devoted to various other purposes, which help them to compensate for their blindness. For example, regions of the occipital lobe that in sighted people are involved in the visual analysis of three-dimensional space become devoted, in the blind, to the task of identifying the locations from which sounds are coming (Gougoux et al., 2005). In Braille readers, large parts of the occipital cortex become devoted to analyzing tactile input from the fingers in the finely graded way needed to read Braille (Pascual-Leone et al., 2005). Blind people also commonly develop superior verbal memory to compensate for their inability to look up information easily or to find objects by looking. In one fMRI study, blind and sighted people were given lists of nouns to memorize as their brains were scanned (Amedi et al., 2003). The blind subjects showed marked activation of portions of the occipital cortex during this task, which did not occur in the sighted people, and they also showed superior memory. Moreover, those blind subjects who scored best on the memory test showed the most activity in the occipital cortex.

Alvaro Pascual-Leone and his colleagues (2005) found that at least some of these brain changes began to occur in sighted people who had been blindfolded for just 5 days. When the blindfolds were removed, the changes quickly reversed themselves.

Spatial Learning and Growth of the Hippocampus

The hippocampus is involved in many forms of memory, especially memory for spatial locations. Some bird species hide seeds in multiple locations and retrieve them in the winter. As one example, Clark's nutcrackers (native to western North America) bury food in literally thousands of different sites, to which they return during the winter when the food is needed (Gould-Beierle & Kamil, 1999). Various bird species that hide seeds have been found to remember spatial locations better than do species that don't hide seeds and to have an enlargement of an area of the hippocampus (Papini, 2002; Shettleworth & Westwood, 2002).

Researchers working with one of these species, the mountain chickadee, have shown that hippocampal enlargement depends at least partly on experience (Clayton, 2001). When caged chickadees are allowed to hide and retrieve seeds, their hippocampi grow, and when they are then prevented from hiding and retrieving seeds for a period of time, their hippocampi shrink again.

Research suggests that extensive spatial learning can increase hippocampal size in humans, too. Taxi drivers in big cities develop remarkable spatial abilities, and this is especially true of London cabbies, who, to get a license, must go through prolonged training and pass a test of their ability to find the shortest route between any two locations in that large city. Brain scans revealed that the

ZUMA Press Inc / Alamy

■ **Restructuring the cerebral cortex** Whenever people learn new skills, regardless of age, neurons in the cerebral cortex form new long-lasting connections, so that more neurons are recruited into performance of the skill.

 FOCUS 37

What evidence, with birds and with humans, indicates that spatial learning can result in growth in the hippocampus?

Michael Dunning/Getty Images

■ London is not an easy place for which to form a mental map. Experienced London taxi drivers had highly developed posterior hippocampus, associated with spatial memory.

posterior (rear) part of the hippocampus (the part most involved in spatial memory) is significantly larger in London cab drivers than in otherwise similar people who do not drive taxis (Maguire et al., 2000). They also revealed a significant positive correlation between years of cab-driving experience and growth in the hippocampus: In general, the longer a person had been driving a cab, the larger was the posterior hippocampus.

Strengthening of Synapses as a Foundation for Learning

Learning undoubtedly involves many types of changes in the brain. But at the cellular level the type of change that has been most clearly linked to learning is the strengthening of synaptic connections between already existing neurons.

The Hebbian Synapse: Neurons That Fire Together Wire Together

FOCUS 38

How has the discovery of long-term potentiation tended to confirm Hebb's theory about synaptic strengthening?

In the 1940s, the Canadian psychologist Donald Hebb (1949) theorized that some synapses in the brain have the property of growing stronger (more effective) whenever the postsynaptic neuron fires immediately after the presynaptic neuron fires (see **Figure 4.33**). Through this means, Hebb suggested, neurons could acquire the capacity to respond to input that they previously didn't respond to. This could provide a basis for classical conditioning and other forms of learning. In the 1970s, Timothy Bliss and Terje Lømo (1973) discovered a phenomenon called ***long-term potentiation***, or ***LTP***, which strongly supports Hebb's theory.

In the laboratory, LTP is produced by artificially stimulating, with a burst of electrical pulses, a bundle of neurons entering a particular region of an animal's brain. This results in the strengthening of the synapses that those neurons form with postsynaptic neurons so that subsequent weak stimulation of the same bundle elicits a stronger response in the postsynaptic neurons than it would have before. This potentiation (strengthening) is *long term*: It lasts for hours or even months, depending on the conditions. Subsequent research has shown that, at least in some brain areas, LTP works in the following manner.

Figure 4.33 depicts a weak synapse between neuron A and neuron C. When neuron A becomes active, some of the neurotransmitter molecules it releases become bound to conventional, fast-acting receptors on the postsynaptic membrane, where they produce a depolarization that is too slight to play a significant role in triggering action potentials. Other transmitter molecules at the same synapse, however, become bound temporarily to special LTP-inducing receptors on the postsynaptic membrane. If neuron C then fires an action potential (due to input from other neurons, such as B in Figure 4.33), the combination of that firing and the presence of transmitter molecules in the LTP-inducing receptors triggers a series of biochemical events that strengthen the synapse (Byrne, 2008). The presynaptic terminal becomes larger, able to release more transmitter substance than it could before, and the postsynaptic membrane develops more conventional receptor sites than it had before.

As a result of such changes, firing in neuron A produces more depolarization in neuron C than it did before and therefore plays a greater role in triggering action potentials in that cell than it did before. Sets of neurons that behave like this have been found in many parts of the mammalian brain, including various areas of the cerebral cortex, the hippocampus, the cerebellum, and the amygdala—all of which are known to be involved in various kinds of learning (Byrne, 2008).

FIGURE 4.33 A Hebbian synapse The synapse between neuron A and neuron C is initially weak, so A is ineffective in stimulating C. However, if C fires (because of the firing of neuron B) immediately after neurotransmitter molecules have been released from A onto C, the synapse between A and C will grow stronger. If this happens a sufficient number of times, the synapse may become sufficiently strong that A will be able to trigger action in C even when B is inactive. This type of synapse is called *Hebbian* because its existence was first postulated by Donald Hebb. Recent research into the phenomenon of long-term potentiation confirms the existence of such synapses.

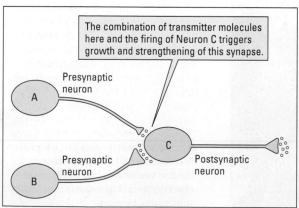

The combination of transmitter molecules here and the firing of Neuron C triggers growth and strengthening of this synapse.

Presynaptic neuron

A

Presynaptic neuron

B

C

Postsynaptic neuron

Evidence That Long-Term Potentiation Is a Basis for Learning

Evidence that LTP is actually involved in learning comes from many experiments showing that disturbing the brain's normal capacity for such potentiation interferes with the animal's ability to learn (Byrne, 2008). In one experiment with mice, a drug that prevents LTP was injected into a portion of the amygdala that is known to be crucial for fear learning. After this treatment, the researchers tried to train the mice to fear a tone that was paired with an electric shock. The LTP-inhibited mice failed to learn such fear. They responded to the shock as did normal mice, but, unlike normal mice, they did not subsequently show fear responses to the tone (Maren, 1999).

Given such evidence that LTP is essential for learning, what would happen if the capacity for LTP were increased above the normal level? Joe Tsien and his colleagues (2000) found a way to answer that question. The postsynaptic receptors that are involved in initiating LTP come in two forms—a strong form, which is highly effective in triggering LTP, and a weak, less effective form. Through genetic engineering, Tsien and his colleagues produced a strain of mice—which they named "Doogie," after the boy genius of the 1990s television show *Doogie Howser, M.D.*—that had many more of the strong receptors and fewer of the weak ones than do normal mice. As predicted, brain neurons in the Doogie mice showed more LTP in response to electrical stimulation than did those in the normal, unaltered mice. Remarkably, but just as predicted, the Doogie mice also showed better memory than the unaltered mice in a series of three widely different tests: maze learning, classical conditioning of a fear response, and object recognition (see **Figure 4.34**). In each case, the altered mice behaved similarly to the unaltered mice during the learning experience but showed significantly better memory when tested a day or more later (Tsien, 2000). More recently, Tsien and his colleagues showed that such genetic modification can also prevent the decline in memory that normally occurs in aged mice (Cao et al., 2007).

The results of these experiments raise many questions that have not yet been fully answered. Will similar results be found with other animals and other forms of learning? Could memory in people be improved through methods that increase LTP? If a simple genetic change can improve memory by increasing LTP, then why hasn't evolution already produced that change through natural selection? Perhaps LTP beyond a certain level, or even memory beyond a certain level, is maladaptive in the conditions of everyday life.

FOCUS 39

What evidence shows that long-term potentiation is involved in learning?

FIGURE 4.34 A genetically altered "smart" mouse being tested for object recognition Mice, like other mammals, explore new objects more than familiar ones. In this test, each mouse was exposed to two objects: one that it had explored in a previous 5-minute session and one that was new. Mice that were genetically altered to produce enhanced LTP explored the new object (in this case, the one on the right) more than the old one even when several days had elapsed since the initial session. In contrast, unaltered mice explored the new object more than the old one only when a shorter period of time had elapsed. These results indicate that the altered mice remembered the original object for a longer period of time than did the unaltered mice.

Bill Ballenberg/Getty Images

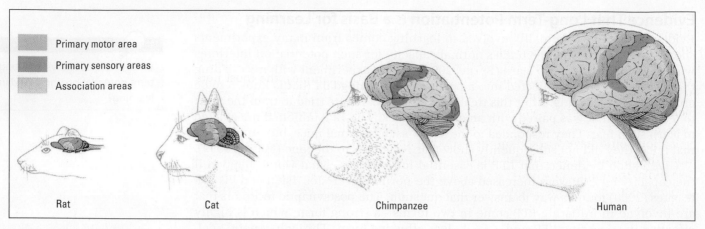

Primary motor area
Primary sensory areas
Association areas

Rat   Cat   Chimpanzee   Human

FIGURE 4.35 Comparison of the brains of four mammals All the brains contain the same structures, but in the chimpanzee and human, proportionately much more cortical space is devoted to association areas than in the rat and cat.
(Information from Rose, 1973.)

 FOCUS 40

What area of the brain shows the most substantial change in humans relative to other mammals?

The Evolution of the Human Brain

As we've just seen, brains change over the course of an individual's development and in response to learning. However, the brain has also changed over longer stretches of time. Here, we briefly discuss the *evolution* of the human brain, particularly how the brain changed over the last 5 to 7 million years, since we last shared a common ancestor with modern chimpanzees and bonobos.

Although most of our discussion to this point has been about human brains, brain organization is very similar in all mammals. What has changed appreciably over evolutionary time is the amount of volume dedicated to the associative areas of the brain relative to the sensory and motor areas. **Figure 4.35** shows that the amount of association cortex, relative to the other two categories, increases dramatically as one goes from simpler mammals, such as the rat and the cat, to more complex ones, such as the chimpanzee and the human.

In fact, the most prominent feature of the human brain is its size. In comparison to other mammals, the human brain is much larger than expected in proportion to human body size. Primates in general have large brains relative to their body size, but humans' brains are especially large. Harry Jerison (1973, 2002) developed a formula for evaluating the expected ratio between brain weight and body weight for animals called the **encephalization** (en-sěf´-ə-lə-**zā**´-shən) **quotient**, or **EQ**. Animals with brains that are the expected weight given their body weight have an EQ of 1.0. Animals with smaller brains than expected for their body weight have an EQ of less than 1.0, and animals with larger brains than expected for their body weight have an EQ of greater than 1.0. Using this measure, humans have an EQ of about 7.6, more than triple that of chimpanzees at 2.3 (Jerison, 1973, 2002; Rilling & Insel, 1999). This change in relative brain size has apparently occurred gradually since humans and chimpanzees last shared a common ancestor. Using fossil evidence, EQs can be derived for human ancestors, and these are provided for three such species (*Australopithecus afarensis*, *Homo habilis*, and *Homo erectus*), along with modern chimpanzees and humans, in **Table 4.3**. As you can see, the EQ for *Australopithecus*

TABLE 4.3 Estimated encephalization quotients (EQ) for chimpanzees (*Pan troglodytes*) and four hominid species

Species	Time	EQ
Pan troglodytes (chimpanzees)	Modern	2.3
Australopithecus afarensis	3.5 mya	3.1
Homo habilis	2.0 mya	4.0
Homo erectus	0.5 mya	5.5
Homo sapiens	Modern	7.6
Note: mya = millions of years ago		

afarensis, an early small-brained species that lived 3 to 4 million years ago, was only slightly greater than that of chimpanzees. From this point on, brain weight relative to body weight increased at a rapid rate.

Although humans are physically different from chimpanzees and other apes in many ways (their digestive tracts are quite different, for example), the most notable difference is in their brains. This is because brains are the eventual source for behavior and cognition—where chimpanzees and humans truly diverge. Chimpanzees and humans have enough in common to give us a glimpse of how natural selection could have worked on the thinking and behavior of ancient apes to produce the human mind. But although contemporary chimpanzees and humans both use tools, transmit information across generations, and form social coalitions, the gap between the two species in executing these skills is enormous. And the primary organ responsible for this gap is the brain.

SECTION REVIEW

The brain physically changes in response to experience.

Growth and Reorganization

- Rats in enriched environments develop thicker cortexes with larger neurons and more and stronger synaptic interconnections. They also generate new neurons at a faster rate.

- Skill learning causes larger portions of the brain to become involved in performing that particular skill.

- The hippocampus, an area critical to spatial memory, grows as a result of spatial learning (as demonstrated in London taxi drivers).

Long-Term Potentiation (LTP)

- LTP strengthens synaptic connections in ways that mediate learning.

- In line with Hebb's theory, the coordinated firing of a presynaptic and postsynaptic neuron strengthens the synaptic connections of the first onto the second.

- LTP involves enlargement of axon terminals and generation of new receptor sites on postsynaptic membranes.

Human brains are substantially larger than expected for their body weight, more so than any other species.

- This difference is greatest in the association ("thinking") cortex.

- Gradual changes in relative brain size can be seen in the line that led to modern humans.

Thinking Critically About Neural Control of Behavior

1. If our goal is to understand typical human behavior, what are the benefits and limitations of studying people with brain damage?

2. Does neuroscience contribute to a better understanding of human psychology? Or should neuroscience and psychology be treated as separate disciplines, each examining a distinct and important phenomenon (the brain and mind, respectively)?

Reflections and Connections

Hippocrates was right: The brain is the organ of the mind. The mind is a set of processes (feeling, thinking, initiating action, etc.) carried out by physical activities in the brain. The brain does not work in isolation from the rest of the body or the environment—it needs input from sensory nerves, is affected by chemicals carried in the blood, and acts through motor nerves and (to a lesser degree) hormones. Yet the brain is the center of all that we call the mind, for it contains the mechanisms needed to analyze all inputs and organize all outputs.

In reviewing this chapter, so full of terms and details, keep the following broad points in mind:

1. The value of a functionalist perspective As you review the structures described in this chapter—ranging from the little ones, such as *synaptic vesicles* and *dendrites,* to the big ones, such as the *cerebellum* and *autonomic nervous system*—ask yourself, for each: What is it for? What did it evolve to do? That is, what role does it play in the workings of the larger machine that is the human being? How is it related to other parts of the machine, and how can variations in it affect human behavior? The structures are much easier to remember, and certainly more interesting, if you think of their roles in a larger system.

2. Brain science relates to the rest of psychology As researchers discover more about the brain, knowledge about it becomes relevant to broader areas of psychology. In later chapters, you will read about the brain in relation to psychology's understanding of basic processes of motivation, sensation, memory, and thought. You will also read of brain-based theories of mental disorders and of drugs that are believed to alleviate specific mental disorders through their interactions with neurotransmitters. Knowledge of the brain and how it relates to thought, emotion, and action will be relevant to almost any aspect of human behavior you choose to study, from art, music, and intimate relationships to philosophy, politics, and religion.

Key Terms

action potentials   105
amygdala   125
androgen   133
aphasia   138
association areas   126
autonomic portion of the peripheral motor system   120
axon   104
axon terminal   104
basal ganglia   124
brainstem   123
Broca's aphasia   138
cell body   104
cell membrane   105
central nervous system   102
cerebellum   124
cerebral cortex   111
corpus callosum   134

cranial nerves   119
dendrites   104
electroencephalogram (EEG)   115
encephalization quotient (EQ)   146
excitatory synapse   109
frontal lobes   126
functional magnetic resonance imaging (fMRI)   116
hippocampus   125
hormones   131
hypothalamus   125
inhibitory synapse   109
interneurons   103
limbic system   125
long-term potentiation (LTP)   144
medulla   123
midbrain   123

mirror neurons   111
motor neurons   103
myelin sheath   104
nerve   102
neurogenesis   110
neurons   102
neuroscience   101
neurotransmitter   108
nucleus   104
occipital lobes   126
parasympathetic division of the autonomic motor system   121
parietal lobes   126
pattern generators   122
peripheral nervous system   102
pons   123
positron emission tomography (PET)   116
prefrontal cortex   128

premotor areas   128
primary motor area   126
primary sensory areas   126
resting potential   106
selective cell death (or apoptosis)   111
sensory neurons   103
somatic portion of the peripheral motor system   120
somatosensation   120
spinal nerves   119
sympathetic division of the autonomic motor system   121
synapse   108
temporal lobes   126
thalamus   124
transcranial magnetic stimulation (TMS)   115
Wernicke's aphasia   139

Find Out More

Norman Doidge (2007). *The brain that changes itself: Stories of personal triumph from the frontiers of brain science.* New York, NY: Viking.

Norman Doidge, a research psychiatrist and psychoanalyst, has written an enthusiastic and engaging book about the brain's ability to regenerate and change. He describes case histories of brain-damaged patients who made remarkable recoveries and the science behind those recoveries. He also introduces us to scientists who have pioneered the study of the brain's regenerative

possibilities—people such as Alvaro Pascual-Leone, whose work is mentioned in this chapter.

Michael S. Gazzaniga (2018). *The consciousness instinct: Unraveling the mystery of how the brain makes the mind.* New York, NY: Farrar, Straus and Giroux.

Pioneering neuroscientist Michael Gazzaniga tackles one of the most persistent and difficult issues of philosophy and psychology—consciousness. As brain science addresses the problem of how awareness can emanate from bundles

of neurons, questions of artificial intelligence and what it means to be human overturn the old model of the brain as a machine.

Michael Shermer (2012). *The believing brain: From ghosts and gods to politics and conspiracies—how we construct beliefs and reinforce them as truths.* New York, NY: St. Martin's.

Psychologist and science historian Michael Shermer takes a new look at how beliefs and evidence are synthesized in the brain. The brain is, Shermer argues, designed to seek out and identify patterns and pieces of information that support already-held beliefs. Through a series of anecdotal examples, he makes the case for why the brain first believes and then constructs explanations.

Sandrine Thuret (2015, June). *You can grow new brain cells. Here's how.* London: TED@BCG 2015.

https://www.ted.com/talks/sandrine_ thuret_you_can_grow_new_brain_cells_ here_s_how

Can the adult brain generate new nerve cells? In this 11-minute TED talk, neuroscientist Sandrine Thuret examines the birth of new neurons—neurogenesis—in the hippocampus and explains how this process relates to memory and mood. She describes research in both mice and humans on factors associated with hippocampal neurogenesis, including diet and exercise.

LaunchPad
macmillan learning

Visit LaunchPad for Psychology 8e launchpadworks.com to access the e-book, videos, activities, additional resources, and LearningCurve quizzes, as well as study aids including flash cards and web quizzes.

Mechanisms of Motivation and Emotion

LEARNING OUTCOMES

After studying this chapter, you should be able to:

- Explain the general principles of motivation.
- Identify and describe the brain's reward mechanisms.
- Explain why hunger is a regulatory drive.
- Summarize what we know about the sleep drive.
- Explain how psychological scientists study emotions.

The kaleidoscope that makes a day or a year of mental life has both fast- and slow-moving components. Sensations, perceptions, thoughts, and muscle movements flit through our consciousness and behavior at speeds measured in milliseconds. But slower changes, measurable in minutes or hours, modulate and help to direct these rapid changes. These slower-changing components of the mind are called *behavioral states;* they include variations in motivation, emotion, and level of arousal.

Are you hungry right now, or angry, or sleepy? As you study this chapter, your mental state affects your capacity to pay attention, and it may direct your attention to some things over others. If you are hungry, thoughts of food may capture most of your attention. If you are sleepy, your reaction even to the most interesting ideas in the chapter might be "oh hmmmm . . . zzzzzz." Clearly, your mental state affects your momentary thoughts and actions. But what affects your mental state? What exactly makes you hungry, sleepy, happy, or angry? These questions link psychology to the study of the brain and its interactions with the body's internal environment as well as the external environment.

This chapter is about the physiological underpinnings of motivation and emotion. It first describes the general concept of motivation from a physiological perspective, then reward mechanisms in the brain, and then hunger, sleep, dreams, and emotionality—in that order. Social and cultural influences on motivation and emotion, which are only touched on here, are discussed more fully in later chapters.

General Principles of Motivation

To *motivate,* in the most general sense of the term, is to set in motion. In psychology, the term **motivation** is often used to refer to the entire constellation of factors, some inside the organism and some outside, that cause an individual to behave in a particular way at a particular time. Defined this way, motivation is a very broad concept—almost as broad as all of psychology. Every chapter in this book deals with motivation in one way or another. Genes, learning, physiological variables, perceptual and thought processes, developmental variables, social experiences, and personality characteristics all have a role in motivation.

A more precise label for the topic at hand is **motivational state**, or **drive**. These terms are used interchangeably to denote an internal condition that orients an individual toward a specific category of goals and that can change over time in a

Vesnaandjic/Getty Images

reversible way (the drive can increase and then decrease). Different drives direct a person toward different goals. Hunger orients one toward food, sex toward sexual gratification, curiosity toward novel stimuli, and so on.

Drives in psychology are considered hypothetical constructs because they can't be directly observed. Instead, the psychologist infers the existence of a state—the state of hunger, thirst, and so on—from the animal's behavior. An animal is said to be hungry if it behaves in ways that bring it closer to food, to be sexually motivated if it behaves in ways that bring it into contact with a sexual partner, and to be curious if it seeks out and explores new environments. The drive varies over time: The animal will work harder, or accept more discomfort, to attain the goal at some times than at others. We infer that something inside the animal changes, causing it to behave differently at different times in the same environment.

FOCUS 1

How do drives and incentives (a) complement one another and (b) influence one another in their contributions to motivation?

But the inside interacts constantly with the outside. Motivated behavior is directed toward *incentives,* the sought-after objects or ends that exist in the external environment. Incentives are also called *reinforcers, rewards,* or *goals.* The motivational state that leads you to stand in line at the cafeteria is presumably hunger, but the incentive for doing so is the sandwich you intend to purchase. Drives and incentives complement one another in the control of behavior; if one is weak, the other must be strong to motivate the goal-directed action. Thus, if you know that the cafeteria's sandwiches taste like cardboard (weak incentive), you are likely to wait in line for a sandwich only if your hunger drive is strong; but if the cafeteria serves really great sandwiches (strong incentive), you are likely to wait even if your hunger drive is weak.

Drives and incentives not only complement each other but also influence each other's strength. A strong drive can enhance the attractiveness (incentive value) of a particular object: If you are very hungry, even a sandwich that tastes like cardboard might seem quite attractive. Conversely, a strong incentive can strengthen a drive: The savory aroma of food might increase your hunger drive as you wait in line, and this in turn might induce you to eat something that previously wouldn't have interested you if, by the time you get to the buffet table, your favorite sandwiches are gone.

Varieties of Drives

In general, drives motivate us toward goals that promote our survival and reproduction. Some drives promote survival by helping us maintain the internal bodily conditions that are essential for life.

Drives That Help Preserve Homeostasis

FOCUS 2

How is the concept of homeostasis related to that of drive? How is this relationship demonstrated in the case of a little boy who craved salt?

In a now classic book titled *The Wisdom of the Body* (1932/1963), the physiologist Walter B. Cannon described the requirements of the tissues of the human body. For life to be sustained, certain substances and characteristics within the body must be kept within a restricted range, going neither above nor below certain levels. These include body temperature, oxygen, minerals, water, and energy-producing food molecules. Physiological processes, such as digestion and respiration, must continually work toward achieving what Cannon termed ***homeostasis*** [ho'-me-o-sta'-sis], the constancy of internal conditions that the body must actively maintain. Cannon pointed out that maintaining homeostasis involves the organism's outward behavior as well as its internal processes. To stay alive, individuals must find and consume foods, salt, and water and must maintain their body temperature through such means as finding shelter. Cannon theorized that the basic physiological underpinning for some drives is a loss of homeostasis, which acts on the nervous system to induce behavior designed to correct the imbalance.

Following Cannon, psychologists and physiologists performed experiments showing that animals indeed do behave in accordance with the needs of their bodily tissues (Woods & Stricker, 2012). For example, if the caloric (energy) content of its food is increased or decreased, an animal will compensate by eating less or more of it, keeping the daily intake of calories relatively constant. As another example, removal of the adrenal glands causes an animal to lose too much salt in its urine (because one of the adrenal hormones is essential for conserving salt). This loss of salt dramatically increases the animal's drive to seek out and eat extra salt, which keeps the animal alive as long as salt is available (Stricker, 1973; Stricker & Verbalis, 2012).

The force of homeostasis in human behavior was dramatically and poignantly illustrated by the clinical case of a boy, referred to as D. W., who when 1 year old developed a great craving for salt (Wilkins & Richter, 1940). His favorite foods were salted crackers, pretzels, potato chips, olives, and pickles; he would also take salt directly from the shaker. When salt was denied him, he would cry until his parents gave in, and when he learned to speak, *salt* was one of his first and favorite words. D. W. survived until the age of 3 1/2, when he was hospitalized for other symptoms and placed on a standard hospital diet. The hospital staff would not yield to his demands for salt, and he died within a few days. An autopsy revealed that his adrenal glands were deficient; only then did D. W.'s doctors realize that his salt craving came from physiological need. His strong drive for salt and his ability to manipulate his parents into supplying it, even though they were unaware that he needed it, had kept D. W. alive for more than 2 years after the onset of the adrenal deficiency—powerful evidence for "the wisdom of the body."

Limitations of Homeostasis: Regulatory and Nonregulatory Drives Homeostasis is a useful concept for understanding hunger, thirst, and the drives for salt, oxygen, and an appropriate body temperature, but not for understanding many other drives. Consider sex, for example. People are highly motivated to engage in sex, and sex serves an obvious evolutionary function, but there is no tissue need for it. No vital bodily substance is affected by engaging in sexual behavior; nobody can die from lack of sex (despite what an admirer may have told you). Psychologists therefore find it useful to distinguish between two general classes of drives—regulatory and nonregulatory. A *regulatory drive* is one, like hunger, that helps preserve homeostasis, and a *nonregulatory drive* is one, like sex, that serves some other purpose. We discussed briefly hormonal influences on sex drive in Chapter 4 and will discuss other aspects of sexuality in later chapters, notably Chapters 6, 8, 12, 14, and 15.

> **FOCUS 3**
>
> What is the distinction between regulatory and nonregulatory drives, and how can mammalian drives be classified into five categories based on function?

A Functional Classification of Mammalian Drives

One way to think about the whole set of drives that we share with other mammals is to categorize them in accordance with their evolutionary functions—their roles in promoting survival and reproduction. From an evolutionary perspective, it is useful to distinguish among the following five categories of mammalian drives:

1. *Regulatory drives.* As already noted, these are drives that promote survival by helping to maintain the body's homeostasis. Hunger and thirst are prime examples.

2. *Safety drives.* These are drives that motivate an animal to avoid, escape, or fend off dangers such as precipices, predators, or enemies. The most obvious safety drive is fear, which motivates individuals to flee from danger. Another is anger, which is manifested when fighting (or threatening to fight) rather than flight is needed to ensure one's safety. We will argue later in this chapter that sleep is also a safety drive. It evolved at least partly as a means of keeping animals tucked quietly away during that part of each 24-hour day when they would be most in danger if they were moving about.

3. *Reproductive drives.* The most obvious of these are the sexual drive and the drive to care for young once they are born. When they are at a peak, these drives can be extraordinarily powerful. Animals (including people) will risk their lives to mate and to protect their offspring. As discussed in Chapter 3, sexual jealousy, including the anger associated with it, also serves the function of reproduction to the degree that it promotes the fidelity of one's sexual partner.

4. *Social drives.* Many mammals, and especially humans, require the cooperation of others to survive. The social drives include the drives for friendship and for acceptance and approval by the social groups of which one is a part. In humans, these drives can be as powerful as the regulatory, safety, and reproductive drives. People will risk their lives for friendship and for social approval.

5. *Educative drives.* These consist primarily of the drives to play and to explore (curiosity). As we will discuss in Chapter 8, the young of nearly all social mammals practice life-sustaining skills through play, and mammals of all ages acquire useful information about their environment by exploring novel objects and territories. When other drives are not too pressing, the drives for play and exploration come to the fore.

Human Drives That Seem Not to Promote Survival or Reproduction

Not all of human motivation is easily understood in terms of survival and reproduction. For instance, humans everywhere like to produce and experience art, music, and literature (including oral stories and poetry). What motivates these activities? Have we evolved special aesthetic drives? If so, what adaptive functions prompted the natural selection of such drives?

At present, these questions are much debated, and there is no firm answer. Our own view is that the pursuits of art, music, and literature are natural extensions of our drives for play and exploration. These pursuits can exercise perceptual and motor skills, imagination, and creative thinking in ways that may be useful in future real-life situations and can also provide us with ideas for governing our own lives. Like other playful and exploratory activities, these pursuits help our minds to grow during periods when there are no more pressing survival needs that must be fulfilled. Developing skills in art, music, and storytelling may also enhance one's status in a social group and impress members of the opposite sex, which would have had survival value for our ancestors.

A somewhat different (but not incompatible) view, presented by Steven Pinker (1997), is that art, music, and literature appeal to us not because we have special drives for them but because they tap into many of our already existing drives and proclivities, which evolved for other purposes. For example, in describing the appeal of fiction, Pinker (1997) writes: "When we are absorbed in a book or movie, we get to see breathtaking landscapes, hobnob with important people, fall in love with ravishing men and women, protect loved ones, attain impossible goals, and defeat wicked enemies" (p. 539). In this example, a book or movie appeals to our drives for sex, love, social esteem, parenting, achievement, and aggression. To suggest that art, music, and literature may be vicarious means of satisfying other drives rather than drives in and of themselves is not to diminish them. These pursuits enrich our lives immensely; they extend us beyond evolution's narrow dictates of mere survival and reproduction.

Of course, some things that people become motivated for are truly harmful. Drug addictions and compulsive gambling are artificial drives, created by human inventions, which can ruin people's lives. Later in this chapter we will examine how these motivations tap artificially into our natural drive mechanisms.

FOCUS 4

What are two possible explanations of the universal human drives for art, music, and literature?

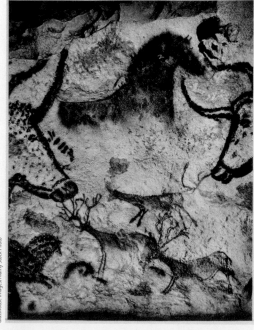

■ **Early art** Did whoever produced this painting—about 18,000 years ago in one of the Lascaux Caves, in France—have a concept of art or a word for it? We have no idea. To the modern eye, however, this is a work of art. It may represent a universal human proclivity.

Glasshouse Images/Alamy Stock Photo

Drives as States of the Brain

We said that drives are normally considered to be hypothetical entities, inferred from observed behavior. Yet, essentially all psychologists would agree that drives are products of physical processes within the body, particularly within the brain. In theory, at least, every drive we experience corresponds with some state of the brain.

According to the ***central-state theory of drives***, which guides much of the discussion in this chapter, different drives correspond to neural activity in different sets of neurons in the brain. A set of neurons in which activity constitutes a drive is called a ***central drive system***. Although the central drive systems for different drives must vary from one another, they may have overlapping components. For example, because hunger and sex are different drives, the neural circuits for them cannot be identical. If they were, hunger and sex would always occur in tandem; the drives would always rise and fall together. But their respective circuits may share components that produce behavioral effects common to both drives, such as increased alertness.

For a set of neurons to serve as a central drive system, first, it must receive and integrate the various signals that can raise or lower the drive state. For hunger, these signals include chemicals in the blood, the presence or absence of food in the stomach, and the sight and smell of food in the environment. Second, a central drive system must act on all the neural processes that would be involved in carrying out the motivated behavior. It must direct perceptual mechanisms toward stimuli related to the goal, cognitive mechanisms toward working out strategies to achieve the goal, and motor mechanisms toward producing the appropriate movements. Refer back to Figure 4.22 (p. 129), which depicts a hierarchical model of the control of action, with mechanisms involved in motivation and planning at the top. The central drive systems are part of that top level of the hierarchy. To affect behavior (e.g., to cause a hungry person to cross a room for some fresh cherries), they must influence the activity of motor systems at lower levels of the hierarchy.

Researchers have sound reasons to believe that the hypothalamus is the hub of many central drive systems (Card & Swanson, 2013). Anatomically, this brain structure is ideally located to play such a role (see **Figure 5.1**). It is centered at the base of the brain, just above the brainstem, and is strongly interconnected with higher areas of the brain. It also has direct connections to nerves that carry input from, and autonomic motor output to, the body's internal organs. It has many capillaries and is more sensitive to hormones and other substances carried by the blood than are other brain areas. Finally, through its connections to the pituitary gland, it controls the release of many hormones (as described in Chapter 4). Thus, the hypothalamus has all the inputs and outputs that central drive systems would be expected to have. And, as you will see later in the chapter, small disruptions in particular parts of the hypothalamus can have dramatic effects on an animal's drives.

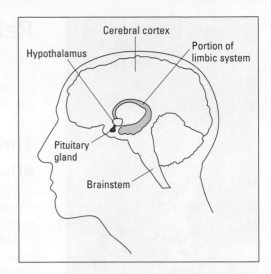

FIGURE 5.1 Location of the hypothalamus The hypothalamus is ideally situated to serve as a hub for central drive systems. It has strong connections to the brainstem below, the limbic system and cerebral cortex above, and the endocrine system (by way of its tie to the pituitary gland).

 FOCUS 5

In theory, what characteristics must a set of neurons have to function as a central drive system? What characteristics of the hypothalamus seem to suit it to be a hub of such a system?

SECTION REVIEW

Drives are reversible internal conditions that orient individuals toward specific types of goals.

Varieties of Drives

- Regulatory drives (such as hunger) promote homeostasis, whereas nonregulatory drives (such as sex) serve other purposes.

- Mammalian drives can be classified by function into regulatory, safety, reproductive, social, and educative categories.

- Humans also exhibit aesthetic drives; the evolutionary functions of these are debated.

Drives as States of the Brain

- According to the central-state theory of drives, different drives correspond to neural activity in different but overlapping central drive systems in the brain.

- The hypothalamus is ideally located to be a hub of central drive systems.

© Image Source/Alamy

FIGURE 5.2 Liking Many species of mammals show a similar facial reaction to tasty foods. The reaction includes a tongue protrusion, which looks as if the individual were lapping up the last bits of the food. This expression has been used as an objective index of "liking" in research involving food rewards in laboratory rats (Berridge & Robinson, 2003).

FOCUS 6

What are three interrelated components of the concept of reward?

From: J. Olds, "Pleasure centers in the brain," Scientific American, October 1956, page 112

FIGURE 5.3 Lever pressing for electrical stimulation to the brain Each time this rat presses the lever, it receives a brief pulse of electrical current through an electrode implanted in its brain. Some of Olds's rats continued to press the lever for 24 hours without rest, as often as 5,000 times per hour (Olds, 1956).

FOCUS 7

How did Olds and Milner identify reward pathways in the brain?

Reward Mechanisms of the Brain

As noted in the previous section, motivated behavior involves the pursuit of *rewards* (also known as incentives, goals, or reinforcers). Let's look more closely at the concept of reward and at research into how rewards act on the brain to promote and reinforce the behaviors that led to them.

Three Components of Reward: Liking, Wanting, and Reinforcement

In psychology, the term *reward* has three interrelated, but in some ways separable, meanings. A reward is something that we *like,* something that we *want,* and something that serves as a *reinforcer* in learning (Berridge & Kringelbach, 2008).

Liking refers to the subjective feeling of pleasure, or satisfaction, that occurs when one receives a reward. We know this feeling from our own experience. We experience pleasure from good food when we are hungry, from water when we are thirsty, from drifting off to sleep when we are tired, and from sexual activity when we are sexually motivated. We also experience pleasure from pay, praise, the company of good friends, play, music, discoveries made through exploration, and our own assessment of a job well done. Most of the things we seek in life bring us pleasure when we obtain them. We cannot know for sure whether other mammals also experience pleasure from the rewards they receive, but their behavior suggests that they do (see **Figure 5.2**).

Wanting refers to the desire to obtain a reward. This is the component of reward that links most clearly to the concept of motivation. To want something is to be motivated to get it. Whereas pleasure occurs when a reward is received, wanting occurs before it is received. Wanting is typically measured by assessing the amount of effort an individual will exert, or the amount of pain the individual will bear, in order to obtain the reward. Usually objects that are wanted are also liked, but it is possible to separate the two.

Reinforcement refers to the effects that rewards have in promoting learning. As discussed in Chapter 8 (in the section on operant conditioning), animals and people learn to attend to stimuli that signal the availability of rewards, and they learn to make responses that bring rewards in the presence of those stimuli. Through its effects on the brain, a reward helps to stamp in, or *reinforce,* the memory of stimuli and actions that occurred just before the reward was received. Such learning helps the individual to become more effective in finding and procuring the same type of reward in the future.

Studies of the brain have provided some clues to the mechanisms of each of these three components of reward.

Identification of Reward Neurons in the Brain

The study of brain mechanisms of reward was initiated in the 1950s, when James Olds and Peter Milner made a remarkable discovery. These researchers observed, by accident at first, that when rats received electrical stimulation through thin wires implanted in certain brain areas, they behaved as if they were trying to get more of that stimulation. For example, if a rat happened to receive the stimulation while exploring a particular corner of the cage, the animal would return repeatedly to that corner. To see if such brain stimulation would serve as a reinforcer for learning, Olds and Milner tested rats in an apparatus in which they could electrically stimulate their own brains by pressing a lever (see **Figure 5.3**). With electrodes placed in certain brain areas, rats learned very quickly to press the lever and continued to press at high rates, sometimes for many hours without stopping (Olds & Milner, 1954).

Subsequent research showed that rats and other animals will work hardest and longest to stimulate a tract in the brain called the ***medial forebrain bundle***. The neurons of this tract that are most crucial for this rewarding effect have their cell bodies in nuclei in the midbrain and synaptic terminals in a large nucleus in the basal ganglia called the **nucleus accumbens** (see **Figure 5.4**). The nucleus accumbens itself has connections to large areas of the limbic system and the cerebral cortex, and it is now understood to be a crucial center for the behavioral effects of rewards, in humans as well as in other mammals.

When Olds and Milner inserted electrodes into the medial forebrain bundle, they were tapping artificially, but very effectively, into the brain's natural reward system. Subsequent research, involving the recording of activity in the brain, has shown that the medial forebrain bundle and the nucleus accumbens become active in all sorts of situations in which an individual receives a reward—whether the reward is food, opportunity to copulate, novel objects to explore, or (in humans) a prize received for winning a game (Breiter et al., 2001; Koob et al., 2012). Moreover, damage to either of these brain structures destroys all sorts of motivated behaviors (Koob et al., 2012). Without a functioning medial forebrain bundle or nucleus accumbens, animals will not work to find or obtain rewards and will die unless they are provided with food and water through a stomach tube.

Separating the "Liking" and "Wanting" Systems

Many of the neurons of the medial forebrain bundle that terminate in the nucleus accumbens release **dopamine** [**dop**'-ə-men'] as their neurotransmitter. This release appears to be essential for the "wanting" component of reward, but not for the "liking" component. Animals that have been well trained to press a lever for some reward (e.g., food) show a release of dopamine into the nucleus accumbens just before they begin to press the lever, but not after they receive the reward (Phillips et al., 2003). This pattern is consistent with the idea that dopamine helps motivate the animal to obtain the reward (promotes "wanting") but is not essential for the

FOCUS 8

What is some evidence that the medial forebrain bundle and nucleus accumbens are essential pathways for the effects of a wide variety of rewards?

FOCUS 9

What is some evidence that the "wanting" and "liking" components of reward involve different neurotransmitters?

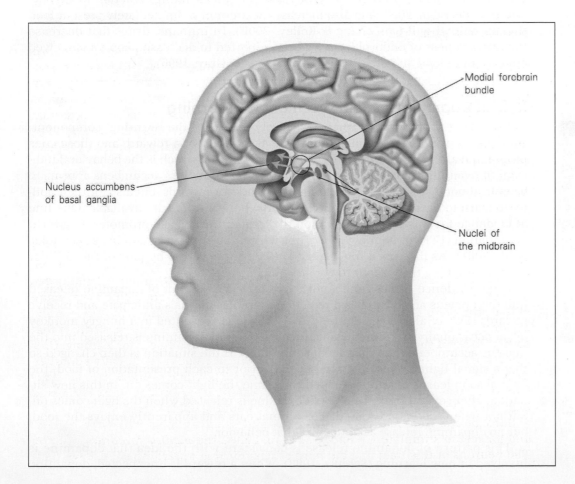

FIGURE 5.4 A reward pathway in the brain The medial forebrain bundle is a neural tract consisting of neurons whose cell bodies are in nuclei in the midbrain and whose synaptic terminals are in the nucleus accumbens of the basal ganglia. Rats will quickly learn to press a lever to electrically stimulate the medial forebrain bundle or the nucleus accumbens.

pleasure ("liking") associated with obtaining the reward. Other research shows that the larger the expected reward, the greater the degree of dopamine release in the nucleus accumbens (Roesch et al., 2007).

More direct evidence that dopamine is involved in "wanting" but not "liking" comes from studies in which rats are treated with drugs that block dopamine's effect in the nucleus accumbens. These animals continue to consume foods, copulate with sexual partners, and explore novel stimuli that are immediately present. They also continue to exhibit the facial "liking" expression (depicted in Figure 5.2) when they taste a sugar solution. However, they do not continue to seek out or work for rewards that are not immediately present (Berridge & Robinson, 2003; Zhang et al., 2003). Their behavior suggests that they continue to enjoy the consumption of rewards but are no longer concerned with (no longer behave as if they want) rewards that are absent. Conversely, drugs that increase the activity of dopamine in the nucleus accumbens increase the rate at which rats and other animals will work for food, but do not increase the facial "liking" response to sucrose or the animal's consumption of food that is immediately available (Berridge & Robinson, 2003).

If dopamine is responsible for the "wanting" component of reward, what is responsible for the "liking" component? Some of the neurons of the medial forebrain bundle that terminate in the nucleus accumbens release not dopamine but a different transmitter, one that is in the **endorphin** family. *Endorphin* is short for "endogenous morphine-like substance" (*endogenous* meaning "created within the body"). Endorphins are chemicals created within the body that have effects similar to those of morphine and other opiate drugs such as opium and heroin; they are best known for their role in inhibiting the sense of pain. They are also associated with pleasurable experiences, both natural (e.g., sex) and artificial (e.g., drug "highs") (Le Merrer et al., 2009). When drugs that activate endorphin receptors are injected into the nucleus accumbens, they increase the facial "liking" reaction to sucrose (Smith & Berridge, 2007) and also increase the amount of immediately present food that an animal will eat (Zhang & Kelley, 2000). In humans, drugs that decrease the effectiveness of endorphins have been reported to decrease people's perceived enjoyment of food and other rewards (Yeomans & Gray, 1996).

Role of Dopamine in Reinforcement for Learning

The learning component of reward is closely related to the "wanting" component. Animals learn that certain cues signal the availability of a reward, and those cues prompt the animal to search for or work for the reward, which is the behavioral indicator of "wanting." The release of dopamine into the nucleus accumbens appears to be crucial not just for motivating animals to work for rewards, but also for their ability to learn to use cues to predict when and where rewards are available. One line of evidence for this is the observation that dopamine release promotes long-term potentiation (LTP) of neural connections within the nucleus accumbens (Reynolds et al., 2001). As discussed in Chapter 4, LTP is believed to be part of the cellular basis for learning throughout the brain.

Other evidence comes from studies in which the amount of dopamine released into the nucleus accumbens is directly measured as animals anticipate and receive rewards (Day et al., 2007; Schultz, 1998). If food is presented to a hungry monkey or rat occasionally, at unpredictable times, a burst of dopamine is released into the nucleus accumbens each time food is presented. If the situation is then changed so that a signal light comes on a few seconds prior to each presentation of food, the animal soon learns to anticipate food each time the light comes on. In this new situation, after several trials, a burst of dopamine is released when the light comes on, but not when food is presented. The animal eats and apparently enjoys the food, but no dopamine release accompanies that behavior.

This pattern of dopamine release is consistent with the idea that dopamine is involved in new learning (Schultz, 1998). When a reward is unexpected, dopamine

FOCUS 10

What evidence suggests that dopamine is crucial to the capacity of rewards to promote new learning—that is, to serve as reinforcers?

release immediately after the reward helps to reinforce an association between the reward and any stimulus or response that happened to precede it. When the cues and responses leading to a reward have already been well learned, however, there is no need for further reinforcement of that learning, and dopamine release in response to the reward (the food) ceases. Dopamine release now occurs in response to the signal preceding reward (the light) because now the animal's interest lies in learning how to predict when the signal will appear or how to make it appear.

Hijacking the Brain's Reward System

When Olds and Milner delivered electrical impulses into the medial forebrain bundle in rats, they were short-circuiting the rats' natural reward systems. When people get "hooked" on drugs or on gambling, they are doing essentially that same thing with their own brains.

Drug Addiction

Cocaine, amphetamine, heroin, opium, and other often-abused drugs exert their euphoric and habit-forming effects through action on the brain's reward pathways (Koob et al., 2012). In various ways, these drugs mimic or promote the effects of dopamine and endorphins in the nucleus accumbens.

Rats fitted with mechanisms for pumping drugs into their bloodstreams will self-administer cocaine and other such drugs, and become addicted, but will stop self-administering the drugs if the nucleus accumbens is destroyed or chemically blocked (Wise, 1996). Rats will work as hard to administer tiny amounts of cocaine or amphetamine through a cannula (tiny tube) directly into the nucleus accumbens as they will to administer much larger amounts into the bloodstream (Hoebel et al., 1983; Wood & Emmett-Oglesby, 1989). These findings are consistent with other evidence that the nucleus accumbens is a key area where drugs act to produce their addictive effects.

Our understanding of the brain's reward mechanisms gives us a clue as to why such drugs are addictive. Not only do they produce an immediate sense of euphoria, but even more significant for the problem of addiction, they strongly activate the dopamine-receiving neurons in the nucleus accumbens that are responsible for promoting reward-based learning. Normal rewards, such as food, activate these neurons only when the reward is unexpected; but cocaine and other addictive drugs, through their direct chemical effects, activate these neurons every time the drug is taken. The result may be a sort of super-learning (Hyman et al., 2006). With each dose of the drug, the dopamine response acts to reinforce, once again, associations between any cues that are present in the environment and the feelings and behaviors of wanting and taking the drug. The result is the buildup of an extraordinarily strong craving and habit, triggered whenever cues that were present during past drug-taking are again present.

It has often been observed that drug addicts gradually lose their "liking" (enjoyment) of the drug over time, even while their "wanting" of the drug (craving) increases (Kelley & Berridge, 2002). The loss in liking occurs, presumably, because of drug-induced changes in the brain that reduce the endorphin-mediated pleasure response. However, because the dopamine response is not reduced, the learned drug craving and habit continue to grow stronger with each dose (Kelley & Berridge, 2002; Nestler & Malenka, 2004). The craving itself, rather than any expected pleasure, becomes the main reason for taking the drug. Drug taking becomes a compulsion rather than something that one freely chooses to do for pleasure. (Other reasons why drug addicts continue to take drugs, having to do with conditioned counteractive responses, are discussed in Chapter 8.)

FOCUS 11

How does an understanding of the brain's reward system help us to understand drug addiction and compulsive gambling?

■ **Wanting without liking** After repeated use, a drug such as cocaine or heroin continues to promote dopamine release in the brain, and thus to reinforce "wanting," but the drug may no longer promote endorphin release, so the "liking" response no longer occurs.

Mediaimage/Science Source

■ **Internet gambling** Whether done on the Internet or at an actual casino, gambling can become compulsive. Because wins are essentially random and unpredictable, each win may result in a new burst of dopamine release, which helps to create the compulsion.

A Brain-Based Theory of Compulsive Gambling

In North America, about 2% of adults suffer from a compulsive, pathological drive to gamble (Kessler et al., 2008), a drive that persists even though it may leave the person and his or her family in financial ruins. Compulsive gambling is in some ways similar to drug addiction (Jazaeri & Bin Habil, 2012). Gamblers claim to feel a euphoric high when they are gaming and winning, and to experience withdrawal symptoms—such as sweating, restlessness, and sleeplessness—when they try to abstain. Every cue in the environment that has been previously associated with gambling elicits in them a strong, often irresistible urge to gamble. Our understanding of the brain's reward mechanisms gives us some clues about the origins of this compulsion.

Brain imaging studies with healthy human subjects (using the fMRI technique, discussed in Chapter 4) have revealed that games of chance with monetary rewards are powerful activators of the nucleus accumbens and other structures known to be part of the brain's reward system (Potenza, 2013). Because the payoff is never predictable, every instance of payoff results in a new burst of dopamine release in the nucleus accumbens, no matter how many times the person plays. Thus, gambling, like drug taking, overrides the brain's dopamine-conserving mechanism—the mechanism that shuts off the dopamine response once the reward has become predictable.

Consciously, the person may know that the game pays off in a way that is unpredictable and uninfluenced by anything that he or she does, but the brain's primitive reward system nevertheless behaves as if it is constantly trying to learn how to predict and produce the reward. Dopamine's repeated reinforcement of associations between payoffs and the cues and behaviors that precede each payoff results in the buildup of an abnormally strong habit.

People who, for genetic reasons, have high levels of dopamine receptors in their brains have an unusually high susceptibility to compulsive gambling (Sabbatini da Silva Lobo et al., 2007). The same is true for people who, because of Parkinson's disease or other disorders, are taking drugs that increase the potency of dopamine transmission in the brain (Giladi et al., 2007; Quickfall & Suchowersky, 2007). These findings are consistent with the theory that compulsive gambling is reinforced by the dopamine response to unpredicted rewards.

SECTION REVIEW

Brain reward systems mediate three aspects of reward: wanting, liking, and reinforcement.

Neurochemistry of Reward

■ The medial forebrain bundle and nucleus accumbens contain essential pathways of the brain's reward system. Animals will work for electrical stimulation in these areas.

■ The release of dopamine into the nucleus accumbens is associated with wanting; the release of endorphins into this area is associated with liking.

■ The release of dopamine into the nucleus accumbens is also crucial to reinforcement; it promotes learning how to predict and obtain a given reward.

Drug Addiction and Compulsive Gambling

■ Addictive drugs cause dopamine release into the nucleus accumbens each time they are taken, which may cause super-learning of cues and actions associated with obtaining the drug; hence, addiction.

■ Because of the unpredictability of rewards in gambling, each reward may stimulate release of dopamine into the nucleus accumbens, resulting in super-learning of cues and actions associated with gambling.

Hunger: An Example of a Regulatory Drive

It is no accident that eating is one of life's great pleasures. Throughout our evolutionary history, the difficulty of finding adequate food was one of the major barriers, if not *the* major barrier, to survival. As a result, natural selection built into us (and other animals) powerful, robust hunger mechanisms that lead us to search for food, to eat when food is available, and to experience pleasure when we eat.

Natural selection also built into us satiety mechanisms, which tend to keep us from overeating and becoming obese. But the satiety mechanisms are not as robust as the hunger mechanisms. In our evolutionary history, food scarcity was a much bigger problem than overabundance. Far more people died of starvation than of obesity—a contrast to the situation in today's postindustrial nations, where obesity has become a major health problem. In what follows, we examine some of the mechanisms that control appetite and then look at the modern problem of obesity.

Neural and Hormonal Control of Appetite

The purpose of hunger and satiety is to regulate the amount of food materials in the body at an appropriate level for survival and well-being. Any regulatory system, whether human-made or organic, makes use of *feedback control*. The substance or quality being regulated feeds back upon the controlling device and inhibits the production of more of that substance or quality when an appropriate level is reached. A home thermostat, which controls the heating system, is a good example. The thermostat is sensitive to temperature. When the temperature is low, a switch closes in the thermostat, which turns on the furnace, which provides heat. When the temperature rises above the set level, the switch opens, and the furnace turns off. Thus heat, produced by the furnace, feeds back onto the thermostat to shut off the source of heat when enough of it is present.

The mammalian brain regulates food intake in a manner that is a bit like the operation of a home thermostat, but far more complicated. Sets of neurons in the brain's hypothalamus raise or lower the animal's drive to eat, and these neurons are themselves regulated by the body's deficit or surfeit of food materials. We might think of these neurons as the brain's "food-o-stat." When food materials are relatively low in the body, the food-o-stat cranks up appetite, which motivates the animal to consume more food. When food materials are plentiful in the body, indicators of that plenitude feed back upon the food-o-stat and turn appetite off, or at least down a bit.

FOCUS 12

What is meant by feedback control, and how does the arcuate nucleus of the hypothalamus serve as a control center for appetite?

A Nucleus in the Hypothalamus Serves as an Appetite-Control Center

The neurons that constitute the food-o-stat exist in several closely interconnected portions of the hypothalamus, but are most concentrated in the **arcuate** [**ark'**-yu¯-ət] **nucleus**, which lies in the center of the lowest portion of the hypothalamus, very close to the pituitary gland (Berthoud & Morrison, 2008). This tiny brain area has been described as the "master control center" for appetite and weight regulation (Marx, 2003). It contains two classes of neurons that have opposite effects on appetite. One class, the *appetite-stimulating neurons,* connect to various parts of the brain and promote all the effects that are associated with increased hunger, including craving for food, increased attention to food-related cues, increased exploration in search of food, and heightened enjoyment of the taste of food. The other class, the *appetite-suppressing neurons,* have effects on various parts of the brain that are opposite to those of the appetite-stimulating neurons.

Both of these classes of arcuate neurons exert their effects on other brain areas through the release of slow-acting neurotransmitters, which have the capacity to alter neural activity for long periods of time—in this case for periods ranging from minutes to several hours.

Many Internal Signals Contribute to Short-Term Regulation of Appetite

Eating a large meal produces a number of physiological changes in the body. Among these are slightly elevated body temperature (resulting from a heightened rate of metabolism), increased blood level of glucose (a simple sugar molecule derived from the breakdown of carbohydrate foods), distention of the stomach and intestines (resulting from food inside those structures), and the release of certain hormones produced by endocrine cells in the stomach and intestines. There is evidence that all these changes can either directly or indirectly incite neurons in the arcuate nucleus and nearby areas of the hypothalamus to activate hunger-suppressing neurons and inhibit hunger-stimulating neurons (Berthoud & Morrison, 2008). When all these effects are operating properly, the result is a decline in appetite for several hours following ingestion of a meal.

One appetite-suppressing hormone that has received considerable attention is *peptide YY$_{3-36}$* (abbreviated *PYY*), which is produced by special endocrine cells in the large intestine. Food entering the intestines after a meal stimulates secretion of PYY into the bloodstream. In humans, blood levels of the hormone begin to increase 15 minutes after a meal is eaten, peak at about 60 minutes, and remain elevated for as long as 6 hours after a large meal (Batterham et al., 2003). Research with rodents shows that one of the target tissues of PYY is the arcuate nucleus, where the hormone excites appetite-suppressing neurons and inhibits appetite-stimulating neurons (Marx, 2003).

In both rats and humans, injection of extra PYY into the bloodstream reduces total food consumed over the next several hours (J. V. Gardiner et al., 2008). In one double-blind experiment with humans, PYY injection reduced the amount of food eaten at a buffet luncheon, by both lean and obese human volunteers, by an average of about 30%, and also reduced reported level of appetite in both groups (Batterham et al., 2003). The same researchers also found that lean subjects had higher baseline levels of naturally produced PYY than did obese subjects and exhibited a much greater increase in PYY following a meal (see **Figure 5.5**). This result suggests that insufficient PYY production may be a contributing cause of obesity. As you can well imagine, pharmaceutical companies are currently investigating the possibility that PYY, or some modified form of it, might be developed and marketed as a weight-control drug (Troke et al., 2014).

Leptin Contributes to the Long-Term Control of Appetite and Body Weight

In the short term, eating provides an immediate supply of building blocks (such as amino acids) and energy molecules (such as glucose) needed to grow, repair, and fuel the body. Over the long term, eating more than is immediately needed adds to the amount of fat that is stored in special fat cells in various tissues of the body. Fat stores provide an extra source of energy that the body can call upon when food is not available in the environment. Too much fat, however, impedes movement and puts stress on all the body's organs. Not surprising, the hunger mechanism, when it is working optimally, is sensitive not just to the short-term indicators of the amount of food recently eaten but also to the amount of fat stored in the body.

Fat cells in mice, humans, and other mammals secrete a hormone called **leptin** at a rate directly proportional to the amount of fat that is in the cells (Woods et al., 2000). Leptin is taken up into the brain and acts on neurons in the arcuate nucleus and other parts of the hypothalamus to reduce appetite. Animals that lack either the gene needed to produce leptin or the gene needed to produce the receptor sites for leptin in the hypothalamus become extraordinarily obese (see **Figure 5.6**) (Friedman, 1997). Some people—though very few—lack the gene needed to produce leptin. Such individuals are extremely obese, but they reduce their eating, lose weight rapidly, and keep it off when given daily injections of leptin (Farooqi et al., 2002).

When the hunger-suppressing effect of leptin was discovered in the 1990s, there was much excitement about the

---

FOCUS 13

What is the evidence that the hormone PYY helps reduce appetite after a meal and that underproduction of PYY may contribute to obesity?

FOCUS 14

How does the hormone leptin contribute to weight regulation, and why isn't leptin a good anti-obesity drug?

FIGURE 5.5 Blood levels of the hormone PYY in obese and lean human subjects Blood levels of PYY were found to be lower in obese subjects than in lean subjects. After eating a meal, lean subjects showed a much larger increase in PYY than did obese subjects. Researchers believe that this difference may be a cause of obesity, as PYY acts on the brain to suppress appetite. (Data from Batterham et al., 2003.)

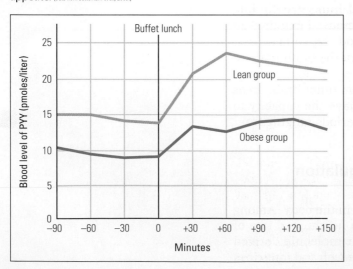

possibility that injections of this hormone could help many people lose weight. Subsequent research, however, found that hunger is reduced by increased leptin up to a certain level, but that most overweight people already have blood concentrations of leptin well above that level and additional leptin has no effect (Marx, 2003). Other research suggests that many obese people feel chronically hungry not because they lack leptin but because their brains are relatively insensitive to the hormone (Berthoud & Morrison, 2008). A drug that helped restore leptin sensitivity might help them lose weight, and such a drug has been found effective in suppressing appetite in mice (Tam et al., 2012), but so far the drug has not been tested with humans.

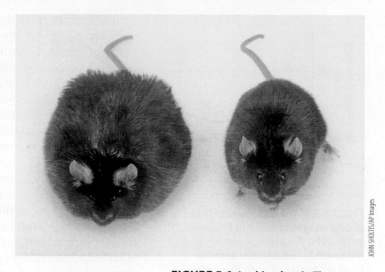

FIGURE 5.6 Lacking leptin The mouse on the left, which lacks the gene needed to synthesize the weight-regulating hormone leptin, greatly outweighs the genetically normal mouse. Without leptin, the animal overeats and becomes obese.

Roles of Sensory Stimuli in Control of Appetite

As you probably know from personal experience, hunger is provoked not just by events inside us but also by sensory stimuli in the environment. Even if you were not initially hungry, the sight or smell of good food might make you hungry. This effect of the environment makes good sense from an evolutionary perspective. For most of our history as a species, food was not always available. Evolution led us and other animals to be opportunists with regard to food; our hunger increases when food is available so that we don't pass up opportunities to eat.

Through classical conditioning (discussed in Chapter 8), any cues that have previously signaled opportunity to eat—such as the sight or smell of good food, the sound of a dinner bell, or the sight of a clock showing it is dinner time—can bring on a sudden surge of appetite. Such conditioning is reflected not just in reports of increased hunger but also in the occurrence of reflexive physiological responses, such as the secretion of saliva and digestive juices, that help to prepare the body for food and add further to the sense of hunger (Woods et al., 2000).

Once a person begins to eat, the taste of the food can influence the reduction or prolongation of appetite during a meal. People and laboratory animals that eat a type of food until they are satiated experience renewed appetite when a different food, with a different taste, is placed before them (Havermans et al., 2009). This phenomenon is referred to as **sensory-specific satiety**, and many experiments show that it is mediated primarily by the sense of taste (Raynor & Epstein, 2001). When people eat one food at a meal, their rating of the taste pleasantness of that food declines relative to their rating of the taste pleasantness of other foods. This effect begins immediately after eating the food and lasts typically for several hours. Experiments with animals show that the sight and smell of a new food can result in renewed activity in appetite-stimulating neurons in the hypothalamus after the animal has been sated on a different food (Rolls et al., 1986). Laboratory animals that can regularly choose from a variety of different-tasting foods eat more, and become fatter, than do animals that have only one food choice, even if the nutritional content of various foods is identical (Raynor & Epstein, 2001). People, too, eat more when offered more food choices (Raynor & Epstein, 2001).

FOCUS 15

How do conditioned stimuli and the availability of many foods, with different flavors, contribute to appetite and obesity?

Problems of Obesity

Human evolution occurred almost entirely in environments where food choices were far fewer, and far lower in fat and sugar, than are the foods available in modern cultures. Natural selection built into us excellent mechanisms to defend against weight loss in times of scarcity, but rather poor mechanisms to maintain a healthy weight in times of plenty.

A measure called the *body mass index,* or *BMI,* is generally used to assess a person's weight. BMI is defined as body weight in kilograms divided by the square of

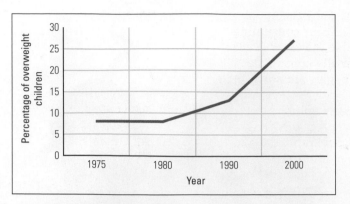

FIGURE 5.7 Trends in percentage of overweight children in England, 1975–2000 The obesity epidemic is not confined to the United States or to adults, but is occurring all over the developed world beginning in infancy and childhood. (Data from International Task Force on Obesity, 2004. [Title of cited publication: Obesity in children and young people, a crisis in public health. www.iotf.org.])

🔍 **FOCUS 16**

What is the evidence that within a culture, differences in body weight result mostly from differences in genes, but across cultures, environment plays a large role?

---

the person's height in meters. A BMI of 25 or more is considered overweight, and one of 30 or more is considered obese. Thus a person who is 1.7 meters (5 feet 7 inches) tall and weighs 73 kilograms (161 pounds) is deemed overweight (BMI = $73/1.7^2$ = 25.3), and a person of that same height who weighs 88 kilograms (194 pounds) is considered obese (BMI = $88/1.7^2$ = 30.4). A "normal" weight at that height would be 118 to 160 pounds; less than 118 pounds would be considered underweight.

BMI does not take into account one's gender, age, or how muscular or flabby a person's body is, thus it provides only a general measure to evaluate obesity. Nevertheless, using the BMI, a survey taken in 2011–2012 reported that 17% of 2- to 19-year-olds and 35% of adults in the United States were obese (Ogden et al., 2014). Comparison with earlier studies (e.g., Hill et al., 2003) reveals that the rate of obesity has risen rapidly over the past few decades and is also rising rapidly in many other parts of the world. (See **Figure 5.7** for changes in childhood obesity in England between 1975 and 2000.) As obesity rises, so does the rate of diseases that are secondary to it, including Type 2 diabetes, coronary heart disease, stroke, and certain types of cancers (Marx, 2003). The immediate causes of this obesity epidemic are clear: People consume more calories and exercise less than they used to.

Effects of Genes and Nutrition on Body Weight

Within the United States, or any other Western culture, the determination of who does or does not become obese depends very much on genes and relatively little on the specific home environment (Barsh et al., 2000). The weights of adopted children correlate much more strongly with the weights of their biological parents than with those of their adoptive parents; identical twins usually have very similar weights, even if raised in different homes; and pairs of biological siblings raised in different homes are, on average, nearly as similar to each other in weight as are pairs raised in the same home (Grilo & Pogue-Geile, 1991; Stunkard et al., 1986). This does not mean that body weight is little influenced by the environment. It simply means that the environmental conditions that promote obesity are fairly constant within Western cultures, so differences in weight have mostly to do with genetic differences in how individuals respond to those conditions.

Across cultures, environmental differences can have a large effect on body weight. As one example, a study in the 1990s found that obesity was very common among Pima Indians living in Arizona but essentially absent among their genetic relatives living in Mexico. The Mexican Pimas subsisted mainly on grains and vegetables; their culture does not include the high-calorie foods available to the Arizona Pimas (Gibbs, 1996). The genes that promote obesity in United States culture apparently do so by increasing the person's attraction to high-calorie foods, by decreasing one or another of the feedback effects that high food intake or fat level has on the hunger mechanisms in the hypothalamus, and by decreasing the body's ability to burn up excess calories quickly (Barsh et al., 2000).

The diets of people in the developed world are different from diets of traditional people in many ways; however, the prevalence of sugars in modern diets, particularly *fructose,* has been a topic of considerable debate. Fructose, which is found in sucrose and high-fructose corn syrup, has been identified by some to be a particularly potent source of calories and a major contributor to the obesity problem. For example, one study investigated the brain's reactions to fructose versus glucose, as well as subjects' perception of satiety after consuming these sugars (Page et al., 2013). The researchers asked 20 healthy, normal-weight young adults to consume 75 grams of either pure fructose or pure glucose and then measured their brains' reactions via fMRI. They reported differences in activation of various areas of the hypothalamus between the fructose and glucose conditions, as well as differences in the striatum, a subcortical area involved in inhibitory responses. More important, subjects reported feelings of fullness and satiety after consuming glucose, but not after consuming fructose. Although this was a preliminary study with a small sample that used levels of sugar ingestion far in excess to what an individual would normally consume at a single time, it illustrates that, at least under some conditions, all sugars are not alike as far as the brain is concerned, and that fructose, found in abundance in many prepared foods, may be a particular problem when it comes to obesity. Other studies suggest that consumption or exposure to high levels of fructose early in life (during the fetal and infancy periods) can alter metabolism, neuroendocrine function, and appetite control, increasing the likelihood of later obesity (Goran et al., 2013).

Modern life is also marked by a decrease in physical activities. Fewer adults work at jobs that require physical exertion, and people spend more time in sedentary recreational activities, such as watching television and playing computer games, than did past generations. This tendency toward a less active lifestyle begins in childhood. Schools have been cutting back on both recess and physical education since the 1960s (Nestle & Jacobson, 2000; Pellegrini, 2005), and outdoor play in general has decreased.

Another factor involved in obesity is prenatal nutrition. Women with poor diets when pregnant are more apt to have children who are overweight. Such infants typically have lower birth weight than infants with better prenatal nutrition. While most eventually catch up to their peers in weight, they show elevated levels of the appetite-regulating hormone leptin. They develop "thrifty phenotypes," storing more fat than children whose prenatal diets were more nutritious. This makes sense from an evolutionary perspective, with fetuses being sensitive to their level of nutrition. When prenatal nutrition is good, brain circuitry that controls appetite and metabolism develops as if food resources will be plentiful in the future; when prenatal nutrition is poor, brain circuitry develops differently, causing individuals to hold on to as many calories as they can in anticipation of limited food resources (see Gluckman & Hansen, 2005). Peter Gluckman and Mark Hanson (2005) refer to fetuses responding to current conditions (in this case poor nutrition) not for immediate advantage but in anticipation of later advantage after birth as *predictive adaptive responses*. The result of this strategy with respect to poor fetal nutrition for people in modern cultures is often obesity.

Problems of Dieting

It might seem that the problem of obesity could be solved by a simple application of willpower, but this is far easier said than done. Weight gained is often very difficult to lose. Decreased food intake not only activates the hunger mechanisms in the brain but can also produce a decline in basal metabolism (the rate at which calories are burned while the individual is at rest). A lower metabolism makes the body convert food to fat more efficiently (Keesey & Corbett, 1984; Leibel et al., 1995). In one extreme case, a woman managed to reduce her weight from 312 pounds to a still-obese but much healthier 192 pounds through diet. She was able to maintain her new weight for at least 18 months without losing any more by eating a total of just 1,000 to 1,200 calories a day—less than half of what most women would have to eat to maintain that weight (Rodin et al., 1989).

Despite the odds, some overweight and obese people do lose significant amounts of weight and avoid regaining it. A study of approximately 3,000 highly successful dieters, who had lost an average of over 60 pounds per person and had kept it off for an average of 5 years at the time of the study, revealed that they succeeded primarily by avoiding high-fat foods and by greatly increasing their exercise (Butler, 2004). Many other studies, too, have shown that a combination of exercise and dieting is far more effective in producing long-term weight loss than is dieting alone (Cudjoe et al., 2007). Regular exercise not only burns up calories immediately but also builds muscle, which, even when resting, burns calories at a higher rate than do other body tissues (Van Itallie & Kissileff, 1990).

Doug James/Shutterstock

■ If the only Pima Indians you ever saw were those living in Mexico and following traditional Pima practices, you might conclude that they are genetically predisposed to be slender. Studies published in the 1990s reported that obesity was almost nonexistent among the Mexican Pima. However, their close relatives living across the border in the United States (like this boy dancing at a holy festival) were often obese. That difference lies not in genes but in the choices of foods available.

 FOCUS 17

On the basis of the reports of successful dieters and the advice of appetite researchers, what can people do to maintain a healthy weight?

SECTION REVIEW

Hunger is a regulatory drive controlled by neural, hormonal, and sensory factors.

Control Mechanisms of Hunger

- The arcuate nucleus of the hypothalamus is a feedback-based appetite control center, with both appetite-stimulating and appetite-suppressing neurons.

- Eating a large meal causes physiological changes, including the release of PYY, that influence the arcuate nucleus and nearby areas to reduce hunger.

- Leptin, a hormone produced by fat cells, helps to regulate body weight by acting on the hypothalamus to reduce appetite.

- Sensory stimuli also affect appetite, as illustrated by sensory-specific satiety and by the appetite-boosting power of learned cues that signal the availability of food.

Obesity

- Within a culture, genetic differences are the primary determinants of who becomes obese, but across cultures, environmental differences play a substantial role.

- Decreasing food intake activates hunger mechanisms in the brain and

can reduce basal metabolism, making weight loss harder.

- Poor prenatal nutrition can lead to fetuses developing "thrifty phenotypes," anticipating future environments of food scarcity by storing more fat than children whose prenatal diets are more nutritious.

- Developing good nutrition habits and engaging in regular exercise are among the techniques that can make it easier to maintain a healthy weight.

The Sleep Drive

Sleepiness is clearly a drive. A sleepy person is motivated to go to sleep and will expend effort to reach a safe and comfortable place to do so. Achieving this goal and drifting off to sleep provides a sense of pleasure analogous to that which comes from eating when hungry or copulating when sexually motivated.

Sleepiness operates in some ways like a regulatory drive. As with hunger, thirst, or other regulatory drives, the longer one goes without satisfying the sleep drive, the stronger the drive becomes. But, unlike other regulatory drives, it is not clear what the sleep drive regulates, except sleep itself. In addition, sleepiness is controlled not just by amount of sleep deprivation but also by a biological clock that keeps time within the 24-hour day–night cycle. Regardless of how much sleep one has had recently, sleepiness tends to increase at night and decrease during daytime hours. Let us examine three questions: (1) What is sleep? (2) What are the functions of sleep? (3) What brain mechanisms control sleepiness and arousal?

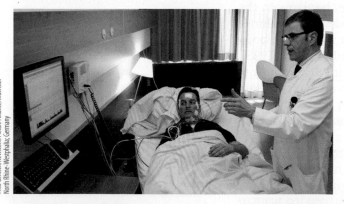

■ **Keeping track of sleep** Using electrodes attached to the patient's scalp and other areas of his body, the researcher monitors EEG, eye movements, breathing rate, and other muscle movements to keep track of the patient's stages of sleep and wakefulness.

Friso Gentsch/Newscom/Picture Alliance/Muenster North Rhine-Westphalia, Germany

Description of Sleep as a Physiological and Behavioral State

Sleep is a condition of relative unresponsiveness to the environment. Because people show little overt behavior and cannot answer questions when they are asleep, scientists who study this state must focus on physiological and subtle behavioral changes.

The most valuable index of sleep is based on the electroencephalogram (abbreviated EEG). As discussed in Chapter 4, the EEG is an amplified recording of the electrical activity of the brain that is picked up by electrodes pasted to the person's skull. These electrical signals can be stored and analyzed by a computer, producing records like those shown in **Figure 5.8**. The EEG recording is a gross index of the electrical activity of the brain, representing an average of the activity of billions of neurons, with the greatest weight given to those lying closest to the recording site.

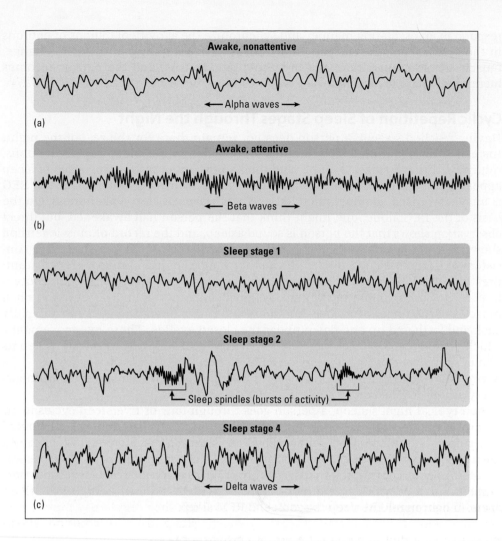

(a) Awake, nonattentive — ← Alpha waves →

(b) Awake, attentive — ← Beta waves →

Sleep stage 1

Sleep stage 2 — ↳ Sleep spindles (bursts of activity) →

(c) Sleep stage 4 — ← Delta waves →

FIGURE 5.8 EEG waves of waking and sleep stages In general, as one goes from an alert to a relaxed state, and then to ever-deeper stages of sleep, the EEG waves become slower in frequency (fewer waves per second) and higher in amplitude (as shown by their greater vertical extent in the EEG record). The brief bursts of rapid waves called sleep spindles that appear in stage 2 are the most distinctive markers of the onset of sleep. Sleep stage 3 is not shown here; it is arbitrarily defined as the period when 10 to 50% of the EEG consists of delta waves. REM sleep, also not shown, is characterized by beta waves that look like those of the awake, attentive state. (Data from Rechtschaffen & Kales, 1968.)

EEG Waves Accompanying Wakefulness and Stages of Sleep

When a person is relaxed but awake, with eyes closed and not thinking of anything in particular, the EEG typically consists of large, regular waves called *alpha waves,* which occur at a frequency of about 8 to 13 cycles per second (see Figure 5.8a). These relatively slow waves stem from a synchronized pulsing of neurons in the thalamus and cerebral cortex that occurs in the absence of focused mental activity or emotional excitement. When a person concentrates on an external stimulus, or tries to solve a problem, or becomes excited, the EEG pattern changes to low-amplitude, fast, irregular waves called *beta waves* (see Figure 5.8b). The low amplitude of these waves indicates that neurons are firing in an unsynchronized manner, such that their contributions to the EEG tend to cancel one another out. Whereas alpha waves are analogous to the large, regular waves that occur on a pond undisturbed by anything but a steady wind, beta waves are more akin to the effect of a million pebbles tossed suddenly onto the surface of the pond. The crests of the ripples created by some pebbles would cancel out the troughs created by others, resulting in a chaotic, high-frequency, low-amplitude pattern of ripples.

When a person falls asleep, the EEG goes through a fairly regular sequence of changes, which are used by researchers to divide sleep into four stages, using the criteria described in the caption to Figure 5.8 (Pace-Schott & Hobson, 2013). Stage 1 is a brief transition stage, when the person is first falling asleep, and stages 2 through 4 are successively deeper stages of true sleep. As sleep deepens, an increased per-centage of the EEG is devoted to slow, irregular, high-amplitude waves called *delta waves*. These waves, like others, are controlled by neurons in the thalamus that

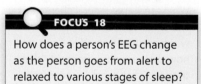

FOCUS 18

How does a person's EEG change as the person goes from alert to relaxed to various stages of sleep?

respond in an oscillating manner and synchronize the activity of billions of neurons in the cerebral cortex (Steriade et al., 1993). Corresponding to this EEG change, muscle tension, heart rate, and breathing rate decline, and the person becomes increasingly hard to awaken.

Cyclic Repetition of Sleep Stages Through the Night

FOCUS 19

How do REM and non-REM sleep differ, and how do they cycle through the night?

Having reached stage 4, a person does not remain there for the rest of the night. Instead, after about 80 to 100 minutes of total sleep time, sleep rapidly lightens, returning through stages 3 and 2, and then a new, quite fascinating stage of sleep appears for a period of about 10 minutes or more. During this new stage the EEG is unsynchronized, looking much like the beta waves of alert wakefulness. On the basis of the EEG alone, one might think that the person had awakened, but direct observation shows that the person is sound asleep, and the record of muscle tension shows that the muscles are more relaxed than at any other sleep stage. Yet, consistent with the unsynchronized EEG, other indices of high arousal are apparent: Breathing and heart rate become more rapid and less regular; penile erection occurs in males (even in infants and young boys); twitching movements occur in the small muscles of the fingers and face; and, most indicative of all, the eyes move rapidly back and forth and up and down under the closed eyelids. These eye movements, which can be recorded electrically along with the EEG, give this stage of sleep its name, *rapid-eye-movement sleep,* or **REM sleep**. As you may have guessed, it is during REM sleep that most dreams occur. Stages 2, 3, and 4 are referred to collectively as **non-REM sleep**.

In a typical night's sleep, a person goes through four or five sleep cycles, each involving gradual descent into deeper stages of non-REM sleep, followed by a rapid lightening of non-REM sleep, followed by REM sleep (Pace-Schott & Hobson, 2013). Each complete cycle takes about 90 minutes. As depicted in **Figure 5.9**, the deepest non-REM sleep occurs in the first cycle or two. With each successive cycle, less time is spent in the deeper stages of non-REM sleep (stages 3 and 4), and more time is spent in light non-REM sleep (stage 2) and REM sleep.

Dreams and Other Mental Activity During Sleep

FOCUS 20

What are some general characteristics of dreams that people describe when aroused from REM sleep, and how do these differ from the "sleep thought" that people more often describe when aroused from non-REM sleep?

When people are awakened during REM sleep, they usually (in about 90% of cases) report a mental experience that researchers call a *true dream* (Foulkes, 1985). Such a dream is experienced as if it were a real event rather than something merely imagined or thought about. The dreamer has the feeling of actually seeing or in other ways sensing various objects and people and of actually moving and behaving in the dream environment. Moreover, a true dream usually involves a progression of such experiences, woven into a somewhat coherent though often bizarre story. The more time the sleeper spends in REM sleep before awakening, the longer and more elaborate is the reported dream. Studies show that nearly everyone dreams several times a night. Even people who believe that they rarely dream, or who can recall only fragments of dreams upon normal awakening in the morning, will describe vivid, detailed dreams if awakened during REM periods.

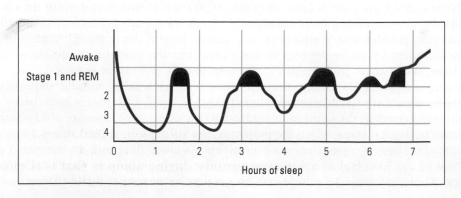

FIGURE 5.9 The cycle of sleep stages through a night People usually go through four or five sleep cycles per night, each ending with a period of REM sleep. With successive cycles, the depth of slow-wave sleep becomes less and the amount of time spent in REM sleep increases. (Data from Snyder & Scott, 1972.)

Analyses of the contents of hundreds of reported dreams reveal a number of generalities about them (Domhoff, 2003; Valli et al., 2008). Most dreams are about people, objects, and activities that are well known and meaningful to the dreamer, but very few dreams are repetitions of events that actually happened in the dreamer's daytime experience. Most dreams involve emotions, especially negative emotions. Dreams involving fear, worry, or embarrassment are more common than joyous dreams. Among college students, dreams of being lost, of being late for an examination, and of being inappropriately dressed (or undressed) in public are common.

People who are awakened during non-REM sleep report some sort of mental activity just before awakening roughly half the time (Foulkes, 1985; Hobson, 1995). Such reports are sometimes of true dreams, but more often they are of *sleep thought,* which lacks the vivid sensory and motor hallucinations of true dreams and is more akin to daytime thinking. Often the subject of sleep thought is some problem that had been of concern during the day. For example, a student who had been cramming for a math exam might report working on a calculus problem while sleeping. A major difference between sleep thought and daytime thought is that the former is usually ineffective. Although the sleeper may feel that he or she is solving a calculus problem, questions upon awakening indicate that no real progress was made (Hobson, 1987).

During sleep a person is less responsive to events in the environment than when awake, but not completely unresponsive. The eyes are closed, but all of the other sensory channels (e.g., hearing) remain open. In one study using fMRI, people's brains were observed to respond to various sounds when they were asleep in much the same way as they did when they were awake (Portas et al., 2000). Whether asleep or awake, the sound of one's own name had effects on emotional centers in the limbic system that did not occur in response to sounds that were less meaningful to the person. The fact that parents can sleep through a thunderstorm but become aroused by the whimpering of their child in the next room is further evidence that the sleeping person's brain sorts out sounds by meaning to some degree.

One characteristic of all mental activity during sleep is that it is quickly forgotten. Dreams, sleep thoughts, and sensory experiences during sleep are lost unless the person wakes up during them and thinks about them while awake. This is fortunate, as such forgetting frees us from carrying around thousands of bizarre and confusing memories.

Theories About the Functions of Sleep

Why must we sleep? Countless children have asked that question to protest being put to bed, and many scientists have asked it, too. Sleep must have come about in the course of evolution to serve some function or functions related to survival and reproduction; otherwise it would not be such a universal and compelling drive. Several theories have been proposed to explain the evolution of the sleep drive. The theories are not incompatible with one another, and they all appear to have some degree of validity (Barone & Krieger, 2015).

The Preservation and Protection Theory

<table>
<tr><td>

FOCUS 21

What evidence supports the preservation and protection theory of sleep?

</td></tr>
</table>

The *preservation and protection theory* of sleep derives primarily from comparison of sleep patterns across different species of animals. It posits that sleep came about in evolution to preserve energy and protect individuals during that portion of each 24-hour day when there is relatively little value and considerable danger in moving about. An animal needs only a certain number of hours per day to do the things that are necessary or useful for survival, and the rest of the time, according to this theory, it is better off asleep—quiet, hidden, and protected from predators and other possible dangers (Meddis, 1977).

Support for this theory comes from evidence that variations in sleep time among different species do not correspond with differences in physical exertion while awake but do correspond with feeding habits and ways of achieving safety (Allison & Cicchetti, 1976; Lima et al., 2005). At one extreme, large grazing animals such as bison and horses average only 2 or 3 hours of sleep per 24-hour day. Because of their large size and because they eat grass and other vegetation, which are extremely low in calories, they must spend most of their time eating, and, therefore, they have little time to sleep. Moreover, because of their size and the fact that they cannot burrow or climb trees, it is difficult for such animals to find safe sleeping places. Thus, they are safer awake.

Even among animals that are roughly the same size as each other, grazing animals sleep less than do meat-eaters. Sheep and goats, for example, sleep only 4 or 5 hours per 24 hours, while lions and tigers sleep 14 to 16 hours (Campbell & Tobler, 1984). Sheep and goats must spend more time eating than lions and tigers, and, because they are more often preyed upon, they are at much greater risk when asleep. At the other extreme in sleep time are opossums and bats, which average about 20 hours of sleep each 24-hour day. These two species need little time to obtain food (such as high-calorie insects or grubs), and they are adapted to hide in out-of-the-way places. According to the preservation and protection theory, they sleep so much because they have no need to be awake for long and are protected from predators while asleep.

In addition to explaining differences in total amount of sleep, the preservation and protection theory also explains differences in the time of day at which different species sleep. Animals that rely heavily on vision generally forage during the day and sleep at night. Conversely, animals such as mice and rats that rely more on other senses, and are preyed upon by animals that use vision, generally sleep during the day and forage at night. The theory also accounts for the fact that infants in most species of mammals sleep much more than adults. Infants who are being cared for by adults do not need to

Kenneth M. Highfill/Science Source

■ **Asleep and protected** According to the preservation and protection theory, a major function of sleep is to keep animals quiet and hidden during that portion of the day or night when it would be most dangerous and least profitable for them to be moving about.

spend time foraging, and sleep protects them from wandering into danger. Their sleep also gives their caregivers an opportunity to rest or attend to other needs.

It is interesting to speculate about the evolutionary conditions behind the 6- to 8-hour nighttime sleep pattern that characterizes adult humans throughout the world. Humans are highly visual creatures who need light to find food and do other things necessary for survival. At night it may have been best for us, during most of our evolution, to be tucked away asleep in a cave or other hiding place, so as not to be tempted to walk about and risk falling over a cliff or being attacked by a nocturnal predator. Only during the past few centuries—an insignificant speck of evolutionary time—have lights and other contrivances of civilization made the night relatively safe for us. Accordingly, our pattern of sleep might be in part a vestigial trait, a carryover from a period when the night was a time of great danger. To the degree that nighttime is still more dangerous than daytime, our pattern of sleep may continue to serve an adaptive function.

The Body-Restoration Theory

The body-restoration theory of sleep function is the theory that most people intuitively believe. It is the theory that your parents probably repeated to you as their reason for sending you to bed at a certain hour. According to this view, the body wears out during the day, and sleep is necessary to put it back in shape.

Scientific support for this theory includes the observation that sleep is a time of rest and recuperation. The muscles are relaxed, metabolic rate is down, and growth hormone, which promotes body repair, is secreted at a much higher rate than during wakefulness (Douglas, 2002; Siegel, 2003). Also consistent with the restoration theory is the observation that prolonged, complete sleep deprivation in rats results in breakdown of various bodily tissues, leading, within about three weeks, to death (Everson, 1993; Everson et al., 1989).

The theory also offers an explanation for the general tendency of small mammals to sleep longer than large ones. Small mammals need to maintain a higher overall level of metabolism than do large mammals because they lose body heat more rapidly, and higher metabolism leads to greater wear and tear on bodily tissues (J. M. Siegel, 2005). However, contrary to this theory, research with birds has failed to show any correlation across species between sleep time and metabolic rate; instead, it has shown a strong correlation between sleep time and risk of predation, which tends to support the preservation and protection theory discussed previously. Thus, birds that are most protected from predators while asleep, sleep longest regardless of their body size or metabolic rate (Roth et al., 2006). The theory also does not explain the large differences in sleep time between grazing animals and meat-eating animals that have similar body sizes and metabolic rates. Nor does it explain the failure of researchers to find consistent positive correlations, either across species or within species, between the amount of time an animal sleeps and the average amount of energy it expends through vigorous activity during the day.

The fact that all vertebrate animals sleep at least an hour or two out of every 24 hours, regardless of the degree to which they are at risk while sleeping, suggests that some amount of sleep is needed for body repair. But the body-restoration theory does not provide a satisfactory explanation of the large differences among species in sleep time, and it offers no explanation for the fact that some animals sleep during the day while others sleep at night. (Chapter 9 discusses an additional apparent function of sleep that involves growth process, that of consolidating new long-term memories into neural circuits in the brain.)

The Brain-Maintenance Theory of REM Sleep

If sleep in itself serves purposes of energy conservation, protection from danger, and bodily restoration, then what is the function of REM sleep? Why is restful non-REM sleep interrupted regularly by these periods of increased brain activity and energy expenditure? This question has generated much debate and research.

FOCUS 22

What evidence supports the body restoration theory of sleep, and what are some limitations of the theory?

FOCUS 23

What evidence supports the theories that REM sleep promotes the maintenance of brain circuits?

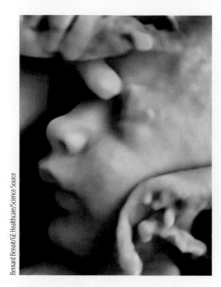

■ **Sweet dreams?** We have no idea whether human fetuses, such as this one of 7 months, experience dream sensations or not, but we do know that they spend most of their time in REM sleep.

FOCUS 24

How might dreams be explained as inevitable consequences of the state of the brain during REM sleep?

One long-standing theory is that REM sleep provides regular exercise to groups of neurons in the brain (Hobson, 1988). Synapses can degenerate if they go too long without being active (Edelman, 1987), so neural activity during REM sleep may help preserve important circuits. One line of evidence for this theory is that the longer a person or animal sleeps, the greater is the proportion of sleep time spent in REM sleep. With longer sleep periods there may be more need to interrupt non-REM sleep with exercise.

The theory also helps explain why REM sleep occurs to a much greater degree in fetuses and infants than in adults, regardless of species (see **Figure 5.10**). In fact, the peak of REM sleep in humans occurs in 30-day-old fetuses, which spend almost 24 hours a day in this state. Perhaps as their brains are developing in the relative isolation of the womb, they need to exercise sensory and motor pathways, and REM sleep is their means for doing that (Hobson, 1988). In the fetus, REM sleep is accompanied by body movements such as kicking and twisting, which are apparently triggered by the bursts of activity in motor areas of the brain, so muscles as well as brain circuits are exercised. By the time of birth a neural inhibitory system matures, which inactivates most motor neurons during REM sleep and thus prevents most movements that would otherwise occur. However, the motor neurons to the eyes and to various internal structures, such as the heart, remain uninhibited, so eye movements and increased heart rate persist as observable effects of the brain's activity.

Do Dreams Have Functions?

As just noted, there is good reason to think that REM sleep serves useful functions, but nobody knows if the dreams that accompany such sleep also serve useful functions. One theory, founded on the observation that dreams so often involve fearful content and negative emotions, is that dreams somehow provide a means of rehearsing and resolving threatening experiences that either have happened or could happen in the person's real life (Valli et al., 2008).

Other sleep researchers, however, have suggested that dreams may not serve any life-promoting functions, but may simply be side effects of the physiological changes that occur during REM sleep (Antrobus, 2000; Hobson, 2004). Neurons in

FIGURE 5.10 Changes in sleep over the course of life As shown here, both the total daily sleep time and the percentage of sleep time spent in REM sleep decrease as a person gets older. If the curves were extended to the left, they would show that prior to birth, REM sleep occupies most of each 24-hour day. (Data from Snyder & Scott, 1972.)

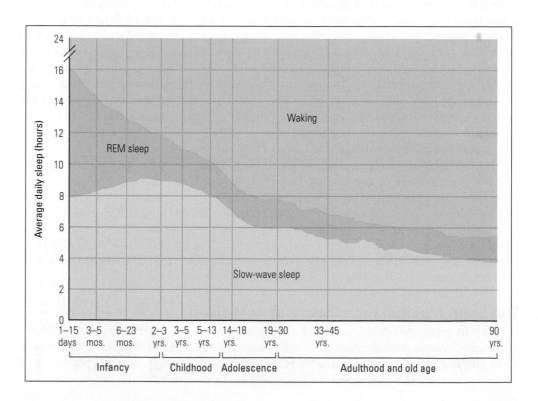

visual and motor areas of the brain become active during REM sleep, and hallucinations of sights and movements may be an inevitable consequence of such activity. Neurons involved in memory retrieval and emotions also become active, and these may bring familiar images and strong emotional feelings into the sleeping person's mind. In research done in the 1960s, electrical stimulation in portions of the cerebral cortex produced dream-like hallucinations in people who were awake (Penfield & Perot, 1963). A similar phenomenon may well occur in REM sleep. In addition to producing hallucinations, the brain continues in REM sleep to engage in some degree of thought, just as it does in non-REM sleep. But now the thought becomes wrapped up in trying to make sense of the hallucinations. The result is the weaving of a story connecting one hallucination to the next—hence, the dream. Because of reduced mental capacity during sleep, the story is less logical than one the awake brain would develop, but it still contains some degree of logic.

Sometimes the side-effect theory just described is interpreted as an argument against the psychoanalytic view that dream analysis can be useful for understanding a person's mind. But that interpretation seems unjustified. Even if dreams are triggered by random events in the brain, the actual images, emotions, and story lines that constitute the dream are not random. They certainly contain elements based on the dreamer's experience, and because they occur at a time of reduced mental capacity, ideas or feelings that are normally suppressed by higher mental processes could emerge and perhaps be useful in psychoanalysis (Reiser, 1991). In fact, in one experiment, people were more likely to dream about a particular person if they were asked to suppress thoughts about that person just before going to sleep than if they were asked to think actively about that person just before going to sleep (Wegner et al., 2004). This finding is at least consistent with the idea that dream analysis might reveal ideas and concerns that a person is actively suppressing during the day.

Individual Variations in the Sleep Drive, and Effects of Failure to Satisfy That Drive

The sleep drive varies from person to person. Some need more sleep than the typical 6 to 8 hours a night to function well, and others need less (Douglas, 2002). At the extreme are rare people, referred to as *nonsomniacs,* who sleep much less than most of us and yet do not feel tired during the day. A study of such people conducted in the 1970s by Ray Meddis (1977) found that they were generally vigorous and healthy. The most extreme nonsomniac in Meddis's sample was a 70-year-old nurse who reported that for most of her life she had slept about 50 minutes per night. She was very active during the day and usually spent the night in quiet activities, such as reading or painting. To verify her nonsomnia, Meddis observed her continuously for a prolonged period in the sleep lab. She slept not at all the first 3 days and nights in the lab, remaining cheerful and talkative throughout. Finally, on the fourth night, she slept a total of 99 minutes and awoke feeling fully rested. A more recent study, of people who did well on an average of 3 to 6 hours of sleep per night, found that these people were unusually energetic and scored higher than average, in a positive direction, on an "Attitude to Life" questionnaire (Monk et al., 2001).

FOCUS 25

How does insomnia differ from nonsomnia? What negative consequences occur when people fail to satisfy their sleep drive?

The fact that nonsomnia is compatible with physical and psychological health adds to the evidence that only a small amount of sleep is needed for body repair and growth of new synapses in the brain. Yet, most of us do need roughly 8 hours of sleep to function well. We need that sleep because we have a sleep drive that overwhelms our mind and makes us tired, miserable, and ineffective at mental tasks when we fail to meet it. The drive for that much sleep may have evolved for reasons other than body repair and brain growth, but that doesn't mean we can ignore it.

The amount of time people sleep each night not only varies among individuals, but has also varied over recent decades. Based on surveys done by the Gallup organization, Americans in 1942 averaged 7.9 hours of sleep per night. That number had fallen to 6.7 hours by 1990 and remained stable for the next 20 years (Jones, 2013), causing some to propose that the United States is facing a public health crisis (Barnes & Drake, 2015). Many people who sleep less believe that they do not get enough sleep, and numerous studies have linked short-term sleep deprivation with a host of moderate cognitive declines, both in adults (Lim & Dinges, 2010) and children (Astill et al., 2012).

One explanation for today's lack of sleep is that we live a very different lifestyle from our ancient ancestors, who, without the benefit of artificial light, likely slept more than modern humans do. This, however, seems not to be the case. A recent study examining sleep patterns of people in three hunter-gatherer societies in South America and Africa suggests that contemporary humans are sleeping about as much as our ancestors did (Yetish et al., 2015). The researchers reported that these people living a traditional lifestyle without artificial lighting go to sleep about three hours after sunset, usually awake before sunrise, sleep an average of about 6 to 7 hours a night, and rarely take naps. Between 1.5% and 2.5% of the hunter-gatherers did experience insomnia about once a year, considerably lower than rates for people from industrial countries, which is about 30% (Doghramji, 2006; Leger et al., 2000).

Unlike someone with nonsomnia, an insomniac is someone who has a normal drive for sleep but who, for some reason (such as worry), has great difficulty sleeping at night. Unlike a nonsomniac, an insomniac feels tired during the day as a result of not sleeping—and so do most people who voluntarily reduce their sleep.

Many laboratory studies have been conducted in which people with normal sleep drives voluntarily stay awake for periods of 3 or 4 days or even longer. After about 72 hours awake, some people begin to experience symptoms such as distorted perceptions and extreme irritability (Borbély, 1986). Sleepiness waxes and wanes during such studies, in accordance with the inner clock that controls it. People find it much harder to stay awake during the late night and early morning hours than they do during the rest of the 24-hour day, even after several days of sleep deprivation. In such experiments, scores on tests of vigilance, judgment, and creative thinking also wax and wane in a 24-hour cycle, keeping pace with sleepiness (Horne, 1988; Jennings et al., 2003). Scores on such tests decline when sleepiness rises, apparently because sleepy people have difficulty attending to the task and because their performance is often interrupted by brief moments of falling asleep, from which they arouse themselves. In general, stimulants such as caffeine, which counteract sleepiness, also remove the negative effects of sleep deprivation on the performance of such tasks. **Figure 5.11** illustrates the effects both of sleepiness and of stimulants on a test of vigilance (Wesensten et al., 2002).

In the real world outside of the laboratory, sleepiness—with its accompanying decline in attention and judgment—is dangerous. Many accidents in the workplace result from it, and sleepiness rivals drunkenness as a leading cause of traffic fatalities (CDC, 2013b; Horne & Reyner, 2001).

Brain Mechanisms Controlling Sleep

In the early years of sleep research, some researchers viewed sleep as the natural state that the brain slips into when not aroused by external stimulation, so they saw no need to posit the existence of special sleep-inducing mechanisms. But we can observe that sometimes sleepiness overwhelms us even when external stimulation is

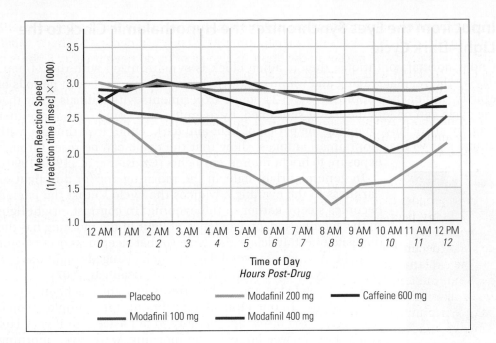

FIGURE 5.11 Decline and rise in vigilance during sleep deprivation In this experiment, university students were kept awake for 42 hours before the start of testing. Just before testing, some received a strong dose of caffeine, others received one of three doses of another stimulant drug, modafinil, and still others received a placebo. In the test of vigilance, conducted every hour, the subjects watched a time display on a computer screen and were instructed to press a button as quickly as possible each time it began to increment. The measure was response speed (the reciprocal of response time). As shown in the graph, in the placebo group vigilance declined steadily from midnight to 8 a.m. and then began to increase. This is consistent with other evidence that the circadian rhythm of sleepiness and wakefulness continues even after long periods of sleep deprivation. There was no such decline in the groups receiving caffeine or in those receiving high doses of modafinil. (Data from Wesensten et al., 2002.)

high, whereas at other times we can't sleep no matter how quiet, dark, and nonstimulating the environment may be. We now know that sleepiness, like other drives, is actively promoted by neural mechanisms located in the hypothalamus and related brain areas. There are several such neural mechanisms (Pace-Schott & Hobson, 2013), an important one being associated with the daily cycles of sleep and wakefulness.

Rhythm-Generating Neurons in the Hypothalamus Control the Daily Cycle of Sleepiness

In all vertebrates, as noted earlier, the sleep drive waxes and wanes in a cyclic manner over the 24-hour day. This cycle of sleepiness and wakefulness continues, in laboratory animals and human volunteers, even after many days in an artificial "time-free environment" where there are no regular changes in lighting or other cues to indicate the time of day. In such an environment, the cycle is typically a few minutes longer or shorter than 24 hours, and it varies from individual to individual, but it is remarkably constant within a given individual (Lavie, 2001).

A repetitive biological change that continues at close to a 24-hour cycle in the absence of external cues is called a ***circadian*** [sir-**ka–d'**-e ̄-ən] ***rhythm*** (from the Latin words *circa,* meaning "about," and *dies,* meaning "day"). The clock that controls the circadian rhythm of sleep in all mammals is located in a specific nucleus of the hypothalamus called the ***suprachiasmatic*** [sup-ra-kı-as-**ma ̆ t'**-ic] ***nucleus*** (Weaver & Emery, 2012). This nucleus contains rhythm-generating neurons that gradually increase and decrease their rate of action potentials over a cycle of approximately 24 hours, even when surgically isolated from other parts of the brain (Herzog, 2007). If this nucleus is damaged, the affected animal or human will lose regular sleep–wake rhythms and instead sleep at rather random times over the 24-hour day (Cohen & Albers, 1991).

In addition to controlling sleepiness, the suprachiasmatic nucleus also controls a daily rhythm of body temperature (which normally declines in the evening and increases in the morning) and of certain hormones. Melatonin is the hormone most directly linked to the circadian clock, and is often used by researchers as an index of the clock's timing. This hormone, produced by the pineal gland, begins to be secreted into the bloodstream in the evening, typically about 2 hours before a person is ready to fall asleep, and is secreted at relatively high levels until approximately the time when the person is ready to awaken naturally in the morning (Dumont & Beaulieu, 2007).

FOCUS 26

What is some evidence that the sleep drive is affected by an internal clock, located in the hypothalamus, that can operate even without external time cues?

FOCUS 27

What is some evidence that the internal clock is continuously reset by daily changes in light? Through what pathway does that resetting occur?

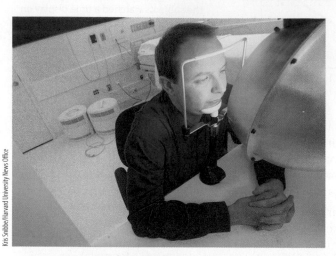

■ **Resetting the circadian clock** Steven Lockley and his colleagues have found that blue light works better than white light in resetting the circadian clock that times the onset of sleepiness. Timed exposures to such light can help shift workers and world travelers adapt their sleep schedules to the requirements of their work or travel.

Input from the Eyes Synchronizes the Hypothalamic Clock to the Light–Dark Cycle

Under normal conditions, the circadian clock is synchronized with the 24-hour day by the regular waxing and waning of daylight, so rhythms occur in periods of exactly (rather than approximately) 24 hours. Experiments with animals show that the cycle can be lengthened or shortened, by as much as a couple of hours either way, by artificially changing the period of light and dark. Other experiments, with humans as well as nonhuman animals, show that the cycle can be reset through exposure to bright fluorescent lights (Czeisler et al., 1989, 1990).

In general, bright light in the morning and/or dim light or darkness in the evening advances the cycle so that the person becomes sleepy earlier in the evening. In contrast, bright light in the evening and/or avoidance of light in the morning has the opposite effect. It delays the cycle so that sleepiness occurs later at night. A series of several days of such changed conditions can alter the cycle significantly (Dumont & Beaulieu, 2007).

This knowledge about the effects of light has been put to practical use. In one clinical experiment, for example, people with *sleep-onset insomnia,* inability to fall asleep until very late at night or the wee hours of the morning, were given morning treatments with bright light. After a week of such exposure, the subjects showed an earlier peak of melatonin than before, earlier sleep onset, and an increase of nearly an hour's more sleep per night, on average, than before treatment. This improvement lasted throughout a 3-week follow-up period after the treatment had ended (Lack et al., 2007). Other research suggests that a tendency to avoid morning light and to use relatively bright lights at home in the evening may be a cause of sleep-onset insomnia in many people today (Dumont & Beauliu, 2007). If you suffer from this problem, you might shift your own cycle to an earlier sleep time by spending some time every morning in sunlight and, in the evening, dimming your room lights and avoiding LCD screens on computers and similar devices.

How does neuroscience explain these findings? Brain researchers have found that changes in lighting influence the rhythm-generating neurons by way of a neural tract that runs from the retinas of the eyes to the suprachiasmatic nucleus. These neurons differ from those that are involved in vision, and they originate from light receptors in the retina that differ from the receptors (rods and cones) essential for vision (Van Gelder, 2008).

SECTION REVIEW

There is a drive for sleep, a state involving relative unresponsiveness to the environment.

Basic Characteristics of Sleep

- Researchers use EEG records to divide sleep into stages, with stage 4 being the deepest.

- A sleeper progresses through the sleep stages, from light to deep and rapidly back to light, in approximately 90-minute cycles.

- REM (rapid-eye-movement) sleep occurs at the transition between stage 4 and the next sleep cycle.

- Most true dreams occur in REM sleep, and sleep thought occurs in non-REM sleep.

Functions of Sleep

- The preservation and protection theory asserts that sleep is needed to conserve energy and increase safety. It is supported by cross-species comparisons of amount and timing of sleep.

- The body-restoration theory contends that the body needs sleep to recover from wear and tear. It is supported by sleep-deprivation studies in animals.

- REM sleep may function to maintain brain circuits and consolidate new learning.

- Different people need different amounts of sleep. Sleep deprivation reduces performance, especially on tests of vigilance.

Brain Mechanisms

- The suprachiasmatic nucleus in the hypothalamus acts as an internal clock for sleepiness and wakefulness.

- Light synchronizes the internal clock with the light–dark cycle.

Foundations for Understanding Emotions

Enough about sleep—now it's time to wake up and face the challenges of the day! Midterm exams are just around the corner, your family is after you to get your life in order, your lover has just left you for another, and a hungry tiger is crouched behind you. Are you awake now? All these events have something in common: All (if you believe them) have the potential to elicit strong emotions.

Emotion, like *motivation,* is a concept that applies to almost all of psychology. Much, if not all, of our thought and behavior is tinged with emotion. Our goal in this section is to introduce you to some ideas about the underlying processes and mechanisms of emotion. You will find more about particular emotions in other chapters.

■ **Delight and its object** An emotion is a subjective feeling directed toward an object that is experienced as the cause of the feeling.

The Nature and Value of Emotions

Emotion is a concept that has been difficult for psychologists to pin down and define in an agreed-upon way. According to one estimate, psychologists have generated at least 90 different definitions of emotion (Plutchik, 2001). Our own preferred definition is one that closely resembles the way the term is used in everyday life: An **emotion** is a subjective feeling that is mentally directed toward some object. That object can be another person ("She feels *angry* with John"), an organism or a thing ("He *fears* snakes"; "She *hates* bottled water"), an idea or concept ("She *loves* freedom"), or even oneself, including *pride, shame, guilt, shyness, jealousy, envy, empathy,* and *embarrassment.* These latter emotions are called *self-conscious emotions,* which seem to depend on an individual's self-awareness (Draghi-Lorenz et al., 2001; Lewis, 2000). Some researchers refer to them as *other-conscious emotions* (Saarni et al., 2006) because they seem to be related to the expectations and opinions of *other* people for one's behavior. These emotions, mature forms of which are not seen until late in the second year of life, seem to require a sophisticated cognitive system, one that may be unique to *Homo sapiens.* Moreover, such emotions are as much a characteristic of human nature as is our advanced cognition. As evolutionary primatologist Sarah Hrdy (1999) wrote: "What makes us humans rather than just apes is the capacity to combine intelligence with articulate empathy" (p. 392). Without "articulate empathy"—a sort of human glue that develops over time—sociability as we know it would not be possible, and we would be a very different species from the one we are today.

The *feeling* associated with emotion, independent of the object, is referred to by some psychologists as **affect** [**aph**-ect]. Such feelings can vary along two dimensions. One dimension has to do with the degree of pleasantness or unpleasantness of the feeling, and the other has to do with the degree of mental and physical arousal. **Figure 5.12** shows one way of describing and depicting various affects. Notice that by moving upward or downward on the circle, one goes toward increasing or decreasing arousal; by moving rightward or leftward, one goes toward increasing degrees of pleasure or displeasure. The terms in the figure do not describe emotions, but rather feelings devoid of objects. An emotion depends on the object as well as the feeling. Thus, a feeling of pleasure may be experienced as the emotion of *pride* when the object is oneself and as the emotion of *love* when the object is someone else.

Emotional feelings are not always attached to objects. Sometimes an emotional feeling is experienced as free-floating rather than directed at a particular object; if it lasts for a sufficiently long period, it is referred to as a **mood**. Moods can last for hours, days, or even longer and can color all aspects of one's thought and behavior.

FOCUS 28

According to the definitions used here, how does *emotion* differ from *affect* and from *mood*?

FIGURE 5.12 Affects Basic affects are shown here arranged in a circle in which the vertical dimension represents degree of perceived arousal and the horizontal dimension represents degree of pleasure or displeasure.

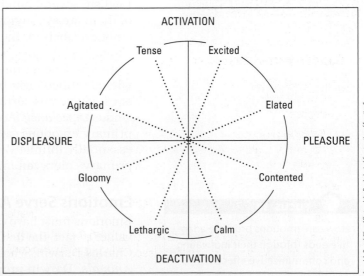

from J.A. Russell, "Core Affect and the Psychological Construction of Emotion," Psychological Review, Vol 110(1), Jan 2003, 145–172. Copyright © American Psychological Association. Reprinted by permission.

"YOU MEAN YOUR BIG SMILE IS BOTTLED-UP AGGRESSION? MINE IS BOTTLED-UP HOSTILITY."

■ Although facial expressions for different emotions are universal, people have some control over their emotional expression, so what you see is not necessarily what a person is actually feeling.

FOCUS 29

Through what strategy did Plutchik arrive at his model of eight primary emotions?

FOCUS 30

How can emotions promote adaptive ends through their motivating and communicative effects?

In some cases, everyday language provides different terms for moods and emotions that have similar underlying feelings. A feeling of being tense, jittery, and unhappy may be labeled as *anxiety* when it is a free-floating mood but as *fear* when it is an emotion associated with an object such as a spider or an upcoming examination. A feeling of being sad and upset may be labeled *depression* when it is free-floating and as *grief* when it is associated with a specific loss.

Emotions have several components, beginning with a behavioral expression. An emotional response, such as a smile, does not always mean that the person is happy; just look at the smiling faces of actors whose names are *not* called for the Oscar ("And the Oscar goes to . . ."). A person may feel one emotion (disappointment upon receiving an unattractive garment for a birthday present) but display another (joy, to the person who gave the gift). This reflects an ability to *regulate emotions,* something that develops over childhood and adolescence (Eisenberg & Spinard, 2004). Second, although facial expressions are perhaps the best way to read people's emotions, we can also recognize other people's emotions by their voice or their body language. We even do this with our pets, inferring that our dog's rapidly wagging tail when given a treat is a sign of happiness (who's to say it's not?). Third, emotions are not independent of cognitions. In fact, the same physiological arousal may represent different emotions depending on how we interpret the situation. For example, a child's increasing heart rate may reflect joy when she receives a jack-in-the-box for a gift; this same increase in heart rate may reflect fear, however, when the clown jumps out of the box and frightens her. As primatologist Robert Sapolsky commented, "based on heart rate measures one never can know for sure if it is a murder or an orgasm that has actually taken place" (quoted in Punset, 2005, p. 131). We'll have more to say about emotions and cognition later in this chapter.

How Many Emotions Are There?

As you might imagine, the answer to this question is arbitrary. It depends on how finely graded a taxonomy (system of classification) we wish to create. Fear, for example, might be understood as one emotion or as a cluster of emotions that all have some things in common. One's fear of heights, fear of death, and fear of others' judgments, for example, may be experienced as qualitatively different from one another.

Some psychologists have attempted to identify a set of primary emotions by analyzing the emotion labels that are common to a language or to several languages. In English, several hundred different words are used as labels for emotions, but many of them are synonyms or near synonyms. By asking people to rate pairs of common emotion labels for the degree of similarity between the emotions they describe, psychologists have found that the labels can be clustered into a relatively small number of groups. One useful classification system was developed by Robert Plutchik (2003), who identified eight primary emotions. They can be arranged as four pairs of opposites: *joy* versus *sorrow, anger* versus *fear, acceptance* versus *disgust,* and *surprise* versus *expectancy.* According to Plutchik's model (depicted in **Figure 5.13**), these primary emotions can mix with one another in any number of ways to produce an essentially infinite variety of different emotional experiences, just as a small set of primary colors can mix to create virtually all the colors the human eye can see.

Emotions Serve Adaptive Functions

Emotions must have come about through natural selection because of their adaptive value. In fact, the first scientific theory and systematic study of emotions came from Charles Darwin, who in 1872 published *The Expression of the Emotions in Man and Animals.* Darwin proposed that emotions are universal and have species-specific

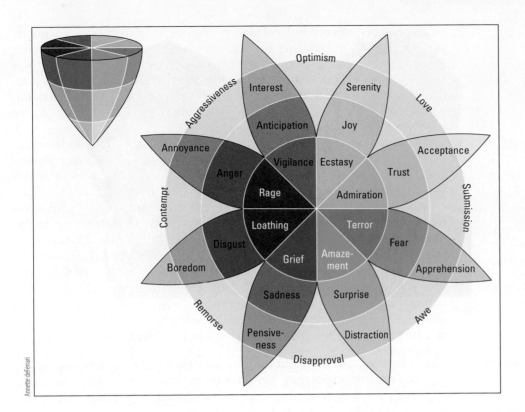

FIGURE 5.13 A model of primary emotions Robert Plutchik has proposed that the spectrum of all emotions can be represented by a cone with eight sectors. The vertical dimension of the cone represents emotional intensity. The eight sectors represent eight primary emotions, arranged such that similar emotions are next to one another and opposite emotions are on opposite sides of the cone. In the exploded view of the cone, with the sectors laid out flat, the emotion labels in the spaces between sectors represent mixtures of the adjacent two primary emotions. (This model of emotions may appear similar to the model of affects shown in Figure 5.12, but it was developed from a different set of observations and premises; the two models are not directly comparable.)

adaptive functions, reflected by facial expressions. Darwin identified six basic emotions based on facial expressions: surprise, anger, sadness, disgust, fear, and happiness. (Compare this to Plutchik's list of basic emotions.) He insisted that each conferred some adaptive benefit to the individual person or animal expressing them (see Fox & Stifter, 2005, for a more detailed discussion). The belief that basic emotions are innate and associated with distinctive bodily and facial reactions is referred to as *discrete emotion theory* (Izard, 1991; Tomkins, 1962) and is an extension of Darwin's functionalist view.

This line of thinking draws attention to the motivating qualities of emotions. Implicit in the positive-negative dimension of emotional feelings is the idea that emotions motivate us to approach objects that can help us, and to avoid or repel objects that hinder us, in our efforts to survive and reproduce. When passionately in love, we behave in all sorts of ways, including ways that under other conditions would seem foolish, to get close to our beloved, a potential partner in reproduction. When fearful, we run away, freeze, or try to look inconspicuous attempting to avoid the dangerous predator or enemy. When angry, we puff ourselves up, threaten, and sometimes even fight, in order to repulse or change the behavior of one who tries to harm us or who stands in the way of what we want or need. Strong emotions of all sorts focus our attention narrowly on the object of the emotion and lead us to ignore, for a time, other events and drives that would distract us from that object.

Carol Saarni and colleagues (2006) proposed that we engage in emotions and take action based on our emotions in order to fulfill adaptive functions. For example, the emotion of disgust serves to keep us away from contamination or illness, and causes us to actively reject the disgusting substance or object. Similarly, the emotion of shame prompts us to behave appropriately and preserve our self-esteem. When we feel shame, we may take action by withdrawing from a situation or avoiding others.

Emotions also promote our survival and reproduction through their capacity to communicate our intentions and needs to others. Our expressions of love may signal to our beloved that we will be faithful mates. Our expressions of fear may signal

■ **Anger serves valuable functions** Sometimes the person we are most angry at is also the person we care most about. This woman's anger is a clear signal to her partner that something in their relationship is out of balance and needs correction.

FIGURE 5.14 Emotional expressions may influence sensory processing In the expression of fear (a), the eyes and nostrils are wide open, which may facilitate vision and smell. In the expression of disgust (b), the eyes and nostrils are partly shut, which may serve to cut off vision and smell.

(a)   (b)

submission to our human attackers and thereby prevent a fight, or they may draw friends to our aid. Hints of anger may, on their own, convince the objects of our anger to change their ways in desired directions. As discussed in Chapter 3, many emotions are automatically and unconsciously expressed facially in universal ways. Such expressions likely came about through natural selection primarily because of their communicative value.

Self-conscious emotions such as pride, shame, guilt, jealousy, and embarrassment are of critical importance for successful social life. Nearly all social interactions involve emotion. Our social situations affect our emotions, and our emotions affect our behavior. As social beings, we are endowed with emotions that help us to connect with others, to coordinate our behavior with that of others, to gain and retain social acceptance, and, at the same time, to avoid being exploited by others. The feelings of guilt, shame, and embarrassment are painful, and the pain may motivate us to make amends when we have offended others or been ineffective in some way. Conversely, the feeling of pride rewards us for behaving effectively and gaining others' approval.

Facial expressions of at least some emotions may serve more than communicative value; they may be part of the body's way of dealing with the emotion-arousing situation. The expression of fear, for example, involves a widening of the eyes and an opening of the nasal passages, which increases the field of vision and sensitivity to odors (see **Figure 5.14a**). In a fear-provoking environment, such increased sensitivity to sights and smells may have been useful to our evolutionary ancestors, and may still be useful, as a means of detecting potential threats (Susskind et al., 2008). Conversely, in the emotion of disgust—which involves a rejection of some object in the environment—the field of vision and the nasal passages narrow, cutting off the offending sight or odor (see **Figure 5.14b**).

Effects of Bodily Responses on Emotional Feelings

Most emotional states are accompanied by peripheral changes in the body. By *peripheral* changes, we mean all changes in the body outside of the central nervous system. These include changes in heart rate, blood pressure, diversion of blood from one set of tissues to another, activation of certain glands, tension in particular muscles, and facial expression of the emotion. The changes, overall, are adaptive because of their communicative function or their role in helping prepare the body for possible action.

Common sense and everyday language tell us that these peripheral changes are caused by our emotions. We say: "My heart pounds and I tremble because I am afraid"; "My face is flushed and my teeth are clenched because I am angry"; "Tears well up in my eyes and a lump forms in my throat because I feel grief." Over 100 years ago, in his classic textbook *The Principles of Psychology*, William James (1890/1950) turned common sense upside down and suggested that bodily reactions precede the emotions and cause them, rather than the reverse.

James's Peripheral Feedback Theory of Emotion

James's evidence for his theory of emotion came not from experiments but from introspection. Looking inward at his own emotions, James concluded that his emotional feelings were really sensations stemming from bodily changes. Thus, his feeling of fear was elicited by a quickened heart, shallow breathing, gooseflesh, and trembling limbs. Similarly, his feeling of anger was elicited by a flushed face, dilated nostrils, and clenched teeth. James believed that he could identify a different constellation of bodily changes for each emotion and that if he could not feel these changes, he would not feel the emotion.

The essence of James's theory is that the bodily reaction to an emotion-provoking stimulus is automatic, occurring without conscious thought or feeling, and that the assessment of one's emotional state follows, based on the perception of the bodily state. In an unexpected encounter with a bear, the brain instantly, at some unconscious level, judges the bear to be dangerous and precipitates a bodily change that helps prepare the person for flight. There is no time, in an emergency, for conscious reflection. The body reacts immediately. Then, later on, when the danger is over or at least reduced, the person may sense his beating heart and trembling knees and conclude that he is or was frightened. The contrast between James's theory and the common-sense theory that he was arguing against is illustrated in the top two portions of **Figure 5.15**.

> **FOCUS 31**
>
> What is James's theory of emotion? What evidence did James supply for the theory, and what modern evidence is consistent with the theory?

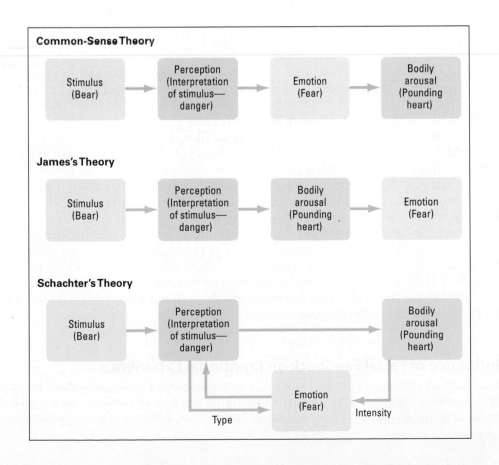

FIGURE 5.15 Three theories of emotion Each theory proposes a different set of causal relationships among perception of the stimulus, bodily arousal, and emotional feeling. According to the common-sense theory (so labeled by James), the emotional feeling precedes and causes the bodily arousal. James's theory reverses that relationship, and Schachter's theory holds that the intensity of the emotional feeling depends on the bodily response, but the type of emotion experienced (such as fear, anger, or love) depends on the person's cognitive assessment of the external stimulus or situation.

A considerable amount of evidence today tends to support James's theory. People throughout the world describe their emotions in terms of bodily changes and are quite consistent in the kinds of changes they associate with each emotion (Cacioppo et al., 1992; Rime et al., 1990). Researchers have also found that people who are particularly good at detecting changes in their own internal condition, such as changes in their heart rate, are more likely than others to detect and report emotional states in themselves (Critchely et al., 2004; Wiens et al., 2000). Moreover, brain imaging studies have shown that a certain portion of the somatosensory area of the cerebral cortex, which becomes active when a person is sensing his or her own bodily state, also becomes active when a person is consciously assessing his or her own emotional state (Critchely et al., 2004; Damasio, 2001).

Schachter's Cognition-Plus-Feedback Theory

FOCUS 32

How does Schachter's theory differ from James's? How did Schachter support his theory with experiments?

In the 1960s, Stanley Schachter developed a theory of emotion that can be understood as a variation of James's theory. According to Schachter, the feeling of an emotion depends not just on sensory feedback pertaining to the body's response but also on the person's perceptions and thoughts (cognitions) about the environmental event that presumably evoked that response. More specifically, he proposed that perception and thought about the environment influence the *type* of emotion felt, and that sensory feedback about the degree of bodily arousal influences the *intensity* of the emotion felt (see the bottom portion of Figure 5.15). Thus, if you see a bear, your perception that it is dangerous leads you to interpret your emotion as fear, and your perception of the degree to which your heart is pounding and your knees are trembling determines the amount of fear you experience. Schachter also proposed that the intensity of the emotional feeling influences the interpretation of the stimulus. Thus, if your bodily arousal was already high—perhaps from drinking too much coffee—that arousal would contribute to your emotional intensity and might lead you to perceive the bear as more dangerous than you otherwise would.

In experiments testing his theory, Schachter (1971) injected people with either epinephrine (a hormone also known as adrenaline, which raises heart rate and produces other effects associated with high arousal) or a placebo (an inactive substance) and then exposed them to various emotion-eliciting conditions. He found that epinephrine alone did not produce any particular emotion (the subjects just said they felt jumpy), but when epinephrine was combined with an emotion-inducing situation, such as a horror film, it increased the intensity of the subject's emotion. As predicted by his theory, the kind of emotion subjects felt depended on the external situation, but the intensity was heightened by epinephrine. The epinephrine-injected subjects manifested and reported more anger when insulted, more fear when watching a frightening film, and more hilarity when watching a slapstick comedy than did placebo-injected subjects. This emotion-enhancing effect occurred only if the subjects had not previously been informed of the physiological effects of epinephrine. Thus, according to Schachter, high physiological arousal increases emotion only when people believe that the arousal is caused by the external situation. Schachter's theory fits well with the modern idea that emotions are defined not just by feelings but also by the perceived objects of those feelings.

Influence of Facial Feedback on Emotional Experience

Paul Ekman (1984) proposed a theory of emotions that is similar to James's peripheral feedback theory but focuses particularly on the role of the face. As discussed in Chapter 3, Ekman and his colleagues found that different basic emotions are associated with different facial expressions. Those expressions are produced rapidly and automatically (though they can be inhibited). According to Ekman, sensory feedback from facial expressions contributes both to emotional feelings and to the production of the full-body reactions that accompany emotions.

If you form your face into a smile, will you feel happier? A suggestion typical of the literary heroine Pollyanna, perhaps—but research indicates there may be some truth to it. In one experiment, for example, some subjects were each asked to hold a pencil tightly between their teeth, which forced their faces into smiling expressions, and others were asked to hold a pencil between their lips in a manner that did not produce smiles (see **Figure 5.16**), as they watched films of happy or funny scenes (Soussignan, 2002). The result was that the former reported more enjoyment of the films than did the latter. In other experiments, subjects have been asked to contract certain facial muscles—in ways (unbeknownst to the subject) designed to mimic the facial expressions of fear, anger, sorrow, or happiness. The results, generally, are that people who hold their faces in these ways subsequently report experiencing more of the specific emotion that their faces were mimicking—whether or not they were aware that they were mimicking a particular emotion (Flack, 2006).

Ekman and his colleagues (1983) found that induced facial expressions not only can alter self-reports of emotion but also can produce physiological responses throughout the body that are consistent with the induced expression. In one experiment, these researchers asked subjects to move specific facial muscles in ways designed to mimic each of six basic emotional expressions (see **Figure 5.17**). For comparison, they asked other subjects to experience each emotion by mentally reliving an event in which that emotion had been strong. As the subjects held the

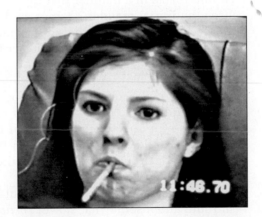

FIGURE 5.16 Forcing a smile In Soussignan's (2002) experiment testing the facial feedback theory of emotion, some subjects were asked to hold a pencil between their teeth in a manner that led to their lips being pulled back and their cheeks raised, similar to a full-faced smile, and others were asked to hold a pencil between their lips, which prevented smiling.

(a) (b) (c)

FIGURE 5.17 Inducing an expression of fear Shown here are frames from a videotape of a man following the instructions used by Ekman and his colleagues (1983) to induce an expression of fear: (a) "Raise your brows and pull them together," (b) "now raise your upper eyelids," and (c) "now stretch your lips horizontally, back toward your ears."

facial expressions or imagined the emotional events, various indices of their physiological arousal were recorded.

The main finding was that different patterns of arousal accompanied different emotions, but the pattern for a given emotion was the same whether the person had been asked to relive that emotion or simply to move certain facial muscles. For instance, anger, whether relived or mimicked by facial molding, was accompanied by increases in skin temperature that did not occur for the other emotions (consistent with evidence that blood tends to flow into the skin during anger). As another example, anger and fear—in both the mimicking and the reliving conditions—increased the subjects' heart rates more than did any other emotion. Researchers subsequently replicated these findings with a wide variety of people, including people in non-Western cultures (Levenson, 1992; Levenson et al., 1992).

Brain Mechanisms of Emotion

Thus far, we have focused on emotional feelings and peripheral bodily changes but have said little about the role of the brain in emotions. Of course the brain is the center both for producing the bodily changes and for experiencing emotional feelings. Research on the brain's emotional systems has focused particularly on two structures: the amygdala and the prefrontal portion of the cerebral cortex.

The Amygdala Assesses the Emotional Significance of Stimuli

In James's classic example (diagrammed in Figure 5.15, p. 181), a person sees a bear and reacts in a manner that the person subsequently interprets as fear. What causes the initial reaction? James assumed that somehow the brain can quickly and unconsciously assess the significance of stimuli and can generate appropriate bodily reactions. We now know that a crucial structure for this capacity of the brain is the amygdala.

Recall from Chapter 4 that the *amygdala*, a cluster of nuclei buried underneath the cerebral cortex, in the temporal lobe, is part of the limbic system. This structure appears to be, among other things, the brain's early warning system. It receives stimulus input from all of the body's sensory systems. It performs continuous, rapid assessments of that input, and alerts the rest of the brain and body if it judges that some sort of whole-body or behavioral reaction may be called for.

The amygdala receives sensory input by way of two routes: a very rapid *subcortical* route and a somewhat slower *cortical* route (diagrammed in **Figure 5.18** for the sense of vision). Through the former, it analyzes incoming information even before that information has been processed by sensory areas of the cerebral cortex. Through the latter, it analyzes, in more detail, information that has been processed by the cerebral cortex. The amygdala sends its output to many other brain structures. Through those outputs it alerts the rest of the brain to pay attention to the stimulus of concern, and it generates such bodily reactions as increased heart rate and muscle tension (Davis, 1992).

In a set of classic experiments with monkeys, removal of the amygdala along with nearby portions of the temporal lobe of the cerebral cortex on both sides of the brain produced a dramatic set of changes in behavior described as *psychic blindness* (Klüver & Bucy, 1937; Weiskrantz, 1956). The monkeys could still see objects and could move in a coordinated fashion, but they seemed indifferent to the psychological significance of objects. They no longer responded fearfully to objects that had previously frightened them or aggressively to objects that

FOCUS 34

What is some evidence that the amygdala initiates emotional reactions to stimuli and that this effect can occur even without conscious awareness of the emotion-eliciting stimuli?

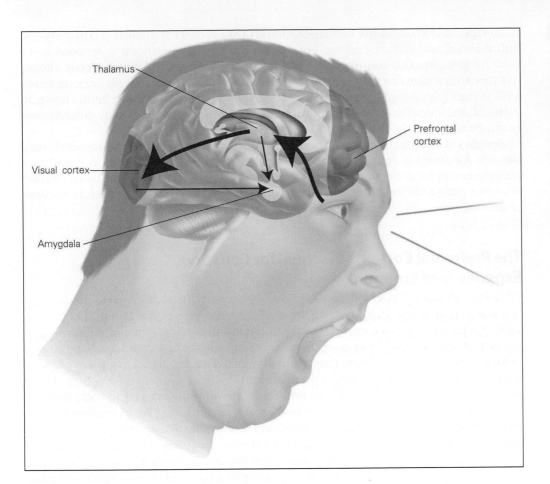

Thalamus

Prefrontal cortex

Visual cortex

Amygdala

FIGURE 5.18 Two routes from the eyes to the amygdala Most visual input goes from relay nuclei in the thalamus to the visual area of the cerebral cortex, and from there to other areas of the brain, including the amygdala. However, some visual input goes directly from the thalamus to the amygdala, bypassing the cerebral cortex. The direct input from the thalamus to the amygdala may be responsible for fast, unconscious emotional responses to visual stimuli.

had previously angered them. They also failed to distinguish in the usual ways between foods and nonfoods or between appropriate and inappropriate objects for sexual attention.

Humans who have suffered even partial damage to the amygdala exhibit striking losses in fear and anger, even though they don't show the other symptoms of psychic blindness (Allman & Brothers, 1994; Berridge, 2003). For instance, one woman with such damage failed to react emotionally, or even to show much concern, when she and her husband were mugged (Bruce & Young, 1998). In experiments, people with damage to the amygdala generally fail to respond emotionally to stimuli—such as pictures of frightening or disgusting scenes—that regularly elicit emotional responses and feelings in people with intact brains (Berntson et al., 2007; Helmuth, 2003).

Moreover, in brain imaging studies with people with intact brains, increased neural activity in the amygdala correlates strongly with increases in fear, anger, or disgust (Hamann et al., 2002; Whalen, 1998). The amygdala may also be activated, but less so, by stimuli that induce positive emotions, and may be more generally involved in processing the relevance of stimuli, both positive and negative (Cunningham & Borsch, 2012). In one brain imaging study with men, the left amygdala (but not the right) became active in response to a variety of appealing pictures, including depictions of attractive seminude women and of appetizing foods (Hamann et al., 2002). People even react emotionally to stimuli—such as angry words or faces—that are flashed on a screen too rapidly for conscious perception (Öhmann, 1999; Ruys & Stapel, 2008). This effect most likely occurs via the subcortical sensory input to the amygdala.

Joseph LeDoux and his colleagues found that rats with lesions destroying the entire visual and auditory cortex, but not the amygdala, continued to respond emotionally to sights and sounds that had previously been paired with electric shock, but rats with lesions destroying the amygdala did not (LeDoux, 1996; LeDoux et al., 1989). Similarly, people who have damage to the visual cortex have been shown to respond emotionally to visual stimuli that they could not consciously see (Anders et al., 2004).

Sensory areas of the cortex are essential for conscious perception of stimuli, but not for unconscious emotional responses to them. The fact that emotional responses can be generated by subcortical pathways to the amygdala helps explain why our emotions are often irrational and difficult to control through conscious reasoning.

The Prefrontal Cortex Is Essential for Conscious Experience of Emotion

FOCUS 35

What is some evidence that the prefrontal cortex is involved in the conscious feeling of emotions, and that the right and left prefrontal cortices are differentially involved with different types of emotional responses?

While the amygdala is essential for unconscious emotional responses, the *prefrontal cortex*—that is, the foremost portion of the frontal lobe of the cerebral cortex (at right in Figure 5.18)—is essential for the full conscious experience of emotions and the ability to act in deliberate, planned ways based on those feelings. One line of evidence for this comes from observations many decades ago of people who were subjected to prefrontal lobotomy—an operation that disconnects the prefrontal area from the rest of the brain and was, before the development of drug treatments, a relatively common treatment for severe mental disorders. The operation usually relieved people of their crippling emotional feelings, but it also left them unable to plan and organize their lives effectively (Valenstein, 1986). The prefrontal cortex receives input from the amygdala and from the somatosensory cortex, and such input provides it with information about the amygdala's assessment of the stimulus and the body's state of arousal.

A good deal of research suggests that, to some degree at least, the two cortical hemispheres are involved in processing different emotions. Much research using EEG or fMRI has shown greater neural activity in the right prefrontal cortex when experiencing negative emotions (especially fear and disgust) and greater activity in the left prefrontal cortex when experiencing positive emotions (Haller et al., 1998; Davidson et al., 2003). Recent studies, however, suggest that this laterality of neural activity has more to do with neural preparation to respond to the emotional stimuli than with actual experience of the emotional feeling (Harmon-Jones et al., 2006; Maxwell & Davidson, 2007). The right prefrontal cortex seems to be most involved in responses that entail *withdrawal*, or moving away from the emotional stimulus. That is why the right prefrontal cortex is most responsive in the emotions of fear and disgust. The left prefrontal cortex seems to be most involved in responses that involve *approach*, or moving toward the emotional stimulus, which is why it is most responsive in happy emotions. The most telling data come from studies involving anger. Anger is a negative emotion, but it tends to evoke approach (to confront or fight) rather than withdrawal. Researchers have found that anger is generally associated with greater activation of the left prefrontal cortex than the right, especially if the subjects are given instructions that lead them to visualize possible responses to the anger-provoking stimulus (Harmon-Jones et al., 2006).

Such research on the brain and emotions illustrates the increasing conjoining of psychological theories with knowledge of physiological mechanisms. Conscious and unconscious assessments of differing emotion-provoking stimuli, and anticipated responses to those stimuli, differ not just in the realm of subjective experience but also in the brain pathways that underlie those assessments and response preparations.

SECTION REVIEW

Emotions are subjective feelings directed toward specific objects.

Nature of Emotion	Peripheral Feedback	Brain Mechanisms
■ An *emotion* is a feeling that is tied subjectively to an object of that feeling, as exemplified by anger at someone who insulted you.	■ James argued that peripheral bodily reactions precede and cause emotions.	■ The amygdala rapidly evaluates sensory information for its significance to survival or well-being and triggers bodily responses.
■ The feeling aspect of emotion, called *affect,* can vary in degree of arousal and degree of pleasantness or unpleasantness.	■ Schachter proposed that peripheral feedback affects emotional intensity, but perceptions and thoughts determine the type of emotion.	■ The prefrontal cortex is crucial for conscious emotional experience and deliberate action based on it.
■ Psychologists have theories, but no consensus, about how to classify emotions.	■ Ekman suggested that feedback from facial muscles can induce feelings and bodily reactions indicative of emotion.	■ The right and left prefrontal cortexes are relatively specialized for emotional responses involving, respectively, withdrawal and approach.
■ Emotions have adaptive value, motivating us and communicating our intentions and needs to others.	■ There is evidence to support all three of these ideas.	

Thinking Critically About Motivation and Emotion

1. How might an understanding of the neural mechanisms of motivation help you get a better night's sleep, stay on a diet, or kick your gambling habit?

2. Are emotions, even negative ones, useful? How might the various emotions be seen as adaptations evolved to solve everyday problems?

Reflections and Connections

As you review the mechanisms of reward, hunger, sleep, and emotions described in this chapter, use the following two points to help organize your thoughts.

1. Relating behavioral states to physiological states Hunger, sleepiness, and emotions are examples of *behavioral states—* sustained but reversible changes in the way a person or animal behaves in a given environment. This chapter includes many examples of research aimed at finding relationships between behavioral states and *physiological states.* The general goals of such work are to identify the changes in the brain that provide the foundations for behavioral states and to identify the various neural and chemical inputs that control those changes. These goals are both fascinating and difficult to achieve because the machine being studied is so extraordinarily complex (not to mention alive and mortal). As you think about each type of behavioral state discussed in this chapter, ask yourself: What changes in the brain correspond to this state, and how are these changes regulated through means that tend to promote the individual's survival? Knowing what you do about the relations between different

behavioral and physiological states, what can you do to take advantage of this knowledge in your own life—to get a better night's sleep, to stick to a diet, or to kick or avoid an addiction?

2. Two kinds of methods in the physiological study of states Like the rest of the book, this chapter is about methods and evidence, not just findings. The specific methods described in the chapter fall into two broad categories. One category involves *intervention* in ongoing physiological processes to see what happens to the behaviorally measured state. What happens to a drive or emotion if a particular part of the brain is destroyed or stimulated, or if the activity of a particular hormone or neurotransmitter is increased or decreased in some way? As you review the chapter, notice how often such methods are mentioned.

Intervention is a powerful way to identify causal relationships between physiology and behavior. But most intervention procedures are harmful or at least risky to the subject, so they are used primarily in studies of nonhuman animals. The intervention approach is approximated, however, in studies of people whose natural physiology has been disrupted through accident or disease. The chapter describes several studies of that sort.

The other category involves the *measurement* of physiological processes and the *correlation* of the measures with changes in behavioral state. What natural changes in brain activity (measured by EEG or by brain imaging methods) or in hormonal secretions, heart rate, or other physiological variables accompany specific changes in behavioral state? Most measurement procedures are safe and can be used with humans. Notice, as you review the chapter, how often this correlational method was used in the human studies

described. This method helps identify reliable relationships but does not, by itself, inform us about cause and effect. The observation that brain waves slow down during sleep, or that skin temperature rises during anger, or that the amygdala is active during fear, tells us about correlations but not necessarily about causality. To test cause–effect hypotheses, researchers seek to manipulate the physiological system and measure the effect on behavior. That is why intervention experiments with nonhuman animals often go hand in hand with correlational studies in humans to get at the full story.

Key Terms

affect 177	discrete emotion theory 179	leptin 162	non-REM sleep 168
arcuate nucleus 161	dopamine 157	medial forebrain bundle 156	nucleus accumbens 157
central drive system 155	drive 151	mood 177	regulatory drive 153
central-state theory of drives 155	emotion 177	motivation 151	REM sleep 168
	endorphin 158	motivational state 151	sensory-specific satiety 163
circadian rhythm 175	homeostasis 152	nonregulatory drive 153	suprachiasmatic nucleus 175

Find Out More

Arianna Huffington (2016). *The sleep revolution: Transforming your life one night at a time.* New York: Harmony.

Modern culture has been treating getting a good night's sleep as something only the lazy do. Nearly half of people in the United States and other first-world countries are chronically sleep-deprived, and this has consequences for physical and mental health as well as economic productivity. Arianna Huffington describes this problem, examines the science and business of sleep, and provides some solutions for living healthier, more restful lives. For those who don't have enough waking hours to read her book, you can get the 4-minute version from her TED talk at https://www.ted.com/talks/arianna_huffington_how_to_succeed_get_more_sleep

Jim Horne (2006). *Sleepfaring: A journey through the science of sleep.* Oxford, UK: Oxford University Press.

In this engaging book, a leading sleep researcher describes what we know about sleep and how we know it. Here you will find chapters on animal sleep, brain control of sleep, measures and stages of sleep, effects of sleep deprivation (including an account of Randy Gardner's record-setting performance of 11 straight days without sleep), dreams, and sleep problems. Horne argues that many people worry more than necessary about lack of sleep; most people, he says, do fine with less sleep than they think they need.

Carl Hart & Maia Szalavitz (2013). *High price: A neuroscientist's journey of self-discovery that challenges everything you know about drugs and society.* New York, NY: HarperCollins.

Trailblazing neuroscientist Carl Hart, along with science writer Maia Szalavitz, takes a personal look at addiction and the brain, exploring his own rough background on the streets in the context of his current research in neuroscience and brain activity. In the process, he shows how drugs, the brain, and motivation interact with each other and how they are affected by our society at large.

Lisa Feldman Barrett (2017). *How emotions are made: The secret life of the brain.* New York, NY: Houghton Mifflin Harcourt.

Determined to challenge classical views of emotion, psychological scientist Lisa Feldman Barrett proposes a theory of emotions that takes into account the moment-by-moment confluence of different networks throughout our bodies that make us feel one way or another at any given instant. She argues that a theory of constructed emotion can inspire us to better understand ourselves and those we interact with.

National Institutes of Health (2017). Calculate your body mass index. https://www.nhlbi.nih.gov/health/educational/lose_wt/BMI/bmicalc.htm

This website provides a quick way to estimate your body mass index based on your height and weight. On this page, you can also find links to a number of weight and health-related topics including assessing your weight and health risks, menu planners, and family resources.

Paul Ekman Videos (2017). Paul Ekman Group.

http://www.paulekman.com/paul-ekman/videos/

Paul Ekman's research on facial expressions has shaped the field in numerous ways as well as influencing popular culture with his work on the TV series "*Lie to*

Me." This site offers a selection of short videos in which Ekman discusses emotion, deception, and compassion. Here you can also find plenty of further readings as well as news about Ekman's current research.

Dan Pink (2009, July). The Puzzle of Motivation. TEDGlobal 2009.

https://www.ted.com/talks/dan_pink_on_motivation

Are monetary rewards a good motivator in the workplace? This 18-minute TED talk by writer and career analyst Daniel H. Pink will help you answer that question as you explore the the science of motivation and its application in the business world.

LaunchPad
macmillan learning

Visit LaunchPad for Psychology 8e launchpadworks.com to access the e-book, videos, activities, additional resources, and LearningCurve quizzes, as well as study aids including flash cards and web quizzes.

PART III

Sensation and Perception

Our senses are the conduits that connect our brains and minds to the rest of the world. Nothing is more fundamental to psychology than an understanding of the senses. All of our perceptions, all that we learn, all of our memories and thoughts, come to us through our senses. How does our nervous system respond to and interpret the patterns of energy in the physical world? How do those responses and interpretations provide us with useful information? In Chapter 6, we apply these questions to smell, taste, pain, and hearing; and in Chapter 7, we apply them to vision.

CHAPTER

Smell, Taste, Pain, Hearing, and Psychophysics

6

LEARNING OUTCOMES

After studying this chapter, you should be able to:

- Distinguish sensation from perception and summarize how our sensory systems function.
- Explain sensory thresholds and how they respond to stimuli.
- Summarize how the sense of smell works.
- Summarize how the sense of taste works.
- Describe the sense of touch and how we perceive pain.
- Explain how we hear sounds.

CHAPTER OUTLINE

Overview of Sensory Processes

Psychophysics

Smell

Taste

Pain

Hearing

Thinking Critically About Smell, Taste, Pain, Hearing, and Psychophysics

Reflections and Connections

Key Terms

Find Out More

What would your mental life be like if you had no senses? What if, from birth, you could not see, hear, touch, taste, smell, or in any other way sense the world around you? You would not be able to react to anything because reaction requires sensory input. You would not be able to learn anything because learning begins with sensory input. Would you be able to think? What could you think about with no knowledge gained from the senses? Philosophers, from Aristotle on, have pondered these questions and have usually concluded that without sensation there would be no mental life. It is no wonder that the study of the senses has always been a fundamental part of the science of psychology.

Sensory systems have evolved in all animals in order to guide their behavior. To survive and reproduce, animals must respond to objects and events in the world in which they live. They must move toward food and mates, for example, and away from predators and precipices. Sensory systems did not evolve to provide full, objective accounts of the world's physical properties. Rather, they evolved to provide the specific kinds of information the animal needs to survive and reproduce. To understand an animal's sensory systems is to understand its way of life. For instance, frogs' eyes contain "bug detectors," neurons that respond only to small, moving dark spots and that trigger tongue movements in the spot's direction; they also contain color detectors that distinguish the hue of a pond from that of grass and lily pads (Muntz, 1964). Many species of migrating birds have a magnetic sense, oriented to the earth's magnetic field, that enables them to fly in the correct direction even on cloudy nights when visual cues are not available (Hughes, 1999). Bats, which fly at night, have tiny, almost useless eyes but huge ears. They emit ultrasonic (beyond the range of human hearing) beeps and hear the echoes, which they use to detect both barriers and prey as they navigate in complete darkness (Griffin, 1986).

This chapter and the next are about sensation and perception. **Sensation** refers to the basic processes by which sensory organs and the nervous system respond to stimuli in the environment and to the elementary psychological experiences that result from those processes (e.g., our experience of the bitterness of a taste, loudness of a sound, or redness of a sight). **Perception**, in contrast, refers to the more complex organizing of sensory information within the brain and to the meaningful interpretations extracted from it (e.g., "This is strong coffee," "My alarm clock is ringing," or "That object is an apple"). Thus, the study of perception is more closely tied to the study of the brain, thought, and memory than is the study of sensation. The distinction is fuzzy, however, because during the earliest steps of taking in stimulus information, we already begin to organize it in ways useful for extracting meaning.

This chapter begins with a brief overview of basic processes involved in sensation. We then discuss psychophysics, an approach to finding and describing reliable relationships between physical stimuli and their sensory experiences. The chapter continues with sections on smell, taste, pain, and hearing. The next chapter deals exclusively with vision, which is by far the most thoroughly studied of the senses.

Overview of Sensory Processes

Most broadly, the process of sensation can be diagrammed as follows:

physical stimulus → physiological response → sensory experience

FOCUS 1

How can the process of sensation be described as a chain of three different kinds of events?

This diagram comprises three classes of events, each of which is entirely different from the others: (1) The *physical stimulus* is the matter or energy of the physical world that impinges on sense organs; (2) the *physiological response* is the pattern of chemical and electrical activity that occurs in sense organs, nerves, and the brain as a result of the stimulus; and (3) the *sensory experience* is the subjective, psychological sensation or perception (e.g., the taste, sound, or sight) experienced by the individual whose sense organs have been stimulated. In sipping a cup of coffee, we encounter molecules of caffeine on our tongue (physical stimulus), and we experience a bitter taste (sensory experience). The bitterness is not a chemical property of the caffeine molecules; it exists only in our sensory experience triggered by the molecules. Similarly, electromagnetic energy of a certain wavelength enters our eyes, and we experience the dark brown color of coffee. The brown color is not a property of the electromagnetic energy but exists only in our sensory experience.

Sensory psychologists are interested in identifying lawful relationships among the three classes of events in the foregoing diagram. Here, before discussing particular senses separately, let's consider some general principles that apply to all sensory systems.

Each Sensory System Has Distinct Receptors and Neural Pathways

Ever since Aristotle, people have spoken of the *five senses:* smell, taste, touch, hearing, and vision. Actually, humans have more than five senses, and any attempt to tally them up to an exact number is arbitrary, because what one person thinks of as one sense may be thought of as two or more by another. For example, our skin is sensitive not just to touch but also to temperature (with separate receptors for sensing hot and cold) and pain, neither of which is included in Aristotle's five. Other

TABLE 6.1 Stimuli, receptors, and the pathways to the brain for various senses

Sense	Stimulus	Receptors	Pathway to the brain
Smell	Molecules dissolved in fluid on mucous membranes in the nose	Sensitive ends of olfactory neurons in the olfactory epithelium in the nose	Olfactory nerve (1st cranial nerve)
Taste	Molecules dissolved in fluid on the tongue	Taste cells in taste buds on the tongue	Portions of facial, glossopharyngeal, and vagus nerves (7th, 9th, and 10th cranial nerves)
Touch	Pressure on the skin	Sensitive ends of touch neurons in skin	Trigeminal nerve (5th cranial nerve) for touch above the neck; spinal nerves for touch elsewhere
Pain	Wide variety of potentially harmful stimuli	Sensitive ends of pain neurons in skin and other tissues	Trigeminal nerve (5th cranial nerve) for pain above the neck; spinal nerves for pain elsewhere
Hearing	Sound waves	Pressure-sensitive hair cells in cochlea of inner ear	Auditory nerve (8th cranial nerve)
Vision	Light waves	Light-sensitive rods and cones in retina of eye	Optic nerve (2nd cranial nerve)

senses omitted by Aristotle have to do with body position and the body's internal environment. We have a sense of balance (vestibular), mediated by a mechanism in the inner ear, and a sense of limb position and movement (proprioception), mediated by receptors in muscles and joints. Each sense has distinct sensory receptors and neural pathways to and within the brain (Hendry & Hsiao, 2013; Schwartz & Krantz, 2016).

Sensory receptors are specialized structures that respond to physical stimuli by producing electrical changes that can initiate neural impulses in sensory neurons. *Sensory neurons* (Chapter 4) are specialized neurons that carry information from sensory receptors into the central nervous system. For some senses, receptors are simply the sensitive ends of sensory neurons; for others, they are separate cells that form synapses upon sensory neurons. For some senses, receptors all exist in a specific, localized sensory organ, such as the ear, eye, or nose; for others, they exist in a wide variety of locations. Pain receptors, for example, exist not just throughout the skin but also in muscles, tendons, joints, and many other places. The stimuli, receptors, and peripheral nerves involved in the most thoroughly studied senses are listed in **Table 6.1**.

Regardless of whether they come from one location or many, the neurons for any given sense lead to pathways in the central nervous system that are unique to that sense. These pathways send messages to many different parts of the brain, including specific ***sensory areas*** of the cerebral cortex—for example, areas devoted to vision, hearing, and touch (see **Figure 6.1**). Although brain structures below the cortex can organize unconscious behavioral reactions to sensory stimuli, conscious sensory experiences depend on activity within the cerebral cortex.

Every sensation that you experience consciously is a product, ultimately, of some pattern of activity within a sensory area of your cerebral cortex. You see light because light receptors in your eyes are connected to visual areas of your cortex, and you hear sound because sound receptors in your ears are connected to auditory areas of your cortex. If we could somehow rewire those connections, sending your

FIGURE 6.1 Primary sensory areas of the cerebral cortex Shown here are the locations of the primary cortical areas for vision, hearing, somatosensation (which includes touch, temperature sensitivity, and pain), taste, and smell. The primary taste area lies in a portion of the cerebral cortex called the *insula,* which is buried in the fold between the parietal and temporal lobes. The primary olfactory area lies in a portion of cerebral cortex called the *piriform cortex,* which wraps underneath the temporal lobe. Secondary sensory processing areas generally lie near the primary areas.

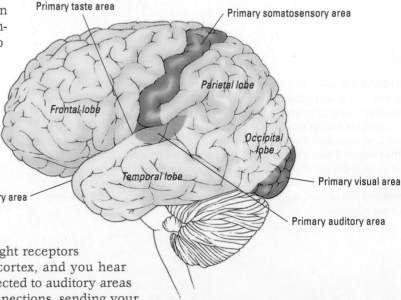

Primary taste area
Primary somatosensory area
Parietal lobe
Frontal lobe
Occipital lobe
Temporal lobe
Primary olfactory area
Primary visual area
Primary auditory area

optic nerves to your auditory brain areas and your auditory nerves to your visual brain areas, you would hear light and see sound. When you bump the back of your head, you may "see stars" because the bump artificially activates neurons in visual areas of your brain.

Sensory Systems Preserve Information About Stimulus Quantity and Quality

FOCUS 2

In general, how do physical stimuli produce action potentials in sensory neurons?

For senses to be useful, they must preserve—in the patterns of neural activity they produce—relevant information about the physical stimuli to which they are responding. That preservation of information is called **sensory coding**.

Every form of energy can vary along at least two dimensions—a quantitative dimension and a qualitative one. The *quantitative variation* refers to the amount or intensity of energy. A sound or light can be weak or strong; molecules stimulating taste or smell can be dilute or highly concentrated. The *qualitative variation* refers to the precise kind of energy. Lights of different wavelengths (which we perceive as different colors) are qualitatively different, as are sounds of different frequencies (which we perceive as different pitches), as are different chemicals (which we perceive as different smells or tastes). Each of our senses relies on **transduction**, the neural process by which a receptor cell produces an electrical change in response to physical stimulation. Transduction occurs in such a way that information about the quantity and quality of the stimulus is preserved in the pattern of action potentials sent to the brain.

FOCUS 3

In general, how do sensory systems code information about the amount and kind of stimulus energy?

Coding of stimulus *quantity* results from the fact that stronger stimuli produce larger **receptor potentials**, which in turn produce faster rates of action potentials in sensory neurons. The brain interprets a fast rate of action potentials as a strong stimulus and a slow rate as a weak stimulus.

In contrast, the coding of stimulus *quality* occurs because qualitatively different stimuli optimally activate different sets of neurons. Different receptors within any given sensory tissue are tuned to respond best to somewhat different forms of energy. In the eye, for example, three different kinds of receptor cells, each most sensitive to a different range of wavelengths of light, provide the basis for color vision. In the ear, different receptors are most sensitive to different sound frequencies. And in the nose and mouth, different receptors are most sensitive to different kinds of molecules. Thus, in general, qualitative variations are coded as different ratios of activity in sensory neurons coming from different sets of receptors. For an illustration of how quantitative and qualitative information about a stimulus can be independently coded for the sense of taste, see **Figure 6.2**. The same principle applies to other senses, as you will discover later in this chapter.

FIGURE 6.2 Quantitative and qualitative coding of taste Shown here are the rates of action potentials in two different taste sensory neurons when a weak or strong solution of sugar or salt is placed on the tongue. Each neuron responds at a faster rate to a strong solution of a given substance than to a weak one (quantitative coding); but neuron A always responds at a faster rate than neuron B when the stimulus is sugar, and the reverse is true when the stimulus is salt (qualitative coding). This illustrates the general principle that sensory quantity is coded in the overall rate of action potentials in sensory neurons and sensory quality is coded in the ratio of activity across different sets of neurons.

(Data are hypothetical, but are based on such findings as those of Nowlis & Frank, 1977.)

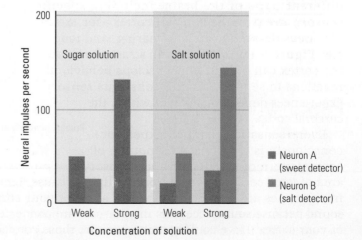

Sensory Systems Respond to Changes More Than to Steady States

Our senses are designed to alert us to changes in our sensory environment and to be relatively oblivious to steady states. When you first put on your wristwatch, you feel the pressure on your skin, but later you don't. When you first wade into a lake, the water may seem terribly cold, but later only slightly cool. When you first enter a chemistry lab, the odor may seem overwhelming, but later you hardly notice it. The change in sensitivity that occurs when a given set of sensory receptors and neurons is either strongly stimulated or relatively unstimulated for a length of time is called *sensory adaptation*. In general, when the amount of stimulation of a sensory system increases for a period of time, the sensory system adapts by becoming less sensitive than it was before; and when the amount of stimulation decreases, the sensory system adapts by becoming more sensitive than it was before.

In many cases, sensory adaptation is mediated by the receptor cells themselves. If a stimulus remains for a period of time, the receptor potential and rate of action potentials are at first great, but over time they lessen, resulting in reduced sensation. However, some adaptation is mediated by changes further inward in the central nervous system.

■ **It's a nice place to work, but I wouldn't want to visit** Can you imagine the pungent smell you would experience if you walked into this cave full of Roquefort cheese? Yet, as suggested by this worker's equable expression, one adapts after a while. In general, our senses are designed to register changes in the environment, not steady states.

FOCUS 4

What is the value of sensory adaptation? How can you demonstrate that adaptation can occur in neurons in the brain, not just in receptors?

SECTION REVIEW

Sensory experiences result from physiological responses to physical stimuli.

Receptors and Pathways

- Sensory receptors respond to physical stimuli with electrical changes, a process called transduction.
- Those electrical changes, called receptor potentials, can trigger action potentials in sensory neurons.
- Activity in a specific sensory area of the cortex (such as visual) produces a corresponding type of sensory experience (such as sight).

Sensory Coding

- Information about physical stimuli is coded in the patterns of neural activity induced by the stimuli.
- Stronger stimuli produce larger receptor potentials and faster rates of firing in sensory neurons.
- Qualitatively different stimuli produce different ratios of activity across different sets of receptors and sensory neurons.

Sensory Adaptation

- In general, continuous stimulation reduces the responsiveness of a sensory system and lack of stimulation increases its responsiveness.
- As a result, senses are more responsive to changing than to unchanging stimulation.

Psychophysics

Psychophysics is the study of relationships between physical characteristics of stimuli and the sensory experiences produced by those stimuli. (You can remember the term by recalling that *psychophysics* relates *psycho*logical sensory experiences to *physic*al characteristics of stimuli.) Sensory experience is typically assessed by asking subjects to make some judgment about each stimulus, such as whether it is present or absent or how it compares to another stimulus. Many experiments discussed later in this chapter are psychophysical, including those assessing people's abilities to detect or identify particular substances by taste or smell and those relating the frequency of a tone to its perceived pitch.

This section describes some psychophysical methods and findings related to (a) the detection of weak stimuli and (b) the detection of small changes in stimuli. Historically, research in psychophysics by such scientists as Ernst Weber and Gustav Fechner played a vital role in the founding of psychology as a science, and many of the questions they raised in the nineteenth century are still topics of research and debate today.

The Absolute Threshold Is a Measure of Sensitivity

Psychophysicists refer to the faintest detectable stimulus of any given type as the *absolute threshold* for that type of stimulus. For example, the weakest intensity of a particular tone (say, middle C on the piano) that you can hear 50% of the time is your absolute threshold for that tone. The weakest solution of sodium chloride (table salt) that you can taste is your absolute threshold for sodium chloride. Absolute thresholds vary from person to person and are used clinically as measures of a person's sensitivity to specific types of stimuli. If you have undergone a clinical test of your hearing, this was a test of your absolute threshold for various sound frequencies. In general, for most senses, absolute thresholds are lower (meaning that sensitivity is greater) for younger adults than for older adults, and, for some senses, women often have greater sensitivity than men. For example, Pamela Dalton and her colleagues (2002) tested women and men repeatedly to determine their absolute thresholds for certain odorous chemicals. As shown in **Figure 6.3**, the women, but not the men, exhibited dramatic increases in sensitivity (declines in absolute thresholds) with repeated testing.

The Difference Threshold Depends on the Magnitude of the Original Stimulus

Another measure of sensitivity is the *difference threshold*, defined as the minimal difference in magnitude (or intensity) between two stimuli that is required for the person to detect them as different. The difference threshold is also called the *just-noticeable difference*, abbreviated *jnd*.

In the early nineteenth century, the German physicist Ernst Weber (1834) conducted a systematic study of just-noticeable differences. Weber asked: What is the relationship between the jnd and the magnitude of the original stimulus? Is the jnd the same for a given type of stimulus regardless of the magnitude of the original stimulus, or does it vary in some systematic way with that magnitude?

In one series of experiments, Weber applied this question to people's abilities to judge differences between weights. On each trial he asked the subjects to pick up each of two weights (the "original" weight and a comparison weight), one at a time, and to judge which was heavier. Weber found that the jnd varied in direct proportion to the original weight. Specifically, he found that for any original weight that he used (within a certain range), the jnd was approximately 1/30 of that weight (Gescheider, 1976). Thus, a typical subject could just barely detect the difference between a 15-gram and a 15.5-gram weight or between a 90-gram and a 93-gram weight. In the first case the jnd was 0.5 gram, and in the second it was 3 grams, but in both cases it was 1/30 of the original weight (which was always the lower of the two weights being compared).

In other experiments, Weber studied people's abilities to discriminate between the lengths of two lines, one presented after the other, and again he found a constant proportionality between the original

FIGURE 6.3 A sex difference in olfactory ability When women and men were tested in repeated sessions for their ability to smell weak concentrations of benzaldehyde (an almond-cherry smell) and citralva (an orange-lemon smell), the women but not the men showed dramatic improvement. By the eighth session, the women's absolute threshold for citralva was more than five log units less than that of the men. In other words, the women were smelling this substance at concentrations less than one hundred-thousandth of the minimal concentration that the men could smell.

(Data from Dalton et al., 2002.)

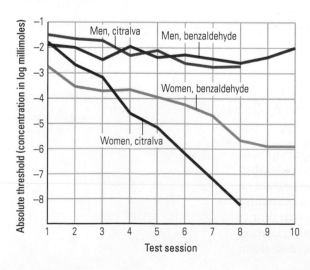

■ **Finding the absolute threshold** In a
sounds of varying frequencies and amp
to one ear at a time. To find the absolu
given frequency, for a given ear, the s
decreasing amplitudes until the person
at increasing amplitudes until the person can detec

stimulus and the difference threshold. For this task, however, the constant fraction was 1/100 rather than 1/30. Thus, a typical subject could just barely detect the difference between a 100- and a 101-millimeter line or between a 1,000- and a 1,010-millimeter line.

On the basis of these and similar experiments, Weber formulated a general law, now called **Weber's law**, stating that *the jnd for stimulus magnitude is a constant proportion of the magnitude of the original stimulus*. The law can be abbreviated as

$$\text{jnd} = kM$$

in which M is the magnitude or intensity of the stimulus used as the original stimulus and k is a proportionality constant referred to as the *Weber fraction*, which is different for different sensory tasks (in the examples just cited, 1/30 for weight judgment and 1/100 for length judgment). Since Weber's time, researchers have confirmed Weber's law for many different types of stimuli, including sounds, sights, tastes, and smells. The law holds up rather well over a wide portion of the possible range of intensities or magnitudes for most types of stimuli, but not at the very low (near the absolute threshold) and very high ends of the range.

Signal Detection Theory

The concept of a sensory threshold implies that beyond a certain level of stimulus intensity (e.g., a specific decibel level of a sound) a person will perceive a stimulus, whereas at a lower intensity the stimulus will not be perceived. It is either perceived or it is not. Yet, it's not quite that simple. Detecting a stimulus depends not only on the strength of the stimulus but also on some characteristics of the perceiver. For example, how alert or motivated is the perceiver? Is it more important never to miss a signal, or will it be more problematic to notice a signal when one was not actually present? To take these psychological factors into consideration, psychologists developed **signal detection theory** (Green & Swets, 1966), which proposes that the detection of a sensory stimulus is dependent upon both the physical intensity of the stimulus and the psychological state (including expectations,

---

FOCUS 5

How did Weber derive a law from data on just-noticeable differences? How can Weber's law be used to predict the degree to which two stimuli must differ for a person to tell them apart?

FIGURE 6.4 Signal detection theory On a series of trials, subjects are to determine whether a stimulus (e.g., a sound) is present or not. This results in four possible outcomes: *Hit* (a stimulus was presented and detected), *Miss* (a stimulus was presented but not detected), *False Alarm* (no stimulus was presented but one was falsely detected), and *Correct Rejection* (no stimulus was presented and none was detected).

		Response	
		Yes (Present)	No (Absent)
Stimulus Signal	Present	Hit	Miss
	Absent	False Alarm	Correct Rejection

motivation, and alertness) of the perceiver. In a signal detection experiment, a stimulus of varying intensity is presented to the subject on some trials and on other trials no stimulus is presented. Subjects' task is merely to say whether a stimulus was presented or not (yes or no) on each trial. This results in one of four outcomes, shown in **Figure 6.4**: *Hit* (a stimulus was presented and detected), *Miss* (a stimulus was presented but not detected), *False Alarm* (no stimulus was presented but one was falsely detected), and *Correct Rejection* (no stimulus was presented and none was detected).

How does such a paradigm help us understand perception? Signal detection theory takes into consideration that people must make judgments about the presence or absence of often ambiguous information, and that judgments are influenced by a host of psychological factors in addition to sensory sensitivity: expectations, motivations, state (e.g., aroused, fatigued), mood, and so on. For example, in diagnosing a possible cancerous lump in a breast, how sensitive is the doctor in identifying a suspicious lump of tissue from a background of normal breast tissue? Does the patient have a family history of breast cancer, raising the doctor's expectation of finding a lump? Given the patient's age and general health, would detecting a lump have greater consequences than not finding one? Using signal detection theory and some statistics, researchers can differentiate a person's sensory sensitivity for detecting a stimulus from the criterion he or she uses to make a "present" or "absent" judgment. There are individual differences both in people's sensory sensitivity and in their criteria for making a "present" judgment, and knowing these differences can have important implications for people performing a host of tasks—for a radar technician identifying "friend" versus "foes" on a screen, a psychiatrist or clinical psychologist making a violence risk assessment ("Is he a risk to himself or others?"), or a doctor making a medical diagnosis, among others (Swets, Dawes, & Monahan, 2000).

SECTION REVIEW

Psychophysics relates sensations to physical characteristics of stimuli.

Sensory Thresholds

- A person's absolute threshold for a specific type of stimulus is the lowest detectable intensity of the stimulus.

- The smallest difference in intensity of a given type of stimulus that a person can detect is a difference threshold, or jnd.

- According to Weber's law, the jnd is a constant proportion of the magnitude of the original stimulus.

Signal Detection Theory

- Detection of a stimulus depends upon both the physical intensity of the stimulus and the psychological state (including expectations, motivation, and alertness) of the perceiver.

Smell

Smell and taste are called chemical senses because the stimuli for them are chemical molecules. The chemical senses are first and foremost systems for warning and attracting. They play on our drives and emotions more than on our intellects. Think of the attraction we feel when we smell a valentine gift of chocolates, perfume, or fresh roses; or the aversive warning sent to us by the stench of feces or rotting meat.

The human sense of smell, or **olfaction**, is much less sensitive than that of many other animals (for example, humans have about 500 genes involved with olfaction, whereas mice have 1,300; Scott, 2013), but it is still remarkably sensitive and useful. We can smell smoke at concentrations well below that needed to trigger even the most sensitive of household smoke detectors. By one recent estimation, humans can distinguish among roughly *1 trillion* different chemicals by smell (Bushdid et al., 2014). Blind people regularly identify individuals by their unique odors, and sighted people can do that too when they try. And smell contributes greatly to what we call "flavor" in foods.

Anatomy and Physiology of Smell

Great progress has been made in recent decades in understanding the sense of smell.

Transduction and Coding for the Sense of Smell

Figure 6.5 illustrates the basic layout of the olfactory (smell) system. The stimuli for smell are molecules that evaporate into the air, are taken with air into the nasal cavity, and then become dissolved in the mucous fluid covering the olfactory epithelium, the sensory tissue for smell, which lines the top of the nasal cavity. The olfactory epithelium contains the sensitive terminals of olfactory sensory neurons

FOCUS 6

How do transduction, qualitative coding, and quantitative coding occur for the sense of smell?

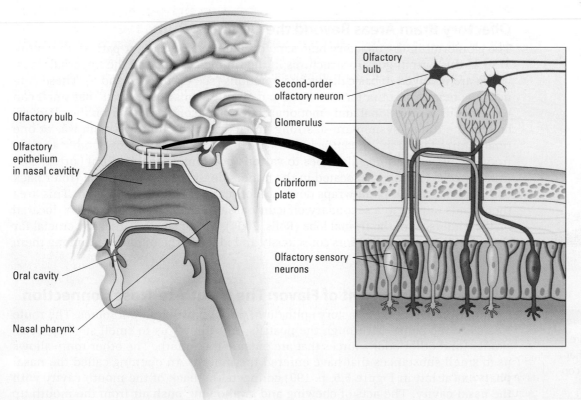

FIGURE 6.5 The anatomy of smell Molecules of odorants enter the nose through the nostrils, become dissolved in the mucous fluid covering the olfactory epithelium, and bind to receptor sites on the sensitive tips of olfactory sensory neurons, where they initiate action potentials. The sensory neurons send their axons through the cribriform plate (a small bone shelf) to form synapses on second-order olfactory neurons in the glomeruli of the olfactory bulb, directly above the nasal cavity. As illustrated in the right-hand diagram by the use of color, each glomerulus receives input from only one type of olfactory sensory neuron (defined by its type of receptor sites). Of the roughly 400 types that exist in the human olfactory system, only two types of such neurons are shown here (depicted as yellow and blue).

(Schwartz & Krantz, 2016) that are capable of binding molecules of specific odorants (odorous substances). The binding of a molecule to a receptor site changes the structure of the cell membrane, which results in an electrical change that tends to trigger action potentials in the neuron's axon. The greater the number of binding sites activated by odorous molecules, the greater the rate of action potentials triggered in the axon.

The olfactory nerve contains roughly 400 different types of sensory neurons, each characterized by a distinctly shaped binding site on its terminals within the olfactory epithelium (Wilson & Mainen, 2006). Any given type of binding site can bind more than one odorant, but any given odorant binds more readily to some types than to others. Thus, each type of olfactory neuron differs from the other types in its degree of sensitivity to particular odorants.

The axons of the olfactory sensory neurons pass through a thin, porous bone into the *olfactory bulb* of the brain, where they form synapses upon other neurons in structures called *glomeruli* [glŏ-**mer**´-ū-lē] (singular *glomerulus*; depicted at right in Figure 6.5). The pattern of these connections is remarkably orderly. Each glomerulus in the olfactory bulb receives input from several thousand olfactory sensory neurons, but all these neurons are of the same type. For each of the 400 different types of olfactory sensory neurons, there is a different receiving glomerulus (or a set of two or three such glomeruli) in the olfactory bulb (Wilson & Mainen, 2006).

From this work, researchers have inferred the process by which qualitative and quantitative coding occurs for the sense of smell. Each odorant that we can distinguish is apparently characterized by its ability to produce a unique pattern of activity across the 400 different types of olfactory neurons and their corresponding glomeruli in the olfactory bulb. Thus, odorant A might trigger much activity in one set of glomeruli, a moderate amount in another set, and very little in others. The greater the amount of odorant A, the greater would be the total amount of activity triggered in each of the glomeruli that it affects, but the ratio of activity across glomeruli would remain relatively constant. Thus, the ratio indicates the type of odorant (quality of the smell), while the total amount of activity indicates the amount of odorant (quantity, or intensity of the smell).

Olfactory Brain Areas Beyond the Olfactory Bulb

The glomeruli in the olfactory bulb send output to various other parts of the brain. Most of this output goes to structures in the limbic system and the hypothalamus, which are involved in basic drives and emotions (see Chapters 4 and 5). These connections help to account for the strong and often unconscious effects that smell can have on our motivational and emotional states. The connections from the olfactory bulb to the limbic system are so strong, in fact, that the limbic system was at one time referred to as the *rhinencephalon,* which literally means "nose brain." Output from the olfactory bulbs also goes to various portions of the cerebral cortex. The primary olfactory area is located in the underside of the temporal lobe (refer back to Figure 6.1, p. 193) and wraps down underneath the rest of the brain. This area then sends output to a secondary olfactory area in the *orbitofrontal cortex,* located on the underside of the frontal lobe (Rolls, 2004). These cortical areas are crucial for the ability to experience odors consciously and identify the differences among them (Buck, 2000a; Rolls, 2004).

Smell as a Component of Flavor: The Mouth-to-Nose Connection

Odorants can reach the olfactory epithelium through two different routes. The route we easily recognize is through the nostrils; this allows us to smell smoke, roses, skunks, and other odor sources that are outside the mouth. The other route allows us to smell substances that have entered the mouth. An opening called the nasal pharynx (at left in Figure 6.5, p. 199) connects the back of the mouth cavity with the nasal cavity. The acts of chewing and swallowing push air from the mouth up into the nose—air that carries volatile molecules of whatever you are eating. Thus,

FOCUS 7

How do we smell foods that are already in our mouths, and what evidence indicates that smell contributes greatly to flavor?

the flavor we perceive in food consists not just of taste (from taste receptors in the mouth) but also of smell that has been triggered through this mouth-to-nose, back-door route. Remarkably, we experience flavor as coming from the mouth, where the food exists, and as indistinguishable from taste, even though it actually comes from the olfactory epithelium (Shepherd, 2006).

If air can't flow out through the nostrils, it can't stream into the nasal cavity from the mouth. Experiments have shown repeatedly that our abilities to identify foods and drinks by flavor decline markedly when our nostrils are shut. You can easily demonstrate this by tasting jelly beans one at a time with your eyes closed (suggested by Schiffman, 1996). You will probably be able to distinguish among flavors such as cherry, grape, orange, and licorice quite easily, until you try it with your nostrils pinched shut. Under that condition, you will most likely find that now all the jelly beans taste the same; all you taste is the sugar. Smell and taste inputs converge in a certain portion of the orbitofrontal cortex, and this area appears to be critical for the psychological experience of flavor (Rolls, 2004).

Differences Among People in Olfactory Sensitivity

General olfactory sensitivity differs greatly from one individual to another. Women are, on average, more sensitive to odors than are men (Doty, 2001), and many women become especially sensitive to odors during pregnancy (Nordin et al., 2004). In both sexes, the number of odor receptors in the nose and sensitivity to odors declines with age (Rosenfeld, 2005), beginning around age 30 and more noticeably around age 65 or 70. By age 65, roughly 11% of women and 25% of men have serious olfactory impairment, and by age 85 those numbers are 60% and 70% (Murphy et al., 2002). Many elderly people complain of loss in ability to taste foods, but tests typically show that their real loss is not taste but smell (Bartoshuk & Beauchamp, 1994). The most dangerous effect of such impairment is the inability to smell smoke or toxic gases in the air. A high proportion of people who die from asphyxiation are elderly people who have lost much or all of their olfactory ability (Doty, 2014).

Many people with otherwise normal olfactory ability are completely unable to smell particular chemicals that others can smell easily. In fact, at least 75 different chemicals have been identified that most people can smell but some cannot (Pierce et al., 2004). These differences are at least partly the result of genetic differences that affect the production of specific olfactory receptors on olfactory neurons. The most fully studied example concerns ability to smell the chemical substance *androstenone,* which is a derivative of testosterone. This chemical is found in human sweat, more so in males than in females, and big differences exist among individuals of both sexes in their ability to smell it. Researchers have found, in different people, three different variants of the gene that codes for the receptor protein for androstenone. People with the most common variant of the gene find androstenone's odor to be strong and putrid; those with the second most common variant find it to be relatively weak and pleasant ("sweet and fruity"); and those with the least common variant cannot smell the chemical at all (Keller et al., 2007).

Sensitivity to specific odors is also very much affected by experience. With repeated tests, people can learn to distinguish the odors of slightly different chemicals that initially smelled identical to them (Li et al., 2008), and to detect specific odors at a much lower concentration than they could initially (Boulkroune et al., 2007). In some cases, such effects of experience have been found for both sexes, but in others it has been found to occur only in women. This was shown in a study described earlier in the chapter (refer back to Figure 6.3, p. 196). In further experiments, Dalton and her colleagues (2002) found the increased sensitivity only for women who were in their reproductive years; it did not occur for prepubescent girls or postmenopausal women. Such findings are consistent with theories that olfaction serves one or more special functions related to reproduction in women, such as choosing mates, avoiding toxins during pregnancy, or bonding with infants.

DAJ/amana images/Getty Images

■ **An excellent bouquet** Professional wine tasters sample the wine's scent through both their noses and their mouths. Through the mouth, odorant molecules reach the nasal cavity by way of a connection called the nasal pharynx. Much of what we think of as taste is actually smell.

FOCUS 8

How do sex, age, genetic differences, and experience affect sensitivity to smells?

Discriminating Among Individuals by Smell

FOCUS 9

What is the evidence (a) that people can identify other individuals by smell; (b) that mothers can identify the scents of their infants very soon after birth; and (c) that infants quickly learn to identify their mother's scent?

As dog owners know, dogs greet and recognize other dogs (and sometimes us) by smell. We humans living in a somewhat odor-phobic culture may not often admit it or even be aware of it, but we too can identify individuals of our species by smell, and along with our other senses, use body odor for social communication (Pazzaglia, 2015). In a typical experiment, one set of subjects wears clean T-shirts for a day without washing or using deodorants or perfumes. Then, another set of subjects is asked to identify by smell alone which shirt was worn by whom. Such experiments have revealed that parents can tell which of their children wore the shirt, children can tell which of their siblings wore it, and people generally can distinguish between the odors of two strangers (Weisfeld et al., 2003).

Role of Smell in Mother–Infant Bonding

Among some mammals, notably goats and sheep, odor recognition is a crucial part of the bond between mother and young (Kendrick et al., 1992). Might smell also play a role in human mother–infant bonding?

In one study conducted in a hospital maternity ward, 90% of mothers who had been exposed to their newborn babies for just 10 to 60 minutes after birth were able to identify by smell alone which of several undershirts had been worn by their own babies (Kaitz et al., 1987). In another study, breast-fed babies as young as 6 days old turned their heads reliably toward cotton breast pads that their own mothers had worn, when given a choice between that and identical-looking pads that had been worn by other lactating women (Macfarlane, 1975). In still another study, babies who were exposed to a particular unusual odor (not that of their mothers) within the first hour after birth turned reliably toward that odor when given a choice between it and another unusual odor 6 days later (Varendi et al., 2002). All such evidence suggests that odor figures into the complex of stimuli that are involved in the attachment between human infants and their mothers.

■ **A sweet aroma** Every human being has a unique, identifiable odor.

Possible Role of Smell in Choosing a Genetically Compatible Mate

FOCUS 10

From an evolutionary perspective, why might mice prefer to mate with others that smell most different from themselves? What evidence suggests that the same might be true of humans?

In mice, odor has been shown to play a role in mating choices. Mice, like dogs and humans, can identify other individuals of their species by smell, and, remarkably, they prefer to mate with opposite-sex mice whose odor is *most different* from their own (Potts et al., 1991; Yamazaki et al., 1988). Why this preference? Researchers have found that the individual differences in odor that determine these mating preferences result from a set of about 50 highly variable genes (genes with many different alleles) referred to collectively as the *major histocompatibility complex* (MHC) (Yamazaki et al., 1994). These same genes also determine the precise nature of the cells used by the immune system to reject foreign substances and kill disease-producing bacteria and viruses. Thus, by choosing mates that smell most different from themselves, mice choose mates that (a) are not likely to be close relatives of themselves, and (b) will add much new genetic variation to the mix of disease-fighting cells that develop in the offspring.

The advantages of mating with someone who has a very different MHC presumably exist in humans as much as in mice (Brennan & Zufall, 2006). In one series of experiments, Claus Wedekind and his colleagues (1995, 1997) asked young men and women to rate the "pleasantness" (and in one study the "sexiness") of the odors of T-shirts that had been worn by young adults of the opposite sex. All the subjects were assessed biochemically for differences in their MHCs. The result was that any given donor's odor was, on average, rated as more pleasant by raters who differed from that person in MHC than by raters who were similar to that person in MHC.

There is some evidence that MHC differences can affect actual sexual behavior in humans. In one study, women who were not using hormonal contraceptives ("the pill") preferred the smell of T-shirts worn by more physically symmetrical (and typically more attractive) men, but only during the middle of their menstrual cycle, a time when women are most fertile. Women during low-fertility times in their cycles and women using hormonal contraception showed no preferences (Gangestad & Thornhill, 1998). These findings suggest that women are capable of using a man's odor in evaluating his potential worth as a mating partner, whether they are conscious of this fact or not.

The sense of smell may also play a role in incest avoidance. Most of us cringe at the thought of having sex with a family member, and, of course, society strongly reinforces that sense of disgust. But one factor that may make such aversion "natural" is the sense of smell. As we noted previously, people can identify their genetic relatives based on smell, and they find the odor of some kin more aversive than others. This was shown in a series of experiments by Glen Weisfeld and his colleagues (2003), who asked people to try to identify by smell T-shirts worn by different family members. Not only could people generally recognize family members on the basis of smell, but the odors of some genetic relatives were particularly negative. Brothers and sisters showed mutual aversion to the odor of their opposite-sex siblings, fathers were aversive to the odor of their daughters (but not their sons), and daughters to the odor of their fathers (but not their mothers). These are the pairings at most risk for incest. Moreover, these patterns were found whether or not the person smelling the T-shirt could accurately recognize who had worn the shirt.

Smell as a Mode of Communication: Do Humans Produce Pheromones?

A *pheromone* [**fer´**-ə-mōn] is a chemical substance that is released by an animal and acts on other members of its species to promote some specific behavioral or physiological response. The most dramatic examples occur in insects. For instance, sexually receptive female cabbage moths secrete a pheromone that attracts male cabbage moths from as far as several miles away (Lerner et al., 1990). Most species of mammals also produce pheromones, which serve such functions as sexual attraction, territorial marking, and regulation of hormone production (Hughes, 1999; Wyatt, 2009). Most species of mammals have in their nasal cavities a structure called the *vomeronasal* [vŏ´-mə-rō-**nā´**-zəl] *organ*, which contains receptor cells specialized for responding to pheromones. Whereas the main olfactory epithelium is designed to distinguish somewhat imprecisely among many thousands of different odorants, the vomeronasal organ appears to be designed for very precise recognition of, and exquisite sensitivity to, a small number of specific substances—the species' pheromones (Buck, 2000b).

Do humans communicate by pheromones? We do have the structures that would make such communication possible. Like other mammals, we have specialized glands in the skin that secrete odorous substances. Such glands are especially concentrated in areas of the body where our species has retained hair—such as in the axillary region (armpits) and genital region (see **Figure 6.6**). One theory is that the function of hair in these locations is to retain the secretions and provide a large surface area from which they can evaporate, so as to increase their effectiveness as odorants (Stoddart, 1990). Some substances secreted by these glands, such as androstenone, are steroid molecules that resemble substances known to serve as pheromones in other mammals. We also have at least a rudimentary vomeronasal organ, but the evidence to date is inconclusive as to whether it functions in our species or is entirely vestigial (Brennan & Zufall, 2006).

FIGURE 6.6 Locations of maximal scent production by humans In humans, specialized scent-producing glands (apocrine glands) are concentrated most highly in the axillary region (underarms) and also exist in high concentrations in the genital area, the area around the nipples, the navel area, on the top of the head, and on the forehead and cheeks (Stoddart, 1990), as shown by the added circles. (The statue here is Michelangelo's *Aurora*, from the tomb of Lorenzo de Medici, in Florence.)

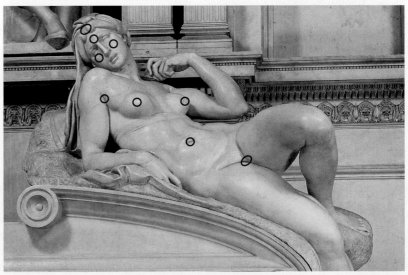

Scala/Art Resource, NY

FOCUS 11

What human anatomical characteristics are consistent with the possibility that we produce and respond to pheromones? What observations and reasoning suggest that we do not produce sex-attractant pheromones?

Motivated partly by the perfume and cologne industry, most human pheromone research has centered on whether or not we produce sex-attractant pheromones. In many experiments, men and women have been exposed to various secretions taken from the other sex and have rated the attractiveness of the odor or changes in their own mood. To date, despite the often lurid claims in ads, such experiments have failed to yield convincing evidence that such pheromones exist (Brennan & Zufall, 2006; Doty, 2014). Certainly some people find some of the odorous substances secreted by other people to be pleasant, but individual differences are great, and no specific human secretion has been found to be consistently attractive to members of the opposite sex. Perhaps that should not be surprising. Sex-attractant pheromones are valuable for animals that mate only at certain times of the year or only when the female is ovulating, as a means of synchronizing the sex drives of males and females to maximize the chance of conception. Humans have taken a different evolutionary route, such that sexual drive and behavior are not tied to a season, cycle, or variable physiological state. For that reason, perhaps, there is little or no need for us to advertise by scent our readiness to mate.

SECTION REVIEW

Smell, one of two human chemical senses, serves functions of warning and attraction.

Basic Facts of Smell

- Roughly 400 different types of sensory neurons exist in olfactory nerves. The receptive ends of each type are most responsive to molecules that reach the olfactory epithelium in the nose.
- These different types of neurons are connected to corresponding parts of the olfactory bulb. Their differential responsiveness allows us to distinguish one scent from another.
- Odorants that enter the nose through a connection from the mouth contribute to the flavor of foods.
- Olfactory sensitivity is generally greater in women than in men, and it declines with age. Sensitivity to specific chemicals varies as a result of both genes and experience.

Telling People Apart by Their Smell

- Humans can identify individuals by smell alone.
- Mothers and their infants quickly learn to recognize the other's smell, a fact that may contribute to bonding.
- Odor allows mice (and perhaps humans) to choose mates that will enhance genetic variety in their offspring.
- Olfaction may play a role in incest avoidance, with pairs of family members at high risk for incest (brothers and sisters) finding each other's odor aversive.

Communicating via Smell

- For most mammals and many other animal species, pheromones serve as chemical messengers between individuals.
- Evidence is mixed regarding the existence of human pheromones. From an evolutionary perspective, humans do not need sex-attractant pheromones.

Taste

Some insects have taste receptors on their feet, which allow them to taste what they are walking on. Fish have taste receptors not just in their mouths but all over their bodies (Hara, 1994). They can taste their prey before they see it, and they use taste to help them track it down. For us and other mammals, taste has a more limited but still valuable function. Our taste receptors exist only in our mouths, and they help us to decide whether a particular substance is good or bad to eat.

Anatomy and Physiology of Taste

The receptors for taste are found on specialized *taste receptor cells,* not directly on the sensory neurons (unlike the case for smell). These cells exist in spherical structures called *fungiform papillae* that contain taste buds. Each bud contains between 50 and 100 receptor cells, arranged something like segments in an orange (see **Figure 6.7**). Most people have between 2,000 and 10,000 taste buds, about two-thirds of which are on the tongue and the rest of which are on the roof of the mouth and in the opening of the throat (Herness & Gilbertson, 1999). People who have more taste buds are typically more sensitive to tastes—especially to bitter tastes—than are people who have fewer taste buds (Bartoshuk & Beauchamp, 1994).

   To be tasted, a chemical substance must first dissolve in saliva and come into contact with the sensitive ends of appropriate taste receptor cells, where it triggers electrical changes that result in action potentials, first in the taste receptor cells and then, by synaptic transmission, in sensory neurons that run to the brain (see Figure 6.7). The specifics of the transduction mechanism vary among taste receptor cells.

FOCUS 12

How does transduction generally occur in taste?

Six Primary Tastes, Five (or Six) Types of Receptor Cells

For many years Western scientists believed that taste receptor cells were of just four types—*sweet, salty, sour,* and *bitter.* Every taste, it was believed, could be understood as a combination of those four primary tastes. Japanese scientists, in contrast, generally spoke of five primary tastes—the four just mentioned plus *umami,* which, loosely translated, means "savory" or "delicious" (Kurihara & Kashiwayanagi, 1998). Umami, they held, is a unique taste, unmatched by any combination of the other primary tastes, and is a major contributor to the taste of many natural foods, especially those that are high in protein, such as meats, fish, and cheese. Umami is also the taste produced by monosodium glutamate (MSG), an amino acid frequently used as a flavor enhancer in Asian cuisine. Taste researchers have recently identified distinct receptor cells and brain areas responsive to MSG, and now even Western taste specialists generally write of five rather than four primary tastes and types of taste receptor cells (Scott, 2013; Shadan, 2009). More recently, *fat* has been suggested as a sixth taste, with its own sensation and class of taste buds (Keast & Costanzo, 2015).

FOCUS 13

What are the six primary tastes? How, in general, does transduction occur in taste receptor cells?

Taste Areas in the Brain

Taste sensory neurons have strong connections to the limbic system and cerebral cortex. The connections to the primary taste area of the cortex (located largely in the *insula,* which is buried in the central fissure that separates the temporal and parietal lobes) are arranged in such a way that different sets of neurons are selectively responsive to each of the basic categories of taste stimuli (Kobayashi, 2006; Rolls, 2004). People with extensive damage to this area lose their conscious experience of taste (Pritchard, 1991), and artificial stimulation here produces experiences of taste in the absence of any stimuli on the tongue (Penfield & Faulk, 1955). The primary taste area in turn sends connections to several other areas of the cortex, including the orbitofrontal cortex, where, as

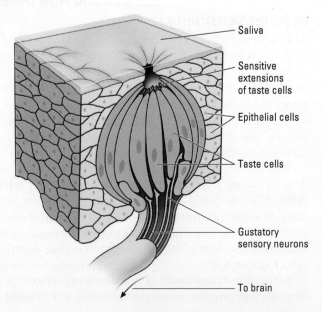

FIGURE 6.7   **A taste bud** Taste buds are found in the surface tissue (epithelium) of the tongue and elsewhere in the mouth. Each one contains 50 or more taste receptor cells. From the tip of each cell, hairlike extensions make contact with the fluid lining the epithelial tissue. These extensions contain binding sites and channels where substances to be tasted exert their effects. The receptor cells produce action potentials in response to such input and, in turn, induce action potentials in taste sensory neurons through synaptic transmission.

Labels in figure:
Saliva
Sensitive extensions of taste cells
Epithelial cells
Taste cells
Gustatory sensory neurons
To brain

mentioned in the section on smell, neural connections for taste and smell intermingle and enable us to experience the mixed taste–smell sensation called flavor.

An Evolutionary Account of Taste Quality

Taste motivates us to eat some substances and avoid others. Generally speaking, salty (at low to moderate intensity), sweet, umami, and fat are pleasant tastes; in the course of evolution, they became attached to substances that fulfilled human nutritional needs. A certain amount of salt intake is required to maintain a proper salt balance in bodily fluids. Natural sugars were a valuable source of energy to our evolutionary ancestors. Protein (the main natural source of umami flavor) is essential for building and restoring tissues. And fats are a valuable source of calories, are used to build new cells, and are critical for normal brain and nerve development. Our ability to taste and enjoy salt, sugars, proteins, and fats is part of the mechanism that helps ensure that we consume adequate amounts of these nutrients.

Still speaking generally, sour and bitter are unpleasant experiences, which natural selection has attached to certain substances that are bad for us. Bacterial decay produces acidic compounds that taste sour. Since decaying substances can cause disease when eaten, natural selection produced a taste system that experiences the sourness of most acids as unpleasant. Many bitter-tasting plants (hemlock is a famous example) and some animals (notably some species of caterpillars), as part of their own evolution, have concentrated toxic substances into their tissues—substances that can harm or kill animals that eat them. As a consequence, our ancestors evolved a taste system that experiences the bitterness of those toxic substances as unpleasant.

To pursue this evolutionary line of thinking, let's consider further the relationship between bitter taste and poisons. A wide variety of chemical substances all taste bitter to us, even though they may be very different chemically from one another, because each is able to bind to one or another of the approximately 25 different types of receptor sites located on bitter receptor cells (Behrens et al., 2007). The receptor sites are specialized protein molecules that bind certain molecules that come into contact with them. The binding of any substance to these sites triggers a chemical change in the cell. This chemical change results in action potentials in the sensory neurons and, ultimately, activity in areas of the brain that produce the bitter sensation, causing the animals to spit out and subsequently avoid these potential foods.

Possible Explanation of Sex and Age Differences in Bitter Sensitivity

Although avoidance of bitter-tasting foods is generally adaptive, too much avoidance of them is not. Plants protect themselves from being eaten not just by producing truly poisonous substances, but also by producing nonpoisonous substances that are sufficiently similar to poisons that they bind to bitter taste receptors and produce bitter taste. Individuals that avoided all bitter tastes would lose the nutritional value of plants that taste bitter but are safe to eat. Through observation and experience, people and other plant-eating animals can learn to eat and enjoy bitter foods that have no toxins or low levels of toxins.

Women are generally more sensitive to bitter taste than are men. In fact, about 35% of women are said to be "supertasters," with a special sensitivity to bitter taste. This is compared to about 15% of men, and about 25% of people cannot taste the specific bitter chemical at all (nontasters). Supertasting (and the lack of it) seems to be controlled by a single dominant gene, with supertasters having an increased number of fungiform papillae (Bartoshuk et al., 1994; Hayes & Keast, 2011) (see **Figure 6.8**).

Although women are generally more sensitive to bitter taste than men, many women become increasingly sensitive to it during the first 3 months of pregnancy

FOCUS 14

From an evolutionary perspective, (a) what is the function of each of the primary tastes, (b) why do so many chemically diverse substances taste bitter, and (c) why does bitter sensation increase in women during pregnancy?

Kathleen Nelson/Alamy

■ **Yuck, bitter** This response may protect children from eating poisonous substances. The mammalian taste system evolved to sense many poisons as bitter. Among humans, young children are especially sensitive to, and rejecting of, bitter taste.

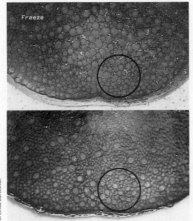

Tongue of supertaster

Tongue of normal taster

Courtesy of Linda Bartoshuk

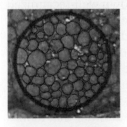
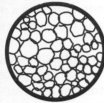

Supertasters can have up to about 60 fungiform papillae in the template area.

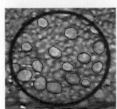
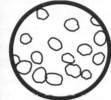

Most individuals have far fewer. This individual has 16 fungiform papillae in the template area.

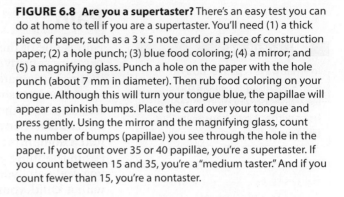

FIGURE 6.8 Are you a supertaster? There's an easy test you can do at home to tell if you are a supertaster. You'll need (1) a thick piece of paper, such as a 3 x 5 note card or a piece of construction paper; (2) a hole punch; (3) blue food coloring; (4) a mirror; and (5) a magnifying glass. Punch a hole on the paper with the hole punch (about 7 mm in diameter). Then rub food coloring on your tongue. Although this will turn your tongue blue, the papillae will appear as pinkish bumps. Place the card over your tongue and press gently. Using the mirror and the magnifying glass, count the number of bumps (papillae) you see through the hole in the paper. If you count over 35 or 40 papillae, you're a supertaster. If you count between 15 and 35, you're a "medium taster." And if you count fewer than 15, you're a nontaster.

(Duffy & Bartoshuk, 1996; Nordin et al., 2004). A possible reason is found in evidence that human fetuses are highly subject to damage by poisons, especially during the first 3 months of their development (Profet, 1992). With the stakes being survival of offspring, the value of avoiding even mild toxins increases. Young children also appear to be highly sensitive to bitter tastes (Cowart, 1981), which may help explain why it is so difficult to get them to eat nutritious but bitter-tasting greens, such as spinach or Brussels sprouts. Children's extra sensitivity to bitterness may help protect them from eating poisonous materials during their early development, before they have learned what is safe to eat and what is not.

SECTION REVIEW

Taste is a chemical sense that helps us decide what is good or bad to eat.

Basic Facts of Taste

- Human taste receptors are specialized cells contained in taste buds on the tongue and other parts of the mouth and throat.

- Six types of taste receptors have been identified, which correspond to six primary tastes—sweet, salty, sour, bitter, umami, and fat.

- Taste receptors can trigger neural impulses in taste sensory neurons, which send input to the primary taste area in the frontal lobe and to other parts of the brain.

Evolution and Taste Quality

- Through evolution, we have generally come to experience beneficial nutrients as pleasant in taste (sweet, salty, umami, or fat) and harmful substances as unpleasant (sour or bitter).

- Bitter receptor cells evolved to respond to many chemically varied substances that are poisonous or chemically similar to poisons.

- Natural selection may explain why children and women, especially pregnant women, are particularly sensitive to bitter tastes.

Pain

FOCUS 15

In what ways is pain a "body" sense, an emotion, and a drive? How does observation of people born without pain sensitivity illustrate pain's value?

Pain is one of the somatosenses (introduced in Chapter 4). That is, like touch, temperature sensitivity, and proprioception (the sense of body position), pain is a sense that can originate from multiple places throughout the body rather than just from specialized sensory organs in the head. (Recall that *soma* means "body.") Pain receptors exist over the whole surface of the skin and in many other bodily tissues.

Pain is a "body" sense in another way, too. When you see, hear, smell, taste, or touch something, you experience the sensation as coming from outside yourself (from the thing you are seeing, hearing, smelling, tasting, or touching); but when you feel pain, you experience it as coming from your own body. If you cut yourself with a knife, your feeling of pain is a sense not of the knife (which you experience with vision and touch) but of your own injured bodily state.

Pain is not only a sense but also a perception, an emotion, and a drive. As an emotion, strong pain overwhelms a person's conscious mind, making it hard to think about anything else; and, like many other emotions, pain has its own well-recognized facial expression (Williams, 2002). As a drive, pain motivates a person both to reduce the pain and to avoid future behaviors like the one that produced it (such as careless handling of knives). In psychology, pain is by far the most thoroughly studied of the somatosenses. That, no doubt, is largely due to the dramatic ways that pain can affect, and be affected by, a person's other psychological experiences.

The evolutionary value of pain—its role in promoting survival—is dramatically illustrated in those rare, unlucky people who are born with a genetic disorder that makes them insensitive to it (Cox et al., 2006). They can experience all other skin sensations—including touch, warmth, cold, tickle, and pressure on the skin—and they can report increasing intensities of those sensations, but pain, with its warning and motivating qualities, is missing. Children with this disorder are not motivated to remove their hands from hot stoves, or to refrain from chewing on their tongues as they eat, or to change their body positions (as most of us do from minute to minute) to relieve the strain on muscles and joints. Even if they are constantly watched throughout childhood, and even if they learn intellectually to avoid certain activities, people with this disorder usually die young from the tissue deterioration and infections that result from their wounds.

Neural Pathways for Pain

The anatomical basis of pain is closely related to that of the other somatosenses, such as touch and temperature sensitivity (Hendry & Hsiao, 2013). For all these senses, the receptor cells are the sensory neurons themselves. These neurons have receptive endings in the skin and long axons that enter the central nervous system. Pain neurons are thinner than other neurons from the skin, and their sensitive terminals, called *free nerve endings,* are not encased in special capsules, or end organs, as are the endings of touch and temperature receptors (see **Figure 6.9**). Free nerve

FIGURE 6.9 Pain receptors in the skin The pain receptors are the sensitive endings of sensory neurons, called free nerve endings. The slower second wave of pain is carried by the very thin C fibers, and the faster first wave is carried by the thicker A-delta fibers. The sense of touch is carried by still thicker (and faster) A fibers, whose endings are not "free" but, rather, are surrounded by a capsule, or end organ, that modifies the pressure stimulus.

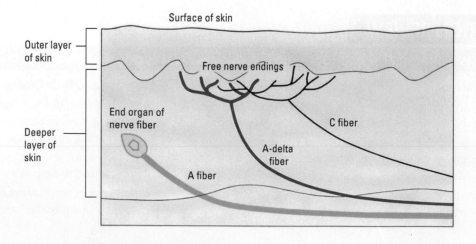

endings can be found in all body tissues from which pain is sensed (Lynn & Perl, 1996)—not just the skin but also the pulp of the teeth (site of the dreaded toothache), muscles (site of cramps and muscle aches), membranes around bones and joints (arthritis pain), and various visceral organs (stomachaches and other inner pains).

Sensory Neurons for Two Waves of Pain

Pain sensory neurons are of two general types—very thin, unmyelinated, slow-conducting neurons called *C fibers* and slightly thicker, myelinated, faster-conducting neurons called *A-delta fibers* (see Figure 6.9). Some A-delta fibers are specialized to respond to strong pressure (such as from a pinprick), while others are specialized to respond to extremes of temperature (hot or cold). C fibers respond to all sorts of stimuli that produce pain, including strong pressure, intense heat or cold, and chemicals that produce pain when applied to the skin (Basbaum & Jessell, 2000). When your skin is pricked or burned, you feel two separate waves of pain: a sharp, highly localized *first pain,* followed (1 or 2 seconds later) by a dull, burning, more diffuse, longer-lasting *second pain.* The first is mediated by A-delta fibers, and the second by the slower C fibers (Basbaum & Jessell, 2000). The C fibers also respond in a more prolonged way to a variety of chemicals that are released by damaged or infected cells, accounting for the persistent pain that accompanies burns, wounds, and infections.

Pain neurons enter the spinal cord (via a spinal nerve) or the brainstem (via a cranial nerve) and terminate there on interneurons. Some of these interneurons promote reflexive responses—such as the automatic withdrawal of the hand from a hot stove—independent of conscious experience. Others send their axons to the thalamus, in the center of the brain, which, in turn, sends output to portions of the brain that are involved in the conscious experience of pain.

Brain Areas for Three Components of Pain Experience

Pain as a psychological experience can be divided meaningfully into three different components, each of which depends most critically on a different portion of the brain (see **Figure 6.10**).

1. The *sensory component* of pain depends largely on the somatosensory cortex, the area of the parietal lobe that receives input for touch and temperature as well as pain (for its location, refer back to Figure 6.1, p. 193). The somatosensory cortex appears to be crucial for the ability to perceive pain as a sensation, to describe its intensity and qualities (e.g., sharp or dull), and to locate it in a particular portion of the body.

2. The *primary emotional and motivational* component of pain, which is experienced immediately, depends on the cingulate cortex and the insular cortex,

FOCUS 16

What is the anatomical basis for a distinction between first and second pain?

FOCUS 17

What are three different components of pain experience, and what evidence links these to three different portions of the brain?

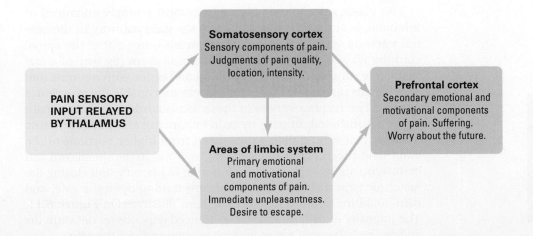

FIGURE 6.10 Brain areas involved in three components of pain experience Pain input from tracts through the spinal cord and midbrain is relayed by one portion of the thalamus to the somatosensory cortex and by another portion to the insular cortex and certain portions of the limbic system. These areas, in turn, send output to the prefrontal cortex. These different areas account for three relatively distinct components of pain experience, described in the figure.

(Based on information reviewed by Price, 2000.)

portions of the limbic system that lie buried in the folds of the brain's frontal lobe. People with damage to the cingulate cortex and the insular cortex experience a condition called *asymbolia for pain* (Price, 2000). They can perceive a painful stimulus and describe it as such, identify the location of the pain, describe its qualities, and rate its intensity; but they do not feel a normal desire to escape the pain. The pain doesn't bother them.

3. Humans experience a third component of pain, the more cognitively based *secondary emotional and motivational* component—the suffering that derives from the person's worrying about the future or about the meaning of the pain. The brain area that is crucial for this troubled state lies in the prefrontal lobe—the front-most portion of the cerebral cortex—which is involved in all aspects of planning and concern for the future (as noted in Chapter 4). People with prefrontal lobe damage feel and respond to the immediate threat and unpleasantness of pain, but they do not worry about it, just as they do not worry about or make plans based on other experiences (Price, 2000).

The experience of pain, with all three of the above components, does not always originate from stimulation of pain receptors. This fact is all too well known by many people who have had a limb amputated. Such people often feel as if the missing limb were still present and full of pain. Such *phantom-limb pain* can persist not only if all the nerves from the limb's stump are destroyed, but even if the pain pathways entering the brain from the spinal cord have been destroyed (Flor et al., 2006). This suggests that the brain's mechanism for experiencing pain and assigning it to a particular body location can be activated without sensory input from that part of the body. In fact, the *lack* of sensory input might trigger phantom-limb pain by removing a source of inhibition to the pain mechanisms of the brain.

The Modulation of Pain

The experience of pain depends not just on the physical stimulus or its damaging effects, but also on other conditions that exist at the time the stimulus or damage occurs. The same degree of wound a person experiences may at one time feel excruciatingly painful and at another time be barely detected. The **gate-control theory** of pain (Melzack & Wall, 1965, 1996) aims at explaining such variability. The theory holds that the experience of pain depends on the degree to which input from pain sensory neurons can pass through a neural "gate" and reach higher pain centers in the brain. Conditions can increase or decrease pain by opening or closing the gate. For example, massage or electrical stimulation can create competing stimulation to a sore back, reducing the perception of pain, just as rubbing the area around your twisted knee will serve to block some of the pain messages.

The major gate, where pain input is most strongly enhanced or inhibited, is at the first way station in the pain pathway in the central nervous system. Pain sensory neurons enter either the spinal cord (by way of a spinal nerve) or the brainstem (by way of a cranial nerve) and terminate there on second-order pain neurons that send signals upward, to higher brain areas that enable the experience of pain. The responsiveness of these second-order neurons to pain input is controlled, in part, by pain-enhancing and pain-inhibiting neurons that extend their axons down from higher portions of the brain. The effects of these descending neurons, in the spinal cord and brainstem, are metaphorically referred to as opening and closing the "gate" for pain. Pain-enhancing neurons tend to open the gate, and pain-inhibiting neurons tend to close it, as illustrated in **Figure 6.11**. The intensity of pain sensation experienced depends on the stimulus and on the balance of forces tending to open or close the gate.

FIGURE 6.11 Gate control of pain
Pain transmission neurons in the spinal cord or brainstem, which receive input from pain sensory neurons coming from the body, can be made more or less excitable by descending connections from the brain. In the figure, + indicates excitatory connections and – indicates inhibitory connections. The excitatory and inhibiting effects on the pain transmission neurons constitute the metaphorical "gate" in the gate-control theory of pain.

(Information from Watkins & Maier, 2000.)

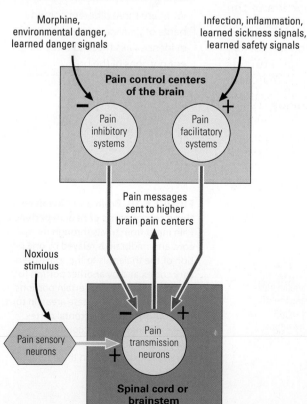

Mechanisms of Pain Enhancement

Recall the last time you were ill. Chances are that you felt increased pain sensitivity all over your body, especially if you had a high fever. Evolutionary psychologists hypothesize that this pain enhancement effect may have evolved to motivate ill individuals to rest rather than move around, in order to conserve energy needed to fight the disease (Kluger, 1991). Although the details are not fully understood, this illness-induced effect is believed to occur through an action of the immune system on pain-enhancing neurons in the brain (again, see Figure 6.11) (Watkins & Maier, 2000; Watkins et al., 2007).

Pain sensitivity can also be increased in specific locations of the body as a result of injury at those locations. This heightened sensitivity occurs partly because of changes in the free nerve endings of C fibers and A-delta fibers that are induced by chemicals released from damaged cells (Basbaum & Jessell, 2000). The sensitized sensory neurons respond to much weaker stimuli than they would have before the injury. In addition, second-order pain neurons in the spinal cord and brainstem become sensitized by intense activation, such that they become more responsive to subsequent input for periods ranging from minutes to weeks (Ji et al., 2003; Woolf & Salter, 2000). The result is that even light touch to a recently burned or wounded area of skin can be intensely painful. Such pain-enhancing systems presumably evolved as a means of motivating individuals to protect damaged areas of their bodies.

Neural and Chemical Mechanisms of Pain Reduction

In addition to understanding the mechanisms that exacerbate pain and pain sensitivity, it is also important to understand how pain can be reduced, or inhibited. A major neural center for pain inhibition exists in a portion of the midbrain called the *periaqueductal gray (PAG)*. Neurons in this area send their axons down into the lower brainstem and spinal cord to inhibit pain input there. Electrical stimulation of the PAG has a powerful *analgesic* (pain-reducing) effect—so powerful, in fact, that abdominal surgery can be performed without drugs in animals that are receiving such stimulation (Mason, 2001). In humans, electrical stimulation of this area has also successfully reduced or abolished chronic pain that could not be relieved by other means (Hosobuchi et al., 1979; Perlmutter & Mink, 2006).

Morphine and other *opiate drugs* (derivatives of opium) exert their well-known analgesic effects partly through direct action in the PAG. Morphine that passes into the brain is taken up at special binding sites on neurons in the PAG, where it increases neural activity and thereby reduces pain (Basbaum & Fields, 1984). Morphine binding sites are also found on neurons in the spinal cord, and injection of a tiny amount of morphine directly into the spinal cord can greatly reduce or eliminate pain in the part of the body that sends its sensory neurons into that spinal cord area (Basbaum & Jessell, 2000).

Of course, the pain-inhibiting system did not evolve to respond specifically to morphine or other foreign substances. Its basic function is to mediate the body's own capacity to reduce pain. The body produces a variety of chemicals that act like morphine, collectively referred to as *endorphins*. (Recall from Chapter 5 that *endorphin* is short for *endogenous morphine-like substance*.) Some endorphins are produced in the brain or spinal cord and serve as neurotransmitters to alter the activity or excitability of neurons to which they bind. Others are secreted from the pituitary and adrenal glands as hormones, which enter the bloodstream and have a variety of effects both peripherally and in the central nervous system (Henry, 1986). Endorphins are believed to inhibit pain by acting both in the PAG and at the places where pain-carrying neurons enter the spinal cord and lower brainstem.

Stress-Induced Analgesia

During his search for the source of the Nile River, the famous explorer David Livingstone was attacked by a lion. He survived the incident and later wrote that

FOCUS 18

How does illness produce a general increase in pain sensitivity, and how does injury produce a localized increase in pain sensitivity?

FOCUS 19

How can pain input be inhibited at its entry into the central nervous system, and how might endorphins be involved in this process?

although the lion shook him "as a terrier does a rat" and crushed his shoulder, he had felt "no sense of pain nor feeling of terror, though quite conscious of all that was happening" (Livingstone, 1857). Other people have had similar experiences. For example, soldiers severely wounded in battle often do not notice their wounds until the battle is over. Faced with a predator or similar threat, a human or other animal cannot afford to nurse a wound or favor it by limping; all the body's resources must be used to fight or flee. The decreased pain sensitivity that accompanies such highly stressful situations is known as ***stress-induced analgesia***.

FOCUS 20

What is some evidence that stress-induced analgesia is at least partly mediated by endorphins?

Many experiments have shown that stress-induced analgesia depends partly, if not entirely, on the release of endorphins. In one experiment, rats that received a series of electric shocks to their feet (the source of stress) became relatively insensitive to pain for several minutes afterward, as indicated by their lack of response to normally painful heat applied to their tails (Lewis et al., 1980). Rats treated with a drug that blocks the action of endorphins did not show this stress-induced analgesia, indicating that the effect must have been mediated by endorphins. In similar experiments, the mere presence of a cat (Lichtman & Fanselow, 1990) produced analgesia in rats, and the presence of biting flies produced analgesia in mice (Kavaliers et al., 1999). In experiments with human subjects, students displayed analgesia upon taking a stressful math test (Bandura et al., 1988), and veterans who had experienced the trauma of war displayed analgesia after watching films depicting combat (Pitman et al., 1990). In all of these cases, the analgesic effect did not occur when subjects were injected with a drug that blocks the actions of endorphins.

Endorphins are also secreted during periods of prolonged, strenuous physical exertion, such as long-distance running, and may account for the pain reduction and euphoric "runner's high" that many people enjoy during and after such exertion. In one experiment both the reduced pain and the sense of euphoria failed to occur in runners who had been treated with an endorphin-blocking drug (Janal et al., 1984).

Belief-Induced Analgesia

FOCUS 21

What is some evidence that pain can be reduced by belief?

In humans, dramatic reduction in pain can also be produced by the power of belief or faith. Some religious groups engage in practices that most of us would regard as torture, yet the participants appear to feel no pain. One group in India, for example, practices a hook-hanging ritual. A man who has been chosen to represent the power of the gods is secured to a rope by two steel hooks that pierce the skin and muscles on his back. He hangs from this rope, swinging back and forth, while he blesses the children and the crops of the village. He feels honored to have been chosen and apparently feels little or no pain (Melzack & Wall, 1996).

A less dramatic example, in cultures where faith is more often placed in science and medicine, is the *placebo effect* on pain. In many cases a pill or injection that contains no active substance (the placebo) can reduce pain in a person who believes that the drug is a painkiller. Experiments have shown that placebo-induced pain reduction depends partly, and in some cases entirely, on the secretion of endorphins (Price et al., 2008). In one of the first such experiments, people who had undergone a tooth extraction reported less pain if given a placebo than if not, and this placebo effect did not occur in subjects who were treated with an endorphin-blocking drug (Levine et al., 1979). Other experiments have shown that various cognitive techniques for relieving pain, such as meditating on the idea that the pain is disconnected from the rest of the body, also work at least partly through endorphins (Bandura et al., 1987). Might the man hanging from hooks in India also be secreting large quantities of endorphins? Nobody knows for sure, but most pain researchers would bet that he is.

SECTION REVIEW

Pain is an emotion and drive as well as a somatosense.

Basic Facts of Pain

- Pain receptors are free nerve endings of pain sensory neurons, located in many parts of the body.
- C fibers and A-delta fibers, two types of pain sensory neurons, mediate two different waves of pain.
- The experience of pain has three identifiable components—sensory, primary emotional and motivational, and secondary emotional and motivational—each relying on different areas of the brain.

Pain Modulation

- The gate-control theory maintains that the degree of pain felt depends on how much input from pain neurons passes through a neural "gate" to higher areas of the brain.
- The enhanced pain sensitivity that accompanies illness or injury helps protect the body from further harm.
- The PAG and endorphins provide the body with a means of pain inhibition.
- Endorphins play a part in stress-induced and belief-induced analgesia.

Hearing

Among mammals, those with the keenest hearing are the bats. In complete darkness, and even if blinded, bats can flit around obstacles such as tree branches and capture insects that are flying in erratic patterns to escape. Bats navigate and hunt by sonar, that is, by reflected sound waves. They send out high-pitched chirps, above the frequency range that humans can hear, and analyze the echoes in a way that allows them to hear such characteristics as the size, shape, position, direction of movement, and texture of a target insect (Feng & Ratnam, 2000). Such *echolocation* is also used by humans (Rowan et al., 2015; Schenkman & Nilsson, 2011), and is better developed in blind than sighted people (Muchnik et al., 1991), but does not come close to matching the ability of bats.

Hearing may not be as well developed or as essential for humans as it is for bats, but it is still enormously effective and useful. It allows us to detect and respond to potentially life-threatening or life-enhancing events that occur in the dark, or behind our backs, or anywhere out of view. We use it to identify animals and such natural events as approaching thunderstorms. And, perhaps most important, it is the primary sensory modality of human language. We learn from each other through our ears.

Merlin D. Tuttle/Science Source

■ **An auditory animal** Bats, which navigate and hunt by sonar, have large, mobile outer ears. This is especially true of some species, such as *Macrotus californicus*, pictured here.

Sound and Its Transduction by the Ear

If a tree falls in the forest and no one is there to hear it, does it make a sound? This old riddle plays on the fact that the term *sound* refers both to a type of physical stimulus and to the sensation produced by that stimulus.

Sound as a Physical Stimulus

As a physical stimulus, sound is the vibration of air or some other medium produced by an object such as a tuning fork, one's vocal cords, or a falling tree. The vibration moves outward from the sound source as a wave (see **Figure 6.12** on page 214). The height of the wave indicates the total pressure exerted by the molecules of air (or another medium) as they move back and forth. This is the sound's **amplitude**, or intensity, which we hear as the sound's *loudness*. Sound amplitude is usually measured in logarithmic units of pressure called *decibels* (*dB*). (See **Table 6.2** on page 214, which further defines decibels and contains the decibel ratings for various common sounds.)

In addition to varying in amplitude, sound waves vary in **frequency**, which we hear as the sound's **pitch**. The frequency of a sound is the rate at which the

FIGURE 6.12 Characteristics of sound The oscillating tuning fork (a) causes air molecules to vibrate in a manner that can be represented as a wave of pressure. Each wave contains an area in which the air molecules are more compressed (the dark regions in the upper diagram) and an area in which they are less compressed (the light regions) than normal. The peak pressure (the highest compression) of each wave defines the amplitude of the sound, and the number of waves that pass a given point per second defines the frequency. The higher the amplitude, the louder the sound; and the higher the frequency, the higher the pitch (b). All the wave drawings in this figure are sine waves, indicative of pure tones.

(Information from Klinke, 1986.)

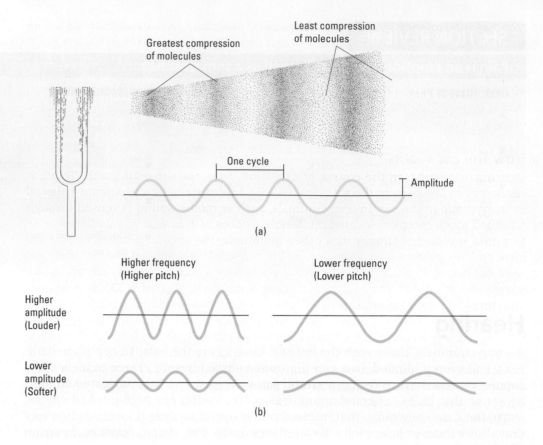

molecules of air or another medium move back and forth. Frequency is measured in *hertz* (*Hz*), which is the number of complete waves (or cycles) per second generated by the sound source. Sounds that are audible to humans have frequencies ranging from about 20 to 20,000 Hz. To give you an idea of the relationship between frequency and pitch, the dominant (most audible) frequency of the lowest note on a piano is about 27 Hz, that of middle C is about 262 Hz, and that of the highest piano note is about 4,186 Hz. The simplest kind of sound is a pure tone,

TABLE 6.2 Sound-pressure amplitudes of various sounds, and conversion to decibels*

Example	P (in sound-pressure units)	Log P	Decibels
Softest detectable sound	1	0	0
Soft whisper	10	1	20
Quiet neighborhood	100	2	40
Average conversation	1,000	3	60
Loud music from a radio	10,000	4	80
Heavy automobile traffic	100,000	5	100
Very loud thunder	1,000,000	6	120
Jet airplane taking off	10,000,000	7	140
Loudest rock band on record	100,000,000	8	160
Spacecraft launch (from 150 ft.)	1,000,000,000	9	180

*One sound-pressure unit (*P*) is defined as 2×10^{-5} newtons/square meter (Klinke, 1986). When measured in sound-pressure units, the amplitude range of human hearing is enormous. A reason for converting to logarithmic units is to produce a smaller range of numbers. The logarithm (log) of a number is the power to which 10 must be raised to produce that number. For example, the log of 10,000 is 4, because $10^4 = 10,000$. A decibel (dB) is defined as 20 log *P*. Thus, 4 log units = 80 dB.

Data from Lindsay, P. H., & Norman, D. A. (1977). *Human information processing* (2nd ed., p. 161). New York, NY: Academic Press; and from Matlin, M. W., & Foley, H. J. (1997). *Sensation and perception* (4th ed., p. 281). Boston, MA: Allyn and Bacon.

a constant-frequency sound wave that can be described mathematically as a sine wave (depicted in Figure 6.12). Pure tones can be produced in the laboratory and are useful in auditory experiments, but they rarely if ever occur in other contexts. Natural sources of sound, including even musical instruments and tuning forks, vibrate at several frequencies at once and thus produce more complex waves than that shown in Figure 6.12. The pitch that we attribute to a natural sound depends on its dominant (largest-amplitude) frequency.

How the Ear Works

Hearing originated, in the course of evolution, from the sense of touch. Touch is sensitivity to pressure on the skin, and hearing is sensitivity to pressure on a special sensory tissue in the ear. In some animals, such as moths, sound is sensed through modified touch receptors located on flexible patches of skin that vibrate in response to sound waves. In humans and other mammals, the special patches of skin for hearing have migrated to a location inside the head, and special organs, the ears, have developed to magnify the pressure exerted by sound waves as they are transported inward. A diagram of the human ear is shown in **Figure 6.13**. To review its structures and their functions, we will begin from the outside and work inward.

The **outer ear** consists of the *pinna,* which is the flap of skin and cartilage forming the visible portion of the ear, and the *auditory canal,* which is the opening into the head that ends at the eardrum. The whole outer ear can be thought of as a funnel for receiving sound waves and transporting them inward. The vibration of air outside the head (the physical sound) causes air in the auditory canal to vibrate, which, in turn, causes the eardrum to vibrate.

The **middle ear** is an air-filled cavity, separated from the outer ear by the eardrum (technically called the *tympanic membrane*). The middle ear's main structures are three tiny bones collectively called *ossicles* (and individually called the *hammer, anvil,* and *stirrup,* because of their respective shapes), which are linked to the eardrum at one end and to another membrane called the *oval window* at the other end. When sound causes the eardrum to vibrate, the ossicles vibrate and push against the oval window. Because the oval window has only about one-thirtieth the area of the tympanic membrane, the pressure (force per unit area) that is funneled to it by the ossicles is about 30 times greater than the pressure on the eardrum.

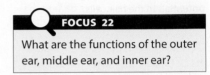

FOCUS 22

What are the functions of the outer ear, middle ear, and inner ear?

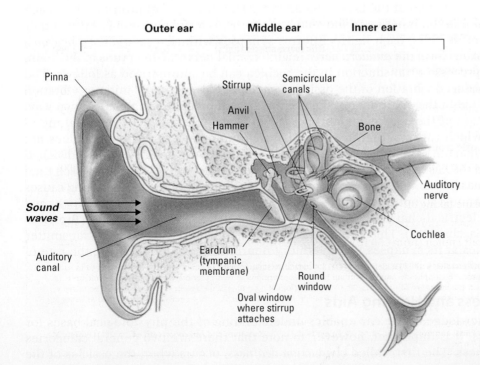

FIGURE 6.13 Parts of the human ear Sound waves (vibrations of air) that enter the auditory canal cause the eardrum to vibrate, which causes the ossicles (the hammer, anvil, and stirrup bones) to vibrate, which causes the oval window to vibrate, setting up waves of motion in the fluid inside the cochlea. The semicircular canals are involved in the sense of balance, not hearing.

FIGURE 6.14 Transduction mechanism in the inner ear This diagram depicts a longitudinal section of the cochlea (partially uncoiled), showing the outer and inner ducts. Sound waves in the fluid of the outer duct cause the basilar membrane to wave up and down. When the basilar membrane moves upward, its hairs bend against the tectorial membrane, initiating receptor potentials in the hair cells.

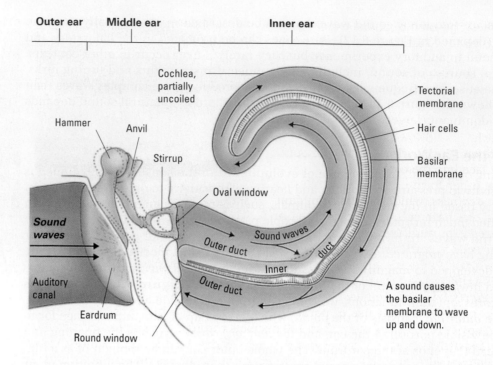

FOCUS 23

How does transduction occur in the inner ear?

FOCUS 24

How do two kinds of deafness differ in their physiological bases and in possible treatment?

Thus, the main function of the middle ear is to increase the amount of pressure that sound waves exert upon the inner ear so that transduction can occur.

The oval window separates the middle ear from the **inner ear**, which consists primarily of the **cochlea**, a coiled structure where transduction takes place. As depicted in the partially uncoiled view in **Figure 6.14**, the cochlea contains a fluid-filled *outer duct*, which begins at the oval window, runs to the tip of the cochlea, and then runs back again to end at another membrane, the *round window*. Sandwiched between the outgoing and incoming portions of the outer duct is another fluid-filled tube, the *inner duct*. Forming the floor of the inner duct is the **basilar membrane**, on which are located the receptor cells for hearing, called **hair cells**. There are four rows of hair cells (three outer rows and one inner row), each row running the length of the basilar membrane. Tiny hairs (*cilia*) protrude from each hair cell into the inner duct and abut against the *tectorial membrane*. At the other end from its hairs, each hair cell forms synapses with several *auditory neurons*, whose axons form the *auditory nerve* (eighth cranial nerve), which runs to the brain.

The process of transduction in the cochlea can be summarized as follows: The sound-induced vibration of the ossicles against the oval window initiates vibration in the fluid in the outer duct of the cochlea, which produces an up-and-down waving motion of the basilar membrane, which is very flexible. The tectorial membrane, which runs parallel to the basilar membrane, is less flexible and does not move when the basilar membrane moves. The hairs of the hair cells are sandwiched between the basilar membrane and the tectorial membrane, so they bend each time the basilar membrane moves toward the tectorial membrane. This bending causes tiny channels to open up in the hair cell's membrane, which leads to a change in the electrical charge across the membrane (the receptor potential) (Brown & Santos-Sacchi, 2013). This in turn causes each hair cell to release neurotransmitter molecules at its synapses upon auditory neurons, thereby increasing the rate of action potentials in those neurons (Hudspeth, 2000b).

Deafness and Hearing Aids

This knowledge of the ear enables understanding of the physiological bases for deafness. It is important, however, to note that there are two general categories of deafness. The first, called *conduction deafness*, occurs when the ossicles of the middle ear become rigid and cannot carry sounds inward from the tympanic membrane to the cochlea. People with conduction deafness can hear vibrations that reach the cochlea by routes other than the middle ear. A *conventional hearing aid* is helpful for such people because it magnifies the sound pressure sufficiently for vibrations to be conducted by other bones of the face into the cochlea.

The other form of deafness is *sensorineural deafness,* which results from damage to the hair cells of the cochlea or damage to the auditory neurons. Damage to hair cells is particularly likely to occur among people who are regularly exposed to loud sounds (see **Figure 6.15**). Indeed, some experts on human hearing are concerned that the regular use of portable music players, which can play music at sound pressure levels of more than 100 decibels through their stock earbuds, may cause partial deafness in many young people today as they grow older (*Nature Neuroscience* editorial, 2007). Congenital deafness (deafness present at birth) may involve damage to either the hair cells or the auditory neurons.

People with complete sensorineural deafness are not helped by a conventional hearing aid, but can in many cases regain hearing with a surgically implanted hearing aid called a *cochlear implant* (Niparko et al., 2000). This device performs the transduction task normally done by the ear's hair cells (though not nearly as well). It transforms sounds into electrical impulses and sends the impulses through thin wires permanently implanted into the cochlea, where they stimulate the terminals of auditory neurons directly. A cochlear implant may enable adults who became deaf after learning language to regain much of their ability to understand speech (Gifford et al., 2008). Some children who were born deaf are able to acquire some aspects of vocal language at a nearly normal rate through the combination of early implantation, improvements in implant technology, and aggressive post-implant speech therapy. However, outcomes remain highly variable, and most children receiving these interventions still do not attain age-appropriate performance in speaking or listening (Ertmer, 2007; Svirsky et al., 2000), and the benefits tend to be greater the earlier the device is implanted (Bond et al., 2009). It is important to note that cochlear implants are effective when deafness has resulted from the destruction of hair cells, but they do not help individuals whose auditory nerve has been destroyed.

Pitch Perception

The aspect of hearing that allows us to tell how high or low a given tone is, and to recognize a melody, is pitch perception. The first step in perceiving pitch is that receptor cells on the basilar membrane respond differently to different sound frequencies. How does that occur? The first real breakthrough in answering that question came in the 1920s, with the work of Georg von Békésy, which eventuated in a Nobel Prize.

The Traveling Wave as a Basis for Frequency Coding

In order to study frequency coding, von Békésy developed a way to observe directly the action of the basilar membrane (von Békésy & Wever, 1960). He discovered that sound waves entering the cochlea set up traveling waves on the basilar membrane, which move from the proximal end (closest to the oval window) toward the distal end (farthest away from the oval window), like a bedsheet when someone shakes it

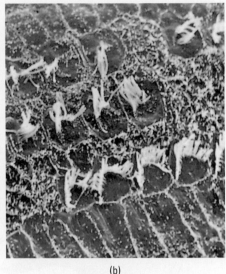

(a)   (b)

Robert S. Preston and J. E. Hawkins, Kresge Hearing Research Institute, University of Michigan

FIGURE 6.15 Warning: Noise can be dangerous These electron micrographs show hair cells on the basilar membrane of a guinea pig (a) before and (b) after exposure to 24 hours of sound at an intensity comparable to a rock concert. The tiny hairs are disarranged on some cells and completely destroyed on others. Notice also that the hair cells exist in four rows—three outer rows and one inner row.

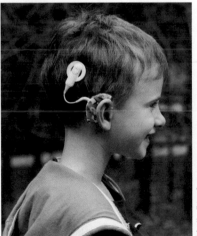

Life in View/Science Source

■ **External portions of a cochlear implant** A microphone hooked around the boy's ear picks up sound waves and sends signals to an auditory processor. The auditory processor converts the signals into electrical pulses, suitable for stimulating the cochlea, and sends those pulses up the cable to a transmitter fastened to the boy's head above and behind his ear. The transmitter sends the pulses through the skin to a receiver implanted in his skull, and from there the pulses are sent by thin wire electrodes to stimulate appropriate sets of auditory neurons in the cochlea of the inner ear.

at one end. As each wave moves, it increases in amplitude up to a certain maximum and then rapidly dissipates. Of most importance, von Békésy found that the position on the membrane at which the waves reach their peak amplitude depends on the frequency of the tone. High frequencies produce waves that travel only a short distance, peaking near the proximal end, not far from the oval window. Low frequencies produce waves that travel farther, peaking near the distal end, nearer to the round window. **Figure 6.16** illustrates the effects that different tones and complex sounds have on the basilar membrane.

From this observation, von Békésy hypothesized that (a) rapid firing in neurons that come from the proximal end of the membrane, accompanied by little or no firing in neurons coming from more distal parts, is interpreted by the brain as a high-pitched sound; and (b) rapid firing in neurons coming from a more distal portion of the membrane is interpreted as a lower-pitched sound. Subsequent research has confirmed the general validity of von Békésy's hypothesis and has shown that the waves on the intact, living basilar membrane are in fact much more sharply defined than those that von Békésy had observed. There is now good evidence that the primary receptor cells for hearing are the inner row of hair cells and that the outer three rows serve mostly a different function. When these outer rows are activated, they stiffen in a manner that amplifies and sharpens the traveling wave (Géléoc & Holt, 2003).

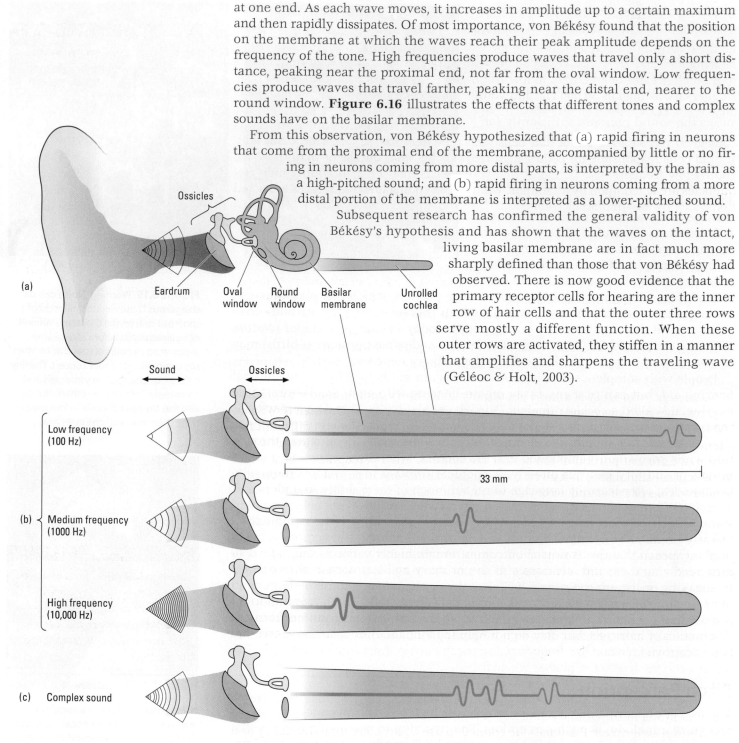

FIGURE 6.16 Waves on the basilar membrane In this highly schematic diagram, the cochlea is uncoiled and stretched out and the basilar membrane is depicted as a line running down the center of the cochlea. Part (b) depicts the back-and-forth movement of the ossicles in response to sound and the traveling wave that that motion sets up on the basilar membrane. The separate parts of (b) illustrate the relationship between the frequency of a tone and the site on the basilar membrane where the traveling wave reaches its peak amplitude. Part (c) shows that a complex sound (that is, a sound made up of more than one frequency) produces wave peaks simultaneously at more than one location on the basilar membrane. The sizes of the wave peaks are greatly exaggerated in the diagram. The waves are shown only at the places where they peak. In fact, each wave must travel the length of the basilar membrane to the site where it reaches its peak. It dies out shortly after that.

(Information from Hudspeth, 2000a.)

Sensory Consequences of the Traveling-Wave Mechanism

The manner by which the basilar membrane responds to differing frequencies helps us make sense of a number of auditory phenomena, among them the pattern of hearing loss that occurs as we get older. We lose our sensitivity to high frequencies to a much greater degree than to low frequencies. Thus, young children can hear frequencies as high as 30,000 Hz, and young adults can hear frequencies as high as 20,000 Hz, but a typical 60-year-old cannot hear frequencies above about 15,000 Hz. This decline is greatest for people who live or work in noisy environments and is caused by the wearing out of hair cells with repeated use (Kryter, 1985). But why should cells responsible for coding high frequencies wear out faster than those for coding low frequencies? The most likely answer is that the cells coding high frequencies are acted upon by all sounds, while those coding low frequencies are acted upon only by low-frequency sounds.

FOCUS 25

How does the traveling-wave theory explain the pattern of hearing loss that occurs as we get older?

Another Code for Frequency

Although the traveling-wave theory of frequency coding has been well validated, it is not the whole story. For frequencies below about 4,000 Hz (which include most of the frequencies in human speech), perceived pitch depends not just on which part of the basilar membrane is maximally active but also on the timing of that activity (Moore, 1997). The electrical activity triggered in sets of auditory neurons tends to be locked in phase with sound waves, such that a separate burst of action potentials occurs each time a sound wave peaks. The frequency at which such bursts occur contributes to the perception of pitch.

Consistent with what is known about normal auditory coding, modern cochlear implants use both place and timing to produce pitch perception (Dorman & Wilson, 2004). These devices break a sound signal into several (typically six) different frequency ranges and send electrical pulses from each frequency range through a thin wire to a different portion of the basilar membrane. Pitch perception is best when the electrical signal sent to a given locus of the membrane is pulsed at a frequency similar to that of the sound wave that would normally act at that location.

FOCUS 26

How does the timing of action potentials code sound frequency? How do cochlear implants produce perception of pitch?

Further Pitch Processing in the Brain

Auditory sensory neurons send their output to nuclei in the brainstem, which in turn send axons upward, ultimately to the primary auditory area of the cerebral cortex, located in each temporal lobe (refer back to Figure 6.1, p. 193). Neurons in the primary auditory cortex are *tonotopically* organized. That is, each neuron there is maximally responsive to sounds of a particular frequency, and the neurons are systematically arranged such that high-frequency tones activate neurons at one end of this cortical area and low-frequency tones activate neurons at the other end. Ultimately, the pitch or set of pitches we hear depends largely on which neurons in the auditory cortex are most active.

As is true of other sensory areas in the cerebral cortex, the response characteristics of neurons in the primary auditory cortex are very much influenced by experience. When experimental animals are trained to use a particular tone frequency as a cue guiding their behavior, the number of auditory cortical neurons that respond to that frequency greatly increases (Bakin et al., 1996). Heredity determines the general form of the tonotopic map, but experience determines the specific amount of cortex devoted to any particular range of frequencies. A great deal of research, with humans as well as with laboratory animals, shows that the brain's response to sound frequencies, and to other aspects of sound as well, is very much affected by previous auditory experience. For example, musicians' brains respond more strongly to the sounds of the instruments they play than to the sounds of other instruments (Kraus & Banai, 2007).

Our capacity to distinguish pitch depends not just upon the primary auditory cortex, but also upon activity in an area of the parietal lobe of the cortex called the

FOCUS 27

How is tone frequency represented in the primary auditory cortex? What evidence suggests a close relationship between musical pitch perception and visual space perception?

intraparietal sulcus, which receives input from the primary auditory cortex. This part of the brain is involved in both music perception and visual space perception. In one research study, people who described themselves as "tone deaf" and performed poorly on a test of ability to distinguish among different musical notes also performed poorly on a visual-spatial test that required them to mentally rotate pictured objects in order to match them to pictures of the same objects from other viewpoints (Douglas & Bilkey, 2007). Perhaps it is no coincidence that we (and also people who speak other languages) describe pitch in spatial terms—"high" and "low." Our brain may, in some way, interpret a high note as *high* and a low note as *low,* using part of the same neural system as is used to perceive three-dimensional space.

Making Sense of Sounds

Think of the subtlety and complexity of our auditory perception. With no cues but sound, we can locate a sound source within about 5 to 10 degrees of its true direction (Hudspeth, 2000a). At a party we can distinguish and listen to one person's voice in a noisy environment that includes not only many other voices but also a band playing in the background. To comprehend speech, we hear the tiny differences between *plot* and *blot*, while ignoring the much larger differences between two different voices that speak either of those words. All sounds set up patterns of waves on our basilar membranes, and from those seemingly chaotic patterns our nervous system extracts all the information needed for auditory perception.

Locating Sounds

The ability to detect the direction of a sound source contributes greatly to the usefulness of hearing. When startled by an unexpected rustling, we reflexively turn toward it to see what might be causing the disturbance. Even newborn infants do this (Muir & Field, 1979), indicating that the ability to localize a sound does not require learning, although this ability improves markedly by the end of the first year (Johnson et al., 2005). Such localization is also a key component of our ability to keep one sound distinct from others in a noisy environment. People can attend to one voice and ignore another much more easily if the two voices come from different locations in the room than if they come from the same location (Feng & Ratnam, 2000).

A key factor in sound localization is the time at which each sound wave reaches one ear compared to the other. A wave of sound coming from straight ahead reaches the two ears simultaneously, but a wave from the right or the left reaches one ear slightly before the other (see **Figure 6.17**). A sound wave that is just slightly to the left of straight ahead reaches the left ear a few microseconds (millionths of a second) before it reaches the right ear, and a sound wave that is 90 degrees to the left reaches the left ear about 700 microseconds before it reaches the right ear. Many auditory neurons in the brainstem receive input from both ears. Some of these neurons respond most to waves that reach both ears at once; others respond most to waves that reach one ear some microseconds—ranging from just a few on up to about 700—before, or after, reaching the other ear. These neurons, presumably, are part of the brain's mechanism for perceiving the direction from which a sound is coming (Recanzone & Sutter, 2008; Thompson et al., 2006).

Analyzing Patterns of Auditory Input

In the real world outside of the laboratory, the sounds we hear, and from which we extract meaning, consist of highly complex patterns of waveforms. How is it that you identify the word *psychology* regardless of whether it is spoken in a high-pitched or low-pitched voice, or spoken softly or loudly? You identify the word not from the absolute amplitude or frequency of the sound waves, but from certain patterns of change in these that occur over time as the word is spoken.

Beyond the primary auditory area are cortical areas for analyzing such patterns (Lombar & Malhotra, 2008; Poremba et al., 2003). For example, some neurons in areas near the primary auditory area respond only to certain combinations of frequencies, others only to rising or falling pitches, others only to brief clicks

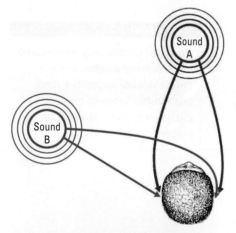

FIGURE 6.17 Locating a sound Sound waves coming from the left (sound B) reach the left ear sooner than the right ear. The converse would be true of sound waves coming from the right. Neurons receiving input from the two ears are sensitive to this difference, which provides a code for sound localization. Without moving the head, it is difficult to distinguish a sound in front of the head from one that is at the same angle in back of the head, but a head rotation quickly resolves that problem.

or bursts of sound, and still others only to sound sources that are moving in a particular direction (Baumgart et al., 1999; Phillips, 1989). In macaque monkeys, some cortical neurons respond selectively to particular macaque calls (Rauschecker et al., 1995). Activity in some combination of neurons in your cerebral cortex must provide the basis for each of your auditory experiences, but researchers are only beginning to learn how this happens.

Phonemic Restoration: An Auditory Illusion

Our auditory system can provide us with the perception of sounds that are not really present as physical stimuli. A well-documented example is the sensory illusion of *phonemic restoration*. **Phonemes** are the individual vowel and consonant sounds that make up words, and phonemic restoration is an illusion in which people hear phonemes that have been deleted from words or sentences as if they were still there. The perceptual experience is that of really *hearing* the missing sound, not that of inferring what sound must be there.

Richard Warren (1970) first demonstrated this illusion in an experiment in which he removed an *s* sound and spliced in a coughing sound of equal duration in the following tape-recorded sentence at the place marked by an asterisk: *The state governors met with their respective legi*latures convening in the capital city.* People listening to the doctored recording could hear the cough, but it did not seem to coincide with any specific portion of the sentence or block out any sound in the sentence. Even when they listened repeatedly, with instructions to determine what sound was missing, subjects were unable to detect that any sound was missing. After they were told that the first "s" sound in "legislatures" was missing, they still claimed to hear that sound each time they listened to the recording. In other experiments, thousands of practice trials failed to improve people's abilities to judge which phoneme was missing (Samuel, 1991). Not surprisingly, phonemic restoration has been found to be much more reliable for words that are very much expected to occur in the sentence than for words that are less expected (Sivonen et al., 2006).

Which sound is heard in phonemic restoration depends on the surrounding phonemes and the meaningful words and phrases they produce. The restored sound is always one that turns a partial word into a whole word that is consistent in meaning with the rest of the sentence. Most remarkably, even words that occur *after* the missing phoneme can influence which phoneme is heard. For example, people heard the stimulus sound **eel* (again, the asterisk represents a cough-like sound) as *peel, heel,* or *wheel,* depending on whether it occurred in the phrase *The *eel was on the orange, The *eel was on the shoe,* or *The *eel was on the axle* (Warren, 1984). The illusory phoneme was heard as occurring at its proper place, in the second word of the sentence, even though it depended on the words that followed it.

One way to make sense of this phenomenon is to assume that much of our perceptual experience of hearing derives from a brief auditory sensory memory, which lasts for a matter of seconds and is modifiable. The later words generate a momentary false memory of hearing, earlier—a phoneme that wasn't actually present—and that memory is indistinguishable in type from memories of phonemes that actually did occur. Illusory restoration has also been demonstrated in music perception. People hear a missing note in a familiar tune as if it were present (DeWitt & Samuel, 1990).

A limiting factor in these illusions is that the gap in the sentence or tune must be filled with noise; it can't be a silent gap. In everyday life the sounds we listen to are often masked by bits of noise, never by bits of silence, so perhaps illusory sound restorations are an evolutionary adaptation by which our auditory system allows us to hear meaningful sound sequences in a relatively uninterrupted stream. When a burst of noise masks a phoneme or a note, our auditory system automatically, after the fact, in auditory memory, replaces that burst with the auditory experience that, according to our previous experience, belongs there. Auditory restoration exemplifies the general principle that our perceptual systems often modify sensory input in ways that help to make sense of that input. We will present more examples of this principle in Chapter 7, which deals with vision.

SECTION REVIEW

Hearing allows us to glean information from patterns of vibrations carried by air.

Basic Facts of Hearing

- Physically, sound is the vibration of air or another medium caused by a vibrating object. A sound wave's amplitude is related to its perceived loudness, and its frequency is related to its perceived pitch.

- The outer ear funnels sound inward, the middle ear amplifies it, and the inner ear transduces and codes it.

- Conduction deafness is due to middle ear rigidity; sensorineural deafness is due to inner ear or auditory nerve damage.

Pitch Perception

- Sounds set up traveling waves on the basilar membrane, which peak at different positions depending on frequency. We decode frequency as pitch.

- The traveling-wave theory helps to explain the asymmetry of auditory masking and the typical pattern of age-related hearing loss.

- For frequencies below 4,000 Hz, the timing of action potentials also codes sound frequency.

- The primary auditory cortex is tonotopically organized. The pitch we hear depends on which cortical neurons become most active.

Making Sense of Sounds

- Brain neurons that compare the arrival time of sound waves at our two ears enable us to locate a sound's source.

- Most sounds are complex waveforms requiring analysis in cortical areas beyond the primary auditory area.

- The phonemic restoration effect illustrates the idea that context and meaning influence sensory experience.

Thinking Critically About Smell, Taste, Pain, Hearing, and Psychophysics

1. What might psychophysics be good for? How might an understanding of psychophysics techniques be useful in the food or cosmetic industries?

2. Are all senses equally important for humans? Why might the senses of humans and nonhuman animals differ in sensitivity? Why don't all animals have "eagle-eye vision" or the keen sense of smell that dogs do?

Reflections and Connections

Two major themes run through this chapter. You will find that details are easier to remember if tied to larger themes, or arguments, than if seen as isolated facts.

1. The mechanisms of transduction and coding All sensory systems respond to physical stimuli by producing action potentials (the process of transduction), and all sensory systems do this in such a way as to preserve useful information about the stimulus (coding).

As a review, for each sense discussed in this chapter—smell, taste, pain, and hearing—consider the following five questions about transduction and coding. Note that the chapter does not answer all these questions completely for each sense (especially not the fifth question), but the questions provide a good framework for organizing and thinking about the information that is provided.

(a) To what type of physical stimulus does this sense respond, and what is the range of stimuli to which it responds?
(b) How is the sensory organ designed for receiving (and possibly concentrating or amplifying) the stimulus?

(c) What are the receptors for the stimulus, and how do they respond in such a way as to generate action potentials in sensory neurons?
(d) How does the transduction process code the different qualities of stimuli to which the sensory system responds?
(e) How do neural mechanisms in the central nervous system alter or reorganize the input, and for what purposes?

2. The survival functions of sensory processes Our sensory systems, like all the basic mechanisms underlying our behavior, evolved through natural selection because they promoted our ancestors' survival and reproduction. They are not unbiased recorders of physical energies but biological tools designed to pick out from the sea of energy around us the information that is potentially most useful. We are sensitive to some kinds of energies and not others, and, within the kinds to which we are sensitive, our senses extract and enhance some relationships and not others.

Here are five examples, described in the chapter, of how sensory processes can be understood in terms of their survival advantages.

(a) Sensory adaptation (the decline in sensitivity to pro-longed, constant stimuli) helps us to ignore stimuli that remain unchanged and to notice changes.

(b) Attraction to the smell of individuals who differ in MHC may help to create genetic diversity and to avoid incest.

(c) Smell and taste work together to produce flavors that are experienced as pleasant or unpleasant, in ways that are gen-erally consistent with what is good for us or bad for us (or for our evolutionary ancestors) to eat. The association of bitter taste with poisons is an example.

(d) Pain is a sensory system for warning us when our actions are damaging our tissues and for motivating us to avoid such actions. Evolved mechanisms increase pain sensitivity at times of illness, when it is best to rest. In contrast, they decrease pain sensitivity at times of threat, when strenuous action without favoring one's wounds may be necessary.

(e) The phonemic-restoration illusion helps us to hear speech in a continuous, meaningful flow and to ignore extraneous noises and interruptions.

Key Terms

absolute threshold   196
amplitude   213
basilar membrane   216
cochlea   216
difference threshold   196
frequency   213
gate-control theory   210
hair cells   216

inner ear   216
just-noticeable difference (jnd)   196
middle ear   215
olfaction   199
outer ear   215
perception   192
pheromone   203

phonemes   221
pitch   213
psychophysics   195
receptor potentials   194
sensation   192
sensory adaptation   195
sensory areas   193
sensory coding   194

sensory receptors   193
signal detection theory   197
stress-induced analgesia   212
transduction   194
Weber's law   197

Find Out More

Daniel J. Levitin (2006). *This is your brain on music: The science of a human obses-sion.* New York, NY: Dutton.

This delightful book about the neuroscience and psychology of music is authored by a former musical performer and producer turned neuroscientist. It deals with ques-tions of how our brains process musical sounds, how such sounds act upon emo-tional mechanisms in our brains, and the reasons for individual differences in musical preferences. In the final chapter, Levitin argues that music played an import-ant evolutionary role in attracting mates and in binding people together into coop-erative groups.

Barb Stuckey (2012). *Taste: Surprising sto-ries and science about why food tastes good.* New York, NY: Simon & Schuster.

Barb Stuckey works as a professional food inventor and knows the five flavor categories with profound fluency. In her easy-to-read book, Stuckey shows readers why we experience foods the way we do, why some people like bitter tastes and others prefer sweet, and how we go from sensing food to perceiving flavor.

Elizabeth O. Johnson & Panayotis N. Soucacos (2010). Proprioception. In J. H. Stone & M. Blouin (Eds.), *Inter-national encyclopedia of rehabilitation.* Retrieved from http://cirrie.buffalo.edu/encyclopedia/en/article/337/

Proprioception is the sense that helps us keep track of the position of our body. It operates through a system of nerve cell receptors (known as proprioceptors) that

allow us to ascertain the angle of our various joints. This article summarizes what we know about how proprioception works, from the outermost receptors to the brain.

Tristram Wyatt (2013, September). The smelly mystery of the human phero-mone. TEDxLeuvenSalon. Retrieved from www.ted.com/talks/tristram_wyatt_the_smelly_mystery_of_the_human_phero-mone#t-878055

Zoologist Tristram Wyatt believes that humans, as all mammals, have phero-mones—but don't rush to buy the latest product claiming to make you sexually irresistible. Scientists can seek evidence of human pheromones by studying our armpits and crotches, and nursing babies and their mothers.

LaunchPad
macmillan learning

Visit LaunchPad for Psychology 8e launchpadworks.com to access the e-book, videos, activities, additional resources, and LearningCurve quizzes, as well as study aids including flash cards and web quizzes.

The Psychology of Vision

LEARNING OUTCOMES

After studying this chapter, you should be able to:

- Describe how the different parts of the eye work, including the functions of rods and cones.
- Identify two major theories of color vision.
- Explain how the visual system develops through the lifespan.
- Discuss various principles related to how we perceive forms, patterns, objects, and faces.
- Describe the mechanisms for depth perception.
- Describe how vision is integrated with other senses.

We are visual creatures. Our eyes are our primary gateway for perceiving and understanding the physical world in which we survive. We say "I see" to mean "I understand," and when we doubt some claim, we say "I'd have to see it to believe it." Our visual system provides us with such rich, clear, solid-looking, and generally useful perceptions of the physical world that it is easy for us to forget that the physical world and our sight of it are not one and the same thing.

In reality, our visual perceptions are subjective, psychological experiences that our brains create from clues that lie in the patterns of light reflected off objects. The machinery that underlies our ability to produce such perceptions is incredibly complex. Brain scientists have estimated that somewhere between 25 and 40% of the human brain is devoted exclusively or primarily to the analysis of input from the eyes (Gross, 1998; Sereno et al., 1995). It is no wonder that vision is the sense to which psychologists have paid the greatest attention.

Vision begins with activity in the eyes, and that is where this chapter begins. From there we examine our abilities to perceive colors, patterns, objects, and depth in three-dimensional space. The chapter concludes by discussing the fascinating phenomenon of multisensory perception.

How the Eye Works

Life on earth evolved in a world illuminated by the sun during the day and by starlight and the moon's reflected sunlight at night. Most forms of earthly life are sensitive in one way or another to that light (Land & Furnald, 1992). Even single-celled organisms contain chemicals that respond to light and alter the organism's activity in survival-promoting ways. In many species of multicellular animals, specialized light-detecting cells called **photoreceptors** evolved and became connected to the animal's nervous system. Earthworms, for example, have photoreceptors distributed throughout their skin. Stimulation of these cells by light causes the worm to wriggle away from the light and back down into the earth, where it finds safety, moisture, and food.

FOCUS 1

How might sophisticated eyes like ours have evolved from primitive beginnings?

Cross-species comparisons, based on homologies (discussed in Chapter 3), suggest that the modern vertebrate eye came about through the evolutionary steps something like the following (Gregory, 1996; Lamb et al., 2007): In some early ancestor to vertebrate animals, photoreceptors became concentrated into groups, forming light-detecting organs, or eye spots, just under the skin. These organs may have initially enabled circadian rhythms—the cyclic biological changes that accompany the day–night light–dark cycle (discussed in Chapter 5). Over successive generations, however, they may have taken on the additional function of responding to shadows, which could help detect predators. With further natural selection, the skin covering the eyespots became transparent, allowing in both more light and clearer shadows. The spots then gradually moved inward, into fluid-filled pits underneath the transparent skin, reducing glare and enabling the animal to detect the direction from which changes in illumination were coming. Subsequent evolution led to the thickening of one of the membranes covering each eyespot to form a crude lens, which may have served merely to magnify the light reaching the photoreceptors. With further evolutionary refinement, the lens became capable of projecting an image onto the lining of photoreceptors. Through such gradual steps, coupled with appropriate changes in the nervous system, primitive organisms' ability to detect shifts in lightness and darkness evolved into the ability to see the shapes of things and eventually into the marvelously complex and precise visual ability that is the subject of this chapter.

Functional Organization of the Eye

The main parts of the human eye are shown in **Figure 7.1**. The photoreceptors lie in the **retina**, a membrane lining the rear interior of the eyeball. The eyeball is filled with a clear gelatinous substance (the vitreous humor) through which light easily passes. The structures at the front of the eye are devices for focusing light reflected from objects in such a way as to form images on the retina.

Structures at the Front of the Eye Focus Images on the Retina

The front of the eyeball is covered by the **cornea**, a transparent tissue that, because of its convex (outward) curvature, helps to focus the light that passes through it. Immediately behind the cornea is the pigmented, doughnut-shaped **iris**, which provides the color of the eye. The iris is opaque, so the only light that enters the interior of the eye is that which passes through a hole called the **pupil**, the black-appearing center in the iris. Muscle fibers in the iris enable it to increase or decrease the diameter of the pupil to allow more or less light to enter.

Behind the iris is the **lens**, which adds to the focusing process begun by the cornea. Unlike the cornea, the lens is adjustable; it becomes more spherical when focusing on objects close to the eye and flatter when focusing on those farther

FOCUS 2

How do the cornea, iris, and lens help to form images on the retina?

FIGURE 7.1 Cross section of the eye, depicting the retinal image The light rays that diverge from any given point on the surface of an object are brought back together (focused) at a distinct point on the retina to create an image of the object on the retina. This drawing shows light rays diverging and being brought together for just two points on the leaf, but the same process is occurring for light rays coming from every point.

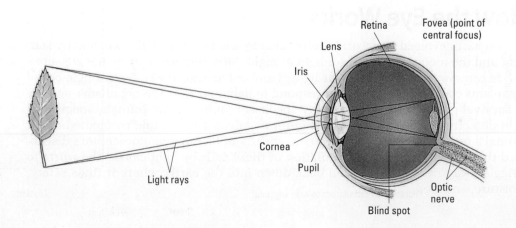

away. Light rays diverge as they move toward the eye from any given point on a visual object. The focusing properties of the cornea and lens bring the light rays back together at a particular point on the retina, thereby forming an image of the object on the retina. The image is upside down (as shown at right in Figure 7.1), but that does not matter, since its only purpose is to trigger patterns of activity in neurons running to the brain. The brain is wired to the retina in such a way that input from lower on the retina is interpreted as up, and input from higher on the retina is interpreted as down.

FIGURE 7.2 Rods and cones This electron micrograph shows that the photoreceptors are aptly named: Rods (stained blue) are rod-shaped; cones (stained blue-green) taper at the ends. Rods are responsible for vision in dim light, and cones for vision in bright light.

Science Source

Transduction Occurs in the Retina

As noted in Chapter 6, the process by which a stimulus from the environment generates electrical changes in neurons is called *transduction*. In vision, transduction is the function of the photoreceptor cells. In each eye millions of photoreceptor cells are arranged, mosaic-like, in one thin layer of the multilayered retina. These cells are of two types: *cones*, which permit sharply focused color vision in bright light, and *rods*, which permit vision in dim light. They are so named because of their shapes (see **Figure 7.2**). Cones are most concentrated in the *fovea*, the pinhead-size area of the retina that is in the most direct line of sight (look again at Figure 7.1), which is specialized for high visual *acuity* (the ability to distinguish tiny details). The concentration of cones decreases sharply with increasing distance from the fovea. Rods, in contrast, exist everywhere in the retina except in the fovea and are most concentrated in a ring about 20 degrees away from the fovea (see **Figure 7.3**). Each human retina contains about 6 million cones and 120 million rods (Wade & Swanston, 1991).

The outer segment of each photoreceptor contains a photochemical—a chemical that reacts to light. The rods' photochemical is called *rhodopsin* [rō-**dŏp´**-sən]. When hit by light, rhodopsin molecules undergo a structural change that triggers a series of chemical reactions in the rod's membrane, which in turn causes a change in the electrical charge across the membrane (Schnapf & Baylor, 1987). The transduction process for cones is similar to that for rods, but it differs in that three varieties of cones exist, each containing a different photochemical (discussed further in this chapter's section on color vision). The electrical changes in rods and cones cause electrical responses in other cells in the retina, which lead to the production

FOCUS 3

How are cones and rods distributed on the retina, and how do they respond to light?

FIGURE 7.3 Distribution of cones and rods in the retina Cones are most concentrated in the fovea. Rods are absent from the fovea and most concentrated in a ring 20 degrees away from it. No receptors at all exist in the blind spot.

(Data from Lindsay & Norman, 1977.)

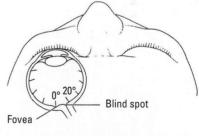

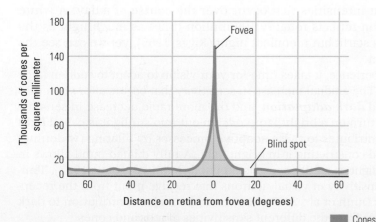

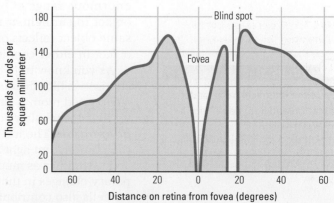

Cones   Rods

FIGURE 7.4 Demonstration of the blind spot Close your left eye and focus on the X with your right eye. Start with the page a little more than a foot from your eye and move it gradually closer, still focusing on the X. At about 10 inches, the bird will disappear. At that location, the image of the bird falls on the blind spot of the retina, shown in Figure 7.3. Yet you will probably still see the bars of the cage running across the area where the bird was located, and the background color may fill the space previously occupied by the bird. The bars and color are perceptually filled in by your visual system.

FOCUS 4

How do cone vision and rod vision differ?

of action potentials (neural impulses) in neurons that form the **optic nerve**, which runs from the back of the eye to the brain. At the place on the retina where the axons of these neurons converge to form the optic nerve there are no receptor cells; this produces a **blind spot** (see Figure 7.3). We normally do not notice the blind spot, but you can demonstrate its existence by following the instructions in **Figure 7.4**.

Differences Between Cone Vision and Rod Vision

Cones and rods provide the starting points for what can be thought of as two separate but interacting visual systems within the human eye. **Cone vision**, also called *photopic vision* or bright-light vision, is specialized for high acuity (the ability to see fine detail) and for color perception. **Rod vision**, also called *scotopic vision* or dim-light vision, is specialized for sensitivity (the ability to see in very dim light). Rod vision lacks acuity and the capacity to distinguish colors, but, according to calculations from laboratory studies, it is sensitive enough to allow a person on a clear night to detect a single candle flame from 30 miles away if no other lights are present (Galanter, 1962). Cone vision came about, through natural selection, to allow us to see fine details during daylight, and rod vision came about to allow us to see at least the vague outlines of objects at night.

In very dim light, you can see objects best when you don't look directly at them—because, as noted before, the fovea (the part of the retina in the direct line of sight) contains no rods. You can demonstrate this in a dark room or on a dark night by identifying an object to look at. The object will disappear if you look straight at it, but reappear when you adjust your gaze just a little off to one side.

Roles of Rods and Cones in Dark Adaptation and Light Adaptation

One of the many problems our visual system has to solve is that of adjusting to the enormous range of light intensities that occur over the course of a day. A white object in sunlight at noon reflects roughly 100 million times as much light as the same object reflects on a starlit but moonless night (Riggs, 1965), yet we can see the object in either condition.

FOCUS 5

What is the chemical basis for dark adaptation and light adaptation? Why do we see mostly with cones in bright light and with rods in dim light?

As you know from experience, it takes time for your vision to adapt to sudden large changes in illumination. The gradual increase in sensitivity that occurs after you enter a darkened room is called **dark adaptation**, and the more rapid decrease in sensitivity that occurs after you turn on a bright lamp or step out into sunlight is called **light adaptation**. The iris contributes to these adaptive processes by dilating (widening) the pupil in dim light and constricting it in bright light. A fully dilated pupil allows in about 16 times as much light as a fully constricted pupil (Matlin & Foley, 1997). Temporary changes in the sensitivity of visual neurons that receive input from the receptor cells also contribute (Dunn et al., 2007). However, the major contribution to dark and light adaptation comes from the different sensitivities of rods and cones.

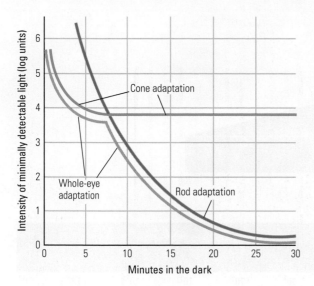

FIGURE 7.5 Dark-adaptation curves The yellow curve depicts the minimal intensity of a spot of light that a person with normal vision can see after varying periods in the dark after having been in bright light. The lower the curve, the greater the sensitivity to light. For the first 7 minutes or so, the cones are more sensitive than the rods, but after that the rods are more sensitive. The two-part nature of the curve can be understood by comparing it to the dark-adaptation curve obtained for a person who has only rods (the blue curve) and to that obtained if the light is presented in such a way that it strikes just the fovea, where only cones exist (the green curve).

(Data from Grusser & Grusser-Cornehis, 1986).

Rhodopsin, the rod photochemical, is much more sensitive to light than are the cone photochemicals. Bright light causes rhodopsin to break down into two inactive substances, making the rods nonfunctional. In sunlight, therefore, you see entirely with your cones, and even in a typical artificially lit room you see mostly with your cones. When you first step from bright light into a dark room, you may see nothing because your rods are still inactive and there isn't enough light to activate your cones. After a few moments in the dark, however, rhodopsin begins to regenerate, your rods regain their sensitivity, and you gradually see more and more. It takes about 25 minutes for rhodopsin to regenerate fully. If you then step out of the dark room into sunlight, you are at first blinded by the dazzling light because your highly sensitive rods are responding maximally and indiscriminately. Within about 5 minutes, however, the rhodopsin breaks down and you begin to see normally with your less sensitive cones. The cone photochemicals also break down somewhat in bright light and regenerate in dim light and thereby contribute to light and dark adaptation, but this change is smaller than that which occurs in rods (see **Figure 7.5**).

SECTION REVIEW

The sophisticated human eye focuses light to form images on photoreceptors in the retina.

Basic Structures and Functions of the Eye

- The cornea and the adjustable lens focus incoming light onto the retina at the back of the eye's interior.
- Light energy is then transduced by two types of photoreceptor cells in the retina—rods and cones—that contain photochemicals that react to light with structural changes.
- These changes can lead to further chemical and electrical changes, ultimately triggering action potentials in neurons that form the optic nerve.

Cone and Rod Vision

- Cones provide color vision, high visual acuity, and ability to see in bright illumination, whereas rods provide the sensitivity that allows vision in dim illumination.
- The rate and degree of dark adaptation and light adaptation are different for rods and cones. A result is that we see only with rods in very dim light and only with cones in bright light.

Seeing Colors

Many animals—including humans, other primates, birds, bees, and most fishes and reptiles— have evolved color vision, which helps to make objects stand out vividly from their backgrounds. The colors that we and other animals see in objects depend on the wavelengths of the light reflected from those objects. The

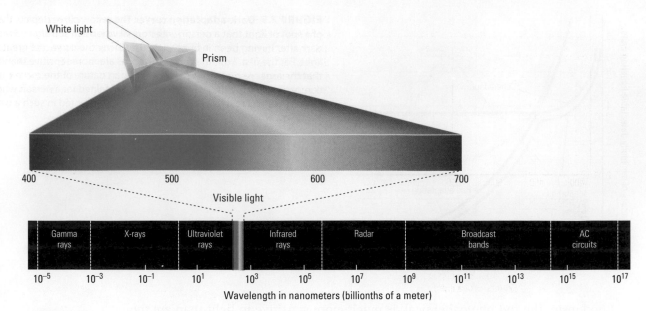

FIGURE 7.6 The electromagnetic spectrum Light is the visible portion of the electromagnetic spectrum. White light, separated according to wavelength with a prism, produces the spectrum of visible colors, extending from violet and blue at the short-wavelength end to red at the long-wavelength end.

wavelengths of light visible to humans range from about 400 to 700 nm (1 nm, or nanometer, is a billionth of a meter). Shorter waves of electromagnetic energy, below our visible range, include ultraviolet rays, X-rays, and gamma rays; longer waves, above our visible range, include infrared rays, radar rays, and radio waves (see **Figure 7.6**).

According to the ***three-primaries law***, three different wavelengths of light (called *primaries*) can be used to match any color that the eye can see if they are mixed in the appropriate proportions. The primaries can be any three wavelengths, provided that one is taken from the long-wave end of the spectrum (red), one from the shortwave end (blue or violet), and one from the middle (green or green-yellow). According to the ***law of complementarity***, pairs of wavelengths can be found that, when added together, produce the visual sensation of white. The wavelengths of light in such a pair are complements of each other.

If you have studied art, you may find this a bit confusing because, although *additive color mixing* works for light (add all colors of light together and you get white), *subtractive color mixing* works when dealing with pigments (add all colors of paint together and you get black). When you were a child playing with paint, you probably proved the basic facts of subtractive color mixing many times. You may remember being disappointed when you mixed all the paints together and produced something pretty close to black rather than the brilliant reddish-yellowish-greenish-blue that you had hoped for. In that experiment, you subtracted essentially all the wavelengths by combining all the pigments, leaving essentially none to be reflected. Our discussion of color vision focuses on additive color mixing.

There are two theories of color vision, both developed in the nineteenth century: the trichromatic theory and the opponent-process theory. For many years these two theories were thought to be contradictory to one another, but we now know that both are true.

The Trichromatic Theory

According to the ***trichromatic theory***, color vision emerges from the combined activity of three different types of receptors, each most sensitive to a different range of wavelengths. This idea was first proposed (in 1802) by Thomas Young and later by Hermann von Helmholtz (1852). Young and Helmholtz reasoned that if every color we see is the result of a unique proportion, or ratio, of activity

FOCUS 6

How does the trichromatic theory explain the three-primaries law? How was the theory validated by the discovery of three cone types?

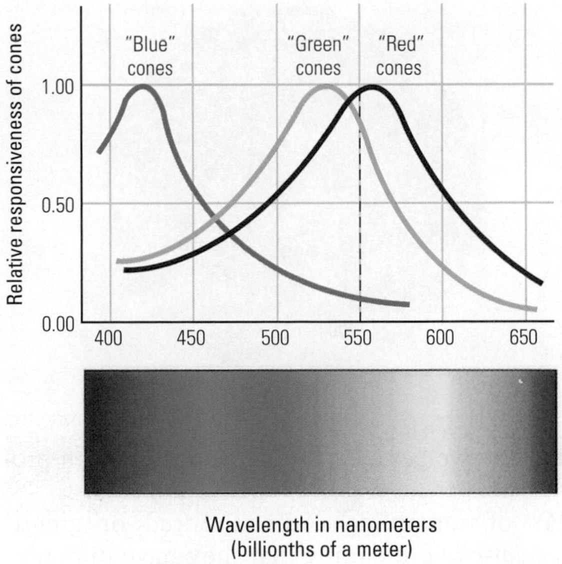

FIGURE 7.7 How the three types of cones respond to different wavelengths of light Any given wavelength produces a unique ratio of activity in the three cone types, and that ratio provides the initial code that permits us to see different wavelengths as different colors. For example, a 550-nm light, which is seen as greenish-yellow, produces a slightly larger response in "red" cones than in "green" cones and very little response in "blue" cones. Any combination of lights that would produce that same ratio of responses would be seen as greenish-yellow.

(For precise data, see Bowmaker & Dartnall, 1980, or Merbs & Nathans, 1992).

among three types of receptors, then the three-primaries law would be an inevitable result: It would be possible to match any visible color by varying the relative intensities of three primary lights, each of which acts maximally on a different type of receptor.

Young and Helmholtz developed their theory purely from behavioral data on the perceptual effects of color mixing, at a time when nothing was known about photoreceptors in the retina. We now know from physiological studies that their theory was correct. Three types of cones indeed exist in the human retina, each with a different photochemical that makes it most sensitive to the light within a particular band of wavelengths.

Figure 7.7 shows an approximation of the actual sensitivity curves for each type of cone. The cones are labeled "blue," "green," and "red," after the color that is experienced when that type of cone is much more active than the other types. Notice that any given wavelength of light produces a unique ratio of activity in the three types of cones. For example, a 550-nm light, which is seen as greenish-yellow, produces a slightly larger response in "red" cones than in "green" cones and a very low response in "blue" cones. That same ratio of response in the three cone types could be produced by shining into the eye a mixture of red, green, and blue primaries, with the first two much more intense than the last. The result would be a perceptual experience of greenish-yellow indistinguishable from that produced by the 550-nm light.

Exceptions to Trichromatic Vision

Some people (one of your authors [David Bjorklund] being one of them) are *dichromats*: They have only two, not three, types of cone photochemicals. These people see according to a two-primaries law of color mixing rather than the three-primaries law. For them, any color that they can see can be matched by varying the proportion of just two different wavelengths of light (see Figure 7.7).

The most common forms of dichromia involve the absence of the normal photochemical for either the "red" or the "green" cones (usually the latter) due to a defect in the gene that produces that photochemical (Neitz et al., 1996). Because the defective gene is recessive and the genes for both the "red" and the "green" photochemicals are located on the X chromosome, this trait appears much more often in men than in women. Men (as discussed in Chapter 3) have only one X chromosome,

> **FOCUS 7**
>
> Why does vision in some people obey a two-primaries law rather than the three-primaries law, and why are these people not good at picking cherries? How does the color vision of most nonprimate mammals, and that of most birds, differ from that of most humans?

FIGURE 7.8 What do you see? The first image (a) serves as a control. Everyone should see the number "12." For the second image (b), people with normal color vision will see the number "26." People with colorblindness (mostly males) will see only the "2," only the "6," or (like one of the book's authors) no numbers at all.

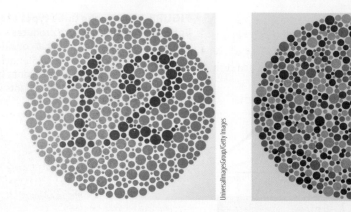

inherited from the mother, so a single defective gene on that chromosome can produce *color blindness* (see **Figure 7.8**).

Approximately 5% of men and 0.25% of women lack either the "red" or "green" cone photochemical and are *red-green color-blind*, meaning that they have difficulty distinguishing colors ranging from green to the red end of the spectrum (Masland, 2001). Figure 7.7 illustrates why this is so. The normal ability to distinguish colors in this range (from about 500 to 700 nm) is mediated almost entirely by differential activity in the "red" and "green" cones, because "blue" cones are quite inactive in this range. If either the "red" or the "green" cone photochemical is missing, then the person has little or no physiological basis for distinguishing one wavelength from another in this range.

Many people who have red-green color blindness don't know it and may wonder why certain perceptual tasks that are hard for them are easy for others. One man's red-green color blindness was not discovered until he told his family how much he admired the perceptual skill of cherry pickers: "After all," he said, "the only thing that tells 'em it's a cherry is . . . that it's round and the leaves aren't. I just don't see how they find 'em in those trees!" (Coren & Ward, 1989). There is an upside to some forms of color blindness, however. Color-blind people are not easily fooled by camouflage; in World War II the U.S. Army even assigned color-blind personnel to detect camouflage colors that people with normal color vision could not see (Reit, 1978).

Most nonprimate mammals, including dogs and cats, have just two types of cones—corresponding to our "blue" and "green" cones—and have the same difficulty discriminating among colors at the long-wavelength end of the spectrum as

■ **The value of color vision** Our sensitivity to the wavelength of reflected light helps us to distinguish objects of interest from their background.

(a)   (b)

do humans who are red-green color-blind (Solomon & Lennie, 2007). Most birds, in contrast, have four types of cones (Dalton, 2004). Birds rely heavily on vision to guide their flight and to locate food, and they have evolved color vision that is better than ours. In addition to "red," "green," and "blue" cones, they have a fourth set of cones that are maximally sensitive to wavelengths in the ultraviolet range (shorter than 400 nm), which we cannot see but are visible to other animals, such as bird species whose hatchlings have ultraviolet mouths.

The Opponent-Process Theory

The trichromatic theory explains the three-primaries law and certain types of color blindness well, but it does not explain the law of complementarity—how certain pairs of wavelengths produce the experience of white. To explain that, Ewald Hering, another nineteenth-century scientist, developed the **opponent-process theory**. Hering was most impressed by the observation that complementary colors of light (blue and yellow, or green and red) seem to swallow each other up, erasing each other's color, when added together. For example, if you begin with blue light and gradually add more of its complement (yellow), the result is not "bluish-yellow" but an ever-paler (more unsaturated) blue, which finally becomes white. To explain such observations, Hering (1878/1964) proposed that color perception is mediated by physiological units (which we now call neurons) that can be either excited or inhibited, depending on the wavelength of light, and that complementary wavelengths have opposite effects (that is, they activate "opposing processes") on these opponent-process units.

More specifically, Hering's proposal was that the ability to see blues and yellows is mediated by blue-yellow opponent neurons, which are excited by wavelengths in the blue part of the spectrum and inhibited by those in the yellow part, or vice versa. Similarly, he proposed that the ability to see greens and reds is mediated by green-red opponent neurons, which are excited by wavelengths in the green part of the spectrum and inhibited by those in the red part, or vice versa. In addition, he proposed that the ability to distinguish bright from dim light, independent of wavelength, is mediated by a third set of neurons (brightness detectors), which are excited by lights of any wavelength. This theory accounts for the facts of complementary colors. A mixture of wavelengths from the blue and yellow parts of the spectrum, or from the green and red parts, appears white (colorless but bright) because the two sets of wavelengths cancel each other out in their effects on color detectors but act in concert to excite brightness detectors.

Color Afterimages Explained by the Opponent-Process Theory

The opponent-process theory also accounts for another psychological phenomenon, the *complementarity of afterimages*. For a demonstration of this phenomenon, follow the instructions in the first paragraph of the caption of **Figure 7.9**. The colors in

■ **Ultraviolet mouths** These starling nestlings' gaping beaks and mouths would appear black to us, but, as shown in this UV photograph, they reflect ultraviolet light intensely. They are ideally designed to attract the attention of the mother starling without attracting that of mammalian predators who cannot see ultraviolet light.

FOCUS 8

How does the opponent-process theory explain (a) the law of complementarity in color mixing and (b) the complementarity of afterimages?

FIGURE 7.9 Complementarity of afterimages Stare at the dot in the middle of the flag for at least half a minute. Then look at the dot on the white space beside the flag. What do you see?

To demonstrate that this effect involves a change within the retina, or at least somewhere early in the visual system before the input from the two eyes converges, repeat the demonstration but this time keep one eye closed as you stare at the middle of the flag. Then look at the dot in the white space first with one eye and then with the other. What happens?

FIGURE 7.10 Reconciliation of the trichromatic and opponent-process theories Shown here is a schematic diagram illustrating how connections from the three types of cones can result in opponent-process cells—cells that are excited by blue and inhibited by yellow (*B+Y−*) and cells that are excited by red and inhibited by green (*R+G−*) Excitatory neural connections are shown as Y-shaped axonal endings, and inhibitory connections are shown as straight lines perpendicular to the axon. The cells marked "I" are inhibitory intermediary neurons. As an exercise, try constructing diagrams that would produce *B−Y+* and *R−G+* opponent neurons.

FOCUS 9

How has the opponent-process theory been validated in studies of the activity of neurons that receive input from cones?

---

the afterimage are the complements of those in the original: What was green becomes red; what was yellow becomes blue; and what was black becomes white.

How does the opponent-process theory explain this phenomenon? Consider the example of green becoming red in the afterimage. As you stare at the picture, the neurons in the retina that respond most strongly to the green-appearing (middle-wavelength) light become fatigued. Therefore, when you shift your eyes to the white paper (which reflects all wavelengths), those neurons don't respond as strongly as they normally would, but other neurons, including those that respond to red-appearing (long-wavelength) light, do respond strongly. Thus, opponent-process neurons that are normally excited by red-appearing light and inhibited by green-appearing light in that part of the retina become excited, resulting in the perception of red. To convince yourself that this adaptive process occurs early in the visual pathway, before the inputs from the two eyes converge, follow the instructions in the second paragraph of the caption of Figure 7.9.

A Physiological Reconciliation of the Two Theories

For many years the trichromatic and opponent-process theories were thought to be contradictory, but in the 1950s and 1960s research showed that both theories are fundamentally correct (De Valois et al., 1966; Hurvich & Jameson, 1957). The retina indeed contains three types of cones, consistent with Young and Helmholtz's trichromatic theory. But the cones feed into ganglion cells (the neurons of the optic nerve) in a pattern that translates the trichromatic code into an opponent-process code, conforming to Hering's theory. Some ganglion cells behave in a red-green opponent manner: They are excited by input from "red" cones and inhibited by input from "green" cones, or vice versa. Others behave in a blue-yellow opponent manner: They are excited by input from "blue" cones and inhibited by input from both "green" and "red" cones (which, in combination, respond best to yellow light), or vice versa. To see how connections from the three cone types could produce such opponent-process cells, look at **Figure 7.10**. Neurons in the cerebral cortex that are most directly involved in color perception maintain these opponent-process characteristics (Dacey, 2000; Solomon & Lennie, 2007).

The research and theories on color vision we have just presented illustrate the value of combining behavioral and physiological research. The trichromatic and opponent-process theories were developed, in the nineteenth century, from behavioral evidence of the perceptual effects of color mixing, before anything was known about the physiology of receptors and neurons. Later, both theories were confirmed physiologically, and neuroscientists and psychologists today are still working out the finer details of the theories.

SECTION REVIEW

The experience of color results from the visual system's response to wavelengths of light.

Wavelength and Color	Trichromatic Theory of Color Vision	Opponent-Process Theory of Color Vision
■ We experience different wavelengths of light as different colors.	■ This theory, derived from the three-primaries law, holds that we have three types of receptors, each most responsive to a particular range of wavelengths.	■ This theory, derived from the law of complementarity, holds that physiological units involved in color vision are affected in opposite ways (excited or inhibited) by complementary wavelengths.
■ Objects appear colored because their pigments absorb some wavelengths from white light and reflect others.	■ The theory was confirmed by the discovery that the retina has three types of cones, each with a different curve of sensitivity to visible wavelengths.	■ The theory explains the complementarity of afterimages.
■ Color mixing involves mixing lights of different wavelengths. It is characterized by the three-primaries law and the law of complementarity.		■ The theory was confirmed by the discovery of visual neurons that behave just as the theory predicted.

Development and Plasticity of the Visual System

"Seeing" is something that is spontaneous and automatic. You don't seem to expend any mental effort seeing—it just happens. You certainly don't "learn" to see, at least the way learning is typically thought of. However, some experience is necessary for vision. We may not learn to see the way a rat learns its way through a maze or the way children learn to behave when in public, but it is also not fully automatic, at least not initially.

Vision at Birth

No one knows for certain what human newborns see, but we can tell how well they see. For example, we know that newborns do not have very good control of the muscles controlling the lens of the eye, limiting their ability to adjust (or *accommodate)* their lens during the first months of life. However, the ability to accommodate improves quickly over the next several weeks and is nearly adultlike by 8 weeks (Candy et al., 2009; Tondel & Candy, 2007, 2008). Also, *convergence* (both eyes looking at the same object) and *coordination* (both eyes following a moving stimulus in a coordinated fashion) are poor at birth, but each develops rapidly and is adultlike by 6 months of age (Aslin & Jackson, 1979).

FOCUS 10

How can you know what an infant sees? What methods can be used to determine visual acuity in young babies?

The visual system of newborns is obviously far from what it will become, but if two stimuli are sufficiently different from one another, even newborns will be able to "see" them and tell them apart. We know this because infants who are shown a visual stimulus decrease their looking time as a result of repeated presentation of that stimulus (this is an example of habituation, to be discussed in Chapter 8). When they are then shown a new stimulus, they will increase their looking time to that stimulus. If they do this, it indicates that the infants can tell the difference between the two stimuli and have at least a very brief memory for the original stimulus. Using procedures such as this, newborns have been shown to discriminate between two highly discrepant stimuli, such as bull's-eye and checkerboard patterns (Friedman, 1972; Slater, 1995).

■ **What do newborns see?** Although newborn's acuity is relatively poor, they are able to see details of their mothers' faces from up to 2 meters away.

This phenomenon of habituation to looking at a stimulus is central to one technique for assessing how clearly newborns can see, in which babies are shown striped patterns like the one in **Figure 7.11**. If infants look at the striped rectangle longer than at a plain gray rectangle, researchers know they can tell the difference, or discriminate, between them. Researchers assess the infants' ability to discriminate by progressively displaying patterns with the stripes closer and closer together. When infants no longer look more at the striped rectangle relative to the solid gray one, this indicates that they cannot discriminate between them. While normal acuity for adults is 20/20 (one can see at a distance of 20 feet what a person with "normal" vision can see at 20 feet), estimates of newborn acuity range from 20/400 to 20/600 (Slater, 1995; Teller, 1997). This would make newborns legally blind in most states. However, there is much that very young infants *can* see with this level of acuity, including details of a parent's face from up to two meters away. Acuity improves substantially during the first year of life, being equivalent to between 20/75 and 20/100 vision at 6 months, and about 20/50 vision at 12 months of age (Teller, 1997), although it does not reach adult levels until about 6 years of age (Mayer & Dobson, 1982; Mayer et al., 1995).

FIGURE 7.11 Determining visual acuity. If infants look at a striped pattern like this one longer than at a plain gray one, we know that they can "see" the lines. When they can no longer tell the difference between the gray pattern and the striped pattern, this reflects the narrowest width of stripes that an infant can discriminate, and this is used to determine their visual acuity.

FOCUS 11

What are experience-expectant processes, and how do they relate to the development of vision?

Is "Experience" Necessary to See?

The visual abilities of newborns improve substantially over the first several months of life, but this does not allow us to conclude that experience is a necessary factor in the ability to see. Is the improvement merely due to neurological maturation? Apparently not: There is evidence that the brain is prepared to make sense of visual information, but that it must receive the proper stimulation to get hooked up properly.

William Greenough and his associates (Black et al., 1998; Greenough et al., 1987) proposed that the nervous system of animals has been prepared by natural selection to expect certain types of stimulation, such as a three-dimensional visual world consisting of moving objects. Accordingly, functions—in this case vision—will develop for all members of a species, given a species-typical environment. Greenough and his colleagues called the processes whereby synapses are formed and maintained when an organism has species-typical experiences as *experience-expectant processes* (or *experience-expectant synaptogenesis*).

But, if that species-typical environment is absent, the animal may not develop normal vision. For instance, when rats or cats are raised in total darkness, they later have difficulty making even simple visual discriminations (Crabtree & Riesen, 1979). Experience with patterned light is necessary for the brain to make sense of the light stimulation falling on the retina. Something similar seems to happen to human adults who have cataracts removed. Shortly after surgery, they can tell the difference between a square and a triangle only by counting the corners (Carlson & Hyvarinen, 1983; Von Senden, 1960). Visual abilities for once-deprived animals and humans improve with time, although the longer the period of deprivation, the less reversible are the effects (Crabtree & Riesen, 1979; Timney et al., 1980).

When kittens first open their eyes, about half of the neurons in the visual cortex respond selectively to direction of movement or orientation of a stimulus—that is, they fire only when an object in their visual field moves in a certain direction or is in a particular orientation, such as diagonal lines or straight lines. (We'll have more to say about feature detection later in the chapter.) After several weeks of normal visual experience, all the cells in the visual cortex become sensitive to the orientation of a stimulus or to direction of movement. These cells "expected" to receive visual input and thus developed "normally" with "normal" experience. However, if kittens are deprived of visual experience immediately after opening their eyes, they gradually lose their sensitivity to orientation. Experience (or lack of experience) changes the structure and organization of their brains. Recovery of normal neuronal structure and responsivity following exposure to patterned light occurs, although the degree of recovery declines with longer periods of deprivation (Blakemore & Van Sluyters, 1975; Cynader et al., 1976).

Of course, experimenters cannot deprive human infants of light as has been done with laboratory animals. However, Daphne Maurer and her colleagues have done research with infants born with cataracts over their eyes, some of whom had them removed shortly after birth (Maurer et al., 2007; see Maurer & Lewis [2013] for a review). The researchers reported that infants who had cataracts removed and new lenses placed in their eyes within several months of birth showed a generally typical pattern of visual development. The longer the delay in removing the cataracts, however, the poorer their vision was. Moreover, even for those babies who had cataracts removed early, some aspects of *face* processing were impaired (Le Grand et al., 2001). This finding suggests that there may be different sensitive periods for the brain areas associated with visual acuity and those associated with processing faces. It also points to the importance of identifying and correcting visual problems early to minimize their long-term effects (Huber et al., 2015).

Seeing Forms, Patterns, Objects, and Faces

The purpose of human vision is not merely to detect the presence or absence of light or different wavelengths, but to identify meaningful objects and actions. As you look at the top of your desk, for example, your retinas are struck by a continuous field of light, varying from point to point in intensity and wavelength. But you see the scene neither as a continuous field nor as a collection of points. Instead, you see objects: a computer, a pencil, a stapler, and a pile of books. Each object stands out sharply from its background. Your visual system has sorted all the points and gradations that are present in the reflected light into useful renditions of the objects on your desk. It has provided you with all the information you need to reach out and touch, or pick up, whichever object you want to use next. How does your visual system accomplish this remarkable feat?

Vision researchers generally consider object perception a type of unconscious problem solving, in which sensory information provides clues that are analyzed using information that is already stored in the person's head. In this section, we explore how our visual system organizes such clues to enable us to see forms, patterns, and objects.

The Detection and Integration of Stimulus Features

Any object that we see can be thought of as consisting of a set of elementary stimulus features, including the various straight and curved lines that form the object's contours, the brightness and color of the light that the object reflects, and the object's movement or lack of movement with respect to its background. Our visual system registers all these features and brings them together to form one unified perception of the object. A major objective of brain research on vision has been to better understand how the brain detects and integrates the elementary stimulus features of objects.

Feature Detection in the Visual Cortex

The primary method of studying feature detection in laboratory animals has been to record the activity of individual neurons in visual areas of the brain while directing visual stimuli into the animals' eyes. As shown in **Figure 7.12**, ganglion cells of the optic nerve run to the thalamus, in the middle of the brain, and form synapses with other neurons that carry their output to the **primary visual area** of the

FIGURE 7.12 Pathway from the eyes to the primary visual cortex Neurons in the optic nerves come together at the optic chiasm at the base of the brain and form the optic tracts, which run to nuclei in the thalamus, where they synapse on neurons that run to the primary visual area of the cerebral cortex.

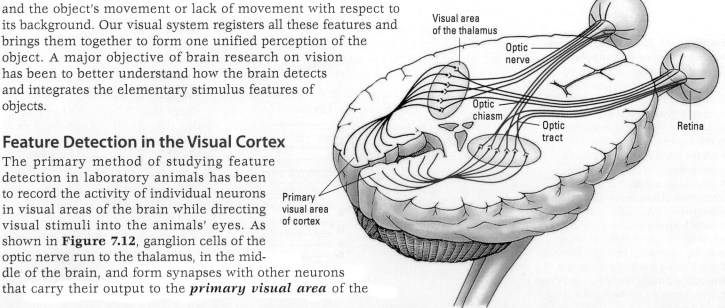

Visual area of the thalamus

Optic nerve

Optic chiasm

Optic tract

Retina

Primary visual area of cortex

cerebral cortex. Within the primary visual area, millions of neurons analyze the sensory input. Researchers have inserted thin electrodes into individual neurons in this area of the animal's cortex in order to record the neurons' rates of action potentials as visual stimuli are presented. The animal—usually a cat or a monkey—is anesthetized, so it is unconscious, but its eyes are kept open and the neural connections from the eyes to the relevant brain neurons are intact.

In a classic series of experiments, David Hubel and Torsten Wiesel (1962, 1979) recorded the activity of individual neurons in the primary visual cortex of cats while the cats' eyes were stimulated by simple black-and-white patterns of various shapes, sizes, and orientations. They found that different neurons responded preferentially to different patterns. For example, some neurons responded best (most strongly) to stimuli that contained a straight contour separating a black patch from a white patch. Hubel and Wiesel called these neurons *edge detectors*. Other neurons, which they called *bar detectors,* responded best to a narrow white bar against a black background, or to a narrow black bar against a white background. Hubel and Wiesel found, moreover, that any given edge detector or bar detector responded best to a particular orientation of the edge or bar. Some responded best when it was oriented vertically, others responded best when it was oriented horizontally, and still others responded best when it was slanted at a specific angle.

Subsequent research showed that neurons in the primary visual cortex are sensitive not just to the orientation of visual stimuli, but also to other visual features, including color and rate of movement. Thus, one neuron might respond best to a yellow bar on a blue background, tilted 15 degrees clockwise and moving slowly from left to right. Taken as a whole, the neurons of the primary visual cortex and nearby areas seem to keep track of all the bits and pieces of visual information that would be available in a scene. Because of their sensitivity to the elementary features of a scene, these neurons are called **feature detectors**.

Treisman's Two-Stage Feature-Integration Theory of Perception

Anne Treisman (1986, 1998) developed a theory of visual perception that she called a *feature-integration theory.* She developed the theory partly from neurophysiological evidence concerning feature detectors, but mostly from behavioral evidence concerning the speed with which people can perceive various stimuli. The theory begins with the assertion that any perceived stimulus, even a simple one such as the X shown in **Figure 7.13**, consists of a number of distinct *primitive sensory features,*

FOCUS 12

What kinds of stimulus features influence the activity of neurons in the primary visual cortex?

FOCUS 13

What is the difference between parallel processing and serial processing? What role does each play in Treisman's feature-integration theory of perception?

FIGURE 7.13 Treisman's theory of feature detection and integration
During stage 1 of visual processing, in Treisman's theory, the primitive features of all stimuli that reach the eyes are registered automatically and simultaneously—that is, in parallel. In this example, all the features of both the X and the V are registered simultaneously in the appropriate feature-mapping areas of the brain. Integration of features occurs at stage 2, during which information is processed serially, from one localized area of the visual field at a time. In this example, only the information from one stimulus, the X, is being processed. An instant later, stage 2 might operate on the V, but it cannot operate on the X and V at the same time.

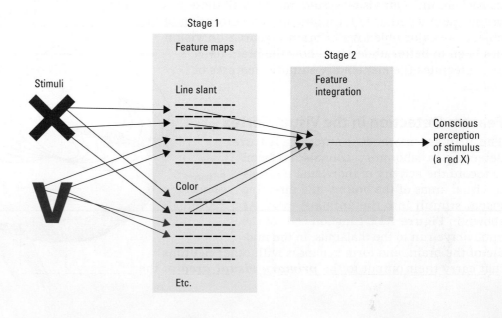

such as its color and the slant of its individual lines. To perceive the stimulus as a unified entity, the perceptual system must detect these individual features and integrate them into a whole. The essence of Treisman's theory is that the detection and integration occur sequentially, in two fundamentally different steps or stages of information processing.

The first stage is the *detection of features,* which occurs instantaneously and involves **parallel processing**. Parallel processing means that this step operates simultaneously on all parts of the stimulus array. That is, our visual system picks up at once all the primitive features of all the objects whose light rays strike our retinas. Even if we are paying attention just to the X in Figure 7.13, our visual system simultaneously picks up the primitive features of the V in that figure and of all other stimuli in our field of view.

The second stage is the *integration of features,* which requires more time and leads eventually to our perception of whole, spatially organized patterns and objects. This step involves **serial processing**, which occurs sequentially, at one spatial location at a time, rather than simultaneously over the entire array. When looking at Figure 7.13, we can integrate the features of the X and then, an instant later, the features of the V, but we cannot integrate the two sets of features simultaneously.

Research Support for Treisman's Theory

To understand some of the evidence on which Treisman based her theory, look at the array of stimuli in **Figure 7.14a**. Notice that no effort is needed to find the single slanted line. You don't have to scan the whole array in serial fashion to find it; it just "pops out" at you. According to Treisman, this is because line slant is one of the primitive features that are processed automatically through parallel processing. Now look at **Figure 7.14b** and find the single slanted green line among the vertical green lines and slanted red lines. In this case the target does not pop out; you have to scan through the array in serial fashion to find it (though you can still find it fairly quickly).

In controlled experiments, Treisman and Stephen Gormican (1988) measured the time it took for people to locate specific target stimuli in arrays like those of Figure 7.14 but with varying numbers of *distractors* (nontarget stimuli). As long as the target differed from all the distractors in one or more of Treisman's list of primitive features—such as slant, curvature, color, brightness, and movement—subjects detected it equally quickly no matter how many distractors were present.

FOCUS 14

How do pop-out phenomena and mistakes in joining features provide evidence for Treisman's theory?

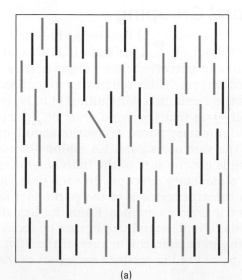

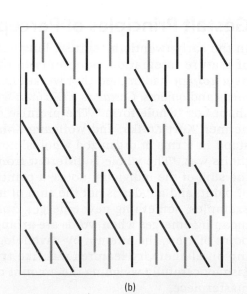

(a)   (b)

FIGURE 7.14 Stimuli that pop out or do not pop out These stimulus arrays are similar to those used by Treisman and Gormican (1988). In (a) the target stimulus (slanted green line) differs from the distractor stimuli in a primitive feature; it is the only slanted line in the array. Here the target pops out at you; you notice it immediately even if you aren't looking for it. In (b) the target stimulus (slanted green line) does not differ from the distractors in a primitive feature; its greenness is matched by some distractors and its slant is matched by other distractors. Rather, this target is distinct in the way its features are conjoined. It is the only line that is both green and slanted. This target does not pop out at you; you have to look for it to notice it.

Maintain speed (next light will be either green or double yellow)

Caution (next light might be single yellow)

Slow down (next light might be red)

Stop

(a)   (b)

FIGURE 7.15 Conjoined features make detection harder Shown here are the light signals used along railroad tracks in the United Kingdom to tell drivers how to proceed. The "slow down" signal is critical, because if a driver misses it there will be insufficient time to come to a full stop when the "stop" signal becomes visible. According to Treisman's theory, however, this signal should be the most difficult to detect, because it is the only signal that is distinguished from the others by a conjoining of two elementary features (color and number) rather than by a single feature. To identify the "slow down" signal as distinct from the others, you have to see that there is only one light *and* that it is yellow. In contrast, the green and red signals are uniquely defined by color alone (no other signal is green or red), and the double-yellow signal is uniquely defined by number alone (no other signal involves illumination of two lights). In an experiment, John Groeger and his colleagues (2005) showed that, indeed, research subjects who had practice identifying the signals were significantly slower at identifying the single-yellow ("slow down") signal than any of the others. According to Groeger, a redesign of the UK railroad signal system could save lives, as accidents do sometimes occur because train drivers misperceive the single-yellow signal.

This lack of effect of the number of distractors on detection time is indicative of parallel processing. In contrast, when the target did not differ from the distractors in any single visual feature, but differed only in its conjoining of two or more features that were present in different sets of distractors, as in Figure 7.14b, the amount of time required to locate the target increased in direct proportion to the number of distractors. This increase in detection time is indicative of serial processing—the necessity to attend separately to each item (or to small groups of items) until the target is found. Identification of a single unique feature can be accomplished with parallel processing (stage 1), but identification of a unique conjoining of two or more features requires serial processing (stage 2).

Treisman also found that subjects who saw simple stimuli flashed briefly on a screen easily identified which primitive features were present but sometimes misperceived which features went together, a phenomenon called *illusory conjunctions*. For example, when shown a straight red line and a green curved one, all subjects knew they had seen a straight line and a curved line, and a red color and a green color, but some were mistaken about which color belonged to which line. Such findings led Treisman to conclude that parallel processing (stage 1) registers features independently of their spatial location and that different features that coincide in space (such as the color and curvature of a given line) are joined perceptually only in serial processing (stage 2), which requires separate attention to each spatial location. Thus, stage 2 operates by assigning primitive features to specific spatial locations and then weaving the features together in patterns that reflect their locations.

Not all research findings are consistent with Treisman's theory. Some researchers have argued, with evidence, that the registration and integration of visual features are not as separate as Treisman proposed (Mordkoff & Halterman, 2008; Roelfsema, 2006). However, researchers continue to find new examples of perceptual phenomenon that fit with predictions from Treisman's theory. For one such example, which could have serious practical consequences, read the caption to **Figure 7.15**.

Gestalt Principles of Perceptual Grouping

In the early twentieth century, long before Treisman had developed her model of feature integration, adherents to the school of thought known as **Gestalt psychology** had argued that we automatically perceive whole, organized patterns and objects. *Gestalt* is a German word that translates roughly as "organized shape" or "whole form." The premise of the Gestaltists—including Max Wertheimer, Kurt Koffka, and Wolfgang Köhler—was that the mind must be understood in terms of organized wholes, not elementary parts. A favorite saying of theirs was, "The whole is different from the sum of its parts." A melody is not the sum of the individual notes, a painting is not the sum of the individual dots of paint, and an idea is not the sum of its elementary concepts. In each of these examples, something new emerges from the arrangement of the parts, just as meaning emerges when words are arranged to form a sentence. From the Gestalt point of view, the attempt by psychologists to understand perception by focusing on elementary features was like trying to explain the beauty of the *Mona Lisa* by carefully weighing the amount of paint used to produce each part of the masterpiece.

Most early Gestalt research was in the area of visual perception. In many laboratory demonstrations, Gestalt psychologists showed that in conscious experience whole objects and scenes take precedence over parts. For example, when looking at a chair, people perceive and recognize the chair as a whole before noticing its arms, legs, and other components. Treisman and other modern perceptual psychologists would not disagree with this point. In our conscious experience, we do typically perceive wholes before we perceive parts; the building up of the wholes from the parts occurs through unconscious mental processes. They would also agree that the whole is different from the sum of its parts because the whole is defined by the way the parts are *organized*, not just by the parts themselves.

Built-in Rules for Organizing Stimulus Elements Into Wholes

The Gestaltists proposed that the nervous system is innately predisposed to respond to patterns in the stimulus world according to certain rules, or *Gestalt principles of grouping*. These principles include the following (Koffka, 1935; Wertheimer, 1923/1938).

1. *Proximity.* We tend to see stimulus elements that are near each other as parts of the same object and those that are separated as parts of different objects. This helps us organize a large set of elements into a smaller set of objects. In **Figure 7.16a**, because of proximity, we see three clusters of dots rather than 13 individual dots.

2. *Similarity.* We tend to see stimulus elements that physically resemble each other as parts of the same object and those that do not resemble each other as parts of different objects. For example, as illustrated in **Figure 7.16b**, this helps us distinguish between two adjacent or overlapping objects on the basis of a change in their texture elements. (Texture elements are repeated visual features or patterns that cover the surface of a given object.)

3. *Closure.* We tend to see forms as completely enclosed by a border and to ignore gaps in the border. This helps us perceive complete objects even when they are partially occluded by other objects. For example, in **Figure 7.16c** we automatically assume that the boundary of the oval is complete, continuing behind the rectangle.

4. *Good continuation.* When lines intersect, we tend to group the line segments to form continuous lines with minimal change in direction. This helps us decide which lines belong to which object when two or more objects overlap. In **Figure 7.16d**, for example, we see two smooth lines, *ab* and *cd*, rather than four shorter lines or two sharply bent lines such as *ac* or *bd*.

5. *Common movement.* When stimulus elements move in the same direction and at the same rate, we tend to see them as part of a single object. This helps us distinguish a moving object (such as a camouflaged animal) from the background. If the dots marked by arrows in **Figure 7.16e** were all moving as a group, you would see them as a single object.

6. *Good form.* The perceptual system strives to produce percepts that are elegant—simple, uncluttered, symmetrical, regular, and predictable (Chater, 1996; Koffka, 1935). This rather unspecific principle encompasses the other principles listed above but also includes other ways by which the perceptual system organizes stimuli into their simplest (most easily explained) arrangement. For example, in **Figure 7.16f**, the left-hand figure, because of its symmetry, is more likely than the middle figure to be seen as a single object. The middle figure, because of its lack of symmetry, is more likely to be seen as two objects, as shown to its right.

FOCUS 15

What are some principles of grouping proposed by Gestalt psychologists, and how does each help explain our ability to see whole objects?

(a) Proximity   (b) Similarity

(c) Closure

(d) Good continuation   (e) Common movement

(f) Good form

FIGURE 7.16 Gestalt principles of grouping These drawings illustrate the six Gestalt principles that are described in the text.

■ **Principle of similarity** When we look at a scene such as this one, we automatically group together portions that contain similar stimulus elements. The similarity may be in color, brightness, texture, or orientation of contours.

Stefano Scatà/AGE Fotostock

Figure and Ground

In addition to proposing the six principles of grouping just listed, the Gestaltists (particularly Rubin, 1915/1958) called attention to our automatic tendency to divide any visual scene into *figure* (the object that attracts attention) and *ground*

FIGURE 7.17 Figure and ground
Because the white form is completely surrounded by the black form, we tend to see the white form as the figure and the black form as the ground.

(the background). As an example, see **Figure 7.17**. The illustration could, in theory, be described as two unfamiliar figures, one white and one black, whose borders happen to coincide, but most people automatically see it as just one white figure against a black background. The figure–ground division is not arbitrary, but is directed by certain stimulus characteristics. In Figure 7.17, the most important characteristic is probably *circumscription*: Other things being equal, we tend to see the circumscribing form (the one that surrounds the other) as the ground and the circumscribed form as the figure.

The figure–ground relationship is not always completely determined by characteristics of the stimulus. With some effort, you can reverse your perception of figure and ground in Figure 7.17 by imagining that the illustration is a black square with an oddly shaped hole cut out of it, sitting on a white background. When cues

FOCUS 16

How do reversible figures illustrate the visual system's strong tendency to separate figure and ground, even in the absence of sufficient cues for deciding which is which?

FIGURE 7.18 Reversible figure
Because it lacks strong cues as to which is figure and which is ground, this image may be seen either as two faces in profile or as a vase. If you stare at it, your perception may alternate between the two.

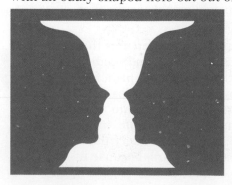

in the scene are sparse or ambiguous, the mind may vacillate in its choice of which shape to see as figure and which as ground. This is illustrated by the **reversible figure** in **Figure 7.18**, where at any given moment you may see either two faces in profile or a vase. In line with the Gestalt figure–ground principle, the same part of the figure cannot simultaneously be both figure and ground, and thus at any instant you may see either the vase or the faces, but not both.

Evidence That Wholes Can Affect the Perception of Parts

When you look at a visual scene, the elementary stimulus features certainly affect your perception of the whole, but the converse is also true: The whole affects your perception of the features. Without your conscious awareness, at a speed measurable in milliseconds, your visual system uses the sensory input from a scene to draw inferences about what is actually present—a process called *unconscious inference*. Once your visual system has hit upon a particular solution to the problem of what is there, it may actually create or distort features in ways that are consistent with that inference. Examples of such creations and distortions are illusory contours and illusory lightness differences.

Illusory Contours

In **Figure 7.19** you probably see a solid white triangle sitting atop some other objects. The contour of the white triangle appears to continue across the white space between the other objects. This is not simply a misperception caused by a fleeting glance. The longer you look at the whole stimulus, the more convinced you may become that the contour (border) between the white triangle and the white background is really there; the triangle seems *whiter* than the background. But if you try to see the contour isolated from the rest of the stimulus, by covering the black portions with your fingers or pieces of paper, you will find that the contour isn't really there. The white triangle and its border are illusions.

The white triangle, with its illusory contour, apparently emerges from the brain's attempt to make sense of the sensory input (Parks & Rock, 1990). The most elegant interpretation of the figure—consistent with the Gestalt principle of good form and with expectations drawn from everyday experience—is to assume that it contains a white triangle lying atop a black triangular frame and three black disks. That is certainly simpler and more likely than the alternative possibility—three disks with wedges removed from them and three unconnected black angles, all oriented with their openings aimed at a common center. According to this unconscious-inference explanation, the perceptual system uses the initial stimulus input to infer that a white triangle must be present (because that makes the most sense), and then it *creates* the white triangle, by influencing contour-detection processes in the brain in such a way as to produce a border where one does not physically exist in the stimulus.

Illusory contours cannot be explained by simple stimulus terms—for example, with the amount of actual lined-up contour existing in the figure. Many experiments have shown that people are more likely to see illusory contours if they are needed to make sense of the figure than if they are not, even when the amount of actual dark-light border is constant (Gillam & Chan, 2002; Hoffman, 1998). For example, compare patterns *a* and *b* in **Figure 7.20**. Most people see an illusory contour, outlining a white square, more clearly in pattern *b* than in pattern *a*, even though the actual black–white borders at the corners of the imagined white square are identical

Q **FOCUS 17**

How do illusory contours illustrate the idea that the whole influences the perception of parts? How are illusory contours explained in terms of unconscious inference?

FIGURE 7.19 Illusory contour In response to this stimulus, the perceptual system creates a white triangle, the borders of which appear to continue across the white page, such that the triangle seems whiter than the white page. (Information from Kanizsa, 1955.)

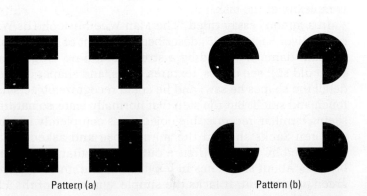

Pattern (a)   Pattern (b)

FIGURE 7.20 Which pattern shows the clearer illusory contour? Most people see an illusory contour (outlining a white square) more clearly in pattern (b) than in pattern (a), a finding that is consistent with the unconscious-inference explanation of pattern perception.

(Information from Kanizsa, 1955, and Hoffman, 1998.)

in the two figures. The unconscious-inference explanation of this is that the white square is more needed in *b* than in *a* to make sense of the stimulus input. The arrangement of four black angular objects is more likely to occur in everyday experience than is the arrangement of four disks with wedges cut out in *b*.

Unconscious Inference Involves Top-Down Control Within the Brain

FOCUS 18

How is unconscious inference described as top-down control within the brain? What is the difference between top-down and bottom-up control?

When psychologists explain perceptual phenomena in terms of unconscious inference, they are not suggesting that these phenomena result from anything other than neural processes in the brain. All reasoning, unconscious or conscious, is a product of neural activity. Unconscious-inference theories imply that the phenomena in question result from neural activity in higher brain areas, which are able to bring together the pieces of sensory information and make complex calculations concerning them.

Neuroscientists have learned that the connections between the primary visual area and higher visual areas in the brain are not one-way. The higher areas receive essential input from the primary visual area, but they also feed back to that area and influence neural activity there (Reid & Usrey, 2013). Thus, complex calculations made in perceptual portions of the temporal, parietal, and frontal lobes (discussed later) can feed back to the primary visual area in the occipital lobe and influence the activity of feature detectors there. For example, visual stimuli that produce illusory contours activate edge-detector neurons in the primary visual cortex that are receiving input from precisely that part of the stimulus where the illusory contour is seen (Albert, 2007; Lee, 2002). In this case, the activity of the edge detector is not the direct result of input from the optic nerve to the edge detector; rather, it is the result of descending connections from higher visual centers that have determined that there *should* be an edge at that location.

Brain scientists and perceptual psychologists refer to control that comes from higher up in the brain as ***top-down control***, and they refer to control that comes more directly from the sensory input as ***bottom-up control***. Perception always involves interplay between bottom-up and top-down control (also called bottom-up and top-down processing) in the brain. Bottom-up processes bring in the sensory information that is actually present in the stimulus. Top-down processes bring to bear the results of calculations based on that sensory information plus other information, such as that derived from previous experience and from the larger context in which the stimulus appears. Remember, all these calculations are being conducted by a calculating machine—the human brain—that is vastly more complex and powerful than any nonbiological computer that humans have developed.

Recognizing Objects

To recognize an object is to categorize it: "It's a bird, it's a plane, it's Superman!" To recognize an object visually, we must form a visual perception of it that we can match to our stored definition, or understanding, of the appropriate object category. We normally do this so naturally and easily that we fail to think of the extraordinary complexity of the task.

In a famous essay titled "The Man Who Mistook His Wife for a Hat," the neurologist Oliver Sacks (1985) described the plight of one of his patients, who, as a result of brain damage caused by a stroke, could no longer recognize objects by sight. He could still see colors, textures, lines, and shapes; he could describe in exquisite detail the shapes he saw; and he could recognize objects using other senses, such as touch and smell. But the step that normally leads so naturally from seeing shapes to seeing familiar, recognizable objects was completely missing in him.

When Sacks showed the man a rose and asked him to identify it, the man responded by trying to figure out, aloud, what it was from the shapes and colors he saw: "About six inches in length," he said. "A convoluted red form with a linear green attachment. It lacks the simple symmetry of the Platonic solids, although it may have a higher symmetry of its own. . . ." After several minutes of such erudite discourse about the object's parts, the man finally guessed, uncertainly, that it might be some kind of flower. Then Sacks asked him to smell it. "Beautiful!" he exclaimed. "An early rose. What a heavenly smell!" He could tell a rose by smell but not by sight, even though he could see and describe each of its parts in terms of geometry and color.

Evidence From People Who Suffer From Visual Agnosias

For us to see and recognize an object such as a rose, the brain must somehow pick up, from the optic nerves' input, the relevant features of the object. Further, it must integrate those features into a perceptual whole that can be matched with stored representations of familiar object categories. Perceptual researchers continue to explore how the normal brain sees and identifies a rose or any other object so easily. Some clues come from observations of people who, after a stroke or other source of brain damage, can still see but can no longer make sense of what they see, a condition called *visual agnosia*. It's interesting to note that the term *agnosia* was coined in the late nineteenth century by Sigmund Freud, who then was a young, little-known neurologist (Goodale & Milner, 2004). Freud derived the term from the Greek words *a*, meaning not, and *gnosia*, meaning knowledge. People with visual agnosia can see, but they do not know what they are seeing.

Visual agnosias have been classified into a number of general types (Farah, 1989; Milner & Goodale, 1995), of which two are most relevant here. People with *visual form agnosia* can see that something is present and can identify some of its elements, such as its color and brightness, but cannot perceive its shape. They are unable to describe or draw the outlines of objects or patterns that they are shown. In contrast, people with *visual object agnosia* can describe and draw the shapes of objects that they are shown, but still cannot identify the objects—such as the patient Oliver Sacks described who was unable to identify a rose, although he could see and describe its parts. When shown an apple and asked to draw it, a person with visual object agnosia might produce a drawing that you and I would recognize as an apple, but they would still be unable to say what it was. As another example, a patient with visual object agnosia described a bicycle that he was shown as a pole and two circles, but he could not identify it as a bicycle or guess what purpose it serves (Hécaen & Albert, 1978).

FOCUS 19

How does the existence of two types of visual deficits caused by brain damage provide support for the idea that the human brain does indeed process objects as distinct entities?

Two Streams of Visual Processing in the Brain

Researchers have learned a great deal about the neural mechanisms involved in higher-order visual processing. The primary visual cortex, which occupies the rearmost part of the occipital lobe, sends its output to (and receives feedback from) many other visual-processing areas, which occupy the rest of the occipital lobe and extend forward into much of the temporal and parietal lobes. The visual areas beyond the primary area exist in two relatively distinct cortical pathways, or "streams," which serve different functions (Konen & Kastner, 2008; Reid & Usrey, 2013). As shown in **Figure 7.21** on the next page, one stream runs into the lower portion of the temporal lobe and the other runs upward into the parietal lobe.

The *"what" pathway,* or the lower, temporal stream, is specialized for identifying objects. Damage in this stream, on both sides of the brain, can result in the types of visual agnosias that we have just been discussing, in which people cannot tell what they are looking at. Experiments involving single-cell recording in monkeys and fMRI in humans have shown that neurons in this pathway typically respond best to complex geometric shapes and to whole objects, in ways that are quite consistent with the recognition-by-components theory (Grill-Spector & Sayres, 2008; Yamane et al., 2008).

The *"where" pathway,* or the upper, parietal stream, maintains a map of three-dimensional space, localizing objects within that space. Researchers have found that

FOCUS 20

What are the anatomical and functional distinctions between two different visual pathways in the cerebral cortex?

FIGURE 7.21 The "what" and "where-and-how" visual pathways Neurons in the primary visual area send output into two relatively distinct streams for further visual processing. The "what" pathway, into the lower temporal lobe, is specialized for perceiving shapes and identifying objects. The "where-and-how" pathway, into the parietal lobe, is specialized for perceiving spatial relationships and for guiding actions.

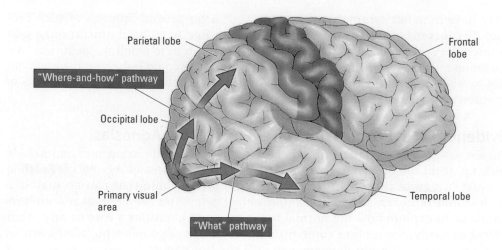

FOCUS 21

What abilities are preserved in people with damage to the "what" pathway but lost in people with damage to the "where-and-how" pathway?

this pathway is also crucial for the use of visual information to guide a person's movements (Goodale, 2007). Neurons in this pathway are concerned not just with *where* the object is located, but also with *how* the person must move in order to pick up the object, or move around it, or interact with it in some other way. For this reason, we use the label "where-and-how," rather than just "where," to refer to the parietal pathway. (Look again at Figure 7.21.)

Effects of Damage in the "What" Pathway People with damage in specific portions of the "what" pathway on both sides of the brain generally suffer from deficits in ability to make conscious sense of what they see, depending on just where the damage is. The examples of visual agnosias previously described resulted from damage in this pathway. An interesting further observation concerning such patients is that they retain the ability to reach accurately for objects and act on them in coordinated ways, guided by vision, even if they can't consciously see the objects.

A dramatic example is the case of a woman known as D. F., extensively studied by Melvyn Goodale (2007) and his colleagues. This woman was diagnosed with very severe visual form agnosia, stemming from carbon monoxide poisoning that destroyed portions of the "what" pathway close to the primary visual area on both sides of her brain. Despite her complete inability to perceive consciously the shapes of objects, D. F. responded to objects in ways that take into account shape as well as size, position, and movement. When she would walk, she moved around obstacles with ease. She was good at catching objects thrown to her, even though she could not consciously see the object coming toward her. When asked to pick up a novel object placed in front of her, she moved her hand in just the correct way to grasp the object efficiently.

In one experiment, D. F. was shown an upright disk with a slot cut through it (Goodale & Milner, 2004). She claimed to be unable to see the orientation of the slot and, indeed, when she was asked to hold a card at the same angle as the slot, her accuracy (over several trials with the slot at varying orientations) was no better than chance. But when asked to slip the card into the slot as if mailing a letter, she did so quickly and accurately on every trial, holding the card at just the right orientation before it reached the slot. She could not use conscious perception to guide her hand, but her hand moved correctly without the use of conscious perception. Apparently the "where-and-how" pathway, which was intact in this woman, is capable of calculating the sizes and shapes of objects, as well as their places, but does not make that information available to the conscious mind.

Effects of Damage in the "Where-and-How" Pathway Damage in the "where-and-how" pathway—in the upper parts of the occipital and parietal lobes of the cortex—interferes most strongly with people's abilities to use vision to guide their actions.

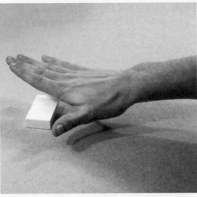

(a)

(b)

FIGURE 7.22 Efficient and inefficient reaching for an object People with damage to the "what" pathway reach for an object in the efficient manner depicted in (a), even though they can't consciously see the object's shape. In contrast, people with damage to the "where-and-how" pathway reach in the inefficient, groping manner depicted in (b), even though they can consciously see the object's shape.

People with damage to this pathway have relatively little or no difficulty identifying objects that they see, and often they can describe verbally where the object is located, but they have great difficulty using visual input to coordinate their movements. They lose much of their ability to follow moving objects with their eyes or hands, to move around obstacles, or to reach out and pick up objects in an efficient manner (Goodale & Milner, 2004; Schindler et al., 2004). Even though they can consciously see and describe an object verbally and report its general location, they reach for it gropingly, much as a blind person does. They frequently miss the object by a few inches, then move their hand around until they touch it (see **Figure 7.22**). Only when they have touched the object do they begin to close their fingers around it to pick it up.

Complementary Functions of the Two Visual Pathways in the Intact Brain These two visual pathways evolved to serve different but complementary functions. The "what" pathway provides most of our conscious vision. It provides the input that allows us to see and identify objects consciously, to talk about those objects, to make conscious plans concerning them, and to form conscious memories of them. In contrast, the "where-and-how" pathway provides the input that is needed for the automatic, rapid, and largely unconscious visual control of our movements with respect to objects. This pathway is able to register the shape of an object to the degree that shape is necessary for effectively reaching for and picking up the object, but it does not register shape in a manner that enters consciousness.

Recognizing Faces

To this point, we've been writing as if people use a single set of psychological and brain mechanisms to identify objects of any kind. The mechanisms are actually quite complicated, and it makes intuitive sense that the brain would have evolved a single set of processes to perform such a task. But might there be one category of objects that are so important to humans, and perhaps to other animals, that specialized psychological and brain mechanisms might have evolved to deal with them? The answer to this question seems to be "yes," and "faces" is that special category.

Faces as "Special" Objects

As highly social animals, humans use faces to identify people, judge their emotions, and often discern their intentions. Although we may also identify people according to their voices or even their odors, we rely more on faces than any other feature for important social information. Humans can recognize and remember thousands of different faces (Schwartz, 2013), even when the faces are seen in different orientations or with different features (e.g., hair style, eyeglasses,

FIGURE 7.23 It doesn't take much for people to see faces in inanimate objects.

Francisco Javier Diaz/Shutterstock

DG Stock/Shutterstock

make-up), and know when a face is unfamiliar (that is, "recognize" an unfamiliar face; Johnston & Edmonds, 2009). And people seem to do this using some specialized brain areas.

How do people even know that a stimulus is a face? That is, what are the physical features that "make a face a face"? Perhaps the most distinguishing features include an oval or round shape, left-right (vertical) symmetry (the right side of the face looks pretty much like the left side), and top-bottom asymmetry, with more elements (the two eyes) at the top and fewer elements (the mouth) at the bottom. We view stimuli that have these features, be they real faces, animated faces, or inanimate objects as faces, or at least as "facelike" (see **Figure 7.23**).

To illustrate that the configuration of elements is important in recognizing faces, consider what happens when we view faces that are presented upside down.

Courtesy of Peter Thompson, from Thompson, P. (1980). Margaret Thatcher: a new illusion. *Perception, 9,* 383–4.

FIGURE 7.24 Thatcherized image
People have difficulty recognizing faces when they are inverted. You may not notice anything particularly strange about these images of Margaret Thatcher when viewing them upside down. But turn the book over and view the photos right-side up. You'll notice that the mouth and eyes have been inverted in one of the photos, giving the image a distorted appearance, something you likely missed when looking at it upside down.

When photographs of faces are inverted, we can still recognize them as faces, but we are no longer able to make fine discriminations among faces as we do when we look at upright faces. For example, look at the two upside down faces in **Figure 7.24**. Are these faces the same or are they different? Other than their inverted presentation, do you see anything peculiar about them? Now rotate the book and look at the photos right-side up. Wow! In the photograph on the left, the eyes and the mouth are inverted, producing a very distorted face. (Such photos are referred to as "Thatcherized" because the alteration was first done with a photograph of British prime minister Margaret Thatcher; Thompson, 1980). In general, people are relatively good at distinguishing between different upright photographs, but they have more difficulty distinguishing between photographs presented upside down (Yin, 1969). So when we say there are special psychological and brain mechanisms people use in processing faces, we mean upright faces—the way people typically see faces every day. This processing of upright faces more effectively than inverted faces is seen early in development, with infants as young as 3 months of age looking longer at upright faces than at inverted faces (Bhatt et al., 2005).

Although humans, and likely other primates (Tsao et al., 2006), seem predisposed to process faces as special stimuli, this does not mean there is no learning involved. As it turns out, although people can discriminate between thousands of different faces, they are better at telling the difference between some types of faces

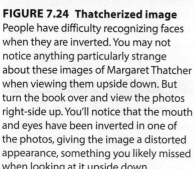

than others. Basically, the more experience people have with certain types of faces, the better they are at discriminating among them. For instance, humans are better at distinguishing between different faces of people than different faces of monkeys (Sigala et al., 2001), although people who see monkey faces on a regular basis show less of this *other-species effect* (Fair et al., 2012).

People not only have trouble discriminating among faces of other species, but also of other races. This **own-race bias** (also known as *cross-race bias, other-race effect,* and *same-race effect*) refers to the fact that people are better able to distinguish between and to remember faces from their own race or ethnic group than from other races or ethnic groups (Meissner & Brigham, 2001). People of European origin, for example, are better able to tell the difference between and remember other European faces than they are African or Asian faces, and vice versa. Rather than reflecting racism, it reflects experience with viewing and remembering faces from one's own versus from different races.

This own-race bias can have consequences for eyewitness testimony. When trying to identify a previously seen person, perhaps in a police lineup in connection with a crime, people are better able to make accurate judgments for people of their own race versus people of different races (Bornstein et al., 2013). In one analysis of 271 cases, witnesses correctly identified 65% of defendants who were the same race as they were, but only 45% of defendants who were a different race from the witnesses (Behrman & Davey, 2001).

This own-race bias is observed in infancy, long before any explicit racial discrimination could develop. Yet, research with young infants indicates it is not innate but is dependent on experience. To assess own-race bias in infants, David Kelly and his colleagues (2009) repeatedly showed 3-, 6-, and 9-month-old Chinese infants a full-face orientation photograph of a single face from one of three different ethnic groups: some saw an Asian face (same race), others saw a Caucasian face (other race), and others saw an African face (other race). After viewing a single face repeatedly, infants' looking time to the face decreased; this is another example of the phenomenon of habituation, mentioned earlier in the chapter. Once their looking time decreased by half of what it had been on the first two trials, infants were shown two new photographs of faces in three-quarters profile, one of a different person and one of the same person they had seen in full-face orientation during the habituation trials (the familiar face). **Figure 7.25** shows two examples of the faces used in these experiments. A common finding in infant memory research is that babies will look longer at a new stimulus than at a familiar (habituated) stimulus, and that this reflects memory of the a familiar stimulus. ("That's the same face I've been looking at for some time; let's look at the new face.") The researchers reported that the 3-month-old Chinese infants looked at the novel face more than the familiar face (that is, displayed recognition memory) for all three races, the 6-month-olds recognized the Chinese (same race) faces and showed marginal recognition for the Caucasian faces, and the 9-month-olds only recognized the faces from their own race (Chinese faces). Kelly and his colleagues (2007) had earlier shown the development of this own-race bias for Caucasian infants, suggesting that this effect is not limited to one race of children but is universal.

Although young infants are not as proficient at recognizing faces as older infants and children, they are able to make distinctions equally well between faces of different races. With age and experience they get better at making discriminations among faces they see frequently (their own race) and relatively less proficient at making discriminations among faces they see less frequently (other races). In other research, 8- and 10-month-old Caucasian infants were shown photographs of Asian female faces for 3 weeks and were later able to distinguish among Asian as well as Caucasian faces (Anzures et al., 2012), suggesting that experience is key in the development of the own-race bias.

The pattern of results discussed in this section indicates that faces are special stimuli and that people seem specially prepared from early in life to be attentive to

Used with permission of Elsevier, from: Kelly, D..., et al., Development of the other-race effect during infancy: Evidence toward universality? *J. Exp Child Psychol,* Vol. 104, Issue 1, September 2009, 105–114; Permission conveyed through the Copyright Clearance Center Inc.

> **FOCUS 24**
>
> How does the own-race bias and its development support the idea that learning is involved in recognizing faces?

FIGURE 7.25 Asian and African faces used in study by Kelly et al. (2009) Infants looked at the single face on top until looking time decreased to 50% relative to early trials. They were then shown the two three-quarters profile faces and their looking time measured. Looking at the new (unfamiliar) face more than the familiar face is an indication of memory for the familiar face. Three-month-olds recognized equally well same-race (Asian) and other-race (African) faces. Nine-month-olds recognized only Asian (same-race) faces, illustrating that the own-race bias develops over infancy.

and to process faces. However, it also suggests that *which* faces are processed most efficiently develops, albeit this developmental process begins quite early. Thus, it appears that the psychological mechanisms used to recognize faces are different from those used for nonface objects. The question then becomes: Are there also different brain mechanisms for recognizing faces and other objects?

Brain Regions Involved in Face Recognition

Earlier in this chapter, we noted that recognition of objects is enabled by many different parts of the brain, including the primary visual cortex of the occipital lobe, the parietal lobe (mostly the "where-and-how" pathway), and the lower portion of the temporal lobe (mostly the "what" pathway; see Figure 7.21, p. 246). When it comes to recognizing faces, those same brain areas are used—especially the occipital and temporal lobes—but some specific regions within the temporal lobe also play a role. Research using brain imaging has identified the *fusiform gyrus* within the temporal lobe as being especially active when people recognize familiar faces (Kanwisher & Dilks, 2013; McCarthy et al., 1997; see **Figure 7.26**).

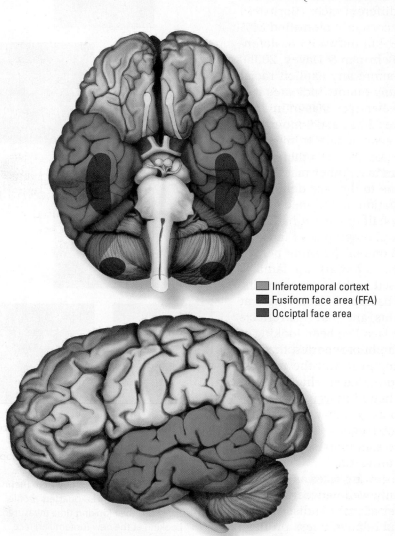

Inferotemporal cortext
Fusiform face area (FFA)
Occiptal face area

FIGURE 7.26 The fusiform face area
The fusiform face area (FFA) plays a central role in recognizing familiar faces, and the occipital face area is involved in identifying new faces and distinguishing faces from other objects.

This finding has been replicated in many different studies, causing researchers to label this area the **fusiform face area** (FFA) (Gazzaniga et al., 2014). Although some research suggests that this area may also be used to recognize any class of stimuli with which people are highly familiar (Gauthier et al., 2000), it is clearly and strongly implicated in the recognition of faces. In contrast, the *occipital face area* appears to be responsible for processing new faces and distinguishing faces from other objects, and is strongly connected to the fusiform face area (Liu et al., 2010).

Further evidence that the fusiform face area is involved in face recognition is provided by a condition called **prosopagnosia**, also known as *face blindness*, in which damage to the fusiform face area results in people having difficulty recognizing familiar faces although they show no deficits in recognizing nonface objects (Moscovitch & Moscovitch, 2000). People with prosopagnosia are unable to recognize the faces of family members or celebrities (and sometimes themselves in a mirror), despite seeing them repeatedly, either in person, in photographs, or on television. People with prosopagnosia can identify familiar people by other cues such as their voice, their posture, gestures, or distinctive facial features such as hairstyle, bushy eyebrows, or a prominent scar. They recognize a face as a face but are unable to identify whose face it is.

Prosopagnosia can be the result of a stroke, although some people are born with the condition (Duchaine & Nakayama, 2006). A 2006 German study revealed that the prevalence of hereditary prosopagnosia is as high as 2% in the population (Kennerknecht et al., 2006). This high rate of the disorder had gone unnoticed mainly because people with this disability as children learn compensatory strategies. According to Ingo Kennerknecht and colleagues (2006), "Many of them had not realized that they were dealing with a specific dysfunction. They have learned to recognize people from voice, gait, habits, gestalt, clothing, accessories, name, and other non-facial cues" (p. 1620).

SECTION REVIEW

To identify a form, pattern, object, or face, we must perceive it well enough to match it to a stored representation.

Integration of Features

- Neurons in the primary visual cortex and nearby areas are maximally responsive to specific visual features (e.g., line orientations, movements, and colors).
- Features are detected through rapid parallel processing and then are integrated spatially through serial processing.

Gestalt Principles

- Gestalt psychologists asserted that whole objects are not merely the sums of their parts and that wholes take precedence in conscious perception.
- The Gestalt principles of grouping describe rules by which we automatically organize stimulus elements into wholes. We also automatically separate figure from ground.

Top-Down Processes

- Wholes influence our perception of parts through unconscious inference, as illustrated by illusory contours and illusory lightness differences.
- The effects of unconscious inference occur through top-down control mechanisms in the brain.

Recognizing Objects

- For us to see and recognize objects, the brain must pick up from the optic nerves the relevant features of the object and integrate those features into a perceptual whole.
- Evidence that the brain does integrate features into perceptual wholes we call "objects" comes from recognition experiments with normal subjects and through observations of people with visual form agnosia and visual object agnosia.

Two Streams of Visual Processing

- Visual processing beyond the primary visual cortex in the occipital lobe takes place through a "what" stream leading into the temporal lobe, and a "where-and-how" stream leading into the parietal lobe.
- Bilateral damage to parts of the "what" stream impairs conscious object recognition but preserves the ability to use vision to direct physical actions with respect to objects, such as grasping or moving around objects. Bilateral damage to the "where-and-how" stream has the opposite effect.

Recognizing Faces

- Humans have evolved special psychological and neurological mechanisms to recognize faces.
- People are better able to discriminate and remember upright as opposed to inverted faces.
- The own-race bias refers to people's abilities to recognize and remember faces from their own race better than faces from other races. This bias develops in infancy.
- The fusiform face area is involved in recognizing familiar faces, whereas the occipital face area appears to be responsible for processing new faces.
- People with prosopagnosia can recognize nonface objects but have difficulty recognizing the faces of familiar people.

Seeing in Three Dimensions

One of the great early puzzles of vision, about which philosophers speculated for centuries, was that of depth perception. We automatically, effortlessly, see the world in three dimensions. Objects occupy and move in space that includes not only a vertical (up-down) and a horizontal (right-left) dimension but also a dimension of depth, or distance from our eyes. Our retinas and the images that are projected on them are two-dimensional. It is relatively easy to understand how our retinas might record the vertical and horizontal dimensions of our visual world, but how do they record the third dimension, that of depth?

A major step toward answering this question was the publication of a treatise on vision by Hermann von Helmholtz (1867/1962), the same German physiologist who developed the trichromatic theory of color vision. According to Helmholtz, seeing is an active mental process. The light focused onto our retinas is not the scene we see but is simply a source of hints about the scene. Our brain infers the characteristics and positions of objects from cues in the reflected light, and those inferences are our perceptions. Helmholtz pointed out that the steps in this inferential process can be expressed mathematically, in equations relating information in the reflected light to conclusions about the positions, sizes, and shapes of objects in the visual scene. We are not conscious of these calculations and inferences; our brain works them out quickly and automatically, without our awareness.

FOCUS 25

How did Helmholtz describe perception as a problem-solving process?

Cues for Depth Perception

Depth perception works best when you use both eyes. You can prove that with a simple demonstration. Pick up two pencils and hold them in front of you, one in each hand, with their points toward each other. Close one eye and move the pencils toward each other to make the points touch at their tips. Chances are, you will miss by a little bit on your first attempt, and your subsequent adjustments will have something of a trial-and-error quality. Now repeat the task with both eyes open. Is it easier? Do you find that now you can see more clearly which adjustments to make to bring the points together and that you no longer need trial and error? You can see depth reasonably well with one eye alone, but you can see it better with both eyes working in concert.

Binocular Cues for Depth

FOCUS 26

How does binocular disparity serve as a cue for depth?

The most important binocular (two-eye) cue for depth perception is *binocular disparity*, which refers to the slightly different (disparate) views that the two eyes have of the same object or scene. Because the eyes are a few centimeters apart, they view any given object from slightly different angles. To see how the degree of binocular disparity varies depending on an object's distance from your eyes, hold your index finger about a foot in front of your eyes with a wall in the background. Look at your finger with just your right eye open, then with just your left eye open, alternately back and forth. As you alternate between the two eyes, your finger appears to jump back and forth with respect to the background wall. That is because each eye views the finger from a different angle. Now move your finger farther away (out to full arm's length), and notice that your view of it jumps a smaller distance with respect to the wall as you again alternate between right-eye and left-eye views. The farther your finger is from your eyes, the smaller is the difference in the angle between each eye and the finger; the two lines of sight become increasingly parallel.

Thus, the degree of disparity between the two eyes' views can serve as a cue to judge an object's distance from the eyes: The less the disparity, the greater the distance. In normal, binocular vision your brain fuses the two eyes' views to give a perception of depth. Helmholtz (1867/1962) showed mathematically how the difference in two objects' distance from the eyes can be calculated from differences in the degree of binocular disparity. More recently, researchers have found that neurons in an area of the visual cortex close to the primary visual area respond best to stimuli that are presented to both eyes at slightly disparate locations on the retina (Thomas et al., 2002). These neurons appear to be ideally designed to permit depth perception. For another demonstration of binocular disparity, see **Figure 7.27**.

Illusions of Depth Created by Binocular Disparity

FOCUS 27

How do stereoscopes provide an illusion of depth?

The ability to see depth from binocular disparity—an ability called stereopsis—was first demonstrated in the early nineteenth century by Charles Wheatstone (described by Helmholtz, 1867/1962). Wheatstone wondered what would happen if he drew two slightly different pictures of the same object or scene, one as seen by the left eye and one as seen by the right, and then viewed them simultaneously, each with the appropriate eye. To permit such viewing, he invented a device called a *stereoscope*. The effect was dramatic. When viewed through the stereoscope, the two pictures were fused perceptually into a single image containing depth.

Stereoscopes became a great fad in the late nineteenth century as they enabled people to see scenes such as Buckingham Palace or the Grand Canyon in full depth by placing cards that contained two photographs of the same scene, shot simultaneously from slightly different angles, into their stereoscope. The Viewmaster, a once-popular child's toy, is a modern example of a stereoscope. Three-dimensional motion pictures and comic books employ the same general principle. In the simplest versions, each frame of the film or comic strip contains an overlapping pair of

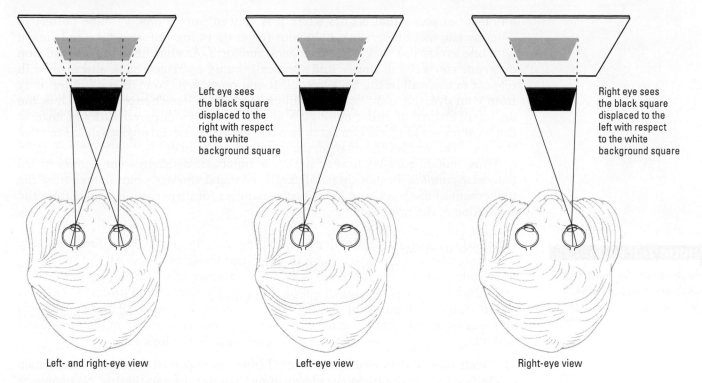

Left eye sees the black square displaced to the right with respect to the white background square

Right eye sees the black square displaced to the left with respect to the white background square

Left- and right-eye view

Left-eye view

Right-eye view

FIGURE 7.27 Demonstration of binocular disparity The two eyes see somewhat different views of the relationship between the closer figure and the more distant figure. The disparity (degree of difference) between the two views is proportional to the distance between the two objects, and that information is used by the perceptual system to perceive the depth between them.

similar images, each in a different color, one slightly displaced from the other, and the viewer wears colored glasses that allow only one image to enter each eye. You can demonstrate stereopsis without any special viewer by looking at the two patterns in **Figure 7.28** in the manner described in the caption.

Monocular Cues for Depth
Although depth perception is most vivid with two eyes, it is by no means absent with one. People who have just one functioning eye can drive cars, shoot basketballs, and reach out and pick objects up without fumbling around.

Motion Parallax Among the monocular (one-eye) cues for depth, perhaps the most valuable is **motion parallax**. (The word *parallax* refers to the apparent change in

(a)   (b)

FOCUS 28

How does motion parallax serve as a cue for depth, and how is it similar to binocular disparity?

FIGURE 7.28 A depth illusion created by binocular disparity The two patterns are constructed to appear as they would to the left and right eye, respectively, if the dark square were actually a certain distance in front of the white square (like that shown in Figure 7.27). In order to experience the three-dimensional effect, hold the book about a foot in front of your eyes and let your eyes drift in an unfocused way until you see double images of everything. You will see four renditions of the white frame with a darker square center—two renditions of (a) and two of (b). When all four of these images are clear, converge or diverge your eyes a little in order to get the right-hand image of (a) to sit right atop the left-hand image of (b). You have fused your left-eye view of (a) and your right-eye view of (b) into a single image, which now appears to be three-dimensional: The dark square seems to float in space in front of the white square.

an object or scene that occurs when it is viewed from a new vantage point.) To demonstrate motion parallax, hold your finger up in front of your face and view it with one eye as you rock your head back and forth. As your head moves, you gain different views of the finger, and you see it being displaced back and forth with respect to the wall in the background. If you now move your finger farther away from your eye, the same head movement produces a less-changed view. Thus, the degree of change in either eye's view at one moment compared with the next, as the head moves in space, can serve as a cue for assessing the object's distance from the eyes: The smaller the change, the greater the distance.

Thus, motion parallax is very similar to binocular disparity—sometimes called *binocular parallax*. In motion parallax, the changed vantage point comes from the movement of the head, and in binocular parallax (or disparity), it comes from the separation of the two eyes.

Pictorial Cues Motion parallax depends on the geometry of true three-dimensionality and cannot be used to depict depth in two-dimensional pictures. All the remaining monocular depth cues, however, can provide a sense of depth in pictures as well as in the real three-dimensional world, and thus they are called ***pictorial cues for depth***. You can identify some of these by examining **Figure 7.29** and considering all the reasons why you see some objects in the scene as standing in the foreground and others as more distant. The pictorial cues include the following:

1. ***Occlusion.*** The trees occlude (cut off from view) part of the mountains, which indicates that the trees are closer to us than are the mountains. Near objects occlude more distant ones.

2. ***Relative image size for familiar objects.*** The image of the woman (both in the picture and on the viewer's retina) is taller than that of the mountains. Because we know that people are not taller than mountains, we take the woman's larger image as a sign that she must be closer to us than are the mountains.

3. ***Linear perspective.*** The rows of plants converge (come closer together) as they go from the bottom toward the mountains, indicating that objects toward the mountains are farther away. Parallel lines appear to converge as they become more distant.

4. ***Texture gradient.*** Texture elements in the picture—specifically, the individual dots of color representing the flowers—are smaller and more densely packed near the trees and mountains than they are at the bottom of the picture. In general, a gradual decrease in the size and spacing of texture elements indicates depth.

FOCUS 29

What are some cues for depth that exist in pictures as well as in the actual, three-dimensional world?

FIGURE 7.29 Pictorial cues for depth
Depth cues in this picture include occlusion, relative image size for familiar objects, linear perspective, texture gradient, position relative to the horizon, and differential lighting of surfaces.

Shaun Egan/Getty Images

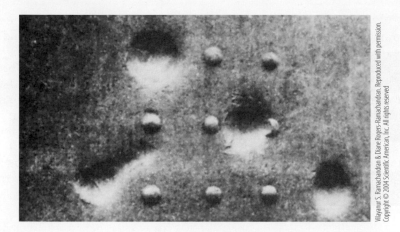

FIGURE 7.30 Depth perception created by light and shade Because we automatically assume that the light is coming from above, we see the smaller disruptions on the surface here as bumps and the larger ones as pits. Turn the picture upside down and see what happens. (The bumps and pits reverse.)

5. *Position relative to the horizon.* The trees are closer to the horizon than is the woman, indicating that they are farther away. In outdoor scenes, objects nearer the horizon are usually farther away than those that are displaced from the horizon in either direction (either below it or above it). If there were clouds in this picture, those seen just above the edge where the earth and sky meet (close to the horizon) would be seen as farther away than those seen farther up in the picture (farther from the horizon).

6. *Differential lighting of surfaces.* In real three-dimensional scenes the amount of light reflected from different surfaces varies as a function of their orientation with respect to the sun or other source of light. The fact that the sides of the rows of lavender are darker than the tops leads us to see the rows as three-dimensional rather than flat. We see the brightest parts of the plants as their tops, closest to us (as we look down on them); and we see the darker parts as their sides, shaded by the tops, and farther from us. For a more dramatic demonstration of an effect of lighting, see **Figure 7.30** and follow the directions in its caption.

FOCUS 30

Why does size perception depend on distance perception?

The Role of Depth Cues in Size Perception

The ability to judge the size of an object is intimately tied to the ability to judge its distance. As **Figure 7.31** illustrates, the size of the retinal image of an object is inversely proportional to the object's distance from the retina. Thus, if an object is moved twice as far away, it produces a retinal image half the height and width of

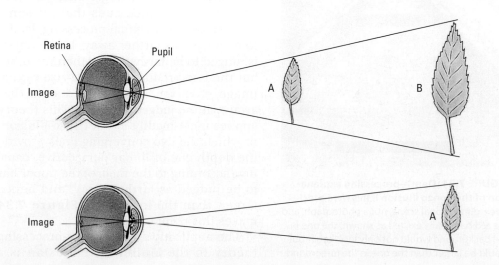

Retina
Pupil
Image

A
B

Image
A

FIGURE 7.31 Relationship of retinal-image size to object size and distance If, as in the upper sketch, object B is twice as tall and wide as object A and also twice as far from the eye, the retinal images that the two objects produce will be the same size. If, as in the lower sketch, object A is moved twice its former distance from the eye, the retinal image produced will be half its former height and width.

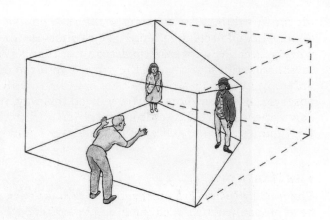

Susan Schwartzenberg, © The Exploratorium, www.exploratorium.edu

FIGURE 7.32 A size-distance illusion
We know that these young women must be approximately the same size, so what explains this illusion? The room they are standing in is distorted. The back wall and both windows are actually trapezoidal in shape, and the wall is slanted so that its left-hand edge is actually twice as tall and twice as far away from the viewer as its right-hand edge (see drawing at right). When we view this scene through a peephole (or the camera's eye), we automatically assume that the walls and window are normal, that the occupants are the same distance away, and therefore that their size is different. This distorted room is called an Ames room, after Adelbert Ames, who built the first one.

the one it produced before. You don't see the object as smaller, though; it just looks farther away. The ability to see an object as unchanged in size, despite change in the image size as it moves farther away or closer, is called *size constancy*. For familiar objects, such as a pencil or a car, previous knowledge of the object's usual size may contribute to size constancy. But size constancy also occurs for unfamiliar objects if cues for distance are available, and even familiar objects can appear to be drastically altered in size if misleading distance cues are present (for an example, see **Figure 7.32**).

Unconscious Depth Processing as a Basis for Size Illusions

It is not difficult to produce drawings in which two identical lines or objects appear to be different in size. Two classic examples are the *Ponzo illusion* (first described by Mario Ponzo in 1913) and the *Müller-Lyer illusion* (first described by F. C. Müller-Lyer in the mid-nineteenth century), both illustrated in **Figure 7.33**. In each illusion two horizontal bars appear to be different in length; but if you measure them, you will discover that they are identical.

Richard Gregory (1968) offered a *depth-processing theory* to account for these and various other size illusions. This theory—consistent with everything said so far about the relation between size and distance—maintains that one object in each illusion appears larger than the other because of distance cues that, at some early stage of perceptual processing, lead it to be judged as farther away. If one object is judged to be farther away than the other but the two produce the same-size retinal image, then the object judged as farther away will be judged as larger. This theory applies most readily to the Ponzo illusion, in which the two converging lines provide the depth cue of linear perspective, causing (according to the theory) the upper bar to be judged as farther away, and hence larger, than the lower one. **Figure 7.34** makes this point clear.

The application of the depth-processing theory to the Müller-Lyer illusion is a

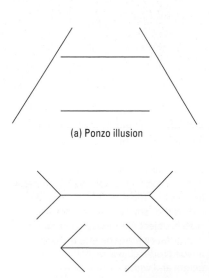

(a) Ponzo illusion

(b) Müller-Lyer illusion

FIGURE 7.33 The Ponzo and Müller-Lyer illusions In both (a) and (b), the top horizontal bar looks longer than the bottom one, although they are actually the same length.

Sorapop Udomsri/Shutterstock

FIGURE 7.34 Depth-processing explanation of the Ponzo illusion If this were a real, three-dimensional scene, not a photograph, and the red bars really existed as shown, the one in the background would not only look larger but would be larger than the one in the foreground.

bit more subtle. The assumption is that people register the figures as three-dimensional objects, something like sawhorses viewed from above. The object with wings extending outward (top drawing in **Figure 7.35**) resembles an upside-down sawhorse, with legs toward the viewer, and the one with inward wings (bottom drawing) resembles a right-side-up sawhorse, with its horizontal bar closer to the observer. If real sawhorses were viewed this way, the horizontal bar of the upside-down one would be farther from the observer than that of the right-side-up one, and if it produced the same-size retinal image, it would in fact be longer.

The Moon Illusion

The **moon illusion** has provoked debate since ancient Greek and Roman times. You have probably noticed that the moon looks huge when it is near the earth's horizon, just above the trees or buildings in the distance, but looks much smaller when it is closer to the zenith (directly overhead). This difference is truly an illusion. Objectively, the moon is the same size, and the same distance from us, whether it is at the horizon or the zenith. If you view the horizon moon through a peephole so that you see it in isolation from other objects such as trees and buildings, the illusion disappears and the moon looks no larger than it does at the zenith.

A depth-processing account of this illusion was first proposed by the Greek astronomer Ptolemy in the second century, was revived by Helmholtz (1867/1962) in the nineteenth century, and has been supported in modern times through research conducted by Lloyd Kaufman and his colleagues (Kaufman et al., 2007; Kaufman & Rock, 1962). The account can be summarized as follows: Our visual system did not evolve to judge such huge distances as that from the earth to the moon, so we automatically assess its distance in relation to more familiar earthly objects. Most objects that we see near the earth's horizon are farther away than objects that we see farther from the horizon (as noted earlier, in the discussion of pictorial cues for depth). For example, birds or clouds seen near the horizon are usually farther away than are those seen closer to the zenith. Thus, our perceptual system assumes that the moon is farther away at the horizon than at the zenith, even though in reality it is the same distance away from us in either position. As in the case of the Ponzo and Müller-Lyer illusions, when two objects produce the same-size retinal image and are judged to be different distances away, the one that is judged to be farther away is seen as larger than the other.

Even today, the main objection to this explanation of the moon illusion is that people do not consciously see the horizon moon as farther away than the zenith moon (Hershenson, 2003). When people see the large-appearing horizon moon and are asked whether it seems farther away or closer than usual, they usually say closer. Again, however, as with the Ponzo and Müller-Lyer illusions, Kaufman and Irving Rock (1989) contend that we must distinguish between unconscious and conscious assessments. From their perspective, the sequence of perceptual assessments about the horizon moon might be described as follows:

1. Unconscious processes judge that the moon is farther away than usual (because objects near the horizon are usually farthest away).

2. Unconscious processes judge that the moon is larger than usual (because if it is farther away but produces the same-size retinal image, it must be larger), and this judgment enters consciousness.

3. If asked to judge distance, most people say that the horizon moon looks closer (because they know that the moon doesn't really change size, so its large apparent size must be due to closeness). This explanation has been called the *farther-larger-nearer theory* (Ross & Plug, 2002).

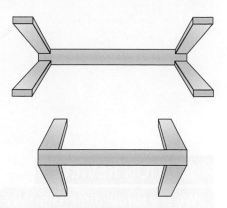

FIGURE 7.35 Depth-processing explanation of the Müller-Lyer illusion Compare these sawhorses with the Müller-Lyer drawings in Figure 7.33b. If these were real sawhorses, viewed from above in the three-dimensional world, the upside-down one would be longer than the right-side-up one.

 The moon illusion The moon at the horizon sometimes looks huge, much bigger than it ever looks when it is higher up in the sky. This is an unaltered photo; the moon really looked this big.

FOCUS 31

How might the unconscious assessment of depth provide a basis for the Ponzo, Müller-Lyer, and moon illusions?

Not all perceptual psychologists agree with the depth-processing account of the moon illusion, or with that of the Ponzo or Müller-Lyer illusions, but that account is supported by more evidence and logic than any other explanations that have been offered to date (Kaufman & Kaufman, 2000; Ross & Plug, 2002).

Although perceptual psychologists have made great strides since the days of Ptolemy, we are still a long way from a full account of the calculations that our brains make to infer the sizes, distances, and shapes of all the objects in our field of view.

SECTION REVIEW

We see three-dimensionally—that is, with depth—even though the retina is two-dimensional.

Depth-Perception Cues

- Our visual system uses various cues to infer the depth (distance) of objects or parts of objects.

- Binocular disparity is a major depth cue that derives from the fact that the two eyes, because of their different spatial positions, receive somewhat different images of an object.

- Another depth cue, motion parallax, is similar to binocular disparity but can occur with just one eye. It makes use of the different images of an object that either eye receives as the head moves right or left.

- Pictorial depth cues, such as linear perspective, do not depend on actual three-dimensionality. They allow us to infer depth even in two-dimensional pictures.

Size Perception

- Size perception depends on depth perception; the size of an object's retinal image is inversely proportional to its distance from the viewer.

- Size constancy is the ability to perceive an object as the same size when its retinal image size varies due to changes in its distance.

- The Ponzo, Müller-Lyer, and moon illusions are based at least partly on unconscious inferences about depth. If two objects create identical retinal images, the one that is unconsciously judged to be farther away will be seen as larger.

Multisensory Perception: Combining Senses

This chapter and the previous one have discussed the senses as if they were independent and separable. We smell a rose, hear a voice, and see a face. Yet, in everyday experience we rarely experience an event with only a single sense. Rather, most of our experiences are *multisensory*. Moreover, we usually experience these inputs to our various systems not as a chaotic mish-mash, but as an integrated whole. *Multisensory integration* (or *multimodal integration*) is the integration of information from different senses by the nervous system.

Multisensory Integration

FOCUS 32

What is the *McGurk effect* and how does it demonstrate visual dominance?

Have you ever tried to watch a movie or television show when the audio and video did not match? Most people find this mildly disconcerting and often have trouble figuring out what exactly is being said by whom. We also are more likely to understand what a speaker says if we can see his or her lips. The correlation between speech and lip movements is so consistent that infants as young as 2 months of age are able to match a person's lip movements to the corresponding sounds (Kuhl & Meltzoff, 1982), although this ability improves with age and experience (see Soto-Faraco et al., 2012).

Of course, when we receive conflicting information from two senses—sight and sound, for example—the result is not necessarily an average of the two senses. For humans (and pigeons, Randich et al., 1978), when sight and sound are put in conflict with one another, vision usually "wins." This is called the *visual dominance effect* (Colavita, 1974; Posner et al., 1976). In one set of studies, subjects were presented with a tone, lights, or, on a few trials, both tones and lights. They were instructed to press one key, as quickly as possible, when a tone was presented and another key when a light was presented. Subjects were told that the bimodal trials (tones and lights) were simply mistakes made by the experimenter. When the bimodal trials were presented, subjects pressed the "light key" on 49 of 50 trials (Colavita, 1974).

Another example of vision having greater influence on audition than vice versa is the *McGurk effect* (McGurk & MacDonald, 1976). This is experienced when one hears a person speak one sound (the phoneme "ba," for example), but watches a face articulating a different sound (the phoneme "ga," for example). Although the exact same sound is impinging upon your ears, in one case you will hear "ba" (what is actually being said), while in the other you will hear a different sound. In the "ba/ga" example most people hear "da" when listening to "ba" but watching a person mouthing "ga." You've really got to watch this in action to appreciate it: Look up "McGurk effect" online to see it for yourself.

FIGURE 7.36 The "Bouba/Kiki" effect Which of these figures is called "bouba" and which is called "kiki"? Most people from a diversity of different language groups pick the rounded figure as "bouba" and the jagged figure as "kiki," showing that the relation between an object and what it is called is not arbitrary.

Neuroscience of Multisensory Integration

For someone to experience multisensory integration, the brain must somehow be able to respond appropriately to stimuli from two sensory modalities, such as sound and vision. Multisensory neurons are neurons that are influenced by stimuli from more than one sense modality, such as those discovered in the superior colliculus of cats, and later of other mammals (Stein & Meredith, 1993; Wallace et al., 2012). Based on single-cell recording with nonhuman animals, researchers determined that multisensory integration is most apt to occur when the individual sensory stimuli (1) come from the same location, (2) arise at approximately the same time, and (3) evoke relatively weak responses when presented in isolation.

Multisensory neurons are found throughout the brain, but multisensory integration also occurs when the outputs of unimodal neurons (those that respond only to a single type of sensory stimulation) are integrated (Wallace et al., 2012).

The "Bouba/Kiki" Effect

Before reading further, look at the shapes in **Figure 7.36**. If you had to guess, which shape do you think is called "bouba" and which is called "kiki"? Most people would guess that the rounded shape on the right was "bouba" and the jagged shape on the left was "kiki." This was first demonstrated in 1929 by the German Gestalt psychologist Wolfgang Köhler, who tested Spanish speakers using the made-up words "takete" and "baluba." It has since been repeated a number of times (Hung et al., 2017), with Vilayanur S. Ramachandran and Edward Hubbard (2001) reporting that greater than 95% of American college students and Tamil speakers from India selected the jagged figure as "kiki" and the rounded figure as "bouba."

Why? One of the defining characteristics of language is the arbitrariness of what we call things; as Shakespeare's Juliet observed: "A rose by any other name would smell as sweet." But it seems that what we call some objects is not totally arbitrary. Ramachandran and Hubbard (2001) proposed that the more rounded stimulus corresponds to the rounded way one must form one's mouth when saying "bouba," whereas the sharper-looking stimulus corresponds to the way one forms one's mouth when saying "kiki." In other words, there is an implicit multisensory match between a visual stimulus and sound, or perhaps the muscle patterns we use to make those sounds. The fact that 2.5-year-old toddlers—who can't yet read—also show the Bouba/Kiki effect indicates that it is not due to the appearance of the letters, but to the sounds of the words (Maurer et al., 2006).

Synesthesia

When you listen to music, do you see color? Or perhaps you taste music, or you see numbers and letters in specific colors. If you do, you are one of the about 1 in 20 people with **synesthesia** (sĭ-nəs-thē´-zhə), meaning literally "joined perception" (from Greek), a condition in which sensory stimulation in one modality induces

FOCUS 33

What are the defining features of synesthesia? Might synesthesia have any adaptive value?

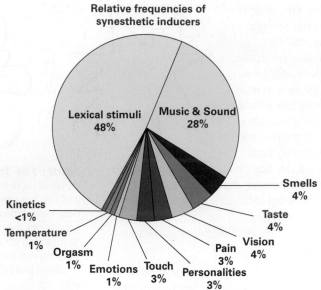

Relative frequencies of synesthetic inducers

Lexical stimuli 48%
Music & Sound 28%
Smells 4%
Taste 4%
Vision 4%
Pain 3%
Personalities 3%
Touch 3%
Emotions 1%
Orgasm 1%
Temperature 1%
Kinetics <1%

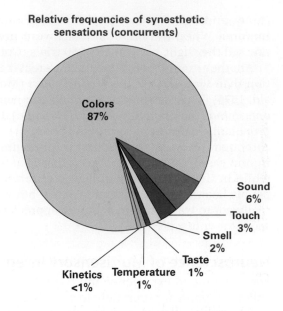

Relative frequencies of synesthetic sensations (concurrents)

Colors 87%
Sound 6%
Touch 3%
Smell 2%
Taste 1%
Temperature 1%
Kinetics <1%

FIGURE 7.37 Frequency of synesthesia These are the relative frequencies of synesthetic inducers (stimuli that induce synesthesia) and concurrents (the sensory system in which one experiences the synesthesia). As you can see, music and lexical (numbers or letters) stimuli are most apt to induce synesthesia, and the vast majority of the synesthesia effect is in terms of colors (for example, "hearing colors" or seeing specific numbers as specific colors). However, many other experiences can induce synesthesia and they can be expressed in just about all of one's senses (for example, "tasting numbers" or "smelling sounds").

(Data from Hochel & Milán, 2008; and Day, 2007.)

FIGURE 7.38 Number–color associations for one synesthete. Notice that the numbers 7 and 8 are composed of two colors each.

a sensation in a different modality. Though known for centuries, synesthesia was more a curiosity than a topic of serious scientific investigation until recently. Few people claimed to be *synesthetes* (people with synesthesia), and little wonder. Several hundred years ago such claims would brand one as a witch, and in more enlightened times experiences such as "seeing sounds" were apt to be viewed as hallucinations and perhaps a sign of schizophrenia. Since the 1980s or so, however, the situation has changed substantially, as modern science has taken the phenomenon of synesthesia seriously. Current estimates are that between 1 and 4% of the population are synesthetes, and, unlike schizophrenia, synesthesia does not interfere with normal functioning and is not classified as a mental disorder (Hochel & Milán, 2008; Simner et al., 2006).

Synesthesia can come in many forms. Researchers have identified more than 60 different types of synesthesia, with the most common being grapheme-color (Simner, 2012; Simner et al., 2006). **Figure 7.37** shows the frequencies of the types of stimuli that evoke synesthesia (called *inducers*) and the types of synesthetic sensations (called *concurrents*). As you can see, letters and/or numbers (lexical stimuli) are the most common inducers of synesthesia, followed by music and sound (adapted from Hochel & Milán, 2008). **Figure 7.38** shows how one grapheme-color synesthete views the numbers 0 through 8.

How do you know if you're a synesthete? As currently defined, synesthetic perception is: (a) involuntary and automatic; (b) consistent (for example, if you see "5" as red today, you will see it as red in 2 weeks); (c) spatially extended (see how the numbers are distributed in Figure 7.37); (d) memorable; and (e) emotional (Cytowic, 2002). Most people with synesthesia find their synesthetic experiences to be emotionally positive. They report that they have been synesthetic since childhood, and it apparently is a stable characteristic, lasting a lifetime (Hochel & Milán, 2008). There is evidence that, for some synesthetes, specific grapheme-color pairings are linked to childhood toys containing colored letters (Witthoft & Winawer, 2013). Synesthesia runs in families, suggesting a genetic component, but it often skips generations. Moreover, monozygotic (genetically identical) twins do not always share the trait (Smilek et al., 2005), indicating that the genetic route to synesthesia is not a simple one. In one large-scale study, synesthesia was found to be disproportionally frequent in artists (Rich et al., 2005), something that had been anecdotally reported earlier.

A number of different theories about the origins of synesthesia have been proposed, and neuroscience has shown that the brains of synesthetes are different from those of "typical" perceivers. Variants of the most common interpretation of synesthesia, the *sensory cross-activation hypothesis,* propose that it is due to cross-activation between different areas of the brain (Hubbard et al., 2011; Ramachandran & Hubbard, 2001). For the most common type of synesthesia, grapheme-color, the cross-activation is proposed to occur within the fusiform gyrus, between one area that represents the visual appearance of graphemes (numbers and letters) and an adjacent area associated with color vision, called V4 (Ramachandran & Hubbard, 2001; see **Figure 7.39**). One hypothesis related to the cross-activation theory was originally proposed by Daphne and Charles Maurer (1988), who suggested that human infants are synesthetes, having many neural connections between different sensory areas. As children develop, most of these synaptic connections get pruned, resulting in increased segregation of the senses (Holcombe et al., 2009; Maurer & Mondloch, 2005). Adult synesthetes are people who fail to display the typical pruning of these cross-modal connections. In support of this, we know that for typically developing children the number of synapses in the sensory and association areas of the brain peak in childhood and decline thereafter (Huttenlocher & Drbaholkar, 1997).

A finding consistent with Maurer and Maurer's interpretation is that adult synesthetes have greater structural connectivity (as reflected by patterns of white matter, the myelin coating on axons, described in Chapter 4) for different parts of the brain than non-synesthetes (Rouw & Scholte, 2007). Other brain imaging research has shown differences in gray matter (neurons) between different areas of the brains of synesthetes and non-synesthetes (Banissy et al., 2012). Much is still to be learned about the neuroscience of synesthesia, but the more we learn, the more complex the picture becomes. For example, a recent review of the neuroscience literature concluded that a network of brain areas, rather than just a single area, is involved in synesthesia (Rouw et al., 2011).

Why is synesthesia so common? Why hasn't natural selection weeded out people with excessive connections between different sensory areas? To put it another way, might people with synesthesia have some adaptive advantage? Ramachandran and his colleagues (Ramachandran & Brang, 2008; Ramachandran & Hubbard, 2001) proposed that the cross-wiring that seems to occur in synesthesia may play a role in seeing connections between higher-order concepts, such as metaphors ("Juliet is the sun," "soft blue"). The fact that artists are more likely to be synesthetes than the general population is consistent with this theory.

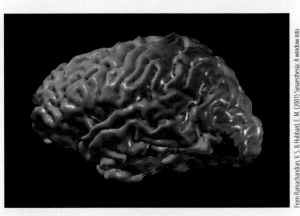

From Ramachandran, V. S. & Hubbard, E. M. (2001) Synaesthesia: A window into perception, thought and language. *Journal of Consciousness Studies*, 8(12), 3–34.

FIGURE 7.39 Regions thought to be cross-activated in grapheme-color synesthesia (green=grapheme recognition area, red=V4 color area).

SECTION REVIEW

Most of our sensory experiences are multisensory and integrated.

Multisensory Integration

- Vision and audition are usually well integrated, with even 2-month-old infants being able to match a person's lip movements to the corresponding sound.

- When vision and audition are in conflict, vision usually "wins"; this is referred to as the visual dominance effect and reflected by the McGurk effect.

- There are some neurons in the superior colliculus of some mammals that respond to multiple sensory stimuli.

- The "Bouba/Kiki" effect reflects the integration of shapes and sounds, attributed to how the mouth is rounded for making some sounds (associated with round shapes) relative to others (jagged shapes).

Synesthesia

- Synesthesia is a condition in which sensory stimulation in one modality induces a sensation in a different modality.

- The sensory cross-activation hypothesis proposes that synesthesia is due to cross-activation between different areas of the brain.

Thinking Critically About The Psychology of Vision

1. Is vision/seeing automatic, or must we "learn" to see?

2. How might the visual system have been shaped by natural selection to foster social relationships?

3. In appreciating or creating works of visual art, would you say we rely more on top-down processing or bottom-up processing, or equally on both? Explain your answer.

Reflections and Connections

As you review this chapter, you may find it useful to think about the following three themes.

1. The survival functions of vision Our visual system, like all the basic mechanisms underlying behavior, evolved to promote our ancestors' survival and reproduction. Our visual system is not an unbiased recorder of physical patterns of light. Rather, it is a biological tool designed to pick out the information in patterns of light that is potentially most useful. Most of the "illusions" that our visual system produces are useful in helping us to recognize and interact effectively with objects in the real world. As you review, think about the survival advantage of each of the various visual abilities discussed in the chapter. Perhaps especially relevant to a highly social species such as *Homo sapiens* is our ability to recognize faces. Think of the ease with which you recognize the faces of familiar people—even those whom you haven't seen in years—and the memories that sometimes come to mind when you see a familiar face.

2. The interaction of bottom-up and top-down processes in vision The neural processes that bring sensory information into the brain and move it along to higher centers of analysis are called bottom-up processes. Those that bring information down from higher centers to contribute to the analysis occurring at lower centers are called top-down processes. Bottom-up processes discussed in this chapter include: (a) the coding of variations in light by rods and cones; (b) the organization of that information to register elementary sensory features such as color, lightness, contour orientations, and degree of binocular disparity; and (c), in Treisman's theory, the integration of sensory features that occupy a given spatial location. Top-down processes are assumed to be involved whenever the analysis of the sensory information hinges on perceptions of the whole or expectations generated by the context.

The phenomena discussed in this chapter that are assumed to involve top-down control include illusory contours, illusory lightness differences that cannot be explained by lateral inhibition, and size judgments that are based on unconscious assessments of depth.

3. The integration of behavioral and neurophysiological discoveries Hermann von Helmholtz realized long ago that all our perceptions result from the interaction between physical properties of the external world and physiological processes occurring in our sensory organs and brain. His trichromatic theory of color vision is an example of his attempts to explain perceptual phenomena—in this case, the three-primaries law of color mixing—in physiological terms. Recent research has made great strides in carrying out the general program of inquiry pioneered by Helmholtz.

This chapter presents many examples of modern explanations of perceptual phenomena that are in the direct tradition of Helmholtz. Consider: (a) the explanation of differences between bright-light vision and dim-light vision in terms of differences between cones and rods in their photochemicals; (b) the explanations of the two laws of additive color mixing in terms of three varieties of cones and the pattern of neural wiring of those cones to opponent-process neurons; (c) the explanation of rapid stimulus feature detection in terms of the properties of individual neurons in the primary visual cortex; (d) the explanation of distinctions between conscious visual perception and unconscious use of visual input to guide movement in terms of two separate pathways of visual processing; (e) the explanation of the role of components in object perception in terms of processes occurring in the "what" pathway of visual processing; and (f) the explanation of binocular disparity as a depth cue in terms of neurons that receive input from slightly different locations on the retinas of the two eyes.

Key Terms

binocular disparity   252

blind spot   228

bottom-up control   244

closure principle   241

common movement
    principle   241

cone vision   228

cones   227

cornea   226

dark adaptation   228

differential lighting of
    surfaces   255

experience-expectant processes
    (experience-expectant
    synaptogenesis)   236

feature detectors   238

figure   242

fovea   227

fusiform face area   250

Gestalt principles of
    grouping   241

Gestalt psychology   240

good continuation
    principle   241

good form principle   241

ground   242

iris   226

law of complementarity   230

lens   226

light adaptation   228

linear perspective   254

moon illusion   257

Find Out More

Simon Ings (2008). *A natural history of seeing: The art and science of vision.* New York, NY: Norton.

This book is a fun, and sometimes funny, intelligent presentation of much about the physics and psychology of vision—including its evolution, its chemistry, and how we see in color. The author, who is a science writer and novelist, will get you thinking at least as much about the unsolved mysteries of sight as about the facts we know.

Dale Purves & R. Beau Lotto (2011). *Why we see what we do redux: A wholly empirical theory of vision* (2nd ed.). Sunderland, MA: Sinauer.

This controversial book examines the relation between physical patterns of light and the perceptions that our visual system generates in response to those patterns. It is filled with illusions—of lightness, color, depth, and motion—that are not readily explained in terms of bottom-up neural wiring or straightforward logical calculations. According to the authors' empirical theory, learning has shaped the visual system such that what we perceive is strongly influenced by our experience with similar stimuli—both individually and in evolutionary terms.

Richard E. Cytowic & David M. Eagleman (2011). *Wednesday is indigo blue: Discovering the brain of synesthesia.* Cambridge, MA: MIT Press.

After years of being mostly a curiosity, synesthesia has become a serious topic for psychologists and neuroscientists. Cytowic and Eagleman present the latest research in synesthesia, arguing that "normal" perception is already multisensory and that synesthesia is a window to the mind and brain. There is an afterword by Dmitri Nabokov, whose famous father, the author Vladimir Nabokov, was a synesthete.

Saad Shaikh (2007). *Eyes on ice & no blind mice: Visions of science from the science of vision.* Bloomington, IN: Author House.

Saad Shaikh is a practicing retinal surgeon whose book helps the lay reader understand why humans are so dependent upon the ability to see. Using everything from important events in medical history to examples from his practice, Shaikh explores the importance of vision and how the effort to make clear sight possible for everyone has changed American history. This is an excellent read for anyone interested in eyesight or the medicine behind healthy vision.

Oliver Sacks (1985). *The man who mistook his wife for a hat and other clinical tales.* New York, NY: Summit Books.

Through a series of case studies, this classic bestseller discusses patients experiencing everything from visual agnosia—as described in this chapter—to hallucinations, to aphasia, to neurosyphilis.

In his career as a neurologist Sacks treated numerous patients, and this book describes both his more interesting cases as well as his interpretation of cases seen throughout history.

Scientific American (2010). *169 best illusions—A sampling.*

https://www.scientificamerican.com/article/169-best-illusions/

This website provides examples of fun and effective optical illusions. Along with each example, the website explains what is known of how the illusion works, which environmental stimuli and sensory phenomena are at play, and who discovered (or made famous) the illusion.

J. Purkinge (2017). *Deceptions of the senses are the truths of perception.* http://people.cornellcollege.edu/dsherman/illusions/

You can find several more optical illusions on this fun website. Along with examples of each visual trick are explanations of how it works and the people key to the development and understanding of the illusion. The site also provides several links to further information and resources for understanding the tricks our eyes can play. From Escher's waterfall to impossible triangles, this website will keep you entertained with optical illusions—and the science behind them—for hours.

LaunchPad
macmillan learning

Visit LaunchPad for Psychology 8e launchpadworks.com to access the e-book, videos, activities, additional resources, and LearningCurve quizzes, as well as study aids including flash cards and web quizzes.

PART IV

Learning and Thinking

The effectiveness of our behavior depends on what we have learned about the environment and on knowledge we have stored as memory. It also depends on our ability to call up and combine the portions of that knowledge that are useful for the task at hand. How do we learn? How do we store and organize our memories? How do we recall memories when we need them? How do we manipulate knowledge in our minds in order to reason and solve problems? What causes individual differences in problem-solving ability? These big questions concern us in Chapter 8 on learning, Chapter 9 on memory and attention, and Chapter 10 on intelligence and reasoning.

CHAPTER

Basic Processes of Learning

8

LEARNING OUTCOMES

After studying this chapter, you should be able to:

- Define classical conditioning and give examples of how it works.
- Define operant conditioning and give examples of how it works.
- Describe how learning takes place through play, exploration, and socialization.
- Identify several species-typical behaviors and their relationship with learning.

To survive, animals must adapt to their environments. Evolution by natural selection, discussed in Chapter 3, is the slow, long-term adaptive process that equips each species for life within a certain range of environmental conditions. But the environment is never constant; it changes from place to place and from time to time, and individuals must adapt to these changes over their lifetimes. To be efficient in finding foods, finding mates, avoiding predators, and carrying out the other necessities of survival and reproduction, animals must adjust to the ever-changing conditions of the specific environments in which they live. In other words, they must learn.

The term ***learning*** is used in various ways by different psychologists to refer to a wide variety of phenomena. For our purposes, we can define it broadly as *any process through which experience at one time can alter an individual's behavior at a future time. Experience* in this definition refers to any effects of the environment that are mediated by the individual's sensory systems (vision, hearing, touch, and so on). *Behavior at a future time* refers to any subsequent behavior that is not part of the individual's immediate response to the sensory stimulation during the learning experience. If I make a clicking sound just before flashing a bright light into your eyes, your immediate response to the click or to the light (such as blinking) does not exemplify learning. But your increased tendency to blink to the click alone, the next time I present that sound, does exemplify learning.

Most of psychology is concerned with the effects of experience on subsequent behavior. For example, social psychologists try to explain people's beliefs and social behaviors in terms of their past experiences, clinical psychologists try to explain people's emotional problems in such terms, and cognitive psychologists try to understand the basic mental processes that are involved in people's ability to learn. Thus, most chapters in any introduction to psychology, including this one, are about learning in one way or another.

andrea/E+/Getty Images

From an evolutionary perspective, learning is a very ancient set of abilities. All animals that have any kind of nervous system have acquired, through natural selection, some abilities to learn. We humans are in some ways unique but in many ways similar to other species in our basic mechanisms of learning.

We begin this chapter with discussions of two very general varieties of learning: classical conditioning and operant conditioning. Then we examine the roles of play, exploration, and observation in learning; and finally, we look at some very specialized forms of learning, such as learning what foods are good or bad to eat.

Classical Conditioning

FOCUS 1

What is a reflex, and how can it change through habituation?

Classical conditioning is a form of learning in which organisms learn to predict events based on relationships between events. At its most basic, classical conditioning is a learning process that creates new reflexes. A **reflex** is a simple, relatively automatic, stimulus–response sequence mediated by the nervous system. If your knee is tapped with a rubber mallet as you sit on an examining table, your lower leg will jerk forward. If a bright light is flashed in your eyes, you will blink. If lemon juice is squirted into your mouth, you will salivate. If a loud alarm suddenly clangs, your muscles will tighten. In each of these examples, a particular well-defined event in the environment, a **stimulus**, results in a particular well-defined behavior, a **response**. The tap on the knee, the flash of light, the squirt of lemon juice, and the sudden alarm are stimuli (note that *stimuli* is the plural form of *stimulus*). The leg jerk, the eye blink, the salivation, and the muscle tightening are responses.

To be considered a reflex, the response to a stimulus must be mediated by the nervous system. Messages carried by nerves from the eyes, ears, skin, or other sensory organs enter the spinal cord or brain and act there to produce messages in nerves running outward to muscles and glands. If something hits you and you fall down as a result of the direct force of the impact, that is not a reflex. If something hits you and your muscles respond in a way that tends to keep you from falling down, that *is* a reflex. Because reflexes are mediated by the nervous system, they can be modified by experience.

One simple effect of experience on reflexes is **habituation**, defined as a decline in the magnitude of a reflexive response when the stimulus is repeated several times in succession. Simply put, habituation occurs when we get *used* to something. Habituation is one of the simplest forms of learning. It does not produce a new stimulus–response sequence but only weakens one that previously existed. For instance, we (David Bjorklund) have a cuckoo clock in our house, with birds chirping followed by Bavarian music on the hour and half hour. It's right outside our bedroom and it never wakes us up at night. When we have houseguests, however, and forget to turn the clock "off," we hear about it the next morning. We have habituated to the repeated event that has no consequence for us, whereas our houseguests have not. It makes good survival sense to be alert to novel stimulation. However, when that stimulation is repeated and nothing is associated with it, it makes further good sense to ignore it, permitting our limited attention to be allocated elsewhere.

Not all reflexes undergo habituation, for example, the knee-jerk reflex discussed earlier. One reflex that does is the startle response to a sudden loud sound. You might jump the first time the sound occurs, but each time the sound is repeated and nothing bad happens, you respond less, and soon you show no visible response at all.

Fundamentals of Classical Conditioning

Classical conditioning, unlike habituation, is a form of reflex learning that does produce a new stimulus–response sequence. It was first described and most extensively studied by a Russian physiologist, Ivan Pavlov. Like many innovations in science, the discovery of classical conditioning was accidental. Its discoverer was not looking to explain a major form of learning, but rather was interested in reflexes involved in digestion. In fact, Ivan Petrovich Pavlov (1849–1936) received the 1904 Nobel Prize in Physiology and Medicine for his work on digestive reflexes in dogs before he turned his attention to learning.

Pavlov's Initial Discovery of Classical Conditioning

Pavlov's initial discovery of what we now call classical conditioning emerged from his earlier studies of digestive reflexes in dogs. Using permanently implanted tubes to collect salivary and stomach juices from dogs (see **Figure 8.1**), he and his team of researchers found, for example, that a dog salivates differently when different kinds of food are placed in its mouth. Juicy meat triggers a very thick saliva; dry bread, a wetter saliva; and acidic fluids, a wetter one yet. In a fine-grained analysis, these represent three different reflexes, with three different stimuli eliciting measurably different salivary secretions.

In the course of these studies, Pavlov encountered a problem. Dogs that had been given food on previous occasions in his experiments would salivate before they received any food. Apparently, signals that regularly preceded food, such as the sight of the food or the sound associated with its delivery, alerted the dogs to the upcoming stimulation and caused them to salivate. At first Pavlov was content to treat this simply as a source of experimental error. He called it "psychic secretion," implying that it was outside the physiologist's realm of study, and he attempted to eliminate it by developing ways to introduce the food into the dog's mouth without any warning. But then it occurred to Pavlov that the premature salivation might be a phenomenon that could be studied physiologically. Rather than call it psychic secretion, perhaps he could consider it a reflex and analyze it objectively, just as he had analyzed the reflexive salivary response to food in the mouth. This insight led Pavlov (1927/1960) to his first experiments on conditioned reflexes.

The Procedure and Generality of Classical Conditioning

To study such reflexes, Pavlov deliberately controlled the signals that preceded food. In one experiment he sounded a bell just before placing food in the dog's mouth. After several such pairings of a bell with food, the dog would salivate in response to the bell sound alone; no food was necessary. Pavlov called the stimulus (the bell sound, in this case) a ***conditioned stimulus***, and he called the response to that stimulus (salivation) a ***conditioned response***. Likewise, the original stimulus (food placed in the mouth) and response (salivation) are referred to as an ***unconditioned stimulus*** and ***unconditioned response***, respectively.

For a diagram of Pavlov's basic procedure and an opportunity to review all of these terms, see **Figure 8.2**. The procedure today is called *classical conditioning*, or sometimes *Pavlovian conditioning*.

In other experiments, Pavlov and his colleagues varied the stimuli used as the conditioned stimulus. They concluded that, essentially, any environmental event that the animal could detect could become a conditioned stimulus for salivation. Sounds produced by bells, buzzers, or tuning forks were highly effective and used most often because they were the easiest to control. But Pavlov's group also produced conditioned responses to visual stimuli, such as a black

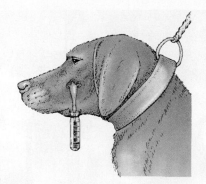

FIGURE 8.1 Pavlov's method for measuring salivation One of the dog's salivary ducts is surgically connected to a glass tube. In his early experiments, Pavlov learned that dogs produce different salivary secretions in response to different foods. Later he found that the dogs could be conditioned to produce these secretions in response to stimuli that reliably precede food.

FOCUS 2

How did Pavlov discover the conditioned response?

FOCUS 3

After his initial discovery, how did Pavlov systematize the process of conditioning, and what names did he give to the relevant stimuli and responses?

FIGURE 8.2 Classical-conditioning procedure A neutral stimulus initially does not elicit a response. After it is paired for several trials with an unconditioned stimulus, however, it becomes a conditioned stimulus and does elicit a response.

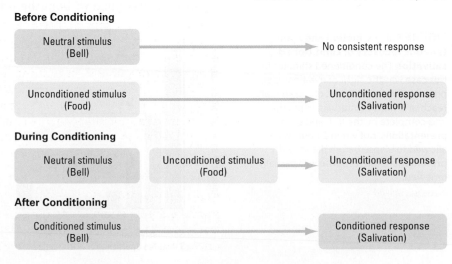

Before Conditioning

| Neutral stimulus (Bell) | → | No consistent response |

| Unconditioned stimulus (Food) | → | Unconditioned response (Salivation) |

During Conditioning

| Neutral stimulus (Bell) | Unconditioned stimulus (Food) | → | Unconditioned response (Salivation) |

After Conditioning

| Conditioned stimulus (Bell) | → | Conditioned response (Salivation) |

Sovfoto

■ **Pavlov conducting an experiment** Pavlov was the personification of the dedicated scientist. His research so engulfed his life that he is said to have hardly noticed such events as the Bolshevik Revolution of 1917, which radically transformed his country. One former co-worker (Gantt, in 1975, as quoted by Hothersall, 1995) recalled Pavlov's angry scolding of an assistant who arrived 10 minutes late to start an experiment: "But Professor," exclaimed the assistant, "there's a revolution going on, with shooting in the streets." To which Pavlov replied, "What the _____ difference does that make when you've work to do in the laboratory? Next time there's a revolution, get up earlier!"

square; to olfactory stimuli, such as the odor of camphor; and to tactile (touch) stimuli, such as pressure applied to a spot on the animal's skin. In each case, the stimulus did not initially elicit the salivary response, but it did so after having been paired with food a number of times.

Of course, classical conditioning is not limited to salivary responses. Researchers have demonstrated this in hundreds of laboratory experiments, and you have experienced countless examples of such conditioning in your everyday life. The sound of a dentist's drill may elicit a conditioned cringing response because of its previous pairing with pain. The sight of the toilet when you enter a bathroom to comb your hair may elicit a previously unfelt urge to urinate due to previous pairings of that sight with that urge. If you once had an automobile accident at a curve in the road on a wet day, each new encounter with such a curve on such a day may elicit a conditioned tensing of muscles. If you go through a day recording instances of conditioned responses, you will soon have a very long list.

Extinction of Conditioned Responses, and Recovery from Extinction

FOCUS 4

How can a conditioned response be extinguished? What evidence led Pavlov and others to conclude that extinction does not return the animal to its original, untrained state?

One question that interested Pavlov had to do with the permanence of a conditioned response. Once a dog has learned to salivate to the sound of a bell, does this reflex still occur if the bell is sounded for many trials *without* the unconditioned food-in-mouth stimulus? Pavlov's group found that without food, the bell elicited less and less salivation on each trial and eventually none at all, a phenomenon they labeled ***extinction***. But they also found that extinction does not return the animal fully to the unconditioned state. The mere passage of time following extinction can partially renew the conditioned response, a phenomenon now known as ***spontaneous recovery*** (see **Figure 8.3**). Moreover, a single pairing of the conditioned stimulus with the unconditioned stimulus can fully renew the conditioned response, which can be extinguished again only by another series of trials in which the conditioned stimulus is presented without the unconditioned stimulus.

FIGURE 8.3 Extinction and spontaneous recovery of conditioned salivation The conditioned stimulus in this case was the sight of meat powder, presented repeatedly out of the animal's reach at 3-minute intervals. Extinction was complete by the fifth and sixth presentations, but when 2 hours were allowed to elapse before the seventh presentation, the response was partially renewed.

(Data from Pavlov, 1927/1960.)

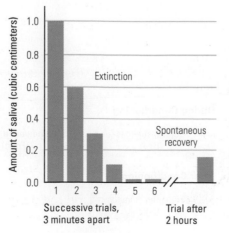

On the basis of such findings, Pavlov concluded that the conditioned response is not truly lost during extinction, but is somehow inhibited, and that it can be disinhibited by such means as the passage of time or the recurrence of the unconditioned stimulus. This conclusion has been validated in many experiments since Pavlov's time (Bouton et al., 2006). In research with conditioned eye-blink reflexes in rabbits, researchers have shown that conditioning and extinction involve different sets of neurons in the brain (Medina et al., 2002). Neurons involved in the conditioning of this response excite other neurons that promote eye blinking. Neurons involved in extinction inhibit those same eye-blink neurons, thereby counteracting but not abolishing the conditioned neural response, just as Pavlov would have predicted.

Generalization and Discrimination in Classical Conditioning

Pavlov and his colleagues found that, after conditioning, animals would show the conditioned response not just to the original conditioned stimulus but also to new stimuli that resembled that stimulus. This phenomenon is called ***generalization***. They found, further, that the magnitude of the response to the new stimulus depended on the degree of similarity between the new stimulus and the original conditioned stimulus. Thus, a dog conditioned to salivate to a 1,000-hertz (cycles-per-second) tone also salivated to tones of other frequencies, but the further the tone's frequency was from the original conditioned stimulus, the less the dog salivated to it.

Generalization between two stimuli can be abolished if the response to one is reinforced while the response to the other is extinguished, a procedure called ***discrimination training***. As an example, Pavlov's group used a dog whose conditioning to the sight of a black square had generalized to a gray square. After a series of trials in which presentations of the gray square were never followed by food and presentations of the black square were always followed by food, the dog stopped salivating to the gray square but continued to salivate to the black one. The researchers continued this procedure with ever-darker shades of gray, until they eventually conditioned the dog to discriminate a black square from a gray one that was so nearly black that a human observer had difficulty telling them apart (Pavlov, 1927/1960).

Generalization as an Index of Subjective Similarity

In experiments with human subjects, researchers following Pavlov discovered that generalization occurs not just when two stimuli are physically similar to one another but also when they are similar in their subjective meaning to the person.

In one experiment, Gregory Razran (1939) used college students as subjects, printed words as conditioned stimuli, and a squirt of lemon juice into the mouth as the unconditioned stimulus. By pairing each word with lemon juice, Razran conditioned students to salivate to the words *style, urn, freeze,* and *surf.* He then tested the students to see if the conditioned response would generalize to other words that had never been paired with lemon juice. Of most interest, he found that the students salivated more to the words *fashion, vase, chill,* and *wave* than to the words *stile, earn, frieze,* and *serf.* That is, the conditioned response generalized more to printed words that resembled the original conditioned stimuli in meaning than to those that resembled the originals in physical appearance or sound. Thus, the true conditioned stimuli in this case were not the physical sights or sounds of the words but the subjects' interpretations of them.

Relevance of Pavlov's Work to the Emergence of Behaviorism

Early in the twentieth century, psychologists in North America were struggling to develop scientific methods appropriate for psychology. Some followed a school of thought known as ***behaviorism***, which avoided terms that refer to mental entities (thoughts, emotions, motives, etc.), because such entities cannot be directly observed. Behaviorists believed that psychology should focus on the relationship between observable events in the environment (stimuli) and observable behavioral reactions to those events (responses). While behaviorism can still address complex human behavior such as cognition and language, it does so from a behavioral perspective.

The principal founder of behaviorism, John B. Watson (1913), put it this way: "In a system of psychology completely worked out, given the response the stimuli can be predicted, and given the stimuli the response can be predicted." In Watson's view, all of behavior is, in essence, reflex-like in nature. Watson did not deny the existence of mental processes, but he believed that these are too obscure to

FOCUS 5

How can generalization in classical conditioning be abolished through discrimination training? How can discrimination training be used to assess an animal's sensory capacities?

FOCUS 6

How do we know that generalization in classical conditioning can be based on the meaning of a stimulus, not just on its physical characteristics?

FOCUS 7

What were the characteristics of early, North American behaviorism? Why were Pavlov's findings on conditioning particularly appealing to behaviorists?

S-R Theory of Classical Conditioning

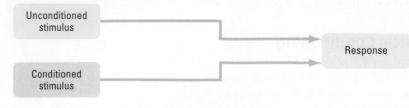

S-S Theory of Classical Conditioning

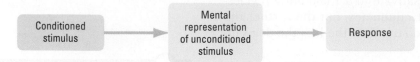

FIGURE 8.4 Comparison of S-R and S-S theories of classical conditioning According to the S-R theory, conditioning produces a direct bond between the conditioned stimulus and the response. According to the S-S theory, conditioning produces a bond between the conditioned stimulus and a mental representation of the unconditioned stimulus, which, in turn, produces the response. Support for the S-S theory comes from experiments showing that weakening the unconditioned response (through habituation), after conditioning, also weakens the conditioned response.

FOCUS 8

How did Pavlov's S-S theory of classical conditioning differ from Watson's S-R theory? How does an experiment involving habituation of the unconditioned stimulus support the S-S theory?

be studied scientifically; instead, he argued that behavior could be understood and described without reference to mental processes.

In addition to developing objective, stimulus–response descriptions of behavior, the early behaviorists established learning as their main explanatory concept. They maintained that a person's behavior at any given time is determined by that person's past experiences with the environment. Watson and the other early behaviorists were much inspired by Pavlov's work on conditioning. In contrast to the empiricist philosophers (discussed in Chapter 1), who talked about learning in terms of unseen associations occurring in the mind, Pavlov seemed to provide an objective, stimulus–response way of studying and understanding learning. If all behavior is essentially reflexive, and if most behavior is learned, and if conditioning is the process by which reflexes are learned, then conditioning would appear to be psychology's most basic explanatory concept. In one of his early books, Watson (1924) attempted to describe even complex examples of human learning in terms of what we now call classical conditioning.

What Is Learned in Classical Conditioning?

We now return to the question raised earlier: What, really, is learned in classical conditioning? Watson's (1924) and other early behaviorists' answer to that question was simply that a new stimulus–response connection is learned. From their perspective, Pavlov's conditioned dog salivated to the bell sounding because of a direct, learned connection between that sound and salivation. This *stimulus-response (S-R)* theory of classical conditioning is diagrammed in the top part of **Figure 8.4**. Pavlov himself, however, had a different theory.

Evidence That Stimulus–Stimulus Associations Are Learned

Pavlov (1927/1960) believed that the animal does not learn a direct stimulus–response connection but, rather, learns a connection between two stimuli—the conditioned stimulus and the unconditioned stimulus. Because the bell and food have been paired in past experience, a neural bond is formed between their representations in the brain such that the sound of the bell now activates the part of the brain that was formerly activated by food, and that, in turn, elicits salivation. Using mental rather than neural terms, we could say that the dog salivates to the bell because the bell sound elicits in the dog a mental representation of food (bell → mental representation of food → salivation). This *stimulus-stimulus (S-S)* theory of classical conditioning is illustrated in the bottom part of Figure 8.4.

The S-S theory did not appeal to Watson and his followers because it posited the existence of an unobserved event in the animal's mind, the mental representation of the original unconditioned stimulus. However, contrary to the early behaviorists' claims, reference to unseen events can be very useful in science if it leads to clear-cut predictions about events that can be seen. Gravity cannot be seen, yet theories of gravity can be developed and tested with experiments on falling objects. The S-S and S-R theories make different predictions about how animals will behave under certain conditions, so it is possible to test the theories with experiments. Many such experiments have been conducted by now, and the weight of the evidence favors the S-S theory for most examples of conditioning in mammals and birds (Anderson, 2000).

Consider a classic experiment conducted by Robert Rescorla (1973) using rats as subjects, a loud sound as the unconditioned stimulus, and a signal light as the conditioned stimulus. The loud sound elicited "freezing" (a fear response in which the rat stands motionless) as an unconditioned response. By pairing the signal light with the loud sound, Rescorla conditioned rats to freeze when the signal light came on. Now, the question was: Did the rats freeze in response to the signal light because of a direct, learned connection between the light and freezing, in accordance with the S-R theory (light → freezing)? Or did they freeze because of a learned connection between the light and the loud sound, in accordance with the S-S theory (light → mental representation of loud sound → freezing)?

To answer the question, Rescorla habituated the response to the loud sound in half of the conditioned rats. That is, he presented the loud sound many times without the signal light until the rats no longer froze in response to it. Then he again tested the rats with the signal light. Would the rats that no longer froze in response to the loud sound continue to freeze in response to the light? The S-R and S-S theories make different predictions. According to the S-R theory, the habituated rats should continue, as before, to freeze in response to the light because conditioning would have produced a direct connection between the light and freezing. But according to the S-S theory, the habituated rats should *not* freeze in response to the light. Why? Because conditioning would have produced a connection between the light and a representation of the loud sound, which itself no longer elicits freezing. Rescorla's results supported the S-S theory: Habituation to the sound greatly reduced the degree to which the rats froze in response to the light.

Classical Conditioning Interpreted as Learned Expectancy

The S-S theory of classical conditioning, by its nature, is more *cognitive* than the S-R theory. As explained in Chapter 1, the term *cognition* refers to knowledge, or information, held in the mind. Cognitive theories are theories in which hypothesized, unobserved entities within the mind are used to explain and predict behavior, contrary to the dictates of behaviorism. The S-S theory is cognitive because it holds that the observed stimulus–response relation is mediated by an inner, mental representation of the original unconditioned stimulus. Cognitive theorists have argued that this mental representation may be best understood as an *expectation* of the unconditioned stimulus. According to this view, Pavlov's dogs learned to expect food when they heard the bell.

Expectancy theory helps make sense of the observation that a conditioned response is often quite different from the unconditioned response. Consider again a dog being conditioned to a sounding bell that precedes food. In response to food, the dog not only salivates but also chews (if it is solid food) and swallows. Salivation becomes conditioned to the bell, but chewing and swallowing usually do not. Moreover, the bell comes to elicit not only salivation but also responses that do not usually occur in response to the food-in-mouth stimulus—such as tail wagging, food begging, and looking in the direction of the usual source of food (Jenkins et al., 1978). According to expectancy theory, all these responses, including salivation, occur not because they were previously elicited by the unconditioned stimulus but because they are the dog's responses to the expectation of food:

bell → expectation of food → tail wagging, food begging, salivation, etc.

Rescorla summed up his cognitive view of classical conditioning as follows: "[Classical] conditioning is not a stupid process by which the organism willy-nilly forms associations between any two stimuli that happen to co-occur. Rather, the organism is best seen as an information seeker using logical and perceptual relations among

Jeffrey Sylvester/Getty Images

■ **Learned expectancy** There is nothing inscrutable about this young tiger cat. The sound of the can being attached to the opener permits her to predict the arrival of food. Her response is not identical to her response to food itself, but one of rapt attention.

FOCUS 9

How does the cognitive construct of expectancy help explain the ways in which conditioned responses differ from unconditioned responses?

events, along with its own preconceptions, to form a sophisticated representation of its world" (1988, p. 154). By this, Rescorla does not mean that animals spend time consciously deliberating about these relationships. Rather, he means that animals have built-in neural mechanisms that automatically make the appropriate calculations.

Conditioning Depends on the Predictive Value of the Conditioned Stimulus

FOCUS 10

What are three conditions in which the pairing of a new stimulus with an unconditioned stimulus does *not* result in classical conditioning? How do these observations support the idea that classical conditioning is a process of learning to predict the onset of the unconditioned stimulus?

Support for the expectancy theory of classical conditioning comes from research showing that conditioning occurs only, or at least mainly, when the new stimulus provides information that truly helps the animal predict the arrival of the unconditioned stimulus. Here are three classes of such findings:

1. *The conditioned stimulus must precede the unconditioned stimulus.* Classical conditioning is most effective if the onset of the conditioned stimulus comes immediately before the unconditioned stimulus. Conditioning commonly doesn't occur at all if the conditioned stimulus comes either simultaneously with or just after the unconditioned stimulus (Lieberman, 2000). (See **Figure 8.5a** and **b.**) This observation makes sense if the animal is seeking predictive information; a stimulus that does not precede the unconditioned stimulus is useless as a predictor and thus is ignored by the animal. Trying to achieve conditioning by placing the conditioned stimulus after the unconditioned stimulus is like trying to reduce traffic accidents by placing "Dangerous Curve" signs after the curves in the road rather than before them.

2. *The conditioned stimulus must signal heightened probability of occurrence of the unconditioned stimulus.* Conditioning depends not just on the total number of pairings of the conditioned stimulus and unconditioned stimulus, but also on the number of times that either stimulus occurs without being paired with the other. As the number of pairings increases, conditioning is strengthened; but as the number of stimulus occurrences *without* pairing increases, conditioning is weakened (Rescorla, 1988). (See **Figure 8.5c.**) The animal's behavior suggests that in some way its nervous system computes two probabilities—the probability that the unconditioned stimulus will immediately follow any given occurrence of the conditioned stimulus and the probability that the unconditioned stimulus will occur at other times—and accepts the conditioned stimulus as a predictor only if the first probability is greater than the second.

   If dangerous curves in the road are no more likely to occur right after "Dangerous Curve" signs than they are to occur in the absence of such signs, the signs would be useless to us as predictors of curves, and we would be well advised to ignore them and try to predict curves using other means. This would be true no matter how many times, in our driving experience, we happened to come across such a sign right before an actual curve. Rats in conditioning experiments behave as if they have that insight.

3. *Conditioning is ineffective when the animal already has a good predictor.* If one conditioned stimulus already reliably precedes an unconditioned stimulus, a new stimulus, presented simultaneously with the original conditioned stimulus, generally does not become a conditioned stimulus. Even after many such pairings the new stimulus fails to elicit the conditioned response if it is presented alone. This failure of conditioning is called the *blocking effect*; the already-conditioned stimulus *blocks* conditioning to the new stimulus that has been paired with it (Kamin, 1969). (See **Figure 8.5d.**) A cognitive interpretation of this is that the animal has already solved the problem of predicting the unconditioned stimulus and has no reason to look for a new predictor.

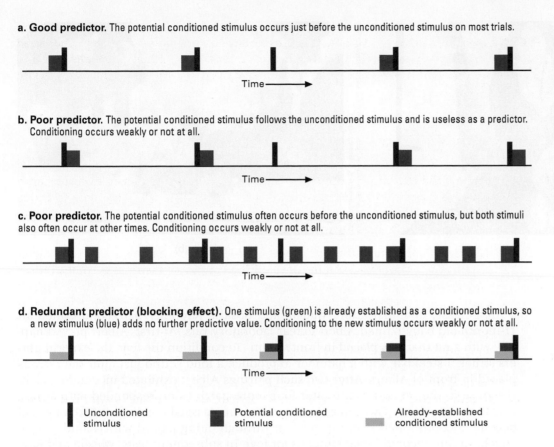

a. Good predictor. The potential conditioned stimulus occurs just before the unconditioned stimulus on most trials.

Time ⟶

b. Poor predictor. The potential conditioned stimulus follows the unconditioned stimulus and is useless as a predictor. Conditioning occurs weakly or not at all.

Time ⟶

c. Poor predictor. The potential conditioned stimulus often occurs before the unconditioned stimulus, but both stimuli also often occur at other times. Conditioning occurs weakly or not at all.

Time ⟶

d. Redundant predictor (blocking effect). One stimulus (green) is already established as a conditioned stimulus, so a new stimulus (blue) adds no further predictive value. Conditioning to the new stimulus occurs weakly or not at all.

Time ⟶

| | Unconditioned stimulus | | Potential conditioned stimulus | | Already-established conditioned stimulus |

FIGURE 8.5 Patterns of stimulus presentation in which conditioning does or does not occur The top time line illustrates a pattern of stimulus presentation in which conditioning occurs. The three lower time lines illustrate patterns in which poor or no conditioning occurs even though the potential conditioned stimulus (blue) and unconditioned stimulus (red) are often paired. Strong conditioning occurs when the potential conditioned stimulus is a reliable and nonredundant predictor of the unconditioned stimulus.

Cognitive psychologists often emphasize that their use of terms such as *expectation* and *prediction* does not imply anything mystical. The terms describe the type of information that underlies the animal's behavior but say nothing about the physical form of that information, which presumably results from computations automatically made by neurons in the brain. Some psychologists develop computer models to explain how such computations might be made.

Conditioned Fear, Liking, Hunger, and Sexual Arousal

From an evolutionary perspective, classical conditioning is a way for individuals to learn to prepare themselves for imminent events that are biologically significant. A conditioned stimulus preceding a painful or startling event can elicit fear and bodily reactions that help brace the individual for that event; a conditioned stimulus preceding delivery of food can elicit hunger and bodily responses that help prepare the gastrointestinal tract for food; and a conditioned stimulus preceding an opportunity for sex can elicit high sex drive and bodily responses that help prepare the body for copulation. Here we'll elaborate on these ideas.

Watson's Classic Demonstration of Fear Conditioning

John B. Watson was the first psychologist to show that the emotion of fear can be conditioned in human beings. Consistent with his behavioral perspective, Watson (1924) defined fear not as a feeling but as a set of observable responses: "a catching of the breath, a stiffening of the whole body, a turning away of the body from the source of stimulation, a running or crawling from it." On the basis of this definition, Watson found two unconditioned stimuli for fear in human infants—sudden loud sound and sudden loss of support (as when a baby slips out of an adult's hands). Other stimuli, he argued, come to elicit fear as a result of conditioning.

 FOCUS 11

How did Watson demonstrate that the emotion of fear can be conditioned?

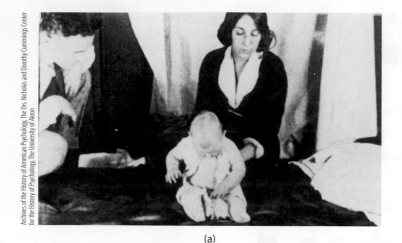

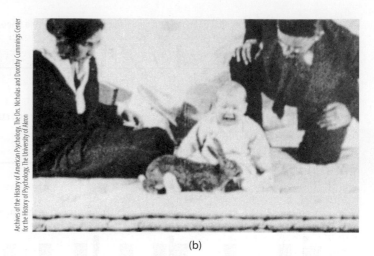

(a)   (b)

FIGURE 8.6 Little Albert with Watson, Rayner, and furry animals Prior to the conditioning experience, 11-month-old Albert played happily with a live laboratory rat (left). After he was conditioned to respond fearfully to the rat, he also cried at the sight of other furry objects, including a rabbit, thereby exhibiting generalization (right).

In a classic demonstration, Watson and Rosalie Rayner (1920) conditioned an 11-month-old baby named Albert to fear laboratory rats. At first, Albert played happily with a rat that was placed in front of him. To condition the fear, the experimenters struck a steel bar with a hammer to produce a loud sound just after the rat was placed in front of Albert. After two such pairings Albert exhibited moderate fear in response to the rat alone, and after four more pairings he responded with strong fear to the rat alone. Thus, in the terminology of classical conditioning, the rat had become a conditioned stimulus for fear through being paired with a loud sound, which was an unconditioned stimulus for fear. In subsequent tests, Watson and Rayner showed that Albert's conditioned fear generalized to other furry objects, such as a rabbit (see **Figure 8.6**).

You might (very appropriately) wonder about the ethics of this experiment. The experiment most likely would not be approved by a modern ethics review committee and would not be allowed today. In fairness to Watson, however, there is no reason to believe that Albert's experience in this demonstration was any more frightening than are the countless startling events that everyone experiences in the normal course of growing up. Moreover, Watson was far more interested in how to eliminate unwanted fears than in how to produce them.

Fear, of course, is not the only emotional response that can be conditioned through Pavlovian procedures. When beer, cigarette, and car advertisers pair their products with scenes of beautiful people having wonderful times, they are trying to get you to drool with anticipated pleasure, like Pavlov's dogs, whenever you see their products.

Liking

People acquire preferences for (and against) things throughout life. Some preferences seem to be instinctive, or species-typical—such as the human preferences for sweet flavors and social stimulation. Most, however, are learned; and this learning seems to occur primarily through classical conditioning. *Evaluative conditioning* refers to changes in the strength of liking or disliking of a stimulus as a result of being paired with another positive or negative stimulus. Modern research is based on a study by A. B. Levey and Irene Martin (1975), in which college students were shown picture postcards and asked to select their two favorite and their two least favorite. These cards served as the unconditioned stimuli. They were then paired with neutral cards (the conditioned stimuli)—some with the liked cards and others with the "disliked" cards—and the subjects were later asked to rate the cards

■ **Conditioning young humans to love beer** The unconditioned stimulus is the happy, sexually suggestive scene. The conditioned stimulus is the beer label.

again. The researchers found that subjects' ratings for the neutral cards changed as a function of which cards they had been earlier paired with: Cards paired with the liked pictures were rated more positively than before, and cards paired with the disliked pictures were rated more negatively than before. This effect, using variants of this procedure for a wide range of stimuli, has been reported in hundreds of studies (De Houwer et al., 2001; Hoffman et al., 2010). It suggests that our likes and dislikes, which motivate much of our behavior, are governed to a significant degree by classical conditioning.

Conditioned Hunger

A signal that reliably precedes food becomes a conditioned stimulus not just for salivation, but for a whole set of responses that help prepare the body for food and induce a state of hunger: the secretion of digestive juices into the stomach, the secretion of certain hormones into the bloodstream, and so on (Woods et al., 2000). Thus, we find in humans the well-known appetizer effect. The taste of a small morsel of food, the smell of food, a dinner bell, a clock indicating that it is dinnertime, or any other signal that reliably precedes a meal can rather quickly cause us to feel much hungrier than we were feeling just before the signal. Other animals, too, begin to act as if they are hungry, as indicated by their food-seeking behavior, when subjected to stimuli that have preceded food in the past (Pavlov, 1927/1960).

In cases where a conditioned stimulus always precedes a specific kind of food, the conditioned hunger that occurs may be specific for that food. For example, in one series of experiments, rats that were made hungry through food deprivation underwent conditioning in which a tone always preceded the delivery of a certain kind of food. Later, when they were not food deprived, they would seek out and eat that same kind of food, but not other foods, when the tone sounded (Petrovich & Gallagher, 2007). The rats behaved as if the tone elicited a sudden craving for that specific, previously tone-paired food. Such findings help us understand why the golden arches of McDonald's, spotted on road signs, can cause a sudden craving for foods we have previously eaten at McDonald's. Purveyors of fast foods are capitalizing on classical conditioning when they plaster the environment with specific symbols that are associated over and over again with their specific foods.

Conditioned Sexual Arousal

A number of experiments have demonstrated that sexual arousal can be conditioned in nonhuman (Pfaus et al., 2012) and human subjects (Both et al., 2011; Hoffman et al., 2012). Typically, a previously neutral stimulus is used as the conditioned stimulus (a photo showing a jar of pennies was used in one experiment) and an erotic, sexually arousing film clip or sexually arousing vibration applied mechanically to the genitals is used as the unconditioned stimulus. Sexual arousal is measured in men by a strain gauge that indicates erection of the penis and in women by a device that responds to increased blood flow to the vagina. As classical conditioning principles would predict, a stimulus that initially does not elicit arousal comes to elicit it after several pairings with the unconditioned stimulus.

Experiments on sexual conditioning in nonhuman animals have generally used males as subjects, with either the sight of a sexually receptive female or physical access to such a female as the unconditioned stimulus. The usual result is that a signal that reliably precedes the presentation of the female becomes a conditioned stimulus for a set of responses that help prepare the male for courtship and mating (Domjan, 2003; Pfaus et al., 2012). Experiments have shown that such conditioning is biologically adaptive in the most direct sense of the term: It increases the number of offspring the animal produces.

In one experiment with domesticated quail, those male birds that received a conditioned stimulus prior to the opportunity to copulate with a hen fathered many

FOCUS 12

How can the appetizer effect and sudden cravings for specific foods be explained in terms of classical conditioning?

FOCUS 13

How has sexual arousal been conditioned in humans and other animals? What is the evidence, from experiments with nonhuman animals, that such conditioning promotes success in reproduction?

more offspring than did those who were presented with a hen without forewarning (Matthews et al., 2007). In this case, the improved fertilization rate apparently resulted from an increase in the number of sperm cells released by the male birds during ejaculation. The conditioned stimulus apparently mobilized the sperm-release mechanism prior to the presentation of the hen so that more sperm were available at the time of copulation.

Conditioned Drug Reactions

As you have just seen, bodily reactions associated with natural emotions and drives can be conditioned. In their early experiments, Pavlov's group showed that bodily reactions to drugs can also be conditioned. In one demonstration with a dog, they paired a tone with injection of a drug that elicited restlessness and vomiting. After repeated pairings, the dog began to exhibit those responses to the tone alone (Pavlov, 1927/1960). Since then, many experiments have shown that drug reactions can be conditioned. Researchers have found, for example, that for habitual coffee drinkers the mere smell and taste of coffee can produce increased alertness, apparently because of the previous pairings of that smell and taste with the effects of caffeine (Flaten & Blumenthal, 1999).

Conditioned Compensatory Reactions to Drugs

● FOCUS 14

Why is the conditioned response to a drug-related stimulus often the opposite of the direct effect of the drug?

Many drugs produce two effects: a direct effect followed by a compensatory reaction that counteracts the direct effect and tends to restore the normal bodily state. In such cases it is often found (for reasons to be explained shortly) that only the compensatory reaction becomes conditioned. As a result, a stimulus that reliably precedes delivery of the drug produces a conditioned response that is opposite to the drug's direct effect. An example of such a drug is morphine. A direct effect of morphine is reduction in sensitivity to pain, but this is counteracted by reflexive responses in the body that tend to restore normal pain sensitivity. When rats are repeatedly injected with morphine in a distinctive environment, that environment becomes a conditioned stimulus for the counteractive response. When the rats are subsequently placed in that environment without morphine, the conditioned reaction occurs: The rats become temporarily hypersensitive to pain (Hinson et al., 1986).

The explanation of such effects rests on the fact that only responses that occur in a reflexive manner, involving the central nervous system (spinal cord and brain), can be conditioned (Siegel, 1999). The direct effects of some drugs are not reflexes and therefore cannot be conditioned, but the counteractive effects are reflexes. As an analogy, consider what would happen if a bell sound (conditioned stimulus) reliably preceded a shove from the front (unconditioned stimulus). The shove would tend to push you backward, but you would counter that with a reflexive movement forward. Only the reflexive movement forward would be conditioned, so if the bell were sounded without the shove, you might fall on your face—a reaction opposite to the direct (nonreflexive) effect of the shove. The body protects itself with counteractive reflexes to all sorts of interventions (such as shoves and drugs) that disrupt its normal functioning. The conditioning of such reflexes is normally useful because it allows the counteraction to begin even before the potentially harmful stimulus strikes.

Conditioned Reactions as Causes of Drug Tolerance

● FOCUS 15

How does classical conditioning contribute to the development of drug tolerance? Why is it dangerous for a drug addict to take his or her usual drug dose in an unusual environment?

Shepard Siegel and his colleagues in Canada have shown that the phenomenon of drug tolerance depends at least partly on conditioning. *Drug tolerance* refers to the decline in physiological and behavioral effects that occur with some drugs when they are taken repeatedly. Because of tolerance, people who regularly take a drug have to increase their doses over time to continue to achieve the original effects. To some degree, tolerance is a result of long-term buildup of physiological systems in the body that help to counteract the drug's effects (Poulos & Cappell, 1991). However, it is also to some degree the result of conditioning. Because of conditioning, stimuli that normally precede drug intake cause the conditioned compensatory reaction to begin before the drug is actually taken, and that reaction counteracts the direct effect of the drug. For example, a conditioned increase in heart rate would counteract the effect of a drug whose direct effect is to slow the heart.

Siegel and his colleagues have found that many cases of "overdose" in heroin addicts are actually cases in which addicts took their usual drug doses in unusual environments (Siegel, 1984; Siegel & Ramos, 2002). When an addict takes a drug in the usual drug-taking environment, cues in that environment produce a conditioned compensatory reaction that allows the addict's body to tolerate a large dose of the drug. If the addict takes the same amount of the drug in a novel environment, where the conditioned cues aren't present, the full impact of the drug kicks in before a counteractive reaction begins, and the result can be severe illness or even death. Consistent with this interpretation, rats that had received many morphine injections in a specific highly distinctive cage were much more likely to survive a high dose of the drug if it was given to them in that same cage than if it was given in a different setting (S. Siegel, 2005). Similar effects have been shown in animal experiments using alcohol (Melchior, 1990) and various other drugs (Goudie, 1990).

■ **A powerful conditioned stimulus for a heroin addict** The stimuli associated with drug preparation become strong conditioned stimuli for bodily responses that are opposite to the direct effect of the drug. Such responses help protect the body from the drug's harmful effects, but they also produce intense drug craving and contribute to relapse in people who have gone through a period of drug withdrawal.

Conditioned Reactions as Causes of Drug Relapse After Withdrawal

Another drug phenomenon that is at least partly explained by conditioned compensatory reactions is that of relapse by addicts who have undergone periods of drug withdrawal (Siegel, 1999). Many addicts withdraw from drugs during a stay at a residential treatment center that is quite unlike their home environment. After some period of drug-free living at the center, they no longer experience withdrawal symptoms or feel a craving for the drug. However, when they return to their own homes and neighborhoods, they are once again surrounded by many cues that, for them, are associated with drug use. These cues elicit compensatory drug reactions, which feel like withdrawal symptoms and elicit a strongly felt need for the drug—a felt need that is all too often irresistible.

> **FOCUS 16**
>
> How does classical conditioning help explain drug relapse after an addict returns home from a treatment center?

In an effort to prevent such relapse, some drug treatment programs attempt to extinguish the effects of conditioning by repeatedly presenting addicts with stimuli associated with drug intake without the drug itself. Such programs have met with only partial success, however (Siegel & Ramos, 2002). It is impossible to identify and present all of the cues that have become conditioned stimuli for compensatory drug reactions for each addict in his or her home environment. Moreover, as you recall, effects of extinction can be quickly undone. Even one exposure to the unconditioned stimulus (the drug, in this case) can renew the conditioned responses to cues associated with it.

An addict's best hope for overcoming a long-term addiction may be to move permanently, if possible, to an entirely new environment. During the Vietnam War, many American soldiers became addicted to heroin in Vietnam. When they returned home, a surprisingly large number overcame their addiction immediately and never took heroin again (Robins et al., 1975). According to Siegel's analysis, this observation makes sense in view of the fact that they had left behind the cues that had become triggers for drug compensatory reactions and returned to an environment that contained none or few of those cues (Siegel, 1999).

SECTION REVIEW

Classical conditioning is the process involved in learning a new response; it enables prediction of and preparation for unconditioned stimuli.

Conditioning Procedure	Extinction	Generalization and Discrimination	What Is Learned?	Conditioned Emotion and Motivation	Conditioned Drug Reactions
■ Classical conditioning begins with an unconditioned response (e.g., food → salivation). ■ During conditioning, a neutral stimulus (e.g., bell sound) is presented just before the unconditioned stimulus (e.g., food). ■ After sufficient pairings, the neutral stimulus becomes a conditioned stimulus, which by itself elicits a response (e.g., bell sound → salivation).	■ If a conditioned stimulus is repeatedly presented without the unconditioned stimulus, the conditioned response stops occurring. ■ The conditioned response is not unlearned in extinction; it is merely suppressed, as shown by spontaneous recovery. ■ Conditioning and extinction apparently involve different sets of neurons, one promoting the conditioned response, the other inhibiting it.	■ Generalization occurs when a stimulus similar to the conditioned stimulus also elicits the conditioned response. ■ Discrimination (reduced generalization) results from repeatedly presenting the unconditioned stimulus followed by the conditioned stimulus and the similar stimulus followed by nothing.	■ According to the S-R theory, supported by early behaviorists, a link between the conditioned stimulus and response is learned. ■ According to the S-S theory, an association between the conditioned and unconditioned stimulus is learned. ■ The S-S theory implies expectancy and is supported by Rescorla's experiment. ■ Consistent with the expectancy idea, conditioning occurs best when the conditioned stimulus is a reliable predictor of the unconditioned stimulus.	■ Examples are the conditioning of fear (in little Albert), the conditioning of hunger (the appetizer effect), the conditioning of liking (evaluative conditioning), and the conditioning of sexual arousal. ■ In general, conditioned stimuli trigger responses that help prepare the individual for a biologically significant event.	■ With some drugs, repeated pairing with a conditioned stimulus causes that stimulus to elicit the same type of response as the drug. ■ With some other drugs, the conditioned stimulus elicits a response that is opposite to the drug response. Such conditioned compensatory reactions contribute to drug tolerance and drug relapse.

Operant Conditioning

We are pulled as well as pushed by events in our environment. That is, we do not just respond *to* stimuli, we also respond *for* stimuli. We behave in ways that are designed to *obtain* certain stimuli, or changes in our environment. My dog rubs against the door to be let out. I flip a switch to illuminate a room, press keys on my computer to produce words on a screen, and say, "Please pass the potatoes" to get potatoes. Most of my day seems to consist of behaviors of this sort—and I expect that most of my dog's day would, too, if there were more things that he could control. Surely, if Pavlov's dogs had had some way to control the delivery of food into their mouths, they would have done more than salivate; they would have pushed a lever, bitten open a bag, or done whatever was required to get the food.

Such actions are called ***operant responses*** because they *operate* on the world to produce some effect. They are also called *instrumental responses* because they function like instruments, or tools, to bring about some change in the environment. The process by which people or other animals learn to make operant responses is called ***operant conditioning***, or *instrumental conditioning*. Operant conditioning can be defined as a learning process by which the effect, or consequence, of a response influences the future rate of production of that response. In general, operant responses that produce effects that are favorable to the animal increase in rate, and those that produce effects that are unfavorable to the animal decrease in rate.

From the Law of Effect to Operant Conditioning: From Thorndike to Skinner

Although the labels "operant" and "instrumental" were not coined until the 1930s, this learning process was studied well before that time, most notably by E. L. Thorndike.

Thorndike's Puzzle-Box Procedure

At about the same time that Pavlov began his research on conditioning, a young American student of psychology, Edward Lee Thorndike (1898), published a report on his own learning experiments with various animals, including cats. Thorndike's training method was quite different from Pavlov's, and so was his description of the learning process. His apparatus, which he called a puzzle box, was a small cage that could be opened from inside by some relatively simple act, such as pulling a loop or pressing a lever (see **Figure 8.7**).

In one experiment, Thorndike deprived cats of food long enough to make them hungry and then placed them inside the puzzle box, one at a time, with food just outside it. When first placed inside, a cat would engage in many actions—such as clawing at the bars or pushing at the ceiling—in an apparent attempt to escape from the box and get at the food. Finally, apparently by accident, the cat would pull the loop or push the lever that opened the door to freedom and food. Thorndike repeated this procedure many times with each cat. He found that in early trials the animals made many useless movements before happening on the one that released the latch, but, on average, they escaped somewhat more quickly with each

FOCUS 17

How did Thorndike train cats to escape from a puzzle box? How did this research contribute to Thorndike's formulation of the law of effect?

FIGURE 8.7 One of Thorndike's puzzle boxes Thorndike designed the puzzle box so that a cat placed inside could open the door by stepping on the tab that pulls down on the string hanging from the ceiling. This in turn would pull up the bolt and allow the door to fall forward.

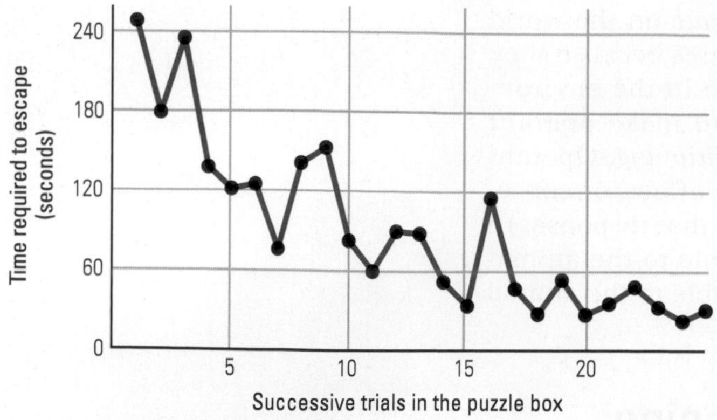

[Graph: Time required to escape (seconds) on y-axis from 0 to 240, Successive trials in the puzzle box on x-axis from 5 to 20]

FIGURE 8.8 Typical learning curve for a cat in Thorndike's puzzle box As illustrated here for a single cat, Thorndike found that cats usually took less time to escape from the box on successive trials, although a great deal of variability occurred from trial to trial.

(Data from Thorndike, 1898.)

successive trial. After about 20 to 30 trials, most cats would trip the latch to freedom and food almost as soon as they were shut in (see **Figure 8.8**).

An observer who joined Thorndike on trial 31 might have been impressed by the cat's intelligence; but, as Thorndike himself suggested, an observer who had sat through the earlier trials might have been more impressed by the creature's stupidity. In any event, Thorndike came to view learning as a trial-and-error process, through which an individual gradually becomes more likely to make responses that produce beneficial effects.

Thorndike's Law of Effect

Thorndike's basic training procedure differed fundamentally from Pavlov's. Pavlov produced learning by controlling the relationship between two stimuli in the animal's environment so that the animal learned to use one stimulus to predict the occurrence of the other. Thorndike, in contrast, produced learning by altering the consequence of some aspect of the animal's behavior. Thorndike's cats, unlike Pavlov's dogs, had some control over their environment. They could do more than merely predict when food would come; they could gain access to it through their own efforts.

Partly on the basis of his puzzle-box experiments, Thorndike (1898) formulated the ***law of effect***, which can be stated briefly as follows: *Responses that produce a satisfying effect in a particular situation become more likely to occur again in that situation, and responses that produce a discomforting effect become less likely to occur again in that situation.* In Thorndike's puzzle-box experiments, the *situation* presumably consisted of all the sights, sounds, smells, internal feelings, and so on that the hungry animal in the box experienced. None of the cats elicited the latch-release response in reflex-like fashion; rather, taken as a whole, they set the occasion for many possible responses to occur, only one of which would release the latch. Once the latch was released, the satisfying effect, including freedom from the box and access to food, caused that response to strengthen; so the next time the cat was in the same situation, the probability of that response's recurrence was increased (see **Figure 8.9**).

Skinner's Method of Studying and Describing Operant Conditioning

The psychologist who did the most to extend and popularize the law of effect for more than half a century was B. F. (Burrhus Frederic) Skinner. Like Watson, Skinner was a confirmed behaviorist. He believed that principles of learning are the most fundamental principles in psychology, and he wanted to study and describe learning in ways that do not entail references to mental events. Unlike Watson, however, Skinner did not consider the stimulus–response reflex to be the fundamental unit of all of behavior. Thorndike's work provided Skinner with a model of how nonreflexive behaviors could be altered through learning.

FIGURE 8.9 Thorndike's law of effect According to Thorndike, the stimulus situation (being inside the puzzle box) initially elicits many responses, some more strongly than others, but the satisfying consequence of the successful response (pressing the lever) causes that response to be more strongly elicited on successive trials.

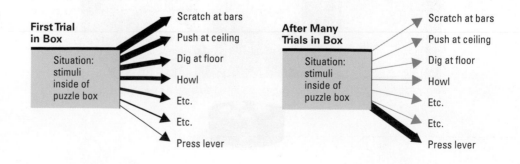

As a graduate student at Harvard University around 1930, Skinner developed an apparatus for studying animals' learning that was considerably more efficient than Thorndike's puzzle boxes. His device, commonly called a "Skinner box," is a cage with a lever or another mechanism in it that the animal can operate to produce some effect, such as delivery of a pellet of food or a drop of water (see **Figure 8.10**). The advantage of Skinner's apparatus is that the animal, after completing a response and experiencing its effect, is still in the box and free to respond again. With Thorndike's puzzle boxes and similar apparatuses such as mazes, the animal has to be put back into the starting place at the end of each trial. With Skinner's apparatus, the animal is simply placed in the cage and left there until the end of the session. Throughout the session, there are no constraints on when the animal may or may not respond. Responses (such as lever presses) can easily be counted automatically, and the learning process can be depicted as changes in the rate of responses (see **Figure 8.11**). Because each pellet of food or drop of water is very small, the hungry or thirsty animal makes many responses before becoming satiated.

Skinner developed not only a more efficient apparatus for studying such learning but also a new vocabulary for talking about it. He coined the terms *operant response* to refer to any behavioral act that has some effect on the environment and *operant conditioning* to refer to the process by which the effect of an operant response changes the likelihood of the response's recurrence. Thus, in a typical experiment with a Skinner box, pressing the lever is an operant response, and the increased rate of lever pressing that occurs when the response is followed by a pellet of food exemplifies operant conditioning. Applying the same terms to Thorndike's experiments, the movement that opens the latch is an operant response, and the increase from trial to trial in the speed with which that movement is made exemplifies operant conditioning.

Skinner (1938) proposed the term **reinforcer**, as a replacement for such words as *satisfaction* and *reward,* to refer to a stimulus change that follows a response and increases the subsequent frequency of that response. Skinner preferred this term because it makes no assumptions about anything happening in the mind; it merely refers to the effect that the presentation of the stimulus has on the animal's subsequent behavior. Thus, in a typical Skinner-box experiment, the delivery of a pellet of food or drop of water following a lever-press response is a reinforcer. In Thorndike's experiment, escape from the cage and access to the food outside it were reinforcers. Some stimuli, such as food for a food-deprived animal or water for a water-deprived one, are naturally reinforcing. Other stimuli have reinforcing value only because of previous learning, and Skinner called these *conditioned reinforcers.* An example of a conditioned reinforcer for humans is money. Once a person learns what money can buy, he or she will learn to behave so as to gain more of it.

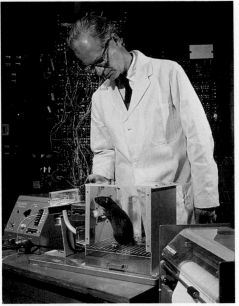

FIGURE 8.10 B. F. Skinner and his operant-conditioning chamber To study operant behavior in rats and other animals, Skinner invented an apparatus widely known as the Skinner box. When the rat shown here presses the lever, it activates an electrical relay system that causes the delivery of a food pellet into a cup next to the lever. Each lever press can be automatically recorded to produce a cumulative record, such as that shown in Figure 8.11.

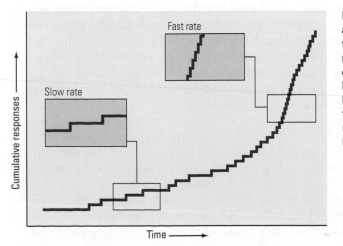

FIGURE 8.11 Typical cumulative response curve for a rat learning to press a lever in a Skinner box This graph is called a *cumulative response curve* because the height of the curve at any point indicates the total (cumulative) number of responses that the rat has made up to that time. The graph is automatically produced, while the rat is responding, by a recording machine outside the Skinner box. A pen moves horizontally across a roll of paper at a constant rate, and each lever press made by the rat produces a slight vertical movement of the pen. Thus, the degree to which the curve slopes upward is a measure of the animal's response rate. Note that early in learning the response rate was very low and then gradually increased to a fast, steady rate.

There is one fundamental difference between Skinner's theory of operant conditioning and Pavlov's theory of classical conditioning: In operant conditioning the individual *emits,* or generates, a behavior that has some effect on the environment, whereas in classical conditioning a stimulus *elicits* a response from the organism. Like Darwin's theory of evolution, Skinner's theory of learning is a *selectionist theory* from this perspective (Skinner, 1974). Animals (including humans) emit behaviors, some of which get reinforced (selected) by the environment. Those that get reinforced increase in frequency in those environments, and those that do not get reinforced decrease in frequency in those environments. Skinner's adoption of selectionist thinking is a clear demonstration of the application of Darwin's ideas to changes, not over evolutionary time, but over the lifetime of an individual.

Operant Conditioning Without Awareness

To Skinner and his followers, operant conditioning is not simply one kind of learning to be studied; it represents an entire approach to psychology. In his many books and articles, Skinner argued that essentially all the things we do, from the moment we arise in the morning to the moment we fall asleep at night, can be understood as operant responses that occur because of their past reinforcement. In some cases, we are clearly aware of the relationship between our responses and reinforcers, as when we place money in a vending machine for a candy bar or study to obtain a good grade on a test. In other cases, we may not be aware of the relationship, yet it exists and, according to Skinner (1953, 1966), is the real reason for our behavior. Skinner argued that awareness—which refers to a mental phenomenon—is not a useful construct for explaining behavior. We can never be sure what a person is aware of, but we can see directly the relationship between responses and reinforcers and use that to predict what a person will learn to do.

An illustration of conditioning without awareness is found in an experiment conducted many years ago, in which adults listened to music over which static was occasionally superimposed (Hefferline et al., 1959). Unbeknownst to the subjects, they could turn off the static by making an imperceptibly small twitch of the left thumb. Some subjects (the completely uninformed group) were told that the experiment had to do with the effect of music on body tension; they were told nothing about the static or how it could be turned off. Others (the partly informed group) were told that static would sometimes come on, that they could turn it off with a specific response, and that their task was to discover that response.

The result was that all subjects in both groups learned to make the thumb-twitch response, thereby keeping the static off for increasingly long periods. But, when questioned afterward, none were aware that they had controlled the static with thumb twitches. Subjects in the uninformed group said that they had noticed the static decline over the session but were unaware that they had caused the decline. Most in the partly informed group said that they had not discovered how to control the static. Only one participant believed that he had discovered the effective response, and he claimed that it involved "subtle rowing movements with both hands, infinitesimal wriggles of both ankles, a slight displacement of the jaw to the left, breathing out, and then waiting" (Hefferline et al., 1959, p. 1339)! While he was consciously making this superstitious response, he was unconsciously learning to make the thumb twitch.

If you think about it, the results of this experiment should not come as a great surprise. We constantly learn finely tuned muscle movements as we develop skill at riding a bicycle, hammering nails, making a jump shot, playing a musical instrument, or any other activity. The probable reinforcers are, respectively, the steadier movement on the bicycle, the straight downward movement of the nail we are pounding, the "swoosh" when the ball goes through the hoop, and the improved sound from the instrument; but often we do not know just what we are doing differently to produce these good effects. Our knowledge is often similar to that of the neophyte carpenter who said, after an hour's practice at hammering, "The nails you're giving me now don't bend as easily as the ones you were giving me before."

FOCUS 19

How do we know that people can be conditioned to make an operant response without awareness of the conditioning process? How is this relevant for understanding how people acquire motor skills?

Principles of Reinforcement

Skinner and his followers identified and studied many behavioral phenomena associated with operant conditioning, including the ones described in this section.

Shaping of New Operant Responses

Suppose you put a rat in a Skinner box, and it never presses the lever. Or you place a cat in a puzzle box, and it never pulls the loop. Or you want to train your dog to jump through a hoop, but it never makes that leap. In operant conditioning, if the desired response never occurs, it can never be reinforced because the reinforcer doesn't occur until after the subject produces that response. The solution to this problem is a technique called *shaping*, in which successively closer approximations to the desired response are reinforced until the desired response finally occurs and can be reinforced.

Imagine that you want to shape a lever-press response in a rat whose initial rate of lever pressing is zero. To begin, you might present a reinforcer (such as a pellet of food) whenever the rat goes anywhere near the lever. The rat will soon be spending most of its time near the lever and occasionally will touch it. When that begins to happen, you might withhold the reinforcer until each time the rat touches the lever, which will increase the rate of touching. Some touches will be more vigorous than others and produce the desired lever movement. When that has happened a few times, you can stop reinforcing any other response; your animal's lever pressing has now been shaped.

Animal trainers regularly use this technique in teaching domestic or circus animals to perform new tricks or tasks (Pryor, 2006), and we all tend to use it, more or less deliberately and not always skillfully, when we teach new skills to other people. For example, when teaching a novice to play tennis, we tend at first to offer praise for any swing of the racket that propels the ball in the right general direction, but as improvement occurs, we begin to bestow our praise only on closer and closer approximations of an ideal swing.

FOCUS 20

How can we use operant conditioning to get an animal to do something that it currently doesn't do?

■ An effect of operant shaping
Through the process of rewarding gradual approximations to the desired behavior, animals can be trained to do things that they would never do without such training.

Extinction of Operantly Conditioned Responses

If we cease giving a reinforcer to an operantly conditioned response, it will decline in rate and eventually disappear. Rats stop pressing levers if no food pellets appear, cats stop scratching at doors if nobody responds by letting them out, and people stop smiling at those who don't smile back. The absence of reinforcement of the response and the consequent decline in response rate are both referred to as *extinction*. Extinction in operant conditioning is analogous to extinction in classical conditioning. Just as in classical conditioning, extinction in operant conditioning is not true "unlearning" of the response. Passage of time following extinction can lead to spontaneous recovery of responding, and a single reinforced response following extinction can lead the individual to respond again at a rapid rate.

FOCUS 21

In what ways is extinction in operant conditioning similar to extinction in classical conditioning?

Schedules of Partial Reinforcement

In the real world as well as in laboratory experiments, a particular response may only produce a reinforcer some of the time. This is referred to as *partial reinforcement*, to distinguish it on the one hand from *continuous reinforcement*, where the response is always reinforced, and on the other hand from *extinction*, where the response is never reinforced. In initial training, continuous reinforcement is most efficient, but once trained, an animal will continue to perform for partial reinforcement. Skinner and other operant researchers have described the following four basic types of partial-reinforcement schedules:

🔍 **FOCUS 22**

How do the four types of partial-reinforcement schedules differ from one another, and why do responses generally occur faster to ratio schedules than to interval schedules?

- In a ***fixed-ratio schedule*** a reinforcer occurs after every *n*th response, where *n* is some whole number greater than 1. For example, in a *fixed-ratio 5 schedule* every fifth response is reinforced.

- A ***variable-ratio schedule*** is like a fixed-ratio schedule except that the number of responses required before reinforcement varies unpredictably around some average. For example, in a *variable-ratio 5 schedule* reinforcement might come after 7 responses on one trial, after 3 on another, and so on, in random manner, but the average number of responses required for reinforcement would be 5.

- In a ***fixed-interval schedule*** a fixed period of time must elapse between one reinforced response and the next. Any response occurring before that time elapses is not reinforced. For example, in a *fixed-interval 30-second schedule* the first response that occurs at least 30 seconds after the last reinforcer is reinforced.

- A ***variable-interval schedule*** is like a fixed-interval schedule except that the period that must elapse before a response will be reinforced varies unpredictably around some average. For example, in a *variable-interval 30-second schedule* the average period required before the next response will be reinforced is 30 seconds.

The different schedules produce different response rates in ways that make sense if we assume that the person or animal is striving to maximize the number of reinforcers and minimize the number of unreinforced responses (see **Figure 8.12**). Ratio schedules (whether fixed or variable) produce reinforcers at a rate that is directly proportional to the rate of responding, so, not surprisingly, such schedules typically induce rapid responding. With interval schedules, in contrast, the maximum number of reinforcers available is set by the clock, and such schedules result—also not surprisingly—in relatively low response rates that depend on the length of the fixed or average interval.

Behavior that has been reinforced on a variable-ratio or variable-interval schedule is often very difficult to extinguish. If a rat is trained to press a lever only on continuous reinforcement and then is shifted to extinction conditions, the rat will typically make a few bursts of lever-press responses and then quit. But if the rat has been shifted gradually from continuous reinforcement to an ever-stingier variable schedule and then finally to extinction, it will often make hundreds of unreinforced responses before quitting. Rats and humans who have been reinforced on stingy variable schedules have experienced reinforcement after long, unpredictable periods of no reinforcement, so they have learned (for better or worse) to be persistent.

🔍 **FOCUS 23**

How do variable-ratio and variable-interval schedules produce behavior that is highly resistant to extinction?

Skinner (1953) and others (Rachlin, 1990) have used this phenomenon to explain why gamblers often persist at the slot machine or dice game even after long periods of losing: They are hooked by the variable-ratio schedule of payoff that characterizes nearly every gambling device or game. From a cognitive perspective, we could say that the gambler keeps playing because of his or her knowledge that the very next bet or throw of the dice might be the one that pays off.

Distinction Between Positive and Negative Reinforcement

In Skinner's terminology, ***reinforcement*** refers to any process that increases the likelihood that a particular response will occur. Reinforcement can be positive or negative. ***Positive reinforcement*** occurs when the *arrival* of some stimulus following a response makes the response more likely to recur. The stimulus in this case is called a ***positive reinforcer***. Food pellets, money, words of praise, and anything else that organisms will work to obtain can be used as positive reinforcers. ***Negative reinforcement***, in contrast, occurs when the *removal* of some stimulus following a response makes the response

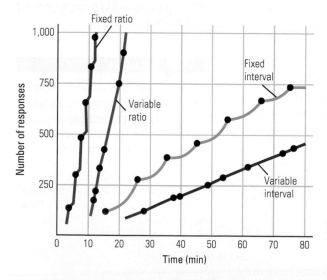

FIGURE 8.12 Different schedules of reinforcement produce different patterns of responding In both fixed- and variable-ratio schedules of reinforcement, subjects respond rapidly to reach their goals. Subjects respond at slower rates with fixed- and variable-interval schedules of reinforcement. Note the scalloping pattern for the fixed-interval schedules. Here, the subject only starts responding toward the end of the interval, when the time for reinforcement is near.

■ **Partial reinforcement in daily life** Winning at slot machines occurs on a variable-ratio schedule, which produces a rapid and steady style of play. Success at reaching a previously busy telephone number that goes straight to voicemail occurs on a variable-interval schedule, which results in a slow and steady rate of redialing.

more likely to recur. The stimulus in this case is called a ***negative reinforcer***. Electric shocks, loud noises, unpleasant company, scoldings, and everything else that organisms will work to get away from can be used as negative reinforcers. The one example of negative reinforcement discussed so far was the experiment in which a thumbtwitch response was reinforced by the temporary removal of unpleasant static.

Notice that *positive* and *negative* here do not refer to the direction of change in the response rate; that increases in either case. Rather, the terms indicate whether the reinforcing stimulus appears (positive) or disappears (negative) as a result of the operant response. Negative reinforcement is not the same a punishment, a mistake that many students of psychology make.

Distinction Between Reinforcement and Punishment

In Skinner's terminology, ***punishment*** is the opposite of reinforcement. It is the process through which the consequence of a response *decreases* the likelihood that the response will recur. As with reinforcement, punishment can be positive or negative. In ***positive punishment***, the arrival of a stimulus, such as electric shock for a rat or scolding for a person, decreases the likelihood that the response will occur again. In ***negative punishment***, the removal of a stimulus, such as taking food away from a hungry rat or money away from a person, decreases the likelihood that the response will occur again. Both types of punishment can be distinguished from extinction, which, you recall, is the decline in a previously reinforced response when it no longer produces any effect.

To picture the distinction between positive and negative punishment, and to see their relation to positive and negative reinforcement, look at **Figure 8.13**. The terms are easy to remember if you recall that *positive* and *negative* always refer to the arrival or removal of a stimulus and that *reinforcement* and *punishment* always refer to an increase or decrease in the likelihood that the response will recur.

The figure also makes it clear that the same stimuli that can serve as positive reinforcers when presented can serve as negative punishers when removed, and the same stimuli that can serve as positive punishers when presented can serve as negative reinforcers when removed. It is easy to think of the former as "desired" stimuli and the latter as "undesired," but Skinner avoided such mentalistic terms. He argued that the only way to tell whether a stimulus is desired or undesired is by observing its reinforcing or punishing effects, so these mentalistic terms add nothing to our understanding. For instance, an adult who scolds a child for misbehaving may think that the scolding is an undesired stimulus that will punish the behavior, but, in fact, it may

FOCUS 24

How does negative reinforcement differ from positive reinforcement?

FOCUS 25

How does punishment differ from reinforcement, and how do the two kinds of punishment parallel the two kinds of reinforcement?

FIGURE 8.13 Two types of reinforcement and two types of punishment Reinforcement (whether positive or negative) increases the response rate, and punishment (whether positive or negative) decreases the response rate. The terms positive and negative refer to whether the reinforcing stimulus arrives or is removed when the response is made.

		Response rate	
		Increases	Decreases
Response causes stimulus to be	Presented	Positive reinforcement (Lever press→food pellet)	Positive punishment (Lever press→shock)
	Removed	Negative reinforcement (Lever press→turns off shock)	Negative punishment (Lever press→removes food)

be a desired stimulus to the child who seeks attention. To Skinner, the proof is in the result. If scolding causes the undesired behavior to become less frequent, then scolding is acting as a positive punisher; if scolding causes the behavior to become more frequent, it is acting as a positive reinforcer.

Discrimination Training in Operant Conditioning

FOCUS 26

How can an animal be trained to produce an operant response only when a specific cue is present?

Through *discrimination training,* an animal can be conditioned to make an operant response to a stimulus more specific than the entire inside of a Skinner box. Discrimination training in operant conditioning is analogous to discrimination training in classical conditioning. The essence of the procedure is to reinforce the animal's response when a specific stimulus is present and to extinguish the response when the stimulus is absent. Thus, to train a rat to respond to a tone by pressing a lever, a trainer would alternate between reinforcement periods with the tone on (during which the animal gets food pellets for responding) and extinction periods with the tone off. After considerable training of this sort, the rat will begin pressing the lever as soon as the tone comes on and stop as soon as it goes off. The tone in this example is called a **discriminative stimulus**.

Operant discrimination training, like the analogous procedure in classical conditioning, can be used to study the sensory abilities of animals and human infants, who cannot describe their sensations in words. In one experiment, for example, researchers trained newborns to change their sucking rate on a nipple to hear (through headphones) a story their mothers had read to them during the last few weeks of the fetal period versus another story (DeCasper & Spence, 1986). Thus, the babies learned to make two different responses (increase or decrease sucking rate) to two different discriminative stimuli. This demonstrated, among other things, that the newborns could hear the difference between the two sounds and would alter their sucking rate to hear the story that their mothers had read to them while they were still in the womb. Operant discrimination training can also be used to study animals' understanding of concepts.

Discrimination and Generalization as Indices of Concept Understanding

In classical conditioning, as you may recall, animals that have learned to respond to a conditioned stimulus will also respond to new stimuli that they perceive as similar to the original conditioned stimulus, a phenomenon referred to as *generalization*. Generalization also occurs in operant conditioning. After operant discrimination training, animals will respond to new stimuli that they perceive as similar to the discriminative stimulus. Such generalization can be used to test an animal's understanding of a concept.

Consider an experiment conducted by Richard Herrnstein (1979), who operantly conditioned pigeons to peck a key for grain, using photographs of natural scenes as discriminative stimuli. Herrnstein divided the photos into two categories—those that had at least one tree or portion of a tree somewhere in the scene and those that didn't. The pigeons received grain (on a variable-ratio schedule of reinforcement) for pecking the key whenever a "tree" photo was shown and nothing when a "no tree" photo was shown. In the first phase, 80 photos were presented each day, 40 of which contained trees and 40 of which didn't. By the end of 5 days of such training—that is, after five presentations of all 80 photos—all the birds were successfully discriminating between the two categories of photos, pecking when the photo contained a tree and not pecking otherwise (see **Figure 8.14**).

Now, the question is: What had Herrnstein's pigeons learned? Did they learn each photo as a separate stimulus, unrelated to the others, or did they learn a rule for categorizing the photos? Such a rule might be stated by a person as follows: "Respond whenever a photo includes a tree or part of a tree, and don't respond otherwise." To determine whether the pigeons had acquired such a rule, Herrnstein

From: E. Wasserman, "The Conceptual Abilities of Pigeons," 83:246–255, American Scientist

FIGURE 8.14 It's a flower Researchers have developed various means to test animals' ability to categorize complex objects. In the experiment illustrated here, Edward Wasserman (1995) trained pigeons to peck a different one of four keys depending on whether the photo shown was of a car, cat, chair, or flower. The birds proved to be quite accurate at classifying objects that they had never seen before.

■ **Tree pictures similar to those used to study concepts in pigeons** Pigeons that had been trained to peck whenever a photo contained a tree, or part of a tree, pecked when they saw photos like these, even though these trees are not green. The pigeons refrained from pecking when they saw a photo that did not include a tree, even if it contained green grass or leaves.

tested them with new photos, which they had never seen before, under conditions in which no grain was given. He found that the pigeons immediately pecked at a much higher rate when a new photo contained a tree than when it did not. In fact, the pigeons were as accurate with new photos as they were with photos that had been used during training. The birds apparently based their responses on a ***concept*** of trees (Herrnstein, 1990). A concept, as the term is used here, can be defined as a rule for categorizing stimuli into groups. The pigeons' tree concept, in this case, must have guided their decision to peck or not to peck.

How might one describe the pigeons' tree concept? That question is not easily answered. It is not the case, for example, that the pigeons simply learned to peck at photos that included a patch of green. Many of the "no tree" photos had green grass, and some of the tree photos were of fall or winter scenes in New England, where the trees had red and yellow leaves or none at all. In some photos, only a small portion of a tree was apparent or the tree was in the distant background. So the method by which the pigeons distinguished tree photos from others cannot be easily stated in stimulus terms, although ultimately it must have been based on the birds' analysis of the stimulus material. Similar experiments have shown that pigeons can acquire concepts pertaining to such objects as cars, chairs, the difference between male and female human faces, and even abstract symbols (Cook & Smith, 2006; Loidolt et al., 2003; Wasserman, 1995). The point is that, even for pigeons—and certainly for humans—sophisticated analysis of the stimulus information occurs before the stimulus is used to guide behavior.

FOCUS 27

How was discrimination training used to demonstrate that pigeons understand the concept of a tree?

When Rewards Backfire: The Overjustification Effect in Humans

In human beings, rewards have a variety of effects, either positive or negative, depending on the conditions in which they are used and the meanings that they engender in those who receive them.

Consider an experiment conducted with nursery-school children (Lepper & Greene, 1978). Children in one group were rewarded with attractive "Good Player" certificates for drawing with felt-tipped pens. This had the immediate

FOCUS 28

Why might a period of reward lead to a subsequent decline in response rate when the reward is no longer available?

effect of leading them to spend more time at this activity than did children in the other group (who were not rewarded). Later, however, when certificates were no longer given, the previously rewarded children showed a sharp drop in their use of the pens—to a level well below that of children in the unrewarded group. So, the long-term effect of the period of reward was to decrease the children's use of felt-tipped pens.

Many subsequent experiments, with people of various ages, have produced similar results. For example, explicitly rewarding children to share leads to *less*, not more, sharing later on. In studies with 20-month-old toddlers (Warneken & Tomasello, 2008) and with 6- to 12-year-old children (Fabes et al., 1989), children who were rewarded for sharing (for example, permitted to play with a special toy) later shared less when given the opportunity compared to children who received only praise or no reward. Other research shows that rewards tied to specific performance or completion of a task are negatively associated with creativity (Byron & Khazanchi, 2012). The drop in performance following a period of reward is particularly likely to occur when the task is something that is initially enjoyed for its own sake and the reward is given in such a manner that it seems to be designed deliberately to motivate the participants to engage in the task (Lepper & Henderlong, 2000). This decline is called the ***overjustification effect*** because the reward presumably provides an unneeded extra justification for engaging in the behavior. The result is that people come to regard the task as something that they do for an external reward rather than for its own sake—that is, as work rather than play. When they come to regard the task as work, they stop doing it when they no longer receive a payoff for it, even though they would have otherwise continued to do it for fun.

Such findings suggest that some rewards used in schools may have negative long-term effects. For example, rewarding children for reading might cause them to think of reading as work rather than fun, which would lead them to read less on their own. The broader point is that one must take into account the cognitive consequences of rewards in predicting their long-term effects, especially when dealing with human beings.

■ **When does play become work?** Athletic games can be great fun for children, but when the focus is on winning trophies and pleasing parents and coaches, what was previously play can become work.

Behavior Analysis

FOCUS 29

How are Skinner's techniques of operant conditioning being used to deal with problem behaviors?

Following in the tradition of Skinner, the field of ***behavior analysis*** uses principles of operant conditioning to predict behavior (Baer et al., 1968). Recall from earlier in this chapter that, in operant conditioning, discrimination and generalization serve as indicators of whether the subject has acquired concept understanding. From this perspective, one has achieved "understanding" to the degree to which one can predict and influence future occurrences of behavior. Behavioral techniques are frequently used to address a variety of real-world situations and problems, including dealing with phobias, developing classroom curricula (for college courses such as *General Psychology*; Chase & Houmanfar, 2009), educating children and adults with special needs (e.g., behavioral techniques used with children with autism and intellectual impairments), helping businesses and other organizations run more effectively (Dickinson, 2000), and helping parents deal with misbehaving children. When behavior analysis is applied specifically to modify problem behaviors, especially as part of a learning or treatment process, it is referred to as *applied behavior analysis* (often abbreviated as *ABA*; Bijou & Baer, 1961).

Consider the behavior analysis implications of "reality" TV programs in which experts (and TV cameras) go into people's homes to help them deal with their unruly children or pets. In one show, *Supernanny*, parents are taught to establish and enforce rules. When giving their child a "time-out," for example, they are told to make certain that the child spends the entire designated time in the "naughty corner." To accomplish this, parents have sometimes had to chase the escaping child repeatedly until the child finally gave in. By enforcing the time-out period, even if it took over an hour to do so, the child's "escape" behavior was extinguished, and—coupled with warmth and perhaps something to distract the child from the offending behavior—discipline became easier.

The first thing one does in behavior analysis is to define some socially significant behaviors that are in need of changing. These target behaviors may be studying for tests by a fourth-grade student, dressing oneself by a person with intellectual impairment, discouraging nail biting by a school-age child, or reducing occurrences of head banging by a child with autism. Then, a schedule of reinforcement is implemented to increase, decrease, or maintain the targeted behavior (Baer et al., 1968).

Teachers use behavioral techniques as a way of managing their classrooms (Alberto & Troutman, 2005). For instance, experienced teachers know that desirable behavior can be modeled or shaped through a series of reinforcements (*successive approximations*), initially providing praise when a child improves his or her performance in a subject by a marginal amount ("That's great! Much better than before!"), then insisting on improved performance before subsequent reinforcement (in this case, social praise) is given, until eventually performance is mostly correct. Other times, teachers learn to remove all possible reinforcement for disruptive behavior, gradually extinguishing it and possibly using praise to reinforce more desirable behavior.

Behavioral techniques have been especially useful for working with people with certain developmental disabilities, including intellectual impairment, attention-deficit with hyperactivity disorder (ADHD), and autism. For example, *token economies* are often used with people with intellectual impairment. In these systems, teachers or therapists deliver a series of tokens when a target behavior is performed. Tokens can be given for brushing one's teeth, making eye contact with a therapist, or organizing the contents of one's desk. The tokens can later be redeemed for products or privileges (e.g., 3 tokens for a pad of paper; 6 tokens for a snack; 20 tokens for an excursion out of school).

Applied behavior analysis has been extensively used in treating children with autism. Recall from Chapter 2 that autism is a disorder characterized by deficits in emotional connections and communication. In severe cases, it may involve absent or abnormal speech, low IQ, ritualistic behaviors, aggression, and self-injury. Ivar Lovaas and his colleagues were the first to develop behavioral techniques for dealing with children with severe autism (Lovaas, 1987, 2003; McEachin et al., 1993). For example, Lovaas reported that 47% of children with severe autism receiving his behavioral intervention attained first-grade level academic performance and a normal level of IQ by 7 years of age, in contrast to only 2% of children with autism in a control group.

Applied behavior analysis has been used in dozens, if not hundreds, of programs for treating children with autism, and most studies report positive effects on cognition for young children with autism compared to control groups of children with autism (Howlin et al., 2009; Reichow & Wolery, 2009), as well as for adaptive behavior and social skills for older children (Dawson & Bruner, 2011). However, researchers also report substantial individual differences in program effectiveness, with some children showing no benefit of participating in ABA programs compared to children in control groups (Spreckley & Boyd, 2009).

Behavior analysis provides an excellent framework for assessing and treating many "problem" behaviors, ranging from the everyday difficulties of parents dealing with a misbehaving child, to the often self-destructive behaviors of children with severe developmental disabilities.

■ Applied behavior analysis is used frequently by therapists to shape the behavior of children with autism.

SECTION REVIEW

Operant conditioning is a type of learning in which the recurrence of a behavior is controlled by the behavior's consequences.

Work of Thorndike and Skinner

- An operant response is an action that produces an effect.
- Thorndike's puzzle box experiments led him to postulate the law of effect.
- Skinner defined *reinforcer* as a stimulus change that follows an operant response and increases the frequency of that response.
- Operant conditioning can occur with or without awareness.

Variations in Availability of Reinforcement

- Shaping occurs when successive approximations to the desired response are reinforced.
- Extinction is the decline in response rate that occurs when an operant response is no longer reinforced.
- Partial reinforcement can be contrasted with continuous reinforcement and can occur on various schedules of reinforcement. The type of schedule affects the response rate and resistance to extinction.

Reinforcement Versus Punishment

- Reinforcement increases response rate; punishment decreases response rate.
- Reinforcement can be either positive (e.g., praise is given) or negative (e.g., a loud noise stops).
- Punishment can be either positive (e.g., a reprimand is given) or negative (e.g., computer privileges are taken away).

Operant conditioning entails learning about conditions and consequences.

Discrimination Training

- If reinforcement is available only when a specific stimulus is present, that stimulus becomes a discriminative stimulus. Subjects learn to respond only when it is present.

Discrimination and Generalization as Indices of Concept Understanding

- Learners generalize to stimuli that they perceive as similar to the discriminative stimulus, but can be trained to discriminate.
- Discrimination and generalization of an operantly conditioned behavior can be used to identify concepts a subject has learned.

Overjustification

- In humans, rewards can have a positive or negative effect, depending on the conditions in which they are used and the meanings that they engender in those who receive them.
- In the overjustification effect, previously reinforced behavior declines because the reward presumably provides an unneeded extra justification for engaging in the behavior.

Behavior Analysis Uses Skinner's Principle of Operant Conditioning

- Teachers use behavioral techniques as a way of managing their classrooms.
- Token economies involve delivering a series of tokens, or artificial reinforcers, for performing target behaviors. They are often used with people with intellectual impairment.
- Work by Lovaas and his colleagues demonstrated the usefulness of behavior analysis for children with severe forms of autism.
- Applied behavior analysis has been shown to have an overall positive effect on children with autism, although there can be substantial individual differences in program effectiveness.

Beyond Classical and Operant Theories of Learning: Play, Exploration, and Observation

Classical and operant conditioning have long been popular research topics in psychology, partly because they truly are ubiquitous learning processes and partly because they are relatively easy to study in the laboratory. By tightly controlling an animal's environment and motivational state, a researcher can induce predictable changes in the animal's behavior. Indeed, the very word *conditioning* implies an active researcher (or trainer) and a passive animal. The researcher *conditions* the animal. The idea that learning is imposed by external conditions rather than controlled by the learner accords closely with the philosophy of early behaviorism.

In nature, however, animals (especially mammals) are active learners. Through *play,* young animals learn how to control their own behavior in effective ways. Through *exploration,* animals of all ages keep track of significant changes in their environment. In addition, animals acquire useful information through *observing* the behavior of others of their kind. Play, exploration, and observation are species-typical behavioral tendencies, or drives, that came about through natural selection precisely because they promote learning. Unlike operant conditioning as studied in laboratories, these activities occur most fully when the animal is free of any strong, immediate need state, such as hunger or thirst, and is free to move about at will.

Play: How the Young Learn How

Play is behavior, engaged in apparently for its own sake, that serves no obvious immediately useful purpose. The demeanor of the playing animal, just like that of a playing child, is often high-spirited and bouncing, which suggests that the animal is having fun. The young of all social mammals spend considerable portions of their time playing. Play is clearly species-typical: Nobody has to teach them to play; they just do it.

Why do young mammals play? It is not enough to say that they play because play is *fun.* That answer only begs us to ask, "Why are young mammals constructed in such a manner that they enjoy playing?" Natural selection does not create species-typical behaviors or pleasures that serve no purpose. So, what is the purpose of play?

Play clearly has some costs. It uses energy, which must be made up for in additional food, and it is sometimes directly dangerous. Young chimpanzees playfully chasing one another in trees sometimes fall and hurt themselves; goat kids frolicking on cliffs have been observed to slip and fall to their deaths; young fur seal pups are more likely to be snatched and eaten by predatory sea lions when they are at play than when they are at rest; and the play of cheetah cubs sometimes spoils their mothers' attempts to stalk and capture game (Bjorklund & Pellegrini, 2002; Byers, 1998; Caro, 1995). The value of play must outweigh such costs, or natural selection would have weeded it out. What is that value?

■ **Young predators at play** These lion cubs are playfully practicing maneuvers that will serve them well as they grow older.

> **FOCUS 30**

What is Groos's theory about the evolutionary function of animals' play, and what are five lines of evidence supporting that theory?

Groos's Theory: Play Is Practice of Species-Typical Skills

The first theorist to write about play from an evolutionary perspective was the German philosopher and naturalist Karl Groos. In a book entitled *The Play of Animals,* published in 1898, Groos argued that the primary purpose of play is to provide a means for young animals to practice their instincts—their species-typical behaviors.

Groos was strongly influenced by the writings of Charles Darwin and had a sophisticated, modern understanding of instincts. He recognized that animals, especially mammals, must to varying degrees *learn* to use their instincts. Young mammals come into the world with biological drives and tendencies to behave in certain ways, but to be effective such behaviors must be practiced and refined. Play, according to Groos, provides that practice. This theory, even today, is the most widely accepted explanation of play among people who study it in animals.

Evidence for Groos's Theory

Much of what we know about play in animals makes sense in the light of Groos's theory and thereby provides evidence supporting that theory. Here are five categories of such evidence:

- *Young animals play more than do adults of their species.* Among the most obvious evidence for Groos's practice theory is the simple fact that young animals, of all species that play, are much more playful than their elders. Young animals have more to learn than do adults of their species, so the fact that they are motivated to play more is no coincidence according to the practice theory.

- *Species of animals that have the most to learn play the most.* Another accurate prediction of Groos's practice theory is that those animal species that have the most to learn play the most (Power, 2000). Young mammals play more than do the young of any other animal class, and mammals, more than any other class, depend on learning in order to survive. Among mammals, primates (monkeys and apes) are the most flexible and adaptable order, and the most dependent on learning; they are also the most playful of all animal orders. Among primates, human beings, chimpanzees, and bonobos are the most flexible and adaptable species, and they appear to be the most playful of all species. Also among mammals, those in the carnivore order (which includes the dog-like and cat-like species) are more playful than herbivores, which is consistent with the observation that success in hunting requires more practice than does success in grazing.

- *Young animals play most at those skills that they most need to learn.* To a considerable degree it is possible to predict the activities that a young animal will play at by knowing what skills it must develop to survive and thrive. Young carnivores play at chasing, stalking, and pouncing—skills they will need in obtaining food (Schaller, 1972). Young herbivores do not play at grazing; that skill is easy to develop and can be practiced through serious grazing, so play is not needed. But young herbivores do play at fleeing and dodging, skills they need for evading predators (Špinka et al., 2001). The young of almost all mammals play at fighting. Among most species of mammals, young males playfight more than do young females (Pellegrini & Smith, 1998), and this corresponds with the fact that among most mammals fighting is a more essential adult skill for males than it is for females. At least among some species of primates, young females, but not young males, engage in playful care of infants (Maestripieri & Roney, 2006).

- *Play involves much repetition.* To practice something is to do it over and over again; and repetition is one of the hallmarks of play. Think of the difference between a cat seriously preying on a mouse and a cat *playing* at preying on a mouse. The *preying* cat pounces once, in its most efficient manner; it then kills the mouse and either eats it or takes it to its den. The *playing* cat, in contrast, lets the mouse go after catching it, so it can stalk and pounce again—and again, and again, until the poor mouse dies of fright and exhaustion. Similarly, bear cubs playing chase games repeatedly chase one another, taking turns being the pursued and the pursuer, like children playing tag. And monkeys, playing at swinging from branch to branch in a tree, sometimes swing repeatedly between the same two branches (Symons, 1978). The repetition is not stereotyped; each repetition may be a little different from the previous one. It is as if the young animal is trying out, each time, a different way of preying, chasing, or swinging.

- *Play is challenging.* In play, young animals seem deliberately to put themselves into situations that challenge their abilities. In playfighting, whether among rats or monkeys, the stronger of the two will allow the weaker one to pin it, and then will struggle to get out of the pinned position. In playful leaping and running, the young of many species seem to make deliberately awkward motions, from which they then have to recover skillfully to avoid a fall (Špinka et al., 2001). When young monkeys practice swinging from branch to branch, they commonly choose branches that are at such a distance that they often can't make it, but low enough that a fall doesn't hurt. Mountain goat kids that can already run well on flat ground tend to concentrate their playful running on steep slopes, where running is more difficult (Byers, 1977).

Applying the Theory to Humans

In a second book, entitled *The Play of Man* (1901), Groos extended his theory of play to human beings. Groos recognized basic differences between humans and other mammals. We humans have at least as many species-typical behaviors as other mammals have, but ours are even less rigid, more modifiable by experience, enabling us to adapt to a wider range of environmental niches than is true of other mammals. Moreover, we are the only truly cultural species. *Culture,* by definition, is the set of learned skills, knowledge, beliefs, and values that characterize a group of interconnected individuals and are passed along from generation to generation. To do well as human beings we must learn not just the skills that are common to the whole species, but also those that are unique to the specific culture in which we are developing.

So, according to Groos, in the evolution of our species the basic mammalian drive to play was elaborated upon, by natural selection, to include a heavy component of imitation. We are motivated to play not just at those activities (such as two-legged walking and running) that people everywhere do in pretty much the same way, but also to play at the very specific activities that we see are crucial to success in the particular culture in which we are growing up. Children in a hunting culture play at hunting, using and elaborating upon the particular methods of hunting that they see among their elders. Children in our present-day culture play at writing and computers. In the evolution of human beings, those individuals who were born with a genetic tendency to pay attention to and play at the human activities around them, especially those activities that are difficult yet crucial to success, were more likely to survive and reproduce than those born without such a tendency.

For Groos, and for most theorists since, play has been seen as a preparation for adulthood, and surely it is. But play also provides some immediate benefits for the players, be they human or nonhuman (Bjorklund & Green, 1992; Pellegrini, 2013). Some aspects of play serve to adapt children to the niche of childhood and not necessarily (or only) to prepare them for adulthood. Rough-and-tumble play provides opportunities for vigorous physical exercise that is important for skeletal and muscle development (Bruner, 1972; Dolhinow & Bishop, 1970). Children can also develop a sense of mastery during play when experimenting with new activities, including tool use, which can have benefits both for their immediate survival and for their future (Bjorklund & Gardiner, 2011). Moreover, the rough-and-tumble play characteristic of young males serves as a way for them to learn and practice social signaling (Martin & Caro, 1985), with exaggerated movements and a play face communicating playful intent. Males also use rough-and-tumble play to establish leadership in their peer group and assess others' strength (Pellegrini & Smith, 1998), both important in dealing with one's peers in the here and now, not just in some unspecified future.

One type of play may be unique to humans and seems to serve an important role in cognitive development. **Symbolic play**, which is also called *fantasy, pretend* or *make-believe play,* includes an "as if" orientation to objects, actions, and other people and increases during early childhood as a result of children's growing abilities to use symbols to represent something as other than itself (Carlson et al., 2014; Lillard, 2015). A number of researchers have shown that children who engage in more symbolic play, especially when playing with others, have higher levels of language development, perspective taking, and executive-function abilities (Berk et al., 2006; Pierucci et al., 2014). Executive functions refers to a set of basic cognitive abilities including working memory, inhibition, and mental flexibility, that play an important role in planning and regulating behavior. (Executive functions are discussed in greater detail in Chapter 9.) According to Clancy Blair and Adele Diamond (2008), "During social pretend play, children must hold their own role and those of others in mind (working memory), inhibit acting out of character (employ inhibitory control), and flexibly adjust to twists and turns in the evolving plot (mental flexibility); all three of the core executive functions thus get exercise" (p. 907). In fact, Mark Nielsen (2012) proposed that symbolic play is a critical feature of human childhood and, along with imitation, has a central role in the evolution of human cognition. According to Nielsen (2012, p. 176), "By pretending children thus develop a capacity to generate and reason with novel suppositions and imaginary scenarios, and in so doing may get to practice the creative process that underpins innovation in adulthood."

Exploration: How Animals Learn What and Where

Play is not the only drive that came about in evolution to promote active learning. The other great one is curiosity, or the drive to explore. Groos (1898) considered exploration to be a category of play, but most students of play and exploration now consider the two to be distinct (Pellegrini, 2013). Learning can be divided at least roughly into two broad categories—learning *to do* (skill learning) and learning *about* (information learning). Play evolved to serve the former, and exploration evolved to serve the latter.

Exploration is a more primitive and widespread category of behavior than is play. Animals whose activities are rather rigidly controlled by their genetic makeup so that they don't have much to learn in the *to do* category must nevertheless learn *about* their environment. They must learn where food, shelter, mates, and other necessities for life and reproduction are located. Fish don't play, at least not in any way that is reliably identified as such by researchers, but they do regularly approach and explore novel objects (Ward et al., 2003). Even insects explore to find food and other necessities of life, although they do so in rather inflexible ways (Gordon, 1995). Mammals of all species, regardless of age, explore novel environments and objects with which they are confronted.

The Nature of Mammalian Exploration

Exploration, unlike play, is often mixed with a degree of fear. Exploration is elicited by novel stimuli, and novel stimuli often induce fear until they are fully explored. In fact, one purpose of exploration, in animals and people, is to determine whether or not an unfamiliar object or place is safe.

Explorers are often caught in a balance between curiosity, which drives them toward the unfamiliar terrain or novel object, and fear, which drives them away. A rat placed in a novel test arena with various objects in it will first cower in a corner. Then it will take a few steps out from the corner, along a wall, and dash back. Then it will venture a bit farther along the wall before dashing back again. Gradually, the rat will get bolder. It will eventually approach and explore—by smell, sight, and touch—the entire arena and all the objects within it. Once the rat is thoroughly familiar with the arena, it will reduce its movement but will continue periodically to tour the arena as if looking to see if anything has changed—a behavior referred to as *patrolling*. During its patrolling, the animal periodically rears up on its hind legs to get a better view. If a new object has been placed in the arena, the rat will attend to that rather than to old objects and will explore it at first gingerly and then more

Sam Gross The New Yorker Collection/The Cartoon Bank

"Well you don't look like an experimental psychologist to me."

boldly (Inglis et al., 2001). Similar behaviors have been described in many other species of mammals.

Some of the earliest research on exploration came from studies of rats in mazes. Researchers learned that rats' movements through mazes are governed not just by their drive for the food in the goal box, but also by their drive to explore all of the maze's alleys (Dember & Fowler, 1958; Winfield & Dennis, 1934). Rats that have already learned the most direct route to the goal will often persist in exploring round-about routes and dead-end alleys. Rats that are prevented from entering a particular alley, by a block placed at its entrance, will typically explore that alley first as soon as the block is removed. Not surprisingly, the hungrier a rat is (that is, the longer it has been deprived of food), the more directly it will run to the food-containing goal box; the less hungry it is, the more time it will spend exploring the other alleys in a maze. But even very hungry rats will often spend some time exploring (Inglis et al., 2001). In other research, Harry Harlow and his colleagues demonstrated that rhesus monkeys would solve complex mechanical puzzles in the absence of any obvious rewards (Harlow, 1953). Apparently, and counter to the dictates of learning theory of the time, animals (and people) will explore novel objects and even figure out how to operate them, not for some explicit reward, but to satisfy their curiosity.

■ **A curious monkey** Sometimes naturalists find that the animals they study are as curious about them and their equipment as they (the naturalists) are about the animals. Here a woolly monkey explores a camera.

Evidence That Animals Acquire Useful Information Through Exploration

In a now classic experiment, Edward Tolman and C. H. Honzik (1930) showed that rats can learn about the pathways in a maze even if no food or other such reward is provided for doing so. These researchers tested three groups of rats in a complex maze under different reward conditions. Group 1 received one trial per day in the maze with no food or other reward in the goal box. As expected, this group showed little improvement from day to day in the time they took to reach the goal box (the goal box contained no "goal" for them). Group 2 received one trial per day with food in the goal box. As expected, this group improved considerably from day to day in their rate of movement to the goal box. The most interesting group was group 3. Rats in this group received one trial per day with no reward for 10 days, like group 1; but, beginning on the 11th day, they received one trial per day with a food reward, like group 2. These rats improved dramatically between days 11 and 12. On day 11, they were no better than the other unrewarded group (group 1), but on day 12, after just one experience with the reward, they were as fast at reaching the goal box as the rats that had been rewarded all along (see **Figure 8.15**).

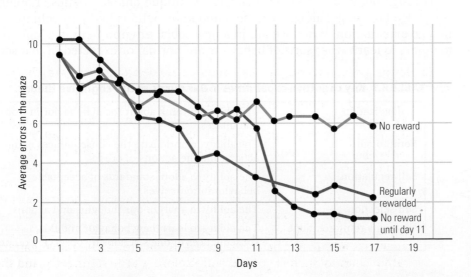

FIGURE 8.15 Latent learning of a maze Each rat received one trial per day in the maze, with or without a food reward in the goal box. The group that received its first reward on day 11 performed as well on day 12 (and thereafter) as the group that had received a reward every day. From this, Tolman and Honzik concluded that the rats had learned the spatial layout of the maze even without a reward, but the rats did not use that knowledge until the changed conditions made it worthwhile for them to do so.

(Data from Tolman & Honzik, 1930.)

On the basis of this and other experiments, Tolman (1948) argued that rewards affect what animals *do* more than what they *learn*. Animals learn the locations of distinctive places in their environment through exploration, whether or not they have ever found rewards there, but they do not run directly to those places unless they have found rewards there. Tolman used the term **latent learning** to refer to learning that is not immediately demonstrated in the animal's behavior. In the experiment just described, the rats in group 3 learned the spatial layout of the maze in the first 10 trials, but that learning remained latent, not manifested in their behavior, until the addition of a reward gave the rats a reason to run straight to the goal box.

Latent learning has been demonstrated in many experiments since Tolman's time. Through exploration, without rewards, rats learn the layouts of mazes and then are able to take the shortest route to a reward when a reward is introduced (Roberts et al., 2007). There is also evidence, from experiments with mice, that animals that explore the most are the same animals that learn the most in a wide variety of tests of learning (Matzel et al., 2006).

In nature it is likely that most learning about the environment is latent. Animals learn about many aspects of their surroundings through exploration, but only an unpredictable portion of that knowledge becomes useful at a later time and affects the animal's behavior.

Social Learning: Learning by Watching and Interacting With Others

The objects of most intense exploration, for most of us, are other people. By watching others we learn an enormous amount about people, about how to do things, and about the human significance of the rest of our environment. **Social learning** is broadly defined as occurring in a situation "in which one individual comes to behave similarly to another" (Boesch & Tomasello, 1998). This is usually done simply by watching others and is referred to by psychologists as **observational learning**.

An early (and continuing) advocate of the importance of observational learning in humans is Albert Bandura (1962, 1986). In his *social learning* (later renamed *social cognitive*) *theory*, Bandura argued that children learn important social behaviors from observing others through a process of **vicarious reinforcement**, the ability to learn from the consequences of others' actions. It is not necessary for a person's behavior to be explicitly reinforced to learn; rather, it is enough to observe another person reinforced for some action. As Bandura modified his theory over nearly 50 years, his outlook became increasingly more cognitive, deviating from its original roots in behaviorism. For example, in addition to vicarious reinforcement, Bandura proposed four other key cognitive capabilities—symbolization, forethought, self-regulation, and self-selection—which are described in **Table 8.1**.

Through observation we learn about the unique characteristics of others, so we can judge how to get along with them and know who is likely to help us or hurt us in a given situation. When we are in a new social environment, we look frequently to others to learn what sorts of behaviors are normal or expected in that setting—so

TABLE 8.1 Key cognitive capabilities in Bandura's social-cognitive theory

Symbolization	The ability to think about social behavior in words and images.
Forethought	The ability to anticipate the consequences of our actions and the actions of others.
Self-regulation	The ability to adopt standards of acceptable behavior for ourselves.
Self-selection	The ability to analyze our thoughts and actions.
Vicarious reinforcement	The ability to learn new behavior and the consequences of one's actions by observing others.

Palladino
Handelsman
& Butler
© Psi Chi

■ Different theorists have emphasized different ways in which human and non-human animals learn.

when in Rome, we can do as the Romans do. We also look frequently to others to see what they are looking at and how they are responding to what they are looking at. In that way we learn some of what they already know about the surrounding environment. To learn a new skill—whether it's a new dance step, driving a car, or performing surgery—we usually begin by observing the actions of a person who has already mastered the skill. Thank goodness for that; imagine what the world would be like if people learned driving and surgery only by trial and error!

Learning How by Watching Skilled Performers

Many experiments have shown that animals can learn or partially learn how to perform a new task by watching others do it. Kittens learned more quickly to press a lever for food if they had seen their mother do so than if they had not (Chesler, 1969). Dogs were better at moving around a barrier to get food if they had seen another dog or human being do it first than if they hadn't (Pongrácz et al., 2008). Mice who had observed a well-trained mouse make a sequence of two movements to get a food pellet learned that sequence of movements more readily than those who hadn't (Carlier & Jamon, 2006).

It is tempting to interpret such results as evidence that mammals in general are able to learn by imitating the actions of others of their kind. But, if you think about it, you realize that imitation is cognitively complex. To *imitate*, an animal must observe, remember, and reproduce the specific pattern of movements that were produced by the model. To reproduce the movements, the learner must map the observed actions onto its own movement control system. Many researchers argue, with evidence, that real imitation does not occur in mammals other than primates (and perhaps only in humans; Bjorklund et al., 2010; Whiten et al., 2004). Further, they point to evidence that observational learning by nonprimates involves simpler means, including stimulus enhancement and goal enhancement (Byrne & Russon, 1988; Zentall, 2006).

Stimulus enhancement refers to an increase in the salience or attractiveness of the object that the observed individual is acting upon. *Goal enhancement* refers to an increased drive to obtain rewards similar to what the observed individual is receiving. Thus, a kitten that sees its mother pressing a lever for food pellets may become attracted to the lever (stimulus enhancement) and motivated to eat food pellets (goal enhancement). In this case, stimulus enhancement increases the likelihood that the kitten will press the lever, goal enhancement increases the reward value of the pellets, and the two combined help the kitten learn very quickly to press the lever for pellets. By this account, the kitten is not imitating the movements of its mother but is going to the lever because that was made salient, pushing it more or less accidentally, and then eating the pellets because they too were made salient.

Chimpanzees clearly learn by observation, but they seem not to engage in true imitation, at least not much. Rather, they are more apt to learn by *emulation,* which involves observing another individual achieve some goal (picking up and dropping

🔍 **FOCUS 33**

How does observation of skilled performers help animals learn new operant tasks? How does imitation differ from stimulus enhancement, goal enhancement, and emulation?

a log to reveal tasty ants, for instance), then reaching that same goal by their own means (bouncing up and down on the log). For example, in one study, 3- and 4-year-old children and chimpanzees were shown a series of three actions, two of which were necessary and one of which was not, to open an opaque puzzle box. Both the children and the chimpanzees copied all three behaviors and got the reward. However, when they were then shown a transparent puzzle box, the children still copied all three actions, even when they could readily see that one of these actions was irrelevant. The chimpanzees, however, skipped the irrelevant action and copied only the necessary ones to achieve their goal (Horner & Whiten, 2005). In this and other studies (Tomasello, 2000), the chimpanzees seem to be more focused on the goal and less on the means used to achieve it, a characteristic of emulation.

There is at least one exception to this pattern, and that is for chimpanzees that have been raised as if they were children, called *enculturated chimpanzees*. In several studies, such animals display true imitation, even imitating the behaviors of a model up to 24 hours after originally observing it (Bjorklund et al., 2002; Buttlemann et al., 2007; Tomasello et al., 1993). Apparently, something associated with a human-like rearing environment altered young chimpanzees' social-learning abilities, causing them to be more like 4-year-old human children in some ways than mother-raised chimpanzees.

Cultural Transmission in Chimpanzees

FOCUS 34

What is the evidence that chimpanzees transmit cultural traditions from generation to generation?

We humans are the supremely cultural animal. *Culture,* as we said before, refers to the beliefs and traditions that are passed along from generation to generation. Because of culture we do not have to invent the wheel anew, or figure out how to grow crops or how to build houses; we merely improve on what our ancestors invented. Observational learning appears to be a prerequisite for human culture. The skills and rituals acquired by each generation are passed on to the next not so much because the older generation deliberately trains the younger (though that is part of it) but more because members of the younger generation intently observe their elders and learn to behave as they do (Lancy, 2015).

The species that comes second to humans in exhibition of culture—though a far distant second—is, not surprisingly, the chimpanzee. Wild chimpanzees living in different groups, geographically isolated from one another, have different cultural traditions, which pass from generation to generation. Researchers studying wild chimpanzees at seven different field stations have identified at least 39 different behaviors, ranging from tool design to mating displays, that are distinct to specific groups and that seem to arise from cultural tradition rather than from constraints imposed by the environment (Whiten, 2007; Whiten et al., 1999).

For example, chimpanzees in some colonies crack hard-shelled nuts by placing a nut on a carefully selected rock and hitting it with another carefully selected rock (see **Figure 8.16**; Mercader et al., 2002). The young in these colonies learn this skill by observing their elders and practicing elements of it over a period of several months (Inoue-Nakamura & Matsuzawa, 1997). In other colonies, however, chimpanzees have never been observed to crack nuts, even though plenty of nuts and stones are available. Apparently, in those colonies the discovery that nuts can be cracked was never made, so it could not be passed along. Research conducted with chimpanzees living in a wildlife sanctuary has shown that the introduction of one nut-cracking chimp can lead quickly to the spreading of that skill throughout the colony (Marshall-Pescini & Whiten, 2008).

The most sophisticated form of social learning is teaching, which involves the teacher modifying his or

FIGURE 8.16 Chimpanzees learn through observation to crack nuts with rocks. The infant sitting beside her mother is too young to work seriously at nut cracking, but may be learning something about it through watching the older master.

Fiona Rogers/Nature Picture Library

her behavior in order that the "student" acquire new knowledge. Teaching requires that the learner appreciate the perspective of the teacher and that the teacher be sensitive to the knowledge, motivations, and emotions of the learner. Parents begin "teaching" their children in infancy, although true learning from teaching likely doesn't occur until sometime later. Although we frequently talk of nonhuman animals teaching their offspring, teaching in the animal world is rare. It has been shown in meerkats (Thorton & McAuliffe, 2006), dolphins (Bender et al., 2009), and chimpanzees (Boesch, 1991), but the situations in which it is observed are far more limited than in humans. For example, when mother Atlantic spotted dolphins are foraging with their calves, they orient their bodies to the prey they are chasing and delay eating the prey (Bender et al., 2009). Mother chimpanzees make exaggerated movements while cracking nuts when in the presence of their infants (Boesch, 1991). However, at least in chimpanzees, teaching is rarely observed, and it appears that most social learning in our close genetic relatives is not achieved by teaching but by other less complex forms of observational learning, such as emulation (Bering & Povinelli, 2003). In fact, despite the ubiquity of teaching in modern cultures, David Lancy (2015) notes that direct teaching of children by adults in traditional cultures is rare and was likely rare for our ancestors. Instead, children seem especially prepared to learn from others by watching. In fact, Lancy (2016) has suggested that whereas observational learning is an evolved, universal feature of humans, teaching is not, but rather is primarily a result of recent cultural changes and the emergence of modern economies.

As we've seen, many species engage in social learning, but none does so to the extent and level of proficiency as *Homo sapiens*. Many have suggested that human minds were shaped by natural selection to be especially attentive to social relations— to infer the goals, intentions, and thoughts of others— that permitted our ancestors to more effectively cooperate and compete with, and especially learn from one another (Shafto et al., 2012; Tomasello, 2009). You can think of humans' propensity for social learning as a broad type of specialized learning mechanism, and we will examine the centrality of social cognition for our species in later chapters of this book. But now we turn to some narrower forms of specialized learning, both in humans and other animals.

SECTION REVIEW

In the natural environment, learning is promoted by play, exploration, and observation.

Play	Exploration	Social Learning
■ In line with a theory originated by Karl Groos, young mammals appear to play in ways that help them to develop crucial survival skills. Play is most frequent in those species that have the most to learn.	■ Exploration is more primitive than play, occurring in many more species and at all ages. It promotes learning about the environment.	■ Albert Bandura's social learning (later social cognitive) theory emphasized the role of vicarious reinforcement in social learning.
■ Human children play not just at skills that are crucial to people everywhere, but also at those unique skills that are crucial to the culture in which they develop.	■ Curiosity motivates exploration of novel objects and places, but is balanced by fear.	■ Stimulus enhancement, goal enhancement, and emulation are simpler forms of observational learning than imitation.
■ Children's symbolic play may promote the development of language, perspective taking, and executive-function abilities.	■ Latent learning experiments show that exploration alone, without external reward, produces useful knowledge.	■ The most sophisticated form of social learning is teaching, which humans do readily but is rare (though not nonexistent) in other animals.

Specialized Learning Abilities: Filling the Blanks in Species-Typical Behavior Patterns

Thus far we have been examining learning processes and activities that are general in the sense that they operate in a wide variety of contexts. Animals can learn many different things through classical conditioning, operant conditioning, play, exploration, and observation. But natural selection has also endowed animals with specialized learning abilities that have quite limited domains of operation. We may think of these as adjuncts to particular species-typical behavior patterns. Each such learning ability helps to mesh some aspect of the animal's species-typical behavior with particular variable characteristics of the animal's environment.

In Chapter 3, we cited the white-crowned sparrow's learning of its local song dialect as an example of specialized learning. That ability does not stem from a general capacity of sparrows to imitate. Instead, it results from a special learning mechanism that is specific to song learning and narrow in scope. It allows the bird to learn any given white-crowned sparrow song dialect, but does not allow the bird to learn the song of another bird species. In this section, we look at special learning abilities related to food preferences and then at a few other examples of specialized learning mechanisms.

Special Abilities for Learning What to Eat

For some animals, learning what to eat is a relatively simple matter. Koalas, for instance, eat only the leaves of eucalyptus trees. Through natural selection, koalas evolved a food-identifying mechanism that tells them that eucalyptus leaves are food and everything else is not. That simplifies their food choice, but if eucalyptuses vanish, so will koalas. Other animals are more flexible in their diets. Most flexible of all are omnivorous creatures, such as rats and humans, which treat almost all organic matter as potential food and must *learn* what is safe to eat. Such animals have evolved special mechanisms for learning to identify healthful foods and to avoid potential poisons.

Food-Aversion Learning: How It Differs From Typical Classical Conditioning

If rats become ill after eating a novel-tasting food, they subsequently avoid that food. In experiments demonstrating this, researchers induce illness by adding a toxic substance to the food or by administering a drug or a high dose of X-rays (inducing radiation sickness) to the animals after they have eaten (Garcia et al., 1972). Similarly, people who by chance get sick after eating an unusual food often develop a long-term aversion to the food (Bernstein, 1991). For years as a child, I (Peter Gray) hated the taste and smell of a particular breakfast cereal, because once, a few hours after I ate it, I happened to develop a bad case of stomach flu. I knew, intellectually, that the cereal wasn't the cause of my illness, but that didn't help. The learning mechanism kicked in automatically and made me detest that cereal.

Some psychologists choose to describe such cases of food-aversion learning in terms of classical conditioning. In that description, the feeling of illness or nausea induced by the X-ray treatment or drug is the unconditioned stimulus for a reaction of aversion or revulsion, and the taste and smell of the food become conditioned stimuli for that reaction. For example, many patients receiving chemotherapy or radiation therapy for cancer report acquiring aversions to foods that became associated with the nausea accompanying these therapies (Mattes et al., 1992). This is why such patients are often counseled to avoid eating favorite foods before treatment: Whatever aversions they acquire, those favorite foods won't be affected. But

FOCUS 35

What are two ways in which food-aversion learning differs from typical examples of classical conditioning? How do these differences make sense in terms of the function of such learning?

John Garcia, the researcher who pioneered the study of food-aversion learning, argues that such learning is markedly different from standard cases of classical conditioning (Garcia et al., 1989).

One special characteristic of food-aversion learning has to do with the optimal delay between the conditioned and unconditioned stimuli. In typical cases of classical conditioning, such as the salivary reflex studied by Pavlov, conditioning occurs only when the unconditioned stimulus follows immediately (within a few seconds) after the conditioned stimulus. But food-aversion learning has been demonstrated even when X-rays were administered as long as 24 hours after the animals had eaten the food (Etscorn & Stephens, 1973).

Another special characteristic has to do with the sorts of stimuli that can serve as conditioned stimuli for such learning. In typical cases of classical conditioning, almost any kind of detectable stimulus can serve, but in food-aversion learning the stimulus must be a distinctive taste or smell (and taste generally works better than smell). Rats that become ill after eating a particular food subsequently avoid any food that tastes or smells like what they had eaten, even if it looks different, but they do not avoid a food that looks like what they had eaten if it tastes and smells different (Garcia et al., 1968, 1989). Also, when the X-ray–induced radiation sickness was paired with flashing lights or sounds, it was very difficult for the rats to relate the two experiences. But not when novel food was involved.

These distinguishing characteristics of food-aversion learning make excellent sense when considered in the light of the function that such learning serves in the natural environment. In general, poisons and spoiled foods do not make an individual ill immediately, but only after many minutes or several hours. Moreover, it is not the visual quality of the food that produces illness, but rather its chemical quality, detectable in its taste and smell. For example, a food that has begun to rot and makes an animal sick may look identical to one that has not begun to rot, but its taste and smell are noticeably different. Thus, to be effective, a learning mechanism for food aversion must tolerate long delays and be tuned especially to those sensory qualities that correspond with the food's chemistry.

Counter to the conventional wisdom of his day, Garcia argued that the rats were *prepared* to make an association between nausea and food consumption (especially novel food), something that would be adaptive in the wild. A few years after Garcia published his work, Martin Seligman (1970) extended this idea, proposing that all associations between events and behavior are not equally learnable. Rather, there is a continuum of preparedness, such that animals (including people) are prepared by natural selection to make some associations and unprepared, or even contraprepared, for others. *Prepared behaviors* include the association between food ingestion and nausea, as shown by Garcia in rats, as well as learned behaviors that are vital to an organism's survival, such as imprinting in ducks and geese (an infant bird forming an attachment to a moving and/or vocalizing stimulus, usually its mother), which is most easily acquired hours after hatching (see discussion of imprinting later in this chapter). *Unprepared behaviors* are those acquired through the normal processes of operant conditioning and usually take repeated trials to acquire. *Contraprepared behaviors,* in contrast, are those that are impossible or difficult to learn despite extensive training, such as the association between nausea and patterns of light and sounds in rats.

Seligman's three-part classification shows that the rules of operant conditioning are not as uniform, or general, as Skinner and other behavioral theorists proposed; rather, there are some *biological constraints on learning,* shaped over the course of evolution, that make some associations more easily acquired than others.

Food-Preference Learning

The other side of the coin of learning to avoid harmful foods is learning to choose foods that satisfy a specific nutritional requirement. Just as rats can learn to associate the taste of a food with subsequent illness and thereafter avoid that food, they can also associate a taste with a subsequent improvement in health and thereafter prefer that food.

A number of experiments have shown that when rats are deprived of a mineral (such as calcium) or a vitamin that is essential for health, they will learn to prefer the flavor of a new food that contains that mineral or vitamin (Rozin & Schull, 1988; Tordoff, 2002). In one series of experiments, researchers deprived rats of thiamine (one of the B vitamins, essential for health) for a period of time and then offered them a choice of foods, only one of which contained thiamine (Overmann, 1976; Rozin & Kalat, 1971). Each food had a distinct flavor, and thiamine—which itself has no flavor—was added to a different food for different rats. The result was that, within a few days of experience with the foods, most rats strongly preferred the thiamine-containing food.

How did the rats "figure out" which food contained the thiamine? Close inspection of their eating patterns suggests a possible answer (Rozin & Kalat, 1971). When first presented with the choices, a rat usually ate just one or two of the foods. Then, typically after several hours, the rat would switch to a different food or two. Such behavior—eating just one or two foods at a time—seems ideally suited for isolating particular foods that lead to an increase or a decrease in health. If the rat had sampled all the foods at once, it would have had no basis for knowing which one had affected its health.

We don't know if humans have a similar ability to learn which foods have a vitamin or mineral that we need, as no controlled experiments have been conducted to find out. It would not be ethical to deprive people of necessary nutrients for the sake of such research. However, there is evidence that people, as well as rats, learn to prefer a food that is high in calories (Brunstrom, 2005). This learning mechanism, which was no doubt valuable both to our evolutionary ancestors and to some people today, may have an unfortunate effect on those of us who are overweight and surrounded by wide choices of foods.

In the typical human flavor-preference learning experiment, college students are presented each day with one of two differently flavored foods, which is either laced with a high-calorie substance or not so laced. Initially the two foods are rated as equally pleasant (or unpleasant) in taste, but, over the course of days, the students' average rating of the high-calorie food goes up, while their rating of the low-calorie food stays the same or declines (Brunstrum, 2005; Brunstrom & Mitchell, 2007). Apparently some delayed satisfying effect of the calories causes the students to develop a preference for the high-calorie version.

Learning From Others What to Eat

In addition to learning from their own experiences with foods, rats learn what to eat from one another. Newly weaned wild rats generally limit their diets to foods that older rats in the colony regularly eat. Through this means, they can avoid even tasting a food that older animals have learned is poisonous (Galef & Clark, 1971) and can choose, from the beginning, a nutritious food that older animals have learned to prefer (Beck & Galef, 1989). Similar results have been found with kittens (Wyrwicka, 1996). Even in adulthood, rats are strongly influenced by one another's food choices. Bennett Galef (1990, 2002) has found that rats in a colony sniff near the mouth of a rat that has recently eaten and then show a strong preference for the food they had smelled on the demonstrator rat's breath. Through this and other means, adult rats introduced into a new colony acquire the colony's food preferences. The tendency to eat what others of one's kind have been eating has been demonstrated in many other species of animals as well (Galef & Giraldeau, 2001).

We humans don't learn food preferences by smelling one another's breath (at least not consciously), but we are certainly influenced by our observations of what those around us eat. In one experiment, children between 1 and 4 years old were more willing to taste a new food if they saw an adult eat it first than if they had never seen anyone eat it (Harper & Sanders, 1975). Other research suggests

FOCUS 36

How has flavor-preference learning been demonstrated in humans?

FOCUS 37

How do rats and people learn food preferences by attending to others of their kind?

that children are most open to new foods from about 1 to 2 years of age, which is when they are most likely to be closely watched and fed by adults, and are least willing to try new foods between about 4 and 8 years of age, a time when they have greater freedom of movement and are not so closely watched but have not yet learned to distinguish foods from poisons (Cashdan, 1994). From this point of view, the finicky eating of 4- to 8-year-olds is an evolutionary adaptation that reduces the chance of eating something poisonous. However, positive reinforcement in the form of decorative stickers or other tokens has been successful in encouraging children to try new foods, including vegetables. Children reinforced in this way have developed a liking for the new foods that lasted at least 3 months after rewards ceased (Cook et al., 2011).

Mitch York/Getty Images

■ **Observational learning has its limits** Children acquire the food preferences of their culture by observing their elders, but sometimes it takes a while.

Food preferences can even begin while still in the womb. For example, in one experiment pregnant women ate anise-flavored food while others did not. (Anise tastes like licorice.) At birth and 4 days later, infants born to anise-consuming mothers showed a preference for anise odor, whereas those born to non–anise-consuming mothers displayed aversion or neutral responses to anise (Schaal et al., 2000).

Summary of Rules for Learning What to Eat

Suppose that you were a wise teacher of young omnivorous animals and wanted to equip your charges with a few rules for food selection that could be applied no matter what food was available. Two that you would probably come up with are these: (1) When possible, eat what your elders eat. Such food is probably safe, given that your elders have most likely been eating it for some time and are still alive. (2) When you eat a new food, remember its taste and smell. If the food is followed within a few hours by feelings of improved health, continue choosing foods of that taste and smell, but if you feel sick, avoid such foods.

Notice that these rules do not specify what to eat, but specify *how to learn* what to eat. The first rule describes a specific variety of observational learning, and the second describes a specific, efficient variety of associative learning. As you have just seen, rats do in fact behave in accordance with these rules, and humans may also. Of course, we assume that these rules have been imparted not by a wise teacher of young omnivores but by natural selection, which has shaped the brain to operate automatically in accordance with the rules.

FOCUS 38

In sum, what has natural selection imparted to young omnivores about food selection?

Other Examples of Special Learning Abilities

Food selection is by no means the only domain in which special learning abilities have apparently come about through evolution. Here are some other well-studied examples.

Prepared Fear-Related Learning

Earlier in the chapter we described a demonstration by Watson and Rayner (1920), in which a young boy named Albert was conditioned to fear a white rat by pairing it with a loud noise. Several years later, a graduate student working with Thorndike named Elsie Bregman (1934) tried to repeat that demonstration with one important modification. Instead of using a rat as the conditioned stimulus, she used various inanimate objects, including wooden blocks and pieces of cloth. Despite numerous attempts, with 15 different infants as subjects, she found no evidence of conditioning. What are we to make of this apparent discrepancy? One possibility, suggested by Martin Seligman (1971), is that people are biologically predisposed to acquire fears of situations and objects, such as spiders and snakes, that posed a threat to our evolutionary ancestors and are less disposed to acquire fears of other situations and objects.

FOCUS 39

What is some evidence that people and monkeys are biologically predisposed to learn to fear some things more easily than other things?

FIGURE 8.17 A biologically pre-pared learned reaction Monkeys that have never been harmed by snakes nevertheless learn quickly to fear them through watching the fearful reactions of other monkeys.

More recently, Susan Mineka and her colleagues (1984) showed that rhesus monkeys are not afraid of snakes when first exposed to them but easily learn to fear them. In one experiment, monkeys raised in the laboratory did not react fear-fully to snakes until they saw a monkey that had been raised in the wild do so. After that, they showed strong fear reactions themselves when a snake was present (see **Figure 8.17**). In subsequent experiments, Michael Cook and Mineka (1989, 1990) used splicing to produce films in which a monkey was shown reacting fearfully in the presence of various objects, including toy snakes, flowers, and a toy rabbit. Through observing the films, monkeys that previously feared none of these objects developed a fear of toy snakes (and real snakes) but not of flowers or toy rabbits.

From an evolutionary perspective, this learning bias makes a good deal of sense. In some regions where rhesus monkeys live there are dangerous snakes, but in other regions all of the snakes are harmless. In places where snakes are harmless, an inflexible instinctive fear of them would be maladaptive. Thus, the learning mecha-nism may have evolved because it allows monkeys living in areas where snakes are dangerous to learn quickly to fear and avoid them, while it allows monkeys living elsewhere to go about their business relatively oblivious to snakes. We humans also vary greatly in the degree to which we fear snakes. Research suggests that we learn to fear snakes and other objects that posed threats to our evolutionary ancestors—such as spiders, rats, and angry faces—more readily than we learn to fear equally dangerous objects that were not present in our early evolutionary history, such as electrical outlets, guns, and automobiles (Mineka & Öhman, 2002; Seligman, 1971).

How early do such fears develop? In a clever study, Judy DeLoache and Vanessa LoBue (2009) showed 7- to 9-month-old infants and 14- to 16-month-old toddlers vid-eos of snakes and other animals (giraffes, rhinoceroses). The infants initially showed no greater fear to the snakes than to the other animals, suggesting that a fear of snakes is not inborn. (In fact, other research [LoBue et al., 2013; Thrasher & LoBue, 2016] has shown that infants and young children without previous negative experience with spiders and snakes are often highly interested in these animals.) The infants and tod-dlers then saw brief video clips of snakes and other animals associated with either a happy or fearful voice. Both the infants and toddlers looked longer at the snakes when they heard the fearful voice than when they heard the happy voice. There was no difference in looking times to the two voices when they saw videos of other ani-mals. DeLoache and LoBue suggested that, much like Mineka's monkeys, human chil-dren are prepared to acquire a fear of snakes (see also LoBue & Rakison, 2013).

Other research has found that people who provide social support for an individual can serve as *prepared safety stimuli*. For example, in a series of studies Erica Hornstein and her colleagues (2016) reported that people are less likely to associate social-support figures (for example, a photo of one's mother) with fear than to associate strangers or to other familiar but neutral stimuli (for example, professors in a course the participant was currently taking). The authors suggested that, just as people are prepared to make fearful associations with some evolutionarily relevant stimuli (for example, spiders and snakes), they are also prepared *not* to make such associations to social-support figures.

Imprinting in Precocial Birds: Learning to Identify One's Mother

Some of the earliest evidence for specialized learning abilities came from studies of young precocial birds. *Precocial* birds are those species—such as chickens, geese, and ducks—in which the young can walk almost as soon as they hatch. Because they can walk, they can get separated from their mother. To avoid that, they have acquired, through natural selection, an efficient means to determine who their mother is and a drive to remain near her. The means by which they learn to recognize their mother was discovered by Douglas Spalding near the end of the nineteenth century.

Spalding (1873/1954) observed that newly hatched chicks that were deprived of their mother, and that happened to see him (Spalding) walk by shortly after they were hatched, would follow him as if he were their mother. They continued to follow him for weeks thereafter, and once attached in this way they would not switch to following a real mother hen. Some 60 years later, Konrad Lorenz (1935/1970) made the same discovery with newly hatched goslings. Lorenz labeled the phenomenon ***imprinting***, a term that emphasizes the very sudden and apparently irreversible nature of the learning process involved. It's as if the learning is immediately and indelibly stamped in.

One interesting feature of imprinting is the rather restricted ***critical period*** during which it can occur. Spalding (1873/1954) found that if chicks were prevented from seeing any moving object during the first 5 days after hatching and he then walked past them, they did not follow. Instead, they showed "great terror" and ran away. In more detailed studies, Eckhard Hess (1958, 1972) found that the optimal time for imprinting mallard ducklings is within the first 18 hours after hatching.

Although early studies suggested that young birds could be imprinted on humans or other moving objects as easily as on their mothers, later studies proved otherwise. Given a choice between a female of their species and some other object, newly hatched birds invariably choose to follow the former. Experiments with chicks indicate that this initial preference centers on visual features of the head. Newly hatched chicks will follow a box with a chicken head attached to it as readily as they will a complete stuffed chicken and more readily than any object without a chicken head (Johnson & Horn, 1988). The experience of following the object brings the imprinting mechanism into play, and this mechanism causes the chicks to be attracted thereafter to all the features of the moving object (Bateson, 2000). Under normal conditions, of course, the moving object is their mother, so imprinting leads them to distinguish their mother from any other hen.

FOCUS 40

What aspects of a young fowl's ability to follow its mother depend on learning, and how is that learning guided by inborn biases?

■ **Konrad Lorenz and followers** Lorenz conducted research on imprinting and many other aspects of behavior in ducks and geese. These geese, which were hatched by Lorenz in an incubator, followed him everywhere, as if he were their mother.

Nina Leen/Getty Images

It's not just sight that is involved in imprinting, but also sound (Grier et al., 1967). If you put precocial birds such as ducks in a circular tub and play the maternal call of their species from a speaker on one side and the maternal call of another species from a speaker on the opposite side, they will invariably approach the speaker playing the call from their own species. It's easy to look at these findings and infer that imprinting is a classic example of an instinct—something that is under strong genetic control and requires no experience for its expression. But are these young birds really devoid of all experience? They've actually heard their mother's call while still in the egg. However, when ducklings are removed from their mothers and hatched in an incubator, they still approach their maternal call, even though they had never heard it before. But they have heard the peeping of the other ducklings in the brood of eggs, and their own peeps, for that matter. (Ducklings start peeping several days before hatching.) When this auditory experience is removed by means of a pre-hatch surgical procedure that prevents the ducklings from peeping until several days after hatching, the ducklings then approach the speakers randomly. These experiments, done by Gilbert Gottlieb (1991), show that even something that looks like a clear-cut instinct such as auditory imprinting still involves some experience. Natural selection has worked so that the brain, sensory organs (in this case, those associated with hearing), and experience are coordinated to produce a valuable adaptive behavior. For the most part, it's only the surgically altered duckling hatched in Gottlieb's lab that will fail to get the appropriate experience for imprinting. But as we stressed in Chapter 3, behavior is always the product of both genes and experience, and it sometimes takes a lot of effort to discover what those experiences are.

In sum, we have here a learning process for which the timing (the critical period), the stimulus features (characteristics typical of a mother bird of the species), and the behavioral response (following) are all prepared by genes in interaction with the environment; and this learning process promotes its specific adaptive function (staying near the mother).

Sexual Imprinting and the Westermarck Effect

FOCUS 41

What is the Westermarck effect, and what evidence is there that it is based on early cohabitation?

Lorenz also noted that an animal's early experiences could influence subsequent sexual preferences; that is, which species an animal is sexually attracted to, or the characteristics of a same-species individual that an animal will find most attractive. This phenomenon is known as *sexual imprinting*. For example, male zebra finch's sexual preferences for mates as adults are related to features of their mothers (for example, beak color) (Ten Cate, et al., 2006). Similarly, domesticated animals from falcons to panda bears have been known to show no interest in members of their own species for mates but to make sexual presentations to their human caretakers.

Although sexual imprinting such as that observed in zebra finches has not been observed in humans, people do seem to acquire an *aversion* to having sex with close relatives. All sexually reproducing species have evolved mechanisms for incest aversion in order to avoid inbreeding. Offspring born to close genetic relatives are more likely to share recessive alleles (genes) that increase the chance of developing deleterious physical or mental disorders. In humans, early experience has been found to influence whom people develop an aversion to having sex with, chiefly their siblings. Evidence suggests that this aversion is based on living in the same household during the early years of life. The Finnish anthropologist Edward Westermarck (1891) observed that people in all cultures who are raised together from early in childhood rarely ever marry, whether they are siblings, cousins, or unrelated adoptive or foster siblings. He proposed that the early familiarity of growing up together results in a lack of sexual attraction when the children become adolescents and adults.

Evidence in support of the **Westermarck effect** comes from several sources. The first is from the work of Wolf (1995), who studied the tradition of *minor marriages* in Taiwan during the late nineteenth and early twentieth centuries. As in many cultures, Taiwanese families sometimes arranged the marriage of their young children years before reaching adulthood. The tradition was that the bride-to-be would move into the home of the boy's family and the future bride and groom would be reared together as brother and sister. This arrangement permitted the boy's family to keep tabs on his future wife, increasing paternity certainty when they were ready to marry. Wolf noted that when the girl moved in with the boy's family before she was 30 months of age, she often later objected to marrying her "brother." When these minor marriages did happen, the divorce rate was three times greater, produced 40% fewer children, and the wives admitted to having more extramarital affairs, all relative to "major marriages."

Another source of evidence for the Westermarck effect comes from studies of people reared together from early childhood in Israeli cooperative communities (kibbutzim). Shepher (1983) observed that such children, although frequently engaging in heterosexual play during childhood, rarely engaged in sexual intercourse as adolescents and adults, and there were no marriages between 2,769 couples from 211 kibbutzim.

■ Boys and girls raised together on Israeli kibbutzim rarely engage in sexual intercourse with each other as adolescents and adults. Marriages between individuals raised from early childhood on the same kibbutz are extremely rare.

These studies suggest that genetically unrelated people who are raised together in childhood do not find one another sexually attractive as adults. But what about siblings? Are the same mechanisms in play for them as well? This question was addressed by Bevc and Silverman (1993, 2000), who interviewed people about the incidence of post-childhood sex with siblings. Because such activities are associated with the stigma of incest, the researchers recruited volunteers by placing ads in newspapers in a large city to answer survey questions about sexual relations between brothers and sisters (Bevc & Silverman, 2000). They classified sexual activity as either "mature," which included completed or attempted genital, anal, or oral intercourse; or "immature," which included fondling, exhibitionism, and touching. From this sample, they found 54 cases of people who had admitted having intercourse with a sibling. Similar to the results of an earlier survey of college students (Bevc & Silverman, 1993), they reported that siblings who had been separated during early childhood were more likely to have engaged in genital intercourse than nonseparated pairs. There was no effect of separation, however, for "immature" sexual behaviors. Bevc and Silverman (2000) suggested that early cohabitation results in a so-called *incest inhibition effect*, such that the incidence of reproductive sexual behavior (that is, intercourse) is reduced, but non-reproductive sexual behaviors (such as fondling and exhibitionism) are not necessarily reduced. They also hypothesized, consistent with Wolf (1995), that the sensitive period for the incest-inhibition effect is before the age of 3. Consistent with these findings, there is anecdotal evidence that siblings who were separated early in childhood (e.g., raised in foster or adoptive homes) often have feelings of sexual attraction for one another when they meet as adults. One survey of post-adoption counselors in London indicated that about 50% of clients who had been reunited with siblings as adults experienced "strong, sexual feelings" (Greenberg & Littlewood, 1995).

What is the mechanism for the effect of early cohabitation and subsequent incest avoidance? To avoid inbreeding, people have to be able to (1) detect kin, and (2) regulate sexual motivation based on the likelihood that another person of the opposite sex is a close relative. A number of mechanisms have been suggested (see Tal & Lieberman, 2007). One likely candidate is olfactory (smell) cues. In fact, there is evidence that people can identify their genetic relatives based on smell and find the odor of some kin more aversive than others. In a series of studies, Glenn Weisfeld and his colleagues (2003) had family members wear T-shirts on two consecutive nights and to avoid using perfumes or scented soaps. People were then given the T-shirts and asked to identify on the basis of smell who had worn each shirt. Immediate family members exhibited particular patterns of aversions to each other's odors. Fathers showed aversions to their daughters' (but not to their sons') odors, whereas mothers did not display any aversions; opposite-sex (but not same-sex) sibling pairs showed aversions to each other's odors; and daughters displayed aversions to their fathers' odors. The only cases in which aversion was mutual was the brother–sister and father–daughter pairs, which represent the greatest danger of incest. These patterns of aversion were found whether or not the person smelling the T-shirt could recognize who had worn the shirt. The findings by Weisfeld and his colleagues make a strong argument that the Westermarck effect is governed, at least in part, by the sense of smell.

SECTION REVIEW

Specialized learning abilities have evolved related to species-typical behaviors.

Choosing Food	Objects of Fear	Imprinting on Mother	Sexual Imprinting and the Westermarck Effect
■ Rats and people avoid foods that they had eaten some minutes or hours before becoming ill. Such food-avoidance learning differs in significant ways from general classical conditioning. ■ Rats, and possibly humans, can learn to prefer foods associated with health improvement or nutritional gain. ■ Observation of what others eat influences food choice, differently in rats and people. ■ Some taste preferences can be acquired before birth.	■ We (and other species) are prepared by natural selection to learn to fear objects or situations that were threatening in the species' evolutionary past. ■ In experiments, monkeys learned to fear real and toy snakes, but not flowers or toy rabbits, by observing others' fearful reactions. ■ Human infants and toddlers are more attentive to snakes when they hear a fearful voice than a happy voice.	■ Ducklings and goslings follow the first moving object they see within a critical period, and continue to follow it. ■ Certain characteristics of imprinting help to ensure that, under normal conditions, the young of these species will learn to identify and follow their own mothers. ■ Ducklings will approach the maternal call of their species shortly after hatching, and auditory experience while still in the egg is critical for this adaptive behavior to develop.	■ Sexual imprinting is the process by which some animals' mate preferences as adults are influenced by their early rearing experiences. ■ Incest aversion in humans is related to early cohabitation; this is called the Westermarck effect.

Thinking Critically About Processes of Learning

1. Can research on conditioning using rats and pigeons as subjects really tell us anything about how humans learn? Why or why not?

2. Is play "childish" and essentially useless other than for keeping children amused? Modern schools are increasingly reducing opportunities to play during the day. From an educational perspective, why might this be a good or not so good thing?

Reflections and Connections

In this chapter we refer to three different perspectives on learning: the *behavioral, cognitive,* and *evolutionary* perspectives. A perspective is a point of view, a framework, a set of ground rules and assumptions that scientists bring to the topic studied. The perspective helps determine the kinds of questions asked, the kinds of evidence regarded as important, the kinds of studies conducted, and the vocabulary used to describe the observations. Here are some thoughts about these perspectives.

1. Did the cognitive revolution really replace behaviorism? Behaviorism was one of the first overarching perspectives in psychology, attempting to account for nearly all important psychological phenomena. It assumed that (1) behavior is shaped by the environment and (2) all aspects of behavior, including learning, are best described in terms of observable stimuli and responses, without reference to unseen mental events. Although behaviorism dominated research and serious thought in psychology through much of the first half of the twentieth century, critics argued that behaviorism ignored the richness that is human thought. Behaviorism was overshadowed in the latter part of the twentieth century by the cognitive perspective. When I (David Bjorklund) was a student of psychology at the height of this transition, my teachers told me cognitive psychology broke the "stranglehold" behaviorism had had upon psychology, and that

cognitive psychology was behaviorism's death knell. At the time, I bought it. However, it became apparent that even if the cognitive revolution introduced a new way of thinking about behavior and thought, it did not negate the findings of behaviorism. Much learning *is* done via associations, reinforcement *does* alter the frequency of an individual's behavior, and different schedules of reinforcement *do* produce different patterns of behavior. Cognitivism may have replaced behaviorism as the principal explanatory mechanism for understanding behavior, but it did not make behaviorism's findings any less legitimate. Although behaviorism's assumption of a mindless organism is no longer fashionable, the principles of learning and the many findings it produced are real and exist alongside cognitive interpretations when we attempt to understand human actions or to modify behavior, such as in the use of techniques of applied behavior analysis for dealing with unruly children or people with autism.

2. The evolutionary perspective This is the perspective that most clearly unites the material in Chapter 3 on evolution and the material on learning in the present chapter. Behaviorism and cognitivism have roots in philosophy, which strives to understand human behavior and the human mind in terms of widely applicable general principles (e.g., principles of mental associations and the law of effect). In contrast, the evolutionary perspective grew out of biology, which recognizes the diversity of life processes. The view that learning mechanisms are products of natural selection implies that they should be specially designed to solve biologically significant problems of survival and reproduction. Evolutionary interpretations of learning are not contradictory to behavioral or cognitive interpretations. Rather, they represent different levels of analysis or causation—*distal* for evolutionary interpretations and immediate, or *proximal*, for behavioral and cognitive interpretations. In fact, behavioral and cognitive mechanisms for learning have their own evolutionary history.

In this chapter, the evolutionary perspective manifested itself most clearly in research on the value of conditioning in helping animals to predict biologically significant events (e.g., foods, dangers, and opportunities for sex); the role of play in motivating animals to practice life-sustaining skills; the special human adaptations for observational learning; the specialized, domain-specific learning mechanisms (e.g., food preferences, fear learning, imprinting on the mother, and place learning); and sexual-preference learning such as the Westermarck effect (which leads to avoidance of inbreeding), that are unique to certain species.

Key Terms

behavior analysis 288
behaviorism 269
classical conditioning 266
concept 287
conditioned response 267
conditioned stimulus 267
continuous reinforcement 283
critical period 305
discrimination training 269
discriminative stimulus 286
drug tolerance 276
evaluative conditioning 274

extinction 268
fixed-interval schedule 284
fixed-ratio schedule 284
generalization 269
habituation 266
imprinting 305
latent learning 296
law of effect 280
learning 265
negative punishment 285
negative reinforcer 285
negative reinforcement 284

observational learning 296
operant conditioning 279
operant responses 279
overjustification effect 288
partial reinforcement 283
positive punishment 285
positive reinforcement 284
positive reinforcer 284
punishment 285
reflex 266
reinforcement 284
reinforcer 281

response 266
shaping 283
social learning 296
spontaneous recovery 268
stimulus 266
symbolic play 293
unconditioned response 267
unconditioned stimulus 267
variable-interval schedule 284
variable-ratio schedule 284
vicarious reinforcement 296
Westermarck effect 306

Find Out More

John Alcock (2013). *Animal behavior: An evolutionary approach* (10th ed.). Sunderland, MA: Sinauer.

This very popular text focuses first on the evolutionary basis of behavior, followed by the proximate mechanisms underlying animal behavior. Beautifully illustrated and easy to read, the book explores the evolutionary puzzles provided by developmental and neurophysiological mechanisms.

Stephen Ray Flora (2004). *The power of reinforcement*. Albany, NY: State University of New York Press.

Flora, in the tradition of Skinner, is an unabashed advocate for the deliberate use of positive reinforcement (rewards) to improve people's behavior. In this clearly written,

well-argued work, Flora advocates the intelligent use of reinforcement in parenting, educational settings, correctional institutions, and health improvement programs.

Peter Gray (2014, May 10). The decline of play and the rise of mental disorders. Lesson created by Jose G. Lepervanche using video from the TEDx Talks YouTube channel. Monmouth County, NJ.

http://ed.ted.com/on/bt6AeE9S

Inspired by his own son's unhappy experience with "imprisonment schooling," the senior author of this textbook launched an initiative to advocate for free play as an essential way for children to gain an internal sense of control, build emotional resilience, and learn skills for

solving problems and getting along with others. This site offers not only the TED talk, but also a set of resources to explore and a guided discussion.

HelpGuide.org (n.d.) Understanding addiction: How addiction hijacks the brain.

https://www.helpguide.org/harvard/how-addiction-hijacks-the-brain.htm

This site provides down-to-earth, practical insights into the pleasure centers in the brain, the learning process, and the development of compulsion that leads to addiction. The content is adapted with permission from the *Harvard Mental Health Letter* and *Overcoming Addiction: Paths toward recovery*, a special health report published by Harvard Health Publications.

LaunchPad
macmillan learning

Visit LaunchPad for Psychology 8e www.launchpadworks.com to access the e-book, videos, activities, additional resources, and Learning Curve quizzes, as well as study aids including flash cards and web quizzes.

Memory, Attention, and Consciousness

LEARNING OUTCOMES

After studying this chapter, you should be able to:

- Describe the information-processing model of the mind and how it applies to sensory, short-term, and long-term memory, and to "fast" and "slow" thinking.

- Explain how the brain enables us to focus attention on significant stimuli.

- Describe how working memory functions.

- Define executive functions and identify their neurological basis.

- Contrast explicit and implicit memory.

- Summarize how memories are encoded and consolidated.

- Outline the process of retrieving long-term memories.

Repeatedly, while working on this book, I (Peter Gray) have lamented my seeming lack of memory. I can't remember who did that experiment. I forgot to copy my list of the articles I need for this section. Now, where did I put my laptop?

Like digestion, memory is one of those abilities that we tend to take for granted except when it fails us. We are usually more aware of forgetting than of remembering. But if we stop to think about it, we realize that our remembering is far more impressive than our forgetting. Every waking moment is full of memories. Every thought, every learned response, every act of recognition is based on memory. We use memory not just to think about the past but also to make sense of the present and plan for the future. One can argue that memory *is* the mind. Memory plays center stage in our lives, and recollections of our past serve as the basis of our personal identity.

Memory is intimately tied to learning. Memory is often thought of as the change within an individual, brought on by learning, that can influence the individual's future behavior: Learning $\longrightarrow$ memory $\longrightarrow$ effect on future behavior. In Chapter 8 we examined basic learning processes, focusing on the relation between observable aspects of the learning experience (the training conditions) and subsequent behavior, with little concern for the inner change— memory—that mediates that relation. This chapter, in contrast, is primarily about that inner change, and it deals with types of learning and memory, some of which may be unique to human beings. Our main focus here is on the conscious, self-aware human mind.

Although memory is the "star" of this chapter, it cannot be studied in isolation from other basic cognitive abilities. Equally important is the phenomenon of *attention*. William James (1890/1950) stated, "Everyone knows what attention is. It is the taking possession of the mind, in clear and vivid form, of one out of what may seem several simultaneously possible objects or trains of thought. . . . It implies withdrawal from some things in order to deal effectively with others." Modern definitions of attention are not much different, even though attention and related abilities, such as executive functions, are viewed through the lens of more contemporary theories, as well as with the benefit of nearly 100 years of behavioral, and more recently neuropsychological, research.

Consciousness is a word that different philosophers and psychologists use in different ways and about which they often debate. For practical purposes, many psychologists define consciousness, or more properly self-consciousness (or self-awareness), as the experiencing of one's own mental events in such a manner that one can report on them to others (Baars & Franklin, 2003). The value of this definition, which is the one we use throughout this book, is that it provides an objective criterion for identifying conscious experiences. If you tell me, correctly, that a picture I show you has a bluebird in it, then I assume that you consciously see the bluebird. If, sometime later, you say, "a bluebird," when I ask you what was in the picture, then I assume you have consciously recalled the bluebird. Defined this way, *consciousness* and *awareness* are synonyms. Consciousness may be unique to humans, and in fact, many scholars have proposed that becoming self-aware played a major role in human cognitive evolution (Bering & Bjorklund, 2007; Donald 2000; Humphrey, 1976).

This chapter begins with a general model of information processing that psychologists have long used as a framework for talking and thinking about the human mind. It then discusses issues of attention, working memory, executive functions—cognitive processes involved in the regulation of thought and behavior—memory as the representation of knowledge, and the formation and recall of long-term memories. Throughout the chapter we also examine the neural bases of these processes.

Overview: An Information-Processing Model of the Mind

Cognitive psychologists commonly look at the mind (or brain) as a processor of information, analogous to a computer. Yet there is no single information-processing theory of cognition. Rather, information-processing theories are built on a set of assumptions concerning how humans acquire, store, and retrieve information. One core assumption of information-processing approaches is that an individual has limited mental resources in processing information; we only have so much mental energy, storage space, or time to devote to the processing of information. A second core assumption is that information moves through a system of stores, as depicted in **Figure 9.1**. Information is brought into the mind by way of the sensory systems, and then it can be manipulated in various ways, placed into long-term storage, and retrieved when needed to solve a problem.

This information-processing model, first proposed in the 1960s (Atkinson & Shiffrin, 1968; Waugh & Norman, 1965), serves as a general framework for thinking and

FOCUS 1

What are the main components of the information-processing model of the mind presented here?

FIGURE 9.1 An information-processing model of the mind This model has long served as a framework for thinking about the human mind, and we will use it for that purpose throughout the chapter.

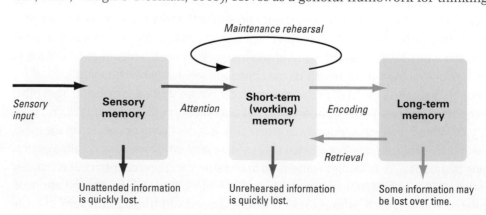

Maintenance rehearsal

Sensory input → Sensory memory → *Attention* → Short-term (working) memory → *Encoding* → Long-term memory

Retrieval

Unattended information is quickly lost.

Unrehearsed information is quickly lost.

Some information may be lost over time.

talking about the mind. As you use this model throughout this chapter, remember that it is simply a way of trying to make sense of the data from many behavioral studies. Like any model, it is a metaphor—if taken literally, it can place blinders on thought and research.

The information-process model portrays the mind as containing three types of **memory stores**—sensory memory, short-term (or working) memory, and long-term memory—conceived of metaphorically as places (boxes in the diagram) where information is held and operated on. Each store type is characterized by its *function* (the role it plays in the overall workings of the mind), its *capacity* (the amount of information it can hold at any given instant), and its *duration* (the length of time it can hold an item of information). In addition to the stores, the model specifies a set of **control processes**, including *attention, rehearsal,* *encoding,* and *retrieval,* which govern the processing of information within stores and the movement of information from one store to another. Following is a brief description of the three stores and the control processes.

Erich Hartmann/Magnum Photos

■ **Why don't we see this way?** If you're wondering why multiple sensory-memory representations of a scene don't overlap and distort your view of the world, the answer is that each new image from instant to instant overrides the sensory memory of the previous image.

Sensory Memory: The Brief Prolongation of Sensory Experience

When lightning flashes on a dark night, you can still see the flash and the objects it illuminated for a split second beyond its actual duration. Similarly, when a companion says, "You're not listening to me," you can still hear those words, and a few words of the previous sentence, for a brief time after they are spoken. Thus, you can answer (falsely), "I was listening. You said . . ."—and then you can repeat your annoyed companion's last few words even though, in truth, you weren't listening when the words were uttered. These examples demonstrate that some trace of sensory input stays in your information-processing system for a brief period—less than 1 second for sights and up to several seconds for sounds—even when you are not paying attention to the input. This trace and the ability to hold it are called **sensory memory**.

A separate sensory-memory store is believed to exist for each sensory system (vision, hearing, touch, smell, and taste). Each sensory store is presumed to hold, very briefly, all the sensory input that enters that sensory system, whether or not the person is paying attention to that input. The function of the store, presumably, is to hold on to sensory information, in its original sensory form, long enough for it to be analyzed by unconscious mental processes and for a decision to be made about whether or not to bring that information into the short-term store. Most of the information in our sensory stores does not enter into our consciousness. We become conscious only of those items that are transformed, by the selective process of *attention,* into working memory.

 FOCUS 2

What is the function of sensory memory?

The Short-Term Store: Conscious Perception and Thought

Information in the sensory store that is attended to moves into the next compartment, which is called the **short-term store** (the central compartment in Figure 9.1); each item fades quickly and is lost within seconds if it is no longer actively attended to or thought about. Conceived of as the major workplace of the mind, the short-term store is sometimes referred to as **working memory**. More recently, researchers use *working memory* to refer to the process of storing and

 FOCUS 3

What are the basic functions of the short-term store, and how is this memory store equated with consciousness? How does working memory resemble the central processing unit of a computer?

■ **The passing moment** The flow of thought through working memory is not unlike the flow of scenery past the window of a moving train.

transforming information being held in the short-term store, and we will examine working memory from this perspective later in this chapter. Short-term store is, among other things, the seat of conscious thought—the place where all conscious perceiving, feeling, comparing, computing, and reasoning take place.

As depicted by the arrows in Figure 9.1, information can enter the short-term store from both the sensory-memory store (representing the present environment) and the long-term-memory store (representing knowledge gained from previous experiences). In this sense, the short-term store is analogous to the central processing unit of a computer. Information can be transmitted into the computer's central processing unit from a keyboard (comparable to input from the mind's sensory store), or it can be entered from the computer's hard drive (comparable to input from the mind's long-term store). The real work of the computer—computation and manipulation of the information—occurs within its central processing unit.

The sensory store and long-term store both contribute to the continuous flow of conscious thought that constitutes the content of the short-term store. *Flow* is an apt metaphor here. The momentary capacity of the short-term store is very small—about seven plus or minus two items (Miller, 1956); only a few items of information can be perceived or thought about at once. Yet the total amount of information that moves through the short-term store over a period of minutes or hours can be enormous, just as a huge amount of water can flow through a narrow channel over time.

Long-Term Memory: The Mind's Library of Information

Once an item has passed from sensory memory into the short-term store, it may or may not then be encoded into **long-term memory** (again, see Figure 9.1, p. 312). Long-term memory corresponds most closely to most people's everyday notion of memory. It is the stored representation of all that a person knows. As such, its capacity must be enormous. Long-term memory contains the information that enables us to recognize or recall the taste of an almond, the sound of a banjo, the face of a grade-school friend, the names of the foods eaten at supper last night, the words of a favorite song, and the spelling of the word *song*. We are not conscious of the items of information in our long-term store except when they have been activated and moved into the short-term store. According to the model, the items lie dormant, or relatively so, like books on a library shelf or digital patterns on a computer disk, until they are called into the short-term store and put to use. **Table 9.1** summarizes what we've learned about memory thus far.

Control Processes: The Mind's Information Transportation Systems

According to the information-processing model presented in Figure 9.1, the movement of information from one memory store to another is regulated by the control processes of *attention, encoding,* and *retrieval,* indicated by arrows between

FOCUS 4

In the information-processing model, what are the functions of attention, encoding, and retrieval?

TABLE 9.1 Characteristics of Short-Term and Long-Term Memory

Short-Term Memory	Long-Term Memory
Active (information is thought about)	Relatively passive (repository of information)
Short duration (items disappear within seconds if no longer thought about)	Long duration (items can last a lifetime)
Limited capacity (7 +/− 2 items)	Unlimited capacity (all long-lasting knowledge)

the boxes. Control processes can be thought of as strategies for moving information through the system and enhancing performance.

Attention, in this context, is the process that controls the flow of information from the sensory store into the short-term store. Because the capacity of sensory memory is large and that of the short-term store is small, attention must restrict the flow of information from the first into the second.

Encoding is the process that controls movement from the short-term store into the long-term store. When you deliberately memorize a poem or a list of names, you are consciously encoding it into long-term memory. Most encoding, however, is not deliberate; rather, it occurs incidentally, as a side effect of the special interest that you devote to certain items of information. If you become interested in, and think about, ideas in this book, you will incidentally encode many of those ideas into long-term memory, along with the new terms relating to them.

Retrieval is the process that controls the flow of information from the long-term store into the short-term store. Retrieval is what we commonly call *remembering* or *recalling*. Like attention and encoding, retrieval can be either deliberate or automatic. Sometimes we actively search our long-term store for a particular piece of information. More often, however, information seems to flow automatically into the working store from the long-term store. One image or thought in working memory seems to call forth the next in a stream that is sometimes logical, sometimes fanciful.

As mentioned previously, the short-term store has a limited capacity. We can only encode, retrieve, or attend to so much information at any one time. Any control process can be viewed as requiring a certain proportion of the system's limited capacity for its execution. One way of thinking about this is to ask how much mental energy any particular process takes. Although we can't compute brain energy consumption as we can compute the number of miles per gallon our car uses, researchers can use neuroimaging techniques to measure how much glucose is consumed executing a mental operation. Glucose is a source of energy for the brain, and the amount of glucose used to execute a given operation indicates how much energy that operation requires. Research has shown that glucose consumption in brain areas associated with cognitive processing is greater (i.e., more resource consuming) when executing more difficult tasks relative to those that are easier (i.e., less resource consuming) (Haier et al., 1992). This provides convincing evidence that the "energy" metaphor for the information-processing system's limited capacity is an apt one.

Individual mental operations can also be placed on a continuum with respect to how much of one's limited capacity each requires for its execution (Hasher & Zacks, 1979). At one extreme are *effortful processes*, which require the use of mental resources for their successful completion; at the other extreme are *automatic processes*, which require little or none of the short-term store's limited capacity. In addition to not requiring any mental effort, truly automatic processes are hypothesized: (1) to occur without intention and without conscious awareness; (2) not to interfere with the execution of other processes; (3) not to improve with practice; and (4) not to be influenced by individual differences in intelligence, motivation, and education (Hasher & Zacks, 1979). In contrast, effortful processes are hypothesized to: (1) be available to consciousness; (2) interfere with the execution of other effortful processes; (3) improve with practice; and (4) be influenced by individual differences in intelligence, motivation, and education.

Processes closer to the automatic end of the continuum, such as keeping track of the approximate frequency of certain events or understanding sentences that are spoken to you, may develop without any explicit practice. Others, such as reading or driving a car, can develop with practice. These operations are at first very effortful and require your full attention,

■ **Control processes at play** The player who best manages her control processes of attention, encoding, and retrieval is likely to win this game—unless, of course, she was dealt a lousy hand.

Corina Marie Howell/ImageSource/AGE Fotostock

but with practice are done "effortlessly." Of course, some mental effort is expended even on these well-learned tasks, as reading rate or driving performance will decline when there are distractions or the reader/driver engages in a secondary task (e.g., texting while driving). Everyday cognition involves a constant combination of automatic (and unconscious) and effortful (and conscious) processes, some of which we will examine in this and the following chapter.

"Fast" and "Slow" Thinking: Dual-Processing Theories of Cognition

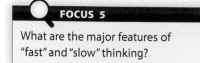

FOCUS 5

What are the major features of "fast" and "slow" thinking?

Following from the description of control processes just provided, many psychologists have proposed that, when solving problems, people have two general ways of proceeding. Such **dual-processing theories** typically place one way of thinking on the automatic end of the information-processing continuum, with processing being fast, automatic, and unconscious. The second way of thinking is placed on the effortful side of this continuum, with processing being slow, effortful, and conscious. Different theorists have provided different labels for the two types of thinking, including implicit/explicit, heuristic/analytic, associative/rule-based, verbatim/gist, automatic/controlled, or System 1/System 2, among others (Evans & Stanovich, 2013; Stanovich & West, 2000).

Cognitive psychologist Daniel Kahneman, who won the Nobel Prize in Economics in 2002 for his work done in collaboration with Amos Tversky on human decision-making, refers to these two types of processing in his 2011 book *Thinking Fast and Slow* as "fast" and "slow" thinking. "Fast" thinking is intuitive, with little or no sense of voluntary control. People think and remember by processing inexact, "fuzzy" memory representations rather than working logically from exact, verbatim representations (Brainerd & Reyna, 2015). In contrast, "slow" thinking involves the conscious self deciding which aspects of a problem to attend to, deciding which cognitive operations to execute, and then deliberately solving the problem.

For example, when given the over-learned problem 2 + 2 = ?, you automatically answer "4," without thought. In fact, if you wanted to provide a wrong answer, you would first have to inhibit the correct one, the one you've been giving to this problem since you were in kindergarten. You need a different approach, however, to answer the problem 14 × 39 = ? You would likely immediately know that it is a multiplication problem and that you have the mental tools to solve it. You may also know that 90 and 73,936 are unlikely answers, but to get the precise answer would require a good deal of mental effort, using strategies you learned in elementary school, and maybe even a calculator. You would need to stop doing other tasks, such as paying attention to the television or to a conversation with a friend, while you're computing the answer. You solved the first problem (2 + 2) using the "fast" thinking system, whereas you needed the "slow" system to solve the second problem.

In many cases, when presented with a problem, you cannot shut off the "fast" system, even if it may interfere with your arriving at the correct solution to a problem via the "slow" system. This is illustrated in the **Stroop interference effect**, named after J. Ridley Stroop (1935), the first to describe it. Stroop presented words or shapes printed in colored ink to subjects and asked them to name the ink color of each as rapidly as possible. In some cases each word was the name of the color in which it was printed (e.g., the word *red* printed in red ink); in others it was the name of a different color (e.g., the word *blue* printed in red ink); and in still others it was not a color name. Stroop found that subjects were slowest at naming the ink colors for words that named a color different from the ink color. To experience this effect yourself, follow the instructions in the caption of **Figure 9.2**. Automatic processing of the

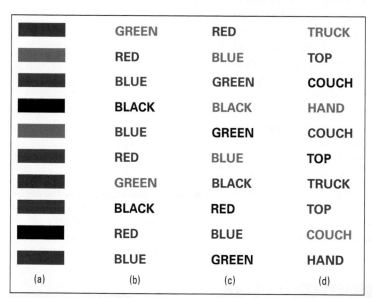

(a)	(b)	(c)	(d)
	GREEN	RED	TRUCK
	RED	BLUE	TOP
	BLUE	GREEN	COUCH
	BLACK	BLACK	HAND
	BLUE	GREEN	COUCH
	RED	BLUE	TOP
	GREEN	BLACK	TRUCK
	BLACK	RED	TOP
	RED	BLUE	COUCH
	BLUE	GREEN	HAND

FIGURE 9.2 The Stroop interference effect Time yourself or a friend on each of the following tasks: (1) Name the colors in each box in column (a). (2) Name the ink colors used to print the words in columns (b), (c), and (d), timing each column separately. Column (c) will take the longest, because the color words interfere with naming the ink colors—that is the Stroop interference effect. Column (d) may also take somewhat longer than either (a) or (b), because the non-color words interfere somewhat with naming the ink colors. Column (b) should be quickest, because there the words facilitate naming the ink colors.

"fast" system is also responsible for many visual illusions, such as the Müller-Lyer illusion presented in Chapter 7, in which lines of identical length appear to differ in size depending on how they are framed. One line appears longer to us (via "fast" processing), even though we know (via "slow" processing) it is not.

Our "fast" processing is similar to the type of cognition seen in preverbal infants and nonhuman animals. Although some degree of "slow," conscious processing may be found in some nonhuman animals, no other species comes close to the effortful, explicit, conscious cognition displayed by *Homo sapiens*. Much of this chapter and the next is devoted to looking at such "slow" processing, including recalling information from the past, reasoning, and general intelligence. However, you should keep in mind that the second "fast" system—the one we share with other animals—is also operating and often influences how we solve everyday problems.

SECTION REVIEW

The standard information-processing model posits three memory stores and various control processes.

Sensory Memory

- A separate sensory store for each sensory system (vision, hearing, etc.) holds brief traces of all information registered by that system.
- Unconscious processes may operate on these traces to determine which information to pass on to working memory.

The Short-Term Store

- This store is where conscious mental work takes place on information brought in from sensory memory and long-term memory.
- It is called short-term memory because information in it that is no longer attended to quickly disappears.

Long-Term Memory

- This is the repository of all that a person knows.
- Information here is dormant, being actively processed only when it is brought into the short-term store.

Control Processes

- Attention brings information from sensory memory into the short-term store.
- Encoding brings information from the short-term store into long-term memory.
- Retrieval brings information from long-term memory into the short-term store.
- Cognitive processes can be placed on a continuum from effortful to automatic.

"Fast" and "Slow" Thinking: Dual-Processing Theories of Cognition

- Fast thinking is unconscious and intuitive.
- Slow thinking is conscious and deliberate.

Attention: The Portal to Consciousness

Imagine one of our prehistoric hunting-and-gathering ancestors foraging for nutritious roots. Most of her conscious attention is devoted to perceiving and analyzing visual stimuli in the soil that tell her where the roots might be. At the same time, however, at some level of her mind, she must monitor many other sensory stimuli. The slight crackling of a twig in the distance could signal an approaching tiger. The stirring of the infant on her back could indicate that the baby needs comforting before it begins to cry and attract predators. A subtle darkening of the sky could foretell a dangerous storm. On the positive side, a visual clue in the foliage, unrelated to stimuli she is focusing on, could indicate that an even more nutritious form of vegetation exists nearby.

Natural selection endowed us with mechanisms of attention that can meet two competing needs. One need is to focus mental resources on the task at hand and not be distracted by irrelevant stimuli. The other, opposing need is to monitor stimuli that are irrelevant to the task at hand and to shift attention immediately to anything that signals some danger or benefit that outweighs that task. Cognitive psychologists have been concerned with the question of how our mind manages these two competing needs.

> **FOCUS 6**
>
> What two competing needs are met by our attentional system? How do the concepts of preattentive processing and top-down control of the attentive gate pertain to these two needs?

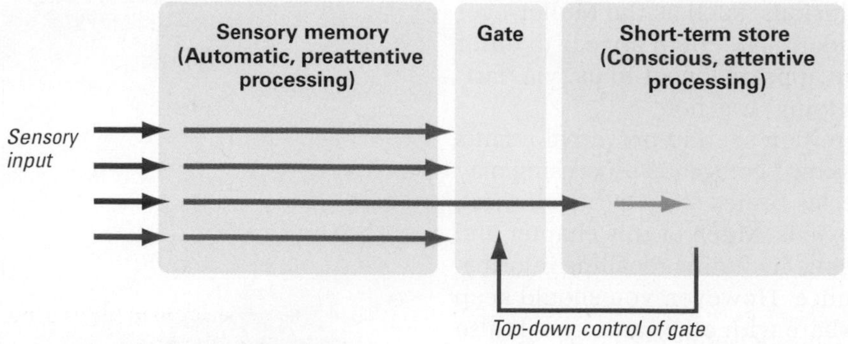

FIGURE 9.3 A generalized model of attention All sensory input enters the sensory memory store, where it is processed preattentively. Then some of it is selected to pass through the gate into conscious, working memory. The arrow going from working memory to the gate indicates top-down control of the selection criteria.

Figure 9.3 depicts a very general model, in which attention is portrayed as a gate standing between sensory memory and the short-term store. According to this model, all information that is picked up by the senses enters briefly into sensory memory and is analyzed to determine its relevance to the ongoing task and its potential significance for the person's survival or well-being. That analysis occurs at an unconscious level and is called ***preattentive processing***. Logically, such processing must involve some comparison of the sensory input to information already stored in short-term or long-term memory. Without such comparison, there would be no basis for distinguishing what is significant from what is not. The portions of the brain that are involved in preattentive processing must operate on the attention gate to help determine what items of information will be allowed to pass into the limited-capacity, conscious, short-term compartment at any given moment. In Figure 9.3, that top-down control is depicted by the arrow at the bottom which runs from the short-term store compartment to the gate. The degree and type of preattentive processing that occurs, and the nature of the top-down control of the gate, are matters of much speculation and debate (Knudsen, 2007; Pashler, 1998).

Although emerging theories view attention as a dynamic system, with attention both influencing and being influenced by aspects of the environment and the traits and behavior of a person (Ristic & Enns, 2015), this classic model explains important research findings that bear on the two competing problems the attention system must solve: focusing attention narrowly on the task at hand and monitoring all stimuli for their potential significance.

The Ability to Focus Attention and Ignore the Irrelevant

We are surprisingly good at attending to a relevant train of stimuli and ignoring stimuli that are irrelevant to the task we are performing. Here is some evidence for that.

Selective Listening

The pioneering research on attention, beginning in the 1940s and 1950s, centered on the so-called *cocktail-party phenomenon,* the ability to pick up important information (e.g., someone saying your name) while focusing on other information (e.g., a conversation with someone at a noisy cocktail party). People's ability to do this implies that information was being unconsciously processed on an unattended channel while consciously processing other information. In the laboratory, this ability is usually studied by playing recordings of two spoken messages at once and asking the subject to shadow one message—that is, to repeat immediately each of its words as they are heard—and ignore the other message. The experiments showed that people perform well at this as long as there is some physical difference between the two voices, such as in their general pitch levels or in the locations in the room from which they are coming (Haykin & Chen, 2005). When asked immediately after the shadowing task about the unattended voice, the subjects could usually report whether it was a woman's voice or a man's but were usually unaware of any of the message's meaning or even whether the speaker switched to a foreign language partway through the session (Cherry, 1953; Cherry & Taylor, 1954). Yet, people will remember hearing some salient information from the unattended channel, such as their own name, indicating that the unattended information was being processed at some level (Moray, 1959).

FOCUS 7

What evidence from research shows that people very effectively screen out irrelevant sounds and sights when focusing on difficult perceptual tasks?

Selective Viewing

Selective viewing seems to be a simpler task than selective listening; we can control what we see just by moving our eyes, whereas we have no easy control over what we hear. But we can also attend selectively to different, nearby parts of a visual scene without moving our eyes, as demonstrated in a classic experiment by Irvin Rock and Daniel Gutman (1981). These researchers presented, in rapid succession, a series of images to viewers whose eyes were fixed on a spot at the center of the screen. Each image contained two overlapping forms, one green and one red (see **Figure 9.4**), and subjects were given a task that required them to attend to just one color. Most of the forms were nonsense shapes, but some were shaped like a familiar object, such as a house or a tree. After viewing the sequence, subjects were tested for their ability to recognize which forms had been shown. The result was that they recognized most of the forms that had been presented in the attended color but performed only at chance level on those that had been presented in the unattended color, regardless of whether the form was nonsensical or familiar.

The most dramatic evidence of selective viewing comes from experiments in which subjects who are intent on a difficult visual task fail to see large, easily recognized objects directly in their line of sight. In one such experiment (Simons & Chabris, 1999), college students watched a 75-second video in which three black-shirted players tossed a basketball among themselves, and three white-shirted players tossed another basketball among themselves, while all six moved randomly around in the same small playing area. Subjects were asked to count the number of passes made by one of the two groups of players while ignoring the other group. You can take this test for yourself. Before reading further about the results of this experiment, go to https://www.youtube.com/results?search_query=Simons+%26+Chabris%2C+1999 or do an Internet search for "Simons & Chabris, 1999." Watch the video, and count the number of times the players wearing white pass the basketball. Go ahead, we'll wait.

Perhaps you noticed that midway through the video a woman dressed in a gorilla costume walked directly into the center of the two groups of players, faced the camera, thumped her chest, and then, several seconds later, continued walking across the screen and out of view. Remarkably, when questioned immediately after the video, 50% of the subjects claimed they had not seen the gorilla. When these subjects were shown the video again, without having to count passes, they expressed amazement—with such exclamations as, "I missed *that?!*"—when the gorilla came on screen. This effect is even found when experts search for information. For example, radiologists looked at X-ray images to detect nodules in lung tissue. An image of a gorilla, 48 times the size of a normal nodule, was inserted in the last slide. Despite the familiarity of the task, 83% of the radiologists failed to see the gorilla (Drew et al., 2013).

Stage magicians and pickpockets have long made use of this phenomenon of *inattentional blindness* (Macknik et al., 2008). The skilled magician dramatically releases a dove with his right hand, while his left hand slips some new object into his hat. Nobody notices what his left hand is doing, even though it is in their field of view, because their attention is on the right hand and the dove. The skilled pickpocket creates a distraction with one hand while deftly removing your wallet with the other.

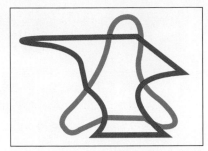

FIGURE 9.4 Overlapping forms used in an experiment on attention To assess the degree to which vision can be selective, Rock and Gutman (1981) directed subjects to attend to either just the red or just the green shape in slides such as this and then tested their recognition of both shapes in each slide.

(From: Rock, I., & Gutman, D. (1981). The effect of inattention on form perception. *Journal of Experimental Psychology: Human Perception and Performance, 7*, 275–285. Copyright © American Psychological Association. Reprinted by permission.)

The Ability to Shift Attention to Significant Stimuli

There are limits to inattentional blindness. If our hunter-gatherer ancestors frequently missed real gorillas, or lions or tigers, because of their absorption in other tasks, our species would have become extinct long ago. For example, one recent study showed that subjects did *not* display inattentional blindness when spiders, an evolutionarily relevant threat stimulus, served as the distracting stimuli (New & German, 2015). Similarly, we would not be alive today if we didn't shift our attention to unexpected dangers while crossing the street. We are good at screening out irrelevant stimuli when we need to focus intently on a task, but we are also good at shifting our attention to stimuli that signal danger or are otherwise significant to us.

Our ability to shift attention appears to depend, in part, on our capacity to listen or look backward in time and "hear" or "see" stimuli that were recorded a moment earlier in sensory memory. A major function of sensory memory is to hold onto fleeting, unattended stimuli long enough to allow us to turn our attention to them and bring them into consciousness if they prove to be significant (Lachter et al., 2004). Here is some evidence for that idea.

Shifting Attention to Meaningful Information in Auditory Sensory Memory

Auditory sensory memory is also called ***echoic memory***, and the brief memory trace for a specific sound is called the *echo*. Researchers have found that the echo fades over a period of seconds and vanishes within at most 10 seconds (Cowan et al., 2000; Gomes et al., 1999).

In a typical experiment on echoic memory, subjects are asked to focus their attention on a particular task, such as reading a prose passage that they will be tested on, and to ignore spoken words that are presented as they work. Occasionally, however, their work on the task is interrupted by a signal, and when that occurs they are to repeat the spoken words (usually digit names, such as "seven, two, nine, four") that were most recently presented. Sometimes the signal comes immediately after the last word in the spoken list, and sometimes it comes after a delay of several seconds. The typical result is that subjects can repeat accurately the last few words from the spoken list if the signal follows immediately after the last word of the list, but performance drops off as the delay is increased, and it vanishes at about 8 to 10 seconds (Cowan et al., 2000). The subjective experience of people in such experiments is that they are only vaguely aware of the spoken words as they attend to their assigned task, but when the signal occurs, they can shift their attention back in time and "hear" the last few words as if the sounds were still physically present.

Shifting Attention to Meaningful Information in Visual Sensory Memory

Visual sensory memory is also called ***iconic memory***, and the brief memory trace for a specific visual stimulus is called the *icon*. The first psychologist to suggest the existence of iconic memory was George Sperling (1960). In experiments on visual perception, Sperling found that when images containing rows of letters were flashed for one twentieth of a second, people could read the letters, as if they were still physically present, for up to one third of a second after the image was turned off. For instance, if an image was flashed containing three rows of letters and then a signal came on that told the subjects to read the third row, subjects could do that if the signal occurred within a third of a second after the image was flashed (see **Figure 9.5**). Such findings led Sperling to propose that a memory store must hold visually presented information, in essentially its original sensory form, for about a third of a second beyond the termination of the physical stimulus.

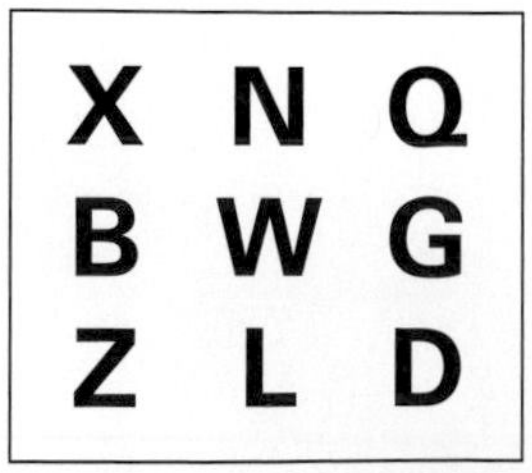

A number of experiments have shown that people who are attending to one set of visual stimuli and successfully ignoring another set will tend to notice stimuli in the ignored set that have special meaning to them. This is analogous to the cocktail party effect in the auditory mode (i.e., hearing your name while carrying on a conversation during a noisy party). For example, if the task is to identify names of types of animals in sets of words and to ignore pictures, people are more likely to notice a picture of an animal than other pictures (Koivisto & Revonsuo, 2007). Similarly, people commonly notice their own written name in a set of stimuli that

FOCUS 8

How does sensory memory permit us to hear or see, retroactively, what we were not paying attention to? How have experimenters measured the duration of auditory and visual sensory memory?

FIGURE 9.5 Sample of slide used to demonstrate iconic memory When slides like this were flashed for one twentieth of a second, followed by a pointer indicating which row to read, subjects could still read the letters in that row because of iconic memory.

they are supposed to ignore (Frings, 2006; Mack et al., 2002). In such cases, preattentive processes apparently analyze the picture or name, recognize it as significant, and shift the person's attention to it while it is still available in sensory memory.

Unconscious, Automatic Processing of Stimulus Input

The information-processing model (Figure 9.1, p. 312) is a useful starting point for thinking about the mind, but it is far from complete. Perhaps its greatest deficiency is its failure to account for unconscious effects of sensory input. In the model, sensory information can influence behavior and consciousness only if it is attended to and enters the conscious short-term store; otherwise, it is simply lost from the system. In fact, however, there is evidence that sensory input can alter behavior, and even conscious thought, without itself becoming conscious. One means by which it can do this is called *priming*.

■ **Learning to split attention** Action video games require players to notice target stimuli that can appear at any time while they are attending to other stimuli. Researchers have found that playing such games increases people's ability to attend to many stimuli at once.

Unconscious Priming of Mental Concepts

Priming is the activation, by sensory input, of information that is already stored in long-term memory. The activated information then becomes more available to the person, altering the person's perception or chain of thought. The activation is not experienced consciously, yet it influences consciousness. There is good evidence that such activation can occur even when the priming stimulus is not consciously perceived.

One of the earliest demonstrations of unconscious priming was an experiment in which researchers showed students either of two visual stimuli similar to those depicted in **Figure 9.6** (Eagle et al., 1966). In this experiment, the left-hand stimulus contained the outline of a duck, formed by the tree trunk and its branches (similar to the rabbit outline in Figure 9.6). The researchers found that subjects who were shown the duck-containing stimulus, in three 1-second flashes on a screen, did not consciously notice the duck. Yet when all subjects were subsequently asked to draw a nature scene, those who had been shown the duck-containing stimulus were significantly more likely to draw a scene containing a duck or a duck-related object (such as a pond) than were the other subjects.

FOCUS 9

What is some evidence that concepts stored in long-term memory can be primed by stimuli that are not consciously perceived?

FIGURE 9.6 Tree with and without a rabbit If you briefly view the tree on the left, you may not consciously see a rabbit, but may subsequently be more likely to draw a scene having to do with rabbits than would someone who briefly viewed the tree on the right.

Another early example involves a selective-listening procedure (MacKay, 1973). Subjects wore headphones that presented different messages to each ear and were instructed to shadow (repeat) what they heard in one ear and ignore what was presented to the other ear. The shadowed message included sentences, such as *They threw stones at the bank*, that contained words with two possible meanings. At the same time, the other ear was presented with a word that resolved the ambiguity (*river* or *money* in this example). After the shadowing task, the subjects were asked to choose from a pair of sentences the one that was most like the shadowed sentence. In the example just cited, the choice was between *They threw stones at the savings and loan association* and *They threw stones toward the side of the river*. Although the subjects could not report the non-shadowed word, they usually chose the sentence that was consistent with the meaning of that word. Thus, the unattended word influenced their interpretation of the shadowed message, even though they were unaware of having heard that word.

In everyday life, priming provides a means by which contextual information that we are not attending to can help us make sense of information that we are attending to. I might not consciously notice a slight frown on the face of a person I am listening to, yet that frown might prime my concept of sadness and cause me to experience more clearly the sadness in what he is saying. As you will discover later in the chapter, priming also helps us retrieve memories from our long-term store at times when those memories are most useful.

Automatic, Obligatory Processing of Stimuli

A wonderful adaptive characteristic of the mind is its capacity to perform routine tasks automatically, which frees its limited, effortful, conscious working memory for more creative purposes or for dealing with emergencies. Such automatization depends at least partly on the mind's ability to process relevant stimuli preattentively (unconsciously) and to use the results of that processing to guide behavior. When you were first learning to drive, for example, you probably had to devote most of your attention to such perceptual tasks as monitoring the car right ahead of you, watching for traffic signals, and manipulating the steering wheel, brake, and accelerator. With time, however, these tasks became automatic, allowing you to devote ever more attention to other tasks, such as carrying on a conversation or looking for a particular street sign.

Another example of a skill at which most of us are experts is reading. When you look at a common printed word, you read it automatically, without any conscious effort. You unconsciously (preattentively) use the word's individual letters to make sense of the word. Because of that, when you read a book you can devote essentially all of your attention to the meaningful words and ideas in the book and essentially no attention to the task of recognizing the individual letters that make up the words. In fact, researchers have found that, in some conditions at least, reading is not only automatic but also obligatory (impossible to suppress). In certain situations, people can't refrain from reading words that are in front of their open eyes, even if they try. Recall the Stroop interference effect, discussed earlier in this chapter, in which adult readers find it impossible not to read a color name they are looking at, and that interferes with their ability to think of and say quickly the ink color name when the two are different. However, this doesn't mean that we always understand everything we read. We've all had the experience of reading a sentence over and over, each time realizing we have no idea what it said. Getting at the meaning of a sentence requires mental effort—but once we become proficient at identifying individual letters and words, more of our limited mental resources can be used to derive meaning. Compare your reading to that of a beginner who may expend so much effort sounding out individual letters to identify words that a sentence's meaning is lost (if it was ever found) by the time the young reader gets to the period.

FOCUS 10

How is the concept of automatic, unconscious processing of stimuli used to help explain (a) people's ability to do more than one task at once, and (b) the Stroop interference effect?

Brain Mechanisms of Preattentive Processing and Attention

For many years psychologists were content to develop hypothetical models about mental compartments and processes, based on behavioral evidence, without much concern about what was physically happening in the brain. The advent of fMRI and other new methods for studying the intact brain have changed that. Many studies have been conducted to see how the brain responds during preattentive processing of stimuli, during attentive processing of stimuli, and at moments when shifts in attention occur. Much is still to be learned, but so far three general conclusions have emerged:

1. *Stimuli that are not attended to nevertheless activate sensory and perceptual areas of the brain.* Sensory stimuli activate specific sensory and perceptual areas of the cerebral cortex whether or not the person consciously notices those stimuli. Such activation is especially apparent in the primary sensory areas, but it also occurs in areas farther forward in the cortex that are involved in analyzing stimuli for meaning. In several fMRI studies, words that were flashed on a screen too quickly to be consciously seen activated neurons in portions of the occipital, parietal, and frontal cortex that are known, from other studies, to be involved in reading (Dehaene et al., 2001, 2004). Apparently, the unconscious, preattentive analysis of stimuli for meaning involves many of the same brain mechanisms that we use to analyze consciously perceived stimuli.

2. *Attention magnifies the activity that task-relevant stimuli produce in sensory and perceptual areas of the brain, and it diminishes the activity that task-irrelevant stimuli produce.* Attention, at the neural level, seems to temporarily sensitize the relevant neurons in sensory and perceptual areas of the brain, increasing their responsiveness to the stimuli they are designed to analyze, while having the opposite effect on neurons whose responses are irrelevant to the task (Reynolds et al., 2012). In a task that requires attention to dots moving upward and inattention to dots moving downward, neurons in the visual system that respond to upward motion become more responsive, and neurons that respond to downward motion become less responsive, than they normally are (Yantis, 2008).

3. *Neural mechanisms in anterior (forward) portions of the cortex are responsible for control of attention.* Many studies have shown that areas in the frontal lobe and in anterior portions of the temporal and parietal lobes become active when shifts in attention occur (Ruff et al., 2007; Shipp, 2004). Other studies have shown that the prefrontal cortex (the most anterior portion of the frontal lobe) is especially active during tasks, such as the Stroop task, that require intense concentration on relevant stimuli and screening out of irrelevant stimuli (van Veen & Carter, 2006). Such findings suggest that these anterior regions control attention by acting in a top-down fashion on sensory and perceptual areas farther back in the cerebral cortex.

Other research has shown that some forms of brain damage can cause people to ignore, or not see, information in half of their visual field. Lesions in the parietal lobe, the frontal lobe, and the anterior cingulate cortex in one hemisphere can result in *spatial neglect,* with individuals being unable to "see" things in the contralateral visual field (the side opposite the brain injury) (Vallar, 1993). In such cases, a patient with a lesion on the left side of her brain may not see the food on the right side of her plate, the numbers on the right side of a clock, or the objects pictured on the right side of a photograph. **Figure 9.7** (page 324) shows the drawing of a patient with spatial neglect. In both cases, the subject was asked to copy the model exactly (from Reynolds et al., 2012).

The effects of spatial neglect are also found in how people represent time. Most people in Western cultures mentally represent events on a timeline, with past events to the left and future events to the right. When subjects without brain lesions

FOCUS 11

What three general conclusions have emerged from studies of brain mechanisms of preattentive processing and attention?

FIGURE 9.7 Spatial neglect People with spatial neglect are unable to process information in the visual field opposite to the brain hemisphere in which they have a lesion. Here, a patient with a lesion on the right side of his brain neglected to include most information on the left side of his drawing.

(From Reynolds, J. H., Gottlieb, J. P., & Kastner, S. (2012). "Attention," In L. R. Squire, D. Berg, F. E. Bloom, S. du Lac, A. Ghosh, & N. C. Spitzer (Eds.), *Fundamental neuroscience* (4th ed.) (pp. 989–1007). New York: Elsevier.)

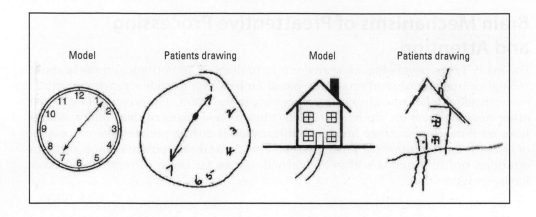

were told a story about a character, they recalled and recognized events associated with the future and past equally well. Subjects who had right-hemisphere strokes causing left spatial neglect remembered items associated with the future (and thus the right side of a mental number line) as well as did subjects without spatial neglect. However, patients with left-hemisphere damage resulting in right spatial neglect remembered past events (associated with the left side of a mental number line) poorly, much as they neglected visual objects in the left visual field. This suggests that spatial representations are related to the same brain areas as some types of temporal representations (Saj et al., 2014).

In sum, attention is a state of the brain in which neural resources are shifted such that more resources are devoted to analyzing certain selected stimuli and fewer resources are devoted to analyzing other stimuli that are picked up by the senses. The more neural activity a stimulus produces, the more likely it is that we will experience that stimulus consciously.

SECTION REVIEW

Attention is the means by which information enters consciousness.

Focused Attention

- Selective listening and viewing studies show that we can effectively focus attention, screening out irrelevant stimuli.
- In general, we are aware of the physical qualities, but not the meaning, of stimuli that we do not attend to.

Shifting Attention

- We unconsciously monitor unattended stimuli in sensory memory so that we can shift our attention if something significant occurs.
- Such monitoring includes preattentive processing for meaning.

Preattentive Processing

- Through preattentive processing, unattended sensory information can affect conscious thought and behavior.
- For example, in unconscious priming, stimuli that are not consciously perceived can activate information in long-term memory, which can influence conscious thought.
- Preattentive processing is automatic and in some cases obligatory, as exemplified by the Stroop interference effect.

Brain Mechanisms

- Many of the same brain areas are involved in preattentive processing and conscious processing of stimuli for meaning.
- However, attention causes greater activation of the relevant sensory and perceptual areas.
- Shifts in attention are controlled by areas of the cerebral cortex anterior to (forward of) sensory and perceptual areas.
- Damage to areas in the left or right hemisphere of the brain can cause spatial neglect.

Working Memory: The Active, Conscious Mind

We've used the concept of the short-term store to refer to the metaphorical space in which information is held for brief periods and "worked on." As mentioned earlier, working memory refers to the process of storing and transforming information being held in the short-term store. Working memory is the center of conscious perception and thought; it thinks, makes decisions, and controls such processes as attention and retrieval of information from long-term memory.

The most influential psychological model of working memory to date is that developed by Alan Baddeley (1986, 2006), which divides working memory into a number of separate but interacting components. The components in Baddeley's model include a ***phonological loop***, responsible for holding verbal information; a ***visuospatial sketchpad***, responsible for holding visual and spatial information; and a ***central executive***, responsible for coordinating the mind's activities and for bringing new information into working memory from the sensory and long-term stores. (Baddeley added a fourth component, the episodic buffer, to the model in 2000, but we will not discuss this here.) Here we'll focus on the phonological loop.

"To find out if you're someone who could benefit from our Memory Improvement Seminar press 15973622283095217061 0137."

Verbal Working Memory: The Phonological Loop

As a test of one aspect of your own working memory, read the digits at the end of this sentence and then close your eyes and try to keep them in mind for a minute or so: 2 3 8 0 4 9 7. What did you do to keep them in mind? If you are like most people, you repeated the digit names over and over to yourself in the order you read them: *two three eight zero four nine seven*. Some IQ tests (discussed in Chapter 10) include a measure of *digit span,* the number of digits that a person can keep in mind for a brief period and report back accurately. Most people have a digit span of about seven digits. More generally, the number of pronounceable items—such as digits, other words, or nonsense syllables—that a person can keep in mind and report back accurately after a brief delay is called the ***short-term memory span***, or simply *memory span*. According to Baddeley's model, it might better be called the *span of the phonological loop of working memory*. The phonological loop is the part of working memory that holds on to verbal information by subvocally repeating it.

Generally, people can subvocally keep in working memory about as much verbal material as they can state aloud in 2 seconds (Baddeley et al., 1975). Items that are not rehearsed through subvocal repetition fade quickly; some of them begin to disappear within about 2 seconds or slightly longer. People who can speak rapidly have larger spans than people who cannot speak so rapidly. The span for single-syllable words is greater than that for multiple-syllable words. Try repeating aloud from memory the following seven-word list, with eyes closed, immediately after reading it: *disentangle appropriation gossamer anti-intellectual preventative foreclosure documentation.* Now try repeating it aloud after 10 seconds of subvocal repetition. In each case, was that list harder than the list of digits?

Any manipulation that interferes with a person's ability to articulate the words to be remembered interferes with verbal short-term memory (Baddeley, 2003). Try to hold seven digits in mind while repeating over and over, out loud, the word *the*. You probably can't do it; the act of saying *the* interferes with your ability to articulate to yourself the digit names.

How do we know that memory span is affected by the time it takes to articulate words? Some evidence comes from research examining digit spans for people speaking different languages. For example, Chinese speakers have longer digit spans than English speakers do, a difference that is apparent as early as 4 years of age and extends into adulthood (Chen & Stevenson, 1988; Geary et al., 1993). This

FOCUS 12

What is some evidence that people keep information in the phonological loop through subvocal repetition?

FIGURE 9.8 An analogy to the phonological loop of working memory Holding several items of information in the phonological loop is a bit like spinning several plates on the ends of sticks. Just as you have to go back to each plate and renew its spin before it falls, you have to go back to each item in the phonological loop and repeat it before it vanishes from working memory.

FOCUS 13

Why is working-memory span usually two items less than memory span?

difference is due to differences in the rate with which number words (one, two, and so on) in the two languages are spoken. The digit names in Chinese are all one syllable and can be articulated more quickly than the longer digit words of the English language. A similar pattern has been found between English and Welsh, with digit span being greater for English digits than for Welsh digits, which take longer to pronounce than those in English. This was true even for subjects whose first language was Welsh (Ellis & Hennelley, 1980).

Keeping a list of memory items in the phonological loop is a bit like a circus performer's keeping a set of plates spinning on the ends of sticks (see **Figure 9.8**). As the number of plates increases, the performer must work more frantically to get back to each and renew its spinning before it falls. Performers who can move quickly can spin more plates than performers who move slowly. Larger plates take longer to set in motion than smaller ones, so the performer can't spin as many large plates as small ones. If the performer attempts to do another task at the same time that involves his or her arms and hands—such as building a tower of cups and saucers—the number of plates he or she can spin decreases.

Of course, in everyday life we don't normally use our phonological loop to keep nonsensical lists in mind, any more than we use our hands to keep plates spinning. Rather, we use it for useful work. We say words silently to ourselves, and we bring ideas together in the form of words, as we reminisce about our experiences, solve problems, make plans, or in other ways engage in verbal thought. We don't just hold material in working memory; we stream material through it, in an often-logical fashion.

Working-Memory Span

As useful as memory span is for assessing cognitive performance, in recent years cognitive psychologists have found that an even better measure for assessing cognitive abilities is to examine how many items a person can keep in mind while performing some "work." In *working-memory-span* tasks, subjects are asked to remember a set of items while doing something with those items. For example, in a reading-span task subjects may be asked to read a set of short sentences (e.g., "In the summer it is very hot"; "The horse jumped over the fence"). After hearing several such sentences, subjects are asked to recall the last word in each sentence, in the order they were presented. Or subjects may be given a series of simple arithmetic problems to solve (8 + 1 = ?; 4 + 3 = ?) and asked to remember the sum (9, 7) of each problem, in the order they were presented. Working-memory span is typically about two items shorter than memory span, and also shows improvements over childhood and declines in older adulthood (Cowan & Alloway, 2009; Dykiert et al., 2012). Apparently, the mental resources required to process or "work" on information compete with the mental resources needed to store information (Barrouillet & Camos, 2012). One reason for the increased interest in working-memory-span tasks is that, compared to memory-span tasks, they are more strongly associated with (and predictive of) important higher-level abilities, including reading, writing, mathematics, memory strategies, and IQ, among others (Bjorklund, 2013; Kane & Engle, 2002).

One way of demonstrating the importance of working memory on task performance is to examine what happens when someone tries to engage in two tasks at once (i.e., to multitask). Consider, for example, the dual tasks of driving a car and talking on a cell phone. Although both driving and speaking are highly developed and automated skills, they each consume a portion of working memory; performing one interferes with performing the other. In a correlational study involving only drivers who sometimes used their cell phones while driving, the accident rate during phone use was four times that for the same group when they did not

■ **Simulated driving while talking on hands-free cell phone** In their simulated-driving experiments, Strayer and Drews (2007) found that talking on a cell phone created more driving errors, regardless of whether or not the phone was hands-free.

■ Although developing expertise in something like driving often permits one to "dual-task"—doing two things at once—texting while driving shouldn't be one of them. In a simulation of drivers (17 to 24 years of age) in the United Kingdom, texting while driving reduced the drivers' reaction times by 35%. This compares to reductions of 12% due to alcohol consumption and 21% when smoking marijuana (Reed & Robbins, 2008), making texting a greater accident risk than driving while intoxicated.

use their phones (Redelmeier & Tibshirani, 1997). In a simulated-driving experiment in the laboratory, conversing on a phone doubled the number of driving errors made (Strayer & Johnston, 2001). Moreover, it is important to note that in both studies, the disruptive effect on driving was just as great for hands-free phones as for hand-held phones. The interference is a mental one, involving competing uses of working memory, not a motor one, involving competing uses of the hands.

Subsequent simulated-driving experiments showed that drivers whose minds were occupied with cell phone conversations frequently missed road signs because of inattentional blindness, the same reason that people in the basketball pass-counting experiment missed seeing the gorilla (Strayer & Drews, 2007). Conversations with passengers did not have the deleterious effects that cell phone conversations had. Why? Because passengers, unlike phone partners, experience the driving conditions that the driver experiences, so the conversation becomes synchronized with the driving; when the driving gets difficult, the conversation temporarily stops. The effects of texting while driving may be even more substantial, as this behavior combines cognitive distraction with manual and visual distractions (CDC, 2013). Indeed, as of 2017, 47 states and the District of Columbia had enacted texting bans for all drivers.

Multitasking also has negative consequences on less life-threatening activities, such as preparing for an exam. In one study of nearly 700 college students, researchers measured the incidence of using social media (e.g., watching television or Youtube, reading or sending text messages, checking Facebook) while studying (Patterson, 2017). **Figure 9.9** shows the average performance on the exam both for students who studied a lot for the test (High-Study group) and those who studied less (Low-Study group) as a function of level of multitasking (low, medium, and high). As you can see, the more multitasking with media students did while studying, the lower was their score on the exam.

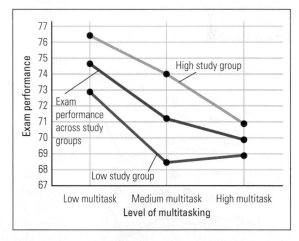

FIGURE 9.9 Exam performance The graph shows students' performance on an exam in Low-Study (< 120 minutes), High-Study (> 120 minutes), and the average scores across both groups, for students who engaged in low, medium, and high multitasking while studying. The more students multitasked, the worse they did on the exam, regardless of how much they studied.

(Data from Patterson, 2017.)

Executive Functions

FOCUS 14

What are the three subcomponents of executive functions?

Cognitive psychologists today see working memory not as an isolated process but as part of **executive functions**—relatively basic and general-purpose information-processing mechanisms that, together, are important in planning, regulating behavior, and performing complex cognitive tasks (Miyake & Friedman, 2012; Miyake et al., 2000). (Don't confuse these executive functions with the central executive of the Baddeley model, discussed earlier.) Most researchers agree that executive functions consist of three related components: (a) *working memory*, or *updating*, monitoring, and rapidly adding/deleting the contents of working memory; (b) *switching*, shifting flexibly between different tasks or mindsets; and (c) *inhibition*, preventing a cognitive or behavioral response, or keeping unwanted information out of mind. Individual differences in executive functions are related to performance on other cognitive tasks, such as IQ, reasoning, and school grades (Friedman et al., 2006; Richland & Burchinal, 2013), as well as important socioemotional phenomena such as faithfulness to a romantic partner (Klauer et al., 2010) and sticking with diet and exercise regimes (Hall et al., 2008). The various components of executive function have been assessed by a variety of tasks.

An example of a switching task is the Wisconsin Card Sorting Test (WCST), in which subjects are given sets of cards with different objects on them (e.g., squares, stars, and circles) that vary in color and number (see **Figure 9.10**). Subjects are asked to sort the cards into specific categories (e.g., according to color, number, or shape), and accurate sorting is reinforced by the examiner. After several trials and without notice, the examiner switches reinforcement to another category. For instance, the initial category may be color, in which case subjects would be reinforced for sorting all the green cards in one group, the red ones in another, and so on, regardless of the number or shape of the items on the cards. The examiner may then switch from color to number, so that all target cards are now to be placed according to number (one, two, three, or four), with color and shape being irrelevant. Subjects are given feedback after a mistake, so they should presumably be able to learn a new classification scheme after only a few trials.

Inhibition has also been assessed by a variety of relatively simple tasks. For example, the Stroop task discussed earlier in this chapter (see Figure 9.2, p. 316) is used to assess inhibition. To what extent can people inhibit the dominant response (e.g., to say the color word "**blue**") and instead identify the color the word is written in (in this case, green)?

Updating, or working memory, is assessed by tasks like those described in the previous section looking at working-memory span, as well as some dual tasks, such as those assessing the effects of talking on the phone and driving.

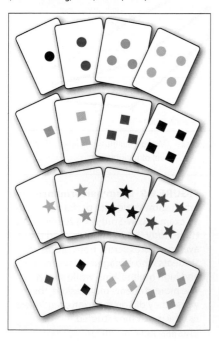

FIGURE 9.10 The Wisconsin Card Sorting Test Subjects start sorting cards by one dimension (color, for instance) then, without notice, they are reinforced for sorting by another dimension (shape, for instance). The number of errors following "switch" trials is a measure of the executive function of switching.

(Data from Berg, 1948; Milner, 1964).

Four General Conclusions About Executive Functions

Akira Miyake and Naomi Friedman (2012) looked at more than a decade of research and arrived at four general conclusions about executive functions. First, executive functions show both unity and diversity. This means that performance on the various types of executive functions (updating, switching, and inhibition) all correlate with one another. That is, people who perform well on updating tasks are likely to perform well on switching and inhibition tasks as well. This suggests that the various tasks are tapping some common underlying cognitive ability. However, these correlations are not perfect, indicating that each type of executive function is also assessing some unique abilities.

Second, there is a substantial genetic component to executive functions. For example, by looking at performance of different types of executive functions by people with different degrees of genetic relatedness (e.g., identical twins, biological siblings, and adopted siblings), one can get an estimate of the *heritability* of a trait, or the degree to which individual differences in a trait can be attributed to inheritance. Research by Friedman and her colleagues (2008) showed that the heritability of executive functions was quite high—higher than what is typically reported for IQ or personality. Similarly high estimates of heritability were reported for measures of executive function in childhood (Engelhardt et al., 2015).

This does not mean, however, that executive functions cannot be altered by experience. When people experience different environments (including training environments), the level of a trait can vary even when heritability is high. A number of studies have trained people ranging in age from preschoolers to adults in various aspects of executive functions and have reported significant improvements (Best, 2011; Dahlin et al., 2008; Diamond, 2012). However, other studies have failed to find significant benefits of training, or suggest that training effects are limited to specific tasks (e.g., training on a particular working-memory task), calling into question the effectiveness of such training on everyday functioning (Melby-Lervåg et al., 2016; Shipstead et al., 2012; Wass et al., 2012). Other studies, with both children (Diamond, 2012) and older adults (Colcombe & Kramer, 2003), report that increases in physical exercise are related to improvements in executive functions, and that people who exercise more have better executive functions (Hillman et al., 2009).

Third, executive functions are related to and predictive of important clinical and societal outcomes. For example, externalizing behaviors (where one "acts out" such that one's behavior adversely affects other people, including conduct disorder and oppositional defiant disorder), attention-deficit/hyperactivity disorder (ADHD), excessive risk taking, and substance abuse are all related to low levels of behavioral inhibition and are associated with executive functions, such that people who perform better on tasks of executive functions have fewer behavior problems (Young et al., 2009). More generally, executive functions are related to the ability to regulate one's behavior and emotions (i.e., to display self-discipline), beginning in early childhood (Kochanska et al., 2000), through adulthood (Pronk et al., 2011), and into old age (von Hippel & Dunlop, 2005).

Fourth, there is substantial developmental stability of executive-function abilities. Although all aspects of executive functions improve over childhood, children (and even infants) who perform well on executive-function tasks tend to develop into adults with high executive-function abilities.

Executive functions can be thought of as a set of low-level cognitive abilities that, in combination, make it possible for people to regulate their thoughts, emotions, and behavior. These abilities improve with age, decline in old age, and at all ages are associated with psychological functioning. Several researchers have speculated that the evolution of executive functions was an important component in the emergence of the modern human mind (Causey & Bjorklund, 2011; Geary, 2005a). The abilities to keep an increasing number of items in mind at one time,

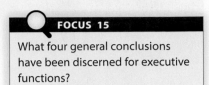

FOCUS 15

What four general conclusions have been discerned for executive functions?

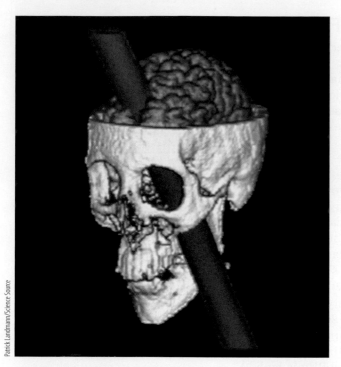

FIGURE 9.11 Phineas Gage This reconstruction of the injury suffered by Phineas Gage shows how the metal rod destroyed much of his frontal lobes and disconnected them from other parts of his brain. Although Gage's intelligence was presumably unchanged after the accident, his personality and ability to plan and make decisions was radically affected.

FOCUS 16

How does the case of Phineas Gage show that the prefrontal cortex is related to executive functions?

FOCUS 17

What general roles does the prefrontal cortex play in working memory?

resist distractions, inhibit inappropriate behavior, and regulate one's emotions and actions are critical to effective functioning in any social group, as well as for carrying out tasks such as making tools, hunting, and preparing meals, among many others. These abilities are better developed in humans than in other primates and may be a key to understanding both human cognition and human evolution.

Neurological Basis of Executive Functions

Research has also found correlates of executive functions with brain function and structure, especially the prefrontal cortex. There is no single area of the brain that is responsible for the various components of executive functions, but the prefrontal cortex has been identified as a critical area for the control of thought and behavior (Miller & Wallis, 2013). The prefrontal cortex appears to be the neural hub for executive functions (Huey et al., 2006). It is the part of the brain that somehow organizes the efforts of the other portions of the brain and keeps them focused on the task. The prefrontal cortex receives information from the sensory cortex and is connected to structures in the motor system, the limbic system (important in memory, motivation, and emotional expression), and the basal ganglia. It is thus well placed to play a major role in the control of behavior and cognition.

One of the earliest cases in the medical annals demonstrating the role of the prefrontal cortex in emotional regulation is that of Phineas Gage (Damasio et al., 1994). Gage, a railroad employee, was in the wrong place at the wrong time, when an explosion sent a metal bar through his cheek and out the top of his head (see **Figure 9.11**). The accident destroyed much of his prefrontal cortex, but, surprisingly, he survived and seemed not to have lost any of his intellectual abilities. However, in many other respects, Gage was a changed man. He was unable to plan the work he and his crew needed to accomplish and frequently spoke in a profane, rude, and irreverent manner, all counter to his preinjury personality. In essence, he was unable to control his impulses. Patients with prefrontal lobe damage, like Gage, often lack empathy, show alterations in mood and emotional expressions, have difficulty planning and making decisions, and generally have difficulty inhibiting thoughts and behaviors. For example, patients with frontal lobe damage perform poorly on the Wisconsin Card Sorting Tests discussed earlier. When the rules change (sort by color, not by number), they are unable to make the switch, but rather continue to sort by the previous rule.

ADHD is associated with delays in the development of the frontal cortex. For instance, in one study, development of the frontal cortex of 7- to 13-year-old children with ADHD lagged about 3 years behind those of children without ADHD, whereas their motor areas developed slightly earlier (Shaw et al., 2007). This uneven pattern of brain development may account for the increased fidgeting and restlessness seen in children with ADHD.

More specific brain regions can also be identified that are associated with particular aspects of executive functions. For example, working-memory tasks involve the anterior portion of each prefrontal lobe. In neuroimaging studies, increased activity in the prefrontal cortex occurs when a person deliberately holds either verbal or visual information in mind (Nee et al., 2008).

Although the prefrontal cortex's relation to behavior regulation has been known at least since the days of Phineas Gage, new neuroimaging techniques are permitting scientists to get a closer look at important brain/cognition relations.

SECTION REVIEW

Executive functions enable regulation of thoughts, emotions, and behavior.

Executive Functions

- Executive functions involve processes of working memory (updating), switching, and inhibition.

- Executive functions (a) show both unity and diversity, (b) have a substantial genetic component, (c) are related to and predictive of important clinical and societal outcomes, and (d) are developmentally stable.

Neurological Basis of Executive Functions

- The prefrontal cortex serves as the neural hub for executive functions.

- Patients with damage to the prefrontal cortex have difficulty planning and making decisions, regulating emotions, and inhibiting thought and behavior.

Memory as the Representation of Knowledge

Memory, broadly defined from the perspective of cognitive psychology, refers to all of the information in a person's mind and to the mind's capacity to store and retrieve that information. Here, we examine memory as the *representation of knowledge*. In the next section, we examine memory as the act of remembering.

When we think of "memories" we typically think of things that have happened to us in the past. In fact, it's not too much of a stretch to say that "we are what we remember." Our memories tell us who we are, who we love, our entire life history. They are all available to consciousness, or self-awareness, and are autobiographical in nature.

But there is more to "memories" than this. Some aspects of our memories are available to consciousness but are not related to our personal histories. Your knowledge of the language you speak, the rules of arithmetic and multiplication, and perhaps basic facts about how the world works (e.g., objects fall when they are dropped) are also "memories" of a sort, and although you may remember being taught arithmetic in third grade, your knowledge of arithmetic is represented differently from your recollection of being instructed in the process. Many of your memories are also nonverbal. You know how to ride a bike, how to throw a ball, and maybe how to ski, but you'd probably have a tough time explaining in words exactly how these skills are performed. Different types of information are represented differently in the brain, and we will examine some of these differences in this section, following mostly from the theorizing of Endel Tulving (2000, 2005).

Explicit and Implicit Memory

Explicit memory is the type of memory that can be brought into a person's consciousness. It provides the content of conscious thought, and it is highly flexible. Explicit memories can be called to mind even in settings quite different from those in which they were acquired, and they can be combined with other explicit memories for purposes of reflection, problem solving, and planning. Such memory is termed *explicit* because it is assessed through tests in which the person is asked to report directly (explicitly) what he or she remembers about a particular entity or event. It is also called *declarative memory* because the remembered information can be declared (stated in words).

Implicit memory, in contrast, is the type of memory that cannot be verbalized. It consists of all the nonverbal and unconscious means through which previous experiences can influence a person's actions and thoughts. Tulving called such

---

FOCUS 18

What are the differences between explicit and implicit memory, and how is each memory type assessed? In what sense are implicit memories more context-dependent than explicit memories?

FIGURE 9.12 Types of long-term memory Explicit- and implicit-memory systems follow different rules and involve different neural systems in the brain. The explicit and implicit categories can be further subdivided into narrower memory categories that may also involve different neural systems.

(Information from Tulving, 1985, and Squire et al., 1993.)

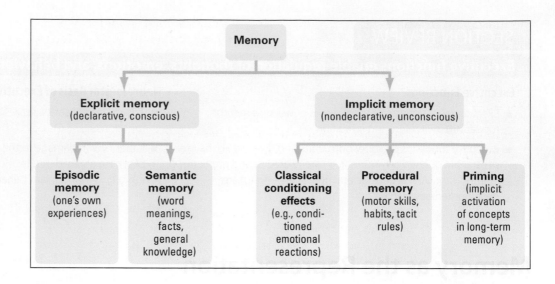

knowledge *anoetic,* or not subject to conscious attention. Such memory is called *implicit* because it is assessed through tests in which the memory is not explicitly reported but is implicitly inferred from behavioral responses. We would test your memory for balancing on a bicycle not by asking you *how* to do it but by asking you *to* do it. Your good performance on the bicycle would imply that you know how to balance on it. Because people do not report in words the relevant information, implicit memory is also called *nondeclarative memory.* Implicit memories are much more closely tied to the contexts in which they were acquired than are explicit memories. Whereas explicit memories can be called forth voluntarily outside of their original context, implicit memories exert their effects automatically in the context of the specific stimuli, tasks, or problems to which they pertain.

In addition to distinguishing between explicit and implicit memories, cognitive psychologists also distinguish among subclasses of each type, along the lines depicted in **Figure 9.12**.

Varieties of Explicit Memory: Episodic and Semantic

FOCUS 19

How do the two subclasses of explicit memory differ from one another?

As shown in Figure 9.12, explicit memory is divisible into two subclasses. *Episodic memory* is explicit memory of one's own past experiences. Your memory of what you did and how you felt on your 16th birthday, or of what you ate for dinner last night, or of any other specific event in your life, is episodic memory. Because episodic memories have a personal quality, they are sometimes called *autobiographical memories.* An integral part of your episodic memory of an event is your memory of yourself experiencing that event—as participant, witness, or learner. Tulving referred to episodic memory as *autonoetic,* or "self-knowing," permitting the placement of the self into a particular set of circumstances at a specific time in the past for the purpose of mentally recreating it. According to Tulving (2002), "Time's arrow is bent into a loop" (p. 2) by the uniquely human ability to mentally travel in time and consciously transport oneself into the past.

Semantic memory, by contrast, is explicit memory that is not tied mentally to a particular past experience. It includes knowledge of word meanings (which is one definition of *semantics*) plus the myriad facts, ideas, and schemas that constitute one's general understanding of the world. It also includes knowledge of oneself that is not mentally tied to the re-experiencing of a particular episode in one's life. Your memories that apples are red, that penguins are birds, that you were born on a certain date, and that psychology is the most fascinating of all academic subjects are examples of semantic memory. Of course, all such information had to have been acquired through past experiences in your life, but your memory of the information does not depend on remembering those experiences. To remember your birth date, or that penguins are birds, you do not have to remember anything about the circumstances in which you learned that fact. Although semantic memory is still conscious and within awareness, it is not tied to any specific event in time. Tulving called such knowledge *noetic,* or knowing.

Here is a test question: *What is classical conditioning?* After answering the question, think about *how* you answered it. Did you think back to your experience of reading about classical conditioning in Chapter 8 of this book, or to your experience of hearing your professor define classical conditioning, and try to reconstruct the definition from your memory of that reading or classroom experience? Or did you just *know* the answer, without having to reflect on any particular past experience? If the first is the case, then your memory of the definition of classical conditioning is an episodic memory (or at least partly so); if the second is the case, it is a semantic memory.

In general, episodic memories are more fleeting, and less stable, than semantic memories. Over time, we forget most of our memories of specific past experiences, but the general knowledge that we extract from those experiences often stays with us.

Network Models of Memory Organization

Recalling an item from semantic memory is like looking for information in an encyclopedia. To find an item that doesn't come easily to mind, you probe your mind with terms or concepts that have meaningful associations to that item. Many cognitive psychologists today depict the mind's storehouse of knowledge as a vast network of mental concepts linked by associations. **Figure 9.13** illustrates such a model. Allan Collins and Elizabeth Loftus (1975) developed this diagram to explain the results of experiments concerned with people's abilities to recognize or recall specific words very quickly after exposure to other words. For example, a person can recognize the word *apple* more quickly if the previous word was *pear* or *red* than if it was *bus.* Collins and Loftus assumed that the degree to which one word speeds up the ability to recognize or recall another reflects the strength of the mental association between the two words or concepts. Similar experiments have shown that many types of memory items—including memories for famous people—can be organized in networks based on strengths of association among them (Stone & Valentine, 2007).

In Figure 9.13, the strength of association between any two concepts is represented by the length of the path between them; the shorter the path, the stronger the association. Notice how the diagram incorporates the idea that common properties of objects often provide a basis for their link in memory. *Roses, cherries, apples, sunsets,* and *fire engines* are all linked to the concept *red,* and through that common tie they are all linked to one another. The model is called a *spreading-activation model* because it proposes that the activation of any one concept initiates a spread of activity to nearby concepts in the network, which primes those concepts so they become temporarily more retrievable than they were before. The spreading activity declines with distance, so concepts that are closely linked with the active concept receive more priming than those that are more distantly linked. Such models are convenient ways to depict the results of many memory experiments, and they help us to visualize the patterns of associations that make up the mind.

Modern brain theories posit that memories for concepts, such as those depicted in Figure 9.13, are stored in overlapping neural circuits in the cerebral cortex (Fuster, 2006; Patterson et al., 2007). Some of the neurons that are part of the circuit for one concept are part of the circuit for other concepts as well. The more overlap there

FOCUS 20

What sorts of experimental results was Collins and Loftus's spreading-activation model designed to explain? How does the model expand on the idea that mental associations provide a basis for memory and thought?

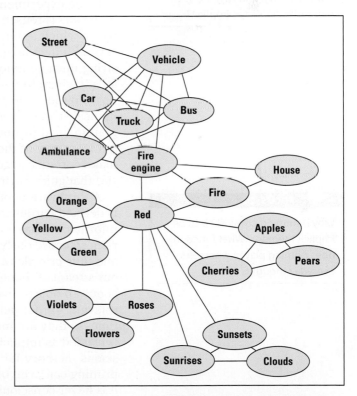

FIGURE 9.13 A network model of memory organization This diagram depicts schematically some of the links, or associations, among a tiny fraction of the thousands of different concepts that are stored in a typical person's long-term semantic memory.

(From Collins, A., & Loftus, E. (1975). A spreading-activation theory of semantic processing. *Psychological Review, 82,* 407–428. Figure 1, p. 412. Copyright © American Psychological Association.)

pixland/Corbis

■ **Procedural memory** The learned skill of balancing on a bicycle is retained as implicit procedural memory. You can't say just how you do it, but you don't forget it.

FOCUS 21

What are some examples of procedural memory, and why are such memories classed as implicit?

FOCUS 22

Why is priming considered to be implicit memory? What function does priming play in a person's everyday thought?

is between the circuits for two concepts, the more closely they are associated in the person's mind. According to these theories, priming occurs because the activation of the circuit for one concept literally activates part of the circuit for another, making that whole circuit more easily activated than it was before.

Varieties of Implicit Memory

Implicit memory can also be divided into subclasses, as depicted in the right-hand portion of Figure 9.12. One subclass consists of the memories resulting from classical conditioning—the internal changes that lead a person or animal to respond to conditioned stimuli. Recall that consciousness is not required for classical conditioning to occur. A second subclass is a broad one known as ***procedural memory***, which includes motor skills, habits, and unconsciously learned (tacit) rules. With practice you improve at a skill such as riding a bicycle, hammering nails, or weaving a rug. The improvement is retained (remembered) from one practice session to the next, even though you are unaware of the changes in muscle movements that make the difference. You can even learn to make decisions based on complex rules without ever becoming aware of the rules (Greenwald, 1992), and that phenomenon, too, exemplifies procedural memory.

Some experiments demonstrating rule-based procedural memories use *artificial grammars* (Frensch & Rünger, 2003; Reber, 1989), which consist of sets of rules specifying which letters may or may not follow certain other letters in strings that are several letters long. For example, one rule might be that an *X* at the beginning of a string must be followed by either another *X* or a *V*, and another rule might be that a *J* anywhere in the middle of a string must be followed by a *B*, *K*, or *T*. Subjects are not told the rules. Instead, they are shown examples of grammatical and nongrammatical strings, labeled as such, and then are asked to categorize new examples as grammatical or not, on the basis of their "gut feelings." The subjects typically do not learn any of the rules explicitly—they cannot state the rules—yet they learn to make correct categorizations at a rate significantly better than chance. The memories that guide their correct choices are implicit.

A third variety of implicit memory is priming (Tulving, 2000). Recall that *priming* is defined earlier in this chapter (on p. 321) as the activation, by sensory input, of information that is already stored in long-term memory. This activation is not experienced consciously, yet it influences subsequent conscious perception and thought and thus provides a link between implicit and explicit memory. Priming helps keep our stream of thought running along consistent, logical lines. When we see or think about an object, event, or idea, those elements of our semantic memory that are relevant to that perception or thought become activated (primed) for a period of time, so they are more easily retrievable into conscious, working memory. Priming is classed as implicit memory because it occurs independently of the person's conscious memory for the priming stimulus. As noted in the discussion of attention, priming can even occur when the priming stimulus is presented in such a way that it is never consciously perceived.

Neuropsychological Evidence for Separate Memory Systems

Further evidence for multiple, distinct memory systems comes from studies of people who have impaired memory resulting from brain damage. Brain damage can destroy one kind of memory while leaving another kind intact.

Implicit Memory Remains Intact in Temporal-Lobe Amnesia: The Case of H. M.

Imagine what life would be like if, as a result of brain damage, you became unable to form new explicit (conscious) long-term memories. At any given moment you would be fully aware of your environment and able to think about it, but you would have no idea how you arrived at that moment. You would live first in one moment, then in another, with no memory of the previous moments. If you made a plan for the future—even the future of just a few minutes ahead—you would forget the plan the instant you stopped thinking of it. Your life would be like that of the late Henry Molaison—known for decades in the psychological literature as H. M.—who indeed did lose his ability to form new explicit long-term memories.

In 1953, at age 27, H. M. underwent surgery as treatment for severe epilepsy. A portion of the temporal lobe of the cortex and underlying parts of the limbic system, including the hippocampus, on each side of his brain were removed. The surgery was effective against the epilepsy, but it left him unable to encode new explicit long-term memories. Between the time of his surgery and his death in 2008, H. M. participated in hundreds of memory experiments.

Throughout his life, H. M. could remember events that occurred well before the operation. His long-term-memory store was full of knowledge acquired largely in the 1930s and 1940s. He could converse, read, solve problems, and keep new information in mind as long as his attention remained focused on it. He had an excellent vocabulary and was a skilled solver of crossword puzzles (Scotko et al., 2008). But the minute his attention was distracted, he would lose the information he had just been thinking about, and he would be unable to recall it later.

To hold information in mind for a period of time, H. M. sometimes used elaborate memory schemes. In one test, for example, he successfully kept the number 584 in mind for 15 minutes, and when asked how he did this, he replied: "It's easy. You just remember 8. You see, 5, 8, 4 add to 17. You remember 8; subtract from 17 and it leaves 9. Divide 9 by half and you get 5 and 4, and there you are—584. Easy." Yet a few minutes later, after his attention had shifted to something else, he could not remember the number or the memory scheme he had used, or even that he had been given a number to remember (Milner, 1970).

H. M.'s memory impairment made it impossible for him to live independently. He had to be accompanied wherever he went and needed constant reminders of what he was doing (Hilts, 1995). He was aware of his memory deficit and once described it in the following way (Milner, 1970): "Right now, I'm wondering, have I done or said anything amiss? You see, at this moment everything looks clear to me, but what happened just before? That's what worries me. It's like waking from a dream. I just don't remember."

There have been many other studies of people who have a memory loss like H. M.'s, though usually not as complete, after strokes or other sources of brain damage. Any loss of long-term memory, usually resulting from some sort of physical disruption or injury to the brain, is called *amnesia*. H. M.'s particular disorder is **temporal-lobe amnesia**, which is most strongly correlated with damage to the *hippocampus,* a limbic-system structure buried within the temporal lobe (see **Figure 9.14** on page 336 and discussion in Chapter 4), and discussion in Chapter 4), and cortical and subcortical structures closely connected to it (Gold & Squire, 2006; Squire, 1992).

Neuroimaging studies complement the evidence from brain-damage research. When people with undamaged brains are given new information to memorize, they manifest increased activity in the hippocampus and adjacent parts of the temporal lobe, and the degree of that increase correlates positively with the likelihood that they will recall the information successfully in a later test (Otten et al., 2001; Reber et al., 2002). Apparently, activity in the hippocampus is essential for the formation of at least some types of long-term memories.

FOCUS 23

How does the case of H. M. support the idea of a sharp distinction between working memory and long-term memory?

FOCUS 24

What evidence indicates that the hippocampus and temporal-lobe structures near it are involved in encoding explicit long-term memories?

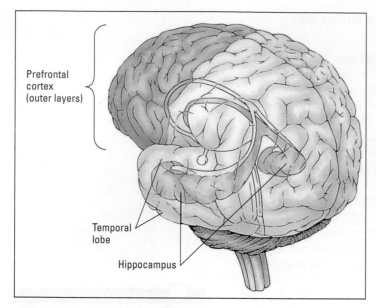

Prefrontal
cortex
(outer layers)

Temporal
lobe

Hippocampus

FIGURE 9.14 Brain areas involved in temporal-lobe amnesia The hippocampus, buried within the temporal lobe, is critically involved in long-term memory encoding. The most severe form of amnesia occurs when this structure and some of the surrounding areas of the temporal lobe are destroyed on both sides of the brain. As discussed later in the chapter, the prefrontal cortex is also involved in long-term memory encoding.

H. M.'s deficits had to do entirely with explicit memory; he and other patients with similar damage have generally behaved normally on implicit-memory tests. If classically conditioned to blink their eyes in response to a conditioned stimulus, they show the conditioned response as strongly in subsequent tests as do subjects who do not have amnesia (Daum et al., 1989). If given practice with a new motor skill, such as tracing a pattern that can be seen only in its mirror image, they show normal improvement from session to session and retain the effects of previous learning, even if months elapse between one session and the next (see **Figure 9.15**; Gabrieli et al., 1993; Milner, 1965). Similarly, they can learn and retain artificial grammars and tacit rules for grouping objects into categories (Knowlton et al., 1992; Poldrack & Foerde, 2008), and they show as much activation of long-term semantic memories in response to priming stimuli as do normal subjects (Gabrieli, 1998; Levy et al., 2004).

In all these examples, the subjects with amnesia manifest implicit memory even when they cannot consciously remember anything about the learning experience. In one experiment, a patient with severe amnesia learned to program a computer over a series of sessions. At each session, his programming ability was better than it was in the previous session, even though he had no explicit memory of ever having programmed a computer before (Glisky et al., 1986).

FIGURE 9.15 Implicit memory without explicit memory As shown in the graph, the temporal-lobe-amnesic patient H. M. improved from session to session in a mirror-tracing task, even though at each session he could not remember having performed the task before. The task was to trace a star under conditions in which the star and hand could be seen only in a mirror, so that movements had to be made oppositely from the way in which they appeared. An error was counted whenever the stylus moved off the star's outline. The data points on the graph represent the average number of errors per trial for the seven trials that occurred in each session. Sessions occurred on three successive days and then after delays of 1 week, 15 days, and nearly a year.
(Data from Gabrieli et al., 1993.)

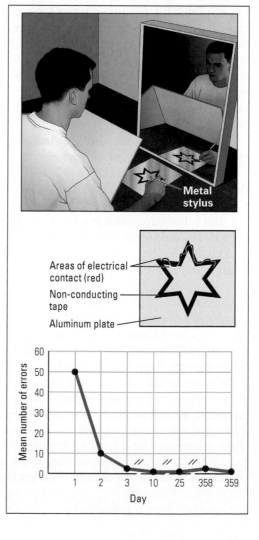

Semantic Memory Without Episodic Memory

The most severe cases of temporal-lobe amnesia, like that of H. M., entail loss of both episodic- and semantic-memory encoding. H. M. not only failed to remember anything about his own experiences that occurred after his surgery (in 1953) but also failed to remember almost all factual information that he had experienced after that date (Corkin, 2002). He could not name new world leaders or entertainers, and if asked to draw a car or a radio from memory, he would draw a 1940s or early 1950s version (Milner, 1984).

People with severe brain damage are not the only ones who can remember new information without remembering the experience of learning that information. It happens to all of us. With a little poking around in your own semantic store, you will find many facts that you yourself know but can't relate to any episodes in your life. I (Peter Gray) know that kumquats are a kind of fruit, but I can't recall any instance in my life of ever seeing, reading about, or hearing of kumquats.

Older people are especially familiar with the phenomenon of knowing without knowing how they know. In old age, the capacity to form new episodic memories generally declines more rapidly than does the capacity to form new semantic memories (Johnson et al., 1993). Young children also show excellent semantic memory and poor episodic memory. During their first 4 years of life, children acquire an enormous amount of semantic information—including word meanings and facts about their world—that will stay with them throughout their lives. But children under 4 are relatively poor at recalling specific episodes in their lives, and none of us in adulthood can recall much about our own childhood prior to about age 4 (West & Bauer, 1999). Apparently the human ability for episodic-memory encoding develops more slowly and unravels more quickly than that for semantic-memory encoding.

The inability to remember events from infancy and early childhood is not just due to the length of time between experiencing the event and trying to recall it. Even 4- and 5-year-old children fail to remember events in their lives from just 1 and 2 years earlier (Peterson et al., 2011). The inability to remember events from infancy and early childhood is called *infantile amnesia* and marks the beginning of true autobiographical memory—personal and long-lasting memories that are the basis for one's personal life history (Nelson, 1996). Yet, some people can provide one or two vivid memories of life as an infant, including one of your authors (David Bjorklund):

> My memory is of me as a sick baby. I had the croup (something like bronchitis). When I recall this memory I can feel the congestion in my chest, hear the vaporizer whir, smell the Vicks VapoRub, and see the living room of my grandparents' house while looking through the bars of my crib. The memory is like a multisensory snapshot. I have no story to tell, only the recall of an instant of my life as a sickly baby. My mistake was relating this vibrant and personally poignant memory to my mother. She listened carefully and then told me that I had never had the croup; my younger brother Dick had the croup as an infant. I was about 4 years old at the time. My "memory" was a reconstruction—and of an event I had only *observed*, not one I had actually *experienced*. (Bjorklund & Causey, 2018, p. 300)

Most people who have recollections from infancy and early childhood can be explained as this one was—a reconstruction based on what one heard, experienced, or imagined later.

Why can't we remember events from early childhood? There have been several explanations, but most modern ones focus on how early memories were encoded and represented and how we try to remember them years later (Howe et al., 2009). For instance, Gabrielle Simcock and Harlene Hayne (2002) showed 27- to 39-month-old children a sequence of actions in their homes about a "Magic Shrinking Machine." They then interviewed the children 6 and 12 months later and asked them to remember as much as they could about the novel (and seemingly memorable) event. The children's memory for the earlier event was related to their level of vocabulary development *at the time of the original experience*. Children with higher

FOCUS 25

Why does infantile amnesia cease around the age of 4?

verbal scores at the initial testing were able to remember aspects of the event 6 and 12 months later, whereas children of the same age but with poorer language skills were not. According to the authors, "children's verbal reports were frozen in time, reflecting their verbal skill at the time of encoding, rather than at the time of test" (p. 229). Overall, the research evidence indicates that infantile amnesia reflects important changes that occur during early childhood—changes that permit autobiographical memory and that separate our species from all others.

The relatively poor episodic memory at both ends of the life span may be related to prefrontal cortical functioning (Li et al., 2005; Wheeler et al., 1997). The prefrontal cortex develops more slowly in childhood and tends to suffer more damage in old age than does the rest of the brain. People with prefrontal cortical damage typically experience a much greater loss in episodic-memory encoding than in semantic-memory encoding (Wheeler, 2000). This brain area, which is much larger in humans than in other species and is crucial for planning and complex thought, may be essential for our sense of self, including our sense of our own past experiences.

We are not only a conscious species but also a self-conscious species. Unlike other animals, humans reminisce about our past, think about our position in the present, and project ourselves into the future as we make plans and contemplate their consequences. In fact, one explanation for infantile amnesia is that, until about age 4, children do not have a well-developed sense of self (Howe et al., 2009). This evolutionarily recent addition to the mammalian cognitive machinery is apparently more fragile—more destructible by aging and injuries—than is the more ancient semantic-memory system or the still more ancient implicit-memory system (Tulving, 2002; Wheeler et al., 1997).

FOCUS 26

How might the relative lack of episodic memory in early childhood and old age be explained? How does episodic memory seem to distinguish humans from other species?

SECTION REVIEW

Our brain has various memory systems.

Explicit and Implicit Memory

- Information in explicit (declarative) memory can be brought into consciousness, whereas information in implicit (nondeclarative) memory cannot, though it can influence thought and behavior.

- Explicit memory includes two subclasses: episodic memory, which is memory of particular past experiences; and semantic memory, which is one's store of general knowledge and beliefs.

- Subclasses of implicit memory include the learning that arises from classical conditioning, procedural memories, and priming.

- Network models describe long-term memory as a vast web of associations that vary in strength. Activation can spread along associative pathways in a way that enables memory retrieval and thought.

Neuropsychological Evidence

- People with temporal-lobe amnesia, such as H. M., exhibit normal capacities to form and use all sorts of implicit memories but lack the ability to form new episodic memories.

- Damage to the hippocampus disrupts the acquisition of new memories, as reflected by the case of H. M.

- Infantile amnesia is attributed to differences in how early memories were encoded and represented and how we try to remember them years later.

- Children under 4 and older adults generally exhibit poorer episodic memory than semantic memory, which may be related to immaturity of or damage in the prefrontal cortex.

Memory as the Process of Remembering

There is more to memory than "memories." Memory also refers to the processes of encoding, storing, and retrieving information, and it is to that aspect of memory that we now turn.

Encoding Information Into Long-Term Memory

As you read a book, or attend to a conversation, or admire scenery, some of the sensory information that reaches your conscious mind enters your long-term-memory store, allowing you to recall it later. Why does some but not all of the information that reaches the short-term store get encoded into the long-term store?

As discussed earlier, verbal information can be maintained in working memory simply by repetition. Repetition is not, however, a good way to encode information into long-term memory. People who participate in a digit-span test—holding a list of digits in mind by reciting them over and over—rarely remember the digits even a minute after the test ends.

Everyday life also has many examples of the failure of repetition as a rehearsal technique to promote long-term memory. In the early twentieth century, Edmund Sanford (1917/1982) illustrated this point by describing his own poor memory of four short prayers that he had read aloud thousands of times over a 25-year period as part of his daily religious practice. He found, when he tested himself, that he could recite, on average, no more than three or four successive words of each prayer from memory before having to look at the printed text for prompting. I myself (Peter Gray) have looked up certain telephone numbers dozens of times and held them in working memory long enough to dial them, without ever encoding them into long-term memory. Yet I remember some other numbers that I have looked up only once or twice. The ones I remember are the ones I thought about in some way that helped me encode them into long-term memory.

Cognitive psychologists today distinguish between two kinds of rehearsal. **Maintenance rehearsal** is the process by which a person holds information in working memory for a period of time, and **encoding rehearsal** is the process by which a person encodes information into the long-term store. The rehearsal activities that are effective for maintenance are not necessarily effective for encoding. Research suggests that some of the most effective activities for encoding involve elaboration, organization, and visualization.

Elaboration Promotes Encoding

Most of what we learn and remember in our everyday lives does not come from consciously trying to memorize. Rather, we remember things that capture our interest and stimulate our thought. The more deeply we think about something, the more likely we are to remember it later. To think deeply about an item is to do more than simply repeat it; it is to tie that item to a structure of information that already exists in long-term memory. Psychologists who study this process call it **elaboration**, or *elaborative rehearsal*. The immediate goal of elaboration is not to memorize but to understand—and attempting to understand is perhaps the best way to encode information into long-term memory.

Elaborative rehearsal capitalizes on the tendency to remember things that conform to some sort of logic, even if the logic is fictional. There is no obvious logic to the fact that stone formations hanging down in a cave are called *stalactites* while those pointing up are called *stalagmites*. But you can invent a logic: A stalactite has a *c* in it, so it grows from the *c*eiling; a stalagmite has a *g*, so it grows from the *g*round. Or a *stalactite* holds *tight* to the ceiling, whereas a *stalagmite might* eventually reach the ceiling. A person's name can be better remembered by devising a logical relation between the name and some characteristic of the person. Thus, you might remember Mr. Longfellow's name by noting that he is tall and thin or, if he is actually short and stout, by recalling that he is definitely not a long fellow. Students may remember the name of a Professor Gray or Professor Brown by relating it to the color of the professor's hair.

Laboratory Evidence for the Value of Elaboration In a classic experiment demonstrating the value of elaboration, Fergus Craik and Endel Tulving (1975) showed subjects a long series of printed words, one at a time, and for each word asked a

FOCUS 27

What is some evidence, from the laboratory and from the classroom, that the more deeply a person thinks about an item of information, the more likely it is to be encoded into long-term memory?

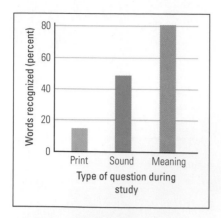

FIGURE 9.16 Superior memory resulting from meaningful elaboration Subjects were shown a long sequence of words and, for each, were asked questions that required them to focus on the way the word was printed, how it sounded, or what it meant. The type of question dramatically affected the subjects' later ability to recognize words as ones that had appeared in the sequence.

(Data from Craik & Tulving, 1975.)

question that required a different form of thought about the word. In some cases, the question was simply about the printing of the word ("Is it in capital letters?"). In other cases, the question asked about the word's sound ("Does it rhyme with *train?*"). In still others, the question referred to the word's meaning ("Would it fit in the sentence, *The girl placed the ___ on the table?*"). As shown in **Figure 9.16**, subjects remembered many more words when they had been asked questions that focused on meaning than they did in the other conditions.

Many experiments have confirmed the idea that thinking about meaning promotes long-term memory. For example, the best memory for a list of objects occurred in a group of subjects who were asked to think about how each object might help them to survive if they were stranded in the grasslands of a foreign country (Nairne et al., 2008). In another experiment, on memory for lines from a play, the best memory was shown by those who were asked to study the lines in the manner that professional actors study their lines—by thinking about the meanings that each line is meant to convey and how best to convey those meanings in reading the lines (Noice & Noice, 2006). In both of these experiments, those given the thought instructions performed better on a subsequent test of memory than did those who were asked to memorize the words or lines deliberately. This was despite the fact that the "think" groups, unlike the "memorize" groups, did not know that the experiment was concerned with memory and that they would be tested later.

The Value of Elaboration for School Learning In a study of fifth graders, John Bransford and his colleagues (1982) found that students who received high marks in school were far more likely to use elaborative rehearsal than were those who received lower marks. The researchers gave the children written passages to study for a test and asked them to explain what they did as they studied each passage. For example, one passage described two different kinds of boomerangs, a returning kind and a nonreturning kind, each used for different purposes. Academically successful students often reported that they rehearsed the material by asking themselves questions about it. They might wonder what a nonreturning boomerang looks like or why it is called a boomerang if it doesn't return, and this caused them to think deeply about what a boomerang really is and about the information in the passage. Less successful students, in contrast, usually studied the passages simply by rereading them.

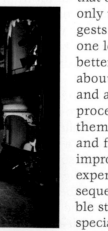

■ **Thinking through the lines** It is not exactly clear how performers commit long passages to memory, but they apparently do much more than repeat the passages over and over. Instead, they likely engage in a form of elaborative rehearsal.

Bransford's study was correlational, so it does not prove that elaborative study caused better test performance; it shows only that the two tended to go together. But other research suggests that elaborative study can improve students' grades. In one long-standing program aimed at helping students perform better in college, students are taught to write down questions about every textbook section that they read as they read it and about the lecture notes they take as they take them. The process of generating these questions and trying to answer them presumably deepens students' thought about the ideas and facts that they are reading about or hearing and thereby improves both understanding and memory. In a series of field experiments, students who were taught these techniques subsequently achieved higher grades than did otherwise comparable students who received either subject-matter tutoring or no special help (Heiman,1987).

Such findings are compatible with the following advice for studying this or any other textbook:

- Don't passively highlight or copy passages as you read for later rereading. Focus on the ideas, not the author's exact words.

- Constantly ask yourself questions such as these: Do I understand the idea that the author is trying to convey here? Do I agree with it? Is it relevant to my own life experiences? (Research has shown that people remember new information better when they relate it to themselves; Symons & Johnson, 1997.) Has the author given evidence supporting it? Does the evidence seem reasonable? How is this idea relevant to the larger issues of the chapter? (In this textbook, the numbered focus questions that appear in the margins give you a start on this task.)

- As you ask such questions, jot down notes in the margins that bear on your answers, such as "This idea seems similar to . . . ," or "I don't understand what my instructor means by . . . ."

- Through this active process, you will encode the material in a far richer and more lasting way than you could accomplish by simple rereading. In the process, you will also generate questions to ask other students or your instructor.

Organization Promotes Encoding

As a memory strategy, organization is closely tied to elaboration. Organizing items to be remembered is itself a means of elaboration; you must think about the items, not just repeat them, in order to organize them. Moreover, organization can improve memory by revealing or creating links among items that would otherwise be perceived as separate.

One way to increase the number of items one can retain in the short-term store is to group adjacent items that are at first perceived as separate, thus making them a single item. This procedure, known as **chunking**, decreases the number of items to be remembered and increases the amount of information in each item (Miller, 1956). As a simple illustration, if you had to memorize the series *M D P H D R S V P C E O I H O P*, your task would be made easier if you saw the series not as a string of 16 independent letters but as a set of five common abbreviations—M.D., Ph.D., RSVP, CEO, and IHOP. You could make your task still easier if you then chunked these five abbreviations into one sentence: "The M.D. and Ph.D. RSVPed to the CEO of IHOP." In developing such a story, you would not only be chunking but also elaborating—making the information more meaningful by adding some new information of your own.

Beginning music students find it easier to remember the notes on the lines of the treble clef as one sentence, "*Every Good Boy Does Fine,*" than as the senseless string of letters *E G B D F*. Similarly, physiology students can recall the seven physiological systems (skeletal, circulatory, respiratory, digestive, muscular, nervous, and reproductive) by matching their first letters to the consonants in *SACRED MANOR*. Both devices involve chunking. In the first example, the five notes are chunked into one meaningful sentence, and in the second the seven systems are chunked into two meaningful words. By reducing the number of separate items, and by attaching more meaning to each item, chunking provides an advantage both for maintaining information in working memory and for encoding it into long-term memory.

The Role of Chunking in Expert Memory We are all much better at forming long-term memories for information that is within rather than outside our realm of expertise. For example, master chess players can look for just a few seconds at a chess game in progress and form a long-term memory of the locations of all the pieces on the board (de Groot, 1965). Similarly, football coaches have excellent memories for diagrams of football plays (Garland & Barry, 1991), architects have excellent memories for floor plans (Atkin, 1980), and physicians have excellent memories for information gained in diagnostic interviews of patients (Coughlin & Patel, 1987).

As a step toward explaining the expertise advantage in memory, K. Anders Ericsson and his colleagues have posited the existence of a special kind of long-term memory, called *long-term working memory* (Ericsson & Delaney, 1999; Ericsson & Kintsch, 1995). They conceive of this as memory for the interrelated set of items (such as a patient's case history or the pieces on a chess board) that is crucial for solving the problem or completing the task at hand. Such memories are encoded

FOCUS 28

How can chunking be used to increase the amount of information that can be maintained in short-term memory or encoded into long-term memory?

FOCUS 29

How does chunking figure into experts' excellent memories for information that is within their realm of expertise?

FIGURE 9.17 Chess memory The top drawings exemplify the types of chess layouts used in chess memory research. On the left is a board taken from a master's game, and on the right is one with randomly arranged pieces. The graph shows the memory performance (averaged over 13 experiments) of chess players of various skill levels who studied either a game board or a random board for 10 seconds or less. The average number of pieces per board was 25. Skill level is measured in ELO points: 1600 is Class B, 2000 is Expert, and 2200 is Master.

Republished with permission of Elsevier, from Gobet, F., Lane, P. C. R., Croker, S., Cheng, P. C.-H., Jones, G., Oliver, I., et al. (2001). "Chunking mechanisms in human learning." *Trends in Cognitive Sciences, 5*, 236–243; permission conveyed through Copyright Clearance Center.

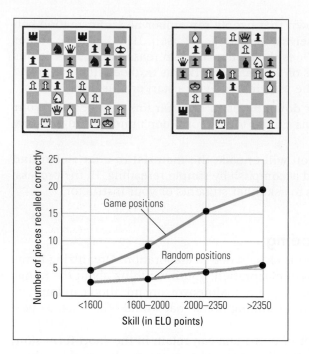

 FOCUS 30

What is a hierarchical organization, and how can such an organization facilitate encoding into long-term memory?

into long-term storage in a manner that makes the entire structure of information easily accessible to working memory, at least until the problem is solved or the task is finished. Such memories allow a physician to puzzle over a particular patient's symptoms while driving home from work, or a chess master to mull over the possibilities inherent in a particular set of chess positions while away from the game. Such memories are not lost as a result of interruptions, as short-term working memories are, so they allow the person to go back to a previous task after time spent on another task (Oulasvirta & Saariluoma, 2006).

Chunking plays a major role in the formation of long-term working memories. In order to form such a memory of, say, a particular arrangement of pieces on a chess board, a person must already have in long-term storage a great deal of well-established information about possible and likely ways that such items might be arranged. This knowledge provides a foundation for the efficient chunking of new items of information. Chess games normally progress in certain logical ways, so logical relationships exist among the pieces, which experts can chunk together and remember as familiar formations rather than as separate pieces. If the chess pieces are arranged randomly rather than in ways that could occur in a real game, masters are scarcely any better than novices at remembering their locations (Gobet et al., 2001; see **Figure 9.17**). Experts in other realms also lose their memory advantage when information is presented randomly rather than being grouped in ways that make sense to them (Vicente & Wang, 1998; Weber & Brewer, 2003).

Hierarchical Organization Promotes Encoding The most useful format for organizing some kinds of information is the hierarchy. In a hierarchy, related items are clustered together to form categories, related categories are clustered to form larger (higher-order) categories, and so on.

In an experiment demonstrating the advantage of hierarchical organization for long-term memory, Andrea Halpern (1986) gave subjects a chart listing 54 well-known song titles to be memorized. In some cases the chart was organized in a hierarchical manner, with songs arranged according to meaningful categories and subcategories; for example, patriotic or rock-and-roll songs. In other cases a similar chart was used but organized randomly, with no systematic relation among categories, subcategories, and song titles. When tested later for their memory of the song titles, subjects who had studied the organized chart recalled accurately many more titles than did those who had studied the disorganized chart. During the test the

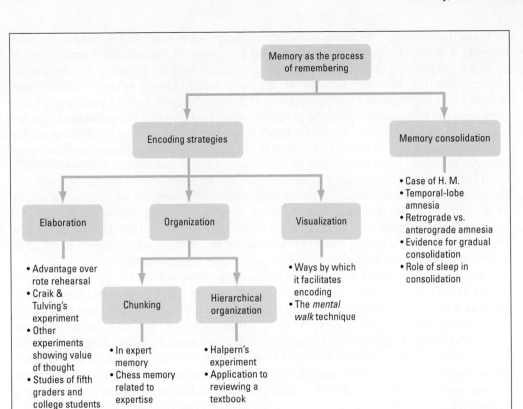

FIGURE 9.18 Hierarchical summary of a textbook section Summarized here are the ideas and evidence presented in this section (pp. 338–348) of the textbook. Such a chart is an aid to thought and memory because it reveals the logical connections among the items of information. Notice that some of the boxed items correspond to headings within the section.

former group of subjects would first recall a category name and then the songs that had been listed under that name.

As pointed out in Chapter 1, the information in this textbook (like that in nearly all textbooks) is hierarchically arranged: Each main heading refers to a set of related ideas, and each subheading refers to a smaller subset of ideas within the larger set. An efficient way to summarize the information in almost any textbook chapter is to sketch it out according to its hierarchical organization. As an illustration, a hierarchical sketch of the section you are now reading appears in **Figure 9.18**. Notice that the top node indicates in key words the theme of the section, the nodes subordinate to it indicate the main ideas pertaining to that theme, and the comments under them indicate the examples or evidence provided for each idea. You could summarize the whole chapter with seven such diagrams, one for each of the chapter's main sections. This would be a more efficient aid in helping you remember the information for a test than would a string of terms and names that does not connect the ideas to each other or to supportive evidence. The section reviews of this textbook also preserve the hierarchical organization of ideas and evidence within each section (see Chapter 1).

Visualization Promotes Encoding

Our discussion of encoding so far has centered mostly on memory for verbal information. But we can also encode pictures or visual scenes into long-term memory, apparently in a nonverbal form, which can be recalled later into the visuospatial sketchpad of working memory. Visual and verbal memories interact and supplement one another in our everyday experience. If we asked you to describe your living room, you would probably summon a pictorial memory of that room and then find the words to describe it.

A good deal of research suggests that people can improve their memory for verbally presented information if they encode that information visually as well as verbally. For example, memory for information in news stories improves if relevant pictures accompany the stories (Prabu, 1998). Lacking pictures, people can improve their memory for verbally presented information by visualization: constructing "mental pictures" to represent that information (Paivio, 1986).

FOCUS 31

How might visualization help improve memory for verbally presented information?

Visualization may improve memory through several different means. It may provide a distinct visual memory trace to supplement the verbal memory trace, thereby increasing the chance that the memory will be recalled in the future (Paivio, 1986). It may also provide an efficient way to chunk several verbally presented ideas together. For example, a verbal description of a person you haven't met may contain many separate items of information that you can combine into a single visual image. In addition, visual imagery may improve memory by linking newly learned information to information that is already well encoded in long-term memory. An example of that is found in a memory technique called the *mental walk,* used by nearly all contestants in the annual World Memory Championships when they are asked to memorize, in order, the names of a long list of objects (Maguire et al., 2003). As they hear the list of objects, they imagine themselves taking a walk along a familiar route and leaving each object next to a familiar landmark on the route. Then, during recall, they mentally walk the route again, inspect each landmark, and "see" each item that they had previously deposited there.

People are very good at recognizing images (Shepard, 1967; Standing, 1973). Think of all the faces you can recognize, even if you can't always put a name to a face, and the countless specific objects you've seen perhaps only once but recognize when seen again. In one experiment, Timothy Brady and his colleagues (2008) showed subjects 2,500 real-world objects for 3 seconds each. Subjects were told that they should try to remember the details of each object; then, 5.5 hours later, their recognition memory for the objects was tested. At the time of testing, subjects were shown pairs of objects and had to determine which object in the pair had been presented earlier (the "old" picture). For some subjects, the "old" items were paired with an object from another, novel category (e.g., a parcel of paper vs. a gage); for a second group of subjects, the "old" items were paired to a different exemplar of the same type of item (e.g., two different mirrors); and for a third group of subjects the "old" items were paired with the same object but in a different state (e.g., the same basket, but one upright and the other on its side). **Figure 9.19** presents

FIGURE 9.19 Example test pairs (one "old" and one "new") used in each of three conditions (novel, exemplar, and state). After seeing 2,500 pictures, subjects were shown pairs of pictures and had to identify which picture they had seen before (that is, which was the "old" one).

Brady, T. F., Konkle, T., Alvarez, G. A., & Oliva, A. (2008). Visual long-term memory has a massive storage capacity for object details. *Proceedings of the National Academy of Science*, 105, 14325–14329. Figure 1. Copyright (2008) National Academy of Sciences, U.S.A

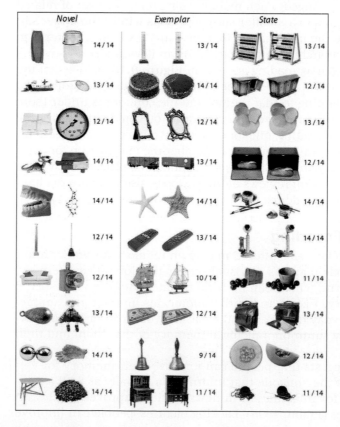

examples of the items used in this experiment. Brady and colleagues reported high levels of performance for all groups (chance is 50%), as illustrated in **Figure 9.20**. Performance was highest when "old" items were paired with novel objects (93% correct), but only slightly higher than performance in the other two conditions (88% and 87% correct for the Exemplar and State conditions). Thus, subjects could correctly recognize thousands of objects after viewing them for a single, brief time for up to 5.5 hours. According to the authors, this suggests that visual memory is a *massive store*.

Memory Consolidation

According to the information-processing model we've been following in this chapter, once information has been attended to in short-term memory and encoded, it becomes part of permanent, long-term memory. However, the process is not quite as simple as that. Initial long-term memories are quite fragile and must be consolidated. As you'll see, some memories fade quickly, whereas others are strengthened or even modified over time.

Retrograde Amnesia as Evidence for Gradual Consolidation of Long-Term Memories

Earlier in this chapter we discussed temporal-lobe amnesia, suffered by the patient H. M. As we noted then, destruction of the hippocampus resulted in an inability to encode new episodic memories, although such patients can still form new implicit memories. This most dramatic type of amnesia observed in H. M. and other patients with temporal-lobe damage is ***anterograde*** [ăn´-tə-rō-grād´] ***amnesia***, the loss of capacity to form long-term memories of events occurring after the injury. However, these patients also show a considerable degree of ***retrograde amnesia***, loss of memories of events that occurred before the injury.

Retrograde amnesia is generally time graded; it is greatest for memories acquired just before the injury and least for those acquired long before (Manns & Buffalo, 2012; Wixted, 2004, 2005). H. M., for example, lost all his memories of events that occurred within several days of his surgery, some of his memories of events that occurred within a few years of his surgery, and essentially none of his memories of events that occurred in his childhood, many years before the surgery (Eichenbaum, 2001). Such time-graded retrograde amnesia is also seen in people who have suffered a severe blow to the head.

The time-graded nature of retrograde amnesia suggests that long-term memories are encoded in the brain in at least two forms: a labile, easily disrupted form and a stable, not easily disrupted form. Long-term memories appear to be encoded first in the labile form. Then, gradually over time, they apparently are either re-encoded in the stable form or lost (forgotten). ***Consolidation*** occurs when the labile memory form is converted into the stable form.

According to a prominent theory, the labile form of long-term memory involves neural connections in the hippocampus and the stable form involves neural connections in various parts of the cerebral cortex, without dependence on the hippocampus (Eichenbaum, 2001; Medina et al., 2008). This theory is supported by the time-graded retrograde amnesia observed after loss of the hippocampus, and it is also supported by neuroimaging research with people who have intact brains and normal memories. When people recall memories that were acquired relatively recently, neural activity in the hippocampus increases; but when they recall memories that were first acquired many years earlier, increased activity occurs in parts of the cerebral cortex but not in the hippocampus (Haist et al., 2001).

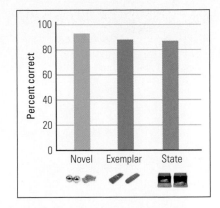

FIGURE 9.20 Memory for pictures Memory performance for each of the three test conditions (Novel, Exemplar, and State). Performance was high even in the most difficult (State) condition. (Data from Brady et al., 2008.)

FOCUS 32

What evidence supports the theory that long-term memories first exist in a labile (unstable), hippocampal-dependent state— and then, if not lost, that they are gradually consolidated into a more stable form that doesn't depend on the hippocampus?

Role of Retrieval in Memory Consolidation and Modification

Nobody knows just how memory consolidation occurs, though it apparently involves modification of existing synaptic connections and growth of new synaptic connections in the brain. It is also not clear why some memories appear to consolidate relatively quickly (within days) and others much more slowly (over years) or why many memories are forgotten within minutes, hours, or days and never become consolidated. There is, however, evidence that memories that are recalled and used repeatedly, over relatively long time periods, are the ones most likely to be consolidated into a form that resists disruption.

Research, mostly with nonhuman animals, suggests that every time a memory is recalled and put to use, the neural trace for that memory enters temporarily into a new labile stage—that is, a stage when it can be modified (Lee, 2008; Tronson & Taylor, 2007). Depending on what happens when the memory is recalled, that memory may be strengthened, or weakened, or changed by the addition of some new content to it (Altmann & Gray, 2002). From this point of view, long-term memories are not static, like words on a page, but are dynamic entities, changing in some ways every time they are used. Recent research using fMRI in humans has been able to observe brain-related changes when a memory is reactivated, and although this research has yet to show convincingly that reactivation of a memory enhances the strength of that memory, it provides a way of assessing such questions not easily afforded by behavioral methods (Levy & Wagner, 2013).

From a functional point of view, the fact that memories are modifiable during retrieval makes sense. Cues that my brain might use to consolidate memories into a very long-lasting form include the frequency and time course of my retrieving them. At the end of today, when I go to my car, I will retrieve for the last time the information about where I parked this morning. There may even be something about my mental attitude in retrieving it that signals my memory system that I won't need this memory again, so it can fade. I will, however, continue for a long time to retrieve memories of more enduring value, such as information about what my car looks like, so those memories are likely to consolidate into forms that resist disruption and are not dependent on my hippocampus. Moreover, each time that I retrieve my memory of what my car looks like, in the presence of my car, that memory may be updated to include any modifications in the car's appearance. Researchers are only barely beginning to learn about the kinds of cues that the long-term memory system uses to strengthen, weaken, or modify memories in useful ways.

That active retrieval of information can consolidate memory and facilitate learning is nicely shown in a series of experiments by Jeffrey Karpicke and Henry Roediger (Karpicke, 2012; Karpicke & Roediger, 2010; Roediger & Karpicke, 2006). For example, in one experiment (Roediger & Karpicke, 2006, Experiment 2), after reading two educational texts ("The Sun," "Sea Otters"), college students either studied the material for four study periods (SSSS), studied the material for three study periods and then recalled the items (SSSR), or studied the material once then practiced retrieving the material for three periods (SRRR). At the end of the learning phase, subjects were asked to estimate how well they thought they had learned the material. A week later subjects recalled the material again. The results of this experiment are shown in **Figure 9.21**.

As you can see, subjects predicted that their performance would be greatest in the condition that afforded the most chances to study (SSSS) and worst in the condition in which students studied the material only once but practiced recalling it repeatedly (SRRR). Yet, the results were in the exact opposite direction, with actual recall being greatest on the multiple retrieval condition (SRRR) and poorest in multiple study condition (SSSS). These findings, and others like them (see Karpicke, 2012), demonstrate the central role that retrieval has in consolidating memory and promoting meaningful learning, and also provide students with a simple technique to improve their academic learning.

FOCUS 33

What might be the value of the increased modifiability of long-term memories that occurs during retrieval?

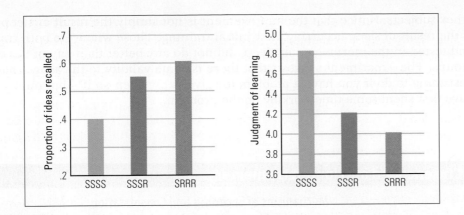

FIGURE 9.21 Final recall College students read educational texts and either studied them for four study periods (SSSS), studied for three study periods and then recalled the items (SSSR), or studied once then practiced retrieving the material for three periods (SRRR). The graph in (a) shows the actual recall, whereas (b) shows predicted recall. As you can see, students' predictions were opposite to their actual performance.

(Data from Roediger & Karpicke, 2006.)

The Role of Sleep in Memory Consolidation

Have you ever found that your memory for, and maybe even your understanding of, some newly learned information was better after a period of sleep than it was before? Many recent experiments have shown that sleep, shortly after learning, helps to consolidate newly acquired memories, making them more easily retrievable and less susceptible to disruption than they were before the sleep (Rasch & Born, 2008; Stickgold, 2005). A similar period of wakefulness does not have this effect. The effect seems to occur no matter what time of day the sleep occurs, as long as it occurs within a few hours after the learning experience. Some of these experiments used paired-associate tasks, in which subjects were presented with pairs of words and then were tested for their ability to recall the second member of each pair after seeing just the first member (Backhaus et al., 2008). But improved memory after sleep has been shown with many other tasks as well, and for children as well as adults (Gömez & Edgin, 2015).

Recall from Chapter 5 that sleep occurs in a series of stages, each associated with certain brain wave patterns. For paired-associate tasks and other tasks involving conscious recall, the type of sleep that seems most valuable is slow-wave, non-REM sleep (Rasch & Born, 2008). The improved learning correlates positively with the amount of slow-wave sleep, not the amount of REM sleep. There is also evidence that the hippocampus becomes activated at various times during slow-wave sleep. One prominent theory is that the hippocampal activity represents activation of the memory trace, which allows consolidation of the memory into a new, more stable form.

Sleep may improve not just the durability of new memories, but also their quality, leading to new insights. Ullrich Wagner and his colleagues (2004) demonstrated this when they trained people to solve a certain type of mathematical problem by following a series of seven steps. Unbeknownst to the subjects, the problems could also be solved by a simpler method, involving just two steps. In the experiment, the subjects were given a small amount of training on the task and then, 8 hours later, were tested with a long series of the same type of problems to see how quickly they could solve them. Some subjects were trained in the morning and then tested in the evening, after no sleep; others were trained in the evening and tested the next morning after a night's sleep; and still others were trained in the evening but kept awake during the night before testing in the morning. For comparison, two other groups received their training and testing all in one block, occurring either in the morning after sleep or in the evening after a period awake.

The results of the study are shown in **Figure 9.22**. As you can see, the subjects who had a period of sleep between training and testing were more than twice as likely to discover the simpler way of solving the problem than were any of the

FOCUS 34

What is some evidence that sleep promotes the durability and quality of long-term memories?

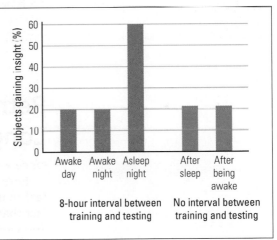

FIGURE 9.22 Sleep after training improved insight Subjects were trained, in the morning or in the evening, to follow a 7-step procedure for solving a type of mathematical problem. Then they were tested, either immediately after training or 8 hours after training. The crucial measure was the percentage who discovered an easier, 2-step way to solve the problem (achieved "insight"). As the graph shows, the 8-hour interval increased insight only if subjects slept during that period. An 8-hour interval spent awake, whether it was during the day or during the night, did not increase insight.

(Data from Wagner et al., 2004.)

other subjects. Notice that the improvement is not simply the result of sleep, but is the result of sleep occurring after initial training. Those who were both trained and tested in the morning, after sleep, did not do any better than any of the other groups. The experiment suggests that there is some validity to the adage that the best thing to do if you have a problem to solve is to "sleep on it"—but only if you have first spent some time working on the problem.

SECTION REVIEW

For later recall, information must be encoded into long-term memory.

Thoughtful Means of Encoding

- Elaboration involves actively extending one's understanding of something, thereby connecting it with information already in long-term memory. Its effectiveness has been demonstrated in field research (such as school learning) as well as in the laboratory.

- Chunking facilitates encoding by grouping separate items into one higher-level unit. Experts use previously learned chunks to create long-term working memories in areas of their expertise.

- Organizing information into a logical hierarchy facilitates encoding and retrieval.

- Visualizing verbally presented information may improve memory by creating an additional memory trace, by chunking separate items together into one image, and by forming links to information already in long-term memory.

Mechanisms of Encoding and Consolidation

- The time-graded nature of retrograde amnesia suggests that long-term memories exist first in a labile form, becoming gradually more stable through consolidation.

- Frequent recall of memories can promote both their modification and their consolidation.

- Sleep shortly after learning helps to consolidate memories and in some cases may reorganize memories in ways that promote new insights.

Retrieving Information From Long-Term Memory

Once we encode an item into long-term memory, we may or may not be able to find it there when we need it. Why are we sometimes unable to remember a name or fact that we "know" that we know? Why do we at other times remember a name or fact that we thought we had long since forgotten? Why do we sometimes remember an event differently each time we retell it, or remember an event that didn't really happen as if it did? These are some of the questions that cognitive psychologists have addressed in research and theories concerning the retrieval of information from long-term memory.

The Internet contains billions of pages of textual information, sitting in hundreds of thousands of servers throughout the world. All that information would be useless to you were it not for search engines, such as Google, that can rapidly scan the pages and find what you are looking for. The long-term-memory store of your brain likewise contains vast quantities of information (though not as much as the Internet), which is useful only to the degree that we can call information forth at the moment we need it.

Retrieval of specific items from any information-storage system depends on how the stored information is organized. Books in a library are organized by topic, making it easier for us to find all there is about, say, the Civil War or flower gardening. Words in a dictionary are organized alphabetically, so we can find them on the basis of their spelling. Web pages on the Internet contain links to other pages that deal with related issues, and efficient search engines take advantage of those links to rank pages in the order of their relevance to the search terms that we have typed in. In the human mind, long-term memories are stored not in isolation, but in networks in which each item is linked to many others through connections called **associations**, somewhat analogous to the links among websites (Griffiths et al., 2007). When any one memory is activated by an appropriate stimulus or thought, other memories associated with it become temporarily activated, or *primed,* to become more easily retrievable. A stimulus or thought that primes a particular memory is a **retrieval cue** for that memory.

The evidence for these ideas about memory organization and retrieval comes not from knowledge of how memories are stored physically in the brain, but from behavioral studies.

Mental Associations as Foundations for Retrieval

Speculation about mental associations goes back at least to the time of Aristotle. Aristotle considered two concepts to be associated if the thought of one tends to evoke (call forth from long-term memory) the thought of the other, and he proposed several principles of association, the most central of which are contiguity and similarity.

According to Aristotle's principle of **association by contiguity**, some concepts are associated because they have occurred contiguously (i.e., together) in the person's previous experience. Thus, *napkin* and *plate* might be associated in your mind because you have frequently seen napkins and plates together. When you see the face of someone you know, his or her name leaps to your mind because you have often experienced that face and that name together in the past. The contiguity principle also accounts for our ability to bring quickly to mind the various properties of an object when we hear its name. If you hear *apple,* you can immediately think *red, round, sweet, tart, grows on trees, good in pies* because you have experienced all those properties of apples contiguously with apples themselves and with the word *apple.*

According to the principle of **association by similarity**, items that share one or more properties in common are linked in memory whether or not they were ever experienced together. Your thought *apple* might evoke the thought *rose* because both are red, even if you have never seen an apple and a rose together.

Why Elaborative Rehearsal Creates Easily Retrievable Memories

Earlier in this chapter we discussed network models of memory organization, describing how concepts such as *red, roses, cherries, apples, sunsets,* and *fire* are organized in semantic memory. How you place new information into your network of associations has a big effect on your ability to retrieve it. This brings us back to the role of elaborative rehearsal in memorization, discussed earlier. The more mental associations you create in learning a new item of information, the more ways will be available for you to retrieve it.

Suppose you are learning for the first time that the capital of Vermont is Montpelier. You might notice, as you encode this new fact, that the syllable *mont* appears in both the capital name and the state name, and you might then think about the fact that *mont* is French for mountain, that Vermont is known as the Green Mountain state, and that many of the early settlers were French. More imaginatively, you might notice that *Montpelier* sounds like *mount peeler* and you might think of a strong wind peeling the snow off one of Vermont's mountains. Through such observations and thoughts you are setting up many possible retrieval cues for remembering, later, that the capital of Vermont is Montpelier. The last syllable of *Vermont,* or the thought of Vermont's mountains, or of French settlers, or of wind, or of snow, or of anything that can be peeled, could prime the name Montpelier in your memory store.

In an experiment that demonstrated the value of retrieval cues generated by elaborative encoding, Timo Mäntylä (1986) presented subjects with 500 nouns one by one in a single very long session. He did not ask the subjects to memorize the

FOCUS 35

What do the principles of association by contiguity and association by similarity say about retrieval from long-term memory? According to James, how does the second principle depend on the first?

FOCUS 36

How might elaborative encoding facilitate retrieval? How is this idea supported by a memory-testing experiment?

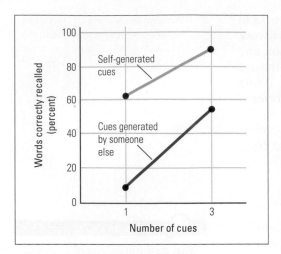

FIGURE 9.23 Value of self-generated retrieval cues Subjects generated either one or three single-word properties related to each of 500 nouns. Later they were tested for their ability to recall each noun, using either their own self-generated properties or another subject's self-generated properties as retrieval cues.

(Data from Mäntylä, 1986.)

FOCUS 37

How is the effect of context on memory adaptive? What is some evidence that retrieval is best when the retrieval context is similar to the encoding context?

FOCUS 38

What does it mean to say that memories are constructed?

nouns but asked them to write down either one or three words that they regarded as properties of the object named by each noun. For example, for the word *barn* a subject might write *large, wooden, red*. He then surprised the subjects with a test of their ability to recall all 500 nouns. As cues, he gave them either their own self-generated properties or those generated by a different subject in the same experiment. Subjects who received three self-generated properties for each word were able to recall correctly more than 90% of the 500 nouns. When only one property was available or when the properties had been generated by someone else, recall was much poorer (see **Figure 9.23**).

Contextual Stimuli as Retrieval Cues

The environmental context that we find ourselves in at any given moment provides retrieval cues that prime our memories for our past experiences in that context. Such priming is generally adaptive because our past experiences in a given context are often relevant to our future experiences in that context. Sitting behind the steering wheel of an automobile primes my memories relevant to driving, the sight and smell of a gymnasium prime my memories of basketball rules and strategies, and standing at a podium primes my memories of lecture techniques that were helpful in the past.

Many experiments have shown that people who are given facts or word lists to memorize in a particular context do better at recalling that information if tested in that same context than if tested in a different context (Smith & Vela, 2001). The context might be a particular room, or it might be a single very noticeable stimulus that seems to be incidental to the learning task. In one series of experiments, people who studied a list of words in a room that smelled of chocolate or cinnamon/apple or mothballs performed better on a recall test if that same smell was present than they did if a different smell, or no smell, was present (Schab, 1990). Other experiments have shown that even instructions to imagine the context that was present during learning can facilitate recall (Smith & Vela, 2001).

Memory Construction as a Source of Distortion

Remembering is not just a process of retrieving traces that were laid down during the original encoding. The brain is not a tape recorder, video camera, or CD burner that records information; and remembering is not a matter of finding the right apparatus to play it back. Instead, remembering is an active, inferential process guided by a person's general knowledge and intuitions about the world and by cues in the present environment. When you hear a story or experience an event, your mind encodes into long-term memory only some parts of the available information. Later, when you try to recount the story or event, you retrieve the encoded fragments and fill in the gaps through your logic and knowledge, which tell you what must have happened even if you can't quite remember it. With repeated retelling, it becomes harder to distinguish what was present in the original encoding from what was added later. Thus, memory of the story or experience is not a simple readout of the original information but a *construction* built and rebuilt from various sources. Our ability to construct the past is adaptive because it allows us to make logical and useful sense of our incompletely encoded experiences. But the process can also lead to distortions.

Effects of Preexisting Beliefs: Fitting Memories to Schemas and Scripts

British psychologist Frederick Bartlett was among the first to call attention to the role of people's general knowledge or beliefs in their more specific memories. Bartlett (1932) used the term ***schema*** to refer to one's generalized mental representation, or

Stockbroker/Alamy

■ **Following the script** Years from now, these children may construct memories of this birthday party largely from their knowledge of the typical birthday-party script.

concept, of any given class of objects, scenes, or events. He used the term especially in relation to concepts that may vary from culture to culture and that involve spatial or temporal relationships among the individual units of the object, scene, or event. For example, in mainstream Western culture people might share a relatively common schema of a living room, perhaps including a couch, an easy chair, and a rocking chair, all oriented around a television set, with a coffee table in front of the couch. When we enter a new living room, we recognize it as a living room and assess its unique features by comparing it with our already-existing schema. Schemas that involve the organization of events in time, rather than of objects in space, are commonly called *scripts* by today's cognitive psychologists (Schank & Abelson, 1977). The typical children's birthday party is a good example: The celebration involves the presentation of the cake, the singing of "Happy Birthday," and the blowing out of the candles; birthday presents may also be opened.

According to Bartlett and the results of many studies since his time, schemas do not just help us recognize and label the objects, scenes, and events that we encounter in daily life; they also affect the way we remember them later. We tend to remember any particular living room or birthday party as being more like the standard living room or birthday party than it really was. That is because we fill gaps in our memories for specific scenes and events with information drawn from our more general schemas and scripts.

In a classic demonstration of the effect of general knowledge on memory for the specific, Bartlett (1932) asked British university students to listen to a Native American story entitled "The War of the Ghosts" and later asked them to retell the story from memory. He found that the story often changed in the retelling, and he found certain consistencies in those changes. Details not essential to the plot tended to drop out, and those that were essential were often exaggerated. Also, points in the story that were consistent with Native American beliefs but not with the students' own beliefs were often changed to be more consistent with the latter. For example, the protagonist's obligation to certain spirits—a key component of the original story—tended to be transposed into an obligation to his parents. The changes were not deliberate; the students were trying to retell the story accurately, but they inevitably used their own ways of understanding things—their own schemas—to fill the gaps in their memory.

 FOCUS 39

How did Bartlett demonstrate that culture-specific schemas affect the way that people remember a story?

"Well, I'm here to develop some false memories so I can forget about my own rotten past!"

False memories of childhood abuse can sometimes be developed in therapy by well-intentioned therapists.

> ### FOCUS 40
> What is some evidence that eye-witnesses' memories, even when very confidently expressed, are not always reliable? What is some evidence that suggestions made after the event can influence eye-witnesses' memories?

False Eyewitness Memories: Effects of Suggestion

Memory construction is affected not just by preexisting schemas, but also by events that occur after the event being remembered was encoded. Such constructions can have serious consequences when recounted in courtrooms or psychotherapists' offices.

Perhaps the most egregious of false memories are those that send innocent persons to prison or, sometimes, to death. In the 1990s, when DNA testing began to identify dozens of people who had been convicted of serious crimes they did not commit, the U.S. Attorney General's office ordered a study to discover the causes of those injustices. That study, and similar studies since then, concluded that the great majority of those convictions came about because of highly confident eyewitness identifications (Wells et al., 2002, 2006). In many cases the eyewitness was not confident early in the investigative process, but became so over time. An example is the case of Larry Mayes, who spent 21 years in prison for a rape he did not commit (Loftus, 2004). The victim failed to pick Mayes in two initial police lineups, but then became confident that he was the rapist after police helped her "recover" her memory of him through hypnosis. By the time of trial, the face of Larry Mayes was clearly embedded in her mind, and she was certain he was the rapist.

Hypnosis is a state of high suggestibility; psychologists have shown repeatedly that false memories can be created relatively easily through suggestions or encouragement made in that state (Lynn et al., 1997; Steblay & Bothwell, 1994). People who hold steadfastly to truly bizarre memories—such as having been abducted by aliens from another planet—often first recalled or became confident about those memories when questioned under hypnosis by investigators who believe in such phenomena (Newman & Baumeister, 1996). Many experiments—some involving simulated crimes—have shown that memories can also be altered or created through suggestions and encouragement without hypnosis (Spinney, 2008). In one study, simply saying, "Good job, you are a good witness," dramatically increased witnesses' confidence in their memories of who committed the simulated crime, whether or not the memories were accurate (Wells & Bradfield, 1999). Other studies have shown that leading questions can alter people's memories not just of who was involved in an incident, but also of what happened.

In a classic experiment, Elizabeth Loftus and J. C. Palmer (1974) had adults view a film depicting a traffic accident. Later, the researchers asked some of the subjects how fast the cars were going when they *hit* each other, and they asked others how fast the cars were going when they *smashed into* each other. The question with the word *smashed* elicited estimates of faster speed than did the question with the word *hit*. Moreover, when the subjects returned a week later and were asked to remember the film and say whether there was any broken glass in the accident, those who had heard the word *smashed* were more likely to say they saw broken glass (though actually there was none in the film) than were those who had heard the word *hit*. In subsequent studies, Loftus and others showed that such memory distortion is especially likely if the misinformation is introduced in just the manner that a clever but biased detective or cross-examiner is likely to introduce it—repeatedly but subtly, in the context of recounting aspects of the event that really did occur (Loftus, 1992; Zaragoza & Mitchell, 1996).

False Memories of Childhood Experiences: Effects of Suggestion and Imagination

If an adult in psychotherapy begins to recall instances of having been abused in childhood, does the memory necessarily reflect the truth, or might it have been constructed from ideas implanted by a well-intentioned but misguided therapist?

In the 1980s, a number of high-profile court cases centered on this question. Some people were suing their parents for past, horrible abuses discovered in therapy, and some parents were suing therapists for implanting false memories in their offspring. The cases led to a spate of psychological research showing that techniques of suggestion, encouragement, and imagination indeed can create false memories of childhood experiences.

In one such study, Elizabeth Loftus and Jacqueline Pickrell (1995) led adults to believe that at age 5 they had been lost in a certain shopping mall and had been helped and comforted there by an elderly woman—an experience that in fact had never happened, according to the subjects' parents and other close relatives who served as informants. Yet 25% of the subjects maintained—both at initial questioning and in follow-up interviews 1 and 2 weeks later—that they could remember the event. Some even elaborated upon it with details beyond those supplied by the researchers. Using a similar technique, adults were falsely led to believe that they had committed a crime (assault or theft) that led to contact with the police when they were young adolescents (Shaw & Porter, 2015). Subjects were interviewed three times and asked to try to recall details of the event, along with events that actually had happened in their childhoods. Although none of the subjects recalled the false criminal activity during the first interview, by the third interview 70% of the subjects remembered being involved in a criminal activity involving the police!

Subsequent studies showed that false-memory construction can be abetted by imagination. In one experiment, researchers told each subject (falsely) that according to the subject's parents, a particular embarrassing incident had occurred in his or her childhood (Hyman & Pentland, 1996). The made-up incident was one in which the subject, at age 5, had been running around at a wedding reception and had knocked over the punch bowl, spilling punch on the bride's parents. Subjects in the *imagination condition* were asked, in two successive sessions, to form vivid mental images of this event to help them remember it, and others, in the *control condition*, were asked just to think about the event as a way of remembering it. The result was that mental imagery sharply increased reported memory (see **Figure 9.24**). In an interview conducted after the second imagery session, 38% of the subjects in the imagery condition, compared to only 12% in the control condition, claimed to remember the punch-spilling incident.

Other experiments have shown that imagery alone, even without misleading suggestions from the researcher, can create false memories. In one, adults were simply asked to imagine a certain painful medical procedure—a procedure that in fact is never performed—and then, later, were asked to try to remember whether that procedure had ever been done to them in their childhood. The result was that over 20% of those in the imagination condition, compared to about 5% in the control condition, said they could remember enduring that procedure (Mazoni & Memon, 2003). Similar studies done with preschool and early school-age children have shown that they are even more susceptible to the effects of imagining ("Do you remember getting your finger caught in a mousetrap?") (Ceci et al., 1994) and will create memories of unusual and unlikely events (a rabbit getting loose in their classroom) simply by overhearing other children talk about it (Principe et al., 2010). Some children will even create memories about their infancy, based on experiences they had or things they hear years later. Recall my (David Bjorklund's) memory as a sickly baby sitting in a crib at his grandparents' house (p. 337).

Such research should not lead us to conclude that all our childhood memories are false constructions. The research does, however, suggest strongly that childhood memories are even more subject to distortion by suggestion and imagination than are memories acquired later in life.

FOCUS 41

How have false memories for childhood experiences been implanted in experiments? What evidence indicates that imagination can facilitate false-memory construction?

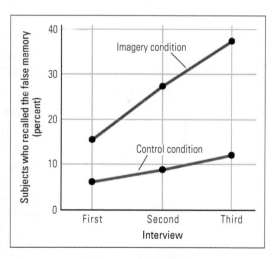

FIGURE 9.24 Effect of imagery on development of a false memory Adult subjects were told (falsely) about an incident that happened in their childhood. They were asked to try to remember it either by thinking about it (control condition) or by vividly imagining what might have happened (imagery condition). This procedure was repeated the next day, and the subjects' memories were again assessed in a third session, 2 days after the first. The graph shows the percentage of subjects in each condition, at each interview, who claimed to remember the incident.
(Data from Hyman & Pentland, 1996.)

FOCUS 42

How might source confusion and social pressure contribute to false-memory construction?

Source Confusion and Social Pressure as Causes of False-Memory Construction

According to some theorists, a basic cause of most cases of false-memory construction is *source confusion* (Lindsay, 2008). We acquire information from various sources—including firsthand experiences, stories we have heard, and scenes we have imagined—and our minds reorganize the information in ways that may be meaningful but that obscure the ties between each item and its original source. Events that are conceptually linked but came from different sources may become confounded in memory. The memory of the actual traffic accident witnessed becomes confounded with the memory of what the cross-examiner implied about the accident. The memory of an actual event in childhood becomes confounded with a story heard from others or with an imagined scene constructed by free association in a psychotherapy session.

Social pressure also, no doubt, figures into many cases of false memory (Loftus, 1997). In most of the experiments just described, subjects were in one way or another led to believe that they should remember the suggested events. Similar pressure occurs in crime investigations, where the investigator acts as if any normal person should remember the incident's details. And it sometimes occurs in psychotherapists' offices, where a misguided therapist conveys the message that certain kinds of incidents, such as childhood abuse, must have happened and that the patient's task is to remember those incidents (McNally, 2003; Pendergrast, 1995). A person who feels pressured, even gently so, to come up with a memory is more likely than an unpressured person to identify a vague, possible memory as an actual memory; and the more often the memory is repeated, and the more praise the person receives for recalling it, the more confident the person becomes that the memory is true (Brainerd & Reyna, 2005). The opposite is probably true also: A person who feels pressured by family members or an abuser to believe that certain memories are exaggerated, or even figments of his or her imagination, may come to doubt memories that are in fact accurate.

Prospective Memory and Mental Time Travel

To this point we have been talking about remembering things in the past, called *retrospective memory*. But we also sometimes use memory to remember to do things in the future, termed ***prospective memory*** (Einstein & McDaniel, 2005). For example, on my way home today, I need to remember to stop at the store and pick up some milk, otherwise I will have dry cereal for tomorrow morning's breakfast. Prospective memory is a type of episodic memory, but what is retrieved is not a past event but a future intent. Researchers have distinguished two types of prospective memory. *Event-based* prospective memory involves remembering to perform a particular action when cued by a target event (e.g., giving a message to a friend when you next see him or her), whereas *time-based* prospective memory involves remembering to execute an intended action after the passage of a certain amount of time or at a specific moment (e.g., answering e-mails in 10 minutes). Unlike retrospective memory, in prospective memory "no one is there to put you in a retrieval mode when the target event occurs . . . thus, a key question in the prospective memory arena is how, in the absence of a direct request to search memory, the cognitive system supports retrieval of the intended action at the appropriate moment" (Einstein & McDaniel, 2010, p. 1082). Like retrospective memory, prospective memory is relatively poor in children, increases in adolescents and young adulthood, and declines in older adults (Kvavilashvili et al., 2009). In fact, failures of prospective memory are a frequent complaint for older adults. People of all ages complain about failures of prospective memory, and such failures can have serious consequences in many workplaces, including aviation and medicine (Dismukes, 2013; Loft, 2014).

There are three phases in prospective memory: (a) first, a subject forms an intention (buy milk on the way home); (b) second, the intention must be maintained;

FOCUS 43

Why might differences in executive functions affect one's prospective memory abilities?

and (c) third, there must be a "switch" from the ongoing task (driving home) to execute the intention (stopping at the store and buying milk) (Ellis, 1996). The *executive functioning* account of prospective memory proposes that each phase requires using a limited pool of cognitive resources in an effective way (Wong & Leboe, 2009). People need to be able to plan (phase 1) and regulate their thinking and behavior, particularly during the "switch" phase (phase 3), and each phase uses cognitive resources. Support for this position comes from tasks in which subjects who are given a prospective memory task ("Remember to put the sign on the door when we leave") perform more poorly on ongoing problem-solving tasks than subjects not given a future-oriented task to perform (Smith, 2003). Thus, like the dual tasks discussed in the section on working memory, having to remember to do something in the future reduces performance on a simultaneous task, presumably because the tasks compete for a limited set of resources in the short-term store. Further evidence for the role of executive functions in prospective memory comes from studies in which performance on the prospective memory task declines as the cognitive demands of the ongoing task increase (Marsh & Hicks, 1998).

Some researchers call prospective memory *mental time travel* (Suddendorf & Corballis, 2010; Tulving, 2005). Seamlessly transporting oneself (mentally) to not only different places but also different times is a hallmark of human cognition. Similar to Tulving's conceptualization of episodic memory, this ability requires an autonoetic (self-knowing) component, reaching beyond simple general procedural memory, permitting individuals to represent the self in the future. This has resulted in this type of memory being called *episodic future thought* (Quon & Atance, 2010; Szpunar, 2010).

Other species, including chimpanzees and scrub jays, display a form of prospective memory. For example, scrub jays are able to cache and later locate hundreds of hidden food morsels (Clayton & Dickinson, 1999), and chimpanzees will keep a tool for later use for up to an hour (Osvath & Osvath, 2008). However, these abilities seem not to require the autonoetic, or self-knowing, abilities characteristic of human episodic memory (Salwiczek et al., 2010; Suddendorf & Corballis, 2010), suggesting that the ability to anticipate and act on future needs or drive states sets human cognition apart from that of other species.

SECTION REVIEW

To use information held in long-term memory, we must be able to retrieve it.

Mental Associations and Retrieval	Memory Construction and Distortion	Prospective Memory
■ Mental associations are links among items of information in long-term memory, which provide a basis for retrieval.	■ Memories are not passive, complete records like photographs or video recordings; instead, they are constructed and reconstructed.	■ Failures of prospective memory are common complaints for people of all ages and have serious consequences in some workplaces.
■ The principles of contiguity and similarity underlie the formation of mental associations. Similarity is a derivative of contiguity.	■ Schemas and scripts, which represent our general knowledge and beliefs, can affect memory construction at both encoding and retrieval, assisting memory but also sometimes distorting it.	■ Remembering to do things in the future requires good executive functions, as well as a well-developed sense of self.
■ Elaborative rehearsal affects the number and meaningfulness of associations to new information and thereby its retrievability.	■ Leading questions, suggestions (especially those made under hypnosis), imagination, source confusion, and social pressures can distort memories or create false ones by influencing the constructive process of memory.	
■ The environmental context of learning can provide useful retrieval cues resulting from associations created at the time of encoding.		

Thinking Critically About Memory, Attention, and Consciousness

1. To what extent do you think your behavior is governed by unconscious versus conscious thought?

2. The philosopher René Descartes said "I think, therefore I am" ("Cogito ergo sum"). Does cognitive research and theory address Descartes' statement?

3. How might knowing that much of your behavior is motivated by unconscious processes help you modify your behavior to make you a more effective (or self-aware) person?

Reflections and Connections

Memory is the central topic of cognitive psychology. It is relevant to all aspects of both conscious and unconscious mental activity. Consider the following thoughts to help organize the ideas in this chapter, elaborate upon them, and thereby encode them into your long-term memory.

1. A model of information processing provides a functional representation of the mind. In the functionalist view, each store and process in the mind represents not a different part (or structure) but a different job that the mind performs in its overall task of acquiring and using information. What is the main function of each mental process—how does it contribute to normal, everyday thought and behavior? What special characteristics help it serve that function? Think also how you can use your knowledge of memory and information processing to learn, retain, and retrieve information about all aspects of your life, not just for getting a better grade on your next psychology test, but for learning how to play a musical instrument, keeping the plot line of a novel in mind, or avoiding crashing your car.

2. Unconscious supports for conscious thought and behavior. Sigmund Freud (1933/1964) drew an analogy between the human mind and an iceberg. Consciousness, he suggested, is the small visible tip of the mind that is supported by massive unconscious portions that are invisible, submerged under the ocean's surface. Although Freud's view of the functions of the unconscious mind (discussed in Chapter 14) was different from that presented here, the analogy remains apt. We are conscious only of the perceptions and thoughts that course through our limited-capacity working memory. We are unconscious of all the preattentive analysis of information and of the top-down control of selective attention that help determine which stimuli make it into working memory. We are also unconscious of the vast store of information we

have in long-term memory and of the priming processes that determine which portions of that store will, at a given moment, be most available for retrieval into consciousness. And we are unconscious of the vast set of procedural memories and effects of conditioning that allow us to carry out routine tasks and respond adaptively to stimuli without conscious attention. As you review the chapter, think about all the ways in which unconscious information and processes support that small part of your mental activity that enters your consciousness.

3. The mind as a product of the brain. In cognitive psychology the term *mind* refers to the entire set of processes—unconscious as well as conscious—by which information is acquired and used within a person to organize and direct the person's behavior. The mind is entirely a product of the brain. In recent years, the field of cognitive neuroscience has arisen from the merging of cognitive psychology with neuroscience. Neuroimaging methods allow psychologists to identify which parts of the brain become most active as people engage in specific mental tasks.

Of course, there is a big difference between knowing *where* in the brain a particular task is accomplished and knowing *how* it is accomplished. At this point we are far from knowing how neural activity in the brain provides the basis for memories, thoughts, and decisions. We have long known that the brain is the seat of the mind, and merely demonstrating that different areas of the brain light up when performing different tasks or showing that the brains of people with and without intellectual disabilities show different activation patterns, by themselves, provide little new insight into cognitive functioning. The best neuroscience research not only identifies sections of the brain associated with a particular type of cognition but, combined with behavioral data, provides insight into the psychological mechanisms involved.

Key Terms

anterograde amnesia 345	echoic memory 320	maintenance rehearsal 339	scripts 351
association 349	effortful processes 315	memory 331	semantic memory 332
association by contiguity 349	elaboration 339	memory stores 313	sensory memory 313
association by similarity 349	encoding 315	phonological loop 325	short-term memory span 325
attention 315	encoding rehearsal 339	preattentive processing 318	
automatic processes 315	episodic memory 332	priming 321	short-term store 313
central executive 325	executive functions 328	procedural memory 334	Stroop interference effect 316
chunking 341	explicit memory 331	prospective memory 354	
consciousness 312	iconic memory 320	retrieval 315	temporal-lobe amnesia 335
consolidation 345	implicit memory 331	retrieval cue 349	visuospatial sketchpad 325
control processes 313	infantile amnesia 337	retrograde amnesia 345	working memory 313
dual-processing theories 316	long-term memory 314	schema 350	

Find Out More

Larry R. Squire & Eric R. Kandel (2009). *Memory: From mind to molecules*, 2nd ed. Greenwood Village, CO: Roberts & Company.

Larry Squire is a leader in the cognitive neuroscience of memory, and Eric Kandel is a Nobel laureate known especially for his research on the neural and molecular basis of memory in invertebrates. In this beautifully illustrated 250-page book they combine their two realms of expertise to explain the nature and neuronal basis of implicit and explicit memory systems.

Suzanne Corkin (2013). *Permanent present tense*. New York, NY: Basic Books.

Suzanne Corkin is one of the neuroscientists who spent much of her career working directly with famed memory patient H. M. In this biography, Corkin describes how H. M. contributed to scientists' growing understanding of how memory works and what happens when it fails. Through retellings of specific conversations with H. M. and descriptions of experiments conducted with him,

Corkin helps us understand how H. M.'s misfortune benefited humankind at large.

Maryanne Garry & Harlene Hayne (Eds.) (2014). *Do justice and let the sky fall: Elizabeth F. Loftus and her contributions to science, law, and academic freedom.* Mahwah, NJ: Psychology Press.

A great deal of what we know about how the environment influences memories is the result of research conducted by Elizabeth F. Loftus and her colleagues. This collection of chapters by Loftus and many other notable scientists examines how memories are constructed, deconstructed, and reconstructed. It outlines the progression of not only Loftus's career but the lines of empirical study she inspired and the cognitive theories that grew out of that research.

Adam Gazzaley (2011, March). *Brain: Memory and multitasking.* TEDxSanJoseCA. https://youtu.be/tiANn5PZ4BI

Adam Gazzaley is Director of the Neuroscience Imaging Center at the

University of California-San Francisco Memory and Aging Center. In this talk, he provides a great overview of memory, attention, and executive processes. He ties this into our ability to multitask and the role of interference and capacity on information processing systems.

Elizabeth Loftus (2013, June). *How reliable is your memory?* TEDGlobal 2013. http://www.ted.com/talks/elizabeth_loftus_the_fiction_of_memory.html

Memory researcher Elizabeth Loftus begins with the tragic story of Steve Titus, who was mistakenly accused and convicted of rape. Loftus describes how she worked on the case and how she studies false memories. She explores other fascinating cases and examines how memory can be constructed and reconstructed—and how false memories can have serious repercussions.

Visit LaunchPad for Psychology 8e launchpadworks.com to access the e-book, videos, activities, additional resources, and LearningCurve quizzes, as well as study aids including flash cards and web quizzes
Visit LaunchPad For Psychology 8e
www.macmillanhighered.com/launchpad/graybjork8e
to access the e-book, videos, activities, additional resources, and LearningCurve quizzes, as well as study aids including flashcards and web quizzes.

Solving Problems: Reasoning and Intelligence

LEARNING OUTCOMES

After studying this chapter, you should be able to:

- Explain how people use analogies and inductive reasoning to solve problems.

- Describe how deductive reasoning and insight are used in problem solving.

- Provide examples of how cross-cultural differences affect perception and reasoning.

- Recount how intelligence tests were first developed, how their validity is assessed, and what evidence supports the existence of general intelligence.

- Identify various genetic and environmental factors in terms of their contributions to intelligence.

Life is full of problems and always has been. Solving some of these problems is a matter of life and death—finding food, avoiding becoming food for another animal, identifying friends and enemies—while other problems we face are of lesser importance—deciding what to wear to a party, navigating to and from home, answering exam questions. Solving each of these problems requires intelligence. Compared with other species, humans are not the most graceful, nor the strongest, nor the swiftest, nor the fiercest, nor the gentlest, nor the most long-lived. We do, however, fancy ourselves to be the most intelligent of animals; and, at least by our own definitions of intelligence, our fancy is apparently correct. We are the animal that knows and reasons; that classifies and names the other animals; that tries to understand all things, including ourselves. We are also the animal that tells one another what we know, with the effect that each generation of our species starts off with more knowledge, if not more wisdom, than the previous one.

In Chapter 9 we defined memory broadly as all the information we store, whether for long periods or only fleetingly, and all the mechanisms we have for manipulating that information. But what is the purpose of memory, thus defined? From an evolutionary perspective, there is no value in reminiscence for its own sake. We can't do anything about the past. We can, however, influence our future. The evolutionary functions of memory are to understand our present situation, recognize and solve problems posed by that situation, anticipate the future, and make plans that will help us to prepare for and in some ways alter that future for our own (or our genes') well-being. Our memory of the past is useful to the degree that it helps us to understand and to deal adaptively with the present and the future. The processes by which we use our memories in these adaptive ways are called *reasoning,* and our general capacity to reason is *intelligence*. In this chapter we explore reasoning and intelligence, beginning with the ways in which people approach problems.

Another theme in Chapter 9 was the importance of conscious awareness in human thought and memory, while also noting that much cognition goes on without such awareness. We continue this theme in the present chapter. As you'll see, much reasoning and intelligent decision making is done with the "slow," explicit, and conscious system as described in dual-process theories of human cognition. However, you'll also learn that many aspects of problem solving involve the "fast," implicit, and unconscious system, which sometimes helps us solve problems efficiently but at other times leads us to "illogical" decisions.

How People Reason I: Analogies and Induction

To a large extent, we reason by using our memories of previous experiences to make sense of present experiences or to plan for the future. To do so, we must perceive the similarities among various events we have experienced. Even our most basic abilities to categorize experiences and form mental concepts depend on our ability to perceive such similarities.

When you see dark clouds gathering and hear distant thunder, you know from past experiences that rain is likely, so you take precautions against getting wet. If you saw an object with wheels on it, based on your past experiences, you might assume it was designed to convey things from place to place. Can you imagine any plan, any judgment, any thought that is not founded in some way on your ability to perceive similarities among different objects, events, or situations? Our bet is that you can't.

Most of our everyday use of similarities to guide our thinking comes so easily and naturally that it doesn't seem like reasoning. In some cases, however, useful similarities are not so easily identified. As William James (1890) pointed out, the ability to see similarities where others don't notice them is what, more than anything else, distinguishes excellent reasoners from the rest of us. Two kinds of reasoning that depend explicitly on identifying similarities are *analogical reasoning* and *inductive reasoning*. These are the topics of this section.

Analogies as Foundations for Reasoning

Generally speaking, an *analogy* is any perceived similarity between otherwise different objects, actions, events, or situations. Psychologists, however, use the term more narrowly to refer just to certain types of similarities. In this more restricted sense, an ***analogy*** refers to a similarity in behavior, function, or relationship between entities or situations that are in other respects, such as in their physical makeup, quite different from each other (Gentner & Kurtz, 2006).

■ **Analogies are often mothers of invention** The Wright brothers succeeded in developing the first functional airplane (left-hand photo) because of many analogies they perceived to both large soaring birds (such as eagles) and bicycles (they were bicycle mechanics by profession) (Johnson-Laird, 2006). Bringing together many of the attributes of birds and bikes, they built a plane that was light and highly maneuverable, had a broad wingspan, and could be easily tilted to facilitate turns and counter buffeting winds. Their competitors, who failed, had instead been focusing on building heavy planes with powerful engines, based more on analogies to automobiles than to birds and bikes.

By this narrower definition, we would not say that two baseball gloves are analogous to one another because they are too obviously similar and are even called by the same name. But we might say that a baseball glove is analogous to a butterfly net. The analogy here lies in the fact that both are used for capturing some category of objects (baseballs or butterflies) and both have a funnel-like shape that is useful for carrying out their function. If you saw some brand-new object that is easily maneuverable and has a roughly funnel-like shape, you might guess, by drawing an analogy to either a baseball glove or a butterfly net, that it is used for capturing something.

One type of analogical reasoning problem you're likely familiar with is one that is stated A: B :: C: ?. For example, *man* is to *woman* as *boy* is to? The answer here, of course, is *girl*. One can use the knowledge of the relation between the first two elements in the problem (a *man* is an adult *male*, a *woman* is an adult *female*) to complete the analogy for a new item (*boy*). Analogies are thus based on *similarity relations*. One must understand the similarity between men and women and boys and girls if one is to solve the above analogy.

Here are two examples that are a bit more complicated than the *man* is to *woman* example:

1. PLANE is to AIR as BOAT is to (a) submarine, (b) water, (c) oxygen, (d) pilot.

2. SOON is to NEVER as NEAR is to (a) close, (b) far, (c) nowhere, (d) seldom.

To answer such questions correctly, you must see a relationship between the first two concepts and then apply it to form a second pair of concepts that are related to each other in the same way as the first pair. The relationship between PLANE and AIR is that the first *moves through* the second, so the correct pairing with BOAT is WATER. The second problem is a little more difficult. Someone might mistakenly think of SOON and NEVER as opposites and might therefore pair NEAR with its opposite, FAR. But *never* is not the opposite of *soon*; it is, instead, the negation of the entire dimension that *soon* lies on (the dimension of time extending from now into the future). Therefore, the correct answer is NOWHERE, which is the negation of the dimension that *near* lies on (the dimension of space extending outward from where you are now). If you answered the second problem correctly, you might not have consciously thought it through in terms like those we just presented; you may have just intuitively seen the correct answer. But your intuition must have been based, unconsciously if not consciously, on your deep knowledge of the concepts referred to in the problem and your understanding of the relationships among those concepts.

Another mental test that makes exclusive use of analogy problems is Raven's Progressive Matrices test, which is often used by psychologists as a measure of fluid intelligence, a concept discussed later in this chapter. In this test, the items are visual patterns rather than words, so knowledge of word meanings is not essential. **Figure 10.1** illustrates a sample Raven's problem. The task is to examine the three patterns in each of the top two rows to figure out the rule that relates the first two patterns in each row to the third pattern. The rows are analogous to one another in that the same rule applies to each, even though the substance of the patterns is different from row to row. Once the rule is figured out, the problem is solved by applying that rule to the bottom row. In Figure 10.1, the rule for each row is that the first pattern is superimposed onto the second pattern to produce the third pattern. Applying that rule to the third row shows that the correct solution to this problem, chosen from the eight pattern choices at the bottom, is number 8.

Analogies can be complicated but, if the similarity relations are familiar to the individual, even young children can solve them. The first study to test analogical reasoning of the A: B :: C: ? type with young children was conducted by Keith Holyoak and his colleagues (1984). They gave preschool and kindergarten children

FOCUS 1

How would you construct a test to assess a person's ability to perceive analogies?

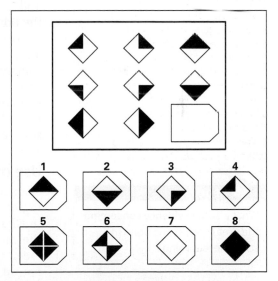

FIGURE 10.1 Sample Raven's problem The task is to infer the rule describing how the pattern changes within each of the first two rows and then to apply that rule to the third row to arrive at the correct solution. The solution is one of the eight choices at the bottom.

(From *Raven's Progressive Matrices (Standard Parallel, Sets A-E).* Copyright © 1998 by NCS Pearson, Inc. Reproduced with permission. All rights reserved. "*Raven's Progressive Matrices and Vocabulary Scales*" is a trademark, in the US and/or other countries, of Pearson Education, Inc., or its affiliates.)

■ Analogies are only as good as the similarity relationships on which they are based.

some gumballs in a bowl and asked them to move the gumballs to another, out-of-reach bowl without getting out of their chairs. Available to the children were a number of objects they could use to help them solve the task including scissors, an aluminum cane, tape, string, and a sheet of paper. Before solving the problem, children heard a story about a genie with a similar problem. The genie had to move some jewels from one bottle within his reach to another bottle, out of his reach. To solve this problem the genie used his magic staff to pull the second bottle closer to him. Children were then told to think of as many ways as they could to solve *their* problem—to get the gumballs from one bowl to another. About half of the preschool and kindergarten children solved the problem by using the aluminum cane to pull the bowl closer, and the remainder did so after a hint, illustrating that these young children were capable of reasoning by analogy. However, when children were given a different analogy (the genie rolled up his magic carpet and used it as a tube to transport jewels from one bottle to another), they were much less successful. This shows that success on analogical reasoning problems is highly dependent on the similarity between objects. If someone is not familiar with one set of relations (e.g., how electricity is transmitted through wires), the similarity with another relationship (e.g., how nervous impulses are transmitted in the brain) will not be useful.

Use of Analogies in Scientific Reasoning

Scientists often attempt to understand and explain natural phenomena by thinking of analogies to other phenomena that are better understood. As pointed out in Chapter 3, Charles Darwin came up with the concept of natural selection as the mechanism of evolution partly by seeing the analogy between the selective breeding of plants and animals by humans and the selective breeding that occurs in nature. Since the former type of selective breeding could modify plants and animals over generations, it made sense to Darwin that the latter type could too. Similarly, the astronomer Johannes Kepler developed his theory of the role of gravity in planetary motion by drawing analogies between gravity and light, both of which can act over long distances but have decreasing effects as distance becomes greater (Gentner & Markman, 1997). Neuroscientists have made progress in understanding some aspects of the brain through analogies to such human-made devices as computers.

In an analysis of discussions held at weekly meetings in many different biology labs, Kevin Dunbar (1999, 2001) discovered that biologists use analogies regularly to make sense of new findings and to generate new hypotheses. In a typical 1-hour meeting, scientists generated anywhere from 2 to 14 different analogies as they discussed their work. Most of the analogies were to other biological findings, but some were to phenomena completely outside the realm of biology.

FOCUS 2

What is some evidence concerning the usefulness of analogies in scientific reasoning?

Analytical thinking not only provides scientists with analogies to assist their understanding of the natural world, but is also associated with a more skeptical, scientific view of the world in general, even for nonscientists. For example, researchers have shown that people who engage more in analytical thinking are more skeptical about religious, paranormal, and conspiratorial theories than those less apt to engage in such thinking (Pennycook et al., 2015).

Use of Analogies in Judicial and Political Reasoning and Persuasion

Lawyers, politicians, and ordinary people frequently use analogies to convince others of some claim or course of action they support. The following example is taken from a novel (Bugliosi, 1978, cited by Halpern, 1996), but it certainly could occur in real life. At the end of a trial involving much circumstantial evidence, the defense attorney, in his summation to the jury, said that evidence is like a chain: it is only as strong as its weakest link. If one piece of evidence is weak, the chain breaks and the jurors should not convict the accused. The prosecutor then stood up and told the jurors that evidence is not like a chain, but is like a rope made of many separate strands twisted together. The strength of the rope is equal to the sum of the individual strands. Even if some of the weaker strands break, the strong ones still hold the rope together. The prosecutor had the more convincing analogy and won the case.

Researchers have found that university students are good at generating analogies to defend political viewpoints. In one study, in Canada, some students were asked to defend the position that the Canadian government should eliminate deficit spending even if that would require a sharp reduction in such social programs as health care and support for the needy, and other students were asked to defend the opposite position (Blanchette & Dunbar, 2000). Students arguing on either side developed many potentially convincing analogies. Not surprisingly, many of the analogies were from the closely related realm of personal finances—comparing the national debt to one's personal debt, or comparing a reduction in social programs to a failure to invest one's personal money for future gain. But many other analogies were taken from more distant realms. For instance, failure to eliminate the debt was compared to failure to treat a cancer, which grows exponentially over time and becomes uncontrollable if not treated early; and failure to provide care for the needy was compared to a farmer's failure to care for crops that have been planted, which ruins the harvest.

The next time you become involved in, or listen to, a political discussion, tune your ears to the analogies presented and, for each, ask yourself whether it helps to clarify the issue or misleads. You may be surprised at how regularly and easily analogies slip into conversations; they are a fundamental component of human thought and persuasion. We reason about new or complicated issues largely by comparing them to more familiar or less complicated issues, where the answer seems clearer. Such reasoning is useful to the degree that the structural relationships in the analogy hold true; it is misleading to the degree that those relationships don't hold true. Good reasoners are those who readily see the structural relationships between one kind of event and another, allowing them to determine when an analogy holds true and when or how it breaks down.

Neurological Basis of Analogical Reasoning

As you might guess, research indicates that the prefrontal cortex is involved in analogical reasoning. However, unlike relatively simple semantic retrieval (for example, determining whether two words are semantically related), analogical reasoning calls upon multiple prefrontal brain areas. For example, Silvia Bunge and her colleagues (2005) presented subjects with two tasks while their brains were being scanned via fMRI. For both tasks, subjects were initially shown a pair of words (for example, "rain/drought" or "bouquet/flowers") and asked to determine how the two words in each pair were related (see **Figure 10.2**). About half

FOCUS 3

How are analogies useful in judicial and political reasoning? What distinguishes a useful analogy from a misleading one?

FIGURE 10.2 Example of analogy and semantic task For both tasks, subjects judged how the first pair of words was related. For the analogy problems, subjects were to determine whether or not the second pair of words was related to each other along the same dimension (here, both part/whole) as was the first pair. For the semantic problems, subjects were to determine only whether the words in the second pair were related to each other or not along any dimension.

From Bunge, S. A., Wendelken, C., Badre, D., & Wagner, A. D. (2005). Analogical reasoning and prefrontal cortex: Evidence for separable retrieval and integration mechanisms. *Cerebral Cortex, 15,* 239–249.

a second later, subjects were shown a second pair of words. In the *analogy condition*, subjects had to determine whether the two words were related on the basis of the same dimension as were the word pairs from the first pair. In the example provided in Figure 10.2, subjects had to determine whether the "chain/link" relation in the second pair (a chain is composed of individual links) is the same or different than the "bouquet/flowers" relation (a bouquet is composed of individual flowers) from the first pair. In the *semantic condition*, subjects merely had to determine whether the words in the second pair were related to one another on the basis of any dimension.

The researchers reported that the anterior left inferior prefrontal cortex was activated when making semantic decisions, but multiple areas of the prefrontal cortex were activated when making analogical decisions. Subsequent research demonstrated that extensive training in analogical reasoning (i.e., a preparatory course for the Law School Admission Tests [LSAT] that emphasized reasoning skills) resulted in changes in the distribution of white matter (mostly myelinated axons, see Chapter 4) connecting frontal cortices and in the frontal and parietal lobes. Further, subjects who showed larger gains on the LSAT displayed greater white-matter changes in some parts of the brain (Mackey et al., 2012, 2013).

This research shows that analogical reasoning involves brain areas involved in the integration of information. Moreover, other research has shown that, at least by the age of 6 years, children use the same brain regions as adults to solve analogical reasoning problems, although aspects of the patterns of brain activation change with age (Wendelken et al., 2011; Wright et al., 2008). Thus, at least some aspects of analogical reasoning develop early, with experience altering both cognition and underlying brain structures with age.

Despite the early development of analogical reasoning abilities in childhood and the frequent use of analogies in everyday situations by adults, people do not readily use analogies to solve novel problems. Both adults and children show little spontaneous transfer between analogical contexts in laboratory settings (Gick & Holyoak, 1980, 1983). Young children's ability to engage in analogical reasoning and the effects that practice can have on both how well one reasons and on the underlying brain structures suggest that formal instruction in analogical reasoning could provide substantial educational benefits (Richland & Simms, 2015; Vendetti et al., 2015). Michael Vendetti and his colleagues (2015, p. 104) have suggested several things that educators can do to support students in making analogical comparisons:

1. Provide students with opportunities to make comparisons between newly learned concepts and previously learned ones.

2. Present source and target analogies simultaneously so that the student may visualize ways in which they are related.

3. Provide additional cues, such as gestures, that move between the two contexts being compared in order to highlight analogical mappings.

4. Highlight both the similarities and differences between sources and targets. If the difference can lead to an incorrect inference, indicate explicitly where the analogy "breaks down."

5. Use relational language to facilitate attention to shared relationships.

Inductive Reasoning and Some Biases in It

Inductive reasoning, or *induction*, is the attempt to infer some new principle or proposition from observations or facts that serve as clues. Induction is also called *hypothesis construction* because the inferred proposition is at best an educated guess, not a necessary conclusion from the available evidence. Scientists engage in inductive reasoning as they try to infer rules of nature from their observations of specific events in the world. Psychologists reason inductively when they make guesses about the workings of the human mind on the basis of observing human behavior under varied conditions. Detectives reason inductively when they piece together bits of evidence to make inferences as to who might have committed a crime. In everyday life we all use inductive reasoning regularly to make sense of our experiences or predict new ones. When you look outside in the morning, see that the ground is wet, and say, "It probably rained last night," you are basing that guess on inductive reasoning. Your past observations of relationships between rain and wet ground have led you to induce the general rule that wet ground usually results from rain.

All the examples of reasoning by use of analogies, discussed earlier, are also examples of inductive reasoning. In fact, in general, inductive reasoning is reasoning that is founded on perceived analogies or other similarities. The evidence from which one induces a conclusion is, ultimately, a set of past experiences that are in some way similar to one another or to the experience one is trying to explain or predict.

In general, we are very good at inductive reasoning—certainly far better at it than is any other species of animal (Gentner, 2003). However, most psychologists who study inductive reasoning have focused not on our successes but on our mistakes. Such research has led to the identification of several systematic biases in our reasoning, based primarily on our "fast" and unconscious cognitive system. Knowledge of such biases is useful to psychologists for understanding the cognitive processes that are involved in reasoning and to all of us who would like to reason more effectively.

FOCUS 4

What is inductive reasoning, and why is it also called hypothesis construction? Why is reasoning by analogy inductive?

The Availability Bias

The *availability bias* is perhaps the most obvious bias in inductive reasoning. When we reason, we tend to rely too strongly on information that is readily *available* to us and to ignore information that is less available. For example, when students were asked whether the letter *d* is more likely to occur in the first position or the third position of a word, most people said the first (Tversky & Kahneman, 1973). In reality, *d* is more likely to be in the third position; but, of course, people find it much harder to think of words with *d* in the third position than to think of words that begin with *d*.

As another example, when asked to estimate the percentage of people who die from various causes, most people overestimate causes that have recently been emphasized in the media, such as terrorism, murders, and airplane accidents, and underestimate less-publicized but much more frequent causes, such as heart disease and traffic accidents (Brase, 2003). The heavily publicized causes are more available to conscious recall than are the less-publicized causes.

The availability bias can have serious negative consequences when it occurs in a doctor's office. In a book on how doctors think, Jerome Groopman (2007) pointed out that many cases of misdiagnosis are the result of the availability bias. For example, a doctor who has just treated several cases of a particular disease, or who has been thinking about that disease, may be predisposed to perceive that disease in a new patient who has some of the expected symptoms. If the doctor then fails to ask the questions that would rule out other diseases that produce those same symptoms, the result may be misdiagnosis and mistreatment. Research has shown that the availability bias with respect to misdiagnosis is most likely to be observed in younger, less experienced physicians (Mamede et al., 2010).

FOCUS 5

What kinds of false inferences are likely to result from the availability bias?

The Confirmation Bias

Textbooks on scientific method (in this book, Chapter 2) explain that scientists should design studies aimed at *disconfirming* their currently held hypotheses. One can never prove absolutely that a hypothesis is correct, but one can prove absolutely that it is incorrect. The most credible hypotheses are those that survive the strongest attempts to disprove them. Nevertheless, research indicates that people's natural tendency is to try to confirm rather than disconfirm their current hypotheses (Lewicka, 1998).

In an early demonstration of this **confirmation bias** (or *myside bias*), Peter Wason (1960) engaged subjects in a game in which the aim was to discover the experimenter's rule for sequencing numbers. On the first trial the experimenter presented a sequence of three numbers, such as *6 8 10*, and asked the subject to guess the rule. Then, on each subsequent trial, the subject's task was to test the rule by proposing a new sequence of three numbers to which the experimenter would respond *yes* or *no*, depending on whether the sequence fit the rule. Wason found that subjects overwhelmingly chose to generate sequences consistent with, rather than inconsistent with, their current hypotheses and quickly became confident that their hypotheses were correct, even when they were not. For example, after hypothesizing that the rule was *even numbers increasing by twos*, a person would, on several trials, propose sequences consistent with that rule—such as *2 4 6* or *14 16 18*—and, after getting a *yes* on each trial, announce confidently that his or her initial hypothesis was correct. Such persons never discovered that the experimenter's actual rule was *any increasing sequence of numbers*.

In contrast, the few people who discovered the experimenter's rule proposed, on at least some of their trials, sequences that contradicted their current hypothesis. A successful subject who initially guessed that the rule was *even numbers increasing by twos* might offer the counterexample *5 7 9*. The experimenter's *yes* to that would prove the initial hypothesis wrong. Then the subject might hypothesize that the rule was any sequence of numbers increasing by twos and test that with a counterexample, such as *4 7 10*. Eventually, the subject might hypothesize that the rule was any increasing sequence of numbers and, after testing that with counterexamples, such as *5 6 4*, and consistently eliciting *no* as the response, announce confidence in that hypothesis.

In other experiments demonstrating a confirmation bias, subjects were asked to interview another person to discover something about that individual's personality (Skov & Sherman, 1986; Snyder, 1981). Typically, some were asked to assess the hypothesis that the person is an *extravert* (socially outgoing), and others were asked to assess the hypothesis that the person is an *introvert* (socially withdrawn). The main finding was that subjects usually asked questions for which a *yes* answer would be consistent with the hypothesis they were testing. Given the extravert hypothesis, they tended to ask such questions as "Do you like to meet new people?" And given the introvert hypothesis, they tended to ask such questions as "Are you shy about meeting new people?" This bias, coupled with the natural tendency of interviewees to respond to all such questions in the affirmative, gave most subjects confidence in the initial hypothesis, regardless of which hypothesis that was or whom they had interviewed.

One interesting and somewhat surprising finding about the confirmation bias is that it is *not* related to intelligence. High-IQ people are just as likely to fall prey to the bias as people with lower IQs (Stanovich et al., 2013).

The Predictable-World Bias

We are so strongly predisposed to find order in our world that we are inclined to "see" or anticipate order even where it doesn't exist. Superstitions often arise because people fail to realize that coincidences are often

FOCUS 6

What are two different ways by which researchers have demonstrated the confirmation bias?

■ **Reasoning that matters** Doctors use inductive reasoning to diagnose medical problems on the basis of evidence that they gain from interviewing patients about their symptoms. The availability bias and confirmation bias can sometimes result in false diagnoses.

Jose Luis Pelaez/Getty Images

just coincidences. Some great event happens to a man when he is wearing his green shirt and suddenly the green shirt becomes his "lucky" shirt.

The ***predictable-world bias*** is most obvious in games of pure chance. Gamblers throwing dice or betting at roulette wheels often begin to think that they see reliable patterns in the results. This happens even to people who consciously "know" that the results are purely random. Part of the seductive force of gambling is the feeling that you can guess correctly at a better-than-chance level or that you can control the odds. In some games such a belief can lead people to perform *worse* than they should by chance. Here's an example.

Imagine playing a game with a 6-sided die that has 4 red sides and 2 green sides. You are asked to guess, on each trial, whether the die will come up red or green. You will get a dollar every time you are correct. By chance, over the long run, the die is going to come up red on four-sixths (two-thirds) of the trials and green on the remaining one-third of trials. Each throw of the die is independent of every other throw. No matter what occurred on the previous throw, or the previous 10 throws, the probability that the next throw will come up red is two chances in three. That is the nature of chance. Thus, the best strategy is to guess red on every trial. By taking that strategy you will, over the long run, win on about two-thirds of the trials. That strategy is called *maximizing*.

But most people who are asked to play such a game do not maximize (Stanovich & West, 2003, 2008). Instead, they play according to a strategy referred to as *matching*; they vary their guesses over trials in a way that matches the probability that red and green will show. Thus, in the game just described, they guess red on roughly two-thirds of the trials and green on the other one-third. They know that, over the long run, about two-thirds of the throws will be red and one-third will be green, and they behave as if they can predict which ones will be red and which ones will be green. But in reality they can't predict that, so the result is that they win less money over the long run than they would if they had simply guessed red on every trial.

Thus, you could say that the typical players in such a game are either too smart for their own good, or not smart enough. Rats, in analogous situations—where they are rewarded more often for pressing a red bar than for pressing a green one—quickly learn to press the red one all the time when given a choice. Presumably, their maximizing derives from the fact that they are not smart enough to figure out a pattern; they just behave in accordance with what has worked best for them. People with the highest IQ scores also typically maximize in these situations, but for a different reason (Stanovich & West, 2003, 2008): They do so because they understand that there is no pattern, so the best bet always is going to be red.

The predictable-world bias is, in essence, a tendency to engage in inductive reasoning even in situations where such reasoning is pointless because the relationship in question is completely random. Not surprisingly, researchers have found that compulsive gamblers are especially prone to this bias (Toplak et al., 2007). They act as if they can beat the odds, despite all evidence to the contrary and even if they consciously know that they cannot.

Outside of gambling situations, a tendency to err on the side of believing in order rather than randomness may well be adaptive. It may prompt us to seek order and make successful predictions where order exists, and that advantage may outweigh the corresponding disadvantage of developing some superstitions or mistaken beliefs. There's no harm in the man's wearing his lucky green shirt every day, as long as he takes it off to wash it now and then.

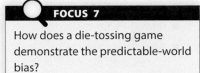

FOCUS 7

How does a die-tossing game demonstrate the predictable-world bias?

Hilary Jane Morgan/age fotostock/Superstock

■ **What is your lucky number?** The predictable-world bias may operate consciously or unconsciously to lead gamblers, in games of pure chance, to believe that they have some control over the outcome. Some might bet their "lucky numbers," for example, in the belief that those numbers will come up more often than other numbers.

SECTION REVIEW

We reason largely by perceiving similarities between new events and familiar ones.

Analogies as a Basis for Reasoning

- Analogies are similarities in behavior, functions, or relationships in otherwise different entities or situations.

- Both scientists and nonscientists often use analogies to make sense of observations and generate new hypotheses.

- Analogies are commonly used in legal and political persuasion.

- Analogical thinking involves multiple parts of the prefrontal cortex, with extensive practice using analogies altering brain structure.

Inductive Reasoning

- In inductive reasoning, or hypothesis construction, a new principle or proposition is inferred on the basis of specific observations or facts. We are generally good at inductive reasoning, but are susceptible to certain biases.

- True scientific reasoning is a form of inductive reasoning.

- The availability bias is our tendency to give too much weight to information that comes more easily to mind than to other relevant information.

- The confirmation bias leads us to try to confirm rather than disconfirm our current hypothesis. Logically, a hypothesis cannot be proven, only disproven.

- The predictable-world bias leads us to arrive at predictions through induction even when events are actually random.

How People Reason II: Deduction and Insight

> "Let me run over the principal steps. We approached the case, you remember, with an absolutely blank mind, which is always an advantage. We had formed no theories. We were simply there to observe and to draw inferences from our observations."
>
> Sherlock Holmes—"The Adventure of the Cardboard Box" (Conan Doyle, 1917)

Sir Arthur Conan Doyle's famous detective, Sherlock Holmes, is likely the king of deduction. Rather than starting with a theory, or hypothesis, which is tested and modified as a result of observations, Holmes starts with facts and only then does he logically draw inferences from his observations.

Deductive reasoning, or *deduction*, is the attempt to derive logically the consequences that must be true if certain premises are accepted as true. Whereas inductive reasoning is reasoned guesswork, deductive reasoning (when done correctly) is logical proof, assuming that the premises really are true. In everyday life we reason deductively to derive the logical implications of statements that we hear. If you tell me that everyone in your family is over 6 feet tall, then I can deduce that everyone in your family is also over 5 feet tall. If you studied plane geometry, then you engaged in deductive reasoning that is more complex than most everyday examples as you tried to prove or disprove various correlates based on axioms that were given to you. In fact, all of mathematics is deduction. One starts, in mathematics, with certain givens and deduces the consequences.

Table 10.1 presents deductive problems that are typical of the types of problems used by psychologists who study such reasoning. Before looking at the answers, try solving each problem. The first is a *series problem,* which requires you to organize items into a series on the basis of a set of comparison statements and then arrive at a conclusion that was not contained in any single statement. The second is a *syllogism,* which presents a major premise, or proposition, and a minor premise that you must combine mentally to see if a particular conclusion is true, false, or indeterminate (cannot be determined from the premises). Did you get the correct answer to each problem? If you did, you deduced correctly.

FOCUS 8

How does deductive reasoning differ from inductive reasoning? How is it illustrated by series problems and syllogisms?

TABLE 10.1 Deductive-reasoning problems

Series problem	Syllogism	
John is taller than Henry.	All chefs are violinists (major premise).	*Answers:*
John is shorter than Mary.	Mary is a chef (minor premise). Is Mary a violinist?	(·ou 'ǝʇɐuᴉɯɹǝʇǝpuᴉ 'ǝʇɐuᴉɯɹǝʇǝpuᴉ :*suɹoɟ ǝʌᴉʇɐuɹǝʇ∀*)
Mary is shorter than Billy.	*Alternative forms, based on different minor premises:*	·sǝʎ :*wsᴉƃolʃʎS* ·ou :*wǝlqoɹd sǝᴉɹǝS*
Is Billy shorter than Henry?	Mary is a violinist. Is she a chef? Mary is not a chef. Is she a violinist? Mary is not a violinist. Is she a chef?	

The Concrete Nature of Deductive Reasoning

There was a time when many psychologists believed that deductive reasoning is fundamentally a logical process best understood in mathematical terms. For example, the highly influential Swiss developmental psychologist Jean Piaget believed that people who are roughly 13 years of age or older reason deductively by applying abstract logical principles, which can be expressed mathematically (Inhelder & Piaget, 1958). According to that view, problems are solved by a sort of mental algebra, in which the specific contents of the problem are mapped onto the xs and ys of logical equations, the equations are solved, and the answers are delivered.

Today relatively few psychologists accept the "abstract logic" or (to use Piaget's term) "formal operational" view of deductive reasoning (Evans, 2005). One reason for rejecting that view is that study after study—with people all over the world, including highly educated people in universities—has revealed that we are much better at solving problems put to us in concrete terms than problems put to us in terms of xs and ys or other abstract symbols. Research has repeatedly shown that our natural inclination is to solve deductive problems by reflecting on our real-world knowledge, not by thinking about laws of logic. One reason Sherlock Holmes's deductive methods were so successful was that his world knowledge was so extensive. With training, people can learn laws of logic, but even those who learn them well rarely apply them to the problems of daily life.

Deductive Problems: Logic or Content?

If people used formal logic to solve syllogisms, then it should not matter whether the statements in the problem are consistent with everyday experience, violate everyday experience, or are nonsensical. All that should matter is the formal structure of the problem. But numerous experiments show that the content does matter. Consider, for example, the following two syllogisms. In each, you are instructed to use logic alone, not your knowledge of the real world. Assume for each that the first two propositions are valid, and judge whether or not the conclusion follows logically from those propositions.

1. All living things need water.
   Roses need water.
   Therefore, roses are living things.

FOCUS 9

What is the evidence that the tendency to rely on real-world knowledge can overwhelm our deductive-reasoning ability?

2. All insects need oxygen.
Mice need oxygen.
Therefore, mice are insects.

Structurally, these two problems are identical. In each case, the conclusion is not valid. It does not necessarily follow, from the first two premises of the first problem, that roses are living things, or, from the first two premises of the second problem, that mice are insects. The correct conclusion for both of these syllogisms is "indeterminate." According to the premises, roses may be living things but they don't have to be, and mice may be insects but they don't have to be. The premises do not say that all things that need water are living, or that all things that need oxygen are insects.

When university students were given these problems, only about 30% got the first problem correct, but nearly all of them got the second problem correct (Stanovich, 2003). Even though the students understood that these are logic problems, not questions about real-world facts, they apparently could not resist being influenced by their knowledge of the real world. Their knowledge that roses are living things led them to believe that the conclusion to the first problem is logically valid, and their knowledge that mice are not insects led them to believe that the conclusion to the second problem is logically not valid. When the same type of problem is put to students using nonsense terms—such as "All schniezels need quisics"—typically around 70% get it correct (Stanovich, 2003). In that case, the content neither helps nor hinders.

The bias for using knowledge rather than formal logic in answering deductive reasoning questions can be construed as a bias for thinking inductively rather than deductively. Our natural tendency is to reason by comparing the current information with our previous experience, and, outside the mathematics classroom or psychology experiment on logic, that tendency generally serves us well. Part of the skill in solving problems that contradict our knowledge gained from past experience lies in our ability or willingness to suppress that knowledge.

Another "logical" task in which prior knowledge greatly influences performance is Wason's (1966) selection task. In the abstract version of the task, subjects are shown four cards on a table, such as the ones displayed below, and given the following rule: "If a card has a vowel on one side, then it must have an even number on the other side."

A   G   2   7

Their task is to determine whether or not the set of cards in front of them conforms to the rule. To find out, they should turn over the fewest number of cards possible to determine the truth of the rule. Try it before reading on.

This is a difficult task, with fewer than 10% of subjects selecting the correct cards, the "A" and the "7" (Stanovich & West, 2000). Most subjects select the "A" and the "2." According to the rule, a card with a vowel on one side must have an even number on the other side, and the only way to test this is to turn over the "A" card. But turning over the "2" card is incorrect. The rule does not state that all cards with an even number on one side must have a vowel on the other, so knowing what's on the other side of the "2" cannot prove or disprove the rule. The critical card here is the "7." If there is a vowel on the other side of the "7," the rule is violated.

The problem becomes much easier, however, when instead of numbers and letters, the problem is stated in terms of relationships people know, particularly those involving social rules—what people ought to do in certain situations. Take, for example, the following set of cards (Cosmides & Tooby, 1992):

Beer   Coke   16 years old   25 years old

Subjects are now asked to test the following rule: "If a person is drinking alcohol, then he or she must be at least 21 years old." Which cards do you turn over to solve this problem? The answer will likely be obvious to you, as it is to most adults: the

"Beer" and "16 years old" cards. What is on the other side of the "Coke" card is irrelevant because anyone, regardless of age, can drink Coke. The same is true for is what's on the other side of the "25 years old" card because 25-year-olds, being more than 21 years old, can drink either Coke or beer. So by changing the abstract task to one based on familiar relationships, this very difficult problem becomes much easier.

Cosmides and Tooby (1992, 2016) proposed that it is not just familiarity that makes the "drinking problem" easy; it is also easy because it is in the form of a social contract. They propose that humans evolved to be sensitive to being cheated when dealing with others and developed "cheater detectors" relative to social contracts. From a similar perspective, the social-contract problems reflect *deontic reasoning,* which is reasoning about what one may, should, or ought to do; whereas the abstract problems reflect descriptive, or indicative reasoning, which implies only a description of "facts" without any violation of social rules. Consistent with Cosmides and Tooby's argument, even preschool children are able to solve simple deontic reasoning problems better than similar description problems (Cummins, 2013; Harris & Núñez, 1996).

Elements of Insight

Sometimes a problem will stymie us for hours, or days, and then suddenly, "Aha!"— we see the solution. What causes such flashes of insight? What do we do to bring them about? What might we do to achieve such insights more quickly and regularly? To address these questions, psychologists have studied people's performance on **insight problems**, problems that are specially designed to be unsolvable until one looks at them in a way that is different from the usual way. Insight problems often entail a mix of inductive and deductive reasoning. Sometimes the crucial insight involves perceiving some similarity or analogy that one didn't perceive before, and sometimes it involves a new understanding of the problem's propositions or of the steps that could or could not lead to a solution.

An Example of an Insight Problem

One problem that psychologists have used in insight experiments is the *candle problem*. Subjects are given a candle, a book of matches, and a box of tacks and are asked to attach the candle to a bulletin board in such a way that the candle can be lit and will burn properly. They are allowed to use only the objects they have been given.

Before reading the next section, spend a few minutes trying to solve this problem, depicted in **Figure 10.3**. As you work on it, pay attention to your own thought processes. If you solved the problem, how did you do it? What thoughts led you to insight? If you did not solve the problem, join the crowd. Relatively few people solve it and others like it without hints or clues of some kind. We'll come to the solution shortly.

Breaking Out of a Mental Set: Broadening Perception and Thought

Insight problems tend to be difficult because their solution depends on abandoning a well-established habit of perception or thought, referred to as a **mental set**, and then viewing the problem in a different way.

The candle problem is difficult because people see the objects that they are given in too narrow a way. They see the tacks and matches as potentially useful, and they try to find ways of tacking the candle to the board, or using a match to melt wax to stick the

FIGURE 10.3 The candle problem
Using only the objects shown here, attach the candle to the bulletin board in such a way that the candle can be lit and will burn properly.

candle to the board in such a way that it tilts out from the board so it can be lit. None of those methods work. Most subjects fail to see that the box containing the tacks could help them solve the problem. Their mental set is to see the box as just a container for the tacks, not as something that can be used to help solve the problem. Karl Duncker (1945), who invented the candle problem and performed the first experiments with it, referred to this type of mental set as **functional fixedness**, the failure to see an object as having a function other than its usual one. We'll have more to say about functional fixedness later in this section.

Research in which subjects describe their thoughts aloud as they try to solve such problems shows that the first step to insight, generally, is to realize that the method they are trying is not likely to work and that a new method must be found. This realization leads people to re-examine the objects of the problem more broadly, to notice aspects of those objects that they didn't notice before, to think more broadly about possible ways of solving the problem, and in some cases to say, "Aha!" Before reading the next section, try again to solve the candle problem if you haven't already solved it.

Discovering a Solution

For the candle problem, people might overcome functional fixedness by trying a different way of thinking about the problem. Instead of thinking, "How can I solve the problem with the materials I have?" they might step mentally back a bit and think, "What would I need to solve this problem?" The latter question might lead them to think, "I need something like a shelf, which can be tacked to the bulletin board." This might then lead them to look again at the materials to see if there is anything that could serve as a shelf, and—Aha!—they see that the tack box will make an adequate shelf if the tacks are removed. They remove the tacks, tack the box to the bulletin board so it forms a shelf, melt some wax onto the shelf, and stick the candle to it. By thinking about the problem differently, they were able to see the analogy between the tack box and a shelf, and that solved the problem. Researchers have shown that the candle problem becomes easier if the tacks are placed next to the box rather than in it (Adamson, 1952). Seeing the tack box empty makes it more obvious to subjects that it could be used for something other than holding tacks. Other techniques, such as encouraging subjects *not* to fixate on distracting surface properties of a problem (Chrysikou & Weisberg, 2005), have also been shown to decrease functional fixedness.

Functional Fixedness and Tools: A Special Case?

FOCUS 10

To what extent is the design stance with respect to tools a limitation of human cognition or an adaptation?

Functional fixedness is a common phenomenon, found not just in college students in first-world countries, but also in children (German & Johnson, 2002) and in people who live in traditional societies (German & Barrett, 2005). It seems to be particularly prevalent when tools are used to solve problems. Humans are not the only species to make and use tools, but no other animal makes as much use of tools, and from an early age, as *Homo sapiens*. Think of your day, from the time you get out of bed until you're back in it again many hours later. How many tools did you use today? Your meals likely involved silverware, plates, or bowls. You probably used pen and paper sometime during the day, perhaps paperclips, staples, and rubber bands—all things your grandparents likely used when they were your age—and, of course, you likely used some electronics, from television to smartphones and computers. Your ancient ancestors also used tools in their everyday lives: perhaps spears, axes, and digging sticks for hunting and gathering, as well as baskets to carry food and slings to carry babies. What these tools, both ancient and modern, have in common is that they were all manufactured by people for a specific purpose, something that we tool users seem implicitly aware of. From an early age, people readily assume that tools are designed for an intended function, which the philosopher Daniel Dennett (1990) called the *design stance*. Thus, forks are for eating, axes for chopping, and objects that resemble forks and axes were likely made for eating and chopping as well.

Functional fixedness is typically seen in a negative light, reflecting a lack of creativity and flexible thinking, and to some extent it surely is. However, given the central role of tools in human life and throughout human evolution, functional fixedness with respect to tools may be an adaptation. Once a tool has been invented and used for a specific purpose, it develops special status. It can be used for that purpose effectively without having to go through a trial-and-error process. Knowing what a tool is "for" and using it exclusively for that purpose thus provides the user increased efficiency, although at the cost of some flexibility. In the end, however, the tradeoff seems reasonable.

Two pieces of evidence support the contention that the design stance with respect to tools, and human artifacts in general, may be an adaptation. First, it is seen early in development. For instance, Clark Barrett and his colleagues (2007) showed 12- and 18-month-old infants a box with a light display and a small hole on its side (see **Figure 10.4**). The infants then watched as the experimenter grasped the round end of a spoon or of a novel spoon-like object and inserted the object's straight end into the box, turning on the light. When infants were given an opportunity ("Now it's your turn") with the novel object, they grasped the round end about 60% of the time, successfully turning on the light. However, when they were given the spoon, fewer than 25% grasped the round end, failing to insert the tool into the box and turn on the light. Thus, even 1-year-olds had developed a "spoon" category, knew how a spoon should be used (hold it by the straight end), and were reluctant to use it in a nonconventional way. Other studies with 2- and 3-year-old children have found that when they are shown a function for a novel tool, they are later less apt to use it for a different task, even though it would be well suited for it—a classic demonstration of functional fixedness (Bloom & Markson, 1998; Casler & Kelemen, 2005).

The other source of evidence that the design stance with respect to tools may be an adaptation is that it is not found in other tool-using animals (Ruiz & Santos, 2013). For example, how chimpanzees, bonobos, gorillas (Buttelmann et al., 2007), and monkeys (Cummins-Sebree & Fragaszy, 2005) use a tool seems uninfluenced by having used the tool to solve a previous problem. They are just as likely to use a familiar tool used to solve a new problem as an equally effective novel tool. They seem to make their selection based on what will likely work, regardless of whether they have had prior experience with a tool. Thus, they behave more flexibly with respect to tools, but such flexibility likely has a cost in using a familiar tool efficiently.

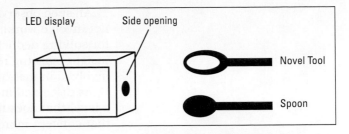

FIGURE 10.4 The light box and tools used in the study by Barrett, Davis, and Needham (2007) Twelve- and 18-month-old children used the novel tool to turn on the light, but displayed "functional fixedness" with the spoon, failing to use it in a novel way.

From Barrett, Tracy M.; Davis, Evan F.; Needham, Amy Developmental Psychology, Vol 43(2), Mar 2007, 352–368. Copyright © American Psychological Association.

Unconscious Mental Processes May Lead to Insight

A good deal of research suggests that the mental capacities required for solving insight problems are different from those required for deductive reasoning. One study showed that people's ability to solve insight problems, but not their ability to solve syllogisms, correlated positively with their *creativity,* measured by their ability to think of clever titles for jokes (Niu et al., 2007). Another study found that working-memory capacity, which correlates positively with the ability to solve deductive reasoning problems, did not correlate at all with the ability to achieve insight in insight problems (Ash & Wiley, 2006). Researchers have also found that people commonly solve insight problems best if they take some time off from the problem, do something else, and then come back to it (Sio & Ormerod, 2009). The time off is referred to as an *incubation period.* The assumption is that during incubation the person is unconsciously reorganizing the material related to the problem while consciously doing and thinking about other things. Incubation appears to facilitate insight, but does not seem to help in deduction. Deduction requires conscious attention to the problem; it is a form of effortful, "slow" thinking.

FOCUS 11

What evidence suggests that solving insight problems is qualitatively different from deductive reasoning? How might mental priming be involved in achieving insight?

All such observations suggest that unconscious, "fast" mental processes, which do not involve working memory, are more important for solving insight problems than for solving deductive reasoning problems. Although the mechanisms involved in insight learning remain "mysterious" (Bowden et al., 2005), one mechanism likely involved in insight is unconscious priming.

As discussed in Chapter 9, *priming* refers to the activation of a mental concept to a level that does not reach the level of consciousness, but that nevertheless makes that concept more available for forming connections to other concepts. During an incubation period, all of the elementary concepts related to an unsolved problem may remain primed, even though the person is not consciously thinking about them. As the person goes about other activities and thinks about other things, some of those primed concepts may form new associations, and, eventually, some new association may create a solution. For example, a person who has failed to solve the candle problem may, during an incubation period, come into contact with a small shelf, which may create an association to the primed concept of the tack box. Either immediately or sometime later (when the person returns to thinking about the problem), that new association may cause the solution to leap into the person's conscious mind—"Aha! A tack box can be a shelf!"

The Value of a Happy, Playful Frame of Mind

FOCUS 12

What evidence suggests that happiness or playfulness helps to solve insight problems? According to the "broaden-and-build" theory, how do positive emotions differ from negative emotions in their effects on perception and thought?

In a classic series of experiments, Alice Isen and her colleagues showed that people are better at solving insight problems if they are made to feel happy than if they are in a serious or somber mood (Isen, 2001). For example, college students who had just watched a comedy film were far more successful in solving the candle problem than were those who had seen either a serious film or no film (Isen et al., 1987). In another experiment, physicians were quicker to arrive at the correct diagnosis of a liver disease, based on evidence provided by the experimenter, if they had first been given a bag of candy (Estrada et al., 1997). Those who had received the candy reasoned more flexibly, took into account all the evidence more readily, and were less likely to get stuck on false leads than those who had not received candy. Other experiments have shown that a happy mood improves people's performance on various tests of creativity and on the ability to see whole patterns, rather than just the parts, in tests of visual perception (Fredrickson, 2003).

From the results of such research, Barbara Fredrickson (2001, 2006) developed what she called the *broaden-and-build theory* of positive emotions. Negative emotions, such as fear and anger, tend to narrow one's focus of perception and thought. Those emotions lead people to focus only on the specific emotion-evoking objects and to think only of routine, well-learned ways of responding. As pointed out in Chapter 5, such narrowing may be adaptive. A moment of emergency is not the right time to test creative new ideas; it is a time for action that has proven effective in the past. In contrast, according to Fredrickson, positive emotions—such as joy and interest—broaden one's scope of perception and thought and increase creativity. Positive emotions are felt when there is no imminent danger and one's immediate biological needs are relatively well satisfied. That is the time to think creatively and to come up with new ideas and ways of dealing with the world. From an evolutionary perspective, the building of ideas and knowledge during periods of safety and happiness is adaptive; those ideas may prove useful in satisfying future needs or preventing future emergencies.

Our own interpretation is that it is not so much happiness per se but the feeling of playfulness that is conducive to learning and creativity (Gray & Chanoff, 1984). We suspect that the comedy films and bags of candy used by Isen and her colleagues put their subjects not just in a happy frame of mind, but in a playful one. Play is a time when people regularly view objects and information in new ways. In play, a tack box can easily be something other than a box for tacks. In play, one is open to considering all the information available, not just that which would seem at first glance to be most useful. A good problem solver may be one who combines the creative spirit of play with a serious search for a solution that really works.

SECTION REVIEW

Deduction and insight contribute to problem-solving ability.

Concrete Nature of Deductive Reasoning

- Deduction is the derivation of conclusions that must be true if the premises are true. Syllogisms are classic examples of deductive-reasoning problems.

- Older theories suggested that we solve such problems with formal logic, whereas newer theories recognize that we are biased toward using content knowledge even when told not to.

Insight

- The candle problem has been used to study insight, where sudden solutions come from seeing things in a new way.

- Our tendency to see tools as designed for a specific purpose leads to functional fixedness, but may also result in more efficient use of tools.

- Insight often derives from abandoning a mental set (a habitual way of perceiving or thinking) and paying attention to aspects of the problem and materials that might otherwise be overlooked.

- Insight may also be promoted by an incubation period or by a happy or playful frame of mind.

Cross-Cultural Differences in Perception and Reasoning

Most studies of reasoning have been conducted in Western cultures, usually with university students as subjects. Thus, the studies may tell us more about how schooled Westerners think than about how human beings in general think. Researchers who have compared reasoning across cultures have found some interesting differences.

Responses of Unschooled Non-Westerners to Western-Style Logic Questions

Some psychologists have administered standard tests of reasoning, prepared originally for Westerners, to people in non-Western cultures. A general conclusion from such research is that the way people approach such tests—their understanding of what is expected of them—is culturally dependent. Non-Westerners, who haven't attended Western-style schools, often find it absurd or presumptuous to respond to questions outside their realm of concrete experiences (Cole & Means, 1981; Scribner, 1977). Thus, the logic question, "If John is taller than Carl, and Carl is taller than Henry, is John taller than Henry?" is likely to elicit the polite response, "I'm sorry, but I have never met these men." Yet the same person has no difficulty solving similar logic problems that present themselves in the course of everyday experience.

Research also found that non-Westerners are more likely than Westerners to answer logic questions in practical, functional terms rather than in terms of abstract properties (Hamill, 1990). To solve classification problems, for example, Westerners generally consider it smarter to sort things by taxonomic category than by function, but people in other cultures do not. A taxonomic category, here, is a set of things that are similar in some property or characteristic; and a functional group is a set of things that are often found together, in the real world, because of their functional relationships to one another. For instance, consider this problem: Which of the following objects does not belong with the others: *ax, log, shovel, saw*? The correct answer, in the eyes of Western cognitive psychologists, is *log* because it is the only object that is not a tool. But when the Russian psychologist Alexander Luria (1971) presented this problem to unschooled Uzbekh peasants, they consistently

---

FOCUS 13

How do unschooled members of non-Western cultures typically perform on classification problems? Why might we conclude that differences in classification are based more on preference than on ability?

chose *shovel* and explained their choice in functional terms: "Look, the saw and the ax, what could you do with them if you didn't have a log? And the shovel? You just don't need that here." It would be hard to argue that such reasoning is any less valid than the reasoning a Westerner might give for putting all the tools together and excluding the log.

Here are two other examples from one of Luria's subjects, Rakmat, a 38-year-old illiterate peasant who was shown pictures of three adults and one boy (from Luria, 1976):

> The examiner said, "Look, here you have three adults and one child. Now clearly the child doesn't belong in this group."
>
> [Rakmat answered] "Oh, but the boy must stay with the others! All three of them are working, you see, and if they have to keep running out to fetch things, they'll never get the job done, but the boy can do the running for them. . . The boy will learn; that'll be better, then they'll be able to work well together." (p. 55)
>
> Subject is then shown drawing of: *bird-rifle-dagger-bullet.*
>
> [Rakmat answered] "The swallow doesn't fit here. . . . No . . . this is a rifle. It's loaded with a bullet and kills the swallow. Then you have to cut the bird up with the dagger, since there's no other way to do it. . . . What I said about the swallow before is wrong! All these things go together." (pp. 56–57)

This difference in reasoning may be one of preference more than of ability. Michael Cole and his colleagues (1971) described an attempt to test a group of Kpelle people in Nigeria for their ability to sort pictures of common objects into taxonomic groups. No matter what instructions they were given, the Kpelle persisted in sorting the pictures by function until, in frustration, the researchers asked them to sort them the way stupid people do. Then they sorted by taxonomy!

An East–West Difference: Focus on Wholes Versus Parts

Richard Nisbett and his colleagues have documented a number of differences in the perception and reasoning of people in East Asian cultures, particularly in Japan and China, compared to that of people in Western cultures, particularly in North America (Nisbett et al., 2001; Varnum et al., 2010). According to these researchers, East Asians perceive and reason more holistically and less analytically than do Westerners. In perceptual tests, East Asians tend to focus on and remember the whole scene and the interrelationships among its objects, whereas Westerners tend to focus on and remember the more prominent individual objects of the scene as separate entities, abstracted from their background.

In one experiment, Japanese students at Kyoto University and American students at the University of Michigan viewed animated underwater scenes such as that depicted in **Figure 10.5** (Masuda & Nisbett, 2001). Each scene included one or more large, active fish, which to the Western eye tended to dominate the scene, but also included many other objects. After each scene, the students were asked to describe fully what they had seen. The Japanese, on average, gave much more complete descriptions than did the Americans. Whereas the Americans often described just the large fish, the Japanese described also the smaller and less active creatures, the water plants, the flow of current, the bubbles rising, and other aspects of the scene.

FOCUS 14

How have researchers documented a general difference between Westerners and East Asians in perception and memory? How might this difference affect reasoning?

FIGURE 10.5 Sample scene viewed differently by Japanese and American students This is a still from one of the animated scenes used by Masuda and Nisbett (2001) to study cultural differences in perception and memory. While American students generally attended to and remembered the large "focal fish," the Japanese students generally attended to and remembered the whole scene. (Data from Masuda et al., 2001.)

The Japanese were also much more likely than the Americans to recall the relationships among various elements of the scene. For instance, they would speak of the large fish as swimming against the water's current, or of the frog as swimming underneath one of the water plants. Subsequently, the students were shown pictures of large fish and were asked to identify which ones they had seen in the animated scenes. Some of the fish were depicted against the same background that had existed in the original scene, and some were depicted against novel backgrounds. The Japanese were better at recognizing the fish when the background was the same as the original than when it was different, whereas the Americans' ability to recognize them was unaffected by the background. Apparently the Japanese had encoded the fish as integrated parts of the whole scene, whereas the Americans had encoded them as entities distinct from their background.

In other research Japanese and American adults were shown a box with a line drawn in it (see **Figure 10.6**), and, in a smaller box, had to reproduce either the absolute length of the line (bottom left) or the relative length of the line (bottom right) (Kitayama et al., 2003). As you might expect, the American subjects were more accurate in performing the absolute task, reflective of analytic processing, whereas the Japanese subjects were more accurate in performing the relative tasks, reflective of holistic processing. This cross-national pattern is found as early as 6 years of age (Duffy et al., 2009; Vasilyeva et al., 2007). However, both American and Japanese 4- and 5-year-old children find the absolute task more difficult (Duffy et al., 2009), suggesting that children over the world begin life with a more "relational/holistic" bias. But, depending on cultural practices, some time around 6 years of age, American children become socialized to *focus* their attention, whereas Japanese children become socialized to *divide* their attention.

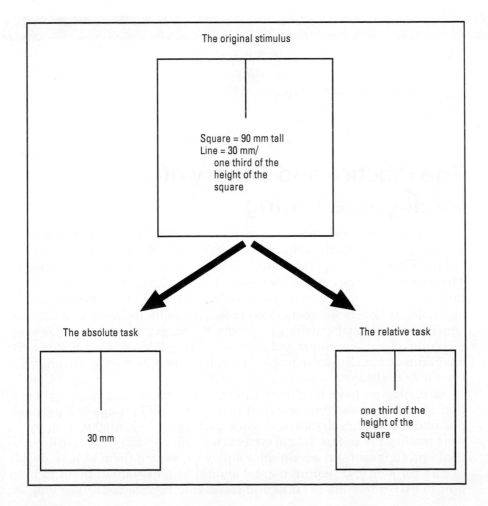

FIGURE 10.6 The frame-line test
Children are asked to draw the line in the boxes at the bottom that is either the same absolute length as the line in the top box (absolute task) or the same relative length (relative task). Beginning at age 6, Americans perform better on the absolute task and Japanese perform better on the relative task. However, 4- and 5-year-old children in both America and Japan make more errors on the absolute task.

East Asians' attention to background, context, and interrelationships apparently helps them to reason differently in some ways from the way Westerners do (Nisbett & Masuda, 2007; Nisbett et al., 2001). When asked to describe why an animal or a person behaved in a certain way, East Asians more often than Americans talk about contextual forces that provoked or enabled the behavior. Americans, in contrast, more often talk about internal attributes of the behaving individual, such as motivation or personality. Thus, in explaining a person's success in life, East Asians might talk about the supportive family, the excellent education, the inherited wealth, or other fortunate circumstances that made such success possible, while Americans are relatively more likely to talk about the person's brilliant mind or capacity for hard work.

Nobody knows for sure why these differences in perception and reasoning between Westerners and East Asians came about. The difference certainly is not the result of genetic differences. Within a generation or two, the offspring of East Asians who have emigrated to North America begin to perceive and think more like other Americans than like East Asians (Nisbett et al., 2001). Nisbett and his colleagues suggest that the roots of the difference are in ancient philosophies that underlie the two cultures. Western ways of thinking have been much influenced, historically, by ancient Greek philosophy, which emphasizes the separate, independent nature of individual entities, including individual people. East Asian ways of thinking have been much influenced by ancient Asian philosophies, such as Confucianism, which emphasize the balance, harmony, and wholeness of nature and of human society.

SECTION REVIEW

There are cultural differences in perception and reasoning.

- Non-Westerners who lack formal schooling apply rules of logic that are more closely tied to everyday, practical function than to abstract concepts.

- East Asian subjects tend to focus on the entire context of a problem or situation, as do very young children in both Western and East Asian cultures.

The Practice and Theory of Intelligence Testing

People differ from one another in many ways. Some are stronger, some are braver, some are more sociable, some are more dependable, some are kinder, and some are more mentally adept than others. It is that last difference that interests us here. The variable capacity that underlies individual differences in reasoning, solving problems, and acquiring new knowledge is referred to as *intelligence*. Cognitive psychologist Robert Sternberg (1997) offered a more technical definition of intelligence as "the mental activities necessary for adaptation to, as well as shaping and selecting of, any environmental context . . . Intelligence is not just reactive to the environment but also active in forming it. It offers people an opportunity to respond flexibly to challenging situations" (p. 1030).

Psychologists have long been interested in measuring intelligence. Much of that interest comes from practical concerns. The first applied psychologists— practitioners who try to solve real-world problems using insights from psychology— were intelligence testers. School systems wanted intelligence tests to determine who could profit most from education; employers wanted them to help decide whom to hire for jobs that require mental ability; armies wanted them to help decide how to assign recruits to ranks and tasks. Intelligence tests have long served all these functions. But psychologists have also been interested in intelligence testing for theoretical, scientific reasons. By correlating individual differences in intelligence test scores with other characteristics of people and their experiences, psychologists have aimed to understand the biological and experiential factors that contribute to intelligence.

A Brief History of Intelligence Testing

Let's begin historically. Although a number of researchers, notably British scientist Sir Francis Galton (1822–1911), investigated the relation between intellectual achievement and a range of basic sensory and cognitive abilities, modern intelligence tests have their ancestry in a test called the *Binet-Simon [Bǐ-nā´-Sǐ-mōn´] Intelligence Scale,* which was developed in France in 1905 by Alfred Binet (1857–1911) and his assistant Theophile Simon. Binet believed that intelligence is best understood as a collection of various higher-order mental abilities that are only loosely related to one another (Binet & Henri, 1896). He also believed that intelligence is nurtured through interaction with the environment and that the proper goal of schooling is to increase intelligence. In fact, the major purpose of Binet and Simon's test—developed at the request of the French Ministry of Education—was to identify children who were not profiting as much as they should from their schooling so that they might be given special attention.

Binet and Simon's test was oriented explicitly toward the skills required for schoolwork. It included questions and problems designed to test memory, vocabulary, common knowledge, use of numbers, understanding of time, and ability to combine ideas. To create the test, problems were pretested with schoolchildren of various ages, and the results were compared with teachers' ratings of each child's classroom performance (Binet & Simon, 1916/1973). Items were kept in the test only if more of the high-rated than low-rated children answered them correctly; otherwise, they were dropped. Binet was aware of the circularity of this process: His test was intended to measure intelligence better than existing measures did, but to develop it, he had to compare results with an existing measure (teachers' ratings). Yet, once developed, the test would presumably have advantages over teachers' ratings. Among other things, it would allow for comparison of children who had had different teachers or no formal schooling at all.

By 1908, the Binet-Simon test was widely used in French schools. Not long after that, English translations of the test appeared, and testing caught on in England and North America even more rapidly than in France.

The first intelligence test commonly used in North America was the *Stanford-Binet Scale,* a modification of Binet and Simon's test that was developed in 1916 at Stanford University. The Stanford-Binet Scale has been revised over the years and is still used, but the most common individually administered intelligence tests today are variations of a test that was developed by David Wechsler in the 1930s and was modeled after Binet's. The descendants of Wechsler's tests that are most widely used today are the Wechsler Adult Intelligence Scale, Fourth Edition (WAIS-IV), the Wechsler Intelligence Scale for Children, Fourth Edition (WISC-IV) for children 7 to 16 years old, and the Wechsler Preschool and Primary Scale of Intelligence, Fourth Edition (WPPSI-IV) for children 2 to 7 years old.

Table 10.2 on page 380 summarizes the core subtests of the WAIS-IV used in computing the *full-scale* IQ score. (There are five supplemental, or optional, subtests to the WAIS-IV, but they are not used in computing the full-scale IQ score and so are not listed here.) As indicated in the table, the subtests are grouped into four categories. The *verbal comprehension* category provides an index of verbal abilities and includes three core subtests: *Vocabulary; Similarities,* the ability to explain how similar concepts are alike; and *Information,* general knowledge and general understanding of the social and physical

 FOCUS 15

What sorts of subtests make up modern IQ tests, such as the Wechsler tests, and how is IQ determined?

■ **An elementary school student taking an IQ test** In IQ tests such as the WISC and Stanford-Binet, children are tested individually and are often required to explain their answers.

TABLE 10.2 Core subtests of the Wechsler Adult Intelligence Scale, Fourth Edition (WAIS-IV).

Verbal Comprehension
Vocabulary Words to be defined.
Similarities On each trial, the person must say how two objects or concepts are alike.
Information Questions about generally well-known people, places, events, and objects.

Perceptual Processing
Block Design Blocks are to be arranged to match specific designs.
Matrix Reasoning Geometric shapes that change according to some rule are presented in an incomplete grid. From a set of choices, the person selects the shape that best completes the grid.
Visual Puzzles Detect and combine visual patterns.

Working Memory
Digit Span String of orally presented digits must be repeated verbatim (and, in a second phase, in reverse order).
Arithmetic Arithmetic problems to be solved mentally.

Processing Speed
Symbol Search On each trial a target set and a search set of symbols are presented. The person says as quickly as possible whether or not a target symbol appears in the search set.
Digit–Symbol Coding The person translates a series of single-digit numbers into symbols as quickly as possible, using a code that is provided.

Source: Information from Lichtenberger & Kaufman, 2013.

world. The *perceptual processing* category subtests depend much less than the verbal comprehension subtests on verbal skills and already-acquired knowledge and more on spatial and quantitative reasoning. This category includes the core subtests of: *Block Design*, the ability to match visual designs; *Matrix Reasoning* (similar to the problem shown in Figure 10.1 on p. 361); and *Visual Puzzles*, which assesses the ability to detect and combine visual patterns. The *working memory* category includes two core subtests: *Digit Span*, the number of randomly presented digits than can be remembered in a row; and *Arithmetic*, in which subjects must concentrate while manipulating mental mathematical problems. Finally, the *processing speed* category includes two core subsets: *Symbol Search*, the ability to spot target symbols quickly in arrays of visual symbols; and *Digit–Symbol Coding*, assessing the ability to transform digits according to the rules of a code.

The scoring system for every modern intelligence test uses results obtained from large samples of individuals who have already taken the test. These results are used as normative data to translate each individual's raw score on an intelligence test into an **IQ** (*intelligence quotient*) score. A person whose performance is exactly average for the comparison group is assigned an IQ score of 100. People whose performance is above or below average receive scores above or below 100, assigned in such a way that the overall distribution of scores fits the bell-shaped curve known as a normal distribution, depicted in **Figure 10.7**. (For a more precise description of normal distributions and the method for standardizing test scores, see the Statistical Appendix at the end of the book.) For children, the comparison group for determining IQ is always a set of children who are the same age as the child being scored.

The Validity of Intelligence Tests as Predictors of Achievement

Recall from Chapter 2 that a test is *valid* if it measures what it is intended to measure. If intelligence tests measure intellectual ability, then IQ scores should correlate with other indices of a person's intellectual functioning. For the most part, researchers have assessed IQ validity in terms of the tests' abilities to predict success in school and careers. Not surprisingly—given that most modern intelligence tests

FOCUS 16

How have psychologists assessed the validity of IQ tests? What are the general results of such assessments?

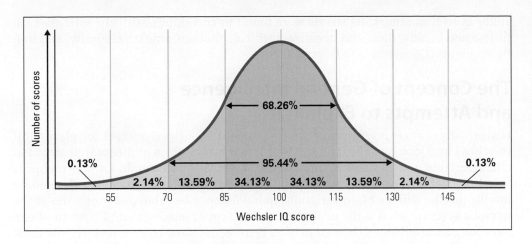

FIGURE 10.7 Standardized scoring of Wechsler IQ tests The scoring system for Wechsler IQ tests is based on the assumption that intelligence is distributed in the population according to a normal distribution (represented by the bell-shaped curve). Thus raw scores on the test are converted into IQ scores in such a way as to produce a normal distribution. Notice that with this system about 68% of IQ scores are between 85 and 115 and about 95% are between 70 and 130.

are direct or indirect descendants of Binet's, which was explicitly designed to measure school abilities—IQ scores do correlate moderately well with grades in school; the correlation coefficients in various studies range from 0.3 to 0.7 (Neisser et al., 1996; White, 2000).

How well do IQ scores predict achievement outside of school? Many studies have shown that people with higher IQ scores are much more likely than those with lower scores to gain employment in intellectually demanding occupations such as medicine, law, science, and business management (Bergman et al., 2015; Neisser et al., 1996). This is true even if the comparison is just among people who were raised in the same or similar families, originating from the same socioeconomic background (Schmidt & Hunter, 2004). Still, the conclusions one can draw from such studies are limited by the fact that intellectually demanding jobs generally require high educational attainment. Thus, in theory, the relation between IQ and employment could be secondary to the fact that people with high IQs perform better in school.

A better index of the relation between IQ and career success comes from research correlating IQ with on-the-job performance as measured by supervisors' ratings, colleagues' ratings, or direct observations. Many such studies have been conducted, and they regularly show moderate positive correlations (Schmidt & Hunter, 2004). Not surprisingly, the strength of the correlations depends on the type of job. For jobs that require relatively little judgment and reasoning—such as assembly-line work—the average correlation is about 0.2; for jobs that require a great deal of judgment and reasoning—such as scientist, accountant, and shop manager—the correlation is typically about 0.5 to 0.6 (Schmidt & Hunter, 2004). For jobs in the high-mental-complexity category, IQ tests are better predictors of performance than any other measures that have been developed, including measures aimed at testing specific knowledge and skills related to the job (Gottfredson, 2002; Schmidt & Hunter, 2004).

In addition to predicting school and work performance, IQ scores are positively related to better physical (Batty et al., 2006) and mental (Deary et al., 2010) health, fewer non-intentional and intentional (including suicide) injuries, and a lower incidence of late-onset dementia (Deary et al., 2010). IQ scores are also related to longevity (Deary, 2008; Leon et al., 2009). A study in Scotland, for example, revealed that people who scored high on an IQ test that was given to all 11-year-olds in the nation were significantly more likely to still be alive at age 76 than were those who scored lower on the test (Deary, 2008; Deary & Der, 2005). This was true even for people who were similar in education and socioeconomic status. The numbers were such that a 15-point difference in IQ was associated with a 21% difference in survival rate. At least one reason for longer survival, apparently, is better self-care. In that

"Do you have 'Intelligence for Idiots'?"

study as well as others, IQ scores were found to correlate positively with physical fitness and healthy diets and negatively with alcoholism, smoking, obesity, and traffic accidents (Gottfredson & Deary, 2004).

The Concept of General Intelligence and Attempts to Explain It

Historically, concern with the practical uses of intelligence tests for placement in school and jobs has always been paralleled by theories and research aimed at characterizing and explaining intelligence. What is the rationale for conceiving of "intelligence" as a unitary, measurable entity? How broadly, or narrowly, should intelligence be defined? Can variations in intelligence be related to properties of the nervous system? What is the evolutionary function of intelligence? These questions have long been subject to heated debate. Here is the most common story, told most often by those who are most centrally concerned with these questions.

General Intelligence (*g*)

FOCUS 17

What was Spearman's concept of general intelligence, or *g*? Why did Spearman think that *g* is best measured with a battery of tests rather than with any single test?

In the early twentieth century, the British psychologist and mathematician Charles Spearman (1927) conducted many research studies in which he gave dozens of different mental tests to people—all of whom were members of the same broad cultural group—and found that the scores always correlated positively with one another if his sample was large enough. This has been confirmed by decades of research and is termed the *positive manifold*. That is, people who scored high on any one mental test also, on average, tended to score high on all other tests. Scores on tests of simple short-term memory span correlated positively with scores on tests of vocabulary, which correlated positively with scores on tests of visual pattern completion, which correlated positively with scores on tests of general knowledge, and so on. Most of the correlations were of moderate strength, typically in the range of 0.3 to 0.6.

From this observation—coupled with a mathematical procedure called *factor analysis,* which he invented for analyzing patterns of correlations—Spearman concluded that some common factor is measured, more or less well, by every mental test. Spearman labeled that factor *g*, for ***general intelligence***.

To Spearman and many other researchers, general intelligence is the underlying ability that contributes to a person's performance on all mental tests (Jensen, 1998). In their view, every mental test is partly a measure of *g* and partly a measure of some more specific ability that is unique to that test. Accordingly, the best measures of *g* are derived from averaging the scores on many diverse mental tests. That is exactly the logic that lies behind the use of many very different subtests in standard intelligence tests such as the WAIS-IV, to determine the full-scale IQ score (refer back to Table 10.2).

Fluid Intelligence and Crystallized Intelligence

Raymond Cattell was a student and research associate of Spearman's in England until he moved to the United States in 1937. Cattell (1971) agreed with Spearman that scores on mental tests reflect a combination of general intelligence and a specific factor that varies from test to test, but he contended that general intelligence itself is not one factor but two. More specifically, he proposed that Spearman's *g* is divisible into two separate *g*s: *fluid intelligence* and *crystallized intelligence*.

Fluid intelligence, as defined by Cattell (1971), is the ability to perceive relationships among stimuli independently of previous specific practice or instruction concerning those relationships. It is best measured by tests in which people identify similarities and differences between stimulus items that they have never previously experienced, or between items so common that everyone in the tested population would have experienced them. According to Cattell, *fluid abilities* are biologically determined and reflected by tests of memory span, speed of processing, and spatial thinking. An example of a test assessing fluid intelligence is *Raven's*

FOCUS 18

What evidence led Cattell to distinguish between fluid intelligence and crystallized intelligence?

Progressive Matrices test, discussed earlier and illustrated in Figure 10.1 (on p. 361). Verbal analogy problems constructed only from common words that essentially all speakers of the language would know, such as the two problems presented back on page 361, are a second example of tasks that tap fluid intelligence.

A verbal analogy problem that would *not* be a good measure of fluid intelligence is the following (modified from Herrnstein & Murray, 1994):

> RUNNER is to MARATHON as OARSMAN is to (a) boat, (b) regatta, (c) fleet, or (d) tournament.

Solving this problem is limited not just by ability to perceive relationships but also by knowledge of uncommon words (especially *regatta*), and such knowledge reflects crystallized intelligence, not fluid intelligence.

Crystallized intelligence, according to Cattell (1971), is mental ability derived directly from previous experience. It is best assessed in tests of knowledge, such as knowledge of word meanings (*What is a regatta?*), cultural practices (*Do forks go to the right or left of plates in a proper table setting?*), and how particular tools or instruments work (*How does a mercury-filled thermometer work?*). Although people may differ in the domains of their knowledge (one person may know a lot of words but little about tools, for example), Cattell considered crystallized intelligence to be a component of general intelligence. One's accumulated knowledge can be applied broadly to solve a wide variety of problems (see Blair, 2006).

Like Spearman, Cattell based his theory largely on the factor analysis of scores on many different mental tests. Cattell's analysis indicated that mental tests tend to fall into two clusters: those that depend mostly on raw reasoning ability and those that depend mostly on previously learned information. Test scores within each cluster correlate more strongly with one another than with scores in the other cluster (see **Figure 10.8**). In addition, Cattell (1971) found that measures of fluid and crystallized intelligence change differently with age. Fluid ability typically peaks at about age 20 to 25 and declines gradually after that, while crystallized ability typically continues to increase until about age 50 or even later.

Many research studies have corroborated Cattell's conclusions about the differences between fluid and crystallized intelligence in their variation with age. **Figure 10.9** shows the combined results from many such studies for four mental

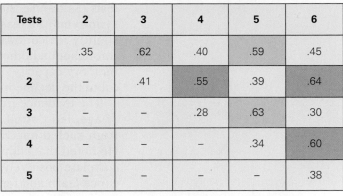

Tests	2	3	4	5	6
1	.35	.62	.40	.59	.45
2	–	.41	.55	.39	.64
3	–	–	.28	.63	.30
4	–	–	–	.34	.60
5	–	–	–	–	.38

FIGURE 10.8 Hypothetical correlations among test scores, suggestive of two underlying intelligences Each coefficient in the matrix is the correlation between the two tests indicated by its row and column. Thus, .35 is the correlation between test 1 and test 2. All the correlations are positive. Notice, however, that the correlations among tests 1, 3, and 5 (in gold) and among tests 2, 4, and 6 (in purple) are higher than any of the other correlations. This pattern of correlations suggests that the tests measure two different but somewhat overlapping abilities. Tests 1, 3, and 5 are the best measures of one ability, and tests 2, 4, and 6 are the best measures of the other. This result could be taken as support for Cattell's theory if the items in one cluster of tests seem to measure raw reasoning (fluid intelligence) and those in the other seem to measure learned information (crystallized intelligence).

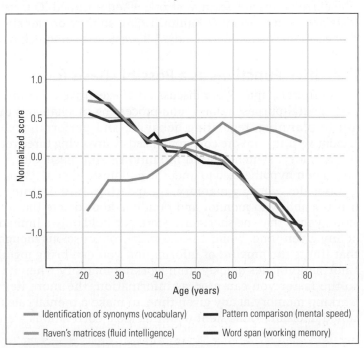

FIGURE 10.9 Average scores on four mental tests as a function of age The scores on each test are normalized (by the method described in the Appendix at the back of this book) such that 0 is the average for all subjects combined. A score of +1 or more would place a person in the top 16% of all subjects tested, and a score of –1 or less would place one in the bottom 16%. (Data from Salthouse, 2004.)

tests (Salthouse, 2004). As you can see in the figure, vocabulary (ability to identify synonyms) increases steadily until the mid-50s and then levels off or decreases slightly. In contrast, ability to solve Raven's matrix problems decreases steadily throughout adulthood. The figure also shows that word span (a measure of working memory capacity) and mental speed decline in a manner that is essentially identical to the decline in scores on Raven's Progressive Matrices.

The evidence from the analysis of correlation patterns, and the differing effects of age, led Cattell to argue that fluid and crystallized intelligences are distinct from each other. He did not, however, think that they are entirely independent. He noted that within any given age group crystallized- and fluid-intelligence scores correlate positively. This, he suggested, is because people with higher fluid intelligence learn and remember more from their experiences than do people with lower fluid intelligence. In that sense, he claimed, crystallized intelligence depends on fluid intelligence. Researchers indeed have found significant correlations between measures of fluid intelligence and at least some measures of verbal learning ability (Tamez et al., 2008).

Mental Speed as a Possible Basis for *g*

FOCUS 19

What findings have revived Galton's idea of mental quickness as a basis for general intelligence?

Might some basic cognitive abilities underlie general intelligence? This was an idea originally proposed by Francis Galton in the nineteenth century, and revived in the latter part of the twentieth century, using more sophisticated measures and measuring devices (Coyle et al., 2011; Sheppard & Vernon, 2008). Several literature reviews of the evidence from both children and adults reported modest correlations (between about –.30 and –.50) between speed of responding and intelligence, with faster responding (and, thus, presumably faster information processing) being associated with higher IQs (Fry & Hale, 2000; Jensen, 1998).

One measure of mental speed is *inspection time*—the minimal time that subjects need to look at or listen to a pair of stimuli to detect the difference between them. In one common test of inspection time, two parallel lines, one of which is 1.4 times as long as the other, are flashed on a screen and subjects must say which line is longer. The duration of the stimulus varies from trial to trial, and inspection time is the shortest duration at which a subject can respond correctly at some level significantly above chance. Studies correlating inspection time with IQ scores have typically revealed correlation coefficients of about .3 for measures of fluid intelligence and about .2 for measures of crystallized intelligence (Sheppard & Vernon, 2008). The correlations are about as strong when untimed IQ tests are used as when timed tests are used (Vernon & Kantor, 1986), so they do not simply result from the fact that the subtests of some standard IQ tests require quick reaction.

Executive Functions as a Possible Basis for *g*

FOCUS 20

How might executive functions provide a basis for individual differences in intelligence, and how might mental quickness affect that capacity? What evidence supports this logical possibility?

Recall from Chapter 9 our discussion of executive functions, a set of relatively basic and general-purpose information-processing mechanisms that, together, are important in planning, regulating behavior, and performing complex cognitive tasks. Executive functions are conceptualized as involving three related components (working memory, switching, and inhibition), and these, either together or separately, have been hypothesized to underlie *g* (Shipstead et al., 2016; Žebec et al., 2015).

Consider working memory, or updating. In the context of executive functions it is the ability to monitor and rapidly add or delete the contents of the short-term store. Recall that the short-term store can hold only a limited amount of information at any given time. While it is the center of conscious thought, it is also a bottleneck that limits the amount of information you can bring together to solve a problem. Information fades quickly from working memory when it is not being acted upon, so the faster you can process information, the more items you can maintain in working memory at any given time, to make a mental calculation or arrive at a reasoned decision. Consistent with this idea, correlations are high between measures of mental speed and working memory; according to some psychologists, this is why mental speed correlates positively with fluid intelligence (Miller & Vernon, 1992).

Recall from Chapter 9 that the capacity of the short-term store is assessed by *working-memory-span* tasks, in which subjects must remember information while performing some "work" on that information. For example, subjects are asked to solve a series of simple addition problems and then to recall, in order, the sum of each problem. Such working-memory-span problems are better predictors of cognitive abilities than simpler memory-span measures that ask the subjects to recall some information (such as a series of digits) without having to perform any "work" simultaneously. In fact, in one study, working-memory span at age 5 predicted academic performance at age 11 better than IQ, measured either at age 5 or at age 11 (Alloway & Alloway, 2010).

Researchers have also found that people with different levels of intellectual attainment differ in executive functions. For example, children and adults with intellectual impairment perform more poorly on executive-function tasks (Kittler et al., 2008) than people without intellectual impairment, and gifted children have higher levels of executive functions than nongifted children do (Arffa, 2007; Mahone et al. 2002). In other research, children's ability to self-regulate their emotions and behaviors accounted for more than twice as much of individual differences in subsequent measures of academic performance (e.g., school grades, school attendance, hours spent doing homework) as did IQ (Duckworth & Seligman, 2005).

The finding of a connection between individual differences in executive functions and intelligence is consistent with Robert Sternberg's concept of intelligence as "mental self-government." By this he means that people who perform well on intelligence tests are those who can control their mental resources in a way that allows for efficiency in problem solving (i.e., who use effectively the "slow" thinking system discussed in Chapter 9). To perform well on most cognitively demanding tasks, one must remain focused, avoid distraction, and distinguish between relevant and irrelevant information. These skills also seem to be involved in most if not all IQ tests and subtests, especially those that tap fluid intelligence more than crystallized intelligence. Some psychologists, in fact, consider fluid intelligence and executive functions to be essentially the same concept (Gray et al., 2003; Kane & Engle, 2002).

General Intelligence as an Evolutionary Adaptation for Novelty

General intelligence is sometimes equated with a general ability to cope adaptively with one's environment (Snyderman & Rothman, 1987). In the opinion of most intelligence researchers, however, that definition is far too broad. Cockroaches cope very well with their environment but perform poorly on IQ tests. All basic human capacities, like the basic capacities of any other species, came about through natural selection because they helped individuals adapt to the prevailing conditions of life. For example, human emotionality and sociability are valuable, evolved characteristics that help us survive in our social environments. People vary in measures of social and emotional competence, and these measures generally do not correlate reliably with measures of either fluid or crystallized intelligence (Kanazawa, 2004). A person can be intellectually brilliant but emotionally and socially incompetent, or vice versa.

From an evolutionary perspective, it is reasonable to assume that general intelligence evolved in humans as a means of solving problems that are evolutionarily novel (Geary & Berch, 2016; Kanazawa, 2004). People, more than other creatures, are capable of dealing

FOCUS 21

What reasoning suggests that general intelligence is an adaptation for dealing with evolutionarily novel problems?

■ **Intelligent species** Dr. Robert Shumaker of the Indianapolis Zoo works with Azy, an orangutan, in research on cognition using computer-generated symbols. Apes and, to a much greater degree, human beings have the capacity to solve novel problems—problems that were not regularly posed by the environment in which the species evolved. Some theorists consider this capacity to be the essence of intelligence.

National Geographic Creative/Alamy Stock Photo

effectively with a wide range of environmental conditions, including conditions that were never regularly faced by our evolutionary ancestors. Our capacity to see analogies, to reason inductively, to deduce the logical consequences of statements, to achieve creative insights, and to predict and plan for future events all help us to cope with the novelties of life and to find ways to survive in a variety of unexpected conditions. The same intelligence that allowed hunter-gatherers to find new ways of hunting game, or processing roots to make them edible, allows us to figure out how to operate computers.

SECTION REVIEW

Efforts to characterize and measure intelligence have both practical and theoretical goals.

History and Validity of Intelligence Testing

- Binet regarded intelligence as a loose set of higher-order mental abilities that can be increased by schooling. His tests used school-related questions and problems.

- Most modern intelligence tests are rooted in Binet's approach and use a variety of verbal and nonverbal subtests.

- IQ scores correlate moderately well with school grades and job performance. Such correlations are commonly used as indices of IQ validity.

Nature of General Intelligence

- Spearman proposed that general intelligence, or *g*, is a single factor that contributes to all types of mental performance.

- Cattell argued that *g* consists of two factors—fluid and crystallized intelligence.

- Modern measures of mental quickness and executive functions correlate significantly with IQ.

- Sternberg proposed that the efficiency of mental self-government accounts for individual differences in intelligence.

- General intelligence may have been selected for in human evolution because it helps us deal with novel problems.

Genetic and Environmental Contributions to Intelligence

Although not everyone considers IQ an adequate measure of intelligence, it would be hard to disagree that people exhibit substantial individual differences in intelligence. But what are the origins of these differences? Within psychology, researchers have often looked at two seemingly opposing contributions: *nature* (biology, genes) and *nurture* (learning, culture). The **nature–nurture debate**, which has persisted throughout psychology's history in various guises, poses this question: *Are psychological differences among people primarily the result of differences in their genes (nature) or in their environments (nurture)?* The psychological differences that have been most often subjected to this debate are differences in personality (see Chapter 14), in susceptibility to mental disorders (see Chapter 15), and, especially, in intelligence as measured by IQ. As you will discover, the answer to the nature–nurture question concerning IQ is, *it depends*. It depends on just whose IQs you are comparing.

Nature, Nurture, and IQ Differences

FOCUS 22

What is the difference between the absurd form of the nature–nurture question and the reasonable form? Why is one absurd and the other reasonable?

A common misunderstanding is that the nature–nurture question has to do with the degree to which a particular trait, in an individual, results from genes or environment. Some might ask, for example, "Does a person's intelligence result more from genes or from environment?" But if you think about that question, you will realize it is absurd. Without genes there would be no person and hence no intelligence, and without environment there would also be no person and no intelligence. Given that genes and environment are both essential for any trait to develop, it would be absurd to think that one contributes more than the other to the trait. But it is not absurd to ask whether *differences* in a trait among individuals result more from *differences* in their genes or *differences* in their environments. An alternative way of expressing the nature–nurture debate is *how do nature and nurture interact to produce a particular pattern of development or of intelligence?* As we saw in Chapter 3, genes are always expressed in an environment, and the effect those genes will have on any outcome, including intelligence, will differ depending on the environment in which they find themselves.

A useful analogy (suggested by Hebb, 1949) concerns the contribution of length and width to the areas of rectangles. It is absurd to ask whether the area of any given rectangle results more from its length or its width because both dimensions are essential to the area. If you shrink either to zero, there is no rectangle and no area. But it is not absurd to ask whether the differences in area among a given set of rectangles result more from differences in their length or in their width. As illustrated in **Figure 10.10**, the answer could be length or it could be width, depending on the specific set of rectangles asked about.

Similarly, when we ask whether differences in intelligence derive primarily from differences in genes or in environment, the answer might be genes for one set of people and environment for another. Logic tells us, for example, that IQ differences are likely to result more from environmental differences if the people we are studying live in very diverse environments than if they live in similar environments. If you were raised in an ideal upper-middle-class home and I was raised in a dysfunctional low-income family, the difference between us in IQ would be attributable mostly to differences in our environments; but if we were both raised in typical middle-class environments, then whatever difference exists between us in IQ might result mostly from differences in our genes.

■ **Like parent, like child** People often pass on traits and talents to their offspring. Pianist Ellis Marsalis is the father of four musicians. Here he accompanies his son Wynton, receiving the French Legion of Honor award in 2009.

The Concept of Heritability

The central concept in any modern scientific discussion of the nature–nurture question is **heritability**. Heritability is the degree to which variation in a particular trait, within a particular population of individuals, stems from genetic differences as opposed to environmental differences. Heritability is often quantified by a statistic called the *heritability coefficient,* which ranges from 0 (none of the differences in a trait are attributed to inheritance) to 1.0 (100% of the differences in a trait are attributed to inheritance). It reflects the proportion of differences in an observed trait that is due to genetic variability.

Heritability does not say anything about how much of any trait is due to genetic factors, only what percentage of the difference in a trait within a specific population can be attributed to inheritance, on average. As an example, assume that individual differences in weight are due to just two factors: inheritance (genetics) and diet (environment). Now assume that every person living in an isolated mountaintop community gets 100% of his or her nutritional needs. The average weight of men in this community is 150 pounds. If you meet two men from the community, one weighing 155 pounds and the other 160 pounds, 100% of their 5-pound difference would be due to genetics, and the heritability coefficient would be 1.0. This is

FOCUS 23

How is heritability defined? Why would we expect heritability to be higher in a population that shares a similar environment than in an environmentally diverse population?

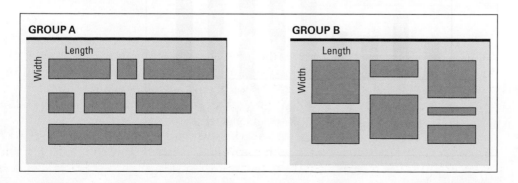

FIGURE 10.10 A geometric analogy to heritability It is senseless to say that a given rectangle's area results more from its length than from its width, or vice versa. However, differences in area among rectangles can result primarily or entirely from differences in length (as shown in group A) or in width (as shown in group B). Similarly, one can imagine one group of people in which IQ variation results mostly from their differing genes and another group in which it results mostly from their differing environments.

GROUP A

Length

Width

GROUP B

Length

Width

"I don't know anything about the bell curve, but I say heredity is everything."

because their diets are identical—no differences in environment exist—meaning that all differences must be attributed to genes.

But now assume that a famine hits this community, changing the number of calories people consume and thus the average weight (say from 150 to 140 pounds). If everyone experienced the same reduction of calories (say a 20% decrease), environments would still be identical and heritability would still be 1.0, despite the 10-pound difference in the population average. But suppose the dietary changes were not uniform among the mountaintop inhabitants—instead, some people received a greater percentage of their dietary needs (say, 100%) than others (say, 75%). The *average* population weight change may still be 10 pounds, but now some percentage of a 5-pound difference in weight between any two men would likely (on average) be due to environment, and thus heritability would be something less than 1.0. The more variable the environments are between people in a population, the lower heritability will be. Heritability is thus relative, varying with the environmental conditions in which people within the population live.

Family Studies of the Heritability of Intelligence

How might one estimate heritability, given that there is no direct way to measure individual differences in genes or environments? The general answer is to compare groups of people who differ in their degree of genetic relationship to see how much they differ in the trait in question. To the degree that a trait is heritable, people who are closely related to each other genetically should be more similar to each other than are people who are related more distantly.

A difficulty with using this logic, however, is that related people also typically share similar environments. Thus, the observation that siblings are, on average, more similar to each other in IQ than are unrelated people does not, by itself, tell us the degree to which their similarity results from similarities in their genes or in their environment. For this reason, many large-scale and tightly controlled studies of adoptees and twins have been conducted over the past half-century. Their findings are quite consistent and summarized in **Figure 10.11** (Bouchard & McGue, 1981).

Note that in Figure 10.11 some correlations are between "family" members that either do not share genes (parents and adopted offspring; adoptive siblings), or between genetically related people who are not reared in the same home environment (siblings reared apart; parents and adopted-away offspring; identical twins reared apart). As you can imagine, twins are especially valuable subjects in such studies because some pairs of twins are genetically identical (monozygotic)

> **FOCUS 24**
>
> What is the logic of comparing identical and fraternal twins to study the heritability of traits? What difference is observed between identical and fraternal twins in IQ correlation?

FIGURE 10.11 Average correlations of family studies of intelligence
Correlations generally increase as genetic similarity between pairs of people increases.

(Data from Bouchard & McGue, 1981.)

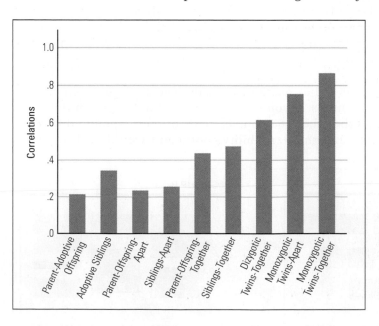

and other pairs (fraternal twins; dizygotic) are, like nontwin siblings, only 50% genetically related. A common way to estimate the heritability of IQ is to compare the correlation in IQ scores of identical twins with that of fraternal twins.

As explained in Chapter 2, correlation coefficients can run from 0.00 to either plus or minus 1.00. As shown in Figure 10.11, correlations generally increase as genetic similarity increases, suggesting a significant role for genetics. Heritability estimates can be derived from these correlations. The easiest way to compute a heritability coefficient is by using data from twin studies. The correlation (denoted as *r*) based on data from nonidentical twins is subtracted from the correlation based on data from identical twins, and the difference is doubled, or,

Heritability = (r identical twins − r nonidentical twins) × 2

The precise logic behind this method involves extensive mathematical detail, but you can get a sense of that logic without the mathematics. The assumption is that the environment is equally similar for the two categories of twins, so the difference between the two in IQ correlation must stem from the difference in their degree of genetic relatedness; that is, the difference must reflect heritability. Because fraternal twins are themselves 50% genetically related, the difference between the two correlation coefficients is assumed to reflect only half the difference that would be observed if the comparison were between identical twins and completely unrelated individuals. Therefore, the difference is doubled to arrive at an estimate of the heritability coefficient.

Taking the correlations of the IQs of identical (monozygotic) twins reared together shown in Figure 10.11 (.86) and those of fraternal (dizygotic) twins reared together (.60), the resulting computation is $H = (.86 − .60) × 2 = .52$. This means that the heritability of intelligence (at least based on this data set) is .52, or that 52% of the difference in intelligence between people is attributed to genetics.

Another way to assess heritability of IQ is to study the IQ correlation of pairs of identical twins who were adopted at an early age into separate homes. On the assumption that the environments of raised-apart identical twins are no more similar to each other than are the environments of any two members of the study population chosen at random, the correlation coefficient for raised-apart identical twins is itself an estimate of the heritability coefficient (Loehlin et al., 1988). The average coefficient determined from many such studies is .73 (McGue et al., 1993; see Figure 10.11). So, using this method, the estimated heritability for IQ is .73. Most of the twin pairs in those studies were adults, but a few were adolescents, and no attempt was made to determine the coefficient separately for different age groups.

Every procedure for assessing heritability involves assumptions that may not be entirely true, so any heritability coefficient should be taken as only a rough estimate. But the studies suggest, overall, that genetic differences account for roughly 30% to 50% of the IQ variance among children and for considerably more than 50% of the IQ variance among adults in the populations that were studied (McGue et al., 1993; Nisbett et al., 2012).

Heritability of IQ does *not* represent some biological feature of people that is impervious to experience. Rather, heritability estimates of IQ vary with environmental factors for people in the same population (Hanscombe et al., 2012; Rowe et al., 1999). For instance, in one study David Rowe and his colleagues (1999) gathered verbal IQ scores from 3,139 adolescent sibling pairs from economically diverse backgrounds. The sample included sets of monozygotic and dizygotic twins, and adopted siblings. Rowe and his colleagues reported that, for all the subjects, the heritability of verbal IQ was .57, similar to what other researchers have reported. Rowe and his colleagues next divided the sample into a high-education group (parents had greater than a high school education) and a low-education group (parents had less than a high school education). The heritability for the

FOCUS 25

How can IQ heritability be estimated using the correlation coefficients for the IQs of identical and fraternal twins raised together?

FOCUS 26

How can IQ heritability be estimated by studying identical twins who were adopted into different homes?

FOCUS 27

How can a person's rearing environment influence the heritability of IQ?

FIGURE 10.12 Genetic and shared-environment effects of IQ for adolescents for the overall sample, and for the low-education and the high-education families. Genetic and shared-environment effects changed substantially when education of the parents was considered, illustrating the important role that environment has on estimates of the heritability of IQ.

(Data from Rowe et al., 1999.)

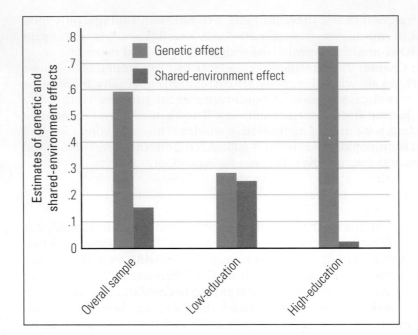

FOCUS 28

What is the evidence that the effect of a shared family environment on IQ correlations is lost in adulthood? How might this loss be explained?

■ **Identical twins learning together**
Whether they are raised together or apart, identical twins tend to exhibit similar mental abilities. Genetic dispositions to enjoy certain classes of activities may promote similarity in their development.

high-education group jumped to .74, but decreased to .26 for the low-education group. These results are graphically illustrated in **Figure 10.12**.

These results indicate that heritability increases with improved environmental conditions, here as reflected by level of parental education. According to Sandra Scarr (1992), this is because harmful environments (reflected in Rowe's research by a low level of education for the adolescents' parents) have an especially strong impact on the development of certain traits, whereas average or above-average environments will have little influence beyond that contributed by genetics.

Contrary to what might be expected, studies that have assessed fluid and crystallized intelligence separately indicate that the two are about equally heritable (Horn, 1985). Apparently, within the populations that have been studied, genetic differences influence the amount of factual knowledge that people have learned just as much as they influence people's ability to think quickly or to see relationships in novel stimuli. Genetic differences could have such an effect in a variety of ways. Genes can influence curiosity, reading ability, long-term memory, or any of countless other traits that influence the acquisition and recall of facts.

The Short-Lived Influence of Family Environment

It seems reasonable to expect that the IQs of children raised in the same family would be more similar than average, not just because of shared genes but also because of shared environments. After all, children in the same family are exposed to the same parents, the same neighborhoods, the same schools, and the same learning opportunities at home. But is this expectation correct?

The most direct way to assess the degree to which a shared family environment leads to similarity in IQ is to study pairs of adoptive siblings who are genetically unrelated but are raised together. Assuming that such pairs are genetically no more similar to each other than any two random people from the study population, any correlation greater than zero in their IQs must stem from their shared environment. Several such studies have been done, and the results tell a remarkably consistent story. As long as the unrelated siblings are still children, their IQs do correlate positively with each other; but the correlation is lost completely by the time they reach adulthood.

Taking all such studies together, the average IQ correlation for genetically unrelated children living in the same family is .25, and the average for genetically unrelated adults who had been raised in the same family is –.01, or essentially zero (McGue et al., 1993). Other studies have shown that the IQ correlations for other categories of children raised in the same family also decline as the children enter adulthood, but the greater the degree of genetic relationship, the smaller the decline (Plomin & Daniels, 1987). Similarly, a meta-analysis of twin studies found that IQ correlations for fraternal twins declined at adulthood while that for identical twins did not (McGue et al., 1993). Apparently, families have a moderately strong early influence on children's IQ, but the effect fades as the children become adults.

The transient nature of the effect of the family on IQ is perhaps the most surprising result that has emerged from studies of IQ correlations. Before such studies were done, many, if not most, psychologists believed that even subtle differences in the early environments of children would give some an advantage in intellectual development that would last a lifetime. But the research has shown conclusively that the advantage or disadvantage of being raised in a particular home, within the range of homes the researchers sampled, disappears by early adulthood.

One way to explain this finding is to assume that as children grow into adulthood, they increasingly choose their own environments, and their genetic differences influence the kinds of environments they choose (Dunn & Plomin, 1990; Scarr & McCartney, 1983). Those who are genetically similar, and therefore more similar in interests and temperament, may choose more similar environments than do those who are genetically different, and so they remain more similar in intelligence. If you think of intelligence as analogous to muscle strength, which can vary depending on exercise, then you can understand why an adult's IQ may be more influenced by adult environment than by childhood environment.

Blend Images/Alamy Stock Photo

■ **Seeking her own path** This young woman's mental development may have been considerably influenced up until now by her parents and the home they provided. From now on, however, that influence will be reduced. Her own dispositions will play a greater role in determining what she learns and how her mind develops. This may help explain why the heritability coefficients for IQ are greater for adults than for children.

Effects of Personality and Life Experiences on Intelligence

Intelligence is maintained and strengthened through active, intellectual engagement with the world. It is not surprising that people who score high on a personality test designed to measure openness to experience have, on average, higher IQs than do those who score lower on that personality measure (Ackerman & Heggestad, 1997; Gignac et al., 2004). Openness to experience includes the characteristics of curiosity, independence of mind, and broad interests. Presumably, people who have these characteristics choose intellectually engaging styles of life, and that choice tends to raise their intelligence. Openness appears to correlate at least as strongly with measures of fluid intelligence as with measures of crystallized intelligence. Intellectual engagement apparently does not just increase one's store of knowledge, but also increases one's capacity for mental gymnastics.

 FOCUS 29

What evidence suggests that intellectual involvement can increase a person's fluid intelligence over time?

More direct evidence that activities can alter intelligence is found in a long-term study, conducted by Melvin Kohn and Carmi Schooler, of the effects of men's occupations on their intellectual development. Kohn and Schooler periodically tested a large sample of men, throughout their careers, with a test of *intellectual flexibility*. The test included a number of subtests that are quite similar to those found on standard IQ tests, and it was later shown to correlate strongly with fluid intelligence as measured by standard IQ tests (Kohn & Schooler, 1978; Schooler, 2001).

The most general finding was that the men's intellectual flexibility tended to change when their job demands changed. When they were in jobs that required them to handle a great deal of information and make complex decisions, their intellectual flexibility increased over time. When they were in routine jobs that depended more on brawn and/or tolerance of drudgery, their intellectual flexibility decreased over time. In subsequent research, done with both men and women,

Schooler and his colleagues found that engagement in intellectually challenging leisure-time activities, even without career change, can also increase intellectual flexibility (Schooler, 2007; Schooler & Mulatu, 2001). These effects—both of occupation and of leisure-time activities—were greater for older adults (age 58 and older) than for younger adults (Schooler, 2001, 2007).

Here, again, the analogy between mental strength and physical strength seems to hold. Young people can maintain relatively strong muscles without much exercise, but as we get older our muscles begin to atrophy unless we increase their use. The same, apparently, is true for brain power.

■ **Use it and keep it** Older adults who have careers or interests that keep them intellectually active retain their full intelligence longer than those who retire to a non-intellectual life. Shown here is Phil Aune, nicknamed "PaPa Alpha," who retired at age 70 as the world's oldest air-traffic controller. Mr. Aune worked for 47 years at California's Van Nuys Airport, the world's busiest general-aviation airport.

Origins of IQ Differences Between Cultural Groups

The conclusions about the high heritability of IQ discussed so far in this chapter were properly qualified by the phrase "for the population that was studied." In almost all cases that population was white, North American or European, and in the upper two-thirds of the socioeconomic scale (Stoolmiller, 1999). Heritability coefficients are always limited to the population that was studied. The more uniform the environment of that population, the smaller is the proportion of IQ variance that stems from environmental variation and the greater is the heritability coefficient (look back at the formula on p. 389). If heritability studies included people occupying the entire range of human environments rather than just a slice of that range, the resultant heritability coefficients would be smaller than those presented earlier.

Comparisons of racial or cultural groups routinely reveal average differences in IQ. The difference that has attracted the most attention, and on which we will focus here, is that between blacks and whites in the United States: Blacks, on average, score about 12 points lower than whites on standard IQ tests (Dickens & Flynn, 2006). The question is why. Some people who have heard of the heritability studies that you have just read about assume that those studies can be applied to understand the black–white difference. They assume that if IQ is highly heritable within a group, then any IQ difference between two groups must also be largely the result of genetic differences. But that assumption is false.

FOCUS 30

Why can't heritability coefficients found within groups be used to infer the source of differences between groups?

Why Within-Group Heritability Coefficients Can't Be Applied to Between-Group Differences

The heritability of a trait within a group, in fact, tells us nothing about differences between groups. To understand why, consider the example illustrated in **Figure 10.13**. Imagine two wheat fields, each planted from the same package of genetically diverse wheat seeds. Imagine further that the soil fertility is relatively constant within each field but quite different between the two—one has richer topsoil than the other. Within either field, differences in the sizes of individual plants would be the result primarily of genetic differences in the seeds, yet the average difference between the two fields would almost certainly be due entirely to the difference in the environment (the richness of the soil).

To take another example, height in people is more than 90% heritable when measured for a given cultural group, yet group differences in height can be found that are clearly the result of the environment (Ceci, 1996). In the 1950s researchers found that men of full Japanese ancestry born in California were nearly 3 inches taller, on average, than Japanese men born in Japan (Greulich, 1957). That difference almost certainly resulted from differences in diet between the two groups during their childhoods. (Read again the hypothetical example about the heritability of weight we gave on pp. 387–388.)

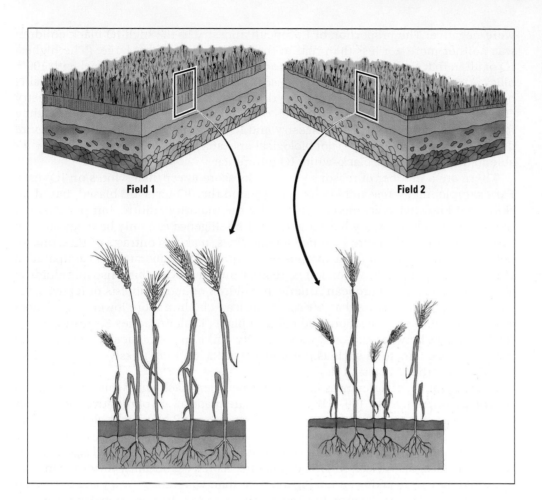

FIGURE 10.13 Why high within-group heritability tells us nothing about group differences In this example the same genetically diverse mix of wheat seeds was planted in two fields. Within each field the environment is quite uniform (same thickness of topsoil), so the differences in plant size are mostly the result of differences in genes (high heritability). However, the difference between the two fields in average plant size in this case cannot result from genes, because genetic differences would cancel out in the averages; it must result from differences in the environment.

Evidence That Black–White IQ Differences Are Cultural in Origin

In the examples just given, we could be quite certain that the group differences were environmental in origin because there was reason to believe that the members of the two groups (of wheat plants and of Japanese men) did not differ genetically, on average. In contrast, many people automatically think of differences between the so-called black and white "races" as racial differences, and they automatically assume that racial means "genetic."

In the United States and many other countries, however, blacks and whites are not truly distinct races in a biological sense but, rather, are different cultural groups. We generally classify people as "black" who have any detectable black African ancestry, no matter how small a proportion it is. Thus, a person who is half English, one-fourth French, and one-fourth African is called "black," whereas that person's cousin, who is half English, one-fourth French, and one-fourth Polish, is called "white." While some average genetic differences exist between the two groups—which show up in skin pigmentation, for example—the amount of genetic variation *within* each group is far greater than the average difference *between* them.

Researchers who have attempted to separate the effect of black African ancestry from the effect of the social designation "black" have consistently failed to find evidence that genetic ancestry plays a role in the black–white IQ difference. In the first such study, Paul Witty and Martin Jenkins (1935) attempted to determine if high-IQ black children have more European and less African ancestry than blacks who have lower IQs. They identified a sample of black children in Chicago who had IQs in the superior range (125 or better) and then interviewed their parents to see if they had more European ancestry than the average black person. The results

FOCUS 31

What evidence suggests that the average IQ difference between black and white Americans derives from the environment, not genes?

were negative: The proportion of European ancestry in the high-IQ black children was neither more nor less than that in the black population at large. (The highest IQ of all in that study, incidentally, was a remarkable 200 scored by a girl with 100% black African ancestry.) Later, other researchers performed similar studies, using biochemical methods to determine the degree of black African and other ancestry (Loehlin et al., 1973; Scarr & Carter-Saltzman, 1983). Like Witty and Jenkins, they found no relationship between ancestry and IQ, and they concluded that the *social* designation of black or white, not biological ancestry, is most likely the critical variable in determining the black–white IQ difference.

There are a number of reasons why blacks score lower than whites on IQ tests. For example, many researchers have suggested that IQ tests are biased, based on skills and knowledge deemed important by the majority culture, but perhaps not the minority culture. Many have argued that intelligence can only be meaningfully assessed within the culture in which a child lives, making contrasts of IQ scores of people with different cultural experiences inappropriate (Laboratory of Comparative Human Cognition, 1983; Miller-Jones, 1989). Consistent with this, Hispanic children also score lower than European American children on most subtests of IQ tests, for many of the same reasons that African American children score lower (e.g., factors associated with SES, education, and cultural bias) (Thaler & Jones-Forrester, 2013). IQ differences between minority and majority children are reduced when they are given "culture fair" tests such as the nonverbal Raven's Progressive Matrices Test mentioned earlier (Anastasi, 1988).

Another source of differences in IQ scores between blacks and whites is related to ***stereotype threat*** (Steele, 1997). When people are made aware of negative stereotypes for their particular social group, such as the stereotypical belief that blacks perform poorly on tests of intelligence, they tend to confirm them. For example, when groups of African and European American college students were administered a test of verbal intelligence, the African American students scored significantly lower when they were told they were taking an intelligence test than when they were told the test did not assess people's intelligence. In contrast, the scores of the European American students did not differ between the two conditions (Steele & Aronson, 1995). Although the stereotype threat does not account for the entirety of the black–white IQ difference (Sackett et al., 2004), its presence suggests that IQ tests may be assessing not just people's intelligence, but also people's tendency to "choke" under situations in which a stereotype threat was activated.

Different Types of Minority Status Can Have Different Effects on IQ

How might the social designation of black or white affect IQ? Nobody knows for sure, but John Ogbu (1986; Ogbu & Stern, 2001) suggested an interesting line of thought. On the basis of cross-cultural research, Ogbu distinguished between *voluntary minorities* and *involuntary* or *castelike minorities*. Voluntary minorities are groups, such as Italian Americans and Chinese Americans, who emigrated in hopes of bettering themselves, who typically see themselves as well off compared with those they left behind, and who see themselves as on their way up, regardless of how the dominant majority may see them. In contrast, involuntary minorities are groups, such as African Americans and Native Americans, who became minorities through being conquered, colonized, or enslaved. They are people who for long periods were, and in many ways still are, treated as if they are a separate, inferior class. According to research summarized by Ogbu, involuntary minorities everywhere perform more poorly in school, and score an average of 10 to 15 points lower on IQ tests, than the dominant majority.

FOCUS 32

What is stereotype threat, and how does it explain differences in IQ between white and black Americans?

FOCUS 33

What evidence suggests that the status of being an involuntary minority may be particularly detrimental to IQ development?

■ Some theorists believe that IQ tests are culturally biased and that one always has to consider the context in which intelligence is assessed.

"YOU CAN'T BUILD A HUT, YOU DON'T KNOW HOW TO FIND EDIBLE ROOTS AND YOU KNOW NOTHING ABOUT PREDICTING THE WEATHER. IN OTHER WORDS, YOU DO TERRIBLY ON OUR I.Q. TEST."

■ **The Buraku of Japan** Descendants of people who worked as tanners and butchers—jobs that were traditionally believed to be unclean and worthy only of lowly people—the Buraku are no longer legally categorized as outcasts, but continue to be discriminated against. Here, Buraku workers perform hazardous tasks in the cleanup of the Fukushima-Daiichi nuclear plant after it was damaged by an earthquake and tsunami in 2011. Like outcast groups elsewhere, Buraku in Japan perform more poorly in school and have lower average IQ scores than other citizens of their nation. However, when they emigrate to America, where most people do not know their caste status, the IQ difference between them and other Japanese Americans vanishes.

Particularly informative in Ogbu's work is the comparison of the Buraku outcasts of Japan with blacks of the United States. The Buraku, who are a purely cultural class, not racially distinct from other Japanese, were emancipated from official outcast status by a royal edict in 1871, just 8 years after blacks in the United States were emancipated from slavery; yet, both groups, to this day, often occupy menial positions and are implicitly, if not explicitly, perceived as inferior by many members of the dominant majority. The gap in school achievement and IQ between the Buraku and the majority group in Japan is about the same as that between blacks and whites in the United States—but the gap disappears when Buraku move to the United States. Most people in the United States do not know the difference between Buraku and other Japanese, and the two groups of immigrants are treated the same and perform equally well in school and on IQ tests. According to Ogbu, it is the sense that one is an outcast, and that standard routes to achievement are cut off, that oppresses castelike minorities and depresses their scholastic achievements and IQs.

The Historical Increase in IQ

Perhaps the most dramatic evidence of cultural influence on intelligence is the improved performance on IQ tests that has been observed worldwide over the years since they were invented. As previously discussed (see Figure 10.7), IQ tests are graded on a bell-shaped curve, with the average score for the population at any given time in history assigned a value of 100. But the average score keeps rising, indicating that the tests become easier for each successive generation, so researchers periodically modify the scoring system and increase the difficulty of the questions.

James Flynn (1987, 2007, 2012) has compiled data on norm adjustments for many different countries, from the dawn of IQ testing to the present, and has found that the increase in IQ has occurred at a rather steady rate of about 9 to 15 points every

Yoshikazu Tsuno/ZUMAPRESS/Newsroom

FOCUS 34

How does history provide further evidence that IQ is highly susceptible to cultural influence? On which measures has IQ increased the most?

FIGURE 10.14 Examples of gains in intelligence-test scores Shown here are IQ gains from 1948 to 2002, in the United States, as measured by Raven's Progressive Matrices, by the Wechsler Intelligence Scale for Children (Full Scale), and by several subtests of the Wechsler Intelligence Scale for Children. These are the gains that would have occurred if the tests were not made more difficult and the scoring systems were not adjusted at each test revision. (Data from Flynn, 2007.)

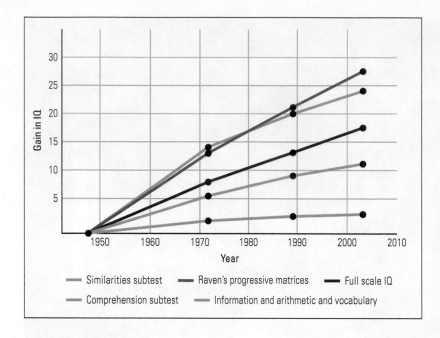

30 years, depending on the type of test. This so-called *Flynn effect* has occurred for people of all races and ethnicities and has occurred in countries as varied as the United States, Belgium, Argentina, and Kenya (Daley et al., 2003; Trahan et al., 2014). The greatest increases, interestingly, are in the tests geared toward fluid intelligence, such as Raven's Progressive Matrices—the very tests that were originally conceived of as least affected by cultural experience and most indicative of raw reasoning ability.

As an example, **Figure 10.14** illustrates the gains in IQ scores that would have occurred in the United States between 1948 and 2002 if the tests and scoring system had not been periodically adjusted. The graph depicts data for various subtests of a standard IQ test (the WISC), for the full-scale IQ score, and for Raven's Progressive Matrices. Notice that the biggest gains are for Raven's Matrices and the Similarities subtest of the WISC, both of which are deemed to be excellent measures of fluid intelligence. (In the Similarities subtest, the person is presented on each trial with the names of two common objects or events, such as *mouse* and *crow*, and has to say what is similar about them; a correct answer might be that they are both animals.)

FOCUS 35

How might the historical increase in fluid intelligence scores be explained?

What accounts for these massive gains in IQ from one generation to the next? Flynn (2007, 2012) argues that the increase is due mainly to changes in modern life. Improvements in education, greater use of technology, and more people being engaged in intellectually demanding work have all led to a greater proportion of people with experience manipulating abstract concepts than was the case in decades past. This, in turn, is responsible for elevated IQ scores for people of all ages.

Partly because of television, computers, and other such technology, we are constantly being presented with new ideas, new information, new problems to solve. Fluid IQ tests require us to answer questions or solve problems on the spot, based upon information that we have just been given. In today's world, that is something that we do all the time, so we have become good at it.

Even television, so often disparaged as intellectually stifling, may promote the kind of thinking that leads to good performance on fluid IQ tests. As Steven Johnson (2005) has demonstrated with quantitative analyses, television programs have, over time, grown immensely in complexity and pace. Programs that have been popular relatively recently—such as *Game of Thrones, NCIS,* and *House of Cards*—require viewers to keep many subplots and different characters in mind and to shift mental set frequently as the action jumps quickly from one time and place to another and the dialogue provides only hints about what is going on. Compare that to the simpler progression of events in, say, the 1950s show *I Love Lucy*. Moreover, fast-paced video games exercise attention and working-memory capacity, which are the aspects of mind that contribute most to measures of fluid intelligence. We aren't necessarily any better than our grandparents were at solving real-world problems, but we are definitely better at the game-like problems that make up the fluid components of IQ tests.

SECTION REVIEW

Nature–nurture questions about intelligence have no simple answers.

IQ Differences Within a Cultural Group

- The reasonable version of the nature–nurture question asks whether genetic or environmental variation contributes more to observed IQ variation within a population.

- Heritability is the extent to which variation in a trait (e.g., IQ), within a particular population, derives from genetic differences among the individuals.

- Twin studies have shown that, within a population, genetic variation accounts for about half of IQ variance.

- Effects of the shared family environment on IQ are temporary; they disappear in adulthood.

- There is evidence that a person's job or leisure activities can alter his or her fluid intelligence.

IQ Differences Between Cultural Groups

- Heritability coefficients for IQ *within* groups cannot be legitimately used to explain the source of average IQ differences *between* groups.

- The average black–white IQ difference found in the United States is related to the social designation of black or white rather than to the degree of African or European ancestry.

- Involuntary minority status is particularly likely to reduce a group's IQ.

- The Flynn effect may result from changes in technology as well as cultural factors.

Thinking Critically About   Reasoning and Intelligence

1. What is meant by "intelligence," and to what extent are levels of intellectual functioning influenced by nature versus nurture?

2. Is it reasonable to contrast the cognitive abilities of people from different cultures? What aspects of human thinking are characteristics of the species (species universal) versus dependent upon the culture one is brought up in (culture specific)?

Reflections and Connections

In reflecting on what you have learned in this chapter, think about its content in relation to each of the following four themes.

1. The concrete nature of human reasoning For most of us formal reasoning, as found in mathematics, plays a relatively small role in our everyday reasoning. Instead, we typically reason by comparing the current problem with memories that seem relevant to that situation. Consider how this tendency applies to the following: (a) reasoning by analogy; (b) biases in inductive reasoning; (c) the content bias and use of mental models in deductive reasoning; and (d) the role of mental sets, and overcoming mental sets, in solving insight problems.

2. Cultural and other environmental influences on reasoning Just as people reason concretely, different people are likely to develop different reasoning abilities based on different experiences they have had. Consider the different experiences, and associated differences in reasoning patterns, that may result from: (a) cross-cultural differences in responses to classification problems; (b) East–West differences in holistic versus analytic perception and thought; (c) evidence that scores on IQ tests vary across cultures and have been increasing over time as a result of cultural changes; and (d) evidence that a person's IQ can increase or decrease over time, depending on the work environment.

3. Concepts of intelligence are rooted in correlational research Research on intelligence makes heavy use of correlational methods. For example, if people who tend to score high (or low) on one test or measure also tend to score high (or low) on the other, this correlation suggests that the two measures are assessing the same underlying characteristic, though it may not be clear just what that characteristic is. As you think about intelligence testing, note how correlation patterns have been used to support (a) the concept of general intelligence; (b) the claim that intelligence tests are valid predictors of academic and employment success; (c) the distinction between fluid and crystallized intelligence; and (d) the ideas that variations in mental speed, working memory, and central executive processes may contribute to variations in intelligence.

4. Limitation of the concept of heritability Heritability is a valuable concept because it brings clarity to the long-standing nature–nurture question. However, heritability does not tell us about the relative roles of genes and environment in the development of a trait within an individual; it only informs us about their relative roles in contributing to the variability of the trait within a population. If you understand how the formula for heritability operates, you should be able to explain: (a) why heritability for a trait might be different for one population than for another; (b) why heritability decreases when the environmental diversity of the population increases; (c) why heritability of a trait can be greater for adults than for children; and (d) why high heritability within a culture at a particular time is compatible with strong environmental effects across cultures and over historical time.

Key Terms

analogy 360
availability bias 365
confirmation bias 366
crystallized intelligence 383
deductive reasoning 368

fluid intelligence 382
Flynn effect 396
functional fixedness 372
general intelligence (g) 382
heritability 387

inductive reasoning 365
insight problems 371
intelligence 378
IQ 380
mental set 371

nature–nurture debate 386
predictable-world bias 367
stereotype threat 394

Find Out More

Philip N. Johnson-Laird (2007). *How we reason*. Oxford, UK: Oxford University Press.

This book by a leading researcher on the psychology of reasoning is sophisticated but clearly written and enjoyable. Johnson-Laird expands on his mental-models view of reasoning and shows how we reason well and how we sometimes reason poorly.

Richard E. Nisbett (2009). *Intelligence and how to get it*. New York, NY: Norton.

Nisbett is a leading social psychologist who has devoted much of his career to understanding how intelligence is influenced by the social and cultural environment. In this book for general readers, he clearly describes such influences, including schooling and cultural

differences—particularly the differences between Asian and Western cultures.

Daniel Kahneman (2011). *Thinking fast and slow*. New York, NY: Farrar, Straus, & Giroux.

Nobel laureate Daniel Kahneman looks at the basics of human problem solving, reasoning, and decision making, based chiefly on four decades of research with his close collaborator Amos Tversky. Kahneman proposes, as have many others, that there are two basic processing systems: one "fast," intuitive, and automatic; and the other "slow," logical, and effortful. He reviews research on many of the topics covered in this chapter as well as other heuristics and biases the human mind is prone to. This engaging book is an excellent way for a beginner to

get an idea of what cognitive psychology is all about.

Alex Wissner-Gross (2013, November). *A new equation for intelligence*. TEDxBeaconStreet. https://www.ted.com/talks/alex_wissner_gross_a_new_equation_for_intelligence?utm_source=tedcomshare&utm_medium=referral&utm_campaign=tedspread

Physicist/computer scientist Wissner-Gross provides an interesting take on what intelligence is. He discusses what has been learned from gameplay research and AI and the role of future freedom of action in entropy. He argues that intelligence is a physical process that can be discerned in part through the use of simulations and AI.

Eliza Lambert (Producer) (*2017, April 5*). *Could solving this one problem solve all the others?* [Audio podcast]. http://freakonomics.com/podcast/solving-one-problem-solve-others/

In this engaging podcast, psychologist Angela Duckworth (University of Pennsylvania) and business and computer scientist Katharine Milkman (Wharton School at University of Pennsylvania) explore how humans often make poor decisions that result in self-sabotaging behavior. With a team of academic researchers working with corporate and institutional partners, they developed a project called "Making Behavior Change Stick" with the goal of perfecting the science of behavior change. Listen to this fascinating podcast to find out if it will work.

Visit LaunchPad for Psychology 8e launchpadworks.com to access the e-book, videos, activities, additional resources, and LearningCurve quizzes, as well as study aids including flash cards and web quizzes.

PART V

Growth of the Mind and Person

One way to understand any complex entity, whether it's a building under construction or a person growing, is to watch it develop over time. This is the approach taken by developmental psychologists, who study the changes through which human behavior becomes increasingly complex and sophisticated from the prenatal period to adulthood. The topic of this unit is developmental psychology: Chapter 11 describes the development of body, thought and language, and Chapter 12 explores the development of social relationships and their role in promoting other aspects of development.

CHAPTER

The Development of Body, Thought, and Language

11

LEARNING OUTCOMES

After studying this chapter, you should be able to:

- Summarize the physical changes that take place before birth and during puberty.

- Describe how infants explore the environment and learn basic physical principles.

- Define and differentiate Piaget's theory, Vygotsky's theory, and the information-processing model of cognitive development.

- Explain theory of mind and how it applies to the typical development of young children and to individuals with autism.

- Identify the characteristics of human language and describe how infants and children learn language.

- Identify theories of language acquisition and name some advantages and disadvantages of bilingualism.

CHAPTER OUTLINE

Physical Development

How Infants Learn About the Environment

Three Theories of Children's Mental Development

Children's Understanding of Minds

The Nature of Language and Children's Early Linguistic Abilities

Internal and External Supports for Language Development

Thinking Critically About the Development of Body, Thought, and Language

Reflections and Connections

Key Terms

Find Out More

When I (Peter Gray) first saw my newborn son, my words did not match my thought. I said something like, "Oh, he's beautiful," but my thought was, "My goodness, will he turn into a real human being?" Of course, I knew intellectually that he already was a human being, but at the moment he looked more like a cross between that and a garden slug.

Over the next weeks, months, and years, the little slug's mother and I watched in amazement as he grew not only to look increasingly human but also to do the things that humans everywhere do. He began to smile in response to our smiles; he began eventually to walk upright on two legs and to talk, sometimes incessantly; and, true to his species' name (*Homo sapiens*, where *sapiens* means "wise"), he manifested from early on an insatiable curiosity and soon developed a remarkable store of knowledge and theories about his world.

This chapter is about the millions of new human beings who enter the world every year. More specifically, it is the first of two chapters concerned with ***developmental psychology***, the study of changes that occur in people's abilities and dispositions as they grow older. Some developmental psychologists study changes that occur in adulthood, but the most prominent changes are those that occur in infancy and childhood. Researchers find infants and children fascinating and worthy of understanding for their own sake, but also because they see in

FatCamera/Getty Images

infants and children the origins of adult abilities. Human thought and language in particular are extraordinarily complex, and developmental psychologists have learned a great deal about them by watching them grow in infants and children.

Another reason to study development is to gain an understanding of the mechanisms underlying behavior. Are animals, including people, the product of their genes, or are they shaped by their environments? Clearly, as we've already seen in other chapters in this book (especially Chapter 10 in discussing intelligence), neither extreme version of this nature–nurture debate is plausible. It is plausible, however, to ask, *"How do nature and nurture interact to produce a particular psychological outcome?"* and the only way to answer this question is by looking at development.

This chapter begins by focusing on the physical development that takes place before we are born and then on the changes that occur during puberty. We then examine how infants learn about the physical world. We turn next to some theories and research concerning the development of reasoning, including reasoning about people's minds as well as about physical objects. Finally, we discuss the acquisition of language. A theme throughout is that children's own exploratory and playful activities are prime forces for their mental development. Through play and exploration, in a responsive social environment, children acquire the abilities and knowledge that enable them to survive and thrive in the world into which they are born.

Physical Development

FOCUS 1

What are the three phases of prenatal development and what are the major milestones of each phase?

Human development begins with conception, progresses for 9 months in the protection of the womb, and continues after birth when infants face a radically different environment—one in which they must eat, drink, deal with an amazing number of sights and sounds, and interact with other members of their own species. This section begins with a description of prenatal development, followed by an examination of another period of dramatic development in the course of the life span: puberty and adolescence.

■ Many sperm may reach the egg (ovum), but only one can fertilize it.

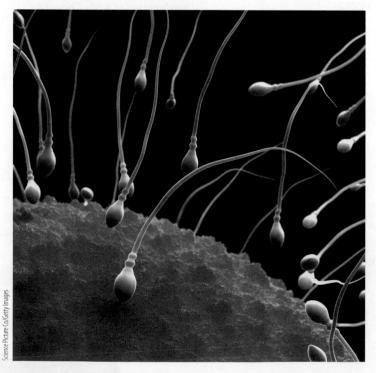

Science Picture Co/Getty Images

Prenatal Development

Humans, like all mammals, are a sexually reproducing species, requiring the joining of male sperm with a female egg to begin a new life. Women typically release one egg (ovum) from one of their ovaries each month, whereas men release approximately 250 million sperm in each ejaculation (Baker & Bellis, 2007). Only one of these many millions of sperm, however, will impregnate the egg, and this will occur in the *fallopian tube,* which connects the ovaries to the uterus, or womb.

Zygotic, Embryonic, and Fetal Phases

Researchers divide the prenatal period into three phases: the *zygotic* (or germinal), *embryonic*, and *fetal phases*. When sperm joins egg, combining 23 nuclear genes from the mother with 23 from the father (review the basics of genetics in Chapter 3), the zygote begins its journey to the uterus. During this time, which lasts about two weeks, the zygote divides many times, eventually implanting in the uterine wall, ending the zygotic phase and beginning the embryonic phase. However, it is estimated that 40% of zygotes do not survive this earliest phase of prenatal development, and as many as one-third of those that do become implanted are lost in later phases by spontaneous abortions, also known as miscarriages (O'Rahilly & Müller, 2001). While a miscarriage is often emotionally traumatic for the expectant parents, it is important to realize that it is a very common occurrence, often with no known cause.

The embryonic period extends from the third to about the eighth week after conception. During this time, the embryo's major organ systems develop. The embryo receives nutrition from the mother's bloodstream via the umbilical cord through the *placenta,* which develops inside the uterus during pregnancy. The placenta also exchanges oxygen, antibodies, and wastes between the mother and embryo.

The final phase of the prenatal period, the fetal, extends from about nine weeks until birth, which usually takes place about 38 weeks after conception. The most prominent feature of the fetal period is growth and refinement of organs and body structure. At 3 months, the fetus is about 2.5 inches long and weighs about half an ounce. Six months later, at birth, the average newborn is about 20 inches long and weighs about 7.5 pounds. The fetus also changes in proportion. The head of the fetus at 9 weeks is proportionally large relative to the rest of the body, and this decreases, with the body catching up, so to speak, by the time a baby is born. However, even at birth, an infant's head accounts for about 20% of its body. In comparison, in the average adult the head is about only 12% of the body (Tanner, 1990). This change in proportions, with development progressing essentially from head to foot, is termed *cephalocaudal development.*

By the end of the 12th week after conception, all the organs are formed, though not functioning well, and are in same proportion to each other as in a full-term newborn, just smaller. The external genitalia begin to differentiate between males and females around the 9th week but are not fully formed until about the 12th week. As early as the 8th week, the embryo begins to move, and activity increases by 12 weeks. The mother may be able to detect some of these movements, although most mothers don't feel the baby move until the 4th or 5th month of pregnancy (Fifer, 2005).

Fetuses "behave" and are able to perceive some stimuli. For example, ultrasounds reveal that some fetuses suck their thumbs and respond to touch. By 6 months, fetuses respond to their mothers' heartbeat and sounds from outside the womb, including language. In fact, research has shown that infants show a preference for their mothers' voices immediately after birth, an indication that their auditory system is functioning reasonably well before birth (DeCasper & Fifer, 1980; Kisilevsky et al., 2003).

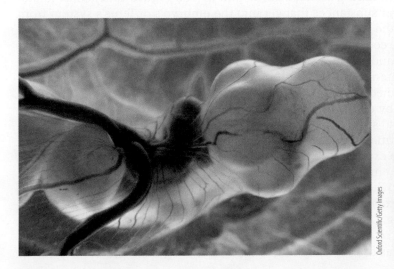

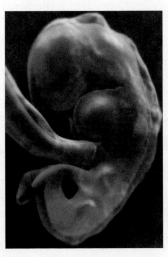

■ Development of internal organs occurs rapidly during the embryonic phase. Development during the fetal phase involves mostly increases in size and perfecting the functioning of organs.

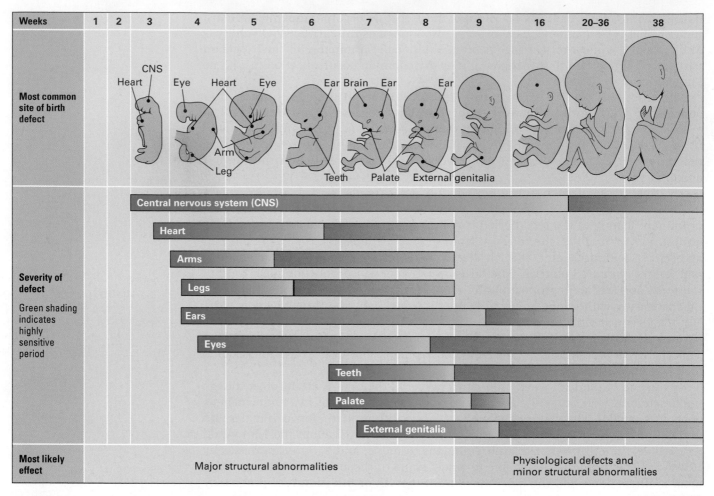

| Weeks | 1 | 2 | 3 | 4 | 5 | 6 | 7 | 8 | 9 | 16 | 20–36 | 38 |

FIGURE 11.1 Prenatal development and sensitivity to teratogenic effects As indicated by the green shading, organ systems and limbs are most sensitive to the effects of teratogens during the early weeks of prenatal development, while the central nervous system remains vulnerable later into pregnancy.

(Information from Moore & Persaud, 2003.)

The Effects of Experience During the Prenatal Period

Although embryos and fetuses are sheltered from the outside world, they are none-theless subject to the effects of experience. The types of experience that researchers have most thoroughly studied are the effects of *teratogens*, environmental agents that cause harm during prenatal development (see **Figure 11.1**). Most teratogens are in the form of substances that get into the embryo's or fetus's system from the mother through the umbilical cord. These include both legal and illegal drugs, including marijuana, cocaine, and heroin, and prescription drugs such as antibiotics, antidepressants, and sex hormones; as well as alcohol and tobacco—substances that a pregnant woman may not think of as "drugs." The developing embryo or fetus can also be harmed by diseases, such as AIDS, rubella (German measles), and herpes simplex; and by environmental pollutants, such as mercury, lead, and nicotine (from secondhand smoke).

A teratogen's potential effect on prenatal development depends on how early or late in pregnancy the exposure occurs. Recall that development of organ systems is most rapid during the embryonic period, between the 3rd and 8th weeks after conception. This is the time when an agent can most substantially alter the course of development; it may, for example, prevent an organ from developing properly, or fingers and toes from forming. Once an organ such as the kidney or hands or feet have been developed, exposure to a potential teratogen will have little or no effect on future development. This was dramatically illustrated by the drug thalidomide, which was

FOCUS 2

When is the unborn child most susceptible to the effects of teratogens and why?

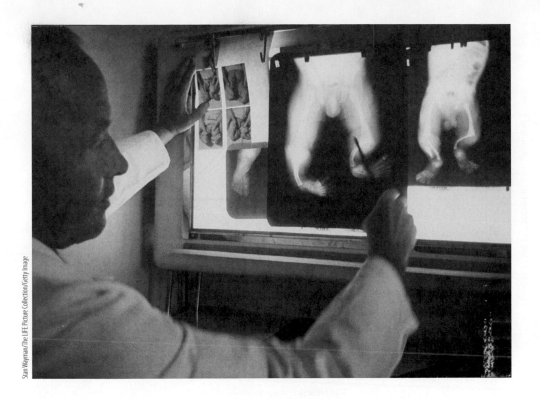

■ Pregnant women who took the drug thalidomide early in pregnancy gave birth to babies with malformed limbs. Women who took the drug later had physically normal babies, illustrating the sensitivity of the embryo to the effects of teratogens.

prescribed to some women in Europe and Asia in the early 1960s to combat morning sickness. (Thalidomide was not approved for use in the United States.) When women took thalidomide during the first 8 weeks of pregnancy, the result was often babies born with deformed limbs, as well as damage to other organ systems. The drug interfered with the development of limb formation and hands and feet. However, these deformations were not found in babies born to women who took the drug later in pregnancy, after limbs and their appendages had already been developed.

It is not just teratogens that embryos and fetuses respond to, but other aspects of experience, such as nutrition and maternal stress. For example, we noted in Chapter 5 that women with poor diets during pregnancy tend to have low-birth-weight infants who then grow to become overweight or obese during childhood. These babies developed "thrifty phenotypes," storing more fat than children whose prenatal diets were more nutritious. In other situations, children who were prenatally exposed to high levels of stress hormones show higher anxiety and fearfulness, temperamental difficulty, impulsivity, reduced executive functions, impaired attention, higher aggression, and risk taking (Glover, 2011; Pluess & Belsky, 2011). Although these can all be viewed as negative consequences of prenatal stress, some of these characteristics (e.g., high levels of aggression and risk taking) may be well suited for children growing up in high-stress environments. Along these lines, Marco Del Giudice (2012) suggests, "The developing fetus can use this information as a 'forecast' of the environmental conditions it will eventually face after birth, and start adjusting its physiological and behavioral profile to match the requirements of the world it will probably encounter" (p. 1615).

Infancy, roughly the first 18 to 24 months after birth, is the time of most rapid developmental change, change that lays the foundation for further development. Human infants are born especially immature in comparison to other primates, in large part because of their big brains. If prenatal development lasted much longer, a newborn's brain would be too large to fit through the birth canal. This means that much brain development that occurs prenatally in other primates occurs after birth in humans. But before we discuss how infants learn about the world into which they emerge, let's look at physical development after birth, focusing on another period of dramatic physical change: puberty and adolescence.

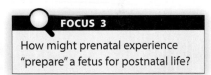

FOCUS 3

How might prenatal experience "prepare" a fetus for postnatal life?

FIGURE 11.2 Growth curves for different parts of the body, expressed in terms of percentage of eventual adult growth Different organ systems and parts of the body develop at different rates.

(Data from Scammon, 1930.)

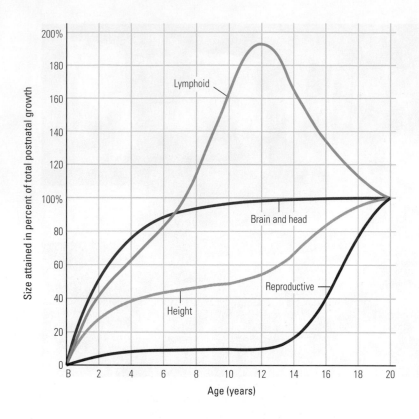

Physical Development: Puberty and Adolescence

FOCUS 4

To what extent do different parts of the body develop at different rates? Why might this be so?

When we think of physical growth, we think of body height and weight, and people certainly get taller and heavier with age. It is not difficult to observe that body growth is relatively rapid during infancy and the preschool years, becomes more gradual over childhood, and accelerates in adolescence. However, there are other parts of the body that are less obviously visible, and they develop at different rates than height, as shown in **Figure 11.2**. As you can see, the curve for height displays the pattern we just described, but the head and brain grow rapidly over the first 5 or 6 years and approach adult levels by age 10. The lymphoid system, which includes the thymus and lymph glands, develops rapidly early in life, greatly exceeding adult dimensions by about age 12, and just as rapidly decreases during adolescence. At the bottom of the graph is the reproductive system, which shows little growth until adolescence.

It is this dramatic upswing in reproductive development that characterizes some of the most studied changes in physical development—those that occur with the onset of **puberty**. Puberty refers to the developmental stage leading up to adolescence when glands associated with the reproductive system begin to enlarge, bringing about changes in physical appearance and behavior. Increases in hormones in both males (androgens, especially testosterone) and females (estrogens and progesterone) contribute to changes in physical stature (the adolescent growth spurt, which typically begins about a year earlier in girls than boys), reproductive ability (the production of sperm in males and viable eggs in females), and emotions and behavior related to sexual attraction.

■ Physical development occurs rapidly during puberty, with girls beginning their growth spurt before boys. Two children with the same birthdays can differ substantially in appearance during adolescence.

Puberty does not happen all at once, but is actually a series of related events, typically spanning 4 or 5 years. For example, in females, initial breast development begins at about 11 years and is mostly completed by 15 or 16 years. A girl's first menstrual period (termed *menarche*) typically occurs at about 13 years of age, although many girls do not become fertile (able to conceive a child) until

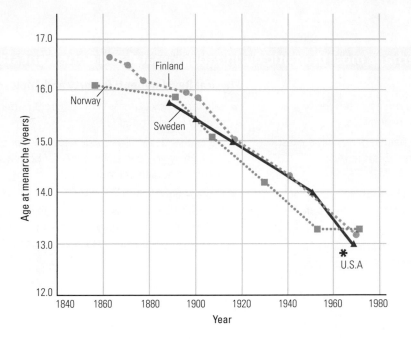

FIGURE 11.3 Historical trends in menarche Data from countries where historical records are available demonstrate that the average age of menarche decreased sharply from the middle of the nineteenth to the middle of the twentieth century. The average age of menarche has not changed appreciably in the past 50 years.

(Data from Tanner, 1990.)

about age 15 or 16 because eggs are not always produced in the first 2 or 3 years of menstrual cycles. A girl's growth spurt starts around age 12, with skeletal growth being complete between 14 and 15 years of age. Similarly, for boys, testes begin to increase in size between 11 and 12 years of age, and the penis increases in size beginning about 13 years, shortly before the male adolescent growth spurt begins. Boys typically have their first nocturnal emission at 14 and develop facial hair between the ages of 15 and 16 (Tanner, 1990). The male voice change begins on average at about age 13, and by age 15 most boys have developed their adult male voice.

These are all average age-of-attainment values, of course, with individual boys and girls showing very wide variation. Nevertheless, on average, the age of menarche has shown substantial decreases over recent historical times. This is illustrated in **Figure 11.3**, which shows the average age of menarche in three European countries over the past 150 years or so, along with the average age in the United States around 1965. As you can see, there was a steady decline in the average age of menarche from 1860 to about 1960 (Tanner, 1990). This trend is generally attributed to better nutrition; indeed, today girls who are overweight attain menarche sooner than other girls, and diet may be associated with other signs of earlier puberty. However, the average age of menarche has not changed substantially in the last 50 years or so. In the United States today, the average age of menarche is 12.6 years for Caucasian females and 12.1 years for African-American females (Steingraber, 2007).

Other pubertal events continue to change over time, most notably breast development. This is clearly shown in a large-scale study conducted by Marcia Herman-Giddens and her colleagues (1997), who studied pubertal development in more than 17,000 girls in the United States between the ages of 3 and 12 years of age. They reported that although the age of menarche remained unchanged since the 1950s, the average age of breast development and presence of pubic hair continues to decline. For example, they found that the average age for breast development was 9.96 years for white girls and 8.87 years for African-American girls, with some girls (1% of white girls and 3% of African-American girls) showing signs of breast development as early as age 3. Researchers have identified several candidates for the cause of this accelerated development, including exposure to passive tobacco smoke, insecticides, arsenic, polybrominated biphenyls (a fire retardant), and chemicals used in common plastics (Blanck et al., 2000; Herman-Giddens et al., 1997). However, as with menarche, hormonal changes associated with obesity are the top potential cause of early breast development.

FOCUS 5

How has the emergence of different aspects of puberty changed over historical time, and what is responsible for these changes?

Physical development is perhaps most dramatic during the prenatal and pubescent stages of life.

Prenatal Development

- The prenatal period is divided into three phases: the zygotic (or germinal), the embryonic, and the fetal.

- Development is most rapid in the head region, with the rest of the body catching up in size later; this is termed *cephalocaudal development*.

- The effects of teratogens are apt to be most severe during the embryonic phase because major organ systems are being formed at this time.

- Other prenatal experiences, such as the availability of nutrition and experiencing high levels of stress, seem to prepare the fetus for postnatal life.

Physical Development: Puberty and Adolescence

- Different body systems show different patterns of change from infancy to adulthood.

- Major changes in physical development occur at puberty, with different aspects of puberty for both boys and girls occurring at different times.

- Average age of menarche decreased from the mid-1800s to about 1960 and has remained stable since. Breast growth and other aspects of pubertal development have accelerated in recent decades, with obesity being a major cause.

How Infants Learn About the Environment

When an infant emerges from the womb, he or she is confronted by a world of sights, sounds, and other sensations that William James (1890/1950) termed "one great blooming, buzzing confusion" (p. 488). How do infants learn about the environment that surrounds them? What do they know, early on, about that world?

The Infant as Explorer

Infants' sensory systems all function at birth (although one sense, vision, is still quite immature). On the day they are born, infants will turn toward sounds, turn toward anything that touches their face, turn away from unpleasant odors, suck a nipple more readily for a sweet liquid than for a sour one, and orient their eyes toward high-contrast or moving visual stimuli (Maurer & Maurer, 1988). Within a short time after birth, they not only respond to stimuli but do so selectively, in ways that seem well designed for learning.

Infants Look Selectively at Novel Objects

FOCUS 6

How does infants' behavior reveal that they are actively exploring their environments with their eyes and that they remember what they have seen?

Hundreds of experiments have shown that babies gaze longer at new stimuli than at familiar ones. When shown a pattern, they look at it intently at first and then, over the course of minutes, look at it less and less—a phenomenon referred to as *habituation*. This decline in attention does not stem from general fatigue; if a new pattern is substituted for the old one, infants immediately increase their looking time—a phenomenon called *dishabituation*. Similarly, if shown the new and old patterns at the same time, they look more at the new one than the old one. This preference for novelty makes sense if we assume that infants are actively trying to learn about their world. They look at new stimuli because they have more to learn from them than from old stimuli, which they have already explored. Be careful interpreting the word "preference" here, however. Infants do not necessarily "like" the novel stimulus more; they merely have a bias to pay attention to what is less familiar.

Infants' bias for looking at novel stimuli is so reliable that developmental psychologists use it to assess infants' abilities to perceive and remember. Babies who look significantly longer at a new stimulus than at one they have already seen must perceive the difference between the two and must, at some level, remember having seen the old one before. In one such experiment, infants as young as 1 day old perceived the difference between two checkerboards with different-sized squares and remembered that difference over the seconds that separated one trial from the next (Friedman, 1972). This was shown by the fact that they looked longer at the checkerboard that they had not seen before when they were given a choice. Later, you will read about research in which infants' selective looking is used to assess their knowledge and expectations about the physical world.

Infants Seek to Control Their Environments

Within a few weeks after birth, infants begin to show a special interest in aspects of the environment that they can control. In one experiment, 2-month-olds smiled and attended much more to a mobile that moved in response to their own bodily movement than to a motor-driven mobile that they could not control (Watson, 1972). In another experiment, 4-month-olds learned quickly to make a particular movement to turn on a small array of lights, but lost interest and responded only occasionally after they became good at this task. When the conditions were changed so that a different movement was needed to turn on the lights, the infants regained interest and made another burst of responses (Papousek, 1969). Their renewed interest must have been generated by the new relationship between a response and the lights, because the lights themselves were unchanged. Apparently, the babies were interested not so much in the lights per se as in their ability to control them.

In still another experiment, infants as young as 2 months, who had learned to turn on a video and sound recording of the *Sesame Street* theme song by pulling strings tied to their wrists, showed facial expressions of anger when the device was disconnected so that they could no longer control it (Lewis et al., 1990). In subsequent, similar experiments, 4- and 5-month-old babies showed facial expressions of both anger and sadness at losing control of their ability to turn on the recording, even when the recording still came on as often as before but under the control of the experimenter rather than themselves (Sullivan & Lewis, 2003). Apparently, it was the loss of control, not the loss of opportunities to see and hear the recording, that upset the infants. The desire to control our environment seems to be a facet of human nature that exists in every phase of development, and its function seems obvious: We, more than any other species, survive by controlling our environment.

Infants Explore Increasingly With Hands and Eyes Together

During their first 3 or 4 months of life, babies, like puppies and other young mammals, put practically anything that they can reach into their mouths. They mouth objects in ways that seem designed to test the objects' properties. With time, however, they gradually give up their puppy ways and explore increasingly in the more uniquely human way, with hands and eyes together, rather than with mouths (Rochat, 1989).

By 5 or 6 months, babies regularly manipulate and explore objects in the sophisticated manner that researchers label *examining* (Ruff, 1986). They hold an object in front of their eyes, turn it from side to side, pass it from one hand to the other, rub it, squeeze it, and in various other ways act as if they are deliberately testing its properties.

FOCUS 7

How does infants' behavior reveal that they are motivated to control their environments and are emotionally involved in retaining control?

■ **A small scientist** By 5 to 6 months of age, infants learn about the properties of objects by manipulating them with their hands while watching intently to observe the effects.

Ariel Skelley/Blend Images/Getty Images

Such actions decline dramatically as the infant becomes familiar with a given object but return in full force when a new object, differing in shape or texture, is substituted for the old one (Ruff, 1986, 1989). As evidence that examining involves focused mental activity, researchers have found that babies are more difficult to distract with bright visual stimuli when they are examining an object than at other times (Oakes & Tellinghuisen, 1994).

Infants do not have to be taught to examine objects. They do it in every culture, whenever objects are in their reach, whether or not such behavior is encouraged. Roger Bakeman and his colleagues (1990) studied the exploratory behavior of infants among the !Kung San, a hunting-and-gathering group of people in Botswana, Africa, who have been relatively uninfluenced by industrialized cultures. (The !K in !Kung stands for a click-like sound that is different from the pronunciation of "K" in the Roman alphabet.) !Kung adults do not make toys for infants or deliberately provide them with objects for play. Yet !Kung babies examine objects that happen to be within their reach—stones, twigs, food items, cooking utensils—in the same manner as do babies in industrialized cultures; and, as in industrialized cultures, their examining increases markedly in frequency and intensity between about 4 and 6 months of age. !Kung adults do not encourage such behavior because they see no reason to, yet they recognize its value and do not discourage it. Their view of child development seems to be well summarized by one of their folk expressions, which can be translated roughly as "Children teach themselves" (Bakeman et al., 1990).

Infants Use Social Cues to Guide Their Exploration

Although babies act upon and explore their environments independently of adult encouragement, they often use cues from adults to guide such actions. Beginning in the latter half of their first year of life, babies regularly exhibit *gaze following*—that is, they watch the eyes of a nearby person and move their own eyes to look at what that person is looking at (Woodward, 2003). Such behavior really does depend on attention to the eyes; if the adult's eyes are closed or covered, the baby does not look preferentially in the direction the adult is facing (Brooks & Meltzoff, 2002). Gaze following ensures that infants will attend to those objects and events that are of greatest interest to their elders, which may be the most important things to attend to and learn about for survival within their culture. It also helps to promote language development. If the adult is naming an object, it is useful to the child to know what object the adult is looking at and naming. Researchers have found that babies who show the most reliable gaze following learn language faster than those who exhibit less gaze following (Brooks & Meltzoff, 2008).

Another achievement during the latter part of the first year is infants' ability to view other people as *intentional agents*—individuals who *cause* things to happen and whose behavior is designed to achieve some goal (Bandura, 2006). This is first clearly seen around 9 months of age when infants engage in **shared attention** (sometimes called *joint attention*) with another person (Tomasello, 2009; Tomasello & Carpenter, 2007). This involves a three-way interaction between the infant, another person, and an object. It usually begins with the adult pointing out objects that both the infant and adult can see. By 12 months of age, infants will point to alert others to objects they are not attending to (Liszkowski et al., 2007), and between 12 and 18 months of age they will point to direct an adult's attention to an object the adult is searching for (Liszkowski et al., 2006).

By the time they can crawl or walk freely on their own (toward the end of their first year), infants engage in what is called **social referencing**—they look at their caregivers' emotional expressions for clues about the possible danger of their own actions (Walden, 1991). In an experiment with 12-month-olds, not one crawled over a slight visual cliff (an apparent 30-centimeter drop-off under a solid glass surface; see **Figure 11.4**) if the mother showed a facial expression of fear, but most crawled over it if her expression was one of joy or interest (Sorce et al., 1985).

How do infants, beginning before 12 months of age, use their observations of adults' behavior to guide their own explorations?

FIGURE 11.4 Is it safe? Babies refused to crawl over the "visual cliff" if they saw an expression of fear on their mother's face, but most crawled over it if her expression showed joy or interest.

In another experiment, 12-month-olds avoided a new toy if the mother showed a facial expression of disgust toward it, but they played readily with it otherwise (Hornik et al., 1987).

Infants' Knowledge of Core Physical Principles

We all share certain assumptions about the nature of physical reality. We assume, for example, that objects continue to exist even when they disappear from view; that two solid objects cannot occupy the same space at the same time; and that if an object moves from one place to another, it must do so along a continuous path. We expect these principles always to be true, and when they seem to be violated, we usually assume that our senses have been somehow deceived, not that the principles have been overturned.

At what age do people begin to make these core assumptions about physical reality? Some theorists, such as Elizabeth Spelke and her colleagues (Spelke, 2000; Spelke & Kinzler, 2007) propose that infants possess *core knowledge* about the physical world, needing relatively little experience with their physical environment to arrive at these insights. Similarly, David Geary (2005) proposed that infants are born with a small set of *skeletal competencies* specialized to make sense of the physical world. Stated another way, this position argues that infants are not born as blank slates, as the seventeenth-century philosopher John Locke argued, but are prepared by evolution to make sense of their physical world so that some things are more easily learned than others.

■ **Peek-a-boo** The results of selective-looking experiments suggest that babies even younger than this one know that objects continue to exist when out of view. Nevertheless, they take delight in having that understanding confirmed, especially when the object is a familiar, friendly person.

Infants Reveal Core Knowledge in Selective-Looking Experiments

Just as babies look longer at novel objects than at familiar ones, they also look longer at unexpected events than at expected ones. Researchers have capitalized on this with many experiments that have used selective looking to assess what infants expect to happen in specific conditions (Baillargeon, 2004, 2008).

A classic example of such a *violation-of-expectation experiment* is illustrated in **Figure 11.5**. First, in the habituation phase, the baby is repeatedly shown a physical event until he or she is bored with it, as indexed by reduced time spent looking at it. In the example shown in the figure, that event is the back-and-forth movement of a hinged screen over a 180-degree arc. Then, in the test phase, the infant is shown one of two variations of the original event. One variation, the *impossible event,* is an illusion, arranged with mirrors or other trickery, that appears to violate one or more core physical principles. In the example, this event is one in which an object placed behind the rotating screen fails to prevent the screen from rotating all the way back. It is as if the object magically disappears each time the screen rotates back and then magically reappears each time the screen rotates forward. The other event, the *possible event,* does not violate any physical principle. In the example, this event is one in which the rotating screen stops in each rotation at the place where it would bump into the object behind it.

Notice that the two test events are designed so that, on purely sensory grounds, the possible event differs more from the original

⦿ FOCUS 9

What is the violation-of-expectation method for studying infants' knowledge of physical principles? With this method, what have researchers discovered about the knowledge of 2- to 4-month-olds?

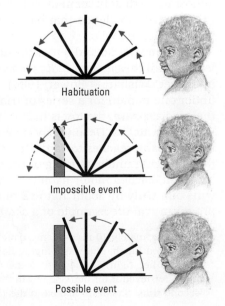

Habituation

Impossible event

Possible event

FIGURE 11.5 Evidence for understanding of object permanence in very young infants After being habituated to the back-and-forth movement of the screen, infants as young as 3.5 months looked longer at the impossible event, in which the screen seemed to go through and obliterate a solid object, than they did at the possible event.

(Research by Baillargeon, 1987.)

habituation event than does the impossible one. Thus, if infants respond simply on the basis of sensory novelty, they should look longest at the possible event. But if they respond from knowledge of physical principles, they should look longest at the impossible event because that differs most from what they would expect to happen. In fact, using the setup shown in Figure 11.5, Renée Baillargeon (1987) found that infants as young as 3.5 months old looked longer at the impossible event than at the possible event. This result is strong evidence that even such young infants understand, in some way, that solid objects do not normally pass through and temporarily obliterate other solid objects.

Similar experiments have demonstrated infants' knowledge of other core principles. For instance, babies as young as 2.5 to 3 months expect an object to appear behind the screen where it was originally placed, not behind a different screen (Baillargeon, 2004); expect a rolling ball to stop at a solid barrier rather than pass through it (Spelke et al., 1992); and expect a stationary ball to remain stationary unless pushed by another object (Spelke et al., 1994). Of course, young infants do not manifest entirely the same expectations about the physical world that adults, or even 2-year-olds, do. Core principles may be present early on, but nuances related to them are acquired with age and experience (Baillargeon, 2008). For example, Baillargeon (1994, 1998) found that 4-month-olds expected a box to fall to the ground when it was released in midair, but did not expect it to fall when it was set on the edge of a shelf with most of its weight hanging off the shelf or when completely unsupported but in contact with a finger. Only by 6 to 7 months did babies show evidence that they expected the unbalanced box to fall, presumably due to their increasing experience with falling (and supported) objects.

Infants Reveal Less Knowledge in Search Tasks Than in Selective-Looking Tasks

The findings supporting infants' early knowledge of core principles surprised many developmental psychologists. Previous research, using a different procedure, had suggested that infants under about 5 months of age lack even the most basic understanding of **object permanence**, the principle that objects continue to exist when out of view. The pioneer of that research was the famous Swiss developmental psychologist Jean Piaget (1954), who tested infants' understanding by having them search for hidden objects. In the simplest of his tests, the *simple hiding problem,* an attractive toy is shown to a baby and then is placed under a napkin as the baby watches. Babies younger than about five months typically follow the toy with their eyes as it disappears under the napkin, but do not reach for it once it is there; they almost immediately seem to lose interest in it. Piaget and his successors interpreted this result as evidence that babies this age completely lack the concept of object permanence.

Between about 6 and 9 months of age, most infants solve the simple hiding problem but fail the *changed-hiding-place problem, or the A-not-B problem,* also developed by Piaget (Wishart & Bower, 1984). In the first phase of this test, the toy is hidden under one napkin for a series of trials, and the baby retrieves it each time. Then, in the crucial phase, the toy is hidden under another napkin, right next to the first, as the baby watches. Despite having watched the object disappear under the new napkin, the baby reaches toward the original napkin. Piaget concluded that at this age the emerging understanding of object permanence is still very fragile; when pitted against a learned motor habit (reaching toward the original hiding place), the habit wins out. Only by about 10 to 12 months do most infants solve this problem. Let us provide a real-life example of a *changed-hiding-place problem*:

> At approximately 10 months, my daughter Heidi was seated in her high chair, having just completed lunch. She was banging her spoon on the tray of the chair when it fell to the floor to her right. She leaned to the right, saw the spoon on the floor, and vocalized to me; I retrieved it for her. She began playing with the spoon again, and it fell to the right a second time. She again leaned to the right, saw the spoon on the floor, and vocalized until

FOCUS 10

How did Jean Piaget test infants' understanding of object permanence? What might explain the discrepancy between Piaget's results and the results of selective-looking experiments?

I returned it to her. Again, she played with the spoon, and again it fell to the floor, but this time to her left. After hearing the clang of the spoon hitting the floor, Heidi leaned to the right to search for the spoon, and she continued her search for several seconds before looking at me with a puzzled expression. Heidi had been watching the spoon at the time it fell. Thus, when it fell the third time, she had both visual and auditory cues to tell her where it must be. But she searched where she had found the vanished object before. She trusted her past experience with the fallen spoon more than her perceptions. At this age, children still understand objects by their actions on them, in these cases by their prior actions (Bjorklund & Causey, 2018, pp. 133–134).

Why do infants younger than 5 months, who appear to understand object permanence in selective-looking experiments, fail even the simplest of Piaget's tests of object permanence? Nobody knows for sure, but a number of researchers have suggested that the difficulty in Piaget's tests has to do with the ability to plan the correct arm and hand movement to obtain the hidden object (Baillargeon, 1998; Keen, 2003). In order to retrieve a hidden object, the baby not only must know where the object is, but also must be able to use that knowledge to guide his or her reaching movement. Babies under 5 months of age have no difficulty reaching for objects that are in full view, but may be unable to use mental images of hidden objects to guide their reaching. Consistent with this interpretation, researchers have found that infants as young as 3 to 4 months old who fail to reach for a hidden object nevertheless *look* at the location where the object was hidden, even after a moment's distraction (Ruffman et al., 2005).

Dramatic improvement in infants' search abilities occurs shortly after they learn to crawl or in other ways move about on their own (Campos et al., 2000). In one experiment, 8-month-olds were tested in a series of search tasks, including a version of Piaget's classic changed-hiding-place problem (Kermoian & Campos, 1988). One group had learned to crawl at least 9 weeks before the tests; a second group had not learned to crawl but had at least 9 weeks of experience moving around in walkers at home; and a third group had neither learned to crawl nor been provided with walkers. Approximately 75% of the babies in the first two groups succeeded on the changed-hiding-place problem, compared with only 13% of those in the third group. For infants to move about on their own, they need to coordinate their vision with their muscular movements in new ways to avoid bumping into objects; as they move, they also see objects from new and varied perspectives. Such experiences may well help them learn to plan all sorts of effective movements, including those involved in retrieving hidden objects.

> **🔍 FOCUS 11**
>
> What evidence suggests that self-produced locomotion promotes rapid development of infants' search abilities?

■ **Self-produced locomotion promotes cognitive development** When babies learn to crawl and are able to move around on their own, they gain new perspectives on their world and make rapid gains in their ability to solve Piagetian search problems.

SECTION REVIEW

Infants actively explore their physical world and know some of its core principles.

Exploring the World Around Them

- Infants prefer novel stimuli, as demonstrated by the fact that they look longer at them. This reliable tendency is used to study infant perception and memory.

- Infants exhibit a strong drive to control their environment; they become upset when control is taken away.

- By 5 or 6 months, infants examine objects with their hands and eyes, focusing on the objects' unique properties.

- From 6 to 12 months of age, infants use their observations of adults to mimic adults' actions, look where adults are looking, use adults' emotional expressions to identify danger or safety, and engage in shared attention.

Knowledge of Core Physical Principles

- Infants as young as 2.5 to 4 months of age have knowledge of core physical principles, revealed by the fact that they look longer at physically impossible events than at physically possible events.

- Search tasks that involve manual reaching appear to show later development of the concept of object permanence, perhaps because reaching requires the infant to form a plan to obtain the hidden object.

- Experience with self-produced locomotion promotes the ability to solve manual search problems.

Three Theories of Children's Mental Development

As children grow from infancy toward adulthood, their thinking becomes ever more logical, ever more effective in solving problems. How can these changes be characterized, and what are the processes through which they develop? Here we shall address these questions from three theoretical perspectives. The first is Piaget's theory, which focuses on the child's actions on the physical world as a driving force for cognitive development. The second is Lev Vygotsky's sociocultural theory, which focuses on the child's interactions with other people as a driving force. The third is the information-processing perspective, which accounts for mental development in terms of maturational changes in basic components of the child's mind.

Piaget's Theory: Role of the Child's Own Actions in Mental Growth

In his long career at the University of Geneva (from the 1920s until his death in 1980), Jean Piaget wrote more than 50 books and hundreds of articles on children's reasoning. His goal was to understand how the adult mind, particularly its capacity for objective reasoning, develops from the child's more primitive abilities. His primary methods were those of observation, testing, and questioning. From his observations of children's conversations and play, he would extract clues about their understanding. He would also present children with specific tasks to solve and question them about their reasons for the solutions they offered. From this work, Piaget developed an elaborate, comprehensive theory of cognitive development.

Piaget's fundamental idea was that mental development derives from the child's own actions on the physical environment. According to Piaget, children in their play and exploration are constantly striving to figure out what they can do with the various objects that exist in their world. By acting on objects, children develop mental representations, called **schemes**, which are mental blueprints for actions. More specifically, Piaget used the term *schemes* to refer to a mental representation of a bodily movement or of something that a person can *do* with an object or category of objects. The earliest schemes, according to Piaget, are closely tied to specific objects and are called forth only by an object's immediate presence. Thus, a young infant might have a sucking scheme most applicable to nipples, a grasping and shaking scheme most applicable to rattles, and a smiling scheme most applicable to human faces. As children grow older, they develop new, more sophisticated, more abstract schemes that are less closely tied to the immediate environment or to actual physical actions. They become schemes for mental actions.

Schemes Develop Through Assimilation and Accommodation

Piaget conceived of the growth of schemes as involving two complementary processes: assimilation and accommodation.

Assimilation is the process by which new experiences are incorporated into existing schemes. Piaget was a biologist by training, and he considered the assimilation of experiences to be analogous to the assimilation of food. Two people may eat the same type of food, but the food will be assimilated into the tissues differently, depending on the inner structures involved in digestion and building the body. Moreover, just as nondigestible foods will not result in body growth, new experiences that are too different from existing schemes to be mentally digested will not result in mental growth. A calculator given to an infant will not contribute to the child's arithmetic skills because the infant has no calculating scheme into which to assimilate the calculator's functions. Instead, the infant will probably assimilate the calculator into his or her already well-developed sucking scheme or banging scheme.

Few new stimuli perfectly fit an existing scheme. Assimilation usually requires that existing schemes expand or change somewhat to accommodate the new object or event. Appropriately, Piaget referred to this process as *accommodation*. In Piaget's theory, the mind and its schemes are not like a brick wall, which just grows bigger as each new brick (unit of knowledge) is added; they are more like a spider's web, which changes its entire shape somewhat as each new thread is added. The web accommodates to the thread while the thread is assimilated into the web. The addition of new information to the mind changes somewhat the structure of schemes that are already present.

Bill Anderson/Science Source

FOCUS 12

In Piaget's theory, how do schemes develop through assimilation and accommodation?

■ **Jean Piaget** Because of his interest in the influence of the environment on children's cognitive development, Piaget preferred to observe children in natural settings. Here he is shown during a visit to a nursery school.

Children Behave Like Little Scientists

In Piaget's view, infants and children at play behave like little scientists. Their exploratory play—in which they manipulate objects in all sorts of ways to see what happens—can be thought of as experimentation. They are most strongly motivated to explore those objects and situations that they partly but do not fully understand. Stated differently, in Piaget's terms, they are most drawn to experiences that can be *assimilated* into existing schemes, but not too easily, so that *accommodation* is required. This natural tendency leads children to direct their playful activities in ways that maximize their mental growth.

Consider, for example, an infant who already has a scheme for stacking objects, which includes the notion that an object placed on top of another will remain on top. One day this infant happens to place an object above an open container and, instead of remaining on top, the object falls into the container. This observation is intriguing to the infant because it seems to violate his stacking scheme. As a result, the infant may spend lots of time dropping various objects into various containers. Such exploration eventually leads the infant to modify (accommodate) his

FOCUS 13

What is Piaget's "little scientist" view of children's behavior? How is it illustrated by the example of an infant playing with containers and by an experiment with preschool children allowed to play with a two-lever toy?

■ **Accommodation** This 11-month-old may be accommodating her "stacking scheme" to assimilate the experience of one object fitting inside another. From such experiences, a new "fits inside" scheme may develop.

FOCUS 14

In Piaget's theory, what is the special value of operations?

FOCUS 15

In Piaget's theory, what are the four stages and the ages roughly associated with each?

---

stacking scheme to include the notion that if one object is hollow and open-topped, a smaller object placed over its top will fall inside. At the same time, other schemes that include the notion that two objects cannot occupy the same place at the same time may also undergo accommodation.

As another illustration of the little scientist concept, consider an experiment performed by Laura Schulz and Elizabeth Bonawitz (2007). These researchers presented preschool children (ages 4 to 5), one at a time, with a box that had two levers sticking out of it. Pressing one lever caused a toy duck to pop up through a slit on top of the box, and pressing the other lever caused a puppet made of drinking straws to pop up. The box was demonstrated to different children in two different ways. In one demonstration condition, each lever was pressed separately, so the child could see the effect that each lever produced when pressed. In the other condition, the two levers were always pressed simultaneously, so the child could not know which lever controlled which object. After the demonstration, each child was allowed to play with the two-lever box or with a different toy.

The result was that children who had only seen the two levers operated simultaneously chose to play much more with the demonstrated box than with the new toy, while the opposite was true for the other children. The logical interpretation is this: The children who could see, from the demonstration, what each lever did were no longer much interested in the box because they had little more to learn from it. In contrast, those who had only seen the two levers pressed simultaneously wanted to play with the box so they could try each lever separately and discover whether it moved the duck, or the puppet, or both. In related work, preschool children learned more about the functions of a novel toy when they were simply allowed to play with the toy than when they were shown one function of the toy (Bonawitz et al., 2011). Consistent with Piaget's theory, the children's play was oriented toward discovery, not toward repetition of already known effects.

Reversible Actions (Operations) Promote Development

As children grow beyond infancy, according to Piaget, the types of actions most conducive to their mental development are those called **operations**, defined as *reversible actions*—actions whose effects can be undone by other actions. Rolling a ball of clay into a sausage shape is an operation because it can be reversed by rolling the clay back into a ball. Turning a light on by pushing a switch up is an operation because it can be reversed by pushing the switch back down. Young children perform countless operations as they explore their environments, and in doing so, they gradually develop *operational schemes*—mental blueprints that allow them to think about the reversibility of their actions.

Understanding the reversibility of actions provides a foundation for understanding basic physical principles. The child who knows that a clay ball can be rolled into a sausage shape and then back into a ball of the same size as it was before has the basis for knowing that the amount of clay must remain the same as the clay changes shape—the principle of *conservation of substance*. The child who can imagine that pushing a light switch back down will restore the whole physical setup to its previous state has the basis for understanding the principle of cause and effect, at least as applied to the switch and the light.

Four Types of Schemes, Four Stages of Development

Piaget conceived of four types of schemes, which represent increasingly sophisticated ways of understanding the physical environment. His research convinced him that the four types develop successively, in stages roughly correlated with the child's age (see **Table 11.1**).

The Sensorimotor Stage The most primitive schemes in Piaget's theory are ***sensorimotor schemes***, which provide a foundation for acting on objects that are present but not for thinking about objects that are absent. During the sensorimotor

TABLE 11.1 Piaget's theory: Periods and characteristics

Period and approximate age range	Major characteristics
Sensorimotor: birth to 2 years	Intelligence is limited to the infant's own actions on the environment. Cognition progresses from the exercise of reflexes (for example, sucking, visual orienting) to the beginning of symbolic functioning.
Preoperations: 2 to 7 years	Intelligence is symbolic, expressed via language, imagery, and other modes, permitting children to mentally represent and compare objects out of immediate perception. Thought is intuitive rather than logical and is egocentric, in that children have a difficult time taking the perspective of another.
Concrete operations: 7 to 11 years	Intelligence is symbolic and logical. (For example, if A is greater than B and B is greater than C, then A must be greater than C.) Thought is less egocentric. Children's thinking is limited to concrete phenomena and their own past experiences; that is, thinking is not abstract.
Formal operations: 11 to 16 years	Children are able to make and test hypotheses; possibility dominates reality. Children are able to introspect about their own thought processes and, generally, can think abstractly.

Source: With permission from Bjorklund, D. F., & Causey, K. (2018). *Children's thinking: Cognitive development and individual differences* (sixth edition). San Francisco: Sage, p. 160.

stage (from birth to roughly 2 years of age), thought and overt physical action are one and the same. The major task in this stage is to develop classes of schemes specific for different categories of objects. Objects the child explores become assimilated into schemes for sucking, shaking, banging, squeezing, twisting, dropping, and so on, depending on the objects' properties. Eventually the schemes develop in such a way that the child can use them as mental symbols to represent particular objects and classes of objects in their absence, and then they are no longer sensorimotor schemes.

The Preoperational Stage *Preoperational schemes* emerge from sensorimotor schemes and enable the child to think beyond the here and now. Children in the preoperational stage (roughly from age 2 to 7) have a well-developed ability to symbolize objects and events that are absent, and in their play they delight in exercising that ability (Piaget, 1962). Put a saucepan into the hands of a preschooler, and it is magically transformed into a ray gun or a guitar—the saucepan becomes a symbol in the child's play. The schemes at this stage are called preoperational because, although they can represent absent objects, they do not permit the child to think about the reversible consequences of actions.

According to Piaget, understanding at the preoperational stage is based on appearances rather than principles. If you roll a ball of clay into a sausage shape and ask the child if the shape now contains more than, less than, or the same amount of clay as before, the child will respond in accordance with how the clay looks. Noting that the sausage is longer than the ball was, one preoperational child might say that the sausage has more clay than the ball had. Another child, noting that the sausage is thinner than the ball, might say that the sausage has less clay. (For another test of operational thinking, see **Figure 11.6** on page 418.)

What does it mean to say that preoperational children are now able to use symbols? In everyday language, the word *symbol* typically refers to external referents for objects and events. For example, a photograph of an object is a substitute for the real thing—it is a symbolic representation of an object that is not physically present. Think of the magnets in the shape of candy bars, apples, and miniature beer mugs that adorn many refrigerator doors; they are, in actuality, only magnets that

FIGURE 11.6 A test of conservation of liquid Although she knew that the two tall glasses contained the same amount of liquid and watched the contents of one glass being poured into the short glass, this child still points to the tall glass when asked, "Which has more?" She uses perception rather than logic to answer the question.

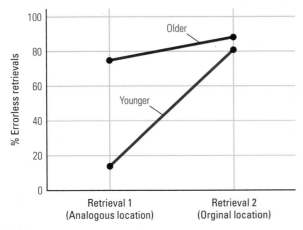

FIGURE 11.7 The number of errorless retrievals (correctly locating the hidden toy) for 2.5-year-olds (younger) and 3-year-olds (older) on a model task. Retrieval 1 refers to finding the toy in the real room, and Retrieval 2 refers to finding the toy in the original location (i.e., remembering where the toy was hidden in the scale model). Although the younger children remembered where the toy in the scale model was hidden, they were not able to use the model to guide their search in the "real" room.

(Data from DeLoache, 1987).

symbolize something else. Judy DeLoache (2010; DeLoache & Marzolf, 1992) has referred to the knowledge that an entity can stand for something other than itself as ***representational insight***, and she and others have shown that young children's ability to use symbols increases gradually over the toddler and preschool years. For example, in one set of experiments, Deloache (1987) asked 2- and 3-year-old children to find a toy hidden in a room. Before searching in the room, however, an experimenter pointed out the hiding place of the toy to the children using a scale model of the real room. Children were then given the opportunity to find the toy in the real room. The results of this study are shown in **Figure 11.7**, separately for older (3-year-old) and younger (2.5-year-old) children. As you can see, both the younger and older children performed well when retrieving the toy from the scale model, showing that there was nothing wrong with their memory. However, only the 3-year-old children were successful in retrieving the toy in the real room.

Why was this task so difficult for the young children? In subsequent studies by DeLoache and others (DeLoache, 1991; Jowkar-Baniani & Schmuckler, 2011; Preissler & Bloom, 2007), it was found that young children had a difficult time treating the scale model as a symbol (i.e., something that represents what's in the real room) because it is a salient and interesting object on its own. They were unable to engage in *dual representation*, treating an object as *both* a symbol and an object itself. Young children were better able to find the toy in the real room when photographs were used—photographs being less interesting than scale models—or by making the model less interesting (e.g., by viewing it through a window).

This and related research suggests that, as Piaget proposed, young children are able to use one object to represent another, but their ability to do so improves with age and is shown in some contexts but not others. Concerning the development of dual representation, DeLoache and Donald Marzolf (1992) summarize the research findings: "Young children are capable of responding to a single entity either concretely, as an object itself, or abstractly, as a representation of something else. It is very difficult for them to do both at once, that is, to achieve dual representation" (p. 328).

The Concrete-Operational Stage Although (or perhaps because) preoperational children have not yet internalized an understanding of operations, they continually produce operations as they explore their environment. As they push, pull, squeeze, mix, and so on, they gradually develop ***concrete-operational schemes*** and eventually enter the *concrete-operational stage* (roughly from age 7 to 11). These schemes permit a child to think about the reversible consequences of actions and thereby provide the basis for understanding physical principles such as conservation of substance and cause and effect (Piaget, 1927).

A concrete-operational child who has had experience with clay will correctly state that the sausage has the same amount of clay as the ball from which it was rolled because it can be rolled back into that ball. A concrete-operational child who has had experience with bicycles will correctly say that the chain is crucial to the bicycle's movement but the fender is not because the child can picture the reversible consequences of removing each and knows that the pedals can move the wheels only if there is a physical connection between the two.

The earliest schemes for operations are referred to as *concrete* because they are still tied closely to the child's actual experiences in the world. The child might have schemes, for example, for the conservation of clay rolled into various shapes and of fluids poured from one container to another, yet still lack an understanding of conservation of substance as a general principle that applies regardless of the type of substance.

Although the effective use of operations and the reversibility of thought may be the hallmark differences between preoperational and concrete-operational children, Piaget described several other features of cognition that differentiate preoperational from concrete-operational children. One such difference is **centration** versus **decentration**. According to Piaget, preoperational children's attention is focused on the most salient aspect of their perceptual fields, which Piaget called centration. In contrast, concrete-operational children can separate themselves from specific aspects of a perceptual array and attend to and make decisions based on the entire perceptual field, which Piaget called decentration. Consider, for example, the conservation of liquid task (Figure 11.6, p. 418). Children are shown two identical tall, thin glasses of liquid. They then watch as the liquid in one glass is poured into a shorter, stouter glass, with the result that the liquid level in the new glass is much lower than in the original glass. When asked if both glasses now have the same amount of liquid, young children typically say "no," there is more in the taller glass. They cannot ignore the difference in height when making their decision. In contrast, concrete operational children can ignore the perceptual difference (that is, they can decenter), making it easier for them to realize that the amount of liquid in the two glasses must be the same despite the difference in appearance.

Perceptual centration of preoperational children can also be seen in how they often judge the age of a person by his or her height (Piaget, 1929). Consider, for instance, the 5-year-old who told her 35-year-old, 4-foot-11-inch mother that she was the "youngest mommy in the whole neighborhood." In actuality, she was the shortest mommy in the whole neighborhood and, if truth be known, one of the oldest among her daughter's friends. Here's another example (from Bjorklund & Causey, 2018, p. 168):

> As a young graduate student, I (DB) was finishing a day of testing at a kindergarten when I ran into the mother of one of the children. We talked for a while about the project, and then she said she was surprised to see that I was so young. She had questioned her son about me, and he had told her that I was older than his mother and much older than his teacher. In reality, I was 22 years old at the time, the child's mother looked to be in her early 30s, and his teacher was a woman nearing retirement. How could a 5-year-old child be so far off? The answer is that I am about 6 feet tall, the boy's mother was about 5-feet-3-inches, and his teacher was a petite woman, likely no more than 5-feet tall. To this child's mind (and eyes), I was a good "foot older" than his teacher.

Another feature that differentiates preoperational and concrete-operational thinkers is **egocentricity**. Piaget used the term *egocentricity* to describe young children's intellectual perspective. Young children interpret the world through their own perspective and generally assume that others see the world as they do. Concrete-operational children, in contrast, are better able to take the point of view of others. According to Piaget, this egocentric perspective permeates young children's entire cognitive life, influencing their perceptions, their language, and their social interactions. For example, 6-year-old Alese is in first grade and has an older brother; therefore, she

FOCUS 16

What are two ways, other than reversibility of operations, that preoperational and concrete-operational children differ?

assumes that all first-graders have older siblings and can never be the eldest child in their family.

Although egocentric thinking is usually viewed negatively (it's immature, after all), it may provide some advantages for young children in some contexts (Bjorklund, 1997b; Bjorklund & Green, 1992). People in general learn and remember information better when it is referenced to themselves (for example, when one is asked to determine how words on a list or events in a story relate to you) than when no self-referencing is done (Mood, 1979; Ross et al., 2011). Young children's tendencies to relate new information to themselves might thus give them a learning advantage (see Bjorklund & Sellers, 2014).

The Formal-Operational Stage During the concrete-operational stage, the child begins to notice certain similarities about the operations that can be performed on different entities. For instance, the child who understands that the amount of clay remains the same no matter what shape it is molded into, and that the amount of water remains the same no matter what the shape of the glass it is poured into, may begin to understand the principle of conservation of substance as a general principle, applicable to all substances. In this way, according to Piaget, the child develops *formal-operational schemes*, which represent abstract principles that apply to a wide variety of objects, substances, or situations. When such schemes characterize a significant portion of a person's thinking, the person is said to be in the *formal-operational stage* (which begins roughly at the onset of adolescence and continues throughout adulthood). Formal-operational schemes permit a person to think theoretically and apply principles even to actions that cannot actually be performed (Inhelder & Piaget, 1958).

With formal operations, adolescents can contemplate not just things that "are" (i.e., concrete entities), but also things that might be, such as world peace, universal religion, or changes in the legal system. They can "think about thinking" and extend principles into hypothetical realms that neither they nor anyone else has actually experienced. While the concrete-operational reasoner is limited to empirical (fact-based) science and arithmetic, the formal-operational reasoner is capable of theoretical (principle-based) science and formal mathematics.

For Piaget, formal-operational thinking is the epitome of logical thought. However, subsequent research has shown that most adults do not use formal-operational abilities even though they can (Capon & Kuhn, 1979), and such thinking is rare in cultures where formal schooling is not the norm (Cole, 1990; Dasen, 1977). In addition, people are more apt to display formal-operational thought in areas in which they are more knowledgeable. For example, in one study college students solved a series of formal-operational problems, and they performed best when the problems were in their area of expertise—physics majors on physics problems, political science majors on political problems, and English majors on literary problems (De Lisi & Staudt, 1980; see **Figure 11.8**). Thus, although many people are able to use formal-operational logic as described by Piaget, most of us usually fail to do so. In the words of Peter Wason and Philip Johnson-Laird (1972): "At best, we can all think like logicians: At worst, logicians all think like us" (p. 245).

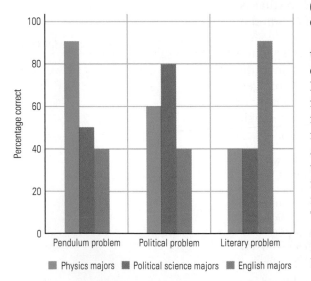

FIGURE 11.8 Percentage of college students displaying formal thought College students performed best on formal-operational problems in their area of expertise: physics majors on physics problems, political science majors on political science problems, and English majors on English problems. (Data from De Lisi & Staudt, 1980).

Criticism of Piaget's Theory of Stages

Piaget's theory has played a dominant role in motivating developmental psychologists to focus more closely than they had before on children's actions and on the ways that those actions promote mental growth. The concepts of assimilation and accommodation and the idea that operations contribute significantly to cognitive development are still much valued by many developmental psychologists. Especially valued is the general idea that children actively build their own minds through their exploration of the world around them.

The most frequent criticisms of Piaget's theory today center on his concept of developmental stages (Kohler, 2008). Piaget himself acknowledged that the transitions from stage to stage are gradual, not abrupt. His own research convinced him that each new type of scheme develops slowly, over the course of years, and that a child at any given point in development might use a more advanced type of scheme for one class of problems while still using a more primitive type for other problems. Subsequent research, however, has led many developmental psychologists to reject the whole concept that people think in fundamentally different ways at different ages.

Much research suggests that Piaget underestimated the mental abilities of infants and young children and overestimated those of adolescents and adults. Earlier in this chapter you read about violation-of-expectation experiments showing that infants as young as 3 months expect objects to continue to exist when out of view, contrary to Piaget's assertion that infants in the sensorimotor stage cannot think of absent objects. Children as young as 4 or 5 years can pass at least some tests of concrete-operational reasoning if the problems are presented clearly, without distracting information, and with words that the child understands (McGarrigle & Donaldson, 1975; Siegler & Svetina, 2006); and other researchers have successfully trained concrete-operational children to perform formal-operational tasks (Adey & Shayer, 1992; Stone & Day, 1978).

Piaget has had a greater impact on developmental psychology than any other person. As one scholar quoted by Harry Beilin (1992) put it, "assessing the impact of Piaget on developmental psychology is like assessing the impact of Shakespeare on English literature or Aristotle on philosophy—impossible" (p. 191). Although many details of Piaget's theory are questioned today, he uncovered many important phenomena, and while his account of development is not fully accurate, it provides a reasonable picture of the behavior of most children most of the time and a good jumping-off point for further investigation.

FOCUS 17

Why do many of today's developmental psychologists doubt Piaget's theory of stages of mental development?

Vygotsky's Theory: Role of the Sociocultural Environment in Mental Growth

Children do not develop in a social vacuum. They develop in a sociocultural milieu in which they interact constantly with other people and with products of their cultural history. The person most often credited with originating the sociocultural perspective on cognitive development is Lev Vygotsky, a Russian scholar who died in 1934 at age 38, after devoting just 10 years to formal research and writing in psychology.

Vygotsky (1934/1962) agreed with Piaget that the main force for development is the child's active interaction with the environment, but he disagreed with Piaget's conception of the relevant environment. Whereas Piaget emphasized the child's interaction with the physical environment, Vygotsky emphasized the child's interaction with the social environment. Vygotsky proposed that children's thinking does not develop in a vacuum but is inherently *sociocultural*. It is affected by the values, beliefs, and tools of intellectual adaptation found in a child's culture. Because these values and intellectual tools can vary substantially from culture to culture, and within a culture over time, Vygotsky believed that neither the course nor the content of intellectual growth was as "universal" as Piaget and others had assumed. In Vygotsky's view, cognitive development is largely a matter of internalizing the symbols, knowledge, ideas, and modes of reasoning that have evolved over the course of history and constitute the culture into which the child is born.

The distinction between Vygotsky's and Piaget's perspectives can be illustrated by applying those perspectives to a story, told by Piaget (1970), about how a mathematician friend of his had, as a child, become fascinated by mathematics:

FOCUS 18

How does Vygotsky's perspective on cognitive development differ from Piaget's?

> When he was a small child, he was counting pebbles one day; he lined them up in a row, counted them from left to right, and got to ten. Then, just for fun, he counted them from

right to left to see what number he would get, and was astonished that he got ten again. He put the pebbles in a circle and counted them, and once again there were ten. And no matter how he put the pebbles down, when he counted them, the number came to ten. He discovered there what is known in mathematics as commutativity—that is, the sum is independent of the order.

The story is prototypically Piagetian. The child, through acting on physical objects (pebbles), discovers and is exhilarated by a core principle of mathematics (commutativity). As Piaget goes on to explain, "The knowledge that this future mathematician discovered that day was drawn, then, not from the physical properties of the pebbles, but from the actions that he carried out on the pebbles."

How might Vygotsky have reacted to this story? It was told long after Vygotsky had died, but we imagine him asking: "Where did that young boy learn to count in the first place? Of all the things he might do with pebbles, why did he decide that counting them was worthwhile?" Vygotstky might have gone on to say that the answer lies in the boy's social environment. He was growing up in a culture where number words are in the air and people value counting. He may have discovered with pebbles that day the principle of commutativity, but his social environment had prepared him to make that discovery.

Although Vygotsky saw cognitive development as inseparable from its cultural context, neither he nor modern advocates of sociocultural theory would consider culture and development to be independent of biology. Quite the opposite. This is captured in Mary Gauvain's (2001) statement that "cognitive development is an active, constructive process that involves beings who are evolutionarily predisposed to live and learn in social context with other 'like-minded' beings. They are like-minded in terms of both the neurological system available and the social requirements that are in place" (p. 63).

Tools of Intellectual Adaptation

FOCUS 19

What is Vygotsky's concept of tools of intellectual adaptation? How can such tools influence the course of cognitive development?

Vygotsky believed that children learn to think, in part, as a function of the ***tools of intellectual adaptation*** that their culture provides. Such tools include number words, alphabets; and objects like pencils, books, abacuses, calculators, and computers. Children may still discover concepts such as commutativity through their active manipulation of objects as Piaget suggested, but they do so with the tools their culture provides them, and usually with the implicit assistance of significant others in their local environment.

Consider the way a culture's language represents numbers and how that may influence quantitative thinking. The languages of some hunter-gatherer groups contain very few number words. For instance, the language of the Pirahã of Brazil has only three number words, which, translated to English, are *one, two,* and *more than two*. The Pirahã do not count. In one experiment, tribe members were shown sets of nuts containing from one to nine nuts. Then the researcher placed the nuts in a can and drew them out one by one while asking, as each nut was removed, if any nuts were left in the can. Most of the tribe members were correct for one, two, or three nuts, but were incorrect for larger sets (Gordon, 2004). If the Pirahã wanted to keep exact counts of things or to think mathematically, they would have to start by inventing or learning number words. However, Pirahã children who learn Portuguese (the dominant language in Brazil) are able to do addition and subtraction with larger quantities. This supports the view that the language's ability to represent numbers is responsible for the pattern of numerical thinking in these cultures (Gordon, 2004).

A more subtle linguistic effect on numerical reasoning may lie in the comparison of people who speak English or certain other European languages with those who speak Asian languages such as Chinese, Japanese, and Korean. Asian children greatly outperform American and European children in mathematics at every stage of their schooling. Usually that effect is attributed to differences in how mathematics is taught, but some researchers have argued that the difference may stem at least partly from a difference in language (Miller et al., 1995; Miura & Okamoto, 2003).

In English and other European languages the number words do not precisely mirror the base-10 number system that is used in all of arithmetic, but they do so in Chinese, Japanese, and Korean. While we count *one, two, . . . , nine, ten, eleven, twelve, thirteen, . . . , twenty, twenty-one, . . .*, the speakers of the Asian languages count (if their words were translated literally into English) *one, two, . . . , nine, ten, ten one, ten two, ten three, . . . , two-tens, two-tens one, ...* The words *eleven* and *twelve* give the English-speaking child no clue at all that the number system is based on groups of 10, whereas *ten one* and *ten two* make that fact abundantly clear to the Asian child. Even many English-speaking adults do not know that *teen* means "ten" (Fuson & Kwon, 1992), and children do not automatically think of *twenty* as "two tens." Because the Asian words make the base-10 system transparent, Asian children might develop an implicit grasp of that system and thereby gain an advantage in learning arithmetic.

Consider children learning to add two-digit numbers—say, 34 plus 12. English-speaking children pronounce the problem (aloud or to themselves) as "*thirty-four* plus *twelve*," and the words give no hint as to how to solve it. Chinese-speaking children, however, pronounce the problem (in effect) as "*three-tens four* plus *ten two*," and the words themselves point to the solution. In the two numbers together, there are four tens (*three tens* plus *one ten*) and six ones (*four* plus *two*), so the total is *four-tens six* (forty-six).

Consistent with this view, a number of experiments have shown that children who speak Asian languages have a much better implicit understanding of the base-10 system, even before they begin formal mathematics training, than do children who speak European languages. In one experiment, for example, 6-year-olds in the United States, and in France and Sweden (where number words contain irregularities comparable to those in English) were compared with 6-year-olds in China, Japan, and Korea on a task that directly assessed their use of the base-10 system (Miura et al., 1994). All the children had recently begun first grade and had received no formal training in mathematics beyond simple counting.

Each was presented with a set of white and purple blocks and was told that the white blocks represented units (ones) and the purple blocks represented tens. The experimenter explained, "Ten of these white blocks are the same as one purple block," and set out 10 whites next to a purple one to emphasize the equivalence. Each child was then asked to lay out sets of blocks to represent specific numbers—11, 13, 28, 30, and 42. The results were striking. The Asian children made their task easier by using the purple blocks correctly on over 80% of the trials, but the American and European children did so on only about 10%. While the typical Asian child set out four purples and two whites to represent 42, the typical American or European child laboriously counted out 42 white blocks. When they were subsequently asked to think of a different method to represent the numbers, most of the American and European children attempted to use the purple blocks, but made mistakes in about half the trials.

Differences in the way languages represent numbers actually reflect subtle differences in how a culture's tools of intellectual adaptation can influence how children learn to think. Consider the drastic changes in technology that occurred over the latter part of the twentieth century and into the current one. Computers and the many related devices (smartphones, iPads) and formats change the way children learn to think and transform them into very different adults. Recall our discussion in Chapter 10 of the Flynn effect, the continual increase in IQ scores over the course of the twentieth century. Flynn (2012) argued that the increase is due mainly to changes in modern life, including greater use of technology.

Most college students today, and certainly nearly all who will follow them, are *digital natives,* people who grew up with digital media and take them for granted. Older people who grew up in the age before desktop computers (including your two authors) can learn to use the new technology, but rarely find that it comes easily or spontaneously to them. Computer (and smartphone) literacy is like a first language

FOCUS 20

How might the number words of Asian languages help children learn the base-10 number system more easily than American and European children? What evidence suggests that they do learn the base-10 system earlier?

■ American children lag behind East Asian children in mathematical ability. Although there are numerous reasons for this difference, one seems to be the way European and Asian languages represent numbers.

"Big deal, an A in math. That Would be a D in any other country."

FOCUS 21

How might being a "digital native" influence how children today learn to think?

for most people under 40 today, whereas it is like a second language to most people over 40. Such differences in the availability of computers at an early age surely affect how people learn to think.

Access to digital media varies not only between generations but also between developed and developing cultures and within a culture. For instance, a 2012 survey of American homes revealed that 80% of white and 83% of Asian adults 25 years and older used the Internet, compared to 68% for black and 64% for Latino adults (U.S. Census Bureau, 2014). Such differences in access to the Internet likely translate to differences in the ability to use and take advantage of modern technology.

The Role of Collaboration and Dialogue in Mental Development

FOCUS 22

What is the "zone of proximal development," and how does it relate to children's cognitive development?

Vygotsky's fundamental idea is that development occurs first at the social level and then at the individual level. People learn to converse with words (a social activity) before they learn to think with words (a private activity). People also learn how to solve problems in collaboration with more competent others before they can solve the same kinds of problems alone. Vygotsky (1935/1978) coined the term *zone of proximal development* to refer to the realm of activities that a child can do in collaboration with more competent others but cannot yet do alone. According to Vygotsky, children's development is promoted most efficiently through their behavior within their zones of proximal development (Gauvain, 2013; Gauvain & Perez, 2016).

In research at an alternative, age-mixed school, Jay Feldman and I (Peter Gray) found many examples of collaboration between adolescents and younger children that illustrate Vygotsky's concept of a zone of proximal development (Gray & Feldman, 2004). In one case, a teenage boy helped a 5-year-old girl find her lost shoes by asking her to think of all the places she had been that day and all the places where she had already looked. Through such suggestions, the teenager added structure to the little girl's thinking, enabling her to think and search more systematically than she could have done on her own. Such collaboration not only helped the child to find her shoes but also probably promoted her mental development by suggesting questions that she might ask herself to guide future searches for missing objects.

Related to the concept of the zone of proximal development is the concept of *scaffolding* (Wood et al., 1976). Scaffolding occurs when experts are sensitive to the abilities of a novice and provide responses that guide the novice to gradually increase his or her understanding of a problem. Imagine that 4-year-old Sage is trying to assemble a puzzle. She appears to understand that the pieces interlock in some way, but her seemingly random attempts get her nowhere. Sage's mother notices this and places pieces with matching parts close together and points this out to Sage, who puts the two pieces together. Sage's mother then collects several pieces that have the same color and asks Sage to put some of these pieces together. After several failed attempts, Sage succeeds. Her mother repeats the process and Sage continues to put the puzzle pieces together, looking for help from her mother less often. Now, rather than collecting potentially matching pieces, her mother merely tells Sage to look for pieces with matches. Sage's mother reduces the amount of support as Sage improves and is able to do more of the task on her own.

From a Vygotskian perspective, critical thinking—in adults as well as children—derives largely from the social, collaborative activity of dialogue. In actual dialogue, one person states an idea and another

Clarissa Leahy/Getty Images

■ **In the zone** This boy may not be quite ready to repair his bicycle himself, but he can with a little help and advice from his dad. Vygotsky pointed out that skill development often occurs best when children collaborate with more skilled others to do things that are within the child's *zone of proximal development*.

responds with a question or comment that challenges or extends the idea. In the back-and-forth exchange, the original statement is clarified, revised, used as the foundation for building a larger argument, or rejected as absurd. From many such experiences we develop the capacity for internal self-dialogue so that we (or what may seem like voices within us that represent our friends and critics) question and extend our own private thoughts and ideas and in that way improve them or throw them out. Consistent with Vygotsky's view, researchers have found that students who engage in covert dialogues with authors as they read, or who explain ideas they are studying or logic problems they are working on to other people, real or imagined, acquire a more complete understanding of what they are reading or studying than do students who do not engage in such activities (Chi et al., 1994; Mercer & Littleton, 2007).

The Child as Apprentice

While Piaget's child can be characterized as a little scientist performing experiments on the world and discovering its nature, Vygotsky's child can be characterized as an apprentice (Rogoff, 1990, 2003). In Vygotsky's view, children are born into a social world in which people routinely engage in activities that are important to the culture. Children are attracted to those activities and seek to participate. At first their roles are small, but they grow as the children gain skill and understanding. From this view, cognitive development is a progression not so much from simple tasks to more complex ones as from small roles to larger roles in the activities of the social world. Barbara Rogoff (1990, 2003) has documented many ways by which children in various cultures involve themselves in family and community activities and learn from those activities.

■ **Working in the zone** Parents working in their children's zone of proximal development scaffold children's problem solving, giving them more support early on, and less support as children take more responsibility for task performance.

One prediction of the apprenticeship analogy is that people who grow up in different cultures will acquire different cognitive abilities. A child surrounded by people who drive cars, use computers, and read books will not learn the same mental skills as a child surrounded by people who hunt game, weave blankets, and tell stories far into the night. The apprenticeship analogy also reminds us that logic itself is not the goal of mental development; the goal is to function effectively as an adult in one's society. To achieve that goal, children must learn to get along with other people and to perform economically valuable tasks. In our society, such tasks may involve for some people the kind of mathematical and scientific reasoning that Piaget labeled *formal-operational*; but in another society, they may not.

FOCUS 23

How does Vygotsky's "apprentice" view of the child contrast with Piaget's "scientist" view?

An Information-Processing Perspective on Mental Development

As you have just seen, developmental psychologists in the tradition of Piaget and Vygotsky attempt to understand how children's interactions with their physical or social environment increase their knowledge and lead to new ways of thinking about the world around them. In contrast, developmental psychologists who adopt the *information-processing perspective* attempt to explain children's mental development in terms of operational changes in basic components of their mental machinery.

FOCUS 24

What is the information-processing perspective on cognitive development, and how does it differ from Piaget's and Vygotsky's perspectives?

The information-processing approach to cognition, as described in Chapter 9, begins with the assumption that the mind is a system, analogous to a computer, for analyzing information from the environment. According to the standard information-processing model (refer back to Figure 9.1 on p. 312), the mind's machinery includes attention mechanisms for receiving information, working memory for actively manipulating (or thinking about) information, and long-term memory for passively holding information so that it can be used in the future. As children grow, from birth to adulthood, their brains continue to mature in various ways, resulting in changes in their abilities to attend to, remember, and use information gleaned through their senses.

Development of Long-Term Memory Systems: Episodic Memory Comes Last

In Chapter 9 we discussed the phenomenon of *infantile amnesia,* the inability to remember events and experiences before the age of 3 or 4 years. The reason for this is that before this age, children do not have well-developed *explicit,* or *declarative, memory,* which requires a degree of self-awareness and abstract encoding that develop gradually over childhood. However, *implicit memories,* which affect behavior even though the person is unable to report them, are available even to young infants. Implicit memories include procedural memories, such as how to pound with a hammer or ride a bicycle, and effects of classical and operant conditioning, which are demonstrated in nonverbal behavior.

As a demonstration of implicit memory in young infants, consider a study by Carolyn Rovee-Collier and her colleagues. A 2-month-old who learns to kick with one leg to move a mobile and who then, a day later, kicks again as soon as the mobile appears, demonstrates implicit memory of how to operate the mobile (see **Figure 11.9**). Rovee-Collier and her colleagues gave 2-month-olds just a few minutes' experience with moving a mobile by kicking. As much as 4 months later, these infants remembered the kicking action if given occasional reminders in which they saw the mobile but did not have a chance to operate it (Rovee-Collier & Cuevas, 2009). The length of time infants can remember specific actions on this and similar tasks increases steadily over the first 2 years of life, so that by 18 months infants can remember actions for as long as 13 weeks (Rovee-Collier, 1999).

Most research suggests that young children must develop the ability to encode their experiences into words before they can form episodic memories of those experiences (Bauer, 2013; Richardson & Hayne, 2007). Recall our earlier discussion of the "Magic Shrinking Machine" study by Simcock and Hayne (2002) in Chapter 9, in

---

FOCUS 25

Through what developmental steps do young children develop the capacity to form episodic memories?

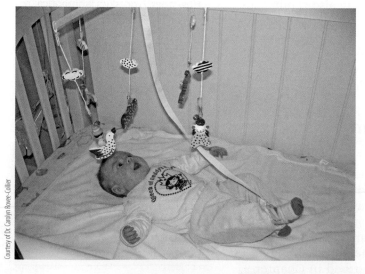
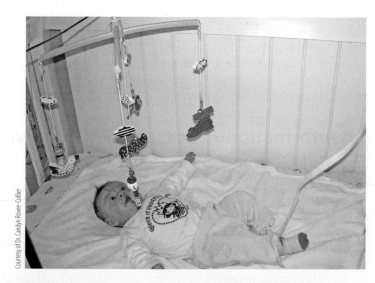

FIGURE 11.9 A test of infants' implicit procedural memories The infant, as young as 2 months of age, learns to operate the mobile by kicking one leg (a). During the test, on another day, the mobile is again presented, but now the ribbon is connected to another hook, so the infant can't control the mobile (b). The infant's immediate kicking in this condition is a sign of long-term memory for how to control the mobile.

which toddlers remembered a novel event only if they had a sufficiently sophisticated vocabulary at the time of the experience, irrespective of their language ability 6 months later when they were questioned about the event.

There is evidence, however, that preverbal infants can form some types of episodic memories when testing is done via *deferred imitation* of previously observed actions. Deferred imitation refers to reproducing the behavior of a model some significant time (usually hours or days) after watching the model. If subjects are able to do this, it implies that they developed a mental representation of the action that they were able to retrieve some significant time later when given the appropriate context. Piaget (1945/1962) had proposed that deferred imitation required symbolic representation and thus was not observed until about 18 to 24 months of age, beginning with the period of preoperations. More recent research, however, has shown that infants as young as 9 months old will copy the actions of a model (e.g., put a toy on an apparatus and then pull a lever) up to 5 weeks later (Carver & Bauer, 1999). The possibility that deferred imitation is a form of explicit memory is supported by the fact that people (such as H.M., discussed in Chapter 9) with brain damage causing anterograde amnesia—the inability to form new episodic memories—are also unable to learn new actions via deferred imitation (McDonough et al., 1995).

At about age 3 children begin, with some reliability, to talk about their experiences as they experience them. Such talk seems to help them make sense of what they are doing, as we noted earlier, and it may also be essential to the formation of episodic memories. At first such talk depends on the existence of an older conversation partner who can help the child organize the experience in a coherent way and find the appropriate words for it. In one study, researchers recorded the conversations of mothers and their 3-year-old children at visits to a natural history museum and then, a week later, asked the children to recall what they had seen at the museum (Tessler & Nelson, 1994). The result was that the children correctly recalled only those items that had been commented on jointly by both the mother and child in conversation. Items that had been commented on just by the mother or just by the child were not recalled. In general, preschool children whose mothers provide evaluations of their children's memory performance, and who use more elaborative language when talking about memory with their children, have children who remember past events better than do children with less elaborative mothers (Fivush, Haden, & Reese, 2006; Wenner et al., 2008).

■ **Forming episodic memories** To form long-term episodic memories, young children must encode their experiences verbally. Such encoding is facilitated by adults who share the experience and, through conversation, help the child to find words for what he or she sees.

Many other research studies have shown that the ability to form detailed, long-lasting episodic memories increases gradually throughout the years of childhood and reaches a plateau in late adolescence or young adulthood (Ofen et al., 2007; Schneider, 2015). This improvement is accompanied by continued maturation of the brain, particularly in the prefrontal lobes (Ofen et al., 2007; Riggins et al., 2015). Connections between the prefrontal lobes and other portions of the brain seem to be crucial to the formation and recall of episodic memories.

The Development of Basic-Level Processes: Executive Function

Recall from Chapters 8, 9, and 10 that *executive functions* are mental processes involved in the regulation of thought and behavior, and most researchers propose that there are three related components to executive function: *working memory* (or updating); *inhibition*; and *switching* (or cognitive flexibility) (Miyake & Friedman, 2012). Related to each of these is the speed with which we can process information. These basic-level cognitive abilities play a critical role in most higher-level cognitive tasks, and so understanding how they develop during childhood is important for understanding how children acquire culturally important abilities such as reading and mathematics (Carlson et al., 2013; Zelazo, 2015).

FOCUS 26

How do executive functions and speed of processing change with age during childhood and early adolescence? How might working-memory capacity depend on speed of processing?

Many experiments, using many different sorts of measures, have shown that the amount of either verbal or visual information that a person can hold in working memory at any given time increases steadily throughout childhood and reaches adult levels at about age 15. For instance, the number of digits or random single-syllable words that a person can hold in mind and repeat, after hearing them just once, increases from about three at age 4 to about seven at age 15 (Gathercole et al., 2004). These increases are accompanied by improved performance on standard tests of fluid intelligence (Kail, 2007; Swanson, 2008).

Children's inhibition abilities, as well as the ability to resist interference, show marked improvements over childhood. Inhibition tasks used with young children include variants of the familiar game "Simon Says" (children must only perform an action when Simon says so—for example, "Simon says, 'Touch your nose'"); the tapping task, in which children must tap once each time the examiner taps twice and tap twice each time the examiner taps once; and the opposites task, pointing to one of two pictures an interviewer did *not* point to (Baker et al., 2010).

Young children often have a difficult time inhibiting their speech. For instance, in one study children were shown a picture book and asked to name only certain pictures on a page—pictures of people, for example—and not to name others, such as pictures of animals (Kipp & Pope, 1997). Kindergarten children showed no tendency to inhibit their responses, mentioning one set of items (animals) as frequently as the other (people), despite seeming to understand the instructions to do otherwise. One 4-year-old we know had particular difficulty with inhibiting his speech. While relating what had happened at preschool that day, he quickly shifted to talking about something on a TV show he had seen recently. Realizing his sudden change of topic, he said, "Oops, I interrupted myself."

One way of assessing inhibition is to present people with an attractive option they are supposed to avoid to see how well they are at resisting temptation. We do this when we diet. The chocolate cake in the refrigerator "calls" to you; can you resist, or do you succumb to the temptation and promise to start your diet for real tomorrow?

One classic series of studies of resistance to temptation has been over 40 years in the making (Mischel, 2012; Mischel & Ayduk, 2011; Mischel et al., 1972). In these studies, 4-year-old children sat at a table with an experimenter. On the table were a bell and two treats (marshmallows in the original studies). The experimenter explained to the children that they would eventually receive a treat, but first he had to leave the room for a while. Children were then told "if you wait until I come back by myself then you can have this one [two marshmallows]. If you don't want to wait you can ring the bell and bring me back any time you want to. But if you ring the bell then you can't have this one [two marshmallows], but you can have that one [one marshmallow]" (Shoda et al., 1990, p. 980). Some children waited for up to 15 minutes, but most rang the bell, or in other studies ate a single marshmallow after some delay rather than waiting to get two. What's special about these studies, however, is that the researchers reevaluated many of the child subjects again as adolescents (Eigsti et al., 2006; Shoda et al., 1990) and a third time when they were in their early 30s (Ayduk et al., 2000, 2008; Schlam et al., 2013). The longer 4-year-olds were willing to wait before taking their treat, the higher were their SAT scores and school grades, the better they were able to concentrate and deal with stress as teenagers, and, as adults, they had healthier body mass indexes, a higher sense of self-worth, and were less vulnerable to psychosocial maladjustment. Interestingly, these simple latency measures taken at 4 years of age predicted self-regulating abilities nearly 30 years later. Similar findings, predicting adult outcomes with respect to physical health, substance dependence, personal finances, and criminal behavior based on childhood measures of self-control, have been reported in a 30-year longitudinal study of more than 1,000 subjects from Dunedin, New Zealand (Moffitt et al., 2011).

Young children also have difficulty shifting from one task or set of rules to another (Hanania & Smith, 2009). In a simplified variant of the Wisconsin Card Sorting Test (Chapter 9, p. 328), called the *Dimensional Card Sorting Task,* developed

■ **Preschoolers had a difficult time resisting eating one marshmallow for the chance of getting two** Four-year-old children who were better at resisting temptation in this simple task fared better as adolescents and adults on a host of physical and psychological factors than those who were not as good at resisting temptation.

by Philip Zelazo and his colleagues (1996), children are shown a set of cards with simple pictures drawn on them, much like those shown in **Figure 11.10**. The cards depict either automobiles or flowers, which are either red or blue. In the "shape game," children are to put all the automobile cards in one pile and the flowers in the other. In the "color game," they are to put all the red cards in one pile and the blue ones in the other. Three-year-olds easily can play either the shape or the color game, but things become more complicated when, after playing one game, they are told to switch to the other: If they had been sorting by shape, they are now told to sort by color and vice versa. They are reminded of the rule and even asked to state it, which they can do. Nevertheless, most 3-year-olds continue to sort by the old rule, failing to switch to the new rule despite being able to state it. Most 4-year-olds, however, can switch rules appropriately.

We should also note that changes in executive function occur at the other end of the life-span continuum. In older adults, declines have been observed in each aspect of executive functions—working memory, inhibition, and task switching (Goh et al., 2012; Passow et al., 2012; Wasylyshyn et al., 2011).

Closely correlated with each of these measures of executive function is *speed of processing*—the speed at which elementary information-processing tasks can be carried out. Speed of processing is usually assessed with reaction-time tests that require a very simple judgment, such as whether two letters or shapes flashed on a screen are the same or different, or whether an arrowhead is pointing right or left. Such tests consistently reveal age-related improvement in speed up to about 15 years of age (Kail, 1993, 2007; Wassenberg et al., 2008; see **Figure 11.11** on page 430). As discussed in Chapter 10, faster processing speed permits faster mental movement from one item of information to another, which improves one's ability to keep track of (and thereby hold) a number of different items in working memory at once. Faster processing speed may result at least partly from the physical maturation of the brain that occurs throughout childhood, independent of specific experiences. Consistent with that view, 9- and 10-year-old boys who were judged as physically mature for their age—on the basis of

FIGURE 11.10 Dimensional Card Sorting Task Children are asked to sort cards initially by one dimension (for example, color) and later by a second dimension (for example, shape). Children much younger than 4 years of age have difficulty on the "switch" trials, and usually continue to sort by the original dimension.

(Research by Zelazo et al., 1996.)

FIGURE 11.11 Reaction time for simple tasks decreases with age Children and adolescents were tested for their speed on six different tests, including a test of elementary reaction time (releasing a button in response to a signal) and a test of picture matching (judging whether two pictures are identical or not). Each person's average time for the six tests was converted by dividing it by the average time achieved by young adults, and the results were then averaged for each age group. Note that a decline in reaction time implies an increase in speed.

(Data from Kail, 1993.)

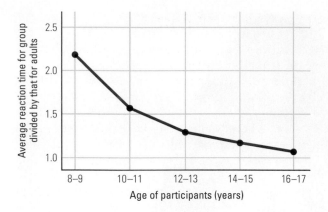

their height as a percentage of their predicted adult height—exhibited significantly faster reaction times than did boys of the same age who were judged as physically less mature (Eaton & Ritchot, 1995).

As we mentioned in Chapter 9, the prefrontal cortex plays a major role in executive functions (Miller & Wallis, 2012); it is one of the last brain areas to fully develop. Performance on a variety of executive-function tasks has been found to be significantly correlated with the development of the prefrontal cortex from infancy through adolescence (Bell et al., 2007; Luna et al., 2001). For example, neuroscientist Beatriz Luna and her colleagues (2001) examined brain activity using fMRI of subjects between the ages of 8 and 30 years while they performed a variety of inhibition tasks. The researchers reported that the adolescents showed greater levels of neural activity in the prefrontal cortex than in either children or adults. Although task performance increased gradually with age, brain activation in the frontal cortex on this task increased sharply between childhood and adolescence, only to decrease again in adulthood.

SECTION REVIEW

Three complementary perspectives help us understand children's mental growth.

Piaget: The Child as Little Scientist	Vygotsky: The Child as Apprentice	The Information-Processing Perspective
■ Piaget believed that cognitive development occurs through the child's actions on the physical environment, which promote the development of schemes (mental blueprints for actions).	■ Vygotsky considered the child's interaction with the social and cultural environment to be the key to cognitive development, leading to internalization of symbols, ideas, and ways of thinking.	■ Children exhibit implicit long-term memory from early infancy on, but we cannot assess their explicit memory capacity until they have sufficient language skills.
■ Piaget held that mental growth involves assimilation (fitting new experiences into existing schemes) and accommodation (modifying those schemes to fit with new experiences).	■ Through dialogue and collaboration with more competent others, children acquire skills socially before being able to perform them individually. Such learning takes place within the child's zone of proximal development.	■ Episodic long-term memory apparently requires that the child encode personal experiences verbally, which begins to happen with some regularity at about age 3.
■ Operational schemes (schemes for reversible actions) are particularly important to cognitive development, according to Piaget.		■ Executive functions, including working memory, inhibition, and shifting, increase as the child grows older, up to about age 15. A parallel increase in processing speed accompanies this increase in capacity.
■ Piaget described four successive stages of cognitive development (sensorimotor, preoperational, concrete-operational, and formal-operational), each employing an increasingly sophisticated type of scheme.		

Children's Understanding of Minds

To develop as fully functional humans, we must learn not just about the physical world but also about the social world around us. Most of us—adults and children alike—spend more time trying to understand other people than trying to understand inanimate objects, and we apply entirely different explanatory concepts to the two endeavors. In our explanatory frameworks, billiard balls move because they are hit by other balls or cue sticks, but people move because they want to get somewhere. We are all psychologists in our everyday lives, continually trying to account for people's behavior in terms of their minds; psychologists sometimes refer to this as *folk psychology*. We attribute emotions, motives, feelings, desires, goals, perceptions, and beliefs to people, and we use those attributes to explain their actions. This is referred to as ***theory of mind***—a person's concept of mental activity; the ability to understand one's thoughts, feelings, and behaviors and those of others. Theory of mind implies having some causal-explanatory framework to attribute intention to and to predict the behavior of others (Astington & Hughes, 2013; Wellman, 1990).

David Premack (1990) suggested that beginning at a very early age, humans automatically divide the world into two classes of entities—those that move on their own and those that don't—and attribute psychological properties to the former but not the latter. When 3- to 5-year-olds saw videos of balls moving like billiard balls, only in response to physical impacts, they described the movements in purely physical terms; but when they saw videos of balls moving and changing direction on their own, they immediately regarded the balls as representing people or animals and described the movements in mental terms (Premack, 1990). A child described one sequence of movements as one ball trying to help another ball get out of a hole.

Even Very Young Children Explain Behavior in Mental Terms

By the time children have learned language sufficiently to offer verbal explanations—that is, by about 2 to 3 years of age—they already explain people's behavior in terms of mental constructs, especially in terms of perceptions, emotions, and desires (Hickling & Wellman, 2001; Lillard & Flavell, 1990). Even preverbal 18-month-olds will help an adult achieve a goal based on what they think that adult understands (Buttelmann et al., 2015). They expect others to respond to objects that they (the others) can see but not to objects that they cannot see. They describe a crying person as sad. They say that a person filling a glass with water is thirsty and wants a drink. In one experiment (Repacholi & Gopnik, 1997), 2-year-olds demonstrated an understanding that another person's desires could be different from their own. Having learned that a particular adult preferred broccoli to crackers as a snack, they gave that adult broccoli, even though their own preference was for crackers. Unlike the 2-year-olds, however, 14-month-olds gave crackers to the broccoli-loving adult.

In another experiment, researchers showed that even 12-month-olds can display a remarkable understanding of what is in another person's mind (Tomasello & Haberl, 2003). In that experiment, each infant played with two adults and three new toys, one toy at a time. One of the two adults left the room while one of the three toys was being played with and therefore did not see or play with that toy. Then, at the end of the play session, all three toys were brought into the room on a tray and the adult who had missed playing with one of them looked in the direction of the three toys and said, "Wow! Cool! Can you give it to me?" In response, the majority of infants gave the adult the toy that that adult had not played with before, not one of the two toys with which the adult was already familiar. To perform in this way, the infants must have known which toy was new to the adult, even though it wasn't new to them, and must also have known that people are more excited by new things than by familiar ones.

FOCUS 27

What do children younger than 3 years old understand about other people's minds?

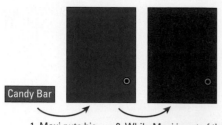

1. Maxi puts his candy bar in the blue cupboard

2. While Maxi is out of the room, his mother moves the candy bar into the red cupboard.

3. Maxi returns to the room to get his candy bar. Which cupboard will he look in first?

FIGURE 11.12 A test of ability to understand false belief In this test, which is usually presented with the help of puppets that act out the sequence, most children under age 4 say that Maxi will look in the red cupboard.

(Research by Wellman et al., 2001.)

FOCUS 28

What evidence suggests that children younger than age 4 usually do not understand that people can hold false beliefs? Why might false beliefs be particularly difficult for young children to understand?

FOCUS 29

What logic and evidence suggest that engagement in pretend play, especially in role-play with other children, may help children acquire an understanding of false beliefs?

Delay in Understanding Beliefs, Especially False Beliefs

As adults, we explain people's behavior not just in terms of their perceptions, emotions, and desires but also in terms of their *beliefs,* and we know that beliefs can be mistaken. For example, if we see a man carrying an umbrella on a sunny day, we might explain that he believed it was going to rain that day. Three-year-olds, however, rarely offer explanations in terms of beliefs (Colonnesi et al., 2008; Saxe et al., 2004), and tests indicate that they do not clearly understand that beliefs can differ from reality (Wellman et al., 2001).

A typical test of false-belief understanding is the following (illustrated in **Figure 11.12**). The child is told a story, which is also acted out with puppets for clarity, in which Maxi puts his candy bar in a blue cupboard. Then Maxi leaves the room and his mother comes in, finds the candy bar, and moves it into the red cupboard. Then Maxi reenters the room to get his candy bar, and the child is asked: "In which cupboard will Maxi look first?" Most 4-year-olds answer, just as you would, "In the blue cupboard," but most 3-year-olds insist that he'll look in the red cupboard (Wimmer & Perner, 1983). The problem isn't poor memory because the 3-year-olds in these experiments have no difficulty reporting accurately on all the factual details of the story when questioned. Rather, they seem not to understand that someone can believe something that isn't true.

Three-year-olds' denials of false belief apply even to their own false beliefs. In one experiment, 3-year-olds were shown a crayon box and asked to say what they believed was inside (Atance & O'Neill, 2004). Each of them said, "Crayons." Then the children (who were tested individually) were told that they could get some paper to draw on with the crayons if they wanted to. When the children returned with drawing paper, the box was opened, and it proved to have candles inside rather than crayons. When asked what they thought the box had in it when they first saw it, most said, "Candles." When asked why they had gotten the paper if they thought the box contained candles, most had no plausible explanation.

Perhaps the concept of false belief is particularly difficult to grasp because of its inherent contradiction. False beliefs are both false and true at the same time. They are false in reality but true in the minds of the believers. In this way they differ from the products of make-believe.

Make-Believe as a Precursor to the Belief–Reality Distinction

Three-year-olds may have difficulty understanding false beliefs, but they have no difficulty understanding pretense. Toddlers who are 2 and 3 years old, as well as older children, engage in an enormous amount of pretend play, and researchers have found that even 1.5-year-old infants differentiate between make-believe and reality (Leslie, 1994; Rakoczy, 2008). An 18-month-old who turns a cup filled with imaginary water over a doll and says, "Oh oh, dolly all wet," knows that the doll isn't really wet.

Alan Leslie (1987, 1994) has suggested that children's understanding of false beliefs emerges from their earlier understanding of pretense. Pretense is similar to false belief. Both, by definition, are mental conceptions that depart from reality. The only difference between the two is that pretenders know that their conception doesn't match reality, whereas believers think that theirs does. Three-year-olds, who fail false-belief tests such as the one in which a crayon box actually holds candles, do not fail analogous tests in which they are asked to report what either they or another person had *pretended* was in the box before it was opened (Lillard & Flavell, 1992; Woolley, 1995).

Children everywhere engage in pretend play, whether or not they are encouraged to do so (Carlson et al., 1998; Pellegrini & Bjorklund, 2004). Piaget (1962) regarded such play as an expression and exercise of the child's ability to symbolize objects in their absence, but many developmental psychologists today ascribe even further significance to it. Leslie (1991) suggests that the brain mechanisms that enable and motivate pretend play came about in evolution because such play provides a foundation for understanding nonliteral mental states, including false beliefs. A child who understands that pretense differs from reality has the foundation for understanding that people's beliefs (including the child's own beliefs) can differ from reality and that people can fool others by manipulating their beliefs. Mark Nielsen (2012) goes even further, proposing that pretense and counterfactual thinking involved in fantasy play, along with imitation, are not only essential components of childhood but actually responsible for the emergence of the human mind. According to Nielsen (2012), "By pretending children thus develop a capacity to generate and reason with novel suppositions and imaginary scenarios, and in so doing may get to practice the creative process that underpins innovation in adulthood" (p. 176).

■ These 3-year-olds may not understand false beliefs but they certainly understand pretense. Pretend play helps children acquire the belief–reality distinction and also helps them learn to reason hypothetically.

Evidence for the view that pretend play promotes false-belief understanding comes from research showing strong correlations between the two. Children who have engaged in lots of pretend role-play with other children pass false-belief tests at a higher rate than do children who have engaged in less (Jenkins & Astington, 1996). Other research has shown that children who have child-age siblings at home, especially older siblings, pass false-belief tests at a much higher rate than do same-age children who lack such siblings (McAlister & Peterson, 2007; Ruffman et al., 1998; see **Figure 11.13**). Children with siblings engage in much more role-play than do those without siblings, because their siblings are always-present potential playmates (Youngblade & Dunn, 1995). Social role-play (role-play with another child) may be more valuable for development of false-belief understanding than is solo role-play because in social role-play children must respond appropriately to the pretend statements of the other child, not just to their own pretend statements: *I'm your mommy, and you must obey me,* or *Bang, I got you.* They get used to the idea that other people can hold concepts in their heads that do not reflect reality.

Autism: A Disorder in Understanding Minds

Suppose you were oblivious to the minds of other people. You would not feel self-conscious or embarrassed in others' presence because you would have no understanding of, or concern for, their thoughts about you. You would not ask others about their thoughts or inform them of yours because you would have no reason to. You would not look where others look, attend to their words, or in any way try to fathom their perceptions and beliefs. People would serve the same function to you as inanimate objects or machines. You might try to get a bigger person's attention to help you get a cookie from the top shelf in the kitchen, but that person's attention would have no value to you in and of itself.

If you had these characteristics, you would almost certainly be diagnosed as having **autism**, or **autism spectrum disorder (ASD)**, a disorder which, as mentioned in Chapters 2 and 8, is characterized by severe deficits in social interaction and language acquisition, a tendency toward repetitive actions, and a narrow focus of interest (American Psychiatric Association, 2013). Among the earliest signs of autism in infants are failure to engage in prolonged eye contact, failure to synchronize emotional expressions with those of another person, and failure to follow another person's gaze (Baron-Cohen, 1995; Mundy et al., 1990). The deficit in language seems to be secondary to the lack of interest in communication. Unlike children who fail to learn language because of deafness, children with autism rarely use gestures as an alternative form of communication, and when they do, it is almost always for instrumental purposes (e.g., to get someone to help them reach

FOCUS 30

How does research on people with autism support the premise that the understanding of minds and the understanding of physical objects are fundamentally different abilities?

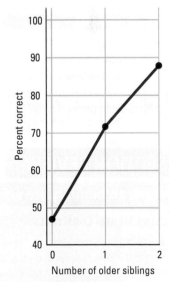

FIGURE 11.13 Older siblings promote false-belief understanding Three- and 4-year-old children with older siblings succeeded on a standard test of understanding of false belief at a much higher rate than did those who had no older siblings.

(Data from Ruffman et al., 1998.)

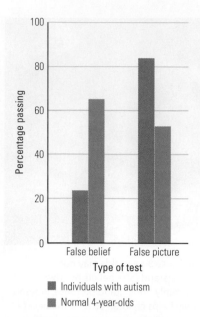

FIGURE 11.14 Performance of individuals with autism and typically developing 4-year-olds on false-belief and false-picture tests Individuals with autism were much more likely to understand that a picture could misrepresent current reality than to understand that a person's belief could misrepresent current reality. In contrast, typically developing 4-year-olds performed better on the false-belief tests than on the false-picture tests.

(Data from Leslie & Thaiss, 1992.)

 FOCUS 31

How does research on autism support the idea that an understanding of false beliefs may derive, in part, from prior engagement in pretend play?

a cookie). Those with the more severe forms of ASD, if they learn language at all, learn it late, almost invariably with the help of deliberate teaching, and their language always contains peculiarities that seem to reflect a lack of sensitivity to other people's minds and perspectives.

As you might expect, people with autism perform poorly on false-belief tests and on tests of ability to either deceive or detect deception (Tager-Flusberg, 2007; Yirmiya et al., 1996). In fact, Simon Baron-Cohen (1995) proposed that the primary deficit of these children is an inability to read minds, or what he calls *mindblindness*. Stated another way, people with autism lack a fully developed theory of mind—the ability to understand our own thoughts, feelings, and behaviors and those of others. In one experiment (Leslie & Thaiss, 1992), relatively high-functioning children with autism and adolescents whose verbal abilities were equivalent to those of typically developing 6-year-olds were compared with typically developing 4-year-olds on two false-belief tests and two "false-picture" tests. The false-belief tests were versions of the changed-location and container tests described previously, and the false-picture tests were constructed to assess the understanding that a photograph, rather than a belief, might misrepresent reality. In one false-picture test, for example, the child saw a photograph being taken of an object at one location. Then the object was moved to a new location, and the child was asked where the object would be in the photograph when it was viewed. The results of the experiment are shown in **Figure 11.14**. As you can see, the individuals with autism performed much worse than the typically developing 4-year-olds on the false-belief tests, but much better than they did on the false-picture tests. This experiment not only demonstrates the specificity of the intellectual impairment in autism but also suggests that the human capacity to understand mental representations (beliefs) is distinct from the capacity to understand physical representations (pictures).

In line with Leslie's theory that make-believe play is a developmental precursor to understanding false beliefs and other nonliteral mental representations, children with autism have consistently been found to lack such play (Mastrangelo, 2009; Wulff, 1985). Children with autism explore the real physical properties of objects, as do typically developing children, but they do not make one object stand for another or pretend that an object has properties different from those it actually has. In contrast, children with developmental disorders such as Down syndrome, despite often having lower IQs than some children with autism, do engage in pretend play (Hill & McCune-Nicolich, 1981) and eventually develop a much better understanding of false beliefs and deception than do children with autism (Baron-Cohen et al., 1985; Yirmiya et al., 1996).

SECTION REVIEW

Children begin quite early to understand not only physical reality but also the mind.

Using Mental Constructs	**Make-Believe**	**Autism**
■ Young children seem to automatically ascribe psychological characteristics to objects that move on their own.	■ Children everywhere engage in make-believe play; even toddlers distinguish between reality and pretense.	■ People with autism have impaired motivation and skills for making connections with other people.
■ Well before the age of 3, children use such mental constructs as perception, emotion, and desire to explain people's behavior.	■ Make-believe play, especially role-play, may provide a foundation for the later understanding of false beliefs.	■ Children with autism typically do not engage spontaneously in make-believe play, do not develop false-belief understanding, and think literally rather than hypothetically.
■ The understanding that beliefs can be false (i.e., not congruent with reality) takes longer to develop, appearing at about age 4.		

The Nature of Language and Children's Early Linguistic Abilities

Of all the things that people can do, none seems more complex than understanding and speaking a language. Thousands of words and countless subtle grammatical rules for modifying and combining words must be learned. Yet nearly all people master their native language during childhood; in fact, most are quite competent with language by the time they are 3 or 4 years old. How can children too young to tie their shoes or to understand that 2 plus 2 equals 4 succeed at such a complex task? Most developmentalists agree that language learning requires biological mechanisms that predispose children to it, coupled with an environment that provides adequate models and opportunity to practice. In this section, we first consider the question of what language is and then chart the normal course of its development. Then, in the next section, we will explore the biological and environmental requirements for language development.

Universal Characteristics of Human Language

Just what is it that children learn when they learn a language? Linguists estimate that at least 6,000 separate languages exist in the world today, all distinct enough that the speakers of one cannot understand those of another (Grimes, 2000). Yet these languages are all so fundamentally similar to one another that we can speak of *human language* in the singular (Pinker & Bloom, 1992). Moreover, although other animals have communication systems, they differ from humans in at least three important ways (Tomasello, 2006): Human language is *symbolic, grammatical,* and although all biologically typical people acquire language, *the particular language children learn to speak varies with culture.*

All Languages Use Symbols (Morphemes) That Are Arbitrary and Discrete

Every language has a vocabulary consisting of a set of symbols, entities that represent other entities. The symbols in a language are called **morphemes**, defined as the smallest meaningful units of a language—that is, the smallest units that stand for objects, events, ideas, characteristics, or relationships. In all spoken languages, morphemes take the form of pronounceable sounds. Most morphemes are words, but others are prefixes or suffixes used in consistent ways to modify words. Thus, in English, *dog* is both a word and a morpheme, *-s* is a morpheme but not a word, and *dogs* is a word consisting of two morphemes (*dog* and *-s*). The word *antidisestablishmentarianism* contains six morphemes (*anti-dis-establish-ment-arian-ism*), each of which has a separate entry in an English dictionary.

Morphemes in any language are both arbitrary and discrete. A morpheme is *arbitrary* in that no similarity need exist between its physical structure and that of the object or concept for which it stands. Nothing about the English morpheme *dog,* or the Spanish morpheme *perro,* or the French morpheme *chien,* naturally links it to the four-legged, barking creature it represents. This is in contrast to nonverbal signals (discussed in Chapter 3) that typically develop from and bear physical resemblance to such actions as fighting or fleeing; such signals communicate intentions to engage in the actions that they resemble. Because morphemes are arbitrary, new ones can be invented whenever needed to stand for newly discovered objects or ideas, or to express newly important shades of meaning. This characteristic gives language great flexibility. A morpheme is *discrete* in that it cannot be changed in a graded way to express gradations in meaning. For example, you cannot say that one thing is bigger than another by changing the morpheme *big.* Rather, you must add a new morpheme to it (such as *-er*) or replace it with a different morpheme (such as *huge*).

FOCUS 32

What are the universal characteristics of morphemes? How do morphemes differ from nonverbal signals?

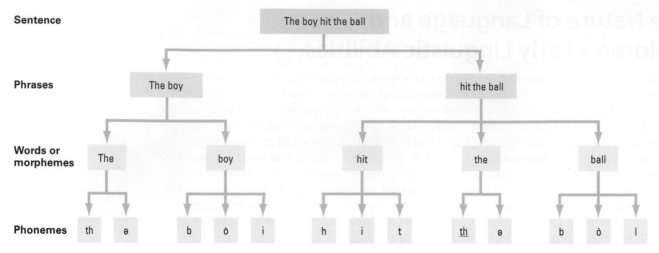

Sentence — The boy hit the ball

Phrases — The boy | hit the ball

Words or morphemes — The | boy | hit | the | ball

Phonemes — th ə | b ȯ i | h i t | th ə | b ȯ l

FIGURE 11.15 The hierarchical structure of language These four levels of organization characterize every spoken language.

All Languages Are Hierarchically Structured in a Similar Way

FOCUS 33

How can any sentence, in any language, be described as a four-level hierarchy? How can rules of grammar be described in relation to that hierarchy?

In addition to commonalities in their symbol systems, all languages share a particular hierarchical structure of units (see **Figure 11.15**). The top level (largest unit) is the sentence, which can be broken down into phrases, which can be broken down into words or morphemes, which can be broken down into elementary vowel and consonant sounds called **phonemes**. The power of this four-level organization is that the relatively few phonemes (anywhere from 15 to 80 occur in any given language) can be arranged in different ways to produce an enormous number of possible words, which themselves can be arranged in different ways to produce a limitless number of possible phrases and sentences.

Every language has rules—collectively referred to as the **grammar** of the language—that specify permissible ways to arrange units at one level to produce the next higher level in the hierarchy. Grammar includes rules of *phonology*, which specify how phonemes can be arranged to produce morphemes; rules of *morphology*, which specify how morphemes can be combined to form words; and rules of **syntax**, which specify how words can be arranged to produce phrases and sentences. These rules differ from language to language, but every language has them, and similarities exist across languages in the fundamental nature of the rules (Pinker & Bloom, 1992; Pinker & Jackendoff, 2005).

Grammatical Rules Are Usually Learned Implicitly, Not Explicitly

FOCUS 34

What does it mean to say that knowledge of grammar is usually implicit rather than explicit?

People often think of grammar as something they learned (or tried to learn) in elementary school (which used to be called *grammar* school, perhaps for that very reason). But grammar is learned implicitly, without conscious effort, long before formal schooling. The fact that 4-year-olds can carry on meaningful conversations with adults, producing and understanding new and unique sentences, indicates that by age 4 children have already acquired much of the essential grammar of their native language. Four-year-olds can't name or describe the rules of grammar (nor can most adults), yet they use them every day. Indeed, even professional linguists fall short of describing the full grammar of the world's languages (Jackendoff, 2003). Grammatical rules in this sense are like the rules that underlie the sequence and timing of specific muscle movements in walking or running; both sets of rules are encoded in implicit rather than explicit memory. We generally can't state them, but we use them when we walk, run, or carry on a conversation.

People's implicit knowledge of grammar is demonstrated in their ability to distinguish acceptable from unacceptable sentences. Nearly every English speaker can identify *The mouse crawled under the cabinet* as a grammatical sentence and

The crawled cabinet mouse the under as nongrammatical, although few can explain exactly why. The ability to distinguish grammatical from nongrammatical sentences is not based simply on meaning. As linguist Noam Chomsky (1957) pointed out, English speakers recognize *Colorless green ideas sleep furiously* as grammatically correct but absurd.

The Course of Language Development

In a remarkably short time, infants progress from cries, coos, and babbles to uttering words, sentences, and narratives, becoming "linguistic geniuses" over the course of just a few years. Children across the world, although learning different languages, achieve this impressive cognitive and communicative feat in very similar ways.

Early Perception of Speech Sounds

Infants seem to treat speech as something special as soon as they are born, and maybe even before (Werker & Gervain, 2013). In experiments in which newborns, just 1 to 4 days old, could produce sounds by sucking on a nipple, the babies sucked more vigorously to produce the sound of a human voice than to produce any other sounds that were tested (Butterfield & Siperstein, 1974; Vouloumanos & Werker, 2007).

The ability of very young infants to hear the differences among speech phonemes has been demonstrated in many experiments. One technique is to allow an infant to suck on a pacifier that is wired to trigger the playing of a particular sound each time a sucking response occurs. When the baby becomes bored with a sound, as indicated by a reduced rate of sucking, the sound is changed (maybe from *pa* to *ba*). Typically, the rate of sucking increases immediately thereafter, which indicates that the infant hears the new sound as different from the previous one. Another method, which can be used with infants 5 months old and older, involves rewarding the baby with an interesting sight for turning his or her head when the sound changes. The baby soon learns to look to the right—where the interesting visual display appears—each time the sound changes. This response serves as an index that the baby distinguishes the new sound from the old one.

The results of such experiments suggest that babies younger than 6 months old hear the difference between any two sounds that are classed as different phonemes in any of the world's languages (Saffran et al., 2006; Tsao et al., 2004). At about 6 months of age, however, two kinds of changes begin to occur in their ability to discriminate between similar speech sounds: They become relatively *better* at discriminating between sounds that represent different phonemes in their native language, and they become *worse* at discriminating between sounds that are classed as the same phoneme in their native language (Kuhl et al., 2008). For example, infants growing up in English-speaking cultures gradually become better than they were before at distinguishing between the English /l/ and /r/, which are distinct phonemes in English but not in Japanese, and they gradually *lose* the ability to distinguish among the subtly different /t/ sounds that constitute different phonemes in

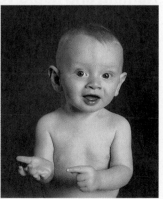

Jeffrey Debelle/© Dr. Laura Ann Petitto

■ **Manual babbling** Deaf or hearing infants whose deaf parents communicate by sign language go through a stage of babbling with their hands. Their babbling gestures resemble the signs of the language but do not yet express meaning.

FOCUS 35

How have researchers shown that very young infants can distinguish between subtly different speech sounds? How do infants' abilities to distinguish among such speech sounds change during the second half-year of their lives? What is the value of these changes?

Hindi but not in English (Kuhl et al., 2008; Werker & Tees, 1999). In contrast, Japanese infants gradually lose the ability to distinguish among /l/ and /r/, and Indian infants in Hindi-speaking homes become better at distinguishing among the /t/ sounds relevant to their language.

Cooing and Babbling

FOCUS 36

What is the distinction between cooing and babbling? What are the reasons for thinking that these vocalizations are precursors to language production?

Beginning at birth, infants can cry and produce various other vocal signs of distress, but at about 2 months they begin to produce a new, more speech-like category of sounds called *cooing,* which consists of repeated drawn-out vowels (*oooh-oooh, eeeh-eeeh*). At about 6 months, cooing changes gradually to *babbling,* which consists of repeated consonant-and-vowel sounds such as *paa-paa-paa* or *tooda-tooda* (Masataka, 2003). Cooing and babbling occur most often when the infant is happy. They seem to be forms of vocal play that have evolved to help the infant exercise and refine the complex muscle movements needed to produce coherent speech.

Coos and the earliest babbles do not depend on the infant's hearing spoken sounds. Deaf infants coo and begin to babble at about the same age and in the same manner as hearing infants (Petitto, 2000), and early babbles are as likely to contain foreign-language sounds as native-language sounds (Locke, 1983). By 8 months of age, however, hearing infants begin to babble in ways that mimic the rhythm and pitch patterns of the language they hear around them; the babbling of a French baby becomes recognizably French, and that of a British baby becomes recognizably British (de Boysson-Bardies, 1999). Beginning at about 10 months of age, hearing infants produce babbled sounds that increasingly resemble syllables and words of their native language (de Boysson-Bardies, 1999; Locke, 1983). Also at this age, deaf babies who are exposed to a sign language begin to babble with their hands—repeating over and over hand movements that are similar in form and rhythm to those of the language they see around them (Petitto et al., 2001). Eventually, recognizable words appear in the hearing infant's vocal babbling and the deaf infant's manual babbling.

Word Comprehension Precedes Word Production

FOCUS 37

What is the evidence that babies begin to understand words well before they begin to speak?

During the babbling phase of life, before the first production of recognizable words, infants begin to show evidence that they understand some words and phrases that they hear regularly. In one experiment, 6-month-olds were shown side-by-side videos of their parents. When they heard the word "Mommy" or "Daddy," they looked reliably more at the video of the named parent than at the unnamed parent (Tincoff & Jusczyk, 1999). Other experiments have revealed that 9-month-olds can respond to a number of common words by looking at the appropriate object when it is named (Balaban & Waxman, 1997) and can follow simple verbal commands, such as "Get the ball" (Benedict, 1979). By the time that they say their first word, at about 10 to 12 months of age, infants may already know the meaning of dozens of words (Swingley, 2008).

Naming and Rapid Vocabulary Development

Babies' first words are most often produced in a playful spirit. The child at first uses words to point things out, or simply to name them for fun, not generally to ask for them (Bloom & Lahey, 1978). For instance, my (Peter Gray's) son used the word *ba* joyfully to name his bottle, after he received it; it was not until weeks later that he began using *ba* to ask for his bottle when he wanted it.

New words come slowly at first, but then, typically at about 15 to 20 months of age, the rate begins to accelerate, known as the *word spurt* (Mervis & Bertrand, 1994). Between the ages of 2 and 17 years, the typical person learns about 60,000 words, an average of about 11 new words per day (Bloom, 2001). Relatively few of these are explicitly taught; most often, the child must infer the meaning of a new word from the context in which others use it. How do young children, early in the language-learning process, draw these inferences?

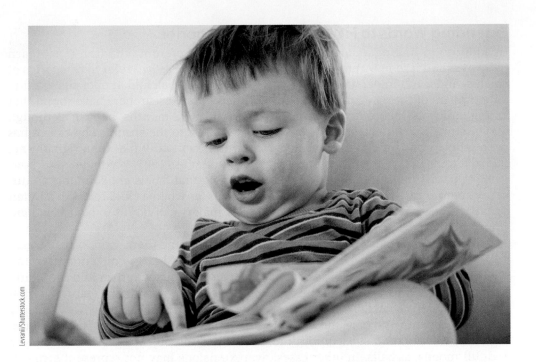

Lewramii/Shutterstock.com

■ **First words** Naming objects is an important step in the mastery of language. It is also a source of great delight to infants and their caregivers.

Most of the earliest words learned, in any language culture, are nouns that refer to categories of objects in the child's environment (Golinkoff et al., 1994). Young children's tendency to look at whatever an older person is looking at (shared attention, discussed earlier) no doubt helps them identify objects that the older person is referring to when speaking. Infants are especially likely to follow an adult's gaze when the adult is labeling an object in the environment (Baldwin, 2000). Researchers have found that those infants who show the most reliable gaze following, when tested at 10 and 11 months of age, show the greatest gains in vocabulary over the next several months (Brooks & Meltzoff, 2008).

In addition, young children seem to have a number of cognitive biases, or built-in assumptions, that help them narrow down the likely referent to a new word they hear (Golinkoff et al., 1994; Regier, 2003). One of these is a strong tendency to link new words with objects for which they do not already know a name, known as the *mutual exclusivity assumption*. Other things being equal, young children assume that a new word is not a synonym for a word they already know but a label for something whose name they don't know. In one experiment, 3- and 4-year-olds were presented with toy animals that they could name (a pig, a sheep, and a cow) plus one that they could not name (a tapir). When they heard the novel word *gombe* in the presence of these objects, all the children applied it to the novel animal (Clark, 1987). Other research indicates that toddlers begin to manifest this bias at about the same time—in their second year of life—at which their rate of vocabulary learning begins to increase rapidly (Mervis & Bertrand, 1994). Although the bias leads to some mistakes, it is apparently more helpful than harmful to their acquisition of words.

By the time they can understand multiword sentences, young children are able to use their tacit knowledge of grammar to help them infer the meaning of new words, including verbs and other parts of speech as well as nouns (Bernal et al., 2007; MacWhinney, 2016). Thus, if they are shown a videotaped scene and told, "The duck and bunny are biffing," 2-year-olds—who understand *duck* and *bunny* and know implicitly that words ending in *-ing* refer to actions—infer that *biffing* means whatever the duck and bunny are both doing (Naigles, 1990). If told, instead, "The duck is biffing the bunny," they infer that *biffing* means whatever the duck is doing to the bunny. As another example, 2-year-olds who heard "Mommy feeds the ferret" inferred that a ferret is an animal, not an inanimate object (Goodman et al., 1998). This is referred to as *syntactic bootstrapping* (Gleitman, 1990; Hoff & Naigles, 2002).

<hr />

FOCUS 38

How do young children make the link between new words that they hear and appropriate referents in their environments?

Extending Words to Fit Appropriate Categories

In addition to linking a new word to its immediate referent, children must learn how to extend it to new referents. Common nouns such as *ball* refer to categories of objects, and a full understanding is demonstrated when a child applies the word to all members of the category and not to nonmembers. Researchers have found that young children, including even infants as young as 12 months, behave as though they assume that a newly heard label applies not just to the specific object that has been labeled but also to other objects that are perceptually like the original one, referred to as the *taxonomic assumption* (Golinkoff et al., 1995; Waxman & Markow, 1995). That is, infants are biased toward assuming that labels are common nouns, not proper nouns. The bias leads to some mistakes, as when a child refers to all men as *Daddy,* but is useful overall because the vast majority of nouns to be learned are common nouns.

Children sometimes overextend common nouns, using them more broadly than adult usage would allow. On the basis of an analysis of a large collection of examples, Eve Clark (1973) proposed that *overextension* results when a child implicitly defines a new word in terms of just one or a few of the prominent features of the original referent object. Thus a child who hears *ball* in association with a specific ball might take the object's most prominent feature—its roundness—as the defining characteristic and subsequently refer to all round objects, including oranges and full moons, as balls. In other cases, overextensions may not represent errors at all but simply derive from children's attempts to communicate about objects that they have not yet learned to name (Clark, 1995). A toddler who says, "Look doggie," while pointing to a cat, may in essence be saying, "Look at that thing that is something like a doggie." The same child, when asked which animals in a set of pictures are dogs, may pick the actual dogs and not the cats (Thomson & Chapman, 1977).

What is remarkable, however, is not that children make errors in their extensions but that they usually extend new words appropriately (Bloom, 2001). Somehow they figure out quickly the categories that are referred to by the words they hear adults and older children using.

Using Grammatical Rules

As babies are learning to speak, they go through a period when each of their utterances is only one word long. Typically at about 18 to 24 months of age they begin to put words together. At this stage they use content words almost exclusively, especially nouns and verbs, and usually arrange them in the grammatically correct

FOCUS 39

What are two reasons why children might overextend common nouns that they have learned?

FOCUS 40

How do children demonstrate knowledge of grammatical rules in their early speech? How do some of their "mistakes" in grammar confirm that they know the rule and are not just mimicking?

■ **Ohh, Kermit** When young children overextend common nouns and proper nouns to apply to objects beyond the appropriate category, they may not always be making mistakes. A child who sees an alpine marmot for the first time and says, "Ohh, Kermit," may really be saying, "Ohh, there is an animal that looks like Kermit the Frog from *Sesame Street.*" The drive to speak and communicate is so strong that, lacking the appropriate word, children will come up with the closest approximation they know.

blickwinkel/Alamy

sequence for simple, active sentences (Brown, 1973). For an English-speaking child, this means that subjects are placed before verbs, and verbs before objects. A child at the two-word stage will say "Billy kick" to mean that Billy is kicking something, and "Kick Billy" to mean that someone is kicking Billy. During this early stage of language development, children are economical in their word choice, using only concrete and high-information words that are most important in conveying meaning. Such speech has been described as *telegraphic speech*: It is performed much as telegrams were once written and text messages are written today, including only the high-content words and omitting all the *if*s, *and*s, and *but*s.

When children acquire a new grammatical rule, such as adding *-ed* to the end of a verb to create the past tense, they almost invariably overgeneralize it at first (Kuczaj, 1977; Marcus et al., 1992). The 3-year-old who says "kicked," "played," and "laughed" also says "goed," "thinked," and "swimmed." Similarly, children who have just learned to add *-s* to pluralize nouns will talk about many *mouses, sheeps,* and *childs*. This overgeneralization, called *overregularization*, confirms that children really know the rule. If they followed the rule only when adults did, their usage might be attributed to simple imitation. As further evidence suggesting that their grammar is based on rules, young children have been shown to use the rules with made-up words that they had never heard before, as illustrated in **Figure 11.16**.

Children are not taught the rules of grammar explicitly; nobody sits a 2-year-old down and tries to explain how to create infinitives, possessives, or past-tense verbs. Some parents correct their children's grammar, but even this is rare (Brown & Hanlon, 1970), and long-term experiments in preschools have shown that deliberate programs of correcting grammar have little effect on rule acquisition (de Villiers & de Villiers, 1979). Through their own devices, children actively (and mostly unconsciously) infer grammatical rules from examples of rule-based language spoken around them and to them.

This is a wug.

Now there is another one.
There are two of them.
There are two _____.

Jen Berko (Gleason). "The Child's Learning of English Morphology." Word, 1958. By permission of the author.

FIGURE 11.16   One wug and two _____ ? With this test, Jean Berko found that children who had just begun to use the rule of forming plurals by adding *-s* would use the rule correctly even for words they had never heard before.

SECTION REVIEW

Children rapidly acquire the complex tools of language, beginning in infancy.

Linguistic Universals

- The smallest meaningful units in all languages are a set of symbols called morphemes; morphemes are arbitrary and discrete.

- All languages are hierarchically structured, with sentences at the top of the hierarchy and phonemes (elementary vowel and consonant sounds) at the bottom.

- Every language has a grammar—a set of rules that specify the permissible ways to combine units at one level of the hierarchy to create a unit at the next higher level.

- Knowledge of grammar is generally more implicit than explicit.

The Course of Language Development

- Babies under 6 months can distinguish phonemes. After that, they become better at distinguishing different phonemes in their native language, but worse at distinguishing between sounds that represent the same phoneme in their native language.

- Infants coo and later babble as a form of vocal play that helps to prepare the vocal apparatus for speech. By 8 months, their babbling starts to mimic their native language.

- The first recognizable words appear at about 10 to 12 months; vocabulary growth accelerates soon after and continues for years, though children sometimes overextend words.

- Children first combine words at about 18 to 24 months, demonstrating knowledge of word-order rules. Knowledge of other grammatical rules is demonstrated in overgeneralizations of them (e.g., saying *deers* or *goed*).

Internal and External Supports for Language Development

How is it that children can learn language so early, with so little apparent conscious effort and without deliberate training? There is no doubt that humans enter the world equipped in many ways for language. We are born with

- anatomical structures in the throat (the larynx and pharynx) that enable us to produce a broader range of sounds than any other mammal can produce (Lieberman, 2007);

- brain areas specialized for language (including Broca's and Wernicke's areas, discussed in Chapter 4);

- a preference for listening to speech and an ability to distinguish among the basic speech sounds of any language; and

- mechanisms that cause us to exercise our vocal capacities through a period of cooing and babbling.

There is also no doubt that most of us are born into a social world that provides rich opportunities for learning language. We are surrounded by language from birth, and when we begin to use it, we achieve many rewards through this extraordinarily effective form of communication.

The Idea of Special Inborn Mechanisms for Language Learning

Chomsky's Concept of an Innate Language-Learning Device

FOCUS 41

How did Noam Chomsky link the study of grammar to psychology? What did he mean by a language-acquisition device?

The linguist Noam Chomsky, more than anyone else, was responsible for drawing psychologists' attention to the topic of language. In his highly influential book *Syntactic Structures* (1957), Chomsky characterized grammatical rules as fundamental properties of the human mind. In contrast to an earlier view, held by some psychologists, that sentences are generated in chain-like fashion, with one word triggering the next in a sequence, Chomsky emphasized the hierarchical structure of sentences. He argued convincingly that a person must have some meaningful representation of the whole sentence in mind before uttering it and then must apply grammatical rules to that representation in order to fill out the lower levels of the hierarchy (phrases, morphemes, and phonemes) to produce the utterance.

Chomsky (1957, 1965, 1968) conceived of grammatical rules as aspects of the human mind that link spoken sentences ultimately (through one or more intermediary stages) to the mind's system for representing meanings. Although specific grammatical rules vary from one language to another, they are all, according to Chomsky, based on certain fundamental principles, referred to as ***universal grammar***, that are innate properties of the human mind. These properties account for the universal characteristics of language (discussed earlier) and for other, more subtle language universals (Pinker, 1994). To refer to the entire set of innate mental mechanisms that enable a child to acquire language quickly and efficiently, Chomsky coined the term ***language-acquisition device***, or ***LAD***. The LAD includes the inborn foundations for universal grammar plus the entire set of inborn mechanisms that guide children's learning of the unique rules of their culture's language. Support for the concept of an innate LAD comes partly from observations of language-learning deficits in people who have suffered damage to particular brain areas (discussed in Chapter 4) or who have a particular genetic disorder (specific language impairment), characterized primarily by difficulty in articulating words, distinguishing speech sounds from other sounds, and learning grammatical rules (Gopnik, 1999; Vargha-Khadem & Liégeois, 2007).

Children's Invention of Grammar

Further support for the LAD concept comes from evidence that young children invent grammar when it is lacking in the speech around them. Here are two examples of such evidence.

Children's Role in Development of Creole Languages New languages occasionally arise when people from many different language cultures simultaneously colonize an area and begin to communicate with one another. These first-generation colonists communicate through a primitive, grammarless collection of words taken from their various native languages—a communication system referred to as a ***pidgin language***. Subsequently, the pidgin develops into a true language, with a full range of grammatical rules, at which point it is called a ***creole language***. Derek Bickerton (1984) studied creole languages from around the world and found that at least some of them were developed into full languages within one generation by the children of the original colonists. Apparently, the children imposed grammatical rules on the pidgin they heard and used those rules consistently in their own speech—powerful evidence, in Bickerton's view, that children's minds are innately predisposed to grammar.

Deaf Children's Invention of a Grammatical Sign Language Bickerton's evidence of children's role in creating new languages was necessarily indirect, as he was studying languages that emerged many years ago. More recently, Ann Senghas and her colleagues have documented directly the emergence of a new sign language among deaf children in Nicaragua (Senghas & Coppola, 2001; Senghas et al., 2004). Prior to 1977, deaf Nicaraguans had little opportunity to meet other deaf people. There was no deaf community or common sign language, and the deaf were typically treated as though they were intellectually impaired. In 1977 the first Nicaraguan school for the deaf was founded, so deaf children for the first time came into extended contact with one another. On the basis of outmoded ideas, the school did not at first teach any sign language but, instead, attempted to teach the deaf to speak and lip-read the nation's vocal language (Spanish), an approach that rarely succeeds. Despite the official policy, the students began to communicate with one another using hand signs.

At first their signing system was a manual pidgin, an unstructured and variable amalgam of the signs and gestures that the individuals had been using at home. But over the course of a few years the signs became increasingly regularized and efficient, and a system of grammar emerged. All this occurred naturally, with no formal teaching, simply through the students' desires to communicate with one another. Of most significance for our discussion, the new grammar was produced not by the oldest, wisest members of the community but by the youngest. In fact, those who were more than about 10 years old when the deaf community was formed not only failed to contribute to the development of a grammar but learned little of the one that did develop. The sign language invented by the children has since become the official sign language of Nicaragua (*Idioma de Señas de Nicaragua*). It is a true language, comparable to American Sign Language, in which the morphemes are elementary hand movements and grammatical rules stipulate how the morphemes can be combined and sequenced into larger units.

Children's improvement of grammar may be viewed by us as a creative act, but it is almost certainly not experienced as that by the children themselves. Children tacitly assume that language has grammar, so they unconsciously read grammar into language even where it doesn't exist. Just as children learning English overregularize grammatical rules when they say things like *goed* and *mouses*, and thereby temporarily make English grammar more consistent and elegant than it really is, children exposed to a pidgin language

FOCUS 42

How have studies of creole languages and studies of deaf children in Nicaragua supported the idea that children invent grammar in the absence of a preexisting grammatical language?

■ **Creating a language** When deaf children in Nicaragua were brought together for the first time, in a school community, they gradually created a new sign language. The youngest children contributed most to the grammatical structure of the language.

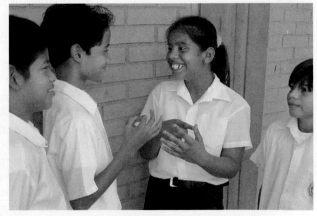

Ann Senghas

or to an early version of the Nicaraguan sign language may accept the slightest random hint of a grammatical rule as a true rule and begin to use it as such. In the case of a newly emerging language—unlike the case of a long-established language such as English—the children's rules are incorporated into the language and are learned by the next generation.

Critical Period for Learning the Grammar of One's First Language

FOCUS 43

What evidence supports the view that grammar is learned more readily in early childhood than later in life?

The LAD apparently functions much more effectively during the first 10 years of childhood than later in life. Children who are deprived of the opportunity to hear and interact with a language during their first 10 years have great difficulty learning language later on and never master the grammar of the language they learn. That is one of the lessons learned from observations of deaf children who were not exposed to a true language until adolescence or late in childhood (Mayberry et al., 2002; Senghas et al., 2004). Much more rarely, a hearing person is discovered who was deprived of language throughout childhood, and in every such case that has been documented, the person was subsequently unable to learn language fully (Curtiss, 1977).

The most thoroughly studied language-deprived hearing person is a woman known as Genie. She was rescued in 1970, at age 13, from the inhuman conditions in which her violently abusive father and partly blind and submissive mother had raised her (Curtiss, 1977; Rymer, 1993). From shortly after birth until her rescue, Genie had been locked in a tiny room and exposed to almost no speech. At the time of her rescue, she understood a few words but could not string words together and had learned no grammar. She was then placed in a foster home where she was exposed to English much as infants normally are and received tutorial help. In this environment, she eventually acquired a large vocabulary and learned to produce meaningful, intelligent statements; but even after 7 years of language practice, at age 20, her grammar lagged far behind other indices of her intelligence (Curtiss, 1977). A typical sentence she produced was "I hear music ice cream truck," and she often misunderstood sentences whose meaning depended on grammar. Over subsequent years of adulthood, her grammar showed little improvement (Rymer, 1993).

Learning within the critical period is much less important for second-language learning than for first-language learning. People who learned their first language within the critical period can learn a second language reasonably well at any time in life, although not quite as well as they could have if they had learned it earlier. Those who learn a second language after the age of about 10 or 11 almost always speak with an accent and generally do not acquire the grammar of the language as fully or easily as do those who learn the language at a younger age (Au et al., 2002; Johnson & Newport, 1989).

The Language-Acquisition Support System

FOCUS 44

How do parents in our culture modify their speech to infants?

Children come into the world predisposed to acquire language, but they do not acquire it in a social vacuum. Neither Genie nor any other child has ever invented language alone. Normal language development requires not just the LAD but also the **LASS**—the **language-acquisition support system**—provided by the social world into which the baby is born (Bruner, 1983).

In Western culture and most others, adults regularly simplify their speech to infants and young children in ways that might help the children learn words and some aspects of grammar. They enunciate more clearly than when speaking to adults, use a more musical tone of voice with greater pitch variation, use short sentences that focus on the here and now, repeat and emphasize salient words, and use gestures to help convey meaning (Snow, 1984; Soderstrom, 2007). A 6-month-old playing with a ball might be told, "Oh, you have a *ball*. A nice *ball*. What a pretty *ball*." Such speech is often referred to as *motherese* (although it is not just mothers who speak this way to babies), and more generally as *infant-directed speech*.

Researchers have found that such speech does help infants to distinguish individual words and to make connections between words and their referents (Soderstrom, 2007; Thiessen et al., 2005).

Adults also frequently treat infants' early vocalizations as if they were verbal statements. For instance, a mother or father might respond to the baby's *ba-ba-ga-goo-goo* with, "Oh, yes, very interesting!" Such responsiveness can lead to back-and-forth, conversation-like exchanges between infant and adult. It is interesting that mothers of deaf infants also use a form of infant-directed signing, using more repetitions and greater exaggerations of movements to their deaf infants than to their deaf adult friends (Masataka, 1996).

Parents' Speech to Infants Affects Language Acquisition

Several research studies have shown positive correlations between the degree to which mothers speak to their infants, using appropriately simplified language, and the rate at which the infants develop language (Furrow et al., 1979; Tamis-LeMonda et al., 2001). A problem with such studies, however, is that the observed correlations might derive more from genetic similarities between mothers and their children than from differences in the language environments that the mothers provide. Genetically verbal mothers may produce genetically verbal children.

Better evidence for an effect of mothers' influence on language development comes from a study involving infants who were adopted at birth (Hardy-Brown et al., 1981). In that study, adopted infants' rates of language development correlated more strongly with their biological mothers' verbal abilities than with their adoptive mothers' verbal abilities, but the linguistic environments provided by the adoptive mothers also played a significant role. In particular, infants whose adoptive mothers often responded verbally to their early vocalizations developed language more rapidly than did those whose adoptive mothers were less responsive. Further evidence comes from a series of studies in which parents were trained to engage frequently in back-and-forth verbal play with their infants, from age 3 months to 15 months (Fowler et al., 2006). Those children developed language considerably sooner than did children in otherwise comparable families without such training. Apparently, parents' verbal responsiveness to infants' vocalizations plays a significant role in the rate of language acquisition.

Cross-Cultural Differences in the LASS

Cross-cultural research shows that children all over the world acquire language at roughly similar rates, despite wide variations in the degree and manner of adults' verbal interactions with infants (Ochs & Schieffelin, 1995). For example, the Kalikuli people of the New Guinea rainforest believe that there is no reason to speak to babies who cannot yet speak themselves. These babies hear no motherese, and little speech of any kind is directed toward them. However, unlike infants in our culture, they go everywhere with their mothers and constantly overhear the speech not only of their mothers but of other adults and children around them. This rich exposure to others' conversations may compensate for the lack of speech directed to them. Apparently, large variations can occur in the LASS without impairing infants' abilities to learn language.

Bilingualism

Most of our discussion has implicitly assumed that a child is learning just one language—his or her "mother tongue." However, many people over the globe are bi- or multilingual, speaking two or more languages from early in life. For example,

■ **Taking account of the listener** Most people automatically simplify their speech when talking to infants and young children. Even young children addressing younger children deliberately slow their rate of speech, choose simple words and grammatical structures, and gesture broadly.

 FOCUS 45

What evidence suggests that differences in the language environments provided by parents can affect the rates at which infants acquire language?

FOCUS 46

What light has been shed on the LASS by cross-cultural research?

in some European countries, such as Switzerland and Luxembourg, it is typical for people to speak three or four languages, and it is not uncommon for people on the island of New Guinea to be fluent in five or more languages (Diamond, 2013).

There are many factors that influence how easily and how well a child will acquire a second language. Generally speaking, the earlier children are exposed to a second language, the greater the chances that they will become proficient in it. Also, the more similar two languages are to one another (such as English and German versus English and Chinese), the easier it is to learn the second language (Snow & Yusun Kang, 2006).

Simultaneous and Sequential Bilinguals

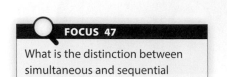

FOCUS 47

What is the distinction between simultaneous and sequential bilinguals?

The timing of learning a second language makes a difference in proficiency, even when the individual is fully fluent in both languages. Some people are exposed from birth to two languages and are typically equally (or nearly so) fluent in both languages; they are known as *simultaneous bilinguals*. Other people, called *sequential bilinguals*, learn a second language *after* mastering their first. Although sequential bilinguals can gain proficiency in a second language, their first language is usually the dominant (that is, most proficient) one. They typically retain an accent, for example (Myers-Scotton, 2008).

Some neuroimaging research supports the idea that people who master a second language relatively late in life (in adolescence, for example) do so in a different way, neurologically speaking, than people who acquire two languages in childhood (likely simultaneously). For instance, in one study the brains of bilingual adults who learned two languages early in development were contrasted with adults who learned their first language in childhood but their second language in adolescence. For the former group (early bilinguals), the same areas of the brain "lit up" when speaking sentences in both languages. This was not the case, however, for the "late bilinguals," who had learned their second language in adolescence or adulthood. Instead, the pattern of brain activation was different when speaking their first versus their second languages (see **Figure 11.17**). This pattern is consistent with the theory that children's brains are "prepared" early in life for processing language, but, with age, they lose this special ability. It is still possible to learn a second language

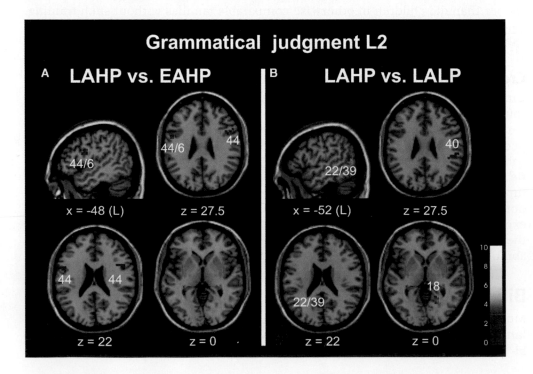

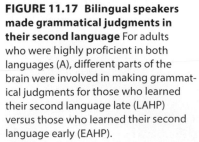

FIGURE 11.17 Bilingual speakers made grammatical judgments in their second language For adults who were highly proficient in both languages (A), different parts of the brain were involved in making grammatical judgments for those who learned their second language late (LAHP) versus those who learned their second language early (EAHP).

(Republished with permission of Elsevier, from Wartenburger, I., et. al., "Early setting of grammatical processing in the bilingual brain," *Neuron*, (2003):37, 159–170; Permission conveyed through the Copyright Clearance Center, Inc.)

later in life, but it is not done as easily and is accomplished using different (though overlapping) parts of the brain (Wartenburger et al., 2003).

Costs and Benefits of Bilingualism

Although there are some obvious advantages of speaking two languages, there has also been considerable debate, especially in education circles, about the costs and benefits of bilingualism (see Bialystok & Craik, 2010). One disadvantage of bilingualism is that children learning two languages at once typically show a delay in syntactic development and have smaller vocabularies in each language relative to monolingual children (Gathercole, 2013). However, bilingual children's total vocabularies (unique words known in language 1 plus language 2) are comparable to that of monolingual children (Hoff et al., 2012). Other research has shown that bilinguals of all ages are also slower at retrieving individual words from their long-term memories than monolinguals (Bialystok et al., 2008).

On the plus side, in addition to be being able to communicate effectively in two languages, bilinguals are able to recognize a wider range of phonemes than monolinguals (MacWhinney, 2005), and often are more sensitive toward the cultural values of the speakers of both the languages they have mastered (Snow & Yusun Kang, 2006). Research has also found that bilingualism conveys the advantage of enhanced executive functions (Bialystok & Craik, 2010; Bialystock & Feng, 2011). Learning two languages at once is more effortful than learning just one, and bilingual children must work at minimizing interference between their languages. As a result, bilingual children show greater levels of task switching and inhibition than monolinguals (Bialystok & Craik, 2010). There is even evidence that 7-month-old infants growing up in bilingual households show better inhibition and switching abilities (judged by looking time in a study that required infants to look to the right or left to see a dancing puppet, then switching the sides where the puppet was shown) than infants from monolingual homes (Kovács & Mehler, 2009). Finally, bilingualism has been found to postpone the decline in executive function that typically occurs in old age (Bialystok et al., 2007).

FOCUS 48

What are some of the costs and benefits of bilingualism relative to speaking only one language? Do you think the costs outweigh the benefits?

SECTION REVIEW

Inborn mechanisms and the social context jointly support children's acquisition of language.

Innate Mechanisms for Language Acquisition

- Chomsky hypothesized the existence of an innate language-acquisition device (LAD), consisting of a universal grammar and mechanisms that guide native-language learning.

- The reality of the LAD is supported by children's imposition of grammatical rules to create creole languages and, in Nicaragua, a sign language.

- The LAD appears to function most effectively in the first 10 years of life. Children deprived of sufficient exposure to language during that period do not fully learn language later.

External Support for Language Acquisition

- The social context provides children with a language-acquisition support system (LASS).

- Caregivers in most cultures assist language acquisition by speaking "motherese," or infant-directed speech, and by being responsive to early linguistic efforts.

- Children acquire language at roughly the same rate everywhere, despite wide cross-cultural variation in the LASS.

Bilingualism

- Many people around the world speak two or more languages.

- A distinction is made between simultaneous bilinguals, who learn both languages in childhood, and sequential bilinguals, who learn their second language after acquiring their first.

- There are both costs and benefits to bilingualism. Bilingual children have smaller vocabularies in each language than monolingual children, but develop greater executive functions than monolinguals.

Thinking Critically About The Development of Body, Thought, and Language

1. How can we know what an infant is thinking about? Why or why not might it be worthwhile to study perception and cognition in preverbal infants?

2. How are the child's capacities and limitations at each of Piaget's stages of development related to the kind of scheme that is most prominent? How does the child's behavior at each stage promote advancement to the next stage?

3. Some theorists propose that children play an active role in their own mental development, whereas others emphasize the role of a child's sociocultural environment in influencing cognitive development. Are these approaches complementary or antagonistic to one another?

4. To what extent is language development supported by inborn mechanisms and/or the social context?

Reflections and Connections

Thinking and talking are—to use a term from Chapter 3—*species-typical* activities of humans. We are biologically predisposed for thought and language, just as we are predisposed to smile and walk on two legs. The human brain has been specialized for these activities in the course of evolution; people everywhere, in every culture, think and talk in ways that are recognizably human and distinguishable from the activities of any other species. Yet, despite their universality, these abilities must develop anew in each human being.

1. Why thought and language must develop Why aren't these species-typical abilities fully present at birth? An immediate answer is that birth occurs in humans at a relatively early stage in the body's growth. The brain, including the pathways required for thought and language, continues to mature after birth. A more profound answer, however, lies in the ultimate functions of thought and language.

Thought serves to make sense of the environment so that we can navigate safely through it and use parts of it to promote our survival and reproduction. We can survive in a wide range of conditions because we can think of ways to modify them to suit our needs. Similarly, to communicate effectively in our particular cultural group, we must acquire the specific linguistic elements (the words and grammar) that represent concepts crucial to survival in that group. Thought and language must be fine-tuned to the unique physical and social environment in which each individual must survive, and such adjustment is best accomplished when thought and language develop in that environment.

2. Biological foundations for development Evolution could not endow human beings with the specific knowledge and skills needed to survive in every human environment, but it could and did endow the species with a solid foundation for acquiring them. This theme, of evolved and inherited foundations for development, can help tie together many of the ideas and research findings described in this chapter. As you review, consider the following questions: What inborn assumptions may help each new person make sense of his or her physical, social, and linguistic worlds? What universal aspects of babies' and children's explorations and play may help them learn about the particulars of their native environments and languages?

3. Social supports for development The inherited tendencies and drives that promote development can only flourish in a responsive environment. Babies need solid surfaces against which to exercise their muscles in order to learn to walk, objects to explore in order to learn about the physical world, and people to listen to and with whom to exercise their linguistic play in order to learn to talk. Young children may, as Piaget contended, choose what to assimilate from the array of information around them, but adults help provide that array.

As you review the chapter, consider the specific ways in which the child uses and is influenced by the social environment. How do infants employ gaze following, shared attention, and social referencing to guide their explorations? What does Vygotsky's theory tell us about the roles of the tools of intellectual adaptation, dialogue, and cooperative action in the development of thought? What is the role of the language-acquisition support system in language development?

Key Terms

accommodation 415
assimilation 415
autism (autism spectrum disorder) 433
centration 419

concrete-operational schemes 418
creole language 443
decentration 419

developmental psychology 401
egocentricity 419
embryonic phase 402
fetal phase 402

formal-operational schemes 420
grammar 436
language-acquisition device, or LAD 442

Find Out More

Tiffany Field (2007). *The amazing infant.* Malden, MA: Blackwell.

A leading researcher on infant development, Field has made valuable contributions about the role of touch in infants' emotional and physical growth. This highly readable book presents fascinating basic information about infant cognitive, linguistic, social, and emotional development.

Jean Piaget (1929). *The child's conception of the world.* London, UK: Routledge.

A historical foundation not just for Piaget's subsequent work but also for the whole subfield of cognitive development, this book is far more accessible than many of Piaget's other writings. In the introduction, he spells out his method of learning about children's thinking through interviewing them. The book is devoted to Piaget's findings about children's conceptions of reality, expressed in such issues as where the names of things come from, where rain comes from, and what it means to think.

David F. Bjorklund & Kayla B. Causey (2018). *Children's thinking: Cognitive development and individual differences* (6th edition). Thousand Oaks, CA: Sage.

This succinct and accessible textbook on cognitive development describes what we know—and *how* we know—about the various cognitive processes involved in children's thinking, including each of the topics discussed in this chapter.

Annie Murphy Paul (2011, July). *What we learn before we're born.* TEDGlobal. https://www.ted.com/talks/annie_murphy_paul_what_we_learn_before_we_re_born

In this TED talk, science writer Annie Paul discusses cutting-edge research on nativism and in utero learning. Among other findings, she cites evidence that fetuses take cues from their intrauterine environment that affect their physiology— they prepare themselves for conditions they will encounter once they are born.

Steven Pinker (2015). *How we speak reveals what we think* (video and transcript). Bigthink.com

http://bigthink.com/videos/how-we-speak-reveals-how-we-think-with-steven-pinker

In this full-length lecture, cognitive psychologist Steven Pinker discusses the relationship between thinking and language, expanding on Chomsky's nativist perspective.

LaunchPad
macmillan learning

Visit LaunchPad for Psychology 8e launchpadworks.com to access the e-book, videos, activities, additional resources, and LearningCurve quizzes, as well as study aids including flash cards and web quizzes.

Social Development

LEARNING OUTCOMES

After studying this chapter, you should be able to:

- Describe ways in which attachment and culture influence infant development.

- Define prosocial behavior and social learning, and give some examples of each.

- Identify some different styles and theories related to parenting.

- Explain the roles of play and of gender differences in social development.

- Describe some developmental milestones related to adolescence.

- Describe adult development with regard to relationships, careers, and aging.

The natural human environment is a social environment. We are adapted to survive with the help of others. Natural selection has endowed us with brain mechanisms that enable us to make the kinds of connections with other people—at each stage in our lives—that are essential to our survival and reproduction.

In Chapter 11 we described human development with emphasis on the individual; in this chapter we shift our focus to how the individual interacts with others. Over the span of our lives we are involved continuously in interpersonal relationships that sustain, enhance, and give meaning to our existence. As *infants* we depend physically and emotionally on adult caregivers. As *children* we learn to get along with others and to abide by the rules and norms of society. As *adolescents* we begin to explore romantic relationships and consider how we will take our place in the adult world. As *adults* we assume responsibility for the care and support of others and contribute, through work, to the broader society.

Social development refers to the changing nature of our relationships with others over the course of life. What characterizes our ties to other people at each phase of life? How do those relationships promote our survival and influence our subsequent development? How variable is social development from culture to culture and between males and females? These are some of the principal questions of this chapter, which begins with infancy and then proceeds, section by section, through childhood, adolescence, and adulthood.

Infancy: Using Caregivers as a Base for Growth

In the mid-twentieth century, the psychoanalytically oriented child psychologist Erik Erikson (1963) developed an elaborate theory of social development. Erikson's theory posited that each stage of life is associated with a particular crisis, or problem, to be resolved through interactions with other people. It also posited that the way the person resolves each problem influences how he or she approaches subsequent life stages. In infancy, according to Erikson, the primary problem is that of developing a sense of *trust*—that is, a secure sense that other people, or certain other people, can be relied upon for care and help.

Other theorists have focused on the infant's need for care and on the psychological consequences of the manner in which care is provided. One such theorist was British psychologist John Bowlby, who brought an evolutionary perspective to bear on the issue of early child development. Bowlby (1958, 1980) contended that the emotional bond between human infant and adult caregiver—especially the mother—is promoted by a set of instinctive tendencies in both partners. These include the infant's crying to signal discomfort, the adult's distress and urge to help on hearing the crying, the infant's smiling and cooing when comforted, and the adult's pleasure at receiving those signals.

Human infants are completely dependent on caregivers for survival, but, consistent with Bowlby's theory, they are not passively dependent. They enter the world biologically prepared to learn who their caregivers are and to elicit from them the help they need. By the time they are born, babies already prefer the voices of their own mothers over other voices (discussed in Chapter 11), and shortly thereafter they also prefer the smell and sight of their own mothers (Bushnell et al., 1989; Macfarlane, 1975). Newborns signal distress through fussing or crying. By the time they are 3 months old, they express interest, joy, sadness, and anger through their facial expressions, and they respond to such expressions in others (Izard et al., 1995; Lavelli & Fogel, 2005).

In these ways, infants take an active role in building emotional bonds between themselves and those on whom they most directly depend. They also use those caregivers as a base from which to explore the world. In the 1950s, Bowlby began to use the term **attachment** to refer to such emotional bonds, and since then the study of infants' attachment to caregivers has become a major branch of developmental psychology.

Attachment to Caregivers

At about the same time that Bowlby was beginning to write about attachment, Harry Harlow initiated a systematic program of research on attachment with rhesus monkeys. Harlow controlled the monkeys' living conditions experimentally to learn about the developmental consequences of raising infants in isolation from their mothers and other monkeys. Most relevant to our present theme are experiments in which Harlow raised infant monkeys with inanimate surrogate (substitute) mothers.

Harlow's Monkeys Raised with Surrogate Mothers

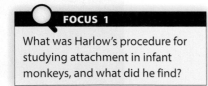

FOCUS 1

What was Harlow's procedure for studying attachment in infant monkeys, and what did he find?

In one experiment, Harlow raised infant monkeys individually in isolated cages, each containing two surrogate mothers—one made of bare wire and the other covered with soft terry cloth (see Harlow & Zimmerman, 1959; **Figure 12.1**). The infants could feed themselves by sucking milk from a nipple that was affixed either to the wire surrogate or to the cloth surrogate. Harlow's purpose was to determine if the infants would become attached to either of these surrogate mothers as they would to a real mother; he also wanted to know which characteristic—the milk-providing nipple or the soft cloth exterior—was most effective in inducing attachment.

Harlow's main finding was that regardless of which surrogate contained the nipple with milk, all the infant monkeys treated the cloth-covered surrogate, not the wire one, as a mother. They clung to it for much of the day and ran to it when frightened by a strange object (see **Figure 12.2**). They also were braver in exploring an unfamiliar room when the cloth surrogate was present than when it was absent, and they pressed a lever repeatedly to look at it through a window in preference to other objects. This work demonstrated the role of contact comfort in the development of attachment bonds, and it helped to revolutionize psychologists' thinking

FIGURE 12.1 Harlow's motherless monkeys Harlow raised infant monkeys with two surrogate (substitute) mothers, one wire and one cloth. The monkey shown here received its nourishment from a bottle attached to the wire surrogate but went to the cloth surrogate for comfort, affection, and reassurance.

about infants' needs. Provision of adequate nutrition and other physical necessities is not enough; infants also need close contact with comforting caregivers.

The Form and Functions of Human Infants' Attachment

Bowlby (1969, 1973, 1980) observed attachment behaviors in young humans, aged 8 months to 3 years, that were similar to those that Harlow observed with monkeys. He found that children showed distress when their mothers (the objects of their attachment) left them, especially in an unfamiliar environment; showed pleasure when reunited with their mothers; showed distress when approached by a stranger unless reassured or comforted by their mothers; and were more likely to explore an unfamiliar environment when in the presence of their mothers than when alone. Many research studies have since verified these general conclusions (see Thompson, 2013).

Bowlby contended that attachment is a universal human phenomenon with a biological foundation that derives from natural selection. Infants are potentially in danger when out of sight of caregivers, especially in a novel environment. During our evolutionary history, infants who scrambled after their mothers and successfully protested their mothers' departure, and who avoided unfamiliar objects when their mothers were absent, were more likely to survive to adulthood and pass on their genes than were those who were indifferent to their mothers' presence

FOCUS 2

According to Bowlby, what infant behaviors indicate strong attachment, and why would they have come about in natural selection?

FIGURE 12.2 Evidence of infant monkeys' preference for the cloth surrogate These graphs show (a) the average number of hours that Harlow's monkeys spent on each of the surrogate mothers and (b) the percentage of time that they ran to each when they were frightened by a strange object. Notice that the preference for the cloth surrogate was as strong for the monkeys that were fed on the wire surrogate as for those fed on the cloth surrogate. (Data from Harlow, 1959.)

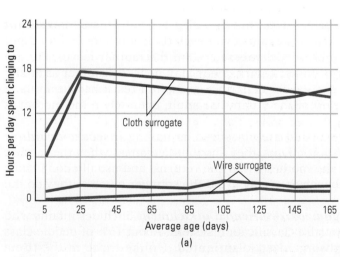

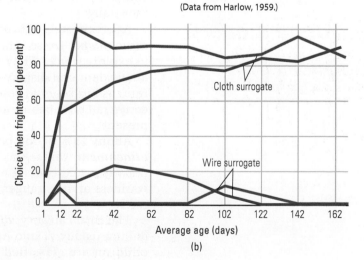

FOCUS 3

From an evolutionary perspective, why does attachment strengthen at about 6 to 8 months of age?

FOCUS 4

How does the strange-situation test assess the security of attachment?

or absence. Evidence that similar behaviors occur in all human cultures (Konner, 2010) and in other species of mammals (Kraemer, 1992) supports Bowlby's evolutionary interpretation.

Also consistent with the evolutionary explanation is the observation that attachment begins to strengthen at about the age (6 to 8 months) when infants begin to move around on their own. A crawling or walking infant—who for good evolutionary reasons is intent on exploring the environment—can get into more danger than an immobile one. For safety's sake, exploration must be balanced by a drive to stay near the protective caregiver. As was noted in Chapter 11, infants who can crawl or walk exhibit much *social referencing*; that is, they look to their caregivers for cues about danger or safety as they explore. To feel most secure in a novel situation, infants require not just the presence of their attachment object but also that person's emotional availability and expressions of reassurance. Infants who cannot see their mother's face typically move around her until they can (Carr et al., 1975), and infants who are approached by a stranger relax more if their mother smiles cheerfully at the stranger than if she doesn't (Broccia & Campos, 1989).

The Strange-Situation Measure of Attachment Quality

In order to assess attachment systematically, Mary Ainsworth—who originally worked with Bowlby—developed the ***strange-situation test*** (Ainsworth et al., 1978). Briefly, the strange-situation test begins with a mother and her infant, between the ages of 12 and 18 months, entering a small room (although fathers and infants of other ages are sometimes tested, too). The mother shows the baby some toys and allows the child to explore or play freely. This is followed by a series of 3-minute periods of various activities by the adults in the study. First, an unfamiliar adult enters the room, talks to the mother, and interacts with the infant. Three minutes later, the mother goes out of the room, leaving the child with the stranger. Finally, the mother returns. The behaviors that are most important for evaluating attachment are those of the baby when the mother returns. Based on babies' responses, Ainsworth and her colleagues developed three attachment classifications: secure, insecure-resistant, and insecure-avoidant. A fourth type, disorganized/disoriented (Main & Solomon, 1986) was included later.

Using the strange situation and based on mostly middle-class samples (see van IJzendoorn et al., 1999), about 60% of the babies tested by Ainsworth and by others are classified as having ***secure attachment***, at least in the United States. These infants actively explore while in the room with their mothers, and they become upset when their mothers leave them. When the mother returns, a securely attached baby will often run or crawl to her, greeting her warmly. The mother is able to soothe the child to the extent that sometimes the child returns to play with the stranger.

Approximately 10% of the babies tested are classified as having ***insecure-resistant attachment***. These infants appear anxious even with their mothers and tend not to explore much. They become very distressed when the mother leaves, but are ambivalent and display anger on her return. They stay near the mother after she returns but seem to resent her earlier departure and often resist her attempts at contact. These babies are wary of the unfamiliar adult, even when the mother is present.

About 15% of the babies tested are classified as having ***insecure-avoidant attachment***. Unlike the resistant infants, they show little distress when the mother departs, avoid contact with the mother when she returns, and usually don't show wariness of the stranger, although they may avoid the stranger much as they do the mother.

The final category, ***disorganized/disoriented attachment***, includes infants who did not readily fit into Ainsworth's classification system. About 15% of middle-class children are classified as disorganized/disoriented. Unlike those in the three standard classifications, disorganized/disoriented infants show no coherent strategy for dealing with stress during separation and reunion in the strange-situation test. Disorganized/disoriented infants seek to be close to their mothers in erratic ways, often showing patterns typical of secure, avoidant, and/or resistant infants simultaneously (e.g., strong approach to the mother followed by strong avoidance). They may sometimes look dazed and disoriented upon reunion with their mothers. They may freeze in the middle of movement, approach her backwards, or wait an inordinate amount of time before deciding to approach her. Unlike other infants, disorganized/disoriented infants seem to have developed no consistent way of handling separation and reunion with their mothers.

Sensitive Care Correlates With Secure Attachment and Positive Later Adjustment

Ainsworth hypothesized that infants would become securely attached to mothers who provide regular contact comfort, respond promptly and helpfully to the infant's signals of distress, and interact with the infant in an emotionally synchronous manner—a constellation of behaviors referred to today as *sensitive care*. Consistent with that hypothesis, Ainsworth and other researchers subsequently found significant positive correlations between ratings of the mother's sensitive care and security of the infant's attachment to the mother (Ainsworth, 1979; Posada et al., 2004). In most such studies, the mother's style of parenting was assessed through home visits early in infancy and attachment was assessed with the strange-situation test several months later, after the baby could move about on its own.

Ainsworth (1989) also predicted that secure attachment would lead to positive effects later on in life. This view was very much in line with that of Bowlby (1973), who proposed that infants develop an internal "working model," or cognitive representation, of their first attachment relationship and that this model affects their subsequent relationships throughout life. It was also consistent with Erikson's (1963) theory that secure attachment in infancy results in a general sense of trust of other people and oneself, allowing the infant to enter subsequent stages of life in a confident, growth-promoting manner. Consistent with such views, children judged to be securely attached in infancy have been found, on average, to be more confident, better at solving problems, emotionally healthier, and more sociable later in childhood than those who had been found to be insecurely attached (Ainsworth, 1989; Raikes & Thompson, 2008). In fact, the positive effects of secure attachment are so many and so rich that Teresa McDevitt and Jeanne Ormond (2004) described secure attachment as a "multivitamin" that prevents problems and fosters healthy development. The results of a longitudinal study by K. Lee Raby and his colleagues (2015) reported positive effects of secure attachment through 32 years of age, as reflected in measures of social adjustment (e.g., effective romantic relationships) and educational attainment.

How do we know that maternal sensitivity is truly causing infants to become securely attached to their mothers rather than some third factor such as infant temperament? The answer is found in the results of several training studies. For example, mothers with temperamentally irritable babies—babies who by disposition are unusually fussy, easily angered, and difficult to comfort—participated in a 3-month training program, beginning when their infants were 6 months old, designed to help and encourage the mothers to perceive and respond appropriately to their babies' signals, especially signals of distress. When the infants were 12 months old, all of them were tested with their mothers in the strange-situation test. The result was that 62% of the infants with trained mothers showed secure attachment, whereas only 22% of the infants in a control condition did (van den Boom, 1991). Other experiments have shown that parental training for foster parents can result in more sensitive parenting, more secure attachment, reduced physiological evidence of distress in the child, and fewer reported problem behaviors in the child (Dozier et al., 2006; Fisher et al., 2006).

FOCUS 5

What evidence suggests that sensitive parenting correlates with secure attachment and subsequent emotional and social development? How did Ainsworth interpret the correlations, and how else might they be interpreted?

■ Mothers' sensitivity to their babies' signals of physical and social needs is associated with secure attachment.

FOCUS 6

What experimental evidence supports the theory that sensitive care promotes secure attachment?

Some Children Are More Susceptible to Parental Effects Than Are Others

FOCUS 7

What evidence suggests that some infants are relatively invulnerable to negative effects of insensitive parenting?

Several studies have suggested that the relationship between parental care and infants' attachment depends, at least partly, on the genetic makeup of the child (Bakermans-Kranenburg & van Ijzendoorn, 2007; Belsky et al., 2007). The most dramatic effect comes from an experiment involving infants who differ in a certain gene that is involved in the manner by which the brain uses the neurotransmitter serotonin.

The gene at issue (called the 5-HTTLLPR gene) comes in two forms (or *alleles*, as defined in Chapter 3), a short (*s*) form and a long (*l*) form. The *l* allele results in greater uptake of serotonin into brain neurons than does the *s* allele. Previous research had shown that children who are homozygous for the *l* allele (i.e., have *l* on both paired chromosomes, as discussed in Chapter 3) are less affected by negative environmental experiences than are other children. For example, they are less likely to become depressed or highly fearful as a result of living in abusive homes (Kaufman et al., 2006). In a study of attachment, parents were assessed for their level of sensitive care when their infants were 7 months old, and then the infants' attachment behavior was assessed using the strange-situation test when the infants were 15 months old (Barry et al., 2008). A genetic test revealed that 28 of the 88 infants had the *ll* genotype and the rest had either *ss* or *sl*.

The results of the study are shown in **Figure 12.3**. Attachment security increased significantly and rather sharply with increased maternal sensitivity for the *ss/sl* group but was not significantly affected by maternal sensitivity for the *ll* group. The *ll* infants showed highly secure attachment regardless of the level of maternal sensitivity. As technologies continue to advance, much new research is exploring this and other relationships between parenting and children's genetic makeup.

Cross-Cultural Differences in Infant Care

FOCUS 8

What are some differences in the way cultures care for young infants?

Beliefs and practices regarding infant care vary considerably from culture to culture. Our Western, Euro-American culture is in many ways less indulgent of infants' desires than are other cultures. Are such differences in care associated with any differences in infant social behavior and subsequent development?

During most of our species' history, our ancestors lived in small groups, made up mostly of close relatives, who survived by gathering and hunting food cooperatively in the forest or savanna. The biological underpinnings of infants' and caregivers' behaviors evolved in the context of that way of life. Partly for that reason, an examination of infant care in the few hunter-gatherer cultures that have survived into recent times is of special interest.

Melvin Konner (1976, 2010) studied the !Kung San people, who live in Africa's Kalahari Desert. He observed that !Kung infants spend most of their time during their first year in direct contact with their mothers' bodies. At night the mother sleeps with the infant, and during the day she carries the infant in a sling at her side. The sling is arranged in such a way that the infant has constant access to the mother's breast and can nurse at will—which, according to Konner, occurs on average every 15 minutes. This position also enables the infant to see what the mother sees and in that way to be involved in her activities. When not being held by the mother, the infant is passed around among others, who cuddle, fondle, kiss, and enjoy

FIGURE 12.3 Interaction between genes and environment Security of attachments to their mothers was positively correlated with the sensitivity of maternal care for most infants, but not for those with the *ll* genotype, who showed secure attachment regardless of quality of care. Attachment security was scored numerically, based on each infant's behavior in the strange situation, and the scores were standardized, such that 0 is the average overall of the infants combined. (Standardized scores are explained in the Statistical Appendix.) The upward slope for the *ss/sl* infants is statistically significant; the slight downward slope for the *ll* infants is not significant.

(Data from Barry et al., 2008.)

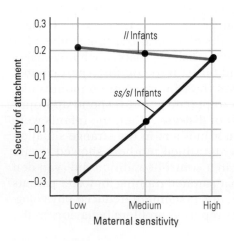

the baby. According to Konner, the !Kung never leave an infant to cry alone, and usually they detect the distress and begin to comfort the infant before crying even begins.

Studies of other hunter-gatherer cultures have also shown a high degree of indulgence toward infants (Lamb & Hewlett, 2005), but the people who provide the care can vary. Among the Efe (*Eff-ay*), a traditional hunter-gatherer society native to the Ituri forest of central Africa, infants are in physical contact with their mothers for only about half the day (Ivey Henry et al., 2005; Morelli & Tronick, 1991). During the rest of the day they are in direct contact with other caregivers, including siblings, aunts, and unrelated women. Efe infants nurse at will, not just from their mothers but also from other lactating women in the group. However, at about 8 to 12 months of age—the age at which research in many cultures has shown that attachment strengthens—Efe infants begin to show increased preference for their own mothers. They are less readily comforted by other people and will often reject the breast of another woman and seek the mother's. Such "indulgence" of their infants by hunter-gatherer mothers apparently does *not* lead to greater dependence or prevent them from learning to cope with life's frustrations. Rather, Konner (1976, 2010) contends that !Kung children are extraordinarily cooperative and brave. In a cross-cultural test, !Kung children older than 4 years explored more and sought their mothers less in a novel environment than did their British counterparts (Blurton-Jones & Konner, 1973).

In no culture yet studied is the average father nearly as involved as the average mother in direct care of infants and young children; but, in general, paternal involvement appears to be greater in hunter-gatherer cultures than in agricultural or industrial cultures (Hewlett, 1988). The record on this score seems to be held by the Aka of central Africa, a hunter-gatherer group closely related to the Efe (Hewlett, 1988). Aka fathers have been observed to hold their infants an average of 20% of the time during daylight hours and to get up with them frequently at night. Among the Aka, the whole family—mother, father, infant, and other young children—sleep together in the same bed.

FOCUS 9

What observations suggest that hunter-gatherers are highly indulgent toward infants? What parenting styles distinguish the !Kung, Efe, and Aka?

Dr. Gilda Morelli

■ **An Efe girl and her infant brother**
In hunter-gatherer cultures, infants are in direct physical contact with a caregiver almost constantly. Efe infants spend about half of each day with their mothers and the rest of the day with other members of the group.

SECTION REVIEW

Infants develop emotional attachment bonds with the caregivers on whom they depend.

Attachment to Caregivers

- Harlow found that infant monkeys became attached to a cloth surrogate mother but not to a wire one, even if the latter provided milk. They turned to the cloth "mother" for contact comfort and explored the environment more fully in its presence.

- Bowlby found that human infants also exhibit attachment behaviors. Such behaviors, which help protect the baby from danger, intensify when the baby can move around on its own.

- Secure attachment of infants to caregivers, measured by the strange-situation test, correlates with the caregiver's responsive, emotionally sensitive care. Parent-training experiments indicate that sensitive care promotes secure attachment.

- Security of attachment in infancy and early childhood predicts psychological adjustment later in life.

- Some infants, who have a particular genotype, appear to develop secure attachment regardless of the sensitivity or insensitivity of care.

Infant Care in Different Cultures

- Hunter-gatherer societies such as the Efe and Aka treat infants with indulgence, keeping them in nearly constant physical contact, permitting nursing at will, and responding quickly to signs of distress.

Helping, Comforting, and Learning From Others in Childhood

As children grow from infancy into toddlerhood and beyond, they become increasingly mobile and capable of a wide variety of actions in their physical and social worlds. In his life-span theory of social development, Erikson (1963) divided the years from age 1 to 12 into three successive stages; these are concerned, respectively, with the development of *autonomy* (self-control), *initiative* (willingness to initiate actions), and *industry* (competence in completing tasks). These characteristics are all closely related to one another in that they involve the child's ability to control his or her own actions.

As Erikson pointed out, however, children's actions frequently bring them into conflict with caregivers and others around them. According to Erikson, caregivers' responses to children's actions, and the ways by which caregivers and children resolve their conflicts, influence children's social development. On the positive side, children may develop the ability to behave appropriately, with confidence, in ways that are satisfying both to themselves and to others. On the negative side, children may develop feelings of shame, doubt, and inferiority that interfere with autonomy, initiative, and industry. The psychologically healthy person, in Erikson's theory, is one who responds appropriately to others' needs without sacrificing his or her own sense of self-control. Developmental psychologists refer to such actions as ***prosocial behavior***, voluntary behavior intended to benefit other people (Eisenberg et al., 2013; Paulus, 2014), and it is to this topic we now turn.

The Development of Prosocial Behavior

As we've noted several times in this book, infants and young children are predisposed to be social. Infants prefer to look at faces and seem to have a special ability to process and make sense of faces; they view others as intentional agents who do things "on purpose" with specific goals in mind; and they easily form attachments with multiple people (but especially their mothers) early in life. Infants and young children are not simply oriented toward social stimuli, however, but are disposed to behave positively, or prosocially, toward other people, and we will look at three aspects of young children's prosocial behavior here: helping, comforting, and sharing.

The Early Emergence of Empathy and Empathic Comforting

FOCUS 10

According to Hoffman, how does empathy develop during infancy and early toddlerhood?

Newborn babies, as young as 2 or 3 days old, reflexively cry and show other signs of distress in response to another baby's crying. Martin Hoffman (2007) has suggested that this tendency to feel discomfort in response to another's expressed discomfort is a foundation for the development of empathy. Over time, the response gradually becomes less reflexive and more accompanied by thought. By about 6 months of age, babies may no longer cry immediately in response to another's crying, but rather turn toward the distressed individual, look sad, and whimper.

Until about 15 months of age, the child's distress when others are distressed is best referred to as *egocentric* empathy (Hoffman, 2007). The distressed child seeks comfort for himself or herself rather than for the other distressed person. At about 15 months, however, children begin to respond to another's discomfort by attempting to comfort that person, and by 2 years of age they begin to succeed at such comforting (Knafo et al., 2008). Hoffman described a case in which 2-year-old David first attempted to comfort his crying friend by giving him his (David's) own teddy bear. When that didn't work, David ran to the next room and returned with his friend's teddy bear and gave it to him. The friend hugged the bear and immediately stopped crying. To behave in such an effective manner, the child must not only feel bad about another's discomfort, but must also understand enough about the other person's mind to know what will provide comfort.

The Young Child's Natural Tendency to Give and Help

Near the end of their first year, infants routinely begin to voluntarily give objects to their caregivers and to delight in games of give-and-take, in which the child and caregiver pass an object back and forth. In a series of experiments conducted in the United States, nearly every one of more than 100 infants, aged 12 to 18 months, spontaneously gave toys to an adult during brief sessions in a laboratory room (Hay & Murray, 1982; Rheingold et al., 1976). They gave not just to their mothers or fathers but also to unfamiliar researchers, and they gave new toys as frequently as familiar ones. They gave when an adult requested a toy by holding a hand out with palm up, and they gave when no requests were made. Infants in a !Kung hunter-gatherer community were likewise observed to give objects regularly, beginning near the end of their first year of life (Bakeman et al., 1990).

In addition to liking to give, young children enjoy helping with adult tasks. In one study, children between 18 and 30 months old were frequently observed joining their mothers, without being asked, in such household tasks as making the bed, setting the table, and folding laundry (Rheingold, 1982). In other research, experimenters sat across from 18- and 24-month-old toddlers performing tasks such as reaching for a marker or stacking books (Warneken & Tomasello, 2006). Occasionally, a mishap would occur and the marker or book would fall to the floor. Children spontaneously retrieved the fallen objects, and did so more often when it looked as if the adult had made a mistake (e.g., intended to stack the book but it slipped out of his hand) than when the experimenter intentionally dropped the object to the floor.

One might argue that young children's early giving, sharing, and helping are largely self-centered rather than other-centered, motivated more by the child's own needs and wishes than by the child's perception of others' needs and wishes. But the very fact that such actions seem to stem from the child's own wishes is evidence that our species has evolved prosocial (socially beneficial) drives, which motivate us—with no feeling of sacrifice—to involve ourselves in positive ways with other people. Giving and helping become increasingly other-focused as they become linked to another species-typical capacity in the child, that of *empathy*, the ability to perceive and feel the emotions that another person is feeling.

In their relationships with caregivers, young children are most often on the receiving end of acts of giving, helping, and comforting. They therefore have ample opportunity not only to witness such behaviors but also to feel their pleasurable and comforting consequences. Correlational studies indicate that children who have received the most sensitive care, and who are most securely attached to their caregivers, also demonstrate the most giving and comforting to others (Bretherton et al., 1997; Kiang et al., 2004).

FOCUS 11

What evidence suggests that young children naturally enjoy giving? How do the !Kung use that enjoyment for moral training?

■ **Giving is natural** Infants and young children all over the world delight in games of give-and-take with adults or older children. Sharing appears to be an aspect of human nature that begins to be exercised as soon as the child's capacity for motor coordination makes it possible.

Sharing

Closely related to giving is sharing. Young children are notoriously poor sharers, with the word *mine* being a frequent refrain between two toddlers trying to play with a single toy. In one study, 84% of all disputes between pairs of 21-month-old children involved conflict over toys (Hay & Ross, 1982). Sharing is more common with older children, with the amount of sharing increasing with age. For example, when 5- to 14-year-old children had earned five candy bars and were told they could share some of their candy with "poor children," a majority of children at all ages shared at least one candy bar, and the number of candy bars shared increased with age. Specifically, 60% of 5- and 6-year-olds shared, 92% of 7- and 8-year-olds shared, as did 100% of 9- and 10-year-olds and 13- and 14-year-olds (Green & Schneider, 1974).

However, even young children will share in many contexts. Celia Brownell and her colleagues (2009) had 18- and 25-month-old toddlers take part in a food-sharing task with an adult. Children were at one end on an apparatus and could pull on a handle to deliver a treat for themselves; or, if they chose, they could pull another

FOCUS 12

At about what age and under what conditions do children share?

handle and deliver a treat both for themselves and for the adult on the other side of the apparatus. On some trials the adult said, "I like crackers. I want a cracker." Although the 18-month-olds responded randomly on all trials, the 25-month-olds shared on about 70% of the trials when the adult vocalized such a wish.

Young children seem especially likely to share in situations in which they need to collaborate to achieve a goal. In one study, 3-year-old children were shown how to operate an apparatus in which two people must pull on ropes in order to deliver a prize. Under these conditions, children cooperated on 70% of the trials, and shared the rewards equally on more than 80% of these trials (Warneken et al., 2011).

In other situations in which an adult distributes resources (stickers or food) among children, even 3-year-olds realize when they are getting an unfair deal, although they are less apt to complain when they get the lion's share of the resources (LoBue et al., 2010). When children are in control of the resources and can choose to share or not, most 4- and 5-year-old children share, but continue to keep more resources for themselves than they give to others (Benenson et al., 2007). As they get older, children are increasingly likely to see fairness in terms of equitable distributions (i.e., rewards according to merit or effort expended), although this tendency varies with culture, as children from traditional and hunter-gatherer cultures are less apt to consider effort/merit in making distribution decisions than children from Western cultures (Schäfer et al., 2015).

Young children's fair distribution of resources is also related to theory of mind. In several studies, preschool children who passed false-belief tasks (see Chapter 11) were more likely to make a fair distribution of resources between themselves and a peer than children who failed such tasks (Takagishi et al., 2010; Wu & Su, 2014).

Social Learning

Given the extent to which children are oriented toward their social environment, it should not be surprising that much of what they learn is accomplished in a social context. We discussed social learning in Chapter 8, providing an outline of Bandura's social learning theory (renamed social cognitive theory). Here we expand on our earlier discussion, focusing on the phenomenon of overimitation and how children learn from observing other children.

Overimitation

Like chimpanzees, children of about 2 years of age and younger frequently engage in *emulation* (see Chapter 8.) They seem to understand the goal a model has in mind, but do not restrict themselves to using the same behaviors as the model did to achieve that goal (Nielsen, 2006; McGuigan & Whiten, 2009). Things begin to change around the child's third birthday, however. Several studies have convincingly demonstrated that beginning about this time most children faithfully repeat the actions of a model, even if many of those actions are irrelevant and if there is a more efficient way to solve the problem (Hoehl et al., 2014; Nielsen et al., 2015). Such **overimitation** was observed in a study by Derek Lyons and his colleagues (2007), who showed preschool children how to open a transparent container to get a toy that was locked inside. Some of the actions of the model were clearly relevant to opening the container, such as unscrewing its lid, whereas others were clearly irrelevant, such as tapping the side of the container with a feather. When later given a chance to retrieve the toy themselves, most children copied both the relevant and irrelevant actions, even though they were able to tell the experimenter which were actions necessary and which were "silly"; they even did so if they were asked to avoid the "silly" ones. Overimitation is not limited to children from Western culture but has also been observed in 2- to 6-year-old Kalahari Bushman children (Nielsen & Tomaselli, 2010; Nielsen et al., 2014). In contrast, researchers have found no evidence that chimpanzees engage in overimitation (Nielsen, 2012).

Although we might think older children and adults should know better, even they engage in overimitation. In one study using a transparent container that had

FOCUS 13

What is overimitation, who engages in it, and why might it be adaptive?

to be opened to retrieve an object, 3- and 5-year-old children and adults observed models performing both relevant and irrelevant actions on the container. Copying irrelevant actions actually increased with age, with the adults displaying less efficient performance than the children (McGuigan et al., 2011).

Children (and adults) are not necessarily blind mimics, however. For example, 3-, 4-, and 5-year-old children in one study were less apt to copy irrelevant actions in attempting to get a toy out of a container when the adult model made it clear that such actions were accidental (saying, "Whoops! I didn't mean to do that!") than when the actions were cued as intentional (saying "There!") (Gardiner et al., 2011).

Why should children (and adults) copy irrelevant actions? One explanation is that humans age 3 and older generally believe that models are trustworthy and that each action has a purpose. Recall from Chapter 11 that infants and toddlers see other people as *intentional agents*, doing things "on purpose" to achieve specific goals. In most cases, what a model does is important to attaining a goal, and any effort children expend beyond what is necessary to complete a task is more than compensated by the greater efficiency that social learning, as opposed to trial-and-error learning, affords. This may be especially adaptive for humans relative to other social animals, because children must learn about thousands of artifacts, all cultural inventions (Whiten et al., 2009). Children may understand that some actions are relevant and others are irrelevant for completing a task, but they believe all of the actions are important for the "bigger overarching action sequence" (Keupp et al., 2013, p. 393). Consistent with this interpretation, children seem to think that modeled actions on objects are normative. For example, 3- to 5-year-old children corrected a puppet that omitted unnecessary actions previously performed by an adult, protesting that the puppet was "doing it wrong" (Kenward, 2012).

Learning From Other Children

Although children surely learn much from watching adults, they also learn from other children. In one study by Lydia Hopper and her colleagues (2010), one preschooler was shown how to work the panpipes apparatus, shown in **Figure 12.4**, using a stick to retrieve a treat. There are three ways to successfully operate the panpipes to get the reward: (a) the Lift method, in which the stick is inserted into a hole to lift the T-bar; (b) the Poke method, in which the stick is inserted into

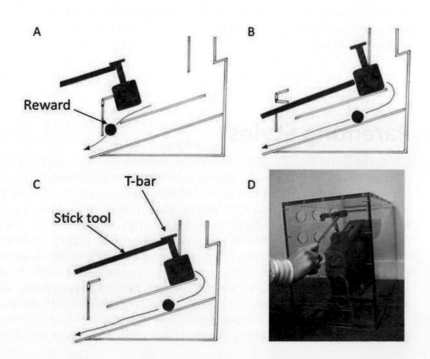

FIGURE 12.4 Panpipes apparatus
(A) The stick-tool inserted under the T-bar for the lift method, (B) the stick-tool inserted into the top hole for the poke method, and (C) the push-lift method by using the stick-tool pushing the T-bar back. In (D) the panpipes are viewed from the child's perspective, inside the clear plastic box with the access holes, with lift being demonstrated.

(Whiten, A., & Flynn, E. G. (2010). The transmission and evolution of experimental 'microcultures' in groups of young children. *Developmental Psychology, 46,* 1694–1709.)

a different hole, poking the T-bar; and (c) the Push-Lift method, in which the stick is used to push and then slide the T-bar. One child was shown the Lift method. This child then served as the model for another child, who in turn served as a model for another child, and so on for a total of 20 children. All 20 children successfully learned the Lift method, demonstrating the fidelity with which children can transmit information from one to another. In contrast, when another group of children was shown the panpipes and asked to figure out how to get the treat out, only 3 of 16 succeeded.

But preschool children do not often deliberately teach a skill to another child. A more common occurrence in a preschool classroom is one child performing some task while their classmates happen to see the outcome. This was examined in a study by Andrew Whiten and Emma Flynn (2010), who taught one child in each of two preschool classrooms either the Lift or the Poke method for working the panpipes. They then placed the panpipes into the child's classroom and watched what happened. Most of the children in a classroom tried to operate the panpipes, usually after watching the trained child receive a treat, and 83% of children who did so were successful. However, after a few days, several children learned alternate ways of operating the panpipes (Lift if they had originally used Poke and vice versa), and this new method, too, spread to other children in the classroom. Not surprisingly, in addition to simply modeling how to get a treat from the panpipes, many children talked about what they were doing, trying to teach other children how to operate the apparatus. This research shows that young children have a number of social-learning abilities at their disposal and that a skill learned by one child will be transmitted to other children, sometimes with fidelity and sometimes with modifications.

FOCUS 14

What evidence is there that children learn new skills from watching other children?

SECTION REVIEW

The child's species-typical drives and emotions, and interactions with caregivers, promote social development.

The Development of Prosocial Behavior

- Young children are predisposed to give; they give objects spontaneously to others beginning near the end of their first year.

- The development of empathy during the second year causes children to base their giving, helping, sharing, and comforting on an understanding of and concern for others' needs and feelings.

Social Learning

- Children learn much in social contexts; by 3 years of age they tend to imitate all actions a model displays, both relevant and irrelevant (overimitation).

- Children transmit skills to one another, usually with high fidelity.

Parenting Styles

For some animals, the offspring are on their own after birth. This, of course, is not the case with mammals, whose sole source of food is their mother's milk. Yet, once infants are weaned the young of many mammals must fend for themselves, whereas for other mammals, including all primates, mom (and for a handful of primates, dad) continues to have some "parenting" obligations. This is especially true for humans, whose extended period of immaturity makes it necessary for them to be cared for long after they are no longer dependent on mother's milk for survival. But there are many ways in which parents interact with the children on the way to adulthood, and these are often characterized as ***parenting styles***. Psychologists describe parenting style in terms of two dimensions: (1) the degree of *warmth* a parent shows toward a child, reflected by being loving and attentive to children and their needs, and (2) the degree of *control* a parent attempts to exert over

TABLE 12.1 Parenting styles can be classified according to warmth (high versus low) that parents display and the amount of control (high versus low) they try to impose on their children's behavior

Control	Warmth	
	High (warm, responsive)	**Low** (rejecting, unresponsive)
High (demanding, restrictive)	Authoritative	Authoritarian
Low (undemanding, permissive)	Permissive	Uninvolved

Source: Information from Maccoby & Martin, 1983.

a child's behavior. Parenting style can be divided into four general types, depending where a parent falls (high versus low) on these two dimensions (see **Table 12.1**).

Correlations Between Disciplinary Styles and Children's Behavior

The best-known, pioneering study of parenting styles was conducted by Diana Baumrind (1967, 1971). Baumrind assessed the behavior of young children by observing them at nursery schools and in their homes, and she assessed parents' behaviors toward their children through interviews and home observations. On the basis of the latter assessments, she classed parents into three groups:

- *Authoritarian* parents strongly value obedience for its own sake and use a high degree of power assertion to control their children (low warmth, high control).

- *Authoritative* parents are less concerned with obedience for its own sake and more concerned that their children learn and abide by basic principles of right and wrong (high warmth, high control).

- *Permissive* parents are most tolerant of their children's disruptive actions and least likely to discipline them at all. The responses they do show to their children's misbehavior seem to be manifestations of their own frustration more than reasoned attempts at correction (high warmth, low control).

Eleanor Maccoby and John Martin (1983) added *uninvolved* (or *neglectful*) *parenting* to the matrix. Uninvolved parents are disengaged from their children, emotionally cold, and demand little from their offspring (low warmth, low control).

Baumrind and others (see Collins & Steinberg, 2006) found that children of authoritative parents exhibit the most positive qualities. They are friendlier, happier, more cooperative, and less likely to disrupt others' activities than are children of either authoritarian or permissive parents. In a follow-up study of the same children, the advantages for those with authoritative parents were still present at age 9 (Baumrind, 1986). In contrast, children of authoritarian parents often perform poorly in school, have low self-esteem, and are more apt to be rejected by their school peers (Pettit et al., 1988), whereas children of permissive parents tend to be impulsive and aggressive, often acting out of control (Lamborn et al., 1991). Children of uninvolved parents typically fare the worst. In adolescence, they often show a broad range of problem behaviors, including sexual promiscuity, antisocial behavior, drug use, and internalizing problems such as depression and social withdrawal (Baumrind, 1991; Lamborn et al., 1991).

The Cause–Effect Problem in Relating Parenting Style to Children's Behavior

As always, we must be cautious in drawing causal inferences from correlational research. It is tempting to conclude from studies such as Baumrind's that the positive parenting style caused the good behavior of the offspring, but the opposite

---

FOCUS 15

What are the four general parenting styles psychologists have identified, and how do they affect children's psychological development?

causal relationship may be just as plausible. Some children are temperamentally, for genetic reasons, less cooperative and more disruptive than others, and that behavior may elicit harsh, power-assertive discipline and reduced warmth from parents. Several studies have shown that children with different temperaments do, indeed, elicit different disciplinary styles from their parents (Jaffee et al., 2004; O'Connor et al., 1998). Also, children's behavior and style of discipline interact over time, each influencing the others. In one longitudinal study, early spanking of children by their mothers was associated with later externalizing (acting out) behavior by their children, while early externalizing behavior by children elicited more spanking over time by their mothers (Gershoff et al., 2012).

The best evidence that parenting styles influence children's development comes from experiments that use training to modify the styles of one group of parents and then compare their offspring to those of similar parents who did not receive such training. In one experiment, divorced mothers of 6- to 8-year-old sons were assigned either to a training condition, in which they were taught how to use firm but kind methods of discipline, or to a comparison condition, in which no such training was given. Assessments a year later showed that the sons whose mothers had undergone training had better relationships with their mothers, rated themselves as happier, and were rated by their teachers as friendlier and more cooperative than was the case for the sons of the comparison mothers (Forgatch & DeGarmo, 1999). Further assessment, three years later, revealed significantly less delinquent behavior by sons of the trained mothers compared to those of the untrained mothers.

SECTION REVIEW

Parenting Styles

- Baumrind's correlational research found that children of parents with an authoritative disciplinary style were happier, friendlier, and more cooperative than children of parents with either authoritarian or permissive styles.

- Experimental research supports Baumrind's ideas about an authoritative disciplinary style promoting better outcomes for children.

The Roles of Play and Gender in Development

Parents play important roles in children's social development, but so do peers. Indeed, if developmental psychology were an endeavor pursued by children rather than by adults, we suspect that research would focus more on children's relationships with one another than on their relationships with adults. Parents and other caregivers provide a base from which children grow, but peers are the targets toward which children are oriented and about which they often have the most conscious concerns. A mother and father want their daughter to wear a certain pair of shoes, but the neighborhood children think the shoes are "geeky" and a different style is "cool." Which shoes will the girl want to wear? From an evolutionary perspective, children's strong orientation toward peers makes sense: It is the peer group, not the parental group, that will provide the child's most direct future collaborators in life-sustaining work and reproduction.

Across cultures and over the span of history, a child's social world is composed largely of other children. In most cultures for which data are available, children above the age of 4 or 5 spend more of their daytime hours with other children than with adults (Lancy, 2015; Whiting & Edwards, 1988). What are they doing together? Mostly they are playing. In every culture that has been studied, children play when they have the opportunity, and their play takes certain universal forms (Pellegrini & Bjorklund, 2004). It is also true that in every culture studied, children tend to segregate themselves by sex when they play: Boys play mostly with boys, and girls play mostly with girls (Maccoby, 1998; Whiting & Edwards, 1988). Through playing with others of their own sex, children develop the gender-specific skills and attitudes of their culture.

Developmental Functions of Play

Let us take a closer look at the subject of play, first discussed in Chapter 8. Young mammals—including human children—play at fleeing, chasing, fighting, stalking, and nurturing. What are some universal forms of human play, and what developmental functions do they seem to serve?

Play Is a Vehicle for Acquiring Skills

Chapter 8 presented evidence that play evolved in mammals as a means to ensure that the young of the species will practice and become expert at skills that are necessary for their long-term survival and reproduction. The play of young humans is often like that of other young mammals and appears to serve many of the same functions. Children all over the world play chase games, which promote physical stamina, agility, and the development of strategies to avoid getting caught. Play nurturing and play fighting are also universal, and everywhere the former is more prevalent among girls and the latter is more prevalent among boys (Eibl-Eibesfeldt, 1989).

Other universal forms of human play help children develop human-specific skills (Pellegrini, 2013). Children everywhere become good at making things with their hands through constructive play, become skilled with language through word play, and exercise their imaginations and planning abilities through social fantasy play. In cultures where children can directly observe the sustenance activities of adults, children focus much of their play on those activities (Gray, 2009; Kamei, 2005). For instance, young boys in hunter-gatherer cultures spend enormous amounts of time at play hunting, such as shooting at butterflies with bows and arrows, and develop great skill in the process.

■ **Tag, you're it!** Children, like all young mammals, enjoy chase games. Such play promotes physical development and skill in escaping from predators and enemies.

In a study of two Mexican villages, Douglas Fry (1992) showed how children's play reflects and may help transmit a culture's values and skills. The two villages were alike in many ways, and the similarity was reflected in aspects of the children's play. In both communities, boys made toy plows with sticks and used them to furrow the earth as their fathers worked at real plowing in the fields, and girls made pretend tortillas, mimicking their mothers. In one respect, however, the two communities differed markedly.

For generations in La Paz the people had prided themselves on their peacefulness and nonviolence, but the same was not true in San Andrés (the villages' names are pseudonyms). Often in San Andrés, but rarely in La Paz, children saw their parents fight physically, heard of fights or even murders among men stemming from sexual jealousy, and were themselves victims of beatings administered by their parents. In his systematic study of the everyday activities of 3- to 8-year-olds, Fry observed that

FOCUS 16

How do observations of two Mexican villages illustrate the role of play in transmitting cultural skills and values from one generation to the next? How might play promote cultural advancement?

the San Andrés children engaged in about twice as much serious fighting, and about three times as much play fighting, as the La Paz children. When fighting is common in a culture, fighting will apparently be understood intuitively by children as a skill to be practiced not just in anger but also in play, for fun.

Children's play can help create and advance culture as well as reflect it. When the computer revolution began in North America, children—who usually had no use for computers other than play—were in many families the first to become adept with the new technology. They taught their parents how to use computers. Some of the same children—as young adults, but still in the spirit of play—invented new and better computers and computer programs. The Dutch cultural historian Johan Huizinga (1944/1970) wrote a book contending that much of what we call "high culture"—including art, literature, philosophy, and legal systems—arose originally in the spirit of play where play was extended from childhood into adulthood.

Play as a Vehicle for Learning About Rules and Acquiring Self-Control

In addition to practicing species-typical and culturally valued skills, children may, through play, acquire more advanced understandings of rules and social roles and greater self-control. Both of the famous developmental psychologists introduced in Chapter 11, Jean Piaget and Lev Vygotsky, proposed theories along these lines.

In his book *The Moral Judgment of the Child*, Piaget (1932/1965) argued that unsupervised play with peers is crucial to moral development. He observed that adults use their superior power to settle children's disputes, but when adults are not present, children argue out their disagreements and acquire a new understanding of rules based on reason rather than authority. They learn, for example, that rules of games such as marbles are not immutable but are human contrivances designed to make the game more interesting and fair and can be changed if everyone agrees. By extension, this helps them understand that the same is true of the social conventions and laws that govern life in democratic societies. Consistent with Piaget's theory, Ann Kruger (1992) found that children showed greater advances in moral reasoning when they discussed social dilemmas with their peers than when they discussed the same dilemmas with their parents. With peers, children engaged actively and thoughtfully in the discussions, which led to a higher level of moral reasoning; with parents they were far more passive and less thoughtful.

■ **A helping hand** In age-mixed play, older children enable younger children to do things that they would not be able to do alone. As a result, younger children acquire new physical and intellectual skills and older children acquire nurturing skills. Age-mixed play is also more frequently gender-mixed than is same-age play.

In an essay on the value of play, Vygotsky (1933/1978) theorized that children learn through play how to control their own impulses and to abide by socially agreed-upon rules and roles—an ability that is crucial to social life. He pointed out that, contrary to common belief, play is not free and spontaneous but is always governed by rules that define the range of permissible actions for each participant. In real life, young children behave spontaneously—they cry when they are hurt, laugh when they are happy, and express their immediate desires. But in play they must suppress their spontaneous urges and behave in ways prescribed by the rules of the game or the role they have agreed to play. Consider, for example, children playing a game of "house," in which one child is the mommy, another is the baby, and another is the dog. To play this game, each child must keep in mind a conscious conception of how a mommy, a baby, or a dog behaves, and must govern his or her actions in accordance with that conception.

Play, then, according to Vygotsky, has this paradoxical quality: Children freely enter into it, but in doing so they give up some of their freedom. In Vygotsky's view, play in humans evolved at least partly as a means of practicing self-discipline of the sort that is needed to follow social conventions and rules.

Consistent with Vygotsky's view, researchers have found that young children put great effort into planning and enforcing rules in their social fantasy play

(Furth, 1996; Garvey, 1990). Children who break the rules—who act like themselves rather than the roles they have agreed to play—are sharply reminded by the others of what they are supposed to do: "Dogs don't sit at the table; you have to get under the table." Also in line with Vygotsky's view, researchers have found positive correlations between the amount of social fantasy play that children engage in and subsequent ratings of their social competence and self-control (Berk et al., 2006; Pierucci et al., 2014).

The Special Value of Age-Mixed Play

In age-graded school settings, such as recess, children play almost entirely with others who are about the same age as themselves. But in neighborhood settings in our culture, and even more so in cultures that don't have age-graded schools (Whiting & Edwards, 1988), children often play in groups with age spans of several years. Indeed, as Konner (1975) pointed out, the biological underpinnings of human play must have evolved under conditions in which age-mixed play predominated. Hunter-gatherer communities are small and births within them are widely spaced, so a given child rarely has more than one or two potential playmates who are within a year of his or her own age.

Psychologists have paid relatively little attention to age-mixed play, but the work that has been done suggests that such play is often qualitatively different from play among age mates (see Gray, 2013). One difference is that it is less competitive; there is less concern about who is best (Feldman & Gray, 1999). An 11-year-old has nothing to gain by proving him- or herself stronger, smarter, or more skilled than a 7-year-old, and the 7-year-old has no chance of proving the reverse. Konner (1972) noted that age-mixed rough-and-tumble play among the !Kung children whom he observed might better be called "gentle-and-tumble," because an implicit rule is that participants must control their movements so as not to hurt a younger child.

I (Peter Gray) have studied age-mixed play at an alternative school in the United States, where children from age 4 to 18 intermingle freely. At this school, age mixing appears to be a primary vehicle of education (D. Greenberg, 1992). Young children acquire more advanced interests and skills by observing and interacting with older children, and older children develop skills at nurturing and consolidate some of their own knowledge by helping younger children. I observed this happening in a wide variety of forms of play, including rough-and-tumble, sports of various types, board games, computer play, constructive play (such as play with blocks or with art materials), and fantasy play (Gray & Feldman, 2004). In each of these contexts, to make the game more fun, older children helped younger children understand rules and strategies. Studies of play among siblings who differ by several years in age have yielded similar findings (Brody, 2004).

Gender Differences in Social Development

Life is not the same for girls and boys. That is true not just in our culture but in every culture that has been studied (Maccoby, 1998; Whiting & Edwards, 1988). To some degree, the differences are biological in origin, mediated by hormones (Else-Quest & others, 2006). But, as the anthropologist Margaret Mead (1935) noted, the differences also vary from culture to culture and over time within a given culture in ways that cannot be explained by biology alone.

Gender Differences in Interactions with Caregivers

Even in early infancy, boys and girls, on average, behave somewhat differently from each other (Alexander & Wilcox, 2012). On average, newborn boys are more irritable and less responsive to caregivers' voices and faces than are newborn girls (Hittelman & Dickes, 1979; Osofsky & O'Connell, 1977). By 6 months, boys squirm more and show more facial expressions of anger than do girls when confined in an infant seat, and girls show more facial expressions of interest and less

FOCUS 18

What features of age-mixed play may make it particularly valuable to children's development?

■ **My tough little boy** Researchers have found that fathers generally play more vigorously with their infant sons than with their infant daughters.

TABLE 12.2 Several frequently reported sex differences

Physical and mental health

Morbidity and mortality rates (Females have lower mortality rates than males.)

Mental disorders (Males are more apt to display externalizing problems, females internalizing problems.)

School adaptation (Girls adapt better than boys.)

Aggressive behaviors (Boys are more physically aggressive than girls.)

Physical development

Activity level (Boys are more active than girls.)

Motor skills and muscle strength (Boys can throw farther than girls; girls have better fine-motor coordination and flexibility than boys.)

Growth rate and neurological development (Girls exhibit earlier neurological development than boys.)

Cognitive development

Spatial abilities (Boys are better at mental rotation and spatial perception than girls.)

Mathematical abilities (Girls get better grades than boys in math classes; boys perform better on standardized math tests than girls.)

Linguistic abilities (Girls develop language sooner, have higher reading literacy and verbal fluency than boys; boys are more apt to have language and reading disabilities than girls.)

Socioemotional development

Emotional patterns (Females are more socially oriented and sensitive and emotionally expressive than males.)

Risk-taking behaviors (Boys exhibit more risk-taking behaviors than girls.)

Interest areas and activities (Boys show a higher interest in mechanical, inanimate objects and how they work than girls; girls show a higher interest in people and human relationships than boys.)

Play style and social organization (Boys' play is characterized by rough-and-tumble play and an interest in attaining dominance, whereas girls are more cooperative and enabling of others.)

Source: With permission from Bjorklund, D. F., & Hernández Blasi, C. (2012). *Cengage Advantage Books: Child and adolescent development: An integrative approach, 1/e.* ©2012 South-Western, a part of Cengage Learning, Inc. Reproduced by permission: www.cengage.com/permissions. Data from Benenson, 2005; and Ruble et al., 2006.

fussing than do boys when interacting with their mothers (Weinberg et al. 1999). By 13 to 15 months, girls are more likely than are boys to comply with their mothers' requests (Kochanska et al., 1998). By 17 months, boys show significantly more physical aggression than do girls (Baillargeon et al., 2007).

Table 12.2 presents a list of several frequently reported sex differences in each of four general areas: (a) physical and mental health; (b) physical development; (c) cognitive development; and (d) socioemotional development. In most of these cases, the differences between boys and girls are small, with much overlap (e.g., many boys adapt better to school than the average girl, although, on average, girls have an advantage). The presence of reliable sex differences cannot address the origins of the differences (i.e., whether they are mainly biological or mainly cultural), only that they exist and are usually found across cultures.

Parents and other caregivers behave differently toward girls and boys, beginning at birth. They are, on average, more gentle with girls than with boys; they are more likely to talk to girls and to jostle boys (Maccoby, 1998). Such differences in treatment may in part reflect caregivers' sensitivity and responsiveness to actual differences in the behaviors and preferences of the infant girls and boys, but it also reflects adult expectations that are independent of the infants' behaviors and preferences. In one study, mothers interacted more closely with, talked in a more conversational manner to, and gave fewer direct commands to their infant daughters than to their infant sons, even though the researchers could find no differences in the infants' behavior (Clearfield & Nelson, 2006). In another study, mothers were asked to hold a 6-month-old female infant, who in some cases was dressed as a girl and introduced as Beth, and in other cases was dressed as a boy and introduced as Adam. The mothers talked to Beth more than to Adam, and gave Adam more direct gazes unaccompanied by talk (Culp et al., 1983).

Other research suggests that, regardless of the child's age, adults offer help and comfort more often to girls than to boys and more often expect boys to solve problems on their own. In one experiment, college students were quicker to call for help for a crying infant if they thought it was a girl than if they thought it was a boy (Hron-Stewart, 1988). In another study, mothers of 2-year-old daughters helped their toddlers in problem-solving tasks more than did mothers of 2-year-old sons (Hron-Stewart, 1988). Theorists have speculated that the relatively warmer treatment of girls and greater expectations of self-reliance for boys may lead girls to

FOCUS 19

What are some of the ways that girls and boys are treated differently by adults in our culture, and how might such treatment promote different developmental consequences?

become more affectionate and sociable and boys to become more self-reliant than they otherwise would (Dweck et al., 1978; MacDonald, 1992).

Adults' assumptions about the different interests and abilities of girls and boys may play a role in the types of careers that the two sexes eventually choose. In particular, parents and teachers often express the belief that math and science are harder and less interesting for girls than for boys. A number of studies suggest that such different expectations influence the way that adults talk about science and math to boys and girls, even when measures of children's abilities and self-reported interests show no such differences (Lindberg et al., 2008; Tenenbaum & Leaper, 2003).

In one study, parents and their young children were observed at interactive exhibits at a science museum (Crowley et al., 2001). The main finding was that parents, both fathers and mothers, were far more likely to explain something about the workings of the exhibits, or the underlying principles being demonstrated, to their sons than to their daughters. This occurred regardless of the age of the child (see **Figure 12.5**) and despite the fact that the researchers could find no evidence, from analyzing the children's behavior and questions, that the sons were more interested than were the daughters in the exhibits or in the principles being demonstrated. Perhaps such differential treatment helps explain why many more men than women choose careers in the physical sciences.

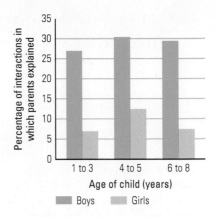

FIGURE 12.5 More explanations to boys than to girls At a science museum, parents were much more likely to explain the mechanisms or principles of interactive exhibits to sons than to daughters, regardless of age.
(Data from Crowley et al., 2001.)

Gender Identity and Its Effects on Children's Behavior

Children's gender development may be influenced by adults' differential treatment, but children also actively mold themselves to behave according to their culture's gender conceptions. By age 4 or 5, most children have learned quite clearly their culture's stereotypes of male and female roles (Martin & Ruble, 2004; Williams & Best, 1990) and recognize that they themselves are one gender or the other and always will be, an understanding referred to as *gender identity* (Kohlberg, 1966). Once they have this understanding, children in all cultures seem to become concerned about projecting themselves as clearly male or female. They attend more closely to people of their own gender and model their behavior accordingly, often in ways that exaggerate the male–female differences they see. When required to carry out a chore that they regard as gender-inappropriate, they often do so in a style that clearly distinguishes them from the other gender. For example, in a culture where fetching water is considered women's work, young boys who are asked to fetch water carry it in a very different manner from that used by women and girls (Whiting & Edwards, 1988).

From a biological perspective, gender is not an arbitrary concept but is linked to sex, which is linked to reproduction. A tendency toward gender identity may well have evolved as an active assertion of one's sex as well as a means of acquiring culture-specific gender roles. By acting "girlish" and "boyish," girls and boys clearly announce that they are on their way to becoming sexually viable women and men. Researchers have found that young children often create or overgeneralize gender differences (Martin & Ruble, 2004). For example, when preschoolers were told that a particular boy liked a certain sofa and a particular girl liked a certain table, they generalized this to assume that all boys would like the sofa and all girls would like the table (Bauer & Coyne, 1997). Children's active imposition of gender roles upon their world has been likened to their active imposition of grammatical rules upon the language that they hear (Martin et al., 2002).

Children's Self-Imposed Gender Segregation

In all cultures that have been studied, boys and girls play primarily with others of their own sex (Maccoby, 1998; Pellegrini et al., 2007). In North American culture, such segregation is more common in activities structured by children themselves than in activities structured by adults (Berk & Lewis, 1977). Even 3-year-olds have been observed to prefer same-sex playmates to opposite-sex playmates (Maccoby & Jacklin, 1987), but the peak of gender segregation, observed in many

FOCUS 20

How do children mold themselves according to their understanding of gender differences?

FOCUS 21

What function might children's self-segregation by gender serve? In our culture, why might boys avoid playing with girls more than the reverse?

different settings and cultures, occurs in the age range of 8 to 11 years (Gray & Feldman, 1997; Whiting & Edwards, 1988). In their separate playgroups, boys practice what they perceive to be the masculine activities of their culture, and girls practice what they perceive to be the feminine activities of their culture.

In some settings, children reinforce gender segregation by ridiculing those who cross gender lines, but this ridicule is not symmetrical. Boys who play with girls are much more likely to be teased and taunted by both gender groups than are girls who play with boys (Petitpas & Champagne, 2000; Thorne, 1993). Indeed, girls who prefer to play with boys are often referred to with approval as "tomboys" and retain their popularity with both sexes. Boys who prefer to play with girls are not treated so benignly. Terms like *sissy* or *pansy* are never spoken with approval. Adults, too, express much more concern about boys who play with girls or adopt girlish traits than they do about girls who play with boys or adopt boyish traits (Martin, 1990). Perhaps the difference reflects the culture's overall view that male roles are superior to female roles, which might also help to explain why, over the past several decades, many women in Western culture have moved into roles that were once regarded as exclusively masculine, while relatively fewer men have moved into roles traditionally considered feminine.

Gender Differences in Styles of Play

Girls and boys tend to play differently as well as separately, and the differences are in some ways consistent from culture to culture (Rose & Rudolph, 2006; Whiting & Edwards, 1988). Some social scientists consider boys' and girls' peer groups to be so distinct that they constitute separate subcultures, each with its own values, directing its members along different developmental lines (Maccoby, 1998; Maltz & Borker, 1982).

The *world of boys* has been characterized as consisting of relatively large, hierarchically organized groups in which individuals or coalitions attempt to prove their superiority through competitive games, teasing, and boasting. A prototypical boys' game is king of the hill, the goal of which is to stand on top and push everyone else down. The *world of girls* has been characterized as consisting of smaller, more intimate groups, in which cooperative forms of play predominate and competition is more subtle. A prototypical girls' game is jump rope, the goal of which is to keep the action going as long as possible through the coordinated activities of the rope twirlers and the jumper.

The "two-worlds" concept may exaggerate the typical differences in the social experiences of boys and girls. Most research supporting the concept has been

■ **Sex-stereotypical play** By age 4 or 5, most children have learned their culture's stereotypes of male and female roles. Choosing to play with "masculine" or "feminine" toys demonstrates this learning.

kali9/Getty Images

■ **A lack of symmetry** We are much more accepting of the little girl who dresses and acts like a boy than we are of the little boy who dresses and acts like a girl. Why?

conducted in age-segregated settings, such as school playgrounds and summer camps, but at home and in neighborhoods children often do play in age-mixed groups. As noted earlier, age-mixed play generally centers less on winning and losing than does same-age play, so age mixing reduces the difference in competitiveness between boys' and girls' play. Moreover, several studies indicate that boys and girls play together more often in age-mixed groups than in age-segregated groups (Ellis et al., 1981; Gray & Feldman, 1997).

Whether or not they play together, boys and girls are certainly interested in each other. On school playgrounds, for example, the separate boys' and girls' groups interact frequently, usually in teasing ways (Thorne, 1993). That interest begins to peak, and interactions between the sexes take on a new dimension, as children enter adolescence.

SECTION REVIEW

The child's development is influenced by play with other children and by gender.

Developing Through Play

- Children everywhere play in ways that promote the development of skills needed for their survival. These include culture-specific skills, acquired by observing adults.

- Piaget contended that children learn about rules and become better moral reasoners through play, and Vygotsky contended that children develop self-control through play. Contemporary research supports these ideas.

- Age-mixed play appears to be less competitive and more conducive to teaching, learning, and development of nurturing skills than is play among age mates.

Gender and Social Development

- There are many reliable sex differences in mental and physical health, physical development, cognitive development, and socioemotional development, although the magnitude of these differences is often quite small.

- Adults treat girls and boys differently beginning at birth, at least partly on the basis of socially grounded beliefs about gender. This may help to create or widen some gender differences.

- Once gender identity is established, by years 4 or 5, children attend to and mimic the culturally appropriate behaviors for their gender. They also exaggerate gender stereotypes and play increasingly with same-sex peers.

- Boys' and girls' groups are in some ways different subcultures. Boys tend to play competitively, in relatively large, hierarchical groups. Girls play more cooperatively, in smaller, more intimate groups. These differences may be muted in age-mixed play.

Adolescence: Breaking Out of the Cocoon

Adolescence is the transition period from childhood to adulthood. It begins with the first signs of puberty (the physical changes leading to reproductive capacity; see Chapter 11), and it ends when the person is viewed by him- or herself, and by others, as a full member of the adult community. Defined this way, adolescence in our culture begins earlier and ends later than it did in times past or still does in many other cultures.

Acceptance by self and others into adulthood—the end of adolescence—comes gradually in our culture and has no clear-cut markers. In traditional societies, where adult roles are clearly defined and are learned through the child's direct involvement in the adult world, the transition to adulthood may coincide with one or another of the physical changes near the end of puberty and be officially marked by rites of passage or other celebrations. But our culture lacks such rites, and our laws dole out adult privileges and responsibilities inconsistently over a wide age span. In most states of the United States, young people are first allowed to drive a car at 16, enlist in the military at 17, vote at 18, and purchase alcohol at 21. Although the average age for first marriage is currently about 29 for men and 27 for women in the United States (and many other industrialized countries), the *legal* age for marriage varies from 13 to 21, depending on state of residence, sex, and whether parental permission has been granted. More important, the age at which people actually begin careers or families, often seen as marks of entry into adulthood, varies greatly.

This variability in defining what it means to be an adult has resulted in some developmental psychologists proposing a new stage of development – ***emerging adulthood***, which ranges from about 18 years to the mid-20s and precedes one's settling into routines of career or family (Arnett, 2000, 2004). In the United States and many other developed countries, often because of the need for extended schooling, young people are taking longer to establish their own households, get married and have children, and establish permanent careers than did their parents and grandparents. More young men and women also continue to live (or have returned to live) with their parents than was the case in previous decades (U.S. Census Bureau, 2011). Although emerging adulthood can be viewed as an extension of adolescence (Steinberg, 2015), in many ways people in this stage have the independence of full-fledged adults while still not seeing themselves as "grown up" members of the community.

In Erikson's life-span theory, adolescence is the stage of *identity crisis,* the goal of which is to give up one's childhood identity and establish a new identity—including a sense of purpose, a career orientation, and a set of values—appropriate for entry into adulthood (Erikson, 1968). Many developmental psychologists today disagree with Erikson's specific definition of identity and with his idea that the search for identity necessarily involves a "crisis," but nearly all agree that adolescence is a period in which young people act in ways designed to move themselves from childhood toward adulthood, whether consciously or unconsciously. With a focus on adolescents' and young adults' emerging self-identities, we look here at the developmental processes of breaking away from parents, forming closer relationships with peers, risk taking, delinquency, bravery, morality, and sexual explorations.

Shifting From Parents to Peers for Intimacy and Guidance

A big part of growing up is becoming independent, and this typically involves breaking away from parental control and becoming more involved with peers and "peer life." This often results in conflict between adolescents and their parents, as adolescents simultaneously form closer bonds with peers.

Breaking Away From Parental Control

"I said, 'Have a nice day,' to my teenage daughter as she left the house, and she responded, 'Will you *please* stop telling me what to do!'" That joke, long popular among parents of adolescents, could be matched by the following story, told by an adolescent: "Yesterday, I tried to really communicate with my mother. I told her how important it is that she trust me and not try to govern everything I do. She responded, 'Oh, sweetie, I'm so glad we have the kind of relationship in which you can be honest and tell me how you really feel. Now, please, if you are going out, wear your warmest coat and be back by 10:30.'"

Adolescence is often characterized as a time of rebellion against parents, but it rarely involves out-and-out rejection. Surveys taken over the past several decades have shown that most adolescents admire their parents, accept their parents' religious and political convictions, and claim to be more or less at peace with them (Offer & Schonert-Reichl, 1992; Steinberg, 2001). The typical rebellion, if one occurs at all, is aimed specifically at some of the immediate controls that parents hold over the child's behavior. At the same time that adolescents are asking to be treated more like adults, parents may fear new dangers that can accompany this period of life—such as those associated with sex, alcohol, drugs, and automobiles—and try to tighten controls instead of loosening them. So adolescence is often marked by conflicts centering on parental authority.

For both sons and daughters, increased conflict with parents is linked more closely to the physical changes of puberty than to chronological age (Steinberg, 1989). If puberty comes earlier or later than is typical, so does the increase in conflict. Such conflict is usually more intense in the early teenage years than later (Steinberg, 2001); by age 16 or so, most teenagers have achieved the balance of independence and dependence they are seeking.

FOCUS 23

What is the typical nature of the so-called adolescent rebellion against parents?

Establishing Closer Relationships With Peers

As adolescents gain more independence from their parents, they look increasingly to their peers for emotional support. In one study, fourth graders indicated that their parents were their most frequent providers of emotional support, seventh graders indicated that they received almost equal support from their parents and friends, and tenth graders indicated that they received most of their emotional support from friends (Furman & Buhrmester, 1992).

Conforming to Peers

As children approach and enter their teenage years, they become increasingly concerned about looking and behaving like their peers. Self-report measures indicate that young people's tendency to conform peaks in the years from about age 10 to 14 and then declines gradually after that (Steinberg & Monahan, 2007). The early teenage years are, quite understandably, the years when parents worry most about possible negative effects of peer pressure. Indeed, teenagers who belong to the same friendship groups are more similar to one another with regard to risky behaviors (e.g., smoking, drinking, drug use, and sexual promiscuity) than they are to teenagers who are not among their group of friends (Steinberg, 2008). Such similarity is at least partly the result of selection rather than conformity; people tend to choose friends who have interests and behaviors similar to their own. Still, a number of research studies have shown that, over time, friends become more similar to one another in frequency of risky or unhealthful behaviors than they were originally (Curran et al., 1997; Jaccard et al., 2005).

Western parents and researchers tend to emphasize the negative influences of peers, but adolescents themselves often describe positive peer pressures, such as encouragement to avoid unhealthful behaviors and engage in healthful ones (Steinberg, 2015). On the basis of extensive studies in China, Xinyin Chen and his

FOCUS 24

What evidence suggests that peer pressure can have negative and positive effects? What difference in attitude about peer pressure is reported to exist in China compared to the United States?

colleagues (2003) reported that Chinese parents, educators, and adolescents view peer pressure much more as a positive force than as a negative one. In China, according to Chen, young people as well as adults place high value on academic achievement, and adolescent peer groups do homework together and encourage one another to excel in school. In the United States, in contrast, peer encouragement for academic achievement is relatively rare (Steinberg, 1996).

Increased Rates of Recklessness and Delinquency

Statistically, people worldwide are much more likely to engage in disruptive or dangerous actions during adolescence than at other times in life (Defoe et al., 2014). In Western cultures, rates of theft, assault, murder, reckless driving, unprotected sex, illicit drug use, and general disturbing of the peace all peak between the ages of 15 and 25 (Archer, 2004; Arnett, 2007). The adolescent peak in recklessness and delinquency is particularly sharp in males, as exemplified in the graphs in **Figure 12.6**.

What causes the increased recklessness and delinquency? Some psychologists have tried to address this question by exploring the underlying cognitive, motivational, or brain characteristics of adolescents that differentiate them from adults. Adolescents have been described as having a *myth of invulnerability*—that is, a false sense that they are protected from the mishaps and diseases that can happen to other people (Elkind, 1978). They have also been described as *sensation seekers,* who enjoy the adrenaline rush associated with risky behavior; as having heightened *irritability* or *aggressiveness,* which leads them to be easily provoked; and as having *immature inhibitory control centers* in the prefrontal lobes of their brains (Martin et al., 2004; Steinberg, 2015). Reasonable evidence has been compiled for all of these ideas, but such concepts leave one wondering why adolescents have such seemingly maladaptive characteristics, which can lead to their deaths. Why would natural selection not have weeded out such traits?

Explanations That Focus on Adolescents' Segregation from Adults

One line of explanation focuses on aspects of adolescence that are relatively unique to modern, Western cultures. In this view, adolescent recklessness is largely an aberration of modern times, not a product of natural selection. Terrie

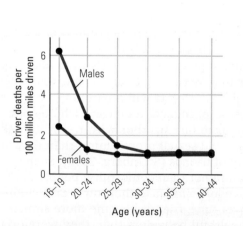
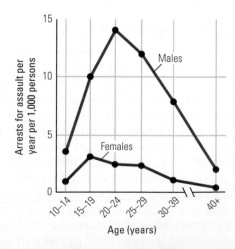

FIGURE 12.6 Evidence of heightened recklessness and aggressiveness in adolescence and youth
The "Driver deaths" graph is based on an analysis of traffic fatalities in the United States in 1970 by Wilson and Daly (1985, p. 69). The high rate of death for young drivers is probably due to inexperience as well as recklessness, but inexperience can't explain why the rate is so much higher for young men than for young women. The "Arrests for assault" graph, from Campbell (1995, p. 100), shows the rate of arrests for assault in 1989 in the United States, as reported by the U.S. Department of Justice.

(Data from Wilson & Daly, 1985 [Driver deaths]; and Campbell, 1995 [Arrests for assault].)

Moffitt (1993), for example, suggests that the high rate of delinquency is a pathological side effect of the early onset of puberty and delayed acceptance into legitimate adult society. She cites evidence that the adolescent peak in violence and crime is greater in modern cultures than in traditional cultures, where puberty usually comes later and young people are more fully integrated into adult activities. According to Moffitt, young people past puberty, who are biologically adults, are motivated to enter the adult world in whatever ways are available to them. Sex, alcohol, and crime are understood as adult activities. Crime, in particular, is taken seriously by adults and brings adolescents into the adult world of lawyers, courtrooms, and probation officers. Crime can also bring money and material goods that confer adult-like status.

FOCUS 25

What are two theories about how adolescents' segregation from adults might contribute to their recklessness and delinquency?

Moffitt's theory makes considerable sense, but it does not account well for risky adolescent activities that are decidedly not adult-like. Adults do not "surf" on the tops of fast-moving trains or drive around wildly in stolen cars and deliberately crash them, as adolescents in various cities have been observed to do (Arnett, 1995).

In a theory that is in some ways the opposite of Moffitt's, Judith Harris (1995, 1998) suggests that adolescents engage in risky and delinquent activities not to join the adult world but to set themselves apart from it. Just as they dress differently from adults, they also act differently. According to Harris, their concern is not with acceptance by adults but with acceptance by their own peers—the next generation of adults. Harris agrees with Moffitt that our culture's segregation of adolescents from adult society contributes to adolescents' risky and sometimes delinquent behavior, but she disagrees about the mechanism. To Moffitt, such segregation reduces the chance that adolescents can find safe, legitimate ways to behave as adults; to Harris it does so by producing adolescent subcultures whose values are relatively unaffected by those of adults. Moffitt's and Harris's theories may each contain part of the truth. Perhaps adolescents seek adult-like status while, at the same time, identifying with the behaviors and values of their adolescent subculture.

The Neurological Basis of Risk Taking in Adolescence

Although the psychological reasons for adolescents' high levels of risk-taking behavior are debatable, such behavior is surely governed by underlying changes in adolescents' brains. Lawrence Steinberg (2015; Albert et al., 2013) has proposed that adolescent risk taking reflects a competition between two developing brain systems, the *cognitive-control network,* involved in planning and regulating behavior and located primarily in the frontal lobes, and the *socioemotional network,* located primarily in the limbic system (see Chapter 4). According to Steinberg, although adolescents are able to make logical decisions as well as young adults under "neutral" conditions, the socioemotional brain network becomes dominant under conditions of emotional or social arousal or when in the presence of peers. The result is that, although adolescents may "know better" than to engage in some forms of risky behavior, the presence of peers interferes with their cognitive-control network, increasing the incidence of risky behaviors in social settings.

"Young man, go to your room and stay there until your cerebral cortex matures."

The impact of peers on risky behavior in adolescents is demonstrated in research using a simulated driving task (Gardner & Steinberg, 2004). Adolescents (13 to 16 years old), young (emerging) adults (average age = 19 years), and adults (average age = 37 years) were equally able to avoid "crashes" during the video simulations when driving alone, but the pattern was substantially different when driving in the presence of friends. As shown in **Figure 12.7** on page 476, the number of crashes for adults was about the same whether they were alone or with friends. In contrast, the number of crashes for adolescents was substantially greater in the social situation, and it was moderately greater for young adults. In a subsequent brain imaging experiment, where adolescents performed the

FIGURE 12.7 Adolescents take significantly more risks and are involved in more "crashes" in a video-driving game when playing with friends than when playing alone The effect is smaller for young adults, and playing with friends has no effect on the driving of adults.

(Data from Steinberg, 2007, and Gardner & Steinberg, 2004.)

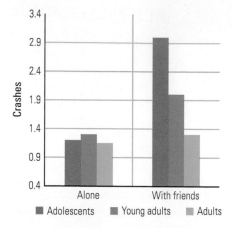

Crashes

3.4 2.9 2.4 1.9 1.4 0.9 0.4

Alone   With friends

■ Adolescents ■ Young adults ■ Adults

FOCUS 26

How have Wilson and Daly explained the recklessness and delinquency of adolescent males in evolutionary terms?

■ **Pure recklessness** Risk taking reaches a peak in adolescence and young adulthood, especially among males.

driving task either with or without a peer watching them, reward-related areas of the brain were more active when peers were watching them then when they were not. There was no difference in the activation of the cognitive control areas between the two conditions (Chein et al., 2011). The results of these laboratory simulations are similar to actual driving statistics. The rate of vehicular deaths for 16- and 17-year-old drivers more than doubles when there are three or more passengers in the car compared to when adolescents drive alone. In contrast, there is no relationship between vehicular deaths and the number of passengers for older drivers (Chen et al., 2000).

An Evolutionary Explanation of the "Young-Male Syndrome"

Neither Moffitt nor Harris addresses the question of why risky and delinquent activities are so much more readily pursued by young males than by young females or why they occur, at least to some degree, in cultures that do not segregate adolescents from adults. Even in hunter-gatherer communities, young males take risks that appear foolish to their elders; they also die at disproportionate rates from such mishaps as falling from trees that they have climbed too rapidly (Hewlett, 1988). To address such issues, Margo Wilson and Martin Daly (1985; Daly & Wilson, 1990) have discussed what they call "the young-male syndrome" from an evolutionary perspective, focusing on the potential value of such behavior for reproduction.

As discussed in Chapter 3, among mammals in general, the number of potential offspring a male can produce is more variable than the number a female can produce and is more closely tied to status. In our species' history, males who took risks to achieve higher status among their peers may well have produced more offspring, on average, than those who didn't, so genes promoting that tendency may have been passed along. This view gains credibility from studies in which young women report that they indeed are sexually attracted to men who succeed in risky, adventurous actions, even if such actions serve no social good (Kelly & Dunbar, 2001; Kruger et al., 2003). In hunter-gatherer times, willingness to take personal risks in hunting and defense of the tribe and family may well have been an especially valuable male trait. According to Wilson and Daly, train surfing, wild driving, careless tree climbing, and seemingly senseless acts of violence are best understood as ways in which young men gain status by demonstrating their fearlessness and valor.

In support of their thesis, Wilson and Daly point to evidence that a high proportion of violence among young men is triggered by signs of disrespect or challenges to status. One young man insults another, and the other responds by punching, knifing, or shooting him. Such actions are more likely to occur if other young men are present than if they aren't. No intelligent person whose primary goal was murder would choose to kill in front of witnesses, but young men who commit murder commonly do just that.

Of course, not all young males are reckless or violent, but that does not contradict Wilson and Daly's thesis. Those who see safer paths to high status—such as through college, inherited wealth, or prestigious jobs—have less need to risk their lives for prestige and are less likely to do so (Ellis et al., 2012).

Females also exhibit a peak in violence during adolescence and youth, although it is a much smaller peak than men's (refer back to Figure 12.6). Anne Campbell (1995, 2002) has argued that when young women do fight physically, they do so for reasons that, like the reasons for young men's fighting, can be understood from an evolutionary perspective. According to Campbell's evidence, young women fight most often in response to gossip or insults about their alleged sexual activities, which could tarnish their standing with men, and in instances when one woman appears to be trying to attract another's boyfriend.

An Expanded Moral Vision and Moral Sense of Self

Adolescence seems to bring out both the worst and the best in people. Adolescents can be foolhardy and violent, but they can also be heroic and work valiantly toward making the world better. Adolescence is, among other things, a period of rapid growth in the sophistication of moral reasoning and a time in which many people develop moral self-images that guide their actions.

Advancement on Kohlberg's Scale of Moral Reasoning

Since the 1970s and 1980s, most research on moral development has been based on a theory and methods developed originally by Lawrence Kohlberg. Kohlberg assessed moral reasoning by posing hypothetical dilemmas to people—primarily to adolescents—and asking them how they believed the protagonist should act and why. For example, a man must decide whether to steal a certain drug under conditions in which that theft is the only way to save his wife's life. To evaluate the level of moral reasoning, Kohlberg was concerned not with whether people answered yes or no to such dilemmas but with the reasons they gave to justify their answers. Drawing partly on his research findings and partly on concepts gleaned from the writings of moral philosophers, Kohlberg (1984) proposed that moral reasoning develops through a series of stages, which are outlined in **Table 12.3**.

As you study Table 12.3, notice the logic underlying Kohlberg's theory of moral reasoning. Each successive stage takes into account a broader portion of the social world than does the previous one. The sequence begins with thought of oneself alone (Stage 1) and then progresses to encompass other individuals directly involved in the action (Stage 2), others who will hear about and evaluate the action (Stage 3), society at large (Stage 4), and, finally, universal principles that concern all of humankind (Stage 5).

According to Kohlberg, the stages represent a true developmental progression in the sense that, to reach any given stage, a person must first pass through the preceding ones. Thinking within one stage and discovering the limitations of that way of thinking provide the impetus for progression to the next. Kohlberg did not claim that everyone goes through the entire sequence; in fact, his research suggested that few people go beyond Stage 4, and many stop at Stage 2 or Stage 3. Nor did he link his stages to specific ages, but he did contend that adolescence and young

FOCUS 27

How did Kohlberg assess moral reasoning? How can his stages be described as the successive broadening of one's social perspective? How does research using Kohlberg's system help explain adolescent idealism?

TABLE 12.3 Kohlberg's stages of moral reasoning

The quotations in each stage description exemplify how a person at that stage might justify a man's decision to steal an expensive drug that is needed to save his wife's life.

Stage 1: Obedience and punishment orientation
Reasoners in this stage focus on direct consequences to themselves. An action is bad if it will result in punishment, good if it will result in reward. "If he lets his wife die, he will get in trouble."

Stage 2: Self-interested exchanges
Reasoners here understand that different people have different self-interests, which sometimes come into conflict. To get what you want, you have to make a bargain, giving up something in return. "It won't bother him much to serve a little jail term if he still has his wife when he gets out."

Stage 3: Interpersonal accord and conformity
Reasoners here try to live up to the expectations of others who are important to them. An action is good if it will improve a person's relationships with significant others, bad if it will harm those relationships. "His family will think he's an inhuman husband if he doesn't save his wife."

Stage 4: Law-and-order morality
Reasoners here argue that to maintain social order, each person should resist personal pressures and feel duty-bound to follow the laws and conventions of the larger society. "It's a husband's duty to save his wife. When he married her he vowed to protect her."

Stage 5: Human-rights and social-welfare morality
Reasoners here balance their respect for laws with ethical principles that transcend specific laws. Laws that fail to promote the general welfare or that violate ethical principles can be changed, reinterpreted, or in some cases flouted. "The law isn't really set up for these circumstances. Saving a life is more important than following this law."

Note: The quotations are based on examples in Kohlberg (1984) and Rest (1986). A sixth stage, which emphasized universal ethical principles almost to the exclusion of other considerations, has been dropped in current versions, because of failure to find people who reason in accordance with it.

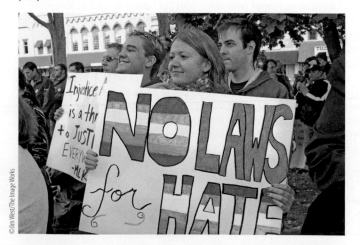

FIGURE 12.8 Changes in moral reasoning from age 10 to 24 This graph, based on a longitudinal study of males from a relatively high socio-economic background, shows the percentage of subjects at each age who were reasoning at each of Kohlberg's stages. Notice the sharp decline of Stages 1 and 2 reasoning during early adolescence, the rise and fall of Stage 3 reasoning, and the consistent increase of Stage 4 reasoning during adolescence and young adulthood. Little Stage 5 reasoning was found, but it, too, increased with age.

(Data from Colby et al., 1983.)

■ **Morality and social causes** Being moral and setting a good example for others is a strong aspect of adolescents' self-image. Morality may include advocating for the rights of minorities, including sexual minorities. Adolescents who exhibited the highest levels of moral reasoning were also the most likely to help others, to volunteer to work for social causes, or to refrain from taking part in actions that harm other people.

adulthood are the times when advancement to the higher stages is most likely to occur. **Figure 12.8** illustrates the results of one long-term study that supports Kohlberg's claim about the rapid advancement of moral reasoning during adolescence.

Kohlberg's theory is about moral reasoning, which is not the same thing as moral action. Kohlberg recognized that one can be a high-powered moral philosopher without being a moral person, and vice versa, yet he argued that the ability to think abstractly about moral issues does help account for the idealism and moral commitment of youth. In line with this contention, several research studies found that adolescents who exhibited the highest levels of moral reasoning were also the most likely to help others, to volunteer to work for social causes, or to refrain from taking part in actions that harm other people (Haan et al., 1968; Kuther & Higgins-D'Alessandro, 2000; Muhlberger, 2000).

Sexual Explorations

When we think of adolescence, our first mental image is typically that of sexual blooming. By definition, this is the stage of life when pubertal hormones act on the body to make it reproductively functional (discussed in Chapter 11) and on the brain to heighten greatly the level of sexual desire. Girls and boys who previously watched and teased each other from the safety of their same-sex groups become motivated to move closer together, to get to know each other, to touch in ways that aren't just teasing. The new thoughts and actions associated with all these changes can bring on fear, exhilaration, dread, pride, shame, and bewilderment—sometimes all at once.

In their early dating, teenagers who were previously more or less separate in the "world of boys" and the "world of girls" come together and learn how to communicate with one another. For boys it may be a matter of learning how to pay closer attention to another's needs and to speak in a more accommodating, less assertive manner. For girls it may often be a matter of learning to be more assertive. One study found that 10th graders' discussions with their romantic partner were more difficult than their discussions either with a close same-sex friend or with their own mother (Furman & Shomaker, 2008). More negativity was expressed, and there was more failure in communication. Yet, when asked, teenagers commonly regard their romantic relationship as their closest relationship and their most important source of emotional support (Collins et al., 2009). Longitudinal studies indicate that success in developing emotional intimacy in early romantic relationships is highly predictive of eventual success in marriage (Karney et al., 2007).

The Development of Sexuality and Sexual Behavior in Adolescence

As a culture, we glorify sex and present highly sexual images of teenagers in advertisements and movies; yet, at the same time, we typically disapprove of sex among the real teenagers of everyday life. Teenage sex is associated in the public mind with delinquency, and, indeed, the youngest teenagers to have sexual intercourse are often those most involved in delinquent or antisocial activities (Capaldi et al., 1996). Earliest intercourse usually occurs surreptitiously, often without benefit of adult advice, and often without a condom or other protection against pregnancy and sexually transmitted diseases. Yet, sexuality in adolescence is normative, and engaging in sexual intercourse as a teenager is not necessarily associated with poor psychological functioning (Harden, 2014).

Sexual Attraction Sexual behavior follows a typical pattern for adolescents in developed countries. Adults recall their earliest feelings of sexual attraction occurring between 10 and 12 years of age, although this varies with sex, culture, and sexual orientation (Herdt & McClintock, 2000). This is typically followed about a year later by first sexual fantasies, which are actually adolescents' most common sexual experience, and by the beginning of masturbation (Collins & Steinberg, 2006; DeLamater & Friedrich, 2002). Many adolescents move on to sexual behavior with a partner, typically beginning with "making out" and "petting" and, for many, sexual intercourse. **Figure 12.9** shows the percentage of American males and females who reported having had sexual intercourse between the ages of 14 and 19 years. As you can see, although few young teenagers report having sex, this increases to about 70% by age 19 (Guttmacher Institute, 2006).

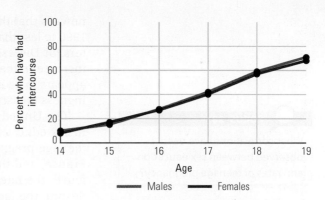

FIGURE 12.9 The percentage of U.S. male and female teenagers who have had sexual intercourse by age Rates are nearly identical for boys and girls.

(Data from Alan Guttmacher Institute, 2006.)

Sexual-Minority Development For those whose sexual orientation is not the culture's ideal, the sexual awakening of adolescence can be especially difficult. The developmental process of sexual identity for gay and lesbian (*sexual-minority*) youth is similar to that for heterosexual youth. Many children become aware of same-sex attraction when they are approximately 8 to 10 years old (Savin-Williams, 1998), years before most children display mature sexual feelings or behaviors, although for others, such awareness is not attained until adolescence. In fact, it is not uncommon for women's first awareness of being a lesbian or bisexual to occur only after years of maintaining heterosexual relationships and even motherhood (D'Augelli & Patterson, 2001).

The average age that people identify themselves as a sexual minority is about 15, although, again, this is highly variable (Savin-Williams & Cohen, 2004). Girls are likely to have labeled themselves as lesbian or bisexual before engaging in sexual behavior with another female, whereas boys often do not label themselves as gay until after they have had sex with another male (Savin-Williams & Diamond, 2000). It is typically several more years, usually between 17 and 19 years of age, before sexual-minority youth "go public," first telling their siblings and close friends of their sexual orientation, and later their parents (usually their mothers rather than their fathers). "Coming out" can often lead to loss of some heterosexual friends, disappointment from one's parents, physical and verbal abuse from peers, and an increase in mental and physical health problems (Lick et al., 2013). These effects can be especially strong in some ethnic groups (more so in Latin and Asian American than European American groups) and in some conservative religions (D'Augelli, 2005). However, when youth truly accept their sexual identity and receive the support of family and friends (which does not always happen), psychological adjustment is apt to be good (D'Augelli, 2004) despite the cultural stigmatization that continues to exist in certain segments of some societies.

Sexually Transmitted Diseases and Pregnancy Sexual intercourse can sometimes lead to sexually transmitted diseases (STDs) and to pregnancy. The rates of STDs in American teenagers and young adults are exceptionally high. Although 15- to 24-year-olds represent only about a quarter of sexually experienced people in the United States, they account for nearly half of the new cases of STDs (CDC, 2015). Based on a 2008 report by the CDC, approximately 3.2 million girls between the ages of 14 and 19 (26% of that population) were infected with at least one of the most common STDs. The rate of infection increased to 40% for sexually active girls (Forhan et al., 2008).

Concerning pregnancy, in the United States in recent times, roughly 7% of teenage females aged 15 to 19 became pregnant in any given year (Kost & Henshaw, 2013). About a quarter of these pregnancies were terminated by abortion, and most of the rest resulted in births. Most teenage pregnancies occurred outside of marriage, often to mothers who were not in a position to care for their babies adequately. The good news is that the rate of teenage pregnancy has fallen, from a peak of about 12% in 1990 to less than 3% in 2013 (Martin et al., 2015), and it is declining further still (Centers for Disease Control, 2017). The decline apparently stems primarily from a sharp increase in teenagers' use of condoms and other birth control methods, which itself appears to be a result of increased sex education in schools and parents' greater willingness to discuss sex openly with their children and teenagers (Abma et al., 2004).

The United States, however, still lags behind the rest of the industrialized world in sex education and in use of birth control by teenagers, and still has the highest teenage pregnancy rate of any industrialized nation. Such countries as Germany, France, and the Netherlands have teenage pregnancy rates that are less than one fourth the rate in the United States (Guttmacher Institute, 2002; World Bank, 2016), despite the fact that their rates of teenage sexual activity are equivalent to that in the United States.

A long-standing problem arises from the persistent double standard regarding sexuality for girls and boys, which probably stems from biological as well as cultural influences. Not just in Western culture, but in most cultures worldwide, boys are more often encouraged in their sexual adventures, and are more likely to feel proud of them, than are girls (Gordon & Gilgun, 1987; Michael et al., 1994). Boys, more often than girls, say that they are eager to have sex for the sheer pleasure of it, and girls, more often than boys, equate sex with love or say that they would have intercourse only with someone they would marry. One index of this difference is depicted in **Figure 12.10**, which shows results of a survey conducted in the United States in 2002 (Abma et al., 2004). Far more young women than young men reported that they did not want their first sexual intercourse to happen at the time that it did happen. A separate analysis showed that the younger a teenage female was when she had her first intercourse, the less likely she was to have wanted it to happen.

FOCUS 28

What correlations have been observed between sex education and rates of teenage pregnancy?

FIGURE 12.10 A difference in desire
This graph shows differences in the degree to which young males and females wanted their first sexual intercourse to happen when it did happen, according to their own reports.
(Data from Abma et al., 2004.)

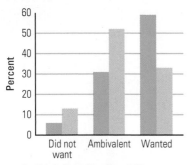

Feelings about first sexual intercourse

■ Males   ■ Females

FOCUS 29

How can the sex difference in desire for uncommitted sex be explained in evolutionary terms?

Evolutionary Explanation of Sex Differences in Sexual Eagerness

In culture after culture, young men are more eager than young women to have sexual intercourse without a long-term commitment (Buss, 1995; Schmitt, 2003). Why? The standard evolutionary explanation is founded on the theory of parental investment, developed by Robert Trivers (1972) to account for sex differences in courtship and mating in all animal species. According to the theory (discussed more fully in Chapter 3), the sex that pays the greater cost in bearing and rearing young will—in any species—be the more discriminating sex in choosing when and with whom to copulate, and the sex that pays the lesser cost will be the more aggressive in seeking copulation with multiple partners.

The theory can be applied to humans in a straightforward way. Sexual intercourse can cause pregnancy in women but not in men, so a woman's interest frequently lies in reserving intercourse until she can afford to be pregnant and has found a mate who will help her and their potential offspring over the long haul. In contrast, a man loses little and may gain much—in the amoral economics of natural selection—through uncommitted sexual intercourse with many women. Some of those women may succeed in raising his children, sending copies of his genes into the next generation, at great cost to themselves and no cost to him. Thus natural selection may well have produced a tendency for women to be more sexually restrained than men.

FOCUS 30

How can sexual restraint and promiscuity, in both sexes, be explained as adaptations to different life conditions? What evidence suggests that the presence or absence of a father at home, during childhood, may tip the balance toward one strategy or the other?

Teenage Sexuality May Depend on Conditions of Rearing

A key word in the last sentence of the preceding paragraph is *tendency*. Great variation on the dimension of sexual restraint versus promiscuity exists within each sex, both across cultures and within any given culture (Belsky et al., 1991). As in any game of strategy, the most effective approach that either men or women can take in courtship and sex depends very much on the strategy taken by the other sex.

■ **The dilemma of teenage sex** As a culture, we glorify sex and present highly sexual images of teenagers in advertisements and movies. At the same time, adults typically disapprove of sex among the real teenagers of everyday life.

In communities where women successfully avoid and shun men who seek to behave promiscuously, promiscuity proves fruitless for men and the alternative strategy of fidelity works best. Conversely, in communities where men rarely stay around to help raise their offspring, a woman who waits for "Mr. Right" may wait forever. Cross-cultural studies have shown that promiscuity prevails among both men and women in cultures where men devote little care to young, and sexual restraint prevails in cultures where men devote much care (Barber, 2003; Draper & Harpending, 1988; Marlowe, 2003).

Some researchers have theorized that natural selection may have predisposed humans to be sensitive to cues in childhood that predict whether one or the other sexual strategy (restraint vs. promiscuity) will be more successful. One such cue may be the presence or absence of a caring father at home. According to a theory originated by Patricia Draper and Henry Harpending (1982), the presence of a caring father leads girls to grow up assuming that men are potentially trustworthy providers and leads boys to grow up assuming that they themselves will be such providers; these beliefs promote sexual restraint and the seeking of long-term commitments in both sexes. If a caring father is not present, according to the theory, girls grow up assuming that men are untrustworthy "cads" rather than "dads," and that assumption leads them to flaunt their sexuality to extract what they can from men in short-term relationships. For their part, boys who grow up without a caring father tend to assume that long-term commitments to mates and care of children are not their responsibilities, and that assumption leads them to go from one sexual conquest to another. These assumptions may not be verbally expressed or even conscious, but are revealed in behavior.

In support of their theory, Draper and Harpending (1982, 1988) presented evidence that even within a given culture and social class, adolescents raised by a mother alone are generally more promiscuous than those raised by a mother and father together. In one early study, teenage girls who were members of the same community playground group and were similar to one another in socioeconomic class were observed for their degrees of flirtatiousness, both with boys on the playground and with an adult male interviewer. Girls who were raised by a mother alone—after divorce early in the girl's childhood—were, on average, much more flirtatious than girls who still had a father at home (Hetherington, 1972). More recent studies have revealed that girls raised by a mother alone are much more likely to become sexually active in their early teenage years and to become pregnant as teenagers than are girls raised by a mother and father (Ellis, 2004; Ellis et al., 2003). The results of two studies, conducted in the United States and New Zealand, are depicted in **Figure 12.11** (Ellis et al., 2003).

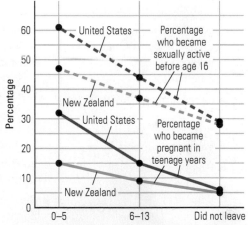

Daughter's age in years when father left the home

FIGURE 12.11 Effect of fathers' absence on daughters' rates of early sexual activity and teenage pregnancy These data came from two large-scale studies, one in the United States and one in New Zealand. The rates of early sexual activity and teenage pregnancy were statistically adjusted to factor out possible confounding variables, including race, socioeconomic class, the mother's age at first birth, family life stress, parental discipline style, degree of parental monitoring, and neighborhood dangers.

(Data from Ellis et al., 2003.)

Researchers have also found that girls raised in father-absent homes tend to go through puberty earlier than do those raised in homes where a father is present (Ellis, 2004; Webster et al., 2014). This difference has even been shown within families, in a study comparing the age of menarche for full sisters (Tither & Ellis, 2008). In cases where the father left the family, the younger sisters—the ones who were still young children when the father left—reached menarche at an earlier age than did the older sisters. Since the sisters in each pair had the same mother and father, this consistent difference must have been the result of a difference in experience, not a difference in genes. Early puberty may be part of the mechanism through which experiences at home affect the onset of sexual activity.

Draper and Harpending's theory is still controversial, though an increasing amount of evidence supports it (Ellis et al., 2012). Regardless of whether the theory eventually proves to be true, it illustrates the attempt of many contemporary psychologists to understand the life course in terms of alternative strategies that are at least partly prepared by evolution but are brought selectively to the fore by life experience.

SECTION REVIEW

Adolescence is a period of breaking away and developing an adult identity.

Shifting From Parents to Peers	**Recklessness and Delinquency**	**The Moral Self**	**Sexual Explorations**
■ Adolescent conflict with parents generally centers on the desire for greater independence from parental control. ■ Increasingly, adolescents turn to one another rather than to their parents for emotional support. ■ Peer pressure can have positive as well as negative influences.	■ Risky and delinquent behaviors are more frequent in adolescence than in other life stages. ■ Segregation from adults may promote delinquency by depriving adolescents of positive adult ways to behave, or by creating an adolescent subculture divorced from adult values. ■ Risky and delinquent behavior is especially common in young males. It may serve to enhance status, ultimately as part of competition to attract females.	■ In Kohlberg's theory, moral reasoning develops in stages, progressing in breadth of social perspective. Rapid advancement in moral reasoning often occurs in adolescence.	■ Sexual attraction, to members of the opposite sex or to same-sex peers, develops gradually over adolescence, with the first feelings of sexual attraction usually beginning between 10 and 12 years of age. ■ The rates of sexually transmitted diseases and pregnancy in American teenagers and young adults are high relative to rates in other industrialized countries. ■ Sex differences in eagerness to have sex can be explained in terms of differences in parental investment. ■ An evolution-based theory, supported by correlational research, suggests that the presence or absence of a father at home may affect the sexual strategy—restraint or promiscuity—chosen by offspring.

Adulthood: Finding Satisfaction in Love and Work

In his life-span theory, Erikson (1963) proposed that establishing intimate, caring relationships and finding fulfillment in work are the main tasks of early and middle adulthood. In this respect he was following the lead of Sigmund Freud (1935/1960), who defined emotional maturity as the capacity to love and to work. Some psychologists believe that adult development follows a predictable sequence of crises or problems to be resolved (Erikson, 1963; Levinson, 1986), while others contend that the course of adulthood in our modern culture is extraordinarily variable and unpredictable (Neugarten, 1979, 1984). But in essentially every psychological theory of adult development, caring and working are the two threads that weave the fabric of adulthood.

Love

We are a romantic species. In every culture for which data are available, people describe themselves as falling in love (Fisher, 2004). We are also a marrying species. In every culture, adults of child-producing age enter into long-term unions sanctioned by law or social custom, in which the two members implicitly or explicitly promise to care for each other and the offspring they produce (Rodseth et al., 1991), although cultures vary greatly in the degree to which people abide by those promises. Love and marriage do not necessarily go together, but they often do, and in most cultures their combination is considered ideal. In some cultures people fall in love and then get married; in others they get married—through an arrangement made by the couple's parents—and then, if fate works as hoped for, fall in love. Researchers have attempted to understand the underlying psychological elements of romantic love and to learn why some marriages are happy and others are not.

Romantic Love Viewed as Adult Attachment

Romantic love is similar in form, and perhaps in underlying mechanism, to the attachment that infants develop with their parents (Diamond, 2004; Hazan & Shaver, 1994). Close physical contact, caressing, and gazing into each other's eyes are crucial to the early formation of both types of relationships, and lovers' communications often include cooing and baby talk. A sense of fusion with the other reigns when all is well, and a feeling of exclusivity—that the other person could not be replaced by anyone else—prevails. The partners feel most secure and confident when they are together and may show physiological evidence of distress when separated (Feeney & Kirkpatrick, 1996).

The emotional bond is not simply a by-product of shared pleasures. In long-married couples it may exist even when the two have few interests in common. Sometimes the bond reveals its full intensity only after separation or divorce or the death of one partner. The experience of losing one's partner typically involves intense anxiety, depression, and feelings of loneliness or emptiness that are not relieved even by highly supportive friends and an active social life (Stroebe et al., 1996).

As with infants' attachments with their caregivers, the attachments that adults form with romantic partners can be classified as *secure* (characterized by comfort), *anxious* (characterized by excessive worry about love or lack of it from the partner), or *avoidant* (characterized by little expression of intimacy or by ambivalence about commitment) (Kirkpatrick, 2005). Studies using questionnaires and interviews have revealed continuity between people's descriptions of their adult romantic attachments and their recollections of their childhood relationships with their parents (Fraley, 2002; Mikulincer & Shaver, 2007). People who recall their relationships with parents as warm and secure typically describe their romantic relationships

FOCUS 31

How is romantic love like infant attachment? What evidence suggests continuity in attachment quality between infancy and adulthood?

in similar terms, and those who recall anxieties and ambiguities in their relationships with parents tend to describe analogous anxieties and ambiguities in their romances. Such continuity could stem from a number of possible causes, including a tendency for adult experiences to color the person's memories of childhood. Most attachment researchers, however, interpret it as support for a theory developed by Bowlby (1980), who suggested that people form mental models of close relationships based on their early experiences with their primary caregivers and then carry those models into their adult relationships (Fraley & Brumbaugh, 2004).

Ingredients of Marital Success

In the sanitized version of the fairy tale (but not in the Grimm brothers' original), love allows the frog prince and the child princess to transform each other into perfect human adults who marry and live happily ever after. Reality is not like that. Roughly half of new marriages in North America are predicted to end in divorce (Bramlett & Mosher, 2002), and even among couples who don't divorce, many are unhappy in marriage. Why do some marriages work while others fail?

In interviews and on questionnaires, happily married partners consistently say that they like each other; they think of themselves not just as husband and wife but also as best friends and confidants (Buehlman et al., 1992; Lauer & Lauer, 1985). They use the term *we* more than *I* as they describe their activities, and they tend to value their interdependence more than their independence. They also talk about their individual commitment to the marriage, their willingness to go more than halfway to carry the relationship through difficult times.

Happily married couples apparently argue as often as unhappily married couples do, but they argue more constructively (Gottman, 1994; Gottman & Krokoff, 1989). They genuinely listen to each other, focus on solving the problem rather than "winning" or proving the other wrong, show respect rather than contempt for each other's views, refrain from bringing up past hurts or grievances that are irrelevant to the current issue, and intersperse their arguments with positive comments and humor to reduce the tension. Disagreement or stress tends to draw them together, in an effort to resolve the problem and to comfort each other, rather than to drive them apart (Murray et al., 2003).

In happy marriages, both partners are sensitive to the unstated feelings and needs of the other (Gottman, 1998; Mirgain & Cordova, 2007). In contrast, in unhappy marriages, there is often a lack of symmetry in this regard; the wife perceives and responds to the husband's unspoken needs, but the husband does not perceive and respond to hers (Gottman, 1994, 1998). Perhaps this helps explain why, in unhappy marriages, the wife typically feels more unhappy and manifests more physiological distress than does her partner (Gottman, 1994; Levenson et al., 1993). Such observations bring to mind the differing styles of interaction and communication shown by girls and boys in their separate playgroups. Researchers have found that in all sorts of relationships, not just marriages, women are on average better than men at attending to and understanding others' unspoken emotions and needs (Thomas & Fletcher, 2003). Success in marriage may often depend on the husband's willingness and ability to acquire some of the intimacy skills that he practiced less, as a child, than did his wife.

The impact of negative interactions between married couples has been documented in longitudinal studies by John Gottman and his colleagues. For instance, Gottman and Clifford Notarius (2000) were able to identify couples who would divorce by looking at patterns of positive and

FOCUS 32

What are some characteristics of happily married couples? Why might marital happiness depend even more on the husband's capacity to adjust than on the wife's?

"CURLY HERE SAYS I'M 'TOO SARCASTIC'..."

■ Having negative styles of talking and arguing and difficulty communicating are risk factors for divorce. Fortunately, such behavior can be changed.

negative interactions. Gottman (2011) even claims that he can predict with 94% accuracy whether a couple will divorce within 4 years based on an interview with the couple. In the interview, Gottman asks the couple to tell him "a story about us," and looks for five key components: (1) *fondness and admiration*; (2) *"we-ness" versus "me-ness"*—do they use "us" and "we" more than "I" and "me"; (3) *love maps*— the degree to which the couple describes the history of their relationships in detail with positive versus negative energy; (4) *purpose and meaning instead of chaos*—the degree to which the couple talks about shared goals and aspirations; and (5) *satisfaction instead of disappointment*. If the negatives outweigh the positives, it is unlikely the couple will be together in 4 years' time.

In their research at the University of Denver, Howard Markman and his colleagues (2004; Markman & Rhodes, 2012) identified several risk factors for unhappy marriages and divorce. Some of these factors are beyond the individual's control, such as experiencing serious money problems or having divorced parents. Personality can also play a role; individuals who react defensively to problems and disappointments are at risk. Other risk factors include marrying someone from a different religious background, marrying very young, getting married after knowing each other for only a short time, and having unrealistic beliefs about marriage. Perhaps paradoxically, couples that live together before marriage also have a higher rate of marital conflict and divorce than those who wait until marriage to live together (Hewitt & de Vaus, 2009). If a partner has been divorced, this increases the risk of marital difficulties, especially if he or she also has children from the prior marriage.

However, Markman and colleagues also identified relationship patterns that can be changed for the better if the couple is willing to work on them. These include:

- Use a positive style of talking and resolving arguments (e.g., avoid putdowns, yelling, and name calling)
- Make an effort to communicate when you disagree (e.g., don't sulk or give the "silent treatment")
- Learn to handle disagreements as a team (e.g., capitalize on each other's strengths to resolve conflicts)
- Be honest with yourself and your partner: Are you completely committed to each other for the long term?

Employment

Work, of course, is first and foremost a means of making a living, but it is more than that. It occupies an enormous portion of adult life. Work can be tedious and mind numbing or exciting and mind building. At its best, work is for adults what play is for children. It brings them into social contact with their peers outside the family, poses interesting problems to solve and challenges to meet, promotes development of physical and intellectual skills, and is fun.

The Value of Occupational Self-Direction

In surveys of workers, people most often say they enjoy their work if it is (a) complex rather than simple, (b) varied rather than routine, and (c) not closely supervised by someone else (Galinsky et al., 1993; Kohn, 1980). Sociologist Melvin Kohn refers to this much-desired constellation of job characteristics as *occupational self-direction*. A job high in occupational self-direction is one in which the worker makes many choices and decisions throughout the workday. Self-direction is a key characteristic of entrepreneurship (starting one's own business) and is also typical of jobs in small businesses, as well as top-level management positions in larger organizations. Research suggests that jobs of this sort, despite their high demands, are for most people less stressful—as measured by effects on workers' mental and physical health—than are jobs in which workers make few choices and are closely supervised (Spector, 2002). Research also suggests that such jobs promote certain positive personality changes.

In a massive, long-term study conducted in both the United States and Poland, Kohn and his colleague Kazimierz Slomczynski found that workers who moved into jobs that were high in self-direction, from jobs that were low in that quality, changed psychologically in certain ways, relative to other workers (Kohn & Slomczynski, 1990). Over their time in the job, they became more intellectually flexible, not just at work but in their approaches to all areas of life. They began to value self-direction more than they had before, in others as well as in themselves. They became less authoritarian and more democratic in their approaches to child rearing; that is, they became less concerned with obedience for its own sake and more concerned with their children's abilities to make decisions. Kohn and Slomczynski also tested the children. They found that the children of workers in jobs with high self-direction were more self-directed and less conforming than children of workers whose jobs entailed less self-direction. Thus the job apparently affected the psychology not just of the workers but also of the workers' children.

All these effects occurred regardless of the salary level or prestige level of the job. In general, blue-collar jobs were not as high in self-direction as white-collar jobs, but when they were as high, they had the same effects. Kohn and Slomczynski contend that the effects they observed on parenting may be adaptive for people whose social class determines the kinds of jobs available to them. In settings where people must make a living by obeying others, it may be sensible to raise children to obey and not question. In settings where people's living depends on their own decision making, it makes more sense to raise children to question authority and think independently.

FOCUS 33

What evidence suggests that the type of job one has can alter one's way of thinking and style of parenting and can influence the development of one's children?

FOCUS 34

What difference has been found between husbands' and wives' enjoyment of out-of-home and at-home work? How did the researchers explain that difference?

■ **Occupational self-direction** Self-employed people, and others who make most of their own decisions throughout a typical workday, learn to think independently and question authority, and they tend to raise their children to do the same. They are also far more likely to enjoy their work than are people who work under the thumb of a micromanaging boss.

Balancing Out-of-Home and At-Home Work

Women, more often than men, hold two jobs—one outside the home and the other inside. Although many men today spend much more time at housework and child care than they did in decades past, the average man is still less involved in these tasks than the average woman (although the gender difference becomes much smaller when home maintenance and repair is included) (Foster & Kreisler, 2012). Moreover, in dual-career families, women typically feel more conflict between the demands of family and those of work than do men (Bagger et al., 2008; McElwain et al., 2005).

Despite the traditional stereotype of who "belongs" where—or maybe because of it—some research suggests that wives enjoy their out-of-home work more than their at-home work, while the opposite is true for husbands. Reed Larson and his colleagues (1994) asked 55 working-class and middle-class married parents of school-age children to wear pagers as they went about their daily activities. The pagers beeped at random times during the daytime and evening hours, and at each beep the person filled out a form to describe his or her activity and emotional state just prior to the beep. Over the whole set of reports, wives and husbands did not differ in their self-rated happiness, but wives rated themselves happier at work than at home and husbands rated themselves happier at home than at work. These results held even when the specific type of activity reported at work or at home was the same for the two. When men did laundry or vacuumed at home, they said they enjoyed it; when women did the same, they more often said they were bored or angry. Why this difference?

The men's greater enjoyment of housework could stem simply from the fact that they did it less than their wives, but that

Michael Pole/Corbis/Getty Images

explanation doesn't hold for the women's greater enjoyment of out-of-home work. Even the wives who worked away from home for as many hours as their husbands did, at comparable jobs, enjoyed that work more than their husbands did. Larson and his colleagues suggest that both differences derived from the men's and women's differing perceptions of their choices and obligations. Men enjoyed housework because they didn't really consider it their responsibility; they did it by choice and as a gallant means of "helping out." Women did housework because they felt that they had to; if they didn't do it, nobody else would, and visitors might assume that a dirty house was the woman's fault. Conversely, the men had a greater sense of obligation, and reduced sense of choice, concerning their out-of-home work. They felt that it was their duty to support their family in this way. Although the wives did not experience more actual on-the-job choice in Kohn's sense of occupational self-direction than their husbands did, they apparently had a stronger global belief that their out-of-home work was optional. As Larson and his colleagues point out, the results do match a certain traditional stereotype: Men "slave" at work and come home to relax, and women "slave" at home and go out to relax. What's interesting is that the very same activity can be slaving for one and relaxing for the other, depending apparently on the feeling of obligation or choice.

Growing Old

According to current projections of life expectancy, and taking into account the greater longevity of college graduates compared with the rest of the population, the majority of students reading this book will live past the age of 80. How will today's young adults change as they grow into middle adulthood and, later, into old age?

■ **Socioemotional satisfaction** As people grow older, they tend to become more interested in enjoying the present and less future-oriented than they were when they were younger.

Some young people fear old age. There is no denying that aging entails loss. We gradually lose our youthful looks and some of our physical strength, agility, sensory acuity, mental quickness, and memory. We lose some of our social roles (especially those related to employment) and some of our authority (as people take us less seriously). We lose loved ones who die before we do, and, of course, with the passing of each year we lose a year from our own life span.

Yet, if you ask older adults, old age is not as bad as it seems to the young. Research studies, using a variety of methods, have found that older adults, on average, report greater current enjoyment of life than do middle-aged people, and middle-aged people report greater enjoyment than do young adults (Mroczek, 2001; Sheldon & Kasser, 2001). This finding has been called the "paradox of aging": Objectively, life looks worse in old age—there are more pains and losses—but subjectively, it feels better. As we age, our priorities and expectations change to match realities, and along with losses there are gains. We become in some ways wiser, mellower, and more able to enjoy the present moment.

A Shift Toward Focus on the Present and the Positive

Laura Carstensen (1992; Carstensen & Mikels, 2005; Reed & Carstensen, 2012) has developed a theory of aging—called the *socioemotional selectivity theory*—which helps explain why older adults commonly maintain or increase their satisfaction with life despite losses. According to Carstensen, as people grow older—or, more precisely, as they see that they have fewer years left—they become gradually more concerned with enjoying the present and less concerned with activities to prepare for the future. Young people are motivated to explore new pathways

FOCUS 35

How does the socioemotional selectivity theory account for elderly people's generally high satisfaction with life?

and meet new people, despite the disruptions and fears associated with the unfamiliar. Such activities provide new skills, information, social contacts, and prestige that may prove useful in the future. But with fewer years left, the balance shifts. The older one is, the less sense it makes to sacrifice present comforts and pleasures for possible future gain. According to Carstensen, this idea helps us understand many of the specific changes observed in older adults.

As people grow older, they tend to devote less attention and energy to casual acquaintances and strangers and more to people with whom they already have close emotional ties (Fung et al., 2001; Löckenhoff & Carstensen, 2004). Long-married couples grow closer. Husbands and wives become more interested in enjoying each other and less interested in trying to improve, impress, or dominate each other, and satisfaction with marriage becomes greater (Henry et al., 2007; Levenson et al., 1993). Older adults typically show less anger than do younger adults, in response to similar provocations, and become better at preserving valued relationships (Blanchard-Fields, 2007). Ties with children, grandchildren, and long-time friends grow stronger and more valued with age, while broader social networks become less valued and shrink in size. Such changes have been observed not just among older adults but also among younger people whose life expectancy is shortened by AIDS or other terminal illnesses (Carstensen & Fredrickson, 1998).

People who continue working into old age typically report that they enjoy their work more than they did when they were younger (Levinson, 1978; Rybash et al., 1995). They become, on average, less concerned with the "rat race" of advancement and impressing others and more concerned with the day-to-day work itself and the pleasant social relationships associated with it.

Selective Attention to and Memory for the Positive

In several experiments, Carstensen and her colleagues found that older people, unlike younger people, attend more to emotionally positive stimuli than to emotionally negative stimuli and show better memory for the former than the latter (Mather & Carstensen, 2003; St. Jacques et al., 2009). In one experiment (Charles et al., 2003), young adults (age 18–29), middle-aged adults (41–53), and old adults (65–80) were shown pictures of positive scenes (e.g., happy children and puppies), negative scenes (e.g., a plane crash and garbage), and neutral scenes (e.g., a runner and a truck). Then they were asked to recall and briefly describe, from memory, as many of the pictures as they could. One predictable result was that older people recalled fewer of the scenes, overall, than did younger people; memory for all information declines as we age. The other, more interesting finding was that the decline in memory with age was much sharper for the negative scenes than for the positive scenes (see **Figure 12.12**). Apparently, selective attention and memory is one means by which older people regulate their emotions in a positive direction.

FOCUS 36

How might selective attention and selective memory contribute to satisfaction in old age?

FIGURE 12.12 Effect of age on memory for positive, negative, and neutral scenes Memory for depictions of emotionally negative scenes declined much more sharply between middle age and old age than did memory for depictions of positive or neutral scenes. (Data from Charles, Mather, & Carstensen, 2003.)

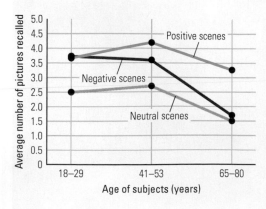

This *positivity bias* extends beyond memory. For instance, older adults are more likely than younger adults to direct their attention away from negative stimuli (Mather & Carstensen, 2003), have greater working memory for positive than for negative emotional images (Mikels et al., 2005), and evaluate events in their own lives more positively than younger adults (Schryer & Ross, 2012). In general, older adults are more emotionally positive than younger adults.

Approaching Death

The one certainty of life is that it ends in death. Surveys have shown that fear of death typically peaks in the person's fifties, which is when people often begin to see some of their peers dying from such causes as heart attack and cancer (Karp, 1988; Riley, 1970). Older people have less fear of death (Cicirelli, 2001). They are more likely to accept it as inevitable; and death in old age, when a person has lived a full life, seems less unfair than it did earlier.

Various theories have been offered regarding the stages or mental tasks involved in preparing for death. On the basis of her experience with caring for dying patients, Elisabeth Kübler-Ross (1969) proposed that people go through five stages when they hear that they are incurably ill and will soon die: (1) *denial*—"The diagnosis can't be right," or "I'll lick it"; (2) *anger*—"Why me?"; (3) *bargaining*—"If I do such and such, can I live longer?"; (4) *depression*—"All is lost"; and (5) *acceptance*—"I am prepared to die." Another theory is that preparation for death consists of reviewing one's life and trying to make sense of it (Butler, 1975).

As useful as such theories may be in understanding individual cases, research shows that there is no universal approach to death. Each person faces it differently. One person may review his or her life; another may not. One person may go through one or several of Kübler-Ross's stages but not all of them, and others may go through them in a different order (Kastenbaum, 1985). The people whom I (Peter Gray) have seen die all did it in pretty much the way they did other things in life. When my mother discovered that she would soon die—at the too-young age of 62—it was important to her that her four sons be around her so that she could tell us some of the things she had learned about life that we might want to know. She spent her time talking about what, from her present perspective, seemed important and what did not. She reviewed her life, not to justify it but to tell us why some things she did worked out and others didn't. She had been a teacher all her life, and she died one.

SECTION REVIEW

Love and work are the major themes of adulthood.

Love

- Romantic love has much in common with infant attachment to caregivers. The attachment style developed in infancy—secure, anxious, or avoidant—seems to carry forward into adult attachments.

- Happy marriages are generally characterized by mutual liking and respect, individual commitment to the marriage, and constructive means of arguing.

- Wives are generally better than husbands at perceiving and responding to their spouse's unspoken needs, so marital happiness often depends on the husband's developing those abilities.

Employment

- Jobs that permit considerable self-direction are enjoyed more than other jobs. Workers with such jobs become more self-directed in their overall approach to life and may, through their parenting, pass this trait on to their children.

- When husbands and wives both work outside the home, wives generally enjoy the out-of-home work more, and husbands enjoy the at-home work more. Perhaps the nonstereotypical task seems more a matter of choice, which promotes greater enjoyment.

Growing Old

- The elderly generally report greater life satisfaction than do middle-aged and young adults, despite the objective losses that accompany aging.

- Elderly people focus more on the present and less on the future than do younger people. They also attend to and remember emotionally positive stimuli more than negative ones.

- Though various theories make general statements about what people do as they approach death, it is really a highly individual matter.

Thinking Critically About Social Development

1. What is attachment and why might it be so important for human development? Why might attachment early in life affect social relations in adulthood?

2. Do psychological differences in gender have a basis in biology or are they entirely socially constructed?

3. Is adolescence a "true" developmental stage, characteristic of our species, or is it primarily a social construction, invented by cultures in which additional education is required before taking on adult roles?

Reflections and Connections

This chapter has run the life course, from birth to death. As you review it, you might organize your thinking around the following two themes.

1. Development as a product of evolution The universal characteristics of human beings at each life phase are evolved adaptations that promote survival and reproduction, either immediately within that phase or through helping the individual prepare for challenges ahead (Bjorklund et al., 2016). Think about how this idea might apply to each of the main topics in the chapter, from the nature of infants' attachments to caregivers to the changes in priorities that arise in old age.

As you think about each of these topics, you may well decide that the evolutionary accounts offered for some are more complete or compelling than those offered for others. You may think of alternative explanations, either founded in evolutionary theory or not.

2. Development as adaptation to the specifics of one's social environment Evolution has endowed us not with rigid instincts but with tendencies, drives, and alternative strategies that are facilitated, inhibited, selected, or redirected in accordance with our experiences in our social environments.

Researchers have found many reliable correlations between aspects of a person's social environment and the person's development. How might these correlations be understood as adaptive changes that help the person to meet the specific social conditions of his or her life?

Think about this question as it might apply to behavioral changes or differences associated with (a) caregiver responsiveness or unresponsiveness to infants' signs of distress; (b) cultural and individual differences in sleeping arrangements for infants and young children; (c) differing styles of parental discipline of children; (d) age-mixed compared with age-segregated play environments; (e) cultural differences in the degree to which children witness violence among adults; (f) social-class differences that alter the chance of adolescents' achieving status through nonrisky means; (g) good parental models for moral development in adolescence; (h) conditions that may alter sexual strategy toward either promiscuity or restraint; and (i) occupational self-direction in adulthood.

As you review, you may find that some of the explanations just called for are lacking or incomplete, or you may decide that the correlational evidence does not warrant the cause–effect inference implied. In such cases, how might future research fill the gaps and establish causal relationships?

Key Terms

attachment 452

disorganized/disoriented
   attachment 454

emerging adulthood 472

gender identity 469

insecure-avoidant
   attachment 454

insecure-resistant
   attachment 454

overimitation 460

parenting styles 462

prosocial behavior 458

secure attachment 454

strange-situation test 454

Find Out More

Catherine Salmon & Todd K. Shackelford (Eds.) (2008). *Family relationships: An evolutionary perspective.* Oxford, UK: Oxford University Press.

This scholarly book consists of chapters that are each written by a different expert or set of experts—leading theorists from evolutionary psychology and related disciplines. The book provides insights based on an evolutionary view of parent–child relationships, sibling relationships, domestic violence, and all aspects of family dynamics.

Elizabeth Marshall Thomas (2006). *The old way: A story of the first people.* New York, NY: Farrar, Straus and Giroux.

Thomas was only 19 years old when she ventured into Africa's Kalahari Desert with the rest of her family in search of the !Kung hunter-gatherers. This book is a wonderfully written, vivid account of the lives and ways of these peaceful people. We can learn much about ourselves by examining our "old way"— our hunter-gatherer way—of living.

Alan M. Slater & Paul C. Quinn (Eds.) (2012). *Developmental psychology: Revisiting the classic studies.* London, UK: SAGE Publications.

As the saying goes, hindsight is 20/20— and that holds true for this look back at some of the most important and influential developmental studies of our time.

This 14-chapter book, with contributions from prominent psychologists, conducts critical analyses of landmark studies such as Harlow's monkeys, Little Albert, and Bandura's Bobo doll research. It brings the concepts from these classic studies into current context and shows how they influenced research in subsequent years.

Sarah-Jayne Blakemore (2012, June). *The mysterious workings of the adolescent brain.* TEDGlobal. https://www.ted.com/talks/sarah_jayne_blakemore_the_mysterious_workings_of_the_adolescent_brain?utm_source=tedcomshare&utm_medium=referral&utm_campaign=tedspread

Cognitive neuroscientist Blakemore discusses how the development of the brain relates to impulsivity as well as decision making in adolescents. She reviews the current research on neurodevelopment of the prefrontal cortex and its relation to teen social behavior.

Peter Gray (2013). *Free to learn: Why unleashing the instinct to play will make our children happier, more self-reliant, and better students for life*. New York, NY: Basic Books.

The senior author of this textbook, Peter Gray, presents his provocative argument that modern society and schooling ignore the evolutionary value of play, which is taken for granted in hunter-gatherer societies. He argues, with evidence, that many of the problems of contemporary education can be resolved if we liberate our children to pursue their own interest through self-directed play, essentially entrusting them with their own education. Although you may not agree will all of Gray's conclusions, the book provides much food for thought.

Peter Gray (2014, May). *The decline of play*. TEDxNavesink.

https://www.youtube.com/watch?v= Bg-GEzM7iTk&feature=youtu.be

Peter Gray argues that the decline in children's freedom to play with other children, without adult direction, is correlated with clinical disorders, decreased creativity, and external locus of control. He documents why free play is essential for children's healthy social and emotional development and outlines steps through which we can bring free play back to children's lives.

LaunchPad
macmillan learning

Visit LaunchPad for Psychology 8e launchpadworks.com to access the e-book, videos, activities, additional resources, and LearningCurve quizzes, as well as study aids including flash cards and web quizzes.

We humans are social beings through and through. We are motivated to understand others, and our understanding of ourselves is strongly affected by our perceptions of what others think of us. Chapter 13 is about the mental processes involved in understanding others, ourselves, and the social world in general, as well as some of the ways in which other people influence our behavior. Chapter 14 is about personality—a person's general style of interacting with the world. We all vary in our emotions, motives, and styles of thinking and behaving, and these differences give each of us a unique personality.

CHAPTER

Social Psychology

13

LEARNING OUTCOMES

After studying this chapter, you should be able to:

- Describe how people perceive others and make attributions about them.

- Explain self-perceptions and attitudes and how they influence our behavior.

- Define stereotypes and discuss ways in which they influence interpersonal and group behavior.

- Summarize some effects of being observed and evaluated by others.

- Describe several lines of research on how examples, opinions, and requests can influence behavior.

- Compare prosocial behavior with aggression and competition, giving some examples of each.

CHAPTER OUTLINE

Forming Impressions of Other People

Perceiving and Evaluating the Self

Perceiving Ourselves and Others as Members of Groups

Effects of Being Observed and Evaluated

Effects of Others' Examples, Opinions, and Requests

To Cooperate or Not: Prosocial Behavior and the Dilemma of Social Life

Thinking Critically About Social Psychology

Reflections and Connections

Key Terms

Find Out More

Humans are intensely social animals. Natural selection has designed us to depend on one another for even our most basic needs. To obtain food, for example, we benefit greatly from the help of others and the knowledge shared by members of a human community. Throughout our evolutionary history, to be thrown out of the tribe was tantamount to death. We are also thinking social animals. Most of what we think about is other people, ourselves, our relationships with other people, and the social conventions and norms that are essential aspects of life in any human society.

This chapter is about **social psychology**, the subfield of psychology that deals most explicitly with how we view one another and are influenced by one another. The first sections of this chapter focus on *person perception*, the processes by which we perceive and understand one another and ourselves, and on *attitudes*, the evaluative beliefs that we have about our social world and the entities within it. Further sections focus on the effects that those perceptions and beliefs have on our emotions and actions. Relationships are also a central topic in social psychology. However, since we discussed various types of relationships (infant-mother, peer, marital) in the previous chapter on social development, relationships will not be discussed further here.

xavierarnau/Getty Images

Forming Impressions of Other People

FOCUS 1

In what sense are people natural psychologists?

One of social psychology's pioneers, Fritz Heider (1958), pointed out that human beings are natural psychologists—or *naïve psychologists,* to use his term. We are practitioners of *folk psychology,* a means by which people "naturally" come to understand the psychological world. Consistent with Heider's view, researchers have found that people untrained in psychology often make remarkably accurate observations and judgments about other people's behavior (Carney et al., 2007).

Yet, as Heider himself pointed out, our judgments of others sometimes suffer from certain consistent mistakes, or *biases.* Such biases interest social psychologists for two reasons. First, they provide clues about the mental processes that contribute to accurate as well as inaccurate perceptions and judgments. In this regard, social psychologists' interest in biases is analogous to perceptual psychologists' interest in visual illusions, which (as discussed in Chapter 7) provide clues to understanding normal, accurate visual perception. Second, an understanding of biases can promote social justice. By helping people understand the psychological tendencies that contribute to prejudice and unfair treatment of other people, social-psychological findings can help people overcome such biases.

Making Attributions from Observed Behavior

Actions are directly observable, but thoughts are not. Therefore, our judgments about the personalities of people we encounter are based largely on what we observe of their actions. As naïve psychologists, in our everyday experiences we intuitively form impressions of people's personalities on the basis of their actions.

For example, if a new acquaintance smiles at you, you do not simply register the fact that she smiled; rather, you interpret the smile's meaning and use that interpretation to infer something about the kind of person she is. Depending on the context, the precise form of the smile, and any prior information you have about her, you might decide that the smile represents friendliness, or smugness, or guile. What you carry away from the encounter is not so much a memory that the person smiled as a memory that she was friendly, smug, or deceitful. That memory is added to your growing impression of her and may affect—fairly or unfairly—your future interactions with her.

Any such judgment about another person is, in essence, a claim about causation. It is an implicit claim that the person's behavior is caused in part by some more or less permanent characteristic of the person, such as friendliness or deceitfulness. In common English usage, any claim about causation is called an *attribution.* In the study of person perception, an **attribution** is a claim about the cause of someone's behavior. As Heider (1958) pointed out, we naturally make judgments about others' personalities on the basis of their behavior, but for these judgments to be meaningful we must distinguish actions that tell us something lasting and unique about the person from those that do not.

The Person Bias in Attributions

FOCUS 2

What evidence supports the existence of a person bias in attributions?

In his original writings about attribution, Heider (1958) noted that people tend to give too much weight to personality and not enough to the environmental situation when they make attributions about others' actions. For example, imagine that we are caught in a traffic jam and Susan, our driver, is expressing a great deal of anger. Does her anger tell us something useful about her as a person? Most people tend to ignore the traffic jam as cause and attribute Susan's anger too heavily to her character. Many researchers have confirmed the existence of this **person bias** in attribution.

Some of the most dramatic examples of the person bias occur in situations in which a person is socially pressured or required to behave in a certain way.

In one experiment, for example, college students listened to a student who was assigned to read a political statement written by someone else (Gilbert & Jones, 1986). Even when the assignment was made by the observers themselves, so they could be sure that the reader had not chosen it himself, observers tended to rate the reader as politically liberal when the statement he read was liberal and as politically conservative when the statement was conservative. Even though there was no logical reason to assume that the statement had anything to do with the reader's own political beliefs, the students still made that attribution.

Other research has shown that a person's social role can have undue effects on the attributions that others make about that person. When we observe a police officer, nurse, teacher, or student carrying out his or her duties, we tend—in accord with the person bias—to attribute the action to the individual's personality and to ignore the constraints that the role places on how the person can or must act. We might develop quite different impressions of the same person if we saw him or her in out-of-role situations.

In one experiment demonstrating this effect of roles, Ronald Humphrey (1985) set up a simulated corporate office and randomly assigned some volunteers to the role of manager and others to that of clerk. The managers were given interesting tasks and responsibilities, and the clerks were given routine, boring tasks. At the end of the study, the subjects rated various aspects of the personalities of all subjects, including themselves. Compared with those in the clerk role, those in the manager role were judged by others more positively; they were rated higher in leadership, intelligence, assertiveness, supportiveness, and likelihood of future success. In keeping with the person bias, the subjects apparently ignored the fact that the role assignment, which they knew was random, had allowed one group to manifest characteristics that the other group could not. The bias did not hold when the subjects rated themselves—people tend to view their abilities and psychological attributes more positively than as judged by others (Sheppard et al., 2013)—but it did hold when they rated others who had been assigned to the same role as themselves.

By the mid-1970s so much evidence had appeared to support the person bias that Lee Ross (1977) called it the *fundamental attribution error*, a label designed to signify the pervasiveness and strength of the bias and to suggest that it underlies many other social-psychological phenomena. That label is still in use despite growing evidence that the bias may not be as fundamental as Ross and others thought (Uleman et al., 2008). People are much more likely to make this error if their minds are occupied by other tasks or if they are tired than if they devote their full attention to the task (Gilbert, 1989). Also, in many cases, the apparent demands of the experiment may artificially produce the person bias. Research subjects who are told that their task is to judge someone's personality are much more likely to exhibit the person bias than are those who are asked to explain the observed behavior in whatever terms they wish (Malle, 2006).

Prior to the 1980s, social-psychological studies of attributions had been conducted only in Western cultures, mostly in North America and Western Europe. This observation led some to suggest that the person bias in attributions might be a product of a predominantly Western way of thinking. To test this theory, Joan Miller (1984) asked middle-class children and adults in the United States and in a Hindu community in India to think of an action by someone they knew and then to explain why the person had acted in that way. As predicted, the Americans made more attributions to personality and fewer to the situation than did the Indians. This difference was greater for adults—who would presumably incorporate cultural norms more strongly—than it was for children (see **Figure 13.1** on page 496).

■ **Is she a careless person or just having a moment of distraction?** According to the person bias (or fundamental attribution error), people tend to attribute other people's behavior to a trait, or disposition, whereas they are more likely to attribute their own behavior to the context.

FOCUS 3

Why is the person bias often called the "fundamental attribution error"? In what conditions does the bias most often occur?

FOCUS 4

What logic and evidence suggest that the person bias may be a product of Western culture and may not exist in Eastern cultures?

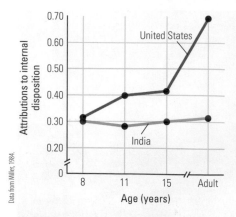

FIGURE 13.1 **Cultural difference in making attributions** When asked to explain another person's behavior, the proportion of attributions to internal disposition (personality or attitude) was greater among people in the United States than it was among Hindus in India, and this difference was greater for adults than for children. (The proportions were determined by dividing the number of person attributions by the total number of person-plus-situation attributions for each group.)

FOCUS 5

How have researchers documented biasing effects of physical attractiveness on perceptions of personality?

■ **Luckily for them, they're cute** Researchers have found that good-looking children are less likely to be blamed for their misbehavior than are children who are not so good looking. The teacher here may be more inclined to attribute this disruptive behavior to the merriment of the situation than he would if the boys were not so cute.

In the years since Miller's pioneering work, similar results have been found in dozens of studies comparing attributions made by people raised in North America with those raised in various Far Eastern countries, including China, Japan, and Korea (Lehman et al., 2004; Norenzayan & Nisbett, 2000). Although there are many possible reasons for this cultural difference (language, genes), Michael Varnum and his colleagues (2010) argue that the most likely explanation is social orientation. That is, Western cultures emphasize personal independence whereas Eastern cultures emphasize greater interdependence among people.

Effects of Facial Features on Person Perceptions

"Don't judge a book by its cover" goes the saying, but we have the saying precisely because we know that people do just that. Similarly, we caution ourselves against judging people by their facial features because we know that we do tend to make such judgments, often falsely and unfairly. The two most researched biases that derive from perceptions of facial features are the *attractiveness bias* and the *baby-face bias*.

Consistent with folktales in which the good people (the princesses and princes) are beautiful and the bad people (the witches and ogres) are ugly, experiments have shown that physically attractive people are commonly judged as more intelligent, competent, sociable, and moral than less attractive people (Dion, 2002; Langlois et al., 2000).

In one experiment, fifth-grade teachers were given report cards and photographs of children whom they did not know and were asked to rate each child's intelligence and achievement. The teachers rated physically attractive children as brighter and more successful than unattractive children with identical report cards (Clifford & Walster, 1973). In another study, which analyzed actual court cases, judges regularly gave longer prison sentences to unattractive people than to attractive people convicted of comparable crimes (Stewart, 1985). There is also evidence that East Asians are less susceptible to the attractiveness bias than are Westerners (Dion, 2002). Just as they are less inclined than Westerners to judge a person's character from a brief glimpse of the person's behavior, they are also less inclined to judge it from the person's physical attractiveness. Apparently, the attractiveness bias is at least partly a result of an influence of Western culture.

But is there any evidence that more attractive people actually *are* more intelligent than less attractive people? Leslie Zebrowitz and her colleagues (2002) obtained archival photographs and IQ scores of people born between 1920 and 1929 who had participated in three longitudinal studies and asked a panel of judges to estimate their attractiveness and intelligence based on photos. Photographs had been taken at five different times in the life span: childhood, puberty, adolescence, mid-adulthood, and later adulthood. **Figure 13.2** shows the correlations between rated attractiveness and (a) IQ and (b) perceived intelligence. As you can see, the correlations between perceived attractiveness and perceived intelligence were quite high and similar for all ages judged (median correlation = .57). The correlations with IQ, however, were much lower (median correlation = .21), although still greater than expected by chance for all but the older adults.

One explanation for the significant, though small (accounting for only about 4% of the individual differences in IQ) relation between IQ and physical attractiveness is the "good genes" theory. Basically, attractiveness signals "good genes," and people have evolved to judge good-looking people as high-quality (i.e., intelligent) potential mates (Buss, 1989; Thornhill & Gangestad, 1999). Alternatively, facial attractiveness is related to symmetry (the right side of the face being similar to the left side), and symmetry is related to prenatal experiences: The more problems a fetus experiences, the less symmetrical his or her body is, and the less fit overall he or she can be expected to be (Furlow et al., 1997). Even if the relation between actual IQ and attractiveness is reliable (and some research suggests it is not; Mitchem et al., 2015), it accounts for only a small portion of the variance in IQ and is significantly less than what people perceive (mostly incorrectly) the relation between attractiveness and intelligence to be.

Another pervasive, although less well-known, bias concerns a person's facial maturity. Some people, regardless of their age, have facial features that resemble those of a baby: a round rather than elongated head, a forehead protruding forward rather than sloping back, large eyes, and a small jawbone. In a series of experiments conducted in both the United States and Korea, baby-faced adults were perceived as more naïve, honest, helpless, kind, and warm than mature-faced adults of the same age and sex—even though the subjects could tell that the baby-faced persons were not really younger (McArthur & Berry, 1987; Zebrowitz et al., 1993).

In one study, Leslie Zebrowitz and Susan McDonald (1991) found that the baby-face bias influenced the outcomes of actual cases in a small-claims court. Baby-faced defendants were much more frequently found innocent in cases involving intentional wrongdoing than were mature-faced defendants, but they were neither more nor less frequently found innocent in cases involving negligence (such as performing a contracted job incompetently). Apparently, judges find it hard to think of baby-faced persons as deliberately causing harm but do not find it difficult to think of them as incompetent or forgetful.

Another study, with enormous practical implications, showed that facial features play a big role in determining the results of U.S. Congressional elections. Alexander Todorov and his colleagues (2005) prepared black-and-white facial photographs of the two top candidates for each of 95 Senate races and 600 House of Representatives races taking place between the years 2000 and 2004. They showed each pair of photos for just 1 second to adult subjects who were not familiar with the candidates, asking them to judge, for each pair, which candidate looked more competent. The result was striking. The competence judgments, based on that 1-second viewing, correctly predicted the winner of 72% of the Senate races and 67% of the House races! Other evidence indicates that those judgments were probably founded primarily on assessments of facial maturity (Zebrowitz & Montepare, 2005). Apparently, people vote for the mature-faced person, who looks more competent, over the baby-faced person, who looks more naïve. Consistent with that interpretation, another research study showed that when photographs of former U.S. presidents Reagan and Kennedy were digitally altered to increase their baby-facedness, their perceived leadership qualities declined (Keating et al., 1999).

Konrad Lorenz (1943, 1971) suggested long ago that human beings intuitively respond to infants' facial features with feelings of compassion and care, a characteristic that helps promote the survival of our offspring. Immature facial features may provide adults with cues regarding a child's health and overall maturity level that in turn may influence the amount of time and resources they devote to a child. In support of this, perceptions of cuteness and attractiveness (which is associated with a greater display of immature features) are the single best predictors of the likelihood of people making hypothetical adoption decisions (Volk et al., 2007; Waller et al., 2004). He also noted that the infant-like features of some animal species (such as rabbits and pandas) lead us to perceive them as particularly cute, innocent, and needing care, regardless of the animals' actual needs or behaviors. The work of Zebrowitz and others suggests that we generalize this response not just to babies and animals but also to adult humans whose faces resemble those of babies. We may want to cuddle and comfort the more baby-faced candidate, but we don't choose him or her as our leader.

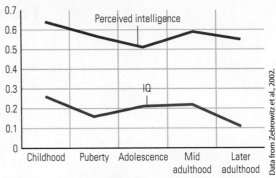

FIGURE 13.2 Correlations between ratings of physical attractiveness and IQ and perceived intelligence at five different points in the lifespan The high correlations between attractiveness and perceived intelligence reflect the attractiveness bias. The lower correlations between physical attractiveness and IQ show that the connection is not nearly as strong as people think, although physical attractiveness may account for about 4% of the individual differences in IQ.

FOCUS 6

How have researchers documented biasing effects of a babyish versus a mature-looking face? What practical consequences have been shown to result from this bias?

Forming Impressions on the Internet

The Internet, like the telephone before it and postal services before that, has added new dimensions to human communication. More than any other communication tool, the Internet allows people to locate and "meet" other people who have similar interests—through chat rooms, social networking sites, news groups, special-interest e-mail lists, dating services, and the like. While some research conducted in the early days of the Internet suggested that Internet use was socially detrimental, studies conducted more recently generally report positive correlations between Internet use and overall sociability and emotional well-being (Valkenburg & Peter, 2009). Here we focus on the role of the Internet in meeting new people. Many friendships and valued acquaintanceships today involve people who first met in cyberspace. Some of these relationships remain confined to cyberspace, but in other cases Internet friends eventually meet in person, and the friendship extends into the tangible world.

In several experiments, randomly formed pairs of opposite-sex college students who did not know each other were assigned to participate in get-acquainted meetings, either online (through an Internet chat room) or in face-to-face encounters. The most striking general result is that those who had met online reported more liking of each other than did those who had met face-to-face (Bargh & McKenna, 2004). In one such experiment, this first meeting was followed by a second meeting, in which all pairs met face-to-face (McKenna et al., 2002). As you can see in **Figure 13.3**, the degree of liking between those who first met on the Internet increased even more in the face-to-face meeting, while the lesser degree of liking between those who first met face-to-face was not significantly affected by the second meeting.

How can such results be explained? Researchers have found that get-acquainted meetings over the Internet are more intimate, more revealing of what each person considers to be his or her "true self," than are such meetings conducted face-to-face (Bargh & McKenna, 2004; Valkenburg & Peter, 2009). Apparently, the relative anonymity of the Internet, along with the lack of visual and auditory contact, reduces social anxiety and frees people to reveal more about themselves than they would if they met face-to-face. Also, without knowledge of the physical features of the other person, the biasing effects of attractiveness, or lack thereof, are absent. Communication is not shut down by early negative judgments or anxieties based on physical features. When and if the two partners do meet, they already know a good deal about each other and may feel something of an emotional bond, which may lead them to see each other as more attractive than they would have if they were complete strangers.

Not only can people show their "true" selves on the Internet, they can also "try out" new identities. This happens especially during adolescence. In this context, identity can be defined as "the aspect of the self that is accessible and salient in a particular context and that interacts with the environment" (Finkenhauer et al., 2002, p. 2). Sometimes teenagers conduct *identity experiments* online, pretending to be someone they are not. This was investigated in one study of Dutch children and adolescents ranging in age from 9 to 18 years (Valkenburg et al., 2005). The researchers asked the subjects if they had ever pretended to be someone else online and why. About half of the adolescents admitted to this, with "pretending" being more frequent for the younger than the older subjects (9- to 12-year-olds: 72%; 13- to 14-year-olds: 53%; 15- to 18-year-olds: 28%). Both boys and girls admitted to some false representation online, with boys exaggerating their masculinity and girls pretending to be prettier and older than they really were.

Used wisely, the Internet apparently is a valuable tool for making friends. But, as is often pointed out, the Internet's seductive nature also creates potential dangers. People can easily create false impressions of themselves over the Internet. For the sake of personal safety, the first few face-to-face meetings with an Internet acquaintance should be in a safe, public place; it is also advisable to use the Internet to verify the information a would-be friend has provided about him- or herself.

FOCUS 7

What evidence suggests that strangers who meet on the Internet like each other more than do strangers who meet in person? How might this phenomenon be explained?

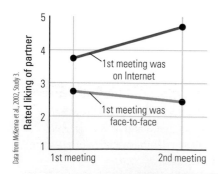

FIGURE 13.3 Getting acquainted on the Internet Randomly selected opposite-sex pairs of students met for 20 minutes either on the Internet or face-to-face, and then all pairs met face-to-face for a second 20-minute period. After each meeting, subjects anonymously rated their liking of their partners using a scale in which 7 was maximal liking.

SECTION REVIEW

We are constantly forming impressions of others and judging the causes of their behavior.

Basing Attributions on Observed Behavior	Effects of Physical Appearance	Forming Impressions on the Internet
■ Logically, we might attribute a person's behavior primarily to characteristics of the person or the situation. ■ The person bias is the tendency to give undue weight to personality and not enough to the situation in making attributions.	■ A common bias is the tendency to see physically attractive people as more intelligent, social, competent, and moral than less attractive people. ■ We tend to see baby-faced individuals as more honest, naïve, helpless, and warm—but less competent—than otherwise comparable people with mature faces.	■ In experiments, people who met initially on the Internet liked each other more than people who initially met face-to-face. ■ This tendency may result from people on the Internet being less anxious, more intimate, and freed from the biasing effects of physical appearance. ■ Adolescents are especially prone to conducting identity experiments online, pretending to be someone they are not.

Perceiving and Evaluating the Self

Few concepts are more important to people than the personal sense of self, or **self-concept**. Self-concept refers to the way that a person defines him- or herself. Many psychologists and sociologists have argued that the self-concept is fundamentally a *social* product. To become aware of yourself, you must first become aware of others of your species and then become aware, perhaps from the way others treat you, that you are one of them. Self-awareness includes awareness not just of the physical self, but also of one's own personality and character, reflected psychologically in the reactions of other people.

Seeing Ourselves Through the Eyes of Others

Many years ago the sociologist Charles Cooley (1902/1964) coined the term *looking-glass self* to describe what he considered to be a very large aspect of each person's self-concept. Cooley's "looking glass" is not an actual mirror; it is a metaphor for other people who react to us. He suggested that we all naturally infer what others think of us from their reactions, and we use those inferences to build our own self-concepts. Cooley's basic idea has been supported by much research showing that people's opinions and attitudes about themselves are very much affected by the opinions and attitudes of others.

FOCUS 8

According to Cooley, what is the "looking glass" with which we evaluate ourselves?

Effects of Others' Appraisals on Self-Understanding and Behavior

The beliefs and expectations that others have of a person—whether they are initially true or false—can to some degree create reality by influencing that person's self-concept and behavior. Such effects are called **self-fulfilling prophecies** or **Pygmalion effects**.

Pygmalion was the mythical Roman sculptor who created a statue of his ideal woman and then brought her to life by praying to Venus, the goddess of love. More relevant to the point being made here, however, is George Bernard Shaw's revision of the myth in his play *Pygmalion* (upon which the musical *My Fair Lady* was based). In the play, an impoverished Cockney flower seller, Eliza Doolittle, becomes a "fine lady" largely because of the expectations of others. Professor Higgins assumes that she is capable of talking and acting like a fine lady, and Colonel Pickering assumes that she is truly noble at heart. Their combined actions toward Eliza lead her to change her own understanding of herself, and therefore her behavior, so that the

FOCUS 9

What are Pygmalion effects in psychology, and how were such effects demonstrated in elementary school classrooms?

assumptions become reality. Psychological research indicates that such effects are not confined to fiction.

In a classic experiment, Robert Rosenthal and Lenore Jacobson (1968) led elementary school teachers to believe that a special test had predicted that certain students would show a spurt in intellectual growth during the next few months. Only the teachers were told of the supposed test results, not the students. In reality, the students labeled as "spurters" had been selected not on the basis of a test score but at random. Yet, when all the students were tested 8 months later, the "spurter" students showed significantly greater gains in IQ and academic performance than did their classmates. These were real gains, measured by objective tests, not just perceived gains. Somehow, the teachers' expectations that certain children would show more intellectual development than other children created its own reality.

Subsequent replications of this *Pygmalion in the classroom effect* provided clues concerning its mechanism. Compared to their behavior toward non-"spurter" students, teachers became warmer toward the "spurters," gave them more time to answer difficult questions, gave them more challenging work, and noticed and reinforced their self-initiated efforts (Cooper & Good, 1983; Rosenthal, 1994). In short, either consciously or unconsciously, they created a better learning environment for the selected students than for other students. Through their treatment of them, they also changed the selected students' self-concepts. The students began to see themselves as more capable academically than they had before, and this led them to work harder to live up to that perception (Cole, 1991; Jussim, 1991).

More recently, many experiments have demonstrated the Pygmalion effect with adults in various business and management settings as well as with children in school. When supervisors are led to believe that some of their subordinates have "special promise," those randomly selected subordinates in fact do begin to perform better than they did before (Eden, 2003; Natanovich & Eden, 2008). Again, these effects appear to occur partly from the extra attention and encouragement that the selected subordinates get and partly from the change in the subordinates' self-concepts in relation to their work.

Self-Esteem as an Index of Others' Approval and Acceptance

Our self-concepts have a strong evaluative component, which psychologists refer to as self-esteem. *Self-esteem*, by definition, is one's feeling of approval, acceptance, and liking of oneself. It is usually measured with questionnaires in which people rate the degree to which they agree or disagree with such statements as, "On the whole, I am satisfied with myself" and "I feel that I have a number of good qualities" (Tafarodi & Milne, 2002).

We experience self-esteem as being rooted in our own judgments about ourselves, but, according to an influential theory proposed by Mark Leary (1999, 2005), these judgments actually derive primarily from our perceptions of others' attitudes toward us. The theory is referred to as the *sociometer theory* because it proposes that self-esteem acts like a meter to inform us, at any given time, of the degree to which we are likely to be accepted or rejected by others. According to the sociometer theory, what you experience as your self-esteem at this very moment largely reflects your best guess about the degree to which other people, whom you care about, respect and accept you. As partial support of the sociometer theory, Leary and others have cited the following lines of evidence:

- Individual differences in self-esteem correlate strongly with individual differences in the degree to which people believe that they are generally accepted or rejected by others (Leary et al., 2001).

- In experiments, and in correlational studies involving real-life experiences, people's self-esteem increased after praise, social acceptance, or other satisfying social experiences and decreased after evidence of social rejection (Baumeister et al., 1998; Leary et al., 2001).

FOCUS 10

What is the sociometer theory of self-esteem, and what evidence supports it?

- Feedback about success or failure on a test had greater effects on self-esteem if the person was led to believe that others would hear of this success or failure than if the person was led to believe that the feedback was private and confidential (Leary & Baumeister, 2000). This may be the most compelling line of evidence for the theory because if self-esteem depended just on our own judgments about ourselves, then it shouldn't matter whether or not others knew how well we did.

The sociometer theory was designed to offer an evolutionary explanation of the function of self-esteem. From an evolutionary perspective, other people's views of us matter a great deal. Our survival depends on others' acceptance of us and willingness to cooperate with us. A self-view that is greatly out of sync with how others see us could be harmful. If I see myself as highly capable and trustworthy, but nobody else sees me that way, then my own high self-esteem will seem foolish to others and will not help me in my dealings with them. A major evolutionary purpose of our capacity for self-esteem, according to the sociometer theory, is to motivate us to act in ways that promote our acceptance by others. A decline in self-esteem may lead us to change our ways in order to become more socially acceptable, or it may lead us to seek a more compatible social group that approves of our ways. Conversely, an increase in self-esteem may lead us to continue on our present path, perhaps even more vigorously than before.

Actively Constructing Our Self-Perceptions

Although other people's views of us play a large role in our perceptions of ourselves, we do not just passively accept those views. We actively try to influence others' views of us, and in that way we also influence our own self-perceptions. In fact, rather than viewing the self as a static entity, some theorists view it as a dynamic one, shifting from one state to another at times when the self-structure is poorly integrated, but resisting the tendency to change in the face of inconsistent information when the self-structure is well integrated (Nowak et al., 2000; Vallacher et al., 2015).

In addition, we compare ourselves to others as a way of defining and evaluating ourselves, and we often bias those comparisons by giving more weight to some pieces of evidence than to others. For example, to see oneself as tall, or conscientious, or good at math, is to see oneself as having that quality *compared with other people*. The process of comparing ourselves with others in order to identify our unique characteristics and evaluate our abilities is called **social comparison**. A direct consequence of social comparison is that the self-concept varies depending on the **reference group**, the group against whom the comparison is made.

In one series of studies illustrating the role of the reference group, children's self-descriptions were found to focus on traits that most distinguished them from others in their group (McGuire & McGuire, 1988). Thus, children in racially homogeneous classrooms rarely mentioned their race, but those in racially mixed classrooms often did, especially if their race was in the minority. Children who were unusually tall or short compared with others in their group mentioned their height, and children with opposite-gender siblings mentioned their own gender more frequently than did other children (see **Figure 13.4**). Such evidence suggests that people identify themselves largely in terms of the ways in which they perceive themselves to be different from those around them.

Other research conducted in many different countries has shown that academically able students at nonselective schools typically have higher academic self-concepts than do equally able students at very selective schools (Marsh et al., 2008), a phenomenon aptly called the *big-fish-in-small-pond effect*. The effect reflects the difference in the students' reference groups, and a change of reference group, therefore, can dramatically affect our self-esteem. Many first-year college students who earned high grades in high school feel crushed when their marks are only average or less compared with those of their new, more selective reference group of college classmates.

FOCUS 11

What is some evidence that people construct a self-concept by comparing themselves with a reference group? How can a change in reference group alter self-esteem?

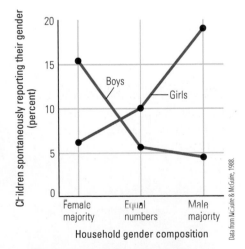

FIGURE 13.4 Evidence that children define themselves in terms of differences from their reference group As shown here, children were more likely to mention their gender when describing themselves if their gender was in the minority in their household than they were if it was in the majority.

Despite the fact that our self-image may change with the reference group, most of us think relatively well of ourselves, often unrealistically so. Repeated surveys have found that most college students rate themselves as better students than the average college student, and in one survey 94% of college instructors rated themselves as better teachers than the average college instructor (Alicke et al., 1995; Cross, 1977). Indeed, at least in North America and Western Europe, people tend to rate themselves unduly high on practically every dimension that they value (Roese & Olson, 2007). Adults' overestimation of their abilities (which is even greater in children; see Bjorklund, 2007) is termed a *positive illusory bias*, which is associated with greater psychological well-being, at least in the short term (Robins & Beer, 2001; Taylor & Brown, 1994). Although it is useful to have relatively accurate views of ourselves, it feels good to think well of ourselves, so most of us skew our self-evaluations in positive directions. We maintain our unduly high self-evaluations by treating evidence about ourselves differently from the way we treat evidence about others.

One way that we maintain a high view of ourselves is to systematically skew the attributions we make about our successes and failures. Earlier in this chapter we described the *person bias*—the general tendency to attribute people's actions, whether good or bad, to internal qualities of the person and to ignore external circumstances that constrained or promoted the actions. That bias applies when we think about other people's actions, but not when we think about our own actions. When we think about our own actions a different bias takes over, the **self-serving attributional bias**, defined as a tendency to attribute our *successes* to our own inner qualities and our *failures* to external circumstances. This bias has been demonstrated in countless experiments, with a wide variety of different kinds of tasks (Mezulis et al., 2004).

In one demonstration of this bias, students who performed well on an examination attributed their high grades to their own ability and hard work, whereas those who performed poorly attributed their low grades to bad luck, the unfairness of the test, or other factors beyond their control (Bernstein et al., 1979). In another study, essentially the same result was found for college professors who were asked to explain why a paper they had submitted to a scholarly journal had been either accepted or rejected (Wiley et al., 1979).

Another means by which most of us maintain inflated views of ourselves involves selective memory. Research has shown that people generally exhibit better long-term memory for positive events and successes in their lives than for negative events and failures (D'Argembeau & Van der Linden, 2008). The same bias does not occur in memory for the successes and failures of other people. This positivity bias is especially strong in older adults (Mather et al., 2004).

Although having a slightly inflated sense of ourselves may be adaptive, when one's self-concept is far in excess of one's accomplishments, the outcome may be maladaptive. This can happen when a child's parents provide nothing but praise to their children—deserved or not—resulting in an overinflated sense of self and an unrealistically high level of self-esteem (Lamborn et al., 1991).

Over the past several decades the professed self-esteem of American adolescents has been increasing, promoted in large part by a societal emphasis on building self-esteem (Twenge, 2006; Twenge & Campbell, 2001). Although self-esteem is generally associated with better academic achievement and psychological health, an unrealistically high level of self-esteem can backfire. For example, American adolescents' self-esteem with respect to academic performance has increased over recent decades but has been accompanied by *declines* in actual academic performance and increases in adjustment problems, including depression (Berk, 2005). For instance, in a comparison of 40 developed countries, American teenagers ranked slightly below the average in mathematics achievement but they were first in math self-concept (OECD, 2012). Overinflated self-esteem and its negative consequences seem to be especially prevalent among children from more affluent homes, whose

---

FOCUS 12

What are two means by which people build and maintain inflated views of themselves?

parents strive to protect their offspring from feelings of failure in order to promote their sense of self-worth (Levine, 2006).

According to Martin Seligman (1998), the "self-esteem movement" in the United States resulted in young people who felt good about themselves without achievements to warrant their feelings. This is an unstable foundation on which to build a personality and can lead to depression when they encounter failure.

Attitudes, Explicit and Implicit: Their Origins and Their Effects on Behavior

When we discuss the ways in which people evaluate other people and themselves, we are implicitly discussing attitudes. An **attitude** is any belief or opinion that has an evaluative component—a judgment or feeling that something is good or bad, likable or unlikable, moral or immoral, attractive or repulsive. Our attitudes tie us both cognitively and emotionally to our entire social world. We all have attitudes about countless objects, people, events, and ideas, ranging from our feelings about a particular brand of toothpaste to those about democracy or religion. Our most central attitudes, referred to as *values,* help us judge the appropriateness of whole categories of actions.

Social psychologists first began to study attitudes as a way of predicting how individuals would behave in specific situations. They conceived of attitudes as mental guides that people use to make behavioral choices (Allport, 1935). Over the years much research has been conducted to determine the degree to which people's attitudes do relate to their actual behavior and to understand the conditions in which that relationship is strong or weak. One clear finding is that the attitude–behavior relationship depends very much upon the way in which the attitude is assessed.

One important distinction is between *explicit* and *implicit* attitudes. **Explicit attitudes** are conscious, verbally stated evaluations. They are measured by traditional attitude tests in which people are asked, in various ways, to state their evaluation of some object or form of behavior. For example, to assess explicit attitudes about eating meat, people might be asked to respond, on a scale ranging from *strongly agree* to *strongly disagree,* to items such as "In general, I like to eat meat."

Implicit attitudes, by definition, are attitudes that are manifested in automatic mental associations (Fazio & Olson, 2003; Nosek, 2007). They are measured by **implicit association tests** (Greenwald et al., 1998), which are based on the fact that people can classify two concepts together more quickly if they are already strongly associated in their minds than if they are not strongly associated. In such a test—which is administered with a stopwatch or timer—the score is based on the speed of associations. For example, if you are faster at associating *meat* and meat-related words or pictures with good terms (such as *wonderful*) than with bad terms (such as *terrible*), this indicates that you have a positive implicit attitude toward meat. If the opposite is true, then you have a negative implicit attitude toward meat.

Implicit attitudes are gut-level attitudes. The object of the attitude automatically elicits mental associations that connote "good" or "bad," and these influence our bodily emotional reactions. In this sense, implicit attitudes automatically influence our behavior. The *less* we think about what we are doing, the more influence our implicit attitudes have. In contrast, our explicit attitudes require thought; the *more* we think about what we are doing, the more influence our explicit attitudes have. In many cases, people's implicit and explicit attitudes coincide, and in those cases behavior generally corresponds well with attitude. But quite often implicit and explicit attitudes do not coincide (Nosek, 2007).

Suppose you have become convinced that eating meat is a bad thing—bad for animals, bad for the planet, maybe bad for your health. You have developed, therefore, a *negative explicit* attitude toward eating meat. But suppose, from your long history of enjoying meat, you have a *positive implicit* attitude toward eating meat. If meat is put before you, your implicit attitude will win out unless you consciously think

---

FOCUS 13

What is the difference between implicit and explicit attitudes in their manner of influencing behavior?

about your explicit attitude and use restraint. Your implicit attitude automatically makes you want to eat the meat. Not surprising, people who successfully maintain a vegetarian diet generally have negative implicit as well as negative explicit attitudes toward eating meat, and positive implicit as well as positive explicit attitudes toward eating vegetables (De Houwer & De Bruycker, 2007).

Experiments using fMRI have shown that people's implicit attitudes are reflected directly in portions of the brain's limbic system that are involved in emotions and drives. In contrast, explicit attitudes are reflected in portions of the prefrontal cortex that are concerned with conscious control. In cases where an explicit attitude counters an implicit attitude, the subcortical areas respond immediately to the relevant stimuli, in accordance with the implicit attitude, but then downward connections from the prefrontal cortex may dampen that response (Stanley et al., 2008). If you have a positive implicit but negative explicit attitude about eating meat, pleasure and appetite centers might respond immediately to meat put before you; but then, if you think about your explicit attitude, those responses might be overcome through connections from your prefrontal cortex.

Attitudes as Rationalizations to Attain Cognitive Consistency

A century ago, Sigmund Freud began developing his controversial theory that human beings are fundamentally irrational. What pass for reasons, according to Freud, are most often rationalizations designed to calm our anxieties and boost our self-esteem. A more moderate view, to be pursued here, is that we are rational but the machinery that makes us so is far from perfect. The same mental machinery that produces logic can produce pseudo-logic.

In the 1950s, Leon Festinger (1957) proposed what he called ***cognitive dissonance theory***, which ever since has been one of social psychology's most central ideas (Cooper, 2012). According to the theory, we have a mechanism built into the workings of our mind that creates an uncomfortable feeling of dissonance, or lack of harmony, when we sense some inconsistency among the various explicit attitudes, beliefs, and items of knowledge that constitute our mental store. Just as the discomfort of hunger motivates us to seek food, the discomfort of cognitive dissonance motivates us to seek ways to resolve contradictions or inconsistencies among our conscious cognitions.

Such a mechanism could well have evolved to serve adaptive functions related to logic. Inconsistencies imply that we are mistaken about something, and mistakes can lead to danger. Suppose you have a favorable attitude about sunbathing, but you learn that overexposure to the sun's ultraviolet rays is the leading cause of skin cancer. The discrepancy between your preexisting attitude and your new knowledge may create a state of cognitive dissonance. To resolve the dissonance in an adaptive way, you might change your attitude about sunbathing from positive to negative, or you might bring in a third cognition: "Sunbathing is relatively safe, in moderation, if I use a sunscreen lotion." But the dissonance-reducing mechanism, like other mechanisms, does not always function adaptively. Just as our hunger drive can lead us to eat things that aren't good for us, our dissonance-reducing drive can lead us to reduce dissonance in illogical and maladaptive ways. Those are the effects that particularly intrigued Festinger and many subsequent social psychologists.

Avoiding Dissonant Information

I (Peter Gray) once heard someone cut off a political discussion with the words, "I'm sorry, but I refuse to listen to something I disagree with." People don't usually come right out and say that, but have you noticed how often they seem to behave that way? Given a choice of books or articles to read, lectures to attend, or documentaries to watch, people generally choose those that they believe will support their

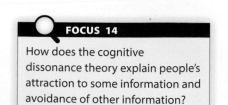

FOCUS 14

How does the cognitive dissonance theory explain people's attraction to some information and avoidance of other information?

existing views. (The proliferation of television and Internet news sources aimed at people with specific political views has made it increasingly easy to do this. People get their information from news sources that share their worldviews, making it less likely that they obtain an unbiased perspective on important issues.) That observation is consistent with the cognitive dissonance theory. People don't always avoid dissonant information, but a considerable body of research indicates that they very often do (Frey, 1986; Jonas et al., 2001).

A good, real-world illustration of the avoidance of dissonant information is found in a research study conducted in 1973, the year of the Senate Watergate hearings, which uncovered illegal activities associated with then-President Richard Nixon's 1972 reelection campaign against George McGovern (Sweeney & Gruber, 1984). The hearings were extensively covered in all of the news media at that time. By interviewing a sample of voters before, during, and after the hearings, Sweeney and Gruber discovered that (a) Nixon supporters avoided news about the hearings (but not other political news) and were as strongly supportive of Nixon after the hearings as they had been before; (b) McGovern supporters eagerly sought out information about the hearings and were as strongly opposed to Nixon afterward as they had been before; and (c) previously undecided voters paid moderate attention to the hearings and were the only group whose attitude toward Nixon was significantly influenced (in a negative direction) by the hearings. So, consistent with the cognitive dissonance theory, all but the undecideds approached the hearings in a way that seemed designed to protect or strengthen, rather than challenge, their existing views.

Firming Up an Attitude to Be Consistent With an Action

We make most of our choices in life with less-than-absolute certainty. We vote for a candidate not knowing for sure if he or she is best, buy one car even though some of the evidence favors another, or choose to major in psychology even though some other fields have their attractions. After we have irrevocably made one choice or another—after we have cast our ballot, made our down payment, or registered for our courses and let the deadline for schedule changes pass—any lingering doubts would be discordant with our knowledge of what we have done. So, according to the cognitive dissonance theory, we should be motivated to set those doubts aside.

Many studies have shown that people do tend to set their doubts aside after making an irrevocable decision. Even in the absence of new information, people suddenly become more confident of their choice after acting on it than they were before. For example, in one study, bettors at a horse race were more confident that their horse would win if they were asked immediately after they had placed their bet than if they were asked immediately before (Knox & Inkster, 1968). In another study, voters who were leaving the polling place spoke more positively about their favored candidate than did those who were entering (Frenkel & Doob, 1976).

Changing an Attitude to Justify an Action: The Insufficient-Justification Effect

Sometimes people behave in ways that run counter to their attitudes and then are faced with the dissonant cognitions, "I believe *this*, but I did *that*." They can't undo their deed, but they can relieve dissonance by modifying—maybe even reversing— their attitudes. This change in attitude is called the *insufficient-justification effect*, because it occurs only if the person has no easy way to justify the behavior, given his or her previous attitude.

One requirement for the insufficient-justification effect to occur is that there be no obvious, high incentive for performing the counter-attitudinal action. In a classic experiment that demonstrates the low-incentive requirement, Festinger and James Carlsmith (1959) gave college students a boring task (loading spools

FOCUS 15

How does the cognitive dissonance theory explain why people are more confident of a decision just after they have made it than just before?

FOCUS 16

In theory, why should the insufficient-justification effect work best when there is minimal incentive for the action and the action is freely chosen? How was this theory verified by two classic experiments?

into trays and turning pegs in a pegboard) and then offered to "hire" them to tell another student that the task was exciting and enjoyable. Some students were offered $1 for their role in recruiting the other student, and others were offered $20 (a princely sum at a time when the minimum wage in the United States was $1 an hour). The result was that those in the $1 condition changed their attitude toward the task and later recalled it as truly enjoyable, whereas those in the $20 condition continued to recall it as boring. Presumably, students in the $1 condition could not justify their lie to the other student on the basis of the little money they were promised, so they convinced themselves that they were not lying. Those in the $20 condition, in contrast, could justify their lie: *I said the task was enjoyable when it was actually boring, but who wouldn't tell such a small lie for $20?*

Another essential condition for the insufficient-justification effect is that subjects must perceive their action as stemming from their own free choice. Otherwise, they could justify the action—and relieve dissonance—simply by saying, "I was forced to do it."

In an experiment demonstrating the free-choice requirement, students were asked to write essays expressing support for a bill in the state legislature that most students personally opposed (Linder et al., 1967). Students in the free-choice condition were told clearly that they didn't have to write the essays, but they were encouraged to do so, and none refused. Students in the no-choice condition were simply told to write the essays, and all complied. After writing the essays, all students were asked to describe their personal attitudes toward the bill. Only those in the free-choice condition showed a significant shift in the direction of favoring the bill; those in the no-choice condition remained as opposed to it as did students who had not been asked to write essays at all. In this case, attitude change in the free-choice condition apparently occurred because the students could justify their choice to write the essays only by deciding that they did, after all, favor the bill.

SECTION REVIEW

The social world around us profoundly affects our understanding of ourselves.

Seeing Ourselves Through Others' Eyes

- Classroom experiments have demonstrated Pygmalion effects, in which adults' expectations about children's behavior created the expected behavior. Such effects occur at least partly by altering the children's self-concepts.

- A variety of evidence supports the sociometer theory, which states that self-esteem reflects the level of acceptance or rejection we believe we can expect from others.

Active Construction of Self-Perceptions

- We perceive ourselves largely through social comparison—comparing ourselves to others. Our judgments and feelings about ourselves depend on the reference group to which we compare ourselves, as illustrated by the big-fish-in-small-pond effect.

- At least in North America and Western Europe, people tend to enhance their views of themselves through such means as making self-serving attributions (attributing success to the self and failure to the situation), remembering successes more than failures, and defining their own criteria for success.

Attitudes and Behavior

- An attitude is a belief or opinion that includes an evaluative component.

- Explicit attitudes are conscious, verbally stated evaluations.

- Implicit attitudes—those formed through direct experience or repeated associations—influence behavior automatically.

Attitudes and Cognitive Dissonance

- We are motivated to reduce cognitive dissonance—a discomforting lack of accord among our explicit beliefs, knowledge, attitudes, and actions.

- The desire to prevent or reduce cognitive dissonance often leads people to avoid dissonant information and to set aside doubts about a decision once it has been made.

- When we freely and with little incentive do something contrary to an attitude, we may alter the attitude to better fit the action; this is called the insufficient-justification effect.

Perceiving Ourselves and Others as Members of Groups

In the previous section you read that the self-concept is social; others are involved in its construction. We see ourselves reflected in others' reactions to us, and we understand ourselves by comparing our attributes with other people's. But the self-concept is also social in terms of the groups to which we belong and with which we identify—*I am a Brazilian-American, Roman Catholic, member of the university marching band*. Self-descriptions that pertain to the person as a separate individual are referred to as **personal identity**, and those that pertain to the social categories or groups to which the person belongs are referred to as **social identity** (Tajfel, 1972). We spend much of our lives interacting in groups, and group behavior is an important area within social psychology. In this section we examine some consequences of viewing ourselves and others in terms of the groups to which we and they belong.

In-Groups and Out-Groups and Their Effects on Perception and Behavior

We can switch between personal and social identities in our perceptions of others as well as ourselves. When we view others in terms of their personal identities, we see them as unique individuals. When we view others in terms of their social identities, we gloss over individual differences and see all members of a group as similar to one another. This is particularly true when we view members of **out-groups**—that is, members of groups to which we do not belong. (Conversely, groups we belong to are called **in-groups**.)

The schema, or organized set of knowledge or beliefs, that we carry in our heads about any group of people is referred to as a ***stereotype***. You may have stereotypes for men, women, Asians, African Americans, Californians, Catholics, and college professors. We gain our stereotypes largely from the ways our culture as a whole depicts and describes each social category. A stereotype may accurately portray typical characteristics of a group, or exaggerate those characteristics, or be a complete fabrication based on culture-wide misconceptions.

We can hold stereotypes about in-groups as well as out-groups, and stereotypes are useful to the degree that they provide us with some initial, valid information about a person. However, they are also sources of prejudice and social injustice. Our stereotypes can lead us to prejudge others on the basis of the group to which they belong, without seeing their qualities as individuals. In the United States, research on stereotyping has focused primarily on European Americans' stereotypes of African Americans, which are part and parcel of a long history of racial bias that began with the institution of slavery.

Distinction Between Explicit and Implicit Stereotypes

FOCUS 17

What is the distinction among public, private, and implicit stereotypes? What are two means by which researchers identify implicit stereotypes?

Just as there are explicit and implicit attitudes—as described in the preceding section of this chapter—there are also explicit and implicit stereotypes. Many people are sensitized to the harmful effects of stereotypes and are therefore reluctant to admit to holding them. Partly for that reason, social psychologists find it useful to distinguish among three levels of stereotypes: public, private, and implicit (Dovidio et al., 1994). The *public* level is what we say to others about a group. The *private* level is what we consciously believe but generally do not say to others. Both public and private stereotypes are referred to as ***explicit stereotypes*** because the person consciously uses them in judging other people. Such stereotypes are measured by questionnaires on which people are asked to state their views about a particular group, such as immigrants, women, or older adults. Responses on such questionnaires are easy to fake, but the hope is that research subjects who fill them out anonymously will be honest in their responses.

A			B			C		
Male		Female	Male or Violent		Female or Nonviolent	Male or Nonviolent		Female or Violent
___	John	___	___	Henry	___	___	Jill	___
___	Hank	___	___	War	___	___	Hug	___
___	Joan	___	___	Fight	___	___	Punch	___
___	David	___	___	Joan	___	___	Bill	___
___	Mary	___	___	Help	___	___	Hank	___
___	Jill	___	___	Mary	___	___	Fight	___
___	Susan	___	___	David	___	___	Susan	___
___	Bill	___	___	Hank	___	___	Help	___
___	Henry	___	___	Love	___	___	Joan	___
___	Amy	___	___	Jill	___	___	Kill	___
___	David	___	___	Punch	___	___	John	___
___	Hank	___	___	John	___	___	David	___
___	Joan	___	___	Susan	___	___	Hit	___
___	Jill	___	___	Care	___	___	Care	___
___	John	___	___	Hit	___	___	War	___
___	Mary	___	___	Bill	___	___	Henry	___
___	Amy	___	___	Amy	___	___	Amy	___
___	Bill	___	___	Peace	___	___	Love	___
___	Susan	___	___	Kill	___	___	Mary	___

Research from Gladwell, 2005.

FIGURE 13.5 An implicit association test How long does it take you to classify the items in each of these columns? Time yourself, in seconds, separately on each column. For column A, place a check to the left of each male name and to the right of each female name. For column B, place a check to the left of each male name or term that has to do with violence, and place a check to the right of each female name or term that has to do with nonviolence. For column C, place a check to the left of each male name or term that has to do with nonviolence, and place a check to the right of each female name or term that has to do with violence.

Implicit stereotypes, in contrast, are sets of mental associations that operate more or less automatically to guide our judgments and actions toward members of the group in question, even if those associations run counter to our conscious beliefs. Most psychological research on stereotyping today has to do with implicit stereotypes. These stereotypes are measured with tests in which the person's attention is focused not on the stereotyped group per se, but on performing quickly and accurately an objective task that makes use of stimuli associated with the stereotype. One type of test commonly used in this way is the *implicit association test*.

As described earlier with regard to implicit attitudes, implicit association tests are based on the fact that people can classify two concepts together more quickly if they are already strongly associated in their minds than if they are not strongly associated. To get an idea of how such a test works, complete the paper-and-pencil version that is presented in **Figure 13.5**, following the instructions in the caption. You will need a watch or clock that can count seconds to time yourself.

How did you perform? If you are like everyone we know who has taken this test, it took you longer to go through List C, where nonviolent terms are classified with male names and violent terms with female names, than it took you to go through List B, where violent terms go with male names and nonviolent terms with female names. Nearly everyone shares the stereotype that males are relatively violent and females are relatively nonviolent.

Implicit association tests used in research are usually presented on a computer. Each individual stimulus appears on the screen, one at a time, and the person must respond by pressing one of two keys on the keyboard, depending on the category of the stimulus. If you wish to take such a test, you might find examples on the Internet at *https://implicit.harvard.edu/implicit,* where you can take part in an ongoing experiment involving implicit associations. (This site has been active for several years and may or may not still be active at the time that you are reading this.)

In implicit association tests having to do with race, a typical procedure is to use photographs of white and black faces, along with "good" words (such as love, happy, truth, terrific) and "bad" words (such as poison, hatred, agony, terrible) as the stimuli. In one condition, the job is to categorize white faces and "good" words together by pressing one key on the keyboard whenever one of them appears, and to classify black faces and "bad" words together by pressing another key whenever one of those appears. In the other condition, the job is to classify white faces and "bad" words together and black faces and "good" words together. The typical result is that white college students take about 200 milliseconds longer per key press, on average, in the latter condition than in the former (Aberson et al., 2004; Cunningham et al., 2001). White American children as young as 6 years of age perform similarly to adults (Baron & Banaji, 2006; Qian et al., 2016), and a same-race bias has also been found in Japanese children (Dunham et al., 2006), suggesting such a bias is universal and emerges early in development (see Dunham et al., 2008, for a review).

Implicit Stereotypes Can Be Deadly

In 2015 in West Palm Beach, 20-year-old Contrell Stephens was riding his bike when he was stopped by a police officer who believed he was behaving "suspiciously." Contrell reached into his back waistband to retrieve his cell phone, which the police offer thought was a gun. The officer shot him four times, paralyzing Stephens for life. In 2016 in Las Vegas, 23-year-old Keith Childress, who was wanted in another state for failing to attend a sentencing hearing, was shot dead by police when he reached for his cell phone that the police mistook for a gun. In 2016 in San Antonio 36-year-old Antronie Scott, who was wanted on two felony warrants for gun and drug possession, was shot and killed by police as he exited his car holding a cell phone that the police officer believed was a gun. And in 1999 in New York City, 23-year-old Amadou Diallo, was who standing on the stoop of his apartment building when police approached him, was shot and killed by four undercover police officers when he reached into his pocket and withdrew his wallet, which the police officers mistook for a gun. What these four men had in common, besides possessing an object that was mistaken for a gun, was that they were black and the police officers were white or, in the Stephens case, Asian.

Would these men have been shot if they had been white? In the cases of Stephens and Diallo, would the officers have seen them as suspicious and approached them in the first place if they had been white? And if they had approached them, would they have mistaken Stephens's cell phone and Diallo's wallet for a gun? We can never know the answers for these individual cases, but there are grounds for believing that skin color can play a large role in such situations. Many research studies have shown that white people implicitly view unfamiliar black people as more hostile, violent, and suspicious looking than unfamiliar white people, and several experiments, inspired by the Diallo case, reveal that white people implicitly associate black faces more strongly with guns and violence than they do white faces (Payne, 2006; Plant & Peruche, 2005). For example, in one study, white subjects categorized threatening and nonthreatening objects after being shown brief pictures of white and black faces. Subjects made faster decisions and fewer errors categorizing threatening objects when they were preceded by black faces than by white faces, even if those faces were of 5-year-old children (Todd et al., 2016).

Most such experiments have used college students as subjects, but one was conducted with actual police officers (Plant & Peruche, 2005). In this experiment,

FOCUS 18

What evidence suggests that implicit prejudice can cause police officers to shoot at black suspects more readily than at white suspects?

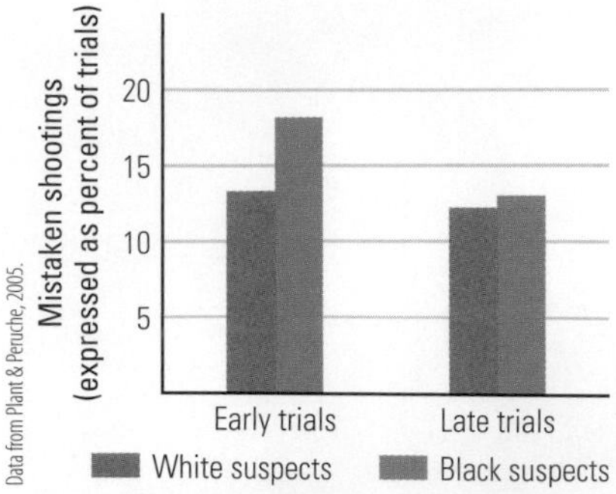

Data from Plant & Peruche, 2005.

FIGURE 13.6 Race of suspect affects decision to shoot in computer simulations During the first 80 trials of a computer simulation game, police officers who had to make split-second decisions "shot" more often at unarmed black suspects than at unarmed white suspects. With practice, however, this bias disappeared.

FOCUS 19

What sorts of learning experiences are most effective in reducing (a) explicit and (b) implicit prejudice?

---

which involved computer simulations of self-defense situations, the instructions to each officer included the following words:

> Today your task is to determine whether or not to shoot your gun. Pictures of people with objects will appear at various positions on the screen. . . . Some of the pictures will have the face of a person and a gun. These people are the criminals, and you are supposed to shoot at these people. Some of the pictures will have a face of a person and some other object (e.g., a wallet). These people are not criminals and you should not shoot at them. Press the "A" key for "shoot" and press the "L" key on the keyboard for "don't shoot." (p. 181)

During the experiment, each picture appeared on the screen until the officer responded or until a 630-millisecond time limit had elapsed. As shown in **Figure 13.6**, during the first 80 trials the officers mistakenly shot unarmed black suspects significantly more often than they shot unarmed white suspects. With practice, during which they received immediate feedback as to whether they had shot an armed or unarmed person, they gradually overcame this bias. They did not show the bias during the final 80 trials of the 160-trial game. The researchers hope that such training will reduce officers' bias in real-life encounters with criminal suspects.

Defeating Explicit and Implicit Negative Stereotypes

People often hold implicit stereotypes at odds with their explicit beliefs about the stereotyped group. Whereas explicit stereotypes are products of conscious thought processes, modifiable by deliberate learning and logic, implicit stereotypes appear to be products of more primitive emotional processes, modifiable by such means as classical conditioning (Livingston & Drwecki, 2007). White people who have close black friends exhibit less implicit prejudice than do those without black friends (Aberson et al., 2004), and there is evidence that exposure to admirable black characters in literature, movies, and television programs can reduce implicit prejudice in white people (Rudman, 2004). Apparently, the association of positive feelings with individual members of the stereotyped group helps reduce automatic negative responses toward the group as a whole.

In one long-term study, Laurie Rudman and her colleagues (2001) found that white students who volunteered for a diversity-training course showed significant reductions in both explicit and implicit prejudice toward black people by the end of the course. However, the two reductions correlated only weakly with each other: Those students who showed the greatest decline in explicit prejudice did not necessarily show much decline in implicit prejudice, and vice versa. Further analysis revealed that those students who felt most enlightened by the verbal information presented in the course, and who reported the greatest conscious desire to overcome their prejudice, showed the greatest declines in explicit prejudice. In contrast, those who made new black friends during the course, or who most liked the African American professor who taught it, showed the greatest declines in implicit prejudice.

SECTION REVIEW

The groups we belong to can be a major determinant of how we perceive ourselves and others.

In-Groups and Out-Groups

- We tend to have more positive associations with in-groups (groups we belong to) than with out-groups (groups we don't belong to).

Explicit and Implicit Stereotypes

- Stereotypes—the schemas that we have about groups of people—can be explicit (available to consciousness) or implicit (unconscious but able to affect our thoughts, feelings, and actions). Implicit stereotypes are measured through implicit association tests.

- Studies reveal that negative implicit stereotypes can promote prejudiced behavior even without conscious prejudice.

- Implicit prejudices are based on primitive emotional processes, modifiable by classical conditioning. Positive associations with members of the stereotyped group can help to reduce implicit prejudice.

Effects of Being Observed and Evaluated

A central theme of social psychology is that human behavior is influenced powerfully by the social environment in which it occurs. We behave as we do—sometimes heroically, sometimes villainously, more often somewhere in between—not just because of who we are, but also because of the social situations in which we find ourselves. Social norms and the examples, expectations, requests, and demands of those around us influence our behavior essentially every waking moment of every day. None of us is such an individualist as to be uninfluenced by others.

A general concept that runs through the remainder of this chapter is that of **social pressure**, a set of psychological forces that are exerted on us by others' judgments, examples, expectations, and demands, whether real or imagined. At any given moment, we are most strongly influenced by those people who are physically or psychologically closest to us.

Social pressure arises from the ways we interpret and respond emotionally to the social situations around us. Such pressure is useful because it promotes our social acceptability and helps create order and predictability in social interactions. But it can also lead us to behave in ways that are objectively foolish or even morally repugnant.

We begin by considering a minimal form of social pressure—the mere presence of other people who can observe us perform. We do not behave in exactly the same way when others can see us as we do when we are alone. As social beings, we are concerned about the impressions we make on other people, and that concern influences our behavior.

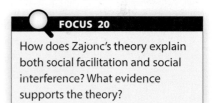

FOCUS 20

How does Zajonc's theory explain both social facilitation and social interference? What evidence supports the theory?

Facilitating and Interfering Effects of an Audience

Having an audience affects how well people perform tasks. In some cases, being observed improves performance (termed **social facilitation**), whereas in other cases, an audience hinders performance (termed **social interference** or *social inhibition*).

Why does an audience sometimes improve a person's performance and other times worsen it? In reviewing the experiments, Robert Zajonc (rhymes with "science") (1965) noticed that social facilitation usually occurred with relatively simple or well-learned tasks and that social interference usually occurred with complex tasks or tasks that involved new learning. From this observation, Zajonc proposed the following generalization: *The presence of others facilitates performance of dominant actions and interferes with performance of nondominant actions.* In this statement, the term *dominant actions* refers to actions that are so simple, species-typical, or well learned that they can be produced automatically, with little conscious thought; and *nondominant actions* refers to actions that require considerable conscious thought or attention.

To explain both effects, Zajonc further proposed that the presence of an audience increases a person's level of drive or arousal. The heightened drive increases the person's effort, which facilitates dominant tasks where the amount of effort determines degree of success. However, the heightened drive also interferes with controlled, calm, conscious thought and attention; it thereby worsens performance of nondominant actions (see **Figure 13.7**).

Much subsequent research has supported Zajonc's theory. The presence of observers does increase drive and arousal, as measured by self-reports and by physiological indices such as increased heart rate and muscle tension (Cacioppo et al., 1990; Zajonc, 1980). Other studies have shown, just as Zajonc predicted, that either facilitation or interference can occur in the very same task, depending on the performers' skill. In one experiment, expert pool players performed better when they were watched conspicuously by a group of four observers than when they thought

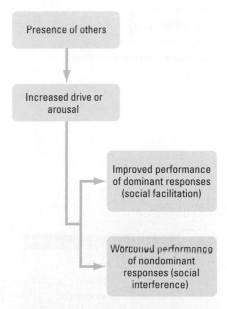

FIGURE 13.7 Zajonc's theory of social facilitation and interference This theory relates social facilitation and interference to a more general effect of high arousal or drive on dominant (habitual, cognitively easy) and nondominant (nonhabitual, cognitively difficult) responses.

■ **Social facilitation** When the performer is an expert, like Serena Williams, the presence of an audience improves performance. Such an audience would worsen performance for a novice.

Henk Koster / Alamy Stock Photo

they were not being observed, and the opposite occurred for novice pool players (Michaels et al., 1982). Facilitation and interference are not limited to experts. In one study, college students were asked to explain something they had just learned (e.g., classical conditioning, evolution, or research methods) to another student. Interference increased when subjects were given negative feedback just before the test to make them feel unconfident and more anxious about their ability; in contrast, interference decreased or was abolished when subjects were given positive feedback designed to make them feel very confident about their ability (Klehe et al., 2007).

Choking Under Pressure: The Working-Memory Explanation

Social interference can be thought of as a subcategory of a more general phenomenon commonly referred to as *choking under pressure*. The highly aroused mental state produced by any strong form of pressure to perform well can, ironically, cause performance to worsen.

Using the terminology of modern cognitive psychology, "choking" is especially likely to occur with tasks that make strong demands on working memory. Working memory, as described in Chapter 9, is the part of the mind that controls conscious attention and holds, in consciousness, those items of information that are needed to solve a problem. The kinds of tasks that Zajonc referred to as involving nondominant responses are, in general, tasks that make heavy demands on working memory. Pressure and accompanying anxiety can worsen performance on such tasks by creating distracting thoughts—thoughts about being evaluated, about the difficulty of the task, about the consequences of failing, and so on—which usurp much of the limited capacity of working memory and thereby interfere with concentration on the problem to be solved.

The role of working memory on choking can be seen in research on test taking. With sufficient pressure, choking can occur even in students who normally do not suffer from test anxiety, and researchers have found that it occurs specifically with test items that make the highest demands on working memory.

In one series of experiments, for example, students were given math problems that varied in difficulty and in the degree to which students had an opportunity to practice them in advance (Beilock et al., 2004). Pressure to perform well was manipulated by telling some students that they were part of a team and that if they failed to perform above a certain criterion neither they nor their teammates—who had already performed above the criterion—would win a certain prize. They were also told they would be videotaped as they worked on the problems, so that math teachers and professors could examine the problem-solving process. Students in the low-pressure group, in contrast, were simply asked to solve the problems as best they could. The result was that the high-pressure group performed significantly worse than the low-pressure group on the unpracticed difficult problems, but not on the easy or thoroughly practiced problems, which were less taxing on working memory.

FOCUS 21

What evidence supports the view that choking on tests occurs because distracting thoughts interfere with working memory?

FOCUS 22

How can the activation of a stereotype influence test performance? What evidence suggests that this effect, like other forms of choking, involves increased anxiety and interference with working memory?

Stereotype Threat as a Special Cause of Choking

Stereotype threat, a particularly potent cause of choking on academic tests, was first described by Claude Steele (1997). It is the threat that test-takers experience when they are reminded of the stereotypical belief that the group to which they belong is not expected to do well on the test. In a series of experiments, Steele found that African American college students, but not white college students, performed worse on various tests if the tests were referred to as "intelligence tests" than if the same tests were referred to by other labels. He found, further, that this drop in performance became even greater if the students were deliberately reminded of their race just before taking the test. The threat in this case came from the common stereotype that African Americans have lower intelligence than white Americans. Essentially all African American college students are painfully aware of this stereotype.

Subsequently, stereotype threat has been demonstrated with other stigmatized groups as well (Mazerolle et al., 2012; Schmader et al., 2008). For example, older adults perform worse on working-memory tests when they know they are being contrasted with a group of young adults than when they are told that the tasks are "age fair" and do not vary with age (Mazerolle et al., 2012; see **Figure 13.8**). In other situations, women consistently perform worse on problem-solving tests that are described as "math tests" than on the same tests when given other names, and this effect is magnified if attention is drawn to the stereotype that women have lower math aptitude than do men (Johns et al., 2005; Wheeler & Petty, 2001). This effect has been observed for elementary and middle-school children (Muzzatti & Agnoli, 2007), and even in girls as young as 5 years (Ambady et al., 2001). White males have also been shown to exhibit stereotype threat in math, when the stereotype that whites have less math ability than do Asians is made salient to them (Aronson et al., 1999). And Christians, who in the United States are a majority, perform more poorly on science-related tests when reminded of the stereotype that Christians are less competent in science than non-Christians (Rios et al., 2015). The effect of stereotype threat is an example of what was described earlier in the chapter as a *self-fulfilling prophecy:* The expectation that you will perform badly in fact causes you to perform badly.

As in the case of other examples of choking, stereotype threat seems to produce its effects by increasing anxiety and mental distraction. People report higher levels of felt anxiety and manifest greater physiological evidence of anxiety (e.g., heart-rate increase) when taking a test in the stereotype-threat condition than when taking the same test in the nonthreat condition (Johns et al., 2008; Osborne, 2007). The threat seems to undermine confidence, while at the same time increasing motivation to do well (so as not to confirm the stereotype), resulting in increased anxiety. The increased anxiety apparently reduces performance at least in part by occupying working memory with worrisome thoughts, thereby reducing the amount of working memory capacity available to solve the problems. Researchers have found that stereotype threat reduces performance on problems that tax working memory more than on problems that can be answered largely through recall from long-term memory (Beilock et al., 2007).

It is, however, possible to overcome stereotype threat—often by simply being aware of the stereotype-threat phenomenon (Johns et al., 2005). Apparently, such awareness leads test-takers to attribute their incipient anxiety to stereotype threat rather than to the difficulty of the problems or to some inadequacy in themselves, and this helps them to concentrate on the problems rather than on their own fears. Other research has shown that self-affirming thoughts before the test—such as thoughts created by listing your own strengths and values—can reduce or abolish stereotype threat, apparently by boosting confidence and/or by reducing the importance attributed to the test (Martens et al., 2006).

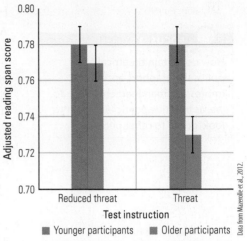

FIGURE 13.8 Older (average age = 69) and younger (average age = 21) adults were given working-memory tests and told that these tests were "fully validated and diagnostic of memory capacity" In the Threat condition, subjects were told that both younger and older adults would be performing these tasks, which is usually enough to remind older adults that memory is typically worse in older than younger adults. In the Reduced Threat condition, subjects were also told that these were "age-fair" tests in which performance does not vary with age. As you can see, the younger and older adults varied minimally in the Reduced Threat condition. In contrast, the older adults performed significantly worse in the Threat condition.

Impression Management: Behavior as Performance

Besides influencing our abilities to perform specific tasks, social pressures influence our choices of what to say and do in front of other people. Because we care what others think of us, we strive to influence their thoughts. To that end, we behave differently when witnesses are present than when we are alone, and differently in front of some witnesses than in front of others. The term ***impression management*** refers to the entire set of ways by which people consciously and unconsciously modify their behavior to influence others' impressions of them (Schlenker, 1980).

FOCUS 23

How do certain theatrical and political metaphors apply to impression management? Why do we, as intuitive politicians, want to look "good" to other people?

Humans as Actors and as Politicians

As Shakespeare put it, "All the world's a stage, and all the men and women merely players." Sociologist Erving Goffman developed an approach to thinking about human behavior based on this metaphor. In a classic book titled *The Presentation of Self in Everyday Life*, Goffman (1959) portrayed us as actors, playing at different times on different stages to different audiences. In Goffman's view, we are not necessarily aware that we are performing. Barry Schlenker and Beth Pontari (2000) expanded on this idea by suggesting that there need not be a division in our minds between the images we try to project and our sincere beliefs about ourselves. At any given moment we may simply be trying to exhibit our best self, or those aspects of our self that seem most appropriate and useful to meet the moment's needs, which change with our audience.

An alternative metaphor is that we are *intuitive politicians* (Tetlock, 2002). We perform in front of others not just to tell a good story or portray a character at a given moment, but also to achieve real-life ends over the long term that may be selfish or noble, or to some degree both. To do what we want to do in life, we need the approval and cooperation of other people—their votes, as it were—and to secure those votes, we "campaign" for ourselves and our interests quite naturally, often without conscious awareness of our political ingenuity and strategies.

Depending on our needs, our capacities, and our audience, we may at any given time portray ourselves as pitiful, enraged, stern, or even irrational and unpredictable. These can be effective strategies for certain ends. For some people these strategies may even become regular ploys. But most of us, most of the time, try to make ourselves look *good* to other people. We want to come across as attractive, friendly, competent, rational, trustworthy, and moral because we know that others will be inclined to collaborate with us if they see those qualities in us. We also want to look modest, so people will think we are understating, not overstating, our virtues. We want to look sincere, not as if we are putting on a show or trying to ingratiate ourselves. And in general, we are more concerned with impression management with new acquaintances than with familiar friends and companions (Leary & Kowalski, 1995; Tice et al., 1995). We may or may not be conscious of our delicate balancing act between showing off and appearing modest, or between sincerity and ingratiation, but the act requires effort.

SECTION REVIEW

Social pressure affects our performance and leads us to try to control how others see us.

Effects of Having an Audience

- The presence of others can cause either social facilitation (improved performance) or social interference (worsened performance).

- The presence of others leads to heightened drive and arousal, which—in line with Zajonc's theory—improves performance on dominant tasks and worsens performance on nondominant tasks.

- Evaluation anxiety is at least part of the cause of social interference.

Choking Under Pressure

- Choking occurs because pressure produces distracting thoughts that compete with the task itself for limited-capacity working memory.

- Stereotype threat is a powerful form of choking that occurs when members of a stigmatized group are reminded of stereotypes about their group before performing a relevant task.

Impression Management

- Because of social pressure, we consciously or unconsciously modify our behavior in order to influence others' perceptions of us.

- This tendency to manage impressions has led social scientists to characterize us as actors, playing roles, or as politicians, promoting ourselves and our agendas.

Effects of Others' Examples, Opinions, and Requests

Other people influence our behavior not just through their roles as observers and evaluators but also through the examples they set. There are two general reasons why we tend to conform to others' examples.

One reason has to do with information and pragmatics. If other people cross bridge A and avoid bridge B, they may know something about the bridges that we don't know. To be safe, we had better stick with bridge A, too. If other people say rhubarb leaves are poisonous, then to be safe, in the absence of better information, we shouldn't eat them, and we should probably tell our children they are poisonous. One of the great advantages of social life lies in the sharing of information. We don't all have to learn everything from scratch; rather, we can follow the examples of others and profit from trials and errors that may have occurred generations ago. Social influence that works through providing clues about the objective nature of an event or situation is called *informational influence*.

FOCUS 24

What are two classes of reasons why people tend to conform to examples set by others?

The other general reason for conforming is to promote group cohesion and acceptance by the group. Social groups can exist only if some degree of behavioral coordination exists among the group members. Conformity allows a group to act as a coordinated unit rather than as a set of separate individuals. We tend to adopt the ideas, myths, and habits of our group because doing so generates a sense of closeness with others, promotes our acceptance by them, and enables the group to function as a unit. We all cross bridge A because we are the bridge A people, and proud of it! If you cross bridge B, you may look like you don't want to be one of us or you may look strange to us. This kind of social influence, which works through the person's desire to be part of a group or to be approved by others, is called *normative influence*.

Conformity to group norms is found early in development. In fact, 2- and 3-year-old children, when shown a demonstration of a puppet performing a novel set of actions, will correct a person who fails to use the same words and actions in performing the task, with some 3-year-olds saying things like, "It doesn't work like that. You have to do it like this" (Kenward, 2012; Keupp et al., 2013). Thus, young children will recognize what is normative and attempt to enforce social norms on others (Schmidt & Tomasello, 2012). Conformity to peer pressure becomes especially important for children during the school years, peaking in early adolescence (Berndt, 1979; Gavin & Furman, 1989).

Asch's Classic Conformity Experiments

Under some conditions, conformity can lead people to say or do things that are objectively ridiculous, as demonstrated in a famous series of experiments conducted

FOCUS 25

How did Asch demonstrate that a tendency to conform can lead people to disclaim the evidence of their own eyes?

■ **A perplexed subject** It is not hard to tell who the real subject is in this photograph taken during a critical trial in one of Asch's experiments

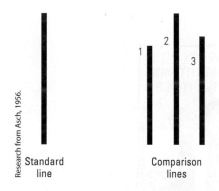

Research from Asch, 1956.

Standard line   Comparison lines

FIGURE 13.9 Sample stimuli used by Asch to study conformity The task on each trial was to select the comparison line that was identical in length to the standard. On critical trials, the confederates unanimously made a specific wrong choice (either 1 or 3, in this example).

by Solomon Asch in the 1950s. Asch's original purpose was to demonstrate the limits of conformity (Asch, 1952). Previous research had shown that people conform to others' judgments when the objective evidence is ambiguous (Sherif, 1936), and Asch expected to demonstrate that they would not conform when the evidence is clear-cut. But his results surprised him and changed the direction of his research.

Asch's (1956) procedure was as follows: A college-student volunteer was brought into the lab and seated with six to eight other students, and the group was told that their task was to judge the lengths of lines. On each trial they were shown one standard line and three comparison lines and were asked to judge which comparison line was identical in length to the standard (see **Figure 13.9**). As a perceptual task, this was absurdly easy. In previous tests, subjects performing the task alone almost never made mistakes. But, of course, this was not really a perceptual task; it was a test of conformity. Unbeknownst to the real subject, the others in the group were confederates of the experimenter and had been instructed to give a specific wrong answer on certain prearranged "critical" trials. Choices were stated out loud by the group members, one at a time in the order of seating, and seating had been arranged so that the real subject was always the next to last to respond. The question of interest was this: On the critical trials, would subjects be swayed by the confederates' wrong answers?

Of more than 100 subjects tested, 75% were swayed by the confederates on at least one of the 12 critical trials. A few of the subjects conformed on every trial, others on only one or two, with most (95%) responding independently at least once. On average, subjects conformed on 37% of the critical trials. That is, on more than one-third of the trials on which the confederates gave a wrong answer, the subject also gave a wrong answer, usually the same wrong answer as the confederates had given. Asch's experiment has been replicated dozens of times, in at least 17 different countries (Bond & Smith, 1996). The results reveal some decline in conformity in North America after the 1950s and some variation across cultures, but they still demonstrate a considerable amount of conformity whenever and wherever the experiment is conducted.

More recent research has shown that conformity to social pressure occurs not only for simple perceptual judgments, but also for moral ones. For example, Payel Kundu and Denise Dellarosa Cummins (2013) presented subjects with hypothetical moral dilemmas, some of which most people think are permissible (e.g., pushing a switch so a runaway trolley is diverted down a track killing one person rather than killing five people if the switch is not pushed) and others which most people think are impermissible (e.g., killing one's oldest son to appease a leader of a clan on whose land you have trespassed). Subjects who rated the dilemmas in the presence of confederates who rated the impermissible dilemmas (sacrificing an oldest son) as permissible were more likely to also rate those actions as permissible than control subjects who were alone when they rated the dilemmas (see also Lisciandra et al., 2013).

Norms as Forces for Helpful and Harmful Actions

In Asch's experiments, the social context was provided by the artificial situation of a group of people misjudging the length of a line. In everyday life, the social context consists not just of what we hear others say or see them do, but also of the various telltale signs that inform us implicitly about which behaviors are normal in the setting in which we find ourselves, and which behaviors are not. The norms established by such signs can have serious consequences for all of us.

Effects of Implicit Norms in Public-Service Messages

Many public-service messages include statements about the large number of people who engage in some undesirable behavior, such as smoking, drunk driving, or littering. According to Robert Cialdini, an expert on persuasion, such messages may undermine themselves. At the same time that they are urging people not to behave in a certain way, they are sending the implicit message that behaving in that way is normal—many people do behave in that way.

Proposing that such messages would be more effective if they emphasized that the majority of people behave in the desired way, Cialdini (2003) developed a public-service message designed to increase household recycling and aired it on local radio and TV stations in four Arizona communities. The message depicted a group of people all recycling and speaking disapprovingly of a lone person who did not recycle. The result was a 25% increase in recycling in those communities—a far bigger effect than is usually achieved by public-service messages.

In another study, Cialdini and his colleagues (described in Cialdini, 2003) created two signs aimed at decreasing the pilfering of petrified wood from Petrified Forest National Park. One sign read, "Many past visitors have removed petrified wood from the Park, changing the natural state of the Petrified Forest," and depicted three visitors taking petrified wood. The other sign depicted a single visitor taking a piece of wood, with a red circle-and-bar symbol superimposed over his hand, along with the message, "Please do not remove the petrified wood from the Park, in order to preserve the natural state of the Petrified Forest." On alternate weekends, one or the other of these signs was placed near the beginning of each path in the park. To measure theft, marked pieces of petrified wood were placed along each path. The results of this experiment are illustrated in **Figure 13.10**. The dramatic result was that 7.92% of visitors tried to steal marked pieces on the days when the first sign was present, compared with only 1.67% on the days when the second sign was present. Previous research had shown that, with neither of these signs present but only the usual park injunctions against stealing, approximately 3% of visitors stole petrified wood from the park. Apparently, by emphasizing that many people steal, the first sign increased the amount of stealing sharply above the baseline rate; and the second sign, by implying that stealing is rare as well as wrong, decreased it to well below the baseline rate.

Conformity as a Basis for Failure to Help: The Passive Bystander Effect

A man lies ill on the sidewalk in full view of hundreds of passersby, all of whom fail to stop and ask if he needs help. A woman is brutally beaten in front of witnesses who fail to come to her aid or even to call the police. How can such incidents occur?

In many experiments, social psychologists have found that a person is much more likely to help in an emergency if he or she is the only witness than if other witnesses are also present. In one experiment, for example, college students filling out a questionnaire were interrupted by the sound of the researcher, behind a screen, falling and crying out, "Oh . . . my foot . . . I . . . can't move it; oh . . . my ankle . . . I can't get this thing off me" (Latané & Rodin, 1969). In some cases the student was alone, and in other cases two students sat together filling out questionnaires. The remarkable result was that 70% of those who were alone went to the aid of the researcher, but only 20% of those who were in pairs did so. Apparently an accident victim is better off with just one potential helper present than with two! Why?

FOCUS 26

According to Cialdini, how can public-service messages best capitalize on normative influences? What evidence does he provide for this idea?

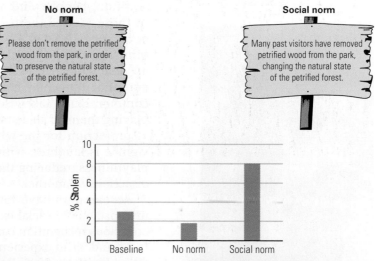

FIGURE 13.10 Signs used in a field experiment in Petrified Forest National Park When Robert Cialdini (2003) used the right-hand sign in a field experiment, visitors actually took more pieces of petrified wood than when there was no sign.

■ **Passing by** The presence of other witnesses decreases each witness's likelihood of helping.

FOCUS 27

How can the failure of multiple bystanders to help a person in need be explained in terms of informational and normative influences?

FOCUS 28

What is the value, for group life, of the spread of sadness, anger, fear, and laughter from person to person? How might emotional contagion figure into the rise of a group leader?

■ **A poker face is hard to keep** We tend automatically to signal our emotions when in the company of others. Only through conscious effort can we refrain from giving away our hand.

Part of the answer probably has to do with diffusion of responsibility. The more people present, the less any one person feels it is his or her responsibility to help (Schwartz & Gottlieb, 1980). But conformity also seems to contribute.

If you are the only witness to an incident, you decide whether it is an emergency or not, and whether you can help or not, on the basis of your assessment of the victim's situation. But if other witnesses are present, you look also at them. You wait briefly to see what they are going to do, and chances are you find that they do nothing (because they are waiting to see what you are going to do). Their inaction is a source of information that may lead you to question your initial judgment: Maybe this is not an emergency, or if it is, maybe nothing can be done. Their inaction also establishes an implicit social norm. If you spring into action, you might look foolish to the others, who seem so complacent. Thus, each person's inaction can promote inaction in others through both informational and normative influences.

Emotional Contagion as a Force for Group Cohesion

A social group is not just a collection of individuals. It is a *unified* collection. People in a social group tend to behave more like one another than the same individuals would if they were not in a group. They tend automatically to mimic one another's postures, mannerisms, and styles of speech, and this imitation contributes to their sense of rapport (Lakin & Chartrand, 2003; van Baaren et al., 2004). They also tend to take on the same emotions.

As noted in Chapter 3, people everywhere express emotions in relatively similar ways. Such facial expressions help members of a group know how to interact with one another. By seeing others' emotional expressions, group members know who needs help, who should be avoided, and who is most approachable for help. In addition, people tend automatically to adopt the emotions that they perceive in those around them, and this helps the group to function as a unit (Hatfield et al., 1994; Wild et al., 2001). Sadness in one person tends to induce sadness in others nearby, and that is part of the mechanism of empathy by which others become motivated to help the one in distress. Anger expressed in the presence of potential allies may lead to shared anger that promotes their recruitment into a common cause. Likewise, fear in one person tends to induce fear in others nearby, placing them all in a state of heightened vigilance and thereby adding a measure of protection for the whole group. One of the most contagious of all emotional signals is laughter, which apparently helps put a group into a shared mood of playfulness, reducing the chance that one person will be offended by the remarks or actions of another.

Researchers have found that the spread of emotions can occur completely unconsciously. Facial expressions of emotions flashed on a screen too quickly for conscious recognition can cause subjects to express the same emotion on their own faces and/or to experience brief changes in feeling compatible with that emotion (Dimberg et al., 2000; Ruys & Stapel, 2008).

Political leaders often achieve their status at least partly through their ability to manipulate others' emotions, and their own emotional expressions are part of that process. Former U.S. presidents Ronald Reagan and Bill Clinton were both known as "great communicators," and much of their communication occurred through their persuasive facial expressions. In a research study conducted shortly after Reagan was elected president, university students watched film clips of Reagan expressing happiness, anger, or fear as he spoke to the American public about events that faced the nation (McHugo et al., 1985). In some cases the sound track was kept on, in others it was turned off, and in all cases the students' own emotional reactions were recorded by measuring their heart rates, their perspiration, and the movements of particular facial muscles. Regardless of whether they claimed to be his supporters or opponents, and regardless of whether they could or could not hear what he was saying, the students' bodily changes indicated that they were responding to Reagan's performance with emotions similar to those he was displaying.

Social Pressure in Group Discussions

When people get together to discuss an idea or make a decision, their explicit goal usually is to share information. But whether they want to or not, group members also influence one another through normative social pressure. Such pressure can occur whenever one person expresses an opinion or takes a position on an issue in front of another: Are you with me or against me? It feels good to be with, uncomfortable to be against. There is unstated pressure to agree.

Group Discussion Can Make Attitudes More Extreme

When a group is evenly split on an issue, the result is often a compromise (Burnstein & Vinokur, 1977). Each side partially convinces the other, so the majority leaves the room with a more moderate view on the issue than they had when they entered. However, if the group is not evenly split—if all or a large majority of the members argue on the same side of the issue—discussion typically pushes that majority toward a more extreme view in the same direction as their initial view. This phenomenon is called *group polarization*.

FOCUS 29

What are some experiments that have demonstrated group polarization?

Group polarization has been demonstrated in many experiments, with a wide variety of problems or issues for discussion. In one experiment, mock juries evaluated traffic-violation cases that had been constructed to produce either high or low initial judgments of guilt. After group discussion, the jurors rated the high-guilt cases as indicating even higher levels of guilt, and the low-guilt cases as indicating even lower levels of guilt, than they had before the discussion (Myers & Kaplan, 1976). In other experiments, researchers divided people into groups on the basis of their initial views on a controversial issue and found that discussions held separately by each group widened the gaps between the groups (see **Figure 13.11**). In one experiment, for example, discussion caused groups favoring a strengthening of the military to favor it even more strongly and groups favoring a paring down of the military to favor that more strongly (Minix, 1976; Semmel, 1976).

Group polarization can have socially serious consequences. When students whose political views are just slightly to the right of center get together to form a Young Conservatives club, their views are likely to shift further toward the right. Similarly, a Young Liberals club is likely to shift to the left. Prisoners who enter prison with little respect for the law and spend their time talking with other prisoners who share that view are likely to leave prison with even less respect for the law than they had before. Systematic studies of naturally occurring social groups suggest that such shifts are indeed quite common (Sunstein, 2003).

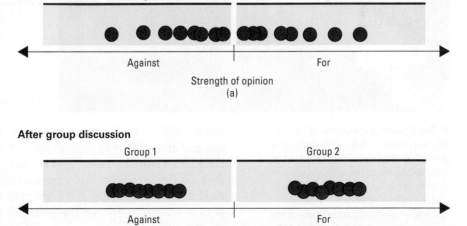

FIGURE 13.11 Schematic illustration of group polarization Each circle represents the opinion of one individual. When the individuals are divided into two groups on the basis of the direction of their initial position (a) and then discuss the issue with other members of their group, most shift toward a more extreme position than they held before (b).

Conditions That Lead to Good or Bad Group Decisions

Decisions made by groups are sometimes better and sometimes worse than decisions made by individuals working alone. To the degree that the group decision arises from the sharing of the best available evidence and logic, it is likely to be better (Surowiecki, 2004b). To the degree that it arises from shared misinformation, selective withholding of arguments on the less-favored side, and participants' attempts to please or impress one another rather than to arrive at the best decision, the group decision is likely to be worse than the decision most group members would have made alone.

In a now-classic book titled *Groupthink,* Irving Janis (1982) analyzed some of the most misguided policy decisions made in the U.S. White House. Among them were the decisions to sponsor the Bay of Pigs invasion of Cuba in 1961 (an invasion that failed disastrously), to escalate the Vietnam War during the late 1960s, and to cover up the Watergate burglary in the early 1970s. Janis contends that each of these decisions came about because a tightly knit clique of presidential advisers, whose principal concerns were upholding group unity and pleasing their leader (Presidents Kennedy, Johnson, and Nixon, respectively), failed to examine critically the choice that their leader seemed to favor and instead devoted their energy to defending that choice and suppressing criticisms of it.

To refer to such processes, Janis coined the term **groupthink**, which he defined as "a mode of thinking that people engage in when they are deeply involved in a cohesive in-group, when the members' striving for unanimity overrides their motivation to realistically appraise alternative courses of action." More recently, many other ill-advised decisions have been attributed to groupthink, including the decision by NASA to launch the U.S. space shuttle Challenger in below-freezing weather, which resulted in the explosion of the vehicle and the deaths of seven crew members, including a high school social studies teacher (Moorhead et al., 1991); the endorsements by corporate boards of shady accounting practices, which led to the downfalls of Enron and several other large corporations (Postmes et al., 2001; Surowiecki, 2004a); and various decisions by the G. W. Bush administration concerning the invasion and occupation of Iraq (Houghton, 2008; McQueen, 2005).

A number of experiments have aimed at understanding the conditions that promote or prevent groupthink. Overall, the results suggest that the ability of groups to solve problems and make effective decisions is improved if (a) the leaders refrain from advocating a view themselves and instead encourage group members to present their own views and challenge one another (Leana, 1985; Neck & Moorhead, 1995), and (b) the groups focus on the problem to be solved rather than on developing group cohesion (Mullen et al., 1994; Quinn & Schlenker, 2002). It is hard to learn this lesson, but a group that values the dissenter rather than ostracizing that person is a group that has the potential to make fully informed, rational decisions.

FOCUS 30

How did Janis explain some White House policy blunders with his groupthink theory? What can groups do to reduce the risk of groupthink?

Bruce Weaver/AP Photo

■ **The Challenger explosion** The flawed decision making that Irving Janis called groupthink has been implicated in the 1986 explosion of the U.S. space shuttle Challenger. In striving for unanimity in the decision to launch, managers ignored engineers' warnings about the dangers of launching after a night of freezing temperatures.

Requests and Sales Pressure: Some Principles of Compliance

One of the least subtle yet most potent forms of social influence is the direct request. If the request is small and made politely, we tend to comply automatically (Langer et al., 1978), we tend to honor requests of people who have done things for us (the *norm of reciprocity*), and we are more apt to honor a request from someone who is a member of our in-group, even if we don't know that person personally. But even if the request is onerous or offensive, people often find it hard to look a requester in the eye and say no. The tendency to comply usually serves us well. Most requests are reasonable, and we know that in the long run doing things for others pays off, as others in turn do things for us. But from time to time we are faced with situations that threaten to exploit our tendency to comply. It is useful to know the techniques that are often used in such situations so that instead of succumbing to pressure we give when we want to give and buy what we want to buy.

Robert Cialdini (1987, 2001) is a social psychologist who has devoted more than lip service to the idea of combining real-world observations with laboratory studies. To learn about compliance from the real-world experts, Cialdini took training in how to sell encyclopedias, automobiles, and insurance; infiltrated advertising agencies and fund-raising organizations; and interviewed recruiters, public-relations specialists, and political lobbyists. He learned their techniques, extracted what seemed to be basic principles, and tested those principles in controlled experiments. The following paragraphs describe a sample of compliance principles taken largely from Cialdini's work but also much studied by other social psychologists.

Throwing the Low Ball: Increasing the Price After Commitment to Buy

One of the most underhanded sales tricks is the *low-ball technique*. The essence of this technique is that the customer first agrees to buy a product at a low price and then, after a delay, the salesperson "discovers" that the low price isn't possible and the product must be sold for more. Experiments conducted by Cialdini and others (1978) suggest that the trick works because customers, after agreeing to the initial deal, are motivated to reduce cognitive dissonance (see discussion earlier in this chapter) by setting aside any lingering doubts they may have about the product. During the delay between the low-ball offer and the real offer, they mentally exaggerate the product's value; they set their heart on the house, or car, or ice cream treat that they had agreed to purchase. Having done this, they are now primed to pay more than they would have initially.

Putting a Foot in the Door: Making a Small Request to Prepare the Ground for a Large One

With some chagrin, I (Peter Gray) can introduce this topic with a true story in which I was outwitted by a clever gang of driveway sealers. While I was raking leaves in front of my house, these men pulled up in their truck and asked if they could have a drink of water. I, of course, said yes; how could I say no to a request like that? Then they got out of the truck and one said, "Oh, if you have some lemonade or soda, that would be even better; we'd really appreciate that." Well, all right, I did have some lemonade. As I brought it to them, one of the men pointed to the cracks in my driveway and commented that they had just enough sealing material and time to do my driveway that afternoon, and they could give me a special deal. Normally, I would never have agreed to a bargain like that on the spot; but I found myself unable to say no. I ended up paying far more than I should have, and they did a very poor job. I had been taken in by what I now see to be a novel twist on the foot-in-the-door sales technique.

The basis of the *foot-in-the-door technique* is that people are more likely to agree to a large request if they have already agreed to a small one (Pascual & Guaguen, 2005). The driveway sealers got me twice on that: Their request for water primed me to agree to their request for lemonade, and their request for lemonade primed me to agree to their offer to seal my driveway. In situations like my encounter with the driveway sealers, the foot-in-the-door technique may work because compliance with the first request induces a sense of trust, commitment, or compassion toward the person making that request. In other situations it may work by inducing a sense of commitment toward a particular product or cause (Burger, 1999).

FOCUS 31

How can the low-ball sales technique be explained in terms of cognitive dissonance? What evidence supports this explanation?

FOCUS 32

How can the foot-in-the-door sales technique be explained in terms of cognitive dissonance?

■ **A foot in the door** By agreeing to a visitor's first request to sign a petition, this homeowner may find it more difficult to refuse a second request, that she donate money or time to the cause.

The technique has proved to be especially effective in soliciting donations for political causes and charities. People who first agree to make a small gesture of support, such as by signing a petition or giving a few minutes of their time, are subsequently more willing than they otherwise would be to make a much larger contribution (Cialdini, 2001; Freedman & Fraser, 1966). During the 2016 presidential election year, I (David Bjorklund) received many email requests to take "short surveys" about my political opinions. I actually like taking surveys, and responded to the first several of them. After completing each survey there was always a request for money. I managed to resist the urge to donate, although felt a bit guilty *not* giving just a few bucks to a cause I had just said I believed in. Apparently a small donation or gesture of support leads the person to develop a firmer sense of support for the cause—"I contributed to it, so I must believe in it"—which in turn promotes willingness to make a larger donation.

Conditions That Promote Obedience: Milgram's Experiments

Obedience refers to those cases of compliance in which the requester is perceived as an authority figure or leader and the request is perceived as an order. Obedience is often a good thing. Obedience to parents and teachers is part of nearly everyone's social training. Running an army, an orchestra, a hospital, or any enterprise involving large numbers of people would be almost impossible if people did not routinely carry out the instructions given to them by their leaders or bosses. But obedience also has a dark side. Most tragic are the cases in which people obey a leader who is malevolent, unreasonable, or sadly mistaken. Cases in which people, in response to others' orders, carry out unethical or illegal actions have been referred to as *crimes of obedience* (Hinrichs, 2007; Kelman & Hamilton, 1989).

Sometimes crimes of obedience occur because the order is backed up by threats; the subordinate's job or life may be at stake. In other cases, they occur because the subordinate accepts the authority's cause and doesn't interpret the action as wrong. In still other cases, however, people follow orders that they believe are wrong, even when there would be no punishment for disobeying. Those are the cases that interest us here because they are the cases that must be understood in terms of psychological pressures. When social psychologists think of such cases, they relate them to a series of experiments performed by Stanley Milgram (1963) at Yale University in the early 1960s, which rank among the most famous of all experiments in social psychology. Milgram's goal was to identify some of the psychological pressures that underlie a person's willingness to follow a malevolent order.

FOCUS 33

How did Milgram demonstrate that a remarkably high percentage of people would follow a series of orders to hurt another person?

Milgram's Basic Procedure and Finding

To understand Milgram's experiments emotionally as well as intellectually, it is useful to imagine yourself as one of his subjects. You enter the laboratory and meet the experimenter and another person, who is introduced to you as a volunteer subject like yourself. The experimenter, a stern and expressionless man, explains that this is a study of the effects of punishment on learning and that one of you will serve as teacher and the other as learner. You draw slips of paper to see who will play which role and find that your slip says "teacher." The other subject, a pleasant middle-aged man, will be the learner.

You watch while the learner's arms are strapped to his chair and electrodes are taped to his wrist (see **Figure 13.12**). The experimenter explains that the straps will prevent excessive movement while the learner is shocked and that the electrode paste on the skin has been applied "to avoid blisters and burns." While he is being strapped in, the learner expresses some apprehension, saying that he is concerned because he has a heart condition.

FIGURE 13.12 The "learner" in Milgram's obedience experiments While being strapped into a chair and fitted with electrodes, this pleasant man—the "learner"— mentioned that he had a heart condition.

After observing this part of the procedure, you—the teacher—are taken to an adjoining room, from which you can communicate with the learner through an inter-com. Your job is to read off the questions on a test of verbal memory and to give the learner an electric shock whenever he gives a wrong answer. The shock generator in front of you has 30 switches, labeled with voltage designations from 15 to 450 volts. Additional labels next to the switches describe the shocks as ranging from "Slight shock" to "Danger, severe shock," followed by two switches labeled "XXX."

As the experiment progresses, the learner makes frequent mistakes, and at each mistake the experimenter instructs you to give him a stronger shock than you gave before. The learner receives the early shocks silently, but when you get to 75 volts, he responds with an audible "unghh," and at stronger shocks his protests become more vehement. At 150 volts he cries out, "Experimenter, get me out of here! I won't be in the experiment any more! I refuse to go on!" At 180 volts he hollers, "I can't stand the pain!" By 270 volts his response to each shock is an agonized scream, and at 300 volts he shouts in desperation that he will no longer provide answers in the memory test. The experimenter instructs you to continue anyway and to treat each nonresponse as a wrong answer. At 315 and 330 volts the learner screams violently, and then, most frightening of all, from 345 volts on, the learner makes no sound at all. He does not respond to your questions, and he does not react to the shock.

At various points you look to the experimenter and ask if he should check on the learner or if the experiment should be terminated. You might even plead with the experimenter to let you quit giving shocks. At each of these junctures, the experimenter responds firmly with well-rehearsed prompts. First, he says, "Please continue." If you still protest, he responds, "The experiment requires that you continue." This is followed, if necessary, by "It is absolutely essential that you continue" and "You have no other choice; you must go on." These prompts are always used in the sequence given. If you still refuse to go on after the last prompt, the experiment is discontinued.

In reality—as you, serenely reading this book, have probably figured out—the learner receives no shocks. He is a confederate of the experimenter, trained to play his role. But you, as a subject in the experiment, do not know that. You believe that the learner is suffering, and at some point you begin to think that his life may be in danger. What do you do? If you are like the majority of people, you will go on with the experiment to the very end and eventually give the learner the strongest shock on the board—450 volts, "XXX." In a typical rendition of this experiment, 65% (26 out of 40) of the subjects continued to the very end of the series. They did not find this easy to do. Many pleaded with the experimenter to let them stop, and almost all of them showed signs of great tension, such as sweating and nervous tics, yet they went on.

Why didn't they quit? There was no reason to fear retribution for halting the experiment. The experimenter, although stern, did not look physically aggressive. He did not make any threats. The $5 pay (worth about $50 in today's money) for participating was so small as to be irrelevant, and all subjects had been told that the $5 was theirs just for showing up. So why didn't they quit?

Explaining the Finding

Upon first hearing about the results of Milgram's experiment, people are tempted to suggest that the volunteers must have been in someway abnormal to give painful, perhaps deadly, shocks to a middle-aged man with a heart condition. But that explanation doesn't hold up. The experiment was replicated dozens of times, using many different groups of subjects, and yielded essentially the same results each time. Milgram (1974) himself found the same results for women as for men and the same results for college students, professionals, and workers of a wide range of ages and backgrounds. Others repeated the experiment outside the United States, and the consistency from group to group was far more striking than the differences (Miller, 1986). It is tempting to believe that fewer people would obey today than in Milgram's time, but a recent partial replication casts doubt on that belief (Burger, 2009). In the replication, the experiment stopped, for ethical reasons, right after

 FOCUS 34

Why does Milgram's finding call for an explanation in terms of the social situation rather than in terms of unique characteristics of the subjects?

the 150-volt point for each subject, but nearly as many went to that point as had in Milgram's original experiments.

Another temptation is to interpret the results as evidence that people in general are sadistic. But nobody who has seen Milgram's film of subjects actually giving the shocks would conclude that. The subjects showed no pleasure in what they were doing, and they were obviously upset by their belief that the learner was in pain. How, then, can the results be explained? By varying the conditions of the experiment, Milgram (1974) and other social psychologists (Miller, 1986) identified a number of factors that contributed, in these experiments, to the psychological pressure to obey:

FOCUS 35

How might the high rate of obedience in Milgram's experiments be explained in terms of (a) the norm of obedience, (b) the experimenter's acceptance of responsibility, (c) the proximity of the experimenter, (d) the lack of a model for rebellion, and (e) the incremental nature of the requests?

- *The norm of obedience to legitimate authorities.* The volunteer comes to the laboratory as a product of a social world that effectively, and usually for beneficent reasons, trains people to obey legitimate authorities and to play by the rules. Social psychologists refer to this as the *norm of obedience* (Cialdini & Goldstein, 2004). An experimenter, especially one at such a reputable institution as Yale University, must surely be a legitimate authority in the context of the laboratory, a context that the subject respects but doesn't fully understand. Consistent with the idea of perceived legitimacy, Milgram found that when he moved the experiment from Yale to a downtown office building, under the auspices of a fictitious organization called Research Associates of Bridgeport, the percentage who were fully obedient dropped somewhat—from 65 to 48%. Presumably, it was easier to doubt the legitimacy of a researcher at this unknown office than that of a Yale scientist.

- *The experimenter's self-assurance and acceptance of responsibility.* Obedience is predicated on the assumption that the person giving orders is in control and responsible and that your role is essentially that of a cog in a machine. The experimenter's unruffled self-confidence during what seemed to be a time of crisis no doubt helped subjects to continue accepting the cog-in-machine role as the experiment progressed. To reassure themselves, they often asked the experimenter questions like "Who is responsible if that man is hurt?" and the experimenter routinely answered that he was responsible for anything that might happen. The importance of attributing responsibility was shown directly in an experiment conducted by another researcher (Tilker, 1970), patterned after Milgram's. Obedience dropped sharply when subjects were told beforehand that they, the subjects, were responsible for the learner's well-being.

- *The proximity of the experimenter and the distance of the learner.* In Milgram's original experiment, the experimenter was standing in the same room with the subject, while the learner was in another room, out of sight. To test the importance of physical closeness, Milgram (1974) varied the placement of the experimenter or the learner. In one variation, the experimenter left the room when the experiment began and communicated with the subject by telephone, using the same verbal prompts as in the original study; in this case, only 23% obeyed to the end, compared with 65% in the original condition. In another variation, the experimenter remained in the room with the subject, but the learner was also brought into that room; in this case, 40% obeyed to the end. In still another variation, the subject was required to hold the learner's arm on the shock plate while the shock was administered (see **Figure 13.13**), with the result that only 30% obeyed to the end. Thus, any change that moved the experimenter farther away from the subject, or the learner closer to the subject, tended to tip the balance away from obedience.

- *The absence of an alternative model of how to behave.* Milgram's subjects were in a novel situation. Unlike the subjects in Asch's experiments, they saw no other subjects who were in the same situation as they, so there were no examples of how to respond to the experimenter's orders. In two variations, however, Milgram provided a model in the form of another ostensible subject (actually a confederate

From the film *Obedience* © 1963 by Stanley Milgram, © renewed 1993 by Alexandra Milgram, distributed by Alexander Street Press.

FIGURE 13.13 Giving a shock while in close proximity to the learner In one of Milgram's experiments, subjects were required to hold the learner's arm on the shock plate each time a shock was given. Fewer obeyed in this condition than when the learner received shocks in another room, out of sight of the subjects.

of the experimenter) who shared with the real subject the task of giving shocks (Milgram, 1974). When the confederate refused to continue at a specific point and the experimenter asked the real subject to take over the whole job, only 10% of the real subjects obeyed to the end. When the confederate continued to the end, 93% of the real subjects did, too. In an unfamiliar and stressful situation, having a model to follow has a potent effect.

- *The incremental nature of the requests.* At the very beginning of the experiment, Milgram's subjects had no compelling reason to quit. After all, the first few shocks were very weak, and subjects had no way of knowing how many errors the learner would make or how strong the shocks would become before the experiment ended. Although Milgram did not use the term, we might think of his method as a very effective version of the foot-in-the-door technique. Having complied with earlier, smaller requests (giving weaker shocks), subjects found it hard to refuse new, larger requests (giving stronger shocks). The technique was especially effective in this case because each shock was only a little stronger than the previous one. At no point were subjects instructed to do something radically different from what they had already done. To refuse to give the next shock would be to admit that it was probably also wrong to have given the previous shocks—a thought that would be dissonant with subjects' knowledge that they indeed had given those shocks.

For a summary of the results of the variations in Milgram's experiments, see **Figure 13.14**.

FOCUS 36

How has Milgram's research been criticized on grounds of ethics and real-world validity, and how has the research been defended?

Critiques of Milgram's Experiments

Because of their dramatic results, Milgram's experiments immediately attracted much attention and criticism from psychologists and other scholars.

The Ethical Critique Some of Milgram's critics focused on ethics (Baumrind, 1964). They were disturbed by such statements as this one made in Milgram's (1963) initial report: "I observed a mature and initially poised businessman enter the laboratory smiling and confident. Within 20 minutes he was reduced to a twitching, stuttering wreck, who was rapidly approaching a point of nervous collapse." Was the study of sufficient scientific merit to warrant inflicting such stress on subjects, leading some to believe that they might have killed a man?

Milgram took great care to protect his subjects from psychological harm. Before leaving the lab, they were fully informed of the real nature and purpose of the experiment; they were informed that most people in this situation obey the orders to the end; they were reminded of how reluctant they had been to give shocks; and they were reintroduced to the learner, who

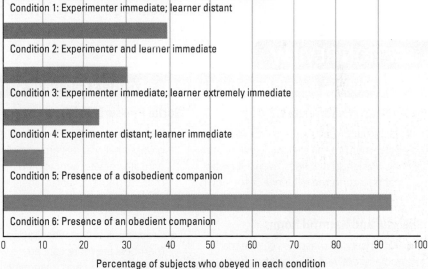

FIGURE 13.14 Results of Milgram's obedience experiments In the first four conditions of the experiment, the greatest degree of obedience occurred when the experimenter and the subject were in the same room and the learner was out of sight in another room. Obedience dropped with decreased proximity of the experimenter and increased proximity of the learner. In conditions 5 and 6, the presence of a disobedient or obedient confederate, masquerading as another subject, dramatically altered the tendency to obey. In each condition, obedience is defined as continuing to give shocks, up through the highest shock level.

offered further reassurance that he was fine and felt well disposed toward them. In a survey made a year after their participation, 84% of Milgram's subjects said they were glad to have participated, and fewer than 2% said they were sorry (Milgram, 1964). Psychiatric interviews of 40 of the former subjects revealed no evidence of harm (Errera, 1972). Still, because of concern for possible harm, a full replication of

Milgram's experiments would not be approved today by the ethics review boards at any major research institution.

The Question of Generalizability to Real-World Crimes of Obedience Other critics have suggested that Milgram's results may be unique to the artificial conditions of the laboratory and have little to tell us about crimes of obedience in the real world, such as the Nazi Holocaust (Miller, 2004). Perhaps Milgram's subjects knew, at some level of their consciousness, that they could not really be hurting the learner because no sane experimenter would allow that to happen (Orne & Holland, 1968). From that perspective, the subjects' real conflict may have been between the belief that they weren't hurting the learner and the possibility that they were. In contrast, Nazis who were actually gassing people could have had no doubt about the effects of their actions. Another difference is that Milgram's subjects had no opportunity, outside the stressful situation in which the orders were given, to reflect on what they were doing, whereas Nazis who were murdering people would go home at night and then return to the gas chambers and kill more people the next day. Historians have pointed to motives for obedience on the part of Hitler's followers—including rampant anti-Semitism and nationalism (Miller, 2004)—that are unlike any motives that Milgram's subjects had.

Most social psychologists would agree that Milgram's findings do not provide full explanations of real-world crimes of obedience, but do shed light on some general principles that apply to such crimes. Preexisting beliefs about the legitimacy of the endeavor, the authority's confident manner, the immediacy of authority figures, the lack of alternative models of how to behave, and the incremental nature of the requests or orders may contribute to real crimes of obedience in much the same way that they contributed to obedience in Milgram's studies, even when the motives are very different. This may be true for crimes ranging from acts of genocide on down to the illegal "cooking of books" by lower-level corporate executives responding to orders from higher-ups (Hinrichs, 2007).

SECTION REVIEW

The opinions, examples, and requests of others can have strong effects on what we say and do.

Conformity Experiments

- Asch found that subjects often stated agreement to the majority view in judging the lengths of lines, even if it meant contradicting the evidence of their own eyes.

Helpful and Harmful Norms

- Public-service messages can be made more effective if they portray the desirable behavior as normative.

- The more bystanders present at an emergency, the less likely any of them are to help. This may result from both informational and normative influences.

- Emotional contagion acts to unite the members of a group, coordinating their actions and promoting bonds of attachment. Successful leaders are often particularly good at expressing emotions in ways that lead others to share those emotions.

Social Pressure Within Groups

- When most or all the people in a group initially agree, group discussion typically moves them toward a more extreme version of their initial view—a phenomenon called group polarization.

- Groupthink occurs when group members are more concerned with group cohesion and unanimity than with genuine appraisal of various approaches to a problem.

Sales Pressure and Compliance

- Salespersons can manipulate us into making purchases through the low-ball and foot-in-the-door techniques, both of which depend on our tendency to reduce cognitive dissonance.

Conditions That Promote Obedience

- In his studies of obedience, Milgram found that most subjects obeyed commands to harm another person, even though it distressed them to do so and there was no real threat or reward involved.

- Factors that help to explain the high rate of obedience in Milgram's experiments include the prevailing norm of obedience to legitimate authorities, the authority's acceptance of responsibility, the proximity of the authority figure, the incremental nature of the requests, and the lack of a model for disobeying.

- Though Milgram took precautions to protect his subjects from psychological harm, some critics object to the studies on ethical grounds. Others question whether the results can be generalized to real crimes of obedience, such as the Nazi Holocaust.

To Cooperate or Not: Prosocial Behavior and the Dilemma of Social Life

Evolutionary theorists have always had difficulty explaining *prosocial behavior,* voluntary behavior intended to benefit other people, introduced in Chapter 12. They've had an easier time explaining aggression or other behaviors that serve to benefit the individual, often at the expense of others. It may not be nice, but stealing a neighbors' property or spouse can have positive consequences for the thief and potentially for his or her genes. Yet, as Michael Tomasello (2009) argued in his book *Why We Cooperate,* prosocial behavior and cooperation are every bit as much a part of evolved human nature as are aggression and competition. Tomasello proposed that there are two components to prosocial behavior, *altruism*—behaviors in which an actor tries to help another individual achieve some goal at some expense (and no obvious benefit) to the actor—and *mutualism,* or *cooperation,* in which two or more individuals coordinate their actions to produce some mutually beneficial outcome, especially one that could not be achieved if working alone. Evidence that both altruism and mutualism are part of humans' evolved nature is that they develop relatively early in childhood, are mediated by empathy, and do not increase with rewards; moreover, hints of such behavior are seen in humans' closest living relatives, chimpanzees (Warneken & Melis, 2012).

However, as we'll see in this section, there is always conflict between cooperating and looking out for Number One. At the same time that they are teammates working for common ends, the members of a group are also individuals with self-interests that can run counter to those of the group as a whole. The tension between acting for the good of the group (cooperation) and acting for one's own selfish good at the expense of the others (detection) is epitomized in **social dilemmas**. A social dilemma exists whenever a particular course of action or inaction will benefit the individual but harm the others in the group and cause more harm than good to everyone if everyone takes that course.

The Tragedy of the Commons: A Social-Dilemma Allegory

The significance of social dilemmas for human survival was dramatically illustrated by the ecologist Garrett Hardin (1968) with an allegory that he called *the tragedy of the commons*. Hardin compared our whole planet with the common grazing land that used to lie at the center of New England towns. When the number of cattle grazing the pasture began to reach the limit that the pasture could support, each farmer was faced with a dilemma: "Should I add another cow to my herd? One more cow will only slightly hurt the pasture and my neighbors, and it will significantly increase my profits. But if everyone adds a cow, the pasture will fail and all the cattle will die." The dilemma becomes a tragedy if all the farmers reason: "It is not my increase in cattle, but the combined increase by everyone, that will determine the fate of the commons. I will lose if others as well as I increase their herd, but I will lose even more if others increase their herd and I do not." So they all add a cow, the pasture gives out, the cattle die, and the townspeople all suffer the loss.

We are all constantly involved in social dilemmas, some so grand in scale as to encompass all members of our species as a single group and others much smaller in scale. Here's a grand one: Sound logic tells me that the pollution I personally add to the Earth's atmosphere by driving a gasoline-burning automobile does not seriously damage the air. It is the pollution of the millions of cars driven by others that causes the serious damage. So I keep driving, everyone else does too, and the pollution keeps getting worse.

FOCUS 37

How does "the tragedy of the commons" illustrate the critical importance of social dilemmas to human survival? What are some examples of real-world social dilemmas?

■ **A modern tragedy of the commons**
The oceans are common fishing grounds where thousands of people make their living. When too many fish are caught, the supply diminishes and valued species may even become extinct. Each fisherman can reason, logically, that his catch contributes very little to the problem; the diminished supply of fish is caused by the thousands of other fishermen.

■ **Should I drive or cycle to work?** For some people it is easy to resolve this dilemma in the cooperative direction. Bicycle commuting not only helps preserve the earth's atmosphere but is also good exercise and more fun than driving.

FOCUS 38

How have laboratory games demonstrated the human sense of justice and willingness to punish even at a personal cost? How does such behavior promote long-term cooperation?

Here's a social dilemma of smaller scale, more typical of the kind that most of us actually experience as a dilemma: If you are part of a team of students working on a project to which everyone is supposed to contribute and for which everyone will receive the same grade, you might benefit by slacking off and letting others do the work. That way you could spend your time on other courses, where your grade depends only on your own effort. But if everyone in your group reasoned that way, the group project would not get done and you, along with the others in your group, would fail.

Every project that depends on group effort or voluntary contributions poses a social dilemma. In each case, *social working,* or *contributing,* is the individual's cooperative solution, and *social loafing,* or *free riding,* is the noncooperative solution. We are all involved in social dilemmas every day. What are the factors that lead us to cooperate or not in any given instance? Let's look at some conditions that promote cooperation in real-life social dilemmas.

Conditions That Promote Cooperation

In real life people cooperate more in social dilemmas than would be expected if their choices were based solely on immediate self-interest (Fehr & Fischbacher, 2004). Many people work hard on group projects even in large groups. Many people contribute to public television. Some people (though not nearly enough) even choose to ride a bicycle or use public transportation, rather than drive a car, to reduce pollution and help save the planet. What are the forces that lead us to cooperate in such "illogical" ways?

Evolution, cultural history, and our own individual experiences have combined to produce in us decision-making mechanisms that are not confined to an immediate cost–benefit analysis. Consciously or unconsciously, thoughtfully or automatically, we take into account factors that have to do with not just our short-term interests but also our long-term interests, which often reside in maintaining good relationships with other people. Many aspects of our social nature can be thought of as adaptations for cooperating in social dilemmas.

Reputation and Reciprocity as Forces for Cooperation

In laboratory situations, and in everyday life, people cooperate with one another because that encourages others to cooperate in return. Such cooperation not only serves to achieve some immediate goal, but it also serves to establish a reputation, and reputation is something that is very important to a highly social species such as *Homo sapiens.* For example, in an economic game in which people can choose to share some, all, or none of their resources (such as money), people behave more generously, or more cooperatively, when they believe that others, who can identify them, will learn about their choices than they do in anonymous conditions (Piazza & Bering, 2008). When players of such games are free to choose the partners with whom they play, they favor those who have already developed a reputation for cooperation (Sheldon et al., 2000).

In some situations, people will spend some of their own resources to punish cheaters. For example, in a *public-goods game,* each player is given a sum of money and then, under conditions of anonymity, must choose whether to keep the money or contribute it to a common pool (the public good). Then, if and only if at least a certain percentage of players (say, 75%) have contributed, all players, including those who haven't contributed, receive a reward that is substantially greater than the amount each person was asked to contribute. The results of a number of experiments have shown that people are willing to give up some of their own earnings in order to punish a player who has contributed substantially less than his or her share to the public good (called *altruistic punishment;* Fehr & Fishbacher, 2004; Krasnow et al., 2016). The punishment, in such cases, involves removing some of the winnings that the "cheater" has garnered. As **Figure 13.15** shows, when the opportunity to punish cheaters is introduced into the rules of such a game, most people stop cheating, so the total amount of cooperation—and thus, the total amount earned by all players combined—increases.

In real life, the consequences of behaving cooperatively spill out everywhere. If I help a person today, that person and others who hear of my help may be disposed to help me in the future, in ways that I cannot even guess at today, and if I get the reputation as a cheater, the long-term consequences may be even greater. Stories of long-range, unanticipated reciprocity are easy to find in everyone's autobiography. Research studies, in various cultures, suggest that people everywhere tend to keep track of the degree to which others are helpful and to offer the greatest help to those who have themselves been most helpful in the past (Fehr, 2004; Gurven, 2004).

Social Identity Promotes Cooperation Within Groups and Competition Across Groups

People everywhere have two different ways of thinking about themselves, which serve different functions. One is *personal identity*, which entails thought of oneself as an independent person with self-interests distinct from those of other people. The other is *social identity*, which entails thought of oneself as a more or less interchangeable member of a larger entity, the group, whose interests are shared by all members. Evolutionarily, the two modes of self-thought may have arisen from our need to survive both as individuals and as groups (Guisinger & Blatt, 1994). If I save myself but destroy the group on which I depend, I will, in the long run, destroy myself. We don't logically think the issue through each time; instead, we automatically cooperate more when we think of the others as members of our group than when we don't.

People are also more likely to feel empathy for in-group than for out-group members. In fact, when groups are in competition with one another, people may experience *schadenfreude,* pleasure at another's pain (Cikara et al., 2011). For example, males, but not females, show activation in reward-related areas of the brain (left ventral striatum) when a competitor receives a painful electric shock (Singer et al., 2006), and both males and females display activation in reward-related areas of the brain (bilateral ventral striatum) when a social competitor has rumors spread about him or her (Takahashi et al., 2009).

Identification with a group increases people's willingness to help members of their own group but decreases their willingness to help members of another group. People are much less likely to trust others and more likely to cheat others when they view those others as part of another group than when they view them as individuals. In real life, as in the laboratory, interactions between groups are typically more hostile than interactions between individuals (Hoyle et al., 1989). All too often the hostility becomes extreme. Such *in-group favoritism* and *out-group discrimination* is evident as early as the preschool years on the basis of sex and race (Buttelmann & Böhm, 2014; Patterson & Bigler, 2006).

Group Against Group: Lessons from Robbers Cave

The most vicious and tragic side of our nature seems to emerge when we see ourselves as part of a group united against some other group. Perhaps because of an evolutionary history of intertribal warfare, we can be easily provoked into thinking of other groups as enemies and as inferior beings, unworthy of respectful treatment. The history of humankind can be read as a sad, continuing tale of intergroup strife that often becomes intergroup atrocity.

There are ethical limits to the degree to which researchers can create the conditions that bring out intergroup hostility for the purpose of study. Muzafer Sherif and his colleagues (1961; Sherif, 1966) approached those limits in a now-famous study, conducted in the 1950s, with 11- and 12-year-old boys at a 3-week camping program in Oklahoma's Robbers Cave Park (so named because it was once used as

FIGURE 13.15 Altruistic punishment increases cooperation In each trial of this social-dilemma game, each player was given 20 money units and could contribute any amount of that to a common pool. The money contributed was then multiplied by 1.4 and redistributed evenly among the four players. In one condition, players could punish low contributors by giving up one of their own money units to have three units taken away from the punished player. With the punishment option, cooperation increased from trial to trial. Without that option, it decreased from trial to trial. At the end of all trials, the players could exchange the money units they had accumulated for real money.

FOCUS 39

What is some evidence that social identity can lead to helping group-mates and hurting those who are not group-mates?

■ **Rattlers versus Eagles** What at first were friendly competitions, such as the tug-of-war shown here, degenerated into serious hostility and aggression between the two groups of boys in Sherif's field study at Robbers Cave.

a hideout by the famous outlaw Jesse James). The researchers were interested in understanding how hostility between groups develops and how it can be resolved.

The Escalation of Conflict

To establish two groups of campers, Sherif and his colleagues divided the boys into two separate cabins and assigned separate tasks to each group, such as setting up camping equipment and improving the swimming area. Within a few days, with little adult intervention, each cabin of boys acquired the characteristics of a distinct social group. Each group established its own leaders, its own rules and norms of behavior, and its own name—the Eagles and the Rattlers.

When the groups were well established, the researchers proposed a series of competitions, and the boys eagerly accepted the suggestion. They would compete for valued prizes in such games as baseball, touch football, and tug-of-war. As Sherif had predicted from previous research, the competitions promoted three changes in the relationships among the boys within and between groups:

1. *Within-group solidarity*. As the boys worked on plans to defeat the other group, they set aside their internal squabbles and differences, and their loyalty to their own group became even stronger than it was before.

2. *Negative stereotyping of the other group*. Even though the boys had all come from the same background (white, Protestant, and middle class) and had been assigned to the groups on a purely random basis, they began to see members of the other group as very different from themselves and as very similar to one another in negative ways. For example, the Eagles began to see the Rattlers as dirty and rough, and in order to distinguish themselves from that group they adopted a "goodness" norm and a "holier-than-thou" attitude.

3. *Hostile between-group interactions*. Initial good sportsmanship collapsed. The boys began to call their rivals names, accuse them of cheating, and cheat in retaliation. After being defeated in one game, the Eagles burned one of the Rattlers' banners, which led to an escalating series of raids and other hostilities. What at first was a peaceful camping experience turned gradually into something verging on intertribal warfare.

FOCUS 40

What changes occurred within and between two groups of boys as a result of intergroup competitions at a summer camp?

Resolving the Conflict by Creating Common Goals

In the final phase of their study, Sherif and his colleagues tried to reduce hostility between the two groups, a more difficult task than provoking it had been. In two previous studies similar to the one at Robbers Cave, Sherif had tried a number of procedures to reduce hostility, all of which had failed. Peace meetings between leaders failed because those who agreed to meet lost status within their own groups for conceding to the enemy. Individual competitions (similar to the Olympic Games) failed because the boys turned them into group competitions by tallying the total victories for each group. Sermons on brotherly love and forgiveness failed because, while claiming to agree with the messages, the boys simply did not apply them to their own actions.

At Robbers Cave, the researchers tried two new strategies. The first involved joint participation in pleasant activities. Hoping that mutual enjoyment of noncompetitive activities would lead the boys to forget their hostility, the researchers brought the two groups together for such activities as meals, movies, and shooting firecrackers. This didn't work either. It merely provided opportunities for further hostilities. Meals were transformed into what the boys called "garbage wars."

The second new strategy, however, was successful. This involved the establishment of **superordinate goals**, defined as goals that were desired by both groups and could be achieved best through cooperation between the groups. The researchers created one such goal by staging a breakdown in the camp's water supply. In response to this crisis, boys in both groups volunteered to explore the mile-long water line to find the break, and together they worked out a strategy to divide their efforts in doing so. Two other staged events similarly elicited cooperation. By the end of this series

FOCUS 41

How did Sherif and his colleagues succeed in promoting peace between the two groups of boys?

of cooperative adventures, hostilities had nearly ceased, and the two groups were arranging friendly encounters on their own initiative, including a campfire meeting at which they took turns presenting skits and singing songs. On their way home, one group treated the other to milkshakes with money left from its prizes.

Research since Sherif's suggests that the intergroup harmony brought on by superordinate goals involves the fading of group boundaries (Bodenhausen, 1991; Gaertner et al., 1990). The groups merge into one, and each person's social identity expands to encompass those who were formerly excluded. The boys at Robbers Cave might say, "I am an Eagle [or a Rattler], but I am also a member of the larger camp group of Eagles plus Rattlers—the group that found the leak in the camp's water supply."

■ **A superordinate task brings people together** When the Red River overflowed in Fargo, North Dakota, the local people worked together to create and stack sandbags to save homes from flooding. None of them could succeed at this task alone; they need one another. Social-psychological theory predicts that this experience will create positive bonds among the volunteers and promote their future cooperation.

If there is hope for a better human future, one not fraught with wars, it may lie in an increased understanding of the common needs of people everywhere and the establishment of superordinate goals. Such goals might include those of stopping the pollution of our shared atmosphere and oceans, the international drug trade, diseases such as AIDS that spread worldwide, and the famines that strike periodically and disrupt the world. Is it possible that we can conceive of all humanity as one group, spinning together on a small and fragile planet, dependent on the cooperation of all to find and stop the leaks?

SECTION REVIEW

Social dilemmas require individuals to decide whether or not to act for the common good.

The Tragedy of the Commons

- In a social dilemma, the choice to behave in a certain way produces personal benefit at the expense of the group and leads to harm for all if everyone chooses that option.
- In the tragedy of the commons, each individual puts one extra cow on the common pasture, thinking his or her cow will make little difference; but the collective effect is disastrous to all.

Roles of Accountability and Social Identity

- Cooperation increases when players are accountable for their actions and can develop reputations as cooperators or cheaters.
- The tendency for people to reject unfair offers and to punish cheaters, even at their own expense, is a force for cooperation.
- Shared social identity among group members increases cooperation within the group but decreases cooperation with other groups.

Group Against Group

- In the Robbers Cave experiment, competition between the two groups of boys led to solidarity within groups, negative stereotyping of the other group, and hostile interactions between groups.
- Hostility was greatly reduced by superordinate goals that required the two groups to cooperate.

Thinking Critically About Social Psychology

1. What evidence was presented for the existence of each of the biases presented in the chapter? For example, how do we know that the person bias exists?

2. How do you think one's implicit attitudes influence one's explicit attitudes? If a person displays racial bias on a test of implicit attitudes but not explicit attitudes, is it appropriate to say that person is a racist?

3. What factors may explain why people experience arousal and a strong drive to do well—leading to either social interference or facilitation—when they know that their performance is being

evaluated? Why might this hold true even if the evaluator is a stranger and the evaluation doesn't count for anything?

4. Why do people find it hard to refuse a direct request? If you were designing an experiment to assess circumstances under which people would refuse a request, how would you go about it?

5. Humans are a highly social species. What social-cognitive abilities might have been selected for in evolution to promote sociality? Might there be any drawbacks in modern culture for some of these evolved abilities?

Reflections and Connections

1. Biases in social perceptions and attitudes can lead people to make judgments that are objectively untrue and unfair Consider the following questions as you think about each bias discussed in the chapter: In what contexts does the bias seem to occur or not occur? What, if any, functions might the bias serve for the person manifesting it? What harm might result from this bias, either to the person who manifests it or to the objects of the biased perception or thought? You will not find the answers to all these questions for every bias described in the chapter, but in most cases you will at least find hints. Apply such questions to the person bias, attractiveness bias, baby-face bias, big-fish-in-little-pond effect, self-serving attributional bias, biasing effects of stereotypes, and insufficient-justification effect.

2. The desire to be accepted by others underlies much of social influence Human beings have a remarkably strong desire to be approved of by others. Why are people so concerned with impression management? Why did subjects in Asch's experiments deny the clear evidence of their own two eyes when it ran counter to what others were saying? Why are people so motivated to abide by social norms? Why do group polarization and groupthink occur? Why do people find it hard not to reciprocate a favor, even one that they did not want in the first place? Why did Milgram's subjects find it hard to tell the

experimenter that he was asking them to do a terrible thing and that they would not do it?

We don't want to oversimplify. The desire to be accepted is surely not the *whole* answer to these questions, but it seems to be a big part of it. As you review each of the phenomena and experiments described in the chapter, you might ask yourself: To what extent (if at all) can this be explained by the desire for acceptance, and what additional explanatory principles seem to be needed?

3. Much of human nature can be understood as adaptation for group living As social beings, we are endowed with characteristics that draw us to other members of our species and help us to function effectively in groups. We feel lonely when separated from companions, pained when rejected, and satisfied or proud when accepted. We tend to adopt the attitudes, behavioral styles, and emotions of others in our group, which helps the group to function as a unit. We also have characteristics that keep us from being exploited by others in the group, as demonstrated by our concern for fairness and our tendency to either punish or avoid those who treat us unfairly. As you review each social-influence phenomenon discussed in this chapter, think about the aspects of human nature that underlie it and help to make group living possible and beneficial.

Key Terms

attitude 503
attribution 494
cognitive dissonance
    theory 504
explicit attitudes 503
explicit stereotypes 508
foot-in-the-door
    technique 521
fundamental attribution
    error 495
group polarization 519

groupthink 520
implicit association tests 503
implicit attitudes 503
implicit stereotypes 508
impression management 513
informational influence 515
in-groups 507
insufficient-justification
    effect 505
low-ball technique 521
normative influence 515

out-groups 507
person bias 494
personal identity 507
Pygmalion effects 499
reference group 501
self-concept 499
self-esteem 500
self-fulfilling prophecies 499
self-serving attributional
    bias 502
social comparison 501

social dilemmas 527
social facilitation 511
social identity 507
social interference 511
social pressure 511
social psychology 493
stereotype 508
stereotype threat 512
superordinate goals 531

Find Out More

Hazel Markus & Alana Conner (2014). *Clash!: How to thrive in a multicultural world.* London, UK: Penguin.

Cultural psychologists Markus and Conner discuss the differences between independence and interdependence and how these differing backgrounds affect our ways of approaching problems. The focus is on how to resolve conflicts both in the workplace and in our relationships by using our diversity and differences not as a hindrance but as a tool.

Elliot Aronson (2018). *The social animal* (12th ed). New York, NY: W. H. Freeman.

In this landmark text, eminent social psychologist Elliot Aronson discusses myriad aspects of social influence and relations including obedience, conformity, prejudice, cults, and terrorism. He uses compelling examples and events like the Milgram obedience studies and Kent State shootings to illustrate how psychology is social and human behavior cannot be studied in a vacuum.

Elliot Aronson (2012). *Not by chance alone: My life as a social psychologist.* New York, NY: Basic Books.

Aaronson is one of social psychology's most influential researchers. He brought cognitive dissonance to the field, exposed a pattern of racial inequalities in the Texas legal system, and defended the right of controversial colleagues to present unpopular arguments. Here, in his autobiography, Aronson recounts the roller-coaster professional life he led from the 1960s through the 1990s and how historical events like the civil rights movements shaped his career.

Mark Leary (2008). *The curse of the self: Self-awareness, egotism, and the quality of human life.* Oxford, UK: Oxford University Press.

Our capacity for self-reflection is a large part of what makes us human. It allows us to think about and learn from our past successes and failures, to see ourselves somewhat as others see us, and to contemplate and plan our futures. However, that same capacity also contributes to human misery. Leary is the social psychologist who developed the sociometer theory of self-esteem. In this book he writes clearly and persuasively about the dark side of too much focus on the self and too little focus on the world outside ourselves.

Paul Bloom (2014, January). *Can prejudice ever be a good thing?* TEDSalon NY2014. https://www.ted.com/talks/paul_bloom_can_prejudice_ever_be_a_good_thing

Using an intentionally provocative title for this TED talk, psychologist Paul Bloom explains why humans are prone to prejudice, how certain situations can exacerbate bias, and how wc can alter our thinking to create a better world.

LaunchPad
macmillan learning

Visit LaunchPad for Psychology 8e launchpadworks.com to access the e-book, videos, activities, additional resources, and LearningCurve quizzes, as well as study aids including flash cards and web quizzes.

Personality

LEARNING OUTCOMES

After studying this chapter, you should be able to:

- Define *personality* and identify the prevailing trait theories of personality.
- Explain how personality confers an adaptive advantage.
- Summarize the psychodynamic and humanistic views of personality.
- Revisit trait theories of personality in light of social-cognitive views.

Personality refers to a person's general style of interacting with the world, especially with other people—whether one is withdrawn or outgoing, excitable or placid, conscientious or careless, kind or stern. Judith Harris (2005) defined personality as: "the development during childhood of chronic patterns of behavior (along with their cognitive and emotional concomitants) that differ from one individual to another. Some individuals are chronically more outgoing, or more aggressive, or more rule-abiding than others" (p. 246). Most chapters of this book emphasize the ways in which we are similar to one another, but in this chapter we turn explicitly to differences among us. A basic assumption of the personality concept is that people do differ from one another in their styles of behavior in ways that are fairly consistent across time and place. In keeping with that view, we define **personality** as the relatively consistent patterns of thought, feeling, and behavior that characterize each person as a unique individual.

Most people are fascinated by human differences. Such fascination is natural and useful. In everyday life we tend to focus on those aspects that distinguish one person from another. Attention to differences helps us decide whom we want for partners and friends and how to deal with the different people that we know. *Personality psychologists* make a scientific study of such differences. Using questionnaires and other assessment tools, they conduct research to measure personality differences and explain their origins. They try to relate personality to the varying roles and habitats that people occupy in the social world, and they try to understand the mental processes that underlie the differences.

This chapter is divided into four main sections. The first is concerned with the basic concept of personality traits and with questions about their validity, stability, and biological bases. The second is concerned with the adaptive functions of personality: How might individual differences prepare people for life within different niches of the social environment? The third and fourth sections are about the unconscious and conscious mental processes that may underlie and help explain behavioral differences among individuals, and the way these are viewed by the psychodynamic, humanistic, and social-cognitive theories of personality.

Personality as Behavioral Dispositions, or Traits

What are the first three adjectives that come to mind concerning your own personality? Do they apply to you in all settings, or only in some? How clearly do they distinguish you from other people you know? Do you have any idea why you have those characteristics?

The most central concept in personality psychology is the *trait*, which can be defined as a relatively stable predisposition to behave in a certain way. Traits are considered to be part of the person, not part of the environment. People carry their traits with them from one environment to another, although the actual manifestation of a trait in the form of behavior usually requires some perceived cue or trigger in the environment. For example, the trait of *aggressiveness* might be defined as an inner predisposition to argue or fight. That predisposition is presumed to stay with the person in all environments, but actual arguing or fighting is unlikely to occur unless the person perceives provocations in the environment. Aggressiveness or kindness or any other personality trait is, in that sense, analogous to the physical trait of "meltability" in margarine. Margarine melts only when subjected to heat (a characteristic of the environment); but some types of margarine need less heat to melt than others do, and that difference lies in the margarine, not in the environment.

Traits are not characteristics that people have or lack in all-or-none fashion but, rather, are dimensions (continuous, measurable characteristics) along which people differ by degree. If we measured aggressiveness or any other trait in a large number of people, our results would approximate a normal distribution, in which the majority are near the middle of the range and few are at the extremes (see **Figure 14.1**).

Traits describe differences among people in their tendencies to behave in certain ways, but they are not themselves explanations of those differences. To say that a person is high in aggressiveness simply means that the person tends to argue or fight a lot, in situations that would not provoke such behavior in most people. The trait is inferred from the behavior. It would be meaningless, then, to say that Harry argues and fights a lot because he is highly aggressive. That would be essentially the same as saying, "Harry argues and fights a lot because he argues and fights a lot"—an example of circular reasoning that does not prove anything.

Mac99/E+/Getty Images

■ **A state is not a trait** This woman is clearly in a state of anger. However, before we judge her as having an aggressive or hostile personality we would have to know how easily she is provoked into anger.

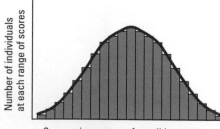

FIGURE 14.1 **Typical distribution of scores measuring a personality trait** When many individuals are tested for a personality trait—such as boldness versus shyness—the majority generally fall in the middle of the range and the frequency tapers off toward zero at the extremes, in a manner that approximates the bell-shaped *normal distribution* depicted here. (For a more complete description of normal distributions, see the Statistical Appendix at the end of the book.)

Trait Theories: Efficient Systems for Describing Personalities

In everyday life we use an enormous number of personality descriptors. Gordon Allport (1937), one of the pioneers of personality psychology, identified 17,953 such terms in a standard English dictionary. Most of them have varying meanings, many of which overlap with the meanings of other terms. Consider, for example, the various connotations and overlapping meanings of *affable, agreeable, amiable, amicable, companionable, congenial, convivial, cordial, friendly, genial, gracious, hospitable, kind, sociable, warmhearted,* and *welcoming*. Personality psychologists have long been interested in devising a more efficient vocabulary for describing personality. **Trait theories of personality** endeavor to specify a manageable set of distinct personality dimensions that can be used to summarize the fundamental psychological differences among individuals.

Factor Analysis as a Tool for Identifying an Efficient Set of Traits

In order to distill all the trait terms of everyday language down to a manageable number of meaningful, different dimensions of personality, trait theorists use a statistical technique called *factor analysis*. Factor analysis is a method of analyzing patterns of correlations in order to extract mathematically defined factors, which underlie and help make sense of those patterns. We will illustrate the technique here, with hypothetical data.

The first step in a factor-analytic study of personality is to collect data in the form of a set of personality measures taken across a large sampling of people. For example, the researcher might present a group of people with a set of adjectives and ask each person to indicate, on a scale of 1 to 5, the degree to which each adjective describes him- or herself. For the sake of simplicity, let us imagine a study in which just seven adjectives are used—*carefree, compliant, dependable, hardworking, kind, rude,* and *trusting.* To get a sense of what it is like to be a subject in such a study, try rating yourself on each of these traits. For each term write a number from 1 to 5, depending on whether you think the term is (1) very untrue, (2) somewhat untrue, (3) neither true nor untrue, (4) somewhat true, or (5) very true of you as a person. Be honest in your ratings; you are doing this anonymously, as are the subjects in actual studies.

Once the data are collected, the researcher statistically correlates the scores for each adjective with those for each of the other adjectives, using the method of correlation described in Chapter 2. The result is a matrix of correlation coefficients, showing the correlation for every possible pair of scores (illustrated in **Table 14.1**).

The next step in a factor analysis is a mathematically complex one called *factor extraction,* in which items (here adjectives) that are strongly related to one another, or that cluster together, are identified. For the data depicted in Table 14.1, such an analysis would identify two rather clear factors. One factor corresponds most closely with the adjectives *carefree, dependable,* and *hardworking;* and the other factor corresponds most closely with the adjectives *compliant, kind, rude,* and *trusting.* The final step is a subjective one, in which the researcher provides a label for the factors. In our hypothetical example, the factor that corresponds with *carefree, dependable,* and *hardworking* might be referred to as the *conscientiousness* dimension; and the factor that corresponds with *compliant, kind, rude,* and *trusting* might be referred to as the *agreeableness* dimension.

What the factor analysis tells us is that these two dimensions of personality are relatively independent of each other. People who are high in conscientiousness are about equally likely to be either high or low in agreeableness, and vice versa. Thus, conscientiousness and agreeableness are useful, efficient trait dimensions because they are not redundant with each other and because each captures at least part of the essence of a set of more specific trait terms.

FOCUS 2

How is factor analysis used to identify trait dimensions that are not redundant with one another?

TABLE 14.1 Hypothetical matrix of correlations among adjectives used as personality self-descriptions

Self-description	Compliant	Dependable	Hard-working	Kind	Rude	Trusting
Carefree	−.11	−.60	−.43	+.01	+.21	+.17
Compliant	−	+.29	+.13	+.39	−.70	+.53
Dependable		−	+.49	+.19	−.13	+.17
Hard-working			−	+.08	−.11	+.09
Kind				−	−.65	+.55
Rude					−	−.48
Trusting						−

Cattell's Pioneering Use of Factor Analysis to Develop a Trait Theory

The first trait theory to be put to practical use was developed by Raymond Cattell (1950). Cattell began his research by condensing Allport's 17,953 English adjectives describing personality down to 170 that he took to be logically different from one another, and eventually identified 16 basic trait dimensions and a questionnaire called the *16 PF Questionnaire* to measure them (Cattell, 1950, 1973). The questionnaire consists of nearly 200 statements about specific aspects of behavior, such as "I like to go to parties."

The Five-Factor Model of Personality

FOCUS 3

Why is the five-factor model of personality generally preferred today over Cattell's trait theory?

Many trait researchers find Cattell's 16-factor theory to be overly complex, arguing that some of its factors are redundant. Today, with computers, it is much easier to perform large-scale factor-analytic studies than it was in Cattell's time. Since the 1970s, hundreds of such studies have been done, with many different measures of personality and many different groups of subjects. Some studies have used self-ratings, based on adjectives or on responses to questions about behavior. Others have used ratings that people make of the personality of someone they know well rather than of themselves. Such studies have been conducted with children as well as with adults, and with people from many different cultures, using questionnaires translated into many different languages (Caspi & Shiner, 2006; McCrae & Terracciano, 2005). Overall, the results have been fairly consistent in supporting what has become known as the ***five-factor model***, or the *Big Five theory*, of personality.

According to the model, a person's personality is most efficiently described in terms of his or her score on each of five relatively independent global trait dimensions: *neuroticism* (vulnerability to emotional upset), *extraversion* (tendency to be socially outgoing), *openness to experience, agreeableness,* and *conscientiousness.* (An easy way to remember the five factors is to observe that their initials spell the acronym OCEAN: *openness to experience, conscientiousness, extraversion, agreeableness,* and *neuroticism.*) Nearly all of the thousands of adjectives commonly used to describe personalities correlate at least to some degree with one or another of these five traits. The model also posits that each global trait dimension encompasses six subordinate trait dimensions referred to as facets of that trait (Costa & McCrae, 1992; Paunonen & Ashton, 2001). The facets within any given trait dimension correlate with one another, but the correlations are far from perfect. Thus, a detailed description of someone's personality would include not just a score for each of the five global traits but also a score for each of the 30 facets. **Table 14.2** presents a brief description of each of the Big Five trait dimensions and a list of the six facets for each.

Other researchers have argued that a sixth trait, *honesty-humility,* should be added to the Big Five, producing the HEXACO Model (**H**onesty-Humility, **E**motionality [comparable to neuroticism in the Five-Factor Mode], e**X**traversion, **A**greeableness, **C**onscientiousness, and **O**penness; Ashton & Lee, 2009).

Grit and the Dark Triad

Still other researchers have focused on a subset of these or related traits associated with a general personality type. Two such sets of traits are *grit* and the *dark triad.*

Grit Angela Duckworth and her colleagues (Duckworth et al., 2007; Duckworth & Quinn, 2009) proposed a higher-order personality trait independent of IQ that is predictive of success in a wide range of domains. Termed ***grit***, it is defined as "perseverance and passion for long-term goals" (Duckworth et al., 2007, p. 1087) and consists of two lower-order factors: *perseverance of effort* and *consistency of interest.* Basically, grit reflects the tendency to work hard at achieving important goals, even in the face of setbacks, and to stick with a particular goal rather than changing goals

TABLE 14.2 The Big Five personality factors and their 30 facets

- **Neuroticism–stability (N):** *High end:* Experience many forms of emotional distress, have unrealistic ideas and troublesome urges.

  Low end: Emotionally stable, do not get upset easily, and are not prone to depression.

  Facets: Anxious–calm; Angry–placid; Depressed–not depressed; Self-conscious–not self-conscious; Impulsive–controlled; Vulnerable–secure.

- **Extraversion–introversion (E):** *High end:* Prefer intense and frequent interpersonal interactions; are energized and optimistic.

  Low end: Reserved and tend to prefer a few close friends to large groups of people.

  Facets: Warm–detached; Gregarious–withdrawn; Assertive–unassertive; Active–contemplative; Excitement-seeking–tranquility-seeking; Positive emotions–modulated emotions.

- **Openness to experience–non-openness (O):** *High end:* Seek out new experiences and have a fluid style of thought.

  Low end: Traditional, conservative, and prefer familiarity to novelty.

  Facets: The six facets refer to openness versus non-openness to experience in each of six realms: Fantasy, Aesthetics, Feelings, Actions, Ideas, and Values.

- **Agreeableness–antagonism (A):** *High end:* Regard others with sympathy and act unselfishly.

  Low end: Not concerned with other people and tend to be antagonistic and hostile.

  Facets: Trusting–suspicious; Straightforward–conniving; Altruistic–selfish; Compliant–noncompliant; Modest–self-aggrandizing; Tender-minded–hard-headed.

- **Conscientiousness–undirectedness (C):** *High end:* Control one's own behavior in the service of one's goals.

  Low end: Have a hard time keeping to a schedule, are disorganized, and are unreliable.

  Facets: Competent–incompetent; Ordered–disordered; Dutiful–neglectful; Achievement-striving–not achievement-striving; Self-disciplined–not self-disciplined; Deliberative–careless.

Note: In this table, the five major traits and the six facets of each trait are indicated as dimensions, using antonyms to indicate the two ends of each dimension. Usually the traits and facets are referred to using just the first term of each of the antonym pairs shown here.

Source: McCrae, R.R., & Sutin, A.R. (2007). New frontiers for the five-factor model: A preview of the literature. *Social and Personality Psychology Compass, 1(1),* 423–440. Republished with permission of John Wiley & Sons Inc. Permission conveyed through Copyright Clearance Center, Inc.

and interests. Duckworth (2016) provides examples of many successful individuals who doggedly pursued their goals despite setbacks and achieved success where equally or more intelligent individuals may have failed. The American inventor Thomas Edison exemplifies grit, as reflected in the statement attributed to him that his successes reflect one percent inspiration and ninety-nine percent perspiration.

Duckworth developed a 12-item, and later an 8-item, scale to measure the two factors of grit. The consistency scale consists of items such as *"I often set a goal but later choose to pursue a different one,"* and the perseverance scale consists of items such as *"I finish whatever I begin"* (see **Table 14.3**). Subjects rate on a 5-point scale how well each statement is like them (1 = *not at all like me* to 5 = *very much like me*). As you can see in the table, consistency of interest items assess the degree to which people are apt to pursue a goal without distraction, whereas perseverance of effort items assess the degree to which people are apt to work hard and persistently at completing a task without being discouraged by setbacks.

In her research, Duckworth and her colleagues (2007) reported that grit accounted for an average of 4% of individual differences beyond other factors such as IQ in predicting success outcomes, including grade-point average among Ivy

TABLE 14.3 Items from the Short-Grit Scale (Grit-S) for *Consistency of Interest* and *Perseverance of Effort* factors

Subjects rate each item on a 5-point scale from 1 = *not at all like me* to 5 = *very much like me*. Subjects who score low on the Consistency of Interest items (not like me) and high on the Perseverance of Effort items (like me) are said to be high in grit.

Consistency of Interest

I often set a goal but later choose to pursue a different one.
I have been obsessed with a certain idea or project for a short time but later lost interest.
I have difficulty maintaining my focus on projects that take more than a few months to complete.
New ideas and projects sometimes distract me from previous ones.

Perseverance of Effort

I finish whatever I begin.
Setbacks don't discourage me.
I am diligent.
I am a hard worker.

Research from Duckworth & Quinn, 2009.

League undergraduate students, the tendency to change jobs, educational attainment, the likelihood of West Point cadets graduating, and ranking in the National Spelling Bee. Although Duckworth et al. reported that grit was associated with the personality trait of conscientiousness as measured in the Big Five model, grit accounted for additional individual differences in outcomes beyond conscientiousness and IQ. The benefits of grit on performance may be due to its association with practice, which has been shown to be important for developing expertise in many domains (Ericcson et al., 1993; Krampe & Ericcson, 1996), as well as success in spelling bees (Duckworth et al., 2011).

Since the publication of Duckworth's initial research, dozens of studies have investigated the effects of grit on various outcomes, with many finding positive effects of grit on success (Duckworth et al., 2011; Strayhorn, 2014), but others failing to do so (see Credé et al., 2016). To get a "big picture" view of the influence of grit on performance, Marcus Credé and his colleagues (2016) examined the effects of grit in a *meta-analysis*, a statistical technique that allows an investigator to evaluate the magnitude of a significant effect across a large number of studies. They looked at the effects of grit in 88 independent samples involving over 65,000 subjects. Credé et al. reported that grit was highly correlated with conscientiousness (correlations in excess of .80), and that the perseverance factor, but not the consistency factor, accounted for individual differences in outcomes beyond the effects of conscientiousness. Similar results were reported for samples of Philippine college and high school students for predicting subjective well-being, with only the perseverance factor predicting outcomes (Datu et al., 2016).

Grit, especially the tendency to persist at difficult tasks, seems to be an important addition to the set of noncognitive personality traits for predicting success on some tasks, but its effects are apparently not as robust as originally proposed. One reason for the mixed results may be because the benefits of grit are limited to certain tasks. For example, grit may be predictive of success for tasks that are difficult and well defined, requiring substantial practice for success. Grit may be less predictive of success on relatively easy tasks or on novel or ill-defined tasks. In fact, persisting with a difficult task too long may be detrimental if it prevents people from seeking help or sticking with a problem when switching to other, more solvable problems would be more beneficial (Credé et al., 2016).

The Dark Triad A number of researchers have examined people with "dark personalities"—people who display often socially offensive traits outside the "normal" range. Researchers have identified people with socially aversive personalities as scoring high on the **dark triad** of personality traits, which consists of narcissism, Machiavellianism, and psychopathy (Book et al., 2016; Jonason et al., 2009). **Narcissism** is defined as extreme selfishness with a grandiose view of one's own abilities and a need for admiration. **Machiavellianism** refers to a personality type in which the person is predisposed to manipulate other people, often through deception. **Psychopathy** involves amoral or antisocial behavior, coupled with a lack of empathy and an inability to form meaningful personal relationships. At its extreme, psychopathy is a personality disorder (antisocial personality disorder, see Chapter 15), but psychopathy can also be expressed at preclinical levels. Some researchers have added "everyday sadism" to the list—people who enjoy inflicting verbal or physical harm (think of bullies)—producing a dark tetrad (Paulhus, 2014).

One may think that such negative personality traits would be highly maladaptive to individuals possessing them, and often they are. People with dark personalities score low on agreeableness and conscientiousness, and often have difficulty getting along with other people (Jackowitz & Egan, 2006). Yet, people with dark personalities can be successful in some contexts. For example, they tend to make good impressions on first dates (Dufner et al., 2013) and brief job interviews (Paulhaus et al., 2013). Although they may make poor long-term mates, men with dark personalities have better luck with exploitative, short-term mating opportunities (Jonason et al., 2009). On the down side, narcissism is associated with overconfidence, deceit, and

FOCUS 4

What is grit, what does it predict, and how is it similar to or different from the personality trait of conscientiousness?

FOCUS 5

What are some of the costs and benefits for people with "dark personalities"?

a seemingly inability to learn from mistakes (Campbell, Goodies, & Foster, 2004); however, it is also associated with leadership and is found in celebrities and political leaders. In one study assessing the degree of narcissism in 42 American presidents (up to and including George W. Bush), Ashley Watts and her colleagues (2013) determined that narcissism was positively associated with overall greatness, public persuasion, crisis management, and agenda setting. However, narcissism was also associated with congressional impeachment and unethical behaviors.

Measurement of the Big Five Traits and Their Facets

Trait theorists have developed many different questionnaires to assess personality. The questionnaire most often used to measure the Big Five traits and their facets is the *NEO Personality Inventory* (where *N, E,* and *O* stand for three of the five major traits), developed by Paul Costa and Robert McCrae (1992). This questionnaire is now in its third revision, referred to as the *NEO-PI-3* (McCrae et al., 2005). In its full form, the person being tested rates 240 statements on a 5-point scale ranging from "strongly disagree" to "strongly agree." Each statement is designed to assess one facet of one of the five major traits.

For example, here are two statements from the NEO-PI-3 designed to assess the sixth facet (values) of openness to experience:

118. *Our ideas of right and wrong may not be right for everyone in the world.*

238. *People should honor traditional values and not question them.*

Agreement with the first statement and disagreement with the second would count toward a high score on the *values* facet of *openness*. In the development of such tests, trait theorists submit the results of trial tests to factor analysis and use the results to eliminate items whose scores do not correlate strongly (positively or negatively) with the scores of other items designed to measure the same facet.

In recent years, shortened versions of the NEO-PI have been available on the Internet for self-testing. You can probably find one or more of these by searching "Big Five personality test" with Google. If you take such a test, you will get feedback regarding your results, and your data may also contribute to an ongoing research study. For one example of research findings using the NEO-PI, see **Figure 14.2**.

One problem with almost all personality questionnaires, which you will discover if you take such a test, is that the questions are quite transparent. A person who wants to present him- or herself as a particular kind of person can easily do so. The usefulness of the questionnaires depends on the honesty and insight of the respondent about his or her own behavior and emotions. In some research studies, and for some clinical purposes, personality inventories are filled out both by the person being evaluated and by others who know that person well. Agreement among the different ratings of the same person adds to the likelihood that the ratings are accurate.

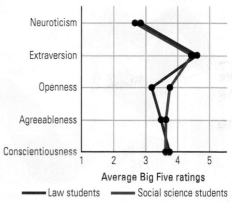

FIGURE 14.2 Personality profiles of law students and social science students at one university Shown here are the average Big Five personality ratings for students studying law and for students studying social sciences at Tel Aviv University, in Israel. The questionnaire used was a Hebrew version of the NEO Personality Inventory. The individual ratings could range from 1 to 5. The differences between the two groups on openness to experience and agreeableness were statistically significant. (Data from Rubinstein, 2005.)

The Relationship of Personality Measures to People's Actual Behavior

How *valid* are personality tests? As discussed in Chapter 2, a test is valid to the degree that its scores are true measures of the characteristics they are meant to measure. A personality test is valid to the degree that scores on each of the traits it measures correlate with aspects of the person's real-world behavior that are relevant to that trait. The validity of personality tests such as the NEO-PI has been supported by countless studies. Here are some examples of correlations between Big Five personality measures and actual behaviors:

- People who score high on *neuroticism,* compared to those who score lower, have been found to (a) pay more attention to, and exhibit better memory of, threats

FOCUS 6

How do researchers assess the validity of personality tests? What are some sample findings that show that measures of the Big Five personality traits are, to at least some degree, valid?

and other unpleasant information (Matthews et al., 2000); (b) manifest more distress when given a surprise math test (Schneider, 2004); (c) experience less marital satisfaction and greater frequency of divorce (Solomon & Jackson, 2014); and (d) be much more susceptible to mental disorders, especially depression and anxiety disorders (Hettema et al., 2004).

● People who score high on *extraversion,* compared to those who score as introverts, have been found to (a) attend more parties and be rated as more popular (Paunonen, 2003); (b) be more often seen as leaders and achieve leadership positions (Roberts et al., 2007); (c) live with and work with more people (Diener et al., 1992); (d) mimic the behavior of others, presumably with the goal of fostering affiliation (Duffy & Chartrand, 2015); and (e) be less disturbed by sudden loud sounds or other intense stimuli (Eysenck, 1990).

"When you lie about yourself, is it to appear closer to or farther away from the middle of the bell curve?"

● People who score high on *openness to experience,* when compared to those who score lower, have been found to (a) be more likely to enroll in liberal arts programs rather than professional training programs in college (Paunonen, 2003); (b) change careers more often in middle adulthood (McCrae & Costa, 1985); (c) perform better in job training programs (Goodstein & Lanyon, 1999); (d) be more likely to play a musical instrument (Paunonen, 2003); (e) be more tolerant of diverse world views (Brandt et al., 2015); and (f) exhibit less racial prejudice (Flynn, 2005).

● People who score high on *agreeableness,* compared to those who score lower, have been found to (a) be more willing to lend money (Paunonen & Ashton, 2001); (b) have fewer behavior problems during childhood (Laursen et al., 2002); (c) manifest less alcoholism or arrests in adulthood (Laursen et al., 2002); (d) are more successful in the workplace (Sackett & Walmsley, 2014); and (e) have more satisfying marriages and a lower divorce rate (Roberts et al., 2007).

● People who score high on *conscientiousness,* compared to those who score lower, have been found to (a) be more sexually faithful to their spouses (Buss, 1996); (b) receive higher ratings for job performance and higher grades in school (Ozer & Benet-Martínez, 2006); (c) put more effort into academic subjects that are uninteresting (Trautwein et al., 2015); and (d) smoke less, drink less, drive more safely, follow more healthful diets, and live longer (Friedman et al., 1995; Roberts et al., 2007).

FOCUS 7

Why might personality traits be most apparent in novel situations or life transitions?

All such findings demonstrate that people's answers to personality test questions reflect, at least to some degree, the ways they actually behave and respond to challenges in the real world.

Personality differences do not reveal themselves equally well in all settings. When you watch people in familiar roles and settings, conforming to well-learned social norms—at their jobs, in the classroom, or at formal functions such as weddings and funerals—the common influence of the situation may override individual personality styles. Personality differences may be most clearly revealed when people are in novel, ambiguous, stressful situations and in life transitions, where cues as to what actions are appropriate are absent or weak (Caspi & Moffitt, 1993). As one pair of researchers put it, in the absence of cues as to how to behave, "the reticent become withdrawn, the irritable become aggressive, and the capable take charge" (Caspi & Moffitt, 1993, p. 250).

■ **A stressful situation** The first day on campus for first-year students is the kind of event that brings out personality differences.

Continuity and Change in Personality Over Time

Does personality change significantly over time in one's life, or is it stable? If you ever have the opportunity to attend the 25th reunion of your high school class, don't miss it; it is bound to be a remarkable experience. Before you stands a person who claims to be your old friend Marty, whom you haven't seen for 25 years. The last time you saw Marty, he was a skinny kid with lots of hair, wearing floppy sneakers and a sweatshirt. What you notice first are the differences: This Marty has a potbelly and very little hair, and he is wearing a business suit. But after talking with him for a few minutes, you have the almost eerie knowledge that this is the same person you used to play basketball with behind the school. The voice is the same, the sparkle in the eyes, the quiet sense of humor, the way of walking. And when it is Marty's turn to stand up and speak to the group, he, who always was the most nervous about speaking before the class, is still most reluctant to do so. There's no doubt about it—this Marty, who now has two kids older than he was when you last saw him, is the same Marty you always knew.

■ **60th reunion of the class of 1941**
After 60 years, these classmates may not have recognized each other at first. But once they began talking and gesturing, so that their personalities came through, they most likely began to see each other as the same individuals they had known as 18-year-old classmates.

But that is all impression. Is he really the same? Perhaps Marty is in some sense *your* construction, and it is your construction that has not changed over the years. Or maybe it's just the situation. This, after all, is a high school reunion held in your old school gymnasium, and maybe you've all been transported back in your minds and are coming across much more like your old selves than you normally would. Maybe you're all trying to be the same kids you were 25 years ago, if only so that your former classmates will recognize you. Clearly, if we really want to answer the question of how consistent personality is over long periods, we've got to be more scientific.

The General Stability of Personality

Many studies have been conducted in which people fill out personality questionnaires, or are rated on personality characteristics by family members or friends, at widely separated times in their lives. The results indicate a rather high stability of personality throughout adulthood. Correlation coefficients on repeated measures of major traits (such as the Big Five) during adulthood typically range from .50 to .70, even with intervals of 30 or 40 years between the first and second tests (Briley & Trucker-Drob, 2014; Terracciano et al., 2006). Such stability apparently cannot be dismissed as resulting from a consistent bias in how individuals fill out personality questionnaires, as similar consistency is found even when the people rating the participants' personalities are not the same in the second test as in the first (Mussen et al., 1980).

 FOCUS 8

What is the evidence that personality is relatively stable throughout adulthood?

Such studies also indicate that personality becomes increasingly stable with increasing age up to about age 50, and it remains at a relatively constant level of stability after age 50 (Caspi et al., 2005; Terracciano et al., 2006). One analysis of many studies, for example, revealed that the average test–retest correlation of personality measures across 7-year periods was .31 in childhood, .54 during young adulthood, .64 at around age 30, and .74 between ages 50 and 70 (Roberts & DelVecchio, 2000). Apparently, the older one gets, up to about age 50, the less one's personality is likely to change. The older you are, the more like "yourself" you become. But some degree of change can occur at any age.

Patterns of Change in Personality With Age

Some of the changes in personality that occur with age are relatively consistent across samplings of individuals and constitute what is commonly thought of as increased *maturity*. Studies in many different cultures on measures of the Big Five indicate that, over the adult years, neuroticism and openness to experience tend to

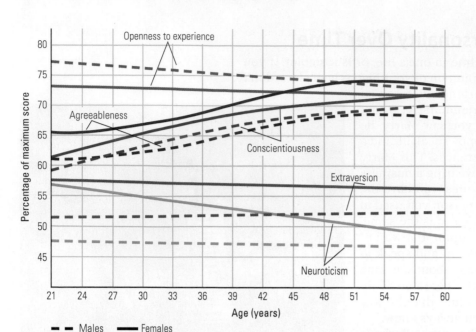

FIGURE 14.3 Average Big Five scores vary somewhat with age and sex This graph depicts the mean scores for men and women on each of the Big Five traits as a function of age. The results are derived from a sample of 132,515 adults, aged 21–60, who completed a version of the Big Five Personality Inventory that was posted on the Internet. Other studies, using more systematically chosen samples, have shown similar results.

(Data from Srivastava et al., 2003)

decline somewhat, and conscientiousness and agreeableness tend to increase somewhat (Caspi et al., 2005; Srivastava et al., 2003). Data from one such study are shown in **Figure 14.3**. Other studies show similar results, but suggest, contrary to the data in the figure, that *agreeableness* continues to increase even into and possibly beyond one's 70s and 80s (Roberts & Mroczek, 2008; Weiss et al., 2005). Such findings are consistent with the general findings of increased life satisfaction in old age, discussed in Chapter 12.

In addition to the general age trends, other research indicates that an individual's personality can change, at least to some degree, in any direction, at any age. The likelihood of change increases when the person experiences a major life change such as a new career, an altered marital status, or the onset of a chronic illness (Helson & Stewart, 1994; Roberts & Mroczek, 2008). Other studies suggest that people who have a particular personality characteristic often make life choices that alter their personality even further in the preexisting direction (Caspi et al., 2005). For example, a highly extraverted person may choose a career that involves a lot of social activity, which may cause the person to become even more extraverted than before.

Genetic Foundations of Personality Traits

Where do traits come from? To some degree, at least, global traits such as the Big Five appear to derive from inherited physiological qualities.

The Heritability of Traits

How heritable are personality traits? As discussed in Chapter 10, *heritability* refers to the degree to which individual differences derive from differences in genes rather than from differences in environmental experiences. Numerous research studies—using the methods described in Chapter 10—have shown that the traits identified by trait theories are rather strongly heritable. The most common approach in these studies has been to administer standard personality questionnaires to pairs of identical twins and fraternal twins (who are no more similar genetically than are ordinary siblings). The usual finding is that identical twins are much more similar than are fraternal twins on every personality dimension measured, similar enough to lead to an average heritability estimate of roughly .50 for most traits, including all of the Big Five (Bouchard, 2004; Bouchard & Loehlin, 2001). Recall from Chapter 10 that a heritability of .50 means that about 50% of the variability among individuals results from genetic differences and the remaining 50% results from environmental differences.

In the past, such findings were criticized on the grounds that parents and others may treat identical twins more similarly than fraternal twins, and similar treatment may lead to similar personality. To get around that possibility, researchers at the University of Minnesota gave personality tests to twins who had been separated in infancy and raised in different homes, as well as to twins raised in the same home (Bouchard, 1991; Tellegen et al., 1988). Their results were consistent with the previous studies: The identical twins were more similar to each other than were

FOCUS 9

How have researchers assessed the heritability of personality traits? What are the general results of such studies?

the fraternal twins on essentially every measure, whether they had been raised in the same home or in different homes, again leading to heritability scores averaging close to .50. Subsequent studies, by other researchers in several different countries, produced similar results (Plomin & Caspi, 1999).

Relative Lack of Shared Effects of the Family Environment

In the past it was common for psychologists to attribute personality characteristics largely to the examples and training that people gain from their mothers and (to a lesser degree) their fathers (Harris, 1998). A common assumption was that people raised in the same family have similar personalities not just because of their shared genes but also because of their shared family environment. Perhaps the most surprising finding in the Minnesota study, confirmed since by other studies, is that this assumption is not true. Being raised in the same family has an almost negligible effect on measures of personality (Bouchard, 2004; Turkheimer & Waldron, 2000). Twin pairs who had been raised in different families were, on average, as similar to—and as different from—each other as were twin pairs who had been raised in the same family.

The contradiction between this finding and long-standing beliefs about the influence of parents is dramatically illustrated by some of the explanations that twins gave for their own behavioral traits (Neubauer & Neubauer, 1996, p. 21). When one young man was asked to explain his almost pathological need to keep his environment neat and clean, he responded, "My mother. When I was growing up she always kept the house perfectly ordered. . . . I learned from her. What else could I do?" When his identical twin brother, who had grown up in a different home in a different country but was also compulsively neat and clean, was asked the same question, he said, "The reason is quite simple. I'm reacting to my mother, who was a complete slob!" In this case the similarity of the twins in their compulsive tendency was almost certainly the result of their shared genetic makeup, yet each one blamed this tendency on his adoptive mother.

The results of such studies of twins do not necessarily mean that the family environment has no influence on personality development. The results do imply, however, that those aspects of the family environment that contribute to personality differentiation are typically as different for people raised in the same family as they are for people raised in different families. Two children raised in the same family may experience that environment very differently from each other.

In work done before the Minnesota twin study, Sandra Scarr and her colleagues (1981) came to a similar conclusion concerning the family environment through a different route. They compared nontwin, adopted children with both their biological siblings (raised in a different home) and with their adoptive siblings (raised in the same home) and found that they were far more similar to their biological siblings than to their adoptive siblings. In fact, for most personality measures, the adoptive siblings, despite being raised in the same home, were on average no more similar to each other than were any two children chosen at random. Later in the chapter we will examine some possible causes of the large individual differences in personality found among children raised in the same family.

Single Genes and the Physiology of Traits

It is reasonable to assume that genes affect personality primarily by influencing physiological characteristics of the nervous system. One likely route by which they might do so is through their influence on neurotransmission in the brain. In line with that view, several laboratories have reported significant correlations between specific personality characteristics and specific genes that alter neurotransmission.

The most consistently replicated such finding concerns the relationship between *neuroticism* and a gene that influences the activity of the neurotransmitter serotonin in the brain. This particular gene (called the 5-HTTLLPR gene, also

FOCUS 10

What evidence suggests that being raised in the same family does not promote similarity in personality?

■ **Identical twins** To study the heritability of personality, researchers at the University of Minnesota located identical twins who had been adopted at an early age and raised in different homes, often in different parts of the country. They paid the twins to come to Minnesota for study, and, as a side effect of the study, reunited twins who had long been separated.

FOCUS 11

How might variation in single genes influence personality?

discussed in Chapter 12) comes in two forms (alleles)—a short (*s*) form and a long (*l*) form. The general finding is that people who are homozygous for the *l* form (that is, have *l* on both paired chromosomes) are on average lower in neuroticism than are people who have at least one *s* allele (Gonda et al., 2009; Schmitz et al., 2007). Serotonin is known to play a role in brain processes involved with emotional excitability, so it is not surprising that variations in serotonin might affect neuroticism.

Other researchers have found a significant relationship between the trait of *novelty seeking*—a more assertive form of openness to experience, which includes elements of impulsiveness, excitability, and extravagance—and alleles that alter the action of the neurotransmitter dopamine (Benjamin et al., 1998; Golimbet et al., 2007). As noted in Chapter 5, dopamine is involved in reward and pleasure systems in the brain, so it is not surprising that alterations in dopamine might affect behaviors that have to do with pleasure seeking.

Such effects are relatively small, and they are not seen in all populations. Variation in personality no doubt derives from the combined effects of many genes interacting with influences of the environment. The effect that any specific gene has on an individual's personality may depend on the mix of other genes that the person carries and on the person's environmental experiences.

SECTION REVIEW

The trait—a relatively stable behavioral predisposition—is a key concept in personality.

Trait Theories

- Factor analysis provides a mathematical means to identify personality traits. Each trait is a continuous dimension, not an all-or-none characteristic.

- Raymond Cattell pioneered this approach, producing a theory with 16 basic traits.

- The most widely accepted trait theory today posits five major traits (neuroticism, extraversion, openness to experience, agreeableness, and conscientiousness), each with six subordinate traits called facets.

- Grit is defined as perseverance and passion for long-term goals and predicts success on task requiring substantial amounts of practice.

- People with "dark" personalities, who score high on the "dark triad" of traits, gain some benefit from their anti-social behavior in some situations.

- Questionnaires designed to measure individuals on the Big Five traits or other traits all require honesty and insight from the respondent to yield accurate results.

Predictive Value of Traits

- All of the Big Five traits have been shown to predict behavior at better-than-chance levels, which helps to establish the validity of the personality measures.

- Studies show that adult personality is relatively stable and becomes more stable with age.

- Correlation coefficients for repeated tests, even many years apart, range from .50 to .70.

- Personality does change, however. Increased age is typically accompanied by increased conscientiousness and agreeableness and decreased neuroticism and openness to experience.

- An individual's personality can change to some extent in any direction at any age, especially in response to life changes.

Genetic Basis of Traits

- Studies comparing pairs of identical and fraternal twins yield heritability estimates for personality averaging about .50.

- The personalities of biological relatives raised in the same family are generally no more similar than those of equally related people raised apart.

- Researchers are searching, with moderate success, for specific gene alleles that contribute to particular traits.

Personality as Adaptation to Life Conditions

Why are people different from one another in personality? Recall from Chapter 3 that psychologists and biologists distinguish between two different types of answers to *why* questions. One type, referred to as *proximate explanation,* focuses on causal mechanisms that operate in the lifetime of the individual to produce the phenomenon in question. Proximate explanations of personality differences focus on ways by which differing genes and experiences work to make us different. The other type of answer, referred to as *distal explanation,* focuses on function, or evolutionary survival value, rather than mechanisms. How might personality differences help individuals survive longer and produce more offspring than they would if all individuals were identical in personality? Why were genetic, developmental, and learning mechanisms that ensure diversity in personality favored by natural selection over mechanisms that would have made us more uniform? These are the questions to which we turn now.

FOCUS 12

How does a distal explanation of personality variability differ from a proximate one?

Advantages of Being Different From One Another

It is conceivable that variability in personality has no adaptive advantage. Perhaps the kinds of differences that personality theorists study simply represent a degree of randomness that could not be weeded out by natural selection. In fact, some evolutionary psychologists have viewed personality traits as by-products or "noise" that have *not* been selected through evolution (Réale et al., 2007; Tooby & Cosmides, 2005). Other evolutionary psychologists think differently, believing that individual differences in personality provide variation among people that may be well suited for a species that lives in a "multi-niche" environment. In this view, natural selection hedges its bets, producing organisms with a range of cognitive and behavioral disposition that may be adaptive for the range of environments it may encounter (Buss, 2009; Ellis et al., 2006). We firmly concur with this latter perspective.

As noted in Chapter 3, sexual reproduction itself seems to be an adaptation that ensures the diversity of offspring. Mixing half of one parent's genes in a random manner with half of the other parent's genes leads to an essentially infinite number of possible new gene combinations in the offspring. From a purely biomechanical point of view, cloning, or asexual reproduction, is a far simpler and less costly form of reproduction than is sexual reproduction, so it is hard to imagine why sexual reproduction would have evolved and persisted if there were no advantage in diversity. It seems equally unlikely that learning mechanisms and other developmental mechanisms that lead us to become different in response to different environmental conditions would have evolved if they didn't produced a survival advantage.

If individual differences in personality are adaptive for survival, we might expect to find them throughout the animal kingdom, and in fact we do. Research on dozens of species of other animals, ranging from ants to fish to chimpanzees, has revealed, in every species tested, individual differences in behavioral styles that can be described in terms similar to those that are used to describe human personality differences (Gosling & John, 1999; Uher, 2008). Many dimensions of personality identified in nonhuman animals have equivalents in the five-factor model (Gosling & John, 1999; Figueredo & King, 2001). For example, *extraversion, neuroticism,* and *agreeableness* have been identified in several species, although *conscientiousness* has only been identified in chimpanzees and humans (see Figueredo et al., 2005).

The conclusion that nonhuman animals have personality probably does not surprise anyone who has owned a dog or a cat. We see personality in our pets. In fact, this is likely one reason these animals were domesticated to be pets. However, the observance of some of the same dimensions of personality in nonhuman animals that we see in ourselves suggests that this variation is not random, that different personalities are likely adapted for certain environmental conditions, and that personality in humans likely has a long evolutionary history. Personality appears to be a basic, biological aspect of animal life.

Diversifying One's Investment in Offspring

One way to think about the value of genetic diversity and personality differences is through an analogy between producing offspring and investing money (Miller, 1997). Investors who put all their money into one company risk going broke if that company suddenly collapses. Smart investors diversify: They invest in a variety of stocks, bonds, and other financial instruments, which are likely to respond differently to economic forces, so that when one goes down, another goes up or at least doesn't go down as rapidly as the first. Diversified investment greatly reduces the potential for dramatic loss while maintaining the potential for substantial gains over the long run.

From the perspective of evolution by natural selection, producing offspring is an investment, the goal of which is to send multiple copies of one's genes into future generations. Since conditions of survival and reproduction vary in unpredictable ways over time, the chance that an individual's genes will die out can be reduced if the offspring differ from one another in some of their characteristics, including their behavioral characteristics. Therefore, over the course of evolution, natural selection would favor mechanisms that ensure diversity of personality in offspring—even the random diversity that results from genetic mixing in sexual reproduction.

The Big Five Traits as Alternative Problem-Solving Strategies

From an evolutionary perspective, personality traits in humans—including the Big Five—can be thought of as alternative general strategies for solving problems related to survival and reproduction (Buss, 1996; Nettle, 2006). Consider, for example, the trait dimension of *extraversion–introversion*. Research has shown that extraverts are more likely than introverts to (a) have many sexual partners, (b) get divorced, and (c) become hospitalized because of accidents (Nettle, 2005). From these data alone, you can well imagine ways in which extraversion could, depending on environmental conditions, either increase or decrease the number of viable offspring a person produces.

Similar analyses can be made of the other Big Five trait dimensions. In terms of psychological health and societal well-being, low *neuroticism* (high emotional stability), high *openness*, high *agreeableness*, and high *conscientiousness* seem to most of us to be more desirable than their opposites. However, you can imagine conditions in which the opposite ends of these dimensions might better promote survival and reproduction.

In truly dangerous conditions, the worry and vigilance shown by individuals high in *neuroticism* could save lives. In some social situations, the conservative values and closed-mindedness of those low in *openness* could lead to more stable family lives and more children than would be achieved by persons high in openness. Much as we all admire *agreeableness,* we must admit that disagreeable people sometimes do get their way, and in some life conditions this could happen often enough to make meanness more viable, in evolutionary terms, than niceness. *Conscientiousness* has to do with pursuing long-term goals and not being distracted by short-term impulses, but in some life conditions long-term goals are not likely to work out anyway and an opportunistic, impulsive approach to life could be more conducive to survival and reproduction.

The finding that individual differences on trait dimensions are partly heritable and partly the product of environmental experience is also consistent with the

■ **A family famous for boldness** The members of the Kennedy clan are well known for their willingness to take risks in their political and personal lives. This photograph, taken in 1938, shows Joseph Kennedy (far left) with his wife Rose (far right) and their children (left to right): Patricia, John (who became the 35th president of the United States), Jean, Eunice, Robert, Kathleen, Edward, Rosemary, and Joseph. The subsequent histories of these people and of their own children offer repeated examples of triumphs and tragedies resulting from risky actions.

evolutionary perspective. In an environment that varies unpredictably, the chances that at least some offspring will survive are enhanced if the offspring are genetically inclined toward different life strategies. Genetic inclinations need to be flexible, however, so that individuals can move along a personality dimension in a direction compatible with their life situation. People who are genetically inclined toward introversion can become more bold and extraverted if their condition of life promotes or requires such adaptation. (If I [Peter Gray] had to make my living selling books rather than writing them, then even I, a prototypical introvert, might become a bit less introverted.)

Differential Susceptibility to Environmental Influence

Personality traits are viewed as relatively stable characteristics of a person. Although context clearly affects how we behave, a trait implies stability, a degree of permanency about an individual. However, researchers have discovered one trait that is associated not with stability but with change: ***differential susceptibility to environmental influence*** (Belsky & Pluess, 2009; Pluess et al., 2013).

Jay Belsky and his colleagues (2007; Belsky, 2005) have proposed that children with fearful, anxious, and "difficult" dispositions are more sensitive to the effects of parenting than other children. According to Belsky, such environmentally sensitive children will readily change their behavior and personalities to novel environments, both positive (lots of family support) and negative (father absence, little family support). As a result, these children may fare especially poorly in less-than-optimal environments, but do particularly well in supportive environments. In other words, such children are affected by their environment both *for better* and *for worse* (Boyce & Ellis, 2005; Ellis & Boyce, 2011). In contrast, other children are more stable and less influenced by extreme environments.

Bruce Ellis and W. Thomas Boyce (2008) described sensitive children (children who are *biologically sensitive to context,* to use their term) as *orchid children*. Like orchids, when they receive loving care they flourish, but they quickly wilt when the environment is not supportive. In contrast, *dandelion children* can survive, and perhaps thrive, in any environment. Through natural selection, parents can unwittingly hedge their bets by producing both types of children, some who will be receptive to change brought about by unanticipated environments, and others who will thrive in an "expected" environment. The relation between positive and negative outcomes in terms of psychological functioning for sensitive and less sensitive children is illustrated in **Figure 14.4**.

Differential susceptibility to environmental influence can be seen in studies assessing the psychological outcomes of highly sensitive and less-sensitive children, living in high-stress or low-stress home environments. For example, in one study by Jelena Obradović and her colleagues (2010), 5- to 6-year-old children were classified as having high or low neurobiological stress reactivity based on their respiratory sinus arrhythmia (RSA), which is a measure of the nervous system's response to stress reflected in variation in heart rate during the respiratory cycle. Changes in RSA are a measure of children's ability to regulate reactions to positive and negative environmental stimuli. Children were further classified with respect to home adversity, with adversity being based on measures of family financial stress, maternal depression, and use of harsh parenting techniques, among others. Measures of psychological adjustment included externalizing behavior (e.g., acting out, conduct disorder,

FOCUS 15

What is meant by orchid and dandelion children, and how do they relate to the idea of differential susceptibility to environmental influences?

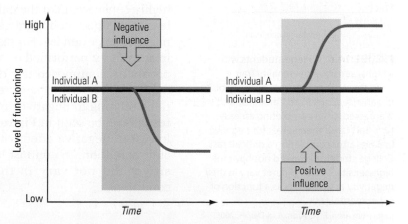

FIGURE 14.4 Differential susceptibility to environmental influences Individual A (orchid child) possesses the "high sensitivity" trait and is thus more adversely affected by negative influences (left side of figure) but also more positively affected by positive influences (right side of figure). Individual B (dandelion child) is less susceptible to environmental influences; his or her psychological functioning is less impacted by both positive and negative events. One would not expect people with low susceptibility to environmental influences to be immune from either positive or negative events, but rather to be less affected by them than highly sensitive individuals.

(Data from Pluess & Belsky, 2012)

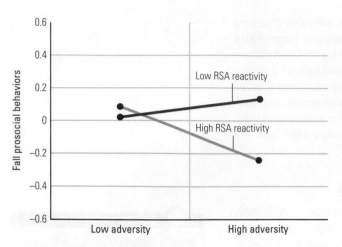

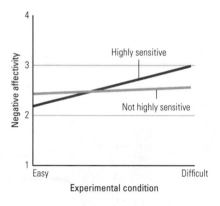

FIGURE 14.5 Highly sensitive children, as reflected by high respiratory sinus arrhythmia (RSA), showed the highest level of prosocial behaviors when growing up in low-adversity homes, but the lowest level of prosocial behaviors when growing up in high-adversity homes.

(Data from Obradović et al., 2010)

FIGURE 14.6 College students with a highly sensitive personality trait rated themselves lower on a survey of negative feelings ("sad," "anxious," and "depressed") after completing an easy task, and rated themselves for negative feelings after completing a difficult task. College students who did not have the high-sensitivity trait did not vary in their negativity assessments as a function of experimental task.

(Data from Aron, E. N., Aron, A., & Davies, 2005)

overt hostility), prosocial behaviors, and school performance. The researchers reported that children high in stress reactivity (the highly sensitive, or orchid, children) displayed poorer adjustment (increased externalizing behavior, decreased prosocial behavior, poor school performance) when growing up in high-adversity environments, but better adjustment when growing up in low-adversity environments. The less-sensitive children (the dandelion children) displayed less change for most measures as a result of level of adversity. This pattern is displayed for prosocial behaviors in **Figure 14.5**. Similar patterns of results have been reported with respect to respiratory infections in high- and low-reactive preschoolers living in high- or low-stress homes (Boyce et al., 1995), and for psychological outcomes in response to supportive and less-supportive parenting for temperamentally prone-to-distress (highly sensitive) infants (Poehlmann et al., 2012).

Behavioral genetic research has identified a gene associated with susceptibility to parental influence (Bakermans-Kranenburg et al., 2008; Goldberg et al., 2013). In one study, parents of 1- to 3-year-old children with high levels of externalizing behavior (e.g., conduct disorder) took part in a "positive parenting" program. One year after completing the program, children who had one version of an allele associated with a dopamine receptor showed significant reductions in externalizing behavior, relative to children in a control group whose parents did not participate in the positive-parenting program. In contrast, children with a different allele displayed no change in externalizing behavior.

In research from a more traditional "personality" tradition, Elaine Aron and her colleagues have identified a *highly sensitive personality* (HSP) trait, in which people are more aware of subtleties in their surroundings, process experiences more deeply, and are more easily overwhelmed in highly stimulating environments (Aron & Aron, 1997; Aron et al., 2012). Elaine Aron and Arthur Aron (1997) developed a questionnaire to identify highly sensitive people. Examples of items on the questionnaire are: "I notice when small things have changed in my environment," "I don't like loud noises," "I find it unpleasant to have a lot going on at once," and "When someone observes me I get nervous. This makes me perform worse than normal." Based on such questionnaires, about 20% of people can be described as highly sensitive. Like the children described in the study by Obradović and her colleagues (2010), such highly sensitive people are more affected by both positive and negative experiences. For example, in one study, college students rated high or low in sensitivity performed either an easy or a difficult task (performing either well or poorly on a supposed test of reasoning abilities, which was "fixed" by the experimenters). The subjects were then given a brief personality survey, with key questions relating to negative emotions (feeling "sad," "anxious," and "depressed"). The results can be seen in **Figure 14.6**. The highly sensitive college students scored the lowest in negative affectivity in the "easy" condition and the highest in the "difficult" condition. In contrast, the college students who were rated as "not highly sensitive" did not vary in their assessments of negative emotions in the two conditions.

Adapting to the Family Environment

The first social environment to which most human beings must adapt is that of the family into which they are born. The first view of other people, the first attempts at communication, the first emotional attachments, the first strivings for acceptance and approval, and the first competitions with others for resources usually occur within the context of the family. Children come into the world with nervous systems predisposed for behaving in certain ways, but those ways of behaving are first exercised and built upon within the family.

Yet, some psychologists contend that the family environment plays little or no role in shaping personality (Harris, 1998; Rowe, 1994). That contention stems primarily from the research indicating that people who were raised in the same home score, on average, just about as differently from one another on personality tests as do equally related people who were raised in different homes. To the degree that siblings are similar to one another in global personality traits, that similarity seems to come mainly from their shared genes, not from their shared home environment.

One response to such findings and arguments has been to suggest that siblings raised in the same home, by the same parents, might nevertheless experience quite different environments (Dunn & Plomin, 1990; Vernon et al., 1997). The same family may influence two siblings in different ways, causing divergence in personalities as often as it causes convergence. Chance events may play a role. For example, one child may have an accident or extended illness that leads to extensive care from the parents not given to the other child. In other cases preexisting differences between siblings may lead to differential parental responses, which magnify the preexisting differences. For example, one child may become labeled as the "good child" and the other as the "problem child," and these may be associated with parental responses that cause the labels to become self-fulfilling prophesies. Preexisting personality differences might also lead siblings to interpret the same objective events quite differently, with different consequences for their further development. For example, a parent's persistent demands that chores be done might be understood by one child as a caring act designed to instill good work habits and by another as harsh discipline. There is evidence that siblings indeed do have different family experiences for all these kinds of reasons (Dunn & Plomin, 1990).

Sibling Contrast: Carving Out a Unique Niche Within the Family

Preexisting small differences between siblings may become exaggerated in part because siblings tend to define themselves as different from one another and tend to accentuate those differences through their own behavioral choices (Lalumière et al., 1996). When people are asked to describe their brother or sister, they commonly begin by saying, in effect, "Oh, he (or she) is entirely different from me," and then proceed to point out how (Dunn & Plomin, 1990). Parents likewise tend to focus more on differences than on similarities when they describe two or more of their children (Schachter, 1982). This within-family emphasis on the differences between siblings is referred to as **sibling contrast**.

Possibly related to sibling contrast is **split-parent identification**, defined as a tendency for each of two siblings to identify with a different one of their two parents. If the first child identifies more strongly with the mother, the second typically identifies more strongly with the father, and vice versa. Sibling contrast and split-parent identification have been documented as highly reliable phenomena in questionnaires filled out by parents as well as in those filled out by the siblings themselves (Schachter, 1982).

"And then, as soon as I had carved out my niche, they went and had another kid."

Why do family members accentuate the differences rather than the similarities between siblings? A possible answer, proposed by Frances Schachter (1982), is that sibling contrast and split-parent identification are devices by which parents and children consciously or unconsciously strive to reduce sibling rivalry, which can be highly disruptive to family functioning. If siblings are seen by themselves and their parents as having very different abilities, needs, and dispositions, then the siblings are less likely to compete with one another and more likely to be valued and rewarded separately for their unique characteristics.

If Aliya is understood to be reserved and scholarly and her sister Brianna is understood to be outgoing and athletic, then Aliya and Brianna can be appreciated by their parents and by each other for their separate traits rather than viewed as

---

FOCUS 16

How might sibling contrast and split-parent identification be useful in reducing sibling rivalry and diversifying parental investment?

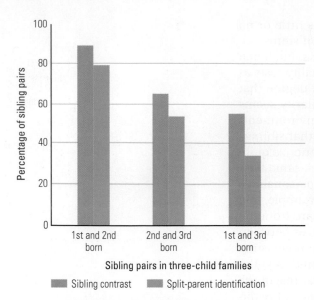

FIGURE 14.7 Sibling contrast and split-parent identification in three-child families Mothers were asked to compare pairs of their children by stating whether the two were similar or different on various personality dimensions and by stating which parent each child identified with more strongly. *Sibling contrast* (orange bars) refers to the percentage of times that the mothers said "different" rather than "alike" in response to personality questions. *Split-parent identification* (blue bars) refers to the percentage of times two siblings were said to identify with different parents rather than with the same parent.

(Data from Schachter, 1982)

competitors on the same dimension—a competition that one of them would have to lose. From an evolutionary perspective, such differentiation may promote the survival of the two siblings and other members of their family not only by reducing rivalry but also by diversifying the parental investment (Lalumière et al., 1996; Sulloway, 1996). To the degree that Aliya and Brianna move into different life niches, they will compete less with each other for limited resources both within the family and in the larger environment outside the family, and they may develop separate skills through which they can help each other and the family as a whole.

In support of the view that sibling contrast and split-parent identification serve to reduce sibling rivalry, Schachter (1982) found that both phenomena are much stronger for adjacent pairs of siblings than for pairs who are separated in birth order (see **Figure 14.7**) and stronger for same-sex pairs of siblings than for opposite-sex pairs. Other researchers have also found greater sibling contrast for siblings who are close in age than for those who are more distant in age (Feinberg & Hetherington, 2000). It seems reasonable that siblings who are the same sex, adjacent to each other in birth order, and close in age would be most subject to implicit comparisons and possible rivalries and would therefore have the greatest need to reduce rivalry through contrast and split-parent identification.

The observation that sibling contrast and split-parent identification are strongest for the first two children in a family (shown in Figure 14.7) is likewise consistent with the rivalry-reduction hypothesis. The first two children are likely to experience the greatest degree of sibling rivalry because, for a period of time, they are the only two children being compared. When third and subsequent children come along, multiple comparisons can be made, so the intensity of comparisons between any two, and the potential for rivalry between them, may be somewhat muted.

Adapting to One's Gender

We do not choose our sex. Pure chance normally decides sex—XX, you're a female; XY, you're a male. Then, throughout life, most of us live with that assignment. What consequences might our biological sex have for personality?

Some Gender Differences in Personality

FOCUS 17

What differences have researchers found between women and men in personality traits?

Standard personality tests reveal relatively consistent differences between men and women in average scores on many personality traits (Costa et al., 2001; Schmitt et al., 2008). These differences hold across diverse cultures (De Bolle et al., 2015), though most are small to moderate in size. One of the largest and most consistent of such differences, found in essentially every culture where tests have been conducted, is that women score higher than men in agreeableness (e.g., refer back to Figure 14.3 on page 544). Many other studies, using a variety of measures, also show that women are, on average, more concerned than men with developing and maintaining positive social relationships (Kashima et al., 1995; Taylor et al., 2000).

Relatively consistent gender differences have also been observed in neuroticism, primarily because women report higher levels of anxiety and feelings of vulnerability than do men (Grijalva et al., 2015). Women also generally score slightly but significantly higher on conscientiousness. Results on the other two Big Five trait dimensions are more varied. Women tend to score considerably higher than men on the warmth and gregariousness facets of extraversion, but considerably lower on the excitement-seeking facet of that trait (McCrae & Terracciano, 2005). Women also tend to score considerably higher than men on the feelings and aesthetics facets of openness to experience, but not on the other four facets of that trait: fantasy, actions, ideas, and values (McCrae & Terracciano, 2005).

Gender not only influences the kind of personality one develops, it also affects the relationship of personality to life satisfaction (Rothbart & Bates, 1998). For example, researchers have found that shyness or behavioral inhibition correlates positively with feelings of emotional distress and unhappiness in young men but not in young women (Gest, 1997). That difference is not present in early childhood but seems to emerge in adolescence and reach a peak in young adulthood. A possible explanation lies in cultural expectations that make life more difficult for shy or inhibited young men than for similarly shy or inhibited young women. In Western culture and all others that have been studied, men are generally expected to initiate romantic and sexual relationships and to be more assertive or dominant in social interactions of all types, whereas shyness or lack of assertion is considered more attractive in women than in men.

"You've had to be kind to survive, and I've had to be nasty."

In other respects, too, personality dispositions that run counter to stereotypes can have social and emotional costs. Women who have a relatively competitive orientation toward others, rather than an orientation emphasizing similarity and agreeableness, typically score lower on measures of self-esteem than do other women, while the opposite is true for men (Josephs et al., 1992). Men who are high in neuroticism are viewed more negatively than are women who are high in that trait (Ozer & Benet-Martínez, 2006).

Evolutionary Foundations of Gender Differences

As noted earlier, personality measures are merely descriptions, not explanations, of psychological differences among people. What accounts for the just-described average differences between women and men on personality measures? In addressing that question, some psychologists focus on evolutionary history, and others focus on the present-day pressures and expectations of the cultures in which we develop.

Personality theorists who favor evolutionary explanations of gender differences (Larsen & Buss, 2008) point to the universality of certain gender differences and to the long history of evolution in which males and females were subject to different reproductive challenges generation after generation. Females' greater role in child care, and perhaps a need for cooperative relationships with other adults in relation to child care, may have led to selection for personality qualities promoting nurturance, cooperation, and caution; whereas males' greater need to compete in order to reproduce may have led to selection for competitiveness, aggressiveness, and risk taking.

Consistent with this evolutionary perspective, Shelley Taylor and her colleagues (2000) have amassed considerable evidence that male and female mammals in general, including humans, tend to respond differently to stressful situations. Whereas males tend to respond to stress by becoming more aggressive, females tend to respond by becoming more nurturant and more motivated to strengthen social connections. According to Taylor, females are more likely than males to attempt to placate their rivals rather than intimidate them, and more likely to seek comfort and support from friends. This difference, of course, is not all or none, but a matter of degree, and there is considerable overlap between the sexes. Taylor also summarizes evidence that sex differences in hormones contribute to these differences in personality (Taylor, 2006; Taylor et al., 2000). Oxytocin, which is at higher levels in females than in males, tends to promote affiliation; and testosterone, which is at higher levels in males, tends to promote aggression.

Cultural Foundations of Gender Differences

Cultural theorists, in contrast, point to the different experiences, expectations, role models, and opportunities provided by the culture for girls and boys (as discussed in Chapter 12). From the cultural perspective, the most relevant niches to think

---

FOCUS 18

How might gender differences in personality be understood in terms of natural selection? What evidence suggests that hormones may provide a basis for such differences?

FOCUS 19

What evidence supports the view that gender differences in personality are at least partly shaped by cultural expectations?

Erik Holladay/NCAA Photos via Getty Images

■ **Becoming assertive** In the 30 years from 1970 to 2000, girls' and women's participation in formal sports increased by nearly tenfold (Twenge, 2001). Perhaps such cultural changes help to explain the increased assertiveness of women, as measured by personality tests that occurred over that same period.

about are not those existing in past generations of humans and prehumans but those in existence right now (Bussey & Bandura, 1999; Wood & Eagly, 2002). The immediate causes of gender differences in personality are social forces that encourage girls to develop the nurturant, agreeable, and conscientious aspects of their nature and boys to develop their competitive, aggressive, and risk-taking aspects.

Consistent with the cultural explanation is evidence that some gender differences in personality have changed, over historical time, in keeping with changing social roles and expectations. In particular, a systematic analysis of scores on various tests of *assertiveness,* given to men and women in the United States between 1931 and 1993, revealed that gender differences in this trait changed over time in keeping with changes in the culture (Twenge, 2001). During the Great Depression and World War II, when women were generally expected to be self-sufficient, personality tests revealed relatively small gender differences in assertiveness. After the war, and through the 1950s and early 1960s, however, women were generally expected to be passive and domestic, and during those years women's scores on assertiveness tests declined considerably while men's scores remained relatively constant. Beginning in the mid-1960s, however, women entered the workforce in ever-increasing numbers and took on roles previously considered to be masculine, and their assertiveness scores subsequently increased. In fact, some studies suggest that by the end of the twentieth century women's average assertiveness scores were as high as men's (Twenge, 2001).

Another route to assessing the role of culture in male–female personality differences is to examine gender differences cross-culturally. In an analysis of Big Five personality scores for men and women in 55 different countries, David Schmitt and his colleagues (2008) found—contrary to what you might expect—that gender differences in personality were *greater* in developed, prosperous, egalitarian countries than in relatively undeveloped, poor, traditional cultures. Overall, women tended to score higher than men in neuroticism, extraversion, agreeableness, and conscientiousness, and this difference was significantly greater in countries such as France, the Netherlands, Canada, and the United States than in countries like Ethiopia, Malaysia, Botswana, and Indonesia. How might this finding be explained?

Schmitt and his colleagues interpret the results as support for the idea of inherent biological personality differences between men and women. They suggest that in wealthier, more egalitarian countries, where people are freer to choose their own routes in life, men and women choose ways of life that are consistent with and reinforce their inborn personality traits. Consistent with this interpretation is evidence that as women have become more accepted in traditionally male roles in developed countries, women have brought a more feminine orientation to those roles. Women business leaders, for example, are on average more likely to lead through nurturance and encouragement, and to exert greater conscientiousness and less aggressiveness, than men occupying similar positions (Eagly, 2007). Thus, increased freedom of occupational choice in wealthier countries may be accompanied by increased flexibility within each occupational role so that people of either gender can bring their personality strengths to bear rather than modify their personalities to fit the job. This explanation of the cross-cultural findings is speculation, but interesting speculation.

SECTION REVIEW

Personality differences may represent alternative adaptations to life's variable conditions.

Advantages of Being Different	Adapting to the Family Environment	Adapting to One's Gender
■ Just as diversified investments help protect one's financial future in a world of unpredictable change, diverse personalities may protect one's genetic investment.	■ Siblings raised together may experience quite different environments, for reasons that include chance events, consequences of their own choices, and differences in how they interpret the same occurrences.	■ On average, women score slightly to moderately higher than men on agreeableness, neuroticism, and conscientiousness.
■ Human variations in the Big Five traits can be viewed as alternative strategies for survival and reproduction.	■ The tendency to exaggerate differences between siblings (sibling contrast) and the tendency for siblings to identify with different parents (split-parent identification) may reduce sibling rivalry and diversify parental investment.	■ Apparently because of cultural pressures, some personality characteristics that run counter to gender stereotypes correlate with unhappiness. For example, shy young men are generally less happy than shy young women.
■ Some individuals are more susceptible to environmental influences than others, often faring the best in highly supportive environments and the worst in nonsupportive environments.		■ Both evolutionary and cultural forces may help to account for gender differences in personality. There is evidence that these differences are greater in modern Western cultures than in more traditional cultures.

Personality as Mental Processes I: Psychodynamic and Humanistic Views

Trait theories, such as the five-factor model, are useful as general schemes for describing human psychological differences and for thinking about possible functions of those differences. Such theories have little to say, however, about the internal mental processes that lead people to behave in particular ways. The rest of this chapter is devoted to ideas about the mental underpinnings of personality.

We begin by examining two very general, classic theoretical perspectives on personality: the psychodynamic and humanistic perspectives. These two perspectives derive largely from the observations and speculations of clinical psychologists, who were attempting to make sense of the symptoms and statements of their clients or patients. These two perspectives also provide much of the basis for the general public's understanding of psychology.

Elements of the Psychodynamic Perspective

The pioneer of clinical psychology, and of the clinical approach to understanding personality, was Sigmund Freud (1856–1939). Freud was a physician who specialized in neurology and, from 1886 on, worked with patients at his private office in Vienna. He found that many people who came to him had no detectable medical problems; their suffering seemed rooted in their memories, especially memories of disturbing events in their childhoods. Many patients could not actually recall such memories consciously, but clues in their behavior led Freud to believe that disturbing memories were present nevertheless, buried in what he referred to as the *unconscious mind*. From this insight, Freud developed a method of treatment in which his patients would talk freely about themselves and he would analyze what they said in order to uncover buried memories and hidden emotions and motives. The goal was to make the patient conscious of his or her unconscious memories, motives, and emotions so that the patient's conscious mind could work out ways of dealing with them.

FOCUS 20

What characteristics of the mind underlie personality differences, according to the psychodynamic perspective?

■ **Sigmund Freud** The founder of psychoanalysis viewed himself as a detective whose task was to use cues in people's behavior to uncover the secrets of their unconscious minds.

Freud coined the term ***psychoanalysis*** to refer both to his method of treatment (discussed in Chapter 16) and to his theory of personality. Freud's psychoanalytic theory was the first of what today are called ***psychodynamic theories***—personality theories that emphasize the interplay of mental forces (the word *dynamic* refers to energy or force and *psycho* refers to mind). Two guiding premises of psychodynamic theories are that (a) people are often unconscious of their motives and (b) processes called *defense mechanisms* work within the mind to keep unacceptable or anxiety-producing motives and thoughts out of consciousness. According to psychodynamic theories, personality differences lie in variations in people's unconscious motives, in how those motives are manifested, and in the ways that people defend themselves from anxiety.

Freud also believed that personality developed in a series of stages: oral, anal, phallic, latency, and genital stages (**see Table 14.4**). He saw the sex drive as a primary instinct, expressed at all stages of life, and proposed that the main source of pleasure satisfaction, or tension reduction, is centered on specific bodily zones, called *erogenous zones*. (We should note that Freud often used the word "sexuality" in a broader sense than laypeople do; in his usage it was often a synonym for "looking for pleasure.") These zones change through the course of development, with erogenous centers shifting from the oral to the anal area in early childhood, and then eventually to the genital area. According to Freud, how parents deal with their children's sexual (or pleasure-seeking) impulses has significant consequences for their later development. Although Freud's stage theory is one of the best known in psychology, there is little research evidence supporting it, and few personality or developmental psychologists today take his stage theory seriously; for that reason we will not discuss it further here.

The Concept of Unconscious Motivation

Freud proposed that the main causes of behavior lie deeply buried in the unconscious mind—that is, in the part of the mind that affects the individual's conscious thought and action but is not itself open to conscious inspection. The reasons people give to explain their behavior often are not the true causes. To illustrate this

TABLE 14.4 Freud's psychosexual stages of development and approximate ages

Freud proposed that the sex drive is a primary instinct, expressed at all stages in life, and is centered on various erogenous zones of the body, with these zones changing with age.	
Oral Stage (birth to 1 year)	During the earliest period of development, sexual excitation is centered around the mouth. Sucking, chewing, eating, and biting produce pleasure. These early forms of gratification become associated with the satisfaction of hunger. The most important accomplishment of the oral stage is the infant's attachment to its mother—the basis for all later intimate relations.
Anal Stage (1 to 3 years)	Beginning around the end of the first year, children's focus changes to the anal area. This does not mark the termination of oral needs; rather the oral needs exist alongside the anal needs, with the latter becoming increasingly important. Freud proposed how parents deal with toilet training at this time has important implications for future personality development.
Phallic Stage (3 to 5 years)	Children's attention is now diverted to the genital area. At this time boys become cognizant that they possess a penis (phallus) and girls become aware they do not. The main accomplishment of this stage is the resolution of the Oedipus complex in boys and the Electra complex in girls, when children's sexual focus becomes the parent of the opposite sex.
Latency Stage (5 years to the beginning of puberty)	Freud proposed that the first three stages of psychosexual development are characterized by constant conflict between children's sexual desires and their parents' wishes to socialize them, with children actively repressing memories from these years. Conflicts diminish during the latency stage, where no part of the body arouses sexual tension and children seem to forget the sexual urges and conflicts of earlier years. Children begin to disengage from family and interact more with peers. They become truly social beings, generally playing in same-sex groups and directing their sexual energy into nonsexual, mainly social areas.
Genital Stage (adolescence and adulthood)	With the onset of puberty, sexual impulses, repressed during the latency stage, come to the fore. These new, more mature sexual urges are directed toward same-age members of the opposite sex.

idea, Freud (1912/1932) drew an analogy between everyday behavior and the phenomenon of posthypnotic suggestion.

In a demonstration of posthypnotic suggestion, a person is hypnotized and given an instruction such as "When you awake, you will not remember what happened during hypnosis. However, when the clock chimes, you will walk across the room, pick up the umbrella lying there, and open it." When awakened, the subject appears to behave in a perfectly normal, self-directed way until the clock chimes. At this signal the subject consciously senses an irresistible impulse to perform the commanded action, and consciously performs it, but has no conscious memory of the origin of the impulse (the hypnotist's command). If asked why he or she is opening the umbrella, the subject may come up with a plausible though clearly false reason, such as "I thought I should test it because it may rain later." According to Freud, the real reasons behind our everyday actions are likewise hidden in our unconscious minds, and our conscious reasons are cover-ups, plausible but false rationalizations that we believe to be true.

Freud believed that to understand his patients' actions, problems, and personalities, he had to learn about the contents of their unconscious minds. But how could he do that when the unconscious, by definition, consists only of information that the patient cannot talk about? He claimed he could do it by analyzing certain aspects of their speech and other observable behavior to draw inferences about their unconscious motives. This is where the term *psychoanalysis* comes from. His technique was to sift the patient's behavior for clues to the unconscious. Like a detective, he collected clues and tried to piece them together into a coherent story about the unconscious causes of the person's conscious thoughts and actions.

Because the conscious mind always attempts to act in ways that are consistent with conventional logic, Freud reasoned that the elements of thought and behavior that are least logical would provide the best clues to the unconscious. They would represent elements of the unconscious mind that leaked out relatively unmodified by consciousness. Freud therefore paid particular attention to his patients' slips of the tongue and other mistakes as clues to the unconscious. He also asked them to describe their dreams and to report in uncensored fashion whatever thoughts came to mind in response to particular words or phrases. These methods are described more fully in Chapter 16.

FOCUS 21

How is the concept of unconscious motivation illustrated by posthypnotic suggestion?

Sex and Aggression as Motivating Forces in Freud's Theory

Unlike most modern psychologists, Freud considered drives to be analogous to physical forms of energy that build up over time and must somehow be released. To live peaceably in society (especially in the Victorian society that Freud grew up in), people must often inhibit direct expressions of the sexual and aggressive drives, so these are the drives that are most likely to build up and exert themselves in indirect ways. Freud concluded from his observations that much of human behavior consists of disguised manifestations of sex and aggression and that personality differences lie in the different ways that people disguise and channel these drives. Over time, Freud (1933/1964) came to define these drives increasingly broadly. He considered the sex drive to be the main pleasure-seeking and life-seeking drive and the aggressive drive to be the force that lies behind all sorts of destructive actions, including actions that harm oneself.

FOCUS 22

How did Freud draw inferences about the content of his clients' unconscious minds?

Social Drives as Motives in Other Psychodynamic Theories

Freud viewed people as basically asocial, forced to live in societies more by necessity than by desire, and whose social interactions derive primarily from sex, aggression, and displaced forms of these drives. In contrast, most psychodynamic theorists since Freud's time have viewed people as inherently social beings whose motives for interacting with others extend well beyond sex and aggression.

*"Of course I'm feeling uncomfortable.
I'm not allowed on the couch."*

For example, Alfred Adler developed a psychodynamic theory that centers on people's drive to feel competent. Adler (1930) contended that everyone begins life with a feeling of inferiority, which stems from the helpless and dependent nature of early childhood, and that the manner in which people learn to cope with or to overcome this feeling provides the basis for their lifelong personalities. According to Adler, people who become overwhelmed by a sense of inferiority will develop either an *inferiority complex,* and go through life acting incompetent and dependent, or a *superiority complex,* and go through life trying to prove they are better than others as a means of masking their inferiority.

Perhaps the most "social" of Freud's followers was Erik Erikson (1950, 1968), who proposed a *psychosocial* theory of development. Erikson believed in the psychosexual stages postulated by Freud (oral, anal, phallic, latency, and genital), as well as the three-part structure of the mind (id, ego, and superego) and the importance of the unconscious. However, unlike Freud, Erikson emphasized the role of society in shaping personality. Other people, and society in general, place demands on people as they develop, and how children (and later adults) handle these demands affects their personalities. In addition, Erikson believed that important developmental milestones extended beyond childhood into adulthood and old age.

Erikson proposed eight stages of psychosocial development, beginning at birth and continuing through the life span. As described in Chapter 12, Erikson believed that people face conflicts, or crises, at each of these stages in their relationships with other people, and how they deal with the crisis at one stage influences how they will deal with crises at the next and following stages. **Table 14.5** summarizes Erikson's eight stages of development.

In all psychodynamic theories, including Freud's, the first few years of life are especially crucial in forming the personality. One's earliest attempts to satisfy drives result in positive or negative responses from others that, taken together, have lifelong effects on how those drives are subsequently manifested.

The Idea That the Mind Defends Itself Against Anxiety

A central idea in all psychodynamic theories is that mental processes of self-deception, known as **defense mechanisms**, operate to reduce one's consciousness of wishes, memories, and other thoughts that would threaten one's self-esteem or in other ways provoke a strong sense of insecurity or anxiety. The theory of defense mechanisms was most thoroughly developed by Anna Freud (1936/1946), Sigmund's daughter, who was also a prominent psychoanalyst. Some examples of defense mechanisms are repression, displacement, reaction formation, projection, and rationalization.

Repression (discussed more fully in the next section) is the process by which anxiety-producing thoughts are pushed out or kept out of the conscious mind. In Freud's theory, repression provides the basis for most of the other defense mechanisms. Freud visualized repression as a damming up of mental energy. Just as water will leak through any crack in a dam, repressed wishes and memories will leak through the barriers separating the unconscious mind from the conscious mind. When such thoughts leak through, however, the mind can still defend itself by distorting the ideas in ways that make them less threatening. The other defense mechanisms are the various means by which we create such distortions.

Displacement occurs when an unconscious wish or drive that would be unacceptable to the conscious mind is redirected toward a more acceptable alternative. For example, a child long past infancy may still have a desire to suck at the mother's breast—a desire that is now threatening and repressed because it violates the child's conscious understanding of what is proper and possible. The desire might be displaced toward sucking on a lollipop, an action that is symbolically equivalent to the original desire but more acceptable and realistic.

In some cases, displacement may direct one's energies toward activities that are particularly valued by society, such as artistic, scientific, or humanitarian endeavors.

FOCUS 23

How do repression, displacement, reaction formation, projection, and rationalization each serve to defend against anxiety?

TABLE 14.5 Erikson's psychosocial stages of development with approximate ages

Stage 1: Basic trust versus mistrust (birth to 1 year)
During the first year, when infants receive warm maternal care and have their needs met as they arise, they develop a sense of basic trust. They come to believe that people are dependable and that the world is a safe place. If such needs are not met, mistrust develops. Developing basic trust prepares the child to deal with the crises that arise as he or she grows older.
Stage 2: Autonomy versus shame and doubt (1 to 3 years)
In the second and third years, parental support and encouragement for the newly developed skills of crawling, walking, climbing, and exploring can promote the child's sense of autonomy. However, children may try new skills but fail to achieve their goals. Also, this stage corresponds to Freud's anal period, and "accidents" with toilet training are common. If parents ridicule children's failures and insist upon doing things for children that they can do for themselves, a sense of shame or doubt may develop.
Stage 3: Initiative versus guilt (3 to 6 years)
Young children learn the roles of society by engaging in fantasy play, setting goals for themselves and attaining them, and competing with other children. Parental support and encouragement for such self-initiated activities promotes the development of a sense of initiative. In contrast, when parents insist on too much self-control and competence in their children, criticize their attempts at adult-like behavior, make fun of their fantasy play, and treat their questions as a nuisance, a sense of guilt can develop.
Stage 4: Industry versus inferiority (6 years to puberty)
School-aged children's increased cognitive abilities motivate them to explore how things work and how they are made, from the mechanisms of a clock and a car engine to the changing seasons. Children who are encouraged to build or make things (birdhouses, cookies, model cars) and who are praised for their accomplishments develop a sense of industry. However, parents who see children's efforts as a nuisance and concentrate on the mess they make rather than the products of their labor may develop a sense of inferiority. Unlike Freud, Erikson believed that social institutions (school, sports, religious organizations, scouting, etc.) influence children's development substantially, beginning with this stage.
Stage 5: Identity versus identity confusion (12 to 18 years)
Each conflict resolution up to this point has contributed to a child's sense of self—his or her identity—but with sexual maturation comes the realization that adult sexual relations and marriage are not too far away. According to Erikson, the major task in adolescence is the integration of various identities brought from childhood into a more complete identity that provides continuity from the past and preparation for the future. This is a period of reorganization. If adolescents cannot come to terms with "who they are" and "who they are to be," the result is identity confusion.
Stage 6: Intimacy versus isolation (young adulthood)
Early adulthood covers the period of courtship, marriage, and early family life. In Erikson's view, young adults who develop the ability to care about and share with another person without fear of losing their own identity have attained intimacy. Intimacy involves not just sexuality in love relationships, but also close friendships, work partnerships, and relationships with fellow members of such organizations as the military, service clubs, and religious congregations. Failure to establish intimacy can result in isolation, the inability to fully share life's experiences with significant others.
Stage 7: Generativity versus stagnation (middle adulthood)
When a middle-aged adult's interests expand beyond his or her immediate family to include the general well-being of younger colleagues, or efforts to improve the future state of society or the world, in Erikson's view the person has developed generativity. Adults who do not have a positive view of the future or a belief in mankind may fall into self-absorption or stagnation.
Stage 8: Integrity versus despair (late adulthood)
When older adults can look back on their lives and the contributions they have made and be satisfied with the life they have led, they form a sense of integrity. They see themselves as part of a bigger picture that includes past and future generations. Others, who look back and see only missed opportunities and regret for what they have done, may experience despair.

In these cases displacement is referred to as **_sublimation_**. A highly aggressive person might perform valuable service in a competitive profession, such as being a trial lawyer, as sublimation of the drive to beat others physically. As another example, Freud (1910/1947) suggested that Leonardo da Vinci's fascination with painting Madonnas was a sublimation of his desire for his mother, which had been frustrated by his separation from her.

Reaction formation is the conversion of a frightening wish into its safer opposite. For example, a young woman who unconsciously hates her mother and wishes her dead may consciously experience these feelings as intense love for her mother and strong concern for her safety. Psychodynamic theorists have long speculated that *homophobia*—the irrational fear and hatred of homosexuals—may often stem from reaction formation. People who have a tendency toward homosexuality, but

■ **Sublimating an unacceptable impulse** Or a person with a (socially unacceptable) unconscious wish to punish others might pursue a (socially approved) career as a trial lawyer or a prosecutor. In that sense, such a career may be a form of sublimation.

fear it, may protect themselves from recognizing it by vigorously separating themselves from homosexuals. In a study supporting that explanation, men who scored highly homophobic on a questionnaire were subsequently found, through direct physical measurement, to show more penile erection while watching a male homosexual video than did other men, even though they denied experiencing any sexual arousal while watching the video (Adams et al., 1996).

Projection occurs when a person consciously experiences an unconscious drive or wish as though it were someone else's. A person with intense, unconscious anger may project that anger onto her friend—she may feel that it is her friend, not she, who is angry. In an early study of projection conducted at college fraternity houses, Robert Sears (1936) found that men who were rated by their fraternity brothers as extreme on a particular characteristic, such as stinginess, but who denied that trait in themselves, tended to rate others as particularly high on that same characteristic.

Rationalization is the use of conscious reasoning to explain away anxiety-provoking thoughts or feelings. A man who cannot face his own sadistic tendencies may rationalize the beatings he gives his children by convincing himself that children need to be disciplined and that he is only carrying out his fatherly duty. Psychodynamic theories encourage us to be wary of conscious logic, since it often serves to mask true feelings and motives. (For discussion of the left-hemisphere interpreter, which seems to be a significant source of rationalization, look back at Chapter 4, pages 137–138.)

Defensive Styles as Dimensions of Personality

Of all of Freud's ideas about the mind, his concept of psychological defense has had the most lasting appeal in psychology and has generated the most research (Cramer, 2000). Some of the cognitive biases discussed in Chapter 13, by which people enhance their own perceptions of themselves and rationalize their own morally questionable actions, can be understood as defense mechanisms. These biased ways of thinking reduce anxiety by bolstering people's images of themselves as highly competent and ethical.

Some people habitually employ certain defenses as their routine modes of dealing with stressful situations in their lives, such that the defense mechanism can be thought of as a dimension of their personality. The most fully researched defensive style is that referred to as *repressive coping*.

Repressive Coping as a Personality Style

FOCUS 24

What evidence exists that some people regularly repress anxious feelings? In general, how do such people differ from others in their reactions to stressful situations?

There is ample evidence that many people regularly repress the emotions that accompany disturbing events in their lives. They are able to recall and describe the events, but they claim that such memories do not make them anxious or otherwise disturb them. Personality researchers refer to these people as *repressors*. For research purposes, repressors are identified by their scores on standardized questionnaires for assessing anxiety and defensiveness. They are people who report experiencing very little anxiety, but who answer other questions in ways that seem highly defensive (Weinberger, 1990). Their questionnaire responses indicate that they have an especially strong need to view themselves in a very favorable light; they do not admit to the foibles that are typical of most people.

Many research studies have identified repressors in this way and compared them with nonrepressors in their reactions to moderately distressing situations in the laboratory. For example, subjects might be asked to complete sentences that contain sexual or aggressive themes, or to describe their least-desirable traits, or to recall fearful experiences that happened to them in the past, or to imagine some unhappy event that could afflict them in the future. The general finding is that repressors report much less psychological distress in these situations than do nonrepressors; but, by physiological indices—such as heart rate, muscle tension, and perspiration—they manifest *more* distress than do nonrepressors (Derakshan et al., 2007; Weinberger, 1990). Research indicates that they are not lying when they say they experience little anxiety; they apparently really believe what they are saying. Somehow they have banished anxious thoughts and feelings from their conscious minds, but have not banished the bodily reactions of anxiety.

In other experiments, compared with nonrepressors, repressors reported less anxiety or other unpleasant emotions in daily diaries, recalled fewer negative childhood experiences, and were less likely to notice consciously or remember emotion-arousing words or phrases presented during an experiment (Cutler et al., 1996; Davis & Schwartz, 1987; Fujiwara et al., 2008). They apparently avoid experiences of anxiety by diverting their conscious attention away from anxiety-arousing stimuli and by dwelling on pleasant rather than unpleasant thoughts.

A good deal of research has centered on the possible benefits and harm of the repressive style of coping. The repressive style may often originate, and be most helpful, at a time when the person is coping with a seriously disturbing life event. For example, this style is common among adolescent cancer survivors, and it seems to help them to maintain a remarkably positive outlook on life (Erickson et al., 2008). Other research indicates that the repressive style helps people who have had heart attacks, or who have lost loved ones to suicide, to cope psychologically (Ginzburg et al., 2002; Parker & McNally, 2008). Laboratory studies suggest that repression may help people in these situations by preserving their conscious minds—their working memories—for rational planning and problem solving. As described in Chapter 13, anxious thoughts occupy space in working memory and thereby interfere with the person's ability to solve problems. Repressors are apparently much less affected by this than are the rest of us (Derakshan & Eysenck, 1998; Parker & McNally, 2008). They continue to function effectively, at work and elsewhere, despite events that would traumatize others.

On the other side of the coin, however, is evidence that repressors may develop more health problems and experience more chronic pain than do nonrepressors (Burns, 2000; Schwartz, 1990). This is consistent with the idea that they experience stress physically rather than as conscious emotion. Repressors may be promoting their cognitive functioning at some cost to their bodies. Like most personality dimensions, repressive coping has benefits and costs; the overall balance between the two depends on the environmental conditions to which the person must adapt.

Distinction Between Mature and Immature Defensive Styles

Other research on defensive styles has focused on the idea that some defenses are more conducive to a person's long-term well-being than are others. The most ambitious and famous such study was begun in the 1930s, with male sophomores at Harvard University as subjects.

Each year until 1955, and less often after that, the Harvard men filled out an extensive questionnaire concerning such issues as their work, ambitions, social relationships, emotions, and health. Nearly 30 years after the study began, when the men were in their late 40s, a research team led by George Vaillant (1995) interviewed in depth 95 of these men, randomly selected. By systematically analyzing the content and the style of their responses in the interview and on the previous questionnaires, the researchers rated the extent to which each man used specific defense mechanisms.

Vaillant divided the various defense mechanisms into categories according to his judgment of the degree to which they would seem to promote either ineffective or effective behavior. *Immature defenses* were those presumed to distort reality the most and to lead to the most ineffective actions. Projection was included in this category. *Intermediate defenses* (referred to by Vaillant as "neurotic defenses"), including

> **FOCUS 25**
>
> What benefit and harm might accrue from the repressive style of coping?

> **FOCUS 26**
>
> What relationships did Vaillant find between defensive styles and measures of life satisfaction?

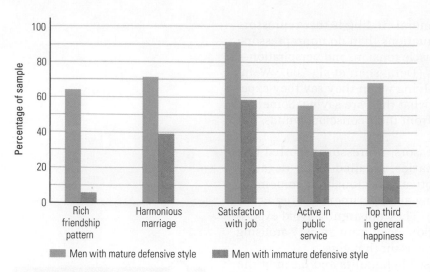

Men with mature defensive style   Men with immature defensive style

FIGURE 14.8 Love, work, and happiness in men with mature and immature defensive styles Harvard alumni classified as using primarily mature defenses were more frequently rated as having rich friendships, a good marriage, satisfaction with their work, active involvement in public service, and a high degree of happiness than were those classified as using primarily immature defenses.
(Data from Vaillant, 1977.)

repression and reaction formation, were presumed to involve less distortion of reality and to lead to somewhat more effective coping. *Mature defenses* were presumed to involve the least distortion of reality and to lead to the most adaptive behaviors. One of the most common of the mature defenses was *suppression,* which involves the conscious avoidance of negative thinking. Suppression differs from repression in that the person has more conscious control over the decision to think about, or not think about, the distressing experience. Another defense in the mature category was *humor,* which, according to Freud and other psychodynamic theorists, reduces fear by making fun of feared ideas.

Consistent with Vaillant's expectations, the men who used the most mature defenses were the most successful on all measures of ability to love and work (Freud's criteria for mature adulthood). They were also, by their own reports, the happiest. **Figure 14.8** depicts some of the comparisons between the men who used mainly mature defenses and those who used mainly immature defenses. Vaillant (1995) also found, not surprisingly, that as the Harvard men matured—from age 19 into their 40s—the average maturity of their defenses increased. Immature defenses such as projection declined, and mature defenses such as suppression and humor increased.

In subsequent research, using more diverse groups of subjects, including women as well as men, Vaillant and others found similar results (Cramer, 2008; Vaillant, 2002). As they grow older, from adolescence on, people rely less on defenses that deny or distort reality and more on defenses that allow them to accept reality. The use of mature rather than immature defenses correlates positively with measures of life satisfaction and success. Such correlations do not prove that mature defenses cause successful coping, but they do at least show that the two tend to go together.

The Humanistic Perspective: The Self and Life's Meanings

Humanistic theories of personality arose, in the mid-twentieth century, partly in reaction to the then-dominant psychodynamic theories. While psychodynamic theories emphasize unconscious motivation and defenses, humanistic theories emphasize people's conscious understanding of themselves and their capacity to choose their own paths to fulfillment. They are called *humanistic* because they center on an aspect of human nature that seems to distinguish us clearly from other animals—our tendency to create belief systems, to develop meaningful stories about ourselves and our world, and to govern our lives in accordance with those stories.

Phenomenological Reality

Phenomenology is the study of conscious perceptions and understandings, and humanistic theorists use the term **phenomenological reality** to refer to each person's conscious understanding of his or her world. Humanistic theorists commonly claim that one's phenomenological reality *is* one's real world; it provides the basis for the person's contentment or lack of contentment and for the meaning that he or she finds in life. In the words of one of the leaders of humanistic psychology, Carl Rogers (1980): "The only reality you can possibly know is the world as you perceive and experience it. . . . And the only certainty is that those perceived realities are different. There are as many 'real worlds' as there are people."

FOCUS 27

How, in general, do humanistic theories differ from psychodynamic theories?

Being One's Self: Self-Actualization and Maslow's Hierarchy of Human Needs

According to most humanistic theories, a central aspect of one's phenomenological reality is the *self-concept,* the person's understanding of who he or she is. Rogers referred to his own version of humanistic theory as *self theory*. He claimed that at first he avoided the construct of self because it seemed unscientific, but was forced to consider it through listening to his clients in therapy sessions. Person after person would say, in effect, "I feel I am not being my real self"; "I wouldn't want anyone to know the real me"; or "I wonder who I am." From such statements, Rogers (1959) gradually came to believe that a concept of self is a crucial part of a person's phenomenological reality and that a common goal of people is to "discover their real selves" and "become their real selves."

Humanistic theorists use the term **self-actualization** to refer to the process of becoming one's full self—that is, of realizing one's dreams and capabilities. The specific route to self-actualization will vary from person to person and from time to time within a person's lifetime, but for each individual the route must be self-chosen.

Rogers (1963, 1977) often compared self-actualization in humans to physical growth in plants. A tree growing on a cliff by the sea must battle against the wind and saltwater and does not grow as well as it would in a more favorable setting, yet its inner potential continues to operate and it grows as well as it can under the circumstances. Nobody can tell the tree how to grow; its growth potential lies within itself. Humanistic theorists hold that full growth, full actualization, requires a fertile environment, but that the direction of actualization and the ways of using the environment must come from within the organism. In the course of evolution, organisms have acquired the capacity to use the environment in ways that maximize growth. In humans, the capacity to make free, conscious choices that promote positive psychological growth is the actualizing tendency. To grow best, individuals must be permitted to make those choices and must trust themselves to do so.

Another pioneer of humanistic psychology, Abraham Maslow (1970), suggested that to self-actualize one must satisfy five sets of needs that can be arranged in a hierarchy (see **Figure 14.9**). From bottom to top, they are (1) *physiological needs* (the minimal essentials for life, such as food and water); (2) *safety needs* (protection from dangers in the environment); (3) *attachment needs* (acceptance and love); (4) *esteem needs* (competence, respect from others and the self); and (5) *self-actualization needs*. In Maslow's view, the self-actualization needs encompass the needs for self-expression, creativity, and "a sense of connectedness with the broader universe." Maslow argued that a person can focus on higher needs only if lower ones, which are more immediately linked to survival, are sufficiently satisfied so that they do not claim the person's full attention and energy.

Maslow's needs hierarchy makes some sense from an evolutionary perspective. The physiological and safety needs are most basic in that they are most immediately linked to survival. If one is starving or dehydrated, or if a tiger is charging, then survival depends immediately upon devoting one's full resources to solving that problem. The social needs for acceptance, love, and esteem are also linked to survival, though not in quite as direct and immediate a fashion. We need to maintain good social relationships with others to ensure their future cooperation in meeting our physiological and safety needs and in helping us reproduce. Continuing in this line of thought, we would suggest that the self-actualization needs are best construed evolutionarily as *self-educative needs*. Playing, exploring, and creating can lead to the acquisition of skills and knowledge that help one later in such endeavors as obtaining food, fending off predators,

Q FOCUS 28

What is Maslow's theory about the relationship among various human needs? How might the theory be reconciled with an evolutionary perspective?

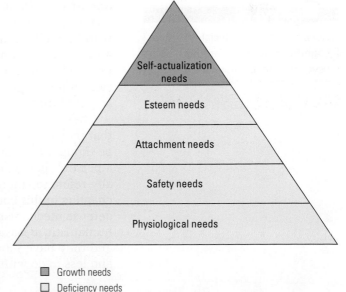

☐ Growth needs
☐ Deficiency needs

FIGURE 14.9 Maslow's hierarchy of human needs According to Maslow, needs at the lower portion of the hierarchy must be satisfied at least to some degree before people can focus on needs higher up. The most psychologically healthy people are those whose deficiency needs are sufficiently satisfied to free their energies for self-actualization.

attracting mates, and securing the goodwill and protection of the community. From this perspective, self-actualization is not in any ultimate sense "higher" than the other needs but is part of the long-term way of satisfying those needs.

SECTION REVIEW

Psychodynamic and humanistic personality theories focus on mental processes.

The Psychodynamic Perspective

- Freud, whose psychoanalytic views originated this perspective, believed that the real causes of behavior lie in the unconscious mind, with sexual and aggressive motives being especially important.

- Other psychodynamic theorists emphasized unconscious effects of other drives. Adler and Erikson emphasized, respectively, competence and the role of society in shaping personality.

- Defense mechanisms serve to reduce conscious awareness of unacceptable or emotionally threatening thoughts, wishes, and feelings.

Defensive Styles as Personality Traits

- People classified as repressors routinely repress disturbing emotional feelings. Though they consciously experience little anxiety, their bodies react strongly to stressful situations. Such repression may help them cope cognitively in times of stress.

- In a longitudinal study of men, Vaillant found that defensive styles that involved less distortion of reality and led to more effective behavior were correlated with greater success in all areas of life.

The Humanistic Perspective

- Humanistic theories emphasize phenomenological reality (the self and world as perceived by the individual).

- In Maslow's hierarchy of needs, self-actualization (becoming one's full self, living one's dreams) is addressed only when more basic needs are adequately met.

Personality as Mental Processes II: Social-Cognitive Views

FOCUS 29

How, in general, do social-cognitive theories differ from psychodynamic theories?

Social-cognitive theories of personality, sometimes called *social-learning* or *social-cognitive-learning* theories, draw both from clinical psychologists' experiences with their clients and from academic psychologists' research on learning, cognition, and social influence. In place of the instinctive, unconscious motives posited by psychodynamic theories as the prime shapers of personality, social-cognitive theories emphasize the roles of *general beliefs* about the nature of the world, which are acquired through one's experiences in the social environment.

These beliefs may be conscious, but they may also be so ingrained and automatic that they exert their influence without the person's conscious awareness. They can be thought of as automatic habits of thought, which can influence many aspects of a person's behavior. Thus, to social-cognitive theorists, the term *unconscious* generally refers to automatic mental processes, in the same sense as discussed in earlier chapters in this book, not to thoughts that are actively barred from consciousness by defense mechanisms. As you will see, social-cognitive ideas overlap very much with humanistic ideas about personality, but they are based more on laboratory research, and they have more to do with predicting people's behavior in specific situations, and less to do with global life choices, than is the case for humanistic theories.

Beliefs Viewed as Personality Traits

The kinds of beliefs that social-cognitive personality theorists have most frequently studied have to do with the value or futility of action. Some beliefs tend to promote an affirmative, take-charge orientation toward the world, while their opposites tend to promote a more passive orientation. Here we describe the dimensions of belief that have been most thoroughly studied as personality traits. As you will see, these belief dimensions seem to overlap considerably with one another, but they have varying shades of meaning, and some social-cognitive theorists think they are quite distinct from one another.

Beliefs About the Locus of Control Over Desired Effects

If there is a principal founder of the social-cognitive perspective on personality, it is Julian Rotter, who wrote the first book explicitly describing a social-cognitive approach to personality (Rotter, 1954). In his early research, Rotter found that people behaved differently at various tasks or games in the laboratory, depending on whether they believed that success depended on skill or luck (Rotter et al., 1961). To the degree that they believed that success depended on skill (which it did), they worked hard and improved. To the degree that they believed it depended on luck, they did not work hard and did not improve. Partly on the basis of these observations, Rotter argued that people's behavior depends not just on the objective relationship between their responses and rewards but also on their subjective beliefs about that relationship.

In many life situations it is not clear to what degree we have control over rewards. For example, we can't be sure whether studying hard will lead to a good grade on an exam, or whether diet and exercise will prevent us from having a heart attack. Rotter (1966) suggested that in such situations people tend to behave according to a generalized disposition (a personality trait), acquired from past experience, to believe that rewards either are or are not usually controllable by people's own efforts. He referred to this disposition as *locus of control* and developed a questionnaire to measure it. **Table 14.6** shows sample test items from Rotter's locus-of-control questionnaire. People whose answers reflect a belief that individuals control their own rewards (and, by extension, their own fate) are said to have an *internal* locus of control. People whose answers reflect a belief that rewards (and fate) are controlled by factors outside themselves are said to have an *external* locus of control.

■ **Skill or luck?** People approach an activity—such as a game of cards—very differently depending on whether they believe its potential rewards are controlled by skill or luck. This insight lies behind Rotter's concept of locus of control.

TABLE 14.6 Sample test items from Rotter's locus-of-control scale

The task on each item is to decide which alternative (a or b) seems more true. The actual test consists of 23 items similar to those shown here.

Item: a. In the long run, people get the respect they deserve in this world.
     b. Unfortunately, an individual's work often passes unrecognized, no matter how hard he or she tries.

Item: a. I have often found that what is going to happen will happen.
     b. Trusting to fate has never turned out as well for me as making a decision to take a definite course of action.

Item: a. In the case of the well-prepared student, there is rarely if ever such a thing as an unfair test.
     b. Many times exam questions tend to be so unrelated to course work that studying is really useless.

Note: For the items shown here, internal locus of control is indicated by choosing a for the first and third items and b for the second item.

Source: Research from Rotter, J. B., 1966. Generalized expectancies for internal versus external locus of control of reinforcement. *Psychological Monographs: General and Applied, 80* (whole no. 609), p. 11. Copyright 1966, published by American Psychological Association.

FOCUS 30

What sorts of behaviors correlate with an internal locus of control?

Since its development, hundreds of studies have shown consistent, though usually not very high, correlations between scores on Rotter's locus-of-control scale and actual behavior in various situations. People who score toward the internal end of the scale are, on average, more likely than others to try to control their own fate. They are more likely to take preventive health care measures (Reich et al., 1997), to succeed in weight-loss programs (Adolfsson et al., 2005), to seek information on how to protect themselves during a tornado warning (Sims & Baumann, 1972), to resist group pressure in laboratory tests of conformity (Crowne & Liverant, 1963), and to prefer games of skill over games of chance (Schneider, 1972). Business leaders who have an internal locus of control implement more innovative, high-risk strategies for growing the business than do those who have an external locus of control, which can be good or bad depending on the economic climate (Wijbenga & van Witteloostuijn, 2007).

Other research indicates that people who score toward the internal end of the scale are, on average, less anxious and more content with life than those who score toward the external end (Phares, 1984). Apparently, the sense of control helps calm people's fears about potential mishaps and dangers.

Of course, as with all correlational research, we cannot be sure what is cause and what is effect. Does a sense of control promote hard work, responsible behavior, innovative action, and general satisfaction with life? Or do hard work, responsible behavior, innovative action, and general satisfaction promote a sense of control? Most social-cognitive theorists would contend that both of these causal hypotheses are correct to some degree. Successful action in any realm tends to lead to a stronger sense of control, which may promote further successful action; and vice versa. Most of us lie somewhere in the middle of the internal–external dimension because, truth be told, we really can control some things and not others, and it's not always clear which things lie in which category.

Beliefs About One's Own Ability to Perform Specific Tasks

Another pioneer of the social-cognitive perspective on personality is Albert Bandura (see discussion of Bandura's social-learning theory in Chapter 8), who, like Rotter, earned a degree in clinical psychology and then went on to a career of laboratory research. Much of Bandura's research centers on *self-efficacy*: people's beliefs about their own abilities to perform specific tasks. People who expect that they can perform a certain task are said to have high self-efficacy about the task, and people who expect the opposite are said to have low self-efficacy about it.

Self-efficacy may seem similar to locus of control, but Bandura (1997) considers the two to be distinct. Self-efficacy refers to the person's sense of his or her own ability, while locus of control refers to the person's belief that ability will produce desired effects. Although self-efficacy and an internal locus of control usually go together, they do not always. If you believe, for example, that you are skilled at math but that the skill is worthless (perhaps because it is unrecognized by your math professor or others in society), then you have high self-efficacy but an external locus of control in that area. Conversely, if you believe that skill at math would bring rewards but that you don't have the skill, then you have low self-efficacy and an internal locus of control in that area. As is the case for locus of control, self-efficacy may be specific to a very narrow range of tasks or more general over a broad range of tasks (Cervone, 1997; Welch & West, 1995).

Bandura and his colleagues have repeatedly demonstrated that improved self-efficacy for a task predicts improvement in actual performance of the task. In one study, for example, various treatments were used to help people overcome their fear of snakes. Those who claimed after treatment that they now expected to be able to pick up and handle a large snake were indeed most likely to succeed at the task, regardless of which treatment they had received (Bandura et al., 1977). Correlations between changes in self-efficacy and changes in performance have likewise been found in such diverse realms as mathematics, physical exertion, tolerance for pain,

FOCUS 31

What evidence supports the theory that high self-efficacy (a) predicts high performance and (b) may help cause high performance?

giving up smoking, and social skills (Bandura & Locke, 2003; Gwaltney et al., 2009; Schunk & Hanson, 1985).

Bandura argues that self-efficacy is not simply a correlate of good performance, but is also a cause of it (Bandura & Locke, 2003). Evidence includes experiments in which false feedback designed to raise or lower a person's self-efficacy improved or worsened performance. In one experiment, for example, some randomly chosen subjects were told that, based on a previous measure, they had much higher than average pain tolerance, and others were told the opposite. When subsequently given a test of pain tolerance, those who were led to believe they had excellent pain tolerance tolerated more pain than did those who were led to believe they had poor pain tolerance (Litt, 1988). Another experiment showed similar results in the realm of problem solving. Those who were led to believe they were good problem solvers worked more persistently, used better strategies, and were more successful at solving problems than were those who were led to believe they were not so good (Bouffard-Bouchard, 1990).

■ **Self-efficacy** According to Albert Bandura, the first step in acquiring a skill like this—or in doing anything that is difficult—is to believe you can do it.

Beliefs About the Possibility of Personal Improvement

Another dimension of belief explored by social-cognitive theorists concerns the degree of malleability of one's own personal qualities. Some people see themselves as rather *fixed* entities. They see themselves as having a certain degree of intelligence, a certain level of athletic ability, and certain rather unchangeable personality traits. In their minds they are what they are and they will always be that. People at the other end of this dimension have a relatively *malleable* view of themselves. They see themselves at any given point, even late in life, as changing, developing, improving. Their intelligence is not fixed, but is something that can grow or atrophy depending on their own efforts or lack of efforts.

Carol Dweck, who has studied this belief dimension extensively, contends that your position on it makes a big difference in your approach to life. Dweck (2006, 2008) and her colleagues have found that people who view themselves as malleable are more likely to strive for self-improvement in all realms of life than are those who see themselves as fixed. They embrace education. They rebound from setbacks, which they interpret as growth experiences rather than failures. They seek out difficult problems to solve so they can learn from them. They strive to improve their personal relationships with others, rather than accept them for what they are. Because of such efforts, they tend to succeed in life.

Several experiments have demonstrated that people can be taught to think of themselves as malleable and that such teaching can change their behavior. In one line of experiments, college students and junior high school students were shown a film depicting how neurons in the brain can make new connections throughout life and how the brain grows, like a muscle, with use. At the end of the semester, those students exhibited more enthusiasm for their academic work and had higher grade-point averages than did otherwise comparable students who had not seen the film (Aronson et al., 2002; Blackwell et al., 2007). People also tend to develop either fixed or malleable views of themselves from the kinds of praise they hear (Mueller & Dweck, 1998). Global praise about attributes, such as "you are intelligent," tend to create a fixed, stagnant view of the self, while praise about effort or choice of strategy for specific tasks—such as "you worked hard and did a great job on that report"—tend to create a malleable, dynamic view of the self.

The Power of Positive Thinking

Much has been written, by psychologists and nonpsychologists alike, about the benefits of a positive, optimistic outlook on life (Cousins, 1977; Seligman, 1990).

Q FOCUS 32

What is the benefit of the belief that the self is malleable? How can people's belief in their own malleability be enhanced, and what effects have been observed of such enhancement?

You have just read about research indicating that people who believe in their own abilities (have high self-efficacy), believe that their abilities will be rewarded (have an internal locus of control), and believe in the possibility of personal improvement (have a malleable self-view) are generally happier and more successful than people who don't have those beliefs.

A number of psychologists have developed questionnaires designed to assess people's general tendency to think either positively or negatively. C. Rick Snyder (1994) and his colleagues developed a questionnaire to assess *hope,* which they construe as a belief in one's ability to solve solvable problems (generalized self-efficacy) combined with a belief that most problems in life are solvable. Martin Seligman (1990) and his colleagues developed a questionnaire to assess the degree to which people explain negative events in their lives in a pessimistic or optimistic manner. Michael Scheier and Charles Carver (1993) developed a questionnaire to assess *dispositional optimism,* the tendency to believe in a rosy future. On the questionnaire, people indicate the degree to which they agree or disagree with such statements as "In uncertain times, I usually expect the best."

Correlational studies using all these questionnaires have shown that, in general, people with an optimistic style of thought are happier and tend to cope more effectively with life's stressors than do people who have a pessimistic style (Nes & Segerstrom, 2006; Snyder, 1994; Taylor et al., 2003). In one such study, Scheier and his colleagues (1989) used their questionnaire to assess dispositional optimism in middle-aged men who were about to undergo coronary artery bypass surgery. They found that those who scored high on optimism before the surgery made quicker recoveries than did those who scored low, even when the medical conditions that led to surgery were equivalent. The optimists were quicker to sit up on their own, to walk, to resume vigorous exercise, and to get back to work full time than were the pessimists.

The most likely explanation for this and other positive correlations with optimism is that optimistic thinking leads people to devote attention and energy to solving their problems or recovering from their disabilities, which in turn leads to positive results. Pessimists are relatively more likely to say, "It won't work out anyway, so why try?"

FOCUS 33

What evidence supports the value of optimism? Through what mechanisms might optimism produce its beneficial effects?

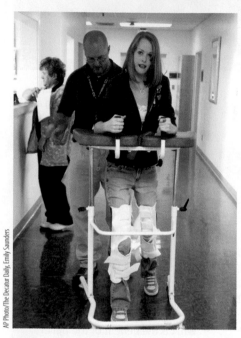

■ **Optimism** The belief that one can overcome adversity may become a self-fulfilling prophecy if that belief leads to effective actions. This young woman, the victim of a head-on automobile collision, works hard at strengthening her legs so she can walk again.

The Optimistic Child

Perhaps the most optimistic of any people on the planet are young children. When preschoolers are asked who are the smartest, most popular, most athletic, most attractive, or toughest kids in their class, they typically list themselves among the top. They typically also list other children whom the teacher and their classmates think are highly popular, attractive, athletic, and so forth, showing that they know talent when they see it. However, they typically include themselves among the list of the "best and the brightest," even if their classmates think otherwise (Boulton & Smith, 1990; Stipek & Daniels, 1988).

Such optimism can be adaptive in young children. Children's tendencies to overestimate their abilities and characteristics enhance their self-efficacy and give them the confidence to try things they would not otherwise try (Bjorklund & Green, 1992; Stipek, 1984). For example, 3- and 4-year-old children who overestimate their abilities to imitate a model ("How well do you think you can juggle three balls like the man is doing?") had higher verbal IQs than more accurate children (Bjorklund et al., 1993). Similarly, 8- to 11-year-old children who overestimated their abilities had higher school grades than did less optimistic children (Lopez et al., 1998), and kindergarten and first-grade children who overestimated how much they had remembered on early trials of a memory task showed greater memory improvement on later trials than more accurate children (Shin et al., 2007). Such patterns are consistent with Deborah Stipek's (1984) proposal that, rather than trying to make young children's self-assessments more accurate, we should "try harder to design educational environments which maintain their optimism and eagerness" (1984, p. 53).

Adaptive and Maladaptive Optimism and Pessimism

Before concluding that optimism is always best, before rushing out to trade the clear lenses on our glasses for rose-tinted ones, we should consider a potential hazard of optimism. Health psychologists have long pointed out the danger of unrealistic, self-delusional forms of optimism. Many people, especially adolescents and young adults, optimistically believe that they are invulnerable to such catastrophes as AIDS, lung cancer, drug addiction, and automobile accidents and fail to take precautions to avoid such dangers (Schwarzer, 1994; Weinstein, 1982). Similarly, an optimistic, inflated belief in their academic or career abilities blinds some people to their own shortcomings and prevents them from taking steps to improve (Dunning et al., 2004). Optimism of this sort, which in the psychodynamic tradition is called *defensive optimism,* may reduce anxiety by diverting thoughts away from fearful possibilities, but it may also lead to serious harm. The optimistic belief that you can control your fate through active self-care and self-improvement usually leads to constructive behaviors, but the optimistic belief that fate will protect you without your participation can lead to dangerously imprudent behaviors.

Just as optimism can be adaptive or maladaptive, depending on whether or not it translates into constructive action, so can pessimism. In research on the cognitive underpinnings of success in college, Julie Norem and her colleagues found students who use apparently opposite mental strategies to perform well academically (Norem & Illingworth, 1993, 2004). Some students use an adaptive form of optimism. They believe they will do well, and that belief, coupled with their thoughts about the positive consequences of doing well, motivates them to work hard and actually do well. Other students, however, use an adaptive form of pessimism. They believe that there is a good chance that they will not do well, despite having done well in the past, and that belief, along with thoughts about the negative consequences of failure, motivates them to work hard to avoid failure. As a result, and apparently to their surprise, they not only pass but achieve high grades. Still, the optimists are probably better off in the long run than the pessimists. One study of adjustment to college life revealed that the pessimists' constant anxiety about failure led them to focus too narrowly on grades and lose the intrinsic pleasure of academic work (Cantor & Harlow, 1994).

What is the difference between those who use either optimism or pessimism constructively and those who do not? We believe it has to do with beliefs about locus of control and personal malleability. People who believe that rewards are controllable (internal locus of control) and that they themselves can improve through effort (malleable self-belief) are likely to work hard and do well regardless of whether or not their focus is on achieving anticipated success (the goal of optimists) or preventing anticipated failure (the goal of pessimists). Consistent with this view, Norem (2008) reports that the defensive pessimists she has studied believe more strongly than do other anxious people that they can improve themselves through effort.

FOCUS 34

What seems to differentiate adaptive from maladaptive optimism and adaptive from maladaptive pessimism?

The Idea of Situation-Specific Personality Traits

Social-cognitive theorists have long contended that global traits—such as those specified by the five-factor model—tell only part of the story of personality. To understand a person, according to these theorists, one must not only know

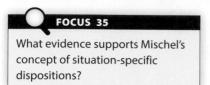

FOCUS 35

What evidence supports Mischel's concept of situation-specific dispositions?

that a person tends to be extraverted or introverted, for example, but must also know the contexts in which the person typically manifests those tendencies. One person might be shy (introverted) at parties but outspoken (extraverted) at formal meetings, while the opposite might be true of another person. One person who scores as disagreeable on the NEO-PI might be most disagreeable to subordinates while another, with the same score, might be most disagreeable to authority figures. The leading advocate for this contextual view of personality is social-cognitive theorist Walter Mischel (1984, 2007).

In one study, Mischel and Phillip Peake (1982) assessed repeatedly, by direct observation, 19 different forms of behavior presumed to be related to the trait of conscientiousness in a group of college students. Included were measures of regularity of class attendance, promptness in completing assignments, bed neatness, and neatness of class notes. They found high consistency within any one of these measures but relatively low consistency across measures. For instance, students who kept neat notes for one class were very likely to keep neat notes for another class but only slightly more likely than average to keep their beds neat.

In another study, Mischel and his colleagues found that children with social adjustment problems at a summer camp were not well described by such global traits as "aggressive" or "withdrawn" but were quite well described and differentiated from one another by terms that referred to the social situations that prompted them to act aggressively or to withdraw (Mischel & Shoda, 1995; Shoda et al., 1994). **Figure 14.10** shows sample results from that study for verbal aggressiveness for two children. As shown in the figure, both children were somewhat more verbally aggressive than the average child at the camp, but the two were very different from each other with regard to the situations in which they exhibited aggression. Child 28 was highly aggressive to peers who approached him in a friendly manner but not particularly aggressive in other situations, and child 9 was highly aggressive to adults but not to peers. Knowledge of that difference is essential to any clinically useful understanding of the children, but that knowledge would be obscured in a global rating of aggressiveness or disagreeableness for the two children.

Since Mischel's early work, psychologists have debated the role of personality traits versus situations, or context, on people's behavior (Funder, 2006; Ross & Nisbett, 2011). Obviously, some "strong" situations (e.g., a funeral) almost require a certain type of behavior, regardless of someone's personality traits. And people with certain personality traits seek out situations in which they feel comfortable, perhaps giving the appearance of greater consistency in behavior across situations than is actually the case. For example, introverts may avoid wild parties but nonetheless behave in a more outward manner when they are compelled to attend one—even if they are not likely to be the "life of the party."

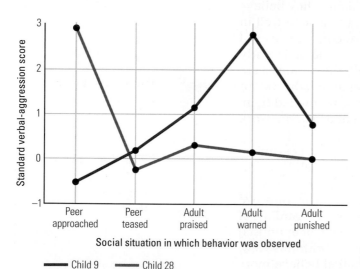

FIGURE 14.10 Situation-specific profiles of verbal aggression for two children Shoda, Mischel, and Wright (1994) recorded various categories of behaviors among emotionally disturbed children in various social situations at a summer camp. Shown here are results concerning verbal aggressiveness for two children. Zero on the y axis represents the average aggressiveness for all the children observed. In overall verbal aggressiveness, these two children were similar, but they were very different with respect to the situations that elicited their aggression.

(Data from Shoda, Mischel, & Wright, 1994.)

Defining Situations

Much research has shown that behavior varies as a function of subtle changes in situations while still maintaining individual consistency across many situations; from this we can see that the dichotomy of "person/personality/trait" versus "situation" in causing someone's behavior is a false one (Funder, 2006). One problem with resolving the "trait versus situation" debate is that although psychologists have spent a lot of time describing personality traits, they have spent less time describing situations. What is a situation, and how do you know when you've moved from one situation to another? Much as personality theorists have formulated five (or six) general personality traits, David Funder and his colleagues set out to formulate a general set of situations that people experience. They developed the Riverside Situational Q-sort (RSQ; Funder, 2016; Sherman et al., 2010; Wagerman & Funder, 2009), in which subjects rated characteristics of situations (e.g., a job needs to be done, a person is being criticized, social interaction is possible) on each of eight dimensions on a scale of 1 (highly characteristic) to 9 (highly uncharacteristic). The resulting scale is called *DIAMONDS* (Rauthmann et al., 2014, Study 1), determined after sampling 100 different features of situations from thousands of subjects, and is described in **Table 14.7**. DIAMONDS consists of the following eight types of situations: **D**uty, **I**ntellect, **A**dversity, **M**ating, p**O**sitivity, **N**egativity, **D**eception, and **S**ociality. Subsequent research showed substantial agreement among subjects concerning which items are highly reflective of different dimensions (for example, "A job needs to be done" as characteristic of Duty; "Situation is playful" as characteristic of pOsitivity) (Rauthmann et al., 2014).

But how does having a reliable measure of situations help us resolve the "trait versus situation" question? One approach is to see how measures of personality relate to the type of situations people experience. For example, people who score high on the personality dimension of Extraversion might be more likely to put themselves in situations that involve social interaction than someone who scores low on Extraversion. Ryne Sherman and his colleagues (2015) tested this hypothesis by giving college students personality tests and relating scores on those tests to the situations the students experienced over the course of a week. Subjects received text messages eight times a day at random intervals over seven days and described, using the DIAMONDS scale, the type of situation they were experiencing at the moment when they received the message (e.g., Duty, "Work needs to be done"; Intellect, "Deep thinking is required"). Sherman and his colleagues reported that subjects' personality traits were partially associated with the situations they reported

TABLE 14.7 The Eight DIAMONDS dimensions of situations and examples of items from the Riverside Situational Q-sort that reflect each dimension

Duty: Does something need to be done?	Items: A job needs to be done. Person is counted on to do something.
Intellect: Is deep information processing needed?	Items: Affords an opportunity to demonstrate intellectual capacity. Situation includes intellectual or cognitive stimuli.
Adversity: Is someone being threatened?	Items: Another person (present or discussed) is under threat. Person is being criticized, directly or indirectly.
Mating: Does the situation involve sexual or romantic content?	Items: Potential romantic partners for person are present. Members of the opposite sex are present.
p**O**sitivity: Is the situation positive?	Items: Situation is playful. Situation is potentially enjoyable.
Negativity: Do negative things taint the situation?	Items: Situation could entail stress or trauma. Situation is potentially anxiety-inducing.
Deception: Is someone being deceptive?	Items: Someone else in this situation might be deceitful. It is possible for person to deceive someone.
Sociality: Does the situation involve social interaction and possible relationship formation?	Items: Members of the opposite sex are present. Social interaction is possible.

Source: Research from Rauthmann, J. F., Gallardo-Pujol, D., Guillaume, E.M., Todd, E., Nave, C. S., Sherman, R., . . . Funder, D. C. (2014). The situational eight DIAMONDS: A taxonomy of major dimensions of situation characteristics. *Journal of Personality and Social Psychology, 107,* 677–718.

experiencing. For example, people scoring high in extraversion were more likely to experience situations high in Sociality, people scoring high in agreeableness were more likely to experience situations high in pOsitivity and low in Deception, and people high in conscientiousness were more likely to experience situations high in Duty. Although relations between personality traits and situations were found in the predicted direction for all traits, the magnitude of the relations was small, and people tended to experience a wide range of situations, independent of their dominant personality characteristics. Thus, personality traits had a significant but small impact on the situations people experience, demonstrating the joint role of personality traits and situations on influencing behavior.

Cross-Cultural Differences in Personality

If personality is, in part, ingrained beliefs and habits of thought that affect behavior, as social-cognitive theorists contend, then we should expect personality to vary across cultures. People growing up in different cultures are exposed to different values, philosophies, economic conditions, and models of how to behave.

Collectivism–Individualism as a Personality Dimension

An important dimension on which cultures vary is the degree to which they have a *collectivist* versus an *individualist* orientation. Collectivist cultures are those that emphasize the interdependence of people and the duties people have to other members of their family and community. Individualist cultures, in contrast, place relatively more emphasis on personal freedom and rights, and relatively less emphasis on responsibilities to others. The cultures of North America, Australia, and Western Europe generally fall on the individualist side of this dimension, and the cultures of East Asia, Africa, and South America generally fall on the collectivist side. Many studies indicate that personalities of people in collectivist and individualist cultures differ from each other in predictable ways. Thus, collectivism and individualism can be thought of as personality traits as well as cultural characteristics (Heine & Buchtel, 2009; Triandis & Suh, 2002).

People with collectivist orientations are highly concerned with personal relationships and promoting the interests of the groups to which they belong. In contrast, those with individualist orientations focus more on their own interests and abilities and less on the interests of the group. While collectivists emphasize the similarities between themselves and other group members, individualists emphasize their own uniqueness. While collectivists see themselves as responding primarily to the conditions of their social environment, individualists see themselves as motivated by their own inner needs and aspirations. The humanistic concept of self-actualization, with its focus on resisting social pressures in order to "be yourself," is a quintessentially individualist concept.

As you would expect, personality tests that are aimed at assessing the collectivist–individualist personality dimension show that people in collectivist cultures generally score as collectivists in personality, and people in individualist cultures generally score as individualists. The differences, however, are by no means all or none; there is lots of overlap. In fact, according to data summarized by Harry Triandis and his colleagues, roughly 40% of people in collectivist cultures score on the individualist side of this personality dimension, and roughly 40% of people in individualist cultures score on the collectivist side (Triandis & Suh, 2002). Collectivists in individualist cultures tend to be loyal members of groups and avoid the "rat race" of individual competition; individualists in collectivist cultures often report feeling oppressed and held back by their culture's demands for conformity and obligations to the group (Triandis & Suh, 2002).

FOCUS 36

In general, how do personalities in collectivist cultures differ from those in individualist cultures? What problems might arise in people whose personalities conflict with the norms of the culture in which they live?

A study comparing personalities in Turkey (a collectivist culture) with those in the United States (an individualist culture) suggests that there is considerable cost to a personality that is too far out of sync with one's culture (Caldwell-Harris & Aycicegi, 2006). The researchers focused on people who scored at either extreme of the collectivism–individualism dimension. Extreme collectivists in Turkey seemed to be well adjusted, but in the United States extreme collectivists tended to be anxious and depressed. Perhaps their strong need for community could not be satisfied in the individualist culture. In contrast, extreme individualists in the United States seemed to be well adjusted, but in Turkey extreme individualists scored high on measures of antisocial tendencies and paranoia (unwarranted suspicion of other people). Perhaps high individualism in a collectivist culture results in rejection by others, which may in turn promote paranoid thoughts and antisocial behavior. Or maybe only those people who for other reasons are paranoid or antisocial become extreme individualists in a collectivist culture. At any rate, the study illustrates the point that the relationship between personality style and life satisfaction depends on the cultural context.

Cultural Differences in Conceptions of Personality

People in different cultures tend to differ not only in their average scores on various personality measures but also in their views about the significance of personality and the relative importance of particular traits. People in collectivist cultures, especially East Asian cultures, place less emphasis on personality than do people in individualist cultures. They are more likely to attribute individual differences in behavior to differences in the environmental situation than to personality differences. East Asians also generally see personality as more malleable than do Westerners (Heine & Buchtel, 2009). Consistent with the theory that belief in a malleable self leads to efforts toward self-improvement, that difference may help explain why East Asians tend to embrace schooling more fully than do Westerners and tend to learn more in school.

When East Asians do talk about personality, they tend to emphasize trait dimensions that are somewhat different from those emphasized in individualist cultures. For example, in China much emphasis is placed on such traits as *harmony* (inner peace of mind and a harmonious way of interacting with others), *face* (a concern with maintaining one's dignity or reputation in relationships with others), and *ren qing* (a relationship orientation that emphasizes the mutual exchange of favors) (Lin & Church, 2004). None of these traits quite matches any of the facets of Western psychologists' five-factor model (the model depicted in Table 14.2). When psychologists in China developed their own indigenous trait theory, using Chinese terms rather than translated versions of Western terms, their analysis produced factors that were in some ways quite different from those of Western psychologists' five-factor model. The most clearly different factor was one that they labeled *interpersonal relatedness,* which includes elements of harmony, concern for reciprocity, and concern for traditional Chinese ways of relating to others (Cheung, 2004; Cheung et al., 2008).

Even today, most personality tests used in non-Western cultures are translated versions of those developed in the West. As many cultural psychologists have pointed out, the results of such tests may often be misleading because people in other cultures may interpret the questions differently than do people in the West and because the questions may not map well onto concepts and dimensions that are meaningful in their culture. Only recently have psychologists in non-Western cultures begun to develop their own personality tests, using their cultures' own terms and concepts. Such research promises to enrich our understanding of the potential ways that human beings can differ from one another and of the value of such differences.

FOCUS 37

What sorts of trait dimensions are emphasized in China more than in Western cultures?

SECTION REVIEW

Social-cognitive theorists stress the roles of beliefs and social contexts in personality.

Beliefs as Personality Traits

- People have an internal or external locus of control, depending on whether they do or do not believe that rewards are controlled by their own efforts.

- People have high or low self-efficacy, depending on whether they do or do not believe they can accomplish the relevant tasks.

- People vary in the degree to which they see themselves as fixed entities or malleable.

- People with an internal locus of control, high self-efficacy, and malleable self-view tend to apply themselves more and to be more successful.

- Young children tend to be overly optimistic about their own abilities, which enhances their self-efficacy and results in improved performance in some situations.

- In general, people with optimistic styles of thought cope better than others with life's demands. However, defensive optimism can cause harm, and some people use pessimism adaptively.

Domain-Specific and Situation-Specific Traits

- Locus of control and self-efficacy beliefs can be general, applying to many tasks, or domain-specific, applying to particular types of tasks. Domain-specific measures of these beliefs have the greatest predictive value.

- Social-cognitive theorists have also shown that traits such as conscientiousness and aggressiveness can vary across contexts, with the pattern of variation depending on the individual. They contend that situation-specific measures of traits have more predictive value than do global trait measures.

- DIAMONDS describes eight general types of situations, and the types of situations in which people find themselves is related to their scores on personality tests.

Cross-Cultural Personality Differences

- Because the social environment differs from one culture to another, social-cognitive theorists expect beliefs and habitual ways of thinking to differ cross-culturally.

- In collectivist cultures, most people have collectivist personality styles, which focus on interdependence; in individualist cultures, most have individualist personality styles, which focus more on individuality and independence.

- In non-Western cultures, the traits that are most useful in characterizing personality may not fully match the five-factor model.

Thinking Critically About Personality

1. To what extent is one's behavior determined by personality traits or by the type of contexts one finds oneself in?

2. To what extent might individual differences in personality reflect adaptive responses to different contexts or different cultures?

Reflections and Connections

Two general ideas might help you organize your thinking as you review how personality can be described, why individuals differ in personality, and how such differences might be understood in terms of mental processes.

1. The varying purposes of personality theories Different personality theories have been developed to serve different purposes. Trait theorists try to distill the essential personality dimensions common to all people, while clinical theorists try to discover the mental processes and beliefs that help or hinder people in coping with life's demands.

Trait theories, such as the five-factor model, are attempts to describe the diversity of human personality objectively and efficiently by identifying sets of nonredundant global traits and ways to measure them. Trait theories do not explain personality; they only describe its elements.

Psychodynamic, humanistic, and social-cognitive theories, in contrast, were designed to explain the particular behaviors,

emotions, and thoughts of individual people, especially of people undergoing psychotherapy. Psychodynamic theories explain personality in terms of unconscious motives and defenses against anxiety. Humanistic theories explain personality in terms of people's subjective understanding of their world and themselves and their strivings for self-actualization. Social-cognitive theories also attempt to explain the behavior of individuals in terms of their beliefs, but they take a less holistic approach. Their interest tends to center more on a specific mental construct (e.g., locus of control) than on individuals as whole entities.

2. Adaptive functions of individual differences Because of the close tie between personality research and clinical research, personality theories have often been concerned with distinctions between healthy (or adaptive) and unhealthy (or maladaptive) personality styles. This concern is reflected in such distinctions as that between mature and immature defenses or between adaptive and maladaptive forms of optimism. An alternative way to think about personality differences, however, is to view them as adaptations to different niches or as different strategies for solving life's problems. In this way of thinking, two quite different styles might be equally healthy or adaptive.

As you review each of the dimensions of personality differences discussed in the chapter—including differences in defensive style, locus of control, optimism versus pessimism, and collectivism versus individualism, as well as the Big Five traits—think about ways in which variation in either direction could be either adaptive or maladaptive, depending on one's life circumstances.

Key Terms

dark triad 540
defense mechanisms 558
differential susceptibility to environmental influence 549
displacement 558
factor analysis 537
five-factor model 538

grit 538
humanistic theories 562
locus of control 565
Machiavellianism 540
narcissism 540
personality 535
phenomenological reality 562
projection 560

psychoanalysis 556
psychodynamic theories 556
psychopathy 540
rationalization 560
reaction formation 559
repression 558
self-actualization 563
self-efficacy 566

sibling contrast 551
social-cognitive theories 564
split-parent identification 551
sublimation 559
trait 536
trait theories of personality 536

Find Out More

David C. Funder & Daniel J. Ozer (Eds.) (2010). *Pieces of the personality puzzle: Readings in theory and research* (5th ed.). New York, NY: Norton.

This collection provides a one-stop tour of the foundations of contemporary personality psychology. Included are articles by historical greats such as Sigmund Freud and Karen Horney (on the psychoanalytic perspective); Abraham Maslow, Carl Rogers, and Dan McAdams (on the humanistic perspective); Walter Mischel and Albert Bandura (on the social-cognitive perspective); and Gordon Allport, Robert McCrae, and Paul Costa (on the trait perspective); as well as new articles on such topics as cross-cultural differences in personality, gender differences in personality, and the relation of personality to happiness.

John D. Mayer (2014). *Personal intelligence: The power of personality and how it shapes our lives.* New York, NY: Scientific American/Farrar, Straus and Giroux.

Mayer came to prominence in psychology through his role in helping to develop the theory of emotional intelligence. In this book, he draws on cognitive psychology research to argue that in order to become our best selves, we use a broader intelligence—which he calls personal intelligence—to understand our own personality and the personalities of the people around us. Illustrating his points with examples from the lives of successful college athletes, police detectives, and musicians, Mayer shows how people who are high in personal intelligence (open to their inner experiences, inquisitive about people, and willing to change themselves) are able to anticipate their own desires and actions, predict the behavior of others, and motivate themselves over the long term and make better life decisions.

Brian Little (2016, July). *Who are you really? The puzzle of personality.* TED Talk. https://youtu.be/qYvXk_bqlBk

Personality researcher Brian Little discusses the "Big 5" and trait psychology as a perspective. He stresses that we are more than a combination of traits; we are agents of free will, possessing the ability to supersede those traits.

Martin Seligman (2008, July). *The new era of positive psychology.* TED Talks. https://youtu.be/9FBxfd7DL3E?list=PL5lo6g_GZWywS23DJJmbs9-ochMLK5EY5

Martin Seligman, past president of the American Psychological Association, has become known as an advocate of optimism and the power of cultivating a positive approach to life that incorporates enjoyment, engagement, and meaning. In this 23-minute presentation he demonstrates how psychology can focus on what makes people happy as well as what makes happy people different from miserable people.

 **LaunchPad** macmillan learning

Visit LaunchPad for Psychology 8e launchpadworks.com to access the e-book, videos, activities, additional resources, and LearningCurve quizzes, as well as study aids including flash cards and web quizzes.

PART VII

Psychological Disorders and Treatment

Sometimes we approach life in ways that create problems for ourselves and those around us. When such problems are persistent and severe enough to interfere with normal functioning, they are considered psychological disorders—the topic of Chapters 15 and 16. Chapter 15 is about identifying disorders and understanding their origins. In Chapter 16, we describe methods to help people overcome or cope with mental problems and disorders.

CHAPTER

Psychological Disorders

15

LEARNING OUTCOMES

After studying this chapter, you should be able to:

- Explain how psychological disorders are defined and categorized, and how culture influences such definitions and categorizations.
- Identify some factors involved in causing psychological disorders.
- Describe anxiety disorders, giving examples.
- Describe obsessive-compulsive disorder and some brain abnormalities that may contribute to it.
- Describe traumatic and stress-related disorders, especially posttraumatic stress disorder, along with their causes.
- Identify the two main categories of mood disorders and compare them.
- Define schizophrenia, explain how it is diagnosed, and identify some of its causal factors.
- Identify the three clusters of personality disorders and describe how such disorders are manifested.

A theme throughout this book is that psychological processes are usually adaptive; they usually promote survival and well-being. Our drives and emotions, including those we experience as uncomfortable or painful, typically motivate survival-enhancing actions. Our perceptions usually provide useful information, and our thoughts usually produce effective plans.

But sometimes these processes, which normally work so well, break down and become maladaptive. Drives become too strong, too weak, or misdirected; emotions become overwhelming; perceptions become distorted; thoughts become confused; and behavior becomes ineffective. We all experience such disturbances occasionally, to some degree, and accept them as a normal part of life. But sometimes such disturbances are so severe, prolonged, or recurrent that they seriously interfere with a person's ability to live a satisfying life. Then the person is said to have a *psychological disorder*.

This chapter begins by discussing the nature and causes of psychological disorders; it then focuses on some of the most familiar classes of disorders, including anxiety disorders, mood disorders, schizophrenia, and personality disorders.

Problems in Identifying Psychological Disorders

Human psychological misery comes in an infinite range of shades and intensities. Before clinicians or researchers can diagnose a psychological disorder, they must evaluate the behavior in terms of four themes, sometimes referred to as the *four Ds*: deviance, distress, dysfunction, and danger. *Deviance* refers to the degree to which the behaviors a person engages in or his or her ideas are considered unacceptable or uncommon in society. For example, being convinced you are being controlled by an alien force would be considered deviant in Western society today. *Distress* refers to the negative feelings a person has because of his or her disorder (e.g., persistent sadness), or the negative feelings of other people (e.g., loss of money due to a spouse's uncontrolled gambling). *Dysfunction* refers to the maladaptive behavior that interferes with a person being able to successfully carry out everyday functions, such as being able to leave the house or to have social relationships with other people. Finally, *danger* refers to dangerous or violent behavior directed at other people or oneself (e.g., suicidal thoughts, self-mutilation).

As you think about the four Ds, you may realize that they do not enable us to make a sharp distinction between "abnormal" misery and "normal" misery—that is, between psychological disorders and normal, run-of-the-mill psychological disturbances. Yet, mental health professionals regularly do make judgments about the presence or absence of a psychological disorder, and they regularly distinguish among and give names to different types of psychological disorders. How do they do it?

In an effort to bring consistency to the language used to talk about psychological disorders, the American Psychiatric Association has developed a manual called the *Diagnostic and Statistical Manual of Psychological Disorders*, abbreviated *DSM*. The manual is continuously a work in progress; its most recent version, **DSM-5**, was published in 2013. The manual specifies criteria for deciding what is officially a disorder and what is not, and it lists many categories and subcategories of disorders along with criteria for identifying them. For better or worse, *DSM-5* provides the current standard language for talking about psychological disorders, so we use that language in this chapter.

What Is a Psychological Disorder?

As the preceding sentences imply, **psychological disorder** has no really satisfying definition. It's a fuzzy concept. Everyone knows that, including the people who wrote *DSM-5*. Yet, in order for researchers and clinicians to communicate with one another, they had to come up with a definition. For one thing, insurance companies demand that patients be diagnosed as having a psychological disorder if there is going to be reimbursement for treatment, so some sort of definition had to be laid out, no matter how fuzzy the concept.

Let us provide the *DSM-5*'s definition of a psychological disorder:

> A psychological disorder is a syndrome characterized by clinically significant disturbance in an individual's cognition, emotion regulation, or behavior that reflects a dysfunction in the psychological, biological, or developmental processes underlying mental functioning. Mental disorders are usually associated with significant distress in social, occupational, or other important activities. An expectable or culturally approved response to a common stressor or loss, such as the death of a loved one, is not a psychological disorder. Socially deviant behavior (e.g., political, religious, or sexual) and conflicts that are primarily between the individual and society are not psychological disorders unless the deviance or conflict results from a dysfunction in the individual, as described above. (American Psychiatric Association, 2013, p. 20)

Although this definition provides a useful guideline for thinking about and identifying psychological disorders, it is arguably ambiguous.

 FOCUS 1

How is *psychological disorder* defined by the American Psychiatric Association? What ambiguities lie in that definition?

Just how much distress or dysfunction must a syndrome entail to be considered "clinically significant"? As all behavior involves an interaction between the person and the environment, how can we tell whether the impairment is really within the person, rather than just in the environment? For example, in the case of someone living in poverty or experiencing discrimination, how can we tell if the person's actions are normal responses to those conditions or represent something more? When people claim that they are deliberately choosing to behave in a way that violates social norms and could behave normally if they wanted to, how do we know when to believe them? A person who starves to protest a government policy may not have a psychological disorder, but what about a person who starves to protest the U.S. government's secret dealings with space aliens who may be planning an invasion? Who has the right to decide whether a person does or does not have a psychological disorder: a *psychiatrist* (a medical doctor specializing in the field of psychological disorders) or psychologist—or perhaps a court of law, or a health insurance administrator who must approve or not approve payment for therapy? Or should the decision be made by the person's family, or the person him- or herself?

These are tough questions that can never be answered strictly scientifically. The answers always represent human judgments, and they are always tinged by the social values and pragmatic concerns of those doing the judging.

■ **Mental distress or psychological disorder?** Feelings of sadness, pessimism, and low self-esteem are evident here, but is the source of the distress the situation or something inside the person? This question is central to defining the concept of psychological disorder.

Categorizing and Diagnosing Psychological Disorders

The dividing lines among different psychological disorders may be fuzzy, but in order to research and treat such disorders scientists and clinicians need a method for categorizing and labeling them. In keeping with the common Western practice of likening psychological disorders to physical diseases, the process of assigning a label to a person's psychological disorder is referred to as *diagnosis*. To be of value, any system of diagnosis must be *reliable* and *valid*.

The Quest for Reliability

The **reliability** of a diagnostic system refers to the extent to which different diagnosticians, all trained in the use of the system, reach the same conclusion when they independently diagnose the same individuals. If you have ever gone to two different doctors with a physical complaint and been given two different, nonsynonymous labels for your disease, you know that diagnosis is by no means completely reliable, even in the realm of physical disorders. Throughout the first several decades after the discipline of psychology came into being, psychiatrists and clinical psychologists had no reliable, agreed-upon method for diagnosing psychological disorders. As a consequence, the same troubled person might be given a diagnosis of schizophrenia by one clinician, depression by another, and neurocognitive disorder by a third.

As a step toward remedying this problem, the American Psychiatric Association published the first edition of *DSM*, in 1952, as a standard system for labeling and diagnosing psychological disorders. The *DSM* was revised in 1968, 1974, 2000, and most recently in 2013, with the goal of defining psychological disorders as objectively as possible, in terms of symptoms that clinicians could observe or could assess by asking relatively simple, straightforward questions of the person being diagnosed or of family members or others who knew that person well. To test alternative ways of diagnosing each disorder, they conducted field studies in which people who might have a particular disorder were diagnosed independently by a number of clinicians or researchers using each of several alternative diagnostic systems. In general, the systems that produced the greatest reliability—that is, the greatest agreement among the diagnosticians as to who had or did not have a particular disorder—were retained. The main categories of disorders identified in *DSM-5* are listed in **Table 15.1**. The first seven categories in the list are the ones that we shall discuss in subsequent sections of this chapter.

As an example of diagnostic criteria specified in *DSM-5*, consider those for *anorexia nervosa*, an eating disorder that can result in self-starvation. The person must (a) refuse to maintain body weight at or above a minimally normal weight for age and height; (b) express an intense fear of gaining weight or becoming fat; (c) manifest a disturbance in the experience of her or his own body weight or shape,

TABLE 15.1 Summary of *DSM-5* categories of psychological disorders

Anxiety Disorders
Disorders in which fear or anxiety is a prominent symptom, including *generalized anxiety disorder, phobias, panic disorder, agoraphobia,* and *social anxiety disorder.*
Trauma- and Stressor-Related Disorders
Disorders associated with exposure to a traumatic or stressful event, including *reactive attachment disorder* and *posttraumatic stress disorder (PTSD).*
Obsessive-Compulsive and Related Disorders
Disorders in which disturbing thoughts, images, or urges invade consciousness, usually accompanied by repetitive actions performed in response to an obsession.
Depressive Disorders
Disorders marked by sad, empty, or irritable mood, including *major depressive disorder* and *dysthymia.*
Bipolar and Related Disorders
Disorders characterized by major fluctuations in mood, from depression to mania, including *bipolar I disorder* and *bipolar II disorder.*
Schizophrenia Spectrum and Other Psychotic Disorders
Disorders on the *schizophrenia spectrum* are marked by disorganized thought and speech, delusions, hallucinations, disorganized behavior, and flattened or inappropriate affect. Another psychotic disorder is *delusional disorder,* which involves persistent delusions not accompanied by other disruptions of thought or mood.
Personality Disorders
Disorders involving inflexible, maladaptive personality traits. *DSM-5* enumerates 10 specific types—such as *paranoid personality disorder, narcissistic personality disorder,* and *avoidant personality disorder*—as well as "other" and "unspecified" personality disorders.
Dissociative Disorders
Disorders characterized by disruption of and/or discontinuity in normal integration of psychological functioning, including *dissociative identity disorder* (previously called "multiple personality disorder").
Feeding and Eating Disorders
Disorders marked by extreme undereating, overeating, or purging; by excessive concern about gaining weight; or by eating nonfood items. Examples include *anorexia nervosa, bulimia nervosa,* and *pica.*
Substance-Related and Addictive Disorders
Disorders brought on by drugs such as alcohol, cocaine, opioids, and tobacco that activate the brain's reward system; as well as non-substance-related disorders such as *gambling disorder.*
Sleep-Wake Disorders
Disorders dealing with disturbances in sleep, including *insomnia disorder, hypersomnolence disorder* (excessive sleepiness), and *narcolepsy* (lapsing into sleep).
Neurodevelopmental Disorders
Early-developing disorders including *intellectual disabilities, communication disorders* (e.g., delayed language, stuttering), *autism spectrum disorder, attention-deficit/hyperactivity disorder (ADHD),* and learning and motor disorders.
Neurocognitive Disorders
Disorders of thinking associated with brain damage or dysfunction due to disease such as *Alzheimer's, Parkinson's,* or *Huntington's* disease, or to traumatic brain injury.

Information from American Psychiatric Association, 2013.

show an undue influence of body weight or shape on self-evaluation, or deny the seriousness of the current low body weight; and (d) if a postpubertal female, have missed at least three successive menstrual periods (a condition brought on by a lack of body fat). If any one of these criteria is not met, a diagnosis of anorexia nervosa would not be made. Notice that all these criteria are based on observable characteristics or self-descriptions by the person being diagnosed; none rely on inferences about underlying causes or unconscious symptoms that could easily result in disagreement among diagnosticians who have different perspectives.

The Question of Validity

The *validity* of a diagnostic system is an index of the extent to which the categories it identifies are useful and meaningful for clinicians. (See Chapter 2, p. 48, for a more general discussion of both validity and reliability.) In theory, a diagnostic system could be highly reliable without being valid. For example, a system that reliably categorizes a group of people as suffering from Disorder X, on the basis of certain superficial characteristics, would not be valid if further work failed to reveal any clinical usefulness in that diagnosis. Do people with the same diagnosis truly suffer in similar ways? Does their suffering stem from similar causes? Does the label help predict the future course of the disorder and help in deciding on a beneficial treatment? To the extent that questions like these can be answered in the affirmative, a diagnostic system is valid.

FOCUS 2

How does validity differ from reliability? How can the validity of the *DSM* be improved through further research and revisions?

The question of validity is much more complicated than that of reliability and must be based on extensive research. In order to conduct the research needed to determine whether or not a diagnosis is valid, by the criteria listed earlier, one must first form a tentative, reliable diagnostic system. For example, the *DSM-5* definition of anorexia nervosa can be used to identify a group of people whose disorder fits that definition, and then those people can be studied to see if their disorders have similar origins and courses of development and respond similarly to particular forms of treatment. The results of such studies may lead to new means of defining and diagnosing the disorder or to new subcategories of the disorder, leading to increased diagnostic validity.

The *DSM* is not the only system for classifying psychological disorders. The World Health Organization (WHO) has developed the *International Classification of Diseases (ICD-10)*, which is used in much of the world to classify psychological disorders, and a group of researchers and clinicians has recently developed the Hierarchical Taxonomy of Psychopathology (HiTOP) to reflect the state-of-the art scientific evidence and to address limitations associated with the *DSM-5* (Kotov et al., 2017). In addition, questions about the validity of the *DSM-5* caused the National Institute of Mental Health (NIMH), the largest source of funding for mental-health research in the United States, to announce plans to develop its own classification system, emphasizing the use of objective laboratory measures, with a focus on biology, genetics, and neuroscience (Insel, 2013). The criticism from the NIMH will not likely end the *DSM*'s authority, but it does underscore the point that there are vigorous controversies over the identification, definition, and classification of psychological disorders, and that perhaps the *DSM* should be considered less of a bible for the field of mental health and more of a dictionary.

Possible Dangers in Labeling

Diagnosing and labeling may be essential for the scientific study of psychological disorders, but labels can be harmful. A label implying a psychological disorder has the potential to interfere with the person's ability to cope with his or her environment through several means: It can stigmatize the person and thereby reduce the esteem accorded to the person by others, it can reduce the labeled person's own self-esteem, and it may even blind clinicians and others to qualities of the person that are not captured by the label.

FOCUS 3

What are some negative consequences of labeling a person as psychologically disordered? What is recommended as a partial solution to this problem?

To reduce the likelihood of such effects, the American Psychiatric Association (2013) recommends that clinicians apply diagnostic labels only to people's disorders, not to people themselves. For example, a client or patient might be referred to as *a person with schizophrenia* or *who suffers from alcoholism* but should not be referred to as *a schizophrenic* or *an alcoholic*. The distinction might at first seem subtle, but if you think about it, you may agree that it is not so subtle in psychological impact. If we say, "John has schizophrenia," we tend to be reminded that John is first and foremost a person, with qualities like those of other people, and that his having schizophrenia is just one of many things we could say about him. In contrast, the statement "John is a schizophrenic" tends to imply that everything about him is summed up by that label.

As we talk about specific disorders in the remainder of this chapter and the next, we will attempt to follow this advice even though it produces some awkward wording at times. We also urge you to add, in your mind, yet another step of linguistic complexity. When we refer to "a person with schizophrenia," you should read this statement as "a person who has been diagnosed by someone as having schizophrenia," keeping in mind that diagnostic systems are never completely reliable.

Medical Students' Disease

The power of suggestion, which underlies the ability of labels to cause psychological harm, also underlies what is sometimes called *medical students' disease*. This disease, which could also be called *introductory psychology students' disease*, is characterized by a strong tendency to relate personally to, and to find in oneself, the symptoms of any disease or disorder described in a textbook. Medical students' disease was described by the nineteenth-century humorist Jerome K. Jerome (1889/1982) in an essay about his own discomfort upon reading a textbook of medical diagnoses. After explaining his discovery that he must have typhoid fever, St. Vitus's dance, and a multitude of diseases he had never heard of before, he wrote, "The only malady I concluded I had not got was housemaid's knee. . . . I had walked into that reading-room a happy, healthy man. I crawled out a decrepit wreck" (p. 6). As you read about specific disorders later in this chapter, brace yourself against medical students' disease. Everyone has at least some of the symptoms, to some degree, of essentially every disorder that can be found in this chapter, in *DSM-5*, or in any other compendium.

Cultural Variations in Disorders and Diagnoses

Psychological disorder is, to a considerable degree, a cultural construct. The kinds of distress that people experience, the ways in which they express that distress, and the ways in which others respond to the distressed person vary from culture to culture and over time in any given culture. Moreover, cultural beliefs and values help determine whether particular syndromes are considered to be disorders or variations of normal behavior.

Culture-Bound Syndromes

The most striking evidence of cross-cultural variation in psychological disorders can be found in *culture-bound syndromes*—expressions of mental distress that are almost completely limited to specific cultural groups (Tseng, 2006). In some cases, such syndromes represent exaggerated forms of behaviors that, in more moderate forms, are admired by the culture.

Examples of culture-related syndromes are the eating disorders *anorexia nervosa* and *bulimia nervosa*. Anorexia nervosa, as noted earlier, is characterized by an extraordinary preoccupation with thinness and a refusal to eat, sometimes to the point of death by starvation. Bulimia nervosa is characterized by periods of extreme binge eating followed by self-induced vomiting, misuse of laxatives or other drugs, or other means to undo the effects of a binge (at least one binge/one purge per week). It is probably not a coincidence that these disorders began to appear with some frequency in the 1970s in North America and Western Europe, primarily among adolescent girls and young women of the middle and upper classes, and that their prevalence increased through the remainder of the twentieth century (Gordon, 1990; Hoek, 2002). During that period, Western culture became increasingly obsessed with dieting and an ideal of female thinness while, at the same time, weight control became more difficult because of the increased availability of high-calorie foods.

Until recently, these eating disorders were almost completely unknown in non-Western cultures. In the early twenty-first century, however, with the increased globalization of Western media and values, anorexia nervosa and bulimia nervosa began to appear throughout the world. Studies in such places as the Pacific Islands and East Africa have shown that the incidence of these disorders correlates directly with the degree of Western media exposure (Becker et al., 2010; Caqueo-Urízar et al., 2011).

An example of a new culturally prepared psychological problem, appearing in various nations, is *Internet addiction*. This has been most fully documented in South Korea, where frighteningly large numbers of young people were found to be dropping out of school or employment, and some were even starving, because of their compulsive game-playing and other uses of the Internet (Tao et al., 2010). To a lesser degree, Internet addiction appears to be a problem also in the United States, and although it did not find its way into the *DSM-5*, "Internet gaming disorder" was listed as recommended for further study.

© Michael Hilgert/age fotostock

■ **Western values and abnormality**
Anorexia nervosa and bulimia nervosa are eating disorders found largely in Western countries. Many clinicians believe that these are culture-bound disorders caused in part by Western society's overemphasis on thinness as the aesthetic ideal for women, a preoccupation on display in Western ads, magazines, movies, and the like.

Role of Cultural Values in Determining What Is a Disorder

Culture does not affect just the types of behaviors and syndromes that people manifest; it also affects clinicians' decisions about what to label as disorders. A prime example has to do with homosexuality. Until 1973, homosexuality was officially—according to the American Psychiatric Association—a psychological disorder in the United States; in that year, the association voted to drop homosexuality from its list of disorders (Minton, 2002). The vote was based partly on research showing that the suffering and impairment associated with homosexuality derived not from the condition itself but from social prejudice directed against homosexuals. The vote was also prompted by an increasingly vocal gay and lesbian community that objected to their sexual orientation being referred to as a disorder, and by gradual changes in attitudes among many in the straight community, who were beginning to accept the normality of homosexuality.

 FOCUS 4

How does the example of homosexuality illustrate the role of culture in determining what is or is not a "disorder"?

Cultural Values and the Diagnosis of ADHD

The American Psychiatric Association has added many more disorders to *DSM* over the past three or four decades than it has subtracted. The additions have come partly from increased scientific understanding of psychological disorders and partly from a general cultural shift toward seeing psychological disorder where people previously saw normal human variation. An example that illustrates both of these trends is *attention-deficit/hyperactivity disorder*, or **ADHD**, which in recent years has been the single most frequently diagnosed disorder among children in the United States (CDC, 2012).

Most diagnoses of ADHD originate because of difficulties in school. Indeed, many of the *DSM-5* symptoms of the disorder refer specifically to schoolwork (American Psychiatric Association, 2013). The manual describes three varieties of the disorder. The *predominantly inattentive type* is characterized by lack of attention to instructions, failure to concentrate on schoolwork or other such tasks, and carelessness in completing assignments. The *predominantly hyperactive impulsive type* is characterized by such behaviors as fidgeting, leaving one's seat without permission, talking excessively, interrupting others, and blurting out answers before the question is

 FOCUS 5

How is ADHD identified and treated? How do critics of the high rate of diagnosis of ADHD explain the high rates?

completed. The *combined type*, which is most common, is characterized by both sets of symptoms.

A prominent but still controversial theory of the neural basis of ADHD is that it involves deficits in, or a slower-than-average rate of maturation of, the prefrontal lobes of the cortex—a portion of the brain responsible for focusing attention on tasks and inhibiting spontaneous activities (Barkley, 2001; Shaw et al., 2007). By far the most common treatment is the drug methylphenidate, sold in various short- and long-acting forms under such trade names as Ritalin and Concerta. Methylphenidate increases the activity of the neurotransmitters dopamine and norepinephrine in the brain, and its effectiveness may derive from its ability to boost neural activity in the prefrontal cortex. This drug reduces the immediate symptoms of ADHD in most diagnosed children, but there are as yet no long-term studies showing that the drug improves children's lives over the long run (Konrad et al., 2007), although benefits in terms of improvements in impulsivity control and perceptual sensitivity as a result of taking methylphenidate over the course of 12 months has been reported in children (Huang et al., 2012). It is also unknown whether it causes long-term negative side effects (Lakhan & Kirchgessner, 2012; Singh, 2008).

During the 1990s, the rate of diagnosis and treatment of ADHD in the United States increased eightfold (LeFever et al., 2003). Currently more than 11% of all U.S. children and adolescents, age 4 to 17, are diagnosed with the disorder (CDC, 2012). Since boys are diagnosed at rates that are at least three times those of girls, this means that the prevalence of ADHD diagnosis among boys is about 16% or more. European Americans, in general, are diagnosed with the disorder more frequently than are African Americans or Latinos, not because they are more disruptive in school but because they are more often referred to clinicians for diagnosis and treatment (LeFever et al., 2003).

Many sociologists and a few psychologists have argued that the explosion in diagnosis of ADHD in the United States and other Western nations derives at least partly from the increased concern about school performance (Rafalovich, 2004), which is manifested in high-stakes standardized testing and competitive admission to magnet schools, advanced-placement programs, and the like. Children everywhere, especially boys, get into trouble in school because of their need for vigorous activity, their impulsiveness, their carelessness about schoolwork, and their willingness to defy teachers and other authority figures. These characteristics vary in a continuous manner, showing the typical bell-shaped distribution of any normal personality dimension (Nigg et al., 2002). Even defenders of the high rate of ADHD diagnosis acknowledge that the characteristics of this disorder exist to some degree in all children, more so in boys than in girls, and that children classed as having the disorder are simply those who have these characteristics to a greater extent than do other children (Maddux et al., 2005; Stevenson et al., 2005). In recent decades, the requirements of schools have become increasingly uniform and have demanded increased levels of docility on the part of children. The ADHD diagnosis and medication of children seems to be the culture's current preferred way of dealing with the lack of fit between the expectations of schooling and the natural activity level of many children. Consistent with this interpretation is the observation that many, if not most, diagnoses of ADHD originate with teachers' recommendations (Graham, 2007; Mayes et al., 2009).

Some critics of the high rate of ADHD diagnosis—including a prominent neuroscientist who has conducted research on brain systems involved in this

■ **Normal playfulness or ADHD?** There is no clear dividing line between normal rambunctious playfulness in children and ADHD. As a result, ADHD is diagnosed at much higher levels in some school districts than in others.

condition (Panksepp, 1998, 2007)—assert that American culture has made it increasingly difficult for children to engage in the sorts of vigorous free play needed by all young mammals, especially young males, for normal development. They contend that, as a culture, we have chosen to treat many children with strong drugs—the long-term consequences of which are still unknown—rather than to design school and neighborhood environments that can accommodate children's needs to express a range of temperaments and behaviors, including impulsivity and rough-and-tumble play.

SECTION REVIEW

Psychological disorder presents numerous conceptual, diagnostic, and social challenges.

Categorizing and Diagnosing Psychological Disorders

- To be considered a psychological disorder by *DSM-5* standards, a syndrome (set of interrelated symptoms) must involve a clinically significant detriment, derive from an internal source, and not be subject to voluntary control. Though these guidelines are useful, "psychological disorder" is still a fuzzy concept.

- Classification and diagnosis (assigning a label to a person's psychological disorder) are essential for clinical purposes and for scientific study of psychological disorders.

- The developers of the *DSM* have increasingly worked on demonstrating reliability (the probability that independent diagnosticians would agree about a person's diagnosis) by using objective symptoms. Validity is a more complex issue.

- Because labeling a person can have negative consequences (e.g., lowering self-esteem or the esteem of others), labels should be applied only to the disorder, not to the person.

- Beware of medical students' disease.

Cultural Variations in Disorders and Diagnoses

- Culture-bound syndromes are expressions of mental distress limited to specific cultural groups. Examples are anorexia and bulimia nervosa (in cultures influenced by modern Western values).

- Culture also affects the types of behaviors or characteristics thought to warrant a diagnosis of psychological disorder. Until 1973, homosexuality was officially classed as a psychological disorder in the United States.

- The great increase in diagnosis of ADHD (attention-deficit/hyperactivity disorder) in the United States may result not just from increased understanding of the disorder but also from the culture's increased emphasis on school performance and reduced opportunities for vigorous play.

Causes of Psychological Disorders

Before examining major categories of psychological disorders, it is worth considering the general question of what causes psychological disorders. In this section we look first at the brain, which is necessarily involved in *all* psychological disorders. We then present a general framework for describing the ways that genes and environment can influence the incidence and onset of psychological disorders. Finally we propose some possible reasons why some disorders occur more often in men than in women, or vice versa.

The Brain Is Involved in All Psychological Disorders

Throughout this book we have emphasized that all thoughts, emotions, and actions—whether they are adaptive or maladaptive—are products of the brain. All the factors that contribute to causing psychological disorders do so by acting, in one way or another, on the brain. These include genes that influence brain development; environmental assaults on the brain, such as those produced by a blow to the head, oxygen deprivation, viruses, or bacteria; and, more subtly, the effects of learning, which are consolidated in pathways in the brain.

The Brain's Role in Irreversible Psychological Disorders

The role of the brain is most obvious in certain chronic psychological disorders—that is, in certain disorders that stay with a person for life once they appear. In these cases the brain deficits are irreversible—or at least cannot be reversed by any methods yet discovered. One example of such a disorder is *autism,* or *autistic spectrum disorder.* Although no definitive cause for autism has been identified, research has found a correlation between autism and a particular brain abnormality that may be caused in some cases primarily by genes and in other cases primarily by prenatal toxins or birth complications that disrupt normal brain development (Kabot et al., 2003). Two other examples are Down syndrome and Alzheimer's disease. We describe them briefly here because they are disorders linked to obvious brain deficits, for which the causes are reasonably well understood.

Down syndrome is a congenital (present at birth) disorder that appears in about 1 out of every 700 newborn babies in the United States (Parker et al., 2010). It is caused by an error in meiosis, which results in an extra chromosome 21 in the egg cell or (less often) the sperm cell (the numbering of chromosomes is depicted in Figure 3.3, p. 63). The extra chromosome is retained in all cells of the newly developing individual. Through a variety of means, it causes damage to many regions of the developing brain, such that the person goes through life with moderate to severe intellectual disability and with difficulties in physical coordination.

Alzheimer's disease, found primarily in older adults, has become increasingly prevalent as ever more people live into old age. It occurs in about 1% of people who are in their 60s, 3% of those in their 70s, 12% of those in their 80s, and 40% of those in their 90s (Alzheimer's Association, 2013). The disorder is characterized psychologically by a progressive deterioration, over the final years of the person's life, in all cognitive abilities—including memory, reasoning, spatial perception, and language—followed by deterioration in the brain's control of bodily functions.

Neurologically, Alzheimer's disease is characterized by certain physical disruptions in the brain, including the presence of *amyloid plaques*. The plaques are deposits of a particular protein, called *beta amyloid*, which form in the spaces between neurons and may disrupt neural communication (Clark et al., 2011; Nicoll et al., 2004). The disorder appears to be caused by a combination of genetic predisposition and the general debilitating effects of old age. Among the genes that may contribute are those that affect the rate of production and breakdown of beta amyloid (Bertram & Tanzi, 2008). Age may contribute partly through the deterioration of blood vessels, which become less effective in carrying excess beta amyloid out of the brain (Nicoll et al., 2004). Although old age is the greatest risk factor for Alzheimer's disease, there are others, which are listed in **Table 15.2**.

> ### FOCUS 6
>
> How are Down syndrome and Alzheimer's disease characterized as brain diseases?

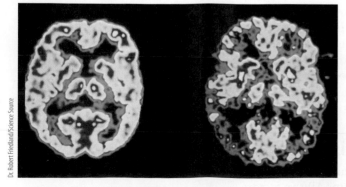

■ Alzheimer's disease affects brain activity. The blue and the black areas in the right image reflect reduced neural activity resulting from Alzheimer's disease.

Dr. Robert Friedland/Science Source

TABLE 15.2 Risk factors for Alzheimer's disease

High cholesterol levels*
High blood pressure*
Sedentary lifestyle*
Tobacco use*
Obesity*
Being over 50
Head injury
Family history of Alzheimer's disease

*Can be modified or prevented.

Information from Alzheimer's Association, 2013.

Role of the Brain in Episodic Psychological Disorders

Many disorders, including all the disorders discussed in the remaining sections of this chapter, are *episodic,* meaning that they are reversible. They may come and go, in episodes. Episodes of a disorder may be brought on by stressful environmental experiences, but the predisposition for the disorder nevertheless resides in one way or another in the brain.

Most psychological disorders, including those that are episodic, are to some degree heritable. The more closely related two people are genetically, the more likely it is that they share the same psychological disorder or disorders, regardless of whether or not they were raised in the same home (Howland, 2005; Rutter, 2006). In most cases it is not known just which genes are involved or how they influence the likelihood of developing the disorder, but it is reasonable to assume that such effects occur primarily through the genes' roles in altering the biology of the brain. Environmental assaults to the brain and the effects of learning can also contribute to the predisposition for episodic disorders.

A Framework for Thinking About Multiple Causes of Psychological Disorders

Most psychological disorders derive from the joint effects of more than one cause. Most disorders are not present at birth, but first appear at some point later in life, often in early adulthood. The subsequent course of a disorder—its persistence, its severity, its going and coming—is influenced by experiences that one has after the disorder first appears. It is useful, therefore, to distinguish among three categories of causes of psychological disorders: predisposing, precipitating, and perpetuating causes—the *three Ps*.

Predisposing causes of psychological disorders are those that were in place well before the onset of the disorder and make the person susceptible to the disorder. Genetically inherited characteristics that affect the brain are most often mentioned in this category. Predispositions for psychological disorders can also arise from damaging environmental effects on the brain, including effects that occur before or during birth. Such environmental assaults as poisons (including alcohol or other drugs consumed by the mother during pregnancy), birth difficulties (such as oxygen deprivation during birth), and viruses or bacteria that attack the brain can predispose a child for the subsequent development of one or more psychological disorders.

Prolonged psychologically distressing situations—such as living with abusive parents or an abusive spouse—can also predispose a person for one or another psychological disorder. Other predisposing causes include certain types of learned beliefs and maladaptive patterns of reacting to or thinking about stressful situations. A young woman reared in upper-class Western society is more likely to acquire beliefs and values that predispose her for an eating disorder than is a young woman from a rural community in China. Highly pessimistic habits of thought, in which one regularly anticipates the worst and fails to think about reasons for hope, predispose people for mood disorders (particularly depression) and anxiety disorders.

Precipitating causes of psychological disorders are the immediate events in a person's life that bring on the disorder. Any loss, such as the death of a loved one or the loss of a job; any real or perceived threat to one's well-being, such as physical disease; any new responsibility, such as might occur as a result of marriage or job promotion; or any large change in the day-to-day course of life can, in the sufficiently predisposed person, bring on the mood or behavioral change that leads to diagnosis of a psychological disorder. **Figure 15.1** on page 588 shows how the recent economic recession served as a precipitating event for an increase in suicides in the United States.

Precipitating causes are often talked about under the rubric of *stress,* a term that sometimes refers to the life event itself and sometimes to the worry, anxiety, hopelessness, or other negative experiences that accompany the life event (Lazarus, 1993). When the predisposition is very high, an event that seems trivial to others

FOCUS 7

How can the causes of psychological disorders be categorized into three types—"the three Ps"?

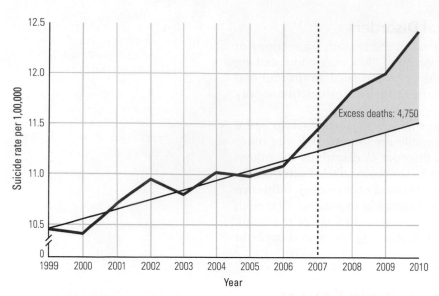

FIGURE 15.1 Trend in suicide rating in United States between 1999 and 2010 Although the rate of suicide showed a steady gradual increase between 1999 and 2008, it spiked in 2008 and increased even further with the onset of the economic recession. The dotted line between 2007 and 2010 indicates the expected trend in suicides, given the trend for the previous 8 years. As you can see, the total number of suicidal deaths far exceeded the expected trend, making the recession a precipitating cause of suicides. (Data from Reeves et al., 2012).

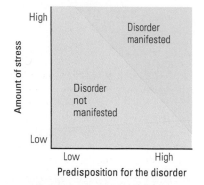

FIGURE 15.2 Relationship between predisposition and stress needed to trigger a psychological disorder The amount of stress needed to bring on a psychological disorder decreases as the predisposition for the disorder increases.

can be sufficiently stressful to bring on a psychological disorder. When the predisposition is very low, even an extraordinarily high degree of loss, threat, or change may fail to bring on a psychological disorder. **Figure 15.2** depicts this inverse relationship.

When looking at early environments as precipitating causes, the standard assumption is that positive environments—those that provide adequate resources and social and emotional support—produce "good" developmental outcomes such as educational success, emotional regulation, and mental health, whereas negative environments—characterized by high levels of stress and inadequate emotional and social support—produce "bad" developmental outcomes such as poor performance in school, poor self-regulation, and mental illness. The negative effects of an adverse environment are proposed to be especially harmful if an individual has a biological predisposition to respond especially strongly to stress. Essentially, early negative experience disturbs the typical course of development, leading to maladaptive behavior and poor mental health. The more risk factors an individual experiences, the greater the deficits in functional behavior (see **Figure 15.3**).

Although there is much research to support this contention (Evans & Cassells, 2014; Sameroff et al., 1993), it ignores the fact that, from an evolutionary developmental perspective, humans evolved to respond to different environmental contexts—good and bad—in an adaptive manner, and that some of the dysfunctional outcomes observed when some children grow up in high-stress environments may reflect their development being *directed* or *regulated* toward acquiring adaptive strategies to cope in these stressful environments (Del Giudice, 2014, 2016; Ellis et al., 2012). For example, Jeffrey Simpson and his colleagues (2012) reported that children whose first 5 years of life could be described as highly unpredictable (e.g., changes in residences, parental job changes, different adult males living in the household), had their first sexual intercourse sooner, more sex partners, and higher levels of aggression, risk taking, and delinquent behaviors at 23 years of age than children growing up in more predictable homes. Although these are all signs of maladjustment in modern society, they reflect what has been called a "fast life history strategy," in which people engage in more risky behaviors, which is adaptive (or would have been adaptive for our ancestors) in uncertain and stressful environments (Ellis et al., 2009).

Perpetuating causes of psychological disorders are those consequences of a disorder that help keep it going once it begins. In some cases, a person who behaves maladaptively may gain rewards, such as extra attention, which helps perpetuate the behavior. More often, the negative consequences of the disorder help perpetuate it. For example, a sufferer of depression may withdraw from friends, and lack of friends can perpetuate the depression. Behavioral changes brought on by a disorder, such as poor diet, irregular sleep, and lack of exercise, may also contribute to prolonging the disorder. Expectations associated with a particular disorder may play a perpetuating role as well. In a culture that regards a particular disorder as incurable, a person diagnosed with that disorder may simply give up trying to change for the better.

Possible Causes of Sex Differences in the Prevalence of Specific Disorders

Little difference occurs between men and women in the prevalence of psychological disorder when all disorders are combined, but large differences are found for specific disorders (American Psychiatric Association, 2013). Women are diagnosed with *anxiety disorders* and *depression* at rates that are nearly twice as great as those for men. Men are diagnosed with *intermittent explosive disorder* (characterized by relatively unprovoked violent outbursts of anger) and with *antisocial personality disorder* (characterized by a history of antisocial [harmful to others] acts with no sense of guilt) at rates that are three or four times those for women. Men are also diagnosed with *substance-use disorders* (including alcohol dependence and other drug dependence) at rates that are nearly twice as great as those for women. These sex differences may arise from a number of causes, including the following:

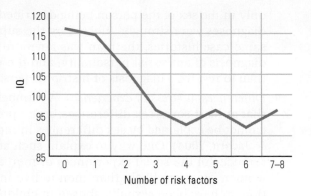

FIGURE 15.3 The relationship between the number of risk factors (for example, low income, father absence, maternal stress) and IQ for a group of 4-year-old children. The greater the number of risk factors, the lower children's IQs tended to be. Similar patterns of *cumulative risk* are found for physical and mental health outcomes (Evans, 2003).

(Data from Sameroff et al., 1993.)

- *Differences in reporting or suppressing psychological distress.* Diagnoses of anxiety disorders and of depression necessarily depend to a great extent on self-reporting. Men, who are supposed to be the "stronger" sex, may be less inclined than women to admit to anxiety and despondency in interviews or questionnaires. Supporting this view, experiments have shown that when men and women are subjected to the same stressful situation, such as a school examination, men report less anxiety than do women even though they show physiological signs of distress that are as great as, or greater than, those shown by women (Polefrone & Manuck, 1987).

- *Clinicians' expectations.* Diagnosticians may, to some degree, find a disorder more often in one sex than in the other because they *expect* to find it. In an experiment demonstrating such an expectancy bias, several hundred clinical psychologists in the United States were asked to make diagnoses on the bases of written case histories that were mailed to them (Ford & Widiger, 1989). For some, the case history was constructed to resemble the *DSM-III* criteria for *antisocial personality disorder* (characterized by disregard or violation of the rights of others; discussed later in the chapter), which is diagnosed more often in men than in women. For others it was constructed to resemble the *DSM-III* criteria for *histrionic personality disorder* (characterized by dramatic expressions of emotion to seek attention; discussed later in the chapter), which is diagnosed more often in women. Each of these case histories was written in duplicate forms, for different clinicians, differing

FOCUS 8

What are four possible ways of explaining sex differences in the prevalence of specific psychological disorders?

■ **Hysterical or angry?** Even today the word "hysterical" may come to mind more quickly when we view an angry woman than when we view an angry man. That same bias may contribute to the more frequent diagnosis of histrionic personality in women than in men.

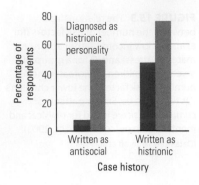

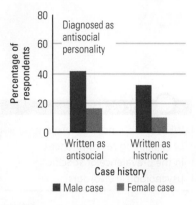

FIGURE 15.4 Evidence of a gender bias in diagnosis In this study, case histories were more likely to be diagnosed as antisocial personality if they described a fictitious male patient and as histrionic personality if they described a fictitious female patient, regardless of which disorder the case history was designed to portray.

(Data from Ford & Widiger, 1989.)

only in the sex of the person being described. As you can see in **Figure 15.4**, the diagnoses were strongly affected by the supposed patient's sex. Given the exact same case histories, the man was far more likely than the woman to receive a diagnosis of antisocial personality, and the woman was far more likely than the man to receive a diagnosis of histrionic personality.

- *Differences in stressful experiences.* A number of well-controlled studies indicate that at least some sex differences in the prevalence of disorders are real—they cannot be explained by sex differences in reporting or by biased diagnoses (Klose & Jacobi, 2004). One way to explain such actual differences is to search for differences in the social experiences of men and women. Throughout the world, women are more likely than men to live in poverty, to experience discrimination, to have been sexually abused in childhood, and to be physically abused by their spouses—all of which can contribute to depression, anxiety, and various other disorders that occur more often in women than in men (Nolen-Hoeksema, 2001; Olff et al., 2007). There is also evidence that the typical responsibilities that women assume in the family, such as caring for children, are more conducive to anxiety and depression than are the typical roles that men assume (Almeida & Kessler, 1998; Barnett & Baruch, 1987).

- *Differences in ways of responding to stressful situations.* The two sexes not only tend to experience different sorts of stressful situations, but also tend to respond differently to objectively similar situations (Kramer et al., 2008). Women tend to "internalize" their discomfort; they dwell mentally (ruminate) on their distress and seek causes within themselves. This manner of responding, in either sex, tends to promote both anxiety and depression (Kramer et al., 2008; Nolen-Hoeksema, 2001). Men, in contrast, more often "externalize" their discomfort; they tend to look for causes outside of themselves and to try to control those causes, sometimes in ways that involve aggression or violence. It is not clear what causes these differences in ways of responding, but it is reasonable to suppose that they are, in part, biologically predisposed. Such differences are observed throughout the world, and there is evidence that male and female hormones influence the typically male and female ways of reacting to stressful situations (Olff et al., 2007; Taylor et al., 2000).

SECTION REVIEW

Though psychological disorders have many possible causes, all exert their effects via the brain.

The Brain's Role in Chronic and Episodic Psychological Disorders

- Chronic psychological disorders such as Down syndrome and Alzheimer's disease arise from irreversible brain deficits.

- Down syndrome derives from an extra chromosome 21, and Alzheimer's disease is correlated with disruptive effects of amyloid plaques in the brain.

- All the other disorders discussed in the chapter are episodic. Causes may include hereditary influences on the brain's biology, environmental assaults on the brain, and effects of learning.

A Framework for Thinking About Multiple Causes

- Predisposing causes include genetic influences, early environmental effects on the brain, and learned beliefs.

- Precipitating causes are generally stressful life experiences or losses.

- Perpetuating causes include poor self-care, social withdrawal, and negative reactions from others.

Causes of Sex Differences in Prevalence of Specific Disorders

- Some diagnoses are much more prevalent in women, and some others are much more prevalent in men.

- Such differences may derive from (a) sex differences in the tendency to report or suppress psychological distress; (b) clinicians' expectations of seeing certain disorders more often in one sex than in the other; (c) sex differences in stress associated with differing social roles; or (d) sex differences in ways of responding to stress.

Anxiety Disorders

The rabbit crouches, frozen in the grass, minimizing its chance of being detected. Its sensory systems are at maximum alertness, all attuned to the approaching fox. With muscles tense, the rabbit is poised to leap away at the first sign that it has been detected; its heart races, and its adrenal glands secrete hormones that help prepare the body for extended flight if necessary. Here we see fear operating adaptively, as it was designed to operate by natural selection.

We humans differ from the rabbit on two counts: Our biological evolution added a massive, thinking cerebral cortex atop the more primitive structures that organize fear, and our cultural evolution led us to develop a habitat far different from that of our ancestors. Our pattern of fear is not unlike the rabbit's, but it can be triggered by an enormously greater variety of both real and imagined stimuli, and in many cases our fear is not adaptive. Fear is not adaptive when it causes a job candidate to freeze during an interview, or overwhelms a student's mind during an examination, or constricts the life of a person who can vividly imagine the worst possible consequence of every action.

Anxiety disorders are those in which fear or anxiety is the most prominent disturbance. The major anxiety disorders recognized by *DSM-5* are *generalized anxiety disorder, phobias,* and *panic disorder*. Genetic differences play a considerable role in the predisposition for all these disorders. Research with twins indicates that roughly 30 to 50% of the individual variability in risk to develop any given anxiety disorder derives from genetic variability (Gelernter & Stein, 2009; Gordon & Hen, 2004). In what follows, we describe the main diagnostic characteristics and precipitating causes of each of these common types of anxiety disorders.

Generalized Anxiety Disorder

Generalized anxiety is called *generalized* because it is not focused on any one specific threat; instead, it attaches itself to various threats, real or imagined. It manifests itself primarily as worry (Turk & Mennin, 2011). Sufferers of **generalized anxiety disorder** worry continuously, about multiple issues, and they experience muscle tension, irritability, and difficulty in sleeping. They worry about the same kinds of issues that most of us worry about—family members, money, work, illness, daily hassles—but to a far greater extent and with much less provocation (Becker et al., 2003).

To receive a *DSM-5* diagnosis of generalized anxiety disorder, such life-disrupting worry must occur on more days than not for at least 6 months and occur independently of other diagnosable psychological disorders (American Psychiatric Association, 2013). Roughly 6% of people in North America could be diagnosed as having this disorder at some time in their lives (Kessler et al., 2005). Generalized anxiety disorder is rarely diagnosed in children; its average age of onset is 31 years (Kessler et al., 2005). In predisposed people, the disorder often first appears at a diagnosable level following a major life change in adulthood, such as getting a new job or having a baby, or after a disturbing event, such as a serious accident or illness (Blazer et al., 1987).

Laboratory research shows that people diagnosed with generalized anxiety disorder are particularly attuned to threatening stimuli. For example, they notice threatening words (such as "cancer" or "collapse") more quickly, reliably, and automatically than do other people, whereas they show no such differences in recognition of nonthreatening words (Mogg & Bradley, 2005). They are also quicker to disengage from negative stimuli than people without the disorder (Yiend et al., 2015). Such heightened attention to potential threat is referred to as *hypervigilance,* and

"Wait a minute—I know there's something we've forgotten to worry about."

FOCUS 9

How can generalized anxiety disorder be understood in terms of hypervigilance, genes, early traumatic experiences, and cultural conditions?

there is evidence that such vigilance begins early in life and precedes the development of generalized anxiety disorder (Eysenck, 1992). Thus, hypervigilance may be a predisposing cause of generalized anxiety disorder as well as a symptom of the disorder.

Hypervigilance may result, in part, from genetic influences on brain development. As noted in Chapter 6, the brain's amygdala responds automatically to fearful stimuli, even when those stimuli don't reach the level of conscious awareness. In most of us, connections from the prefrontal lobe of the cortex help to control the fear reactions, but neuroimaging studies suggest that these inhibitory connections are less effective in people who are predisposed for generalized anxiety (Bishop, 2009). A lifelong tendency toward hypervigilance is also found in many individuals who experienced unpredictable traumatic experiences in early childhood (Borkovec et al., 2004). In an environment where dangerous things can happen at any time, a high degree of vigilance is adaptive.

Surveys taken at various times, using comparable measures, indicate that the average level of generalized anxiety in Western cultures has increased sharply since the middle of the twentieth century (Twenge, 2000). From a cultural perspective, that increase may be attributable to the reduced stability of the typical person's life. In a world of rapid technological change, we can't be sure that today's job skills will still be useful tomorrow. In a world of frequent divorce and high mobility, we can't be sure that the people we are attached to now will be "there for us" in the future. In a world of rapidly changing values and expectations, we have difficulty judging right from wrong or safe from unsafe. Such threats may be felt only dimly and lead not to conscious articulation of specific fears but to generalized anxiety. And, unlike the predatory fox that frightens the rabbit one minute and is gone the next, these threats are with us always.

Phobias

In contrast to generalized anxiety, a *phobia* is an intense, irrational fear that is very clearly related to a particular category of object or event. The fear is of some specific, nonsocial category of object or situation. It may be of a particular type of animal (such as snakes), substance (such as blood), or situation (such as heights or being closed in). For a diagnosis to be given, the fear must be long-standing and sufficiently strong to disrupt everyday life in some way—such as causing one to leave a job or to refrain from leaving home in order to avoid encountering the feared object. Phobias are quite prevalent; surveys suggest that they are diagnosable, at some time in life, in somewhere between 7% and 13% of people in Western societies (Hofmann et al., 2009; Kessler et al., 2005).

Usually a phobia sufferer is aware that his or her fear is irrational but still cannot control it. The person knows well that the neighbor's kitten won't claw anyone to death, that common garter snakes aren't venomous, or that it is safe to look out of a twentieth-floor office window at the cityscape below. People with phobias suffer doubly—from the fear itself and from knowing how irrational they are to have such a fear (Williams, 2005). Laboratory research shows that people with phobias are hypervigilant specifically for the category of object that they fear. For example, people with spider phobias can find spiders

■ **A snake for the hypervigilant**
People who suffer from a specific phobia tend to see the object of their fear even when it is so well camouflaged that most people would miss it. Would you see the snake if you were casually walking by?

in photographs that contain many objects more quickly than can other people. Once they have spotted the object, however, they avert their eyes from it more quickly than do other people (Pflugshaupt et al., 2005).

The Relation of Phobias to Normal Fears

Probably everyone has some irrational fears, and, as in all other anxiety disorders, the difference between the normal condition and the disorder is one of degree, not kind. Phobias are usually of things that many people fear to some extent, such as snakes, spiders, blood, darkness, or heights (Marks, 1987).

Phobias are much more often diagnosed in women than in men (American Psychiatric Association, 2013). In the population as a whole, men and boys are much less likely than women and girls to report fears of such things as spiders and darkness. The sex difference in phobias could stem from the fact that boys are more strongly encouraged than are girls to overcome or to hide their childhood fears (Fodor, 1982).

Phobias Explained in Terms of Learning and Evolution

Relatively little is known about how phobias arise, but learning certainly plays some role (Mineka & Zinbarg, 2006). Approximately 40% of people with phobias recall a traumatic situation in which they first acquired the fear (Hofmann et al., 2009). For example, people with dog phobias often recall being severely bitten by a dog. As described in Chapter 8, such experiences may be understood in terms of classical conditioning: The dog is the conditioned stimulus for fear, and the bite is the unconditioned stimulus. After the conditioning experience, the dog elicits fear even without a bite. In such trauma-producing situations, just one pairing of conditioned and unconditioned stimuli may be sufficient for strong conditioning to occur.

But people often develop phobias of objects that have never inflicted damage or been a true threat to them. For example, a survey conducted in Burlington, Vermont—where poisonous snakes are extremely rare—revealed that the single most common phobia there was of snakes (Agras et al., 1969). If phobias are acquired through traumatic experiences with the feared object, then why aren't phobias of such things as automobiles, electric outlets, or (in Vermont) icy sidewalks more common than phobias of harmless snakes?

According to an evolutionary account of phobias proposed by Martin Seligman (1971), people are genetically prepared to be wary of—and to learn easily to fear—objects and situations that would have posed realistic dangers during our evolutionary history. This idea helps to explain why phobias of snakes, spiders, darkness, and heights are more common than those of automobiles and electric outlets. Research has shown that people can acquire strong fears of such evolutionarily significant objects and situations more easily than they can acquire fears of other sorts of objects (Mineka & Zinbarg, 2006). Simply observing others respond fearfully to them, or reading or hearing fearful stories about them, can initiate or contribute to a phobia.

With respect to snakes, anyway, young children, although not innately fearful of snakes, more easily associate them with fearful responses than other animals. In one study, 7- to 9-month-old infants and 14- to 16-month-old toddlers watched videos of snakes and other animals (giraffes, rhinoceroses) and heard either a fearful or happy voice associated with each animal (DeLoache & LoBue, 2009). Although the children showed no fear of snakes when first watching the video, they looked longer at the snakes when they heard the fearful voice than when they heard the happy voice. There was no difference in their looking times to the two voices when they watched videos of other animals. These findings, along with others showing that monkeys more readily react fearfully after watching another monkey respond with fright to a snake than to a rabbit or a flower (Cook & Mineka, 1989), suggest that infants are prepared to acquire a fear of snakes. To bolster this argument, other research has shown that monkeys (*Macaca fuscata*) have specific neurons that respond selectively to visual images of snakes (Isbell, 2006; Van Le et al., 2013).

FOCUS 10

What evidence links phobias to the kinds of fears that most people have?

FOCUS 11

How might phobias be explained in terms of learning that has been prepared by evolution?

FOCUS 12

Are phobias such as fear of snakes "innate"? Can an evolutionary perspective help us explain some phobias?

Neither children nor monkeys are born with this fear, but rather they seem to possess perceptual biases to attend to certain types of stimuli and to associate them with fearful voices or reactions. In some people, such fears can develop into phobias.

Why do some people acquire phobias and others don't in the face of similar experiences? The answer probably stems from a variety of predisposing factors, including genetic temperament and prior experiences (Craske, 1999). If you had a great deal of safe prior experience with snakes, you would be less likely to develop a snake phobia after a traumatic encounter with a snake than would someone whose first exposure to snakes was traumatic (Field, 2006). As discussed in Chapter 8, classical conditioning of fears is reduced or blocked if the conditioned stimulus is first presented many times in the absence of the unconditioned stimulus.

People with phobias have a strong tendency to avoid looking at or being anywhere near the objects they fear, and this behavior pattern tends to perpetuate the disorder. To understand why this is so, recall from Chapter 8 that operant conditioning occurs through reinforcement following a behavior. When confronted with the feared object, even in the form of a photograph or television show, the person experiences anxiety. By avoiding the object, the person experiences the negative reinforcement of reduced anxiety ("Ah! I feel better now!") and thereby learns to avoid (for example) snakes, instead of learning that the vast majority of snakes found in Vermont are harmless. Without exposure to snakes, there is little opportunity to overcome a fear of them.

■ **Panic** This man has a reason to feel panic: He has just been attacked by a thief. People with panic disorder feel panic such as this at unpredictable times, without provocation.

Peter Cade/The Image Bank/Getty Images

Panic Disorder and Agoraphobia

Panic is a feeling of helpless terror, such as one might experience if cornered by a predator. In some people, this sense of terror comes at unpredictable times, unprovoked by any specific threat in the environment. Because the panic is unrelated to any specific situation or thought, the panic victim, unlike the victim of a phobia, cannot avoid it by avoiding certain situations. Panic attacks usually last several minutes and are accompanied by high physiological arousal (including rapid heart rate and shortness of breath) and a fear of losing control and behaving in some frantic, desperate way (Barlow, 2002). People who have suffered such attacks often describe them as the worst experiences they have ever had—worse than the most severe physical pain they have felt.

It is important to distinguish between a panic attack, which is not a psychological disorder, and panic disorder. A panic attack, which many people experience at one time or another, reflects some specific fear—of making a public speech, for instance. In contrast, a panic disorder reflects anxiety that a panic attack may occur. To be diagnosed with ***panic disorder***, by *DSM-5* criteria, a person must have experienced recurrent unexpected attacks, at least one of which is followed by at least 1 month of debilitating worry about having another attack or by life-constraining changes in behavior (such as quitting a job or refusing to travel) motivated by fear of another attack (American Psychiatric Association, 2013). By these criteria, roughly 2% of North Americans suffer from panic disorder at some time in their lives (Kessler et al., 2005).

As with other anxiety disorders, panic disorder often manifests itself shortly after some stressful event or life change (White & Barlow, 2002). Panic victims seem to be particularly attuned to, and afraid of, physiological changes similar to those signifying fearful arousal. In the laboratory or clinic, panic attacks can be brought on in people with the disorder by any of various procedures that increase heart rate and breathing rate: lactic acid injection, a high dose of caffeine, carbon dioxide inhalation, intense physical exercise, among others (Barlow, 2002). Thus a perpetuating cause, and possibly also predisposing cause, of the disorder is a learned tendency to interpret physiological arousal as catastrophic (Woody & Nosen, 2009).

Agoraphobia is a fear of public places. People with agoraphobia are commonly afraid that they will be trapped or unable to obtain help in a public setting. Agoraphobia develops at least partly because of the embarrassment and humiliation that might follow loss of control (panic) in front of others (Craske, 1999).

○ **FOCUS 13**

What learned pattern of thought might be a perpetuating cause of panic disorder?

SECTION REVIEW

Anxiety disorders have fear or anxiety as their primary symptom.

Generalized Anxiety Disorder	Phobias	Panic Disorder

Generalized Anxiety Disorder

- This disorder, characterized by excessive worry about real or imagined threats, may be predisposed by genes or childhood trauma and brought on by disturbing events in adulthood.
- Hypervigilance—automatic attention to possible threats—may stem from early trauma and may lead to generalized anxiety.
- Levels of generalized anxiety have risen sharply in Western culture since the mid-twentieth century.

Phobias

- Phobias involve intense fear of specific nonsocial objects (e.g., spiders) or situations (e.g., heights).
- Phobia sufferers usually know that the fear is irrational but still cannot control it.
- The difference between a normal fear and a phobia is one of degree.
- Natural selection may have prepared us to fear some objects and situations more readily than others.

Panic Disorder

- People with this disorder experience bouts of helpless terror (panic attacks) unrelated to specific events in their environment, but experiencing a panic attack does not mean one has panic disorder.
- The disorder may be predisposed and perpetuated by a learned tendency to regard physiological arousal as catastrophic.
- Caffeine, exercise, or other ways of increasing heart and breathing rates can trigger panic attacks in susceptible people.

Obsessive-Compulsive Disorder

An *obsession* is a disturbing thought that intrudes repeatedly on a person's consciousness even though the person recognizes it as irrational. A *compulsion* is a repetitive action that is usually performed in response to an obsession. Most people experience moderate forms of these, especially in childhood (Mathews, 2009). I (Peter Gray) remember a period in sixth grade when, while I was reading in school, the thought would repeatedly enter my mind that reading could make my eyes fall out. The only way I could banish this thought and go on reading was to close my eyelids down hard—a compulsive act that I fancied might push my eyes solidly back into their sockets. Of course, I knew that both the thought and the action were irrational, yet the thought kept intruding, and the only way I could abolish it for a while was to perform the action. Like most normal obsessions and compulsions, this one did not really disrupt my life, and it simply faded with time.

MentalHealthHumor.com   By: Chato B. Stewart

THINGS-TO-DO
☐ CHECK OVEN
☐ CHECK LOCKS
☐ WASH HANDS
☐ KILL DUST BUNNIES
☐ FLUSH TOILET
☐ REPEAT
☐ REPEAT
☐ REPEAT
☐ REPEAT
☐ REPEAT

Obsessive-Compulsive Disorder to Do list

Characteristics of OCD

People who are diagnosed with **obsessive-compulsive disorder (OCD)** are those for whom such thoughts and actions are severe, prolonged, and disruptive of normal life. To meet *DSM-5* criteria for this disorder, the obsessions and compulsions must consume more than an hour per day of the person's time and seriously interfere with work or social relationships (American Psychiatric Association, 2013). By these criteria, the disorder occurs in roughly 1 to 2% of people at some time in their lives (Kessler et al., 2005).

Obsessive-compulsive disorder is similar to a phobia in that it involves a specific irrational fear. It is different from a phobia primarily in that the fear is of something that exists only as a thought and can be reduced only by performing some ritual. People with obsessive-compulsive disorder, like those with phobias, suffer also from their knowledge of the irrationality of their actions and often go to great lengths to hide them from other people.

The obsessions experienced by people diagnosed with this disorder are similar to, but stronger and more persistent than, the kinds of obsessions experienced

---

🔍 **FOCUS 14**

How are obsessive-compulsive disorders similar to phobias? How do they differ? What kinds of obsessions and compulsions are most common?

by people in the general population (Mathews, 2009). The most common obsessions concern disease, disfigurement, or death, and the most common compulsions involve checking or cleaning. People with checking compulsions may spend hours each day repeatedly checking doors to be sure they are locked, the gas stove to be sure it is turned off, automobile wheels to be sure they are on tight, and so on. People with cleaning compulsions may wash their hands every few minutes, scrub everything they eat, and sterilize their dishes and clothes in response to their obsessions about disease-producing germs and dirt. Some compulsions, however, bear no apparent logical relationship to the obsession that triggers them. For example, a woman obsessed by the thought that her husband would die in an automobile accident could in fantasy protect him by dressing and undressing herself in a specific pattern 20 times every day (Marks, 1987).

Brain Abnormalities Related to OCD

Although all psychological disorders are brain related, the role of the brain in obsessive-compulsive disorder has been relatively well documented. In some cases, the disorder first appears after known brain damage, from such causes as a blow to the head, poisons, or diseases (Berthier et al., 2001; Steketee & Barlow, 2002). Brain damage resulting from a difficult birth has also been shown to be a predisposing cause (Vasconcelos et al., 2007), and in many other cases, neural imaging has revealed brain abnormalities stemming from unknown causes (Szeszko et al., 2004).

The brain areas that seem to be particularly involved include portions of the frontal lobes of the cortex and parts of the underlying limbic system and basal ganglia (Britton & Rauch, 2009); these normally work together in a circuit to control voluntary actions, the kinds of actions that are controlled by conscious thoughts. One theory is that damage in these areas may produce obsessive-compulsive behavior by interfering with the brain's ability to produce the psychological sense of closure or safety that normally occurs when a protective action is completed. Consistent with this theory, people with obsessive-compulsive disorder often report that they do not experience the normal sense of task completion that should come after they have washed their hands or inspected the gas stove, so they feel an overwhelming need to perform the same action again (Szechtman & Woody, 2004).

These brain areas are also associated with executive function. Recall from Chapter 9 that executive functions are important in planning, regulating behavior, and performing complex cognitive tasks. Executive function comprises three components: working memory, inhibition, and task switching. People with obsessive-compulsive disorder may have deficits in executive function, as they are less able to inhibit an undesirable behavior or to switch from one task to another than people without the disorder. Although findings vary, the results of *meta-analyses* (a statistical technique used to evaluate the magnitude of a significant effect across a large number of studies) clearly suggest that people with obsessive-compulsive disorder display impairments in all aspects of executive function relative to control subjects (Abramovitch et al., 2013; Snyder et al., 2015).

<hr />

FOCUS 15

How might damage to certain areas of the brain result in obsessive-compulsive disorder?

SECTION REVIEW

Obsessive-compulsive disorder involves repetitive, disturbing thoughts (obsessions) and repeated, ritualistic actions (compulsions).

- Obsessive-compulsive disorder is associated with abnormalities in an area of the brain that links conscious thought to action.
- Obsessions and compulsions are often extreme versions of normal safety concerns and protective actions, which the sufferer cannot shut off despite being aware of their irrationality.
- People with obsessive-compulsive disorder show impairments in executive function.

Traumatic and Stress-Related Disorders: Posttraumatic Stress Disorder

The *DSM-5* includes five disorders in which exposure to traumatic or stressful events are explicitly listed in the diagnosis. These include two disorders of childhood, in which children have experienced neglect, abuse, or insufficient care: *reactive attachment disorder*, in which children are inhibited or emotionally withdrawn from their caregivers; and *disinhibited social engagement disorder*, in which children are overly familiar with unfamiliar adults. The remaining three disorders all involve exposure to traumatic events, or threats of trauma. They include *acute stress disorder*, in which individuals experience distressing memories, negative mood, memory loss, and sleep disturbances, among other symptoms, that persist for at least 3 days; *adjustment disorder*, in which individuals experience emotional distress out of proportion to the severity of the stressor in response to an identifiable event, such as a death or the termination of a romantic relationship; and *posttraumatic stress disorder*. It is this last disorder that has received the most attention both from the general public and the medical and psychological community, and is the topic of the remainder of this section.

Posttraumatic stress disorder (**PTSD**) is *necessarily* brought on by stressful experiences. By definition, the symptoms of PTSD must be linked to one or more emotionally traumatic incidents that the affected person has experienced. The disorder is found in people who have survived horrific or life-threatening experiences, including anything from a car accident to battlefield mayhem, torture, rape or other violent assault, or involuntary confinement in a concentration camp or as a prisoner of war.

PTSD is characterized by three major symptoms: uncontrollable re-experiencing, heightened arousal, and avoidance of trauma-related stimuli. *Re-experiencing* of the traumatic event often involves nightmares, "flashbacks" when awake, and distress when reminded about the traumatic event. *Heightened arousal* involves sleeplessness, irritability, exaggerated startle responses, and difficulty concentrating. Finally, sufferers of PTSD attempt to actively *avoid thoughts and situations* that remind them of the trauma and often experience emotional numbing and social withdrawal (American Psychiatric Association, 2013).

It is difficult to assess the prevalence of this disorder because such assessments depend on the population sampled. In the United States, approximately 60% of men and 50% of women experience a least one traumatic event in their lives. Of these, about 8% of men and 20% of women will develop PTSD (National Center for PTSD, 2010). In contrast, in Algeria, where nearly everyone has been a victim of terrorist attacks, 40% of a random sample of adults were found to suffer from this disorder (Khaled, 2004). Similarly, rates of PTSD ranging from 15 to 30% have been found in war-torn regions of Cambodia, Ethiopia, and Palestine (de Jong et al., 2003).

PTSD is especially common in soldiers returning from war. The National Center for PTSD (2010) estimates that PTSD affects 10% of Gulf War veterans, 11 to 20% of Iraq and Afghanistan War veterans, and 30% of Vietnam War veterans. Moreover, the problems of veterans with PTSD are often compounded by other behaviors and conditions. Relative to other veterans, veterans with PTSD are more likely to abuse alcohol and other substances (Jacobsen et al., 2001; Tanielian & Jaycox, 2008), to be involved in domestic violence (Tanielian & Jaycox, 2008), and to experience depression and other anxiety disorders (Foa et al., 2013).

People with PTSD also show deficits in a number of cognitive abilities, including speed of information processing, working memory, verbal learning and memory (Scott et al., 2015), inhibitory control (Catarino et al., 2015), episodic memory (Brewin, 2014), and imagining future events (Kleim et al., 2014). Although it is tempting to conclude that experiencing trauma causes these cognitive deficits, it is also possible that people with lower levels of these cognitive abilities are more

FOCUS 16

How does posttraumatic stress disorder differ from other anxiety disorders?

FOCUS 17

What conditions are particularly conducive to development of posttraumatic stress disorder?

FOCUS 18

Why might some people be more susceptible to PTSD than other people?

FIGURE 15.5 PSTD symptoms in firefighters with low- and high-regulatory flexibility. Firefighters with low emotional-regulation abilities showed increases in PTSD symptoms with repeated exposure to traumatic events. Firefighters with high emotional-regulation abilities displayed no change in the number of PTSD symptoms as a function of repeated traumatic events.

(Data from Levy-Gigi, E., Bonanno, G. A., Shapiro, A. R., Richter-Levin, G., Kéri, S., & Sheppes, G. (2016). Emotion regulation flexibility sheds light on the elusive relationship between repeated traumatic exposure and posttraumatic stress disorder symptoms. *Clinical Psychological Science*, 4, 28–39.)

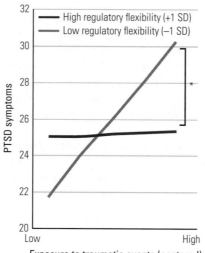

susceptible to the effects of trauma than people with better developed cognitive abilities. It is likely that there is some truth in both of these positions.

People who are exposed repeatedly, or over long periods of time, to distressing conditions are much more likely to develop PTSD than are those exposed to a single, short-term, highly traumatic incident. One study revealed that the incidence of PTSD among Vietnam War veterans correlated more strongly with long-term exposure to the daily stressors and dangers of the war—heat, insects, loss of sleep, sight of dead bodies, risk of capture by the enemy—than with exposure to a single atrocity (King et al., 1995). Another study, of 3,000 war refugees, revealed that the percentage with PTSD rose in direct proportion to the number of traumatic events they had experienced (Neuner et al., 2004). Likewise, children exposed to repeated abuse in their homes are particularly prone to the disorder (Roesler & McKenzie, 1994). Most people can rebound reasonably well from a single horrific event, but the repeated experience of such events seems to wear that resilience down, perhaps partly through long-term debilitating effects of stress hormones on the brain (Kolassa & Elbert, 2007).

Not everyone exposed to repeated highly stressful conditions develops PTSD. One reason for this variability seems to be the ability to regulate one's emotions. As discussed in Chapter 9, executive functions are related to many social and clinical outcomes. Just as people with obsessive-compulsive disorder often have impairments in executive functions (noted earlier in this chapter), executive functions—particularly emotion regulation—are also related to the tendency to experience PTSD. In one study, firefighters who scored low on a test of emotional regulation showed a significant correlation between the number of traumatic events experienced and the incidence of PTSD. Although firefighters low in emotion regulation who experienced few traumatic events showed fewer PTSD symptoms than those who experienced many traumatic events, there was no significant relationship between these variables for firefighters with high emotional self-regulation abilities (Levy-Gigi et al., 2016; see **Figure 15.5**).

Social support, both before and after the stressful experiences, seems also to play a role in reducing the likelihood of PTSD (Ozer et al., 2003). Genes also play a role (Paris, 2000). One line of evidence for that comes from a study of twins who fought in Vietnam, which found that identical twins were considerably more similar to each other in the incidence of the disorder and in the types of symptoms they developed than were fraternal twins (True et al., 1993).

SECTION REVIEW

Posttraumatic stress disorder is characterized by uncontrollable re-experiencing of one or more traumatic events, heightened arousal, and avoidance of trauma-related stimuli.

- People with PTSD are more likely to abuse alcohol and other substances, be involved in domestic violence, experience depression and other anxiety disorders, and display deficits in basic cognitive abilities.

- People with high emotional self-regulation abilities are less apt to display symptoms of PTSD after experiencing multiple traumas than people with low emotional self-regulation abilities.

- Genetic predisposition, repeated exposures to traumatic events, and inadequate social support increase the risk for the disorder.

- Not everyone exposed to repeated highly stressful events develops PTSD.

Mood Disorders

Mood refers to a prolonged emotional state that colors many, if not all, aspects of a person's thought and behavior. It is useful (though oversimplified) to think of mood as a continuum running from *depression* at one end to *elation* at the other. Because we all have tasted both, we have an idea of what they are like. Depression and elation are normal experiences, but at times either of them can become so intense or prolonged as to promote harmful, even life-threatening, actions. Extreme depression can keep a person from working, lead to withdrawal from friends, or even provoke suicide. Extreme elation, called *mania,* can lead to outrageous behaviors that turn other people away or to dangerous acts that stem from a false sense of security and bravado.

DSM-5 identifies two main categories of mood disorders: **depressive disorders**, characterized by prolonged or extreme depression, and **bipolar and related disorders**, characterized usually by alternating episodes of mania and depression.

Depressive Disorders

Depression is characterized primarily by prolonged sadness, self-blame, a sense of worthlessness, and absence of pleasure. Other common symptoms include decreased or increased sleep, decreased or increased appetite, and either retarded or agitated motor symptoms. Retarded motor symptoms include slowed speech and slowed body movements. Agitated symptoms, which are less common than retarded symptoms, include repetitive, aimless movements such as hand wringing and pacing. To warrant a diagnosis of a depressive disorder, the symptoms must be either very severe or very prolonged and not attributable just to a specific life experience, though they may be triggered or exacerbated by such an experience.

Two main classes of depressive disorders are distinguished in *DSM-5*. **Major depression** is characterized by very severe symptoms that last essentially without remission for at least 2 weeks. **Dysthymia** [dĭs-**thī´**-mē-ə], also referred to as *persistent depressive disorder,* is characterized by less severe symptoms that last for at least 2 years. It is not unusual for bouts of major depression to be superimposed over a more chronic state of dysthymia, in which case the person is said to have *double depression.* Surveys in North America suggest that as many as 15% of people suffer from major depression, and 2 to 3% suffer from dysthymia, at some time in their lives (González et al., 2010; Kessler et al., 2005).

■ **Depression** Artists and other creative people who suffer from depression may find inspiration in their depressive moods, even if they are more productive during periods when they feel less depressed.

Gabriele Meerman/dieKleinert / Alamy Stock Photo

Comparisons Between Depression and Generalized Anxiety

Depression and generalized anxiety disorder have many similarities. The two disorders are apparently predisposed by the same genes. The identical twins of people suffering from either generalized anxiety disorder or major depression exhibit equally enhanced rates of either disorder (Kendler et al., 2006). Other studies reveal

FOCUS 19

What are some similarities and differences between depression and generalized anxiety?

TABLE 15.3 Comparison of anxious thoughts with depressed thoughts

Anxious thoughts	Depressed thoughts
What if I get sick and become an invalid?	I'm worthless.
I might offend someone I care about.	I'm offensive to people.
Some might not like how I look.	I'm physically unattractive.
I could lose my job.	Nothing ever works out for me.
I could have a heart attack and die.	Life isn't worth living.

Information from Beck et al., 1987.

that the two disorders often occur in the same individuals. Approximately 60% of people diagnosed with generalized anxiety disorder also suffer from a depressive disorder at some point in their lives (Hettema, 2008; Kessler et al., 2008). Typically, generalized anxiety occurs before onset of major depression (Hunt et al., 2004; Wittchen et al., 2000).

One way to conceive of the difference between generalized anxiety and depression is to think of the former as a frantic, relatively ineffective attempt to cope with life's real and imagined threats through worry and hypervigilance, and to think of the latter as a kind of giving up, despairing of coping and concluding that life is not worth living. Cognitively, anxious individuals worry about what might happen in the future, while depressed individuals feel that all is already lost (see **Table 15.3**). Depressed individuals are much more likely than anxious individuals to stop caring for themselves and to stay in bed all day. The sense of giving up is commonly accompanied by strong feelings of self-blame, of not deserving to live. People with depression frequently have low levels of self-esteem, with some theorists suggesting that low self-esteem contributes to depression (Butler et al., 1994; Orth & Robins, 2013; Sowislo & Orth, 2013).

Negative Thought Pattern as a Cause of Depression

Negative thoughts are characteristic of people who are depressed, and they may also characterize people who are not depressed but are vulnerable to becoming so. Consider two nondepressed college students who have just taken and failed their first test in Introductory Psychology. One responds to the failure by thinking: "I'm stupid. I'm going to fail this course. I'm going to flunk out of college." The other responds by thinking: "Ouch. That was a tough test. I didn't study enough, and I was up too late the night before." The first student illustrates a pattern of thought that is very likely to lead to depression, while the opposite is true of the second.

A prominent modern theory of depression is the *hopelessness theory*, developed by Lyn Abramson and her colleagues (1989). According to this theory, depression results from a pattern of thinking about negative events that has three characteristics:

FOCUS 20

According to the hopelessness theory, what pattern of thinking predisposes a person for depression? What is some evidence for the theory?

- Assuming that the negative event will have disastrous consequences. (The failed test will lead to flunking out of college.)

- Assuming that the negative event reflects something negative about him- or herself. (The failure is proof of stupidity or some such personal inadequacy.)

- Attributing the cause of the negative event to something that is *stable* (will not change) and *global* (capable of affecting many future events). (Stupidity is an unchangeable characteristic that will affect all realms of endeavor.)

FOCUS 21

How might rumination serve to enhance or worsen depression?

In addition, a thinking style used by many people with depression is **rumination**, which involves "repetitively and passively focusing on symptoms of distress and on the possible causes and consequences of these symptoms" (Nolen-Hoeksema et al., 2008, p. 400). Rumination does not lead to problem solving, but rather involves fixation on the one's problems and negative feelings. Rumination is strongly related to depression (Mor & Winquist, 2002; Nolen-Hoeksema et al., 2008) and serves to maintain or worsen depression by maintaining negative thinking and interfering with problem solving (Nolen-Hoeksema, 1991). Jutta Joormann and W. Michael Vanderlind (2014) proposed that rumination is a maladaptive emotional regulation strategy that depressed people use, believing that it provides increased self-understanding and awareness (Papageorgiou & Wells, 2001).

A major controversy concerning the hopelessness theory is whether the three-factor hopeless thought pattern merely *reflects* depression or is also a *cause* of depression (Joormann, 2009). Certainly, depressed people manifest this negative manner of thinking. By *DSM-5* criteria or any other criteria, negative thinking is part of the definition of depression. But Abramson and her colleagues have shown that the hopeless manner of thinking about negative events can also occur in people who are not depressed, and in those people it is predictive of future depression.

In one study, first-year, nondepressed college students with no prior history of clinical depression filled out a questionnaire designed to measure the hopeless style of thinking about negative events and another questionnaire designed to assess their current level of mood. Then they were assessed at various times for depression over a 2.5-year follow-up period (Alloy et al., 2006). Those who had scored high on the measure of negative thinking were over six times as likely to manifest an episode of major depression at some point during the follow-up period than were those who had scored low on that measure. This was true even when just those who were equivalent in mood level at the beginning of the study were compared.

Other evidence that negative thinking is a cause of depression comes from research on cognitive therapy (discussed in Chapter 16). This therapeutic approach, which aims to help people change habitual patterns of thinking, has been shown to reduce depression and the likelihood of its recurrence. Moreover, several studies have shown that children and adolescents who have never been depressed can be at least partially inoculated against future depression by training in which they learn to interpret negative events in hope-promoting ways (Munoz et al., 2009).

Stressful Experiences Plus Genetic Predisposition as Cause of Depression

Many studies have shown that people who have recently suffered a severely stressful experience are much more likely to become depressed than are those who have not (Kessler, 1997; Monroe et al., 2009). The kinds of stressful events that are most strongly associated with depression are *losses* that alter the nature of one's life—loss of a spouse or other close daily companion, loss of a job that one has held for a long time, loss in social status, sharp loss in income, or permanent loss in health. Such events interrupt one's life routines and render ineffective well-established ways of satisfying one's needs and desires. They can promote the kind of hopeless thinking that corresponds with and predicts depression.

Yet, research has also shown very clearly that not everyone becomes depressed in response to such occurrences. Some people are resilient, even in the face of severe losses. They experience sadness, but not major depression, and they put their efforts effectively into restructuring their lives. The difference appears to reside largely in genes.

In a research study dramatically supporting this conclusion, Kenneth Kendler and his colleagues identified over 1,000 women who had twin sisters (Kendler, 1998; Kendler et al., 1995). They studied each to identify (a) whether or not she had recently experienced a highly stressful life event (defined as assault, serious marital problems, divorce or breakup of a marriage or other romantic relationship, or death of a close relative), (b) whether or not a period of major depression began within a month after that stressful event (or within a comparable time period for those who had not experienced a serious stressor), and (c) her level of genetic predisposition for depression. The level of genetic predisposition was judged on the basis

FOCUS 22

How did Kendler demonstrate that the onset of major depression typically requires *both* genetic predisposition and a severely stressful life event?

FIGURE 15.6 Roles of genetic predisposition and stressful experiences in the incidence of depression Women who had recently experienced a severely stressful event were far more likely to experience the onset of major depression than were those who had not. This effect of stress was greater for those who were judged to be more genetically predisposed for depression (based on the status of their twin sisters, as shown in the key) than for those who were judged to be less genetically predisposed.

(Data from Kendler et al., 1995.)

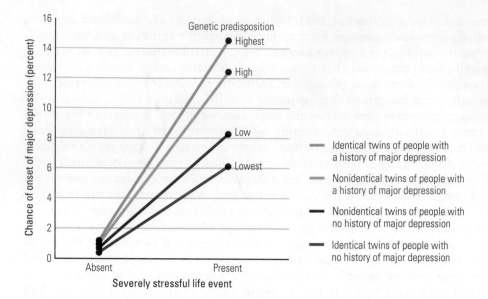

FIGURE 15.7 Adolescent depression and maternal rejection Adolescents who possessed one combination of alleles (TT) experienced significantly greater levels of clinical depression as a result of high levels of maternal rejection than adolescents with alternate combinations of alleles (CC or CT), demonstrating an interaction between genes and environment.

(Data from Haeffel et al., 2008.)

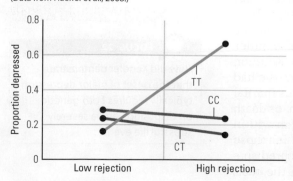

of whether or not the woman's twin sister (co-twin) did or did not have a history of major depression and whether she was an identical twin or a nonidentical twin.

The results of the study are depicted in **Figure 15.6**. Among women who had not recently experienced a highly stressful life event, the incidence of depression was very low regardless of level of genetic predisposition. However, among those who had recently experienced such an event, the incidence of depression was strongly related to the level of genetic predisposition. The results are quite consistent with the idea that major depression generally requires *both* a genetic predisposition for depression *and* some severely stressful event to bring it on.

More recently, research has focused on specific gene alleles that may be conducive to, or protective against, depression. The most consistent findings to date concern a gene (*5-HTTLLPR*) that alters the effects of the neurotransmitter serotonin in the brain. Recall from Chapter 12 that this gene comes in two alleles—a *short* form and the *long* form. In Chapter 12, we describe research indicating that infants who have two copies of the long allele are protected from at least some of the negative effects of insensitive parenting. Several research studies suggest that this allele also tends to protect adults from becoming depressed in response to severe stressful events, but only under certain rearing environments. For example, in research by Avshalom Caspi and his colleagues (2003), people who had the short version of the *5-HTT* gene were more likely to experience depression than people with the long version, but only if they experienced multiple stressful events in childhood. This finding is controversial because, although it has been replicated (Kendler et al., 2005), not all researchers who have looked for this relationship have found it (Risch et al., 2009). In other research looking at different alleles of a gene (called *DAT1*) involved in the transportation of the neurotransmitter dopamine, adolescents were more apt to be classified as clinically depressed if they had experienced high levels of maternal rejection as children than nonrejected adolescents, but only if they had one combination of alleles (TT versus CC or CT; see **Figure 15.7**) (Haeffel et al., 2008). Thus, rather than the *5-HTT* or *DAT1* genes being "for" depression, the research suggests an interaction between genetic disposition and childhood experience in depression.

Possible Brain Mechanisms of Depression

Depression, like every other psychological state, is a product of the brain. Thus, one route to understanding depression is to try to identify changes in the brain that might cause bouts of depression to appear and disappear.

All the drugs that are used regularly to treat depression have the effect of increasing the amount or activity of one or both of two neurotransmitters in the brain: norepinephrine and serotonin. For that reason, an early theory of depression posited that the disorder results from a brain deficiency in one or both of these transmitters (Schildkraut, 1965). Today, however, that simple theory is much doubted (Krishnan & Nestler, 2008). One problem is that it does not explain the delayed effectiveness of drug treatments. Antidepressant drugs begin to enhance the activity of norepinephrine or serotonin (or both) in the brain immediately, yet they typically do not begin to relieve depression until at least 2 weeks of continuous treatment have elapsed. Moreover, by various measures, most depressed people do not appear to have unusually low levels of these neurotransmitters (Cowen, 2005).

Many neuroscientists interested in depression are focusing on the ways that the brain changes during periods of psychological distress. Stress and worry are often associated with an increased release of cortisol, a hormone produced by the adrenal glands. Research with animals shows that cortisol can act on the brain to shut off certain growth-promoting processes. Over periods of weeks or months, a high level of cortisol can result in a small but measurable shrinkage in some portions of the brain, including portions of the prefrontal cortex and the hippocampus (Jacobs, 2004). These brain changes are reversible. During periods of reduced stress, the shrunken brain areas may regain their former size. Moreover, increases in norepinephrine and serotonin over periods of weeks can stimulate growth in these brain areas, and this observation may explain the delayed effects of drug treatments in relieving depression.

Thus, one current theory, which is far from proven, is that depression in humans results at least partly from a stress-induced loss of neurons or neural connections in certain parts of the brain and that recovery from depression results from regrowth in those brain areas (Jacobs, 2004; Martinowich et al., 2007; Perera et al., 2008). This theory is consistent with the evidence that depression often follows a rather prolonged period of anxiety. Anxiety stimulates production of the hormones that interfere with brain growth. The theory is also consistent with the idea that altered ways of thinking can change one's predisposition for depression. Hopefulness reduces psychological distress, which reduces the production of the growth-inhibiting hormones and thereby protects the brain from the changes that lead to depression. It will be interesting to see how well this theory holds up to the tests of future research.

"Thank God they have pills for that now."

 FOCUS 23

What early evidence supported the theory that depression results from a deficit in the neurotransmitters norepinephrine and serotonin? Why is that theory now doubted?

 FOCUS 24

According to a new theory, how might stressful experiences alter the brain in a way that brings on depression?

Possible Evolutionary Bases for Depression

Psychologists viewing depression from an evolutionary perspective have suggested that it may be an exaggerated form of a response to loss that in less extreme form is adaptive (Allen & Badcock, 2006; Nesse, 2000). Only a minority of people develop clinically severe depression, but most of us experience a low mood or moderate depression at some periods in our lives. A depressed mood slows us down, makes us think realistically rather than optimistically, leads us to turn away from goals we can no longer hope to achieve, and signals to others that we are no threat to them and need their help. The signals of helplessness by depressed persons resemble the appeasement displays used by other animals to signal submissiveness and need for care (Price et al., 2004). A depressed mood can also lead to a kind of soul-searching, the end result of which may be the establishment of new, more realistic goals and a new approach to life (Welling, 2003).

Matthew Keller and Randolph Nesse (2005, 2006) have suggested that depressed moods may come in a variety of different forms, each adapted for different survival purposes. Most people who live in northern latitudes experience some degree of depressed mood during the winter (Dam et al., 1998). When it occurs in extreme form, such winter-limited depression is diagnosed as *seasonal affective disorder*,

 FOCUS 25

How might moderate depression, following a loss, be adaptive?

 FOCUS 26

According to Keller and Nesse, how might depressed moods vary, adaptively, depending on the situation?

or *SAD*. This form of depression is accompanied by increased appetite, increased sleepiness, and lethargy—all responses that, in less extreme form, may have been useful to our evolutionary ancestors for building layers of fat and conserving energy to survive the harsh winter. That form of depression is generally not accompanied by the degrees of sadness, crying, and self-reproach that occur in other forms of depression.

In their own research, Keller and Nesse (2006) found that depressed mood following the death of a loved one or the loss of a romantic partner is especially characterized by crying and other expressions of sadness, which may signal the need for help from others. In contrast, they found that depressed mood following repeated failure is especially characterized by self-blame and pessimism, which may motivate the person to withdraw from futile activities and begin a period of realistic reappraisal of life goals. It remains for future research to continue testing the idea that depressed moods come in different forms that serve different adaptive purposes.

Bipolar Disorders

Major depression and dysthymia are sometimes called *unipolar disorders* because they are characterized by mood changes in only one direction—downward from normal. In contrast, bipolar disorders (formerly called manic-depression) are characterized by mood swings in both directions: downward in depressive episodes and upward in manic episodes. Such episodes may last anywhere from a few days to several months, often separated by months or years of relatively normal mood.

DSM-5 identifies two main varieties of bipolar disorders. **Bipolar I disorder** is the classic type, characterized by at least one manic episode, which may or may not be followed by a depressive episode. **Bipolar II disorder** is characterized by a less extreme high phase, referred to as *hypomania* rather than mania. Bipolar I disorder and bipolar II disorder occur, respectively, in about 1% and 2 to 3% of people in the population at some time in life (Merikangas et al., 2011; Kessler et al., 2005). In some cases, episodes of mania may occur without intervening episodes of depression (Belmaker, 2004).

Research with twins and adoptees has shown that the predisposition for bipolar disorder is strongly heritable, more so than unipolar depression or most other psychological disorders (Johnson et al., 2009). Stressful life events may help bring on manic and depressive episodes in people who are predisposed (Ambelas, 1987; Hlastala et al., 2000), but the evidence for such effects is not as strong as it is for unipolar depression. Bipolar disorder, unlike unipolar depression, can usually be controlled with regular doses of the element *lithium*. Lithium seems to work mainly by promoting the survival, development, and function of neurons (Machado-Vieira et al., 2009).

The Manic Condition

FOCUS 27

How are manic states experienced? What is some evidence linking mild manic (hypomanic) episodes to heightened creativity?

Manic episodes are typically characterized by expansive, euphoric feelings; elevated self-esteem; increased talkativeness; decreased need for sleep; and enhanced energy and enthusiasm, which may be focused on one or more grandiose projects or schemes (American Psychiatric Association, 2013). The inordinate feelings of power, confidence, and energy are illustrated by the following quotation from a woman describing her own disorder:

> When I start going into a high, I no longer feel like an ordinary housewife. Instead, I feel organized and accomplished, and I begin to feel I am my most creative self. I can write poetry easily. I can compose melodies without effort. I can paint. . . . I have countless ideas about how the environmental problem could inspire a crusade for the health and betterment of everyone. . . . I don't seem to need much sleep. . . . I feel sexy and men stare at me. Maybe I'll have an affair, or perhaps several. I feel capable of speaking and doing good in politics. (Fieve, 1975, p. 27)

During hypomania and the early stages of a manic episode, the high energy and confidence may lead to an increase in productive work, but, as a manic episode progresses, judgment becomes increasingly poor and behavior increasingly maladaptive. Full-blown mania may be accompanied by bizarre thoughts and dangerous behaviors, such as jumping off a building in the false belief that one can fly; and even hypomania may be accompanied by spending sprees, absence from work, or sexual escapades that the affected person later regrets (Akiskal, 2002). Moreover, not all people with bipolar disorders experience the manic state as euphoric: Some experience it as a time of extraordinary irritability, suspiciousness, or destructive rage (Carroll, 1991).

Possible Relation of Hypomania to Enhanced Creativity

Analyses of biographies and historical documents concerning eminently creative writers, artists, and musicians suggest that a disproportionate percentage of them suffered from a bipolar disorder (Andreasen, 1987; Jamison, 1995). The same studies suggest that those people were most productive during hypomanic phases of their illness—when their mood was elevated, but not to such an extreme as to prevent coherent thought and action. As one example, the composer Robert Schumann—who often suffered from severe depression—produced an extraordinary number of his valued musical works during two episodes of apparent hypomania, one in 1840 and the other in 1849 (Jamison, 1995). As another example, the poet Emily Dickinson wrote much of her best poetry during episodes of apparent hypomania that followed bouts of winter depression (Ramey & Weisberg, 2004).

Such analyses have been criticized on the grounds that the diagnoses of mood disorders and the judgments concerning hypomania were generally made after the fact, on the basis of written material that may not have been fully accurate (Rothenberg, 2001). It is also possible that hypomania in highly creative people is more a result of high creativity than a cause: People who become strongly absorbed in and excited by their work may, as a result, exhibit manic-like behaviors (Ramey & Weisberg, 2004). Still another possibility is that people who suffer from extremes of mood may not, on average, be naturally more creative than others, but may be more drawn to creative activities. Such activities may provide a means for them to deal with or express the unusual feelings and thoughts that accompany their low and high moods.

Further evidence for a correlation between creativity and hypomania—regardless of causal direction—comes from studies of creativity in people who are not famous for their creative accomplishments. This is reflected in the results of a recent meta-analysis that found a significant relationship between creativity and people who were assessed to be at risk for bipolar disorder (Baas et al., 2016). In one study, people who manifested moderate mood swings—states of hypomania alternating with moderate levels of depression—were judged to be more creative in their regular work and home life than were those who exhibited greater stability in their moods (Richards et al., 1988). Another study, of 16-year-olds with no diagnosable mood disorders, revealed positive correlations between tendencies to experience hypomania and high scores on tests of creativity and of openness to experience, a personality trait that itself correlates positively with creativity (Furnham et al., 2008). People with bipolar disorder have also been found, on average, to score higher than others on tests of creativity and openness to experience (Nowakowska et al., 2005; Santosa et al., 2007).

Although not limiting his analyses strictly to hypomania, Dean Simonton (2014) used a previous author's estimates of degree of psychopathology (rated on a 4-point scale: 0 = none, 1 = mild, 2 = marked, 3 = severe; Post, 1994) and an independent measure of eminence (from 1 to 100; Murray, 2003) to examine the relationship between these two factors in 42 scientists, 40 artists, 50 composers, 49 writers,

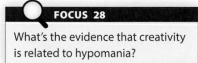

FOCUS 28

What's the evidence that creativity is related to hypomania?

DEA/I. L Charmet/De Agostini/Getty Images

■ **Ups and downs of a composer** Like many highly creative people, composer Robert Schumann suffered from a mood disorder. He attempted suicide twice during bouts of severe depression and eventually died, in 1856, from self-starvation in an asylum. His depression waxed and waned over long cycles, and during two prolonged periods, in 1840 and 1849, he was hypomanic (exhibited moderate mania). Those were his most productive years by far: He composed 24 musical works in 1840 and 27 in 1849. (Jamison, 1995.)

FIGURE 15.8 The eminence-psychopathology functions are graphed for 42 scientists, 40 artists, 50 composers, 49 writers, and 23 thinkers (top to bottom, respectively).

Data from Simonton, D. K. (2014). More method in the mad-genius controversy: A historiometric study of 204 historic creators. *Psychology of Aesthetics, Creativity, and the Arts, 8,* 53–61.

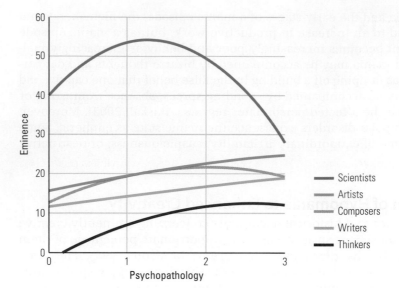

and 23 thinkers (e.g., philosophers). Simonton's results can be seen in **Figure 15.8**. Writers and artists with higher levels of psychopathology were rated as being more eminent, whereas scientists, composers, and thinkers showed an inverted-U relationship between the two factors, with eminence peaking with moderate levels of psychopathology.

All in all, the weight of the evidence seems to favor the idea of a link between hypomanic mood states and heightened creativity, but the causal nature of that link has yet to be determined.

SECTION REVIEW

Mood disorders involve intense, prolonged moods that can disrupt or threaten life.

Depression

- Prolonged sadness, self-blame, a sense of worthlessness, and an absence of pleasure are the hallmarks of depression.

- Rumination, repetitively focusing on symptoms of distress, serves to maintain or worsen depression by maintaining negative thinking and interfering with problem solving.

- The same genes that predispose people for generalized anxiety also predispose them for depression. The two disorders often occur in the same person.

- According to the hopelessness theory, a negative thought pattern—which includes the attribution of negative experiences to stable, global causes—is a predisposing cause of depression.

- A study of twins revealed that major depression is generally brought on by severely stressful life events, in people who are genetically predisposed for depression. Specific genes interact with the environment, affecting the likelihood that a person will experience depression.

- Depression may arise from reversible brain changes that occur during periods of psychological distress.

- Moderate depression may be adaptive, as exemplified by the different kinds of depressed reactions brought on by dark winters, lost loved ones, and repeated failure.

Bipolar Disorders

- Bipolar disorders—marked by mood changes in an upward (manic) as well as downward (depressive) direction—are highly heritable.

- Stressful life events may bring on episodes of bipolar disorder, but the evidence for this is not as clear as it is for unipolar depression.

- Manic episodes commonly involve expansive, euphoric feelings, high energy, extreme talkativeness, and abnormally high self-confidence.

- Full-blown mania involves poor judgment, bizarre thoughts, and self-harmful or dangerous actions; but milder mania (hypomania) may be a time of heightened creativity.

Schizophrenia

John sits alone in his dismal room, surrounded by plastic bags of garbage that he has hoarded during late-night excursions onto the street. He is unkempt and scrawny. He has no appetite and hasn't eaten a proper meal in weeks. He lost his job months ago. He is afraid to go out during the day because he sees in every passing face a spy who is trying to learn, by reading his mind, the secret that will destroy him. He hears voices telling him that he must stay away from the spies, and he hears his own thoughts as if they were broadcast aloud for all to hear. He sits still, trying to keep calm, trying to reduce the volume of his thoughts. John's disorder is diagnosed as schizophrenia.

Schizophrenia is a serious disorder that is found in roughly 0.7% of people worldwide at some time in their lives (Ayuso-Mateos, 2000; Tandon et al., 2008). Schizophrenia accounts for a higher percentage of the in-patient population of mental hospitals than do disorders in any other diagnostic category. The disorder is somewhat more prevalent in men than in women, and it also typically strikes earlier and is more severe in men than in women (Falkenburg & Tracy, 2014). It usually first manifests itself in late adolescence or early adulthood, and the average age for first diagnosis is about 4 years later in women than in men (Riecher-Rossler & Hafner, 2000). Sometimes people make a full recovery from schizophrenia, sometimes they make a partial recovery, and sometimes the disorder takes a deteriorating course throughout the person's life.

The label *schizophrenia* was first used by the Swiss psychiatrist Eugen Bleuler (1911/1950), whose writings are still a valuable source of information and insight about the disorder. Bleuler believed, as do many theorists today, that schizophrenia entails a split among such mental processes as attention, perception, emotion, motivation, and thought, such that these processes operate in relative isolation from one another, leading to bizarre and disorganized thoughts and actions. The term comes from the Greek words *schizo,* which means "split," and *phrenum,* which means "mind," so it literally means "split mind." However, schizophrenia does not refer to "being of two minds" or having a "split (or multiple) personality," even though laypersons and the popular media sometimes misuse the term in that way.

■ **Mental disorder expressed in art** The later-life paintings of British painter Louis Wain (1860–1939) reflect a psychological disorder that may have been schizophrenia. Wain spent the last years of his life in mental institutions.

Kaleidoscope Cats VI (gouache on paper), Wain, Louis (1860–1939) / Bethlem Museum of the Mind, Beckenham, Kent / Bridgeman Images

Diagnostic Characteristics of Schizophrenia

No two sufferers of schizophrenia have quite the same symptoms. But to receive the *DSM-5* diagnosis of **schizophrenia**, the person must manifest a serious decline in ability to work, care for him- or herself, and connect socially with others. The person must also manifest, for at least 1 month, two or more of the following five categories of symptoms: disorganized thought and speech, delusions, hallucinations, grossly disorganized or catatonic behavior, and negative symptoms—all described in this section. These symptoms are usually not continuously present; the person typically goes through episodes of active phases of the disorder, lasting for weeks or months, separated by periods of comparative normalcy.

Disorganized Thought and Speech

Many people with schizophrenia show speech patterns that reflect an underlying deficit in the ability to think in a logical, coherent manner. In some cases, thought and speech are guided by loose word associations. A classic example is this greeting to Bleuler (1911/1950) from one of his patients: "I wish you a happy, joyful, healthy, blessed and fruitful year, and many good wine-years to come as well as a healthy and good apple-year, and sauerkraut and cabbage and squash and seed year." Once the patient's mind hooked onto fruit (in "fruitful year"), it entered into a chain of associations involving fruits and vegetables that had little to do with the original intent of the statement.

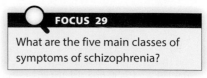

FOCUS 29

What are the five main classes of symptoms of schizophrenia?

In all sorts of formal tests of logic, people with schizophrenia do poorly when in an active phase of their disorder (Docherty et al., 2003; Simpson & Done, 2004). They often encode the problem information incorrectly, fail to see meaningful connections, or base their reasoning on superficial connections having more to do with the sounds of words than with their meanings. People may show disorganized speech or thought long before other symptoms of schizophrenia are apparent (Goldberg et al., 2011).

Delusions

A *delusion* is a false belief held in the face of compelling evidence to the contrary. Common types of delusions in schizophrenia are *delusions of persecution,* which are beliefs that others are plotting against one; *delusions of being controlled,* such as believing that one's thoughts or movements are being controlled in puppet-like fashion by radio waves or invisible wires; and *delusions of grandeur,* which are beliefs in one's own extraordinary importance—for example, that one is the queen of England or is the love object of a famous movie star.

Delusions may result, in part, from a fundamental difficulty in identifying and remembering the original source of ideas or actions (Moritz et al., 2005). For example, delusions of being controlled may derive from a failure to mentally separate voluntary actions from involuntary actions; people with schizophrenia may often find themselves performing actions without remembering that they willfully initiated those actions (Broome et al., 2005). Delusions of persecution may stem, in part, from attempts to make sense of their horrible feelings and confusion. Delusions of grandeur may derive from an inability to separate fantasies from real-world experiences. Moreover, all sorts of delusions may be buttressed by deficits in logical reasoning, as in the case of a woman who supported her claim to be the Virgin Mary this way: "The Virgin Mary is a virgin. I am a virgin. Therefore, I am the Virgin Mary" (Arieti, 1966).

Hallucinations

Hallucinations are false sensory perceptions—hearing or seeing things that aren't there. By far the most common hallucinations in schizophrenia are auditory, usually the hearing of voices. Hallucinations and delusions typically work together to support one another. For example, a man who has a delusion of persecution may repeatedly hear the voice of his persecutor insulting or threatening him.

A good deal of evidence supports the view that auditory hallucinations derive from the person's own intrusive verbal thoughts—thoughts that others of us would experience as disruptive but self-generated. People with schizophrenia apparently "hear" such thoughts as if they were broadcast aloud and controlled by someone else. When asked to describe the source of the voices, they typically say that they come from inside their own heads, and some even say that the voices are produced, against their will, by their own speech mechanisms (Smith, 1992). Consistent with these reports, people with schizophrenia can usually stop the voices by such procedures as humming, counting, or silently repeating a word—procedures that, in everyone, interfere with the ability to imagine vividly any sounds other than those that are being hummed or silently recited (Reisberg et al., 1989). In addition, brain imaging research, using fMRI, has revealed that verbal hallucinations in people with schizophrenia are accompanied by neural activity in the same brain regions that are normally involved in subvocally generating and "hearing" one's own verbal statements (Allen et al., 2008; Shergill et al., 2004).

Grossly Disorganized Behavior and Catatonic Behavior

Not surprising, given their difficulties with thoughts and perceptions, people in the active phase of schizophrenia often behave in very disorganized ways. Many of their actions are strikingly inappropriate for the context—such as wearing many overcoats on a hot day or giggling and behaving in a silly manner at a solemn occasion.

The inability to keep context in mind and to coordinate actions with it seems to be among the basic deficits in schizophrenia (Broome et al., 2005). Even when engaging in appropriate behaviors, such as preparing a simple meal, people with schizophrenia may fail because they are unable to generate or follow a coherent plan of action.

In some cases, schizophrenia is marked by *catatonic behavior*, defined as behavior that is unresponsive to the environment (American Psychiatric Association, 2013). Catatonic behavior may involve excited, restless motor activity that is not directed meaningfully toward the environment; or, at the other extreme, it may involve a complete lack of movement for long periods—a form referred to as a *catatonic stupor*. Such behaviors may be means of withdrawing from a world that seems frighteningly difficult to understand or control.

Negative Symptoms

The so-called *negative symptoms* of schizophrenia are those that involve a lack of, or reduction in, expected behaviors, thoughts, feelings, and drives (American Psychiatric Association, 2013). They include a general slowing down of bodily movements, poverty of speech (slow, labored, unspontaneous speech), flattened affect (reduction in or absence of emotional expression), loss of basic drives such as hunger, loss of the pleasure that normally comes from fulfilling drives, and social withdrawal (Birkett et al., 2011; Pinkham et al., 2012). Although you might expect catatonic stupor to be included in the category of negative symptoms, it is usually not, because the stupor is believed to be actively maintained.

The majority of people with schizophrenia manifest negative symptoms to some degree, and for many these are the most prominent symptoms. I (Peter Gray) once asked a dear friend, who was suffering from schizophrenia and was starving himself, why he didn't eat. His answer, in labored but thoughtful speech, was essentially this: "I have no appetite. I feel no pleasure from eating or anything else. I keep thinking that if I go long enough without eating, food will taste good again and life might be worth living." For him, the most painful symptom of all was an inability to experience normal drives or the pleasure of satisfying them.

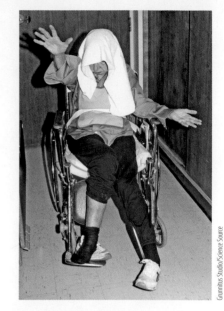

■ **A person in a catatonic stupor**
People with schizophrenia withdraw from their environment in various ways. One of the most extreme forms of withdrawal is the catatonic stupor, in which the person may remain motionless for hours in an uncomfortable position.

Neurological Factors Associated With Schizophrenia

Schizophrenia is characterized primarily as a cognitive disorder, brought on by deleterious changes in the brain (Broome et al., 2005; Heinrichs, 2005). People with schizophrenia appear to suffer from deficits in essentially all the basic processes of attention and memory discussed in Chapter 9 (Dickinson et al., 2008; Reichenberg & Harvey, 2007). They perform particularly poorly at tasks that require sustained attention over time or responding only to relevant information while ignoring irrelevant information (Bozikas et al., 2005; K. Wang et al., 2005). They are abnormally slow at bringing perceived information into their working-memory stores, and poor at holding onto the information once it is there (Barch, 2003; Fuller et al., 2005). All these and other kinds of mental deficits appear to contribute to the whole set of diagnostic symptoms of schizophrenia—disordered thoughts, delusions, hallucinations, disorganized behavior, and negative symptoms (Broome et al., 2005).

Disruptions in Brain Chemistry

By the early 1970s evidence had accrued for the dopamine theory of schizophrenia—the theory that schizophrenia arises from too much activity at brain synapses where dopamine is the neurotransmitter. The most compelling evidence was the observation that the clinical effectiveness of drugs in reducing the positive symptoms of schizophrenia was directly proportional to the drug's effectiveness in blocking dopamine release at synaptic terminals (Seeman & Lee, 1975). Other support came from the finding that drugs such as cocaine and amphetamines, which increase the action of dopamine in the brain, can greatly exacerbate the

 FOCUS 30

What early evidence supported the dopamine theory of schizophrenia? Why is the simple form of that theory doubted today?

symptoms of schizophrenia in people with the disorder and, at higher doses, can even induce such symptoms in people who do not have the disorder (see Abi-Dargham & Grace, 2011).

Today, researchers continue to recognize the role of dopamine in schizophrenia but generally do not accept the original, simple form of the dopamine theory. One major flaw in the theory is that it does not explain the negative symptoms of schizophrenia, which are not well treated by drugs that act solely on dopamine and are not typically exacerbated by drugs that increase that action of dopamine. Modern theories suggest that schizophrenia may involve unusual patterns of dopamine activity. Overactivity of dopamine in some part of the brain, especially in the basal ganglia, may promote the positive symptoms of schizophrenia, and *underactivity* of dopamine in the prefrontal cortex may promote the negative symptoms (Stone et al., 2007).

A good deal of attention has recently been devoted to the role of *glutamate* in schizophrenia (Javitt, 2010; Schobel et al., 2013). Glutamate is the major excitatory neurotransmitter at fast synapses throughout the brain. Some research suggests that one of the major receptor molecules for glutamate is defective in people who have schizophrenia, resulting in a decline in the effectiveness of glutamate neurotransmission (Javitt & Coyle, 2004; Phillips & Silverstein, 2003). Such a decline could account for the general cognitive debilitation that characterizes the disorder. Consistent with this theory, the dangerous, often-abused drug phencyclidine (PCP)—known on the street as "angel dust"—interferes with glutamate neurotransmission and is capable of inducing the full range of schizophrenic symptoms, including the negative and disorganized symptoms as well as hallucinations and delusions, in otherwise normal people (Javitt & Coyle, 2004).

Alterations in Brain Structure

Studies using brain imaging techniques have shown structural differences between the brains of people with schizophrenia and those of other people (Hartberg et al., 2011; Keshavan et al., 2008). The most common finding is enlargement of the cerebral ventricles (fluid-filled spaces in the brain) accompanied by a reduction in neural tissue surrounding the ventricles. Some researchers have detected abnormal blood flow—either too much or too little—to certain areas of the brain in some patients with schizophrenia (Lawrie & Pantelis, 2011; Walther et al., 2011). Other research has found abnormal organization and activation patterns in the cerebellum (Bernard & Mittal, 2015), and decreased neural mass, especially in the hippocampus (involved in memory) and the prefrontal cortex (involved in all sorts of conscious control of thought and behavior), in the brains of individuals with schizophrenia. These differences are relatively small and vary from person to person; they are not sufficiently reliable to be useful in diagnosing the disorder (Heinrichs, 2005; Keshavan et al., 2008).

Some researchers have attempted to explain the timing of the onset of schizophrenia in terms of maturational changes in the brain. During adolescence, the brain normally undergoes certain structural changes: Many neural cell bodies are lost through the process of pruning (see Chapter 4), and many new neural connections grow. The result is a decrease in gray matter (masses of cell bodies) and an increase in white matter (bundles of axons running from one brain area to another) (see **Figure 15.9**). Some researchers have suggested that an abnormality in pruning, which leads to the loss of too many cell bodies, may underlie at least some cases of schizophrenia (Keshavan et al., 2006; Lewis & Levitt, 2002). Consistent with this view, neuroimaging studies of people at risk for schizophrenia revealed a larger decline in gray matter during adolescence or early adulthood in those who subsequently developed the disorder than in those who did not (Lawrie et al., 2008).

Genetic and Environmental Causes of Schizophrenia

Why do the neural and cognitive alterations that bring on and constitute schizophrenia occur in some people and not in others? Genetic differences certainly play a role, and environmental differences do, too.

FOCUS 31

What evidence supports the theory that a defect in glutamate neurotransmission may play a role in schizophrenia?

FOCUS 32

How might an exaggeration of a normal developmental change at adolescence help bring on schizophrenia?

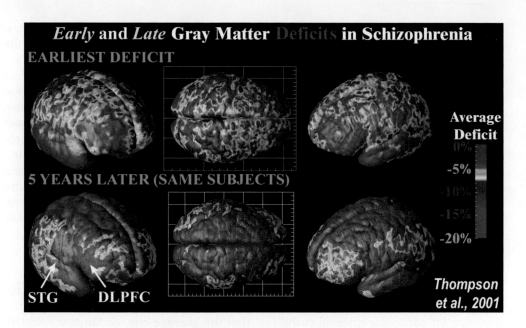

FIGURE 15.9 Mapping brain changes in schizophrenia Derived from MRI scans, these images were created after repeatedly scanning 12 schizophrenia subjects over 5 years, and comparing them with 12 matched healthy controls, scanned at the same ages and intervals. Severe loss of gray matter is indicated by red and pink colors, while stable regions are in blue. STG denotes the superior temporal gyrus, and DLPFC denotes the dorsolateral prefrontal cortex.

(With permission from Thompson, P. M., Vidal, C., Giedd, J. N., Gochman, P., Blumenthal, J., Nicolson, R., . . . Rapoport, J. L. (2001). Mapping adolescent brain change reveals dynamic wave of accelerated gray matter loss in very early-onset schizophrenia. *Proceedings of the National Academy of Sciences of the USA*, *98*, 11650–11655).

Predisposing Effects of Genes

Schizophrenia was one of the first psychological disorders to be studied extensively by behavior geneticists (Gottesman, 1991). In such studies, the first step is to identify a group of people, referred to as *index cases*, who have the disorder. Then the relatives of the index cases are studied to see what percentage of them have the disorder. This percentage is referred to as the **concordance** for the disorder, for the class of relatives studied. The average concordances found for schizophrenia in many such studies, for various classes of relatives, are shown in **Table 15.4**.

All in all, the results indicate that genetic differences among individuals play a substantial role in the predisposition for schizophrenia. The more closely related a person is to an index case, the greater the chance that he or she will develop schizophrenia (Riley & Kendler, 2011). Other research, conducted with people who were adopted at an early age, shows high concordance for schizophrenia between

FOCUS 33

How do the varying rates of concordance for schizophrenia among different classes of relatives support the idea that heredity influences one's susceptibility for the disorder?

TABLE 15.4 Concordance rates for schizophrenia

Relationship to a person who has schizophrenia	Average percentage found to have schizophrenia (concordance)
Relatives in same generation	
Identical twin	48%
Fraternal twin	17%
Nontwin brother or sister	9%
Half sibling	6%
First cousin	2%
Relatives in later generation	
Child of two parents with schizophrenia	46%
Child of one parent with schizophrenia	13%
Grandchild of one person with schizophrenia	5%
Niece or nephew of one person with schizophrenia	4%
Data from Gottesman, 1991.	

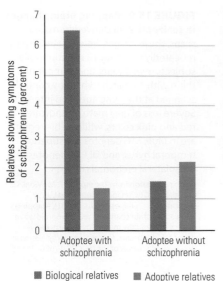

FIGURE 15.10 Results of a classic study of the heritability of schizophrenia The researchers looked for signs of schizophrenia in the biological and adoptive relatives of people who had been adopted at an early age and either did or did not subsequently develop schizophrenia. The results here are the percentage of relatives who showed either schizophrenia or a milder disorder now called schizotypal personality disorder.

(Data from Kety et al., 1976.)

FOCUS 34

What sorts of early disruptions to brain development have been implicated as predisposing causes of schizophrenia?

■ **Identical twins with nonidentical brains** Steven, on the right, has schizophrenia. His genetically identical twin, on the left, does not. Brain scans revealed that Steven's brain has larger cerebral ventricles than does his brother's. Such discordance for schizophrenia in identical twins sometimes occurs when one of the two twins (usually the one born second) suffers from lack of oxygen during the birth process and the other does not.

biological relatives but not between adoptive relatives (Owen & O'Donovan, 2003). The results of one classic study of this type are shown in **Figure 15.10**. Such results indicate that it is the genetic similarity, not the environmental similarity, between relatives that produces high concordance for schizophrenia.

More recently a great deal of research has been aimed at identifying individual genes that contribute to the development of schizophrenia. Many different genes appear to be involved, and no single gene or small set of genes can account for most of the genetic influence in large samples of people with schizophrenia (Bertram, 2008). Consistent with current chemical theories of schizophrenia, at least some of the identified genes are known to influence dopamine neurotransmission, and some are known to influence glutamate neurotransmission (Bertram, 2008; Broome et al., 2005). Recent research has identified genes that influence the major histocompatibility complex, important in the functioning of the immune system (Sekar et al., 2016).

Effects of the Prenatal Environment and Early Brain Traumas

The data in Table 15.4 show that genes are heavily involved in the predisposition for schizophrenia, but they also show that genes are not the only determinants of the disorder. Of particular interest is the fact that the average concordance for schizophrenia for identical twins, 48%, is much less than the 100% that would be predicted if genes alone were involved. Similarly, the concordance for schizophrenia in fraternal twins is considerably higher than that for nontwin pairs of full siblings—17% compared to 9%. This difference cannot be explained in terms of genes, as fraternal twins are no more similar to each other genetically than are other full siblings, but it is consistent with the possibility of a prenatal influence. Twins share the same womb at the same time, so they are exposed to the same prenatal stressors and toxins. That fact, of course, applies to identical twins as well as to fraternal twins, so some portion of the 48% concordance in identical twins may result not from shared genes but from shared prenatal environments.

A number of studies have pointed to specific prenatal variables that can contribute to the likelihood of developing schizophrenia. One such variable is malnutrition (Brown & Susser, 2008). People born in the western Netherlands between October 15 and December 31, 1945, immediately following a severe famine brought on by a Nazi blockade of food supplies, were twice as likely as others born in the Netherlands to have developed schizophrenia (Susser et al., 1996). A more recent study, illustrated in **Figure 15.11,** revealed a similar effect for people who were born in China during or shortly after the Chinese famine of 1960–1961, which resulted from massive crop failures (St. Clair et al., 2005).

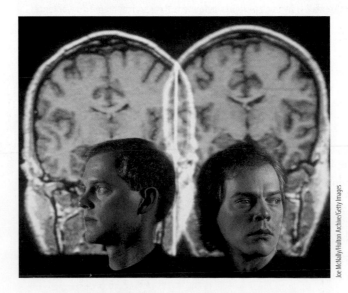

Prenatal viral infections and birth complications may also contribute to a predisposition for schizophrenia. Heightened rates of schizophrenia have been found in people whose mothers had rubella (also known as German measles) or certain other viral diseases during pregnancy and in people who had difficult births, involving oxygen deprivation or other trauma to the brain (Brown & Patterson, 2011; Tandon et al., 2008). There is also evidence that head injury later on in childhood, before age 10, can increase the likelihood of developing schizophrenia (AbdelMalik et al., 2003).

Effects of Life Experiences

The effects discussed so far are predisposing effects. Given a certain level of predisposition, the actual manifestation and course of schizophrenia may be influenced by one's daily experiences. There is strong evidence that various stressful life events can precipitate schizophrenia and exacerbate its symptoms (Pallanti et al., 1997; van Os et al., 2008). Most research on such effects has focused on the family environment.

To date, the most thorough investigation of the effect of the family environment on schizophrenia is a 21-year-long study in Finland of two groups of adopted children (Tienari et al., 2004, 2006). One group of children was at high genetic risk for schizophrenia because their biological mothers were diagnosed with either schizophrenia or a milder schizophrenia-like disorder, and the other group was at low risk because neither of their biological parents showed any evidence of schizophrenia or a related disorder. The main finding was that those high-risk children whose adoptive parents communicated in a relatively disorganized, hard-to-follow, or highly emotional manner were much more likely to develop schizophrenia or a milder disorder akin to schizophrenia than were high-risk children whose adoptive parents communicated in a calmer, more organized fashion. This relationship was not found among the low-risk children. The results suggest that a degree of disordered communication at home that does not harm most children may have damaging effects on those who are genetically predisposed for schizophrenia.

A Cross-Cultural Study of the Course of Schizophrenia

In the 1970s, the World Health Organization (WHO) initiated an ambitious cross-cultural study of schizophrenia that eventually involved locations in 13 different nations. The nations included industrialized, *developed* countries, such as Germany, Japan, Ireland, and the United States; and relatively nonindustrialized, *developing* countries, such as India, Colombia, and Nigeria. Using agreed-upon criteria and cross-cultural reliability checks, the researchers diagnosed new cases of schizophrenia in each location, classed them according to symptom types and apparent severity, and reassessed each case through interviews conducted at various times in subsequent years. Overall, more than 1,000 people with schizophrenia were identified and followed over periods of up to 26 years (Hopper et al., 2007).

The results showed considerable cross-cultural consistency. The relative prevalence of the various symptoms, the severity of the initial symptoms, the average age of onset of the disorder, and the sex difference in age of onset (later for women than for men) were similar from location to location despite wide variations in the ways that people lived. However, the study also led to two overall conclusions that were

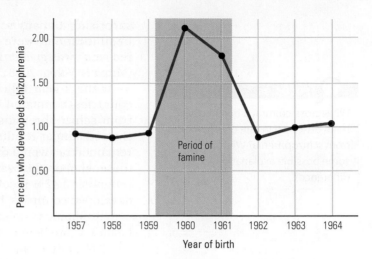

FIGURE 15.11 Effect of malnutrition during pregnancy on rate of schizophrenia in offspring Children who were in their mothers' wombs during the period of great famine in China later developed schizophrenia at roughly twice the usual rate.
(Data from St. Clair et al., 2005.)

 FOCUS 35

What evidence suggests that the family environment may promote schizophrenia, but only in those who are genetically predisposed for the disorder?

■ **Living and playing with schizophrenia** Despite having schizophrenia since he was a young man, Tom Harrell has developed into one of the world's top jazz composers and trumpeters. According to his wife, composing and playing music help to focus Harrell's mind and to reduce the symptoms of schizophrenia.

surprising to many schizophrenia experts. First, quite a high percentage of people, in all locations, were found to *recover* from schizophrenia; and second, the rate of recovery was *greater* in the developing countries than in the developed countries (Vahia & Vahia, 2008).

At the 2-year follow-up, for example, 63% of the patients in the developing countries, compared with 37% in the developed countries, showed full remission from schizophrenic symptoms (Jablensky et al., 1992). Subsequent follow-ups showed similar results and revealed that many of the originally recovered patients remained recovered over the entire study period (Hopper et al., 2007). Even among those who, on the basis of their initial symptoms, were identified as having a "poor prognosis," 42% recovered in the developing countries, compared to 33% in the developed countries, by the WHO criteria.

Why should people in the poorer countries, which have the poorest mental health facilities, fare better after developing schizophrenia than people in the richer countries? Nobody knows for sure, but some interesting hypotheses have been proposed (Jenkins & Karno, 1992; Lin & Kleinman, 1988; López & Guarnaccia, 2005). Family members in less-industrialized countries generally place less value on personal independence and more on interdependence and family ties than do those in industrialized countries, which may lead them to feel less resentful and more nurturing toward a family member who needs extra care. They are more likely to live in large, extended families, which means that more people share in providing the extra care. Perhaps for these reasons, family members in less-industrialized countries are more accepting and less critical of individuals diagnosed with schizophrenia than are those in industrialized countries.

People in developing countries are also less likely to call the disorder "schizophrenia" or to think of it as permanent, and are more likely to refer to it as "a case of nerves," which sounds more benign and ties it to experiences that everyone has had. In contrast, in more developed countries there is a stigma associated with mental illness, and many people with symptoms of schizophrenia are reluctant to seek out therapy or, if they do seek it out, fail to fully engage in it (Corrigan et al., 2014). Finally, in less-industrialized countries those with schizophrenia are more able to play an economically useful role. The same person who could not hold a 9-to-5 job can perform useful chores on the family farm, or at the family trade, or at a local business where everyone knows the family. Being less stigmatized, less cut off from the normal course of human activity, and better cared for by close family members and neighbors may increase the chance of recovery.

Another possible explanation, rarely mentioned in the psychiatric literature, has to do with drugs. Over the course of the WHO study, patients in the developed countries were generally treated with antipsychotic drugs for prolonged periods, as they are today. In contrast, patients in the developing countries were more often not treated with drugs or were treated only for short periods to bring the initial symptoms under control (Jablensky et al., 1992). The authors of the WHO study (Hopper et al., 2007) devote no discussion to the possible role of drugs in promoting or inhibiting recovery, but they do mention, in passing, that the treatment center in Agra, India, which had the highest rate of recovery of all the centers studied, was the only center that used no drugs at all—because they could not afford them.

Some controversial studies in Europe and the United States, some years ago, suggested that prolonged use of antipsychotic drugs, while dampening the positive symptoms of schizophrenia, may impede full recovery (Warner, 1985). This ironic possibility—that the drugs we use to treat schizophrenia might prolong the disorder—has so far not been followed up with systematic research.

A Developmental Model of Schizophrenia

The more scientists learn about schizophrenia, the more apparent it becomes that the disorder has no simple, unitary cause. **Figure 15.12** provides a useful framework

FOCUS 36

What cross-cultural difference has been observed in rate of recovery from schizophrenia? What are some possible explanations of that difference?

(similar to one developed by Tsuang et al., 2001) for thinking about the multiple causes. The disorder is brought on by some combination of genetic predisposition, early physical disruptions to normal brain development, and stressful life experiences. Once the disorder begins, the disorder itself can have effects that help to prolong it, depending at least partly on how family members and others in one's community respond. Distressing effects of the disorder itself, or of others' reactions to it, can cause further deterioration of the brain and a more chronic course for the disorder.

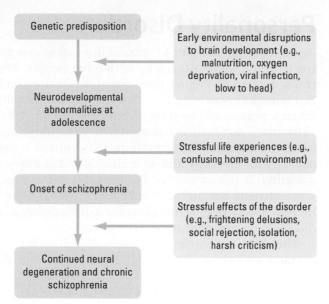

FIGURE 15.12 A developmental model of schizophrenia This model depicts researchers' understanding of the contributions of genes, environmental experiences, and the person's present neural and behavioral condition to the development of schizophrenia and, in some cases, its progression into a chronic condition.

(Research by Tsuang et al., 2001.)

SECTION REVIEW

Schizophrenia is a cognitive disorder with wide-ranging symptoms and multiple causes.

Diagnostic Characteristics

- Schizophrenia is characterized by symptoms classified as positive, disorganized, and negative.

- Positive symptoms include delusions (false beliefs held despite compelling contrary evidence) and auditory hallucinations (which may come from the person's own intrusive verbal thoughts).

- Disorganized symptoms include illogical thought and speech, and behaviors that are inappropriate to the environmental context.

- Negative symptoms include slowed movement, poverty of speech, flattened affect, and the loss of basic drives and the pleasure that comes from fulfilling them.

- Symptoms occur in a great variety of combinations and may change over time in the same person.

Underlying Cognitive and Neural Deficits

- The fundamental deficits in schizophrenia are cognitive, including problems with attention, working memory, and long-term memory.

- Abnormalities in brain chemistry, such as a decline in the effectiveness of glutamate or unusual patterns of dopamine activity, may help to explain the cognitive deficits.

- Structural differences in the brains of people with schizophrenia may include enlarged cerebral ventricles and reduced neural mass in some areas. Excessive pruning of neural cell bodies in adolescence may be a cause of some cases of schizophrenia.

Genetic and Environmental Causes

- Measures of concordance for schizophrenia in identical twins indicate substantial heritability. Some specific genes that appear to be involved have effects consistent with brain chemistry theories of the disorder.

- Predisposition may also arise from early environmental brain injury, including prenatal viruses or malnutrition, birth complications, or early childhood head injury.

- Stressful life experiences and aspects of the family environment can bring on the active phase of schizophrenia or worsen symptoms in predisposed people.

- Recovery from schizophrenia has been found to occur at higher rates in developing countries than in developed countries. Differences in living conditions and cultural attitudes and the lower use of antipsychotic drugs in developing countries may all play a role.

FOCUS 37

What is a personality disorder, and how is it similar to and different from related, more serious disorders?

Personality Disorders

As discussed in Chapter 14, personality refers to a person's general style of interacting with the world, especially with other people. People have different personality traits, and psychologists have spent much time and effort describing these traits. But what happens when someone's personality falls outside of the normal range, when a person's daily style of interaction with other people is viewed as "odd" or extreme? The result is a ***personality disorder***, defined as an enduring pattern of behavior, thoughts, and emotions that impairs a person's sense of self, goals, and capacity for empathy and/or intimacy and is associated with significant stress and disability. It is sometimes difficult to differentiate personality disorders from somewhat extreme but "normal" personality traits on the one hand and serious forms of mental illness (e.g., schizophrenia, social anxiety disorder, or obsessive-compulsive disorder) on the other hand.

The *DSM-5* identifies 10 personality disorders (see **Figure 15.13**), which are divided into three clusters: Cluster A (***paranoid***, ***schizoid***, and ***schizotypal***);

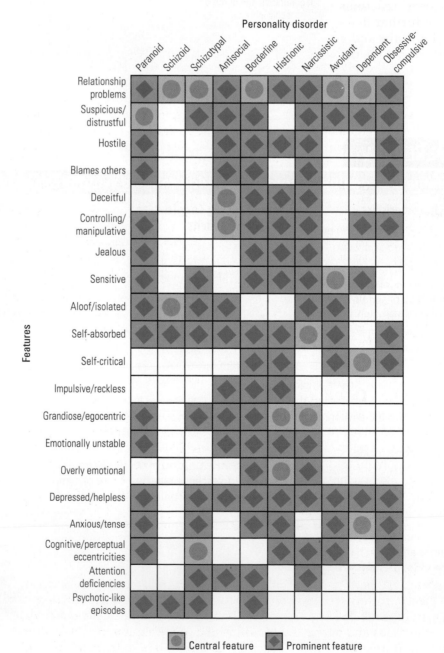

FIGURE 15.13 Prominent and central features of the *DSM-5*'s personality disorders The symptoms of the various personality disorders often overlap, resulting in multiple diagnoses for a given patient.

(Comer, R. J. (2016). *Fundamentals of Abnormal Psychology* (8th ed., p. 423). New York, NY: Worth Publishers.)

Cluster B (*antisocial*, *borderline*, *histrionic*, and *narcissistic*); and Cluster C (*avoid-ant*, *dependent*, and *obsessive-compulsive*). The boxes in the figure containing orange circles reflect the central, or necessary, features for each disorder, according to the *DSM-5*. The purple diamonds in the boxes reflect prominent, though not necessary, features associated with each disorder. We examine each of these disorders briefly in the following sections. We should note that there are limitations and problems with this classification system. Many patients meet criteria for more than one personality disorder, many have personality disorders that do not fall neatly into one of the 10 categories, and personality dysfunction may reflect maladaptive extremes of normal personality trait dimensions.

Cluster A: "Odd" Personality Disorders

This cluster of disorders has much in common with schizophrenia, especially its delusional component. In fact, people with a diagnosis of a Cluster A personality disorder often have close relatives with schizophrenia or are diagnosed themselves with schizophrenia (Chemerinski & Siever, 2011).

 FOCUS 38

Describe the three clusters of personality disorders. Within each cluster, how easy do you think it is to differentiate the symptoms of one disorder from those of others?

Paranoid Personality Disorder

As the name connotes, people with this disorder are deeply distrustful of other people and are suspicious of their motives. They frequently believe that people are "out to get them" and read hostile intentions into the actions of others (Turkat et al., 1990). Most of these attributions are inaccurate, but not so off base as to be considered delusional. They frequently blame others for their failures and tend to bear grudges (Rotter, 2011). Between .5% and 3% of adults display this disorder, and it appears to be more frequent in men than in women (Paris, 2010).

> Mr. W. is a 53-year-old referred for psychiatric evaluation by his attorney to rule out a treatable psychiatric disorder. Mr. W. has entered into five lawsuits in the past 2½ years. His attorney believes that each suit is of questionable validity. Mr. W. has been described as an unemotional, highly controlled person who is now suing a local men's clothing store "for conspiring to deprive me of my consumer rights." He contends that the store manager consistently issued bad credit reports on him. The consulting psychiatrist elicited other examples of similar concerns. Mr. W. has long distrusted his neighbors across the street and regularly monitors their activity since one of his garbage cans disappeared 2 years ago. He took an early retirement from his accounting job a year ago because he could not get along with his supervisor, who he believed was faulting him about his accounts and paperwork. He contends he was faultless. On examination, Mr. W.'s mental status is unremarkable except for constriction of affect and for a certain hesitation and guardedness in his response to questions. (Sperry, 2003, pp. 200–201)

Schizoid Personality Disorder

People with this disorder display little in the way of emotion, either positive or negative, and tend to avoid social relationships. They do not avoid others because they fear or mistrust them, as people with paranoid personality disorders do, but rather because they genuinely prefer to be alone. Many are "loners" who make no effort to initiate or maintain friendships, often including sexual relations and interactions with their families. People with schizoid personality disorder tend to be self centered and are not much influenced by either praise or criticism. This disorder is relatively rare, occurring in fewer than 1% of people in the population (Paris, 2010).

Schizotypal Personality Disorder

People with schizotypal personality disorder show extreme discomfort in social situations, often bizarre patterns of thinking and perceiving, and behavioral eccentricities, such as wearing odd clothing or repeatedly organizing their kitchen shelves. They tend to be anxious and distrustful of others and are often loners. They often see significance in unrelated events, especially as they relate to themselves, and some people with this disorder believe they have special abilities, such as extrasensory perception or magical control over other people. People with this disorder have poor attentional focus, making their conversations vague, often with loose associations (Millon, 2011). They find it difficult to get and keep jobs and often lead idle, unproductive lives. Schizotypal personality disorder occurs in about 2 to 4% of all people, and it is slightly more common in men than in women (Paris, 2010).

Cluster B: "Dramatic" Personality Disorders

This cluster includes four examples, the common link being that individuals with these disorders display highly emotional, dramatic, or erratic behavior that makes it difficult for them to have stable, satisfying relationships.

Antisocial Personality Disorder

People with this disorder consistently violate or disregard the rights of others. They are sometimes (though not in the *DSM-5*) referred to as sociopaths or psychopaths, and the disorder is sometimes called *psychopathy*. They frequently lie, seem to lack a moral conscience, and behave impulsively, seemingly disregarding the consequences of their actions (Kantor, 2006; Millon, 2011). As a result of their reckless behavior and disregard for others, they frequently find themselves in trouble with the law. In fact, it is estimated that approximately 30% of people in the prison population meet the diagnosis criterion for antisocial personality disorder (O'Connor, 2008). People with antisocial personality disorder show poor emotional regulation and deficits in some of the components of executive function (Smith & Lilienfeld, 2015; Rodman et al., 2016). In the broader population, it is estimated that between 3 and 3.5% of people in the United States have antisocial personality disorder, which is about four times more common in men than in women (Paris, 2010).

> Juan G. is a 28-year-old Cuban male who presented late in the evening to the emergency room at a community hospital complaining of a headache. His description of the pain was vague and contradictory. At one point he said the pain had been present for 3 days, whereas at another point it was "many years." He indicated that the pain led to violent behavior and described how, during a headache episode, he had brutally assaulted a medic while he was in the Air Force. He gave a long history of arrests for assault, burglary, and drug dealing. Neurological and mental status examinations were within normal limits except for some mild agitation. He insisted that only Darvon—a narcotic—would relieve his headache pain. The patient resisted a plan for further diagnostic tests or a follow-up clinic appointment, saying unless he was treated immediately "something really bad could happen." (Sperry, 2003, p. 41)

Borderline Personality Disorder

The principal feature of borderline personality disorder is instability, including in emotions—swinging in and out of extreme moods—and self-image, often showing dramatic changes in identity, goals, friends, and even sexual orientation (Westen et al., 2011). Similar to people with antisocial personality disorder, people with borderline personality disorder tend to be impulsive, often engaging in reckless behavior (reckless driving, unsafe sex, substance abuse), sometimes lashing out at others when things don't go right, and other times turning their anger inward, engaging in self-injurious behavior (Chiesa et al., 2011; Coffey et al., 2011). Attempted suicide is common in people with borderline personality disorder, with, according to some estimates, about 75% of people with the disorder attempting suicide at least once in their lives and approximately 10% succeeding (Gunderson, 2011). The relationships of people with borderline personality disorder tend to be intense and stormy, and they often have fears of abandonment, resulting in frantic efforts to head off anticipated separations (Gunderson, 2011). It is estimated that between 1 and 2.5% of people in the population have borderline personality disorder, with most (about 75%) being women (Paris, 2010).

Histrionic Personality Disorder

People with histrionic personality disorder continually seek to be the center of attention—they behave as if they are always "on stage," using theatrical gestures and mannerisms—and are often described as vain, self-centered, and "emotionally charged," displaying exaggerated moods and emotions. People with this disorder constantly seek attention and approval from others and are concerned with how others will evaluate them, often wearing provocative clothing to attract attention. They have a difficult time delaying gratification and may overreact in order to get attention, sometimes to the point of feigning physical illness. Males and females are equally likely to be classified as having histrionic personality disorder, with between 2 and 3% of people in the population having the disorder (Paris, 2010).

> Ms. P is a 20-year-old female undergraduate student who requested psychological counseling at the college health services for "boyfriend problems." Actually, she had taken a nonlethal overdose of minor tranquilizers the day before coming to the health services. She said she took the overdose in an attempt to kill herself because "life wasn't worth living" after her boyfriend had left the afternoon before. She is an attractive, well-dressed woman adorned with make-up and nail polish, which contrasts sharply with the very casual fashion of most coeds on campus. During the initial interview she was warm and charming, maintained good eye contact, yet was mildly seductive. At two points in the interview she was emotionally labile, shifting from smiling elation to tearful sadness. Her boyfriend had accompanied her to the evaluation session and asked to talk to the clinician. He stated the reason he had left the patient was because she made demands on him that he could not meet and that he "hadn't been able to satisfy her emotionally or sexually." Also, he noted that he could not afford to "take her out every night and party." (Sperry, 2003, p. 134)

Narcissistic Personality Disorder

People with this disorder are even more self-centered than people with borderline personality disorder. They seek admiration from others, tend to lack empathy, and are grandiose and overconfident in their own exceptional talents or characteristics. They exaggerate their abilities and achievements and expect others to see the same exceptional qualities in them that they see in themselves. As a result, they are frequently perceived as arrogant. They often make good first impressions (their social skills tend to be relatively good), but these are rarely maintained (Campbell & Miller, 2011). This is due in part to their perceived arrogance, but also to their general lack of interest in other people (Ritter et al., 2011). It is estimated that approximately 1% of people in the population show narcissistic personally disorder, with 75% of them being men (Dhwan et al., 2010).

Some researchers think that family values in Western societies promote narcissism.

Cluster C: "Anxious" Personality Disorders

The common thread for this final cluster of personality disorders is fear and anxiety. People with anxious personality disorders have much in common with people who suffer from depression and anxiety disorder; the difference is one of degree.

Avoidant Personality Disorder

People with this disorder are excessively shy; they are uncomfortable and inhibited in social situations. They feel inadequate and are extremely sensitive to being evaluated, experiencing a dread of criticism. Their extreme fear of rejection causes them to be timid and fearful in social settings and often results in their avoiding social contact, making it impossible for them to be accepted. People with avoidant personality disorder rarely take risks or try out new activities, exaggerating the difficulty of tasks before them (Rodenbaugh et al., 2010). Avoidant personality disorder is similar to generalized anxiety disorder discussed earlier in this chapter (p. 591), and people are sometimes classified with both disorders (Cox et al., 2011). Approximately 1 to 2% of people in the population are afflicted with this disorder, men and women with comparable frequency (Paris, 2010).

Dependent Personality Disorder

People with dependent personality disorder show an extreme need to be cared for. They are clingy and fear separation from significant people in their lives, believing they cannot care for themselves. People with dependent personality disorder fear upsetting relationship partners (their partners may leave them if they do), and as a result tend to be obedient, rarely disagreeing with them, and permitting their partners to make important decisions for them (Millon, 2011). They often feel lonely, sad, and distressed, putting them at high risk for anxiety, depression, and eating disorders (Bornstein, 2007). They are prone to suicidal thoughts, especially when a relationship is breaking up. It is estimated that between 2 and 3% of people in the population suffer from dependent personality disorder, with about the same number of men and women having the disorder (Paris, 2010).

Obsessive-Compulsive Personality Disorder

Like people with obsessive-compulsive disorder, people with obsessive-compulsive personality disorder are preoccupied with order and control, and as a result are inflexible and resist change. They are so highly focused on the details of a task that they often fail to understand the point of an activity. They tend to set excessively high standards for themselves and others, exceeding any normal degree of conscientiousness (Samuel & Widiger, 2011). They often have difficulty expressing affection, and as a result their relations are frequently shallow and superficial. Approximately 1 to 2% of people in the population show obsessive-compulsive personality disorder, with about twice as many men having the disorder as women (Paris, 2010).

Origins of Personality Disorders

There is no lack of theorizing about the origins of personality disorders, but generally less research has been done investigating the causes of these disorders than many other disorders such as depression or schizophrenia (Bernstein & Useda, 2007). Biological explanations, such as possible genetic and neurotransmitter causes, have been proposed for some personality disorders. For example, some studies report a genetic connection for paranoid personality disorder (Kendler et al., 1987), abnormalities in neurotransmitters have been identified for schizotypal and antisocial personality disorders (Patrick, 2007), and abnormalities in brain structures have been found for schizotypal, antisocial, and borderline personality disorders (Hyde et al., 2016; see Comer, 2015). Experiences in childhood have been shown to be related to schizotypal, antisocial, borderline, and dependent personality disorders (see Comer, 2014); and sociocultural explanations have been proposed for narcissistic (family values in Western societies promote narcissism; Campbell & Miller, 2011) and histrionic (some cultures are more accepting of extreme behavior than others; Patrick, 2007) personality disorders. As with other forms of psychological disorders, it is almost certain that there are multiple causes of any single personality disorder, with genes, operating in interaction with the environment at all levels (family, culture, etc.), influencing brain structure (formation of synapses, pruning of neurons, abundance of neurotransmitter receptors) and function (through presence of neurotransmitters such as dopamine, serotonin, and glutamate). Also, although according to the *DSM-5* a person must be at least 18 years old to be diagnosed with a personality disorder, the roots of such disorders are in development, with features of all of these disorders being apparent to lesser degrees during childhood and adolescence.

SECTION REVIEW

Personality Disorders

- Personality disorders refer to stable patterns of behavior that impair a person's sense of self, goals, and capacity for empathy and/or intimacy. They are often divided into three clusters.
- "Odd" personality disorders include paranoid, schizoid, and schizotypal types, all characterized by some degree of delusions and erratic behavior.
- "Dramatic" personality disorders include antisocial, borderline, histrionic, and narcissistic types and are characterized by highly emotional, dramatic, or erratic behavior.
- "Anxious" personality disorders include avoidant, dependent, and obsessive-compulsive types and are characterized by fear and anxiety.
- The origins of personality disorders have not received as much investigation as other psychological disorders, but are likely related to gene-environment interaction affecting the brain over the course of development.

Thinking Critically About Psychological Disorders

1. To what extent might some psychological disorders reflect adaptive behavior taken to an extreme? Or do all (or most) forms of psychological disorders reflect true psychopathology?

2. How might studying psychological disorders help us understand typical (i.e., "normal") behavior and functioning?

3. Are personality disorders actually forms of psychopathology or merely extremes of normal personality differences? Does this distinction make a difference in how we treat people with such disorders?

Reflections and Connections

Here are three final ideas that may help you organize your thoughts as you reflect on what you have read in this chapter:

1. The multiple causes of psychological disorders By this time in your study of psychology, you are no doubt accustomed to the idea that human feelings, thoughts, and actions emerge from the interplay of many causes. This idea also applies to the feelings, thoughts, and actions that lead to the diagnosis of a psychological disorder. The differences among us that are considered disorders—no less than the differences that are considered normal—are caused by differences in our genes and in our past and present environments. Any claim to have found *the* cause of generalized anxiety, depression, schizophrenia, or another major class of disorder is of doubtful validity.

Think about each of the disorders discussed in this chapter in relation to the three classes of causes—predisposing, precipitating, and perpetuating. How might genes and early physical assaults on the brain operate through the person's physiology to predispose him or her for the disorder? How might learned ways of thinking or acting predispose a person for the disorder? How might specific stressful events in life interact with the predisposition to precipitate the disorder? How might the disordered behavior itself, or people's reactions to it, help perpetuate the disorder once it begins? For each disorder, think about the relationship between the research or ideas described and the possible answers to these questions. Note, too, that similar stressful events can result in different kinds of symptoms—and different diagnosed disorders—for different individuals or at different times for any given individual.

2. The continuum between normality and abnormality Although a diagnosis of a psychological disorder is categorical (all or none), the symptoms on which diagnoses are made vary in degree. Thus, any decision as to whether a particular person does or does not have a psychological disorder is based on arbitrary criteria describing how severe or prolonged each symptom must be in order to call the syndrome a disorder.

Think about the disorders described in the chapter in relation to the moods, emotions, thoughts, and behaviors that all of us manifest to some degree. Doing so helps remove some of the mystique from the concept of psychological disorder and helps us identify with people whose troubles are like ours, only stronger. Thinking of disorders as extremes of normal processes has also helped scientists understand them better.

For example, in this chapter you read about evidence relating (a) the symptoms of ADHD to normal childhood impulsiveness and exuberance; (b) the symptoms of general anxiety disorder, phobias, and obsessive-compulsive disorders to normal worries, fears, thoughts, and actions; (c) the symptoms of depression to normal, possibly adaptive mood changes following loss or failure; and (d) the auditory hallucinations experienced in schizophrenia to the intrusive thoughts that all of us experience at times.

3. An evolutionary view of psychological disorder The evolutionary theme running through this book maintains that behavior is generally functional: It promotes survival and reproduction. But psychological disorder is dysfunctional: It reduces one's ability to work and interact with others effectively in survival-promoting ways. Why, then, do psychological disorders exist?

One partial answer may be that psychological disorders are a cost the species pays for the general advantages that come with diversity. Chapter 14, on personality, dealt with individual differences within the range generally considered healthy, or not disordered; it also made the case that natural selection may have favored diversity because those who are different from average can exploit unfilled niches and reap their rewards. Such diversity stems from variations in genes and from behavioral mechanisms that are capable of being modified through experience. Variation in capacity for anxiety, or compulsiveness, or sadness may be beneficial within a certain range; but the coin tosses that distribute genes and experiences will sometimes produce those characteristics at pathological levels.

Key Terms

ADHD 583

agoraphobia 594

Alzheimer's disease 586

antisocial personality disorder 617

anxiety disorders 591

avoidant personality disorder 617

bipolar and related disorders 599

bipolar I disorder 604

bipolar II disorder 604

borderline personality disorder 617

concordance 611

dependent personality disorder 617

depressive disorders 599

Down syndrome 586

DSM-5 578

dysthymia 599

generalized anxiety disorder 591

histrionic personality disorder 617

major depression 599

narcissistic personality disorder 617

obsessive-compulsive disorder (OCD) 595

obsessive-compulsive personality disorder 617

panic disorder 594

paranoid personality disorder 616

perpetuating causes of psychological disorders 588

personality disorder 616

phobia 592

posttraumatic stress disorder (PTSD) 597

precipitating causes of psychological disorders 587

predisposing causes of psychological disorders 587

psychological disorder 578

reliability 579

rumination 600

schizoid personality disorder 616

schizophrenia 607

schizotypal personality disorder 616

validity 581

Find Out More

Kay Jamison (2009). *An unquiet mind.* New York, NY: Random House.

In this autobiography, Kay Jamison—a leading researcher of mood disorders—describes her own experiences as a sufferer of bipolar disorder. The book includes an especially vivid description of her first full-blown manic episode, which occurred during her first year as an assistant professor, as well as a moving account of how she came to terms with the disorder and has managed to live with it.

Jake Wood (2014). *Among you: The extraordinary true story of a soldier broken by war.* London, UK: Mainstream Publishing.

Jake Wood, a military veteran and former business analyst, tells the heartbreaking firsthand account of his struggle with PTSD. After tours in Iraq and Afghanistan, he came home to fight another battle: this one within himself. His book is a brutally frank discussion of the devastating effects of PTSD.

Thomas Insel (2013, April). *Toward a new understanding of mental illness.* Pasadena, California: TEDxCaltech.

https://youtu.be/PeZ-U0pj9LI
Thomas Insel, former director of the National Institutes of Mental Health, discusses the roles of disease and behavior in mental illness. He envisions a future where depression, schizophrenia, and deaths from suicide may be reduced as dramatically as deaths from heart disease have been reduced in recent decades.

Joshua Walters (2011, June). *On being just crazy enough.* TED Full Spectrum Auditions.

https://youtu.be/ruvWiXowiZ8
Joshua Walters, a performance artist who has bipolar disorder, describes how mental illness alters perception and the role medication takes in those with mental illness. In his professional life, mental illness is more like mental "skillness"—the crazier he gets on stage, the more entertaining he becomes. He argues that the key to happiness for all of us may lie in using our own personal craziness to our advantage.

Visit LaunchPad for Psychology 8e launchpadworks.com to access the e-book, videos, activities, additional resources, and LearningCurve quizzes, as well as study aids including flash cards and web quizzes.

Treatment of Psychological Disorders

LEARNING OUTCOMES

After studying this chapter, you should be able to:

- Explain why care for those with psychological disorders is a social issue.

- Identify several biological forms of treatment and the disorders for which they are used.

- Describe the psychodynamic and humanistic approaches to psychotherapy.

- Describe the behavioral and cognitive approaches to psychotherapy.

- Explain and give examples of how psychotherapies are evaluated.

Throughout this book you have read of psychology as a *science*—a vast, complex, fascinating, and sometimes frustrating science in which every finding generates far more questions than it answers. If your experience in reading this book has been anything like ours in writing it, your attitude right now may be one of respect for what psychologists have discovered, combined with awe for the amount that is yet to be learned.

But psychology is not just a science; it is also a *practice*. Practitioners in psychology attempt to apply psychological ideas and findings in ways designed to make life more satisfying for individuals or society as a whole. This last chapter is about **clinical psychology**, the field of practice and research that is directed toward helping people who suffer from psychological problems and disorders. Here you will see how some of the basic knowledge of the brain, mind, and behavior that you have read about has been applied in efforts to help people in psychological need.

We begin with a section on the social problem of providing care for individuals with severe psychological disorders, and then progress through sections that discuss various biological and psychological treatments for psychological disorders. The final section concerns questions about the effectiveness of psychotherapy.

Care as a Social Issue

The existence of mental suffering, like that of physical suffering, raises social and moral questions. Who, if anyone, is responsible for caring for those who cannot care for themselves?

What to Do With Individuals With Severe Psychological Disorders? A Brief History

Through most of history, Western cultures felt little obligation toward people with psychological disorders. As recently as the seventeenth century, people with serious

FOCUS 1

How has Western society's response to people with serious psychological disorders changed over the centuries? What were the goals of the deinstitutionalization movement?

psychological disorders—called "madness" or "lunacy" (and today most often diagnosed as schizophrenia)—were often considered to be in league with the devil, and "treatment" commonly consisted of torture, hanging, or burning at the stake. By the eighteenth century in Europe and North America, people with severe psychological disorders were often "put away" in hospitals and asylums, often under poor conditions. Although reformers in Europe (e.g., Philippe Pinel) and the United States (e.g., Dorothea Dix) campaigned for better treatment, the practice of "warehousing" people with mental illness continued until the middle of the twentieth century. A major change in the treatment of people with severe psychological disorders began in the 1950s, inspired by several factors: an increase in the number of PhD programs in clinical psychology to train psychologists to treat the mental health problems of World War II veterans (Routh, 2013), disenchantment with large state institutions, and especially the development of antipsychotic drugs. That change was *deinstitutionalization*. With medication capable of controlling some of the most severe symptoms of mental illness, people could be returned to the community, many living in transitional homes, receiving outpatient care.

Since the beginning of the deinstitutionalization movement, the number of chronic patients in state mental institutions in the United States has been greatly reduced—from about 600,000 in 1955 to about 100,000 in the early twenty-first century (Torrey et al., 2011)—but it is debatable whether the quality of life of those who would formerly have been in asylums has been improved. They have generally not been integrated into the community but are living on its fringes. Roughly 200,000 of them are homeless, and many more—some 2 million—are in prisons, usually for minor crimes such as trespassing or theft (Fleishman, 2004; Torrey et al., 2011). By one estimate, as many as 16% of people in American prisons have a serious psychological disorder (Torrey et al., 2014).

Most people with a severe psychological disorder do not commit violent crimes, although their rate of engaging in violent behavior is somewhat higher than in the general population (Monahan, 2010). For example, whereas about 2% of people without a severe psychological disorder have assaulted another person, approximately 12% of people with schizophrenia, major depression, or bipolar disorder have done so. Because most people with a psychological disorder are not violent, it is very difficult for mental health professionals to make long-term predictions about who will be violent and who will not (Mills et al., 2011); predictions of imminent violence, however, are more accurate (Otto & Douglas, 2010).

In addition to those who are homeless or incarcerated, many thousands of other people with a psychological disorder are living in rundown rooming houses and understaffed nursing homes (Lamb, 2000). The more fortunate minority are living in long-term residential-care facilities, or group homes, which provide room and board, supervise medication, and offer assistance with problems of daily living (Fleishman, 2004). The alternative to hospitalization that the deinstitutionalization movement envisioned—improved care in a community setting—was never fully realized.

A Positive Development: Assertive Community Treatment

FOCUS 2

How do assertive community treatment programs attempt to help the severely mentally disordered and their families?

Since the 1970s, an increasing number of communities have developed *assertive community treatment (ACT)* or other outreach programs aimed at helping individuals with severe mental illness wherever they are in the community (DeLuca et al., 2008). Each person with mental illness in need is assigned to a multidisciplinary treatment team, which typically includes a case manager, psychiatrist, general physician, nurse, and social workers. Someone on the team is available at any time of the day, seven days a week, to respond to crises. Each patient—whether living on the street or in a boarding house or with family—is visited at least twice a week by a team member, who checks on his or her health, sees if any services are needed, and offers counseling as appropriate. In addition, the team meets frequently with family members to support them in their care for the patient.

A number of well-designed research studies have shown that such programs can be highly effective in reducing the need for hospitalization and increasing patients' satisfaction with life (Coldwell & Bender, 2007; Nelson et al., 2007). Such programs are expensive to operate, but they generally save money in the long run by keeping individuals with mental illness out of hospitals, where their care is much more expensive (The Schizophrenia Patient Outcomes Research Team [PORT], 2004). Despite such evidence, the majority of people with schizophrenia and their families in the United States do not receive such services.

Structure of the Mental Health System

Public concern about mental health generally centers on individuals with the most severe disorders, those who cannot care for themselves and who may commit violent crimes. But most people who seek mental health services have milder problems. The kinds of services they seek depend on such factors as the severity of their disorders, what they can afford, and the services available in their community. They may seek help from mental health professionals, from self-help groups organized by peers who suffer from similar problems or disorders (e.g., Alcoholics Anonymous), from religious organizations, from general practice physicians, or from assistance offered online.

■ **Reaching out** In some communities social workers and medical personnel seek out people who are in need, get to know them as individuals, and help them gain access to useful services and means of support.

Mental Health Professionals

Mental health professionals are those who have received special training and certification to work with people who have psychological problems or psychological disorders. The primary categories of such professionals are the following:

FOCUS 3

What are the major categories of mental health providers?

- *Psychiatrists* have medical degrees, obtained through standard medical school training, followed by special training and residency in psychiatry. They are the only mental health specialists who can regularly prescribe drugs. They typically work in private offices, mental health clinics, and hospitals.

- *Clinical psychologists* usually have doctoral degrees in psychology, with training in research and clinical practice. Some are employed by universities as teachers and researchers in addition to having their own clinical practices. Like psychiatrists, they most often work in private offices, clinics, or hospitals.

- *Counseling psychologists* usually have doctoral degrees in counseling. Their training is similar to that of clinical psychologists but generally entails less emphasis on research and more on practice. More so than psychiatrists or clinical psychologists, counseling psychologists are likely to work with people who have problems of living that do not warrant a diagnosis of psychological disorder.

- *Mental health counselors* usually have master's degrees in counseling or social work. They receive less training in research and psychological diagnostic procedures than do doctoral-level clinical or counseling psychologists. They often work in schools or other institutions, counseling those with school- or job-related problems. They may also conduct psychotherapy in private practice, including specialties such as couples or marriage counseling, career counseling, and child guidance counseling.

- *Psychiatric social workers* usually have master's degrees in social work, followed by advanced training and experience working with people who have psychological problems. They are most often employed by public social-work agencies. They may conduct psychotherapy sessions or visit people in their homes to offer support and guidance.

- *Psychiatric nurses* usually have degrees in nursing, followed by advanced training in the care of patients with mental illness. They usually work in hospitals and may conduct psychotherapy sessions as well as providing more typical nursing services.

Where People With Common Psychological Disorders Go for Treatment

<table>
<tr><td>🔍 **FOCUS 4**</td></tr>
</table>

According to a survey conducted in the United States, where do people with psychological disorders typically find treatment, and what types of treatment do they find?

A large-scale household survey was conducted, in the United States, to find out where people with psychological disorders had sought treatment (P. S. Wang et al., 2005). The survey identified a representative sample of thousands of people who were suffering from clinically significant anxiety disorders, mood disorders (including major depression and bipolar disorders), substance use disorders (alcoholism and other drug abuse or dependence disorders), or intermittent explosive disorder (a disorder involving uncontrolled anger). Of these, 22% had received some form of treatment from a mental health professional within the past year, 59% had received no treatment at all, and most of the remainder had received treatment from a medical doctor or nurse who did not have a mental health specialty.

The survey also revealed that the typical person with a psychological disorder who saw a general practice physician saw that person just once or twice over the course of the year, usually to receive a prescription for drug treatment and/or a few minutes of counseling. In contrast, those who saw a mental health professional met with that person for an average of seven sessions of at least a half hour's length, mostly for counseling or psychotherapy. Not surprisingly, the wealthier and more educated a person with a psychological disorder was, the more likely he or she was to have met for a series of sessions with a mental health professional for psychotherapy (P. S. Wang et al., 2005).

There are many treatment options in the United States for people with psychological disorders, but most people who need the services do not seem to be getting them. Those who have insurance and can afford the deductibles and co-pays are able to see private practice mental health professionals, but most either go untreated or are seen by a care provider without special training in mental health. Community-based programs have proven successful, but they reach only a minority of people with severe psychological disorders. What is somewhat shocking is that prisons may be the country's largest mental health providers, mostly to people who have not committed serious crimes (Torrey et al., 2014). Society has recognized the importance of treating people with psychological disorders, but the cost, the stigma some people associate with seeking treatment, and the difficulty of getting therapy to people who need it make the effective provision of such treatment problematic and not likely to be easily solved.

■ **Support for friends and family of alcohol and drug abusers** The family and friends of people with a debilitating mental or behavioral disorder often need psychological support themselves, in order to be helpful to their loved one while at the same time preserving their own well-being. Al-Anon is a self-help group run by and for people whose lives have been affected by someone else's drinking. Self-help groups are valuable components of the mental health system that are not directed by mental health professionals.

Biological Treatments

A person diagnosed with a psychological disorder might be treated by biological means (most often drugs), psychological means (psychotherapy of one form or another), or both. Biological treatments attempt to relieve the disorder by directly altering bodily processes. In the distant past, such treatments included drilling holes in the skull to let out bad spirits and bloodletting to drain diseased humors. Today, in decreasing order of extent of use, the three main types of biological treatments are drugs, electroconvulsive shock therapy (ECT), and psychosurgery.

Drugs

A new era in the treatment of psychological disorders began in the early 1950s when two French psychiatrists, Jean Delay and Pierre Deniker (1952), reported that they had reduced or abolished the psychotic symptoms of schizophrenia with a drug called chlorpromazine. About the same time, systematic studies of the use of lithium for the treatment of mania were begun (Shorter, 2009). Today, a plethora of drugs is available for treating essentially all major varieties of psychological disorders.

Drugs for psychological disorders have been far from perfect, however. They are not magic bullets that zero in on and correct a disordered part of the mental machinery while leaving the rest untouched—instead, they nearly always produce undesirable side effects. A few of the antianxiety drugs are addictive, and the attempt to withdraw from them sometimes produces symptoms worse than those for which the drug was prescribed. As you read of the three categories of drugs described below, notice their drawbacks as well as their benefits.

Antipsychotic Drugs

Antipsychotic drugs are used to treat schizophrenia and other disorders in which psychotic symptoms (e.g., hallucinations and delusions) predominate. Chlorpromazine (sold as Thorazine) was the first such drug, but now there are many others. Well-designed experiments have shown repeatedly that such drugs reduce and in some cases abolish the hallucinations, delusions, and bizarre actions that characterize the active phase of schizophrenia, thereby reducing the need for hospitalization (Barnes & Marder, 2011; Stroup et al., 2006). All antipsychotic drugs in use today decrease the activity of the neurotransmitter dopamine at certain synapses in the brain, and that effect is believed to be responsible, directly or indirectly, for the reduction in psychotic symptoms.

■ **Madness as possession** This twelfth-century painting probably depicts trephination (piercing the skull to permit evil spirits to escape). With the revival of the medical model in the late Middle Ages, people gave up the use of trephination and other brutal treatments that were based on the belief that abnormal behavior indicates possession.

CCI Archives/Science Source

FOCUS 5

What is known about the mechanisms, effectiveness, and limitations of drugs used to treat schizophrenia, generalized anxiety, and depression?

Since the early 1990s, much research and discussion has centered on reputed differences between two classes of antipsychotic drugs—the so-called *typical* and *atypical* antipsychotics. The typical drugs—of which haloperidol is most used—were the ones first developed, and the atypical drugs—including olanzapine and risperidone—are newer. Early research on the atypical drugs, done mostly by the pharmaceutical companies themselves, suggested that they were more effective than the older drugs in reducing psychotic symptoms and that they produced fewer harmful side effects. However, more recent, unbiased, large-scale studies conducted with public funds have questioned these claims (Carpenter & Buchanan, 2008; Crossly et al., 2010). At present there is no strong evidence that the atypical drugs are better overall than the less-expensive typical drugs. In terms of their biochemical mechanisms, both classes of drugs work by decreasing dopamine activity, although the atypical drugs also affect receptors for other neurotransmitters such as serotonin (Waddington et al., 2011).

Antipsychotic drugs have unpleasant and damaging side effects. They can produce dizziness, confusion, nausea, dry mouth, blurred vision, heart rate irregularities, constipation, weight gain, heightened risk for diabetes, sexual impotence in men, and disrupted menstrual cycles in women (Geddes et al., 2011; Stroup et al., 2012). They also interfere with motor-control processes in the brain and sometimes produce symptoms akin to Parkinson's disease, including shaking and difficulty in controlling voluntary movements. Many patients who take such drugs for many years develop a serious and often irreversible motor disturbance called *tardive dyskinesia,* manifested as involuntary jerking of the tongue, face, and sometimes other muscles.

Given such effects, it is no wonder that many patients diagnosed with schizophrenia stop taking the drugs as soon as the psychotic symptoms decline, or sometimes even before. Clinicians usually regard such "failure to comply" as a serious problem, as there is indeed evidence that, for many patients, such noncompliance means they are more likely to have another psychotic episode and require readmission to the hospital. A fact ignored by many clinicians, however, is that a significant number of patients who stop taking the drugs do quite well without them (Harrow & Jobe, 2007). These patients are frequently unknown to the clinicians because, not needing further treatment, they do not return to the clinic. As far as we can tell—and we have looked—there have been no research studies designed to test the long-term consequences of living without the drugs compared to living with them, or to determine which patients really need the drugs and which ones can do without them, or to test the logically plausible hypothesis that long-term use of the drugs might alter the brain in ways that *prevent* eventual full recovery from schizophrenia. The mental health industry, whose research is financed mostly by pharmaceutical companies, has shown little interest in these questions.

"... so I said," Hold on Doc, later for the family therapy, Let's just put the whole kit n'kaboodle on anti-depressants!"

SIPRESS

Antianxiety Drugs

Drugs used primarily to treat anxiety are commonly referred to as *tranquilizers.* At one time, barbiturates such as phenobarbital were often prescribed as tranquilizers, and many people became seriously addicted to them. During the 1960s, barbiturates were replaced by a new, safer group of antianxiety drugs belonging to a chemical class called *benzodiazepines* [běn´-zō-dī-**ăz**´- -pēns], including chlordiazepoxide (sold as Librium), diazepam (sold as Valium), and alprazolam (sold as Xanax). According to some estimates, by 1975 more than 10% of adults in the United States and Western Europe were taking these drugs on a regular basis (Lickey & Gordon, 1991; Lipman, 1989). In addition to their prescribed use, benzodiazepines are frequently used (and abused) for recreational purposes, primarily by people with primary abuse to other drugs, such as alcohol (The TEDS Report, 2011).

Biochemically, benzodiazepines appear to produce their tranquilizing effects by augmenting the action of the neurotransmitter GABA (gamma-aminobutyric acid) in the brain (Hefti, 2005). GABA is the brain's main inhibitory neurotransmitter, so its increased action decreases the excitability of neurons almost everywhere in the brain. Side effects of benzodiazepines at high doses include drowsiness, a decline in motor coordination, and a consequent increase in accidents. More important, the drugs enhance the action of alcohol; an amount of alcohol that would otherwise be safe can produce a coma or death in people taking a benzodiazepine. In addition, benzodiazepines are now known to be at least moderately addictive, and very unpleasant withdrawal symptoms—sleeplessness, shakiness, anxiety, headaches, and nausea—occur in those who stop taking them after having taken high doses for a long time (Bond & Lader, 1996).

Early research with benzodiazepines tended to show that they were highly effective in relieving generalized anxiety. More recent, more carefully controlled studies, however, have shown them to be of questionable effectiveness (Martin et al., 2007). Such studies have revealed that more than half of the people who were randomly assigned to the benzodiazepine condition dropped out either because of lack of anxiety relief or because of intolerance of the side effects (Martin et al., 2007). Overall, in the more recent studies, those on a placebo (a pill with no active chemicals) did nearly as well as those on a benzodiazepine.

Today benzodiazepines are still often used to treat generalized anxiety disorder and panic disorder, but are rarely used for other anxiety disorders. Their use for all anxiety disorders has declined partly because of growing recognition of their harmful side effects and partly because of evidence that anxiety may be better treated with antidepressant drugs, in the SSRI class, described below (Mathew & Hoffman, 2009). The effectiveness of antidepressant drugs in treating anxiety disorders is consistent with the evidence, discussed in Chapter 15, for a close biological relationship between anxiety and depression.

Antidepressant Drugs

From the 1960s into the mid-1980s, the drugs most commonly used to treat depression belonged to a chemical class referred to as *tricyclics,* of which imipramine (sold as Tofranil) and amitriptyline (sold as Elavil) are examples. Tricyclics block the normal reuptake of the neurotransmitters serotonin and norepinephrine into presynaptic neurons after their release into the synapse, thereby prolonging the action of the transmitter molecules on postsynaptic neurons (Hefti, 2005). Beginning in the mid-1980s, a newer class of antidepressants, referred to as *selective serotonin reuptake inhibitors (SSRIs)*, which block the reuptake of serotonin but not that of other monoamine transmitters, overtook the tricyclic drugs as the first line of treatment for depression (Gitlin, 2009). Among the most-often prescribed of these drugs are fluoxetine (Prozac), citalopram (Celexa), and sertraline (Zoloft). To visualize how such drugs act at the synapse, see **Figure 16.1**.

Many research studies have demonstrated that tricyclics and SSRIs are about equally effective in treating depression (Carr & Lucki, 2011). With either type of drug, only about 50% of people suffering from major depression show a clinically significant improvement in mood, compared with about 30% who improve over the

FIGURE 16.1 How Prozac and other SSRI antidepressant drugs work
(a) When serotonin is released into a synapse, its action is normally cut short by reuptake into the presynaptic neuron. (b) Selective serotonin reuptake inhibitors block this reuptake and thereby increase the action of serotonin on the postsynaptic neuron.

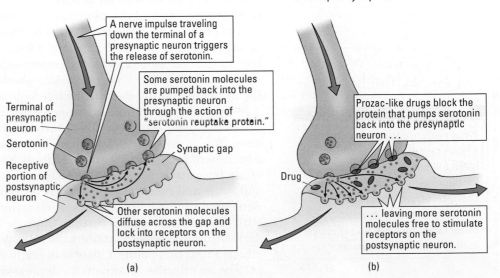

(a)

A nerve impulse traveling down the terminal of a presynaptic neuron triggers the release of serotonin.

Some serotonin molecules are pumped back into the presynaptic neuron through the action of "serotonin reuptake protein."

Terminal of presynaptic neuron

Serotonin

Receptive portion of postsynaptic neuron

Synaptic gap

Other serotonin molecules diffuse across the gap and lock into receptors on the postsynaptic neuron.

(b)

Prozac-like drugs block the protein that pumps serotonin back into the presynaptic neuron . . .

Drug

. . . leaving more serotonin molecules free to stimulate receptors on the postsynaptic neuron.

same time period if given a placebo instead (Hollon et al., 2002). For people with mild or moderate depression, there is even less evidence for the efficacy of antidepressant drugs (Hegerl et al., 2012). In prescribing antidepressants, practitioners must also consider the risk of side effects, which can be severe. Compared with SSRIs, tricyclics are much more likely to be fatal if taken in overdose, and they are also more likely to produce such disruptive and discomforting side effects as fatigue, dry mouth, and blurred vision. Thus, SSRIs are preferred over tricyclics because they have milder side effects—but, ironically, they have been shown to have more negative side effects than the older benzodiazepines (Offidani et al., 2013). Moreover, in some people, SSRIs produce side effects such as reduced sexual drive, headache, nausea, and diarrhea (Gitlin, 2009; Hollon et al., 2002; Uher et al., 2011). Despite such drawbacks, many patients are advised to continue taking antidepressants to maintain the drug's beneficial effects even after a clinical episode lifts.

As noted in Chapter 15, the effects of antidepressant drugs on neurotransmitters occur immediately, but the antidepressant effects take several weeks to develop. This fact suggests that some gradual process—maybe including the growth of new neurons in the brain—underlies the therapeutic effect (Perera et al., 2008). However, despite many theories and much study, researchers still do not know just how antidepressants reduce depression.

Placebo Effects

When drugs are tested for their effectiveness in treating disorders, comparisons are made ideally among at least three different treatment conditions: *no treatment, placebo,* and *drug.* A *placebo* (see Chapter 2) is an inactive substance that is indistinguishable in appearance from the drug. Such experiments are conducted in a double-blind manner (also see Chapter 2)—that is, in such a way that neither the patients nor the researchers who evaluate them are told who is receiving the drug and who is receiving the placebo. Experiments of this sort allow researchers to separate out three different categories of effects through which people improve:

- *Spontaneous remission effect* refers to any improvement shown by those who receive no treatment.
- *Placebo effect* refers to any improvement shown by those receiving the placebo that goes beyond the improvement shown by those receiving no treatment.
- *Drug effect* refers to any improvement shown by those receiving the drug that goes beyond the improvement shown by those receiving the placebo.

When experiments of this sort are conducted with antianxiety or antidepressant drugs, the general finding is that most of the improvement results from spontaneous remission and the placebo effect; only a small amount of improvement can be attributed to the drug itself (Kirsch, 2014; Wampold et al., 2005). For example, in an analysis of such experiments for a variety of antidepressant drugs, Irving Kirsch concluded that about 25% of the improvement in those receiving the drug could be attributed to spontaneous remission, about 50% to the placebo effect, and 25% to the drug's chemical effects (Kirsch & Sapirstein, 1998).

Why is the placebo effect so powerful in treating depression? As discussed in Chapter 15, depression is characterized by feelings of helplessness and hopelessness. In fact, for some people those feelings *are* the disorder. Simply participating in a treatment program—meeting regularly with someone who seems to care and who offers the patient what is believed be a useful drug—may restore feelings of control and hope and produce expectations of improvement. These feelings and expectations may promote life changes, such as improved self-care and more involvement with friends that lead to further improvement in mood. All such effects, which derive from the belief that one's disorder is being treated, contribute to the placebo effect. From this point of view it is really not surprising that a believable placebo may be an effective treatment for depression.

FOCUS 6

What are three different reasons why symptoms of a disorder may decline after being treated with a drug?

FOCUS 7

What evidence suggests that only a small percentage of the improvement following drug treatment for depression results from the chemical effects of the drug? Why might the power of suggestion, or expectancy, be especially effective in the treatment of depression?

Other Biologically Based Treatments

The increased use of drugs, coupled with the increased understanding and acceptance of psychotherapy, has led to the abandonment of most nondrug biological therapies for psychological disorders. Two such treatments still used, however, are electroconvulsive therapy and, in very rare cases, psychosurgery. Psychiatrists are also pioneering newer treatments such as deep brain stimulation and transcranial magnetic stimulation.

Electroconvulsive Therapy

Electroconvulsive therapy, or ***ECT***, is used primarily in cases of severe depression that does not respond to psychotherapy or antidepressant drugs. To the general public this treatment often seems barbaric, and indeed it once was a brutal treatment. The brain seizure induced by the shock would cause muscular contractions so violent that they sometimes broke bones. Today, however, ECT is administered in a way that is painless and quite safe (Keltner & Boschini, 2009; Lisanby, 2007). Before receiving the shock, the patient is put under general anesthesia and given a muscle-blocking drug so that no pain will be felt and no damaging muscle contractions will occur. Then an electric current is passed through the patient's skull, triggering a seizure in the brain that lasts approximately 1 minute. Usually such treatments are given in a series, one every 2 or 3 days for about 2 weeks.

According to most estimates, somewhere between 50 and 80% of people who are suffering from major depression and have not been helped by other forms of treatment experience remission with ECT (Hollon et al., 2002; Lisanby, 2007; Loo, 2010). In some cases, the remission is permanent; in others, depression recurs after several months or more, and then another series of treatments may be given.

Nobody knows how ECT produces its antidepressant effect. In nonhuman animals, such shocks cause immediate release of all varieties of neurotransmitters, followed by longer-lasting changes in transmitter production and in the sensitivity of postsynaptic receptors (Nutt & Glue, 1993). The shocks also stimulate the growth of new neurons in the brain, which some believe may contribute to their antidepressant effect (Jacobs, 2004).

The most frequent side effect of ECT is memory loss, both retrograde amnesia (inability to remember events immediately before the event) and anterograde amnesia (inability to form new memories following the event) (Merkl et al., 2009). In most cases, the memory loss clears up within a few months after the treatment (Squire & Slater, 1983).

Psychosurgery, Deep Brain Stimulation, and Transcranial Magnetic Stimulation

A treatment of last resort today is ***psychosurgery***, which involves surgically cutting or producing lesions in portions of the brain to relieve a psychological disorder. From the late 1930s into the early 1950s, tens of thousands of men and women were subjected to an operation called *prefrontal lobotomy*, in which the anterior (front) portions of the frontal lobes were surgically separated from the rest of the brain. Individuals with severe cases of schizophrenia, bipolar disorder, depression, obsessive-compulsive disorder, and pathological violence were subjected to the operation. Prefrontal lobotomy was so highly regarded that in 1949 the Portuguese neurologist who developed the technique, Egas Moniz, was awarded the Nobel Prize.

By the mid-1950s, however, prefrontal lobotomies had gone out of style, partly because newly developed drug treatments offered an alternative and partly because of mounting evidence that, although lobotomy relieved people of their incapacitating emotions, it left them severely incapacitated in new ways (Valenstein, 1986). As we have mentioned numerous times in earlier chapters, the prefrontal lobes are a critical part of the brain's circuitry for executive functions—the ability to integrate plans with action. Lobotomized patients, having lost the ability to use this part of

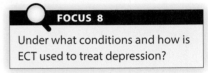

FOCUS 8

Under what conditions and how is ECT used to treat depression?

■ **Electroconvulsive therapy** ECT is the treatment of choice for very severe depression that does not respond to drug therapy. This man has been anesthetized (so he will be unconscious), given a muscle relaxant (so he will not show muscle spasms when the shock is given), and provided with a tube so that his breathing will not be impeded. The shock will be applied to the right side of his brain through the two black leads shown in the photo. Unilateral right-hemisphere ECT disrupts memory much less than does ECT applied across the whole brain.

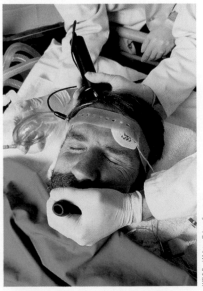

Will & Deni McIntyre/Science Source

FOCUS 9

How are modern, refined forms of psychosurgery sometimes used today in the treatment of obsessive-compulsive disorder?

FOCUS 10

What is the advantage of deep brain stimulation over current forms of psychosurgery?

the brain, could no longer make plans and act according to them. As a consequence, they needed constant care.

Refined versions of psychosurgery were developed in the 1960s and continue to be used in rare cases today. In the new procedures, very small areas of the brain are destroyed by temporarily implanting fine wire electrodes into the targeted areas and applying radiofrequency current through them. Today this procedure is used primarily for treatment of highly incapacitating cases of obsessive-compulsive disorder that have proven, over many years, to be untreatable by any other means.

Obsessive-compulsive disorder is often associated with abnormal amounts of activity in a neural circuit that is involved in converting conscious thoughts into actions. This circuit includes a portion of the prefrontal cortex, a portion of the limbic system called the cingulum, and parts of the basal ganglia. Surgical destruction either of a portion of the cingulum or of a specific neural pathway that enters the basal ganglia reduces or abolishes obsessive-compulsive symptoms in about 50% of people who could not be successfully treated in any other way (Mashour et al., 2005). These procedures produce quite serious side effects in some patients, however, including confusion, weight gain, depression, and, in rare cases, epilepsy (Mashour et al., 2005).

Since the mid-1990s, a number of brain surgeons have been experimenting with a new, safer procedure, called **deep brain stimulation**, for treating intractable cases of obsessive-compulsive disorder (Anderson et al., 2012; Larson, 2008), depression (Mayberg et al., 2005), intractable pain in cancer patients (Young & Brechner, 1986), and some of the motor symptoms associated with Parkinson disease (Kleiner-Fisman et al., 2006). In this procedure a hair-thin wire electrode is implanted permanently into the brain—usually in the cingulum or in a portion of the basal ganglia for patients being treated for obsessive-compulsive disorder. The electrode can be activated in order to electrically stimulate, rather than destroy, the neurons lying near it. High-frequency but low-intensity stimulation through the electrode is believed to desynchronize and disrupt ongoing neural activity, producing an effect comparable to that of a lesion. This effect, unlike that of a lesion, can be reversed just by turning off the electrical current. Trials with deep brain stimulation suggest that it may be as effective as psychosurgery, without the negative side effects (Husted & Shapira, 2004; Larson, 2008).

In Chapter 4 we described the technique of **transcranial magnetic stimulation** as a form of mapping the brain's functions (p. 115). In this method, a technician sends a pulse of electricity through a small copper coil, held just above a person's head. The

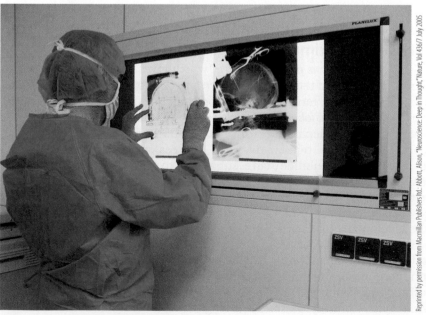

■ **Preparation for deep brain stimulation** As a thin wire electrode is inserted into the patient's brain, the surgeon keeps track of its position through brain imaging.

Reprinted by permission from Macmillan Publishers ltd: Abbott, Alison, "Neuroscience: Deep in Thought," Nature, Vol 436/7 July 2005

magnetic field passes through the scalp and skull and induces an electric current in the neurons immediately below the coil. When focused on the prefrontal cortex, changes in the activity of neurons reduce depression in some patients when it is administered daily over 2 to 4 weeks (Fox et al., 2012; Rosenberg et al., 2011).

SECTION REVIEW

Biological treatments target the brain physically in order to alleviate psychological disorders.

Drugs

- Antipsychotic drugs treat psychotic symptoms, but do not cure people. All such drugs decrease the effectiveness of the neurotransmitter dopamine, and the newer (atypical) drugs also affect other neurotransmitters. They have unpleasant side effects, some quite serious.

- Antianxiety drugs, in a chemical class called benzodiazepines, are used mainly for generalized anxiety disorder and panic disorder. They increase inhibitory activity in the brain, thus reducing excitability; but they are addictive, have potentially harmful side effects, and cause unpleasant withdrawal symptoms.

- Antidepressant drugs include tricyclics and selective serotonin reuptake inhibitors (SSRIs); the former prolong the action of serotonin and norepinephrine in the brain, while the latter affect only serotonin. SSRIs are equally effective in treating depression and have milder side effects, therefore they are more often prescribed. SSRIs are also used to treat anxiety disorders.

- Studies that classify patients' improvement after taking an antidepressant drug into three categories—spontaneous recovery, placebo effect, and drug effect—reveal that much if not most of the improvement is due to the placebo effect. Hope, provided by the sense of being treated, may be the principal ingredient of any treatment for depression.

Other Biological Treatments

- In electroconvulsive therapy (ECT), used to treat depression not helped by other means, electrical current is applied to the skull to induce brain seizures. It is quite safe and effective but can cause memory loss.

- Prefrontal lobotomies, once common, are no longer performed. Today psychosurgery involving small, localized lesions is used occasionally for incapacitating obsessive-compulsive disorder. It is often effective but can produce harmful side effects.

- Deep brain stimulation, a possible alternative to psychosurgery, uses electrical current to disrupt activity rather than destroy tissue at specific brain locations.

- Transcranial magnetic stimulation sends a pulse of electricity through a coil held just above a person's head, inducing an electric current in the neurons immediately below the coil, and can be effective in treating depression.

Psychotherapy I: Psychodynamic and Humanistic Therapies

Biological treatment for psychological disorders aims to improve moods, thinking, and behavior through altering the chemistry and physiology of the brain. Psychological treatment, or *psychotherapy*, aims to improve the same through talk, reflection, learning, and practice.

The two approaches—biological and psychological—are not incompatible. Indeed, most clinicians believe that the best treatment for many people who suffer from serious psychological disorders involves a combination of drug therapy and psychotherapy. In theory as well as in practice, the biological and the psychological are tightly entwined. Changes in the brain can alter the way a person feels, thinks, and behaves; and changes in feeling, thought, and behavior can alter the brain. The brain is not a "hardwired" machine. It is a dynamic biological organ that is constantly growing new neural connections and losing old ones as it adapts to new experiences and thoughts.

Psychotherapy can be defined as any theory-based, systematic procedure, conducted by a trained therapist, for helping people to overcome or cope with

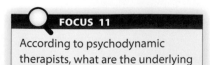

FIGURE 16.2 Theoretical orientation of a sample of psychotherapists
Although there may be as many as 400 different kinds of psychotherapies, most therapists follow one of the orientations in this figure. As you can see, most therapists today consider themselves to be "eclectic" (29%) or cognitive (28%), with many fewer classifying themselves as "client-centered" or "existential" (the humanistic therapies). Note the "psychodynamic" category includes those who labeled their practice as psychodynamic or psychoanalytic.

mental problems through psychological rather than directly physiological means. Psychotherapy usually involves dialogue between the person in need and the therapist, and its aim is usually to restructure some aspect of the person's way of feeling, thinking, or behaving. If you have ever helped a child overcome a fear, encouraged a friend to give up a bad habit, or cheered up a despondent roommate, you have informally engaged in a process akin to psychotherapy.

Psychotherapy takes many different forms—by one count, there are more than 400 types (Corsini & Wedding, 2011). Psychotherapists may work with groups of people, or with couples or families, as well as with individuals. In this chapter we address four classic varieties of individual therapy. We examine *psychodynamic* and *humanistic* therapies together in this section, in part because both of these are holistic in their approach, focusing on the whole person. In contrast, *cognitive* and *behavioral* therapies typically focus more directly and narrowly on the specific symptoms and problems that the client presents.

Decades ago, many psychotherapists believed that their own approach was "right" and other approaches "wrong." As shown in **Figure 16.2**, nearly 30% of today's psychotherapists consider themselves to be "eclectic" or "integrative" in orientation—that is, they do not identify with any one school of thought but use methods gleaned from various schools. Even among those who do identify with a particular school of thought, most borrow techniques and ideas from other schools.

Each major approach in psychotherapy draws on a set of psychological principles and ideas that apply to adaptive as well as to maladaptive behavior.

● The psychodynamic approach focuses on the idea that unconscious memories and emotions influence our conscious thoughts and actions.

● The humanistic approach focuses on the value of self-esteem and self-direction, and on the idea that people often need psychological support from others in order to pursue freely their own chosen goals.

● The behavioral approach focuses on the roles of basic learning processes in the development and maintenance of adaptive and maladaptive ways of responding to the environment.

● The cognitive approach focuses on the idea that people's ingrained, habitual ways of thinking affect their moods and behavior.

Principles of Psychodynamic Therapies

Sigmund Freud, whose theory of personality was discussed in Chapter 14, was the primary founder of psychodynamic psychotherapy. As noted in Chapter 14, Freud used the term *psychoanalysis* to refer to both his theory of personality and his methods of therapy. Today the term **psychoanalysis** is generally used to refer to those forms of therapy that adhere most closely to the ideas set forth by Freud, and the broader term **psychodynamic therapy** is used to include psychoanalysis and therapies that are more loosely based on Freud's ideas. In a 2001 survey, only 10% of those who categorized their therapy as psychodynamic identified their specific method as psychoanalysis (Bechtoldt et al., 2001). Following are some of the main principles and methods that are common to most, if not all, psychodynamic therapies.

Unconscious Conflicts, Often Rooted in Early Childhood Experiences, Underlie Psychological Disorders

The most central, uniting idea of all psychodynamic theories is that mental problems arise from unresolved mental conflicts, which themselves arise from the holding of contradictory motives and beliefs. The motives, beliefs, and conflicts may be

FOCUS 11

According to psychodynamic therapists, what are the underlying sources of psychological disorders?

unconscious, or partly so, but they nevertheless influence conscious thoughts and actions. The word *dynamic* refers to force, and *psychodynamic* refers to the forceful, generally unconscious influences that conflicting motives and beliefs can have on a person's consciously experienced emotions, thoughts, and behavior.

Freud himself argued (e.g., Freud, 1933/1964) that the unconscious conflicts that cause trouble always originate in the first 5 or 6 years of life and have to do with infantile sexual and aggressive wishes, but few psychodynamic therapists today have retained that view. Most psychodynamic therapists today are concerned with conflicts that can originate at any time in life and have to do with any drives or needs that are important to the person. Still, however, most such therapists tend to see sexual and aggressive drives as

"Your mother never read to you and your father never hugged you. That's why you drink from the toilet."

particularly important, as these drives often conflict with learned beliefs and societal constraints. They also see childhood as a particularly vulnerable period during which frightening or confusing experiences can produce lasting marks on a person's ways of feeling, thinking, and behaving. Such experiences might derive from such sources as sexual or physical abuse, lack of security, or lack of consistent love from parents.

In general, psychodynamic theorists see their approach as tightly linked, theoretically, to the field of developmental psychology. Thus, growing up necessarily entails the facing and resolving of conflicts; conflicts that are not resolved can produce problems later in life (Thompson & Cotlove, 2005).

Patients' Observable Speech and Behavior Provide Clues to Their Unconscious Conflicts

To a psychodynamic therapist, the symptoms that bring a person in for therapy and that are used to label a disorder, using *DSM-5* or any other diagnostic guide, are just that— *symptoms*. They are surface manifestations of the disorder; the disorder itself is buried in the person's unconscious mind and must be unearthed before it can be treated.

For example, consider a patient who is diagnosed as having anorexia nervosa (an eating disorder described in Chapter 15). To a psychodynamic therapist, the fundamental problem with the person is not the failure to eat but is something deeper and more hidden—some conflict that makes her want to starve herself. Two people who have similar symptoms and identical diagnoses of anorexia nervosa may suffer from quite different underlying conflicts. One might be starving herself because she fears sex, and starvation is a way of forestalling her sexual development; another might be starving herself because she feels unaccepted for who she is, so she is trying to disappear. To a psychodynamic therapist, the first step in treatment of either patient is finding out why she is starving herself; quite likely, she herself is not conscious of the real reason (Binder, 2004).

To learn about the content of a patient's unconscious mind, the psychodynamic therapist must, in detective-like fashion, analyze clues found in the patient's speech and other forms of observable behavior. This is where Freud's term *psychoanalysis* comes from. The symptoms that brought the patient in for help, and the unique ways those symptoms are manifested, are one source of clues that the therapist considers. What other clues might be useful? Since the conscious mind usually attempts to act in ways that are consistent with conventional logic, Freud reasoned that the elements of thought and behavior that are *least* logical would provide the most useful clues. They would represent elements of the unconscious mind that leaked out relatively unmodified by consciousness. This insight led Freud to suggest that the most useful clues to a patient's unconscious motives and beliefs are found in the patient's free associations, dreams, and slips of the tongue or behavioral errors. These sources of clues are still widely used by psychodynamic therapists.

 FOCUS 12

According to psychodynamic therapists, what is the relationship between symptoms and disorders?

Free Associations as Clues to the Unconscious The technique of *free association* is one in which the patient is encouraged to sit back (or, in traditional psychoanalysis, to lie down on a couch), relax, free his or her mind, refrain from trying to be logical or "correct," and report every image or idea that enters his or her awareness, usually in response to some word or picture that the therapist provides as an initial stimulus. You might try this exercise yourself: Relax, free your mind from what you have just been reading or thinking about, and write down the words or ideas that come immediately to your mind in response to each of the following: *liquid, horse, soft, potato.* Now, when you examine your set of responses to these words, do they make any sense that was not apparent when you produced them? Do you believe that they give you any clues to your unconscious mind?

Dreams as Clues to the Unconscious Freud believed that dreams are the purest exercises of free association, so he asked patients to try to remember their dreams, or to write them down upon awakening, and to describe them to him. During sleep, conventional logic is largely absent, and the forces that normally hold down unconscious ideas are weakened. Still, even in dreams, according to Freud and other psychodynamic therapists, the unconscious is partially disguised. Freud distinguished the underlying, unconscious meaning of the dream (the latent content) from the dream as it is consciously experienced and remembered by the dreamer (the manifest content). The analyst's task in interpreting a dream is the same as that in interpreting any other form of free association: to see through the disguises and uncover the latent content from the manifest content.

Psychodynamic therapists hold that the disguises in dreams come in various forms. Some are unique to a particular person, but some are common to many people. Freud himself looked especially for sexual themes in dreams, and the common disguises that he wrote about have become known as *Freudian symbols,* some of which he described as follows (from Freud, 1900/1953):

> The Emperor and Empress (or King and Queen) as a rule really represent the dreamer's parents; and a Prince or Princess represents the dreamer himself or herself. . . . All elongated objects, such as sticks, tree-trunks, and umbrellas (the opening of these last being comparable to an erection) may stand for the male organ—as well as all long, sharp weapons, such as knives, daggers, and pikes. . . . Boxes, cases, chests, cupboards, and ovens represent the uterus, and also hollow objects, ships, and vessels of all kinds. Rooms in dreams are usually women; if the various ways in and out of them are represented, this interpretation is scarcely open to doubt. In this connection interest in whether the room is open or locked is easily intelligible. There is no need to name explicitly the key that unlocks the room. (p. 353)

■ **Freudian symbols in a work of art painted four centuries before Freud** This is a detail from *The Garden of Earthly Delights,* painted in the late fifteenth century by the Dutch artist Hieronymus Bosch and now housed in the Prado Museum, Madrid. It is believed to represent Bosch's conception of decadence or Hell. Notice the dreamlike (nightmarish) quality and the numerous Freudian symbols—the protruding, phallic-like objects and the womb-like enclosures.

Mistakes and Slips of the Tongue as Clues to the Unconscious Still other clues to the unconscious mind used by psychodynamic therapists are found in the mistakes that patients make in their speech and actions. For example, when having dinner for the first time with his girlfriend's parents, a young man might say "please pass the bed" when he meant to say "please pass the bread." In Freud's rather extreme view, such mistakes are never simply random accidents but are always expressions of unconscious wishes or conflicts. In one of his most popular books, *The Psychopathology of Everyday Life,* Freud (1901/1990) supported this claim with numerous, sometimes amusing examples of such errors, along with his interpretations.

The Roles of Resistance and Transference in the Therapeutic Process

From Freud's time through today, psychodynamic therapists have found that patients often resist the therapist's attempt to bring their unconscious memories or wishes into consciousness (Weiner & Bornstein, 2009). The **resistance** may manifest itself in such forms as refusing to talk about certain topics, "forgetting" to come to therapy sessions, or persistently arguing in a way that subverts the therapeutic process. Freud assumed that resistance stems from the general defensive processes by which people protect themselves from becoming conscious of anxiety-provoking thoughts. Resistance provides clues that therapy is going in the right direction, toward critical unconscious material; but it can also slow down the course of therapy or even bring it to a halt. To avoid triggering too much resistance, the therapist must present interpretations gradually, when the patient is ready to accept them.

Freud also observed that patients often express strong emotional feelings—sometimes love, sometimes anger—toward the therapist. Freud believed that the true object of such feelings is usually not the therapist but some other significant person in the patient's life whom the therapist symbolizes. Thus, *transference* is the phenomenon by which the patient's unconscious feelings about his or her mother or father, or some other significant person in his or her life, are experienced consciously as feelings about the therapist. Psychodynamic therapists to this day consider transference to be especially useful in psychotherapy because it provides an opportunity for the patient to become aware of his or her strong emotions (Weiner & Bornstein, 2009). With help from the analyst, the patient can gradually become aware of the origin of those feelings and their true target.

The Relationship Between Insight and Cure

Psychodynamic therapy is essentially a process in which the analyst makes inferences about the patient's unconscious conflicts and helps the patient become conscious of those conflicts. How does such consciousness help? According to psychodynamic therapists from Freud on, it helps because, once conscious, the conflicting beliefs and wishes can be experienced directly and acted upon; or, if they are unrealistic, they can be modified by the conscious mind into healthier, more appropriate beliefs and pursuits (Thompson & Cotlove, 2005). At the same time, the patient is freed of the defenses that had kept that material repressed and has more psychic energy for other activities. But for all this to happen, the patient must truly accept the insights, viscerally as well as intellectually. The therapist cannot just tell the patient about the unconscious conflicts but must lead the patient gradually to actually experience the emotions and to arrive at the insights him- or herself.

FOCUS 15

According to psychodynamic theories, how do insights into the patient's unconscious conflicts bring about a cure?

Principles of Humanistic Therapy

The humanistic movement in psychology originated in the mid-twentieth century. It grew partly out of existentialist philosophy, which focuses on the idea that human beings create their own life meanings (Hazler & Barwick, 2001), as well as a reaction against the psychodynamic approach, which puts control in the hands of the analyst rather than the patient. From an existentialist perspective, each person must decide for him- or herself what is true and worthwhile in order to live a full, meaningful life; meaning and purpose cannot be thrust upon a person from the outside.

Two fundamental psychological ideas that have been emphasized repeatedly in previous chapters of this book are these: (1) People have the capacity to make adaptive choices regarding their own behavior—choices that promote their survival and well-being; and (2) in order to feel good about themselves and to feel motivated to move forward in life, people need to feel accepted and

"No, I'm not interested in exploring the meaning of my existence; I just want to know whether I actually exist."

FOCUS 16

What is the primary goal of humanistic therapy? How does that goal relate to existentialist philosophy?

■ **Carl Rogers** The inventor of client-centered therapy (second from right) was a charismatic individual who personally embodied the empathy and genuineness that are the essence of his method of therapy.

FOCUS 17

How do the therapist's nondirective approach, empathic listening, and genuine positive regard contribute to the client's recovery, according to humanistic therapists?

approved of by others. No approach to psychotherapy takes these two ideas more seriously than does the humanistic approach.

As described in Chapter 14, the humanistic view of the person emphasizes the inner potential for positive growth—the so-called *actualizing potential*. Recall that the highest level in Maslow's hierarchy of needs (described in Chapter 14) is self-actualization. For this self-actualizing potential to exert its effects, people must be conscious of their feelings and desires, not deny or distort them. Denial and distortion occur when people perceive that others who are important to them consistently disapprove of their feelings and desires. The goal of **humanistic therapy** is to help people regain awareness of their own desires and control of their own lives.

The primary founder of humanistic psychotherapy was Carl Rogers, whose theory of personality was introduced in Chapter 14. Rogers (1951) called his therapeutic approach *client-centered therapy,* a term deliberately chosen to distinguish it from psychodynamic therapies. Client-centered therapy focuses on the abilities and insights of the client rather than those of the therapist. Practitioners of this approach today, however, more often refer to it as ***person-centered therapy*** because they see the therapeutic process as involving a relationship between two unique persons—the client and the therapist (Mearns & Thorne, 2000; Wilkins, 2003). The therapist must attend to his or her own thoughts and feelings, as well as to those of the client, in order to respond in a supportive yet honest way to the client (Raskin et al., 2011).

The core principles of person-centered therapy all have to do with the relationship between the therapist and the client. The therapist lets the client take the lead in therapy, strives to understand and empathize with the client, and endeavors to think positively and genuinely of the client as a competent, valuable person. Through these means, the therapist tries to help the client regain the self-understanding and confidence necessary to control his or her own life.

Allowing the Client to Take the Lead

Humanistic psychotherapists usually refer to those who come to them for help as *clients,* not as patients, because the latter term implies passivity and lack of ability. In humanistic therapy, at least in theory, the client is in charge; it is the therapist who must be "patient" enough to follow the client's lead. The therapist may take steps to encourage the client to start talking, to tell his or her story; but once the client has begun to talk it is the therapist's task to understand, not to direct the discussion or interpret the client's words in ways that the client does not intend. While psychodynamic theorists may strain their patients' credulity with far-reaching interpretations, humanistic therapists more often just paraphrase what the client said, as a way of checking to be sure that they understood correctly.

Listening Carefully and Empathetically

The humanistic therapist tries to provide a context within which clients can become aware of and accept their own feelings and learn to trust their own decision-making abilities. To do so, the therapist must first and foremost truly listen to the client in an empathetic way (Raskin et al., 2011; Rogers, 1951). *Empathy* here refers to the therapist's attempt to comprehend what the client is saying or feeling at any given moment from the client's point of view rather than as an outsider. As part of the attempt to achieve and manifest such empathy, the therapist frequently reflects back the ideas and feelings that the client expresses. A typical exchange might go like this:

> **Client:** *My mother is a mean, horrible witch!*
>
> **Therapist:** *I guess you're feeling a lot of anger toward your mother right now.*

To an outsider, the therapist's response here might seem silly, a statement of the obvious. But to the client and therapist fully engaged in the process, the response serves several purposes. First, it shows the client that the therapist is listening and trying to understand. Second, it distills and reflects back to the client the feeling that seems to lie behind the client's words—a feeling of which the client may or may not have been fully aware at the moment. Third, it offers the client a chance to correct the therapist's understanding. By clarifying things to the therapist, the client clarifies them to him- or herself.

Providing Unconditional but Genuine Positive Regard

Unconditional positive regard implies a belief on the therapist's part that the client is worthy and capable even when the client may not feel or act that way. By expressing positive feelings about the client regardless of what the client says or does, the therapist creates a safe, nonjudgmental environment for the client to explore and express all of his or her thoughts and feelings. Through experiencing the therapist's positive regard, clients begin to feel more positive about themselves, an essential step if they are going to take charge of their lives. Unconditional positive regard does not imply agreement with everything the client says or approval of everything the client does, but it does imply faith in the client's underlying capacity to make appropriate decisions. Consider the following hypothetical exchange:

> **Client:** *Last semester in college I cheated on every test.*
>
> **Therapist:** *I guess what you're saying is that last semester you did something against your values.*

Notice that the therapist has said something positive about the client in relation to the misdeed without condoning the misdeed. The shift in focus from the negative act to the client's positive values affirms the client's inner worth and potential ability to make constructive decisions.

Humanistic therapists must work hard to be both positive and genuine in the feedback they supply to clients. They contend that it is impossible to fake empathy and positive regard; the therapist must really experience them. If the therapist's words and true feelings don't match, the words will not be believable to the client. The capacity for genuine empathy and positive regard toward all clients might seem to be a rare quality, but Rogers suggests that it can be cultivated by deliberately trying to see things as the client sees them.

Although few psychotherapists identify themselves as practicing client-centered therapy today (see Figure 16.2), aspects of the Rogerian approach can be seen in some modern forms of therapy. For example, *emotionally focused therapy* is a brief (8 to 20 sessions) form of therapy that adopts many of the practices of client-centered therapy but emphasizes the importance of emotion, particularly emotions related to attachment (Greenberg & Goldman, 2008; Palmer-Olsen et al., 2011). Emotionally focused therapy, which is often used for couples and family therapy, emphasizes that relationships are attachment bonds and that effective therapy must address the security of those bonds, with change involving new experiences of the self and others, and that emotion is the target of change. Consistent with client-centered therapy, the role of the therapist is to serve as a consultant for the individuals in therapy (Johnson, 2002).

SECTION REVIEW

Talk, reflection, learning, and practice are the tools psychotherapists use to help people.

Principals of Psychodynamic Therapies

- The psychodynamic approach assumes that psychological disorders arise from unresolved mental conflicts that, though unconscious, strongly influence conscious thought and action.

- The psychodynamic therapist's job is to identify the unconscious conflict from observable clues, such as dreams, free association, mistakes, and slips of the tongue. The goal is to help the patient become aware of the conflicting beliefs and wishes and thus be able to deal with them.

- The patient's resistance to the uncovering of unconscious material suggests that the therapist is on the right track. Transference of feelings about significant persons in the patient's life to the therapist helps the patient become aware of these strong emotions.

Principals of Humanistic Therapies

- Humanistic therapists strive to help clients accept their own feelings and desires, a prerequisite for self-actualization (positive, self-directed psychological growth).

- Clients may fail to accept (deny and distort) their feelings and desires because they perceive that these are disapproved of by valued others.

- The humanistic therapist lets clients take the lead, listens carefully and empathetically, and provides unconditional but genuine positive regard.

Psychotherapy II: Behavioral and Cognitive Therapies

As we mentioned earlier, unlike the psychodynamic and humanistic approaches, behavioral and cognitive therapies usually focus on specific symptoms and problems. The symptoms *are* the problem and not necessarily merely a reflection of some deeper underlying cause. Behavioral and cognitive therapists both are also very much concerned with data; they use objective measures to assess whether or not the treatment given is helping the client overcome the problem that is being treated. Many therapists today combine cognitive and behavioral methods, in what is called **cognitive-behavioral therapy** (often abbreviated as **CBT**). Here, however, we will discuss the two separately, as they involve distinct assumptions and methods.

Principles of Behavior Therapy

Behavior therapy is rooted in the research on basic learning processes initiated by such pioneers as Ivan Pavlov, John B. Watson, and B. F. Skinner (discussed in Chapter 8). Unlike all the other psychotherapy approaches we have discussed, behavior therapy is not fundamentally talk therapy. Rather, in behavior therapy clients are exposed by the therapist to new environmental conditions that are designed to retrain them so that maladaptive habitual or reflexive ways of responding become extinguished and new, healthier habits and reflexes are conditioned.

Behavior therapy is very much symptom oriented and concerned with immediate, measurable results. Two of the most common types of treatment in behavior therapy, discussed below, are *contingency management therapy* to modify habits and *exposure therapy* to overcome unwanted fears.

Contingency Management: Altering the Relationship Between Actions and Rewards

The basic principle of operant conditioning, discussed in Chapter 8, is that behavioral actions are reinforced by their consequences. People, like other animals, learn to behave in ways that bring desired consequences and to avoid behaving in ways that do not. When a behavior therapist learns that a client is behaving in ways that are harmful to him- or herself, or to others, the first question the therapist might ask is this: *What reward is this person getting for this behavior, which leads him or her to continue it?* The next step, once the reward is understood, is to modify the behavior–reward contingency so that desired actions are rewarded and undesired ones are not. The broad term for all therapy programs that alter the contingency between actions and rewards is **contingency management**.

For example, if parents complain to a behavior therapist that their child is acting in aggressive and disruptive ways at home, the therapist might ask the parents to keep a record, for a week or more, of each instance of such misbehavior and of how they or others in the family responded. From that record, the therapist might learn that the child is gaining desired attention through misbehavior. The therapist might then work out a training program in which the parents agree to attend more to the child when he is behaving in desired ways and to ignore the child, or provide some clearly negative consequence (such as withdrawing some privilege), when he is behaving in undesired ways. This sort of behavioral work with families, aimed at altering the contingencies between actions and rewards at home, is called *parent management training* (Kazdin, 2003). Contingency management is the principal tool used in *applied behavior analysis*, discussed in Chapter 8 (pp. 288–289), which focuses on changing some target behaviors, such as nail biting, head banging for a child with autism, or study habits for a fourth grader, by changing patterns of reinforcements.

Contingency management has been instituted in many community drug rehabilitation programs through which patients who remain drug free for specified periods of time, as measured by regular urine tests, receive vouchers that they can exchange for prizes. Such programs have proven quite successful in encouraging cocaine and heroin abusers to go many weeks without taking drugs, and these programs are sometimes less expensive than other, more standard treatments (Barry et al., 2009; Higgins et al., 2007).

FOCUS 18

How has contingency management been used to improve children's behavior and motivate abstinence in drug abusers?

Exposure Treatments for Unwanted Fears

Behavior therapy has proven especially successful in treating specific phobias, in which the person fears something well defined, such as high places or a particular type of animal (Emmelkamp, 2004). From a behavioral perspective, fear is a reflexive response, which through classical conditioning can come to be triggered by various nondangerous as well as dangerous stimuli. An unconditioned stimulus for fear is one that elicits the response even if the individual has had no previous experience with the stimulus; a conditioned stimulus for fear is one that elicits the response only because the stimulus was previously paired with some fearful event in the person's experience. Opinions may differ as to whether a particular fear, such as a fear of snakes, is unconditioned or conditioned (unlearned or learned), but in practice this does not matter because the treatment is the same in either case.

A characteristic of the fear reflex, whether conditioned or unconditioned, is that it declines and gradually disappears if the eliciting stimulus is presented many times or over a prolonged period in a context where no harm comes to the person. In the case of an unconditioned fear reflex—such as the startle response to a sudden noise—the decline is called *habituation*. In the case of a conditioned fear reflex, the decline that occurs when the conditioned stimulus is presented repeatedly without the unconditioned stimulus is called *extinction*. For example, if a person fears all dogs because of once having been bitten, then prolonged exposure to various dogs (the conditioned stimuli) in the absence of being bitten (the unconditioned stimulus) will result in reduction or eradication of the fear. Any treatment for an unwanted fear or phobia that involves exposure to the feared stimulus in order to habituate or extinguish the fear response is referred to as an **exposure treatment** (Moscovitch et al., 2009). Behavior therapists have developed three different means to present feared stimuli to clients in such treatments (Krijn et al., 2004).

One means is *imaginal exposure*. A client in this form of treatment is instructed to imagine a particular, moderately fearful scene as vividly as possible until it no

FOCUS 19

What is the theoretical rationale for treating specific phobias by exposing clients to the feared objects or situations?

FOCUS 20

What are three ways of exposing clients to feared objects or situations, and what are the advantages of each?

longer seems frightening. Then the client is instructed to imagine a somewhat more fearful scene until that no longer seems frightening. In this way the client gradually works up to the most feared scene. For example, a woman afraid of heights might be asked first to imagine that she is looking out a second-floor window, then a third-floor window, and so on, until she can imagine, without strong fear, that she is looking down from the top of a skyscraper. The goal is that the ability to imagine the previously feared situation without experiencing fear will generalize so that the person will be able to tolerate—or perhaps even enjoy—the actual situation without fear. Research involving long-term follow-up has shown that imaginal exposure techniques can be quite effective in treating specific phobias (Zinbarg et al., 1992).

The most direct exposure technique is *in vivo exposure*—that is, real-life exposure. With this technique the client, usually accompanied by the therapist or by some other comforting and encouraging helper, must force him- or herself to confront the feared situation in reality. For example, to overcome a fear of flying, the client might begin by going to the airport and watching planes take off and land until that can be done without fear. Then, through a special arrangement with an airline, the client might enter a stationary plane and sit in it for a while, until that can be done without fear. Finally, the client goes on an actual flight—perhaps just a short one the first time. Research suggests that in vivo exposure is generally more effective than imaginal exposure when both are possible (Emmelkamp, 2004). However, in vivo exposure is usually more time consuming and expensive, and is often not practical because the feared situation is difficult to arrange for the purpose of therapy.

Today, with advanced computer technology, a third means of exposure is possible and is rapidly growing in use—*virtual reality exposure*, in which patients wear goggles and experience three-dimensional images that simulate real-world objects and situations. Virtual worlds have been developed for exposure treatments for many different phobias, including fear of heights, fear of flying, claustrophobia (fear of being in small, enclosed spaces), spider phobia, and fear of public speaking (Krijn et al., 2004), as well as anxiety disorders (Antony, 2011). Results to date suggest that virtual reality exposure is reasonably effective (Gonçalves et al., 2012; Krijn et al., 2004; Parsons & Rizzo, 2008). In one research study, for example, all nine participants, who came with strong fears of flying, overcame their fears within six 1-hour sessions of virtual exposure—exposure in which they progressed gradually through virtual experiences of going to an airport, entering a plane, flying, looking out the plane window, and feeling and hearing turbulence while flying (Botella et al., 2004). After the therapy, all of them were able to take an actual plane fight with relatively little fear.

A Case Example: Miss Muffet Overcomes Her Spider Phobia

Our case example of behavior therapy is that of a woman nicknamed Miss Muffet by her therapists (Hoffman, 2004). For 20 years prior to her behavioral treatment, Miss Muffet had suffered from an extraordinary fear of spiders, a fear that had led to a diagnosis not just of spider phobia but also obsessive-compulsive disorder. Her obsessive fear of spiders prompted her to engage in such compulsive rituals as regularly fumigating her car with smoke and pesticides, sealing her bedroom windows with duct tape every night, and sealing her clothes in plastic bags immediately after washing them. She scanned constantly for spiders wherever she went, and she avoided places where she had ever encountered spiders. By the time she came for behavior therapy her spider fear was so intense that she found it difficult to leave home at all.

Miss Muffet's therapy, conducted by Hunter Hoffman (2004) and his colleagues, consisted of ten 1-hour sessions of virtual reality exposure. In the first session she navigated through a virtual kitchen, where she encountered a huge virtual tarantula. She was asked to approach this spider as closely as she could, using a handheld joystick to move forward in the three-dimensional scene. In later sessions, as she

FOCUS 21

How did virtual exposure treatment help Miss Muffet overcome her fear of spiders?

became less fearful of approaching the virtual tarantula, she was instructed to reach out and "touch" it. To create the tactile effect of actually touching the spider, the therapist held out a fuzzy toy spider, which she felt with her real hand as she saw her virtual hand touch the virtual spider.

In other sessions, she encountered other spiders of various shapes and sizes. On one occasion she was instructed to pick up a virtual vase, out of which wriggled a virtual spider. On another, a virtual spider dropped slowly to the floor of the virtual kitchen, directly in front of her, as sound effects from the horror movie *Psycho* were played through her headphones. The goal of the therapy was to create spider experiences that were more frightening than any she would encounter in the real world, so as to convince her, at a gut emotional level, that encountering real spiders would not cause her to panic or go crazy. As a test, after the 10 virtual reality sessions, Miss Muffet was asked to hold a live tarantula (a large, hairy, fearsome looking, but harmless spider), which she did with little fear, even while the creature crawled partway up her arm.

■ **Virtual reality exposure treatment** As treatment for her spider phobia, this woman wears a headset that allows her to walk through a virtual environment in which she confronts spiders, some of which are monstrously large. The screen in the background depicts the scene that she is currently seeing, but her view is three-dimensional. The fuzzy object held in front of her will add a tactile component to her spider experience; she will be asked to touch it with her real hand as she touches the virtual spider with her virtual hand.

Principles of Cognitive Therapy

If a behavior therapist is a trainer, a cognitive therapist is a teacher. While behavior therapy deals directly with maladaptive behaviors, cognitive therapy deals with maladaptive habits of thought. *Cognitive therapy* arose in the 1960s as part of a shift in the overall field of psychology toward greater focus on the roles of thoughts, beliefs, and attitudes in controlling behavior. Like behavior therapists, cognitive therapists use objective measures to determine if the treatment is helping the client. As we mentioned earlier, many therapists combine cognitive and behavioral methods, in cognitive-behavioral therapy.

The field of psychology is filled with evidence that people's beliefs and ingrained, habitual ways of thinking affect their behavior and emotions. Cognitive therapy begins with the assumption that people disturb themselves through their own, often illogical beliefs and thoughts. Maladaptive beliefs and thoughts make reality seem worse than it is, leading to anxiety or depression. The goal of cognitive therapy is to identify maladaptive ways of thinking and replace them with adaptive ways that provide a base for more effective coping with the real world. Unlike psychoanalysis, cognitive therapy generally centers on conscious thoughts, though such thoughts may be so ingrained and automatic that they occur with little conscious effort.

The two best-known pioneers of cognitive therapy are Albert Ellis and Aaron Beck. Both started their careers in the 1950s as psychodynamic therapists but became disenchanted with that approach (Beck & Weishaar, 2011; Ellis, 1986). Each was impressed by the observation that clients seemed to mentally distort their experiences in ways that quite directly produced their problems or symptoms. Ellis referred to his specific brand of cognitive therapy as *rational-emotive therapy,* highlighting his belief that rational thought will improve clients' emotions.

Here we will look at three general principles of cognitive therapy: the identification and correction of maladaptive beliefs and thoughts; the establishment of clear-cut goals and steps for achieving them; and the changing role of the therapist, from that of teacher early in the process to that of consultant later on.

FOCUS 22

How is behavior therapy distinguished from cognitive therapy?

FOCUS 23

According to cognitive therapists, what is the source of clients' behavioral and emotional problems?

Identifying and Correcting Maladaptive Beliefs and Habits of Thought

Different cognitive therapists take different approaches to pointing out their patients' irrational ways of thinking. Beck, as you will see later (in the case example), tends to take a Socratic approach: Through questioning, he gets the patient to discover and correct his or her own irrational thought (Beck & Weishaar, 2011). Ellis, in contrast, took a more direct and blunt approach. He gave humorous names to

FOCUS 24

How did Ellis explain people's negative emotions in terms of their irrational beliefs?

certain styles of irrational thinking. Thus, *musturbation* is the irrational belief that one *must* have some particular thing or *must* act in some particular way in order to be happy or worthwhile. If a client said, "I have to get all A's this semester in college," Ellis might respond, "You're musturbating again." *Awfulizing*, in Ellis's vocabulary, is the mental exaggeration of setbacks or inconveniences. A client who felt bad for a whole week because of a dent in her new car might be told, "Stop awfulizing."

The following dialogue between Ellis (1962) and a client not only illustrates Ellis's blunt style but also makes explicit his theory of the relationship between thoughts and emotions—a theory shared by most cognitive therapists. The client began the session by complaining that he was unhappy because some men with whom he played golf didn't like him. Ellis, in response, claimed that the client's reasoning was illogical—the men's not liking him couldn't make him unhappy.

Client: *Well, why was I unhappy then?*

Ellis: *It's very simple—as simple as A, B, C, I might say. A in this case is the fact that these men didn't like you. Let's assume that you observed their attitude correctly and were not merely imagining they didn't like you.*

Client: *I assure you that they didn't. I could see that very clearly.*

Ellis: *Very well, let's assume they didn't like you and call that A. Now, C is your unhappiness—which we'll definitely have to assume is a fact, since you felt it.*

Client: *Damn right I did!*

Ellis: *All right, then: A is the fact that the men didn't like you, and C is your unhappiness. You see A and C and you assume that A, their not liking you, caused your unhappiness. But it didn't.*

Client: *It didn't? What did, then?*

Ellis: *B did.*

Client: *What's B?*

Ellis: *B is what you said to yourself while you were playing golf with those men.*

Client: *What I said to myself? But I didn't say anything.*

Ellis: *You did. You couldn't possibly be unhappy if you didn't. The only thing that could possibly make you unhappy that occurs from without is a brick falling on your head, or some such equivalent. But no brick fell. Obviously, therefore, you must have told yourself something to make you unhappy.* (Ellis, 1962, pp. 126, 127)

In this dialogue, Ellis invokes his famous *ABC theory of emotions: A* is the *activating event* in the environment, *B* is the *belief* that is triggered in the client's mind when the event occurs, and *C* is the emotional *consequence* of the triggered belief (illustrated in **Figure 16.3**). Therapy proceeds by changing B, the belief. In this example, the man suffers because he believes irrationally that he must be liked by everyone (an example of musturbation), so if someone doesn't like him, he is unhappy. The first step will be to convince the man that it is irrational to expect everyone to like him and that there is little or no harm in not being liked by some people.

FOCUS 25

What is the purpose of homework in cognitive therapy?

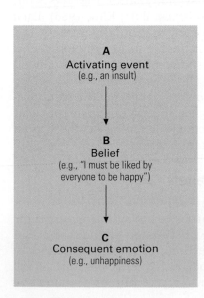

FIGURE 16.3 The ABCs of Ellis's theory Ellis and other cognitive therapists contend that our emotional feelings stem not directly from events that happen to us, but from our interpretation of those events. By changing our beliefs—the cognitions we use for interpreting what happens—we can alter our emotional reactions.

A
Activating event
(e.g., an insult)

B
Belief
(e.g., "I must be liked by everyone to be happy")

C
Consequent emotion
(e.g., unhappiness)

Establishing Clear-Cut Goals and Steps for Achieving Them

Once a client admits to the irrational and self-injurious nature of some belief or habit of thought, the next step is to help the client get rid of that belief or habit and replace it with a more rational

	SITUATION	EMOTION(S)	AUTOMATIC THOUGHT(S)	RATIONAL RESPONSE	OUTCOME
DATE	Describe: 1. Actual event leading to unpleasant emotion, or 2. Stream of thoughts, daydream, or recollection, leading to unpleasant emotion.	1. Specify sad/ anxious/ angry, etc. 2. Rate degree of emotion, 1–100.	1. Write automatic thought(s) that preceded emotion(s). 2. Rate belief in automatic thought(s), 0–100%.	1. Write rational response to automatic thought(s). 2. Rate belief in rational response, 0–100%.	1. Rerate belief in automatic thought(s), 0–100%. 2. Specify and rate subsequent emotions, 0–100.
7/15	Store clerk didn't smile at me when I paid for purchase.	Sad – 60 Anxious – 40	Nobody likes me – 70% I look awful – 80%	Maybe the clerk was having a bad day or maybe she never smiles at customers – 70%	1. 20% 30% 2. Pleasure – 25

Explanation: When you experience an unpleasant emotion, note the situation that seemed to stimulate the emotion. (If the emotion occurred while you were thinking, daydreaming, etc., please note this.) Then note the automatic thought associated with the emotion. Record the degree to which you believe this thought: 0% = not at all, 100% = completely. In rating degree of emotion: 1 = a trace, 100 = the most intense possible.

FIGURE 16.4 Homework sheet for cognitive therapy The purpose of this homework is to enable clients to become aware of and correct the automatic thoughts that contribute to their emotional difficulties.

and adaptive way of thinking. That takes hard work. Long-held beliefs and thoughts do not simply disappear once they are recognized as irrational. They occur automatically unless they are actively resisted.

To help clients overcome their self-injurious ways of thinking, cognitive therapists often assign homework. For example, clients might be asked to keep a diary, or to fill out a form every day such as that depicted in **Figure 16.4**, in which they record the negative emotions they felt that day, describe the situations and automatic thoughts that accompanied those emotions, and describe a rational alternative thought that might make them feel less upset. Such exercises help train clients to become more aware of their automatic thoughts and, through awareness, change them. The diaries or charts also become a record of progress, by which the therapist and client can see if positive ways of thinking are increasing over time and negative emotions are decreasing.

Moving From a Teaching Role to a Consulting Role With the Client

Cognitive therapists, unlike humanistic therapists, are quite directive in their approach. At least at the beginning, the relationship between cognitive therapist and client is fundamentally like that of a teacher and student. The therapist helps the client identify a set of goals, develops a curriculum for achieving those goals, assigns homework, and assesses the client's progress using the most objective measures available. With time, however, as the client becomes increasingly expert in spotting and correcting his or her own maladaptive thoughts, the client becomes increasingly self-directive in the therapy, and the therapist begins to act more like a consultant and less like a teacher (Hazler & Barwick, 2001). Eventually, the client may meet with the therapist just occasionally to describe continued progress and

FOCUS 26

In what sense is a cognitive therapist initially a teacher and later a consultant?

to ask for advice when needed. When such advice is no longer needed, the therapy has achieved its goals and is over.

Although cognitive therapists are directive with clients, most of them acknowledge the value of some of the other tenets of humanistic therapy, particularly the value of maintaining a warm, genuine, and empathic relationship with their clients (Beck & Weishaar, 2011). In fact, increasingly, psychotherapists of all theoretical persuasions are acknowledging that empathy and understanding of the patient are an essential part of the therapeutic process (Hazler & Barwick, 2001; Weiner & Bornstein, 2009).

A Case Example: Beck's Cognitive Treatment of a Depressed Young Woman

Aaron Beck, who at this writing has been applying and researching cognitive therapy for more than 60 years, is by far the most influential cognitive therapist. His earliest and best-known work was with patients with depression, but he has also developed cognitive therapy methods for treating anxiety, uncontrollable anger, and schizophrenia (Bowles, 2004). In the dialogue that follows (from Young et al., 1993, p. 264), we see him at work with a client referred to as Irene—a 29-year-old woman with two young children who was diagnosed with major depression.

Irene had not been employed outside her home since marriage, and her husband, who had been in and out of drug treatment centers, was also unemployed. She was socially isolated and felt that people looked down on her because of her poor control over her children and her husband's drug record. She was treated for three sessions by Beck and then was treated for a longer period by another cognitive therapist.

During the first session, Beck helped Irene to identify a number of her automatic negative beliefs, including: *things won't get better; nobody cares for me;* and *I am stupid*. By the end of the session, she accepted Beck's suggestion to try to invalidate the first of those thoughts by doing certain things for herself before the next session that might make life more fun. She agreed to take the children on an outing, visit her mother, go shopping, read a book, and find out about joining a tennis group—all things that she claimed she would like to do. Having completed that homework, she came to the second session feeling more hopeful. However, she began to feel depressed again when, during the session, she misunderstood a question that Beck asked her, which, she said, made her "look dumb." Beck responded with a questioning strategy that helped her to distinguish between the *fact* of what happened (not understanding a question) and her *belief* about it (looking dumb):

> **Beck:** *OK, what is a rational answer to that* [to why you didn't answer the question]? *A realistic answer?*
>
> **Irene:** *. . . I didn't hear the question right; that is why I didn't answer it right.*
>
> **Beck:** *OK, so that is the fact situation. And so, is the fact situation that you look dumb or you just didn't hear the question right?*
>
> **Irene:** *I didn't hear the question right.*
>
> **Beck:** *Or is it possible that I didn't say the question in such a way that it was clear?*
>
> **Irene:** *Possible.*
>
> **Beck:** *Very possible. I'm not perfect so it's very possible that I didn't express the question properly.*
>
> **Irene:** *But instead of saying you made a mistake, I would still say I made a mistake.*
>
> **Beck:** *We'll have to watch the video to see. Whichever. Does it mean if I didn't express the question, if I made the mistake, does it make me dumb?*

FOCUS 27

How does Beck's treatment of a depressed woman illustrate his approach to identifying and correcting maladaptive, automatic thoughts?

■ **A pioneer of cognitive therapy** Aaron Beck's approach to therapy is gentler then Ellis's, but not less teacher-like. Beck typically leads clients, through a Socratic style of questioning, to discover the irrationality of their thoughts. In this photo (taken in 2008), Beck, at age 87, addresses participants in a training program at the Beck Institute for Cognitive Therapy and Research.

Clem Murray/Newscom/Tribune News Service/Bala Cynwyd/PA/USA

Irene: *No.*

Beck: *And if you made the mistake, does it make you dumb?*

Irene: *No, not really.*

Beck: *But you felt dumb?*

Irene: *But I did, yeah.*

Beck: *Do you still feel dumb?*

Irene: *No. Right now I feel glad. I'm feeling a little better that at least somebody is pointing all these things out to me because I have never seen this before. I never knew that I thought that I was that dumb.* (Young et al., 1993, p. 264)

As homework between the second and third sessions, Beck gave Irene the assignment of catching, writing down, and correcting her own dysfunctional thoughts, using a form similar to the one shown in Figure 16.4. Subsequent sessions were aimed at eradicating each of her depressive thoughts, one by one, and reinforcing the steps she was taking to improve her life. Progress was rapid. Irene felt increasingly better about herself. During the next several months, she joined a tennis league, got a job, took a college course in sociology, and left her husband after trying and failing to get him to develop a better attitude toward her or to join her in couples therapy. By this time, according to Beck, she was cured of her depression, had created for herself a healthy environment, and no longer needed therapy.

Cognitive therapy is the basis for some new types of therapy. For example, *mindfulness-based cognitive therapy* incorporates traditional aspects of cognitive therapy with *mindfulness* and *mindfulness meditation,* which involves becoming aware of all incoming thoughts and feelings, accepting them, but not reacting to them. Mindfulness-based cognitive therapy has been shown to be effective in depression (Barnhofer et al., 2016; Piet & Hougaard, 2011). Similarly, *dialectical behavior therapy* (Linehan & Dimeff, 2001) uses aspects of cognitive therapy plus "mindful awareness" (much like mindfulness) along with training in emotion regulation to successfully treat people with borderline personality disorder, perhaps the first effective therapy for this disorder (Kliem et al., 2010).

SECTION REVIEW

Behavioral and cognitive therapies, both problem centered, are often combined.

Principles of Behavior Therapy

- The goals of behavior therapy are to extinguish maladaptive responses and to condition healthier responses by exposing clients to new environmental conditions.

- Contingency management programs are based on operant-conditioning principles. They modify behavior by modifying behavior–reward contingencies.

- Exposure treatments, based on classical conditioning, are used to habituate or extinguish reflexive fear responses in phobias. Three techniques are imaginal exposure, in vivo (real-life) exposure, and virtual reality exposure.

- In a case example, virtual reality exposure therapy helped "Miss Muffet" overcome a debilitating fear of spiders.

Principles of Cognitive Therapy

- Cognitive therapy is based on the idea that psychological distress results from maladaptive beliefs and thoughts.

- The cognitive therapist works to identify the maladaptive thoughts and beliefs, convince the client of their irrationality, and help the client eliminate them along with the unpleasant emotions they provoke.

- To help the client replace the old, habitual ways of thinking with more adaptive ways, cognitive therapists often assign homework (e.g., writing down and correcting irrational thoughts). Progress is objectively measured. As the client can assume more of the responsibility, the therapist becomes less directive.

- A case example shows Aaron Beck's cognitive treatment of a depressed young woman who came to see how her automatic negative thoughts (e.g., "I am stupid") were affecting her.

Evaluating Psychotherapies

You have just read about four major varieties of psychotherapy. Do they work? That might seem like an odd question at this point. After all, didn't Beck and his associates cure the depressed young woman, and didn't behavior therapy cure Miss Muffet's phobia? But case studies showing that people are better off at the end of therapy than at the beginning—even thousands of them—cannot tell us for sure that therapy works. Maybe those people would have improved anyway, without therapy.

An adage about the common cold goes like this: "Treat a cold with the latest remedy, and you'll get rid of it in 7 days; leave it untreated, and it'll hang on for a week." Maybe psychological problems or disorders are often like colds in this respect. Everyone has peaks and valleys in life, and people are most likely to start therapy while in one of the valleys (see **Figure 16.5**). Thus, even if therapy has no effect, most people will feel better at some time after entering it than they did when they began. The natural tendency for both therapist and client is to attribute the improvement to the therapy, but that attribution may often be wrong.

FOCUS 28

Why must we rely on experiments rather than case studies to assess the effectiveness of psychotherapy?

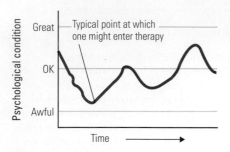

FIGURE 16.5 The peaks and valleys of life If a person enters psychotherapy while in a valley, he or she is likely to feel better after a time even if the therapy is ineffective.

Is Psychotherapy Helpful, and Are Some Types of It More Helpful Than Others?

The only way to know if psychotherapy really works is to perform controlled experiments, in which groups of people undergoing therapy are compared with otherwise-similar control groups who are not undergoing therapy. In fact, in the United States and the United Kingdom, there is a growing movement for *evidence-based treatment*, using only therapies that have been shown empirically to be effective (Carroll, 2012; Sharf, 2012).

A Classic Example of a Therapy-Outcome Experiment

One of the earliest well-controlled experiments on therapy outcome was conducted at a psychiatric outpatient clinic in Philadelphia (Sloane et al., 1975). The subjects were 94 men and women, ages 18 to 45, who sought psychotherapy at the clinic. Most of them suffered from diffuse anxiety, the type that today would probably be diagnosed as generalized anxiety disorder. Each was assigned by a random procedure to one of three groups. Members of one group received once-a-week sessions of *behavior therapy* for 4 months (including such procedures as imaginal exposure to various feared situations and training in assertiveness) from one of three highly experienced behavior therapists. Members of the second group received the same amount of *psychodynamic therapy* (including such procedures as probing into childhood memories, dream analysis, and interpretation of resistance) from one of three highly experienced psychodynamic therapists. The members of the third group, the *no-therapy group*, were placed on a waiting list and given no treatment during the 4-month period but were called periodically to let them know that they would eventually be accepted for therapy.

To measure treatment effectiveness, all subjects, including those in the no-therapy group, were assessed both before and after the 4-month period by psychiatrists who were not informed of the groups to which the subjects had been assigned. As illustrated in **Figure 16.6**, all three groups improved during the 4-month period, but the treatment groups improved significantly more than did the no-treatment group. Moreover, the two treatment groups did not differ significantly from each other in degree of improvement.

This early study anticipated the result of hundreds of other psychotherapy-outcome experiments that have followed it. Overall, such research provides compelling evidence that psychotherapy works, but little if any evidence

FOCUS 29

How did an experiment in Philadelphia demonstrate the effectiveness of behavior therapy and psychodynamic therapy?

Yeah yeah, I know... your therapist has no lines. But is she evidence-based?

DAHLIA CHANG LCSW

Brain-Based Mindfulness Reprocessing

BE HERE NOW!

that one variety of therapy is regularly better than any other standard variety (Lambert & Ogles, 2004; Luborsky et al., 2006; Staines, 2008).

Evidence That Psychotherapy Helps

When hundreds of separate therapy-outcome experiments are combined, the results indicate, very clearly, that therapy helps. In fact, about 75 to 80% of people in the psychotherapy condition in such experiments improved more than did the average person in a nontherapy condition (Lambert & Ogles, 2004; Prochaska & Norcross, 2010). Experiments comparing the effectiveness of psychotherapy with standard drug therapies indicate, overall, that psychotherapy is at least as effective as drug therapy in treating depression and generalized anxiety disorder, and that it is more effective than drug therapy in treating panic disorder (Amick et al., 2015; Imel et al., 2008; Mitte, 2005).

A note of caution should be added, however, for interpreting such findings. Psychotherapy-outcome experiments are usually carried out at clinics associated with major research centers. The therapists are normally highly experienced and, since they know that their work is being evaluated, they are presumably functioning at maximal capacity. It is quite possible that the outcomes in these experiments are more positive than are the average therapy outcomes, where therapists are not always so experienced or so motivated (Lambert & Ogles, 2004). Moreover, just as in the case of drug studies, there is a bias for researchers to publish results that show significant positive effects of psychotherapy and not to publish results that show no effects. This, too, would lead to an overestimation of therapy effectiveness, since the analyses are usually based only on the published findings (Staines, 2008).

Evidence That No Type of Therapy Is Clearly Better, Overall, Than Other Standard Types

There was a time when psychotherapists who adhered to one variety of therapy argued strongly that their variety was greatly superior to others. Such arguments have largely been quelled by the results of psychotherapy-outcome experiments. Taken as a whole, such experiments provide no convincing evidence that any of the major types of psychotherapy is superior to any other for treating the kinds of problems—such as depression and generalized anxiety—for which people most often seek treatment (Lambert & Ogles, 2004; Staines, 2008; Wampold, 2001). Most such experiments have pitted some form of cognitive or cognitive-behavioral therapy against some form of psychodynamic therapy. When the two forms of therapy are given in equal numbers of sessions, by therapists who are equally well trained and equally passionate about the value of the therapy they administer, the usual result is no difference in outcome; people treated by either therapy get better at about the same rate. Relatively few studies have compared humanistic forms of therapy with others, but the results of those few suggest that humanistic therapy works as well as the others (Lambert & Ogles, 2004; Smith et al., 1980), at least for the types of problems that were assessed.

Although research shows that most therapies have comparable benefits, that does not mean that every therapy is equally effective for every disorder. Some experts agree that behavioral exposure treatment is the most effective treatment for phobias (Antony & Barlow, 2002). There is also some reason to believe that cognitive and behavior therapies generally work best for clients who have rather specific problems— problems that can be zeroed in on by the specific techniques of those therapies.

For example, one study contrasted two years of psychodynamic therapy with five months of cognitive-behavioral therapy in 70 patients with the eating disorder bulimia nervosa. The researchers reported that 15% of patients receiving the psychodynamic therapy had stopped binge eating and purging by the end of the therapy, whereas 44% of patients receiving the cognitive-behavioral training had done so (Poulsen et al., 2014). Patients in both treatment groups showed improvements in other areas of

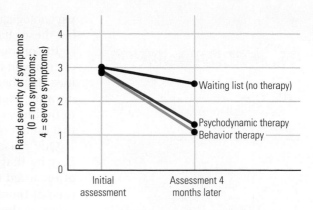

FIGURE 16.6 Results of the Philadelphia experiment Psychiatrists rated the severity of each subject's symptoms before and after a 4-month treatment period. As shown here, those in the two therapy groups improved more than did those who were placed on the waiting list.

(Data from Sloane et al., 1975.)

 FOCUS 30

What is the evidence that psychotherapy works and that for some disorders it works as well as, or better than, standard drug treatments?

 FOCUS 31

What general conclusions have been drawn from research comparing different forms of psychotherapy?

psychological health related to eating (e.g., concern for weight, anxiety, depression), but these changes occurred sooner for the cognitive-behavioral therapy patients.

In contrast, psychodynamic and humanistic therapies may be most effective for clients who have multiple or diffuse problems or problems related to their personalities (Lambert & Ogles, 2004; Siev & Chambless, 2007). And for posttraumatic stress disorder, therapies that focus on patients' trauma memories or that encourage them to find meaning in the traumatic experience produce better results than therapies that do not (Ehlers et al., 2010).

One reason for the general equivalence in effectiveness of different therapies may be that they are not as different in practice as they are in theory. Analyses of recorded therapy sessions have revealed that good therapists, regardless of the type of therapy they claim to practice, often use methods that overlap with other types of therapy. For example, effective cognitive and behavior therapists, who are normally quite directive, tend to become nondirective—more like humanistic therapists—when working with clients who seem unmotivated to follow their lead (Barlow, 2004; Beutler & Harwood, 2000). Similarly, psychodynamic therapists often use cognitive methods (such as correcting maladaptive automatic thoughts), and cognitive therapists often use psychodynamic methods (such as asking clients to talk about childhood experiences), to degrees that seem to depend on the client's personality and the type of problem (Weston et al., 2004).

The Role of Common Factors in Therapy Outcome

Ostensibly different types of psychotherapy are similar to one another not just because the therapists borrow one another's methods but also because, regardless of theoretical orientation, they share certain *common factors*. These factors may be more important to the effectiveness of therapy than are the specific, theory-derived factors that differentiate therapies from one another (Lambert & Ogles, 2004; Sharf, 2012). Many common factors have been proposed, but we find it useful to distill them into three fundamental categories: *support, hope,* and *motivation*.

Support

Support includes acceptance, empathy, and encouragement. By devoting time to the client, listening warmly and respectfully, and not being shocked at the client's statements or actions, any good psychotherapist communicates the attitude that the client is a worthwhile human being. This support may directly enhance the client's self-esteem and indirectly lead to other improvements as well. This makes the emotional interaction between clients and therapists an important component of the therapeutic process: The therapist's responsiveness to the client's behavior increases the likelihood that the client will return for additional sessions and thus the eventual success of the therapy (Liebovitch et al., 2011; Peluso et al., 2012).

Many therapy studies have demonstrated the value of such support. One long-term study, for example, revealed that psychodynamic therapists provide more support and less insight to their clients than would be expected from psychoanalytic theory (Wallerstein, 1989). The same study also showed that support, even without insight, seemed to produce stable therapeutic gains. Another study, of cognitive-behavioral therapy for depression, revealed that the bond of rapport that clients felt with their therapists early in treatment was a good predictor of their subsequent improvement (Klein et al., 2003). In yet another study, college professors with no training in psychology or methods of therapy, but with reputations for good rapport with students, proved able to help depressed college students in twice-a-week therapy sessions as effectively as did highly trained and experienced clinical psychologists (Strupp & Hadley, 1979).

Results such as these led one prominent psychodynamic therapist, Hans Strupp (1989), to the following conclusion: "The first and foremost task for the therapist is to create an accepting and empathic context, which in itself has great therapeutic value because for many people it is a novel and deeply gratifying experience to be accepted and listened to respectfully."

Hope

Hope, for a suffering person, is the expectation that things will get better, that life will become more enjoyable. In psychotherapy, hope may come partly from the sense of support, but it may also come from faith in the therapy process.

Most psychotherapists believe in what they do. They speak with authority and confidence about their methods, and they offer scientific-sounding theories or even data to back up their confidence. Thus, clients also come to believe that their therapy will work. Many studies have shown that people who believe they will get better have an improved chance of getting better, even if the specific reason for the belief is false. As discussed earlier in the chapter, patients who take a placebo are likely to improve if they believe they are taking a drug that will help them. Belief in the process is at least as important for improvement in psychotherapy as it is in drug therapy (Wampold et al., 2005). Hope based on faith in the process is an element that all sought-after healing procedures have in common, whether provided by psychotherapists, medical doctors, faith healers, or folk healers.

Many researchers have designed psychotherapy-outcome experiments that compare accepted forms of psychotherapy with made-up, "false" forms of psychotherapy—forms that lack the specific ingredients that mark any well-accepted type of therapy. For example, in one such study, cognitive-behavioral therapy for problems of anxiety was compared with a made-up treatment called "systematic ventilation," in which clients talked about their fears in a systematic manner (Kirsch et al., 1983). A general problem with such studies is that it is hard for therapists to present the "false" therapy to clients in a convincing manner, especially if the therapists themselves don't believe it will work. Yet, analyses of many such studies indicate that when the "false" therapy is equivalent to the "real" therapy in credibility to the client, it is also generally equivalent in effectiveness (Ahn & Wampold, 2001; Baskin et al., 2003).

■ **Group support** In group therapy, the therapeutic elements of support, hope, and motivation may derive not just from the therapist but also from all of the other participants.

Motivation

Psychotherapy is not a passive process; it is not something "done to" the client by the therapist. The active agent of change in psychotherapy is the client him- or herself. This is an explicit tenet of humanistic therapy and an implicit tenet of other therapies (Hazler & Barwick, 2001). To change, the client must work at changing, and such work requires strong motivation. Motivation for change comes partly from the support and hope engendered by the therapist, which make change seem worthwhile and feasible, but it also comes from other common aspects of the psychotherapy process.

Psychotherapy operates in part by providing options and keeping the client focused on working toward his or her goals, rather than telling the client what the goals should be or the right way to get there. Most caring therapists, regardless of theoretical orientation, will start sessions by asking the client how things have gone since the last meeting. The anticipation of such reporting may cause clients to go through life, between therapy sessions, with more conscious attention to their actions and feelings than they otherwise would so that they can give a full report. Such attention leads them to think more consciously, fully, and constructively about their problems, which enhances their motivation to improve and may also lead to new insights about how to improve. Such reporting may also make the client aware of progress, and progress engenders a desire for more progress.

A Final Comment

Through most of this book our main concern has been with normal, healthy, adaptive human behavior. It is perhaps fitting, though, and certainly humbling, to end on this note concerning psychotherapy: We are *social animals* who need positive regard from other people in order to function well, but sometimes that regard is lacking. We are *thinking animals,* but sometimes our emotions and disappointments get in the way of our thinking. We are *self-motivated and self-directed creatures,* but sometimes we lose our motivation and direction. In these cases, a supportive, hope-inspiring, and motivating psychotherapist can help. The therapist helps not by solving our problems for us, but by providing a context in which we can solve them ourselves.

SECTION REVIEW

Psychotherapy's effectiveness and reasons for its effectiveness have been widely researched.

Determining the Effectiveness of Psychotherapy

- Many controlled experiments, comparing patients in psychotherapy with comparable others not in psychotherapy, have shown that psychotherapy helps.

- Research also indicates that no form of therapy is more effective overall than any other, perhaps because they differ less in practice than in theory.

- Some therapies are better than others for particular situations, however. For example, behavioral exposure therapy is more effective than other treatments for specific phobias.

The Role of Common Factors in Therapy Outcome

- Common factors, shared by all standard psychotherapies, may account for much of the effectiveness of psychotherapy. These include support, hope, and motivation.

- Support (acceptance, empathy, and encouragement) helps to build the client's confidence. Research suggests that support, in and of itself, has considerable therapeutic value.

- Hope comes in part from faith in the process, bolstered by the therapist's own faith in it. People who believe they will get better have a greater chance of getting better.

- The support, hope, and regular reporting of experiences in therapy help to motivate clients toward self-improvement.

Thinking Critically About Treatment of Psychological Disorders

1. Why would a knowledge of research methodology be important for evaluating the effectiveness of different forms of treatments for psychological disorders?

2. By some estimates, prisons may be the largest mental health providers in the United States. What implications, if any, does this have for the diagnosis and treatment of people with psychological disorders?

3. Is psychotherapy a science? Has science shown that psychotherapy works? Give reasons for your answers.

Reflections and Connections

To better understand and remember the different approaches to treatment described in this chapter, think about the principles underlying each approach, about the potential problems of each approach, and about the evidence concerning its effectiveness. In addition, consider two overarching assertions.

1. Biological, behavioral, and cognitive therapies are derivatives of basic approaches to psychological research Biological, behavioral, and cognitive therapies each focus on important features of psychological functioning generated from research in their parent discipline, for example (a) physiological mechanisms, including neurotransmitters; (b) the role of environmental stimuli and learned habits; and (c) the role of cognitive mediators of behavior. Although biological, behavioral, and cognitive therapies focus on different *levels* of causation of behavior, they differ from psychodynamic and humanistic therapies in this way: They each focus more closely on clients' specific symptoms than do psychodynamic and humanistic therapies.

2. Self-knowledge and self-acceptance are goals of psychodynamic and humanistic therapies The psychodynamic and humanistic approaches to treatment focus less on the person's specific symptoms or problems, and more on the person as a whole, than do the other approaches. A psychoanalyst or other psychodynamic therapist who is asked to describe the purpose of therapy might well respond with the Delphic dictum quoted at the very beginning of this book: *Know thyself*. A goal of such therapies is to enable clients to learn about aspects of themselves that were previously unconscious so that they can think and behave in more rational and integrated ways.

While humanistic therapists would agree with the above, they would add, and place greater emphasis on, a second dictum: *Accept thyself*. Humanistic therapists argue that people often learn to dislike or deny important aspects of themselves because of real or imagined criticism from other people. A major task for the humanistic therapist is to help clients regain their self-acceptance so that they can regain control of their lives.

Key Terms

Find Out More

Irving B. Weiner & Robert F. Bornstein (2009). *Principles of psychotherapy: Promoting evidence-based psychodynamic practice* (3rd ed.). Hoboken, NJ: Wiley.

Have you considered psychotherapy as a career? This highly readable textbook, dealing with all phases of the therapy process, will give you a realistic picture of what the job entails. It begins with chapters on assessment and initial interviews; continues with chapters on treatment, including resistance and transference; and ends with a chapter on termination of therapy. The authors represent well the evidence-based, non-doctrinaire spirit of modern-day psychodynamic psychotherapy.

James Bailey (2007). *Man interrupted: Welcome to the bizarre world of OCD, where once more is never enough.* Edinburgh, UK: Mainstream Publishing.

In addition to having a terrific sense of humor, James Bailey has obsessive-compulsive disorder. His main obsession concerns drugs: He constantly fears that someone has put drugs in his food, and needs repeated reassurances that they have not. The book centers on his treatment at a center where the primary treatment is exposure; he must expose himself regularly to the conditions that frighten him and learn to accept them without following through on his compulsion. His descriptions of his own reactions and those of his fellow patients are laugh-out-loud funny. Yet, they portray the terror and the extraordinary life restrictions that accompany this disorder, which is no laughing matter.

American Psychological Association (2017). *How to choose a psychologist.* American Psychological Association Help Center.

http://www.apa.org/helpcenter/choose-therapist.aspx

This online article offers expert advice from the APA Psychology Help Center on how to find and choose a therapist. It explains what psychotherapy is and offers guidelines on what credentials to look for and questions to ask your prospective therapist. The article comes with links to promote sharing on social media.

Eleanor Longden (2013, August). *The voices in my head.* TED Talks.
https://youtu.be/syjEN3peCJw

Eleanor Longden was a promising first-year college student when "antagonistic and dictatorial" voices in her head began to make her life intolerable and led to her being diagnosed with schizophrenia. She recounts the onset of her disorder, being institutionalized, being medicated, and the ups and downs of the mental health care system. She explains how she manages to be fully functional despite the disorder, asserting that the voices in her head are there to be accepted and listened to, not ignored or suppressed.

Melanie Saltzman & Saskia de Melker (2016, September 18). *Can technology help predict who will commit suicide?* Judy Woodruff, anchor & managing editor, *PBS Newshour.* [Podcast]

http://www.pbs.org/newshour/bb/can-technology-help-predict-will-attempt-suicide/

New technological innovations are on the horizon that may identify imminent suicide risk and improve diagnosis and treatment of various psychological disorders. A leading suicide researcher and professor, Dr. Matthew Nock of Harvard University, discusses using computer- and smartphone-based tests that help reveal a person's subconscious thoughts related to suicide. Child psychiatrist Dr. Daniel Dickstein describes his use of video games to help understand the inner workings of the brains of children with bipolar disorder—the disorder most strongly correlated with suicide.

 **LaunchPad**
macmillan learning

Visit LaunchPad for Psychology 8e launchpadworks.com to access the e-book, videos, activities, additional resources, and LearningCurve quizzes, as well as study aids including flash cards and web quizzes.

Statistical Appendix

TABLE A.1 Twenty scores unranked and ranked

Scores in the order they were collected	The same scores ranked
58	17
45	23
23	31
71	36
49	37
36	41
61	43
41	45
37	45
75	49
91	50
54	54
43	57
17	58
63	61
73	63
31	71
50	73
45	75
57	91

Statistical procedures are tools for dealing with data. Some people find them fascinating for their own sake, just as some become intrigued by the beauty of a saw or a hammer. But most of us, most of the time, care about statistics only to the extent that they help us answer questions. Statistics become interesting when we want to know our batting average, or the chance that our favorite candidate will be elected, or how much money we'll have left after taxes. In psychology, statistics are interesting when they are used to analyze data in ways that help answer important psychological questions.

Some of the basics of statistics are described in Chapter 2. The main purpose of the first three sections of this appendix is to supplement that discussion and make it more concrete by providing some examples of statistical calculations. The fourth section (Supplement on Psychophysical Scaling) supplements the discussion of Fechner's work in the section on psychophysics in Chapter 6.

Organizing and Summarizing a Set of Scores

This section describes some basic elements of descriptive statistics: the construction of frequency distributions, the measurement of central tendency, and the measurement of variability.

Ranking the Scores and Depicting a Frequency Distribution

Suppose you gave a group of people a psychological test of introversion-extraversion, structured such that a low score indicates introversion (a tendency to withdraw from the social environment) and a high score indicates extraversion (a tendency to be socially outgoing). Suppose further that the possible range of scores is from 0 to 99, that you gave the test to 20 people, and that you obtained the scores shown in the left-hand column of **Table A.1.** As presented in that column, the scores are hard to describe in a meaningful way; they are just a list of numbers. As a first step toward making some sense of them, you might rearrange the scores in rank order, from lowest to highest, as shown in the right-hand column of the table. Notice how the ranking facilitates your ability to describe the set of numbers. You can now see that the scores range from a low of 17 to a high of 91 and that the two middle scores are 49 and 50.

A second useful step in summarizing the data is to divide the entire range of possible scores into equal intervals and determine how many scores fall in each interval. **Table A.2** presents the results of this process, using intervals of 10. A table of this sort, showing the number

FIGURE A.1 A frequency distribution depicted by a bar graph This graph depicts the frequency distribution shown in Table A.2. Each bar represents a different interval of possible scores, and the height of each bar represents the number of scores that occurred in that interval.

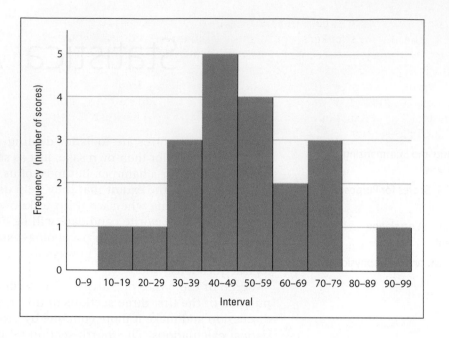

TABLE A.2 Frequency distribution formed from scores in Table A.1

Interval	Frequency
0–9	0
10–19	1
20–29	1
30–39	3
40–49	5
50–59	4
60–69	2
70–79	3
80–89	0
90–99	1

of scores that occurred in each interval of possible scores, is called a *frequency distribution*. Frequency distributions can also be represented graphically, as shown in **Figure A.1**. Here, each bar along the horizontal axis represents a different interval, and the height of the bar represents the frequency (number of scores) that occurred in that interval.

As you examine Figure A.1, notice that the scores are not evenly distributed across the various intervals. Rather, most of them fall in the middle intervals (centering around 50), and they taper off toward the extremes. This pattern would have been hard to see in the original, unorganized set of numbers.

Shapes of Frequency Distributions

The frequency distribution in Figure A.1 roughly approximates a shape that is referred to as a **normal distribution** or *normal curve*. A perfect normal distribution (which can be expressed by a mathematical equation) is illustrated in **Figure A.2a**. Notice that the maximum frequency lies in the center of the range of scores and that the frequency tapers off—first gradually, then more rapidly, and then gradually again—symmetrically on the two sides, forming a bell-shaped curve. Many measures in nature are distributed in accordance with a normal distribution. Height (for people of a given age and sex) is one example. A variety of different factors (different genes and nutritional factors) go into determining a person's height. In most cases, these different factors—some promoting tallness and some shortness—average themselves out so that most people are roughly average in height (accounting for the peak frequency in the middle of the distribution). A small proportion of people, however, will have just the right combination of factors to be much taller or much shorter than average (accounting for the tails at the high and low ends of the distribution). In general, when a measure is determined by several independent factors, the frequency distribution for that measure at least approximates the normal curve. The results of most psychological tests also form a normal distribution if the test is given to a sufficiently large group of people.

But not all measures are distributed in accordance with the normal curve. Consider, for example, the set of scores that would be obtained on a test of English vocabulary if some of the people tested were native speakers of English and others were not. You would expect in this case to find two separate groupings of scores. The native speakers would score high and the others would score low, with relatively few scores in between. A distribution of this sort, illustrated in **Figure A.2b**, is referred to as a *bimodal distribution*. The **mode** is the most frequently occurring score or range of scores in a frequency distribution; thus, a bimodal distribution is one that has two separate areas of peak frequencies. The normal curve is a *unimodal distribution* because it has only one peak in frequency.

Some distributions are unimodal, like the normal distribution, but are not symmetrical. Consider, for example, the shape of a frequency distribution of annual incomes for any randomly selected group of people. Most of the incomes might center around, let's say, $20,000. Some would be higher and some lower, but the spread of higher incomes would be much greater than that of lower incomes. No income can be less than $0, but no limit exists to the high ones. Thus, the frequency distribution might look like that shown in **Figure A.2c**. A distribution of this sort, in which the spread of scores above the mode is greater than that below, is referred to as a *positively skewed distribution*. The long tail of the distribution extends in the direction of high scores.

As an opposite example, consider the distribution of scores on a relatively easy examination. If the highest possible score is 100 points and most people score around 85, the highest score can only be 15 points above the mode, but the lowest score can be as much as 85 points below it. A typical distribution obtained from such a test is shown in **Figure A.2d**. A distribution of this sort, in which the long tail extends toward low scores, is called a *negatively skewed distribution*.

Measures of Central Tendency

Perhaps the most useful way to summarize a set of scores is to identify a number that represents the center of the distribution. Two different centers can be determined—the median and the mean (both described in Chapter 2). The **median** is the middle score in a set of ranked scores. Thus, in a ranked set of nine scores, the fifth score in the ranking (counting in either direction) is the median. If the data set consists of an even number of scores, determining the median is slightly more complicated because two middle scores exist rather than one. In this case, the median is simply the midpoint between the two middle scores. If you look back at the list of 20 ranked scores in Table A.1, you will see that the two middle scores are 49 and 50; the median in this case is 49.5. The **mean** (also called the *arithmetic average*) is found simply by adding up all of the scores and dividing by the total number of scores. Thus, to calculate the mean of the 20 introversion-extraversion scores in Table A.1, simply add them (the sum is 1,020) and divide by 20, obtaining 51 as the mean.

Notice that the mean and median of the set of introversion-extraversion scores are quite close to one another. In a perfect normal distribution, these two measures of central tendency are identical. For a skewed distribution, on the other hand, they can be quite different. Consider, for example, the set of incomes shown in **Table A.3**. The median is $19,500, and all but one of the other incomes are rather close to the median. But the set contains one income of $900,000, which is wildly different from the others. The size of this income does not affect the median. Whether the highest income were $19,501 (just above the median) or a trillion dollars, it still counts as just one income in the ranking that determines the median. But this income has a dramatic effect on the mean. As shown in the table, the mean of these incomes is $116,911.

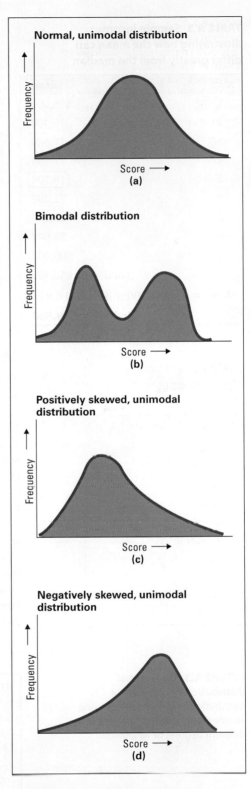

FIGURE A.2 Four differently shaped frequency distributions You can imagine that each of these curves was formed from a set of bars similar to those in Figure A.1, but the bars would be narrower and more numerous (the intervals would be smaller) and the data sets would be much larger.

TABLE A.3 Sample incomes, illustrating how the mean can differ greatly from the median

Rank	Income
1	$15,000
2	16,400
3	16,500
4	17,700
5	19,500
6	21,200
7	22,300
8	23,600
9	900,000

Total = $1,052,200

Mean = $1,052,200 ÷ 9 = $116,911

Median = $19,500

Because the mean is most affected by extreme scores, it will usually be higher than the median in a positively skewed distribution and lower than the median in a negatively skewed distribution. In a positively skewed distribution the most extreme scores are high scores (which raise the mean above the median), and in a negatively skewed distribution they are low scores (which lower the mean below the median).

Which is more useful, the mean or the median? The answer depends on one's purpose, but in general the mean is preferred when scores are at least roughly normally distributed, and the median is preferred when scores are highly skewed. In Table A.3 the median is certainly a better representation of the set of incomes than is the mean because it is typical of almost all of the incomes listed. In contrast, the mean is typical of none of the incomes; it is much lower than the highest income and much higher than all the rest. This, of course, is an extreme example, but it illustrates the sort of biasing effect that skewed data can have on a mean. Still, for certain purposes, the mean might be the preferred measure even if the data are highly skewed. For example, if you wanted to determine the revenue that could be gained by a 5 percent local income tax, the mean income (or the total income) would be more useful than the median.

Measures of Variability

The mean or median tells us about the central value of a set of numbers, but not about how widely they are spread out around the center. Look at the two frequency distributions depicted in **Figure A.3**. They are both normal and have the same mean, but they differ greatly in their degree of spread or variability. In one case the scores are clustered near the mean (low variability), and in the other they are spread farther apart (high variability). How might we measure the variability of scores in a distribution?

One possibility would be to use the *range*—that is, simply the difference between the highest and lowest scores in the distribution—as a measure of variability. For the scores listed in Table A.1, the range is 91 − 17 = 74 points. A problem with the range, however, is that it depends on just two scores, the highest and lowest. A better measure of variability would take into account the extent to which all of the scores in the distribution differ from each other.

One measure of variability that takes all of the scores into account is the *variance*. The variance is calculated by the following four steps: (1) Determine the mean of the set of scores. (2) Determine the difference between each score and

FIGURE A.3 Two normal distributions These normal distributions, superimposed on one another, have identical means but different degrees of variability.

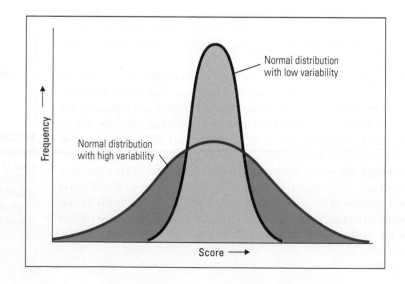

TABLE A.4 Calculation of the variance and standard deviation for two sets of scores that have identical means

First set of scores			Second set of scores		
Score	Deviation (Score − 50)	Squared deviation	Score	Deviation (Score − 50)	Squared deviation
42	−8	64	9	−41	1,681
44	−6	36	19	−31	961
47	−3	9	31	−19	361
49	−1	1	47	−3	9
52	+2	4	56	+6	36
54	+4	16	70	+20	400
55	+5	25	78	+28	784
57	+7	49	90	+40	1,600
Total = 400		Total = 204	Total = 400		Total = 5,832
Mean = 400/8 = 50		Mean = 204/8 = 25.5	Mean = 400/8 = 50		Mean = 5,832/8 = 729

Variance = Mean squared deviation = 25.5

Standard deviation = $\sqrt{\text{Variance}}$ = $\sqrt{25.5}$ = 5.0

Variance = Mean squared deviation = 729

Standard deviation = $\sqrt{\text{Variance}}$ = $\sqrt{729}$ = 27.0

the mean; this difference is called the *deviation*. (3) Square each deviation (multiply it by itself). (4) Calculate the mean of the squared deviations (by adding them up and dividing by the total number of scores). The result—the mean of the squared deviations—is the variance. This method is illustrated for two different sets of scores in **Table A.4**. Notice that the two sets each have the same mean (50), but most of the scores in the first set are much closer to the mean than are those in the second set. The result is that the variance of the first set (25.5) is much smaller than that of the second set (729).

Because the variance is based on the squares of the deviations, the units of variance are not the same as those of the original measure. If the original measure is points on a test, then the variance is in units of squared points on the test (whatever on earth that might mean). To bring the units to their original form, all we need to do is take the square root of the variance. The square root of the variance is the **standard deviation (SD)**, which is the measure of variability that is most commonly used. Thus, for the first set of scores in Table A.4, the standard deviation = $\sqrt{25.5}$ = 5.0; for the second set, the standard deviation = $\sqrt{729}$ = 27.0.

Converting Scores for Purposes of Comparison

Are you taller than you are heavy? That sounds like a silly question, and it is. Height and weight are two entirely different measures, and comparing them is like the proverbial comparison of apples and oranges. But suppose we worded the question this way: Relative to other people of your gender and age group, do you rank higher in height or in weight? Now that is an answerable question. Similarly, consider this question: Are you better at mathematical or at verbal tasks? This, too, is meaningful only if your mathematical and verbal skills are judged relative to those of other people. Compared to other people, do you rank higher in mathematical or in verbal skills? To compare different kinds of scores with each other, we must convert each score into a form that directly expresses its relationship to the whole distribution of scores from which it came.

Percentile Rank

The most straightforward way to see how one person compares to others on a given measure is to determine the person's **percentile rank** for that measure. The percentile rank of a given score is simply the percentage of scores that are equal to that score or lower, out of the whole set of scores obtained on a given measure. For example, in the distribution of scores in Table A.1, the score of 37 is at the 25th percentile because 5 of the 20 scores are at 37 or lower ($5/20 = 1/4 = 25$ percent). As another example in the same distribution, the score of 73 is at the 90th percentile because 18 of the 20 scores are lower ($18/20 = 9/10 = 90$ percent). If you had available the heights and weights of a large number of people of your age and gender, you could answer the question about your height compared to your weight by determining your percentile rank on each. If you were at the 39th percentile in height and the 25th percentile in weight, then, relative to others in your group, you would be taller than you were heavy. Similarly, if you were at the 94th percentile on a test of math skills and the 72nd percentile on a test of verbal skills, then, relative to the group who took both tests, your math skills would be better than your verbal skills.

Standardized Scores

Another way to convert scores for purposes of comparison is to *standardize* them. A **standardized score** is one that is expressed in terms of the number of standard deviations that the original score is from the mean of original scores. The simplest form of a standardized score is called a **z score**. To convert any score to a z score, you first determine its deviation from the mean (subtract the mean from it), and then divide the deviation by the standard deviation of the distribution. Thus,

$$z = \frac{\text{score} - \text{mean}}{\text{standard deviation}}$$

For example, suppose you wanted to calculate the z score that would correspond to the test score of 54 in the first set of scores in Table A.4. The mean of the distribution is 50, so the deviation is $54 - 50 = +4$. The standard deviation is 5.0. Thus, $z = 4/5 = +0.80$. Similarly, the z score for a score of 42 in that distribution would be $(42-50)/5 = -8/5 = -1.60$. Remember, the z score is simply the number of standard deviations that the original score is away from the mean. A positive z score indicates that the original score is above the mean, and a negative z score indicates that it is below the mean. A z score of $+0.80$ is 0.80 standard deviation above the mean, and a z score of -1.60 is 1.60 standard deviations below the mean.

Other forms of standardized scores are based directly on z scores. For example, College Board (SAT) scores were originally (in 1941) determined by calculating each person's z score, then multiplying the z score by 100 and adding the result to 500. That is,

$$\text{SAT score} = 500 + 100(z)$$

Thus, a person who was directly at the mean on the test ($z = 0$) would have an SAT score of 500; a person who was 1 standard deviation above the mean ($z = +1$) would have an SAT score of 600; a person who was 2 standard deviations above the mean would have 700; and a person who was 3 standard deviations above the mean would have 800. (Very few people would score beyond 3 standard deviations from the mean, so 800 was set as the highest possible score.) Going the other way, a person who was 1 standard deviation below the mean ($z = -1$) would have an SAT score of 400, and so on. (Today, a much broader range of people take the SAT tests than in 1941, when only a relatively elite group applied to colleges, and the scoring system has not been restandardized to maintain 500 as the average score. The result is that average SAT scores are now considerably less than 500.)

Wechsler IQ scores (discussed in Chapter 10) are also based on z scores. They were standardized—separately for each age group—by calculating each person's z score on the test, multiplying that by 15, and adding the product to 100. Thus,

$$IQ = 100 + 15(z)$$

This process guarantees that a person who scores at the exact mean achieved by people in the standardization group will have an IQ score of 100, that one who scores 1 standard deviation above that mean will have a score of 115, that one who scores 2 standard deviations above that mean will have a score of 130, and so on.

Relationship of Standardized Scores to Percentile Ranks

If a distribution of scores precisely matches a normal distribution, one can determine percentile rank from the standardized score, or vice versa. As you recall, in a normal distribution the highest frequency of scores occurs in intervals close to the mean, and the frequency declines with each successive interval away from the mean in either direction. As illustrated in **Figure A.4**, a precise relationship exists between any given z score and the percentage of scores that fall between that score and the mean.

As you can see in the figure, slightly more than 34.1 percent of all scores in a normal distribution will be between a z score of +1 and the mean. Since another 50 percent will fall below the mean, a total of slightly more than 84.1 percent of the scores in a normal distribution will be below a z score of +1. By using similar logic and examining the figure, you should be able to see why z scores of −3, −2, −1, 0, +1, +2, and +3, respectively, correspond to percentile ranks of about 0.1, 2.3, 15.9, 50, 84.1, 97.7, and 99.9, respectively. Detailed tables have been made that permit the conversion of any possible z score in a perfect normal distribution to a percentile rank.

Because the percentage of scores that fall between any given z score and the mean is a fixed value for data that fit a normal distribution, it is possible to calculate what percentage of individuals would score less than or equal to any given z score. In this diagram, the percentages above each arrow indicate the percentile rank for z scores of −3, −2, −1, 0, +1, +2, and +3. Each percentage is the sum of the percentages within the portions of the curve that lie under the arrow.

Calculating a Correlation Coefficient

The basic meaning of the term *correlation* and how to interpret a correlation coefficient are described in Chapter 2. As explained there, the correlation coefficient is a mathematical means of describing the strength and direction of the relationship

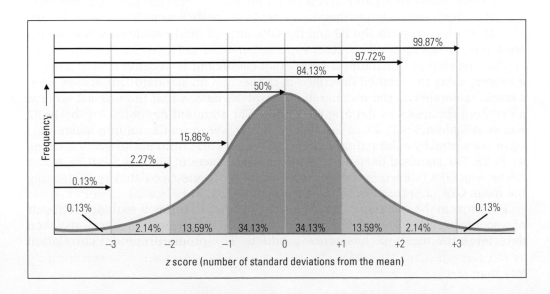

FIGURE A.4 Relationship between z score and percentile rank for a normal distribution.

TABLE A.5 Calculation of a correlation coefficient (*r*)

Students (ranked by IQ)	IQ score	GPA	Z_{IQ}	Z_{GPA}	Cross-products $(Z_{IQ}) \times (Z_{GPA})$
1	82	2.0	−1.77	−0.66	1.17
2	91	1.2	−1.01	−1.71	1.73
3	93	2.3	−0.84	−0.26	0.22
4	97	2.2	−0.51	−0.39	0.20
5	104	3.0	+0.08	+0.66	0.05
6	105	1.8	+0.17	−0.92	−0.16
7	108	3.5	+0.42	+1.32	0.55
8	109	2.6	+0.51	+0.13	0.07
9	118	2.5	+1.26	0.00	0.00
10	123	3.9	+1.68	+1.84	3.09
	Sum = 1,030	Sum = 25.0			Sum = 6.92
	Mean = 103	**Mean = 2.5**			**Mean = 0.69 = *r***
	SD = 11.88	**SD = 0.76**			

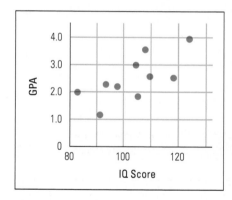

FIGURE A.5 Scatter plots relating GPA to IQ.

between two variables that have been measured mathematically. The sign (+ or −) of the correlation coefficient indicates the direction (positive or negative) of the relationship; and the absolute value of the correlation coefficient (from 0 to 1.00, irrespective of sign) indicates the strength of the correlation. To review the difference between a positive and negative correlation, and between a weak and strong correlation, look back at Figure 2.2 and the accompanying text on p. 43. Here, as a supplement to the discussion in Chapter 2, is the mathematical means for calculating the most common type of correlation coefficient, called the *product-moment correlation coefficient*.

To continue the example described in Chapter 2, suppose you collected both the IQ score and GPA (grade-point average) for each of 10 different high school students and obtained the results shown in the "IQ score" and "GPA" columns of **Table A.5**. As a first step in determining the direction and strength of correlation between the two sets of scores, you might graph each pair of points in a *scatter plot*, as shown in **Figure A.5** (compare this figure to Figure 2.2). The scatter plot makes it clear that, in general, the students with higher IQs tended to have higher GPAs, so you know that the correlation coefficient will be positive. However, the relationship between IQ and GPA is by no means perfect (the plot does not form a straight line), so you know that the correlation coefficient will be less than 1.00.

Each point represents the IQ and the GPA for 1 of the 10 students whose scores are shown in Table A.5. (For further explanation, refer to Figure 2.2 in Chapter 2.)

The first step in calculating a correlation coefficient is to convert each score to a *z* score, using the method described in the section on standardizing scores. Each *z* score, remember, is the number of standard deviations that the original score is away from the mean of the original scores. The standard deviation for the 10 IQ scores in Table A.5 is 11.88, so the *z* scores for IQ (shown in the column marked z_{IQ}) were calculated by subtracting the mean IQ score (103) from each IQ and dividing by 11.88. The standard deviation for the ten GPA scores in Table A.5 is 0.76, so the *z* scores for GPA (shown in the column marked z_{GPA}) were calculated by subtracting the mean GPA (2.5) from each GPA and dividing by 0.76.

To complete the calculation of the correlation coefficient, you multiply each pair of *z* scores together, obtaining what are called the *z-score cross-products*, and then determine the mean of those cross-products. The product-moment correlation coefficient, r, is, by definition, the mean of the z-score cross-products. In Table A.5, the z-score cross-products are shown in the right-hand column, and the mean of them is shown at the bottom of that column. As you can see, the correlation coefficient in this case is $+0.69$—a rather strong positive correlation.

Supplement on Psychophysical Scaling

This section should *not* be read as a supplement to Chapter 2. It concerns an issue discussed in the section on psychophysical scaling in Chapter 6.

Derivation of Fechner's Law From Weber's Law

In Chapter 6, we described Ernst Weber's law, according to which the just-noticeable difference (jnd) between a comparison stimulus and a standard stimulus is directly proportional to the physical magnitude of the standard stimulus (M). As a formula, this is

$$jnd = kM$$

Here, we describe the work of Gustav Fechner, who used Weber's law to derive a law of psychophysical scaling, according to which the magnitude of a sensory experience (S) is directly proportional to the logarithm of the physical magnitude of the stimulus (M). As a formula, this is

$$S = c \log M$$

Here we will use the numbers shown in **Table A.6** to demonstrate the logic of Fechner's derivation of his law from Weber's. The logic begins with the assumption that every jnd is subjectively equal to every other jnd. Thus, the sensory scale in the left-hand column of the table is a jnd scale, and each step in that scale produces an equal change in the magnitude of sensory experience (S). The example is for loudness of a 2000-Hz sound, for which the Weber fraction (k) is 1⁄10 and the minimal intensity that can be heard is 1 sound-pressure unit. With these assumptions, Weber's law predicts that the intensity that will be 1 jnd above the minimum will be 1.10 units ($1 + $ 1⁄10th of $1 = 1.10$). Similarly, the intensity that will be 2 jnd's above threshold will be 1.21 units ($1.10 + $ 1⁄10th of $1.10 = 1.21$).

Continuing in this way, it is possible to derive the physical intensity of the stimulus that would be any given number of jnd's above threshold. The results, for 5 jnd's, are shown in the middle column of the table. Notice that each successive jnd step involves a greater increase in the physical intensity than did the step before. For example, going from 0 to 1 jnd above threshold requires an addition of 0.10 physical unit, whereas going from 4 to 5 jnd's requires an addition of 0.15 physical unit ($1.61 - 1.46 = 0.15$). Thus, the relationship between the first and second columns is not linear. The third column of the table shows the logarithms (to base 10) of the numbers in the middle column. (If you have a calculator, you can check them yourself. The logarithm of 1 is 0, that of 1.1 is 0.041, and so on.) Notice that now, after the logarithmic transformation, the numbers do form a linear relationship with the numbers in the first column. Each jnd step corresponds with an increase of approximately 0.041 log unit. Thus, in line with Fechner's law, each constant step in sensory magnitude corresponds with a constant step in the logarithm of the physical intensity of the stimulus.

TABLE A.6 Demonstration that a jnd sensory scale is linearly related to the logarithm of the physical stimulus (log M)

S in jnd units	M in sound-pressure units if k = 1/10	Log M
0	1.00	0
1	1.10	0.041
2	1.21	0.083
3	1.33	0.124
4	1.46	0.164
5	1.61	0.207

Glossary

absolute threshold In psychophysics, the faintest (lowest-intensity) stimulus of a given sensation (such as sound or light) that an individual can detect. For contrast, see *difference threshold*. (p. 196)

accommodation In Piaget's theory of cognitive development, the change that occurs in an existing mental scheme or set of schemes as a result of the incorporation of the experience of a new event or object. See also *assimilation*. (p. 415)

action potentials Neural impulses; the all-or-nothing electrical bursts that begin at one end of the axon of a neuron and move along the axon to the other end. (p. 105)

adaptation In evolutionary theory, universal and reliably developing inherited feature that arose as a result of natural selection and helped to solve some problem of survival. (p. 78)

ADHD Common acronym for *attention-deficit/hyperactivity disorder*, a frequently diagnosed disorder in children, characterized by impulsiveness and difficulties in focusing attention on tasks. (p. 583)

affect (pronounced **aph**-ect) A noun referring to any emotional feeling. (p. 177)

aggression Fighting and threats of fighting among members of the same species. (p. 93)

agoraphobia A fear of public places. (p. 594)

alleles Different genes that can occupy the same locus on a pair of chromosomes and thus can potentially pair with one another. (p. 64)

altruism A type of helping behavior in which an individual increases the survival chance or reproductive capacity of another individual while *decreasing* its own survival chance or reproductive capacity. For contrast, see *cooperation*. (p. 95)

Alzheimer's disease A disorder found primarily in older adults, characterized by progressive deterioration in cognitive functioning and the presence of deposits in the brain referred to as amyloid plaques. (p. 586)

amplitude The amount of physical energy or force exerted by a physical stimulus at any given moment. For sound, this physical measure is related to the psychological experience of loudness. (p. 213)

amygdala A brain structure that is part of the limbic system and is particularly important for evaluating the emotional and motivational significance of stimuli and generating emotional responses. (p. 125)

analogy In ethology and comparative psychology, any similarity among species that is not due to common ancestry but has evolved

independently because of some similarity in their habitats or lifestyles. For contrast, see *homology*. (p. 84) In problem solving, a similarity in behavior, function, or relationship between entities or situations that are in other respects, such as in their physical makeup, quite different from each other. (p. 360).

androgen A category of hormones, including testosterone, which are produced by the testes in male animals and are normally thought of as "male hormones." These hormones are also produced at lower levels by the adrenal glands, in females as well as in males. (p. 133)

anterograde amnesia Loss, due to injury to the brain, in ability to form new long-term memories for events that occur after the injury. Contrast to *retrograde amnesia*. (p. 345)

antisocial personality disorder A personality disorder in which people consistently violate or disregard the rights of others. People with this disorder are sometimes referred to as sociopaths or psychopaths. (p. 617)

anxiety disorders The class of psychological disorders in which fear or anxiety is the most prominent symptom. It includes *generalized anxiety disorder, panic disorder,* and *phobias*. (p. 591)

aphasia Any loss in language ability due to brain damage. See also *Broca's aphasia, Wernicke's aphasia*. (p. 138)

apoptosis See *selective cell death*.

arcuate nucleus A nucleus (cluster of neural cell bodies) in the hypothalamus of the brain that plays a critical role in the control of appetite. (p. 161)

artificial selection The deliberate selective breeding of animals or plants by humans for the purpose of modifying the genetic makeup of future generations. See *selective breeding*. For contrast, see *natural selection*. (p. 72)

assimilation In Piaget's theory of cognitive development, the process by which experiences are incorporated into the mind or, more specifically, into mental schemes. See also *accommodation*. (p. 415)

association Concerning the mind, a link between two memories or mental concepts, such that recall of one tends to promote recall of the other. (p. 349)

association areas Areas of the cerebral cortex that receive input from the primary or secondary sensory areas for more than one sensory modality (such as vision and hearing) and are involved in associating this input with stored memories, in the processes of perception, thought, and decision making. (p. 126)

association by contiguity Aristotle's principle that if two environmental events (stimuli) occur at the same time or one right after the other (contiguously), those events will be linked together in the mind. (pp. 7, 349)

association by similarity Aristotle's principle that objects, events, or ideas that are similar to one another become linked (associated) in the person's mind (structure of memory), such that the thought of one tends to elicit the thought of the other. (p. 349)

attachment The long-lasting emotional bonds that infants develop toward their principal caregivers. More broadly, the long-lasting emotional bonds that any individual develops toward any other individual or object. (p. 452)

attention The process that controls the flow of information from the sensory store into working memory. More broadly, any focusing of mental activity along a specific track, whether that track consists purely of inner memories and knowledge or is based on external stimuli. (p. 315)

attitude Any belief or opinion that has an evaluative component—a belief that something is good or bad, likable or unlikable, attractive or repulsive. (p. 503)

attribution In social cognition, any inference about the cause of a person's behavioral action or set of actions. More generally, any inference about the cause of any observed action or event. (p. 494)

autism (autism spectrum disorder) An early developing disorder, typically marked by severe deficits in social interaction, severe deficits in language acquisition, a tendency to perform repetitive actions, and a restricted focus of attention and interest. (pp. 49, 433)

automatic processes Cognitive processes that require no mental effort (or mental space) for their execution and are hypothesized (1) to occur without intention and without conscious awareness, (2) not to interfere with the execution of other processes, (3) not to improve with practice, and (4) not to be influenced by individual differences in intelligence, motivation, or education. Contrast with *effortful processes*. (p. 315)

autonomic portion of the peripheral motor system The set of motor neurons that act upon visceral muscles and glands. (p. 120)

availability bias Tendency, in reasoning, to rely too much on information that is readily available to us and to ignore information that is less available. (p. 365)

avoidant personality disorder A personality disorder in which people are excessively shy, being uncomfortable and inhibited in social situations. They feel inadequate and are extremely sensitive to being evaluated, experiencing a dread of criticism. (p. 617)

axon A thin, tube-like extension from a neuron that is specialized to carry neural impulses (action potentials) to other cells. (p. 104)

axon terminal A swelling at the end of an axon that is designed to release a chemical substance (neurotransmitter) onto another neuron, muscle cell, or gland cell. (p. 104)

basal ganglia The large masses of gray matter in the brain that lie on each side of the thalamus; they are especially important for the initiation and coordination of deliberate movements. (p. 124)

basilar membrane A flexible membrane in the cochlea of the inner ear; the wave-like movement of this structure in response to sound stimulates the receptor cells for hearing. See also *hair cells*. (p. 216)

behavior The observable actions of an individual person or animal. (p. 1)

behavior analysis The use of principles of operant conditioning to predict behavior. From this perspective, one has achieved "understanding" to the degree to which one can predict and influence future occurrences of behavior. (p. 288)

behavior therapy Category of treatment methods that use basic principles of learning in order to weaken unwanted behavioral responses or strengthen desired behavioral responses. (p. 642)

behavioral genetics Research specialty that attempts to explain psychological differences among individuals in terms of differences in their genes. (p. 13)

behavioral neuroscience Research specialty that attempts to explain behavior in terms of processes occurring within the nervous system. More specifically, research using invasive techniques (for example, single-cell recordings) with nonhuman animals (p. 11)

behaviorism A school of psychological thought that holds that the proper subject of study is observable behavior, not the mind, and that behavior should be understood in terms of its relationship to observable events in the environment rather than in terms of hypothetical events within the individual. (p. 269)

bias A technical term referring to nonrandom (directed) effects on research results, caused by some factor or factors extraneous to the research hypothesis. (p. 45)

biased sample A subset of the population under study that is not representative of the population as a whole. (p. 46)

binocular disparity The cue for depth perception that stems from the separate (disparate) views that the two eyes have of any given visual object or scene. The farther away the object is, the more similar are the two views of it. (p. 252)

biopsychology The branch of psychology that studies the ways hormones and drugs act on the brain to alter behavior and experience, either in humans or in nonhuman animals. (p. 12)

bipolar and related disorders Mood disorders that are characterized by episodes of abnormally high mood (mania) and abnormally low mood (depression). See *bipolar I disorder* and *bipolar II disorder*. (p. 599)

bipolar I disorder The most severe type of bipolar disorder, characterized by at least one episode of mania and one episode of major depression. See *bipolar and related disorders*. For contrast, see *bipolar II disorder*. (p. 604)

bipolar II disorder The type of bipolar disorder in which the manic phase is less extreme than it is in bipolar I disorder and is referred to as hypomania rather than mania. See *bipolar and related disorders*. For contrast, see *bipolar I disorder*. (p. 604)

blind In scientific research, the condition in which those who collect the data are deliberately kept uninformed about aspects of the study's design (such as which subjects have had which treatment) that could lead them either unconsciously or consciously to bias the results. See also *bias, observer-expectancy effect*. (p. 51)

blind spot The place in the retina of the eye where the axons of visual sensory neurons come together to form the optic nerve. Because the blind spot lacks receptor cells, light that strikes it is not seen. (p. 228)

borderline personality disorder A personality disorder characterized by instability, including in emotions—swinging in and out of extreme moods and self-image—often showing dramatic changes in identity, goals, friends, and even sexual orientation. (p. 617)

bottom-up control In theories of perception, mental processes that bring the individual stimulus features recorded by the senses together to form a perception of the larger object or scene. For contrast, see *top-down control*. (p. 244)

brainstem The primitive, stalk-like portion of the brain that can be thought of as an extension of the spinal cord into the head; it consists of the medulla, pons, and midbrain. (p. 123)

Broca's aphasia A specific syndrome of loss in language ability that occurs due to damage in a particular part of the brain called *Broca's area*; it is characterized by telegraphic speech in which the meaning is usually clear but the small words and word endings that serve grammatical purposes are missing; also called *nonfluent aphasia*. For contrast, see *Wernicke's aphasia*. (p. 138)

cell body The widest part of a neuron, which contains the cell nucleus and the other basic machinery common to all cells. (p. 104)

cell membrane The thin, porous outer covering of a neuron or other cell that separates the cell's intracellular fluid from extracellular fluid. (p. 105)

central drive system According to the central-state theory of drives, a set of neurons in the brain that, when active, most directly promotes a specific motivational state, or drive. (p. 155)

central executive In Baddeley's theory, a component of the mind responsible for coordinating all the activities of working memory and for bringing new information into working memory. (p. 325)

central nervous system The brain and spinal cord. (p. 102)

central-state theory of drives Proposes that the most direct physiological bases for motivational states, or drives, lie in neural activity in the brain. According to most versions of this theory, different drives correspond to activity in different, localizable sets of neurons. See also *central drive system*. (p. 155)

centration In Piaget's theory, the tendency of preoperational children to attend to one aspect of a situation to the exclusion of others; contrast with *decentration*. (p. 419)

cerebellum The relatively large, conspicuous, convoluted portion of the brain attached to the rear side of the brainstem; it is especially important for the coordination of rapid movements. (p. 124)

cerebral cortex The outermost, evolutionarily newest, and (in humans) by far the largest portion of the brain; it is divisible into two hemispheres (right and left), and each hemisphere is divisible into four lobes—the occipital, temporal, parietal, and frontal. (p. 111)

chromosomes The structures within the cell nucleus that contain the genetic material (DNA). (p. 62)

chunking A strategy for improving the ability to remember a set of items by grouping them mentally to form fewer items. (p. 341)

circadian rhythm Any cyclic physiological or behavioral change in a person or other living thing that has a period of about 1 day even in the absence of external cues signaling the time of day. (p. 175)

classical conditioning A training procedure or learning experience in which a neutral stimulus (the conditioned stimulus) comes to elicit a reflexive response through its being paired with another stimulus (usually an unconditioned stimulus) that already elicits that reflexive response; originally studied by Pavlov. See also *conditioned response, conditioned stimulus, unconditioned response, unconditioned stimulus*. (p. 266)

clinical psychology The field of practice and research that is directed toward helping people who suffer from psychological problems and disorders. (p. 625)

closure principle See *Gestalt principles of grouping*. (p. 241)

cochlea A coiled structure in the inner ear in which the receptor cells for hearing are located. (p. 216)

cognitive dissonance theory Festinger's theory proposing that people seek to relieve the discomfort associated with the awareness of inconsistency between two or more of one's own cognitions (beliefs or bits of knowledge). (p. 504)

cognitive neuroscience Research specialty that attempts to explain cognition in terms of processes occurring within the nervous system using noninvasive techniques with humans (p. 11)

cognitive psychology Research specialty that attempts to explain behavior or mental experiences in terms of the cognitions (items of mental information or knowledge) that underlie the behavior or experience. (p. 15)

cognitive therapy An approach to psychotherapy that begins with the assumption that people disturb themselves through their own thoughts and that they can overcome their problems through changing the way they think about their experiences. (p. 645)

cognitive-behavioral therapy (CBT) The psychotherapy approach that stems from a union of cognitive and behavioral theory; it usually characterizes psychological problems as learned habits of thought and action, and its approach to treatment is to help people change those habits. See also *behavior therapy, cognitive therapy.* (p. 642)

common movement principle See *Gestalt principles of grouping.* (p. 241)

concept A rule or other form of mental information for categorizing stimuli into groups. (p. 287)

concordance In behavioral genetics research, an index of heritability found by identifying a set of individuals who have a particular trait or disorder and then determining the percentage of some specific class of their relatives (e.g., identical twins) who have the same trait or disorder. (p. 611)

concrete-operational scheme In Piaget's theory, the type of mental structure that allows a child to think logically about reversible actions (operations) but only when applied to objects with which the child has had direct (concrete) experience. See also *operation.* (p. 418)

conditioned response In classical conditioning, a reflexive response that is elicited by a stimulus (the conditioned stimulus) because of the previous pairing of that stimulus with another stimulus (the unconditioned stimulus) that already elicits a reflexive response. For contrast, see *unconditioned response.* (p. 267)

conditioned stimulus In classical conditioning, a stimulus that comes to elicit a reflexive response (the conditioned response) because of its previous pairing with another stimulus (the unconditioned stimulus) that already elicits a reflexive response. For contrast, see *unconditioned stimulus.* (p. 267)

cone vision The high-acuity color vision that occurs in moderate to bright light and is mediated by cones in the retina; also called *photopic* or *bright-light vision.* See *cones.* For contrast, see *rod vision.* (p. 228)

cones The class of receptor cells for vision that are located in and near the fovea of the retina, operate in moderate to bright light, and are most important for the perception of color and fine detail. For contrast, see *rods.* (p. 227)

confirmation bias Tendency of people to seek evidence that confirms, rather than disconfirms, their current hypotheses. (p. 366)

consciousness In perception, the experiencing of percepts or other mental events in such a manner that one can report on them to others. (p. 312)

consolidation The process by which a new memory becomes solidified in the brain, such that it is not easily forgotten. (p. 345)

contingency management In behavior therapy, any systematic alteration in the relationship (contingency) between actions and rewards that is designed to alter the client's behavior in a desired direction. See *behavior therapy.* (p. 643)

continuous reinforcement In operant conditioning, any condition in which the response is always reinforced. Contrast with *partial reinforcement.* See *reinforcer.* (p. 283)

control processes The mental processes that operate on information in the memory stores and move information from one store to another. See *attention, encoding, retrieval.* (p. 313)

cooperation A type of helping behavior in which interaction among two or more individuals increases the survival chance or reproductive capacity of each individual involved in the interaction. For contrast, see *altruism.* (p. 95)

cornea The curved, transparent tissue at the front of the eyeball that helps to focus light rays as they first enter the eye. (p. 226)

corpus callosum A massive bundle of axons connecting the right and left hemispheres of the higher parts of the brain, including the cerebral cortex. (p. 134)

correlation coefficient A numerical measure of the strength and direction of the relationship between two variables. (p. 42)

correlational study Any scientific study in which the researcher observes or measures (without directly manipulating) two or more variables to find relationships between them. Such studies can identify lawful relationships but cannot determine whether change in one variable is the cause of change in another. (p. 35)

cranial nerve A nerve that extends directly from the brain. See *nerve.* For contrast, see *spinal nerve.* (p. 119)

creole language A new language, with grammatical rules, that develops from a pidgin language in colonies established by people who

had different native languages. See *pidgin language.* (p. 443)

critical period A relatively restricted time period in an individual's development during which a particular form of learning can best occur. See *imprinting.* (p. 305)

crystallized intelligence In Cattell's theory, the variety of intelligence that derives directly from previous experience. It includes one's accumulated knowledge and verbal skills. For contrast, see *fluid intelligence.* (p. 383)

cultural psychology Research specialty that attempts to explain mental experiences and behavior in terms of the culture in which the person developed. (p. 16)

dark adaptation The increased visual sensitivity that occurs when the eyes are exposed for a period of time to dimmer light than was present before the adaptation period. For contrast, see *light adaptation.* (p. 228)

dark triad Three related socially aversive personality traits—narcissism, Machiavellianism, and psychopathy—describing people with "dark personalities." (p. 540)

decentration In Piaget's theory, the ability of concrete operational children to consider multiple aspects of a stimulus or situation; contrast with *centration.* (p. 419)

deductive reasoning Logical reasoning from the general to the specific; the reasoner begins by accepting the truth of one or more general premises or axioms and uses them to assert whether a specific conclusion is true, false, or indeterminate. For contrast, see *inductive reasoning.* (p. 368)

deep brain stimulation A procedure used for treating obsessive-compulsive disorder and depression, in which a hair-thin wire electrode is implanted permanently into the brain and activated to stimulate neurons near the targeted area. (p. 634)

defense mechanisms In psychoanalytic theory, self-deceptive means by which the mind defends itself against anxiety. See *displacement, projection, rationalization, reaction formation, repression, sublimation.* (p. 558)

dendrites The thin, tube-like extensions of a neuron that typically branch repeatedly near the neuron's cell body and are specialized for receiving signals from other neurons. (p. 104)

dependent personality disorder A personality disorder in which people show an extreme need to be cared for. They are clingy and fear separation from significant people in their lives, believing they cannot care for themselves. (p. 617)

dependent variable In an experiment, the variable that is believed to be dependent upon (affected by) another variable (the independent variable). In psychological experiments, it is usually some measure of behavior. (p. 34)

depressive disorders The class of mood disorders characterized by prolonged or frequent bouts of depression. See *dysthymia, major depression*. (p. 599)

descriptive statistics Mathematical methods for summarizing sets of data. (p. 41)

descriptive study Any study in which the researcher describes the behavior of an individual or set of individuals without systematically investigating relationships between specific variables. (p. 37)

developmental psychology The branch of psychology that charts changes in people's abilities and styles of behaving as they get older and tries to understand the factors that produce or influence those changes. (pp. 49, 433)

difference threshold In psychophysics, the minimal difference that must exist between two otherwise similar stimuli for an individual to detect them as different; also called the *just-noticeable difference (jnd)*. (p. 196)

differential lighting of surfaces A pictorial cue for perceiving depth in which the amount of light reflecting on different surfaces indicates the position of objects relative to the light source. (p. 255)

differential susceptibility to environmental influence The idea that people are differentially susceptible to being influenced by their environment. Highly susceptible children (sometimes referred to as *orchid children*) will flourish in good environments and do especially poorly in adverse environments. Less-susceptible children (sometimes referred to as *dandelion children*) are less affected by their rearing conditions so that extreme environments (both good and bad) will have less of an impact on their psychological outcomes. (p. 549)

discrete emotion theory The belief that basic emotions are innate and associated with distinctive bodily and facial reactions. (p. 179)

discrimination training The procedure, in both classical and operant conditioning, by which generalization between two stimuli is diminished or abolished by reinforcing the response to one stimulus and extinguishing the response to the other. See *extinction, generalization, reinforcement*. (p. 269)

discriminative stimulus In operant conditioning, a stimulus that serves as a signal that a particular response will produce a particular reinforcer. (p. 286)

disorganized/disoriented attachment Attachment style in which infants seek to be close to their caregivers in inconsistent ways, often showing patterns typical of secure, avoidant, and/or resistant attachment simultaneously. Compare to *secure, insecure-avoidant*, and *insecure-resistant* attachment. (p. 454)

displacement The defense mechanism by which a drive is diverted from one goal to another that is more realistic or acceptable. Also called *sublimation* in cases where the goal toward which the drive is diverted is highly valued by society. (p. 558)

distal explanations Functional explanations of behavior that state the role that the behavior plays or once played in survival and reproduction, that is, explanations of why the potential for the behavior was favored by natural selection. For contrast, see *proximate explanations*. (p. 76)

DNA Deoxyribonucleic acid; a long, self-replicating molecule that constitutes a gene. (p. 60)

dominant gene A gene that produces its observable effects even if the person is heterozygous for that gene (that is, has that gene allele on only one of the two paired chromosomes). Contrast to *recessive gene*. (p. 64)

dopamine One of many neurotransmitter substances in the brain. It is, among other things, crucial for the "wanting" component of reward. (p. 157)

double-blind experiment An experiment in which both the observer and the subjects are blind with respect to the subjects' treatment conditions. See also *blind*. (p. 52)

Down syndrome A disorder that results from having an extra chromosome 21, characterized by a specific set of physical symptoms and moderate to severe intellectual disability. (p. 586)

drive See *motivational state*.

drug tolerance The phenomenon by which a drug produces successively smaller physiological and behavioral effects, at any given dose, if it is taken repeatedly. (p. 276)

DSM-5 Commonly used abbreviation for the *Diagnostic and Statistical Manual of Mental Disorders, Fifth Edition*, published by the American Psychiatric Association, which defines a wide variety of mental disorders and establishes criteria for diagnosing them. (p. 578)

dualism The philosophical theory proposing that two distinct systems—the material body and the immaterial soul—are involved in the control of behavior. For contrast, see *materialism*. (p. 3)

dual-processing theories Cognitive theories that propose that people have two general ways of processing information. Typically such theories propose that one form of thinking is on the automatic end of the information-processing continuum, with processing being fast, automatic, and unconscious, and the second way of thinking is placed on the effortful side of this continuum, with processing being slow, effortful, and conscious. (p. 316)

dysthymia A psychological disorder characterized by feelings of depression that are less severe than those in major depression but which last for at least a 2-year period. See also *major depression*. (p. 599)

echoic memory Sensory memory for the sense of hearing. (p. 320)

effortful processes Cognitive processes that consume some of the information-processing system's limited capacity and are hypothesized

to (1) be available to conscious awareness, (2) interfere with the execution of other processes, (3) improve with practice, and (4) be influenced by individual differences in intelligence, motivation, or education. Contrast with *automatic processes*. (p. 315)

egocentricity In Piaget's theory, the tendency to interpret objects and events from one's own perspective. (p. 419)

elaboration The process of thinking about an item of information in such a way as to tie the item mentally to other information in memory, which helps to encode the item into long-term memory; also called *elaborative rehearsal*. (p. 339)

electroconvulsive therapy (ECT) A procedure for treating severe depression, in which a patient is anesthetized and given a muscle relaxant, and then an electric current is passed through the patient's skull in such a way as to set up a seizure either in one hemisphere of the brain or in both hemispheres. (p. 633)

electroencephalogram (EEG) A record of the electrical activity of the brain that can be obtained by amplifying the weak electrical signals picked up by recording electrodes pasted to the person's scalp. It is usually described in terms of wave patterns. (p. 115)

embryonic phase Developmental period that extends from the third to about the eighth week after conception in humans, during which all major organ systems develop. (p. 402)

emerging adulthood Period of transition from adolescence to young adulthood (approximately from ages 18 to 25 years). (p. 472)

emotion A subjective feeling that is experienced as directed toward some particular object or event. Contrast to *mood*. (p. 177)

empiricism The idea that all human knowledge and thought ultimately come from sensory experience; the philosophical approach to understanding the mind that is based on that idea. For contrast, see *nativism*. (p. 6)

encephalization quotient (EQ) Formula for evaluating the expected ratio between brain weight and body weight for animals. (p. 146)

encoding The mental process by which long-term memories are formed. See also *long-term memory*. (p. 315)

encoding rehearsal Any active mental process by which a person strives to encode information into long-term memory. For contrast, see *maintenance rehearsal*. (p. 339)

endorphins Chemicals produced in the body that act like morphine in inhibiting pain. (p. 158)

epigenetics Field that examines gene-regulating activity, with no changes to actual DNA, that can have lasting effects for one or more generations. (p. 70)

episodic memory Explicit memory of past events (episodes) in one's own life. For contrast, see *semantic memory, implicit memory*. (p. 332)

evaluative conditioning The changing in the strength of liking or disliking of a stimulus as a result of being paired with another positive or negative stimulus. (p. 274)

evolution The long-term adaptive process, spanning generations, that equips each species for life in its ever-changing natural habitat. (p. 60)

evolutionary psychology Research specialty that attempts to explain how or why specific behavioral characteristics would have come about, by natural selection, in the course of evolution. (p. 13)

excitatory synapse A synapse at which the neurotransmitter increases the likelihood that an action potential will occur, or increases the rate at which they are already occurring, in the neuron on which it acts. For contrast, see *inhibitory synapse.* (p. 109)

executive functions The processes involved in regulating attention and in determining what to do with information just gathered or retrieved from long-term memory. (p. 328)

experience-expectant processes (or experience-expectant synaptogenesis) Processes whereby synapses are formed and maintained when an organism has species-typical experiences; as a result, functions (such as vision) will develop for all members of a species, given a species-typical environment. (p. 236)

experiment A research design for testing hypotheses about cause–effect relationships, in which the researcher manipulates one variable (the independent variable) in order to assess its effect on another variable (the dependent variable). (p. 34)

explicit attitudes Conscious attitudes; that is, attitudes that people are aware of holding and can state verbally. For contrast, see *implicit attitudes.* (p. 503)

explicit memory The class of memory that can be consciously recalled and used to answer explicit questions about what one knows or remembers. See *episodic memory, semantic memory.* For contrast, see *implicit memory.* (p. 331)

explicit stereotypes Stereotypes that people hold consciously. See *stereotypes.* For contrast, see *implicit stereotypes.* (p. 508)

exposure treatment Any method of treating fears—including flooding and systematic desensitization—that involves exposing the client to the feared object or situation (either in reality or imagination) so that the process of extinction or habituation of the fear response can occur. (p. 643)

extinction In classical conditioning, the gradual disappearance of a conditioned reflex that results when a conditioned stimulus occurs repeatedly without the unconditioned stimulus. (p. 268) In operant conditioning, the decline in response rate that results when an operant response is no longer followed by a reinforcer. (p. 283) See *classical conditioning, operant conditioning.*

factor analysis A statistical procedure for analyzing the correlations among various measurements (such as test scores) taken from a given set of individuals; it identifies hypothetical, underlying variables called *factors* that could account for the observed pattern of correlations and assesses the degree to which each factor is adequately measured by each of the measurements that was used in the analysis. (p. 537)

feature detector In vision, any neuron in the brain that responds to a specific property of a visual stimulus, such as its color, orientation, movement, or shape of its contour. More generally, any neuron in the brain that responds to a particular property (feature) of any sensory stimulus. (p. 238)

fetal phase Developmental period that extends from about nine weeks until birth, which usually takes place about 38 weeks after conception in humans. (p. 402)

field study Any scientific research study in which data are collected in a setting other than the laboratory. (p. 38)

figure In perception, the portion of a visual scene that draws the perceiver's attention and is interpreted as an object rather than as the background. For contrast, see *ground.* (p. 242)

five-factor model Model holding that a person's personality is most efficiently described in terms of his or her score on each of five relatively independent global trait dimensions: *neuroticism, extraversion, openness to experience, agreeableness,* and *conscientiousness.* (p. 538)

fixed-interval (FI) schedule In operant conditioning, a schedule of reinforcement in which a fixed period of time must elapse after each reinforced response before it produces a reinforcer. (p. 284)

fixed-ratio (FR) schedule In operant conditioning, a schedule of reinforcement in which a response must be produced a certain fixed number of times (more than once) before it produces a reinforcer. (p. 284)

fluid intelligence In Cattell's theory, the variety of intelligence that enables one to perceive relationships independent of previous specific practice or instruction concerning those relationships. For contrast, see *crystallized intelligence.* (p. 382)

Flynn effect The systematic increase in IQ scores (about 3 points per decade) observed over the twentieth century. (p. 396)

fMRI See *functional magnetic resonance imaging.*

foot-in-the-door technique A technique for gaining compliance in which one first asks for some relatively small contribution or favor before asking for a larger one. Complying with the first request predisposes the person to comply with the second. (p. 521)

formal-operational scheme In Piaget's theory, the type of mental structure that allows a person to reason about abstract concepts and hypothetical ideas. See also *operation, schemes.* (p. 420)

fovea The pinhead-size area of the retina of the eye in which the cones are concentrated and that is specialized for high visual acuity. (p. 227)

fraternal twins Two individuals who developed simultaneously in the same womb, but who originated from separate zygotes (fertilized eggs) and are therefore no more genetically similar to one another than are nontwin siblings; also called *dizygotic twins.* For contrast, see *identical twins.* (p. 64)

free association In psychoanalysis, the procedure in which a patient relaxes, frees his or her mind from the constraints of conscious logic, and reports every image and idea that enters his or her awareness. (p. 638)

frequency For any form of energy that changes in a cyclic or wave-like way, the number of cycles or waves that occur during a standard unit of time. For sound, this physical measure is related to the psychological experience of pitch. (p. 213)

frequency distribution A table or graph depicting the number of individual scores, in a set of scores, that fall within each of a set of equal intervals. (p. A-2)

frontal lobes The frontmost lobes of the cerebral cortex, bounded in the rear by the parietal and temporal lobes; the frontal lobes contain the motor area and parts of the association areas involved in planning and making judgments. (p. 126)

functional fixedness The failure to see an object as having a function other than its usual one. (p. 372)

functional magnetic resonance imagining (fMRI) A method for visually displaying brain activity that is based on the fact that protons in certain molecules can be made to resonate and give off radio waves indicating relative amounts of neural activity in each portion of the brain. (p. 116)

functionalism A school of psychological thought, founded by William James and others, that focuses on understanding the functions, or adaptive purposes, of mental processes. (p. 76)

fundamental attribution error The tendency for people to attribute an action to the individual's personality and to ignore the constraints that the role or situation places on how the person can or must act. (p. 495)

fusiform face area (FFA) Part of the human temporal cortex that is specialized for recognizing familiar faces. (p. 250)

gate-control theory Melzack and Wall's theory proposing that pain will be experienced only if the input from peripheral pain neurons passes through a "gate" located at the point that the pain-carrying neurons enter the spinal cord or lower brainstem. (p. 210)

gender identity A person's subjective sense of being male or female. (p. 469)

gene Component of long molecules of a substance called DNA (deoxyribonucleic acid) that codes for a particular protein; the basic unit of heredity. (p. 60)

general intelligence (g) In Spearman's theory of intelligence (and in other theories based on Spearman's), the underlying mental ability that affects performance on a wide variety of mental tests and accounts for the statistical correlation among scores on such tests. (p. 382)

generalization In classical conditioning, the phenomenon by which a stimulus that resembles a conditioned stimulus will elicit the conditioned response even though it has never been paired with the unconditioned stimulus. (p. 269) In operant conditioning, the phenomenon by which a stimulus that resembles a discriminative stimulus will increase the rate at which the animal produces the operant response, even though the response has never been reinforced in the presence of that stimulus. (p. 286)

generalized anxiety disorder A psychological disorder characterized by prolonged, severe anxiety that is not consistently associated in the person's mind with any particular object or event in the environment or any specific life experience. (p. 591)

genotype The set of genes inherited by the individual. See also *phenotype*. (p. 62)

Gestalt principles of grouping The rules, proposed by Gestalt psychologists, concerning the manner by which the perceptual system groups sensory elements together to produce organized perceptions of whole objects and scenes. They include the principles of (a) *proximity* (nearby elements are grouped together), (b) *similarity* (elements that resemble one another are grouped together), (c) *closure* (gaps in what would otherwise be a continuous border are ignored), (d) *good continuation* (when lines intersect, those segments that would form a continuous line with minimal change in direction are grouped together), (e) *common movement* (elements moving in the same direction and velocity are grouped together), and (f) *good form* (elements are grouped in such a way as to form percepts that are simple and symmetrical). (p. 241)

Gestalt psychology A school of psychological thought, founded in Germany, which emphasizes the idea that the mind must be understood in terms of organized wholes, not elementary parts. (p. 240)

good continuation principle See *Gestalt principles of grouping*. (p. 241)

good form principle See *Gestalt principles of grouping*. (p. 241)

grammar The entire set of rules that specify the permissible ways that smaller units can be arranged to form morphemes, words, phrases, and sentences in a language. (p. 436)

grit A personality trait defined as perseverance and passion for long-term goals, composed of two lower-order factors, *perseverance of effort* and *consistency of interest*. (p. 538)

ground In perception, the portion of a visual scene that is interpreted as the background rather than as the object of attention. For contrast, see *figure*. (p. 242)

group polarization The tendency for a group of people who already share a particular opinion to hold that opinion more strongly—or in a more extreme form—after discussing the issue among themselves. (p. 519)

groupthink A model of thinking in which members of a group are more concerned with group cohesiveness and unanimity than with realistic appraisal of the actions being considered. (p. 520)

habituation The decline in the magnitude or likelihood of a reflexive response that occurs when the stimulus is repeated several or many times in succession. (p. 266)

hair cells The receptor cells for hearing, which are arranged in rows along the basilar membrane of the cochlea in the inner ear. (p. 216)

Hawthorne effect Changes in subjects' behavior as a result of knowing they are being watched, attributed to the special attention they receive. (p. 40)

helping Any behavior that increases the survival chance or reproductive capacity of another individual. See also *altruism, cooperation*. (p. 95)

heritability The proportion of the variability in a particular characteristic, in a particular group of individuals, that is due to genetic rather than environmental differences among the individuals. (p. 387)

hippocampus A structure in the limbic system of the brain that is essential for encoding explicit memories for long-term storage. (p. 125)

histrionic personality disorder A personality disorder in which people continually seek to be the center of attention, behaving as if they are always "on stage," using theatrical gestures and mannerisms; they are often described as "emotionally charged," displaying exaggerated moods and emotions. (p. 617)

homeostasis The constancy in the body's internal environment that must be maintained through the expenditure of energy. (p. 152)

homology In ethology and comparative psychology, any similarity among species that exists because of the species' common ancestry. For contrast, see *analogy*. (p. 84)

hormone Any chemical substance that is secreted naturally by the body into the blood and can influence physiological processes at specific target tissues (such as the brain) and thereby influence behavior. (p. 131)

humanistic theories Personality theories that attempt to focus attention on the whole, unique person, especially on the person's conscious understanding of his or her self and the world. (p. 562)

humanistic therapy Any of several types of psychotherapy that emerged from humanistic personality theories, usually emphasizing the client's own constructions of his or her reality. See *humanistic theories* and *person-centered therapy*. (p. 640)

hypothalamus A small brain structure lying just below the thalamus, connected directly to the pituitary gland and to the limbic system, that is especially important for the regulation of motivation, emotion, and the internal physiological conditions of the body. (p. 125)

hypothesis A specific prediction about what will be observed in a research study, usually derived from a more general conception or theory. See also *theory*. (p. 31)

iconic memory Sensory memory for the sense of vision. (p. 320)

identical twins Two individuals who are genetically identical to one another because they originated from a single zygote (fertilized egg); also called *monozygotic twins*. For contrast, see *fraternal twins*. (p. 64)

implicit association tests Tests of a person's automatic, unconscious mental associations, designed to assess implicit stereotypes or other implicit attitudes. See *implicit stereotypes*. (p. 503)

implicit attitudes Attitudes that are manifested in a person's behavior or automatic mental associations, even though the person may not be conscious of holding those attitudes. For contrast, see *explicit attitudes*. (p. 503)

implicit memory Memory that influences one's behavior or thought but does not itself enter consciousness. See *priming, procedural memory*. (p. 331)

implicit stereotypes Stereotypes that automatically, unconsciously influence people's judgments and actions toward others. See *stereotypes*. For contrast, see *explicit stereotypes*. (p. 508)

impression management The entire set of ways by which people either consciously or unconsciously attempt to influence other people's impressions (perceptions and judgments) of them. (p. 513)

imprinting Ethologists' term for a relatively sudden and irreversible form of learning that can occur only during some critical period of the individual's development. See *critical period*. (p. 305)

independent variable In an experiment, the condition that the researcher varies in order to assess its effect upon some other variable (the dependent variable). In psychology, it is usually some condition of the environment or of the organism's physiology that is hypothesized to affect the individual's behavior. (p. 34)

inductive reasoning Logical reasoning from the specific to the general; the reasoner begins with a set of specific observations or facts and uses them to infer a more general rule to account for those observations or facts; also called *hypothesis construction*. For contrast, see *deductive reasoning*. (p. 365)

infantile amnesia The inability to remember events from infancy and early childhood. (p. 337)

inferential statistics Mathematical methods for helping researchers determine how confident they can be in drawing general conclusions (inferences) from specific sets of data. (p. 41)

informational influence The class of social influence that derives from the use of others' behavior or opinions as information in forming one's own judgment about the objective nature of an event or situation. For contrast, see *normative influence*. (p. 515)

in-groups Groups to which we belong. (p. 507)

inhibitory synapse A synapse at which the neurotransmitter decreases the likelihood that an action potential will occur, or decreases the rate at which they are already occurring, in the neuron upon which it acts. For contrast, see *excitatory synapse*. (p. 109)

inner ear The portion of the ear lying farthest inward in the head; it contains the cochlea (for hearing) and the vestibular apparatus (for the sense of balance). (p. 216)

insecure-avoidant attachment A style of attachment in which infants show little distress when their caregivers depart temporarily, avoid contact with them when they return, and usually do not show wariness of strangers. Compare to *secure, insecure-resistant*, and *disorganized/disoriented attachment*. (p. 454)

insecure-resistant attachment A style of attachment in which infants stay very close to their caregivers and tend not to explore much. They become distressed when their caregivers leave them temporarily, but display anger and initial rejection of contact when they return. Compare to *secure, insecure-avoidant*, and *disorganized/disoriented attachment*. (p. 454)

insight problem A problem that is difficult to solve until it is viewed in a new way, involving a different mental set from that originally taken. See *mental set*. (p. 371)

insufficient-justification effect A change in attitude that serves to justify an action that seems unjustified in the light of the previously held attitude. (p. 505)

intelligence The variable mental capacity that underlies individual differences in reasoning, solving problems, and acquiring new knowledge. (p. 378)

interneuron A neuron that exists entirely within the brain or spinal cord and carries messages from one set of neurons to another. (p. 103)

introspection The personal observations of one's thoughts, perceptions, and feelings. Introspection was used in experimental studies by Wundt and other early psychologists, but the subjective nature of such observations made it an inappropriate source of scientific data. (p. 39)

IQ Abbreviation for *intelligence quotient*, defined as a score on a test of intelligence that is standardized in such a way that the average score for the population is 100 and the distribution of scores around that average matches a normal distribution. See *standardized score* and *normal distribution*. (p. 380)

iris The colored (usually brown or blue), doughnut-shaped, muscular structure in the eye, located behind the cornea and in front of the lens, that controls the size of the pupil and in that way controls the amount of light that can enter the eye's interior. (p. 226)

just-noticeable difference (jnd) See *difference threshold*. (p. 196)

kin selection theory Theory proposing that apparent acts of altruism have come about through natural selection because such actions are disproportionately directed toward close genetic relatives and thus promote the survival of others who have the same genes. See also *altruism*. (p. 95)

laboratory study Any research study in which the subjects are brought to a specially designated area (laboratory) that has been set up to facilitate the researcher's ability to control the environment or collect data. (p. 38)

language-acquisition device (LAD) Chomsky's term for the special, innate characteristics of the human mind that allow children to learn their native language; it includes innate knowledge of basic aspects of grammar that are common to all languages and an innate predisposition to attend to and remember the critical, unique aspects of the language. (p. 442)

language-acquisition support system (LASS) The term used by social-learning theorists to refer to the simplification of language and the use of gestures that occur when parents or other language users speak to young children, which helps children learn language; developed as a complement to Chomsky's concept of the *LAD (language-acquisition device)*. (p. 444)

latent learning Learning that is not demonstrated in the subject's behavior at the time that the learning occurs but can be inferred from its effect on the subject's behavior at some later time. (p. 296)

law of complementarity The observation that certain pairs of limited-wavelength lights that produce different colors (such as red and green) alone will produce the perception of white (no color) when mixed. (p. 230)

law of effect Thorndike's principle that responses that produce a satisfying effect in a particular situation become more likely to recur in that situation, and responses that produce a discomforting effect become less likely to recur in that situation. (p. 280)

learning The process or set of processes through which sensory experience at one time can affect an individual's behavior at a future time. (p. 265)

learning psychology Research specialty in psychology that attempts to understand how the behavior of individuals is shaped through basic learning processes. (p. 14)

lens In the eye, the transparent structure behind the iris that helps focus light that passes through the pupil. (p. 226)

leptin A hormone produced by fat cells that acts in the brain to inhibit hunger and regulate body weight. (p. 162)

level of analysis The type ("level") of causal process that is referred to in explaining some phenomenon. In psychology, a given type of behavior might be explained at the neural, physiological, genetic, evolutionary, learning, cognitive, social, cultural, or developmental level of analysis. (p. 10)

light adaptation The decreased visual sensitivity that occurs when the eyes are exposed for a period of time to brighter light than was present before the adaptation period. For contrast, see *dark adaptation*. (p. 228)

limbic system An interconnected set of brain structures (including the amygdala and hippocampus) that form a circuit wrapped around the thalamus and basal ganglia, underneath the cerebral cortex. These structures are especially important for the regulation of emotion and motivation and are involved in the formation of long-term memories. (p. 125)

linear perspective A pictorial cue for perceiving depth in which the convergence of parallel lines indicates the distance of objects. Parallel lines appear to converge as they become more distant. (p. 254)

locus of control According to Rotter, a person's perception of the typical source of control over rewards. *Internal locus of control* refers to the perception that people control their own rewards through their own behavior, and *external locus of control* refers to the perception that rewards are controlled by external circumstances or fate. (p. 565)

long-term memory Information that is retained in the mind for long periods (often throughout life). For contrasts, see *sensory memory, working memory*. (p. 314)

long-term potentiation (LTP) A process by which repeated activation of synapses results in strengthening of those synapses. (p. 144)

low-ball technique A sales trick in which the salesperson suggests a low price for the item being sold, and then, when the potential customer has agreed to buy it at that price, pretends to discover that the item cannot be sold for that price. (p. 521)

LTP See *long-term potentiation*.

Machiavellianism A personality type in which the person is predisposed to manipulate other people, often through deception. (p. 540)

maintenance rehearsal Any active mental process by which a person strives to hold information in short-term memory for a period of time. For contrast, see *encoding rehearsal*. (p. 339)

major depression A psychological disorder characterized by severe depression that lasts essentially without remission for at least 2 weeks. See also *dysthymia*. (p. 599)

materialism Hobbes's theory proposing that nothing exists but matter and energy. For contrast, see *dualism*. (p. 4)

mean The arithmetic average of a set of scores, determined by adding the scores and dividing the sum by the number of scores. (pp. 41, A-3)

medial forebrain bundle A bundle of neurons that runs from the midbrain to the basal ganglia and other forebrain areas. (p. 156)

median The center score in a set of scores that have been rank-ordered. (pp. 41, A-3)

medulla The lowest portion of the brainstem, bounded at one end by the spinal cord and at the other by the pons. It is responsible, with the pons, for organizing reflexes more complex than spinal reflexes. (p. 123)

meiosis The form of cell division involved in producing egg or sperm cells, which results in cells that are genetically dissimilar and that each have half the number of chromosomes of the original cell. (p. 63)

memory 1. The mind's ability to retain information over time. 2. Information retained in the mind over time. (p. 331)

memory stores In cognitive psychology, hypothetical constructs that are conceived of as places where information is held in the mind. (p. 313)

mental disorder See *psychological disorder.*

mental set A habit of perception or thought, stemming from previous experience, that can either help or hinder a person in solving a new problem. (p. 371)

midbrain The upper portion of the brainstem, bounded at its lower end by the pons and at its upper end by the thalamus, that contains neural centers that organize basic movement patterns. (p. 123)

middle ear The air-filled cavity separated from the outer ear by the eardrum; its main structures are three ossicles (tiny bones) that vibrate in response to sound waves and stimulate the inner ear. (p. 215)

mind 1. The entire set of an individual's sensations, perceptions, memories, thoughts, dreams, motives, emotional feelings, and other subjective experiences. (p. 1) 2. In cognitive psychology, the set of hypothesized information-processing steps that analyze stimulus information and organize behavioral responses. (p. 1)

mirror neurons Neurons in the brain that become active both when the individual makes a particular motion and when the individual sees another individual making that same motion. These neurons are believed to facilitate observational learning. (p. 111)

mitosis The form of cell division involved in normal body growth, which produces cells that are genetically identical to each other. (p. 63)

mode The most frequently occurring score in a set of scores; in a frequency distribution, the interval that contains the highest frequency of scores. (p. A-3)

monogamy A mating system in which one female and one male bond only with each other. For contrast, see *polyandry, polygyny, promiscuity.* (p. 87)

mood A free-floating emotional feeling, not directed at a specific object. Contrast to *emotion.* (p. 177)

moon illusion The illusion by which the moon appears larger when seen near the horizon and smaller when seen near the zenith, even though it is objectively the same size and distance from the viewer in either location. (p. 257)

morphemes The smallest meaningful units of a verbal language; words, prefixes, or suffixes that have discrete meanings. (p. 435)

motion parallax The cue for depth perception that stems from the changed view one has of a scene or object when one's head moves sideways to the scene or object; the farther away an object is, the smaller is the change in view. (p. 253)

motivation The entire constellation of factors, some inside the organism and some outside, that cause an individual to behave in a particular way at a particular time. See also *motivational state.* (p. 151)

motivational state An internal, reversible condition in an individual that orients the individual toward one or another type of goal (such as food or water). This condition is not observed directly but is inferred from the individual's behavior; also called a *drive.* (p. 151)

motor neuron A neuron that carries messages from the brain or spinal cord, through a nerve, to a muscle or gland. (p. 103)

Müller-Lyer illusion A visual size illusion in which a horizontal line looks longer if attached at each end to an outward-extending, V-shaped object, and looks shorter if attached at each end to an inward-extending, V-shaped object. (p. 256)

multisensory integration The integration of information from different senses by the nervous system. (p. 258)

mutations Errors that occasionally and unpredictably occur during DNA replication, producing a "replica" that is different from the original. Mutations are believed to be the original source of all genetic variability. (p. 73)

myelin sheath A casing of fatty cells wrapped tightly around the axon of some neurons. (p. 104)

narcissism An extreme selfishness in which a person has a grandiose view of his or her own abilities and a need for admiration. (p. 540)

narcissistic personality disorder A personality disorder in which people are self-centered, seek admiration from others, tend to lack empathy, and are grandiose and confident in their own exceptional talents or characteristics. (p. 617)

nativism The idea that certain elementary ideas are innate to the human mind and do not need to be gained through experience; the philosophical approach to understanding the mind that is based on that idea. For contrast, see *empiricism.* (p. 7)

natural selection The selective breeding that results from the obstacles to reproduction that are imposed by the natural environment; it is the driving force of evolution. See *selective breeding.* (p. 73)

naturalistic fallacy The mistaken belief that whatever is natural (and particularly whatever is a product of natural selection) is right, good, or moral. (p. 75)

naturalistic observation Any data-collection procedure in which the researcher records subjects' ongoing behavior in a natural setting, without interfering with that behavior. (p. 39)

nature–nurture debate The long-standing controversy as to whether the differences among people are principally due to their genetic differences (nature) or differences in their past and present environment (nurture). (p. 386)

negative punishment In operant conditioning, the type of punishment in which the *removal* of a stimulus (such as taking food or money) when a response occurs decreases the likelihood that the response will recur. For contrast, see *positive punishment.* (p. 285)

negative reinforcement In operant conditioning, the condition in which a response results in *removal* of a negative reinforcer. See *negative reinforcer.* (p. 284)

negative reinforcer In operant conditioning, a stimulus (such as electric shock or loud noise) that is *removed* after a response and whose removal increases the likelihood that the response will recur. (p. 285)

nerve A large bundle containing the axons of many neurons. Located in the peripheral nervous system, nerves connect the central nervous system with muscles, glands, and sensory organs. (p. 102)

neurogenesis The creation of new neurons in which neuronal stem cells divide and replicate themselves by mitosis. (p. 110)

neurons Single cells in the nervous system that are specialized for carrying information rapidly from one place to another and/or integrating information from various sources; also called *nerve cells.* (p. 102)

neuroscience The research specialty that studies the brain. (p. 101)

neurotransmitter A chemical substance released from the axon terminal of a neuron, at a synapse, that influences the activity of another neuron, a muscle cell, or a glandular cell; also called a *transmitter.* (p. 108)

nonregulatory drive Any motivational state (such as the sex drive) that serves some function *other than* that of preserving some constancy of the body's internal environment. For contrast, see *regulatory drive.* (p. 153)

non-REM sleep Stages 2, 3, and 4 of sleep, characterized by the occurrence of slow (delta) waves in the EEG and the lack of rapid eye movements. Contrast to *REM sleep.* (p. 168)

normal distribution A bell-shaped frequency distribution in which the mean, median, and mode are identical and the frequency of scores tapers off symmetrically on both sides, as defined by a specific mathematical equation. See *frequency distribution*. (pp. 68, A-2)

normative influence The class of social influence that derives from people's concern about what others will think of them if they behave in a certain way or express a certain belief. For contrast, see *informational influence*. (p. 515)

nucleus In neuroanatomy, a cluster of cell bodies of neurons within the central nervous system (not to be confused with the cell nucleus within each cell). (p. 104)

nucleus accumbens A nucleus (center of neural cell bodies) in the basal ganglia that is a crucial part of the brain's reward mechanism. (p. 157)

object permanence Piaget's term for the understanding that an object still exists even when it is out of view. (p. 412)

observational learning Learning by watching others. (p. 296)

observational method Any data-collection procedure in which the researcher directly observes the behavior of interest rather than relying on subjects' self-descriptions. (p. 39)

observer-expectancy effect Any bias in research results that derives from the researcher's desire or expectation that a subject or set of subjects will behave in a certain way. See *bias, subject-expectancy effect*. (p. 49)

obsessive-compulsive disorder (OCD) A psychological disorder characterized by a repeated, disturbing, irrational thought (the *obsession*) that can only be terminated (temporarily) by performing some action (the *compulsion*). (p. 595)

obsessive-compulsive personality disorder A personality disorder in which people are preoccupied with order and control, and as a result are inflexible and resist change. (p. 617)

occipital lobes The rearmost lobes of the cerebral cortex, bounded in front by the temporal and parietal lobes; they contain the visual areas of the brain. (p. 126)

occlusion A pictorial cue for perceiving depth in which the closer object occludes (cuts off) part of the view of the more distant object. (p. 254)

olfaction Sense of smell. (p. 199)

operant conditioning A training or learning process by which the consequence of a behavioral response affects the likelihood that the individual will produce that response again; also called *instrumental conditioning*. (p. 279)

operant response Any behavioral response that produces some reliable effect on the environment that influences the likelihood that the individual will produce that response again; also called *instrumental response*. (p. 279)

operation Piaget's term for a reversible action that can be performed either in reality or mentally upon some object or set of objects.

For example, rolling a clay ball into a clay sausage is an operation because the sausage can be rolled back again to form the ball. (p. 416)

operational definition Defining something in terms of the operations by which it could be observed and measured. (p. 48)

opponent-process theory A theory of color vision designed by Hering to explain the law of complementarity, it holds that units (neurons) that mediate the perception of color are excited by one range of wavelengths and inhibited by another (complementary) range of wavelengths. According to the theory, such units cancel out the perception of color when two complementary wavelength ranges are superimposed. See also *law of complementarity*. (p. 233)

optic nerve The cranial nerve that contains the sensory neurons for vision, which run from the eye's retina into the brain. (p. 228)

outer ear The pinna (the visible, external portion of the ear) and the auditory canal (the air-filled opening that extends inward from the pinna to the middle ear). (p. 215)

out-groups Groups to which we do not belong. (p. 507)

overimitation Copying all actions of a model, even those that are irrelevant to achieving a goal. (p. 460)

overjustification effect The phenomenon in which a person who initially performs a task for no reward (except the enjoyment of the task) becomes less likely to perform that task for no reward after a period during which he or she has been rewarded for performing it. (p. 288)

own-race bias The tendency to more easily recognize and remember members of one's own race than members of other races (also known as *cross-race bias, other-race effect,* and *same-race effect*). (p. 249)

panic disorder A psychological disorder characterized by the repeated occurrence of panic attacks at unpredictable times and with no clear relationship to environmental events. Each attack involves an intense feeling of terror, which usually lasts several minutes and is accompanied by signs of high physiological arousal. (p. 594)

parallel processing In perception, the early (unconscious) steps in the analysis of sensory information that act simultaneously on all (or at least many) of the stimulus elements that are available at any given moment. For contrast, see *serial processing*. (p. 239)

paranoid personality disorder A personality disorder in which people are deeply distrustful of other people and are suspicious of their motives. (p. 616)

parasympathetic division of the autonomic motor system The set of motor neurons that act upon visceral muscles and glands and mediate many of the body's regenerative,

growth-promoting, and energy-conserving functions. For contrast, see *sympathetic division of the autonomic motor system*. (p. 121)

parental investment The time, energy, and risk to survival involved in producing, feeding, and otherwise caring for each offspring. (p. 87)

parenting styles The general ways in which parents interact with their children. (p. 462)

parietal lobes The lobes of the cerebral cortex that lie in front of the occipital lobes, above the temporal lobes, and behind the frontal lobes; they contain the somatosensory areas of the brain. (p. 126)

partial reinforcement In operant conditioning, any condition in which the response sometimes produces a reinforcer and sometimes does not. See *reinforcer*. (p. 283)

pattern generators Networks of neurons that stimulate one another in a cyclic manner and thereby produce bursts of action potentials that wax and wane in a regular, repeating rhythm. They help to control rhythmic sequences of muscle movements, such as those involved in walking, running, flying (in birds), or swimming (in fish). (p. 122)

percentile rank For any single score in a set of scores, the percentage of scores in the set that are equal to or lower than that score. (p. A-6)

perception The recognition, organization, and meaningful interpretation of sensory stimuli. For contrast, see *sensation*. (p. 192)

peripheral nervous system The entire set of cranial and spinal nerves that connect the central nervous system (brain and spinal cord) to the body's sensory organs, muscles, and glands. (p. 102)

perpetuating causes of a psychological disorder Those consequences of a psychological disorder—such as the way other people treat the person who has it—that help keep the disorder going once it begins. See *precipitating causes* and *predisposing causes of a psychological disorder*. (p. 588)

person bias The tendency to attribute a person's behavior too much to the person's inner characteristics (personality) and not enough to the environmental situation. (p. 494)

person-centered therapy The humanistic approach to psychotherapy (also called *client-centered therapy*) developed by Carl Rogers, in which the therapist generally refrains from offering advice or leading the course of therapy, but rather listens to the client with empathy and respect and reflects the client's thoughts and feelings back to him or her. See *humanistic therapy* and *humanistic theories*. (p. 640)

personal identity The portion of the self-concept that pertains to the self as a distinct, separate individual. For contrast, see *social identity*. (p. 507)

personality The relatively consistent patterns of thought, feeling, and behavior that characterize each person as a unique individual. (p. 535)

personality disorder Stable pattern of behavior that impairs a person's sense of self, goals, and capacity for empathy and/or intimacy. (p. 616)

PET See *positron emission tomography.*

phenomenological reality Humanistic theorists' term for each person's conscious understanding of his or her world. (p. 562)

phenotype The observable properties of an individual's body and behavior. See also *genotype.* (p. 62)

pheromone A chemical that is released by an animal and that acts on other members of the species to promote some specific behavioral or physiological response. (p. 203)

phobia Any psychological disorder characterized by a strong, irrational fear of some particular category of object or event. (p. 592)

phonemes The various vowel and consonant sounds that provide the basis for a spoken language. (pp. 221, 436)

phonological loop In Baddeley's theory, a component of working memory responsible for holding verbal information. (p. 325)

photoreceptors Specialized light-detecting cells connected to the nervous system in many multicellular animals. In humans and other vertebrates, the photoreceptors are rods and cones. (p. 225)

pictorial cues for depth The depth cues that operate not only when viewing real scenes but also when viewing pictures. They include *occlusion, relative image size for familiar objects, linear perspective, texture gradient, differential lighting of surfaces,* and (for outdoor scenes) *position relative to the horizon.* (p. 254)

pidgin language A primitive system of communication that emerges when people with different native languages colonize the same region; it uses words from the various native languages and has either no or minimal grammatical structure. See also *creole language.* (p. 443)

pitch The quality of the psychological experience (sensation) of a sound that is most related to the frequency of the physical sound stimulus. (p. 213)

placebo In drug studies, an inactive substance given to subjects assigned to the nondrug group. More generally, any treatment that alters a person's behavior or feelings through the power of suggestion. (p. 52)

polyandry A mating system in which one female bonds with more than one male. For contrast, see *monogamy, polygyny, promiscuity.* (p. 87)

polygenic characteristic Any trait or characteristic for which the observed variation is affected by many genes. (p. 68)

polygyny A mating system in which one male bonds with more than one female. For contrast, see *monogamy, polyandry, promiscuity.* (p. 87)

pons The portion of the brainstem that is bounded at its lower end by the medulla and

its upper end by the midbrain and is responsible, with the medulla, for organizing reflexes more complex than spinal reflexes. (p. 123)

Ponzo illusion A visual size illusion in which two converging lines cause objects between the two lines to look larger near the converging ends of the lines and smaller near the diverging ends. (p. 256)

position relative to the horizon A pictorial cue for perceiving depth in which objects nearer the horizon seem farther away than objects displaced from the horizon. (p. 255)

positive punishment In operant conditioning, the type of punishment in which the presentation of a stimulus (such as an electric shock or scolding) when a response occurs decreases the likelihood that the response will recur. For contrast, see *negative punishment.* (p. 285)

positive reinforcement In operant conditioning, the condition in which a response results in a positive reinforcer. (p. 284)

positive reinforcer In operant conditioning, a stimulus (such as food or money) that is presented after a response and that increases the likelihood that the response will recur. (p. 284)

positron emission tomography (PET) A method for visually displaying brain activity that is based upon the uptake of a radioactive form of oxygen into active areas of the brain. (p. 116)

posttraumatic stress disorder (PTSD) A psychological disorder that is directly and explicitly tied to a particular traumatic incident or set of incidents (such as torture) that the affected person has experienced. (p. 597)

preattentive processing The analysis, at an unconscious level, in which the mind determines which stimuli are worth passing into working memory. (p. 318)

precipitating causes of a psychological disorder The events that most immediately bring on a psychological disorder in a person who is sufficiently predisposed for the disorder. See also *perpetuating* and *predisposing causes of a psychological disorder.* (p. 587)

predictable-world bias Tendency to believe that events are more predictable than they actually are. (p. 367)

predisposing causes of a psychological disorder Those conditions that are in place well before the onset of a psychological disorder and that make the person susceptible to the disorder. They may include genetic predisposition, early childhood experiences, and the sociocultural environment in which one develops. See also *perpetuating* and *precipitating causes of a psychological disorder.* (p. 587)

prefrontal cortex The front-most portion of the frontal lobe of the brain's cerebral cortex. (p. 128)

premotor areas Portions of the brain's cerebral cortex that lie directly anterior to (in front of) the motor area. They provide neural programs for producing organized movements. (p. 128)

preoperational scheme In Piaget's theory, mental structures that permit the child to symbolize objects and events that are absent, but do not permit the child to think about the operations that can be performed on objects. See also *operation, schemes.* (p. 417)

primary motor area An area in the rear part of the frontal lobe of the cerebral cortex that is directly involved in the control of movements, especially finely coordinated movements of small muscles, as in the fingers and vocal apparatus. (p. 126)

primary sensory areas Specialized areas of the cerebral cortex that receive input from sensory nerves and tracts by way of the relay nuclei in the thalamus. They include the visual area (in the occipital lobe), auditory area (in the temporal lobe), and somatosensory area (in the parietal lobe). (p. 126)

primary visual area The area in the rear-most part of the occipital lobe that receives input from the optic nerves (by way of the thalamus) and sends output to other visual-processing areas of the brain. (p. 237)

priming The implicit memory process by which a stimulus (the priming stimulus) activates (makes more retrievable) one or more memories that already exist in a person's mind. See *implicit memory.* (p. 321)

procedural memory The class of implicit memory that enables a person to perform specific learned skills or habitual responses. See *implicit memory.* (p. 334)

projection The defense mechanism by which a person consciously experiences his or her own unconscious emotion or wish as though it belongs to someone else or to some part of the environment. (p. 560)

promiscuity A mating system in which members of a group consisting of more than one male and more than one female mate with one another. For contrast, see *monogamy, polygyny, polyandry.* (p. 87)

prosocial behavior Voluntary behavior intended to benefit other people. (p. 458)

prosopagnosia An inability to recognize the faces of familiar people (also known as *face blindness*). (p. 250)

prospective memory Remembering to do something in the future. (p. 354)

proximate explanations Explanations of behavior that state the immediate environmental conditions or the mechanisms within the individual that cause the behavior to occur. For contrast, see *distal explanations.* (p. 76)

proximity principle See *Gestalt principles of grouping.*

psychoanalysis 1. The theory of the mind developed by Freud, which emphasizes the roles of unconscious mental processes, early childhood experiences, and the drives of sex and aggression in personality formation; also called *psychoanalytic theory.* (p. 556) 2. Freud's therapy technique in which such methods as free association, dream analysis, and analysis of transference are used to learn about the person's unconscious mind; the goal is to make the unconscious conscious. (p. 636)

psychodynamic theories Any theory that describes personality and its development in terms of inner mental forces that are often in conflict with one another and are shaped by experiences in early childhood. (p. 556)

psychodynamic therapy Any approach to psychotherapy that is based on the premise that psychological problems are manifestations of inner mental conflicts and that conscious awareness of those conflicts is a key to recovery. See also *psychoanalysis.* (p. 636)

psychological disorder A disturbance in a person's emotions, drives, thought processes, or behavior that (a) involves serious and relatively prolonged distress and/or impairment in ability to function, (b) is not simply a normal response to some event or set of events in the person's environment, and (c) is not explainable as an effect of poverty, prejudice, or other social forces that prevent the person from behaving adaptively, nor as a deliberate decision to act in a way that is contrary to the norms of society. (p. 578)

psychology The science of behavior and the mind. (p. 1)

psychopathy A personality trait involving amoral or antisocial behavior, coupled with a lack of empathy and an inability to form meaningful personal relationships. At its extreme, psychopathy is a personality disorder, but it can also be expressed at preclinical levels. (p. 540)

psychophysics The scientific study of the relationship between physical characteristics of stimuli and the psychological (sensory) experiences that the stimuli produce. (p. 195)

psychosurgery The surgical cutting or production of lesions in a portion of the brain to relieve a psychological disorder. (p. 633)

psychotherapy Any formal, theory-based, systematic treatment for mental problems or disorders that uses psychological means (such as dialogue or training) rather than physiological means (such as drugs) and is conducted by a trained therapist. (p. 635)

PTSD See *posttraumatic stress disorder.*

puberty Period in life in which children attain adult size and physical characteristics, including sexual maturity. (p. 406)

punishment In operant conditioning, the process through which the consequence of a response *decreases* the likelihood that the response will recur. For contrast, see *reinforcement.* (p. 285)

pupil The hole in the center of the iris of the eye through which light passes. See *iris.* (p. 226)

Pygmalion effects See *self-fulfilling prophecies.*

rationalization The defense mechanism by which a person uses conscious reasoning to justify or explain away his or her harmful or irrational behaviors or thoughts. (p. 560)

reaction formation The defense mechanism by which the mind turns a frightening wish into its safer opposite. (p. 559)

receptor potentials Electrical changes in neurons that can trigger action potentials in sensory neurons. (p. 194)

recessive gene A gene that produces its observable effects only if the individual is homozygous for that gene (that is, has that gene allele on both of the two paired chromosomes). Contrast to *dominant gene.* (p. 64)

reciprocity theory Theory proposing that apparent acts of altruism have come about through natural selection because they are actually forms of long-term cooperation rather than true altruism. See also *altruism, cooperation.* (p. 96)

reference group A group of people with whom an individual compares him- or herself for the purpose of self-evaluation. See also *social comparison.* (p. 501)

reflex A simple, relatively automatic, stimulus–response sequence mediated by the nervous system. (p. 266)

regulatory drive Any motivational state (such as hunger or thirst) that helps maintain some constancy of the body's internal environment that is necessary for survival. For contrast, see *nonregulatory drive.* (p. 153)

reinforcement In operant conditioning, the presentation of a positive reinforcer or removal of a negative reinforcer when a response occurs, which increases the likelihood that the subject will repeat the response. See *negative reinforcer, positive reinforcer.* For contrast, see *punishment.* (p. 284)

reinforcer In operant conditioning, any stimulus change that occurs after a response and tends to *increase* the likelihood that the response will be repeated. See *negative reinforcer, positive reinforcer.* (p. 281)

relative image size for familiar objects A pictorial cue for perceiving depth in which one infers the distance of familiar objects on the basis of their known actual sizes and the size of their retinal images. (p. 254)

reliability Degree to which a measurement system produces similar results each time it is used with a particular subject or set of subjects under a particular set of conditions (p. 47). Regarding diagnoses of disorders, the degree to which different diagnosticians, all trained in the use of the diagnostic system, reach the same conclusions when they independently diagnose the same individuals (p. 579)

REM (rapid-eye-movement) sleep The recurring stage of sleep during which the EEG resembles that of an alert person, rapid eye movements occur, the large muscles of the body are most relaxed, and true dreams are most likely to occur. It is sometimes called *emergent stage 1.* (p. 168)

representational insight The knowledge that an entity can stand for something other than itself. (p. 418)

repression The defense mechanism by which the mind prevents anxiety-provoking ideas from becoming conscious. (p. 558)

resistance Attempts by a patient to avoid bringing unconscious memories or wishes into consciousness. (p. 638)

response Any well-defined behavioral action, especially one that is elicited by some form of environmental stimulation or provocation. (p. 266)

resting potential The constant electrical charge that exists across the membrane of an inactive neuron. (p. 106)

retina A thin membrane of cells that lines the rear interior of the eyeball; it contains the receptor cells for vision (rods and cones). (p. 226)

retrieval The mental process by which long-term memories are brought into working memory, where they become part of the flow of thought. See also *long-term memory, working memory.* (p. 315)

retrieval cue A word, phrase, or other stimulus that helps one retrieve a specific item of information from long-term memory. (p. 349)

retrograde amnesia Loss, due to injury to the brain, of long-term memories that had been formed before the injury. Contrast to *anterograde amnesia.* (p. 345)

reversible figure A visual stimulus (usually a picture) in which any given part is seen sometimes as the *figure* and other times as the *ground.* (p. 242)

rhodopsin The photochemical in rods that undergoes structural changes in response to light and thereby initiates the transduction process for rod vision. (p. 227)

rod vision The low-acuity, high-sensitivity, noncolor vision that occurs in dim light and is mediated by rods in the retina of the eye. For contrast, see *cone vision.* (p. 228)

rods The class of receptor cells for vision that are located in the peripheral portions of the retina (away from the fovea) and are most important for seeing in very dim light. For contrast, see *cones.* (p. 227)

rumination Repetitively and passively focusing on symptoms of distress and on the possible causes and consequences of these symptoms. (p. 600)

scaffolding An expert, when instructing a novice, responding contingently to the novice's responses in a learning situation, so that the novice gradually increases his or her understanding of a problem. (p. 424)

schema The mental representation of a concept; the information stored in long-term memory that allows a person to identify a group of different events or items as members of the same category. (p. 350)

schemes Piaget's term for the mental entities that provide the basis for thought and that change in a stage-like way through development.

They contain information about the actions that one can perform on objects, either in reality or symbolically in the mind. (p. 414)

schizoid personality disorder A personality disorder in which people display little in the way of emotion, either positive or negative, and tend to avoid social relationships. (p. 616)

schizophrenia A serious class of psychological disorders that is characterized by disrupted perceptual and thought processes, often including hallucinations and delusions. (p. 607)

schizotypal personality disorder A personality disorder in which people show extreme discomfort in social situations, often bizarre patterns of thinking and perceiving, and behavioral eccentricities. (p. 616)

science An approach to answering questions that is based on the systematic collection and logical analysis of objectively observable data. (p. 1)

script A variety of schema that represents in memory the temporal organization of a category of event (such as the sequence of occurrences at a typical birthday party). (p. 351)

secure attachment Optimal type of attachment in which infants display confidence when their caregivers are present, show mild distress when temporarily left alone, and quickly reestablish contact with caregivers upon their return. Compare to *insecure-avoidant*, *insecure-resistant*, and *disorganized/disoriented attachment*. (p. 454)

selective breeding The mating of those members of a strain of animals or plants that manifest a particular characteristic, which may or may not be done deliberately, to affect the genetic makeup of future generations of that strain; can be used to assess *heritability*. (p. 68)

selective cell death (apoptosis) Early developmental process in which neurons die. (p. 111)

self-actualization In humanistic psychology, the fulfillment of drives that go beyond one's survival needs and pertain to psychological growth, creativity, and self-expression. (p. 563)

self-concept The way a person defines himself or herself. (p. 499)

self-efficacy A person's subjective sense of his or her own ability to perform a particular task or set of tasks. (p. 566)

self-esteem A person's feeling of approval and acceptance of him- or herself. (p. 500)

self-fulfilling prophecies The phenomenon by which beliefs and expectations that others have of a person—whether initially true or false—can to some degree create reality by influencing that person's self-concept and behavior. Also called Pygmalion effects. (p. 499)

self-report method A data-collection method in which the people being studied are asked to rate or describe their own behaviors or mental states. (p. 39)

self-serving attributional bias The tendency of people to attribute their successes to their own qualities and their failures to the situation. (p. 502)

semantic memory One's storehouse of explicit general knowledge, that is, of knowledge that can be expressed in words and is not mentally tied to specific experiences in one's own life. Semantic memory includes, but is not limited to, one's knowledge of word meanings. For contrasts, see *episodic memory*, *implicit memory*. (p. 332)

sensation The psychological experience associated with sound, light, or other simple stimuli and the initial information-processing steps by which sense organs and neural pathways take in stimulus information from the environment. For contrast, see *perception*. (p. 192)

sensorimotor scheme In Piaget's theory, the type of mental structure that enables an infant to act on objects that are immediately present but does not permit thought about objects that are absent. See also *schemes*. (p. 416)

sensory adaptation The temporary decrease in sensitivity to sensory stimulation that occurs when a sensory system is stimulated for a period of time, and the temporary increase in sensitivity that occurs when a sensory system is not stimulated for a period of time. See also *dark adaptation, light adaptation*. (p. 195)

sensory areas Areas of the brain's cerebral cortex that receive and analyze input from the body's senses. Separate sensory areas exist for each distinct sense. See *primary sensory areas*. (p. 193)

sensory coding The process by which information about the quality and quantity of a stimulus is preserved in the pattern of action potentials sent through sensory neurons to the central nervous system. (p. 194)

sensory memory The memory trace that preserves the original information in a sensory stimulus for a brief period (less than 1 second for sights and up to 3 seconds for sounds) following the termination of the stimulus; it is experienced as if one is still sensing the original stimulus. For contrasts, see *long-term memory, working memory*. (p. 313)

sensory neuron A neuron that carries messages from a sensory organ, through a nerve, into the brain or spinal cord. (p. 103)

sensory receptors Specialized biological structures—which in some cases are separate cells and in other cases are the sensitive tips of sensory neurons—that respond to physical stimuli by producing electrical changes that can initiate neural impulses (action potentials) in sensory neurons. (p. 193)

sensory-specific satiety The phenomenon by which a person or animal who is satiated on one food still has an appetite for another food that has a different taste. (p. 163)

serial processing The steps in the processing of sensory information that operate sequentially,

an item at a time, on the available sensory information. For contrast, see *parallel processing*. (p. 239)

shaping An operant-conditioning procedure in which successively closer approximations to the desired response are reinforced until the response finally occurs. See *reinforcement*. (p. 283)

shared attention Two individuals both attending to the same thing or event and sharing that experience. (p. 410)

short-term memory (short-term store) See *working memory*.

short-term memory span The number of pronounceable items of information (such as single, randomly chosen digits) that a person can retain in short-term (working) memory at any given time. (p. 325)

short-term store Memory store that can hold a limited amount of information for a matter of seconds. Cognitive operations are executed in the short-term store and information can be maintained indefinitely in the short-term store through operations such as rehearsal. See also *working memory*. (p. 313)

sibling contrast Tendency to emphasize and exaggerate the differences between siblings. (p. 551)

signal detection theory Proposes that the detection of a sensory stimulus is dependent upon both the physical intensity of the stimulus and the psychological state (including expectations, motivation, and alertness) of the perceiver. (p. 197)

similarity principle See *Gestalt principles of grouping*.

size constancy The perceptual ability to see an object as the same size despite change in image size as it moves farther away or closer. (p. 256)

social comparison Any process in which an individual evaluates his or her own abilities, characteristics, ideas, or achievements by comparing them with those of other people. See also *reference group*. (p. 501)

social dilemma A situation in which a particular action will (a) benefit the individual who takes it, (b) harm the individuals who don't, and (c) cause more harm than benefit to everyone if everyone takes it. (p. 527)

social facilitation The tendency to perform a task better in front of others than when alone. For contrast, see *social interference*. (p. 511)

social identity The portion of the self-concept that pertains to the social categories or groups of which the person is a part. For contrast, see *personal identity*. (p. 507)

social interference The tendency to perform a task worse in front of others than when alone. For contrast, see *social facilitation*. (p. 511)

social learning Learning occurring in a situation in which one individual comes to behave similarly to another. (p. 296)

social pressure The entire set of psychological forces that are exerted on an individual by other people or by the individual's beliefs about other people. (p. 511)

social psychology The branch of psychology that attempts to understand how the behavior and subjective experiences of individuals are influenced by the actual or imagined presence of other people. (pp. 15, 493)

social referencing The process by which infants use the nonverbal emotional expressions of a caregiver as cues to guide their behavior. (p. 410)

social-cognitive theories of personality Theories of personality that emphasize the roles of beliefs and habits of thought that are acquired through one's unique experiences in the social environment. Also called *social-learning* or *social-cognitive-learning theories.* (p. 564)

somatic portion of the peripheral motor system Neurons that act on skeletal muscles of the peripheral motor system. (p. 120)

somatosensation The set of senses that derive from the whole body—such as from the skin, muscles, and tendons—as opposed to those senses that come from the special sensory organs of the head. (p. 120)

species-typical behavior Any behavior pattern that is so characteristic of a given species of animal that it can be used to help identify that species. (p. 80)

spinal nerve A nerve that extends directly from the spinal cord. See *nerve.* For contrast, see *cranial nerve.* (p. 119)

split-parent identification Tendency for each of two siblings to identify with a different one of their two parents. (p. 551)

spontaneous recovery In both classical and operant conditioning, the return—due to passage of time with no further testing or training—of a conditioned response that had previously undergone extinction. (p. 268)

standard deviation A measure of the variability in a set of scores, determined by taking the square root of the variance. (pp. 42, A-5)

standardized score A score that is expressed in terms of the number of standard deviations the original score is from the mean of the original scores. (p. A-6)

statistical significance A statistical statement of how small the likelihood is that an obtained result occurred by chance. By convention, research findings are said to be *statistically significant* if the probability is less than 5 percent that the data could have come out as they did if the research hypothesis were wrong. (p. 44)

stereotype A mental concept by which people characterize one or more specific groups or categories of people. (p. 508)

stereotype threat The threatened feeling that occurs, during the taking of a test, when a person is reminded of the fact that he or she belongs to a group that, according to a culturally prominent stereotype, is expected to perform poorly on the test. See *stereotype.* (pp. 394, 512)

stimulus A well-defined element of the environment that can potentially act on an individual's nervous system and thereby influence the individual's behavior. (p. 266)

strange-situation test A test of an infant's attachment to a particular familiar person, in which the infant's behavior is observed in an unfamiliar room while the familiar person and a stranger move in and out of the room in a preplanned way. (p. 454)

stress-induced analgesia The reduced sensitivity to pain that occurs when one is subjected to highly arousing (stressful) conditions. (p. 212)

Stroop interference effect Named after J. Ridley Stroop, the effect by which a printed color word (such as the word *red*) interferes with a person's ability to name the color of ink in which the word is printed if the ink color is not the same as the color named by the word. (p. 316)

subject-expectancy effect Any bias in research results that derives from subjects' expectations or beliefs about how they should feel or behave in response to the variables imposed in the study. See also *bias, observer-expectancy effect.* (p. 51)

sublimation A form of displacement in which one directs his or her energies toward activities that are particularly valued by society, such as artistic, scientific, or humanitarian endeavors. (p. 559)

superordinate goals The goals shared by two or more groups, which tend to foster cooperation among the groups. (p. 531)

suprachiasmatic nucleus Nucleus (cluster of neurons) in the brain's hypothalamus that controls circadian rhythms of sleep and arousal. (p. 175)

symbolic play A type of play that includes an "as if" orientation to objects, actions, and other people. Symbolic play increases during early childhood as a result of children's growing abilities to use symbols to represent something as other than itself. (p. 293)

sympathetic division of the autonomic motor system The set of motor neurons that act upon visceral muscles and glands and mediate many of the body's responses to stressful stimulation, preparing the body for possible "fight or flight." For contrast, see *parasympathetic division of the autonomic motor system.* (p. 121)

synapse The functional connection through which neural activity in the axon of one neuron influences the action of another neuron, a muscle cell, or a glandular cell. (p. 108)

synesthesia A condition in which sensory stimulation in one modality induces a sensation in a different modality. (p. 259)

syntax The set of grammatical rules for a given language that specifies how words can be arranged to produce phrases and sentences. (p. 436)

temporal lobes The lobes of the cerebral cortex that lie in front of the occipital lobes and below the parietal and frontal lobes and that contain the auditory areas of the brain. (p. 126)

temporal-lobe amnesia The loss in memory abilities that occurs as a result of damage to structures in the limbic system that lie under the temporal lobe of the cerebral cortex. (p. 335)

teratogens External agents, such as drugs and radiation, that can have harmful effects on a developing embryo or fetus. (p. 404)

test In psychology, a data collection method in which stimuli or problems are deliberately presented by the researcher for the subject to respond to. (p. 39)

texture gradient A pictorial cue for perceiving depth in which the gradual change in size and density of textured elements (such as pebbles or blades of grass) indicates depth. (p. 254)

thalamus The brain structure that sits directly atop the brainstem; it functions as a sensory relay station, connecting incoming sensory tracts to special sensory areas of the cerebral cortex. (p. 124)

theory A belief or set of interrelated beliefs that one has about some aspect of the universe, which is used to explain observed facts and to predict new ones. See also *hypothesis.* (p. 31)

theory of mind A person's concepts of mental activity; used to refer to how people conceptualize mental activity and how they attribute intention to and predict the behavior of others. (p. 431)

three-primaries law Three different wavelengths of light (called primaries) can be used to match any color that the eye can see if they are mixed in the appropriate proportions. (p. 230)

TMS See *transcranial magnetic stimulation.*

tolerance See *drug tolerance.*

tools of intellectual adaptation Vygotsky's term for tools a culture provides for thinking and problem solving. (p. 422)

top-down control In theories of perception, mental processes that bring preexisting knowledge or expectations about an object or scene to bear upon the perception of that object or scene. For contrast, see *bottom-up control.* (p. 244)

trait A hypothetical, relatively stable, inner characteristic that influences the way a person responds to various environmental situations. (p. 536)

trait theories of personality Theories of personality that are based on the idea that people can be described and differentiated in terms of hypothetical underlying personality dimensions, called *traits,* which can be measured by questionnaires or other quantitative means. (p. 536)

transcranial magnetic stimulation (TMS) A procedure for temporarily altering the responsiveness of a localized area of the cerebral cortex by creating a magnetic field over that brain area. (p. 115) It is also used as a treatment for depression. (p. 634)

transduction The process by which a receptor cell produces an electrical change in response to physical stimulation. (p. 194)

transference The phenomenon by which a patient's unconscious feelings about a significant person in his or her life are experienced consciously as feelings about the therapist. (p. 639)

trichromatic theory Theory proposed independently by Young and Helmholtz that holds that the human ability to perceive color is mediated by three different types of receptors, each of which is most sensitive to a different range of wavelengths. (p. 230)

unconditioned response A reflexive response that does not depend upon previous conditioning or learning. For contrast, see *conditioned response*. (p. 267)

unconditioned stimulus A stimulus that elicits a reflexive response without any previous training or conditioning. For contrast, see *conditioned stimulus*. (p. 267)

universal grammar In nativist theories of language acquisition, the innate grammar that characterizes all human languages. (p. 442)

validity Degree to which a measurement system actually measures the characteristic that it is supposed to measure (p. 48). Regarding diagnoses of psychological disorders, the degree to which the disorders identified are clinically meaningful; that is, the degree to which the diagnostic labels predict real-world behaviors and treatment outcomes. (p. 581)

variability The degree to which the individual numbers in a set of numbers differ from one another or from their mean. See *variance* and *standard deviation*, which are common measures of variability. (p. 42)

variable Anything that can change or assume different values (p. 33)

variable-interval (VI) schedule In operant conditioning, a schedule of reinforcement in which an unpredictable period of time, varying around some average, must elapse between the receipt of one reinforcer and the availability of another. (p. 284)

variable-ratio (VR) schedule In operant conditioning, a schedule of reinforcement in which the response must be produced a certain *average* number of times before a reinforcer will appear, but the number needed on any given instance varies randomly around that average. (p. 284)

variance A measure of the variability of a set of scores, determined by obtaining the difference (deviation) between each score and the mean, squaring each deviation, and calculating the mean of the squared deviations. (p. A-4)

vestigial characteristics Inherited characteristics of anatomy or behavior that are no longer useful to the species but were presumably useful at an earlier time in evolution. (p. 77)

vicarious reinforcement In Bandura's social cognitive theory, learning from observing others' behaviors and their consequences, without the need to receive specific reinforcement for one's behavior. (p. 296)

visual agnosia A condition caused by damage to specific portions of the occipital and temporal lobes of the cortex, in which people cannot make sense of what they see. (p. 245)

visual dominance effect The phenomenon in which visual stimuli, when presented simultaneously with stimuli from other senses, tend to dominate awareness. (p. 258)

visual form agnosia A variety of agnosia in which people can identify some elements of what they see but cannot perceive an object's shape. (p. 245)

visual object agnosia A variety of agnosia in which people can identify and draw the shapes of objects but cannot identify the objects. (p. 245)

visuospatial sketchpad In Baddeley's theory, a component of working memory responsible for holding visual and spatial information. (p. 325)

Weber's law The idea that, within a given sensory modality (such as vision), the difference threshold (amount that the stimulus must be changed in magnitude to be perceived as different) is a constant proportion of the magnitude of the original stimulus. (p. 197)

Wernicke's aphasia A specific syndrome of loss of language ability that occurs due to damage in a particular part of the brain called *Wernicke's area*. Speech in a person with this disorder typically retains its grammatical structure but loses its meaning due to the speaker's failure to provide meaningful content words (nouns, verbs, adjectives, and adverbs); also called fluent aphasia. For contrast, see *Broca's aphasia*. (p. 139)

Westermarck effect Observation that people who are raised together from early in childhood rarely develop a sexual attraction to one another. (p. 306)

working memory The memory store that is considered to be the main workplace of the mind. Among other things, it is the seat of conscious thought and reasoning. For contrast, see *sensory memory, long-term memory*. (p. 313)

z score The simplest form of a standardized score; it is the score minus the mean divided by the standard deviation. (p. A-6)

zone of proximal development In Vygotsky's theory, the range or set of activities that a child can do in collaboration with more competent others but cannot yet do alone. (p. 424)

zygote The single cell that is formed when an egg and sperm cell unite; the first, single-cell form of a newly developing individual. (p. 64)

zygotic (or germinal) phase Developmental phase lasting approximately two weeks in humans, which starts when an egg is fertilized and ends when the zygote implants in the uterine wall. (p. 402)

References

AbdelMalik, P., Husted, J., Chow, E., & Bassett, A. (2003). Childhood head injury and expression of schizophrenia in multiply affected families. *Archives of General Psychiatry, 60,* 231–236.

Aberson, C. L., Shoemaker, C., & Tomolillo, C. (2004). Implicit bias and contact: The role of interethnic friendships. *Journal of Social Psychology, 144,* 335–347.

Abi-Dargham, A., & Grace, A. A. (2011). Dopamine and schizophrenia. In D. R. Weinberg & P. Harrison (Eds.), *Schizophrenia.* Hoboken, NJ: Wiley.

Abma, J. C., Martinez, G. M., Mosher, W. D., & Dawson, B. S. (2004). Teenagers in the United States: Sexual activity, contraceptive use, and childbearing, 2002. National Center for Health Statistics. *Vital Health Statistics, 23,* 24.

Abramovitch, A., Abramovitch, J. S., & Mittelman, A. (2013). The neuropsychology of adult obsessive-compulsive disorder: A meta-analysis. *Clinical Psychological Review, 33,* 1163–1171.

Abramson, L. Y., Matelsky, G. I., & Alloy, L. B. (1989). Hopelessness depression: A theory-based subtype of depression. *Psychological Review, 96,* 358–372.

Ackerman, P. L., & Heggestad, E. D. (1997). Intelligence, personality, and interests: Evidence for overlapping traits. *Psychological Bulletin, 121,* 219–245.

Adams, H. E., Wright, L. W., & Lohr, B. A. (1996). Is homophobia associated with homosexual arousal? *Journal of Abnormal Psychology, 105,* 440–445.

Adamson, R. E. (1952). Functional fixedness as related to problem solving. *Journal of Experimental Psychology, 44,* 288–291.

Adey, P. S., & Shayer, M. (1992). Accelerating the development of formal thinking in middle and high school students: II. Postproject effects on science achievement. *Journal of Research in Science Teaching, 29,* 81–92.

Adler, A. (1930). Individual psychology. In C. Murchison (Ed.), *Psychologies of 1930.* Worcester, MA: Clark University Press.

Adolfsson, B., Andersson, I., Elofsson, S., Rössner, S., & Undén, A. (2005). Locus of control and weight reduction. *Patient Education & Counseling, 56,* 55–56.

Adolph, K. E., Vereijken, B., & Shrout, P. E. (2003). What changes in infant walking and why? *Child Development, 74,* 475–497.

Agras, S., Sylvester, D., & Oliveau, D. (1969). The epidemiology of common fears and phobias. *Comprehensive Psychiatry, 10,* 151–156.

Ahn, H., & Wampold, B. E. (2001). Where oh where are the specific ingredients? A meta-analysis of component studies in counseling and psychotherapy. *Journal of Counseling Psychology, 48,* 251–257.

Ainsworth, M. D. S. (1979). Attachment as related to mother–infant interaction. *Advances in the Study of Behaviour, 9,* 2–52.

Ainsworth, M. D. S. (1989). Attachments beyond infancy. *American Psychologist, 44,* 709–716.

Ainsworth, M. D. S., Blehar, M. C., Waters, E., & Wall, S. (1978). *Patterns of attachment: A psychological study of the strange situation.* Hillsdale, NJ: Erlbaum.

Akiskal, H. S. (2002). Classification, diagnosis and boundaries of bipolar disorders: A review. In M. Mario, H. S. Akiskal, J. J. López-Ibor, & N. Sartorius (Eds.), *Bipolar disorder* (pp. 1–52). West Sussex, England: Wiley.

Albert, D., Chein, J., & Steinberg, L. (2013). The teenage brain: Peer influences on adolescent decision making. *Current Directions in Psychological Science, 22,* 114–120.

Albert, M. K. (2007). Mechanisms of modal and amodal interpolation. *Psychological Review, 114,* 455–469.

Alberto, P. A., & Troutman, A. C. (2005). *Applied behavior analysis for teachers* (7th ed.). Upper Saddle River, NJ: Prentice Hall.

Alexander, G. M., & Wilcox, T. (2012). Sex differences in early infancy. *Child Development Perspectives, 6,* 400–406.

Alicke, M. D., Klotz, M. L., Breitenbecher, D. L., Yurak, T. J., & Vredenburg, D. S. (1995). Personal contact, individuation, and the better-than-average effect. *Journal of Personality and Social Psychology, 68,* 804–825.

Allen, N. B., & Badcock, P. B. T. (2006). Darwinian models of depression: A review of evolutionary accounts of mood and mood disorders. *Progress in Neuro-Psychopharmacology & Biological Psychiatry, 30,* 815–826.

Allen, P., Laroi, F., McGuire, P. K., & Aleman, A. (2008). The hallucinating brain: A review of structural and functional neuroimaging studies of hallucinations. *Neuroscience & Biobehavioral Reviews, 32,* 175–191.

Allison, T., & Cicchetti, D. V. (1976). Sleep in mammals: Ecological and constitutional correlates. *Science, 194,* 732–734.

Allman, J., & Brothers, L. (1994). Faces, fear and the amygdala. *Nature, 372,* 613–614.

Alloway, T. P., & Alloway, R. G. (2010). Investigating the predictive roles of working memory and IQ in academic attainment. *Journal of Experimental Child Psychology, 106,* 20–29.

Alloy, L. B., Abramson, L. Y., Whitehouse, W. G., Hogan, M. E., Panzarella, C., & Rose, D. T. (2006). Prospective incidence of first onsets and recurrence of depression in individuals at high and low cognitive risk for depression. *Journal of Abnormal Psychology, 115,* 145–156.

Allport, G. W. (1935). Attitudes. In C. Murchison (Ed.), *Handbook of social psychology.* Worcester, MA: Clark University Press.

Allport, G. W. (1937). *Personality: A psychological interpretation.* New York, NY: Holt.

Allport, G. W. (1968). The historical background of modern social psychology. In G. Lindzey & E. Aronson (Eds.), *The handbook of social psychology* (2nd ed., Vol. 1). Reading, MA: Addison-Wesley.

Almeida, D. M., & Kessler, R. C. (1998). Everyday stressors and gender differences in daily distress. *Journal of Personality and Social Psychology, 75,* 670–680.

Altmann, E. M., & Gray, W. D. (2002). Forgetting to remember: The functional relationship of decay to interference. *Psychological Science, 13,* 27–33.

Alzheimers Association. (2013). 10 early signs and symptoms of Alzheimer's. Retrieved from http://www.alz.org/alzheimers_disease_10_signs_of_alzheimers.asp#typical

Ambady, N., Shih, M., Kim, A., & Pittinsky, T. L. (2001). Stereotype susceptibility in children: Effects of identity activation on quantitative performance. *Psychological Science, 12,* 385–390.

Ambelas, A. (1987). Life events and mania: A special relationship? *British Journal of Psychiatry, 150,* 235–240.

Amedi, A., Raz, N., Pianka, P., Malach, R., & Zohary, E. (2003). Early "visual" cortex activation correlates with superior verbal memory performance in the blind. *Nature Neuroscience, 6,* 758–766.

American Psychiatric Association. (2013). *Diagnostic and statistical manual of mental disorders, fifth edition: DSM-5.* Washington, DC: Author.

American Psychological Association. (2002). Ethical principles of psychologists and a code of conduct. *American Psychologist, 57,* 1060–1073.

American Psychological Association. (2010). *Publication manual of the American Psychological Association* (6th ed.). Washington, DC: Author.

Amick, H. R., Gartlehner, G., Gaynes, B. N., Forneris, C., Asher, G. N., Morgan, L. C., . . . Lohr, K. N. (2015). Comparative benefits and harms of second generation antidepressants and cognitive behavioral therapies in initial treatment of major depressive disorder: Systematic review and meta-analysis. *BMJ, 351,* h6019.

Anastasi, A. (1988). *Psychological testing* (6th ed.). New York, NY: Macmillian.

Anders, S., Birbaumer, N., Sadowski, B., Erb, M., Mader, I., Grodd, W., & Lotze, M. (2004). Parietal somatosensory association cortex mediates affective blindsight. *Nature Neuroscience, 7,* 339–340.

Anderson, C. A., Lindsay, J. J., & Bushman, B. J. (1999). Research in the psychological laboratory: Truth or triviality? *Current Directions in Psychological Science, 8,* 3–9.

Anderson, J. R. (2000). *Learning and memory* (2nd ed.). Hoboken, NJ: Wiley.

Anderson, R. J., Frye, M. A., Abulseoud, O. A., Lee, K. H., McGillivary, J. A., Beck, M., Tye, S. J. (2012). Deep brain stimulation for treatment-resistant depression: Efficacy, safety and mechanisms of action. *Neuroscience Biobehavioral Review, 36,* 1920–1933.

Andersson, M. (2005). Evolution of classical polyandry: Three steps to female emancipation. *Ethology, 111,* 1–23.

Andreasen, N. C. (1987). Creativity and mental illness: Prevalence rates in writers and their first-degree relatives. *American Journal of Psychiatry, 144,* 1288–1292.

Antony, M. M. (2011). Recent advances in the treatment of anxiety disorders. *Canadian Psychology/Psychologie canadienne, 52,* 1–9.

Antony, M. M., & Barlow, D. H. (2002). Specific phobias. In D. H. Barlow, *Anxiety and its disorders: The nature and treatment of anxiety and panic* (2nd ed.). New York, NY: Guilford.

Antrobus, J. (2000). Theories of dreaming. In M. H. Kryger, T. Roth, & W. C. Dement (Eds.), *Principles and practice of sleep medicine* (3rd ed.). Philadelphia, PA: W. B. Saunders.

Anzures, G., Wheeler, A., Quinn, P. C., Pascalis, O., Slater, A. M., Heron-Delaney, M., Tanaka, J. W., & Lee, K. (2012). Brief daily exposure to Asian females reverses perceptual narrowing for Asian faces in Caucasian infants. *Journal of Experimental Child Psychology, 112,* 484–495.

Archer, J. (2004). Sex differences in aggression in real-world settings: A meta-analytic review. *Review of General Psychology, 8,* 291–322.

Archer, J. (2006). Testosterone and human aggression: An evaluation of the challenge hypothesis. *Neuroscience and Biobehavioral Reviews, 30,* 319–345.

Arffa, S. (2007). The relationship of intelligence to executive function and non-executive function measures in a sample of average, above average, and gifted youth. *Archives of Clinical Neuropsychology, 22,* 969–978.

Arieti, S. (1966). Schizophrenic cognition. In P. Hook & J. Zubin (Eds.), *Psychopathology of schizophrenia.* New York, NY: Grune & Stratton.

Arnett, J. J. (1995). The young and the reckless: Adolescent reckless behavior. *Current Directions in Psychological Science, 4,* 67–71.

Arnett, J. J. (2000). Emerging adulthood: A theory of development from the late teens through the twenties. *American Psychologist, 55,* 469–480.

Arnett, J. J. (2004). *Emerging adulthood: The winding road from late teens through the twenties.* Oxford, England: Oxford University Press.

Arnett, J. J. (2007). Emerging adulthood: What is it, and what is it good for? *Child Development Perspective, 1,* 68–73.

Aron, E., & Aron, A. (1997). Sensory-processing sensitivity and its relation to introversion and emotionality. *Journal of Personality and Social Psychology, 73,* 345–368.

Aron, E., Aron, A., & Davies, K. M. (2005). Adult shyness: The interaction of temperamental sensitivity and an adverse childhood environment. *Personality and Social Psychology Bulletin, 31,* 181–197.

Aron, E. N., Aron, A., & Jagiellowicz, J. (2012). Sensory processing sensitivity: A review in the light of the evolution of biological responsivity. *Personality and Social Psychology Review, 16,* 262–282.

Aronson, J., Fried, C., & Good, C. (2002). Reducing the effects of stereotype threat on African American college students by shaping theories of intelligence. *Journal of Experimental Social Psychology, 38,* 113–125.

Aronson, J., Lustina, M. J., Good, C., Keough, K., Steele, C. M., & Brown, J. (1999). When white men can't do math: Necessary and sufficient factors in stereotype threat. *Journal of Experimental Social Psychology, 35,* 29–46.

Asch, S. E. (1952). *Social psychology.* Englewood Cliffs, NJ: Prentice Hall.

Asch, S. E. (1956). Studies of independence and conformity: I. A minority of one against a unanimous majority. *Psychological Monographs: General and Applied, 70*(9, Whole No. 416).

Ash, I. K., & Wiley, J. (2006). The nature of restructuring in insight: An individual-differences approach. *Psychonomic Bulletin & Review, 13,* 66–73.

Ashton, M. C., & Lee, K. (2009). The HEXACO-60: A short measure of the major dimensions of personality. *Journal of Personality Assessment, 91,* 340–345.

Aslin, R. N., & Jackson, R. W. (1979). Accommodative-convergence in young infants: Development of a synergistic sensory-motor system. *Canadian Journal of Psychology, 33,* 222–231.

Astill, R. G., Van der Heijden, K. B., Van IJzendoorn, M. H., & Van Someren, E. J. W. (2012). Sleep, cognition, and behavioral problems in school-age children: A century of research meta-analyzed. *Psychological Bulletin, 138,* 1109–1138.

Astington, J. W., & Hughes, C. (2013). Theory of mind: Self-reflection and social understanding. In P. D. Zelazo (Ed.), *Oxford handbook of developmental psychology* (Vol. 2, pp. 398–424). Oxford, England: Oxford University Press.

Atance, C. M., & O'Neill, D. K. (2004). Acting and planning on the basis of a false belief: Its effects on 3-year-old children's reasoning about their own false beliefs. *Developmental Psychology, 40,* 953–964.

Atkin, O. (1980). *Models of architectural knowledge.* London, England: Pion.

Atkinson, R. C., & Shiffrin, R. M. (1968). Human memory: A proposed system and its control processes. In K. W. Spence & J. T. Spence (Eds.), *The psychology of learning and motivation: Advances in research and theory* (Vol. 2, pp. 89–195). San Diego, CA: Academic Press.

Au, T. K., Knightly, L. M., Jun, S.-A., & Oh, J. S. (2002). Overhearing a language during childhood. *Psychological Science, 13,* 238–243.

Ayduk, O., Mendoza-Denton, R., Mischel, W., Downey, G., Peake, P., & Rodriguez, M. L. (2000). Regulating the interpersonal self: Strategic self-regulation for coping with rejection sensitivity. *Journal of Personality and Social Psychology, 79,* 776–792.

Ayuso-Mateos, J. L. (2000). Global burden of schizophrenia in the year 2000. *World Health Organization*. Retrieved July 13, 2016. http://www.who.int/healthinfo/statistics/bod_schizophrenia.pdf

Aziz-Zadeh, L., Wilson, S. M., Rizzolatti, G., & Iacoboni, M. (2006). Congruent embodied representations for visually presented actions and linguistic phrases describing actions. *Current Biology, 16*, 1818–1823.

Baars, B. J., & Franklin, S. (2003). How conscious experience and working memory interact. *Trends in Cognitive Sciences, 7*, 166–172.

Baas, M., Nijstad, B. A., Boot, N. C., & De Dreu, C. K. W. (2016). Mad genius revisited: Vulnerability to psychopathology, biobehavioral approach-avoidance, and creativity. *Psychological Bulletin, 142*, 668–692.

Backhaus, J., Hoeckesfeld, R., Born, J., Hohagen, F., & Junghanns, K. (2008). Immediate as well as delayed post learning sleep but not wakefulness enhances declarative memory consolidation in children. *Neurobiology of Learning and Memory, 89*, 76–80.

Baddeley, A. (1986). *Working memory*. Oxford, England: Clarendon.

Baddeley, A. (2003). Working memory: Looking back and looking forward. *Nature Reviews Neuroscience, 4*, 829–839.

Baddeley, A. (2006). Working memory: An overview. In S. J. Pickering (Ed.), *Working memory and education*. San Diego, CA: Academic Press.

Baddeley, A., Thomson, N., & Buchanan, M. (1975). Word length and the structure of short-term memory. *Journal of Verbal Learning and Verbal Behavior, 14*, 575–589.

Baer, D. M., Wolf, M. M., & Risley, R. R. (1968). Some current dimensions of applied behavioral analysis. *Journal of Applied Behavioral Analysis, 1*, 91–97.

Bagger, J., Li, A., & Gutek, B. A. (2008). How much do you value your family and does it matter? The joint effects of family identity salience, family-interference-with-work, and gender. *Human Relations, 61*, 187–211.

Bagnall, M., du Lac, S., & Mauk, M. (2013). Cerebellum. In L. R. Squire, D. Berg, F. E. Bloom, S. du Lac, A. Ghosh, & N. C. Spitzer (Eds.), *Fundamental neuroscience* (4th ed., pp. 667–696). Boston, MA: Elsevier.

Baillargeon, R. (1987). Object permanence in 3 1/2- and 4 1/2-month-old infants. *Developmental Psychology, 23*, 655–664.

Baillargeon, R. (1994). How do infants learn about the physical world? *Current Directions in Psychological Science, 3*, 133–140.

Baillargeon, R. (1998). Infants' understanding of the physical world. In M. Sabourin, F. Craik, & M. Robert (Eds.), *Advances in psychological science* (Vol. 2, pp. 503–529). Hove, England: Psychology Press.

Baillargeon, R. (2004). Infants' physical world. *Current Directions in Psychological Science, 13*, 89–94.

Baillargeon, R. (2008). Innate ideas revisited. *Perspectives in Psychological Science, 3*, 2–13.

Baillargeon, R. H., Zoccolillo, M., Keenan, K., Côté, S., Pérusse, D., Wu, H.-X., Boivin, M., & Tremblay, R. E. (2007). Gender differences in physical aggression: A prospective population-based survey of children before and after 2 years of age. *Developmental Psychology, 43*, 12–26.

Bakeman, R., Adamson, L. B., Konner, M., & Barr, R. (1990). !Kung infancy: The social context of object exploration. *Child Development, 61*, 794–809.

Baker, R. R., & Bellis, M. A. (2007). Human sperm competition: Ejaculate adjustment by males and the function of masturbation. In T. K. Shackelford & N. Pound (Eds.), *Sperm competition in humans: Classic and contemporary readings* (pp. 141–176). New York, NY: Springer.

Baker, S. T., Friedman, O., & Leslie, A. M. (2010). The opposites task: Using general rules to test cognitive flexibility in preschoolers. *Journal of Cognition and Development, 11*, 240–254.

Bakermans-Kranenburg, M. J., & van IJzendoorn, M. H. (2007). Research review: Genetic vulnerability or differential susceptibility in child development: The case of attachment. *Journal of Child Psychology and Psychiatry, 48*, 1160–1173.

Bakermans-Kranenburg, M. J., van IJzendoorn, M. H., Pijlman, F. T. A., Mesman, J., & Juffer, F. (2008). Experimental evidence for differential susceptibility: Dopamine D4 receptor polymorphism (DRD4 VNTR) moderates intervention effects on toddlers' externalizing behavior in a randomized control trial. *Developmental Psychology, 44*, 293–300.

Bakin, J. S., South, D. A., & Weinberger, N. M. (1996). Induction of receptive field plasticity in the auditory cortex of the guinea pig during instrumental avoidance conditioning. *Behavioral Neuroscience, 110*, 905–913.

Balaban, M. T., & Waxman, S. R. (1997). Do words facilitate object categorization in 9-month-old infants? *Journal of Experimental Child Psychology, 64*, 3–26.

Baldwin, D. A. (2000). Interpersonal understanding fuels knowledge acquisition. *Current Directions in Psychological Science, 9*, 40–45.

Ball, G. F., & Hulse, S. H. (1998). Birdsong. *American Psychologist, 53*, 37–58.

Bandura, A. (1962). *Social learning through imitation*. Lincoln: University of Nebraska Press.

Bandura, A. (1986). *Social foundations of thought and action: A social cognitive theory*. Englewood Cliffs, NJ: Prentice Hall.

Bandura, A. (1997). *Self-efficacy: The exercise of control*. New York, NY: Freeman.

Bandura, A. (2006). Toward a psychology of human agency. *Perspectives on Psychological Science, 1*, 164–180.

Bandura, A., Adams, N. E., & Beyer, J. (1977). Cognitive processes mediating behavioral change. *Journal of Personality and Social Psychology, 35*, 125–139.

Bandura, A., Cioffi, D., Taylor, C. B., & Brouillard, M. E. (1988). Perceived self-efficacy in coping with cognitive stressors and opioid activation. *Journal of Personality and Social Psychology, 55*, 479–488.

Bandura, A., & Locke, E. A. (2003). Negative self-efficacy and goal effects revisited. *Journal of Applied Psychology, 88*, 87–99.

Bandura, A., O'Leary, A., Taylor, C. B., Gauthier, J., & Gossard, D. (1987). Perceived self-efficacy and pain control: Opioid and nonopioid mechanisms. *Journal of Personality and Social Psychology, 53*, 563–571.

Banissy, M. J., Stewart, L., Muggleton, N. G., Griffiths, T. D., Walsh, V. Y., Ward, J., & Kanai, R. (2012). Grapheme-color and tone-color synesthesia is associated with structural brain changes in visual regions implicated in color, form, and motion. *Cognitive Neuroscience, 3*, 29–35.

Barber, N. (2003). Paternal investment prospects and cross-national differences in single parenthood. *Cross-Cultural Research, 37*, 163–177.

Barch, D. M. (2003). Cognition in schizophrenia: Does working memory work? *Current Directions in Psychological Science, 12*, 146–150.

Bargh, J. A., & McKenna, K. Y. A. (2004). The internet in social life. *Annual Review of Psychology, 55*, 573–590.

Barkley, R. A. (2001). Executive function and ADHD: A reply. *Journal of the American Academy of Child and Adolescent Psychiatry, 40*, 501–502.

Barlow, D. H. (2002). The nature of anxious apprehension. In D. H. Barlow, *Anxiety and its disorders* (2nd ed.). New York, NY: Guilford.

Barlow, D. H. (2004). Psychological treatments. *American Psychologist, 9*, 869–877.

Barnes, C. M., & Drake, C. L. (2015). Prioritizing sleep health: Public health policy recommendations. *Psychological Science, 10*, 733–737.

Barnes, T. R. E., & Marder, S. R. (2011). Principles of pharmacological treatment in schizophrenia. In D. R. Weinberg & P. Harrison (Eds.), *Schizophrenia* (pp. 515–524). Hoboken, NJ: Wiley-Blackwell.

Barnett, R. C., & Baruch, G. K. (1987). Social roles, gender, and psychological distress. In R. C. Barnett, L. B. Biener, & G. K. Baruch (Eds.), *Gender and stress*. New York, NY: Free Press.

Barnett, S. A. (1975). *The study of rat behavior* (Rev. ed.). Chicago, IL: University of Chicago Press.

Barnhofer, T., Hubntenburg, J. M., Lifshitz, M., Wild, J., Antonova, E., & Margulies, D. S. (2016). How mindfulness training may help to reduce vulnerability for recurrent depression: A neuroscientific perspective. *Clinical Psychological Science, 4*, 328–343.

Baron, A., & Banaji, M. R. (2006). The development of implicit attitudes. *Psychological Science, 17*, 53–58.

Baron-Cohen, S. (1995). *Mindblindness: An essay on autism and theory of mind*. Cambridge, MA: Bradford Books/MIT Press.

Baron-Cohen, S., Leslie, A. M., & Frith, U. (1985). Does the autistic child have a "theory of mind"? *Cognition, 21*, 37–46.

Barone, D. A., & Krieger, A. C. (2015). The function of sleep. *AIMS Neuroscience, 2*, 71–90.

Barrett, T. M., Davis, E. F., & Needham, A. (2007). Learning about tools in infancy. *Developmental Psychology, 43*, 352–368.

Barrouillet, P., & Camos, V. (2012). As time goes by: Temporal constraints in working memory. *Current Directions in Psychological Science, 21*, 413–419.

Barry, D., Sullivan, B., & Petry, N. M. (2009). Comparable efficacy of contingent management for cocaine dependence among African American, Hispanic, and White methadone maintenance clients. *Psychology of Addictive Behaviors, 23*, 168–174.

Barry, R. A., Kochanska, G., & Philibert, R. A. (2008). G x E interaction in the organization of attachment: Mother's responsiveness as a moderator of children's genotypes. *Journal of Child Psychology and Psychiatry, 49*, 1313–1320.

Barsh, G. S., Farooqi, S., & O'Rahilly, S. (2000). Genetics of bodyweight regulation. *Nature, 404*, 644–651.

Bartlett, F. C. (1932). *Remembering: A study in experimental and social psychology*. Cambridge, England: Cambridge University Press.

Bartoshuk, L. M., & Beauchamp, G. K. (1994). Chemical senses. *Annual Review of Psychology, 45*, 419–449.

Bartoshuk, L. M., Duffy, V. D., & Miller, I. J. (1994). PTC/PROP tasting: Anatomy, psychophysics, and sex effects. *Physiology & Behavior, 56*, 1165–1171.

Basbaum, A. I., & Fields, H. L. (1984). Endogenous pain control systems: Brainstem spinal pathways and endorphin circuitry. *Annual Review of Neuroscience, 7*, 309–338.

Basbaum, A. I., & Jessell, T. M. (2000). The perception of pain. In E. R. Kandel, J. H. Schwartz, & T. M. Jessell (Eds.), *Principles of neuroscience* (4th ed.). New York, NY: McGraw-Hill.

Baskin, T. W., Tierney, S. C., Minami, T., & Wampold, B. E. (2003). Establishing specificity in psychotherapy: A meta-analysis of structural equivalence of placebo controls. *Journal of Consulting and Clinical Psychology, 71*, 973–979.

Bateson, P. (2000). What must be known in order to understand imprinting? In C. Heyes & L. Huber (Eds.), *The evolution of cognition*. Cambridge, MA: MIT Press.

Bateson, P. (2002). The corpse of a wearisome debate. *Science, 297*, 2212–2213.

Batterham, R. L., Cohen, M. A., Ellis, S. M., Le Roux, C. W., Withers, D. J., Frost, G. S., . . . Bloom, S. R. (2003). Inhibition of food intake in obese subjects by peptide YY3–36. *New England Journal of Medicine, 349*, 941–948.

Batty, G. D., Der, G., Macintyre, S., Deary, I. J. (2006). Does IQ explain socioeconomic inequalities in health? Evidence from a population based cohort study in the west of Scotland. *British Medical Journal, 332*, 580–584.

Bauer, P. J. (2013). Memory. In P. D. Zelazo (Ed.), *Oxford handbook of developmental psychology* (Vol. 1, pp. 505–541). Oxford, England: Oxford University Press.

Bauer, P. J., & Coyne, M. J. (1997). When the name says it all: Preschoolers' recognition and use of the gendered nature of common proper names. *Social Development, 6*, 271–291.

Baumard, N., Andre, J. B., & Sperber, D. (2013). A mutualistic approach to morality: The evolution of fairness by partner choice. *Behavioral and Brain Sciences, 36*, 59–122.

Baumeister, R. F., Dori, G. A., & Hastings, S. (1998). Belongingness and temporal bracketing in personal accounts of changes in self-esteem. *Journal of Research in Personality, 32*, 222–235.

Baumgart, F., Gaschler-Markefski, B., Woldorff, M. G., Heinze, H., & Scheich, H. (1999). A movement-sensitive area in auditory cortex. *Nature, 400*, 724–726.

Baumrind, D. (1964). Some thoughts on ethics of research: After reading Milgram's "Behavioral study of obedience." *American Psychologist, 19*, 421–423.

Baumrind, D. (1967). Child care practices anteceding three patterns of preschool behavior. *Genetic Psychology Monographs, 75*, 43–88.

Baumrind, D. (1971). Current patterns of parental authority. *Developmental Psychology Monograph, 4*, 1–103.

Baumrind, D. (1986). *Familial antecedents of social competence in middle childhood*. Unpublished monograph, University of California, Institute of Human Development, Berkeley.

Baumrind, D. (1991). The influence of parenting style on adolescent competence and substance use. *Journal of Early Adolescence, 11*, 56–95.

Beall, A. T., & Tracy, J. L. (2013). Women are more likely to wear red or pink at peak fertility. *Psychological Science, 24*, 1837–1841.

Bechtoldt, H., Norcross, J. C., Wyckoff, L. A., Pokrywa, M. L., & Campbell, L. F. (2001). Theoretical orientations and employment settings of clinical and counseling psychologists: A comparative study. *The Clinical Psychologist, 54*, 3–6.

Beck, A. T., Brown, G., Eidelson, J. I., Steer, R. A., & Riskind, J. H. (1987). Differentiating anxiety and depression: A test of the cognitive content-specificity hypothesis. *Journal of Abnormal Psychology, 96*, 179–183.

Beck, A. T., & Weishaar, M. (2011). Cognitive therapy. In R. J. Corsini & D. Wedding (Eds.), *Current psychotherapies* (9th ed.). Belmont, CA: Brooks/Cole.

Beck, A. T., & Young, J. E. (1985). Depression. In D. H. Barlow (Ed.), *Clinical handbook of psychological disorders: A step-by-step treatment manual*. New York, NY: Guilford.

Beck, D. M. (2010). The appeal of the brain in the popular press. *Perspectives on Psychological Science, 5*, 762–766.

Beck, M., & Galef, B. G. (1989). Social influences on the selection of a protein-sufficient diet by Norway rats (*Rattus norvegicus*). *Journal of Comparative Psychology, 103*, 132–139.

Becker, A. E., Roberts, A. L., Perloe, A., Bainivualiku, A., Richards, L. K., Gilman, S. E., & Striegel-Moore, R. H. (2010). Youth health-risk behavior assessment in Fiji: The reality of global school-based student health survey content adapted for ethnic Fijian girls. *Ethnicity & Health, 15*, 181–197.

Becker, E. S., Goodwin, R., Hölting, C., Hoyer, J., & Margraf, J. (2003). Content of worry in the community: What do people with generalized anxiety disorder or other disorders worry about? *Journal of Nervous and Mental Disease, 191*, 688–691.

Beckerman, S., & Valentine, P. (Eds.). (2002). *Partible paternity: The theory and practice of multiple fatherhood in South America*. Gainsville: University of Florida Press.

Behrens, M., Foerster, S., Staehler, F., Raguse, J.-D., & Meyerhof, W. (2007). Gustatory expression pattern of the human TAS2R bitter receptor gene family reveals a heterogeneous population of bitter taste receptor cells. *Journal of Neuroscience, 27,* 12630–12640.

Behrman, B. W. & Davey, S. L. (2001). Eyewitness identification in actual criminal cases: An archival analysis. *Law and Human Behavior, 25,* 475–491.

Beilin, H. (1992). Piaget's enduring contribution to developmental psychology. *Developmental Psychology, 28,* 191–204.

Beilock, S. L., Kulp, C. A., Holt, L. E., & Carr, T. H. (2004). More on the fragility of performance: Choking under pressure in mathematical problem solving. *Journal of Experimental Psychology: General, 133,* 584–600.

Beilock, S. L., Rydell, R. J., & McConnell, A. R. (2007). Stereotype threat and working memory: Mechanisms, alleviation, and spillover. *Journal of Experimental Psychology: General, 136,* 256–276.

Bell, M. A., Wolfe, C. D., & Adkins, D. R. (2007). Frontal lobe development during infancy and childhood: Contributions of brain electrical activity temperament, and language to individual differences in working memory and inhibition control. In D. Coch, K. W. Fischer, & G. Dawson (Eds.), *Human behavior, learning, and the developing brain: Typical development* (pp. 247–276). New York, NY: Guilford.

Belmaker, R. (2004). Bipolar disorder. *New England Journal of Medicine, 351,* 476–486.

Belsky, J. (2005). Differential susceptibility to rearing influence. In B. J. Ellis & D. F. Bjorklund (Eds.), *The origins of the social mind: Evolutionary psychology and child development* (pp. 139–163). New York, NY: Guilford.

Belsky, J. (2007). Experience in childhood and the development of reproductive strategies. *Acta Psychologica Sinica, 39,* 454–468.

Belsky, J., Bakermans-Kranenburg, M. J., & van IJzendoorn, M. H. (2007). For better *and* worse: Differential susceptibility to environmental influences. *Current Directions in Psychological Science, 16,* 300–304.

Belsky, J., & Pluess, M. (2009). Beyond disthesis-stress: Differential susceptibility to environmental influences. *Psychological Bulletin, 135,* 885–908.

Belsky, J., Steinberg, L., & Draper, P. (1991). Childhood experience, interpersonal development, and reproductive strategy: An evolutionary theory of socialization. *Child Development, 62,* 647–670.

Bender, C. E., Herzing, D. L., & Bjorklund, D. F. (2009). Evidence of teaching in Atlantic Spotted Dolphins (*Stenella frontalis*) by mother dolphins foraging in the presence of their calves. *Animal Cognition, 12,* 43–53.

Benedict, H. (1979). Early lexical development A: Comprehension and production. *Journal of Child Language, 6,* 183–200.

Benenson, J. F. (2005). Sex differences. In B. Hopkins (Ed.), *The Cambridge encyclopedia of child development* (pp. 366–373). New York, NY: Cambridge University Press.

Benenson, J. F., Pascoe, J., & Radmore, N. (2007). Children's altruistic behavior in the dictator game. *Evolution and Human Behavior, 28,* 168–173.

Benham, B. (2008). The ubiquity of deception and the ethics of deceptive research. *Bioethics, 22,* 147–156.

Benjamin, J., Ebstein, R. P., & Lesch, K. (1998). Genes for personality traits: Implications for psychology. *International Journal of Neuropsychopharmacology, 1,* 153–168.

Berg, E. A. (1948). A simple objective technique for measuring flexibility in thinking. *Journal of General Psychology, 39,* 15–22. Reproduced by permission of Taylor & Francis Ltd. http://www.tandf.co.uk/journals and Taylor & Francis LLC http://www.tandfonline.com

Berglund, A., & Rosenqvist, G. (2001). Male pipefish prefer ornamental females. *Animal Behaviour, 61,* 345–350.

Bergman, L. R., Ferrer-Wreder, L., & Žukauskienė, R. (2015). Career outcomes of adolescents with below average IQ: Who succeeded against the odds? *Intelligence, 52,* 9–17.

Bering, J. M., & Bjorklund, D. F. (2007). The serpent's gift: Evolutionary psychology and consciousness. In P. D. Zelazo, M. Moscovitch, & E. Thompson, E. (Eds.), *Cambridge handbook of consciousness* (pp. 595–627). New York, NY: Cambridge University Press.

Bering, J. M., & Povenilli, D. J. (2003). Comparing cognitive development. In D. Maestripieri (Ed.), *Primate psychology*. Cambridge, MA: Harvard University Press.

Berk, L. E. (1986). Relationship of elementary school children's private speech to behavioral accompaniment to task, attention, and task performance. *Developmental Psychology, 22,* 671–680.

Berk, L. E. (2005). Why parenting matters. In S. Olfman (Ed.), *Childhood lost: How American culture is failing our kids* (pp. 19–53). Westport, CT: Praeger.

Berk, L. E., & Lewis, N. G. (1977). Sex role and social behavior in four school environments. *The Elementary School Journal, 77,* 205–217.

Berk, L. E., Mann, T., & Ogan, A. (2006). Make-believe play: Wellspring for development of self-regulation. In D. G. Singer, R. M. Golinkoff, & K. Hirsh-Pasek (Eds.), *Play = learning: How play motivates and enhances children's cognitive and social-emotional growth* (pp. 74–100). New York, NY: Oxford University Press.

Berko, J. (1958). The child's learning of English morphology. *Word, 14,* 150–177.

Bernal, S., Lidz, J., Millotte, S., & Christophe, A. (2007). Syntax constrains the acquisition of verb meaning. *Language Learning and Development, 3,* 325–341.

Bernard, J. A., & Mittal, V. A. (2015). Dysfunctional activation of the cerebellum in schizophrenia: A functional neuroimaging meta-analysis. *Clinical Psychological Science, 3,* 545–566.

Berndt, T. J. (1979). Developmental changes in conformity to peers and parents. *Developmental Psychology, 15,* 608–616.

Bernstein, D. P., & Useda, J. D. (2007). Paranoid personality disorder. In W. O'Donohue, K. A. Fowler, & S. O. Lilienfeld (Eds.), *Personality disorders: Toward DSM-V.* Los Angeles, CA: Sage.

Bernstein, I. L. (1991). Flavor aversion. In R. C. Doty, L. M. Bartoshuk, & J. B. Snow (Eds.), *Smell and taste in health and disease.* New York, NY: Raven.

Bernstein, W. M., Stephan, W. G., & Davis, M. H. (1979). Explaining attributions for achievement: A path analytic approach. *Journal of Personality and Social Psychology, 37,* 1810–1821.

Berntson, G. G., Bechara, A., Damasio, H., Tranel, D., & Cacioppo, J. T. (2007). Amygdala contribution to selective dimensions of emotion. *Social Cognitive and Affective Neuroscience, 2,* 123–129.

Berridge, K. C. (2003). Comparing the emotional brains of humans and other animals. In R. J. Davidson, K. R. Scherer, & H. Hill Goldsmith (Eds.), *Handbook of affective sciences*. Oxford, England: Oxford University Press.

Berridge, K. C., & Kringelbach, M. L. (2008). Affective neuroscience of pleasure: Reward in humans and animals. *Psychopharmacology, 199,* 457–480.

Berridge, K. C., & Robinson, T. E. (2003). Parsing reward. *Trends in Neurosciences, 26,* 507–513.

Bersoff, D. N. (2008). *Ethical conflicts in psychology* (4th ed.). Washington, DC: American Psychological Association.

Berthier, M. L., Kullsevsky, J., Gironell, A., & López, O. L. (2001). Obsessive-compulsive disorder and traumatic brain injury: Behavioral, cognitive, and neuroimaging findings. *Neuropsychiatry, Neuropsychology, and Behavioral Neurology, 14,* 23–31.

Berthoud, H.-R., & Morrison, C. (2008). The brain, appetite, and obesity. *Annual Review of Psychology, 59,* 55–92.

Bertram, L. (2008). Genetic research in schizophrenia: New tools and future perspectives. *Schizophrenia Bulletin, 34,* 806–812.

Bertram, L., & Tanzi, R. E. (2008). Thirty years of Alzheimer's disease genetics: The implications of systematic meta-analysis. *Nature Reviews Neuroscience, 9,* 768–778.

Best, J. R. (2011). Exergaming immediately enhances children's executive function. *Developmental Psychology, 48,* 1501–1510.

Beutler, L. E., & Harwood, M. T. (2000). *Prescriptive therapy: A practical guide to systematic treatment selection.* Oxford, England: Oxford University Press.

Bevc, I., & Silverman, I. (1993). Early proximity and intimacy between siblings and incestuous behavior: A test of the Westermarck theory. *Ethology and Sociobiology, 14,* 171–181.

Bevc, I., & Silverman, I. (2000). Early separation and sibling incest: A test of the revised Westermarck theory. *Evolution and Human Behavior, 21,* 151–161.

Bhatt, R. S., Bertin, E., Hayden, A., & Reed, A. (2005). Face processing in infancy: Developmental changes in the use of different kinds of relational information. *Child Development, 76,* 169–181.

Bialystok, E., & Craik, F. I. M. (2010). Cognitive and linguistic processing in the bilingual mind. *Current Directions in Psychological Science, 19,* 19–23.

Bialystok, E., Craik, F. I. M., & Freedman, M. (2007). Bilingualism as a protection against the onset of symptoms of dementia. *Neuropsychologia, 45,* 459–464.

Bialystok, E., Craik, F. I. M., & Luk, G. (2008). Cognitive control and lexical access in younger and older individuals. *Journal of Experimental Psychology: Learning, Memory, and Cognition, 34,* 859–873.

Bialystok, E., & Feng, X. (2011). Language proficiency and its implications for monolingual and bilingual children. In A.Y. Durgunoglu & C. Goldenberg (Eds.), *Language and literacy development in bilingual settings* (pp. 121–139). New York, NY: The Guilford Press.

Bickerton, D. (1984). The language bioprogram hypothesis. *Behavioral and Brain Sciences, 7,* 173–221.

Bijou, S. W., & Baer, D. M. (1961). *Child development* (Vol. 1). New York, NY: Appleton-Century-Crofts.

Biklen, D. (1990). Communication unbound: Autism and praxis. *Harvard Educational Review, 60,* 291–314.

Binder, J. L. (2004). *Key competencies in brief dynamic psychotherapy: Clinical practice beyond the manual.* New York, NY: Guilford.

Binet, A., & Henri, V. (1896). La psychologie individuelle. *Année Psychologie, 11,* 163–169.

Binet, A., & Simon, T. (1973). *The development of intelligence in children.* New York, NY: Arno Press. (Original work published 1916)

Birkett, P., Clegg, J., Bhaker, R., Lee, K.-H., Mysore, A., Parks, R., & Woodruff, P. (2011). Schizophrenia impairs phonological speech production: A preliminary report. *Cognitive Neuropsychiatry, 16,* 49–49.

Birkhead, T. R., & Moller, A. P. (1992). *Sperm competition in birds: Evolutionary causes and consequences.* San Diego, CA: Academic Press.

Bishop, S. J. (2009). Trait anxiety and impoverished prefrontal control of attention. *Nature Neuroscience, 12,* 92–98.

Bjorklund, D. F. (1997a). In search of a metatheory for cognitive development (or, Piaget is dead and I don't feel so good myself). *Child Development, 68,* 144–148.

Bjorklund, D. F. (1997b). The role of immaturity in human development. *Psychological Bulletin, 122,* 153–169.

Bjorklund, D. F. (2007). *Youth is not wasted on the young: Immaturity in human development.* Oxford, England: Blackwell.

Bjorklund, D. F. (2013). Cognitive development: An overview. In P. D. Zelazo (Ed.), *Oxford handbook of developmental psychology* (pp. 447–476). Oxford, England: Oxford University Press.

Bjorklund, D. F., & Causey, K. (2018). *Children's thinking: Cognitive development and individual differences* (6th ed.). San Francisco, CA: Sage.

Bjorklund, D. F., Causey, K., & Periss, V. (2010). The evolution and development of human social cognition. In P. Kappeler & J. Silk (Eds.), *Mind the gap: Tracing the origins of human universals* (pp. 351–371). Berlin, Germany: Springer Verlag.

Bjorklund, D. F., & Gardiner, A. K. (2011). Object play and tool use: Developmental and evolutionary perspectives. In A. D. Pellegrini (Ed.), *Oxford handbook of play* (pp. 153–171). Oxford, England: Oxford University Press.

Bjorklund, D. F., Gaultney, J. F., & Green, B. L. (1993). "I watch, therefore I can do": The development of meta-imitation over the preschool years and the advantage of optimism in one's imitative skills. In R. Pasnak & M. L. Howe (Eds.), *Emerging themes in cognitive development* (Vol. 1, pp. 79–102). New York, NY: Springer-Verlag.

Bjorklund, D. F., & Green, B. L. (1992). The adaptive nature of cognitive immaturity. *American Psychologist, 47,* 46–54.

Bjorklund, D. F., & Hernández Blasi, C. (2012). *Child and adolescent development: An integrative approach.* Belmont, CA: Wadsworth.

Bjorklund, D. F., Hernández Blasi, C., & Ellis, B. J. (2016). Evolutionary developmental psychology. In D. M. Buss (Ed.), *Evolutionary psychology handbook* (2nd ed., Vol. 2, pp. 904–925). New York, NY: Wiley.

Bjorklund, D. F., & Pellegrini, A. D. (2002). *The origins of human nature: Evolutionary developmental psychology.* Washington, DC: American Psychological Association.

Bjorklund, D. F., & Sellers, P. D. II. (2014). Memory development in evolutionary perspective. In P. Bauer & R. Fivush (Eds.), *Wiley-Blackwell handbook on the development of children's memory* (pp. 126–150). New York, NY: Wiley-Blackwell.

Bjorklund, D. F., Yunger, J. L., Bering, J. M., & Raganb, P. (2002). The generalization of deferred imitation in enculturated chimpanzees (*Pan troglodytes*). *Animal Cognition, 5,* 49–58.

Black, J. E., Jones, T. A., Nelson, C. A., & Greenough, W. T. (1998). Neuronal plasticity and the developing brain. In N. E. Alessi, J. T. Coyle, S. I. Harrison, & S. Eth (Eds.), *Handbook of child and adolescent psychiatry: Vol. 6. Basic psychiatric science and treatment* (pp. 31–53). Hoboken, NJ: Wiley.

Blackwell, L., Trzesniewski, K., & Dwick, C. S. (2007). Implicit theories of intelligence predict achievement across an adolescent transition: A longitudinal study and an intervention. *Child Development, 78,* 246–263.

Blair, C. (2006). How similar are fluid cognition and general intelligence? A developmental neuroscience perspective on fluid cognition as an aspect of human cognitive ability. *Behavioral and Brain Sciences, 29,* 109–160.

Blair, C., & Diamond, A. (2008). Biological processes in prevention and intervention: The promotion of self-regulation as a means of preventing school failure. *Development and Psychopathology, 20,* 899–911.

Blakemore, C., & Van Sluyters, R. C. (1975). Innate and environmental factors in the development of the kitten's visual cortex. *Journal of Physiology, 248,* 663–716.

Blanchard-Fields, F. (2007). Everyday problem solving and emotion: An adult developmental perspective. *Current Directions in Psychological Science, 16,* 26–31.

Blanchette, I., & Dunbar, K. (2000). How analogies are generated: The roles of structural and superficial similarity. *Memory and Cognition, 28,* 108–124.

Blanck, H. M., Marcus, M., Tolbert, P. E., Rubin, C., Henderson, A. K., Hertzberg, V. S., . . . Cameron, L. (2000). Age at menarche and Tanner stage in girls exposed *in utero* and postnatally to polybrominated biphenyl. *Epidemiology, 11,* 641–647.

Blaustein, J. D. (2008). Neuroendocrine regulation of feminine sexual behavior: Lessons from rodent models and thoughts about humans. *Annual Review of Psychology, 59,* 93–118.

Blazer, D., Hughes, D., & George, L. D. (1987). Stressful life events and the onset of a generalized anxiety syndrome. *American Journal of Psychiatry, 144,* 1178–1183.

Bleuler, E. P. (1950). *Dementia praecox, or the group of schizophrenias* (J. Zinkin, Trans.). New York, NY: International Universities Press. (Original work published 1911)

Bliss, T. V. P., & Lømo, T. (1973). Long-lasting potentiation of synaptic transmission in the dentate area of the anaesthetized rabbit following stimulation of the perforant path. *Journal of Physiology (London), 232,* 331–356.

Bloom, L. M., & Lahey, M. (1978). *Language development and language disorders.* Hoboken, NJ: Wiley.

Bloom, P. (2001). Précis of *How children learn the meanings of words. Behavioral and Brain Sciences, 24,* 1095–1103.

Bloom, P., & Markson, L. (1998). Capacities underlying word learning. *Trends in Cognitive Science, 2,* 67–73.

Blurton-Jones, N. G. (1967). An ethological study of some aspects of social behavior of children in nursery school. In D. Morris (Ed.), *Primate ethology.* Chicago, IL: Aldine.

Blurton-Jones, N. G., & Konner, M. J. (1973). Sex differences in the behavior of Bushman and London two- to five-year-olds. In J. Crook & R. Michael (Eds.), *Comparative ecology and behavior of primates.* San Diego, CA: Academic Press.

Bodenhausen, G. V. (1991). Identity and cooperative social behavior: Pseudospeciation or human integration? *World Futures, 31,* 95–106.

Boesch, C. (1991). Teaching among wild chimpanzees. *Animal Behavior, 41,* 530–532.

Boesch, C., & Tomasello, M. (1998). Chimpanzee and human culture. *Current Anthropology, 39,* 591–604.

Bonawitz, E., Shafto, P., Gweon, H., Goodman, N. D., Spelke, E., & Schulz, L. (2011). The double-edged sword of pedagogy: Instruction limits spontaneous exploration and discover. *Cognition, 120,* 322–330.

Bond, A. J., & Lader, M. H. (1996). *Understanding drug treatment in mental health care.* Hoboken, NJ: Wiley.

Bond, M., Mealing, S., Anderson, R., Elston, J., Weiner, G., Taylor, R. S., . . . Stein, K. (2009). The effectiveness and cost-effectiveness of cochlear implants for severe to profound deafness in children and adults: A systematic review and economic model. *Health Technology Assessment, 44*(13).

Bond, R., & Smith, P. B. (1996). Culture and conformity: A meta-analysis of studies using Asch's (1952b, 1956) line judgment task. *Psychological Bulletin, 119,* 111–137.

Book, A., Visser, B. A., Blais, J., Hosker-Field, A., Methot-Jones, T., Gauthier, N. Y., & D'Agata, M. T. (2016). Unpacking more "evil": What is at the core of the dark tetrad? *Personality and Individual Differences, 90,* 269–272.

Boot, W. R., Simons, D. J., Stothart, C., & Stutts, C. (2013). The pervasive problem with placebos in psychology: Why active control groups are not sufficient to rule out placebo effects. *Perspectives on Psychological Science, 8,* 445–454.

Borbély, A. (1986). *The secrets of sleep.* New York, NY: Basic Books.

Borkovec, T. D., Alcaine, O., & Behar, E. (2004). Avoidance theory of worry and generalized anxiety disorder. In R. G. Heimberg, C. L. Turk, & D. S. Mennin (Eds.), *Generalized anxiety disorder: Advances in research and practice.* New York, NY: Guilford.

Bornstein, B. H., Lamb, C. E., Meissner, C. A., & Susan, K. J. (2013). The cross-race effect: Resistant to instructions. *Journal of Criminology,* Article ID 745836.

Bornstein, R. F. (2007). Dependent personality disorder. In W. O'Donohue, K. A. Fowler, & S. O. Lilienfeld (Eds.), *Personality disorders: Toward DSM-V.* Los Angeles, CA: Sage.

Botella, C., Osma, J., Garcia-Palacios, A., Quero, S., & Banos, R. M. (2004). Treatment of flying phobia using virtual reality: Data from a 1-year follow-up using a multiple baseline design. *Clinical Psychology and Psychotherapy, 11,* 311–323.

Both, S., Brauer, M., & Laan, E. (2011). Classical conditioning of sexual response in women: A replication study. *The Journal of Sexual Medicine, 8,* 3116–3131.

Bouchard, T. J. (1991). A twice-told tale: Twins reared apart. In W. M. Gove & D. Cicchetti (Eds.), *Thinking clearly about psychology: Vol. 2. Personality and psychopathology.* Minneapolis: University of Minnesota Press.

Bouchard, T. J. (2004). Genetic influence on human psychological traits: A survey. *Current Directions in Psychological Science, 13,* 148–151.

Bouchard, T. J., Jr., & Loehlin, J. C. (2001). Genes, personality and evolution. *Behavior Genetics, 31,* 243–273.

Bouchard, T. J., Jr., & McGue, M. (1981). Familial studies of intelligence: A review. *Science, 212,* 1055–1059.

Bouffard-Bouchard, T. (1990). Influence of self-efficacy on performance in a cognitive task. *Journal of Social Psychology, 130,* 353–363.

Boulkroune, N., Wang, L., March, A., Walker, N., & Jacob, T. J. (2007). Repetitive olfactory exposure to the biologically significant steroid androstadienone causes a hedonic shift and gender dimorphic changes in olfactory-evoked potentials. *Neuropsychopharmacology, 32,* 1822–1829.

Boulton, M., & Smith, P. K. (1990). Affective bias in children's perceptions of dominance. *Child Development, 61,* 221–229.

Bouton, M. E., Westbrook, R. F., Corcoran, K. A., & Maren, S. (2006). Contextual and temporal modulation of extinction: Behavioral and biological mechanisms. *Biological Psychiatry, 60,* 352–360.

Bowden, E. M., Jung-Beeman, M., Fleck, J., & Kounis, J. (2005). New approaches to demystifying insight. *Trends in Cognitive Science, 9,* 322–328.

Bowlby, J. (1958). The nature of the child's tie to his mother. *International Journal of Psychoanalysis, 39,* 350–373.

Bowlby, J. (1969). *Attachment and loss: Vol. 1: Attachment.* London, England: Hogarth.

Bowlby, J. (1973). *Attachment and loss: Vol. 2: Separation: Anxiety and anger.* New York, NY: Basic Books.

Bowlby, J. (1980). *Attachment and loss* (2nd ed.). New York, NY: Basic Books.

Bowmaker, J. K., & Dartnall, H. J. A. (1980). Visual pigments of rods and cones in a human retina. *Journal of Physiology (London), 298,* 501–511.

Boyack, K.W., Klavans, R., & Börner, K. (2005). Mapping the backbone of science. *Scientometrics, 64,* 351–374.

Boyce, W. T., Chesney, M., Alkon-Leonard, A., Tschann, J., Adams, S., Chesterman, B., . . . Wara, D. (1995). Psychobiologic reactivity to stress and childhood respiratory illnesses: Results of two prospective studies. *Psychosomatic Medicine, 57,* 411–422.

Boyce, W. T., & Ellis, B. J. (2005). Biological sensitivity to context: I. An evolutionary-developmental theory of the origins and functions of stress reactivity. *Development & Psychopathology, 17,* 271–301.

Bozikas, V. P., Andreou, C., Giannakou, M., Tonia, T., Anezoulaki, D., Karavatos, A., . . . Kosmidis, M. H. (2005). Deficits in sustained attention in schizophrenia but not in bipolar disorder. *Schizophrenia Research, 78,* 225–233.

Brady, T. F., Konkle, T., Alvarez, G. A., & Oliva, A. (2008). Visual long-term memory has a massive storage capacity for object details. *Proceedings of the National Academy of Science, 105,* 14325–14329.

Brainerd, C. J., & Reyna, V. F. (2005). *The science of false memory.* Oxford, England: Oxford University Press.

Brainerd, C. J., & Reyna, V. F. (2015). Fuzzy-trace theory and lifespan cognitive development. *Developmental Review, 38,* 89–121.

Bramlett, M. D., & Mosher, W. D. (2002). *Cohabitation, marriage, divorce, and remarriage in the United States* (Vital Health Statistics, Series 23, Number 22). Hyattsville, MD: National Center for Health Statistics.

Brandt, M. J., Crawford, J. T., Chambers J. R., Wetherell, G., & Reyna, C. (2015). Bounded openness: The effect of openness to experience on intolerance is moderated by target group conventionality. *Journal of Personality and Social Psychology, 109,* 549–568.

Bransford, J. D., Stein, B. S., Vye, N. J., Franks, J. J., Auble, P. M., Mezynski, K. J., & Perfetto, G. A. (1982). Different approaches in learning: An overview. *Journal of Experimental Psychology: General, 111,* 390–398.

Brase, G. (2003). The allocation system: Using signal detection processes to regulate representations in a multimodular mind. In D. E. Over (Ed.), *Evolution and the psychology of thinking: The debate.* New York, NY: Psychology Press.

Bregman, E. (1934). An attempt to modify emotional attitude of infants by the conditioned response technique. *Journal of Genetic Psychology, 45,* 169–198.

Breiter, H. C., Aharon, I., Kahnaman, D., Dale, A., & Shizgal, P. (2001). Functional imaging of neural responses to expectancy and experience of monetary gains and losses. *Neuron, 30,* 619–639.

Brennan, P. A., & Zufall, F. (2006). Pheromonal communication in vertebrates. *Nature, 444,* 308–315.

Bretherton, I., Golby, B., & Cho, E. (1997). Attachment and the transmission of values. In J. E. Grusec & L. Kuczynski (Eds.), *Parenting and children's internalization of values: A handbook of contemporary theory.* Hoboken, NJ: Wiley.

Brewin, C. R. (2014). Episodic memory, perceptual memory, and their interaction: Foundations for a theory of posttraumatic stress disorder. *Psychological Bulletin, 140,* 69–97.

Briley, D. A., & Trucker-Drob, E. M. (2014). Genetic and environmental continuity in personality development: A meta-analysis. *Psychological Bulletin, 140,* 1303–1331.

Britton, J. C., & Rauch, S. L. (2009). Neuroanatomy and neuroimaging of anxiety disorders. In M. M. Antony & M. B. Stein (Eds.), *Oxford handbook of anxiety related disorders.* Oxford, England: Oxford University Press.

Broca, P. (1965). Paul Broca on the speech centers (M. D. Boring, Trans.). In R. J. Herrnstein & E. G. Boring (Eds.), *A source book in the history of psychology.* Cambridge, MA: Harvard University Press. (Original work published 1861)

Broccia, M., & Campos, J. J. (1989). Maternal emotional signals, social referencing, and infants' reactions to strangers. In N. Eisenberg (Ed.), *Empathy and related emotional responses* (New Directions for Child Development, No. 44). San Francisco, CA: Jossey-Bass.

Brody, G. H. (2004). Siblings' direct and indirect contributions to child development. *Current Directions in Psychological Science, 13,* 124–126.

Bronner, M., & Hatten, M. E. (2012). Neurogenesis and migration. In L. R. Squire, D. Berg, F. E. Bloom, S. du Lac, A. Ghosh, & N. C. Spitzer (Eds.), *Fundamental neuroscience* (4th ed., pp. 339–361). New York, NY: Elsevier.

Brooks, R., & Meltzoff, A. N. (2002). The importance of eyes: How infants interpret adult looking behavior. *Developmental Psychology, 38,* 958–966.

Brooks, R., & Meltzoff, A. N. (2008). Infant gaze following and pointing predict accelerated vocabulary growth through two years of age: A longitudinal, growth curve modeling study. *Journal of Child Language, 5,* 207–220.

Broome, M. R., Woolley, J. B., Tabraham, P., Johns, L. C., Bramon, E., Murray, G. K., . . . Murray, R. M. (2005). What causes the onset of psychosis? *Schizophrenia Research, 79,* 23–34.

Brown, A. S., & Patterson, P. H. (2011). Maternal infection and schizophrena: Implications for prevention. *Schizophrenia Bulletin, 37,* 284–290.

Brown, A. S., & Susser, E. S. (2008). Prenatal nutritional deficiency and risk of adult schizophrenia. *Schizophrenia Bulletin, 34,* 1054–1063.

Brown, J., Cooper-Kuhn, C. M., Kempermann, G., Van Praag, H., Winkler, J., Gage, F. H., & Kuhn, H. G. (2003). Enriched environment and physical activity stimulate hippocampal but not olfactory bulb neurogenesis. *European Journal of Neuroscience, 17,* 2042–2046.

Brown, J. R., Ye, H., Bronson, R. T., Dikkes, P., & Greenberg, M. E. (1996). A defect in nurturing in mice lacking the immediate early gene fosB. *Cell, 86,* 297–309.

Brown, M. C., & Santos-Sacchi, J. (2013). Audition. In L. R. Squire, D. Berg, F. E. Bloom, S. du Lac, A. Ghosh, & N. C. Spitzer (Eds.), *Fundamental neuroscience* (4th ed., pp. 553–576). New York, NY: Elsevier.

Brown, R. (1973). *A first language.* Cambridge, MA: Harvard University Press.

Brown, R., & Hanlon, C. (1970). Derivational complexity and order of acquisition in child speech. In J. R. Hayes (Ed.), *Cognition and the development of language.* Hoboken, NJ: Wiley.

Brownell, C. A., Svetlova, M., & Nichols, S. (2009). To share or not to share: When do toddlers respond to another's needs? *Infancy, 14,* 117–130.

Bruce, V., & Young, A. (1998). *In the eye of the beholder: The science of face perception.* Oxford, England: Oxford University Press.

Bruner, J. S. (1972). The nature and uses of immaturity. *American Psychologist, 27,* 687–708.

Bruner, J. S. (1983). *Child's talk: Learning to use language.* New York, NY: Norton.

Brunoni, A. R., Michael, A., Nitsche, M. A., Bolognini, N., Bikson, M., Wagner, T., Merabet, L., Edwards, D. J., Valero-Cabre, A., Rotenberg, A., Pascual-Leone, A., Ferrucci, R., Priori, A., Boggio, P. S., & Fregni, F. (2012). Clinical research with transcranial direct current stimulation (tDCS): Challenges and future directions. *Brain Stimulation, 5,* 175–195.

Brunstrom, J. M. (2005). Dietary learning in humans: Directions for further research. *Physiology and Behavior, 85,* 57–65.

Brunstrom, J. M., & Mitchell, G. L. (2007). Flavor-nutrient learning in restrained and unrestrained eaters. *Physiology and Behavior, 90,* 133–141.

Buccino, G., Vogt, G. S., Ritzl, A., Fink, G. R., Zilles, K., Freund, H.-J., & Rizzolatti, G. (2004). Neural circuits underlying imitation learning of hand actions: An event-related fMRI study. *Neuron, 42,* 323–334.

Buck, L. B. (2000a). Smell and taste: The chemical senses. In E. R. Kandel, J. H. Schwartz, & T. M. Jessell (Eds.), *Principles of neuroscience* (4th ed.). New York, NY: McGraw-Hill.

Buck, L. B. (2000b). The molecular architecture of odor and pheromone sensing in mammals. *Cell, 100,* 611–618.

Buehlman, K. T., Gottman, J. M., & Katz, L. F. (1992). How a couple views their past predicts their future: Predicting divorce from an oral history interview. *Journal of Family Psychology, 5,* 295–318.

Bugliosi, V. (1978). *Till death do us part.* New York, NY: Bantam Books.

Bunge, S. A., Wendelken, C., Badre, D., & Wagner, A. D. (2005). Analogical reasoning and prefrontal cortex: Evidence for separable retrieval and integration mechanisms. *Cerebral Cortex, 15,* 239–249.

Burger, J. M. (1999). The foot-in-the-door compliance procedure: A multiple-process analysis and review. *Personality and Social Psychology Review, 3,* 303–325.

Burger, J. M. (2009). Replicating Milgram: Would people still obey today? *American Psychologist, 64,* 1–11.

Burns, J. W. (2000). Repression predicts outcome following multidisciplinary treatment of chronic pain. *Health Psychology, 19,* 75–84.

Burnstein, E., & Vinokur, A. (1977). Persuasive argumentation and social comparison as determinants of attitude polarization. *Journal of Social Psychology, 13,* 315–332.

Bushnell, I. W. R., Sai, F., & Mullin, J. T. (1989). Neonatal recognition of the mother's face. *British Journal of Developmental Psychology, 7,* 3–15.

Buss, D. M. (1989). Sex differences in human mate preferences: Evolutionary hypotheses tested in 37 cultures. *Behavioral and Brain Sciences, 12,* 1–49.

Buss, D. M. (1995). Psychological sex differences: Origins through sexual selection. *American Psychologist, 50,* 164–168.

Buss, D. M. (1996). Social adaptation and five major factors of personality. In J. S. Wiggins (Ed.), *The five-factor model of personality: Theoretical perspectives.* New York, NY: Guilford.

Buss, D. M. (2000). Desires in human mating. *Annals of the New York Academy of Sciences, 907,* 39–49.

Buss, D. M. (2009). How can evolutionary psychology successfully explain personality and individual differences? *Perspectives on Psychological Science, 4,* 359–366.

Buss, D. M. (2011). *The dangerous passion: Why jealousy is as necessary as love and sex.* New York, NY: The Free Press.

Buss, D. M. (Ed.). (2016). *The handbook of evolutionary psychology* (2nd ed.). New York, NY: Wiley.

Buss, D. M., Haselton, M. G., Shackelford, T. K., Bleske, A. L., & Wakefield, J. C. (1998). Adaptations, expectations, and spandrels. *American Psychologist, 53,* 533–548.

Bussey, K., & Bandura, A. (1999). Social cognitive theory of gender development and differentiation. *Psychological Review, 106,* 676–713.

Butler, A. C., Hokanson, J. E., & Flynn, H. A. (1994). A comparison of self-esteem lability and low trait self-esteem as vulnerability factors for depression. *Journal of Personality and Social Psychology, 66,* 166–177.

Butler, D. (2004). Slim pickings. *Nature, 428,* 252–254.

Butler, R. N. (1975). *Why survive?* New York, NY: Harper & Row.

Buttelmann, D., & Böhm, R. (2014). The ontogeny of the motivation that underlies in-group bias. *Psychological Science, 25,* 921–927.

Buttelmann, D., Carpenter, M., Call, J., & Tomasello, M. (2007). Enculturated chimpanzees imitate rationally. *Developmental Science, 10,* F31–F38.

Buttelmann, F., Suhrke, J., & Bettelmann, D. (2015). What you get is what you believe: Eighteen-month-olds demonstrate belief understanding in an unexpected-identity task. *Journal of Experimental Child Psychology, 131,* 94–103.

Butterfield, E. C., & Siperstein, G. N. (1974). Influence of contingent auditory stimulation upon non-nutritional suckle. In *Proceedings of the third symposium on oral sensation and perception: The mouth of the infant.* Springfield, IL: Charles C. Thomas.

Byers, J. A. (1977). Terrain preferences in the play behavior of Siberian ibex kids (*Capra ibex sibirica*). *Zeitschrift für Tierpsychologie, 45,* 199–209.

Byers, J. A. (1998). Biological effects of locomotor play: Getting into shape, or something more specific? In M. Bekoff & J. A. Byers (Eds.), *Animal play: Evolutionary, comparative, and ecological perspectives.* Cambridge, England: Cambridge University Press.

Byrne, J. H. (2003). Postsynaptic potentials and synaptic integration. In L. R. Squire, F. L. Bloom, S. K. McConnell, J. L. Roberts, N. C. Spitzer, & M. J. Zigmond (Eds.), *Fundamental neuroscience* (2nd ed.). San Diego, CA: Academic Press.

Byrne, J. H. (2008). Learning and memory. In L. Squire, D. Berg, F. Bloom, S. du Lac, A. Ghosh, & N. Spitzer (Eds.), *Fundamental neuroscience.* New York, NY: Elsevier.

Byrne, R. W. (2005). Social cognition: Imitation, imitation, imitation. *Current Biology, 15,* R489–R500.

Byrne, R. W., & Russo, A. E. (1998). Learning by imitation: A hierarchical approach. *Behavioral and Brain Sciences, 21,* 667–721.

Byron, K., & Khazanchi, S. (2012). Rewards and creative performance: A meta-analytic test of theoretically derived hypotheses. *Psychological Bulletin, 138,* 809–830.

Cabib, S., Orsini, C., Le Moal, M., & Piazza, P. V. (2000). Abolition and reversal of strain differences in behavioral responses to drugs of abuse after a brief experience. *Science, 289,* 463–465.

Cacioppo, J. (2007, September). Psychology is a hub science. *Observer, 20*(8).

Cacioppo, J. T., Berntson, G. G., & Klein, D. J. (1992). What is an emotion? The role of somatovisceral afference, with special emphasis on somatovisceral "illusions." *Review of Personality and Social Psychology, 14,* 63–98.

Cacioppo, J. T., Rourke, P. A., Marshall-Goodell, B. S., Tassinary, L. G., & Baron, R. S. (1990). Rudimentary physiological effects of mere observation. *Psychophysiology, 27,* 177–186.

Caldwell-Harris, C. L., & Aycicegi, A. (2006). When personality and culture clash: The psychological distress of allocentrics in an individualist culture and idiocentrics in a collectivist culture. *Transcultural Psychiatry, 43,* 331–361.

Campbell, A. (1995). A few good men: Evolutionary psychology and female adolescent aggression. *Ethology and Sociobiology, 16,* 99–123.

Campbell, A. (1999). Staying alive: Evolution, culture, and women's intrasexual aggression. *Behavioral and Brain Sciences, 22,* 203–252.

Campbell, A. (2002). *A mind of her own: The evolutionary psychology of women.* Oxford, England: Oxford University Press.

Campbell, A., & Cross, C. (2012). Women and aggression. In T. K. Shackelford & V. A. Weekes-Shackelford (Eds.), *The Oxford handbook of evolutionary perspectives on violence, homicide, and war* (pp. 197–217). Oxford, England: Oxford University Press.

Campbell, K. (1970). *Body and mind.* Notre Dame, IN: University of Notre Dame Press.

Campbell, S. S., & Tobler, I. (1984). Animals sleep: A review of sleep duration across phylogeny. *Neuroscience and Biobehavioral Review, 8,* 269–300.

Campbell, W. K., Goodies, A. S., & Foster, J. D. (2004). Narcissism, confidence, and risk attitude. *Journal of Behavioral Decision Making, 17,* 297–311.

Campbell, W. K., & Miller, J. D. (Eds.). (2011). *The handbook of narcissistic personality disorder: Theoretical approaches, empirical findings, and treatment.* Hoboken, NJ: Wiley.

Campos, J. J., Anderson, D. I., Barbu-Roth, M. A., Hubbard, E. M., Hertenstein, M. J., & Witherington, D. (2000). Travel broadens the mind. *Infancy, 1,* 149–219.

Candy, T. R., Wang, J., & Ravikumar, S. (2009). Retinal image quality and postnatal visual experience during infancy. *Optometry & Vision Science, 86,* 566–571.

Cannon, W. B. (1963). *The wisdom of the body.* New York, NY: Norton. (Original work published 1932)

Cantor, N., & Harlow, R. E. (1994). Personality, strategic behavior, and daily-life problem solving. *Current Directions in Psychological Science, 3,* 169–172.

Cao, X., Cui, Z., Feng, R., Tang, Y.-P., Qin, Z., Mei, B., & Tsien, J. Z. (2007). Maintenance of superior learning and memory function in NR2B transgenic mice during aging. *European Journal of Neuroscience, 25,* 1815–1822.

Cao-Lei, L., Massart, R., Suderman, M. J., Machnes, Z., Elgbeili, G., Laplante, D. P., Szyf, M., & King, S. (2014). DNA methylation signatures triggered by prenatal maternal stress exposure to a natural disaster: Project Ice Storm. *PLOS One, 9,* e107653–e107653.

Capaldi, D. M., Crosby, L., & Stoolmiller, M. (1996). Predicting the timing of first sexual intercourse for at-risk adolescent males. *Child Development, 67,* 344–359.

Caplan, D. N., & Gould, J. L. (2013). Language. In L. R. Squire, D. Berg, F. E. Bloom, S. du Lac, A. Ghosh, & N. C. Spitzer (Eds.), *Fundamental neuroscience* (4th ed., pp. 1053–1067). Boston, MA: Elsevier.

Capon, N., & Kuhn, D. (1979). Logical reasoning in the supermarket: Adult females' use of a proportional reasoning strategy in an everyday context. *Developmental Psychology, 15,* 450–452.

Caqueo-Urízar, A., Ferrer-García, M., Toro, J., Gutiérrez-Maldonado, J., Peñaloza, C., Cuadros-Sosa, Y., & Gálvez-Madrid, M. J. (2011). Association between sociocultural pressures to be thin, body distress, and eating disorder symptomatology among Chilean adolescent girls. *Body Image, 8,* 78–81.

Card, J. P., & Swanson, L. W. (2013). The hypothalamus: An overview of regulatory systems. In L. R. Squire, D. Berg, F. E. Bloom, S. du Lac, A. Ghosh, & N. C. Spitzer (Eds.), *Fundamental neuroscience* (4th ed., pp. 717–727). Boston, MA: Elsevier.

Cardinal, D. N., & Falvey, M. A. (2014). The maturing of facilitated communication: A means toward independent communication. *Research and Practice for Persons with Severe Disabilities, 39,* 189–194.

Carlier, P., & Jamon, M. (2006). Observational learning in C57BL/6j mice. *Behavioural Brain Research, 174,* 125–131.

Carlson S., & Hyvarinen L. (1983). Visual rehabilitation after long lasting early blindness. *Acta Ophthalmologica* (Copenhagen), *61,* 701–713.

Carlson, S. M., Taylor, M., & Levin, G. (1998). The influence of culture on pretend play: The case of Mennonite children. *Merrill-Palmer Quarterly, 44,* 538–565.

Carlson, S. M., White, R. E., & Davis-Unger, A. C. (2014). Evidence for a relationship between executive function and pretense representation in preschool children. *Cognitive Development, 29,* 1–16.

Carlson, S. M., Zelazo, P. D., & Faja, S. (2013). Executive function. In P. D. Zelazo (Ed.), *Oxford handbook of developmental psychology* (Vol. 1, pp. 706–743). Oxford, England: Oxford University Press.

Carney, D. R., Colvin, C. R., & Hall, J. A. (2007). A thin slice perspective on the accuracy of first impressions. *Journal of Research in Personality, 41,* 1054–1072.

Caro, T. M. (1995). Short-term costs and correlates of play in cheetahs. *Animal Behaviour, 49,* 333–345.

Carpenter, L. L., Tyrka, A. R., McDougle, C. J., Malison, R. T., Owens, M. J., Nemeroff, C. B., & Price, L. H. (2004). Cerebrospinal fluid corticotropin-releasing factor and perceived early-life stress in depressed patients and healthy control subjects. *Neuropsychopharmacology, 29,* 777–784.

Carpenter, W. T., & Buchanan, R. W. (2008). Lessons to take home from CATIE. *Psychiatric Services, 59,* 523–525.

Carr, G. V., & Lucki, I. (2011). The role of serotonin receptor subtypes in treating depression: A review of animal studies. *Psychopharmacology, 213,* 265–287.

Carr, S., Dabbs, J., & Carr, T. (1975). Mother–infant attachment: The importance of the mother's visual field. *Child Development, 46,* 331–338.

Carroll, B. J. (1991). Psychopathology and neurobiology of manic-depressive disorders. In B. J. Carroll & J. E. Barrett (Eds.), *Psychopathology and the brain.* New York, NY: Raven Press.

Carroll, K. M. (2012). Dissemination of evidence-based practices: How far we've come, and how much farther we've got to go. *Addiction, 107,* 1031–1033.

Carstensen, L. L. (1992). Social and emotional patterns in adulthood: Support for socioemotional selectivity theory. *Psychology and Aging, 7,* 331–338.

Carstensen, L. L., & Fredrickson, B. L. (1998). Influence of HIV status and age on cognitive representations of others. *Health Psychology, 17,* 494–503.

Carstensen, L. L., & Mikels, J. A. (2005). At the intersection of emotion and cognition: Aging and the positivity effect. *Current Directions in Psychological Science, 14,* 117–121.

Carter, R. (1999). *Mapping the mind.* Berkeley: University of California Press.

Carver, L. J., & Bauer, P. J. (1999). When the event is more than the sum of its parts: Individual differences in 9-month-olds' long-term ordered recall. *Memory, 2,* 147–174.

Cascio, C. J., Foss-Feig, J. H., Burnette, C. P., Heacock, J. L., & Cosby, A. A. (2012). The rubber hand illusion in children with autism spectrum disorder: Delayed influence of combined tactile and visual input on proprioception. *Autism, 16,* 406–419.

Cashdan, E. (1994). A sensitive period for learning about food. *Human Nature, 5,* 279–291.

Casler, K., & Kelemen, D. (2005). Young children's rapid learning about artifacts, *Developmental Science, 8,* 472–480.

Caspi, A., & Moffitt, T. E. (1993). When do individual differences matter? A paradoxical theory of personality coherence. *Psychological Inquiry, 4,* 247–271.

Caspi, A., Roberts, B. W., & Shiner, R. L. (2005). Personality development: Stability and change. *Annual Review of Psychology, 56,* 453–484.

Caspi, A., & Shiner, R. L. (2006). Personality development. In W. Damon & R. M. Lerner (Gen. Eds.) & N. Eisenberg (Vol. Ed.), *Handbook of child psychology: Vol. 3. Social, emotional, and personality development* (6th ed., pp. 300–365). Hoboken, NJ: Wiley.

Caspi, A., Sugden, K., Moffitt, T. E., Taylor, A., Craig, I. W., Harrington, . . . Poulton, R. (2003). Influence of life stress on depression: Moderation by a polymorphism in the 5-HTT gene. *Science, 301,* 386–389.

Catarino, A., Küooer, C., Werner-Seidler, A., Dalgleish, T., & Anderson, M. C. (2015). Failing to forget: Inhibitory-control deficits compromise memory suppression in posttraumatic stress disorder. *Psychological Science, 26,* 604–616.

Cattell, R. B. (1950). *Personality: A systematic, theoretical, and factual study.* New York, NY: McGraw-Hill.

Cattell, R. B. (1971). *Abilities: Their structure, growth, and action.* Boston, MA: Houghton Mifflin. (Rev. ed.: Amsterdam: North-Holland, 1987.)

Cattell, R. B. (1973). *Personality and mood by questionnaire.* San Francisco, CA: Jossey-Bass.

Causey, K., & Bjorklund, D. F. (2011). The evolution of cognition. In V. Swami (Ed.), *Evolutionary psychology: A critical reader* (pp. 32–71). London, England: British Psychological Society.

CDC (Centers for Disease Control and Prevention). (2012). *Summary health statistics for U.S. children: National Health Interview Survey, 2012.* Atlanta, GA: Author.

CDC (Centers for Disease Control and Prevention). (2013a). *Distracted driving.* Atlanta, GA: Author.

CDC (Centers for Disease Control and Prevention). (2013b). Drowsy driving—19 states and the District of Columbia, 2009–2010. *Morbidity and Mortality Weekly Report, 61,* Nos. 51 & 52.

CDC (Centers for Disease Control and Prevention). (2015). *Sexually transmitted diseases surveillance: 2014.* Retrieved from http://www.cdc.gov/std/stats14/surv-2014-print.pdf

Ceci, S. J. (1996). *On intelligence: A bioecological treatise on intellectual development.* Cambridge, MA: Harvard University Press.

Ceci, S. J., Loftus, E. F., Leichtman, M., & Bruck, M. (1994). The role of source misattributions in the creation of false beliefs among preschoolers. *International Journal of Clinical and Experimental Hypnosis, 62,* 304–320.

Cervone, D. (1997). Social-cognitive mechanisms and personality coherence: Self-knowledge, situational beliefs, and cross-situational coherence in perceived self-efficacy. *Psychological Science, 8,* 43–50.

Cézilly, F., & Zayan, R. (2000). Integrating different levels of analysis in the study of mate choice and mating systems in vertebrates. *Behavioural Processes, 51,* 1–5.

Chagnon, N. A. (1979). Mate competition, favoring close kin, and village fissioning among the Yanomamö Indians. In N. A. Chagnon & W. Irons (Eds.), *Evolutionary biology and human social behavior: An anthropological perspective*. North Scituate, MA: Duxbury Press.

Charles, S. T., Mather, M., & Carstensen, L. L. (2003). Aging and emotional memory: The forgettable nature of negative images for older adults. *Journal of Experimental Psychology: General, 132*, 310–324.

Chase, J. A., & Houmanfar, R. (2009). The differential effects of elaborate feedback and basic feedback on student performance in a modified, personalized system of instruction course. *Journal of Behavioral Education, 18*, 245–265.

Chater, N. (1996). Reconciling simplicity and likelihood principles in perceptual organization. *Psychological Review, 103*, 566–581.

Chein, J., Albert, D., O'Brien, L., Uckert, K., & Steinberg, L. (2011). Peers increase adolescent risk taking by enhancing activity in the brain's reward circuitry. *Developmental Science, 14*, F1–F10.

Chemerinski, E., & Siever, L. J. (2011). The schizophrenia spectrum personality disorders. In D. R. Weinberg & P. Harrison (Eds.), *Schizophrenia*. Hoboken, NJ: Wiley.

Chen, C., & Stevenson, H. W. (1988). Cross-linguistic differences in digit span of preschool children. *Journal of Experimental Child Psychology, 46*, 150–158.

Chen, L-H., Baker, S. P., Braver, E. R., & Li, G. (2000). Carrying passengers as a risk factor for crashes fatal to 16- and 17-year-old drivers. *Journal of the American Medical Association, 283*, 1578–1582.

Chen, X., Chang, L., & He, Y. (2003). The peer group as a context: Mediating and moderating effects of relations between academic and social functioning in Chinese children. *Child Development, 74*, 710–727.

Cherry, E. C. (1953). Some experiments on the recognition of speech, with one and with two ears. *Journal of the Acoustical Society of America, 25*, 975–979.

Cherry, F. C., & Taylor, W. K. (1954). Some further experiments on the recognition of speech with one and two ears. *Journal of the Acoustical Society of America, 26*, 554–559.

Chesler, P. (1969). Maternal influence in learning by observation in kittens. *Science, 166*, 901–903.

Cheung, F., Weigiao, F., & To, C. (2008). The Chinese Personality Assessment Inventory as a culturally relevant personality measure in applied settings. *Social and Personality Psychology Compass, 2*, 74–89.

Cheung, F. M. (2004). Use of Western and indigenously developed personality tests in Asia. *Applied Psychology: An International Review, 53*, 173–191.

Chi, M. T. H., de Leeuw, N., Chiu, M., & LaVancher, C. (1994). Eliciting self-explanations improves understanding. *Cognitive Science, 18*, 439–477.

Chiesa, M., Sharp, R., & Fonagy, P. (2011). Clinical associations of deliberate self-injury and its impact on the outcome of community-based and long-term inpatient treatment for personality disorder. *Psychotherapy and Psychosomatics, 80*, 100–109.

The Chimpanzee Sequencing and Analysis Consortium. (2005). Initial sequence of the chimpanzee genome and comparison with the human genome. *Nature, 437*, 69–87.

Chomsky, N. (1957). *Syntactic structures*. The Hague, Netherlands: Mouton.

Chomsky, N. (1965). *Aspects of a theory of syntax*. Cambridge, MA: MIT Press.

Chomsky, N. (1968). *Language and mind*. New York, NY: Harcourt Brace Jovanovich.

Chrysikou, E. G., & Weisberg, R. W. (2005). Following the wrong footsteps: Fixation effects of pictorial examples in a design problem-solving task. *Journal of Experimental Psychology: Learning, Memory, and Cognition, 31*, 1134–1148.

Chugani, H. T., Phelps, M. E., & Mazziotta, J. C. (1987). Positron emission tomography study of human brain functional development. *Annals of Neurology, 22*, 487–497.

Cialdini, R. B. (1987). Compliance principles of compliance professionals: Psychologists of necessity. In M. Zanna, J. M. Olson, & C. P. Herman (Eds.), *Social influence: The Ontario symposium* (Vol. 5). Hillsdale, NJ: Erlbaum.

Cialdini, R. B. (2001). *Influence: Science and practice* (4th ed.). Boston, MA: Allyn & Bacon.

Cialdini, R. B. (2003). Crafting normative messages to protect the environment. *Current Directions in Psychological Science, 12*, 105–109.

Cialdini, R. B., Cacioppo, J. T., Bassett, R., & Miller, J. A. (1978). The lowball procedure for producing compliance: Commitment then cost. *Journal of Personality and Social Psychology, 36*, 463–476.

Cialdini, R. B., & Goldstein, N. J. (2004). Social influence: Compliance and conformity. *Annual Review of Psychology, 55*, 591–621.

Cicchetti, D., & Toth, S. L. (2006). Developmental psychopathology and preventative intervention. In W. Damon & R. M. Lerner (Gen. Eds.) & K. A. Renninger & I. E. Sigel (Vol. Eds.), *Handbook of child psychology: Vol. 4. Child psychology in practice* (6th ed., pp. 497–547). Hoboken, NJ: Wiley.

Cicirelli, V. G. (2001). Personal meanings of death in older adults and young adults in relation to their fears of death. *Death Studies, 25*, 663–683.

Cikara, M., Bruneau, E. G., & Saxe, R. R. (2011). Us and them: Intergroup failures of empathy. *Current Directions in Psychological Science, 20*, 149–153.

Clark, C. M., Schneider, J. A., Bedell, B. J., Beach, T. G., Bilker, W. B., Mintun, M. A., . . . Skovronsky, D. M. (2011). Use of Florbetpir-PET for imaging ß-Alyloid pathology. *Journal of the American Medical Association, 305*, 275–283.

Clark, E. (1973). What's in a word? On the child's acquisition of semantics in his first language. In T. Moore (Ed.), *Cognitive development and the acquisition of language*. San Diego, CA: Academic Press.

Clark, E. (1987). The principle of contrast: A constraint on language acquisition. In B. MacWhinney (Ed.), *Mechanisms of language acquisition*. Hillsdale, NJ: Erlbaum.

Clark, E. V. (1995). Language acquisition: The lexicon and syntax. In J. L. Miller & P. D. Eimas (Eds.), *Speech, language, and communication*. San Diego, CA: Academic Press.

Clayton, N. S. (2001). Hippocampal growth and maintenance depend on food-caching experience in juvenile mountain chickadees (*Poecile gambeli*). *Behavioral Neuroscience, 115*, 614–625.

Clayton, N. S., & Dickinson, A. (1999). Scrub jays (*Aphelocoma coerulescens*) remember the relative time of caching as well as the location and content of their caches. *Journal of Comparative Psychology, 113*, 403–416.

Clearfield, M. W., & Nelson, N. M. (2006). Sex differences in mothers' speech and play behavior with 6-, 9-, and 14-month-old infants. *Sex Roles, 54*, 127–137.

Clifford, M. M., & Walster, E. (1973). The effects of physical attractiveness on teacher expectation. *Sociology of Education, 46*, 248–258.

Clutton-Brock, T. H. (1991). *The evolution of parental care*. Princeton, NJ: Princeton University Press.

Coffey, S. F., Schumacher, J. A., Baschnagel, J. S., Hawk, L. W., & Holloman, G. (2011). Impulsivity and risk-taking in borderline personality disorder with and without substance use disorders. *Personality Disorders: Theory, Research, and Treatment, 2*, 128–141.

Cohen, R. A., & Albers, H. E. (1991). Disruption of human circadian and cognitive regulation following a discrete hypothalamic lesion: A case study. *Neurology, 41*, 726–729.

Colavita, F. B. (1974). Human sensory dominance. *Perception & Psychophysics, 16*, 409–412.

Colby, A., Kohlberg, L., Gibbs, J., & Lieberman, M. (1983). A longitudinal study of moral judgment. *Monographs of the Society for Research in Child Development, 148* (Whole Nos. 1 & 2).

Colcombe, S., & Kramer, A. F. (2003). Fitness effects on cognitive function in older adults: A meta-analytic study. *Psychological Science, 14,* 125–130.

Coldwell, G. M., & Bender, W. S. (2007). The effectiveness of assertive community treatment for homeless populations with severe mental illness: A meta-analysis. *American Journal of Psychiatry, 164,* 393–399.

Cole, D. A. (1991). Change in self-perceived competence as a function of peer and teacher evaluation. *Developmental Psychology, 27,* 682–688.

Cole, M. (1990). Cognitive development and formal schooling: The evidence from cross-cultural research. In L. C. Moll (Ed.), *Vygotsky and education.* New York, NY: Cambridge University Press.

Cole, M., Gay, J., Glick, J., & Sharp, D. W. (1971). *The cultural context of learning and thinking.* New York, NY: Basic Books.

Cole, M., & Means, B. (1981). *Comparative studies of how people think.* Cambridge, MA: Harvard University Press.

Collins, A., & Loftus, E. (1975). A spreading-activation theory of semantic processing. *Psychological Review, 82,* 407–428.

Collins, W. A., & Steinberg, L. (2006). Adolescent development in interpersonal context. In W. Damon & R. M. Lerner (Gen. Eds.) & N. Eisenberg (Vol. Ed.), *Handbook of child psychology: Vol. 3. Social, emotional, and personality development* (6th ed., pp. 1003–1067). Hoboken, NJ: Wiley.

Collins, W. A., Welsh, D. P., & Furman, W. (2009). Adolescent romantic relationships. *Annual Review of Psychology, 60,* 631–652.

Colonnesi, C., Koops, W., & Terwogt, M. M. (2008). Young children's psychological explanations and their relationship to perception- and intention-understanding. *Infant and Child Development, 17,* 163–179.

Comer, R. J. (2013). *Fundamentals of abnormal psychology,* 7th ed., DSM-5 Update. New York, NY: Worth.

Comer, R. J. (2014). *Abnormal psychology* (8th ed.). New York, NY: Worth.

Comer, R. J. (2015). *Abnormal psychology* (9th ed.). New York, NY: Worth.

Comer, R. J. (2016). *Fundamentals of abnormal psychology.* (8th ed.,). New York, NY: Worth.

Cook, L. J., Chambers, L. C., Añez, E. V., Crocker, H. A., Boniface, D., Yeomans, M. R., & Wardle, J. (2011). Eating for pleasure and profit: The effect of incentives on children's enjoyment of vegetables. *Psychological Science, 22,* 190–196.

Cook, M., & Mineka, S. (1989). Observational conditioning of fear to fear-relevant versus fear-irrelevant stimuli in rhesus monkeys. *Journal of Abnormal Psychology, 98,* 448–459.

Cook, M., & Mineka, S. (1990). Selective associations in the observational conditioning of fear in rhesus monkeys. *Journal of Experimental Psychology: Animal Behavior Processes, 16,* 372–389.

Cook, R. G., & Smith, J. D. (2006). Stages of abstraction and exemplar memorization in pigeon category learning. *Psychological Science, 17,* 1059–1066.

Cooley, C. H. (1964). *Human nature and the social order.* New York, NY: Schocken Books. (Original work published 1902)

Cooper, H. M., & Good, T. L. (1983). *Pygmalion grows up: Studies in the expectation communication process.* New York, NY: Longman.

Cooper, J. (2012). Cognitive dissonance theory. In P. A. M. Van Lange, A. W. Kruglanski, & E. Tory Higgins (Eds.), *Handbook of theories of social psychology* (Vol. 1, pp. 377–397). Los Angeles, CA: Sage.

Corballis, P. M. (1999). The gestural origins of language. *American Scientist, 87,* 138.

Corballis, P. M. (2003). Visuospatial processing and the right-hemisphere interpreter. *Brain and Cognition, 53,* 171–176.

Coren, S., & Ward, L. M. (1989). *Sensation and perception* (3rd ed.). New York, NY: Harcourt Brace Jovanovich.

Corkin, S. (2002). What's new with the amnesic patient H. M.? *Nature Reviews Neuroscience, 3,* 153–160.

Corrigan, P. W., Druss, B. G., & Perlick, D. A. (2014). The impact of mental illness stigma on seeking and participating in mental health care. *Psychological Science in the Public Interest, 15,* 37–70.

Corsini, R. J., & Wedding, D. (Eds.). (2011). *Current psychotherapies* (9th ed.). Belmont, CA: Brooks/Cole.

Cosmides, L., & Tooby, J. (1992). Cognitive adaptations for social exchange. In J. H. Barkow, L. Cosmides, & J. Tooby (Eds.), *The adapted mind: Evolutionary psychology and the generation of culture* (pp. 163–228). New York, NY: Oxford University Press.

Cosmides, L., & Tooby, J. (2016). Adaptations of reasoning about social exchange. In D. M. Buss (Ed.), *Evolutionary psychology handbook* (2nd ed., Vol. 2, pp. 625–668). New York, NY: Wiley.

Costa, P. T., & McCrae, R. R. (1992). *The NEO-PI-R professional manual.* Odessa, FL: Psychological Assessment Resources.

Costa, P. T., Terracciano, A., & McCrae, R. R. (2001). Gender differences in personality traits across cultures: Robust and surprising findings. *Journal of Personality and Social Psychology, 81,* 322–331.

Coughlin, L. D., & Patel, V. L. (1987). Processing of critical information by physicians and medical students. *Journal of Medical Education, 62,* 818–828.

Cousins, N. (1977, May 23). Anatomy of an illness (as perceived by the patient). *Saturday Review, 4–6,* 48–51.

Cowan, N., & Alloway, T. (2009). Development of working memory in childhood. In M. L. Courage & N. Cowan (Eds.), *The development of memory in infancy and childhood* (pp. 304–342). New York, NY: Psychology Press.

Cowan, N., Nugent, L. D., Elliott, E. M., & Saults, J. S. (2000). Persistence of memory for ignored lists of digits: Areas of developmental constancy and change. *Journal of Experimental Child Psychology, 76,* 151–172.

Cowart, B. J. (1981). Development of taste perception in humans: Sensitivity and preference throughout the life span. *Psychological Bulletin, 90,* 43–73.

Cowen, P. J. (2005). The neurobiology of depression. In E. J. L. Griez, C. Faravelli, J. J. Nutt, & J. Zohar (Eds.), *Mood disorders: Clinical management issues.* West Sussex, England: Wiley.

Cowlishaw, G., & Dunbar, R. I. M. (1991). Dominance rank and mating success in male primates. *Animal Behaviour, 41,* 1045–1056.

Cox, B. J., Turnbull, D. L., Robinson, J. A., Grant, B. F., & Stein, M. B. (2011). The effects of avoidant personality disorder on the persistence of generalized social anxiety disorder in the general population: Results from a longitudinal, nationally representative mental health survey. *Depression and Anxiety, 28,* 250–255.

Cox, J. J., Reimann, F., Nicholas, A. K., Thornton, G., Roberts, E., Springell, K., . . . Woods, C. G. (2006). An *SCN9A* channelopathy causes congenital inability to experience pain. *Nature, 444,* 894–898.

Coyle, T. R., Pillow, D. R., Snyder, A. C., & Kochunov, P. (2011). Processing speed mediates the development of general intelligence (*g*) in adolescence. *Psychological Science, 22,* 1265–1269.

Crabbe, J. C., Wahlsten, D., & Dudek, B. C. (1999). Genetics of mouse behavior: Interactions with the laboratory environment. *Science, 284,* 1670–1672.

Crabtree, J. W., & Riesen, A. H. (1979). Effects of the duration of dark rearing on visually guided behavior in the kitten. *Developmental Psychobiology, 12,* 291–303.

Craik, F. I., & Tulving, E. (1975). Depth of processing and the retention of words in episodic memory. *Journal of Experimental Psychology: General, 104,* 268–294.

Cramer, P. (2000). Defense mechanisms in psychology today: Further processes for adaptation. *American Psychologist, 55,* 637–646.

Cramer, P. (2008). Identification and the development of competence: A 44-year longitudinal study from late adolescence to late middle age. *Psychology and Aging, 23,* 410–421.

Craske, M. G. (1999). *Anxiety disorders: Psychological approaches to theory and treatment.* Boulder, CO: Westview.

Credé, M., Tynan, M. C., & Harms, P. D. (2016, June 16). Much ado about grit: A meta-analytic synthesis of the grit literature. *Journal of Personality and Social Psychology.* Advance online publication.

Critchley, H. D., Wiens, S., Rotschtein, P., Öhman, A., & Dolan, R. J. (2004). Neural systems supporting interoceptive awareness. *Nature Neuroscience, 7,* 189–195.

Cross, P. (1977). Not *can* but *will* college teachers be improved? *New Directions for Higher Education, 17,* 1–15.

Crossley, N. A., Constante, M., McGuire, P., & Power, P. (2010). Efficacy of atypical v. typical antipsychotics in the treatment of early psychosis: Meta-analysis. *British Journal of Psychiatry, 196,* 434–439.

Crowley, K., Callanan, M. A., Tenenbaum, H. R., & Allen, E. (2001). Parents explain more often to boys than to girls during shared scientific thinking. *Psychological Science, 12,* 258–261.

Crowne, D. P., & Liverant, S. (1963). Conformity under varying conditions of personal commitment. *Journal of Abnormal and Social Psychology, 66,* 547–555.

Cudjoe, S., Moss, S., & Nguyen, L. (2007). How do exercise and diet compare for weight loss? *Journal of Family Practice, 56,* 841–843.

Culp, R. E., Cook, A. S., & Housley, P. C. (1983). A comparison of observed and reported adult-infant interactions: Effects of perceived sex. *Sex Roles, 9,* 475–479.

Cummins, D. D. (2013). Deontic and epistemic reasoning in children revisited: Comment on Dack and Astington (2011). *Journal of Experimental Child Psychology, 116,* 762–769.

Cummins-Sebree, S. W., & Fragaszy, D. M. (2005). Choosing and using tools: Capuchins (*Cebus apella*) use a different metric than tamarins (*Saguinus oedipus*). *Journal of Comparative Psychology, 119,* 210–219.

Cunningham, W. A., & Brosch, T. (2012). Motivational salience: Amygdala tuning from traits, needs, values, and goals. *Psychological Science, 21,* 54–59.

Cunningham, W. A., Preacher, K. J., & Banaji, M. R. (2001). Implicit attitude measures: Consistency, stability, and convergent validity. *Psychological Science, 12,* 163–170.

Curran, P., Stice, E., & Chassin, L. (1997). The relation between adolescent alcohol use and peer alcohol use: A longitudinal random coefficients model. *Journal of Consulting and Clinical Psychology, 65,* 130–140.

Curtiss, S. (1977). *Genie: A psycholinguistic study of a modern-day "wild child."* San Diego, CA: Academic Press.

Cutler, S. S., Larsen, R. J., & Bunce, S. C. (1996). Repressive coping style and the experience and recall of emotion: A naturalistic study of daily affect. *Journal of Personality, 65,* 379–405.

Cynader, M., Berman, N. M., & Hein, A. (1976). Recovery of function in cat visual cortex following prolonged deprivation. *Experimental Brain Research, 25,* 139–156.

Cytowic, R. E. (2002). *Synaesthesia: A union of the senses* (2nd ed.). Cambridge, MA: MIT Press.

Czeisler, C. A., Johnson, M. P., Duffy, J. E., Brown, E. N., Ronda, J. M., & Kronauer, R. E. (1990). Exposure to bright light and darkness to treat physiologic maladaptation to night work. *New England Journal of Medicine, 322,* 1253–1259.

Czeisler, C. A., Kronauer, R. E., Allen, J. S., Duffy, J. F., Jewett, M. E., Brown, E. N., & Ronda, J. M. (1989). Bright light induction of strong (type O) resetting of the human circadian pacemaker. *Science, 244,* 1328–1333.

Dacey, D. M. (2000). Parallel pathways for spectral coding in primate retina. *Annual Review of Neuroscience, 23,* 743–775.

Dahlin, E., Neely, A. S., Larsson, A., Bäckman, L., & Nyberg, L. (2008). Transfer of learning after updating training mediated by the striatum. *Science, 320,* 1510–1512.

Daley, T. C., Whaley, S. E., Sigman, M. D., Espinosa, M. P., & Neumann, C. (2003). IQ on the rise: The Flynn effect in rural Kenyan children. *Psychological Science, 14,* 215–219.

Dalton, P., Doolittle, N., & Breslin, P. A. S. (2002). Gender-specific induction of enhanced sensitivity to odors. *Nature Neuroscience, 5,* 199–200.

Dalton, R. (2004). True colours. *Nature, 428,* 596–597.

Daly, M., & Wilson, M. (1988). *Homicide.* New Brunswick, NJ: Transaction Publishers.

Daly, M., & Wilson, M. (1990). Killing the competition. *Human Nature, 1,* 81–107.

Dam, H., Jakobsen, K., & Mellerup, E. (1998). Prevalence of winter depression in Denmark. *Acta Psychiatrica Scandinavica, 97,* 104.

Damasio, A. (2001). Fundamental feelings. *Nature, 413,* 781.

Damasio, H., Grabowski, T., Frank, R., Galaburda, A. M., & Damasio, A. R. (1994). The return of Phineas Gage: Clues about the brain from the skull of a famous patient. *Science, 265,* 1102–1105.

Dapretto, M., Davies, M. S., Pfeifer, J. H., Scott, A. A., Sigman, M., Bookheimer, S. Y., & Iacoboni, M. (2006). Understanding emotions in others: mirror neuron dysfunction in children with autism spectrum disorders. *Nature Neuroscience, 9,* 28–30.

D'Argembeau, A., & Van der Linden, M. (2008). Remembering pride and shame: Self-enhancement and the phenomenology of autobiographical memory. *Memory, 16,* 538–547.

Darwin, C. (1963). *The origin of species.* New York, NY: Washington Square Press. (Original work published 1859)

Darwin, C. (1965). *The expression of emotions in man and animals.* Chicago, IL: University of Chicago Press. (Original work published 1872)

Dasen, P. R. (Ed.). (1977). *Piagetian psychology: Crosscultural contributions.* New York, NY: Gardner.

Datu, J. A. D., Valdez, J. P. M., & King, R. B. (2016). Perseverance counts but consistency does not! Validating the Short Grit Scale in a collectivist setting. *Current Psychology, 35,* 121–130.

D'Augelli, A. R. (2005). Stress and adaptation among families of lesbian, gay, and bisexual youth: Research challenges. *Journal of GLBT Family Studies, 1,* 115–135.

D'Augelli, A. R., & Patterson, C. J. (Eds.). (2001). *Lesbian, gay, and bisexual identities and youths: Psychological perspectives.* Oxford, England: Oxford University Press.

Daum, I., Channon, S., & Canavar, A. (1989). Classical conditioning in patients with severe memory problems. *Journal of Neurology and Neurosurgery Psychiatry, 52,* 47–51.

D'Ausilio, A., Pulvermuller, F., Salmas, P., Buflari, I., Begliomini, C., & Fadiga, L. (2009). The motor somatotopy of speech perception. *Current Biology, 19,* 381–385.

Davidson, J. M. (1980). Hormones and sexual behavior in the male. In D. T. Krieger & J. C. Hughes (Eds.), *Neuroendocrinology.* Sunderland, MA: Sinauer.

Davidson, R. J., Pizzagalli, D., Nitschke, J. B., & Kalin, N. H. (2003). Parsing the subcomponents of emotion and disorders of emotion: Perspectives from affective neuroscience. In R. J. Davidson, K. R. Scherer, & H. H. Goldsmith (Eds.), *Handbook of affective sciences.* Oxford, England: Oxford University Press.

Davis, M. (1992). The role of the amygdala in fear and anxiety. *Annual Review of Neuroscience, 15,* 353–375.

Davis, P. J., & Schwartz, G. E. (1987). Repression and the inaccessibility of affective memories. *Journal of Personality and Social Psychology, 52,* 155–162.

Dawson, G., & Burner, K. (2011). Behavioral interventions in children and adolescents with autism spectrum disorder: A review of recent findings. *Current Opinion in Pediatrics, 23,* 616–620.

Day, J. J., Roitman, M. F., Wightman, R. M., & Carelli, R. M. (2007). Associative learning mediates dynamic shifts in dopamine signaling in the nucleus accumbens. *Nature Neuroscience, 10,* 1020–1028.

Day, S. A. (2007). Types of synaesthesia. http://www.daysyn.com/Types-of-Syn.html. Retrieved March 5, 2014.

De Bolle, M., De Fruyt, F., Löckenhoff, C. E., Aguilar-Vafaie, M. E., Ahn, H-N., et al. (2015). The emergence of sex differences in personality traits in early adolescence: A cross-sectional, cross-cultural study. *Journal of Personality and Social Psychology, 108,* 171–185.

de Boysson-Bardies, B. (1999). *How language comes to children.* Cambridge, MA: MIT Press.

de Groot, A. D. (1965). *Thought and choice in chess.* The Hague, Netherlands: Mouton.

De Houwer, J., & De Bruycker, E. (2007). Implicit attitudes towards meat and vegetables in vegetarians and nonvegetarians. *International Journal of Psychology, 42,* 158–165.

De Houwer, J., Thomas, S., & Baeyens, F. (2001). Associative learning of likes and dislikes: A review of 25 years of research on human evaluative conditioning. *Psychological Bulletin, 127,* 853–869.

de Jong, J. T. V. M., Komproe, I. H., & Ommeren, M. V. (2003). Common mental disorders in postconflict settings. *The Lancet, 361,* 2128–2130.

De Lisi, R., & Staudt, J. (1980). Individual differences in college students' performance on formal operations tasks. *Journal of Applied Developmental Psychology, 1,* 163–174.

de Paula, F., Soares, J. M., Haider, M. A., de Lima, G. R., & Baracat, E. C. (2007). The benefits of androgens combined with hormone replacement therapy regarding to patients with postmenopausal sexual symptoms. *Maturitas, 56,* 69–77.

De Valois, R. L., Abramov, I., & Jacobs, G. H. (1966). Analysis of response patterns of LGN cells. *Journal of the Optical Society of America, 56,* 96–97.

de Villiers, J. G., & de Villiers, P. A. (1979). *Language acquisition.* Cambridge, MA: Harvard University Press.

de Waal, F. (2005). *Our inner ape: A leading primatologist explains why we are who we are.* New York, NY: Riverhead Books.

Deary, I. (2008). Why do intelligent people live longer? *Nature, 456,* 175–176.

Deary, I. J., & Der, G. (2005). Reaction time explains IQ's association with death. *Psychological Science, 16,* 64–69.

Deary, I. J., Weiss, A., & Batty, D. (2010). Intelligence and personality as predictors of illness and death: How researchers in differential psychology and chronic disease epidemiology are collaborating to understand and address health inequalities. *Psychological Science in the Public Interest, 11,* 53–79.

DeCasper, A. J., & Fifer, W. P. (1980). Of human bonding: Newborns prefer their mothers' voices. *Science, 208,* 1174–1176.

DeCasper, A. J., & Spence, M. J. (1986). Prenatal maternal speech influences newborns' perception of speech sounds. *Infant Behavior and Development, 9,* 133–150.

Decety, J., & Cacioppo, J. (2010). Frontiers in human neuroscience: The golden triangle and beyond. *Perspectives on Psychological Science, 5,* 767–771.

Defoe, I. N., Dubas, J. S., Figner, B., & van Aken, M. A. G. (2014). A meta-analysis on age differences in risky decisions making: Adolescents versus children and adults. *Psychological Bulletin, 141,* 48–84.

Dehaene, S., Jobert, A., Naccache, L., Ciuciu, P., Poline, J.-B., Le Bihan, D., & Cohen, L. (2004). Letter binding and invariant recognition of masked words. *Psychological Science, 15,* 307–314.

Dehaene, S., Naccache, L., Cohen, L., Le Bihan, D., Mangin, J.-F., Poline, J.-B., & Rivière, D. (2001). Cerebral mechanisms of word masking and unconscious repetition priming. *Nature Neuroscience, 4,* 752–758.

Del Giudice, M. (2012). Fetal programming by maternal stress: Insights from a conflict perspective. *Psychoneuroendocrinology, 37,* 1614–1629.

Del Giudice, M. (2014). An evolutionary life history framework for psychopathology. *Psychological Inquiry, 25,* 261–300.

Del Guidice, M. (2016). The life history model of psychopathology explains the structure of psychiatric disorders and the emergence of the p factor: A simulation study. *Clinical Psychological Science, 4,* 299–311.

DeLamater, J., & Friedrich, R. (2002). Human sexual development. *Journal of Sex Research, 39,* 10–14.

Delay, J., & Deniker, P. (1952). Trente-huit cas de psychoses traitées par la cure prolongée et continué de 4560 RP. *Comptes Rendus Congrès des Médecins Aliénistes et Neurologistes de France et des Pays de Langue Française, 50,* 497–502.

DeLoache, J. S. (1987). Rapid change in the symbolic functioning of very young children. *Science, 238,* 1556–1557.

DeLoache, J. S. (1991). Symbolic functioning in very young children: Understanding of pictures and models. *Child Development, 62,* 736–752.

DeLoache, J. S. (2010). Early development of the understanding and use of symbolic artifacts. In U. Goswami (Ed.), *The Wiley-Blackwell handbook of childhood cognitive development* (2nd ed., pp. 312–336). West Sussex, England: Blackwell.

DeLoache, J. S., & LoBue, V. (2009). The narrow fellow in the grass: Human infants associate snakes and fear. *Developmental Science, 12,* 201–207.

DeLoache, J. S., & Marzolf, D. P. (1992). When a picture is not worth a thousand words: Young children's understanding of pictures and models. *Cognitive Development, 7,* 317–329.

DeLuca, N. L., Moser, L. L., & Bond, G. R. (2008). Assertive community treatment. In K. T. Mueser & D. V. Jeste (Eds.), *Clinical handbook of schizophrenia.* New York, NY: Guilford.

Dember, W. N., & Fowler, H. (1958). Spontaneous alternation behavior. *Psychological Bulletin, 53,* 412–428.

Dennett, D. (1990). The interpretation of texts, people, and other artifacts. *Philosophy and Phenomenological Quarterly, 1*(Supp.), 177–194.

Derakshan, N., & Eysenck, M. W. (1998). Working memory capacity in high trait-anxious and repressor groups. *Cognition and Emotion, 12,* 697–613.

Derakshan, N., Eysenck, M. W., & Myers, L. B. (2007). Emotional information processing in repressors: The vigilance-avoidance hypothesis. *Cognition and Emotion, 21,* 1585–1614.

Desai, D. V., & Dhanani, H. (2004). Sickle cell disease: History and origin. *The Internet Journal of Hematology, 1*(2).

Descartes, R. (1972). *Treatise of man* (T. S. Hall, Trans.). Cambridge, MA: Harvard University Press. (Original work published 1637)

Descartes, R. (1985). *The passions of the soul.* In J. Cottingham, R. Stoothoff, & D. Murdoch (Eds. & Trans.), *The philosophical writings of Descartes* (Vol. 1, pp. 324–404). Cambridge, England: Cambridge University Press. (Original work published 1649)

DeWitt, L. A., & Samuel, A. G. (1990). The role of knowledge-based expectations in music perception: Evidence from musical restoration. *Journal of Experimental Psychology: General, 119,* 123–144.

Dewsbury, D. A. (1988). The comparative psychology of monogamy. In D. W. Leger (Ed.), *Comparative perspectives in modern psychology. Nebraska Symposium on Motivation, 1987.* Lincoln: University of Nebraska Press.

Dhwan, N., Kunik, M. E., Oldham, J., & Coverdale, J. (2010). Prevalence and treatment of narcissistic personality disorder in the community: A systematic review. *Comprehensive Psychiatry, 51,* 333–339.

Diamond, A. (2012). Activities and programs that improve children's executive functions. *Current Directions in Psychological Science, 21,* 335–341.

Diamond, J. (2013). *The world until yesterday: What can we learn from traditional societies?* New York, NY: Viking.

Diamond, L. M. (2004). Emerging perspectives on distinctions between romantic love and sexual desire. *Current Directions in Psychological Science, 13,* 116–119.

Dickens, W. T., & Flynn, J. R. (2006). Black Americans reduce the racial IQ gap: Evidence from standardized samples. *Psychological Science, 17,* 913–924.

Dickinson, A. M. (2000). The historical roots of Organizational Behavior Management in the private sector: The 1950s–1980s. *Journal of Organizational Behavior Management, 20,* 9–58.

Dickinson, D., Ragland, J. D., Gold, J. M., & Gur, R. C. (2008). General and specific cognitive deficits in schizophrenia: Goliath defeats David? *Biological Psychiatry, 64,* 823–827.

Diener, E., Sandvik, E., Pavot, W., & Fujita, F. (1992). Extraversion and subjective well-being in a U.S. national probability sample. *Journal of Research in Personality, 26,* 205–215.

Dillon, K. M. (1993). Facilitated communication, autism, and Ouija. *Skeptical Inquirer, 17,* 281–287.

DiMascio, A., Weissman, M. M., Prusoff, B. A., Neu, C., Zwilling, M., & Klerman, G. L. (1979). Differential symptom reduction by drugs and psychotherapy in acute depression. *Archives of General Psychiatry, 36,* 1450–1456.

Dimberg, U., Thunberg, M., & Elmehed, K. (2000). Unconscious facial reactions to emotional facial expressions. *Psychological Science, 11,* 86–89.

Dion, K. K. (2002). Cultural perspectives on facial attractiveness. In G. Rhodes & L. A. Zebrowitz (Eds.), *Facial attractiveness: Evolutionary, cognitive, and social perspectives.* Westport, CT: Ablex.

Dismukes, R. K. (2013). Prospective memory in workplace and everyday situations. *Current Directions in Psychological Science, 21,* 215–220.

Docherty, N. M., Cohen, A. S., Nienow, T. M., Dinzeo, T. J., & Dangelmaier, R. E. (2003). Stability of formal thought disorder and referential communication disturbances in schizophrenia. *Journal of Abnormal Psychology, 112,* 469–475.

Doghramji, K. (2006). The epidemiology and diagnosis of insomnia. *American Journal of Managed Care, 12,* S214–S220.

Dolhinow, P. J., & Bishop, N. H. (1970). The development of motor skills and social relationships among primates through play. In J. P. Hill (Ed.), *Minnesota Symposia on Child Psychology* (pp. 180–198). Minneapolis: University of Minnesota Press.

Domhoff, G. W. (2003). *The scientific study of dreams: Network analysis, cognitive development, and content analysis.* Washington, DC: American Psychological Association.

Domjan, M. (2003). *The principles of learning and behavior* (5th ed.). Belmont, CA: Wadsworth.

Donald, M. (2000). The central role of culture in cognitive evolution: A reflection on the myth of the "isolated mind." In L. P. Nucci, G. B. Saxe, and E. Turiel (Eds.), *Culture, thought, and development* (pp. 19–38). Mahwah, NJ: Lawrence Erlbaum.

Dorman, M. F., & Wilson, B. S. (2004). The design and function of cochlear implants. *American Scientist, 92,* 436–445.

Doty, R. L. (2001). Olfaction. *Annual Review of Psychology, 52,* 423–452.

Doty, R. L. (2014). Human pheromones: Do they exist? In C. Mucignat-Caretta (Ed), *Neurobiology of chemical communication.* Boca Raton, FL: CRC Press.

Douglas, K. M., & Bilkey, D. K. (2007). Amusia is associated with deficits in spatial processing. *Nature Neuroscience, 10,* 915–921.

Douglas, N. J. (2002). *Clinician's guide to sleep medicine.* London, England: Arnold.

Dovidio, J. F., Johnson, C., Gaertner, S. L., Validzic, A., Howard, A., & Eisinger, N. (1994, April). *Racial bias and the role of implicit and explicit attitudes.* Paper presented at the annual meeting of the Eastern Psychological Association, Providence, RI.

Doyle, A. C. (1917). The adventure of the cardboard box. In *His last bow: A reminiscence of Sherlock Holmes.* New York, NY: George H. Doran.

Dozier, M., Peloso, E., Lindhiem, O., Gordon, M. K., Manni, M., Sepulveda, S., & Ackerman, J. (2006). Developing evidence-based interventions for foster children: An example of a randomized clinical trial with infants and toddlers. *Journal of Social Issues, 62,* 767–785.

Draghi-Lorenz, R., Reddy, V., & Costall, A. (2001). Rethinking the development of "non basic" emotions: A critical review of existing theories. *Developmental Review, 21,* 263–304.

Draper, P., & Harpending, H. (1982). Father absence and reproductive strategy: An evolutionary perspective. *Journal of Anthropological Research, 38,* 255–273.

Draper, P., & Harpending, H. (1988). A sociobiological perspective on the development of human reproductive strategies. In K. B. MacDonald (Ed.), *Sociobiological perspectives on human development.* New York, NY: Springer-Verlag.

Drew, T., Võ, M. L.-H., & Wolfe, J. M. (2013). The invisible gorilla strikes again: Sustained inattentional blindness in expert observers. *Psychological Science, 24,* 1848–1853.

Dronkers, N. F., Pinker, S., & Damasio, A. (2000). Language and the aphasias. In E. R. Kandel, J. H. Schwartz, & T. M. Jessell (Eds.), *Principles of neural science* (4th ed.). New York, NY: McGraw-Hill.

Duchaine, B. C., & Nakayama, K. (2006). Developmental prosopagnosia: A window to content-specific face processing. *Current Opinion in Neurobiology, 16,* 166–173.

Duckworth, A. L. (2016). *Grit: The power of passion and perseverance.* New York, NY: Scribner.

Duckworth, A. L., Kirby, T. A., Tsukayama, E., Berstein, H., & Ericsson, K. A. (2011). Deliberate practice spells success: Why grittier competitors triumph at the National Spelling Bee. *Social Psychological & Personality Science, 2,* 174–181.

Duckworth, A. L., Peterson, C., Matthews, M. D., & Kelly, D. R. (2007). Grit: Perseverance and passion for long-term goals. *Journal of Personality and Social Psychology, 92,* 1087–1101.

Duckworth, A. L., & Quinn, P. D. (2009). Development and validation of the Short Grit Scale (Grit-S). *Journal of Personality Assessment, 91,* 166–174.

Duckworth, A. L., & Seligman, M. E. P. (2005). Self-discipline outdoes IQ in predicting academic performance of adolescence. *Psychological Science, 16,* 939–944.

Duffy, K. A., & Chartrand, T. L. (2015). The extravert advantage: How and when extraverts build rapport with other people. *Psychological Science, 26,* 1795–1802.

Duffy, S., Toriyama, R., Itakura, S., & Kitayama, S. (2009). Development of cultural strategies of attention in North American and Japanese children. *Journal of Experimental Child Psychology, 102,* 351–359.

Duffy, V. B., & Bartoshuk, L. M. (1996). Sensory factors in feeding. In E. D. Capaldi (Ed.), *Why we eat what we eat: The psychology of eating.* Washington, DC: American Psychological Association.

Dufner, M., Rauthmann, J. F., Czarna, A. Z., & Denissen, J. J. (2013). Are narcissists sexy? Zeroing in on the effects of narcissism on short-term mate appeal. *Personality and Social Psychology Bulletin, 39,* 87–882.

Dumont, M., & Beaulieu, C. (2007). Light exposure in the natural environment: Relevance to mood and sleep disorders. *Sleep Medicine, 8,* 557–565.

Dunbar, K. (1999). The scientist in vivo: How scientists think and reason in the laboratory. In L. Magnani, N. Nersessian, & P. Thatard (Eds.), *Model-based reasoning in scientific discovery.* New York, NY: Plenum Press.

Dunbar, K. (2001). The analogical paradox: Why analogy is so easy in naturalistic settings, yet so difficult in the psychology laboratory. In D. Gentner, K. J. Holyoak, & B. N. Kokinov (Eds.), *The analogical mind: Perspectives from cognitive science.* Cambridge, MA: MIT Press.

Duncker, K. (1945). On problem-solving. *Psychological Monographs, 58*(270).

Dunham, Y., Baron, A. S., & Banaji, M. R. (2006). From American city to Japanese village: A cross-cultural investigation of implicit race attitudes. *Child Development, 77,* 1268–1281.

Dunham, Y., Baron, A. S., & Banaji, M. R. (2008). The development of implicit intergroup cognition. *Trends in Cognitive Science, 12,* 248–253.

Dunn, F. A., Lankheet, M. J., & Rieke, F. (2007). Light adaptation in cone vision involves switching between receptor and post-receptor sites. *Nature, 449,* 603–607.

Dunn, J., & Plomin, R. (1990). *Separate lives: Why siblings are so different.* New York, NY: Basic Books.

Dunning, D., Heath, C., & Suls, J. M. (2004). Flawed self-assessment: Implications for health, education, and the workplace. *Psychological Science in the Public Interest, 5,* 69–106.

Dweck, C. S. (2006). *Mindset: The new psychology of success.* New York, NY: Random House.

Dweck, C. S. (2008). Can personality be changed? The role of beliefs in personality change. *Current Directions in Psychological Science, 17,* 391–394.

Dweck, C. S., Davidson, W., Nelson, S., & Enna, B. (1978). Sex differences in learned helplessness: II. The contingencies of evaluative feedback in the classroom. III. An experimental analysis. *Developmental Psychology, 14,* 268–276.

Dykiert, D., Der, G., Starr, J. M., & Deary, I. J. (2012). Sex differences in reaction time mean and intraindividual variability across the lifespan. *Developmental Psychology, 48,* 1262–1276.

Eagle, M., Wolitzky, D. L., & Klein, G. S. (1966). Imagery: Effect of a concealed figure in a stimulus. *Science, 151,* 837–839.

Eagly, A. H. (2007). Female leadership advantage and disadvantage: Resolving the contradictions. *Psychology of Women Quarterly, 31,* 1–12.

Easton, J. A. M., & Shackelford, T. K. (2009). Morbid jealousy and sex differences in partner-directed violence. *Human Nature, 20,* 342–350.

Eaton, W. O., & Ritchot, K. F. M. (1995). Physical maturation and information-processing speed in middle childhood. *Developmental Psychology, 31,* 967–972.

Ecker, W. (2012). Non-delusional pathological jealousy as an obsessive-compulsive spectrum disorder: Cognitive-behavioural conceptualization and some treatment suggestions. *Journal of Obsessive-Compulsive and Related Disorders, 1,* 203–210.

Edelman, G. M. (1987). *Neural Darwinism.* New York, NY: Basic Books.

Eden, D. (2003). Self-fulfilling prophesies in organizations. In J. Greenberg (Ed.), *Organizational behavior: The state of the science* (2nd ed.). Mahwah, NJ: Erlbaum.

Ehlers, A., Bisson, J., Clark, D. M., Creamer, M., Pilling, S., Richards, D., . . . Yule, W. (2010). Do all psychological treatments really work the same in posttraumatic stress disorder? *Clinical Psychology Review, 30,* 269–276.

Eibl-Eibesfeldt, I. (1975). *Ethology: The biology of behavior* (2nd ed.). New York, NY: Holt, Rinehart & Winston.

Eibl-Eibesfeldt, I. (1989). *Human ethology.* New York, NY: de Gruyter.

Eichenbaum, H. (2001). The long and winding road to memory consolidation. *Nature Neuroscience, 4,* 1057–1058.

Eigsti, I.-M., Zayas, V., Mischel, W., Shoda, Y., Ayduk, O., Dadlani, M. B., . . . Casey, B. J. (2006). Predicting cognitive control from preschool to late adolescence and young adulthood. *Psychological Science, 17,* 478–484.

Einstein, G. O., & McDaniel, M. A. (2005). Prospective memory: Multiple retrieval processes. *Current Directions in Psychological Science, 14,* 286–290.

Einstein, G. O., & McDaniel, M. A. (2010). Prospective memory and what costs do not reveal about retrieval processes: A commentary on Smith, Hunt, McVay, and McConnell (2007). *Journal of Experimental Psychology: Learning, Memory, and Cognition, 36,* 1082–1088.

Eisenberg, N., & Spinard, T. L. (2004). Emotion-related regulation: Sharpening the definition. *Child Development, 75,* 334–339.

Eisenberg, N., Spinard, T. L., & Morris, A. S. (2013). Prosocial development. In P. Zelazo (Ed.), *Oxford handbook of developmental psychology* (Vol. 2, pp. 300–325). Oxford, England: Oxford University Press.

Ekman, P. (1973). *Darwin and facial expression: A century of research in review.* Los Altos, CA: Malor.

Ekman, P. (1984). Expression and the nature of emotion. In K. R. Scherer & P. Ekman (Eds.), *Approaches to emotion.* Hillsdale, NJ: Erlbaum.

Ekman, P. (1992). Facial expressions of emotion: New findings, new questions. *Psychological Science, 3,* 34–38.

Ekman, P., & Friesen, W. V. (1975). *Unmasking the face.* Englewood Cliffs, NJ: Prentice Hall.

Ekman, P., & Friesen, W. V. (1982). Measuring facial movements with the facial action coding system. In P. Ekman (Ed.), *Emotion in the human face.* Cambridge, England: Cambridge University Press.

Ekman, P., Friesen, W. V., O'Sullivan, M., Chan, A., Diacoyanni-Tarlatzis, I., Heider, K., . . . Tzavaras, A. (1987). Universals and cultural differences in the judgments of facial expressions of emotion. *Journal of Personality and Social Psychology, 53,* 712–717.

Ekman, P., Levenson, R. W., & Friesen, W. V. (1983). Autonomic nervous system activity distinguishes among emotions. *Science, 221,* 1208–1210.

Elbert, T., Pantev, C., Wienbruch, C., Rockstroh, B., & Taub, E. (1995). Increased cortical representation of the fingers of the left hand in string players. *Science, 270,* 305–307.

Elfenbein, H. A., & Ambady, N. (2003). Universals and cultural differences in recognizing emotions. *Current Directions in Psychological Science, 12,* 159–164.

Elfenbein, H. A., Beaupré, M., Lévesque, M., & Hess, U. (2007). Toward a dialect theory: Cultural differences in the expression and recognition of posed expressions. *Emotion, 7,* 131–146.

Elkind, D. (1978). Understanding the young adolescent. *Adolescence, 13,* 127–134.

Ellis, A. (1962). *Reason and emotion in psychotherapy.* New York, NY: Lyle Stuart.

Ellis, A. (1986). Rational-emotive therapy. In I. L. Kutash & A. Wolf (Eds.), *Psychotherapist's casebook.* San Francisco, CA: Jossey-Bass.

Ellis, B. J. (2004). Timing of pubertal maturation in girls: An integrated life history approach. *Psychological Bulletin, 130,* 920–958.

Ellis, B. J., Bates, J. E., Dodge, K. A., Fergusson, D. M., Horwood, L. J., Pettit, G. S., & Woodward, L. (2003). Does father absence place daughters at special risk for early sexual activity and teenage pregnancy? *Child Development, 74,* 801–821.

Ellis, B. J., & Boyce, W. T. (2008). Biological sensitivity to context. *Current Directions in Psychological Science, 17,* 183–187.

Ellis, B. J., & Boyce, W. T. (Eds.). (2011). Differential susceptibility to context: Toward an understanding of sensitivity to developmental experiences and context. *Development and Psychopathology, 23,* 1–5.

Ellis, B. J., Del Giudice, M., Dishion, T. J., Figueredo, A. J., Gray, P., Griskevicius, V., . . . Wilson, D. S. (2012). The evolutionary basis of risky adolescent behavior: Implications for science, policy, and practice. *Developmental Psychology, 48,* 598–623.

Ellis, B. J., Figueredo, A. J., Brumbach, B. H., & Schlomer, G. L. (2009). Fundamental dimensions of environmental risk: The impact of harsh versus unpredictable environments on the evolution and development of life history strategies. *Human Nature, 20,* 204–268.

Ellis, B. J., Jackson, J. J., & Boyce, W. T. (2006). The stress response systems: Universality and adaptive individual differences. *Developmental Review, 26,* 175–212.

Ellis, J. (1996). Prospective memory of the realization of delayed intentions: A conceptual framework for research. In M. Brandimonte, G. O. Einstein, & M. A. McDaniel (Eds.), *Prospective memory: Theory and application* (pp. 1–22). Mahwah, NJ: Erlbaum.

Ellis, N. C., & Hennelley, R. A. (1980). A bilingual word-length effect: Implications for intelligence testing and the relative ease of mental calculation in Welsh and English. *British Journal of Psychology, 71,* 43–52.

Ellis, S., Rogoff, B., & Cromer, C. (1981). Age segregation in children's social interactions. *Developmental Psychology, 17,* 399–406.

Else-Quest, N. M., Hyde, J. S., Goldsmith, H. H., & Hulle, C. A. (2006). Gender differences in temperament: A meta-analysis. *Psychological Bulletin, 132,* 33–72.

Emmelkamp, P. M. G. (2004). Behavior therapy with adults. In M. J. Lambert (Ed.), *Bergin and Garfield's handbook of psychotherapy and behavior change* (5th ed.). Hoboken, NJ: Wiley.

ENCODE Project Consortium, The. (2012). An integrated encyclopedia of DNA elements in the human genome. *Nature, 489,* 57–74.

Endler, J. A. (1986). *Natural selection in the wild.* Princeton, NJ: Princeton University Press.

Engelhardt, L. E., Briley, D. A., Mann, F. D., Harden, K. P., & Tucker-Drob, E. M. (2015). Genes untie executive functions in childhood. *Psychological Science, 26,* 1151–1163.

Erickson, S. J., Gersle, M., & Montague, E. Q. (2008). Repressive adaptive style and self-reported psychological functioning in adolescent cancer survivors. *Child Psychiatry and Human Development, 39,* 247–260.

Ericsson, K. A., & Delaney, P. F. (1999). Long-term working memory as an alternative to capacity models of working memory in everyday skilled performance. In A. Miyake & P. Shah (Eds.), *Models of working memory: Mechanisms of active maintenance and executive control.* Cambridge, England: Cambridge University Press.

Ericsson, K. A., & Kintsch, W. (1995). Long-term working memory. *Psychological Review, 102,* 211–245.

Ericsson, K. A., Krampe, R. T., & Tesch-Römer, C. (1993). The role of deliberate practice in the acquisition of expert performance. *Psychological Review, 100,* 363–406.

Erikson, E. H. (1950). *Childhood and society.* New York, NY: Norton.

Erikson, E. H. (1963). *Childhood and society* (2nd ed.). New York, NY: Norton.

Erikson, E. H. (1968). *Identity: Youth and crisis.* New York, NY: Norton.

Eriksson, P. E., Perfilieva, E., Bjork-Eriksson, T., Albom, A. M., Nordborg, C., Peterson, D. A., & Gage, F. H. (1998). Neurogenesis in the adult human hippocampus. *Nature Medicine, 4,* 1313–1317.

Errera, P. (1972). Statement based on interviews with forty "worst case" in the Milgram obedience experiments. In J. Katz (Ed.), *Experimentation with human beings: The authority of the investigator, subject, professions, and state in the human experimentation process.* New York, NY: Russell Sage Foundation.

Ertmer, D. J. (2007). Speech intelligibility in young cochlear implant recipients: Gains during year three. *Volta Review, 107,* 85–99.

Essock-Vitale, S. M., & McGuire, M. T. (1980). Predictions derived from the theories of kin selection and reciprocation assessed by anthropological data. *Ethology and Sociobiology, 1,* 233–243.

Estrada, C. A., Isen, A. M., & Young, M. J. (1997). Positive affect facilitates integration of information and decreases anchoring in reasoning among physicians. *Organizational Behavior and Human Decision Processes, 72,* 117–135.

Etscorn, F., & Stephens, R. (1973). Establishment of conditioned taste aversions with a 24-hour CS-US interval. *Physiological Psychology, 1,* 251–253.

Evans, G. W. (2003). A multimethodological analysis of cumulative risk and allostatic load among rural children. *Developmental Psychology, 39,* 924–933.

Evans, G. W., & Cassells, R. C. (2014). Childhood poverty, cumulative risk exposure, and mental health in emerging adults. *Clinical Psychological Science, 22,* 287–296.

Evans, J. St. B. T. (2005). Deductive reasoning. In K. J. Holyoak & R. G. Morrison (Eds.), *Cambridge handbook of thinking and reasoning.* Cambridge, England: Cambridge University Press.

Evans, J. St. B. T., & Stanovich, K. E. (2013). Dual-process theories of higher cognition: Advancing the debate. *Perspectives on Psychological Science, 8,* 223–241.

Everson, C. A. (1993). Sustained sleep deprivation impairs host defense. *American Journal of Physiology, 265,* R1148–R1154.

Everson, C. A., Bergmann, B. M., & Rechtschaffen, A. (1989). Sleep deprivation in the rat: III. Total sleep deprivation. *Sleep, 12,* 13–21.

Eysenck, H. J. (1990). Biological dimensions of personality. In L. A. Pervin (Ed.), *Handbook of personality: Theory and research.* New York, NY: Guilford.

Eysenck, M. W. (1992). *Anxiety: The cognitive perspective.* Hillsdale, NJ: Erlbaum.

Fabes, R. A., Fultz, J., Eisenberg, N., May-Plumlee, T., & Christopher, F. S. (1989). Effects of rewards on children's prosocial motivation: A socialization study. *Developmental Psychology, 25,* 509–515.

Fair, J., Flom, R., Jones, J., & Martin, J. (2012). Perceptual learning: 12-month-olds' discrimination of monkey faces. *Child Development, 83,* 1996–2006.

Falkenburg, J., & Tracy, D. K. (2014). Sex and schizophrenia: A review of gender differences. *Psychosis: Psychological, Social and Integrative Approaches, 6,* 61–69.

Farah, M. J. (1989). *Visual agnosia.* Cambridge, MA: MIT Press.

Farooqi, S., Matarese, G., Lord, G. M., Keogh, J. M., Lawrence, E., Agwu, C., . . . O'Rahilly, S. (2002). Beneficial effects of leptin on obesity, T cell hyporesponsiveness, and neuroendocrine/metabolic dysfunction of human congenital leptin deficiency. *Journal of Clinical Investigation, 110,* 1093–1103.

Fazio, R. H., & Olson, M. A. (2003). Implicit measures in social cognition research: Their meaning and use. *Annual Review of Psychology, 54,* 297–327.

Fecteau, S., Carmant, L., Tremblay, C., Robert, M., Bouthillier, A., & Théoret, H. (2004). A motor resonance mechanism in children? Evidence from subdural electrodes in a 36-month-old child. *Neuroreport, 15,* 2625–2627.

Feder, H. H. (1984). Hormones and sexual behavior. *Annual Review of Psychology, 35,* 165–200.

Feeney, B. C., & Kirkpatrick, L. A. (1996). Effects of adult attachment and presence of romantic partners on physiological responses to stress. *Journal of Personality and Social Psychology, 70,* 255–270.

Fehr, E. (2004). Don't lose your reputation. *Nature, 423,* 449.

Fehr, E., & Fischbacher, U. (2003). The nature of human altruism. *Nature, 425,* 785–791.

Fehr, E., & Fischbacher, U. (2004). Social norms and human cooperation. *Trends in Cognitive Sciences, 8,* 185–190.

Fehr, E., & Gächter, S. (2002). Altruistic punishment in humans. *Nature, 415,* 137–140.

Feinberg, M., & Hetherington, E. M. (2000). Sibling differentiation in adolescence: Implications for behavioral genetic theory. *Child Development, 71,* 1512–1524.

Feldman, J., & Gray, P. (1999). Some educational benefits of freely chosen age mixing among children and adolescents. *Phi Delta Kappan, 80,* 507–512.

Feng, A. S., & Ratnam, R. (2000). Neural basis of hearing in real-world situations. *Annual Review of Psychology, 51,* 699–725.

Festinger, L. (1957). *A theory of cognitive dissonance.* Stanford, CA: Stanford University Press.

Festinger, L., & Carlsmith, J. M. (1959). Cognitive consequences of forced compliance. *Journal of Abnormal and Social Psychology, 58,* 203–210.

Field, A. P. (2006). Is conditioning a useful framework for understanding development and treatment of phobias? *Clinical Psychological Review, 26,* 857–875.

Fieve, R. R. (1975). *Mood swing.* New York, NY: W. Morrow.

Fifer, W. P. (2005). Normal and abnormal prenatal development. In B. Hopkins (Ed.), *The Cambridge encyclopedia of child development* (pp. 173–192). New York, NY: Cambridge University Press.

Figueredo, A. J., & King, J. E. (2001, June). *The evolution of individual differences.* Presentation at the Evolution and Individual Differences Symposium conducted at the annual meeting of the Human Behavior and Evolution Society, London, England.

Figueredo, A. J., Sefcek, J. A., Vasquez, G., Brumbach, B. H., King, J. E., & Jacobs, W. J. (2005). Evolutionary personality psychology. In D. M. Buss (Ed.), *The handbook of evolutionary psychology* (pp. 851–877). Hoboken, NJ: Wiley.

Finkenhauer, C., Engels, R. C. M. E., Meeus, W., & Oosterwegel, A. (2002). Self and identity in early adolescence: The pains and gains of knowing who and what you are. In T. M. Brinthaupt & R. P. Lipka (Eds.), *Understanding early adolescent self and identity: Applications and interventions* (pp. 25–56). Albany: State University of New York Press.

Fins, J. (2015). *Rights come to mind: Brain injury, ethics, and the struggle for consciousness.* New York, NY: Cambridge University Press.

Fisher, H. (2004). *Why we love: The nature and chemistry of romantic love.* New York, NY: Holt.

Fisher, P., Gunner, M., Dozier, M., Bruce, J., & Pears, K. (2006). Effects of therapeutic interventions for foster children on behavioral problems, caregiver attachment, and stress regulatory neural systems. *Annals of the New York Academy of Sciences, 1094,* 215–225.

Fivush, R., Haden, C. A., & Reese, E. (2006). Elaborating on elaborations: Role of maternal reminiscing style in cognitive and socioemotional development. *Child Development, 77,* 1568–1588.

Flack, W. F. (2006). Peripheral feedback effects of facial expressions, bodily postures, and vocal expressions on emotional feelings. *Cognition and Emotion, 20,* 177–195.

Flaten, M. A., & Blumenthal, T. D. (1999). Caffeine-associated stimuli elicit conditioned responses: An experimental model of the placebo effect. *Psychopharmacology, 145,* 105–112.

Fleishman, M. (2004). The problem: How many patients live in residential care facilities? *Psychiatric Services, 55,* 620–622.

Flor, H., Nikolajsen, L., & Jensen, T. S. (2006). Phantom limb pain: A case of maladaptive CNS plasticity. *Nature Reviews Neuroscience, 7,* 873–881.

Flourens, P. J. M. (1965). *Pierre Jean Marie Flourens on the functions of the brain* (M. D. Boring, Trans.). In R. J. Herrnstein & E. G. Boring (Eds.), *A source book in the history of psychology.* Cambridge, MA: Harvard University Press. (Original work published 1824)

Flynn, F. J. (2005). Having an open mind: The impact of openness to experience on interracial attitudes and impression formation. *Journal of Personality and Social Psychology, 88,* 816–826.

Flynn, J. R. (1987). Massive IQ gains in 14 nations: What IQ tests really measure. *Psychological Bulletin, 101,* 171–191.

Flynn, J. R. (2007). *What is intelligence? Beyond the Flynn effect.* Cambridge, England: Cambridge University Press.

Flynn, J. R. (2012). *Are we getting smarter?: Rising IQ in the twenty-first century.* New York, NY: Cambridge University Press.

Foa, E. F., Gillihan, S. J., & Bryant, R. A. (2013). Challenges and successes of evidence-based treatments for posttraumatic stress: Lessons learned from prolonged exposure therapy for PTSD. *Psychological Science in the Public Interest, 14,* 62–111.

Fodor, I. G. (1982). Gender and phobia. In I. Al-Issa (Ed.), *Gender and psychopathology.* San Diego, CA: Academic Press.

Ford, M. R., & Widiger, T. A. (1989). Sex bias in the diagnosis of histrionic and antisocial personality disorders. *Journal of Consulting and Clinical Psychology, 57,* 301–305.

Forgatch, M. S., & DeGarmo, D. S. (1999). Parenting through change: An effective prevention program for single mothers. *Journal of Consulting and Clinical Psychology, 67,* 711–724.

Forhan, S. E., Gottlieb, S. L., Sternberg, M. R., Xu, F., Deblina Datta, S., Berman, S., & Markowitz, L. E. (March, 2008). *Prevalence of sexually transmitted infections and bacterial vaginosis among female adolescents in the United States: Data from the National Health and Nutrition Examination Survey (NHANES) 2003–2004.* Paper presented at meeting of National STD Prevention Conference, Chicago, IL.

Foster, A. C., & Kreisler, C. J. (2012). Beyond the numbers: How parents use time and money. Retrieved from the U.S. Bureau of Labor Statistics website: http//www.bls.gov/opub/btn/volume-1/how-parents-use-time-money.htm

Foulkes, D. (1985). *Dreaming: A cognitive-psychological analysis.* Hillsdale, NJ: Erlbaum.

Fowler, S., Ogston, K., Roberts, G., & Swenson, A. (2006). The effects of early language enrichment. *Early Child Development and Care, 176,* 777–815.

Fox, M. D., Buckner, R. L., White, M. P., Greicius, M. D., & Pascual-Leone, A. (2012). Efficacy of transcranial magnetic stimulation targets for depression is related to intrinsic functional connectivity with the subgenual cingulate. *Biological Psychiatry, 72,* 595–603.

Fox, N. A., & Davidson, R. J. (1988). Patterns of brain electrical activity during facial signs of emotion in 10-month-old infants. *Developmental Psychology, 24,* 230–236.

Fox, N. A., & Stifter, C. A. (2005). Emotional development. In B. Hopkins, R. G. Barr, G. F. Michel, & P. Rochat (Eds.), *The Cambridge encyclopedia of child development* (pp. 234–241). Cambridge, England: Cambridge University Press.

Fraley, R. C. (2002). Attachment stability from infancy to adulthood: Meta-analysis and dynamic modeling of developmental mechanisms. *Personality and Social Psychology Review, 6,* 123–151.

Fraley, R. C., & Brumbaugh, C. C. (2004). A dynamical systems approach to conceptualizing and studying stability and change in attachment security. In W. S. Rholes & J. A. Simpson (Eds.), *Adult attachment: Theory, research, and clinical implications.* New York, NY: Guilford.

Francis, D. D., Diorio, J., Liu, D., & Meaney, M. J. (1999). Nongenomic transmission across generations in maternal behavior and stress response in the rat. *Science, 286,* 1155–1158.

Fredrickson, B. L. (2001). The role of positive emotions in positive psychology: The broaden-and-build theory of positive emotions. *American Psychologist, 56,* 218–226.

Fredrickson, B. L. (2003). The value of positive emotions. *American Scientist, 91,* 330–335.

Fredrickson, B. L. (2006). The broaden-and-build theory of positive emotions. In M. Csikszentmihalyi & I. S. Csikszentmihalyi (Eds.), *A life worth living: Contributions to positive psychology.* Oxford, England: Oxford University Press.

Freedman, J. L., & Fraser, S. C. (1966). Compliance without pressure: The foot-in-the-door technique. *Journal of Personality and Social Psychology, 4,* 195–202.

Frenkel, O. J., & Doob, A. N. (1976). Post-decision dissonance at the polling booth. *Canadian Journal of Behavioural Science, 8,* 347–350.

Frensch, P. A., & Rünger, D. (2003). Implicit learning. *Current Directions in Psychological Science, 12,* 13–18.

Freud, A. (1946). *The ego and the mechanisms of defense* (C. Baines, Trans.). New York, NY: International Universities Press. (Original work published 1936)

Freud, S. (1932). A note on the unconscious in psychoanalysis. In J. Rickman (Ed.), *A general selection from the works of Sigmund Freud.* London, England: Hogarth Press. (Original work published 1912)

Freud, S. (1947). *Leonardo da Vinci: A study in psychosexuality.* New York, NY: Random House. (Original work published 1910)

Freud, S. (1953). *The interpretation of dreams* (J. Strachey, Ed. & Trans.). London, England: Hogarth Press. (Original work published 1900)

Freud, S. (1960). *A general introduction to psychoanalysis.* New York, NY: Washington Square Press. (Original work published 1935)

Freud, S. (1964). *New introductory lectures on psychoanalysis.* In J. Strachey (Ed. & Trans.), *The standard edition of the complete works of Sigmund Freud* (Vol. 20). London, England: Hogarth Press. (Original work published 1933)

Freud, S. (1990). *The psychopathology of everyday life* (A. Tyson, Trans.). In J. Strachey (Ed.), *The standard edition of the complete psychological works of Sigmund Freud.* New York, NY: Norton. (Original work published 1901)

Frey, D. (1986). Recent research on selective exposure to information. *Advances in Experimental Social Psychology, 19,* 41–80.

Friedman, H. S., Tucker, J. S., Schwartz, J. E., Martin, L. R., Tomlinson-Keasey, C., Wingard, D. L., & Criqui, M. H. (1995). Childhood conscientiousness and longevity: Health behaviors and cause of death. *Journal of Personality and Social Psychology, 68,* 696–703.

Friedman, J. M. (1997). The alphabet of weight control. *Nature, 385,* 119–120.

Friedman, N. P., Miyake, A., Corley, R. P., Young, S. E., DeFries, J. C., & Hewitt, J. K. (2006). Not all executive functions are related to intelligence. *Psychological Science, 17,* 172–179.

Friedman, N. P., Miyake, A., Young, S. E., DeFries, J. C., Corley, R. P., & Hewitt, J. K. (2008). Individual differences in executive functions are almost entirely genetic in origin. *Journal of Experimental Psychology: General, 137,* 201–225.

Friedman, S. (1972). Habituation and recovery of visual response in the alert human newborn. *Journal of Experimental Child Psychology, 13,* 339–349.

Frings, C. (2006). Relevant distractors do not cause negative priming. *Psychonomic Bulletin & Review, 13,* 322–327.

Fry, A., & Hale, S. (2000). Relationships among processing speed, working memory and fluid intelligence in children. *Biological Psychology, 54,* 1–34.

Fry, D. P. (1992). "Respect for the rights of others is peace": Learning aggression versus nonaggression among the Zapotec. *American Anthropologist, 94,* 621–639.

Fujiwara, E., Levine, B., & Anderson, A. K. (2008). Intact implicit and reduced explicit memory for negative self-related information in repressive coping. *Cognitive, Affective, & Behavioral Neuroscience, 8,* 254–263.

Fuller, R. L., Luck, S. J., McMahon, R. P., & Gold, J. M. (2005). Working memory consolidation is abnormally slow in schizophrenia. *Journal of Abnormal Psychology, 114,* 279–290.

Funder, D. C. (2006). Towards a resolution of the personality triad: Persons, situations, and behaviors. *Journal of Research in Personality, 40,* 21–34.

Funder, D. C. (2016). Taking situations seriously: The situation construal model and the Riverside Situational Q-Sort. *Current Directions in Psychological Science, 25,* 203–208.

Fung, H. H., Lai, P., & Ng, R. (2001). Age differences in social preferences among Taiwanese and mainland Chinese: The role of perceived time. *Psychology & Aging, 16,* 351–356.

Furlow, B., Armijo-Prewitt, T., Gangestad, S. W., & Thornhill, R. (1997). Fluctuating asymmetry and psychometric intelligence. *Proceedings of the Royal Society (Series B), 264,* 823–829.

Furman, W., & Buhrmester, D. (1992). Age and sex differences in perceptions of networks of personal relationships. *Child Development, 63,* 103–115.

Furman, W., & Shomaker, L. (2008). Patterns of interaction in adolescent romantic relationships: Distinct features and links to other close relationships. *Journal of Adolescence, 31,* 771–788.

Furnham, A., Batey, M., Anand, K., & Manfield, J. (2008). Personality, hypomania, intelligence, and creativity. *Personality and Individual Differences, 44,* 1060–1069.

Furrow, D., Nelson, K., & Benedict, H. (1979). Mothers' speech to children and syntactic development: Some simple relationships. *Journal of Child Language, 6,* 423–442.

Furth, H. G. (1996). *Desire for society: Children's knowledge as social imagination.* New York, NY: Plenum.

Fuson, K. C., & Kwon, Y. (1992). Learning addition and subtraction: Effects of number words and other cultural tools. In J. Bideaud, C. Meljac, & J. Fischer (Eds.), *Pathways to number: Children's developing numerical abilities.* Hillsdale, NJ: Erlbaum.

Fuster, J. M. (1989). *The prefrontal cortex: Anatomy, physiology, and neuropsychology of the frontal lobe.* New York, NY: Raven.

Fuster, J. M. (2006). The cognit: A network model of cortical representation. *International Journal of Psychophysiology, 60,* 25–132.

Futuyma, D. J. (1997). *Evolutionary biology* (3rd ed.). Sunderland, MA: Sinauer.

Gabrieli, J. D. E. (1998). Cognitive neuroscience of human memory. *Annual Review of Psychology, 49,* 87–115.

Gabrieli, J. D. E., Corkin, S., Mickel, S. F., & Growdon, J. H. (1993). Intact acquisition and long-term retention of mirror-tracing skill in Alzheimer's disease and in global amnesia. *Behavioral Neuroscience, 107,* 899–910.

Gaertner, S. L., Mann, J. A., Dovidio, J. F., Murrell, A. J., & Pomare, M. (1990). How does cooperation reduce intergroup bias? *Journal of Personality and Social Psychology, 59,* 692–704.

Galanter, E. (1962). Contemporary psychophysics. In R. Brown, E. Galanter, E. Hess, & G. Mandler (Eds.), *New directions in psychology.* New York, NY: Holt, Rinehart & Winston.

Galef, B. G. (1990). An adaptationist perspective on social learning, social feeding, and social foraging in Norway rats. In D. A. Dewsbury (Ed.), *Contemporary issues in comparative psychology.* Sunderland, MA: Sinauer.

Galef, B. G. (2002). Social influences on food choices of Norway rats and mate choices of Japanese quail. *Appetite, 39,* 179–180.

Galef, B. G., Jr., & Clark, M. M. (1971). Social factors in the poison avoidance and feeding behavior of wild and domesticated rat pups. *Journal of Comparative and Physiological Psychology, 75,* 341–357.

Galef, B. G., Jr., & Giraldeau, L. (2001). Social influences on foraging in vertebrates: Causal mechanisms and adaptive functions. *Animal Behaviour, 61,* 3–15.

Galinsky, E., Bond, J. T., & Friedman, D. E. (1993). *The changing workforce: Highlights of the national study.* New York, NY: Families and Work Institute.

Gallese, V., Gernsbacher, M. A., Heyes, C., Hickock, G., & Iacoboni, M. (2011). Mirror neuron forum. *Perspectives on Psychological Science, 6,* 369–407.

Gangestad, S. W., Simpson, J. A., Cousins, A. J., Garver-Apgar, C. E., & Christensen, P. N. (2004). Women's preference for male behavioral displays change across the menstrual cycle. *Psychological Science, 15,* 203–207.

Gangestad, S. W., & Thornhill, R. (1998). Menstrual cycle variation in women's preferences for the scent of symmetrical men. *Proceedings of the Royal Society, London, B, 265,* 927–933.

Gantt, W. H. (1975, April 25). Unpublished lecture on Pavlov given at Ohio State University, Columbus.

Garcia, J., Brett, L. P., & Rusiniak, K. W. (1989). Limits of Darwinian conditioning. In S. B. Klein & R. R. Mowrer (Eds.), *Contemporary learning theories: Instrumental conditioning theory and the impact of biological constraints on learning.* Hillsdale, NJ: Erlbaum.

Garcia, J., McGowan, B. K., Ervin, F. R., & Koelling, R. A. (1968). Cues—their relative effectiveness as a function of the reinforcer. *Science, 160,* 794–795.

Garcia, J., McGowan, B. K., & Green, K. F. (1972). Biological constraints on conditioning. In A. H. Black & W. G. Prokasy (Eds.), *Classical conditioning II: Current research and theory.* New York, NY: Appleton-Century-Crofts.

Garcia-Moreno, C., Jansen, H., Ellsberg, M., Heise, L., & Watts, C. H. (2006). Prevalence of intimate partner violence: Findings from the WHO multi-country study on women's health and domestic violence. *Lancet, 368,* 1260–1269.

Gardiner, A., Greif, M., & Bjorklund, D. F. (2011). Guided by intention: Preschoolers' imitation reflects inferences of causation. *Journal of Cognition and Development, 12,* 355–373.

Gardiner, J. M., Brandt, K. R., Baddeley, A. D., Vargha-Khadem, F., & Mishkin, M. (2008). Charting the acquisition of semantic knowledge in the case of developmental amnesia. *Neuropsychologia, 46,* 2865–2868.

Gardiner, J. V., Jayasena, C. N., & Blooma, S. R. (2008). Gut hormones: A weight off your mind. *Journal of Neuroendocrinology, 20,* 834–841.

Gardner, H. (1982). *Art, mind, and brain: A cognitive approach to creativity.* New York, NY: Basic Books.

Gardner, M., & Steinberg, L. (2004). Peer influence on risk taking, risk preference, and risky decision making in adolescence and adulthood: An experimental study. *Developmental Psychology, 41,* 625–635.

Garland, D. J., & Barry, J. R. (1991). Cognitive advantage in sports: The nature of perceptual structures. *American Journal of Psychology, 104,* 211–228.

Garvey, C. (1990). *Play* (Enlarged ed.). Cambridge, MA: Harvard University Press.

Gathercole, S. E., Pickering, S. J., Ambridge, B., & Wearing, H. (2004). The structure of working memory from 4 to 15 years of age. *Developmental Psychology, 40,* 177–190.

Gathercole, V. C. M. (2013). *Issues in the assessment of bilinguals.* Bristol, England: Multilingual Matters.

Gauthier, I., Skudlarski, P., Gore, J. C., & Anderson, A. W. (2000). Expertise for cards and birds recruits brain areas involved in face recognition. *Nature Neuroscience, 3,* 191–197.

Gauvain, M. (2001). *The social context of cognitive development.* New York, NY: Guilford.

Gauvain, M. (2013). Sociocultural contexts of development. In P. D. Zelazo (Ed.), *Oxford handbook of developmental psychology* (Vol. 2, pp. 425–251). Oxford, England: Oxford University Press.

Gauvain, M., & Perez, S. (2016). Cognitive development in cultural context. In R. Lerner (Series Ed.), L. Liben & U. Muller (Vol. Eds.), Vol. 2. *Handbook of child psychology and developmental science* (7th ed., pp. 854–896). New York, NY: Wiley.

Gavin, L. A., & Furman, W. (1989). Age differences in adolescents' perceptions of their peer groups. *Developmental Psychology, 25,* 827–834.

Gazzaniga, M. S. (1967, August). The split brain in man. *Scientific American,* 24–29.

Gazzaniga, M. S. (1970). *The bisected brain.* New York, NY: Appleton-Century-Crofts.

Gazzaniga, M. S. (1998, July). The split brain revisited. *Scientific American,* 50–55.

Gazzaniga, M. S. (2000). Cerebral specialization and interhemispheric communication: Does the corpus callosum enable the human condition? *Brain, 123,* 1293–1326.

Gazzaniga, M. S., Ivry, R. B., & Mangun, G. R. (2014). *Cognitive neuroscience: The biology of the mind.* New York, NY: Norton.

Gazzola, V., Aziz-Zadeh, L., & Keysers, C. (2006). Empathy and the somatotopic auditory mirror system in humans. *Current Biology, 16,* 1824–1829.

Ge, S., Yang, C. H., Hsu, K. S., Ming, G. L., & Song, H. (2007). A critical period for enhanced synaptic plasticity in newly generated neurons of the adult brain. *Neuron, 54,* 559–566.

Geary, D. C. (2005). *The origin of mind: Evolution of brain, cognition, and general intelligence.* Washington, DC: American Psychological Association.

Geary, D. C., & Berch, D. B. (2016). Evolution and children's cognitive and academic development. In D. C. Geary & D. B. Berch (Eds), *Evolutionary perspectives on education and child development.* New York, NY: Springer.

Geary, D. C., Bow-Thomas, C. C., Fan, L., & Siegler, R. S. (1993). Even before formal instructions, Chinese children outperform American children in mental arithmetic. *Cognitive Development, 8,* 517–529.

Geary, D. C., DeSoto, M. C., Hoard, M. K., Skaggs Sheldon, M., & Cooper, M. L. (2001). Estrogens and relationship jealousy. *Human Nature, 12,* 299–320.

Geddes, J. R., Stroup, S., & Lieberman, J. A. (2011). Comparative efficacy and effectiveness in drug treatment of schizophrenia. In D. R. Weinberg & P. Harrison (Eds.), *Schizophrenia* (pp. 525–539). Hoboken, NJ: Wiley-Blackwell.

Gee, H. (2002). Aspirational thinking. *Nature, 420,* 611.

Géléoc, G. S. G., & Holt, J. R. (2003). Auditory amplification: Outer hair cells press the issue. *Trends in Neurosciences, 26,* 115–117.

Gelernter, J., & Stein, M. B. (2009). Heritability and genetics of anxiety disorders. In M. M. Antony & M. B. Stein (Eds.), *Oxford handbook of anxiety related disorders.* Oxford, England: Oxford University Press.

Gentner, D. (2003). Why we're so smart. In D. Gentner & S. Goldin-Meadow (Eds.), *Language in mind: Advances in the study of language and thought.* Cambridge, MA: MIT Press.

Gentner, D., & Kurtz, K. J. (2006). Relations, objects, and the composition of analogies. *Cognitive Science, 30,* 609–642.

Gentner, D., & Markman, A. B. (1997). Structure mapping in analogy and similarity. *American Psychologist, 52,* 45–56.

German, T., & Barrett, H. C. (2005). Functional fixedness in a technologically sparse culture. *Psychological Science, 16,* 1–5.

German, T., & Johnson, S. (2002). Function and the origins of the design stance. *Journal of Cognition and Development, 3,* 279–300.

Gersoff, E. T., Langsford, J. E., Sexton, H. R., Davis-Kean, P., & Sameroff, A. (2012). Longitudinal links between spanking and children's externalizing behaviors *Child Development, 83,* 838–843.

Gescheider, G. A. (1976). *Psychophysics: Methods and theory.* Hillsdale, NJ: Erlbaum.

Geschwind, N. (1972, April). Language and the brain. *Scientific American,* 76–83.

Gest, S. D. (1997). Behavioral inhibition: Stability and associations with adaptation from childhood to early adulthood. *Journal of Personality and Social Psychology, 72,* 467–475.

Gibbs, W. W. (1996, August). Gaining on fat. *Scientific American,* 88–94.

Gick, M. L., & Holyoak, K. J. (1980). Analogical problem solving. *Cognitive Psychology, 12,* 306–355.

Gick, M. L., & Holyoak, K. J. (1983). Schema induction and analogical transfer. *Cognitive Psychology, 15,* 1–38.

Gifford, R., Shallop, J. K., & Peterson, A. M. (2008). Speech recognition materials and ceiling effects: Considerations for cochlear implant programs. *Audiology and Neurotology, 13,* 193–205.

Gignac, G., Staough, C., & Loukomitis, S. (2004). Openness, intelligence, and self-reported intelligence. *Intelligence, 32,* 133–143.

Giladi, N., Weitzman, N., Schreiber, S., Shabtai, H., & Peretz, C. (2007). New onset heightened interest or drive for gambling, shopping, eating or sexual activity in patients with Parkinson's disease: The role of dopamine agonist treatment and age at motor symptoms onset. *Journal of Psychopharamacology, 21,* 501–506.

Gilbert, D. T. (1989). Thinking lightly about others: Automatic components of the social inference process. In J. S. Uleman & J. A. Bargh (Eds.), *Unintended thought.* New York, NY: Guilford.

Gilbert, D. T., & Jones, E. E. (1986). Perceiver-induced constraint: Interpretations of self-generated reality. *Journal of Personality and Social Psychology, 50,* 269–280.

Gildersleeve, K., Haselton, M. G., & Fales, M. R. (2014). Do women's mate preferences change across the ovulatory cycle? A meta-analytic review. *Psychological Bulletin, 140,* 1205–1259.

Gillam, B., & Chan, W. M. (2002). Grouping has a negative effect on both subjective contours and perceived occlusion at T-junctions. *Psychological Science, 13,* 279–283.

Ginzburg, K., Solomon, Z., & Bleich, A. (2002). Repressive coping style, acute stress disorder, and posttraumatic stress disorder after myocardial infarction. *Psychosomatic Medicine, 64,* 748–757.

Gitlin, M. J. (2009). Pharmacotherapy and other somatic treatments for depression. In I. H. Gotlib & C. L. Hammen (Eds.), *Handbook of depression* (2nd ed.). New York, NY: Guilford.

Gladue, B. A., Boechler, M., & McCaul, K. (1989). Hormonal response to competition in human males. *Aggressive Behavior, 15,* 409–422.

Gladwell, M. (2005). *Blink: The power of thinking without thinking.* Boston, MA: Little, Brown and Co.

Gleitman, L. R. (1990). The structural sources of verb meanings. *Language Acquisition, 1,* 3–55.

Glisky, E. L., Schacter, D. L., & Tulving, E. (1986). Computer learning by memory-impaired patients: Acquisition and retention of complex knowledge. *Neuropsychologia, 24,* 313–328.

Glover, V. (2011). Prenatal stress and the origins of psychopathology: An evolutionary perspective. *Journal of Child Psychology and Psychiatry, 52,* 356–637.

Gluckman, P., & Hanson, M. (2005). *The fetal matrix: Evolution, development, and disease.* Cambridge, England: Cambridge University Press.

Gobet, F., Lane, P. C. R., Croker, S., Cheng, P. C.-H., Jones, G., Oliver, I., & Pine, J. M. (2001). Chunking mechanisms in human learning. *Trends in Cognitive Sciences, 5,* 236–243.

Goetz, A. T. (2008). Violence and abuse in families: The consequences of paternal uncertainty. In C. A. Salmon & T. K. Shackelford (Eds.), *Family relationships: An evolutionary perspective* (pp. 259–274). Oxford, England: Oxford University Press.

Goetz, A. T., & Romero, G. A. (2012). Intimate partner violence: War at the doorsteps. In T. K. Shackelford & V. A. Weekes-Shackelford (Eds.), *The Oxford handbook of evolutionary perspectives on violence, homicide, and war* (pp. 63–76). Oxford, England: Oxford University Press.

Goffman, E. (1959). *The presentation of self in everyday life.* Garden City, NY: Doubleday.

Goh, J. O., An, Y., & Resnick, S. M. (2012). Differential trajectories of age-related changes in components of executive and memory processes. *Psychology and Aging, 27,* 707–719.

Gold, J. J., & Squire, L. R. (2006). The anatomy of amnesia: Neurohistological analysis of three new cases. *Learning & Memory, 13,* 699–710.

Goldberg, T. E., David, A., & Gold, J. M. (2011). Neurocognitive impairments in schizophrenia: Their character and role in symptom formation. In D. R. Weinberg & P. Harrison (Eds.), *Schizophrenia.* Hoboken, NJ: Wiley.

Goldberg, X., Fatjó-Vilas, M., Alemany, S., Nenadic, I., Cristobal Gastó, C., & Fañanás, L. (2013). Gene–environment interaction on cognition: A twin study of childhood maltreatment and COMT variability. *Journal of Psychiatric Research, 47,* 989–994.

Goldenthal, P., Johnston, R. E., & Kraut, R. E. (1981). Smiling, appeasement, and the silent bared-teeth display. *Ethology and Sociobiology, 2,* 127–133.

Golimbet, V. E., Alfimova, M. V., Gritsenko, I. K., & Ebstein, R. P. (2007). Relationship between dopamine system genes and extraversion and novelty seeking. *Neuroscience and Behavioral Physiology, 37,* 601–606.

Golinkoff, R. M., Mervis, C. B., & Hirsh-Pasek, K. (1994). Early object labels: The case for a developmental lexical principles framework. *Journal of Child Language, 21,* 125–155.

Golinkoff, R. M., Shuff-Bailey, M., Olguin, R., & Ruan, W. (1995). Young children extend novel words at the basic level: Evidence for the principle of categorical scope. *Developmental Psychology, 31,* 494–507.

Gomes, H., Sussman, E., Ritter, W., Kurtzberg, D., Cowan, N., & Vaughan, H. G. (1999). Electrophysiological evidence for developmental changes in the duration of sensory memory. *Developmental Psychology, 35,* 294–302.

Gömez, R. L., & Edgin, J. O. (2015). Sleep as a window into early neural development: Shifts in sleep-dependent learning effects across early childhood. *Child Development Perspectives, 9,* 183–189.

Gonçalves, R., Pedrozo, A. L., Coutinho, E S. F., Figueira, I., & Ventura, P. (2012). Efficacy of virtual reality exposure therapy in the treatment of PTSD: A systematic review. *PLoS One, 7,* e48469.

Gonda, X., Fountoulakis, K. N., Rihmer, Z., Lazary, J., Laszik, A., Akiskal, K. K., . . . Bagdy, G. (2009). Towards a genetically validated new affective temperament scale: A delineation of the temperament 'phenotype' of 5-HTTLPR using the TEMPS-A. *Journal of Affective Disorders, 112,* 19–29.

González, H. M., Tarraf, W., Whitefield, K. E., & Vega, W. A. (2010). The epidemiology of major depression and ethnicity in the United States. *Journal of Psychiatric Research, 44,* 1043–1051.

Goodale, M. A. (2007). Duplex vision: Separate cortical pathways for conscious perception and control of action. In M. Velmans & S. Schneider (Eds.), *The Blackwell companion to consciousness.* Malden, MA: Blackwell.

Goodale, M. A., & Milner, A. D. (2004). *Sight unseen: An exploration of conscious and unconscious vision.* Oxford, England: Oxford University Press.

Goodall, J. (1986). *The chimpanzees of Gombe.* Cambridge, MA: Harvard University Press.

Goodall, J. (1988). *In the shadow of man* (Rev. ed.). Boston, MA: Houghton Mifflin.

Goodman, J. C., McDonough, L., & Brown, N. B. (1998). The role of semantic context and memory in the acquisition of novel nouns. *Child Development, 69,* 1330–1344.

Gopnik, M. (1999). Familial language impairment: More English evidence. *Folia Phoniatrica et Logopaedica, 51,* 5–19.

Goran, M. I., Dumke, K., Bouret, S. G., Kayser, B., Walker, R. W., & Blumber, B. (2013). The obesogenic effect of high fructose exposure during early development. *Nature Reviews Endocrinology 9,* 494–500.

Gordon, D. M. (1995). The expandable network of ant exploration. *Animal Behaviour, 50,* 995–1007.

Gordon, J. A., & Hen, R. (2004). Genetic approaches to the study of anxiety. *Annual Review of Neuroscience, 27,* 193–222.

Gordon, P. (2004). Numerical cognition without words: Evidence from Amazonia. *Science, 306,* 496–499.

Gordon, R. A. (1990). *Anorexia and bulimia: Anatomy of a social epidemic*. Cambridge, MA: Basil Blackwell.

Gordon, S., & Gilgun, J. F. (1987). *Adolescent sexuality*. In V. B. Van Hasselt & M. Hersen (Eds.), *Handbook of adolescent psychology*. New York, NY: Pergamon Press.

Gorelik, G., & Bjorklund, D. F. (2015). The effect of competition on men's self-reported sexual interest. *Evolutionary Psychological Science, 1*, 141–149.

Gosling, S. D., & John, O. P. (1999). Personality dimensions in non-human animals: A cross-species review. *Current Directions in Psychological Science, 8*, 69–75.

Gottesman, I. I. (1991). *Schizophrenia genesis: The origins of madness*. New York, NY: Freeman.

Gottfredson, L. S. (2002). Where and why *g* matters: Not a mystery. *Human Performance, 15*, 25–46.

Gottfredson, L. S., & Deary, I. J. (2004). Intelligence predicts health and longevity, but why? *Current Directions in Psychological Science, 13*, 1–4.

Gottlieb, G. (1991). Experiential canalization of behavioral development: Results. *Developmental Psychology, 27*, 35–39.

Gottman, J. M. (1994). *What predicts divorce? The relationship between marital processes and marital outcomes*. Hillsdale, NJ: Erlbaum.

Gottman, J. M. (1998). Psychology and the study of marital processes. *Annual Review of Psychology, 49*, 169–197.

Gottman, J. M. (2011). *The science of trust: Emotional attunement for couples*. New York, NY: Norton.

Gottman, J. M., & Krokoff, L. J. (1989). Marital interaction and satisfaction: A longitudinal view. *Journal of Consulting and Clinical Psychology, 57*, 47–52.

Gottman, J. M., & Notarius, C. I. (2000). Marital research in the 20th century and a research agenda for the 21st century. *Family Processes, 41*, 159–197.

Goudie, A. J. (1990). Conditioned opponent processes in the development of tolerance to psychoactive drugs. *Progress in Neuro-Psychopharmacology and Biological Psychiatry, 14*, 675–688.

Gougoux, F., Zatorre, R. J., Lassonde, M., Voss, P., & Lepore, F. (2005). A functional neuroimaging study of sound localization: Visual cortex activity predicts performance in early-blind individuals. *PLOS Biology, 3*, 324–333.

Gould, S. J., & Eldredge, N. (1993). Punctuated equilibrium comes of age. *Nature, 366*, 223–227.

Gould-Beierle, K. L., & Kamil, A. C. (1999). The effect of proximity on landmark use in Clark's nutcrackers. *Animal Behaviour, 58*, 477–488.

Graham, L. J. (2007). Out of sight, out of mind, out of site: Schooling and attention-deficit/hyperactivity disorder. *International Journal of Qualitative Studies in Education, 20*, 585–602.

Grant, P. R., & Grant, R. (2006). Evolution of character displacement in Darwin's finches. *Science, 313*, 224–226.

Grant, P. R., & Grant, R. (2008). *How and why species multiply: The radiation of Darwin's finches*. Princeton, NJ: Princeton University Press.

Gray, J. R., Chabris, C. F., & Braver, T. S. (2003). Neural mechanisms of general fluid intelligence. *Nature Neuroscience, 6*, 316–322.

Gray, P. (2008). The value of Psychology 101 in liberal arts education: A psychocentric theory of the university. *APS Observer, 21*, 29–32.

Gray, P. (2009). Play as a foundation for hunter-gatherer social existence. *American Journal of Play, 1*, 476–522.

Gray, P. (2013). *Free to learn: Why unleashing the instinct to play will make our children happier, more self-reliant, and better students for life*. New York, NY: Basic Books.

Gray, P., & Chanoff, D. (1984). When play is learning: A school designed for self-directed education. *Phi Delta Kappan, 65*, 608–611.

Gray, P., & Feldman, J. (1997). Patterns of age mixing and gender mixing among children and adolescents at an ungraded democratic school. *Merrill-Palmer Quarterly, 43*, 67–86.

Gray, P., & Feldman, J. (2004). Playing in the zone of proximal development: Qualities of self-directed age mixing between adolescents and young children at a democratic school. *American Journal of Education, 110*, 108–145.

Green, D. W., & Swets, J. A. (1966). *Signal detection theory and psychophysics*. New York, NY: Wiley.

Green, F. P., & Schneider, F. W. (1974). Age differences in the behavior of boys on three measures of altruism. *Child Development, 45*, 248–251.

Greenberg, D. (1992). Sudbury Valley's secret weapon: Allowing people of different ages to mix freely at school. In *The Sudbury Valley School experience* (3rd ed.). Framingham, MA: Sudbury Valley School Press.

Greenberg, L. S., & Goldman, R. (2008). *Emotion-focused couples therapy: The dynamics of emotion, love and power*. Washington, DC: American Psychological Association.

Greenberg, M., & Littlewood, R. (1995). Post-adoption incest and phenotypic matching: Experience, personal meanings and biosocial implications. *British Journal of Medical Psychology, 68*, 29–44.

Greenough, W. T., & Black, J. E. (1992). Induction of brain structure by experience: Substrate for cognitive development. In M. R. Gunnar & C. A. Nelson (Eds.), *Developmental behavioral neuroscience: The Minnesota Symposia on Child Psychology* (Vol. 24). Hillsdale, NJ: Erlbaum.

Greenough, W. T., Black, J. E., & Wallace, C. S. (1987). Experience and brain development. *Child Development, 58*, 539–559.

Greenwald, A. G. (1992). New look 3: Unconscious cognition reclaimed. *American Psychologist, 47*, 766–779.

Greenwald, A. G., McGhee, D. E., & Schwartz, J. L. K. (1998). Measuring individual differences in implicit cognition: The Implicit Association Test. *Journal of Personality and Social Psychology, 74*, 1464–1480.

Gregory, R. L. (1968, November). Visual illusions. *Scientific American*, 66–76.

Gregory, R. L. (1996). *Eye and brain: The psychology of seeing* (5th ed.). Princeton, NJ: Princeton University Press.

Greulich, W. W. (1957). A comparison of the physical growth and development of American-born and native Japanese children. *American Journal of Physical Anthropology, 15*, 489–515.

Grier, J. B., Counter, S. A., & Shearer, W. M. (1967). Prenatal auditory imprinting in chickens. *Science, 155*, 1692–1693.

Griffin, D. R. (1986). *Listening in the dark: The acoustic orientation of bats and men*. Ithaca, NY: Cornell University Press.

Griffiths, T. L., Steyvers, M., & Firl, A. (2007). Google and the mind. *Psychological Science, 18*, 1069–1076.

Grijalva, E., Newman, D. A., Tay, L., Donnellan, M. B., Harms, P. D., Robins, R. W., & Yan, T. (2015). Gender differences in narcissism: A meta-analytic review. *Psychological Bulletin, 141*, 261–310.

Grillner, S. (2012). Fundamentals of motor systems. In L. R. Squire, D. Berg, F. E. Bloom, S. du Lac, A. Ghosh, & N. C. Spitzer (Eds.), *Fundamental neuroscience* (4th ed., pp. 599–611). New York, NY: Elsevier.

Grill-Spector, K., & Sayres, R. (2008). Object recognition: Insights from advances in fMRI methods. *Current Directions in Psychological Science, s17*, 73–79.

Grilo, C. M., & Pogue-Geile, M. F. (1991). The nature of environmental influences on weight and obesity: A behavior genetic analysis. *Psychological Bulletin, 110*, 520–537.

Grimes, B. F. (Ed.). (2000). *Ethnologue: Languages of the world* (14th ed.). Dallas, TX: SIL International.

Grimm, D. (2015, August 18). Has U.S. biomedical research on chimpanzees come to an end? *Science*. Retrieved from http://news.sciencemag.org/plants-animals/2015/08/has-biomedical-research-chimpanzees-come-end-0

Grodzinsky, Y. (2000). The neurology of syntax: Language use without Broca's area. *Behavioral and Brain Sciences, 23,* 1–71.

Grodzinsky, Y., & Friederici, A. D. (2006). Neuroimaging of syntax and syntactic processing. *Current Opinion in Neurobiology, 16,* 240–246.

Groeger, J. A., Clegg, B. A., & O'Shea, G. (2005). Conjunction in simulated railway signals: A cautionary note. *Applied Cognitive Psychology, 19,* 973–984.

Groopman, J. (2007). *How doctors think.* Boston, MA: Houghton Mifflin.

Groos, K. (1898). *The play of animals.* New York, NY: Appleton.

Groos, K. (1901). *The play of man.* New York, NY: Appleton.

Gross, C. G. (1998). *Brain, vision, memory: Tales in the history of neuroscience.* Cambridge, MA: MIT Press.

Grusser, O. H., & Grusser-Cornehls, U. (1986). Physiology of vision. In R. F. Schmidt (Ed.), *Fundamentals of sensory physiology.* New York, NY: Springer-Verlag.

Guay, A. T. (2001). Decreased testosterone in regularly menstruating women with decreased libido: A clinical observation. *Journal of Sex and Marital Therapy, 27,* 513–519.

Guisinger, S., & Blatt, S. J. (1994). Individuality and relatedness: Evolution of a fundamental dialectic. *American Psychologist, 49,* 104–111.

Gunderson, J. G. (2011). Borderline personality disorder. *New England Journal of Medicine, 364,* 2037–2042.

Gurven, M. (2004). Reciprocal altruism and food sharing decisions among Hiwi and Ache hunter-gatherers. *Behavioral Ecology and Sociobiology, 56,* 366–380.

Guttmacher Institute. (2002). *Teenagers' sexual and reproductive health: Developed countries.* New York, NY: Alan Guttmacher Institute.

Guttmacher Institute. (2006). *Facts on American teens' sexual and reproductive health.* New York, NY: Alan Guttmacher Institute.

Gwaltney, C. J., Meltrik, J., Shiffman, S., & Kahler, C. W. (2009). Self-efficacy and smoking cessation: A meta-analysis. *Psychology of Addictive Behavior, 23,* 56–66.

Haan, N., Smith, M. B., & Block, J. (1968). The moral reasoning of young adults: Political-social behaviour, family background and personality correlated. *Journal of Personality and Social Psychology, 10,* 183–201.

Haeffel, G. J., Getchell, M., Koposov, R. A., Yrigollen, C. Y., DeYoung, C. G., Klinteberg, B., . . . Grigorenko, E. L. (2008). Association between polymorphisms in the dopamine transporter gene and depression: Evidence for a gene–environment interaction in a sample of juvenile detainees. *Psychological Science, 19,* 62–69.

Haier, R. J., Siegel, B., Tang, C., Abel, L., & Buschbaum, M. S. (1992). Intelligence and changes in regional cerebral glucose metabolic rate following learning. *Intelligence, 16,* 415–426.

Haist, F., Gore, J. B., & Mao, H. (2001). Consolidation of human memory over decades revealed by functional magnetic resonance imaging. *Nature Neuroscience, 11,* 1139–1145.

Hall, P. A., Fong, G. T., Epp, L. J., & Elias, L. J. (2008). Executive function moderates the intention–behavior link for physical activity and dietary behavior. *Psychology and Health, 23,* 309–326.

Haller, W., Nitschke, J. B., & Miller, G. A. (1998). Lateralization in emotion and emotional disorders. *Current Directions in Psychological Science, 7,* 26–32.

Halpern, A. R. (1986). Memory for tune titles after organized or unorganized presentation. *American Journal of Psychology, 99,* 57–70.

Halpern, D. F. (1996). *Thought and knowledge: An introduction to critical thinking* (3rd ed.). Hove, England: Erlbaum.

Hamann, S. B., Ely, T. D., Hoffman, J. M., & Kilts, C. D. (2002). Activation of the human amygdala in positive and negative emotion. *Psychological Science, 13,* 135–141.

Hamill, J. F. (1990). *Ethno-logic: The anthropology of human reasoning.* Urbana: University of Illinois Press.

Hamilton, W. D. (1964). The genetical theory of social behaviour, I, II. *Journal of Theoretical Biology, 12,* 12–45.

Hanania, R., & Smith, L. B. (2009). Selective attention and attention switching: Toward a unified developmental approach. *Developmental Science, 12,* 1–14.

Hanscombe, K. B., Trzaskowski, M., Haworth, C. M. A., Davis, O. S. P., Dale, P. S., & Plomin, R. (2012, February 1). Socioeconomic status (SES) and children's intelligence (IQ): In a UK-representative sample SES moderates the environmental, not genetic, effect on IQ. *PLoS One, 7*(2), e30320.

Hara, T. J. (1994). Olfaction and gustation in fish: An overview. *Acta Physiologica Scandinavica, 152,* 207–217.

Harden, K. P. (2014). A sex-positive framework for research on adolescent sexuality. *Perspectives on Psychological Science, 9,* 455–469.

Hardin, G. (1968). The tragedy of the commons. *Science, 162,* 1243–1248.

Hardy-Brown, K., Plomin, R., & DeFries, J. C. (1981). Genetic and environmental influences on the rate of communicative development in the first year of life. *Developmental Psychology, 17,* 704–717.

Harlow, H. F. (1953). Mice, monkeys, men, and motives. *Psychological Review, 60,* 23–32.

Harlow, H. F. (1959, June). Love in infant monkeys. *Scientific American, 68*–74.

Harlow, H. F., & Zimmerman, R. (1959). Affectional responses in the infant monkey. *Science, 130,* 421–432.

Harmon-Jones, E., Lueck, L., Fearn, M., & Harmon-Jones, C. (2006). The effect of personal relevance and approach-related action expectation on relative left frontal cortical activity. *Psychological Science, 17,* 434–439.

Harmon-Jones, E., Peterson, C. K., & Harris, C. R. (2009). Jealousy: Novel methods and neural correlates. *Emotion, 9,* 113–117.

Harper, L. V., & Sanders, K. M. (1975). The effect of adults' eating on young children's acceptance of unfamiliar foods. *Journal of Experimental Child Psychology, 20,* 206–214.

Harris, J. R. (1995). Where is the child's environment? A group socialization theory of development. *Psychological Review, 102,* 458–489.

Harris, J. R. (1998). *The nurture assumption: Why children turn out the way they do.* New York, NY: Simon & Schuster.

Harris, J. R. (2005). Social behavior and personality development: The role of experiences with siblings and with peers. In B. J. Ellis & D. F. Bjorklund (Eds.), *Origins of the social mind: Evolutionary psychology and child development* (pp. 245–270). New York, NY: Guilford.

Harris, P. L., & Núñez, M. (1996). Understanding of permission rules by preschool children. *Child Development, 67,* 1572–1591.

Harrow, M., & Jobe, T. H. (2007). Factors involved in outcome and recovery in schizophrenia patients not on antipsychotic medications: A 15-year multi-follow-up study. *Journal of Nervous and Mental Disease, 195,* 406–414.

Hart, S. L. (2015). *Jealousy in infants: Laboratory research on differential treatment.* New York, NY: Springer.

Hartberg, C. B., Sundet, K., Rimol, L. M., Haukvik, U. K., Lange, E. H., Nesvag, R., . . . Agartz, I. (2011). Subcortical brain volumes relate to neurocognition in schizophrenia and bipolar disorder and healthy controls. *Progress in Neuro-Psychopharmacology & Behavioral Psychiatry, 35,* 1122–1130.

Hasher, L., & Zacks, R. T. (1979). Automatic and effortful processes in memory. *Journal of Experimental Psychology: General, 108,* 356–388.

Hatfield, E., Cacioppo, J. T., & Rapson, R. L. (1994). *Emotional contagion.* Cambridge, England: Cambridge University Press.

Havermans, R. C., Janssen, T., Giesen, J. C. A. H., Roefs, A., & Jansen, A. (2009). Food liking, food wanting, and sensory-specific satiety. *Appetite, 52,* 222–225.

Hay, D. F., & Murray, P. (1982). Giving and requesting: Social facilitation of infants' offers to adults. *Infant Behavior and Development, 5,* 301–310.

Hay, D. F., & Ross, H. S. (1982). The social nature of early conflict. *Child Development, 53,* 105–113.

Hayes, J. E., & Keast, R. S. J. (2011). Two decades of supertasting: where do we stand? *Physiology and Behavior, 104,* 1072–1074.

Haykin, S., & Chen, Z. (2005). The cocktail party problem. *Neural Computation, 17,* 1875–1902.

Hazan, C., & Shaver, P. R. (1994). Attachment as an organizational framework for research on close relationships. *Psychological Inquiry, 5,* 1–22.

Hazler, R. J., & Barwick, N. (2001). *The therapeutic environment: Core conditions for facilitating therapy.* Philadelphia, PA: Open University Press.

Hebb, D. (1949). *The organization of behavior: A neuropsychological theory.* Hoboken, NJ: Wiley.

Hebb, D. (1958). *A textbook of psychology.* Philadelphia, PA: Saunders.

Hécaen, H., & Albert, M. L. (1978). *Human neuropsychology.* Hoboken, NJ: Wiley.

Heckler, S. (1994). Facilitated communication: A response by child protection. *Child Abuse and Neglect, 18,* 495–503.

Hefferline, R. F., Keenan, B., & Harford, R. A. (1959). Escape and avoidance conditioning of human subjects without their observation of the response. *Science, 130,* 1338–1339.

Hefti, F. F. (2005). *Drug discovery for nervous system diseases.* Hoboken, NJ: Wiley.

Hegerl, U., Schönknecht, P., & Mergl, R. (2012). Are antidepressants useful in the treatment of minor depression: A critical update of the current literature. *Current Opinion in Psychiatry, 25,* 1–6.

Heider, F. (1958). *The psychology of interpersonal relations.* Hoboken, NJ: Wiley.

Heiman, M. (1987). Learning to learn: A behavioral approach to improving thinking. In D. N. Perkins, J. Lockhead, & J. Bishop (Eds.), *Thinking: The Second International Conference.* Hillsdale, NJ: Erlbaum.

Heine, S. J., & Buchtel, E. E. (2009). Personality: The universal and the culturally specific. *Annual Review of Psychology, 60,* 369–394.

Heinrichs, R. W. (2005). The primacy of cognition in schizophrenia. *American Psychologist, 60,* 229–242.

Helmholtz, H. von (1962). *Helmholtz's treatise on physiological optics* (J. P. C. Southall, Ed. & Trans.). New York, NY: Dover. (Originally published in the *Handbuch der physiologischen optik,* 1867)

Helmuth, L. (2003). Fear and trembling in the amygdala. *Science, 300,* 568–569.

Helson, R., & Stewart, A. (1994). Personality change in adulthood. In T. F. Heatherton & J. L. Weinberger (Eds.), *Can personality change?* Washington, DC: American Psychological Association.

Hendricks, B., Marvel, M. K., & Barrington, B. L. (1990). The dimensions of psychological research. *Teaching of Psychology, 17,* 76–82.

Hendry, S. H., & Hsiao, S. S. (2013). Fundamentals of sensory systems. In L. R. Squire, D. Berg, F. E. Bloom, S. du Lac, A. Ghosh, & N. C. Spitzer (Eds.), *Fundamental neuroscience* (4th ed., pp. 499–511). New York, NY: Elsevier.

Henrich, J., Heine, S. J., & Norenzayan, A. (2010). The weirdest people in the world. *Behavioral and Brain Sciences, 33,* 61–135.

Henry, J. L. (1986). Role of circulating opioids in the modulation of pain. In D. D. Kelly (Ed.), *Annals of the New York Academy of Sciences: Vol. 467. Stress-induced analgesia.* New York, NY: New York Academy of Sciences.

Henry, N. J. M., Berg, C. A., Smith, T. W., & Florsheim, P. (2007). Positive and negative characteristics of marital interaction and their association with marital satisfaction in middle-aged and older couples. *Psychology and Aging, 22,* 428–441.

Herculano-Houze, S. (2012). The remarkable, yet not extraordinary, human brain as a scaled-up primate brain and its associated cost. *Proceedings of the National Academy of Sciences (USA), 109,* 10661–10668.

Herdt, G., & McClintick, M. (2000). The magical age of 10. *Archives of Sexual Behavior, 29,* 587–606.

Hering, E. (1964). *Outlines of a theory of the light sense* (L. M. Hurvich & D. Jameson, Trans.). Cambridge, MA: Harvard University Press. (Original work published 1878)

Herman-Giddens, M. E., SloraDagger, E. J., Wasserman, R. C., Bourdony, C. J., Bhapkar, M. V., Koch, G. G., & Hasemeier, C. M. (1997). Secondary sexual characteristics and menses in young girls seen in office practice: A study from the Pediatric Research in Office Settings Network. *Pediatrics, 99,* 505–512.

Herness, M. S., & Gilbertson, T. A. (1999). Cellular mechanisms of taste transduction. *Annual Review of Physiology, 61,* 837–900.

Herrnstein, R. J. (1979). Acquisition, generalization, and discrimination reversal of a natural concept. *Journal of Experimental Psychology: Animal Behavior Processes, 5,* 116–129.

Herrnstein, R. J. (1990). Levels of stimulus control: A functional approach. *Cognition, 37,* 133–166.

Herrnstein, R. J., & Murray, C. (1994). *The bell curve: Intelligence and class structure in American life.* New York, NY: Free Press.

Hershenson, M. (2003). A trick of moonlight. *Nature, 421,* 695.

Herzog, E. D. (2007). Neurons and networks in daily rhythms. *Nature Reviews Neuroscience, 8,* 790–802.

Hess, E. H. (1958, March). "Imprinting" in animals. *Scientific American,* 81–90.

Hess, E. H. (1972, August). "Imprinting" in a natural laboratory. *Scientific American,* 24–31.

Hetherington, E. M. (1972). Effects of father absence on personality development in adolescent daughters. *Developmental Psychology, 7,* 313–326.

Hettema, J. M. (2008). The nosologic relationship between generalized anxiety disorder and major depression. *Depression and Anxiety, 25,* 300–316.

Hettema, J. M., Prescott, C. A., & Kendler, K. S. (2004). Genetic and environmental sources of covariation between generalized anxiety disorder and neuroticism. *American Journal of Psychiatry, 161,* 1581–1587.

Hewitt, B., & De Vaus, D. (2009). Change in the association between premarital cohabitation and separation: Australia 1954–2000. *Journal of Marriage and Family, 71,* 353–361.

Hewlett, B. S. (1988). Sexual selection and paternal investment among Aka pygmies. In L. Betzig, M. B. Mulder, & P. Turke (Eds.), *Human reproductive behavior: A Darwinian perspective.* Cambridge, England: Cambridge University Press.

Hickling, A. K., & Wellman, H. M. (2001). The emergence of children's causal explanations and theories: Evidence from everyday conversation. *Developmental Psychology, 37,* 668–683.

Higgins, S. T., Sliverman, K., & Heil, S. H. (Eds.). (2007). *Contingency management in substance abuse treatment.* New York, NY: Guildford.

Hill, J. O., Wyatt, H. R., Reed, G. W., & Peters, J. C. (2003). Obesity and the environment: Where do we go from here? *Science, 299,* 853–855.

Hill, K. (2002). Altruistic cooperation during foraging by the Ache, and the evolved human predisposition to cooperate. *Human Nature, 13,* 105–128.

Hill, P. M., & McCune-Nicolich, L. (1981). Pretend play and patterns of cognition in Down's syndrome children. *Child Development, 52,* 217–250.

Hillman, C. H., Buck, S. M., Themanson, J. R., Pontifex, M. B., & Castelli, D. M. (2009). Aerobic fitness and cognitive development: Event-related brain potential and task performance indices of executive control in preadolescent children. *Developmental Psychology, 45,* 114–129.

Hilts, P. J. (1995). *Memory's ghost.* New York, NY: Simon & Schuster.

Hinrichs, K. T. (2007). Follower propensity to commit crimes of obedience: The role of leadership belief. *Journal of Leadership and Organizational Studies, 14,* 69–76.

Hinson, R. E., Poulos, C. X., Thomas, W., & Cappell, H. (1986). Pavlovian conditioning and addictive behavior: Relapse to oral self-administration of morphine. *Behavioral Neuroscience, 100,* 368–375.

Hippocrates. (1923). The sacred disease. In W. H. S. Jones (Trans.), *Hippocrates* (Vol. 2). London, England: Heinemann.

Hittelman, J. H., & Dickes, R. (1979). Sex differences in neonatal eye contact time. *Merrill-Palmer Quarterly, 25,* 171–184.

Hlastala, S. A., Frank, E., Kowalski, K., Sherrill, J. T., Tu, X. M., Anderson, B., & Kupfer, D. J. (2000). Stressful life events, bipolar disorder, and the "kindling model." *Journal of Abnormal Psychology, 109,* 777–786.

Hobbes, T. (1651/2010). *Leviathan.* Revised Edition. A. P. Martinich & Brian Battiste (Eds.). Peterborough, ON: Broadview Press.

Hobson, J. A. (1987). (1) Sleep, (2) Sleep, functional theories of, and (3) Dreaming. In G. Adelman (Ed.), *Encyclopedia of neuroscience.* Boston, MA: Birkhäuser.

Hobson, J. A. (1988). *The dreaming brain.* New York, NY: Basic Books.

Hobson, J. A. (1995). *Sleep.* New York, NY: Scientific American Library.

Hobson, J. A. (2004). A model for madness? Dream consciousness: Our understanding of the neurobiology of sleep offers insight into abnormalities in the waking brain. *Nature, 430,* 21.

Hochel, M., & Milán, E. G. (2008). Synaesthesia: The existing state of affairs. *Cognitive Neuropsychology, 25,* 93–117.

Hoebel, B. G., Monaco, A. P., Hernandez, L., Aulisi, E. F., Stanley, B. G., & Lenard, L. G. (1983). Self-injection of amphetamine directly into the brain. *Psychopharmacology, 81,* 158–163.

Hoehl, S., Zettersten, M., Schleihauf, H., Grätz, S., & Pauen, S. (2014). The role of social interaction and pedagogical cues for eliciting and reducing overimitation in preschoolers. *Journal of Experimental Child Psychology, 122,* 122–133.

Hoek, H. W. (2002). The distribution of eating disorders. In K. D. Brownell & C. G. Fairburn (Eds.), *Eating disorders and obesity: A comprehensive handbook* (2nd ed.). New York, NY: Guilford.

Hoelzel, A. R., Le Boeuf, B. J., Reiter, J., & Campagna, C. (1999). Alpha-male paternity in elephant seals. *Behavioral Ecology and Sociobiology, 46,* 298–306.

Hoff, E., Core, C., Place, S., Rumiche, R., Señor, M., & Parra, M. (2012). Dual language exposure and early bilingual development. *Journal of Child Language, 39,* 1–27.

Hoff, E., & Naigles, L. (2002). How children use input to acquire a lexicon. *Child Development, 73,* 418–433.

Hoffman, D. D. (1998). *Visual intelligence: How we create what we see.* New York, NY: Norton.

Hoffman, H. (2007). The role of classical conditioning in sexual arousal. In E. Janssen (Ed.), *The Kinsey Institute series: The psychology of sex* (pp. 261–273). Bloomington: Indiana University Press.

Hoffman, H. G. (2004, August). Virtual-reality therapy. *Scientific American, 291,* 58–65.

Hoffman, W., De Houwer, J., Perugini, M., Baeyens, F., & Crombez, G. (2010). Evaluative conditioning in humans: A meta-analysis. *Psychological Bulletin, 136,* 390–421.

Hoffmann, H., Peterson, K., & Garner, H. (2012). Field conditioning of sexual arousal in humans. *Socioaffective Neuroscience & Psychology, 2,* 17336. doi: 10.3402/snp.v2i0.17336

Hofmann, S. G., Alpers, G. W., & Paul, P. (2009). Phenomenology of panic and phobic disorders. In M. M. Antony & M. B. Stein (Eds.), *Oxford handbook of anxiety related disorders.* Oxford, England: Oxford University Press.

Hohmann, G., & Fruth, B. (2000). Use and function of genital contacts among female bonobos. *Animal Behaviour, 60,* 107–120.

Hohmann, G., & Fruth, B. (2003). Intra- and inter-sexual aggression by bonobos in the context of mating. *Behaviour, 140,* 1389–1413.

Holcombe, A. O., Altschuler, E. L., & Over, H. J. (2009). A developmental theory of synesthesia with long historical roots: A comment on Hochel and Milán. *Cognitive Neuropsychology, 26,* 227–229.

Hollon, S. D., Thase, M. E., & Markowitz, J. C. (2002). Treatment and prevention of depression. *Psychological Science in the Public Interest, 3,* 39–77.

Holyoak, K. J., Junn, E. N., & Billman, D. O. (1984). Development of analogical problem-solving skills. *Child Development, 55,* 2042–2055.

Hopper, L. M., Flynn, E. G., Wood, L. A. N., & Whiten, A. (2010). Observational learning of tool use in children: Investigating cultural spread through diffusion chains and learning mechanisms through ghost displays. *Journal of Experimental Child Psychology, 106,* 82–97.

Hopper, L. M., Spiteri, A., Lambeth, S. P., Schapiro, S. J., Horner, V., & Whiten, A. (2007). Experimental studies of traditions and underlying transmission processes in chimpanzees. *Animal Behavior, 73,* 1021–1032.

Horn, J. L. (1985). Remodeling old models of intelligence. In B. B. Wolman (Ed.), *Handbook of intelligence: Theories, measurements, and applications.* Hoboken, NJ: Wilcy.

Horne, J. A. (1988). *Why we sleep: The functions of sleep in humans and other mammals.* Oxford, England: Oxford University Press.

Horne, J. A., & Reyner, L. A. (2001). Sleep-related vehicle accidents: Some guides for road safety policies. *Transportation Research Part F: Traffic Psychology & Behaviour, 4,* 63–74.

Horner, V., & Whiten, A. (2005). Causal knowledge and imitation/emulation switching in chimpanzees (*Pan troglodytes*) and children (*Homo sapiens*). *Animal Cognition, 8,* 164–181.

Hornik, R., Risenhoover, N., & Gunnar, M. (1987). The effects of maternal positive, neutral, and negative affective communications on infant responses to new toys. *Child Development, 58,* 937–944.

Hornstein, E. A., Franselow, M. S., & Eisenberg, N. I. (2016). A safe haven: Investigating social-support figures as prepared safety stimuli. *Psychological Science, 27,* 1051–1060.

Hosobuchi, Y., Rossier, J., Bloom, F. E., & Guillemin, R. (1979). Stimulation of human periaqueductal gray for pain relief increases immunoreactive beta-endorphin in ventricular fluid. *Science, 203,* 279–281.

Hothersall, D. (1995). *History of psychology* (3rd ed.). New York, NY: McGraw-Hill.

Houghton, D. P. (2008). Invading and occupying Iraq: Some insights from political psychology. *Peace and Conflict, 14,* 169–192.

Houk, J. C., & Mugnaini, E. (2003). Cerebellum. In L. R. Squire, F. L. Bloom, S. K. McConnell, J. L. Roberts, N. C. Spitzer, & M. J. Zigmond (Eds.), *Fundamental neuroscience* (2nd ed.). San Diego, CA: Academic Press.

Howe, M. L., Courage, M. L., & Rooksby, M. (2009). The genesis and development of autobiographical memory. In M. L. Courage & N. Cowan (Eds.), *The development of memory in infancy and childhood* (pp. 178–196). New York, NY: Psychology Press.

Howland, R. H. (2005). Biological base in psychopathology. In J. Maddux & B. Winstead (Eds.), *Psychopathology: Foundations for a contemporary understanding.* Mahwah, NJ: Erlbaum.

Howlin, P., Magiati, I., & Charman, T. (2009). Systematic review of early intensive behavioral interventions for children with autism. *American Journal on Intellectual and Developmental Disabilities, 114,* 23–41.

Hoyle, R. H., Pinkley, R. L., & Insko, C. A. (1989). Perceptions of social behavior: Evidence for differing expectations for interpersonal and intergroup interactions. *Personality and Social Psychology Bulletin, 15,* 365–376.

Hrdy, S. B. (1999). *Mother nature: A history of mothers, infants, and natural selection.* New York, NY: Pantheon Books.

Hrdy, S. B. (2009). *Mothers and others: The evolutionary origins of mutual understanding.* Cambridge, MA: Belknap Press.

Hron-Stewart, K. M. (1988, April). *Gender differences in mothers' strategies for helping toddlers solve problems.* Paper presented at the biennial International Conference on Infancy Studies, Washington, DC.

Huang, Y.-S., Wang L.-J., & Chen, C.-K. (2012). Long-term neurocognitive effects of methylphenidate in patients with attention deficit hyperactivity disorder, even at drug-free status. *BioMed Central, 12,* 194.

Hubbard, E. M., Brang, D., & Ramachandran, V. S. (2011). The cross-activation theory at 10. *Journal of Neuropsychology, 5*(2), 152–177.

Hubel, D. H., & Wiesel, T. N. (1962). Receptive fields, binocular interaction, and functional architecture of the cat's visual cortex. *Journal of Physiology (London), 160,* 106–154.

Hubel, D. H., & Wiesel, T. N. (1979, September). Brain mechanisms of vision. *Scientific American,* 150–162.

Huber, E., Webster, J. M., Brewer, A. A., MacLeod, D. I. A., Wandell, B. A., Boynton, G. M., Wade, A. R., & Fine, I. (2015). A lack of experience-dependent plasticity after more than a decade of recovered sight. *Psychological Science, 26,* 393–401.

Hudspeth, A. J. (2000a). Hearing. In E. R. Kandel, J. H. Schwartz, & T. M. Jessell (Eds.), *Principles of neural science* (4th ed.). New York, NY: McGraw-Hill.

Hudspeth, A. J. (2000b). Sensory transduction in the ear. In E. R. Kandel, J. H. Schwartz, & T. M. Jessell (Eds.), *Principles of neural science* (4th ed.). New York, NY: McGraw-Hill.

Huey, E. D., Krueger, F., & Grafman, J. (2006). Representations in the human prefrontal cortex. *Current Directions in Psychological Science, 15,* 167–171.

Huff, D. (1954). *How to lie with statistics.* New York, NY: Norton.

Hughes, H. C. (1999). *Sensory exotica: A world beyond human experience.* Cambridge, MA: MIT Press.

Huizinga, J. (1970). *Homo ludens: A study of the play-element in culture.* London, England: Paladin. (Original work published 1944)

Humphrey, N. K. (1976). The social function of intellect. In P. P. G. Bateson & R. A. Hinde (Eds.), *Growing points in ethology* (pp. 303–317). Cambridge, England: Cambridge University Press.

Humphrey, R. (1985). How work roles influence perception: Structural cognitive processes and organizational behavior. *American Sociological Review, 50,* 242–252.

Hung, S.-M., Styles, S. J., & Hsieh, P.-J. (2017). Can a word sound like a shape before you have seen it? Sound-shape mapping prior to conscious awareness. *Psychological Science, 28,* 263–275.

Hunt, C., Slade, T., & Andrews, G. (2004). Generalized anxiety disorder and major depressive disorder comorbidity in the national survey of mental health and well-being. *Depression and Anxiety, 20,* 23–31.

Hurvich, L. M., & Jameson, D. (1957). An opponent-process theory of color vision. *Psychological Review, 64,* 384–404.

Husted, D. S., & Shapira, N. A. (2004). A review of treatment for refractory obsessive-compulsive disorder: From medicine to deep brain stimulation. *CNS Spectrums, 9,* 833–847.

Huttenlocher, P. R. (1994). Synaptogenesis, synapse elimination, and neural plasticity in human cerebral cortex. In C. A. Nelson (Ed.), *Threats to optimal development. The Minnesota symposium on child psychology* (Vol. 27). Hillsdale, NJ: Erlbaum.

Huttenlocher, P. R., & Dabholkar, A. S. (1997). Regional differences in synaptogenesis in human cerebral cortex. *Journal of Comparative Neurology, 387,* 167–178.

Huxley, J. H., Mayr, E., Osmond, H., & Hoffer, A. (1964). Schizophrenia as a genetic morphism. *Nature, 204,* 220–221.

Hyde, L. W., Shaw, D. S., Murray, L., Gard, A., Hariri, A. R., & Forbes, E. E. (2016). Dissecting the role of amygdala reactivity in antisocial behavior in a sample of young, low-income urban men. *Clinical Psychological Science, 4,* 527–544.

Hyman, I. E., & Pentland, J. (1996). The role of mental imagery in the creation of false childhood memories. *Journal of Memory and Language, 35,* 101–117.

Hyman, S. E., Malenka, R. C., & Nestler, E. J. (2006). Neural mechanisms of addiction: The role of reward-related learning and memory. *Annual Review of Neuroscience, 29,* 565–598.

Iacoboni, M. (2005). Neural mechanisms of imitation. *Current Opinion in Neurobiology, 15,* 632–637.

Iacoboni, M., & Dapretto, M. (2006). The mirror system and the consequences of its dysfunction. *Nature Reviews Neuroscience, 7,* 942–951.

Imel, Z. E., Malterer, M. B., McKay, K. M., & Wampold, B. E. (2008). A meta-analysis of psychotherapy and medication in unipolar depression and dysthymia. *Journal of Affective Disorders, 110,* 197–206.

Inglis, I. R., Langton, S., Forkman, B., & Lazarus, J. (2001). An information primacy model of exploratory and foraging behaviour. *Animal Behaviour, 62,* 543–557.

Inhelder, B., & Piaget, J. (1958). *The growth of logical thinking from childhood to adolescence.* New York, NY: Basic Books.

Inoue-Nakamura, N., & Matsuzawa, T. (1997). Development of stone tool use by wild chimpanzees (*Pan troglodytes*). *Journal of Comparative Psychology, 111,* 159–173.

Insel, T. (April 29, 2013). *Transforming diagnosis.* Retrieved from the National Institute of Mental Health website http://www.nimh.nih.gov/about/director/2013/transforming-diagnosis.shtml

International Human Genome Sequencing Consortium. (2001, Feb. 15). Initial sequencing and analysis of the human genome. *Nature, 409,* 860–921.

International Human Genome Sequencing Consortium. (2004). Finishing the euchromatic sequence of the human genome. *Nature, 431,* 931–945.

International Task Force on Obesity. (2004). Obesity in children and young people, a crisis in public health. *Obesity Reviews, 5,* 4–85.

Isbell, L. A. (2006). Snakes as agents of evolutionary change in primate brains. *Journal of Human Evolution, 51,* 1–35.

Isen, A. M., Daubman, K. A., & Nowicki, G. P. (1987). Positive affect facilitates creative problem solving. *Journal of Personality and Social Psychology, 52,* 1122–1131.

Ivey Henry, P., Morelli, G. A., & Tronick, E. Z. (2005). Child caretakers among Efe foragers of the Ituri Forest. In B. S. Hewlett & M. E. Lamb (Eds.), *Hunter-gatherer childhoods: Evolutionary, developmental, and cultural perspectives.* New Brunswick, NJ: Transaction Publishers.

Izard, C. E. (1991). *The psychology of emotions.* New York, NY: Plenum Press.

Izard, C. E., Fantauzzo, C. A., Castle, J. M., Haynes, O. M., Rayias, M. F., & Putnam, P. H. (1995). The ontogeny and significance of infants' facial expressions in the first 9 months of life. *Developmental Psychology, 31,* 997–1013.

Jablensky, A., Sartorius, N., Ernberg, G., Anker, M., Korten, A., Cooper, J. E., . . . Bertelsen, A. (1992). Schizophrenia: Manifestations, incidence and course in different cultures. A World Health Organization ten-country study. *Psychological Medicine, Monograph Supplements, 20.*

Jaccard, J., Blanton, H., & Dodge, T. (2005). Peer influence on risk behavior: An analysis of the effects of a close friend. *Developmental Psychology, 41,* 135–147.

Jackendoff, R. (2003). Précis of *Foundations of language: Brain, meaning, grammar, evolution. Behavioral and Brain Sciences, 26,* 651–707.

Jackowitz, S., & Egan, V. (2006). The dark triad and normal personality. *Personality and Individual Differences, 40,* 331–339.

Jacobs, B. L. (2004). Depression: The brain finally gets into the act. *Current Directions in Psychological Science, 13,* 103–106.

Jacobsen, L. K., Southwick, S. M., & Kosten, T. R. (2001). Substance use disorders in patients with posttraumatic stress disorder: A review of the literature. *American Journal of Psychiatry, 158,* 1184–1190.

Jacobson, J. W., Mulick, J. A., & Schwartz, A. A. (1995). A history of facilitated communication: Science, pseudoscience, and antiscience. *American Psychologist, 50,* 750–765.

Jaffe, E. (2007). Mirror neurons: How we reflect on behavior. *American Psychological Society Observer, 20,* 20–25.

Jaffee, S. R., Caspi, A., Moffitt, T. E., Polo-Tomas, M., Price, T. S., & Taylor, A. (2004). The limits of child effects: Evidence for genetically mediated child effects on corporal punishment but not on physical maltreatment. *Developmental Psychology, 40,* 1047–1058.

James, W. (1950). *The principles of psychology.* New York, NY: Dover. (Original work published 1890)

Jamison, K. R. (1995, February). Manic-depressive illness and creativity. *Scientific American,* 62–67.

Janal, M. N., Colt, E. W. D., Clark, W. C., & Glusman, M. (1984). Pain sensitivity, mood and plasma endocrine levels in man following long-distance running: Effects of naloxone. *Pain, 19,* 13–25.

Janis, I. (1982). *Groupthink: Psychological studies of policy decisions and fiascoes* (2nd ed.). Boston, MA: Houghton Mifflin.

Javitt, D. C. (2010). Glutamatergic theories of schizophrenia. *Israel Journal of Psychiatry & Related Sciences, 47,* 4–16.

Javitt, D. C., & Coyle, J. T. (2004, January). Decoding schizophrenia. *Scientific American, 290,* 48–55.

Jazaeri, S. A, & Bin Habil, M. H. (2012). Reviewing two types of addiction—Pathological gambling and substance use. *Indian Journal of Psychological Medicine, 34,* 5–11.

Jenkins, H. M., Barrera, F. J., Ireland, C., & Woodside, B. (1978). Signal-centered action patterns of dogs in appetitive classical conditioning. *Learning and Motivation, 9,* 272–296.

Jenkins, J. H., & Karno, M. (1992). The meaning of expressed emotion: Theoretical issues raised by cross-cultural research. *American Journal of Psychiatry, 149,* 9–21.

Jenkins, J. M., & Astington, J. W. (1996). Cognitive factors and family structure associated with theory of mind development in young children. *Developmental Psychology, 32,* 70–78.

Jennings, J. R., Monk, T. H., & van der Molen, M. W. (2003). Sleep deprivation influences some but not all processes of supervisory attention. *Psychological Science, 14,* 473–479.

Jensen, A. R. (1998). *The g factor: The science of mental ability.* Westport, CT: Praeger.

Jerison, H. J. (1973). *Evolution of the brain and intelligence.* San Diego, CA: Academic Press.

Jerison, H. J. (2002). On theory in comparative psychology. In R. J. Sternberg & J. C. Kaufman (Eds.), *The evolution of intelligence* (pp. 251–288). Mahwah, NJ: Erlbaum.

Jerome, J. K. (1982). *Three men in a boat (to say nothing of the dog).* London, England: Pavilion Books. (Original work published 1889)

Ji, R., Kohno, T., Moore, K. A., & Woolf, C. J. (2003). Central sensitization and LTP: Do pain and memory share similar mechanisms? *Trends in Neurosciences, 26,* 696–705.

Johns, M., Inzlicht, M., & Schmader, T. (2008). Stereotype threat and executive resource depletion: Examining the influence of emotion regulation. *Journal of Experimental Psychology: General, 137,* 691–705.

Johns, M., Schmader, T., & Martens, A. (2005). Knowing is half the battle: Teaching stereotype threat as a means of improving women's math performance. *Psychological Science, 16,* 175–180.

Johnson, G. R. (1987). In the name of the fatherland: An analysis of kin term usage in patriotic speech and literature. *International Political Science Review, 8,* 165–174.

Johnson, J. S., & Newport, E. L. (1989). Critical period effects in second-language learning: The influence of maturational state on the acquisition of English as a second language. *Cognitive Psychology, 21,* 60–99.

Johnson, M. H., & Horn, G. (1988). Development of filial preferences in dark-reared chicks. *Animal Behaviour, 36,* 675–783.

Johnson, M. K., Hashtroudi, S., & Lindsay, D. S. (1993). Source monitoring. *Psychological Bulletin, 114,* 3–28.

Johnson, S. (2005). *Everything bad for you is good for you: How today's popular culture is actually making us smarter.* New York, NY: Riverhead Books.

Johnson, S. L., Cuellar, A. K., & Miller, C. (2009). Bipolar and unipolar depression: A comparison of clinical phenomenology, biological vulnerability, and psychosocial predictors. In I. H. Gotlib & C. L. Hammen (Eds.), *Handbook of depression* (2nd ed.). New York, NY: Guilford.

Johnson, S. M. (2002). *Emotionally focused couple therapy with trauma survivors: Strengthening attachment bonds.* New York, NY: Guilford Press.

Johnson, S. P., Hannon, E. E., & Amso, D. (2005). Perceptual development. In B. Hopkins (Ed.), *Cambridge encyclopedia of child development* (pp. 210–216). Cambridge, England: Cambridge University Press.

Johnson-Laird, P. N. (2006). *How we reason.* Oxford, England: Oxford University Press.

Johnston, R. A., & Edmonds, A. J. (2009). Familiar and unfamiliar face recognition: A review. *Memory, 17,* 577–596.

Jonas, E., Schulz-Hardt, S., Frey, D., & Thelen, N. (2001). Confirmation bias in sequential information search after primary decisions: An expansion of dissonance theoretical research on selective exposure to information. *Journal of Personality and Social Psychology, 80,* 557–571.

Jonason, P. K., Li, N. P., Schmitt, D. M., & Webster, G. D. (2009). The Dark Triad: Facilitating a short-term mating strategy in men. *European Journal of Personality, 23,* 5–18.

Jones, J. M. (2013). In U.S., 40% get less than recommended amount of sleep. *Well-Being,* December 19. http://www.gallup.com/poll/166553/less-recommended-amount-sleep.aspx

Joormann, J. (2009). Cognitive aspects of depression. In I. H. Gotlib & C. L. Hammen (Eds.), *Handbook of depression* (2nd ed., pp. 298–321). New York, NY: Guilford.

Joormann, J., & Vanderlind, W. M. (2014). Emotion regulation in depression: The role of biased cognition and reduced cognitive control. *Clinical Psychological Science, 2,* 402–421.

Josephs, R. A., Markus, H. R., & Tafarodi, R. W. (1992). Gender and self-esteem. *Journal of Personality and Social Psychology, 63,* 391–402.

Jowkar-Baniani, G., & Schmuckler, M. (2011). Picture perception in infants: Generalization from two-dimensional to three-dimensional displays. *Infancy, 16,* 211–226.

Jussim, L. (1991). Social perception and social reality: A reflection-construction model. *Psychological Review, 98,* 54–73.

Kaati, G., Bygren, L. O., & Edvinsson, S. (2002). Cardiovascular and diabetes mortality determined by nutrition during parents' and grandparents' slow growth period. *European Journal of Human Genetics, 10,* 682–688.

Kabot, S., Masi, W., & Segal, M. (2003). Advances in the diagnosis and treatment of autism spectrum disorders. *Professional Psychology: Research and Practice, 34,* 26–33.

Kahlenberg, S. M., Thompson, M. E., Muller, M. N., & Wrangham, R. W. (2008). Immigration costs for female chimpanzees and male protection as an immigrant counterstrategy to intrasexual aggression. *Animal Behaviour, 76,* 1497–1509.

Kahneman, D. (2011). *Thinking fast and slow*. New York, NY: Farrar, Straus, & Giroux.

Kail, R. (1993). The role of a global mechanism in developmental change in speed of processing. In M. L. Howe & R. Pasnak (Eds.), *Emerging themes in cognitive development: Vol. 1. Foundations*. New York, NY: Springer-Verlag.

Kail, R. V. (2007). Longitudinal evidence that increases in processing speed and working memory enhance children's reasoning. *Psychological Science, 18*, 312–313.

Kaitz, M., Good, A., Rokem, A. M., & Eidelman, A. I. (1987). Mothers' recognition of their newborns by olfactory cues. *Developmental Psychobiology, 20*, 587–591.

Kamei, N. (2005). Play among Baka children in Camaroon. In B. S. Hewlett & M. E. Lamb (Eds.), *Hunter-gatherer childhoods: Evolutionary, developmental, and cultural perspectives* (pp. 343–359). New Brunswick, NJ: Transaction Publishers.

Kamin, L. J. (1969). Predictability, surprise, attention, and conditioning. In B. A. Campbell & R. M. Church (Eds.), *Punishment and aversive behavior*. New York, NY: Appleton-Century-Crofts.

Kana, R. K., Wadsworth, H. M., & Travers, B. G. (2011). A systems level analysis of the mirror neuron hypothesis and imitation impairment in autism spectrum disorders. *Neuroscience & Biobehavioral Reviews, 53*, 894–902.

Kanazawa, S. (2004). General intelligence as a domain-specific adaptation. *Psychological Review, 111*, 512–523.

Kane, M. J., & Engle, R. W. (2002). The role of the prefrontal cortex in working-memory capacity, executive attention, and general fluid intelligence: An individual-differences perspective. *Psychonomic Bulletin & Review, 9*, 637–671.

Kanizsa, G. (1955). Margini quasi-percettivi in campi con stimolazione omogenea. *Rivista di Psicologia, 49*, 7–30.

Kano, T. (1992). *The last ape: Pygmy chimpanzee behavior and ecology*. Stanford, CA: Stanford University Press.

Kant, I. (1965). *Critique of pure reason* (J. Watson, Trans.). In B. Rand (Ed.), *Modern classical philosophers*. Boston, MA: Houghton Mifflin. (Original work published 1781)

Kantor, M. (2006). The psychopathy of everyday life. In T. G. Plante (Ed.), *Mental disorders of the new millennium: Vol. 1. Behavioral issues*. Westport, CT: Praeger.

Kanwisher, N., & Dilks, D. (2013). The functional organization of the ventral visual pathways in humans. In L. Chalupa & J. Werner (Eds.), *The new visual neuro-sciences* (pp. 733–748). Cambridge, MA: MIT.

Karney, B. R., Beckett, M. K., Collins, R. L., & Shaw, R. (2007). *Adolescent romantic relationships as precursors of healthy adult marriages: A review of theory, research, and programs*. Santa Monica, CA: RAND Corporation.

Karp, D. (1988). A decade of reminders: Changing age consciousness between fifty and sixty years old. *The Gerontologist, 28*, 727–738.

Karpicke, J. D. (2012). Retrieval-based learning: Active retrieval promotes meaningful learning. *Current Directions in Psychological Science, 21*, 157–163.

Karpicke, J. D., & Roediger, H. L., III. (2010). Is expanding retrieval a superior method for learning text materials? *Memory & Cognition, 38*, 116–124.

Kashima, Y., Yamaguchi, S., Kim, U., Choi, S., Gelfand, M. J., & Yuki, M. (1995). Culture, gender, and self: A perspective from individualism-collectivism research. *Journal of Personality and Social Psychology, 69*, 925–937.

Kastenbaum, R. (1985). Dying and death. In J. E. Birren & K. W. Schaie (Eds.), *Handbook of the psychology of aging* (2nd ed., pp. 619–643). New York, NY: Van Nostrand-Reinhold.

Kaufman, J., Yang, B., Douglas-Palumberi, H., Grasso, D., Lipschitz, D., Houshyar, S., . . . Gelernter, J. (2006). Brain-derived neurotrophic factor-5-HTTLPR gene interactions and environmental modifiers of depression in children. *Biological Psychiatry, 59*, 673–680.

Kaufman, L., & Kaufman, J. H. (2000). Explaining the moon illusion. *Proceedings of the National Academy of Sciences (USA), 97*, 500–505.

Kaufman, L., & Rock, I. (1962, July). The moon illusion. *Scientific American*, 120–130.

Kaufman, L., & Rock, I. (1989). The moon illusion thirty years later. In M. Hershenson (Ed.), *The moon illusion*. Hillsdale, NJ: Erlbaum.

Kaufman, L., Vassiliades, V., Noble, R., Alexander, R., Kaufman, J., & Edlund, S. (2007). Perceptual distance and the moon illusion. *Spatial Vision, 20*, 155–175.

Kavaliers, M., Choleris, E., Colwell, D. D., & Ossenkopp, K. (1999). Learning to cope with biting flies: Rapid NMDA-mediated acquisition of conditioned analgesia. *Behavioral Neuroscience, 113*, 126–135.

Kazdin, A. E. (2003). Psychotherapy for children and adolescents. *Annual Review of Psychology, 54*, 253–276.

Keast, R. S. J., & Costanzo, A. (2015). Is fat the sixth taste primary? Evidence and implications. *Flavour, 4(5)*.

Keating, C. F., Randall, D., & Kendrick, T. (1999). Presidential physiognomies: Altered images, altered perceptions. *Political Psychology, 20*, 593–610.

Keen, R. (2003). Representation of objects and events: Why do infants look so smart and toddlers look so dumb? *Current Directions in Psychological Science, 12*, 79–82.

Keesey, R. E., & Corbett, S. W. (1984). Metabolic defense of the body weight set-point. In A. J. Stunkard & E. Stellar (Eds.), *Eating and its disorders* (pp. 87–96). New York, NY: Raven Press.

Keller, A., Zhuang, H., Chi, Q., Vosshall, L. B., & Matsunami, H. (2007). Genetic variation in a human odorant receptor alters odour perception. *Nature, 449*, 468–472.

Keller, M. C., & Nesse, R. M. (2006). The evolutionary significance of depressive symptoms: Different adverse situations lead to different depressive symptom patterns. *Journal of Personality and Social Psychology, 91*, 316–330.

Kelley, A. E., & Berridge, K. C. (2002). The neuroscience of natural rewards: Relevance to addictive drugs. *The Journal of Neuroscience, 22*, 3306–3311.

Kelly, D. J., Liu, S., Lee, K., Quinn, P. C., Pascalis, O., Slater, A. M., & Ge, L. (2009). Development of the other-race effect in infancy: Evidence toward universality? *Journal of Experimental Child Psychology, 104*, 105–114.

Kelly, D. J., Quinn, P. C., Slater, A. M., Lee, K., Ge, L., & Pascalis, O. (2007). The other-race effect develops during infancy. *Psychological Science, 18*, 1084–1089.

Kelly, S., & Dunbar, R. I. M. (2001). Who dares, wins: Heroism versus altruism in women's mate choice. *Human Nature, 12*, 89–105.

Kelman, H. C., & Hamilton, V. L. (1989). *Crimes of obedience*. New Haven, CT: Yale University Press.

Keltner, N. L., & Boschini, D. J. (2009). Electroconvulsive therapy. *Perspectives in Psychiatric Care, 45*, 66–70.

Kendler, K. S. (1998). Major depression and the environment: A psychiatric genetic perspective. *Pharmacopsychiatry, 31*, 5–9.

Kendler, K. S., Gardner, C. O., & Pedersen, G. M. (2006). The sources of co-morbidity between major depression and generalized anxiety disorder in a Swedish national twin sample. *Psychological Medicine, 37*, 453–462.

Kendler, K. S., Heath, A., & Martin, N. G. (1987). A genetic epidemiologic study of self-report suspiciousness. *Comprehensive Psychiatry, 28*, 187–196.

Kendler, K. S., Kessler, R. C., Walters, E. E., MacLean, C., Neale, M. C., Heath, A. C., & Eaves, L. J. (1995). Stressful life events, genetic liability, and the onset of an episode of major depression in women. *American Journal of Psychiatry, 152*, 833–842.

Kendler, K. S., Kuhn, J. W., Vittum, J., Prescott, C. A., & Riley, B. (2005). The interaction of stressful life events and serotonin transporter polymorphism in the prediction of episodes of major depression. *Archives of General Psychiatry, 62,* 529–535.

Kendrick, K. M., Lévy, F., & Keverne, E. B. (1992). Changes in sensory processing of olfactory signals induced by birth in sheep. *Science, 256,* 833–836.

Kennerknecht, I., Grueter, T., Welling, B., Wentzek, S., Horst, J., Edwards, S., & Grueter, M. (2006). First report of prevalence of non-syndromic hereditary prosopagnosia (HPA). *American Journal of Medical Genetics Part A: 140A,* 1617–1622.

Kenward, B. (2012). Over-imitating preschoolers believe unnecessary actions are normative and enforce their performance by a third party. *Journal of Experimental Child Psychology, 112,* 195–207.

Kermoian, R., & Campos, J. J. (1988). Locomotor experience: A facilitator of spatial cognitive development. *Child Development, 59,* 908–917.

Kertes, D. A., Kamin, H. S., Hughes, D. A., Rodney, N. C., Bhatt, S., & Mulligan, C. J. (2016). Prenatal maternal stress predicts methylation of genes regulating the hypothalamic-pituitary-adrenocortical system in mothers and newborns in the Democratic Republic of Congo. *Child Development, 87,* 61–72.

Keshavan, M. S., Gilbert, A. R., & Diwadkar, V. A. (2006). Neurodevelopmental theories. In J. A. Lieberman, T. S. Stroup, & D. O. Perkins (Eds.), *The American Psychiatric Publishing textbook of schizophrenia.* Washington, DC: American Psychiatric Publishing.

Keshavan, M. S., Tandon, R., Boutros, N. N., & Nasrallah, H. A. (2008). Schizophrenia, "just the facts": What we know in 2008. Part 3: Neurobiology. *Schizophrenia Research, 106,* 89–107.

Kessler, R. C. (1997). The effects of stressful life events on depression. *Annual Review of Psychology, 48,* 191–214.

Kessler, R. C., Berglund, P. A., Demler, O., Jin, R., & Walters, E. E. (2005). Lifetime prevalence and age-of-onset distributions of DSM-IV disorders in the National Comorbidity Survey Replication (NCS-R). *Archives of General Psychiatry, 62,* 593–602.

Kessler, R. C., Gruber, M., Hettema, J. M., Hwang, I., Sampson, N., & Yonkers, K. A. (2008). Co-morbid major depression and generalized anxiety disorders in the National Comorbidity Survey follow-up. *Psychological Medicine, 38,* 365–374.

Kessler, R. C., Hwang, I., LaBrie, R., Petukhova, M., Sampson, N. A., Winters, K. C., & Shaffer, J. F. (2008). DSM-IV pathological gambling in the National Comorbidity Survey Replication. *Psychological Medicine, 38,* 1351–1360.

Kety, S. S., Rosenthal, D., Wender, P. H., Schulsinger, F., & Jacobson, B. (1976). Mental illness in the biological and adoptive families of adopted individuals who have become schizophrenic. *Behavior Genetics, 6,* 219–225.

Keupp, S., Behne, T., & Rakocz, H. (2013). Why do children over-imitate? Normativity is crucial. *Journal of Experimental Child Psychology, 116,* 392–406.

Khaled, N. (2004). Psychological effects of terrorist attacks in Algeria. *Journal of Aggression, Maltreatment & Trauma, 9,* 201–212.

Kiang, L., Moreno, A. J., & Robinson, J. L. (2004). Maternal preconceptions about parenting predict child temperament, maternal sensitivity, and children's empathy. *Developmental Psychology, 40,* 1081–1092.

Kiehn, O. (2006). Locomotor circuits in the mammalian spinal cord. *Annual Review of Neuroscience, 29,* 279–306.

Kimmel, A. J. (2007). *Ethical issues in behavioral research: Basic and applied perspectives.* Hoboken, NJ: Wiley-Blackwell.

King, D. W., King, L. A., Gudanowski, D. M., & Vreven, D. L. (1995). Alternative representations of war zone stressors: Relationships to posttraumatic stress disorder in male and female Vietnam veterans. *Journal of Abnormal Psychology, 104,* 184–196.

Kipp, K., & Pope, S. (1997). The development of cognitive inhibition in stream-of-consciousness and directed speech. *Cognitive Development, 12,* 239–260.

Kirkpatrick, L. A. (2005). *Attachment, evolution, and the psychology of religion.* New York, NY: Guilford.

Kirsch, I. (2014). Antidepressants and their placebo effect. *Zeitschrift fur Psychologie, 222,* 128–134.

Kirsch, I., & Sapirstein, G. (1998). Listening to Prozac but hearing placebo: A meta-analysis of antidepressant medication. *Prevention and Treatment, 1,* Article 0002a.

Kirsch, I., Tennen, H., Wickless, C., Saccone, A. J., & Cody, S. (1983). The role of expectancy in fear reduction. *Behavior Therapy, 14,* 520–533.

Kisilevsky, B. S., Sylvia, M. J., Hains, S. M. J., Lee, K., Xie, X., Huang, H., . . . Wang, Z. (2003). Effects of experience on fetal voice recognition. *Psychological Science, 14,* 220–224.

Kitayama, S., Duffy, S., Kawamura, T., & Larsen, J. T. (2003). Perceiving an object and its context in different cultures: A cultural look at new look. *Psychological Science, 14,* 201–206.

Kittler, P. M., Krinsky-McHale, S. J., & Devenny, D. A. (2008). Dual-task processing as a measure of executive function: A comparison between adults with Williams and Down Syndromes. *American Journal on Mental Retardation, 113,* 117–132.

Klauer, K. C., Schmitz, F., Teige-Mocigemba, S., & Voss, A. (2010). Understanding the role of executive control in the Implicit Association Test: Why flexible people have small IAT effects. *Quarterly Journal of Experimental Psychology, 63,* 595–619.

Klehe, U.-C., Anderson, N., & Hoefnagels, E. A. (2007). Social facilitation and inhibition during maximal versus typical performance situations. *Human Performance, 20,* 223–239.

Kleim, B., Graham, B., Fihosy, S., Stott, R., & Ehlers, A. (2014). Reduced specificity in episodic future thinking in posttraumatic stress disorder. *Clinical Psychological Science, 2,* 165–173.

Klein, D. N., Schwartz, J. E., Santiago, N. J., Vivian, D., Vocisano, C., Castonguay, L. G., . . . Keller, M. B. (2003). Therapeutic alliance in depression treatment: Controlling for prior change and patient characteristics. *Journal of Consulting and Clinical Psychology, 71,* 997–1006.

Kleiner-Fisman, G., Herzog, J., Fisman, D. N., Tamma, F., Lyons, K. E., Pahwa, R., . . . Deuschl, G. (2006). Subthalamic nucleus deep brain stimulation: Summary and meta-analysis of outcomes. *Movement Disorders, 21*(Suppl 14), S290–S304.

Klemm, W. R. (1990). Historical and introductory perspectives on brainstem-mediated behaviors. In W. R. Klemm & R. P. Vertes (Eds.), *Brainstem mechanisms of behavior.* Hoboken, NJ: Wiley.

Kliem, S., Kröger, C., & Kossfelder, J. (2010). Dialectical behavior therapy for borderline personality disorder: A meta-analysis using mixed-effects modeling. *Journal of Consulting and Clinical Psychology, 78,* 936–951.

Klinke, R. (1986). Physiology of hearing. In R. F. Schmidt (Ed.), *Fundamentals of sensory physiology.* New York, NY: Springer-Verlag.

Klose, M., & Jacobi, F. (2004). Can gender differences in the prevalence of mental disorders be explained by sociodemographic factors? *Archives of Women's Mental Health, 7,* 133–148.

Kluger, M. J. (1991). Fever: Role of pyrogens and cryogens. *Physiological Reviews, 71,* 93–127.

Klüver, H., & Bucy, P. C. (1937). "Psychic blindness" and other symptoms following temporal lobectomy in rhesus monkeys. *American Journal of Physiology, 119,* 352–353.

Knafo, A., Zahn-Waxler, C., Hulle, C. V., Robinson, J. L., & Rhee, S. H. (2008). The developmental origins of a disposition toward empathy: Genetic and environmental contributions. *Emotion, 8,* 737–752.

Knowlton, B. J., Ramus, S. J., & Squire, L. R. (1992). Intact artificial grammar learning in amnesia: Dissociation of classification learning and explicit memory for specific instances. *Psychological Science, 3,* 172–179.

Knox, R. E., & Inkster, J. A. (1968). Post-decision dissonance at post time. *Journal of Personality and Social Psychology, 8,* 319–323.

Knudsen, E. I. (2007). Fundamental components of attention. *Annual Review of Neuroscience, 30,* 57–78.

Kobayashi, M. (2006). Functional organization of the human gustatory cortex. *Journal of Oral Biosciences, 48,* 244–260.

Kochanska, G., Murray, K. T., & Harlan, E. (2000). Effortful control in early childhood: Continuity and change, antecedents, and implications for social development. *Developmental Psychology, 36,* 220–232.

Kochanska, G., Tjebkes, T. L., & Forman, D. R. (1998). Children's emerging regulation of conduct: Restraint, compliance, and internalization from infancy to the second year. *Child Development, 69,* 1378–1389.

Koffka, K. (1935). *Principles of Gestalt psychology.* New York, NY: Harcourt Brace Jovanovich.

Kohlberg, L. (1966). A cognitive-developmental analysis of children's sex-role concepts and attitudes. In E. E. Maccoby (Ed.), *The development of sex differences.* Stanford, CA: Stanford University Press.

Kohlberg, L. (1984). *The psychology of moral development.* San Francisco, CA: Harper & Row.

Kohler, R. (2008). *Jean Piaget.* New York, NY: Continuum International Publishing Group.

Kohn, M. L. (1980). Job complexity and adult personality. In N. J. Smelser & E. H. Erikson (Eds.), *Theories of work and love in adulthood.* Cambridge, MA: Harvard University Press.

Kohn, M. L., & Schooler, C. (1978). The reciprocal effects of substantive complexity of work and intellectual flexibility: A longitudinal assessment. *American Journal of Sociology, 84,* 24–52.

Kohn, M. L., & Slomczynski, K. M. (1990). *Social structure and self-direction: A comparative analysis of the United States and Poland.* Cambridge, MA: Basil Blackwell.

Koivisto, M., & Revonsuo, A. (2007). How meaning shapes seeing. *Psychological Science, 18,* 845–849.

Kolassa, I.-T., & Elbert, T. (2007). Structural and functional neuroplasticity in relation to traumatic stress. *Current Trends in Psychological Science, 16,* 321–325.

Kolb, B., & Whishaw, I. Q. (2009). *Fundamentals of human neuropsychology* (6th ed.). New York, NY: Worth.

Konen, C. S., & Kastner, S. (2008). Two hierarchically organized neural systems for object information in human visual cortex. *Nature Neuroscience, 11,* 224–231.

Konner, M. (1972). Aspects of the developmental ethology of a foraging people. In N. G. Blurton-Jones (Ed.), *Ethological studies of child behavior.* Cambridge, England: Cambridge University Press.

Konner, M. (2010). *The evolution of childhood: Relationships emotions, mind.* Cambridge, MA: Belknap Press.

Konner, M. J. (1975). Relations among infants and juveniles in comparative perspective. In M. Lewis & L. A. Rosenblum (Eds.), *The origins of behavior: Vol. 4. Friendship and peer relations.* Hoboken, NJ: Wiley.

Konner, M. J. (1976). Maternal care, infant behavior and development among the !Kung. In R. B. Lee & I. DeVore (Eds.), *Kalahari hunter-gatherers: Studies of the !Kung San and their neighbors.* Cambridge, MA: Harvard University Press.

Konrad, K., Neufang, S., Kink, G. R., & Herpertz-Dahlmann, B. (2007). Long-term effects of methylphenidate on neural networks associated with executive attention in children with ADHD: Results from a longitudinal functional MRI study. *Journal of the American Academy of Child and Adolescent Psychiatry, 46,* 1633–1644.

Koob, G. F., Everitt, B. J., & Robins, T. W. (2012). Reward, motivation, and addiction. In L. R. Squire, D. Berg, F. E. Bloom, S. du Lac, A. Ghosh, & N. C. Spitzer (Eds.), *Fundamental neuroscience* (4th ed., pp. 871–898). New York, NY: Elsevier.

Koodsma, D. E., & Byers, B. E. (1991). The functions of bird song. *American Zoologist, 31,* 318–328.

Kost, K., & Henshaw, S. (2013). *U.S. teenage pregnancies, births and abortions, 2008: National trends by age, race and ethnicity.* New York, NY: Guttmacher Institute.

Kotov, R., Krueger, R. F., Watson, D., Achenbach, T. M., Althoff, R. R., Bagby, R. M., . . . Zimmerman, M. (2017, March 23). The Hierarchical Taxonomy of Psychopathology (HiTOP): A Dimensional alternative to traditional nosologies. *Journal of Abnormal Psychology.* Advance online publication. http://dx.doi.org/10.1037/abn0000258

Kovács, A. M., & Mehler, J. (2009, April 21). Cognitive gains in 7-month-old bilingual infants. *Proceedings of the National Academy of Science, 106*(16), 6556–6560.

Kraemer, G. W. (1992). A psychobiological theory of attachment. *Behavioral and Brain Sciences, 15,* 493–541.

Kramer, M. D., Krueger, R. F., & Hicks, B. M. (2008). The role of internalizing and externalizing liability factors in accounting for gender differences in the prevalence of common psychopathological syndromes. *Psychological Medicine, 38,* 51–61.

Krampe, R. T., & Ericsson, K. A. (1996). Maintaining excellence: Deliberate practice and elite performance in young and older pianists. *Journal of Experimental Psychology: General, 125,* 331–359.

Krasnow, M. M., Delton, A. W., Cosmides, L., & Tooby, J. (2016). Looking under the hood of third-party punishment reveals design for personal benefit. *Psychological Science, 77,* 405–418.

Kraus, N., & Banai, K. (2007). Auditory-processing malleability. *Current Directions in Psychological Science, 16,* 105–110.

Krijn, M., Emmelkamp, P. M. G., Olafsson, R. P., & Biemond, R. (2004). Virtual reality exposure therapy of anxiety disorders: A review. *Clinical Psychology Review, 24,* 259–281.

Krishnan, V., & Nestler, E. J. (2008). The molecular neurobiology of depression. *Nature, 455,* 894–902.

Kruger, A. C. (1992). The effect of peer and adult–child transactive discussions on moral reasoning. *Merrill-Palmer Quarterly, 38,* 191–211.

Kruger, D. J., Fisher, M., & Jobling, I. (2003). Proper and dark heroes as dads and cads: Alternative mating strategies in British romantic literature. *Human Nature, 14,* 305–317.

Kruger, D. J., & Fitzgerald, C. J. (2012). Evolutionary perspectives on male-male competition, violence, and homicide. In T. K. Shackelford & V. A. Weekes-Shackelford (Eds.), *The Oxford handbook of evolutionary perspectives on violence, homicide, and war* (pp. 153–170). Oxford, England: Oxford University Press.

Kryter, K. D. (1985). *The effects of noise on man* (2nd ed.). San Diego, CA: Academic Press.

Kübler-Ross, E. (1969). *On death and dying.* New York, NY: Macmillan.

Kuczaj, S. A. (1977). The acquisition of regular and irregular past tense forms. *Journal of Verbal Learning and Verbal Behavior, 16,* 589–600.

Kuhl, P. K., Conboy, B. T., Coffey-Corina, S., Padden, D., Rivera-Gaxiola, M., & Nelson, T. (2008). Phonetic learning as a pathway to language: New data and native language magnet theory expanded (NLM-e). *Philosophical Transactions of the Royal Society B, 363,* 979–1000.

Kuhl, P. K., & Meltzoff, A. N. (1982). The bimodal perception of speech in infancy. *Science, 218,* 1138–1141.

Kukekova, A., Trut, L. N., Chase, K., Shepeleva, D. V., Vladimirova, A. V., Kharlamova, A. V., . . . Acland, G. M. (2008). Measurement of segregating behaviors in experimental silver fox pedigrees. *Behavior Genetics, 38,* 185–194.

Kundu, P., & Cummins, D. D. (2013). Morality and conformity: The Asch paradigm applied to moral decisions. *Social Influence, 8,* 268–279.

Kurihara, K., & Kashiwayanagi, M. (1998). Introductory remarks on umami taste. *Annals of the New York Academy of Sciences, 855,* 393–397.

Kurland, J. A. (1979). Paternity, mother's brother, and human sociality. In N. A. Chagnon & W. Irons (Eds.), *Evolutionary biology and human social behavior: An anthropological perspective.* North Scituate, MA: Duxbury Press.

Kuther, T. L., & Higgins-D'Alessandro, A. (2000). Bridging the gap between moral reasoning and adolescent engagement in risky behavior. *Journal of Adolescence, 23,* 409–422.

Kuther, T. L., & Morgan, R. D. (2012). *Careers in psychology: Opportunities in a changing world* (4th ed.) Belmont, CA: Wadsworth.

Kvavilashvili, L., Kornbrot, D. E., & Mash, V. (2009). Differential effects of age on prospective and retrospective memory tasks in young, young-old, and old-old adults. *Memory, 17,* 180–196.

Laboratory of Comparative Human Cognition. (1983). Culture and cognitive development. In P. H. Mussen (Gen. Ed.) & W. Kessen (Vol. Ed.), *Handbook of child psychology: Vol. 1. History, theory, and methods.* Hoboken, NJ: Wiley.

Lachter, J., Forster, K. I., & Ruthruff, E. (2004). Forty-five years after Broadbent (1958): Still no identification without attention. *Psychological Review, 111,* 880–913.

Lack, L., Wright, H., & Paynter, D. (2007). The treatment of sleep onset insomnia with bright morning light. *Sleep and Biological Rhythms, 5,* 173–179.

Lakhan, S, E., & Kirchgessner, A. (2012). Prescription stimulants in individuals with and without attention deficit hyperactivity disorder: Misuse, cognitive impact, and adverse effects. *Brain and Behaviors, 2,* 661–677.

Lakin, J. L., & Chartrand, T. L. (2003). Using nonconscious behavioral mimicry to create affiliation and rapport. *Psychological Science, 14,* 334–339.

Lalumière, M. L., Quinsey, V. L., & Craig, W. M. (1996). Why children from the same family are so different from one another: A Darwinian note. *Human Nature, 7,* 281–290.

Lamb, H. R. (2000). Deinstitutionalization and public policy. In R. W. Menninger & J. C. Nemiah (Eds.), *American psychiatry after World War II.* Washington, DC: American Psychiatric Press.

Lamb, M. E., & Hewlett, B. S. (2005). Reflections on hunter-gatherer childhoods. In B. S. Hewlett & M. E. Lamb (Eds.), *Hunter-gatherer childhoods: Evolutionary, developmental, and cultural perspectives.* New Brunswick, NJ: Transaction Publishers.

Lamb, T. D., Collin, S. P., & Pugh, E. N. (2007). Evolution of the vertebrate eye: Opsins, photoreceptors, retina and eye cup. *Nature Reviews Neuroscience, 8,* 960–975.

Lambert, M. J., & Ogles, B. M. (2004). The efficacy and effectiveness of psychotherapy. In M. J. Lambert (Ed.), *Bergin and Garfield's handbook of psychotherapy and change* (5th ed.). Hoboken, NJ: Wiley.

Lamborn, S. D., Mounts, N., Steinberg, L., & Dornbusch, S. M. (1991). Patterns of competence and adjustment from authoritative, authoritarian, indulgent, and neglectful families. *Child Development, 62,* 1049–1065.

Lancy, D. (2015). *The anthropology of childhood* (2nd ed.). Cambridge, England: Cambridge University Press.

Lancy, D. (2016). Teaching: Natural or cultural? In D. C. Geary & D. B. Berch (Eds). *Evolutionary perspectives on education and child development* (pp. 33–65). New York, NY: Springer.

Land, M. F., & Furnald, R. D. (1992). The evolution of eyes. *Annual Review of Neuroscience, 15,* 1–29.

Landrum, E., Davis, S., & Landrum, T. (2009). *The psychology major: Career options and strategies for success* (4th ed.). Upper Saddle River, NJ: Prentice Hall.

Langer, E. J., Blank, A., & Chanowitz, B. (1978). The mindlessness of ostensibly thoughtful action. *Journal of Personality and Social Psychology, 36,* 635–642.

Langlois, J. H., Kalakanis, L., Rubenstein, J., Larson, A., Hallam, M., & Smoot, M. (2000). Maxims or myths of beauty? A meta-analytic and theoretical review. *Psychological Bulletin, 126,* 390–423.

Larsen, R. J., & Buss, D. M. (2008). *Personality psychology: Domains of knowledge about human nature* (3rd ed.). New York, NY: McGraw-Hill.

Larson, P. S. (2008). Deep brain stimulation for psychiatric disorders. *Neurotherapeutics, 5,* 50–58.

Larson, R. W., Richards, M. H., & Perry-Jenkins, M. (1994). Divergent worlds: The daily and emotional experience of mothers and fathers in the domestic and public spheres. *Journal of Personality and Social Psychology, 67,* 1034–1046.

Latané, B., & Rodin, J. (1969). A lady in distress: Inhibiting effects of friends and strangers on bystander intervention. *Journal of Experimental Social Psychology, 5,* 189–202.

Lauer, J., & Lauer, R. (1985, June). Marriages made to last. *Psychology Today, 19*(6), 22–26.

Laursen, B., Pulkkinen, L., & Adams, R. (2002). The antecedents and correlates of agreeableness in adulthood. *Developmental Psychology, 38,* 591–603.

Lavelli, M., & Fogel, A. (2005). Developmental changes in the relationship between the infant's attention and emotion during early face-to-face communication: The 2-month transition. *Developmental Psychology, 41,* 265–280.

Lavie, P. (2001). Sleep–wake as a biological rhythm. *Annual Review of Psychology, 52,* 277–303.

Lawrie, S. M., McIntosh, A. M., Hall, J., Owens, D. G. C., & Johnstone, E. C. (2008). Brain structure and function changes during the development of schizophrenia: The evidence from studies of subjects at increased genetic risk. *Schizophrenia Bulletin, 34,* 330–340.

Lawrie, S. M., & Pantelis, C. (2011). Structural brain imaging in schizophrenia and related populations. In K. T. Mueser & D. V. Jeste (Eds.), *Clinical handbook of schizophrenia* (pp. 616–623). New York, NY: Guilford.

Lazarus, J., Inglis, I. R., & Torrance, R. L. L. F. (2004). Mate guarding conflict, extra-pair courtship and signaling in the harlequin duck *Histrionicus histrionicus. Behaviour, 141,* 1061–1078.

Lazarus, R. S. (1993). From psychological stress to the emotions: A history of changing outlooks. *Annual Review of Psychology, 44,* 1–21.

Le Grand, R., Mondloch, C. J., Maurer, D., & Brent, H. P. (2001). Early visual experience and face processing. *Nature, 410,* 890.

Le Merrer, J., Becker, J. A., Befort, K., & Kieffer, B. L. (2009). Reward processing by the opioid system in the brain. *Physiological Reviews, 89,* 1379–1412.

Leana, C. R. (1985). A partial test of Janis' groupthink model. Effects of group cohesiveness and leader behavior on defective decision making. *Journal of Management, 11,* 5–17.

Leary, M. R. (1999). Making sense of self-esteem. *Current Directions in Psychological Science, 8,* 32–35.

Leary, M. R. (2005). Sociometer theory and the pursuit of relational value: Getting to the root of self-esteem. *European Review of Social Psychology, 16,* 75–111.

Leary, M. R., & Baumeister, R. F. (2000). The nature and function of self-esteem: Sociometer theory. In M. Zanna (Ed.), *Advances in experimental social psychology* (Vol. 32, pp. 1–62). San Diego, CA: Academic Press.

Leary, M. R., Cottrell, C. A., & Phillips, M. (2001). Deconfounding the effects of dominance and social acceptance on self-esteem. *Journal of Personality and Social Psychology, 81,* 898–909.

Leary, M. R., & Kowalski, R. M. (1995). *Social anxiety.* New York, NY: Guilford.

LeDoux, J. E. (1996). *The emotional brain: The mysterious underpinnings of emotional life.* New York, NY: Simon & Schuster.

LeDoux, J. E., Romanski, L., & Xagoraris, A. (1989). Indelibility of subcortical emotional memories. *Journal of Cognitive Neuroscience, 1,* 238–243.

Lee, J. L. C. (2008). Memory reconsolidation mediates the strengthening of memories by additional learning. *Nature Neuroscience, 11,* 1264–1266.

Lee, R., Geracioti, T. D., Jr., Kasckow, J. W., & Coccaro, E. F. (2005). Childhood trauma and personality disorder: Positive correlation with adult CSF corticotropin-releasing factor concentrations. *American Journal of Psychiatry, 162,* 995–997.

Lee, T. S. (2002). Top-down influence in early visual processing: A Bayesian perspective. *Physiology and Behavior, 77,* 645–650.

LeFever, G. B., Arcone, A. P., & Antonuccio, D. O. (2003). ADHD among American schoolchildren. *The Scientific Review of Mental Health Practice, 2,* 49–60.

Leger, D., Guilleminault, C., Freyfus, J. P., Delahaye, C., & Paillard, M. (2000). Prevalence of insomnia in a survey of 12,778 adults in France. *European Sleep Research, 9,* 35–42.

Lehman, D. R., Chiu, C., & Schaller, M. (2004). Psychology and culture. *Annual Review of Psychology, 55,* 689–714.

Leibel, R. L., Rosenbaum, M., & Hirsch, J. (1995). Changes in energy expenditure resulting from altered body weight. *New England Journal of Medicine, 332,* 621–628.

Lenroot, R. K., & Giedd, J. N. (2007). The structural development of the human brain as measured longitudinally with magnetic resonance imaging. In D. Coch, K. W. Fischer, & G. Dawson (Eds.), *Human behavior, learning, and the developing brain: Typical development* (pp. 50–73). New York, NY: Guilford.

Leon, D. A., Lawlor, D. A., Clark, H., Batty, G. D., & Macintyre, S. (2009). The association of childhood intelligence with mortality risk from adolescence to middle age: Findings from the Aberdeen children of the 1950s cohort study. *Intelligence, 37,* 520–528.

Lepage, J. F., & Théoret, H. (2006). EEG evidence for the presence of an action observation-execution matching system in children. *European Journal of Neuroscience, 23,* 2505–2510.

Lepper, M. R., & Greene, D. (1978). Overjustification research and beyond: Toward a means-end analysis of intrinsic and extrinsic motivation. In M. R. Lepper & D. Greene (Eds.), *The hidden costs of reward: New perspectives on the psychology of human motivation.* Hoboken, NJ: Wiley.

Lepper, M. R., & Henderlong, J. (2000). Turning "play" into "work" and "work" into "play": 25 years of research on intrinsic and extrinsic motivation. In C. Sansone & J. Harackiewicz (Eds.), *Intrinsic and extrinsic motivation: The search for optimal motivation and performance* (pp. 257–307). San Diego, CA: Academic Press.

Lerner, M. R., Gyorgyi, T. K., Reagan, J., Roby-Shemkovitz, A., Rybczynski, R., & Vogt, R. (1990). Peripheral events in moth olfaction. *Chemical Senses, 15,* 191–198.

Leslie, A. M. (1987). Pretense and representation: The origins of "theory of mind." *Psychological Review, 94,* 412–426.

Leslie, A. M. (1991). The theory of mind impairment in autism: Evidence for a modular mechanism of development? In A. Whiten (Ed.), *Natural theories of mind: Evolution, development and simulation of everyday mindreading.* Cambridge, MA: Basil Blackwell.

Leslie, A. M. (1994). Pretending and believing: Issues in the theory of ToMM. *Cognition, 50,* 211–238.

Leslie, A. M., & Thaiss, L. (1992). Domain specificity in conceptual development: Neuropsychological evidence from autism. *Cognition, 43,* 225–251.

Levenson, R. W. (1992). Autonomic nervous system differences among emotions. *Psychological Science, 3,* 23–27.

Levenson, R. W., Carstensen, L. L., & Gottman, J. M. (1993). Long-term marriage: Age, gender, and satisfaction. *Psychology and Aging, 8,* 301–313.

Levenson, R. W., Ekman, P., Heider, K., & Friesen, W. V. (1992). Emotion and autonomic nervous system activity in the Minangkabau of West Sumatra. *Journal of Personality and Social Psychology, 62,* 972–988.

Levey, A. B., & Martin, I. (1975). Classical conditioning of human "evaluative" responses. *Behaviour Research and Therapy, 13,* 221–226.

Levine, J. D., Gordon, N. C., & Fields, H. L. (1979). The role of endorphins in placebo analgesia. *Advances in Pain Research and Therapy, 3,* 547–550.

Levine, K., Shane, H. C., & Wharton, R. H. (1994). What if . . . : A plea to professionals to consider the risk-benefit ratio of facilitated communication. *Mental Retardation, 31,* 300–307.

Levine, M. (2006). *The price of privilege: How parental pressure and material advantage are creating a generation of disconnected and unhappy kids.* New York, NY: Harper Paperbacks.

Levinson, D. J. (1978). *The seasons of a man's life.* New York, NY: Ballantine.

Levinson, D. J. (1986). The conception of adult development. *American Psychologist, 41,* 3–13.

Levy, B. J., & Wagner, A. D. (2013). Measuring memory reactivation with functional MRI: Implications for psychological theory. *Psychological Science, 8,* 72–78.

Levy, D. A., Stark, C. E. L., & Squire, L. R. (2004). Intact conceptual priming in the absence of declarative memory. *Psychological Science, 15,* 680–683.

Levy-Gigi, E., Bonanno, G. A., Shapiro, A. R., Richter-Levin, G., Kéri, S., & Sheppes, G. (2016). Emotion regulation flexibility sheds light on the elusive relationship between repeated traumatic exposure and posttraumatic stress disorder symptoms. *Clinical Psychological Science, 4,* 28–39.

Lewicka, M. (1998). Confirmation bias: Cognitive error or adaptive strategy of action control? In M. Kofta, G. Weary, & G. Sedek (Eds.), *Personal control in action: Cognitive and motivational mechanisms.* New York, NY: Plenum.

Lewis, D. A., & Levitt, P. (2002). Schizophrenia as a disorder of neurodevelopment. *Annual Review of Neuroscience, 25,* 409–432.

Lewis, J. W., Cannon, J. T., & Liebeskind, J. C. (1980). Opioid and nonopioid mechanisms of stress analgesia. *Science, 208,* 623–625.

Lewis, M. (1993). The emergence of human emotions. In M. Lewis & J. M. Haviland (Eds.), *Handbook of emotions* (pp. 223–235). New York, NY: Guilford.

Lewis, M., Alessandri, S. M., & Sullivan, M. W. (1990). Violation of expectancy, loss of control, and anger expressions in young infants. *Developmental Psychology, 26,* 745–751.

Li, S., Naveh-Benjamin, M., & Lindenberger, U. (2005). Aging neuromodulation impairs associative binding: A neurocomputational account. *Psychological Science, 16,* 445–450.

Li, W., Howard, J. D., Parrish, T. B., & Gottfried, J. A. (2008). Aversive learning enhances perceptual and cortical discrimination of indiscriminable odor cues. *Science, 319,* 1842–1845.

Lichtenberger, E. O., &. Kaufman, A. S. (2013). *Essentials of WAIS-IV assessment* (2nd ed.). New York, NY: Wiley.

Lichtman, A. H., & Fanselow, M. S. (1990). Cats produce analgesia in rats on the tail-flick test: Naltrexone sensitivity is determined by the nociceptive test stimulus. *Brain Research, 553,* 91–94.

Lick, D. J., Durso, L. E., & Johnson, K. L. (2013). Minority stress and physical health among sexual minorities. *Perspectives on Psychological Science, 8,* 521–548.

Lickey, M. E., & Gordon, B. (1991). *Medicine and mental illness: The use of drugs in psychiatry.* New York, NY: Freeman.

Lieberman, D. A. (2000). *Learning: Behavior and cognition* (3rd. ed.). Belmont, CA: Wadsworth.

Lieberman, P. (2007). The evolution of human speech: Its anatomical and neural bases. *Current Anthropology, 48,* 39–66.

Liebovitch, L. S., Peluso, P. R., Norman, M. D., Su, J., & Gottman, J. M. (2012). Mathematical model of the dynamics of psychotherapy. *Cognitive Neurodynamics, 5,* 265–275.

Lillard, A. S. (2015). The development of play. In R. S. Lerner (Gen Ed.), *Handbook of child psychology and developmental science* (Vol. 2). New York, NY: Wiley.

Lillard, A. S., & Flavell, J. H. (1990). Young children's preference for mental state versus behavioral descriptions of human action. *Child Development, 61,* 731–741.

Lillard, A. S., & Flavell, J. H. (1992). Young children's understanding of different mental states. *Developmental Psychology, 28,* 626–634.

Lim, J., & Dinges, D. F. (2010). Sleep deprivation and diligent attention. *Annals of the New York Academy of Sciences, 1129,* 305–322.

Lima, S. L., Rattenborg, N. C., Lesku, J. A., & Amlaner, C. J. (2005). Sleeping under the risk of predation. *Animal Behaviour, 70,* 723–736.

Lin, E. H., & Church, A. T. (2004). Are indigenous Chinese personality dimensions culture-specific? An investigation of the Chinese Personality Assessment Inventory in Chinese American and European American samples. *Journal of Cross-Cultural Psychology, 35,* 586–605.

Lin, K., & Kleinman, A. M. (1988). Psychopathology and clinical course of schizophrenia: A cross-cultural perspective. *Schizophrenia Bulletin, 14,* 555–567.

Lindberg, S. M., Hyde, J. S., & Hirsch, L. M. (2008). Gender and mother–child interactions during mathematics homework: The importance of individual differences. *Merrill-Palmer Quarterly, 54,* 232–255.

Linder, D. E., Cooper, J., & Jones, E. E. (1967). Decision freedom as a determinant of the role of incentive magnitude in attitude change. *Journal of Personality and Social Psychology, 6,* 245–254.

Lindsay, D. S. (2008). Source monitoring. In J. Byrne (Series Ed.) & H. L. Roediger, III (Vol. Ed.), *Learning and memory: A comprehensive reference: Vol. 2. Cognitive psychology of memory.* Oxford, England: Elsevier.

Lindsay, P. H., & Norman, D. A. (1977). *Human information processing* (2nd ed.). San Diego, CA: Academic Press.

Linehan, M. M., & Dimeff, L. (2001). Dialectical behavior therapy in a nutshell. *The California Psychologist, 34,* 10–13.

Lipman, R. S. (1989). Pharmacotherapy of the anxiety disorders. In S. Fischer & R. P. Greenberg (Eds.), *The limits of biological treatments for psychological distress: Comparisons with psychotherapy and placebo.* Hillsdale, NJ: Erlbaum.

Lisanby, S. H. (2007). Electroconvulsive therapy for depression. *New England Journal of Medicine, 357,* 1939–1945.

Lisciandra, C., Postma-Nilsenová, M., & Colombo, M. (2013). Con formorality. A study on group conditioning of normative judgment. *Review of Philosophy and Psychology, 4,* 751–764.

Liszkowski, U., Carpenter, M., Striano, T., & Tomasello, M. (2006). 12- and 18-month-olds point to provide information for others. *Journal of Cognition and Development, 7,* 173–187.

Liszkowski, U., Carpenter, M., & Tomasello, M. (2007). Pointing out new news, old news, and absent referents at 12 months of age. *Developmental Science, 10,* F1–F7.

Litt, M. D. (1988). Self-efficacy and perceived control: Cognitive mediators of pain tolerance. *Journal of Personality and Social Psychology, 54,* 149–160.

Liu, J., Harris, A., & Kanwisher, N. (2010). Perception of face parts and face configurations. An fMRI study. *Journal of Cognitive Neuroscience, 22,* 203–211.

Livingston, R. W., & Drwecki, B. B. (2007). Why are some individuals not racially biased? *Psychological Science, 18,* 816–823.

Livingstone, D. (1857). *Missionary travels and researches in South Africa.* London, England: John Murray.

LoBue, V., Bloom Pickard, M., Sherman, K., Axford, C., & DeLoache, J. S. (2013). Young children's interest in live animals. *British Journal of Developmental Psychology, 31,* 57–69.

LoBue, V., Nishida, T., Chiong, C., DeLoache, J., & Haidt, J. (2010). When getting something good is bad: Even 3 year olds react to inequality. *Social Development, 20,* 154–170.

LoBue, V., & Rakison, D. H. (2013). What we fear most: Developmental advantage for threat-relevant stimuli. *Developmental Review, 33,* 285–303.

Locke, J. (1975). *An essay concerning human understanding* (P. Nidditch, Ed.). Oxford, England: Clarendon. (Original work published 1690)

Locke, J. L. (1983). *Phonological acquisition and change.* San Diego, CA: Academic Press.

Löckenhoff, C. E., & Carstensen, L. L. (2004). Socioemotional selectivity theory, aging, and health: The increasingly delicate balance between regulating emotions and making tough choices. *Journal of Personality, 72,* 1395–1424.

Loehlin, J. C., Vandenberg, S., & Osborne, R. (1973). Blood group genes and Negro–White ability differences. *Behavior Genetics, 3,* 263–270.

Loehlin, J. C., Willerman, L., & Horn, J. M. (1988). Human behavior genetics. *Annual Review of Psychology, 39,* 101–133.

Loft, S. (2014). Applying psychological science to examine prospective memory in simulated air traffic control. *Current Directions in Psychological Science, 23,* 326–331.

Loftus, E. F. (1992). When a lie becomes memory's truth: Memory distortion after exposure to misinformation. *Current Directions in Psychological Science, 1,* 121–123.

Loftus, E. F. (1997). Memory for a past that never was. *Current Directions in Psychological Science, 6,* 60–65.

Loftus, E. F. (2004). Memories for things unseen. *Current Directions in Psychological Science, 13,* 145–147.

Loftus, E. F., & Palmer, J. C. (1974). Reconstruction of automobile destruction: An example of the interaction between language and memory. *Journal of Verbal Learning and Verbal Behavior, 13,* 585–589.

Loftus, E. F., & Pickrell, J. E. (1995). The formation of false memories. *Psychiatric Annals, 25,* 720–725.

Logothetis, N. K. (2008). What we can and what we cannot do with fMRI. *Nature, 453,* 869–878.

Loidolt, M., Aust, U., Meran, I., & Huber, L. (2003). Pigeons use item-specific and category-level information in the identification and categorization of human faces. *Journal of Experimental Psychology: Animal Behavior Processes, 29,* 261–276.

Lombar, S. G., & Malhotra, S. (2008). Double dissociation of "what" and "where" processing in auditory cortex. *Nature Neuroscience, 11,* 609–616.

Loo, C. (2010). ECT in the 21st century: Optimizing treatment: State of the art in the 21st century. *The Journal of ECT, 26*(3), 157.

Lopez, D. F., Little, T. D., Oettingen, G., & Baltes, P. B. (1998). Self-regulation and school performance: Is there optimal level of action-control? *Journal of Experimental Child Psychology, 70,* 54–74.

López, S. R., & Guarnaccia, P. J. (2005). Cultural dimensions of psychopathology: The social world's impact on mental illness. In J. Maddux & B. Winstead (Eds.), *Psychopathology: Foundations for a contemporary understanding.* Mahwah, NJ: Erlbaum.

Lorenz, K. (1970). Companions as factors in the bird's environment (R. Martin, Trans.). In K. Lorenz (Ed.), *Studies in animal and human behavior* (Vol. 1). Cambridge, MA: Harvard University Press. (Original work published 1935)

Lorenz, K. Z. (1943). Die angeborenen Formen möglicher Erfahrung. *Zeitschrift für Tierpsychologie, 5,* 235–409.

Lorenz, K. Z. (1971). *Studies in animal and human behavior* (Vol. 2). Cambridge, MA: Harvard University Press.

Lovaas, O. I. (1987). Behavioral treatment and normal educational and intellectual functioning in young autistic children. *Journal of Consulting and Clinical Psychology, 55,* 3–9.

Lovaas, O. I. (2003). Teaching individuals with developmental delays: Basic intervention techniques. Austin, TX: PRO-ED.

Luborsky, L. B., Barrett, M. S., Antonuccio, D. C., Shoenberger, D., & Stricker, G. (2006). What else materially influences what is represented and published as evidence? In J. C. Norcross, L. E. Beutler, & R. F. Levant (Eds.), *Evidence-based practices in mental health: Debate and dialogue on the fundamental questions* (pp. 257–298). Washington, DC: American Psychological Association.

Lumey, L. H. (1998). Reproductive outcomes in women prenatally exposed to undernutrition: A review of findings from the Dutch famine birth cohort. *Proceeding of the Nutrition Society, 57,* 129–135.

Luna, B., Thulborn, K. R., Monoz, D. P., Merriam, E. P., Garver, K. E., Minshew, N. J., . . . Sweeney, J. A. (2001). Maturation of widely distributed brain function subserves cognitive development. *NeuroImage, 13,* 786–793.

Luria, A. R. (1971). Towards the problem of the historical nature of psychological processes. *International Journal of Psychology, 6,* 259–272.

Luria, A. R. (1976). *Cognitive development: Its cultural and social foundations.* Cambridge, MA: Harvard University Press.

Lynn, B. L., & Perl, E. R. (1996). Afferent mechanisms of pain. In L. Kruger (Ed.), *Pain and touch.* San Diego, CA: Academic Press.

Lynn, S. J., Lock, T. G., Myers, B., & Payne, D. G. (1997). Recalling the unrecallable: Should hypnosis be used to recover memories in psychotherapy? *Current Directions in Psychological Science, 6,* 79–83.

Lyons, D. E., Young, A. G., & Keil, F. C. (2007). The hidden structure of overimitation. *Proceedings of the National Academy of Sciences of the USA, 104,* 19751–19756.

Maccoby, E. E. (1998). *The two sexes: Growing up apart, coming together.* Cambridge, MA: Harvard University Press.

Maccoby, E. E., & Jacklin, C. N. (1987). Gender segregation in childhood. In H. W. Reese (Ed.), *Advances in child development and behavior* (Vol. 20). San Diego, CA: Academic Press.

Maccoby, E., & Martin, J. A. (1983). Socialization in the context of the family: Parent–child interaction. In P. H. Mussen (Series Ed.) & E. M. Hetherington (Vol. Ed.), *Handbook of child psychology* (4th ed., Vol. 4, pp. 1–102). New York, NY: Wiley.

MacDonald, K. (1992). Warmth as a developmental construct: An evolutionary analysis. *Child Development, 63,* 753–773.

Macfarlane, A. J. (1975). Olfaction in the development of social preferences in the human neonate. *Ciba Foundation Symposium, 33,* 103–117.

Machado-Vieira, R., Manji, H. K., & Zarate, C. A., Jr. (2009). The role of lithium in the treatment of bipolar disorder: Convergent evidence for neurotrophic effects as a unifying hypothesis. *Bipolar Disorder, 11*(Suppl 2), 92–109.

Mack, A., Pappas, Z., Silverman, M., & Gay, R. (2002). What we see: Inattention and the capture of attention by meaning. *Consciousness and Cognition, 11,* 488–506.

MacKay, D. G. (1973). Aspects of the theory of comprehension, memory and attention. *Quarterly Journal of Experimental Psychology, 25,* 22–40.

Mackey, A. P., Miller Singley, A. T., & Bunge, S. A. (2013). Intensive reasoning training alters patterns of brain connectivity at rest. *Journal of Neuroscience, 33,* 4796–4803.

Mackey, A. P., Whitaker, K. J., & Bunge, S. A. (2012). Experience-dependent plasticity in white matter microstructure: Reasoning training alters structural connectivity. *Frontiers in Neuroanatomy, 6,* 32.

Macknik, S. L., King, M., Randi, J., Robbins, A., Teller, Thompson, J., & Martinez-Conde, S. (2008). Attention and awareness in stage magic: Turning tricks into research. *Nature Reviews Neuroscience, 9,* 871–879.

MacWhinney, B. (2005). Language evolution and human development. In B. J. Ellis & D. F. Bjorklund (Eds.), *Origins of the social mind: Evolutionary psychology and child development* (pp. 383–410). New York, NY: Guilford.

MacWhinney, B. (2016). Language development. In R. M. Lerner (Gen. Ed.) & L. S. Liben (Vol. Ed.), *Handbook of child psychology and developmental science: Vol. 2. Cognition* (7th ed.). New York, NY: Wiley.

Maddux, J. E., Gosselin, J. T., & Winstead, B. A. (2005). Conceptions of psychopathology: A social constructionist perspective. In J. Maddux & B. Winstead (Eds.), *Psychopathology: Foundations for a contemporary understanding.* Mahwah, NJ: Erlbaum.

Maestripieri, D., & Roney, J. R. (2006). Evolutionary developmental psychology: Contributions from comparative research with nonhuman primates. *Developmental Review, 26,* 120–137.

Magistretti, P. J. (2008). Brain energy metabolism. In L. Squire, D. Berg, F. Bloom, S. du Lac, A. Ghosh, & N. Spitzer (Eds.), *Fundamental neuroscience.* New York, NY: Elsevier.

Maguire, E. A., Gadian, D. G., Johnsrude, I. S., Good, C. D., Ashburner, J., Frackowiak, R. S. J., & Frith, C. D. (2000). Navigation-related structural change in the hippocampi of taxi drivers. *Proceedings of the National Academy of Sciences, 97,* 4398–4403.

Maguire, E. A., Valentine, E. R., Wilding, J. M., & Kapur, N. (2003). Routes to remembering: The brains behind superior memory. *Nature Neuroscience, 6,* 90–95.

Mahone, E. M., Hagelthorn, K. M., Cutting, L. E., Schuerholz, L. J., Pelletier, S. F., Rawlins, C., . . . Denckla, M. B. (2002). Effects of IQ on executive function measures in children with ADHD. *Child Neuropsychology, 8,* 52–65.

Main, M., Hesse, E., & Kaplan, N. (2005). Predictability of attachment behavior and representational processes at 1, 6, and 19 years of age. In K. E. Grossmann, K. Grossmann, & E. Waters (Eds.), *Attachment from infancy to adulthood: The major longitudinal studies* (pp. 245–304). New York, NY: Guilford.

Main, M., & Solomon, J. (1986). Discovery of a disorganized/disoriented attachment pattern. In T. B. Brazelton & M. N. Youngman (Eds.), *Affective development in infancy.* Norwood, NJ: Ablex.

Malcolm, J. R. (1985). Paternal care in Canids. *American Zoologist, 25,* 853–859.

Malle, B. F. (2006). The actor–observer asymmetry in attribution: A (surprising) meta-analysis. *Psychological Bulletin, 132,* 895–919.

Maltz, D. N., & Borker, R. A. (1982). A cultural approach to male–female miscommunication. In J. J. Gumperz (Ed.), *Language and social identity.* Cambridge, England: Cambridge University Press.

Mamede, S., van Gog, T., van den Berge, K., Rikers, R. M. J. P., van Saase, L. C. M., van Guldener, C., & Schmidt, H. G. (2010). Effect of availability bias and reflective reasoning on diagnostic accuracy among internal medicine residents. *Journal of the American Medical Association, 304,* 1198–1203.

Maner, J. K., Miller, S. L., Rouby, D. A., & Gailliot, M. T. (2009). Intrasexual vigilance: The implicit cognition of romantic rivalry. *Journal of Personality and Social Psychology, 97,* 74–97.

Manns, J. R., & Buffalo, E. A. (2012). Learning and memory: Brain systems. In L. R. Squire, D. Berg, F. E. Bloom, S. du Lac, A. Ghosh, & N. C. Spitzer (Eds.), *Fundamental neuroscience* (4th ed., pp. 1029–1051). New York, NY: Elsevier.

Mäntylä, T. (1986). Optimizing cue effectiveness: Recall of 500 and 600 incidentally learned words. *Journal of Experimental Psychology: Learning, Memory, and Cognition, 12*, 66–71.

Marcus, G. F., Pinker, S., Ullman, M., Hollander, M., Rosen, T. J., & Xu, F. (1992). Overregularization in language acquisition. *Monographs of the Society for Research in Child Development, 57*.

Maren, S. (1999). Long-term potentiation in the amygdala: A mechanism for emotional learning and memory. *Trends in Neuroscience, 22*, 561–567.

Markman, H. J., & Rhodes, G. K. (2012). Relationship education research: Current status and future directions. *Journal of Marriage and Family Therapy, 38*, 169–200.

Markman, H. J., Stanley, S. M., Blumberg, S. L., Jenkins, N. H., & Whiteley, C. (2004). *12 hours to a great marriage: A step-by-step guide for making love last.* San Francisco, CA: Jossey-Bass.

Marks, I. M. (1987). *Fears, phobias, and rituals: Panic, anxiety, and their disorders.* Oxford, England: Oxford University Press.

Marler, P. (1970). A comparative approach to vocal learning: Song development in white-crowned sparrows. *Journal of Comparative and Physiological Psychology, 7*, 1–25.

Marlowe, F. (2000). Paternal investment and the human mating system. *Behavioural Processes, 51*, 45–61.

Marlowe, F. W. (2003). The mating system of foragers in the Standard Cross-Cultural Sample. *Cross-Cultural Research: The Journal of Comparative Social Science, 37*, 282–306.

Marsh, H. W., Seaton, M., Trautwein, U., Ladtke, O., Hau, K. T., O'Mara, A. J., & Craven, R. G. (2008). The big-fish-little-pond-effect stands up to critical scrutiny: Implications for theory, methodology, and future research. *Educational Psychology Review, 20*, 319–350.

Marsh, R. L., & Hicks, J. L. (1998). Event-based prospective memory and executive control of working memory. *Journal of Experimental Psychology: Learning, Memory, and Cognition, 24*, 336–349.

Marshall-Pescini, S., & Whiten, A. (2008). Social learning and nut-cracking behavior in East African sanctuary-living chimpanzees (*Pan troglodytes schweinfurthii*). *Journal of Comparative Psychology, 122*, 186–194.

Martens, A., Johns, M., Greenberg, J., & Schimel, J. (2006). Combating stereotype threat: The effect of self-affirmation on women's intellectual performance. *Journal of Experimental Social Psychology, 42*, 236–243.

Martin, C. A., Kelly, T. H., Rayens, M. K., Brogli, B., Himelreich, K., Brenzel, A., . . . Omar, H. (2004). Sensation seeking and symptoms of disruptive disorder: Association with nicotine, alcohol, and marijuana use in early and mid-adolescence. *Psychological Reports, 94*, 1075–1082.

Martin, C. L. (1990). Attitudes and expectations about children with nontraditional and traditional gender roles. *Sex Roles, 22*, 151–165.

Martin, C. L., & Ruble, D. (2004). Children's search for gender cues: Cognitive perspectives on gender development. *Current Directions in Psychological Science, 13*, 67–70.

Martin, C. L., Ruble, D. N., & Szkrybalo, J. (2002). Cognitive theories of early gender development. *Psychological Bulletin, 128*, 903–933.

Martin, J. A., Hamilton, B. E., Osterman, M. J. K., Curtin, S. C., & Mathews, T. J. (2015). Births: Final data for 2013. *National Vital Statistics Report, 64*(1).

Martin, J. L. R., Sainz-Pardo, M., Furukawa, T. A., Martin-Sánchez, E., Seoane, T., & Galán, C. (2007). Benzodiazepines in generalized anxiety disorder: Heterogeneity of outcomes based on a systematic review and meta-analysis of clinical trials. *Journal of Psychopharmacology, 21*, 774–782.

Martin, P., & Caro, T. M. (1985). On the function of play and its role in behavioral development. In J. Rosenblatt, C. Beer, M. Bushnel, & P. Slater (Eds.), *Advances in the study of behavior* (Vol. 15, pp. 59–103). San Diego, CA: Academic Press.

Martinowich, K., Manji, H., & Lu, B. (2007). New insights into BDNF function in depression and anxiety. *Nature Neuroscience, 10*, 1089–1093.

Marx, J. (2003). Cellular warriors at the battle of the bulge. *Science, 299*, 846–849.

Masataka, N. (1996). Perception of motherese in a signed language by 6-month-old deaf infants. *Developmental Psychology, 32*, 874–879.

Masataka, N. (2003). *On the onset of language.* Cambridge, England: Cambridge University Press.

Mashour, G. A., Walker, E. E., & Martuza, R. L. (2005). Psychosurgery: Past, present, and future. *Brain Research Reviews, 48*, 409–419.

Masland, R. H. (2001). The fundamental plan of the retina. *Nature Neuroscience, 4*, 877–886.

Maslow, A. H. (1970). *Motivation and personality* (2nd ed.). New York, NY: Harper & Row.

Mason, P. (2001). Contributions of the medullary raphe and ventromedial reticular region to pain modulation and other homeostatic functions. *Annual Review of Neuroscience, 24*, 737–777.

Mastrangelo, S. (2009). Play and the child with autism spectrum disorder: From possibilities to practice. *International Journal of Play Therapy, 18*, 13–30.

Masuda, T., & Nisbett, R. E. (2001). Attending holistically versus analytically: Comparing the context sensitivity of Japanese and Americans. *Journal of Personality and Social Psychology, 81*, 922–934.

Mather, M., Cacioppo, J. T., & Kanswisher, N. (2013). Introduction to the Special Section: 20 years of fMRI—What has it done for understanding cognition? *Perspectives on Psychological Science, 8*, 41–43.

Mather, M., Canli, T., English, T., Whitfield, S., Wais, P., Ochsner, K., . . . Carstensen, L. L. (2004). Amygdala responds to emotionally valenced stimuli in older and younger adults. *Psychological Science, 15*, 259–263.

Mather, M., & Carstensen, L. L. (2003). Aging and attentional biases for emotional faces. *Psychological Science, 14*, 409–415.

Mathew, S. J., & Hoffman, E. J. (2009). Pharmacotherapy for generalized anxiety disorder. In M. M. Antony & M. B. Stein (Eds.), *Oxford handbook of anxiety related disorders*. Oxford, England: Oxford University Press.

Mathews, C. A. (2009) Phenomenology of obsessive-compulsive disorder. In M. M. Antony & M. B. Stein (Eds.), *Oxford handbook of anxiety related disorders*. Oxford, England: Oxford University Press.

Matlin, M. W., & Foley, H. J. (1997). *Sensation and perception* (4th ed.). Boston, MA: Allyn & Bacon.

Mattes, R. D., Curran, W. J., Jr., Alaviu, J., Powlis, W., & Whittington, R. (1992). Clinical implications of learned food aversions in patients with cancer treated with chemotherapy or radiation therapy. *Cancer, 70*, 192–200.

Matthews, G., Derryberry, D., & Siegle, G. J. (2000). Personality and emotion: Cognitive science perspectives. In S. E. Hampson (Ed.), *Advances in personality psychology* (Vol. 1, pp. 199–237). Philadelphia, PA: Taylor & Francis.

Matthews, R. N., Domjam, M., Ramsey, M., & Crews, D. (2007). Learning effects on sperm competition and reproductive fitness. *Psychological Science, 18*, 758–762.

Matzel, L., Townsend, D. A., Grossman, H., Han, Y. R., Hale, G., Zappulla, M., . . . Kolata, S. (2006). Exploration in outbred mice covaries with general learning abilities irrespective of stress reactivity, emotionality, and physical attributes. *Neurobiology of Learning and Memory, 86*, 228–240.

Maurer, D., & Lewis, T. L. (2013). Sensitive periods in visual development. In P. D. Zelazo (Ed.), *Oxford handbook of developmental psychology* (Vol. 1, pp. 202–234). Oxford, England: Oxford University Press.

Maurer, D., & Maurer, C. (1988). *The world of the newborn*. New York, NY: Basic Books.

Maurer, D., & Mondloch, C. J. (2005). Neonatal synesthesia: A re-evaluation. In C. L. Robertson & N. Sagiv (Eds.), *Synesthesia: Perspectives from cognitive neuroscience*. Oxford, England: Oxford University Press.

Maurer, D., Mondloch, C. J., & Lewis, T. L. (2007). Effects of early visual deprivation on perceptual and cognitive development. *Progress in Brain Research, 164*, 87–104.

Maurer, D., Pathman, T., & Mondloch, C. J. (2006). The shape of boubas: Sound-shape correspondences in toddlers and adults. *Developmental Science, 9*, 316–322.

Maxwell, J. S., & Davidson, R. J. (2007). Emotion and motion: Asymmetries in approach and avoidant actions. *Psychological Science, 18*, 1113–1119.

Mayberg, H. S., Lozano, A. M., Voon, V., McNeely, H. E., Seminowicz, D., Hamani, C., . . . Kennedy, S. H. (2005). Deep brain stimulation for treatment-resistant depression. *Neuron, 45*, 651–660.

Mayberry, R. I., Lock, E., & Kazmi, H. (2002). Linguistic ability and early language exposure. *Nature, 417*, 38.

Mayer, D. L., Beiser, A. S., Warner, A. F., Pratt, E. M., Raye, K. N., & Lang, J. M. (1995). Monocular acuity norms for the Teller Acuity Cards between ages one month and four years. *Investigative Ophthalmology & Visual Science, 36*, 671–685.

Mayer, D. L, & Dobson, V. (1982). Visual acuity development in infants and young children as assessed by operant preferential looking. *Vision Research, 22*, 1141–1115.

Mayes, R., Bagwell, C., & Erkulwater, J. (2009). *Medicating children: ADHD and pediatric mental health*. Cambridge, MA: Harvard University Press.

Mazerolle, M., Régner, I., Morisset, P., Rigalleau, F., & Huguet, P. (2012). Stereotype threat strengthens automatic recall and undermines controlled processes in older adults. *Psychological Science, 23*, 723–727.

Mazoni, G., & Memon, A. (2003). Imagination can create false autobiographical memories. *Psychological Science, 14*, 186–188.

McAlister, A., & Peterson, C. (2007). A longitudinal study of child siblings and theory of mind development. *Cognitive Development, 22*, 258–270.

McArthur, L. Z., & Berry, D. S. (1987). Cross-cultural agreement in perceptions of baby-faced adults. *Journal of Cross-Cultural Psychology, 18*, 165–192.

McCarthy, G., Puce, A., Gore, J. C., & Allison, T. (1997). Face-specific processing in the human fusiform gyrus. *Journal of Cognitive Neuroscience, 9*, 605–610.

McClean, C. Y., Reno, P. L., Pollen, A. A., Bassan, A. I., Capellini, T. D., Guenther, C., . . . Kingsley, D. M. (2011). Human-specific loss of regulatory DNA and the evolution of human-specific traits. *Nature, 471*, 216–219.

McCrae, R. R., & Costa, P. T. (1985). Openness to experience. In R. Hogan & W. H. Jones (Eds.), *Perspectives in personality* (Vol. 1). Greenwich, CT: JAI Press.

McCrae, R. R., Costa, P. T., & Martin, T. A. (2005). The NEO-PI-3: A more readable revised NEO personality inventory. *Journal of Personality Assessment, 84*, 261–270.

McCrae, R. R., & Terracciano, A. (2005). Universal features of personality traits from the observer's perspective: Data from 50 cultures. *Journal of Personality and Social Psychology, 88*, 547–561.

McDevitt, T. M., & Ormond, J. E. (2004). *Child development: Educating and working with children and adolescents* (2nd ed.). Upper Saddle River, NJ: Pearson.

McDonough, L., Mandler, J. M., McKee, R. D., & Squire, L. R. (1995). The deferred imitation task as a nonverbal measure of declarative memory. *Proceedings of the National Academy of Sciences, 92*, 7580–7584.

McEachin, J. J., Smith, T., & Lovaas, O. I. (1993). Long-term outcome for children with autism that received early intensive behavioral treatment. *American Journal on Mental Retardation, 97*, 359–372.

McElwain, A. K., Korabik, K., & Rosin, H. M. (2005). An examination of gender differences in work–family conflict. *Canadian Journal of Behavioral Sciences, 37*, 283–298.

McEwen, B. S. (1989). Endocrine effects on the brain and their relationship to behavior. In G. J. Siegel, B. W. Agranoff, R. W. Albers, & P. B. Molinoff (Eds.), *Basic neurochemistry: Molecular, cellular, and medical aspects* (4th ed.). New York, NY: Raven Press.

McGarrigle, J., & Donaldson, M. (1975). Conservation accidents. *Cognition, 3*, 341–350.

McGue, M., Bouchard, T. J., Iacono, W. G., & Lykken, D. T. (1993). Behavioral genetics of cognitive ability: A life-span perspective. In R. Plomin & G. E. McClearn (Eds.), *Nature, nurture, and psychology*. Washington, DC: American Psychological Association.

McGuigan, N., Makinson, J., & Whiten, A. (2011). From over-imitation to super-copying: Adults imitate causally irrelevant aspects of tool use with higher fidelity than young children. *British Journal of Psychology, 102*, 1–18.

McGuigan, N., & Whiten, A. (2009). Emulation and "over-emulation" in the social learning of causally opaque versus causally transparent tool use by 23- and 30-month-old children. *Journal of Experimental Child Psychology, 104*, 367–381.

McGuire, W. J., & McGuire, C. V. (1988). Content and process in the experience of self. In L. Berkowitz (Ed.), *Advances in experimental social psychology* (Vol. 21). San Diego, CA: Academic Press.

McGurk, H., & MacDonald, J. (1976). Hearing lips and seeing voices. *Nature, 264*, 746–748.

McHugo, G. J., Lanzetta, J. T., Sullivan, D. G., Masters, R. D., & Englis, B. G. (1985). Emotional reactions to a political leader's expressive displays. *Journal of Personality and Social Psychology, 49*, 1513–1529.

McKenna, K. Y. A., Green, A. S., & Gleason, M. E. J. (2002). Relationship formation on the Internet: What's the big attraction? *Journal of Social Issues, 58*, 9–31.

McNally, R. J. (2003). *Remembering trauma*. Cambridge, MA: Harvard University Press.

McQueen, A. (2005). A groupthink perspective on the invasion of Iraq. *International Affairs Review, 14*, 53–80.

Mead, M. (1935). *Sex and temperament in three primitive societies*. New York, NY: William Morrow.

Meaney, M. J. (2010). Epigenetic and the biological definition of gene x environment interactions. *Child Development, 81*, 41–79.

Meaney, M. J. (2013). Epigenetics and the environmental regulation of the genome and its function. In D. Narvaez, J. Panksepp, A. N. Schore, & T. R. Gleason (Eds.), *Evolution, early experience and human development: From research to practice and policy* (pp. 99–128). Oxford, England: Oxford University Press.

Mearns, D., & Thorne, B. (2000). *Person-centred therapy today: New frontiers in theory and practice*. London, England: Sage.

Meddis, R. (1977). *The sleep instinct*. London, England: Routledge & Kegan Paul.

Medina, J. F., Nores, W. L., & Mauk, M. D. (2002). Inhibition of climbing fibers is a signal for the extinction of conditioned eyelid responses. *Nature, 416*, 330–333.

Medina, J. H., Bekinschtein, P., Cammarota, M., & Izquierdo, I. (2008). Do memories consolidate to persist or do they persist to consolidate? *Behavioural Brain Research, 192*, 61–69.

Meisel, R. L., & Sachs, B. D. (1994). The physiology of male sexual behavior. In E. Knobil & J. Neill (Eds.), *The physiology of reproduction.* New York, NY: Raven Press.

Meissner, C. A., & Brigham, J. C. (2001). Thirty years of investigating the own-race bias in memory for faces: A meta-analytic review. *Psychology, Public Policy, and Law, 7,* 3–35.

Melby-Lervåg, M., Redick, T. S., & Hulme, C. (2016). Working memory training does not improve performance on measure of intelligence or other measures of "far transfer": Evidence from a meta-analytic review. *Perspectives on Psychological Science, 11,* 512–534.

Melchior, C. L. (1990). Conditioned tolerance provides protection against ethanol lethality. *Pharmacology Biochemistry and Behavior, 37,* 205–206.

Melzack, R., & Wall, P. D. (1965). Pain mechanisms: A new theory. *Science, 150,* 971–979.

Melzack, R., & Wall, P. D. (1996). *The challenge of pain* (Updated 2nd ed.). New York, NY: Penguin.

Merbs, S. L., & Nathans, J. (1992). Absorption spectra of human cone pigments. *Nature, 356,* 433–435.

Mercader, J., Panger, M., & Boesch, C. (2002). Excavation of a chimpanzee stone tool site in the African rainforest. *Science, 296,* 1452–1455.

Mercer, N., & Littleton, K. (2007). *Dialogue and the development of children's thinking: A sociocultural approach.* New York, NY: Routledge.

Merikangas, K. R., He, J. P., Burstein, M., Swendsen, J., Avenevoli, S., Case, B., . . . Olfso, M. (2011). Service utilization for lifetime mental disorders in U.S. adolescents: Results of the National Comorbidity Survey-Adolescent Supplement (NCS-A). *Journal of the American Academy of Child and Adolescent Psychiatry, 50,* 32–45.

Merkl, A., Heuser, I., & Bajbouj, M. (2009). Antidepressant electroconvulsive therapy: Mechanism of action, recent advances and limitations. *Experimental Neurology, 291,* 20–26.

Mervis, C. M., & Bertrand, J. (1994). Acquisition of the novel name-nameless category (N3C) principle. *Child Development, 65,* 1646–1662.

Mezulis, A. H., Abramson, L. Y., Hyde, J. S., & Hankin, B. L. (2004). Is there a universal positivity bias in attributions? A meta-analytic review of individual, developmental, and cultural differences in self-serving attributional bias. *Psychological Bulletin, 130,* 711–747.

Michael, R. T., Gagnon, J. H., Laumann, E. O., & Kolata, G. (1994). *Sex in America: A definitive survey.* Boston, MA: Little, Brown and Co.

Michaels, J. W., Blommel, J. M., Brocato, R. M., Linkous, R. A., & Rowe, J. S. (1982). Social facilitation and inhibition in a natural setting. *Replications in Social Psychology, 2,* 21–24.

Mikels, J. S., Larkin, G. R., Reuter-Lorenz, P. A., & Carstensen, L. L. (2005). Divergent trajectories in the aging mind: Changes in working memory for affective versus visual information with age. *Psychology and Aging, 20,* 542–553.

Mikulincer, M., & Shaver, P. R. (2007). *Attachment in adulthood: Structure, dynamics, and change.* New York, NY: Guilford.

Milgram, S. (1963). Behavioral study of obedience. *Journal of Abnormal and Social Psychology, 67,* 371–378.

Milgram, S. (1964). Issues in the study of obedience: A reply to Baumrind. *American Psychologist, 19,* 848–852.

Milgram, S. (1974). *Obedience to authority: An experimental view.* New York, NY: Harper & Row.

Mill, J. S. (1875). *A system of logic* (9th ed.). London, England: Longmans, Green, Reader & Dyer. (Original work published 1843)

Miller, A. G. (1986). *The obedience experiments: A case study of controversy in social science.* New York, NY: Praeger.

Miller, A. G. (2004). What can the Milgram obedience experiments tell us about the Holocaust? In A. G. Miller (Ed.), *The social psychology of good and evil.* New York, NY: Guilford.

Miller, E. K., & Wallis, J. D. (2013). The prefrontal cortex and executive functions. In L. R. Squire, D. Berg, F. E. Bloom, S. du Lac, A. Ghosh, & N. C. Spitzer (Eds.), *Fundamental neuroscience* (4th ed., pp. 1069–1089). New York, NY: Elsevier.

Miller, E. M. (1997). Could nonshared environmental variance have evolved to assure diversification through randomness? *Evolution and Human Behavior, 18,* 195–221.

Miller, G. E. (1956). The magic number seven plus or minus two: Some limits on our capacity for processing information. *Psychological Review, 63,* 81–97.

Miller, J. G. (1984). Culture and the development of everyday social explanations. *Journal of Personality and Social Psychology, 46,* 961–978.

Miller, K. F., Smith, C. M., Zhu, J., & Zhang, H. (1995). Preschool origins of cross-national differences in mathematical competence. *Psychological Science, 6,* 56–60.

Miller, L. T., & Vernon, P. A. (1992). The general factor in short-term memory, intelligence, and reaction time. *Intelligence, 16,* 5–29.

Miller-Jones, D. (1989). Culture and testing. *American Psychologist, 44,* 360–366.

Millon, T. (2011). *Disorders of personality: Introducing the DSM/ICD spectrum from normal to abnormal* (3rd ed.). Hoboken, NJ: Wiley.

Mills, J. F., Kroner, D. F., & Morgan, R. D. (2011). *Clinician's guide to violence risk assessment.* Hoboken, NJ: Wiley.

Milner, A. D., & Goodale, M. A. (1995). *The visual brain in action.* Oxford, England: Oxford University Press.

Milner, B. (1965). Memory disturbance after bilateral hippocampal lesions. In P. Milner & S. Glickman (Eds.), *Cognitive processes and the brain.* Princeton, NJ: Van Nostrand.

Milner, B. (1970). Memory and the medial temporal regions of the brain. In K. H. Pribram & D. E. Broadbent (Eds.), *Biology of memory.* San Diego, CA: Academic Press.

Milner, B. (1984). *Temporal lobes and memory disorders.* Paper presented at the American Psychological Association Convention, Toronto, Canada.

Mineka, S., Davidson, M., Cook, M., & Keir, R. (1984). Observational conditional of snake fear in rhesus monkeys. *Journal of Abnormal Psychology, 93,* 355–372.

Mineka, S., & Öhman, A. (2002). Phobias and preparedness: The selective, automatic, and encapsulated nature of fear. *Biological Psychiatry, 52,* 927–937.

Mineka, S., & Zinbarg, R. (2006). A contemporary learning theory perspective on the etiology of anxiety disorders: It's not what you thought it was. *American Psychologist, 61,* 10–26.

Ming, G., & Song, H. (2005). Adult neurogenesis in the mammalian central nervous system. *Annual Review of Neuroscience, 28,* 223–250.

Minix, D. A. (1976). *The rule of the small group in foreign policy decision making: A potential pathology in crisis decisions?* Paper presented to the Southern Political Science Association.

Mink, J. W. (2013). Basal ganglia. In L. R. Squire, D. Berg, F. E. Bloom, S. du Lac, A. Ghosh, & N. C. Spitzer (Eds.), *Fundamental neuroscience* (4th ed., pp. 653–676). Boston, MA: Elsevier.

Minton, H. L. (2002). *Departing from deviance: A history of homosexual rights and emancipatory science in America.* Chicago, IL: University of Chicago Press.

Mirgain, S. A., & Cordova, J. V. (2007). Emotion skills and marital health: The association between observed and self-reported emotion skills, intimacy, and marital satisfaction. *Journal of Social and Clinical Psychology, 9,* 983–1009.

Mischel, W. (1984). Convergences and challenges in the search for consistency. *American Psychologist, 39,* 351–364.

Mischel, W. (2007). Toward a cognitive social learning reconceptualization of personality. In Y. Shoda, D. Cervone, & G. Downey (Eds.), *Persons in context: Building a science of the individual*. New York, NY: Guilford.

Mischel, W. (2012). Self-control theory. In P. A. M. Van Lange, A. W. Kruglanski, & E. Tory Higgins (Eds.), *Handbook of theories of social psychology* (Vol. 2, pp. 1–22). Los Angeles, CA: Sage.

Mischel, W., & Ayduk, O. (2011). Willpower in a cognitive-affective processing system: The dynamics of delay of gratification. In K. D. Vohs & R. F. Baumeister (Eds.), *Handbook of self-regulation: Research, theory, and applications* (2nd ed., pp. 83–105). New York, NY: Guilford.

Mischel, W., Ebbesen, E. B., & Raskoff Zeiss, A. (1972). Cognitive and attentional mechanisms in delay of gratification. *Journal of Personality and Social Psychology, 21,* 204–218.

Mischel, W., & Peake, P. K. (1982). Beyond déjà vu in the search for cross-situational consistency. *Psychological Review, 89,* 730–755.

Mischel, W., & Shoda, Y. (1995). A cognitive-affective system theory of personality: Reconceptualizing situations, dispositions, dynamics, and invariance in personality structure. *Psychological Review, 102,* 246–268.

Mitchem, D. G., Zietsch, B. P., Wright, M. J., Martin, N. G., Hewitt, J. K., & Keller, M. C. (2015). No relationship between intelligence and facial attractiveness in a large genetically informative sample. *Evolution and Human Behavior, 36,* 240–247.

Mitte, K. (2005). Meta-analysis of cognitive-behavioral treatments for generalized anxiety disorder: A comparison with pharmacotherapy. *Psychological Bulletin, 131,* 785–795.

Miura, I. T., & Okamoto, Y. (2003). Language supports for mathematics understanding and performance. In A. J. Baroody & A. Dowker (Eds.), *The development of arithmetic concepts and skills: Constructing adaptive expertise. Studies in mathematical learning* (pp. 229–242). Mahwah, NJ: Erlbaum.

Miura, I. T., Okamoto, Y., Kim, C. C., Chang, C., Steere, M., & Fayol, M. (1994). Comparisons of children's cognitive representation of number: China, France, Japan, Korea, Sweden, and the United States. *International Journal of Behavioral Development, 17,* 401–411.

Miyake, A., & Friedman, N. P. (2012). The nature and organization of individual differences in executive: Four general conclusions. *Current Directions in Psychological Sciences, 21,* 8–14.

Miyake, A., Friedman, N. P., Emerson, M. J., Witzki, A. H., Howerter, A., Wager, T. D. (2000). The unity and diversity of executive functions and their contributions to complex "frontal lobe" tasks: A latent variable analysis. *Cognitive Psychology, 41,* 49–100.

Moffitt, T. E. (1993). Adolescence-limited and life-course-persistent antisocial behavior: A developmental taxonomy. *Psychological Review, 100,* 674–701.

Moffitt, T. E., Arseneault, L., Belsky, D., Dickson, N., Hancox, R. J., Harrington, H., . . . Caspi, A. (2011, Feb. 15). A gradient of childhood self-control predicts health, wealth, and public safety. *Proceedings of the National Academy of Sciences, 108,* 2693–2698.

Mogg, K., & Bradley, B. P. (2005). Attentional bias in generalized anxiety disorder versus depressive disorder. *Cognitive Therapy and Research, 29,* 29–45.

Monahan, J. (2010). The classification of violence risk. In R. K. Otto & K. S. Douglas (Eds.), *Handbook of violence risk assessment* (pp. 187–198). New York, NY: Routledge.

Monk, T. H., Buysse, D. J., Welsh, D. K., Kennedy, K. S., & Rose, L. R. (2001). A sleep diary and questionnaire study of naturally short sleepers. *Journal of Sleep Research, 10,* 173–179.

Monroe, S. M., Slavich, G. M., & Georgiades, K. (2009). The social environment and life stress in depression. In I. H. Gotlib & C. L. Hammen (Eds.), *Handbook of depression* (2nd ed.). New York, NY: Guilford.

Mood, D. W. (1979). Sentence comprehension in preschool children: Testing an adaptive egocentrism hypothesis. *Child Development, 50,* 247–250.

Moore, B. C. J. (1997). *An introduction to the psychology of hearing.* San Diego, CA: Academic Press.

Moore, D. S. (2015). *The developing genome: An introduction to behavioral epigenetics.* New York, NY: Oxford University Press.

Moore, K. L., & Persaud, T. V. N. (2003). *The developing human: Clinically oriented embryology* (7th ed.). Philadelphia, PA: Saunders.

Moorhead, G., Ference, R., & Neck, C. P. (1991). Group decision fiascoes continue: Space shuttle *Challenger* and a revised groupthink framework. *Human Relations, 44,* 539–550.

Mor, N., & Winquist, J. (2002). Self-focused attention and negative affect: A meta-analysis. *Psychological Bulletin, 128,* 638–662.

Moray, N. (1959). Attention in dichotic listening: Affective cues and the influence of instruction. *Quarterly Journal of Experimental Psychology, 11,* 56–60.

Mordkoff, J. T., & Halterman, R. (2008). Feature integration without visual attention: Evidence from the correlated flankers task. *Psychonomic Bulletin & Review, 15,* 385–389.

Morelli, G. A., & Tronick, E. Z. (1991). Parenting and child development in the Efe foragers and the Lese farmers of Zaïre. In M. H. Bornstein (Ed.), *Cultural approaches to parenting.* Hillsdale, NJ: Erlbaum.

Moritz, S., Woodward, T. S., Whitman, J. C., & Cuttler, C. (2005). Confidence in errors as a possible basis for delusions in schizophrenia. *Journal of Nervous and Mental Disease, 193,* 9–16.

Moscovitch, M. & Moscovitch, D. (2000). Super face inversion effects for isolated internal and external features, and for fractured faces. *Cognitive Neuropsychology, 17,* 201–219.

Moser, E. I., Kropff, E., & Moser, M.-B. (2008). Place cells, grid cells, and the brain's spatial representation system. *Annual Review of Neuroscience, 31,* 69–89.

Mostert, M. P. (2001). Facilitated communication since 1995: A review of published studies. *Journal of Autism and Developmental Disorders, 31,* 287–313.

Mroczek, D. K. (2001). Age and emotion in adulthood. *Current Directions in Psychological Science, 10,* 87–90.

Muchnik, C., Efrati, M., Memeth, E., Malin, M., & Hildesheimer, M. (1991). Cetralauditory skills in blind and sighted subjects. *Scandinavian Audiology, 20,* 19–23.

Mueller, C. M., & Dweck, C. S. (1998). Intelligence praise can undermine motivation and performance. *Journal of Personality and Social Psychology, 75,* 33–52.

Muhlberger, P. (2000). Moral reasoning effects on political participation. *Political Psychology, 21,* 667–695.

Muir, D., & Field, J. (1979). Newborn infants orient to sounds. *Child Development, 50,* 431–436.

Mulder, R. A. (1994, November). Faithful philanderers. *Natural History, 103,* 57–62.

Mullen, B., Anthony, T., Salas, E., & Driskell, J. E. (1994). Group cohesiveness and quality of decision making: An integration of tests of the groupthink hypothesis. *Small Group Research, 25,* 189–204.

Müller, J. (1965). *Elements of physiology* (Vol. 2) (W. Baly, Trans.). Excerpted in R. J. Herrnstein & E. G. Boring (Eds.), *A source book in the history of psychology*. Cambridge, MA: Harvard University Press. (Original work published 1838)

Mundy, P., Sigman, M., & Kasari, C. (1990). A longitudinal study of joint attention and language development in autistic children. *Journal of Autism and Developmental Disorders, 20,* 115–128.

Munoz, R. F., Le, H.-N., Clarke, G. N., Barrera, A. Z., & Torres, L. D. (2009). Preventing first onset and recurrence of major depressive episodes. In I. H. Gotlib & C. L. Hammen (Eds.), *Handbook of depression* (2nd ed.). New York, NY: Guilford.

Muntz, W. R. A. (1964, May). Vision in frogs. *Scientific American*, 110–119.

Murdock, G. P. (1981). *Atlas of world cultures*. Pittsburgh, PA: University of Pittsburgh Press.

Murphy, C., Schubert, C. R., Cruickshanks, K. J., Klein, B. E. K., Klein, R., & Nondahl, D. M. (2002). Prevalence of olfactory impairment in older adults. *Journal of the American Medical Association, 288*, 2307–2312.

Murray, C. (2003). *Human accomplishment: The pursuit of excellence in the arts and sciences, 800 B.C. to 1950*. New York, NY: HarperCollins.

Murray, S. L., Bellavia, G. M., Rose, P., & Griffin, D. W. (2003). Once hurt, twice hurtful: How perceived regard regulates daily marital interactions. *Journal of Personality and Social Psychology, 84*, 126–147.

Mussen, P., Eichorn, D. H., Honzik, M. P., Bieher, S. L., & Meredith, W. (1980). Continuity and change in women's characteristics over four decades. *International Journal of Behavioral Development, 3*, 333–347.

Muzzatti, B., & Agnoli, F. (2007). Gender and mathematics: Attitudes and stereotype threat susceptibility in Italian children. *Developmental Psychology, 43*, 747–759.

Myers, D. G., & Kaplan, M. F. (1976). Group-induced polarization in simulated juries. *Personality and Social Psychology Bulletin, 2*, 63–66.

Myers-Scotton, C. (2008). *Multiple voices: An introduction to bilingualism*. Carlton, Victoria, Australia: Blackwell Publishing.

Naigles, L. (1990). Children use syntax to learn verb meanings. *Journal of Child Language, 17*, 357–374.

Nairne, J. S., Pandeirada, J. N. S., & Thompson, S. R. (2008). Adaptive memory. *Psychological Science, 19*, 176–180.

Natanovich, G., & Eden, D. (2008). Pygmalion effects among outreach supervisors and tutors: Extending sex generalizability. *Journal of Applied Psychology, 93*, 1382–1389.

National Center for PTSD. (2010). *Understanding PTSD*. Retrieved from http://www.ptsd.va.gov/public/understanding_ptsd/booklet.pdf

Nature Neuroscience editorial. (2007). More noise than signal. *Nature Neuroscience, 10*, 799.

Neck, C. P., & Moorhead, G. (1995). Groupthink remodeled: The importance of leadership, time pressure, and methodical decision-making procedures. *Human Relations, 48*, 537–557.

Nee, D. E., Berman, M. G., Moore, K. S., & Jonides, J. (2008). Neuroscientific evidence about the distinction between short-term and long-term memory. *Current Directions in Psychological Science, 17*, 102–106.

Neisser, U., Boodoo, G., Bouchard, T. J., Boykin, A. W., Brody, N., Ceci, S. J., . . . Urbina, S. (1996). Intelligence: Knowns and unknowns. *American Psychologist, 51*, 77–101.

Neitz, J., Neitz, M., & Kainz, P. M. (1996). Visual pigment gene structure and the severity of color vision defects. *Science, 274*, 801–804.

Nelson, C. A., Thomas, K. M., & de Haan, M. (2006). Neural bases of cognitive development. In W. Damon & R. M. Lerner (Gen. Eds.) & D. Kuhn & R. S. Siegler (Vol. Eds.), *Handbook of child psychology: Vol. 2. Cognition, perception, and language* (6th ed., pp. 3–57). Hoboken, NJ: Wiley.

Nelson, D. A., Hallberg, K. I., & Soha, J. A. (2004). Cultural evolution of Puget white-crowned sparrow song dialects. *Ethology, 110*, 879–908.

Nelson, G., Aubry, T., & Lafrance, A. (2007). A review of the literature on the effectiveness of housing and support, assertive community treatment, and intensive care management interventions for persons with mental illness who have been homeless. *American Journal of Orthopsychology, 77*, 350–361.

Nelson, K. (1996). *Language in cognitive development: The emergence of the mediated mind*. New York, NY: Cambridge University Press.

Nes, L. S., & Segerstrom, S. C. (2006). Dispositional optimism and coping: A meta-analytic review. *Personality and Social Psychology Review, 10*, 235–251.

Nesse, R. M. (2000). Is depression an adaptation? *Archives of General Psychiatry, 57*, 14–20.

Nestle, M., & Jacobson, M. F. (2000). Halting the obesity epidemic: A public health policy approach. *Public Health Reports, 115*, 12–24.

Nestler, E., & Malenka, R. C. (2004, March). The addicted brain. *Scientific American, 290*, 78–85.

Nettle, D. (2005). An evolutionary approach to the extraversion continuum. *Evolution and Human Behavior, 26*, 363–373.

Nettle, D. (2006). The evolution of personality variation in humans and other animals. *American Psychologist, 61*, 622–631.

Neubauer, P. B., & Neubauer, A. (1996). *Nature's thumbprint: The new genetics of personality* (2nd ed.). New York, NY: Columbia University Press.

Neugarten, B. L. (1979). Time, age, and the life cycle. *American Journal of Psychiatry, 136*, 887–894.

Neugarten, B. L. (1984). Interpretive social science and research on aging. In A. Rossi (Ed.), *Gender and the life course*. Chicago, IL: Aldine.

Neuner, F., Schauer, M., Klaschik, C., Karunakara, U., & Elbert, T. (2004). Comparison of narrative exposure therapy, supportive counseling, and psychoeducation for treating posttraumatic stress disorder in an African refugee settlement. *Journal of Consulting and Clinical Psychology, 74*, 579–587.

New, J. J., & German, T. C. (2015). Spiders at the cocktail party: An ancestral threat that surmounts inattentional blindness. *Evolution and Human Behavior, 36*, 165–173.

Newman, L. S., & Baumeister, R. F. (1996). Toward an explanation of UFO abduction phenomenon: Hypnotic elaboration, extraterrestrial sadomasochism, and spurious memories. *Psychological Inquiry, 7*, 99–126.

Neyer, F., & Lang, F. R. (2003). Blood is thicker than water: Kinship orientation across adulthood. *Journal of Personality and Social Psychology, 84*, 310–321.

Nicoll, J. A. R., Yamada, M., Frackowiak, J., Mazur-Kolecka, B., & Weller, R. O. (2004). Cerebral amyloid angiopathy plays a direct role in the pathogenesis of Alzheimer's disease: Pro-CAA position statement. *Neurobiology of Aging, 25*, 589–597.

Nielsen, M. (2006). Copying actions and copying outcomes: Social learning through the second year. *Developmental Psychology, 42*, 555–565.

Nielsen, M. (2012). Imitation, pretend play, and childhood: Essential elements in the evolution of human culture? *Journal of Comparative Psychology, 126*, 170–181.

Nielsen, M., Moore, C., & Mohamedally, J. (2015). Young children overimitate in third-party contexts. *Journal of Experimental Child Psychology, 112*, 73–83.

Nielsen, M., Mushin, I., Tomaselli, K., & Whiten, A. (2014). Where culture takes hold: "Overimitation" and its flexible deployment in Western, Aboriginal, and Bushmen children. *Child Development, 85*, 2169–2184.

Nielsen, M., & Tomaselli, K. (2010). Over-imitation in the Kalahari Desert and the origins of human cultural cognition. *Psychological Science, 5*, 729–736.

Nigg, J. T., John, O. P., Blasky, L. G., Huang-Pollock, C. L., Willcutt, E. G., Hinshaw, S. P., & Pennington, B. (2002). Big Five dimensions and ADHD symptoms: Links between personality traits and clinical symptoms. *Journal of Personality and Social Psychology, 83*, 451–469.

Niparko, K. K., Kirk, K. I., Mellon, N. K., Robbins, A. M., Tucci, D. L., & Wilson, B. S. (Eds.). (2000). *Cochlear implants: Principles and practices*. Philadelphia, PA: Lippincott Williams & Wilkins.

Nisbett, R. E., Aronson, J., Blair, C., Dickens, W., Flynn, J., Halpern, D. F., & Turkheimer, E. (2012). Intelligence: New findings and theoretical development. *American Psychologist, 67*, 130–159.

Nisbett, R. E., & Masuda, T. (2007). Culture and point of view. *Intellectica, 46–47*, 143–172.

Nisbett, R. E., Peng, K., Choi, I., & Norenzayan, A. (2001). Culture and systems of thought: Holistic versus analytic cognition. *Psychological Review, 108*, 291–310.

Nishida, T. (Ed.). (1990). *The chimpanzees of the Mahale Mountains: Sexual and life history strategies.* Tokyo, Japan: University of Tokyo Press.

Nitsche, M. A., Cohen, L. G., Wassermann, E. M., Priori, A., Lang, N., Antal, A., Paulus, W., Hummel, F., Boggio, P. S., Fregni, F., & Pascual-Leone, A. (2008). Transcranial direct current stimulation: State of the art 2008. *Brain Stimulation, 1*, 206–223.

Niu, W., Zhang, J. X., & Yang, Y. (2007). Deductive reasoning and creativity: A cross-cultural study. *Psychological Reports, 100*, 509–519.

Noice, H., & Noice, T. (2006). What studies of actors and acting can tell us about memory and cognitive functioning. *Current Directions in Psychological Science, 15*, 14–18.

Nolen-Hoeksema, S. (1991). Responses to depression and their effects on the duration of depressive episodes. *Journal of Abnormal Psychology, 100*, 569–582.

Nolen-Hoeksema, S. (2001). Gender differences in depression. *Current Directions in Psychological Science, 10*, 173–176.

Nolen-Hoeksema, S., Wisco, B. E., & Lyubomirsky, S. (2008). Rethinking rumination. *Perspectives on Psychological Science, 3*, 400–424.

Nordin, S., Broman, D. A., Olofsson, J. K., & Wulff, M. (2004). A longitudinal study of self-reported abnormal smell and taste perception in pregnant women. *Chemical Senses, 29*, 391–402.

Norem, J. K. (2008). Defensive pessimism, anxiety, and the complexity of evaluating self-regulation. *Social and Personality Compass, 2*, 121–134.

Norem, J. K., & Illingworth, K. S. S. (1993). Strategy-dependent effects of reflecting on self and tasks: Some implications of optimism and defensive pessimism. *Journal of Personality and Social Psychology, 65*, 822–835.

Norem, J. K., & Illingworth, K. S. S. (2004). Mood and performance among defensive pessimists and strategic optimists. *Journal of Research in Personality, 38*, 351–366.

Norenzayan, A., & Nisbett, R. E. (2000). Culture and cognition. *Current Directions in Psychological Science, 9*, 132–135.

Nosek, B. A. (2007). Implicit–explicit relations. *Current Directions in Psychological Science, 16*, 65–70.

Nowak, A., Vallacher, R. R., Tesser, A., & Borkowski, W. (2000). Society of self: The emergence of collective properties in self-structure. *Psychological Review, 107*, 39–61.

Nowakowska, C., Strong, C. M., Santosa, C. M., Want, P. W., & Ketter, T. A. (2005). Temperamental commonalities and differences in euthymic mood disorder patients, creative controls, and healthy controls. *Journal of Affective Disorders, 85*, 207–215.

Nowlis, G. H., & Frank, M. (1977). Qualities in hamster taste: Behavioral and neural evidence. In J. LeMagnen & P. MacLeod (Eds.), *Olfaction and taste* (Vol. 6). Washington, DC: Information Retrieval.

Numan, M. (2007). Motivational systems and neural circuitry in maternal behavior in the rat. *Developmental Psychobiology, 49*, 12–21.

Nunn, C. L., Gittleman, J. L., & Antonovics, J. (2000). Promiscuity and the primate immune system. *Science, 290*(November 10), 1168–1170.

Nutt, D. J., & Glue, P. (1993). The neurobiology of ECT: Animal studies. In C. E. Coffee (Ed.), *The clinical science of electroconvulsive therapy.* Washington, DC: American Psychiatric Press.

Oakes, L. M., & Tellinghuisen, D. J. (1994). Examining in infancy: Does it reflect active processing? *Developmental Psychology, 30*, 748–756.

Oberman, L. M., Hubbard, E. M., McCleery, J. P., Altschuler, E. L., Pineda, J. A., & Ramachandran, V. S. (2005). EEG evidence for mirror neuron dysfunction in autism spectrum disorder. *Cognitive Brain Research, 24*, 190–198.

Obradović, J., Bush, N. R., Stamperdahl, J., Adler, N. E., & Boyce, W. T. (2010). Biological sensitivity to context: The interactive effects of stress reactivity and family adversity on socioemotional behavior and school readiness. *Child Development, 81*, 270–289.

Ochs, E., & Schieffelin, B. (1995). The impact of language socialization on grammatical development. In P. Fletcher & B. MacWhinney (Eds.), *The handbook of child language.* Cambridge, MA: Basil Blackwell.

O'Connor, P. B. (2008). Other personality disorders. In M. Hersen, & J. Rosqvist (Eds.), *Handbook of psychological assessment, case conceptualization and treatment: Vol. 1. Adults* (pp. 438–462). Hoboken, NJ: Wiley.

O'Connor, T. G., Deater-Deckard, K., Fulker, D., Rutter, M., & Plomin, R. (1998). Genotype–environment correlations in late childhood and early adolescence: Antisocial behavioral problems and coercive parenting. *Developmental Psychology, 34*, 970–981.

OECD. (2012). *Education at a glance 2012: OECD indicators.* OECD Publishing.

Ofen, N., Kao, Y.-C., Sokol-Hessner, P., Kim, H., Whitfield-Gabrieli, S., & Gavrieli, J. D. E. (2007). Development of the declarative memory system in the human brain. *Nature Neuroscience, 9*, 1198–1205.

Offer, D., & Schonert-Reichl, K. A. (1992). Debunking the myths of adolescence: Findings from recent research. *Journal of the American Academy of Child and Adolescent Psychiatry, 31*, 1003–1013.

Offidani, E., Guidi J., Tomba, E., & Fava, G. A. (2013). Efficacy and tolerability of benzodiazepines versus antidepressants in anxiety disorders: A systematic review and meta-analysis. *Psychotherapy and Psychosomatics, 82*, 355–362.

Ogbu, J. U. (1986). The consequences of the American caste system. In U. Neisser (Ed.), *The school achievement of minority children: New perspectives.* Hillsdale, NJ: Erlbaum.

Ogbu, J. U., & Stern, P. (2001). Caste status and intellectual development. In R. J. Sternberg & E. L. Grigorenko (Eds.), *Environmental effects on cognitive abilities.* Mahwah, NJ: Erlbaum.

Ogden, C. L., Carroll, M. D., Kit, B. K., & Flegal, K. M. (2014). Prevalence of childhood and adult obesity in the United States, 2011-2012. *Journal of the American Medical Association, 311*, 806–814.

Öhman, A. (1999). Distinguishing unconscious from conscious emotional processes: Methodological considerations and theoretical implications. In T. Dalgleish & M. Power (Eds.), *Handbook of cognition and emotion.* Chichester, England: Wiley.

Ohyama, T., Nores, W. L., Murphy, M., & Mauk, M. D. (2003). What the cerebellum computes. *Trends in Neurosciences, 26*, 222–227.

Olds, J. (1956, October). Pleasure centers in the brain. *Scientific American*, 105–116.

Olds, J., & Milner, P. (1954). Positive reinforcement produced by electrical stimulation of the septal area and other regions of the rat brain. *Journal of Comparative and Physiological Psychology, 47*, 419–427.

Olff, M., Langeland, W., Draijer, N., & Gersons, B. P. R. (2007). Gender differences in posttraumatic stress disorder. *Psychological Bulletin, 133*, 183–204.

Open Science Collaboration. (2015, August 28). Estimating the reproducibility of psychological science. *Science, 349*, 6251.

Oppenheim, R. W., Milligan, C. E., & von Bartheld, C. S. (2012). Programmed cell death and neurotrophic factors. In L. R. Squire, D. Berg, F. E. Bloom, S. du Lac, A. Ghosh, & N. C. Spitzer (Eds.), *Fundamental neuroscience* (4th ed., pp. 405–435). New York, NY: Elsevier.

O'Rahilly, R., & Müller, F. (2001). *Human embryology and teratology* (2nd ed.). Hoboken, NJ: Wiley-Liss.

Oring, L. W. (1995, August). The early bird gives the sperm: Spotted sandpipers on a Minnesota lake reveal the secrets of their breeding success. *Natural History, 104,* 58–61.

Orne, M. T., & Holland, C. G. (1968). On the ecological validity of laboratory deception. *International Journal of Psychiatry, 6,* 282–293.

Ornstein, R. (1991). *The evolution of consciousness.* Englewood Cliffs, NJ: Prentice Hall.

Orth, U., & Robins, R. W. (2013). Understanding the link between low self-esteem and depression. *Current Directions in Psychological Science, 22,* 455–460.

Osborne, J. W. (2007). Linking stereotype threat and anxiety. *Educational Psychology, 27,* 135–154.

Osofsky, J. D., & O'Connell, E. J. (1977). Patterning of newborn behavior in an urban population. *Child Development, 48,* 532–536.

Osvath, M., & Osvath, H. (2008). Chimpanzee (*Pan troglodytes*) and orangutan (*Pongoabelii*) forethought: Self-control and pre-experience in the face of future tool use. *Animal Cognition, 11,* 661–674.

Otten, L. J., Henson, R. N. A., & Rugg, M. D. (2001). Depth of processing effects on neural correlates of memory encoding: Relationship between findings from across- and within-task comparisons. *Brain, 124,* 399–412.

Otto, R. K., & Douglas, K. S. (2010). (Eds.). *Handbook of violence risk assessment.* New York, NY: Routledge.

Oulasvirta, A., & Saariluoma, P. (2006). Surviving task interruptions: Investigating the implications of long-term memory theory. *International Journal of Human-Computer Studies, 64,* 941–961.

Overmann, S. R. (1976). Dietary self-selection by animals. *Psychological Bulletin, 83,* 218–235.

Owen, M. J., & O'Donovan, M. C. (2003). Schizophrenia and genetics. In R. Plomin, J. C. DeFries, I. W. Craig, & P. McGuffin (Eds.), *Behavioral genetics in the postgenomic era.* Washington, DC: American Psychological Association.

Ozer, D. J., & Benet-Martínez, V. (2006). Personality and the prediction of consequential outcomes. *Annual Review of Psychology, 57,* 401–421.

Ozer, E. J., Best, S. R., Lipsey, T. L., & Weiss, D. S. (2003). Predictors of posttraumatic stress disorder and symptoms in adults. A meta-analysis. *Psychological Bulletin, 129,* 52–73.

Pace-Schott, E. F., & Hobson, A. (2012). The neurobiology of sleep and dreaming. In L. R. Squire, D. Berg, F. E. Bloom, S. du Lac, A. Ghosh, & N. C. Spitzer (Eds.), *Fundamental neuroscience* (4th ed., pp. 847–869). New York, NY: Elsevier.

Page, K. A., Chan, O., Arora, J., Belfort-Deaguiar, R., Dzuira, J., Roehmholdt, B., Cline, G. W., . . . Sherwin, R. S. (2013). Effects of fructose vs glucose on regional cerebral blood flow in brain regions involved with appetite and reward pathways. *Journal of the American Medical Association, 309,* 63–70.

Paivio, A. (1986). *Mental representations: A dual coding approach.* Oxford, England: Oxford University Press.

Pallanti, S., Quercioli, L., & Pazzagli, A. (1997). Relapse in young paranoid schizophrenic patients: A prospective study of stressful life events, P300 measures, and coping. *American Journal of Psychiatry, 154,* 792–798.

Palmer-Olsen, L., Gold, L. L., & Woolley, S. R. (2011). Supervising emotionally focused therapists: A systematic research-based model. *Journal of Marital and Family Therapy, 37,* 411–426.

Panksepp, J. (1998). Attention deficit/hyperactivity disorders, psychostimulants, and intolerance of childhood playfulness: A tragedy in the making? *Current Directions in Psychological Science, 7,* 91–98.

Panksepp, J. (2007). Can PLAY diminish ADHD and facilitate the construction of the social brain? *Journal of the Canadian Academy of Child and Adolescent Psychiatry, 16,* 57–66.

Panksepp, J. (2013). The evolutionary sources of jealousy: Cross-species approaches to fundamental issues. In S. L. Hart & M. Legerstee (Eds.), *Handbook of jealousy: Theory, research, and multidisciplinary approaches* (pp. 101–120). New York, NY: Wiley-Blackwell.

Papageorgiou, C., & Wells, A. (2001). Metacognitive beliefs about rumination in recurrent major depression. *Cognitive and Behavioral Practice, 8,* 160–164.

Papini, M. R. (2002). Pattern and process in the evolution of learning. *Psychological Review, 109,* 186–201.

Papousek, H. (1969). Individual variability in learned responses in human infants. In R. J. Robinson (Ed.), *Brain and early behavior.* San Diego, CA: Academic Press.

Parades, S. H., Ridout, K. K., Seifer, R., Armstrong, D. A., Marisit, C., McWilliams, M. A., & Tyrka, A. R. (2016). Methylation of the glucocorticoid receptor gene promoter in preschoolers: Link with internalizing behavior problems. *Child Development, 87,* 86–97.

Paris, J. (2000). Predispositions, personality traits, and posttraumatic stress disorder. *Harvard Review of Psychiatry, 8,* 175–183.

Paris, J. (2010). *Treatment of borderline personality disorder: A guide to evidence-based practice.* New York, NY: Guilford.

Parish, A. R., & de Waal, F. B. (2000). The other "closest living relative": How bonobos (*Pan paniscus*) challenge traditional assumptions about females, dominance, intra- and intersexual interactions, and hominid evolution. *Annals of the New York Academy of Sciences, 907,* 96–113.

Parker, H. A., & McNally, R. J. (2008). Regressive coping, emotional adjustment, and cognition in people who have lost loved ones to suicide. *Suicide and Life-Threatening Behavior, 38,* 676–687.

Parker, J. G., Low, C. M., Walker, A. R., & Gamm, B. K. (2005). Friendship jealousy in young adolescents: Individual differences and links to sex, self-esteem, aggression, and social adjustment. *Developmental Psychology, 41,* 235–250.

Parker, S. E., Mai, C. T., Canfield, M. A., Rickard, R., Wang, Y., Meyer, R. E., & National Birth Defects Prevention Network. (2010). Updated national birth prevalence estimates for selected birth defects in the United States, 2004–2006. *Birth Defects Research (Part A), 88,* 1008–1016.

Parks, T. E., & Rock, I. (1990). Illusory contours from pictorially three-dimensional inducing elements. *Perception, 19,* 119–121.

Parr, L. A., Waller, B. M., Vick, S. J., & Bard, K. A. (2007). Classifying chimpanzee facial expressions using muscle action. *Emotion, 7,* 172–181.

Parsons, T. D., & Rizzo, A. A. (2008). Affective outcomes of virtual reality exposure therapy for anxiety and specific phobias: A meta-analysis. *Journal of Behavior Therapy and Experimental Psychiatry, 39,* 250–261.

Pascual, A., & Guaguen, N. (2005). Foot-in-the-door and door-in-the-face: A comparative meta-analytic study. *Psychological Reports, 96,* 122–128.

Pascual-Leone, A., Amedi, A., Fregni, F., & Merabet, L. B. (2005). The plastic human brain cortex. *Annual Review of Neuroscience, 28,* 377–401.

Pashler, H., & Wagenmakers, E.-J. (2012). Editors' introduction to the special section on replicability in psychological science: A crisis of confidence? *Perspectives in Psychological Science, 7,* 528–530.

Pashler, H. E. (1998). *The psychology of attention.* Cambridge, MA: MIT Press.

Passow, S., Westerhausen, R., Wartenburger, I., Hugdahl, K., Heekeren, H. R., Lindenberger, U., & Li, S.-C. (2012). Human aging compromises attentional control of auditory perception. *Psychology and Aging, 27,* 99–105.

Patrick, C. J. (2007). Antisocial personality disorder and psychopathy. In W. O'Donohue, K. A. Fowler, & S. O. Lilienfeld (Eds.), *Personality disorders: Toward DSM-V.* Los Angeles, CA: Sage.

Patterson, K., Nestor, P. J., & Rogers, T. T. (2007). Where do you know what you know? The representation of semantic knowledge in the human brain. *Nature Reviews Neuroscience, 8,* 976–987.

Patterson, M. C. (2017). A naturalistic investigation of media multitasking while studying and the effects on exam performance. *Teaching of Psychology, 44,* 51–57.

Patterson, M. M., & Bigler, R. S. (2006). Preschool children's attention to environmental messages about groups: Social categorization and the origins of intergroup bias. *Child Development, 77,* 847–860.

Paukner, A., Anderson, J. R., Borelle, E., Visalberghi, E., & Ferrari, P. F. (2005). Macaques (*Macaca nemestrina*) recognize when they are being imitated. *Biology Letters, 1,* 219–222.

Paulhaus, D. L., Westlake, B. G., Calvez, S. S., & Harms, P. D. (2013). Self-presentation style in job interviews: The role of personality and culture. *Journal of Applied Social Psychology, 43,* 2042–2059.

Paulhus, D. L. (2014). Toward a taxonomy of dark personalities. *Current Directions in Psychological Science, 23,* 421–426.

Paulus, M. (2014). The emergence of prosocial behavior: Why do infants and toddlers, help, comfort, and share? *Child Development Perspectives, 8,* 77–81.

Paunonen, S. V. (2003). Big Five factors of personality and replicated predictions of behavior. *Journal of Personality and Social Psychology, 84,* 411–424.

Paunonen, S. V., & Ashton, M. C. (2001). Big Five factors and facets and the prediction of behavior. *Journal of Personality and Social Psychology, 81,* 524–539.

Pavlov, I. P. (1960). *Conditioned reflexes* (G. V. Anrep, Ed. & Trans.). New York, NY: Dover. (Original work published 1927)

Payne, B. K. (2006). Weapon bias: Split-decisions and unintended stereotyping. *Current Directions in Psychological Science, 15,* 287–291.

Pazzaglia, M. (2015). Body odors: Not just molecules, after all. *Psychological Science, 24,* 329–333.

Pearson, K., & Gordon, J. (2000). Locomotion. In E. R. Kandel, J. H. Schwartz, & T. M. Jessell (Eds.), *Principles of neural science* (4th ed.). New York, NY: McGraw-Hill.

Pellegrini, A. D. (2005). *Recess: Its role in education and development.* Mahwah, NJ: Erlbaum.

Pellegrini, A. D. (2013). Play. In P. Zelazo (Ed.), *Oxford handbook of developmental psychology* (Vol. 2, pp. 276–299). Oxford, England: Oxford University Press.

Pellegrini, A. D., & Bjorklund, D. F. (2004). The ontogeny and phylogeny of children's object and fantasy play. *Human Nature, 15,* 23–43.

Pellegrini, A. D., Long, J. D., Roseth, C. J., Bohn, C. M., & Van Ryzin, M. (2007). A short-term longitudinal study of preschoolers' (*Homo sapiens*) sex segregation: The role of physical activity, sex, and time. *Journal of Comparative Psychology, 121,* 282–289.

Pellegrini, A. D., & Smith, P. K. (1998). Physical activity play: The nature and function of neglected aspect of play. *Child Development, 69,* 577–598.

Peluso, P. R., Liebovitch, L. S., Gottman, J. M., Norman, M. D., & Su, J. (2012). A mathematical model of psychotherapy: An investigation using dynamic non-linear equations to model the therapeutic relationship. *Psychotherapy Research, 22,* 40–55.

Pendergrast, M. (1995). *Victims of memory: Incest accusations and scattered lives.* Hinesburg, VT: Upper Access.

Penfield, W., & Faulk, M. E. (1955). The insula: Further observation on its function. *Brain, 78,* 445–470.

Penfield, W., & Perot, P. (1963). The brain's record of auditory and visual experience. *Brain, 86,* 595–696.

Penycook, G., Fugelsang, J. A., & Koehler, D. J. (2015). Everyday consequences of analytical thinking. *Current Directions in Psychological Science, 24,* 425–432.

Perera, T. D., Park, S., & Nemirovskaya, Y. (2008). Cognitive role of neurogenesis in depression and antidepressant treatment. *The Neuroscientist, 14,* 326–338.

Perlmutter, J. S., & Mink, J. W. (2006). Deep brain stimulation. *Annual Review of Neuroscience, 29,* 229–257.

Petersen, S. E., Fox, P. T., Posner, M. I., Mintun, M., & Raichle, M. E. (1989). Positron emission tomographic studies of the processing of single words. *Journal of Cognitive Neuroscience, 1,* 153–170.

Peterson, C., Warren, K. L., & Short, M. M. (2011). Infantile amnesia across the years: A 2-year follow-up of children's earliest memories. *Child Development, 82,* 1092–1105.

Petitpas, A. J., & Champagne, D. E. (2000). Sports and social competence. In S. Danish & T. P. Gullotta (Eds.), *Developing competent youth and strong communities through after-school programming.* Washington, DC: Child Welfare League of America.

Petitto, L. A. (2000). On the biological foundations of human language. In K. Emmorey and H. Lane (Eds.), *The signs of language revisited: An anthology in honor of Ursula Bellugi and Edward Klima.* Mahwah, N.J.: Lawrence Erlbaum.

Petitto, L. A., Holowka, S., Serio, L. E., & Ostry, D. (2001). Language rhythms in baby hand movements. *Nature, 413,* 35–36.

Petrovich, G. D., & Gallagher, M. (2007). Control of food consumption by learned cues: A forebrain-hypothalamic network. *Physiology & Behavior, 91,* 397–403.

Pettit, G. S., Dodge, K. A., & Brown, M. M. (1988). Early family experience, social problem solving patterns, and children's social competence. *Child Development, 59,* 107–120.

Pfaus, J. G., Kippin, E., Coria-Avila, G. A., Afinso, V. M., Ismall, N., & Parada, M. (2012). Who, what, where, when (and maybe even why)? How the experience of sexual reward connects sexual desire, preference, and performance. *Archives of Sexual Behavior, 41,* 31–62.

Pfennig, D. W., & Sherman, P. W. (1995, June). Kin recognition. *Scientific American,* 98–103.

Pflugshaupt, T., Mosimann, U. P., von Wartburg, R., Schmitt, W., Nyffeler, T., & Müri, R. M. (2005). Hypervigilance-avoidance pattern in spider phobia. *Journal of Anxiety Disorders, 19,* 105–116.

Pfungst, O. (1965). *Clever Hans: The horse of Mr. von Osten* (C. L. Rahn, Trans.). New York, NY: Holt, Rinehart & Winston. (Original work published 1911)

Phares, E. J. (1984). *Introduction to personality.* Columbus, OH: Merrill.

Phillips, D. P. (1989). The neural coding of simple and complex sounds in the auditory cortex. In J. S. Lund (Ed.), *Sensory processing in the mammalian brain: Neural substrates and experimental strategies.* Oxford, England: Oxford University Press.

Phillips, P. E. M., Stuber, G. D., Helen, M. L. A. V., Wightman, R. M., & Carelli, R. M. (2003). Subsecond dopamine release promotes cocaine seeking. *Nature, 422,* 614–618.

Phillips, W. A., & Silverstein, S. M. (2003). Convergence of biological and psychological perspectives on cognitive coordination in schizophrenia. *Behavioral and Brain Sciences, 26,* 65–138.

Piaget, J. (1927). *The child's conception of physical causality* (M. Worden, Trans.). New York, NY: Harcourt, Brace & World.

Piaget, J. (1954). *The construction of reality in the child.* New York, NY: Basic.

Piaget, J. (1962). *Play, dreams and imitation in childhood.* New York, NY: Norton. (Original work published in 1945)

Piaget, J. (1965). *The moral judgment of the child.* New York, NY: Free Press. (Original work published 1932)

Piaget, J. (1969). *The child's conception of the world.* Lanham, MD: Rowman & Littlefield. (Original work published in 1929)

Piaget, J. (1970). *Genetic epistemology* (E. Duckworth, Trans.). New York, NY: Norton. (Original work published in 1945)

Piazza, J., & Bering, J. M. (2008). Concerns about reputation via gossip promote generous allocations in an economic game. *Evolution and Human Behavior, 29,* 172–178.

Pierce, J. D., Cohen, A. B., & Ulrich, P. M. (2004). Responsivity to two odorants, androstenone and amyl acetate, and the affective impact of odors on interpersonal relationships. *Journal of Comparative Psychology, 118,* 14–19.

Pierucci, J. M., O'Brien, C. T., McInnis, M. A., Gilpin, A. T., & Barber, A. B. (2014). Fantasy orientation constructs and related executive function development in preschool: Developmental benefits to executive functions by being a fantasy-oriented child. *International Journal of Behavioral Development, 38,* 62–69.

Piet, J., & Hougaard, E. (2011). The effect of mindfulness-based cognitive therapy for prevention of relapse in recurrent major depressive disorder: A systematic review and meta-analysis. *Clinical Psychology Review, 31,* 1032–1040.

Pinker, S. (1994). *The language instinct.* New York, NY: Morrow.

Pinker, S. (1997). *How the mind works.* New York, NY: Norton.

Pinker, S., & Bloom, P. (1992). Natural language and natural selection. In J. H. Barkow, L. Cosmides, & J. Tooby (Eds.), *The adapted mind: Evolutionary psychology and the generation of culture.* Oxford, England: Oxford University Press.

Pinker, S., & Jackendoff, R. (2005). The faculty of language: What's special about it? *Cognition, 95,* 201–236.

Pinkham, A. E., Mueser, K. T., Penn, D., Glynn, S. M., McGurk, S. R., & Addington, J. (2012). Social and functional impairments. In J. A. Lieberman, T. S. Stroup, & D. O. Perkins (Eds.), *Essentials of schizophrenia* (pp. 93–130). Arlington, VA: American Psychiatric Publishing.

Pitman, R. K., van der Kolk, B. A., Orr, S. P., & Greenberg, M. S. (1990). Naloxone-reversible analgesic response to combat-related stimuli in posttraumatic stress disorder. *Archives of General Psychiatry, 47,* 541–544.

Plant, E. A., & Peruche, B. M. (2005). The consequences of race for police officers' responses to criminal suspects. *Psychological Science, 16,* 180–183.

Pleim, E. T., & Barfield, R. J. (1988). Progesterone versus estrogen facilitation of female sexual behavior by intracranial administration to female rats. *Hormones and Behavior, 22,* 150–159.

Plomin, R., & Caspi, A. (1999). Behavioral genetics and personality. In L. A. Pervin & O. John (Eds.), *Handbook of personality: Theory and research* (2nd ed.). New York, NY: Guilford.

Plomin, R., & Daniels, D. (1987). Why are children in the same family so different from one another? *Behavioral and Brain Sciences, 10,* 1–60.

Pluess, M., & Belsky, J. (2011). Prenatal programming of postnatal plasticity? *Development and Psychopathology, 23,* 29–38.

Pluess, M., & Belsky, J. (2012). Parenting effects in the context of child genetic differences. *ISSBD Bulletin, 62*(2), 3–6. [Supplement to *International Journal of Behavioral Development, 36*(6)]

Pluess, M., Stevens, S., & Belsky, J. (2013). Differential susceptibility: Developmental and evolutionary mechanisms of gene–environment interactions. In M. Legerstee, D. W. Haley, & M. H. Bornstein (Eds.), *The infant mind: Origins of the social brain.* New York, NY: Guilford.

Plutchik, R. (2001). The nature of emotions. *American Scientist, 89,* 344–350.

Plutchik, R. (2003). *Emotions and life: Perspectives from psychology, biology, and evolution.* Washington DC: American Psychological Association.

Poehlmann, J., Hane, A., Burnson, C., Maleck, S., Hamburger, E., & Shah, P. E. (2012). Preterm infants who are prone to distress: Differential effects of parenting on 36-month behavioral and cognitive outcomes. *Journal of Child Psychology and Psychiatry, 53,* 1018–1025.

Poldrack, R. A., & Foerde, K. (2008). Category learning and the memory systems debate. *Neuroscience and Biobehavioral Reviews, 32,* 197–205.

Polefrone, J., & Manuck, S. (1987). Gender differences in cardiovascular and neuroendocrine response to stressors. In R. C. Barnett, L. Biener, & G. K. Baruch (Eds.), *Gender and stress.* New York, NY: Free Press.

Pongrácz, P., Vida, V., Bánhegyi, P., & Miklósa, A. (2008). How does dominance rank status affect individual and social learning performance in the dog (*Canis familiaris*)? *Animal Cognition, 11,* 75–82.

Poremba, A., Saunders, R. C., Crane, A. M., Cook, M., Sokoloff, L., & Mishkin, M. (2003). Functional mapping of the primate auditory system. *Science, 299,* 568–572.

Portas, C. M., Krakow, K., Allen, P., Josephs, O., Armony, J. L., & Frith, C. D. (2000). Auditory processing across the sleep–wake cycle: Simultaneous EEG and fMRI monitoring in humans. *Neuron, 28,* 991–999.

Posada, G., Carbonell, O. A., Alzate, G., & Plata, S. J. (2004). Through Colombian lenses: Ethnographic and conventional analyses of maternal care and their associations with secure base behavior. *Developmental Psychology, 40,* 508–518.

Posada, G., Trumbell, J., Noblega, M., Plata, S., Peña, P., Caronelli, O. A., & Lu, T. (2016). Maternal sensitivity and child secure base use in early childhood: Studies in different cultural contexts. *Child Development, 87,* 297–311.

Posner, M. I., Nissen, M. J., & Klein, R. M. (1976). Visual dominance: An information-processing account of its origins and significance. *Psychological Review, 83,* 157–171.

Post, F. (1994). Creativity and psychopathology: A study of 291 world-famous men. *The British Journal of Psychiatry, 165,* 22–34.

Postmes, T., Spears, R., & Sezgin, C. (2001). Quality of decision making and group norms. *Journal of Personality and Social Psychology, 80,* 918–930.

Potenza, M. N. (2013). How central is dopamine to pathological gambling or gambling disorder? *Frontiers of Behavioral Neuroscience, 7,* Article 206.

Potts, W. K., Manning, C. J., & Wakeland, E. K. (1991). Mating patterns in seminatural populations of mice influenced by MHC genotype. *Nature, 352,* 619–621.

Poulos, C. X., & Cappell, H. (1991). Homeostatic theory of drug tolerance: A general model of physiological adaptation. *Psychological Review, 98,* 390–408.

Poulsen, S., Lunn, S., Danile, S. I. F., Folke, S., Mathiesen, B. B., Katznelson, H., & Fairburn, C. G. (2014). Behavioral therapy for bulimia nervosa. *American Journal of Psychiatry, 171,* 109–116.

Power, T. G. (2000). *Play and exploration in children and animals.* Mahwah, NJ: Erlbaum.

Prabhakar, S., Noonan, J. P., Pääbo, S., & Rubin, E. M. (2006). Accelerated evolution of conserved noncoding sequences in humans. *Science, 314,* 786.

Prabu, D. (1998). News concreteness and visual–verbal association: Do news pictures narrow the recall gap between concrete and abstract news? *Human Communication Research, 25,* 180–201.

Preissler, M. A., & Bloom, P. (2007). Two-year-olds appreciate the dual nature of pictures. *Psychological Science, 18,* 1–2.

Premack, D. (1990). The infant's theory of self-propelled objects. *Cognition, 36,* 1–16.

Price, D. D. (2000). Psychological and neural mechanisms of the affective dimension of pain. *Science, 288,* 1769–1772.

Price, D. D., Finniss, D. G., & Benedetti, F. (2008). A comprehensive review of the placebo effect: Recent advances and current thought. *Annual Review of Psychology, 59,* 565–590.

Price, J. S., Gardner, R., Jr., & Erickson, M. (2004). Can depression, anxiety, and somatization be understood as appeasement displays? *Journal of Affective Disorders, 79,* 1–11.

Prickaerts, J., Koopmans, G., Blokland, A., & Arjan, S. (2004). Learning and adult neurogenesis: Survival with or without proliferation? *Neurobiology of Learning and Memory, 81,* 1–11.

Principe, G. F., Haines, B., Adkins, A., & Guiliano, S. (2010). False rumors and true belief: Memory processes underlying children's errant reports of rumored events. *Journal of Experimental Child Psychology, 107,* 408–422.

Pritchard, T. C. (1991). The primate gustatory system. In T. V. Getchell, R. L. Doty, L. M. Bartoshuk, & J. B. Snow (Eds.), *Smell and taste in health and disease.* New York, NY: Raven Press.

Prochaska, J. O., & Norcross, J. C. (2010). *Systems of psychotherapy: A transtheoretical analysis* (7th ed.). Pacific Grove, CA: Brooks/Cole.

Profet, M. (1992). Pregnancy sickness as adaptation: A deterrent to maternal ingestion of teratogens. In J. H. Barkow, L. Cosmides, & J. Tooby (Eds.), *The adapted mind: Evolutionary psychology and the generation of culture.* Oxford, England: Oxford University Press.

Pronk, T. M., Karremans, J. C., & Wigboldus, D. H. J. (2011). How can you resist? Executive control helps romantically involved individuals to stay faithful. *Journal of Personality and Social Psychology, 100,* 827–837.

Punset, E. (2005). *El viaje a la felicidad: Las nuevas claves científicas* [The journey to happiness: The new scientific cues]. Barcelona, Spain: Destino.

Puumala, S. E., & Hoyme, H. E. (2015). Epigenetics in pediatrics. *Pediatrics in Review, 36,* 14–19.

Qian, M. K., Heyman, G. D., Quinn, P. C., Messi, F. A., Fu, G., & Lee, K. (2016). Implicit racial bias in preschool children and adults from Asia and Africa. *Child Development, 87,* 285–296.

Quickfall, J., & Suchowersky, O. (2007). Pathological gambling associated with dopamine agonist use in restless legs syndrome. *Parkinsonism and Related Disorders, 13,* 535–536.

Quinn, A., & Schlenker, B. R. (2002). Can accountability produce independence? Goals as determinants of the impact of accountability on conformity. *Personality and Social Psychology Bulletin, 28,* 472–483.

Quon, E., & Atance, C. M. (2010). A comparison of preschoolers' memory, knowledge, and anticipation of events. *Journal of Cognition and Development, 11,* 37–60.

Raby, K. L., Roisman, G. I., Fraaley, R. C., & Simpson, J. A. (2015). The enduring predictive significance of early maternal sensitivity: Social and academic competence through age 32. *Child Development, 86,* 695–708.

Rachlin, H. (1990). Why do people gamble and keep gambling despite heavy losses? *Psychological Science, 1,* 249–297.

Rafalovich, A. (2004). *Framing ADHD children: A critical examination of the history, discourse, and everyday experience of attention deficit/hyperactivity disorder.* Lanham, MD: Lexington Books.

Raikes, H. A., & Thompson, R. A. (2008). Attachment security and parenting quality predict children's problem-solving, attributions, and loneliness with peers. *Attachment and Human Development, 10,* 319–344.

Rakoczy, H. (2008). Pretense as individual and collective intentionality. *Mind and Language, 23,* 499–517.

Ramachandran, V. S., & Brang, D. (2008). Synaesthesia. *Scholarpedia, 3,* 3981.

Ramachandran, V. S., & Hubbard, E. M. (2001). Synesthesia: A window into perception, thought, and language. *Journal of Consciousness Studies, 8,* 3–34.

Ramachandran, V. S., & Oberman, L. M. (2006). Broken mirrors: A theory of autism. *Scientific American, 295,* 62–69.

Ramachandran, V. S., & Rogers-Ramachandran, D. (2004, January/February). Seeing is believing: 2-D or not 2-D, that is the question: What shapes formed by shading reveal about the brain. *Scientific American Mind, 14,* 100–101.

Ramey, C. H., & Weisberg, R. W. (2004). The "poetical activity" of Emily Dickinson: A further test of the hypothesis that affective disorders foster creativity. *Creativity Research Journal, 16,* 173–185.

Randich, A., Klein, R. M., & LoLordo, V. M. (1978). Visual dominance in the pigeon. *Journal of the Experimental Analysis of Behavior, 30,* 129–137.

Rasch, B., & Born, J. (2008). Reactivation and consolidation of memory during sleep. *Current Directions in Psychological Science, 17,* 188–192.

Raskin, H. J., Rogers, C., & Witty, M. (2011). Person-centered therapy. In R. J. Corsini & D. Wedding (Eds.), *Current psychotherapies* (9th ed.). Belmont, CA: Brooks/Cole.

Rasmussen, T., & Milner, B. (1977). The role of early left brain injury in determining lateralization of cerebral speech functions. *Annals of the New York Academy of Sciences, 299,* 355–369.

Rauschecker, J. P., Tian, B., & Hauser, M. (1995). Processing of complex sounds in the macaque nonprimary auditory cortex. *Science, 268,* 111–114.

Rauthmann, J. F., Gallardo-Pujol, D., Guillaume, E. M., Todd, E., Nave, C. S., Sherman, R., . . . Funder, D. C. (2014). The situational eight DIAMONDS: A taxonomy of major dimensions of situation characteristics. *Journal of Personality and Social Psychology, 107,* 677–718.

Raynor, H. A., & Epstein, L. H. (2001). Dietary variety, energy regulation, and obesity. *Psychological Bulletin, 127,* 325–341.

Razran, G. A. (1939). A quantitative study of meaning by a conditioned salivary technique (semantic conditioning). *Science, 90,* 89–91.

Réale, D., Reader, S. M., Sol, D., McDougall, P. T., & Dingemanse, N. J. (2007). Integrating animal temperament within ecology and evolution. *Biological Review of the Cambridge Philosophical Society, 82,* 291–318.

Reber, A. S. (1989). Implicit learning and tacit knowledge. *Journal of Experimental Psychology: General, 118,* 219–235.

Reber, P. J., Siwiec, R. M., Gitleman, D. R., Parrish, T. B., Mesulam, M.-M., & Paller, K. A. (2002). Neural correlates of successful encoding identified using functional magnetic resonance imaging. *Journal of Neuroscience, 22,* 9541–9548.

Recanzone, G. H., Merzenich, M. M., Jenkins, W. M., Grajski, K. A., & Dinse, H. R. (1992). Topographic reorganization of the hand representation in cortical area 3b of owl monkeys trained in a frequency-discrimination task. *Journal of Neurophysiology, 67,* 1031–1056.

Recanzone, G. H., & Sutter, M. L. (2008). The biological basis of audition. *Annual Review of Psychology, 59,* 119–142.

Rechtschaffen, A., & Kales, A. (Eds.). (1968). *A manual of standardized terminology, techniques and scoring system for sleep stages of human subjects.* Bethesda, MD: U.S. Department of Health, Education, and Welfare, Public Health Service, National Institutes of Health, National Institute of Neurological Diseases and Blindness, Neurological Information Network.

Redelmeier, M. D., & Tibshirani, R. J. (1997). Association between cellular-telephone calls and motor vehicle collisions. *New England Journal of Medicine, 336,* 453–457.

Reed, A. E., & Carstensen, L. L. (2012). The theory behind the age-related positivity effect. *Frontiers in Psychology, 3,* 339. doi: 10.3389/fpsyg.2012.00339.

Reed, N., & Robbins, R. (2008). The effect of text messaging on driver behavior: A simulator study. *Transport Research Lab Report,* PPR 367.

Reeves, A., Stuckler, D., McKee, M., Gunnell, D., Chang, S.-S., & Basu, S. (2012). Increase in state suicide rates in the USA during economic recession. *Lancet, 380,* 1813–1814.

Regier, T. (2003). Emergent constraints on word-learning: A computational perspective. *Trends in Cognitive Sciences, 7,* 263–268.

Reich, J. W., Erdal, K. J., & Zautra, A. (1997). Beliefs about control and health behaviors. In D. S. Gochman (Ed.), *Handbook of health behavior research: I. Personal and social determinants.* New York, NY: Plenum.

Reichenberg, A., & Harvey, P. D. (2007). Neuropsychological impairments in schizophrenia: Integration of performance-based brain imaging findings. *Psychological Bulletin, 133,* 833–858.

Reichow, B., & Wolery, M. (2009). Comprehensive synthesis of early intensive behavioral interventions for young children with autism based on the UCLA Young Autism Project Model. *Journal of Autism and Developmental Disorders, 39*, 23–41.

Reid, R. C., & Usrey, W. M. (2013). Vision. In L. R. Squire, D. Berg, F. E. Bloom, S. du Lac, A. Ghosh, & N. C. Spitzer (Eds.), *Fundamental neuroscience* (4th ed., pp. 577–595). Boston, MA: Elsevier.

Reisberg, D., Smith, J. D., Baxter, D. A., & Sonenshine, M. (1989). "Enacted" auditory images are ambiguous; "pure" auditory images are not. *Quarterly Journal of Experimental Psychology: Human Experimental Psychology, 41*, 619–641.

Reiser, M. F. (1991). *Memory in mind and brain: What dream imagery reveals.* New York, NY: Basic Books.

Reit, S. (1978). *Masquerade: The amazing camouflage deceptions of World War II.* New York, NY: Hawthorn Books.

Repacholi, B. M., & Gopnik, A. (1997). Early reasoning about desires: Evidence from 14- and 18-month-olds. *Developmental Psychology, 33*, 12–21.

Rescorla, R. A. (1973). Effect of US habituation following conditioning. *Journal of Comparative and Physiological Psychology, 82*, 137–143.

Rescorla, R. A. (1988). Pavlovian conditioning: It's not what you think it is. *American Psychologist, 43*, 151–160.

Rest, J. R. (1986). *Moral development: Advances in research and theory.* New York, NY: Praeger.

Reuter-Lorenz, P. A., & Miller, A. C. (1998). The cognitive neuroscience of human laterality: Lessons from the bisected brain. *Current Directions in Psychological Science, 7*, 15–20.

Reynolds, J. H., Gottlieb, J. P., & Kastner, S. (2012). Attention. In L. R. Squire, D. Berg, F. E. Bloom, S. du Lac, A. Ghosh, & N. C. Spitzer (Eds.), *Fundamental neuroscience* (4th ed., pp. 989–1007). New York, NY: Elsevier.

Reynolds, J. N. J., Hyland, B., & Wickens, J. R. (2001). A cellular mechanism of reward-related learning. *Nature, 413*, 67–70.

Rheingold, H. L. (1982). Little children's participation in the work of adults, a nascent prosocial behavior. *Child Development, 53*, 114–125.

Rheingold, H. L., Hay, D. F., & West, M. J. (1976). Sharing in the second year of life. *Child Development, 47*, 1148–1158.

Rich, A. N., Bradshaw, J. L., & Mattingley, J. B. (2005). A systematic, large-scale study of synaesthesia: Implications for the role of early experience in lexical–colour associations. *Cognition, 98*, 53–84.

Richards, R., Kinney, D. K., Lunde, I., Benet, M., & Merzel, A. P. C. (1988). Creativity in manic-depressives, cyclothymes, their normal relatives and control subjects. *Journal of Abnormal Psychology, 97*, 281–288.

Richardson, R., & Hayne, H. (2007). You can't take it with you: The translation of memory across development. *Current Directions in Psychological Science, 16*, 223–227.

Richland, L. E., & Burchinal, M. R. (2013). Early executive function predicts reasoning development. *Psychological Science, 24*, 87–91.

Richland, L. E., & Simms, N. (2015). Analogy, higher order thinking, and education. *WIREs: Cognitive Science, 6*, 177–192.

Riecher-Rossler, A., & Hafner, H. (2000). Gender aspects in schizophrenia: Bridging the border between social and biological psychiatry. *Acta Psychiatrica Scandinavica Supplement, 102*, 58–62.

Riggins, T., Blankenship, S. L., Mulligan, E., Rice, K., & Redcay, E. (2015). Developmental differences in relations between episodic memory and hippocampal subregion volume during early childhood. *Child Development, 86*, 1710–1718.

Riggs, L. A. (1965). Visual acuity. In C. H. Graham (Ed.), *Vision and visual perception.* Hoboken, NJ: Wiley.

Riley, B., & Kendler, K. S. (2011). Classical genetic studies of schizophrenia. In D. R. Weinberg & P. Harrison (Eds.), *Schizophrenia.* Hoboken, NJ: Wiley.

Riley, J. W., Jr. (1970). What people think about death. In O. B. Brim, Jr., H. E. Freeman, S. Levine, & N. A. Scotch (Eds.), *The dying patient.* New York, NY: Russell Sage Foundation.

Rilling, J. K., & Insel, T. R. (1999). The primate neocortex in comparative perspective using magnetic resonance imaging. *Journal of Human Evolution, 37*, 191–223.

Rilling, J. K., Winslow, J. T., & Kilts, C. D. (2004). The neural correlates of mate competition in dominant male rhesus macaques. *Biological Psychiatry, 56*, 364–375.

Rime, B., Philippot, P., & Cisamolo, D. (1990). Social schemata of peripheral changes in emotion. *Journal of Personality and Social Psychology, 59*, 38–49.

Rios, K., Hadassah Cheng, Z., Totton, R. R., & Shariff, A. F. (2015). Negative stereotypes cause Christians to underperform in and disidentify with science. *Social Psychological and Personality Science, 6*, 959–967.

Risch, N., Herrell, R., Lehner, T., Liang, K., Eaves, L., Hoh, J., . . . Merikangas, K. R. (2009). Interaction between the serotonin transporter gene (5-HTTLPR), stressful life events, and risk of depression: A meta-analysis. *Journal of the American Medical Association, 301*, 2462–2471.

Ristic, J., & Enns, J. T. (2015). The changing face of attentional development. *Current Directions in Psychological Science, 24*, 24–31.

Ritter, K., Dziobek, I., Preissler, S., Rütter, A., Vater, A., Fydrich, T., . . . Roepke, S. (2011). Lack of empathy in patients with narcissistic personality disorder. *Psychiatric Research, 187*, 241–247.

Rizzolatti, G., & Craighero, L. (2004). The mirror neuron system. *Annual Review of Neuroscience, 27*, 169–192.

Rizzolatti, G., Fadiga, L., Fogassi, L., & Gallese, V. (1996). Premotor cortex and the recognition of motor actions. *Cognitive Brain Research, 3*, 131–141.

Roberts, B. W., & DelVecchio, W. F. (2000). The rank-order consistency of personality traits from childhood to old age: A quantitative review of longitudinal studies. *Psychological Bulletin, 126*, 3–25.

Roberts, B. W., Kuncel, N. R., Shiner, R., Caspi, A., & Goldberg, L. R. (2007). The power of personality: The comparative validity of personality traits, socioeconomic status, and cognitive ability for predicting important life outcomes. *Perspectives on Psychological Science, 2*, 313–345.

Roberts, B. W., & Mroczek, D. (2008). Personality trait change in adulthood. *Current Directions in Psychological Science, 17*, 31–34.

Roberts, W. A., Cruz, C., & Tremblay, J. (2007). Rats take correct novel routes and shortcuts in an enclosed maze. *Journal of Experimental Psychology: Animal Behavior Processes, 33*, 79–91.

Robins, L. N., Helzer, J. E., & Davis, D. H. (1975). Narcotic use in Southeast Asia and afterwards. *Archives of General Psychiatry, 32*, 955–961.

Robins, R. W., &. Beer, J. S. (2001). Positive illusions about the self: Short-term benefits and long-term costs. *Journal of Personality and Social Psychology, 80*, 340–352.

Rochat, P. (1989). Object manipulation and exploration in 2- to 5-month-old infants. *Developmental Psychology, 25*, 871–884.

Rock, I., & Gutman, D. (1981). The effect of inattention on form perception. *Journal of Experimental Psychology: Human Perception and Performance, 7*, 275–285.

Rodenbaugh, T. L., Gianoli, M. O., Turkheimer, E., & Oltmanns, T. F. (2010). What kinds of interpersonal problems are unique to avoidant personality disorder when self-report and peer ratings are considered? *Clinicians Research Digest, 28*(8).

Rodin, J., Schank, D., & Striegel-Moore, R. (1989). Psychological features of obesity. *Medical Clinics of North America, 73*, 47–66.

Rodman, A. M., Kastman, E. K., Dorfman, H. M., Baskin-Sommers, A. R., Kiehl, K. A., Newman, J. P., & Buckholtz, J. W. (2016). Selective mapping of psychopathy and externalizing to dissociable circuits for inhibitory self-control. *Clinical Psychological Science, 4*, 550–571.

Rodseth, L., Wrangham, R. W., Harrigan, A. M., & Smuts, B. B. (1991). The human community as a primate society. *Current Anthropology, 32,* 221–252.

Roediger, H. L., III, & Karpicke, J. D. (2006). Test-enhanced learning: Taking memory tests improves long-term retention. *Psychological Science, 17,* 249–255.

Roelfsema, P. R. (2006). Cortical algorithms for perceptual grouping. *Annual Review of Neuroscience, 29,* 203–227.

Roesch, M. R., Calu, D. J., & Schoenbaum, G. (2007). Dopamine neurons encode the better option in rats deciding between differently delayed or sized rewards. *Nature Neuroscience, 10,* 1615–1624.

Roese, N. J., & Olson, J. M. (2007). Better, stronger, faster: Self-serving judgment, affect regulation, and the optimal vigilance hypothesis. *Perspectives in Psychological Science, 2,* 124–141.

Roesler, T. A., & McKenzie, N. (1994). Effects of childhood trauma on psychological functioning in adults sexually abused as children. *Journal of Nervous and Mental Disease, 182,* 145–150.

Roethlisberger, F. J., & Dickson, W. J. (1939). *Management and the worker: An account of a research program conducted by the Western Electric Company, Hawthorne Works, Chicago.* Cambridge, MA: Harvard University Press.

Rogers, C. R. (1951). *Client-centered therapy: Its current practice, implications, and theory.* Boston, MA: Houghton Mifflin.

Rogers, C. R. (1959). A theory of therapy, personality, and interpersonal relationships, as developed in the client-centered frame-work. In S. Koch (Ed.), *Psychology: A study of a science* (Vol. 3). New York, NY: McGraw-Hill.

Rogers, C. R. (1963). The actualizing tendency in relation to "motives" and to consciousness. In M. R. Jones (Ed.), *Nebraska Symposium on Motivation.* Lincoln, NE: University of Nebraska Press.

Rogers, C. R. (1977). *Carl Rogers on personal power.* New York, NY: Delacorte Press.

Rogers, C. R. (1980). *A way of being.* Boston, MA: Houghton Mifflin.

Rogoff, B. (1990). *Apprenticeship in thinking: Cognitive development in social context.* Oxford, England: Oxford University Press.

Rogoff, B. (2003). *The cultural nature of human development.* Oxford, England: Oxford University Press.

Rolls, E. T. (2004). The functions of the orbitofrontal cortex. *Brain and Cognition, 55,* 11–29.

Rolls, E. T., Murzi, E., Yaxley, S., Thorpe, S. J., & Simpson, S. J. (1986). Sensory-specific satiety: Food-specific reduction in responsiveness of ventral forebrain neurons after feeding in the monkey. *Brain Research, 368,* 79–86.

Romens, S. E., McDonald, J., Svaren, J., & Pollak, S. D. (2015). Associations between early life stress and gene methylation in children. *Child Development, 86,* 303–309.

Roney, J. R., Lukaszewski, A. W., & Simmons, Z. L. (2007). Rapid endocrine responses of young men to social interactions with young women. *Hormones and Behavior, 52,* 326–333.

Rose, A. J., & Rudolph, K. D. (2006). A review of sex differences in peer relationship processes: Potential trade-offs for the emotional and behavioral development of girls and boys. *Psychological Bulletin, 132,* 98–131.

Rosenberg, O., Isserles, M., Levkovitz, Y., Kotler, M., Zangen, A., & Dannon, P. N. (2011). Effectiveness of a second deep TMS in depression: A brief report. *Progress in Neuro-Psychopharmacology & Biological Psychiatry, 35*(4), 1041–1044.

Rosenfeld, I. (2005). *Breakthrough health.* Emmaus, PA: Rodale Press.

Rosenthal, R. (1994). Interpersonal expectancy effects: A 30-year perspective. *Current Directions in Psychological Science, 3,* 176–179.

Rosenthal, R., & Jacobson, L. (1968). *Pygmalion in the classroom.* New York, NY: Holt, Rinehart & Winston.

Rosenzweig, M. R., Bennett, E. L., & Diamond, M. C. (1972, February). Brain changes in response to experience. *Scientific American,* 22–29.

Ross, H. E., & Plug, C. (2002). *The mystery of the moon illusion: Exploring size perception.* Oxford, England: Oxford University Press.

Ross, J., Anderson, J. R., & Campbell, R. N. (2011). I remember me: Mnemonic self-reference effects in preschool children. *Monographs of the Society for Research in Child Development, 76* (Number 3, Serial No. 300).

Ross, L. (1977). The intuitive psychologist and his shortcomings: Distortions in the attribution process. In L. Berkowitz (Ed.), *Advances in experimental social psychology.* San Diego, CA: Academic Press.

Ross, L., & Nisbett, R. E. (2011). *The person and the situation: Perspectives of social psychology* (2nd ed.). London, England: Pinter & Martin Ltd.

Roth, T. C., Lesku, J. A., Amlaner, C. J., & Lima, S. L. (2006). A phylogenetic analysis of the correlates of sleep in birds. *Journal of Sleep Research, 15,* 395–402.

Rothbart, M. K., & Bates, J. (1998). Temperament. In N. Eisenberg (Ed.), *Handbook of child psychology: Vol. 3. Social, emotional, and personality development* (5th ed.). Hoboken, NJ: Wiley.

Rothenberg, A. (2001). Bipolar illness, creativity, and treatment. *Psychiatric Quarterly, 72,* 131–147.

Rotter, J. B. (1954). *Social learning and clinical psychology.* New York, NY: Johnson Reprint Co.

Rotter, J. B. (1966). Generalized expectancies for internal versus external locus of control of reinforcement. *Psychological Monographs: General and Applied, 80*(609).

Rotter, J. B., Liverant, S., & Crowne, D. P. (1961). The growth and extinction of expectancies in change of controlled and skilled tasks. *Journal of Psychology, 52,* 161–177.

Rotter, M. (2011). Embitterment and personality disorder. In M. Linden & A. Maercker (Eds.), *Embitterment: Societal, psychological, and clinical perspective* (pp. 177–186). New York, NY: Springer-Verlag.

Routh, D. K. (2013). Clinical psychology. In I. B. Weiner (Ed.), *History of psychology: Vol. 1. Handbook of psychology* (2nd ed., pp. 377–396). Hoboken, NJ: Wiley.

Rouw, R., & Scholte, H. S. (2007). Increased structural connectivity in grapheme–color synesthesia. *Nature Neuroscience, 10,* 792–797.

Rouw, R., Scholte, H. S., & Colizoli, O. (2011). Brain areas involved in synaesthesia: A review. *Journal of Neuropsychology, 5,* 214–242.

Rovee-Collier, C. (1999). The development of infant memory. *Current Directions in Psychological Science, 8,* 80–85.

Rovee-Collier, C., & Cuevas, K. (2009). Multiple memory systems are unnecessary to account for infant memory development: An ecological model. *Developmental Psychology, 45,* 160–174.

Rowan, D., Papadopolos, T., Edwards, D., & Allen, R. (2015). Use of binaural and monaural cues to identify the lateral position of a virtual object using echoes. *Hearing Research, 323,* 32–39.

Rowe, D. C. (1994). *The limits of family influence: Genes, experience, and behavior.* New York, NY: Guilford.

Rowe, D. C., Jacobson, K. C., & van der Oord, E. J. C. G. (1999). Genetic and environmental influences on vocabulary IQ: Parental education level as a moderator. *Child Development, 70,* 1151–1162.

Rozin, P., & Kalat, J. (1971). Specific hungers and poison avoidance as adaptive specializations of learning. *Psychological Review, 78,* 459–486.

Rozin, P., & Schull, J. (1988). The adaptive-evolutionary point of view in experimental psychology. In R. L. Atkinson, R. J. Herrnstein, G. Lindzey, & R. D. Luce (Eds.), *Steven's handbook of experimental psychology* (2nd ed.). Hoboken, NJ: Wiley.

Rubin, E. (1958). Figure and ground. In D. C. Beardslee & M. Wertheimer (Eds.), *Readings in perception.* Princeton, NJ: Van Nostrand. (Original work published 1915)

Rubinstein, G. (2005). The Big Five among male and female students of different faculties. *Personality and Individual Differences, 38,* 1495–1503.

Ruble, D. N., Martin, C. L., & Berenbaum, S. A. (2006). Gender development. In W. Damon & R. M. Lerner (Series Eds.) & N. Eisenberg (Vol. Ed.), *Handbook of child psychology: Vol. 3. Social, emotional, and personality development* (6th ed., pp. 858–932). Hoboken, NJ: Wiley.

Rudman, L. A. (2004). Sources of implicit attitudes. *Current Directions in Psychological Science, 13,* 79–82.

Rudman, L. A., Ashmore, R. D., & Gary, M. L. (2001). "Unlearning" automatic biases: The malleability of implicit stereotypes and prejudice. *Journal of Personality and Social Psychology, 81,* 856–868.

Ruff, C. C., Kristjánsson, Á., & Driver, J. (2007). Readout from iconic memory and selective spatial attention involve similar neural processes. *Psychological Science, 18,* 901–909.

Ruff, H. A. (1986). Components of attention during infants' manipulative exploration. *Child Development, 75,* 105–114.

Ruff, H. A. (1989). The infant's use of visual and haptic information in the perception and recognition of objects. *Canadian Journal of Psychology, 43,* 302–319.

Ruffman, T., Perner, J., Naito, M., Parkin, L., & Clements, W. A. (1998). Older (but not younger) siblings facilitate false belief understanding. *Developmental Psychology, 34,* 161–174.

Ruffman, T., Slade, L., & Redman, J. (2005). Young infants' expectations about hidden objects. *Cognition, 97,* B35–B43.

Ruiz, A. M., & Santos, L. R. (2013). Understanding differences in the way human and non-human primates represent tools: The role of teleological-intentional information. In C. M. Sanz, J. Call, & C. Boesch (Eds.), *Tool use in animals: Cognition and ecology* (pp. 119–133). Cambridge, England: Cambridge University Press.

Russell, J. (2003). Core affect and the psychological construction of emotion. *Psychological Review, 110,* 145–172.

Rutter, M. M. (2006). *Genes and behavior: Nature–nurture interplay explained.* Malden, MA: Blackwell.

Ruys, K. I., & Stapel, D. A. (2008). Emotion elicitor or emotion messenger? Subliminal priming reveals two faces of facial expressions. *Psychological Science, 19,* 593–600.

Rybash, J. M., Roodin, P. A., & Hoyer, W. J. (1995). *Adult development and aging* (3rd ed.). Dubuque, IA: Brown & Benchmark.

Rymer, R. (1993). *Genie: An abused child's flight from silence.* New York, NY: HarperCollins.

Saad, G., & Vongas, J. G. (2009). The effect of conspicuous consumption on men's testosterone levels. *Organizational Behavior and Human Decision Processes, 110,* 80–92.

Saarni, C., Campos, J. J., Camras, L. A., & Witherington, D. (2006). Emotional development: Action, communication, and understanding. In W. Damon & R. M. Lerner (Gen. Eds.) & N. Eisenberg (Vol. Ed.), *Handbook of child psychology: Vol. 3. Social, emotional, and personality development* (6th ed., pp. 226–299). Hoboken, NJ: Wiley.

Sabbatini da Silva Lobo, D., Vallada, H. P., Knight, J., Martins, S. S., Tavares, H., Gentil, V., & Kennedy, J. L. (2007). Dopamine genes and pathological gambling in discordant sib-pairs. *Journal of Gambling Studies, 23,* 421–433.

Sackett, P. R., Hardison, C. M., & Cullen, M. J. (2004). On interpreting stereotype threat as accounting for African American–white differences on cognitive tests. *American Psychologist, 59,* 7–13.

Sackett, P. R., & Walmsley, P. T. (2014). Which personality trait attributes are most important in the workplace? *Perspectives on Psychological Science, 9,* 538–551.

Sacks, O. (1985). *The man who mistook his wife for a hat, and other clinical tales.* New York, NY: Summit Books.

Saffran, J., Werker, J., & Werner, L. A. (2006). The infant's auditory world: Hearing, speech and the beginnings of language. In W. Damon & R. M. Lerner (Gen. Eds.) & D. Kuhn & R. Siegler (Vol. Eds.), *Handbook of child psychology: Vol. 2. Cognition, perception, and language* (6th ed.). Hoboken, NJ: Wiley.

Saj, A., Fuhrman, O., Vuilleumier, P., & Boroditsky, L. (2014). Patients with left side neglect also neglect the "left side" of time. *Psychological Science, 25,* 207–214.

Salthouse, T. A. (2004). What and when of cognitive aging. *American Psychological Society, 13,* 140–144.

Salwiczek, L. H., Watanabe, A., & Clayton, N. S. (2010). Ten years of research into avian models of episodic-like memory and its implications for developmental and comparative cognition. *Behavioural Brain Research, 215,* 221–234.

Sameroff, A., Seifer, R., Baldwin, A., & Baldwin, C. (1993). Stability of intelligence from preschool to adolescence: The influence of social risk factors. *Child Development, 64,* 80–97.

Samuel, D. B., & Widiger, T. A. (2011). Conscientiousness and obsessive-compulsive personality disorder. *Personality Disorders: Theory, Research, and Treatment, 2,* 161–174.

Sanford, E. C. (1982). Professor Sanford's morning prayer. In U. Neisser (Ed.), *Memory observed: Remembering in natural contexts.* New York, NY: Freeman. (Originally written as a letter in 1917)

Santosa, C. M., Strong, C. M., Nowakowska, C., Wang, P. W., Rennicke, C. M., & Ketter, T. A. (2007). Enhanced creativity in bipolar disorder patients: A controlled study. *Journal of Affective Disorders, 100,* 31–39.

Sarra, S., & Otta, E. (2001). Different types of smiles and laughter in preschool children. *Psychological Reports, 89,* 547–558.

Savin-Williams, R. C. (1998). *And then I became gay: Young men's stories.* New York, NY: Routledge.

Savin-Williams, R. C., & Cohen, K. M. (2004). Homoerotic development during childhood and adolescence. *Child and Adolescent Psychiatric Clinics of North America, 13,* 529–549.

Savin-Williams, R. C., & Diamond, L. M. (2000). Sexual identity trajectories among sexual-minority youths: Gender comparisons. *Archives of Sexual Behavior, 29,* 419–440.

Saxe, R., Carey, S., & Kanwisher, N. (2004). Understanding other minds: Linking developmental psychology and functional neuroimaging. *Annual Review of Psychology, 55,* 87–124.

Scammon, R. E. (1930). The ponderal growth of the extremities of the human fetus. *American Journal of Physical Anthropology, 15,* 111–121.

Scarr, S. (1992). Developmental theories for the 1990s: Development and individual differences. *Child Development, 63,* 1–19.

Scarr, S., & Carter-Saltzman, L. (1983). Genetics and intelligence. In J. L. Fuller & E. C. Simmel (Eds.), *Behavior genetics: Principles and applications.* Hillsdale, NJ: Erlbaum.

Scarr, S., & McCartney, K. (1983). How people make their own environments: A theory of genotype–environment effects. *Child Development, 54,* 424–435.

Scarr, S., Weber, P. L., Weinberg, R. A., & Wittig, M. A. (1981). Personality resemblance among adolescents and their parents in biologically related and adoptive families. *Journal of Personality and Social Psychology, 40,* 885–898.

Schaal, B., Marlier, L., & Soussignan, R. (2000). Human foetuses learn odours from their pregnant mother's diet. *Chemical Senses, 25,* 729–737.

Schab, F. R. (1990). Odors and remembrance of things past. *Journal of Experimental Psychology: Learning, Memory, and Cognition, 16,* 648–655.

Schachter, F. F. (1982). Sibling deidentification and split-parent identification: A family tetrad. In M. E. Lamb & B. Sutton-Smith (Eds.), *Sibling relationships: Their nature and significance across the lifespan.* Hillsdale, NJ: Erlbaum.

Schachter, S. (1971). *Emotion, obesity, and crime.* San Diego, CA: Academic Press.

Schäfer, M., Haun, D. B. M., & Tomasello, M. (2015). Fair is not fair everywhere. *Psychological Science, 26,* 1252-1260.

Schaller, G. B. (1972). *The Serengeti lion: A study of predator–prey relations.* Chicago, IL: University of Chicago Press.

Schank, R. C., & Abelson, R. P. (1977). *Scripts, plans, goals and understanding.* Hillsdale, NJ: Erlbaum.

Scheier, M. F., & Carver, C. S. (1993). On the power of positive thinking: The benefits of being optimistic. *Current Directions in Psychological Science, 2,* 26-30.

Scheier, M. F., Matthews, K. A., Owens, J. F., Magovern, G. J., Lefebvre, R., Abbott, R. C., & Carver, C. S. (1989). Dispositional optimism and recovery from coronary artery bypass surgery: The beneficial effects of optimism on physical and psychological well-being. *Journal of Personality and Social Psychology, 57,* 1024-1040.

Schenkman, B. N., & Nilsson, M. E. (2011). Human echolocation: Pitch versus loudness information. *Perception, 40,* 840-852.

Schiff, N. D., Giacino, J. T., Kalmar, K., Victor, J. D., Baker, K., Gerber, M., . . . Rezai, A. R. (2007). Behavioural improvements with thalamic stimulation after severe traumatic brain injury. *Nature, 448,* 600-604.

Schiffman, H. R. (1996). *Sensation and perception: An integrated approach* (4th ed.). Hoboken, NJ: Wiley.

Schildkraut, J. J. (1965). The catecholamine hypothesis of affective disorders: A review of supporting evidence. *American Journal of Psychiatry, 122,* 509-522.

Schindler, I., Rice, N. J., McIntosh, R. D., Rossetti, Y., Vighetto, A., & Milner, A. D. (2004). Automatic avoidance of obstacles is a dorsal stream function: Evidence from optic ataxia. *Nature Neuroscience, 7,* 779-784.

Schizophrenia Patient Outcomes Research Team, The (PORT). (2004). Updated treatment recommendations 2003, *Schizophrenia Bulletin, 30,* 193-217.

Schlam, T. R., Wilson, N. L., Shoda, Y., Mischel, W., & Ayduk, O. (2013). Preschoolers' delay of gratification predicts their body mass 30 years later. *The Journal of Pediatrics, 162,* 90-93.

Schlenker, B. R. (1980). *Impression management: The self-concept, social identity, and interpersonal relations.* Monterey, CA: Brooks/Cole.

Schlenker, B. R., & Pontari, B. A. (2000). The strategic control of information: Impression management and self-presentation in daily life. In A. Tesser, R. B. Felson, & J. M. Suls (Eds.), *Psychological perspectives on self and identity.* Washington, DC: American Psychological Association.

Schmader, T., Johns, M., & Forbes, C. (2008). An integrated process model of stereotype threat effects on performance. *Psychological Review, 115,* 336-356.

Schmidt, F. L., & Hunter, J. (2004). General mental ability in the world of work: Occupational attainment and job performance. *Journal of Personality and Social Psychology, 86,* 162-173.

Schmidt, M., & Tomasello, M. (2012). Young children enforce social norms. *Current Directions in Psychological Science, 21,* 232-236.

Schmitt, D. P. (2003). Universal sex differences in the desire for sexual variety: Tests from 52 nations, 6 continents, and 13 islands. *Journal of Personality & Social Psychology, 85,* 85-104.

Schmitt, D. P. (2005). Fundamentals of human mating strategies. In D. M. Buss (Ed.), *The handbook of evolutionary psychology* (pp. 258-291). Hoboken, NJ: Wiley.

Schmitt, D. P., Realo, A., Voracek, M., & Allik, J. (2008). Why can't a man be more like a woman? Sex differences in Big Five personality traits across 55 cultures. *Journal of Personality and Social Psychology, 94,* 168-182.

Schmitz, A., Hennig, J., Kuepper, Y., & Reuter, M. (2007). The association between neuroticism and the serotonin transporter polymorphism depends on structural differences between personality measures. *Personality and Individual Differences, 42,* 789-799.

Schnapf, J. L., & Baylor, D. A. (1987, April). How photoreceptor cells respond to light. *Scientific American,* 40-47.

Schneider, J. M. (1972). Relationship between locus of control and activity preferences: Effects of masculinity, activity, and skill. *Journal of Consulting and Clinical Psychology, 38,* 225-230.

Schneider, T. R. (2004). The role of neuroticism on psychological and physiological stress responses. *Journal of Experimental Social Psychology, 40,* 795-804.

Schneider, W. (2015). *Memory development from early childhood through emerging adulthood.* New York, NY: Springer.

Schobel, S. A., Chaudhury, N. H., Khan, U. A., Paniagua, B., Styner, M. A., Asllani, I., . . . Smal, S. A. (2013). Imaging patients with psychosis and a mouse model establishes a spreading pattern of hippocampal dysfunction and implicates glutamate as a driver. *Neuron, 78,* 81-93.

Schooler, C. (2001). The intellectual effects of the demands of the work environment. In R. J. Sternberg & E. L. Grigorenko (Eds.), *Environmental effects on cognitive abilities.* Mahwah, NJ: Erlbaum.

Schooler, C. (2007). Use it—and keep it, longer, probably. *Perspectives in Psychological Science, 2,* 24-29.

Schooler, C., & Mulatu, M. S. (2001). The reciprocal effects of leisure time activities and intellectual functioning in older people: A longitudinal analysis. *Psychology and Aging, 16,* 466-482.

Schradin, C., Reeder, D. M., Mendoza, S. P., & Anzenberger, G. (2003). Prolactin and paternal care: Comparison of three species of monogamous new world monkeys (*Callicebus cupreus, Callithrix jacchus,* and *Callimico goeldii*). *Journal of Comparative Psychology, 117,* 166-175.

Schryer, E., & Ross, M. (2012). Evaluating the valence of remembered events: The importance of age and self-relevance. *Psychology and Aging, 27,* 237-242.

Schultz, W. (1998). Predictive signal of dopamine neurons. *Journal of Neurophysiology, 80,* 1-27.

Schulz, L. E., & Bonawitz, E. B. (2007). Serious fun: Preschoolers engage in more exploratory play when evidence is confounded. *Developmental Psychology, 43,* 1045-1050.

Schunk, D. H., & Hanson, A. R. (1985). Peer models: Influence on children's self-efficacy and achievement. *Journal of Educational Psychology, 77,* 313-322.

Schwartz, B. L. (2013). Memory for people: Integration of face, voice, name, and biographical information. In T. J. Perfect, & D. S. Lindsay (Eds.), *The Sage handbook of applied memory* (pp. 3-19). London, England: Sage.

Schwartz, B. L., & Krantz, J. H. (2016). *Sensation & perception.* Los Angeles, CA: Sage.

Schwartz, G. E. (1990). Psychobiology of repression and health: A systems approach. In J. L. Singer (Ed.), *Repression and dissociation: Implications for personality theory, psychopathology, and health.* Chicago, IL: University of Chicago Press.

Schwartz, M. F. (1987). Patterns of speech production of deficit within and across aphasia syndromes: Application of a psycholinguistic model. In M. Coltheart, G. Sartori, & R. Job (Eds.), *The cognitive neuropsychology of language.* Hillsdale, NJ: Erlbaum.

Schwartz, S. H., & Gottlieb, A. (1980). Bystander anonymity and reactions to emergencies. *Journal of Personality and Social Psychology, 39,* 418-430.

Schwartz-Giblin, S., McEwen, B. S., & Pfaff, D. W. (1989). Mechanisms of female reproductive behavior. In F. R. Brush & S. Levine (Eds.), *Psychoendocrinology.* San Diego, CA: Academic Press.

Schwarzer, R. (1994). Optimism, vulnerability, and self-beliefs as health-related cognitions: A systematic overview. *Psychology and Health, 9,* 161-180.

Scotko, B. G., Rubin, D. C., & Tupler, L. A. (2008). H. M.'s personal crossword puzzles: Understanding memory and language. *Memory, 16*, 89–96.

Scott, J. C., Matt, G. E., Wrocklage, K. M, Crnich, C., Hordan, J., Southwick, S. M., . . . Schweinsburg, B. C. (2015). A qualitative meta-analysis of neurocognitive functioning in posttraumatic stress disorder. *Psychological Bulletin, 141*, 105–140.

Scott, J. P. (1963). The process of primary socialization in canine and human infants. *Monograph of the Society for Research in Child Development, 28*, 1–47.

Scott, J. P., & Fuller, J. L. (1965). *Genetics and the social behavior of the dog.* Chicago, IL: University of Chicago Press.

Scott, K. (2013). Chemical senses: Taste and olfaction. In L. R. Squire, D. Berg, F. E. Bloom, S. du Lac, A. Ghosh, & N. C. Spitzer (Eds.), *Fundamental neuroscience* (4th ed., pp. 530). New York, NY: Elsevier.

Scott-Phillips, T. C., Dickins, T. E., & West, S. A. (2011). Evolutionary theory and the ultimate-proximate distinction in the human behaviors sciences. *Perspective on Psychological Science, 6*, 38–47.

Scribner, S. (1977). Modes of thinking and ways of speaking: Culture and logic reconsidered. In P. N. Johnson-Laird & P. C. Wason (Eds.), *Thinking: Readings in cognitive science.* Cambridge, England: Cambridge University Press.

Searle, L. V. (1949). The organization of hereditary maze-brightness and maze-dullness. *Genetic Psychology Monographs, 39*, 279–325.

Sears, R. R. (1936). Experimental studies of projection: I. Attributions of traits. *Journal of Social Psychology, 7*, 151–163.

Sechenov, I. M. (1935). Reflexes of the brain. In A. A. Subkow (Ed. & Trans.), *I. M. Sechenov: Selected works.* Moscow, Russia: State Publishing House for Biological and Medical Literature. (Original work published 1863)

Seeman, P., & Lee, T. (1975). Antipsychotic drugs: Direct correlation between clinical potency and presynaptic action on dopamine neurons. *Science, 188*, 1271–1219.

Sekar, A., Bialas, A. R., de Rivera, H., Davis, A., Hammond, T. R., Kamitaki, N., . . . McCarroll, S. A. (2016). Schizophrenia risk from complex variation of complement component 4. *Nature, 530*, 177–183.

Seligman, M. E. P. (1970). On the generality of the laws of learning. *Psychological Review, 77*, 406–418.

Seligman, M. E. P. (1971). Phobias and preparedness. *Behavior Therapy, 2*, 307–320.

Seligman, M. E. P. (1990). *Learned optimism.* New York, NY: Knopf.

Seligman, M. E. P. (1998). *Learned optimism: How to change your mind and your life* (2nd ed.). New York, NY: Free Press.

Semmel, A. K. (1976). *Group dynamics and foreign policy process: The choice-shift phenomenon.* Paper presented to the Southern Political Science Association.

Senghas, A., & Coppola, M. (2001). Children creating language: How Nicaraguan sign language acquired a spatial grammar. *Psychological Science, 12*, 323–328.

Senghas, A., Kita, S., & Özyürek, A. (2004). Children creating core properties of language: Evidence from an emerging sign language in Nicaragua. *Science, 305*, 1779–1782.

Sereno, M. I., Dale, A. M., Reppas, J. B., Kwong, K. K., Belliveau, J. W., Brady, T. J., . . . Tootell, R. B. H. (1995). Borders of multiple visual areas in humans revealed by functional magnetic imaging. *Science, 268*, 889–892.

Shadan, S. (2009). A taste of umami. *Nature, 457*, 160.

Shafto, P., Goodman, N. D., & Frank, M. C. (2012). Learning from others: The consequences of psychological reasoning for human learning. *Perspectives on Psychological Science, 7*, 341–351.

Sharf, R. S. (2012). *Theories of psychotherapy & counseling: Concepts and cases* (5th ed.). Pacific Grove, CA: Brooks/Cole.

Shaw, J., & Porter, S. (2015). Constructing rich false memories of committing a crime. *Psychological Science, 26*, 291–301.

Shaw, P., Eckstrand, K., Sharp, W., Blumenthal, J., Lerch, J. P., Greenstein, D., . . . Rapoport, J. L. (2007). Attention-deficit/hyperactivity disorder is characterized by a delay in cortical maturation. *Proceedings of the National Academy of Science, 104*, 19649–19654.

Sheldon, K. M., & Kasser, T. (2001). Getting older, getting better? Personal strivings and psychological maturity across the life span. *Developmental Psychology, 37*, 491–501.

Sheldon, K. M., Sheldon, M. S., & Osbaldiston, R. (2000). Prosocial values and group assortation within an *N*-person prisoner's dilemma game. *Human Nature, 11*, 387–404.

Shepard, R. N. (1967). Recognition memory for words, sentences, and pictures. *Journal of Verbal Learning and Verbal Behavior, 6*, 156–163.

Shepher, J. (1983). *Incest: A biosocial view.* New York, NY: Academic Press.

Shepherd, G. M. (2006). Smell images and the flavour system in the human brain. *Nature, 444*, 316–321.

Sheppard, J. A., Klein, W. M. P., Waters, E. A., & Weinstein, N. D. (2013). Taking stock of unrealistic optimism. *Perspectives in Psychological Science, 8*, 395–411.

Sheppard, L. D., & Vernon, P. A. (2008). Intelligence and speed of information-processing: A review of 50 years of research. *Personality and Individual Differences, 44*, 535–551.

Shergill, S. S., Brammer, M. J., Amaro, E., Williams, S. C. R., Murray, R. M., & McGuire, P. K. (2004). Temporal course of auditory hallucinations. *British Journal of Psychiatry, 185*, 516–517.

Sherif, M. (1936). *The psychology of social norms.* New York, NY: Harper.

Sherif, M. (1966). *In common predicament: Social psychology of intergroup conflict and cooperation.* Boston, MA: Houghton Mifflin.

Sherif, M., Harvey, O. J., White, B. J., Hood, W. E., & Sherif, C. S. (1961). *Intergroup conflict and cooperation: The Robbers Cave experiment.* Norman: University of Oklahoma Book Exchange.

Sherman, P. W. (1977). Nepotism and the evolution of alarm calls. *Science, 197*, 1246–1253.

Sherman, R. A., Nave, C. S., & Funder, D. C. (2010). Situational similarity and personality predict behavioral consistency. *Journal of Personality and Social Psychology, 99*, 330–343.

Sherman, R. A., Rauthmann, J. F., Brown, N. A., Serfass, D. S., & Jones, A. B. (2015). The independent effects of personality and situations on real-time expressions of behavior and emotion. *Journal of Personality and Social Psychology, 109*, 872–888.

Shettleworth, S. J., & Westwood, R. P. (2002). Divided attention, memory, and spatial discrimination in food-storing and nonstoring birds, black-capped chickadees (*Poecile atricapilla*) and dark-eyed juncos (*Junco hyemalis*). *Journal of Experimental Psychology: Animal Behavior Processes, 28*, 227–241.

Shin, H.-E., Bjorklund, D. F., & Beck, E. F. (2007). The adaptive nature of children's overestimation in a strategic memory task. *Cognitive Development, 22*, 197–212.

Shipp, S. (2004). The brain circuitry of attention. *Trends in Cognitive Sciences, 8*, 223–230.

Shipstead, Z., Harrison, T. L., & Engle, R. W. (2016). Working memory capacity and fluid intelligence: Maintenance and disengagement. *Perspectives on Psychological Science, 11*, 771–799.

Shipstead, Z., Redick, T. S., & Engle, R. W. (2012). Is working memory training effective? *Psychological Bulletin, 138*, 628–654.

Shoda, Y., Mischel, W., & Peake, P. K. (1990). Predicting adolescent cognitive and social competence from preschool delay of gratification: Identifying diagnostic conditions. *Developmental Psychology, 26*, 978–986.

Shoda, Y., Mischel, W., & Wright, J. C. (1994). Intraindividual stability in organization and patterning of behavior: Incorporating psychological situations into the idiographic analysis of personality. *Journal of Personality and Social Psychology, 67,* 674–687.

Shorter, E. (2009). The history of lithium therapy. *Bipolar Disorder, 11,* 4–9.

Shuster, S. M., & Wade, M. J. (2009). *Mating systems and strategies.* Princeton, NJ: Princeton University Press.

Siegel, J. M. (2003, October). Why we sleep. *Scientific American, 289,* 92–97.

Siegel, J. M. (2005). Sleep phylogeny: Clues to the evolution and function of sleep. In P.-H. Luppi (Ed.), *Sleep: Circuits and functions.* Boca Raton, FL: CRC Press.

Siegel, S. (1984). Pavlovian conditioning and heroin overdose: Reports by overdose victims. *Bulletin of the Psychonomic Society, 22,* 428–430.

Siegel, S. (1999). Drug anticipation and drug addiction: The 1998 H. David Archibald lecture. *Addiction, 94,* 1113–1124.

Siegel, S. (2005). Drug tolerance, drug addiction, and drug anticipation. *Current Directions in Psychological Science, 14,* 296–300.

Siegel, S., & Ramos, B. M. C. (2002). Applying laboratory research: Drug anticipation and the treatment of drug addiction. *Experimental and Clinical Psychopharmacology, 10,* 162–183.

Siegler, R. S., & Svetina, M. (2006). What leads children to adopt new strategies? A microgenetic/cross-sectional study of class inclusion. *Child Development, 77,* 997–1015.

Siev, J., & Chambless, D. L. (2007). Specificity of treatment effects: Cognitive therapy and relaxation for generalized anxiety and panic disorders. *Journal of Consulting and Clinical Psychology, 75,* 513–522.

Sigala, R., Logothetis, N. K., & Rainer, G. (2011). Own-species bias in the representations of monkey and human face categories in the primate temporal lobe. *Journal of Neurophysiology, 105,* 2740–2752.

Silk, J. B. (2002). Kin selection in primate groups. *International Journal of Primatology, 23,* 849–875.

Simcock, G., & Hayne, H. (2002). Breaking the barrier? Children fail to translate their preverbal memories into language. *Psychological Science, 13,* 225–231.

Simner, J. (2012). Defining synaesthesia. *British Journal of Psychology, 103,* 1–15.

Simner, J., Mulvenna, C., Sagiv, N., Tsakanikos, E., Witherby, S. A., Fraser, C., Scott, K., & Ward, J. (2006). Synaesthesia: The prevalence of atypical cross-modal experiences. *Perception, 35,* 1024–1033.

Simons, D. J., & Chabris, C. F. (1999). Gorillas in our midst: Sustained inattentional blindness for dynamic events. *Perception, 28,* 1059–1074.

Simonton, D. K. (2014). More method in the mad-genius controversy: A historiometric study of 204 historic creators. *Psychology of Aesthetics, Creativity, and the Arts, 8,* 53–61.

Simpson, J., & Done, D. J. (2004). Analogical reasoning in schizophrenic delusions. *European Psychiatry, 19,* 344–348.

Simpson, J. A., Griskevicius, V., Kuo, S., Sung, S., & Collins, W. A. (2012). Evolution, stress, and sensitive periods: The influence of unpredictability in early versus late childhood on sex and risky behavior. *Developmental Psychology, 48,* 674–686.

Sims, J. H., & Baumann, D. D. (1972). The tornado threat: Coping styles of the north and south. *Science, 176,* 1386–1392.

Singer, T., Seymour, B., O'Doherty, J. P., Stephan, K. E., Dolan, R. J., & Frith, C. D. (2006). Empathic neural responses are modulated by the perceived fairness of others. *Nature, 439,* 466–469.

Singh, I. (2008). Beyond polemics: Science and the ethics of ADHD. *Nature Reviews Neuroscience, 9,* 957–964.

Sio, U. N., & Ormerod, T. C. (2009). Does incubation enhance problem solving? A meta-analytic review. *Psychological Bulletin, 135,* 94–120.

Skinner, B. F. (1938). *The behavior of organisms.* New York, NY: Appleton-Century-Crofts.

Skinner, B. F. (1953). *Science and human behavior.* New York, NY: Macmillan.

Skinner, B. F. (1966). The phylogeny and ontogeny of behavior. *Science, 153,* 1205–1213.

Skinner, B. F. (1974). *About behaviorism.* New York, NY: Knopf.

Skov, R. B., & Sherman, S. J. (1986). Information-gathering processes: Diagnosticity, hypothesis confirmation strategies and perceived hypothesis confirmation. *Journal of Experimental Social Psychology, 22,* 93–121.

Slater, A. (1995). Visual perception and memory at birth. In C. Rovee-Collier & L. P. Lipsitt (Eds.), *Advances in infancy research* (Vol. 9). Norwood, NJ: Ablex.

Sloane, R. B., Staples, F. R., Cristo, A. H., Yorkston, N. J., & Whipple, K. (1975). *Psychotherapy versus behavior therapy.* Cambridge, MA: Harvard University Press.

Smilek, D., Dixon, M. J., & Merikle, P. M. (2005). Synaesthesia: Discordant *male* monozygotic twins. *Neurocase, 11,* 363–370.

Smith, J. C. (2010). *Pseudoscience and extraordinary claims of the paranormal: A critical thinker's toolkit.* Malden, MA: Wiley-Blackwell.

Smith, J. D. (1992). The auditory hallucinations of schizophrenia. In D. Reisberg (Ed.), *Auditory imagery.* Hillsdale, NJ: Erlbaum.

Smith, K. S., & Berridge, K. C. (2007). Opioid limbic circuit for reward: Interaction between hedonic hotspots of nucleus accumbens and ventral pallidum. *Journal of Neuroscience, 27,* 1594–1605.

Smith, M. L., Glass, G. V., & Miller, T. I. (1980). *The benefits of psychotherapy.* Baltimore, MD: Johns Hopkins University Press.

Smith, R. E. (2003). The cost of remembering to remember in event-based prospective memory: Investigating the capacity demands of delayed intention performance. *Journal of Experimental Psychology: Learning, Memory, and Cognition, 29,* 347–361.

Smith, S. F., & Lilienfeld, S. O. (2015). The response modulation hypothesis of psychopathy: A meta-analysis and narrative analysis. *Psychological Bulletin, 141,* 1145–1177.

Smith, S. M., & Vela, E. (2001). Environmental context-dependent memory: A review and meta-analysis. *Psychonomic Bulletin and Review, 8,* 203–220.

Snow, C. E. (1984). Parent–child interaction and the development of communicative ability. In R. L. Schiefelbusch & J. Pickar (Eds.), *The acquisition of communicative competence.* Baltimore, MD: University Park Press.

Snow, C. E., & Yusun Kang, J. (2006). Becoming bilingual, biliterate, and bicultural. In W. Damon (Gen. Ed.) & K. A. Renninger & I. E. Sigel (Vol. Eds.), *Handbook of child psychology: Vol. 4. Child psychology in practice.* Hoboken, NJ: Wiley.

Snyder, C. R. (1994). *The psychology of hope: You can get there from here.* New York, NY: Free Press.

Snyder, F., & Scott, J. (1972). The psychophysiology of sleep. In S. Greenfield & R. A. Sternbach (Eds.), *Handbook of psychophysiology* (pp. 645–708). New York, NY: Holt, Rinehart & Winston.

Snyder, H. R., Kaiser, R. H., Warren, S. L., & Heller, W. (2015). Obsessive-compulsive disorder is associated with broad impairments in executive function: A meta-analysis. *Clinical Psychological Science, 3,* 301–330.

Snyder, M. (1981). Seek and ye shall find: Testing hypotheses about other people. In E. T. Higgins, C. P. Herman, & M. P. Zanna (Eds.), *Social cognition: The Ontario symposium on personality and social psychology* (pp. 277–303). Hillsdale, NJ: Erlbaum.

Snyderman, M., & Rothman, S. (1987). Survey of expert opinion on intelligence and aptitude testing. *American Psychologist, 42,* 137–144.

Soderstrom, M. (2007). Beyond babytalk: Re-evaluating the nature and content of speech input to preverbal infants. *Developmental Review, 27,* 501–532.

Solomon, B. C., & Jackson, J. J. (2014). Why do personality traits predict divorce? Multiple pathways through satisfaction. *Journal of Personality and Social Psychology, 106,* 978–996.

Solomon, S. G., & Lennie, P. (2007). The machinery of colour vision. *Nature Reviews Neuroscience, 8,* 267–277.

Sommer, S. (2000). Sex-specific predation on a monogamous rat, *Hypogeomys antimena* (Muridae: Nesomyinae). *Animal Behaviour, 59,* 1087–1094.

Sorce, J. F., Emde, R. N., Campos, J., & Klinnert, M. D. (1985). Maternal emotional signaling: Its effect on the visual cliff behavior of 1-year-olds. *Developmental Psychology, 21,* 195–200.

Soto-Faraco, S., Calabresi, M., Navarra, J., Werker, J. F., & Lewkowicz, D. J. (2012). The development of audiovisual speech perception. In A. J. Bremner, D. J. Lewkowicz, & C. Spence (Eds.), *Multisensory development* (pp. 207–228). Oxford, England: Oxford University Press.

Soussignan, R. (2002). Duchenne smile, emotional experience, and autonomic reactivity: A test of the facial feedback hypothesis. *Emotion, 2,* 52–74.

Southgate, V., Johnson, M. H., Osborne, T., & Csibra, G. (2009). Predictive motor activation during action observation in human infants. *Biology Letters, 5,* 769–772.

Sowislo, J. F., & Orth, U. (2013). Does low self-esteem predict depression and anxiety? A meta-analysis of longitudinal studies. *Psychological Bulletin, 139,* 213–240.

Spalding, D. A. (1873; reprinted 1954). Instinct with original observations on young animals. *British Journal of Animal Behavior, 2,* 2–11.

Spear, L. P. (2007). Brain development and adolescent behavior. In D. Coch, K. W. Fischer, & G. Dawson (Eds.), *Human behavior, learning, and the developing brain: Typical development* (pp. 362–396). New York, NY: Guilford.

Spearman, C. (1927). *The abilities of man.* New York, NY: Macmillan.

Spector, P. E. (2002). Employee control and occupational stress. *Current Directions in Psychological Science, 11,* 133–136.

Spelke, E. S. (2000). Core knowledge. *American Psychologist, 55,* 1233–1243.

Spelke, E. S., Breinlinger, K., Macomber, J., & Jacobson, K. (1992). Origins of knowledge. *Psychological Review, 99,* 605–632.

Spelke, E. S., Katz, G., Purcell, S., Ehrlich, S., & Breinlinger, K. (1994). Early knowledge of object motion: Continuity and inertia. *Cognition, 51,* 131–176.

Spelke, E. S., & Kinzler, K. D. (2007). Core knowledge. *Developmental Science, 10,* 89–96.

Spencer, J. P., Blumberg, M. S., McMurray, B., Robinson, S. R., Samuelson. L. K., & Tomblin, J. B. (2009). Short arms and talking legs: Why we should no longer abide the nativist-empiricist debate. *Child Development Perspectives, 3,* 79–87.

Sperling, G. (1960). The information available in brief visual presentations. *Psychological Monographs, 74*(498).

Sperry, L. (2003). *Handbook of diagnosis and treatment of DSM-IV-TR personality disorders* (2nd ed., pp. 200–201). New York, NY: Brunner-Routledge.

Špinka, M., Ruth, C. Newberry, R. C., & Bekoff, M. (2001). Mammalian play: Training for the unexpected. *The Quarterly Review of Biology, 76,* 141–168.

Spinney, L. (2008). Line-ups on trial. *Nature, 453,* 442–444.

Spreckley, M., & Boyd, R. (2009). Efficacy of applied behavioral intervention in preschool children with autism for improving cognitive, language, and adaptive behavior: A systematic review and meta-analysis. *The Journal of Pediatrics, 154,* 338–344.

Squire, L. R. (1992). Memory and the hippocampus: A synthesis from findings with rats, monkeys, and humans. *Psychological Review, 99,* 195–231.

Squire, L. R., Berg, D., Bloom, F. E., du Lac, S., Ghosh, A., & Spitzer, N. C. (Eds.). (2013). *Fundamental neuroscience* (4th ed.). Boston, MA: Elsevier.

Squire, L. R., Knowlton, B., & Musen, G. (1993). The structure and organization of memory. *Annual Review of Psychology, 44,* 453–495.

Squire, L. R., & Slater, P. C. (1983). Electroconvulsive therapy and complaints of memory dysfunction: A prospective three-year follow-up study. *British Journal of Psychiatry, 142,* 1–8.

Srivastava, S., John, O. P., Gosling, S. D., & Potter, J. (2003). Development of personality in early and middle adulthood: Set like plaster or persistent change? *Journal of Personality and Social Psychology, 84,* 1041–1053.

St. Clair, D., Xu, M., Wang, P., Yu, Y., Fang, Y., Zhang, F., . . . He, L. (2005). Rates of adult schizophrenia following prenatal exposure to the Chinese famine of 1959-1961. *Journal of the American Medical Association, 294,* 557–562.

St. Jacques, P. L., Dolcos, F., & Cabeza, R. (2009). Effects of aging on functional connectivity of the amygdala for subsequent memory of negative pictures. *Psychological Science, 20,* 74–84.

Staines, G. L. (2008). The relative efficacy of psychotherapy: Reassessing the methods-based paradigm. *Review of General Psychology, 12,* 330–342.

Standing, L. (1973). Learning 10,000 pictures. *Quarterly Journal of Experimental Psychology, 25,* 207–222.

Stanley, D., Phelps, E., & Banaji, M. (2008). The neural basis of implicit attitudes. *Current Directions in Psychological Science, 17,* 164–170.

Stanovich, K. E. (2003). The fundamental computational biases of human cognition. In J. E. Davidson & R. J. Sternberg (Eds.), *The psychology of problem solving.* Cambridge, England: Cambridge University Press.

Stanovich, K. E., & West, R. F. (2000). Individual differences in reasoning: Implications for the rationality debate? *Behavioral and Brain Sciences, 23,* 645–726.

Stanovich, K. E., & West, R. F. (2003). Evolutionary versus instrumental goals: How evolutionary psychology misconceives human rationality. In D. E. Over (Ed.), *Evolution and the psychology of thinking: The debate.* New York, NY: Psychology Press.

Stanovich, K. E., & West, R. F. (2008). On the relative independence of thinking biases and cognitive ability. *Journal of Personality and Social Psychology, 94,* 672–695.

Stanovich, K. E., West, R. F., & Toplak, M. E. (2013). Myside bias, rational thinking, and intelligence. *Current Directions in Psychological Science, 22,* 259–264.

Steblay, N. M., & Bothwell, R. K. (1994). Evidence for hypnotically refreshed testimony: The view from the laboratory. *Law and Human Behavior, 18,* 635–651.

Steele, C. M. (1997). A threat in the air: How stereotypes shape intellectual identity and performance. *American Psychologist, 52,* 613–629.

Steele, C. M., & Aronson, J. (1995). Stereotype threat and the intellectual test performance of African Americans. *Journal of Social and Personality Psychology, 69,* 797–811.

Stein, B. E., & Meredith, M. A. (1993). The merging of the senses. Cambridge, MA: MIT Press.

Steinberg, L. (1989). Pubertal maturation and parent–adolescent distance: An evolutionary perspective. In G. R. Adams, R. Montemayor, & T. P. Gullota (Eds.), *Biology of adolescent behavior and development.* Newbury Park, CA: Sage.

Steinberg, L. (1996). *Beyond the classroom: Why school reform has failed and what parents need to do.* New York, NY: Simon & Schuster.

Steinberg, L. (2001). We know some things: Adolescent–parent relationships in retrospect and prospect. *Journal of Research on Adolescence, 11,* 1–20.

Steinberg, L. (2007). Risk taking in adolescence: New perspectives from brain and behavioral science. *Current Directions in Psychological Science, 16*, 55–59.

Steinberg, L. (2008). A social neuroscience perspective on adolescent risk-taking. *Developmental Review, 28*, 78–106.

Steinberg, L. (2015). *Age of opportunity: Lessons from the new science of adolescence.* New York, NY: Houghton Mifflin Harcourt.

Steinberg, L., & Monahan, K. C. (2007). Age differences in resistance to peer influence. *Developmental Psychology, 43*, 1531–1543.

Steingraber, S. (2007). *The falling age of puberty in U.S. girls: What we know, what we need to know.* Retrieved from the Breast Cancer Fund website: http://www.breastcancerfund.org/assets/pdfs/publications/falling-age-of-puberty.pdf

Steketee, G., & Barlow, D. H. (2002). Obsessive-compulsive disorder. In D. H. Barlow, *Anxiety and its disorders* (2nd ed.). New York, NY: Guilford.

Steriade, M., McCormick, D. A., & Sejnowski, T. J. (1993). Thalamocortical oscillations in the sleeping and aroused brain. *Science, 262*, 679–685.

Sternberg, R. J. (1997). The concept of intelligence and its role in lifelong learning and success. *American Psychologist, 52*, 1030–1037.

Stevenson, J., Asherson, P., Hay, D., Levy, F., Swanson, J., Thapar, A., & Willcutt, E. (2005). Characterizing the ADHD phenotype for genetic studies. *Developmental Science, 8*, 115–121.

Stewart, J. E., II (1985). Appearance and punishment: The attraction-leniency effect in the courtroom. *Journal of Social Psychology, 125*, 373–378.

Stewart-Williams, S. (2007). Altruism among kin vs. nonkin: Effects of cost of help and reciprocal exchange. *Evolution and Human Behavior, 28*, 193–198.

Stickgold, R. (2005). Sleep-dependent memory consolidation. *Nature, 437*, 1272–1278.

Stiles, J., Brown, T. T., Haist, F., & Jernigan, T. L. (2015). Brain and cognitive development. In R. M. Lerner (Gen. Ed.) & L. S. Liben & U. M. Müller (Vol. Eds.), *Handbook of child psychology and developmental science* (Vol. 2). New York, NY: Wiley.

Stipek, D. (1984). Young children's performance expectations: Logical analysis or wishful thinking? In J. G. Nicholls (Ed.), *Advances in motivation and achievement: Vol 3. The development of achievement motivation.* Greenwich, CT: JAI.

Stipek, D., & Daniels, D. (1988). Declining perceptions of competence: A consequence of changes in the child or the educational environment? *Journal of Educational Psychology, 80*, 352–356.

Stoddart, D. M. (1990). *The scented ape.* Cambridge, England: Cambridge University Press.

Stone, A., & Valentine, T. (2007). The categorical structure of knowledge for famous people (and a novel application of centre-surround theory). *Cognition, 104*, 535–564.

Stone, C. A., & Day, M. C. (1978). Levels of availability of a formal operational strategy. *Child Development, 49*, 1054–1065.

Stone, J., Zeman, A., Simonotto, E., Meyer, M., Azuma, R., Flett, S., & Sharpe, M. (2007). fMRI in patients with motor conversion symptoms and controls with simulated weakness. *Psychosomatic Medicine, 69*, 961–969.

Stoolmiller, M. (1999). Implications of the restricted range of family environments for estimates of heritability and nonshared environment in behavior-genetic adoption studies. *Psychological Bulletin, 125*, 392–409.

Strayer, D. L., & Drews, F. A. (2007). Cell-phone–induced driver distraction. *Current Directions in Psychological Science, 16*, 128–131.

Strayer, D. L., & Johnston, W. A. (2001). Driven to distraction: Dual-task studies of simulated driving and conversing on a cellular telephone. *Psychological Science, 12*, 462–466.

Strayhorn, T. L. (2014). What role does grit play in the academic success of black male collegians at predominantly white institutions? *Journal of African American Studies, 18*, 1–10.

Stricker, E. M. (1973). Thirst, sodium appetite, and complementary physiological contributions to the regulation of intravascular fluid volume. In A. N. Epstein, H. R. Kissileff, & E. Stellar (Eds.), *The neuropsychology of thirst: New findings and advances in concepts.* Washington, DC: Winston.

Stricker, E. M., & Verbalis, J. G. (2012). Water and salt intake and body fluid homeostasis. In L. R. Squire, D. Berg, F. E. Bloom, S. du Lac, A. Ghosh, & N. C. Spitzer (Eds.), *Fundamental neuroscience* (4th ed., pp. 783–797). New York, NY: Elsevier.

Stroebe, W., Stroebe, M., Abakoumkin, G., & Schut, H. (1996). The role of loneliness and social support in adjustment to loss: A test of attachment versus stress theory. *Journal of Personality and Social Psychology, 70*, 1241–1249.

Stroop, J. R. (1935). Studies of interference in serial verbal reactions. *Journal of Experimental Psychology, 18*, 643–662.

Stroup, T. S., Kraus, J. E., & Marder, S. R. (2006). Pharmacotherapies. In J. A. Lieberman, T. S. Stroup, & D. O. Perkins (Eds.), *The American Psychiatric Publishing textbook of schizophrenia.* Washington, DC: American Psychiatric Publishing.

Stroup, T. S., Marder, S. R., & Lieberman, J. A. (2012). Pharmacotherapies. In J. A. Lieberman, T. S. Stroup, & D. O. Perkins (Eds.), *Essentials of schizophrenia* (pp. 173–206). Arlington, VA: American Psychiatric Publishing.

Strupp, H. H. (1989). Psychotherapy: Can the practitioner learn from the researcher? *American Psychologist, 44*, 717–724.

Strupp, H. H., & Hadley, S. W. (1979). Specific vs. nonspecific factors in psychotherapy: A controlled study of outcome. *Archives of General Psychiatry, 36*, 1125–1136.

Stunkard, A., Sorensen, T., Hanis, C., Teasdale, T., Chakraborty, R., Schull, W., & Schulsinger, F. (1986). An adoption study of human obesity. *New England Journal of Medicine, 314*, 193–198.

Suddendorf, T., & Corballis, M. C. (2010). Behavioural evidence for mental time travel in nonhuman animals. *Behavioral Brain Research, 215*, 292–298.

Sullivan, M. W., & Lewis, M. (2003). Contextual determinants of anger and other negative expressions in young infants. *Developmental Psychology, 39*, 693–705.

Sulloway, F. J. (1996). *Born to rebel: Birth order, family dynamics, and creative lives.* New York, NY: Pantheon Books.

Sunstein, C. (2003). *Why societies need dissent.* Cambridge, MA: Harvard University Press.

Surowiecki, J. (2004a, March 8). Board stiffs. *The New Yorker*, 30.

Surowiecki, J. (2004b). *The wisdom of crowds.* New York, NY: Doubleday.

Susser, E., Neugebauer, R., Hoek, H. W., Brown, A. S., Lin, S., Labovitz, D., & Gorman, J. M. (1996). Schizophrenia after prenatal famine. *Archives of General Psychiatry, 53*, 25–31.

Susskind, J. M., Lee, D. H., Cusi, A., Feiman, R., Grabksi, W., & Anderson, A. K. (2008). Expressing fear enhances sensory acquisition. *Nature Neuroscience, 11*, 843–850.

Svirsky, M. A., Robbins, A. M., Kirk, K. I., Pisoni, D. B., & Miyamoto, R. T. (2000). Language development in profoundly deaf children with cochlear implants. *Psychological Science, 11*, 153–158.

Swanson, H. L. (2008). Working memory and intelligence in children: What develops? *Journal of Educational Psychology, 100*, 581–602.

Sweeney, P. D., & Gruber, K. L. (1984). Selective exposure: Voter information preferences and the Watergate affair. *Journal of Personality and Social Psychology, 46*, 1208–1221.

Swets, J. A., Dawes, R. M., Monahan, J. (2000). Psychological science can improve diagnostic decision. *Psychological Science in the Public Interest, 1*, 1–26.

Swingley, D. (2008). The roots of the early vocabulary in infants' learning from speech. *Current Directions in Psychological Science, 17,* 308–312.

Symons, C. S., & Johnson, B. T. (1997). The self-reference effect in memory: A meta-analysis. *Psychological Bulletin, 121,* 371–394.

Symons, D. (1978). *Play and aggression: A study of rhesus monkeys.* New York, NY: Columbia University Press.

Symons, D. (1979). *The evolution of human sexuality.* Oxford, England: Oxford University Press.

Szechtman, H., & Woody, E. (2004). Obsessive-compulsive disorder as a disturbance of security motivation. *Psychological Review, 111,* 111–127.

Szeszko, P. R., MacMillan, S., McMeniman, M., Chen, S., Baribault, K., Lim, K. O., . . . Rosenberg, D. R. (2004). Brain structural abnormalities in psychotropic drug-naïve pediatric patients with obsessive-compulsive disorder. *American Journal of Psychiatry, 161,* 1049–1056.

Szpunar, K. K. (2010). Episodic future thought: An emerging concept. *Perspectives on Psychological Science, 5,* 142–162.

Tafarodi, R. W., & Milne, A. B. (2002). Decomposing global self-esteem. *Journal of Personality, 70,* 443–483.

Tager-Flusberg, H. (2007). Evaluating the theory-of-mind hypothesis of autism. *Current Directions in Psychological Science, 16,* 311–315.

Tajfel, H. (1972). Social categorization. In S. Moscovici (Ed.), *Introduction à la psychologie sociale* [Introduction to social psychology] (Vol. 1). Paris, France: Larousse.

Takagishi, H., Kameshima, S., Schug, J., Koizumi, M., & Yamagishi, T. (2010). Theory of mind enhances preference for fairness. *Journal of Experimental Child Psychology, 105,* 130–137.

Takahashi, H., Kato, M., Matsuura, M., Mobbs, D., Suhara, T., & Okubo, Y. (2009). When your gain is my pain and your pain is my gain: Neural correlates of envy and schadenfreude. *Science, 323,* 937–939.

Takahashi, H., Matsuura, M., Yahata, N., Koeda, M., Suhara T, & Okubo, Y. (2006). Men and women show distinct brain activations during imagery of sexual and emotional infidelity. *Neuroimage, 32,* 1299–1307.

Tal, I., & Lieberman, D. (2007). Kin selection and the development of sexual aversions: Toward an integration of theories on family sexual abuse. In C. Salmon & T. S. Shackelford (Eds.), *Family relationships: An evolutionary perspective.* Oxford, England: Oxford University Press.

Tam, J., Cinar, R., Liu, J., Godlewski, G., Wesley, D., Jourdan, T., . . . Kunos, G. (2012). Peripheral cannabinoid-1 receptor inverse agonism reduces obesity by reversing leptin resistance. *Cell Metabolism, 16,* 167–179.

Tamez, E., Myerson, J., & Hale, S. (2008). Learning, working memory, and intelligence revisited. *Behavioural Processes, 27,* 240–245.

Tamis-LeMonda, C. S., Bornstein, M. H., & Baumwell, L. (2001). Maternal responsiveness and children's achievement of language milestones. *Child Development, 72,* 748–767.

Tandon, R., Keshavan, M. S., & Nasrallah, H. A. (2008). Schizophrenia, "just the facts": What we know in 2008. 2: Epidemiology and etiology. *Schizophrenia Research, 102,* 2–18.

Tanielian, T., & Jaycox, L. H. (Eds.). (2008). *Invisible wounds of war: Summary and recommendations for addressing psychological and cognitive injuries.* Santa Monica, CA: Rand Corporation.

Tanner, J. M. (1990). *Foetus into man: Physical growth from conception to maturity* (Rev. & enlarged ed.). Cambridge, MA: Harvard University Press.

Tao, R., Huang, X., Wang, J., Zhang, H., Zhang, Y., & Li, M. (2010). Proposed diagnostic criteria for Internet addiction. *Addiction, 105,* 556–564.

Tapia, J. C., & Lichtman, J. W. (2012). Synapse elimination. In L. R. Squire, D. Berg, F. E. Bloom, S. du Lac, A. Ghosh, & N. C. Spitzer (Eds.), *Fundamental neuroscience* (4th ed., pp. 437–455). New York, NY: Elsevier.

Taylor, S. E. (2006). Tend and befriend: Biobehavioral bases of affiliation under stress. *Current Directions in Psychological Science, 15,* 273–277.

Taylor, S. E., & Brown, J. D. (1994). Positive illusions and well-being revisited: Separating fact from fiction. *Psychological Bulletin, 116,* 21–27.

Taylor, S. E., Klein, L. C., Lewis, B. P., Gruenewald, T. L., Gurung, R. A. R., & Updegraff, J. A. (2000). Biobehavioral responses to stress in females: Tend-and-befriend, not fight-or-flight. *Psychological Review, 107,* 411–429.

Taylor, S. E., Lerner, J. S., Sherman, D. K., Sage, R. M., & McDowell, N. K. (2003). Are self-enhancing cognitions associated with healthy or unhealthy biological profiles? *Journal of Personality and Social Psychology, 85,* 605–615.

TEDS Report, The. (2011). *Substance abuse treatment admissions for abuse of benzodiazepines.* Retrieved from http://www.samhsa.gov/data/2k11/WEB_TEDS_028/WEB_TEDS-028_BenzoAdmissions_HTML.pdf

Tellegen, A., Lykken, D. T., Bouchard, T. J., Wilcox, K. J., Segal, N. L., & Rich, S. (1988). Personality similarity in twins reared apart and together. *Journal of Personality and Social Psychology, 54,* 1031–1039.

Teller, D. Y. (1997). First glances: The vision of infants. The Friedenwald Lecture. *Investigative Ophthalmology & Visual Science, 38,* 2183–2203.

Ten Cate, C., Verzijden, M. N., & Etman, E. (2006). Sexual imprinting can induce sexual preferences for exaggerated parental traits. *Current Biology, 16,* 1128–1132.

Tenenbaum, H. R., & Leaper, C. (2003). Parent–child conversations about science: The socialization of gender inequities? *Developmental Psychology, 39,* 34–47.

Terracciano, A., Costa, P. T., & McCrae, R. R. (2006). Personality plasticity after age 30. *Personality and Social Psychology Bulletin, 32,* 999–1009.

Tessler, M., & Nelson, K. (1994). Making memories: The influence of joint encoding on later recall by young children. *Consciousness and Cognition, 3,* 307–326.

Tetlock, P. E. (2002). Social functionalist framework for judgment and choice: Intuitive politicians, theologians, and prosecutors. *Psychological Review, 109,* 451–471.

Thaler, N. S., & Jones-Forrester, S. (2013). IQ testing and the Hispanic client. In L. T. Benuto (Ed.), *Guide to psychological assessment with Hispanics* (pp. 81–98). New York, NY: Springer.

Thiessen, E. D., Hill, E. A., & Saffran, J. R. (2005). Infant-directed speech facilitates word segmentation. *Infancy, 7,* 53–71.

Thomas, G., & Fletcher, G. J. O. (2003). Mind-reading accuracy in intimate relationships: Assessing the roles of the relationship, the target, and the judge. *Journal of Personality and Social Psychology, 85,* 1079–1094.

Thomas, O. M., Cumming, B. G., & Parker, A. J. (2002). A specialization for relative disparity in V2. *Nature Neuroscience, 50,* 472–478.

Thompson, J. M., & Cotlove, C. (2005). *The therapeutic process: A clinical introduction to psychodynamic psychotherapy.* Lanham, MD: Rowman & Littlefield.

Thompson, P. (1980). Margaret Thatcher: A new illusion. *Perception, 9,* 483.

Thompson, P. M., Vidal, C., Giedd, J. N., Gochman, P., Blumenthal, J., Nicolson, R., . . . Rapoport, J. L. (2001). Mapping adolescent brain change reveals dynamic wave of accelerated gray matter loss in very early-onset schizophrenia. *Proceedings of the National Academy of Sciences, 98,* 11650–11655.

Thompson, R. A. (2013). Attachment theory and research: Précis and prospect. In P. Zelazo (Ed.), *Oxford handbook of developmental psychology* (Vol. 2, pp. 191–216). Oxford, England: Oxford University Press.

Thompson, R. F. (1985). *The brain: An introduction to neuroscience.* New York, NY: Freeman.

Thompson, S. K., von Kreigstein, K., Deane-Pratt, A., Marquardt, R., Deichmann, R., Griffiths, T. D., & McAlpine, D. (2006). Representation of interaural time delay in the human auditory midbrain. *Nature Neuroscience, 9,* 1006–1008.

Thomson, J. R., & Chapman, R. S. (1977). Who is "Daddy" revisited: The status of two-year-olds' over-extended words in use and comprehension. *Journal of Child Language, 4,* 359–375.

Thorndike, E. L. (1898). Animal intelligence: An experimental study of associative processes in animals. *Psychological Review Monograph Supplements, 2,* 4–160.

Thorne, B. (1993). *Gender play: Girls and boys in school.* New Brunswick, NJ: Rutgers University Press.

Thornhill, R., & Gangestad, S. W. (1999). Facial attractiveness. *Trends in Cognitive Sciences, 3,* 452–460.

Thorton, A., & McAuliffe, K. (2006). Teaching in wild meerkats. *Science, 313,* 227–229.

Thrasher, C., & LoBue, V. (2016). Do infants find snakes aversive? Infants' physiological response to "fear-relevant" stimuli. *Journal of Experimental Child Psychology, 142,* 382–390.

Tice, D. M., Butler, J. L., Muraven, M. B., & Stillwell, A. M. (1995). When modesty prevails: Differential favorability of self-presentation to friends and strangers. *Journal of Personality and Social Psychology, 69,* 1120–1138.

Tienari, P., Wahlberg, K.-E., & Wynne, L. C. (2006). Finnish adoption study of schizophrenia: Implications for family interventions. *Families, Systems, & Health, 24,* 442–451.

Tienari, P., Wynne, L. C., Sorri, A., Lahti, I., Läksy, K., Moring, J., . . . Walhberg, K. E. (2004). Genotype–environment interaction in schizophrenia-spectrum disorder: Long-term follow-up study of Finnish adoptees. *British Journal of Psychiatry, 184,* 216–222.

Tilker, H. A. (1970). Socially responsible behavior as a function of observer responsibility and victim feedback. *Journal of Personality and Social Psychology, 14,* 95–100.

Timney, B., Mitchell, D. E., & Cynader, M. (1980). Behavioral evidence for prolonged sensitivity to effects of monocular deprivation in dark-reared cats. *Journal of Neurophysiology, 43,* 1041–1054.

Tincoff, R., & Jusczyk, P. W. (1999). Some beginnings of word comprehension in 6-month-olds. *Psychological Science, 10,* 172–175.

Tither, J. M., & Ellis, B. J. (2008). Impact of fathers on daughters' age at menarche: A genetically and environmentally controlled sibling study. *Developmental Psychology, 44,* 1409–1420.

Tobias, J., & Seddon, N. (2000). Territoriality as a paternity guard in the European robin, *Erithacus rubecula. Animal Behaviour, 60,* 165–173.

Todd, A. E., Thiem, K. C., & Neel, R. (2016). Does seeing faces of young black boys facilitate the identification of threatening stimuli? *Psychological Science, 27,* 384–393.

Todorov, A., Mandisodza, A. N., Goren, A., & Hall, C. C. (2005). Inferences of competence from faces predict election outcomes. *Science, 308,* 1623–1626.

Tolman, E. C. (1948). Cognitive maps in rats and men. *Psychological Review, 55,* 189–208.

Tolman, E. C., & Honzik, C. H. (1930). "Insight" in rats. *University of California Publications in Psychology, 4,* 215–232.

Tomasello, M. (2000). Culture and cognitive development. *Current Directions in Psychological Science, 9,* 37–40.

Tomasello, M. (2006). Acquiring linguistic constructions. In W. Damon, D. Kuhn, & R. Siegler (Eds.), *The handbook of child psychology: Cognition, perception, and language,* (6th ed., pp. 255–298). New York, NY: John Wiley & Sons, Inc.

Tomasello, M. (2009). *Why we cooperate.* Cambridge, MA: MIT Press.

Tomasello, M., & Carpenter, M. (2007). Shared intentionality. *Developmental Science, 10,* 121–125.

Tomasello, M., & Haberl, K. (2003). Understanding attention: 12- and 18-month-olds know what is new for other persons. *Developmental Psychology, 39,* 906–912.

Tomasello, M., Savage-Rumbaugh, S., & Kruger, A. C. (1993). Imitative learning of actions on objects by children, chimpanzees, and enculturated chimpanzees. *Child Development, 64,* 1688–1705.

Tomkins, S. S. (1962). *Affect, imagery, consciousness: Vol. 1. The positive emotions.* New York, NY: Springer.

Tondel, G. M., & Candy, T. R. (2007). Human infants' accommodation responses to dynamic stimuli. *Investigative Ophthalmology & Visual Science, 48,* 949–956.

Tondel, G. M., & Candy, T. R. (2008). Accommodation and vergence latencies in human infants. *Vision Research, 48,* 564–576.

Toni, N., Teng, E. M., Bushong, E. A., Aimone, J. B., Zhao, C., Consiglio, A., . . . Gage, F. H. (2007). Synapse formation on neurons born in the hippocampus. *Nature Neuroscience, 10,* 727–734.

Tooby, J., & Cosmides, L. (2005). Conceptual foundations of evolutionary psychology. In D. M. Buss (Ed.), *Handbook of evolutionary psychology* (pp. 5–67). Hoboken, NJ: Wiley.

Toplak, M. E., Liu, E., MacPherson, R., Toneatto, T., & Stanovich, K. E. (2007). The reasoning skills and thinking dispositions of problem gamblers: A dual-process taxonomy. *Journal of Behavioral Decision Making, 20,* 103–124.

Tordoff, M. G. (2002). Intragastric calcium infusions support flavor preference learning by calcium-deprived rats. *Physiology and Behavior, 76,* 521–529.

Torrey, E. F., Kennard, A. D., Eslinger, D., Lamb, R., & Pavle, J. (2011). *More mentally ill persons are in jails and prisons than hospitals: A survey of the states. Treatment correction & mental health: An update of the National Institute of Corrections.* Retrieved from http://community.nicic.gov/blogs/mentalhealth/archive/2011/01/28/more-mentally-ill-persons-are-in-jails-and-prisons-than-hospitals-a-survey-of-the-states.aspx

Torrey, E. F., Zdanoxicz, M. T., Kennard, A. D., Lamb, H. R., Eslinger, D. F., Biasotti, M. C., & Fuiller, D. A. (2014). *The treatment of persons with mental illness in prisons and jails: A state survey.* Treatment Advocacy Center. Author.

Torriero, S., Oliveri, M., Koch, G., Caltagirone, C., & Petrosini, L. (2007). The what and how of observational learning. *Journal of Cognitive Neuroscience, 19,* 1656–1663.

Trahan, L. H., Stuebing, K. K., Fletcher, J. M., & Hiscock, M. (2014). The Flynn effect: A meta-analysis. *Psychological Bulletin, 140,* 1332–1360.

Trautwein, U., Nagy, N., Niggli, A., Lüdtke, O., Lenski, A., & Schnyder, I. (2015). Using individual interest and conscientiousness to predict academic effort: Additive, synergistic, or compensatory effects? *Journal of Personality and Social Psychology, 109,* 142–162.

Travers, J. C., Tincani, M. J., & Lang, R. (2014). Facilitated communication denies people with disabilities their voice. *Research and Practice for Persons with Severe Disabilities, 39,* 195–202.

Treisman, A. (1986, November). Features and objects in visual processing. *Scientific American,* 114B–125B.

Treisman, A. (1998). Feature binding, attention and object perception. *Philosophical Transactions of the Royal Society of London, Series B, 353,* 1295–1306.

Treisman, A., & Gormican, S. (1988). Feature analysis in early vision: Evidence from search asymmetries. *Psychological Review, 95,* 15–48.

Triandis, H. C., & Suh, E. M. (2002). Cultural influence on personality. *Annual Review of Psychology, 53,* 133–160.

Trivers, R. L. (1971). The evolution of reciprocal altruism. *Quarterly Review of Biology, 46,* 35–57.

Trivers, R. L. (1972). Parental investment and sexual selection. In B. Campbell (Ed.), *Sexual selection and the descent of man.* Chicago, IL: Aldine.

Troke, R. C., Tan, T. M., & Bloom, S. R. (2014). The future role of gut hormones in the treatment of obesity. *Therapeutic Advances in Chronic Diseases, 5,* 4–14.

Tronson, N. C., & Taylor, J. R. (2007). Molecular mechanisms of memory reconsolidation. *Nature Reviews Neuroscience, 8,* 262–275.

True, W. R., Rice, J., Eisen, S. A., Heath, A. C., Goldberg, J., Lyons, M. J., & Nowak, J. (1993). A twin study of genetic and environmental contributions to liability for posttraumatic stress symptoms. *Archives of General Psychiatry, 50,* 257–264.

Tryon, R. C. (1942). Individual differences. In F. A. Moss (Ed.), *Comparative psychology* (Rev. ed.). Englewood Cliffs, NJ: Prentice Hall.

Tsao, D. W., Freiwald, W. A., Tootell, R. B., & Livingstone, M. S. (2006). A cortical region consisting entirely of face-selective cells. *Science, 311,* 670–674.

Tsao, F.-M., Lui, H.-M., & Kuhl, P. K. (2004). Speech perception in infancy predicts language development in the second year of life: A longitudinal study. *Child Development, 75,* 1067–1084.

Tseng, W.-S. (2006). From peculiar psychiatric disorders through culture-bound syndromes to culture-related specific syndromes. *Transcultural Psychiatry, 43,* 554–576.

Tsien, J. Z. (2000, April). Building a brainier mouse. *Scientific American,* 62–68.

Tsuang, M. T., Stone, W. S., & Faraone, S. V. (2001). Genes, environment, and schizophrenia. *British Journal of Psychiatry, 178,* s18–s24.

Tulving, E. (1985). How many memory systems are there? *American Psychologist, 40,* 385–398.

Tulving, E. (2000). Concepts of memory. In E. Tulving & F. I. M. Craik (Eds.), *The Oxford handbook of memory.* Oxford, England: Oxford University Press.

Tulving, E. (2002). Episodic memory: From mind to brain. *Annual Review of Psychology, 53,* 1–25.

Tulving, E. (2005). Episodic memory and autonoesis: Uniquely human? In H. S. Terrace & J. Metcalfe (Eds.), *The missing link in cognition: Origins of self-reflective consciousness* (pp. 3–56). Oxford, England: Oxford University Press.

Turk, C. L., & Mennin, D. S. (2011). Phenomenology of generalized anxiety disorder. *Psychiatric Annals, 41,* 71–76.

Turkat, I. D., Keane, S. P., & Thompson-Pope, S. K. (1990). Social processing errors among paranoid personalities. *Journal of Psychopathology and Behavioral Assessment, 12,* 263–269.

Turkheimer, E., & Waldron, M. (2000). Nonshared environment: A theoretical, methodological, and quantitative review. *Psychological Bulletin, 126,* 78–108.

Tversky, A., & Kahneman, D. (1973). Availability: A heuristic for judging frequency and probability. *Cognitive Psychology, 5,* 207–232.

Twenge, J. M. (2000). The age of anxiety? Birth cohort change in anxiety and neuroticism, 1952–1993. *Journal of Personality and Social Psychology, 79,* 1007–1021.

Twenge, J. M. (2001). Changes in women's and men's assertiveness in response to status and roles: A cross-temporal meta-analysis, 1931–1993. *Journal of Personality and Social Psychology, 81,* 133–145.

Twenge, J. M. (2006). *Generation Me: Why today's young Americans are more confident, assertive, entitled—and more miserable than ever before.* New York, NY: Free Press.

Twenge, J. M., & Campbell, W. K. (2001). Age and birth cohort differences in self-esteem: A cross-temporal meta-analysis. *Personality and Social Psychology Review, 5,* 321–344.

Uher, J. (2008). Comparative personality research: Methodological approaches. *European Journal of Personality, 22,* 427–455.

Uher, R., Dernovsek, M. Z., Mors, O., Hauser, J., Sourey, D., Zobel, A., . . . Farmer, A. (2011). Melancholic, atypical and anxious depression subtypes and outcome of treatment with escitalopram and nortriptyline. *Journal of Affective Disorders, 132,* 112–120.

Uleman, J. S., Saribay, S. A., & Gonzalez, C. M. (2008). Spontaneous inferences, implicit impressions, and implicit theories. *Annual Review of Psychology, 59,* 329–360.

U. S. Census Bureau. (2011). *More young adults are living in their parents' home: Census Bureau Reports.* Retrieved from https://www.census.gov/newsroom/releases/archives/families_households/cb11-183.html

U.S. Census Bureau. (2014). *Measuring America: Computer and Internet trends in America.* Retrieved from https://www.census.gov/content/dam/Census/library/visualizations/2014/demo/computer_2014_text.pdf

Vahia, V. N., & Vahia,, I. V. (2008). Schizophrenia in developing countries. In K. T. Mueser & D. V. Jeste (Eds.), *Clinical handbook of schizophrenia* (pp. 549–555). New York, NY: Guilford.

Vaillant, G. E. (1977). *Adaptation to life* (1st ed.). Boston, MA: Little, Brown and Co.

Vaillant, G. E. (1995). *Adaptation to life* (2nd ed.). Cambridge, MA: Harvard University Press.

Vaillant, G. E. (2002). *Aging well: Surprising guideposts to a happier life from the Landmark Harvard Study.* Boston, MA: Little, Brown and Co.

Valenstein, E. S. (1986). *Great and desperate cures: The rise and decline of psychosurgery and other radical treatments for mental illness.* New York, NY: Basic Books.

Valkenburg, P. M., & Peter, J. (2009). Social consequences of the Internet for adolescents. *Current Directions in Psychological Science, 18,* 1–5.

Valkenburg, P. M., Schouten, A. P., Jochen, P. (2005) Adolescents' identity experiments on the Internet. *New Media & Society, 17,* 383–402.

Vallacher, R. R., van Geert, P., & Nowak, A. (2015). The intrinsic dynamics of psychological process. *Current Directions in Psychological Science, 24,* 58–64.

Vallar, G. (1993). The anatomical basis of spatial neglect in humans. In I. H. Robertson & J. C. Marshall (Eds.), *Unilateral neglect: Clinical and experimental studies* (pp. 27–62). Hillsdale, NJ: Erlbaum.

Valli, K., Standholm, T., Sillanmäki, L., & Revonsuo, A. (2008). Dreams are more negative than real life: Implications for the function of dreaming. *Cognition and Emotion, 22,* 833–861.

van Baaren, R. B., Holland, R. W., Kawakami, K., & van Knippenberg, A. (2004). Mimicry and prosocial behavior. *Psychological Science, 15,* 71–74.

van den Boom, D. C. (1991). The influence of infant irritability on the development of the mother–infant relationship in the first six months of life. In J. K. Nugent, M. M. Lester, & T. B. Brazelton (Eds.), *The cultural context of infancy* (Vol. 2). Norwood, NJ: Ablex.

Van Gelder, R. N. (2008). How the clock sees the light. *Nature Neuroscience, 11,* 628–630.

van Hooff, J. A. (1976). The comparison of facial expression in man and higher primates. In M. von Cranach (Ed.), *Methods of inference from animal to human behaviour.* Chicago, IL: Aldine.

van IJzendoorn, M. H., Schuengel, C., & Bakermans-Kranenburg, M. J. (1999). Disorganized attachment in early childhood: Meta-analysis of precursors, concomitants, and sequelae, *Development and Psychopathology, 11,* 225–249.

Van Itallie, T. B., & Kissileff, H. R. (1990). Human obesity: A problem in body energy economics. In E. M. Stricker (Ed.), *Handbook of behavioral neurobiology: Vol. 10. Neurobiology of food and fluid intake.* New York, NY: Plenum Press.

Van Le, Q., Isbell, L. A., Matsumoto, J., Nguyen, M., Hori, E., Maior, C., . . . Nishijo, N. (2013). Pulvinar neurons reveal neurobiological evidence of past selection for rapid detection of snakes. *Proceedings of the National Academy of Sciences, 110,* 19000–19005.

van Os, J., Rutten, B. P. F., & Poulton, R. (2008). Gene–environment interactions in schizophrenia: Review of epidemiological findings and future directions. *Schizophrenia Bulletin, 34,* 1066–1082.

van Veen, V., & Carter, C. S. (2006). Conflict and cognitive control in the brain. *Current Directions in Psychological Science, 15,* 237–240.

Vandello, J. A., & Cohen, D. (2008). Gender, culture, and intimate partner violence against women. *Social and Personality Psychology Compass, 2,* 1–16.

Varendi, H., Porter, R. H., & Winberg, J. (2002). The effect of labor on olfactory exposure learning within the first postnatal hour. *Behavioral Neuroscience, 116,* 206–211.

Vargha-Khadem, F., & Liégeois, F. (2007). From speech to gene: The KE family and the FOXP2. In B. Stein (Ed.), *On being moved: From mirror neurons to empathy* (pp. 137–146). Amsterdam, Netherlands: John Benjamins Publishing.

Varnum, M. E., Grossmann, I., Kitayama, S., & Nisbett, R. E. (2010). The origin of cultural differences in cognition: The social orientation hypothesis. *Current Directions in Psychological Science, 19,* 9–13.

Vasconcelos, M. S., Sampaio, A. S., Hounie, A. G., Akkerman, F., Curi, M., Lopes, A. C., & Miguel, E. C. (2007). Prenatal, perinatal, and postnatal risk factors in obsessive-compulsive disorder. *Biological Psychiatry, 61,* 301–307.

Vasilyeva, M., Duffy, S., & Huttenlocher, J. (2007). Developmental changes in the use of absolute and relative information: The case of spatial extent. *Journal of Cognition and Development, 8,* 455–471.

Vendetti, M. S., Matlen, B. J., Richland, L. E., & Bunge, S. A. (2015). Analogical reasoning in the classroom: Insights from cognitive science. *Mind, Brain, and Education, 9,* 100–105.

Venter, J. C., Adams, M. D., Myers, E. W., Li, P. W., Mural, R. J., Sutton, G. G., . . . Zhu, X. (2001, Feb. 16). The sequence of the human genome. *Science, 291,* 1304–1351.

Vernon, P. A., Jang, K. L., Harris, J. A., & McCarthy, J. M. (1997). Environmental predictors of personality differences: A twin and sibling study. *Journal of Personality and Social Psychology, 72,* 177–183.

Vernon, P. A., & Kantor, L. (1986). Reaction time correlations with intelligence test scores obtained under either timed or untimed conditions. *Intelligence, 9,* 357–374.

Vicente, K. J., & Wang, J. H. (1998). An ecological theory of expertise in memory recall. *Psychological Review, 105,* 33–37.

Volk, A. A., Lukjanczuk, J. L., & Quinsey, V. L. (2007). Perceptions of child facial cues as a function of child age. *Evolutionary Psychology, 5,* 801–814.

von Békésy, G., & Wever, E. G. (1960). *Experiments in hearing.* New York, NY: McGraw-Hill Series in Psychology.

von Hippel, W., & Dunlop, S. M. (2005). Aging, inhibition, and social inappropriateness. *Psychology and Aging, 20,* 519–523.

Von Senden, M. (1960). *Space and sight: The perception of space and shape in the congenitally blind before and after operation.* Glencoe, IL: Free Press.

Vouloumanos, A., & Werker, J. F. (2007). Listening to language at birth: Evidence for a bias for speech in neonates. *Developmental Science, 10,* 159–171.

Vygotsky, L. S. (1962). *Thought and language* (E. Haufmann & G. Vaker, Eds. & Trans.). Cambridge, MA: MIT Press. (Original work published 1934)

Vygotsky, L. S. (1978). Play and its role in the mental development of the child. In M. Cole, V. John-Steiner, S. Scribner, & E. Sourberman (Eds.), *Mind in society.* Cambridge, MA: Harvard University Press. (Original work published 1933)

Vygotsky, L. S. (1978). Interaction between learning and development. In M. Cole, V. John-Steiner, S. Scribner, & E. Souberman (Eds.), *Mind in society: The development of higher psychological processes.* Cambridge, MA: Harvard University Press. (Original work published 1935)

Waddington, J. L., O'Tuathaigh, C. M. P., & Remington, G. J. (2011). Pharmacology and neuroscience of antipsychotic drugs. In D. R. Weinberg & P. Harrison (Eds.), *Schizophrenia* (pp. 483–514). Hoboken, NJ: Wiley-Blackwell.

Wade, N. J., & Swanston, M. (1991). *Visual perception: An introduction.* London, England: Routledge.

Wagerman, S. A., & Funder, D. C. (2009). Situations. In P. J. Corr and G. Matthews (Eds.), *Cambridge handbook of personality* (pp. 27–42). Cambridge, England: Cambridge University Press.

Wagner, U., Gals, S., Halder, H., Verleger, R., & Born, J. (2004). Sleep inspires insight. *Nature, 427,* 352–355.

Walden, T. A. (1991). Infant social referencing. In J. Garber & K. A. Dodge (Eds.), *The development of emotion regulation and dysregulation.* Cambridge, England: Cambridge University Press.

Walker, W. I. (1973). Principles of organization of the ventrobasal complex in mammals. *Brain Behavior and Evolution, 7,* 253–336.

Wallace, M. T., Ghose, D., Nidiffer, A. R., Fister, M. C., & Fister, J. K. (2012). Development of multisensory integration in subcortical and cortical brain networks. In A. J. Bremner, D. J. Lewkowicz, & C. Spence (Eds.), *Multisensory development* (pp. 325–341). Oxford, England: Oxford University Press.

Waller, K., Volk, A., & Quinsey, V. L. (2004). The effect of infant fetal alcohol syndrome facial features on adoption preference. *Human Nature, 15,* 101–117.

Wallerstein, R. S. (1989). The psychotherapy research project of the Menninger Foundation: An overview. *Journal of Consulting and Clinical Psychology, 57,* 195–205.

Walther, S., Federspiel, A., Horn, H., Razavi, N., Wuest, R., Dierks, T., . . . Müller, T. J. (2011). Resting state cerebral blood flow and objective motor activity reveal basal ganglia dysfunction in schizophrenia. *Psychiatry Research: Neuroimaging, 192,* 117–124.

Wampold, B. E. (2001). *The great psychotherapy debate: Models, methods, and findings.* Mahwah, NJ: Erlbaum.

Wampold, B. E., Minami, T., Tierney, S. C., Baskin, T. W., & Bhati, K. S. (2005). The placebo is powerful: Estimating effects in medicine and psychotherapy from randomized clinical trials. *Journal of Clinical Psychology, 61,* 835–854.

Wang, K., Fan, J., Dong, Y., Wang, C., Lee, T. M. C., & Posner, M. I. (2005). Selective impairment of attentional networks of orienting and executive control in schizophrenia. *Schizophrenia Research, 78,* 235–241.

Wang, P. S., Lane, M., Olfson, M., Pincus, H. A., Wells, K. B., & Kessler, R. C. (2005). Twelve-month use of mental health services in the United States: Results from the national comorbidity survey replication. *Archives of General Psychiatry, 62,* 629–640.

Ward, N. S., Oakley, D. A., Frackowiak, R. S. J., & Halligan, P. W. (2003). Differential brain activations during intentionally simulated and subjectively experienced paralysis. *Cognitive Neuropsychiatry, 8,* 295–312.

Warneken, F., Lohse, K., Melis, A. P., & Tomasello, M. (2011). Young children share the spoils after collaboration. *Psychological Science, 22,* 267–273.

Warneken, F., & Mclis, A. (2012). The ontogeny and phylogeny of cooperation. In J. Vonk & T. K. Shackelford (Eds.), *The Oxford handbook of comparative evolutionary psychology* (pp. 399–418). Oxford, England: Oxford University Press.

Warneken, F., & Tomasello, M. (2006). Altruistic helping in human infants and young chimpanzees. *Science, 311,* 1301–1303.

Warner, R. (1985). *Recovery from schizophrenia.* London, England: Routledge & Kegan Paul.

Warren, R. M. (1984). Perceptual restoration of obliterated sounds. *Psychological Bulletin, 96*, 371–383.

Wartenburger, I., Heekereb, H. R., Abutalebi, J., Cappa, S. F., Villringer, A., & Perani, D. (2003). Early setting of grammatical processing in the bilingual brain. *Neuron, 37*, 159–170.

Wason, P., & Johnson-Laird, P. (1972). *Psychology of reasoning: Structure and content.* Cambridge, MA: Harvard University Press.

Wason, P. C. (1960). On the failure to eliminate hypotheses in a conceptual task. *Quarterly Journal of Experimental Psychology, 12*, 129–140.

Wason, P. C. (1966). Reasoning. In B. Foss (Ed.), *New horizons in psychology* (pp. 135–151). Harmonsworth, England: Penguin.

Wass, S. V., Scerif, G., & Johnson, M. H. (2012). Training attentional control and working memory—Is younger better? *Developmental Review, 32*, 360–387.

Wassenberg, R., Hendricksen, J. G. M., Hurks, P. P. M., Feron, F. J. M., Keulers, E. H. H., Vles, J. S. H., & Jolles, J. (2008). Development of inattention, impulsivity, and processing speed as measured by the d2 test: Results of a large cross-sectional study in children aged 7–13. *Child Neuropsychology, 14*, 195–210.

Wasserman, E. A. (1995). The conceptual abilities of pigeons. *American Scientist, 83*, 246–255.

Wasylyshyn, C., Verhaeghen, P., & Sliwinski, M. J. (2011). Aging and task switching: A meta-analysis. *Psychology and Aging, 26*, 15–20.

Watkins, L. R., Hutchinson, M. R., Milligan, E. D., & Maier, S. (2007). "Listening" and "talking" to neurons: Implications of immune activation for pain control and increasing efficacy of opioids. *Brain Research Reviews, 56*, 148–169.

Watkins, L. R., & Maier, S. F. (2000). The pain of being sick: Implications of immune-to-brain communication for understanding pain. *Annual Review of Psychology, 51*, 29–57.

Watson, J. B. (1913). Psychology as the behaviorist views it. *Psychological Review, 20*, 158–177.

Watson, J. B. (1924). *Behaviorism.* Chicago, IL: University of Chicago Press.

Watson, J. B., & Rayner, R. (1920). Conditioned emotional reactions. *Journal of Experimental Psychology, 3*, 1–14.

Watson, J. S. (1972). Smiling, cooing, and "the game." *Merrill-Palmer Quarterly, 18*, 323–339.

Watts, A. L., Lilenfeld, S. C., Smith, S. F., Miller, J. D., Campbell, W. K., Waldman, I. D., . . . Faschingbauer, T. J. (2013). The double-edged sword of grandiose narcissism: Implications for successful and unsuccessful leadership among U.S. Presidents. *Psychological Science, 24*, 2379–2389.

Waugh, N. C., & Norman, D. A. (1965). Primary memory. *Psychological Review, 72*, 89–104.

Waxman, S. R., & Markow, D. B. (1995). Words as invitations to form categories: Evidence from 12- to 13-month-old infants. *Cognitive Psychology, 29*, 257–302.

Weaver, D. R., & Emery, P. (2012). Circadian timekeeping. In L. R. Squire, D. Berg, F. E. Bloom, S. du Lac, A. Ghosh, & N. C. Spitzer (Eds.), *Fundamental neuroscience* (4th ed., pp. 819–845). New York, NY: Elsevier.

Weber, E. H. (1834). *De pulen, resorptione, auditu et tactu: Annotationes anatomicae et physiologicae.* Leipzig, Germany: Koehler.

Weber, N., & Brewer, N. (2003). Expert memory: The interaction of stimulus structure, attention, and expertise. *Applied Cognitive Psychology, 17*, 295–308.

Webster, G. D., Graber, J. A., Gesselman, A. N., Crosier, B. S., & Orozco Schember, T. (2014). A life history theory of father absence and menarche: A meta-analysis. *Evolutionary Psychology, 12*, 273–294.

Wedekind, C., & Füri, S. (1997). Body odour preferences in men and women: Do they aim for specific MHC combinations or simply heterozygosity? *Proceedings of the Royal Society of London, Series B, 264*, 1471–1479.

Wedekind, C., Seebeck, T., Bettens, F., & Paepke, A. J. (1995). MHC-dependent mate preference in humans. *Proceedings of the Royal Society of London, Series B, 260*, 245–249.

Wegner, D. M., Fuller, V. A., & Sparrow, B. (2003). Clever hands: Uncontrolled intelligence in facilitated communication. *Journal of Personality and Social Psychology, 85*, 5–19.

Wegner, D. M., Wenzlaff, R. M., & Kozak, M. (2004). Dream rebound: The return of suppressed thoughts in dreams. *Psychological Science, 15*, 232–236.

Weinberg, M. K., Tronick, E. Z., Cohn, J. F., & Olson, K. L. (1999). Gender differences in emotional expressivity and self-regulation during early infancy. *Developmental Psychology, 35*, 175–188.

Weinberger, D. A. (1990). The construct validity of the repressive coping style. In J. L. Singer (Ed.), *Repression and dissociation: Implications for personality theory, psychopathology, and health.* Chicago, IL: University of Chicago Press.

Weiner, R. B., & Bornstein, R. F. (2009). *Principles of psychotherapy: Promoting evidence-based psychodynamic practice* (3rd ed.). Hoboken, NJ: Wiley.

Weinstein, N. D. (1982). Unrealistic optimism about susceptibility to health problems. *Journal of Behavioral Medicine, 5*, 441–460.

Weisfeld, G. E., Czilli, T., Phillips, K. A., Gal, J. A., & Lichtman, C. M. (2003). Possible olfaction-based mechanisms in human kin recognition and inbreeding avoidance. *Journal of Experimental Child Psychology, 85*, 279–295.

Weiskrantz, L. (1956). Behavioral changes associated with ablation of the amygdaloid complex in monkeys. *Journal of Comparative Physiology and Psychology, 49*, 381–391.

Weiss, A., Costa, P. T., Karuza, J., Duberstein, P. R., Friedman, B., & McCrae, R. R. (2005). Cross-sectional age differences in personality among Medicare patients aged 65 to 100. *Psychology of Aging, 20*, 182–185.

Welch, D. C., & West, R. L. (1995). Self-efficacy and mastery: Its application to issues of environmental control, cognition, and aging. *Developmental Review, 15*, 150–171.

Welling, II. (2003). An evolutionary function of the depressive reaction: The cognitive mapping hypothesis. *New Ideas in Psychology, 21*, 147–156.

Wellman, H. M. (1990). *The child's theory of mind.* Cambridge, MA: MIT Press.

Wellman, H. M., Cross, D., & Watson, J. (2001). Meta-analysis of theory-of-mind development: The truth about false-belief. *Child Development, 72*, 655–684.

Wells, G. L., & Bradfield, A. L. (1999). Distortions in eyewitnesses' recollections: Can the postidentification-feedback effect be moderated? *Psychological Science, 10*, 138–144.

Wells, G. L., Memon, A., & Penrod, S. D. (2006). Eyewitness evidence: Improving its probative value. *Psychological Science in the Public Interest, 7*, 45–73.

Wells, G. L., Olson, E. A., & Charman, S. D. (2002). The confidence of eyewitnesses in their identifications from lineups. *Current Directions in Psychological Science, 11*, 151–154.

Wendelken, C., O'Hare, E. D., Whitaker, K. J., Ferrer, E., & Bunge, S. A. (2011). Increased functional selectivity over development in rostrolateral prefrontal cortex. *Journal of Neuroscience, 31*, 17260–17268.

Wenner, J. A., Burch, M. M., Lynch, J. S., & Baer, P. J. (2008). Becoming a teller of tales: Associations between children's fictional narratives and parent-child reminiscence narratives. *Journal of Experimental Child Psychology, 101*, 1–19.

Werker, J. F., & Gervain, J. (2013). Speech perception in infancy: A foundation for language acquisition. In P. D. Zelazo (Ed.), *Oxford handbook of developmental psychology* (Vol. 1., pp. 706–743). Oxford, England: Oxford University Press.

Werker, J. F., & Tees, R. C. (1999). Influences on infant speech processing: Toward a new synthesis. *Annual Review of Psychology, 50,* 509–535.

Wernicke, C. (1977). The aphasia symptom complex: A psychological study on an anatomical basis. In G. H. Eggard (Ed. & Trans.), *Wernicke's works on aphasia.* The Hague, Netherlands: Mouton. (Original work 1874)

Wertheimer, M. (1938). Principles of perceptual organization. In W. D. Ellis (Ed. & Trans.), *A source-book of Gestalt psychology.* New York, NY: Harcourt Brace. (Original work published 1923)

Wesensten, N. J., Belenky, G., Kautz, M. A., Thorne, D. R., Reichardt, R. M., & Balkin, T. J. (2002). Maintaining alertness and performance during sleep deprivation: Modafinil versus caffeine. *Psychopharmacology, 159,* 238–247.

West, T. A., & Bauer, P. J. (1999). Assumptions of infantile amnesia: Are there differences between early and later memories? *Memory, 7,* 257–278.

Westen, D., Betan, E., & Defife, J. A. (2011). Identity disturbance in adolescence: Associations with borderline personality disorder. *Development and Psychopathology, 23,* 305–313.

Westermarck, E. A. (1891). *The history of human marriage.* New York, NY: Macmillan.

Weston, D., Novotny, C. M., & Thompson-Brenner, H. (2004). The empirical status of empirically supported psychotherapies: Assumptions, findings, and reporting in controlled clinical trials. *Psychological Bulletin, 130,* 631–663.

Whalen, P. J. (1998). Fear, vigilance, and ambiguity: Initial neuroimaging studies of the human amygdala. *Current Directions in Psychological Science, 7,* 177–188.

Wheeler, M. A. (2000). Episodic memory and autonoetic awareness. In E. Tulving & F. I. M. Craik (Eds.), *The Oxford handbook of memory.* Oxford, England: Oxford University Press.

Wheeler, M. A., Stuss, D. T., & Tulving, E. (1997). Toward a theory of episodic memory: The frontal lobes and autonoetic consciousness. *Psychological Bulletin, 121,* 331–354.

Wheeler, S. C., & Petty, R. E. (2001). The effects of stereotype activation on behavior: A review of possible mechanisms. *Psychological Bulletin, 127,* 797–826.

White, K. S., & Barlow, D. H. (2002). Panic disorder and agoraphobia. In D. H. Barlow, *Anxiety and its disorders* (2nd ed.). New York, NY: Guilford.

White, S. H. (2000). Conceptual foundations of IQ testing. *Psychology, Public Policy, and Law, 6,* 33–43.

Whiten, A. (2007). Pan African culture: Memes and genes in wild chimpanzees. *Proceedings of the National Academy of Sciences, 104*(Nov. 6), 17559–17560.

Whiten, A., & Flynn, E. G. (2010). The transmission and evolution of experimental "microcultures" in groups of young children. *Developmental Psychology, 46,* 1694–1709.

Whiten, A., Goodall, J., McGrew, W. C., Nishida, T., Reynolds, V., Sugiyama, Y., . . . Boesch, C. (1999). Culture in chimpanzees. *Nature, 399,* 682–685.

Whiten, A., Horner, V., Litchfield, C. A., & Marshall-Pescini, S. (2004). How do apes ape? *Learning & Behavior, 32,* 36–52.

Whiten, A., McGuigan, N., Marshall-Pescini, S., & Hopper, L. M. (2009). Emulation, imitation, over-imitation and the scope of culture for child and chimpanzee. *Philosophical Transactions of the Royal Society of London: Biological Sciences, 364,* 2417–2428.

Whiting, B. B., & Edwards, C. P. (1988). *Children of different worlds: The formation of social behavior.* Cambridge, MA: Harvard University Press.

Widaman, K. F. (2009). Phenylketonuria in children and mothers. *Current Directions in Psychological Science, 18,* 48–52.

Wiens, S., Mezzacappa, E., & Katkin, E. S. (2000). Heartbeat detection and the experience of emotions. *Cognition and Emotion, 14,* 417–427.

Wijbenga, F. H., & van Witteloostruijn, A. (2007). Entrepreneurial locus of control and competitive strategies—the moderating effect of environmental dynamism. *Journal of Economic Psychology, 28,* 566–589.

Wild, B., Erb, M., & Bartels, M. (2001). Are emotions contagious? Evoked emotions while viewing emotionally expressive faces: Quality, quantity, time course and gender differences. *Psychiatry Research, 102,* 109–124.

Wiley, M. G., Crittenden, K. S., & Birg, L. D. (1979). Why a rejection? Causal attributions of a career achievement event. *Social Psychology Quarterly, 42,* 214–222.

Wilkins, L., & Richter, C. P. (1940). A great craving for salt by a child with cortico-adrenal insufficiency. *Journal of the American Medical Association, 114,* 866–868.

Wilkins, P. (2003). *Person-centred therapy in focus.* London, England: Sage.

Wilkinson, G. S. (1988). Reciprocal altruism in bats and other mammals. *Ethology and Sociobiology, 9,* 85–100.

Williams, A. C. (2002). Facial expression of pain: An evolutionary account. *Behavioral and Brain Sciences, 25,* 439–488.

Williams, J. E., & Best, D. L. (1990). *Measuring sex stereotypes: A multination study, revised edition.* Newbury Park, CA: Sage.

Williams, S. L. (2005). Anxiety disorders. In J. Maddux & B. Winstead (Eds.), *Psychopathology: Foundations for a contemporary understanding.* Mahwah, NJ: Erlbaum.

Wilson, M., & Daly, M. (1985). Competitiveness, risk taking, and violence: The young male syndrome. *Ethology and Sociobiology, 6,* 59–73.

Wilson, R. I., & Mainen, Z. F. (2006). Early events in olfactory processing. *Annual Review of Neuroscience, 29,* 161–201.

Wimer, R. E., & Wimer, C. C. (1985). Animal behavior genetics: A search for the biological foundations of behavior. *Annual Review of Psychology, 36,* 171–218.

Wimmer, H., & Perner, J. (1983). Beliefs about beliefs: Representation and constraining function of wrong beliefs in young children's understanding of deception. *Cognition, 13,* 103–128.

Winfield, R. C., & Dennis, W. (1934). The dependence of the rat's choice of pathways upon the length of the daily trial series. *Journal of Comparative Psychology, 18,* 135–147.

Wise, R. A. (1996). Addictive drugs and brain stimulation reward. *Annual Review of Neuroscience, 19,* 319–340.

Wishart, J. G., & Bower, T. G. R. (1984). Spatial relations and the object concept: A normative study. In L. P. Lipsitt & C. Rovee-Collier (Eds.), *Advances in infancy research* (Vol. 3). Norwood, NJ: Ablex.

Wittchen, H. U., Kessler, R. C., Pfister, H., & Lieb, M. (2000). Why do people with anxiety disorders get depressed? A prospective-longitudinal community study. *Acta Psychiatrica Scandinavica, 406,* 14–23.

Witthoft, N., & Winawer, J. (2013). Learning, memory, and synesthesia. *Psychological Science, 24,* 258–265.

Witty, P. A., & Jenkins, M. D. (1935). Intra-race testing and Negro intelligence. *Journal of Psychology, 1,* 179–192.

Wixted, J. T. (2004). The psychology and neuroscience of forgetting. *Annual Review of Psychology, 55,* 235–269.

Wixted, J. T. (2005). A theory about why we forget what we once knew. *Current Directions in Psychological Science, 14,* 6–9.

Wolf, A. (1995). *Sexual attraction and childhood association: A Chinese brief for Edward Westermarck.* Stanford, CA: Stanford University Press.

Wong, J., & Leboe, J. P. (2009). Distinguishing between inhibitory and episodic processing accounts of switch-cost asymmetries. *Canadian Journal of Experimental Psychology, 63,* 8–23.

Wood, D., Bruner, J. S., & Ross, G. (1976). The role of tutoring in problem-solving. *Journal of Child Psychology and Psychiatry, 17,* 89–100.

Wood, D. M., & Emmett-Oglesby, M. W. (1989). Mediation in the nucleus accumbens of the discriminative stimulus produced by cocaine. *Pharmacology, Biochemistry, and Behavior, 33,* 453–457.

Wood, W., & Eagly, A. H. (2002). A cross-cultural analysis of the behavior of women and men: Implications for the origins of sex differences. *Psychological Bulletin, 128,* 699–727.

Woods, S. C., Schwartz, M. W., Baskin, D. G., & Seeley, R. J. (2000). Food intake and the regulation of body weight. *Annual Review of Psychology, 51,* 255–277.

Woods, S. C., & Stricker, E. M. (2012). Food intake and metabolism. In L. R. Squire, D. Berg, F. E. Bloom, S. du Lac, A. Ghosh, & N. C. Spitzer (Eds.), *Fundamental neuroscience* (4th ed., pp. 767–782). New York, NY: Elsevier.

Woodward, A. L. (2003). Infants' developing understanding of the link between looker and object. *Developmental Science, 6,* 297–311.

Woody, S. R., & Nosen, E. (2009). Psychological models of phobic disorders and panic. In M. M. Antony & M. B. Stein (Eds.), *Oxford handbook of anxiety related disorders.* Oxford, England: Oxford University Press.

Woolf, C. J., & Salter, M. W. (2000). Neuronal plasticity: Increasing the gain in pain. *Science, 288,* 1765–1768.

Woolley, J. D. (1995). Young children's understanding of fictional versus epistemic mental representations: Imagination and belief. *Child Development, 66,* 1011–1021.

World Bank. (2016). Adolescent fertility rate (births per 1,000 women ages 15–19). http://data.worldbank.org/indicator/SP.ADO.TFRT

Wrangham, R. W. (1993). The evolution of sexuality in chimpanzees and bonobos. *Human Nature, 4,* 47–79.

Wright, S. B., Matlen, B. J., Baym, C. L., Ferrer, E., & Bunge, S. A. (2008). Neural correlates of fluid reasoning in children and adults. *Frontiers in Human Neuroscience, 8,* 1–8.

Wu, Z., & Su, Y. (2014). How do preschoolers' sharing behaviors relate to their theory of mind understanding? *Journal of Experimental Child Psychology, 120,* 73–86.

Wulff, S. B. (1985). The symbolic and object play of children with autism: A review. *Journal of Autism and Developmental Disorders, 15,* 139–148.

Wyatt, T. D. (2009). Fifty years of pheromones. *Nature, 457,* 262–263.

Wyrwicka, W. (1996). *Imitation in human and animal behavior.* New Brunswick, NJ: Transaction Publishers.

Yamane, Y., Carlson, E. T., Bowman, K. C., Wang, Z., & Connor, C. E. (2008). A neural code for three-dimensional object shape in macaque inferotemporal cortex. *Nature Neuroscience, 11,* 1352–1360.

Yamazaki, K., Beauchamp, G. K., Fung-Win, S., Bard, J., & Boyse, E. A. (1994). Discrimination of odor types determined by the major histocompatibility complex among outbred mice. *Proceedings of the National Academy of Sciences (USA), 91,* 3735–3738.

Yamazaki, K., Beauchamp, G. K., Kupniewski, D., Bard, J., Thomas, L., & Boyse, E. A. (1988). Familial imprinting determines H-2 selective mating preferences. *Science, 240,* 1331–1332.

Yantis, S. (2008). The neural basis of selective attention. *Current Directions in Psychological Science, 17,* 86–90.

Yeomans, M. R., & Gray, R. W. (1996). Selective effects of naltrexone on food pleasantness and intake. *Physiology and Behavior, 60,* 439–446.

Yetish, G., Kaplan, H., Gurven, M., Wood, B., Pontzer, H., Manger P. R., Wilson, C., McGregor, R., & Siegel J. M. (2015). Natural sleep and its seasonal variations in three pre-industrial societies. *Current Biology, 25,* 1–7.

Yiend, J., Mathews, A., Burns, T., Dutton, K., Fernández-Martín, A., Geirgiou, G. A., . . . Fox, E. (2015). Mechanisms of selective attention in generalized anxiety disorder. *Clinical Psychological Science, 3,* 758–771.

Yin, R. K. (1969). Looking at upside-down faces. *Journal of Experimental Psychology, 8,* 141–145.

Yirmiya, N., Solomonica-Levi, D., & Shulman, C. (1996). The ability to manipulate behavior and to understand manipulation of beliefs: A comparison of individuals with autism, mental retardation, and normal development. *Developmental Psychology, 32,* 62–69.

Young, J. E., Beck, A. T., & Weinberger, A. (1993). Depression. In D. H. Barlow (Ed.), *Clinical handbook of psychological disorders: A step-by-step treatment manual* (2nd ed., pp. 240–277). New York, NY: Guilford.

Young, R. F., & Brechner, T. (1986). Electrical stimulation of the brain for relief of intractable pain due to cancer. *Cancer, 57,* 1266–1272.

Young, S. E., Friedman, N. P., Miyake, A., Willcutt, E. G., Corley, R. P., Haberstick, B. C., & Hewitt, J. K. (2009). Behavioral disinhibition: Liability for externalizing spectrum disorders and its genetic and environmental relation to response inhibition across adolescence. *Journal of Abnormal Psychology, 118,* 117–130.

Youngblade, L. M., & Dunn, J. (1995). Individual differences in young children's pretend play with mother and sibling: Links to relationships and understanding of other people's feelings and beliefs. *Child Development, 66,* 1472–1492.

Zajonc, R. B. (1965). Social facilitation. *Science, 149,* 269–274.

Zajonc, R. B. (1980). Compresence. In P. B. Paulus (Ed.), *Psychology of group influence.* Hillsdale, NJ: Erlbaum.

Zaragoza, M. S., & Mitchell, K. J. (1996). Repeated exposure to suggestion and the creation of false memories. *Psychological Science, 7,* 294–300.

Žebec, M. S., Demetriou, A., & Kotrla-Topić, M. (2015). Changing expressions of general intelligence in development: A 2-wave longitudinal study from 7 to 18 years of age. *Intelligence, 49,* 94–109.

Zebrowitz, L. A., Hall, J. A., Murphy, N. A., & Rhodes, G. (2002). Looking smart and looking good: Facial cues to intelligence and their origins. *Personality and Social Psychology Bulletin, 28,* 238–249.

Zebrowitz, L. A., & McDonald, S. M. (1991). The impact of litigants' baby-facedness and attractiveness on adjudications in small claims courts. *Law and Human Behavior, 15,* 603–623.

Zebrowitz, L. A., & Montepare, J. M. (2005). Appearance DOES matter. *Science, 308,* 1565–1566.

Zebrowitz, L. A., Montepare, J. M., & Lee, H. K. (1993). They don't all look alike: Individuated impressions of other racial groups. *Journal of Personality and Social Psychology, 65,* 85–101.

Zeh, J. A., & Zeh, D. W. (2001). Reproductive mode and the genetic benefits of polyandry. *Animal Behaviour, 61,* 1051–1063.

Zelazo, P. D. (2015). Executive function: Reflection, iterative reprocessing, complexity, and the developing brain. *Developmental Review, 38,* 55–68.

Zelazo, P. D., Frye, D., & Rapus, T. (1996). An age-related dissociation between knowing rules and using them. *Cognitive Development, 11,* 37–63.

Zentall, T. R. (2006). Imitation: Definition, evidence, and mechanisms. *Animal Cognition, 9,* 335–353.

Zhang, M., Balmadrid, C., & Kelley, A. E. (2003). Nucleus accumbens opioid, GABAergic, and dopaminergic modulation of palatable food motivation: Contrasting effects revealed by a progressive ratio study in the rat. *Behavioral Neuroscience, 117,* 202–211.

Zhang, M., & Kelley, A. E. (2000). Enhanced intake of high-fat food after striatal mu-opioid stimulation: Microinjection mapping and fos expression. *Neurocience, 99,* 267–272.

Zinbarg, R. E., Barlow, D. H., Brown, T. A., & Hertz, R. M. (1992). Cognitive-behavioral approaches to the nature and treatment of anxiety disorders. *Annual Review of Psychology, 43,* 235–267.

Zohary, E., Celebrini, S., Britten, K. H., & Newsome, W. T. (1994). Neuronal plasticity that underlies improvement in perceptual performance. *Science, 263,* 1289–1292.

Name Index

Subject Index

Notes: Index entries that refer to often-looked-up topics in psychology are boldfaced to make them easier to find.